A Comprehensive Bibliography
of English-Canadian Short Stories, 1950-1983

A Comprehensive Bibliography of English-Canadian Short Stories, 1950-1983

Compiled by Allan Weiss, B.A., M.A., Ph.D.

ECW PRESS

Canadian Cataloguing in Publication Data

Weiss, Allan Barry

A comprehensive bibliography of English-Canadian short stories, 1950-1983

ISBN 0-920763-67-7

1. Short stories, Canadian (English) - Bibliography.*
2. Canadian fiction (English) - 20th century - Bibliography. 3. Authors, Canadian (English) - 20th century - Bibliography. I. Title.

Z1377.F4W44 1988   016.813'01   C87-093357-4

This bibliography was compiled for publication using AUTHEX, a microcomputer-based indexing program developed by Gordon Ripley of *Reference Press*. The publisher is grateful to Mr Ripley for his assistance in the project. Post-processing, design and processing by ECW Production Services, Oakville, Ontario. Cover design by Bette Davies.

Published by ECW PRESS, 307 Coxwell Avenue, Toronto, Ontario.

Table of Contents

Acknowledgements

Since beginning this project, I have referred to it as "*my*" bibliography, implying that I alone was responsible for its compilation. In fact, without the assistance of a great many people this work would never have achieved the degree of comprehensiveness it has attained.

First, I have to thank the authors, editors, and radio producers who took the time to respond to my survey. The number of times "Based on survey response" appears as an annotation attests to how greatly I depended on their help. Special thanks must go to those authors who prepared lengthy and detailed publication lists especially for me: Gertrude Story, Rhoda Elizabeth Playfair Stein, Beatrice E. Fines, Crad Kilodney, Michael Bullock, and Patricia Armstrong. Others kindly photocopied their resumes or sent copies of bibliographies already compiled. To Jane Rule, Margaret Laurence, *et al*, I express my deepest gratitude. I must also thank H. Gordon Green for scanning my list of *Family Herald* authors and marking the ones he knew were Canadians (as well as his own pseudonyms). Like virtually anyone who has written or written on Canadian short stories, I owe a debt of gratitude to Robert Weaver as well; he allowed me to see the files of the radio programme "Anthology," and thereby disrupt his office routine. I regret that those who succeeded him at the CBC do not share his sense of duty towards the public; they seem to have replaced professionalism with paranoia.

My research took me into a number of libraries seeking assistance with large quantities of very specialized periodicals. I therefore became responsible for increasing the workload as well as the statistics of many a librarian. I have to thank those librarians who led me to the names of Canadian periodicals and authors. Thanks to: Michele, Margery, John, and staff at the Thomas Fisher Rare Book Library for not succumbing beneath the torrents of request slips I poured on them; Mary Ann, Mary, Cameron, and the stack-request personnel of the Metro Central Library's Literature Department, who expressed continuing interest in my work; Neil, Mark, Edie, and Mr. Lucas at the United Church of Canada's Archives, where I spent many weeks rummaging through their remarkable and fascinating collection; Mrs. Craddock, Cathy Seguin, and Elizabeth Tilley at the Salvation Army's Heritage Centre Library; Therese, Danny, Lucille, Sharon, and Danica at the National Library; Doris, John, Lorna, Wendy, and Charlie at the Spaced Out Library; Robert Sawyer, John Robert Colombo, and the members of Hydra North; Marion Wyse of the University of Toronto Archives; and Patricia, Patricia, and Ian at the Canadiana Collection.

The editors of some periodicals permitted me to visit their offices and disrupt their workdays with my insistent questioning. Thanks to Betty and staff at the *Companion of St. Francis and St. Anthony*, jwcurry, who graciously allowed me to consult his personal library of little magazines, and Eldon Garnet, who tolerated my not-entirely-anticipated intrusion at the offices of *Impulse*. Thanks as well to Max Ryan of *War Cry*, Lesley McAllister of *Identity*, Fraser Sutherland of *Northern Journey*, Bernice Lever of *Waves*, Eugene McNamara of *University of Windsor Review*, Geoff Hancock of *Canadian Fiction Magazine*, Leslie Choyce of *Pottersfield Portfolio*, Fred Candelaria of *West Coast Review*, and Audrey McKim and Olive Sparling, who worked on *Onward*.

Many other people contributed in various ways to this bibliography. Norman Levine gave me permission to see his papers at York University; Bruce Meyer led me to dozens of fiction-carrying little magazines; Ross Leckie let me see – and own – a complete run of the *Montreal Writers' Forum*; and Crad Kilodney kindly sold me a number of his story collections.

The actual gathering of data, then, required the assistance of so many writers, editors, librarians, and others associated with the Canadian short story that I cannot name them all. On the other hand, transforming masses of notes and countless file cards into a book required the help of others whose expertise – and patience – deserve special mention. Thanks to Robert Lecker for inviting me into the ECW Press fold; Jack David for putting all of the Press's facilities at my disposal; and Paul Davies at ECW Production Services for his hard work in guiding me through the procedures for turning my scribbles into computerese, and otherwise introducing me to the world of DOS, diskettes, and databases. Thanks, too, to Gord Ripley of Reference Press for his efforts in refining and tailoring his database programme to our needs.

Finally, and above all, I must thank the Social Sciences and Humanities Research Council of Canada for showing faith in what one adjudication committee member rightly called "an (almost) unpublished junior scholar." The Council took some risk in funding this project; I only hope that I have justified their faith in me. In any case, it goes without saying that this bibliography would not have been possible without the Council's support.

Introduction

This bibliography, the culmination of about four years' research, is a nearly complete record of English-Canadian short stories first published during the period 1950-1983. The main section of the work [Part II, *Author Index*] contains a total of 19,597 citations, representing the appearances of 14,314 short stories in 1,308 different periodicals, anthologies, and radio productions, as well as 391 author collections published in monograph form. These stories and collections represent the efforts of 4,966 different authors. This number includes work published under names known to be pseudonyms, but excludes works published pseudonymously by known authors (H. Gordon Green, for example, signed his work with 35 different names during his career).

History

In 1982 I began work on my doctoral dissertation, a study of the Canadian short story covering the period 1950 to 1980. To do the kind of study I wanted, I needed a bibliography of Canadian stories initially published during the period. I considered radio broadcasting to be a form of publishing; indeed, many stories that appeared in print were first read on programmes like the CBC's "Anthology."

In my naïveté, I believed that compiling such a bibliography involved little more than taking the listings under "Short Stories" in the annual *Canadian Periodical Index* compilations, and rearranging them by author. I assumed, quite foolishly, that CPI indexed every important Canadian periodical during the period. It was only after producing this rather sparse bibliography that I realized how inadequate CPI would be for my purposes. While it indexed some little magazines in their entirety (e.g. *Fiddlehead* and *Alphabet*), it only began indexing others in the late 1970s (e.g. *Canadian Fiction Magazine, Journal of Canadian Fiction, West Coast Review*, and *Quarry*), and completely ignored the vast majority of fiction-carrying little magazines (e.g. *Malahat Review, Antigonish Review*, and *Prism International*).[1] I did not expect to see very small periodicals like *Alchemist* and *Tide* in CPI, but was surprised to find that even large-circulation magazines like *Liberty, Canadian Home Journal*, and the *Star Weekly* were not indexed at all, and *Chatelaine* was indexed only as of 1969.

I had no choice but to index the stories in the neglected periodicals myself, and began compiling what became the core of the present bibliography. At the same time I collected information on story collections (i.e. books containing stories by single authors), anthologies that published new stories, and some stories by Canadians appearing in foreign books and periodicals. I limited my research on radio broadcasts to the programme "Anthology"; Robert Weaver kindly allowed me to consult the programme's files, which indicated the genre as well as the title of almost every work broadcast each week.

Actually, the *Canadian Periodicals Index*'s general-interest coverage proved to have advantages as well as disadvantages for my bibliography. CPI cited short stories in periodicals where one might not think to find them: *Beaver, Continuous Learning*, and *Canadian Banker*, to name a few. It also cited stories that were published in unusual ways; the Canadian Imperial Bank of Commerce, for example, took it upon itself to publish Canadian short stories in magazines like *Maclean's*, and since these were in the form of advertisements rather than editorial material the stories were not listed in the magazine's table of contents. Despite the shortcomings of CPI, then, the present bibliography owes a great deal to the index's listings.

As I collected my list of authors and their works I ran into

---

1 [Predictably, some of these magazines were indexed by foreign periodical indexes, especially the *American Humanities Index*.]

one major problem: determining whether the writers I found in Canadian periodicals were indeed Canadian. Little magazines usually publish "notes on contributors" that provide much useful information, but the large-circulation magazines of the 1950s and 1960s seldom furnished any sort of biographical data on the authors they published. I decided on the following principles to deal with authors for whom I had no information:

1. If the author appeared in a Canadian little magazine, he or she would be considered Canadian unless the "notes on contributors" indicated otherwise. This rule applied as well to anthologies and the programme "Anthology."

2. If the author appeared in a nationalistic large-circulation magazine like the *Canadian Forum*, he or she would be considered Canadian unless, again, there was information to the contrary.

3. If the author appeared in a large- or small-circulation magazine that published primarily foreign authors – e.g. the *Star Weekly*, *Limbo*, and the *Canadian Home Journal* – he or she would be considered foreign unless specifically identified as Canadian. Magazines of the 1950s made a point of touting the nationality of a Canadian author, since they published so few.

Authors were added to or subtracted from my list according to whatever information I could glean from biographical guides like the invaluable *Contemporary Authors* and, of course, reference books on Canadian literature.

I derived my list of periodicals to be indexed partly from my own knowledge of the field, partly by scanning the shelves of the University of Toronto's Robarts Library, and partly from information supplied by Bruce Meyer, a fellow graduate student who had some familiarity with the little-magazine publishing scene. I usually had little difficulty finding the periodicals I wanted at the Thomas Fisher Rare Book Library, which has had a policy since the 1970s of collecting every Canadian little magazine about which it learned. Unfortunately, for these reasons and others to be discussed later, the bibliography developed a distinct Ontario bias.

After completing my thesis, I applied to the Canadian Studies – Research Tools programme of the Social Sciences and Humanities Research Council of Canada for a grant to expand and update the bibliography. I reasoned that 1983 would be the latest year for which material would be easily obtainable by the time the grant period was over. I was awarded a one-year grant in 1984; included in the total was a travel allowance for a trip to Ottawa to consult the holdings of the National Library.

Methodology

I decided to take three approaches to the problem of gathering data for the bibliography:

1. Indexing Canadian periodicals and books not previously covered, including those from the 1950-1980 period I had not seen as well as those published from 1981-1983. I also extended my coverage to include anthology reprints of previously published stories;

2. Surveying Canadian short-story writers by letter, phone, personal contact, and notices in writers' magazines and newsletters soliciting lists of their short-story publications. I asked that each list supply as much bibliographical information on the publications as possible, in case I was unable to find the publications themselves, and be accompanied by two pieces of biographical information on the author: citizenship status and year of birth;

3. Consulting available bibliographical sources, including foreign indexes and bibliographies of the works of individual authors.

I attempted to locate every Canadian periodical and anthology published during the period that contained short stories written by Canadians. I decided to index university student magazines and anthologies as well, since students at that level are adults (see "Definitions" below); incidentally, many well-known authors published their first stories in such places. My main difficulty was uncovering the titles of Canadian magazines published during the period. I used the available guides, including *The Canadian Writer's Market* and *The Directory of Little Magazines and Small Presses*, looking for magazines large and small that published fiction.

I quickly found, however, that there are simply no adequate guides to Canadian magazines and where they are held. The best way to approach the problem, then, was to go to repositories known to hold large collections of Canadian magazines and consult their card catalogues. Fortunately, Toronto has numerous well-stocked libraries, but of course my geographical limitations only served to reinforce the bibliography's Ontario bias. Following are the libraries I used extensively:

Robarts Library, University of Toronto
Thomas Fisher Rare Book Library, University of
    Toronto
Metro Central Library, Toronto
Canadiana Collection, Fairview Library, North York
United Church of Canada Archives, Emmanuel College,
    University of Toronto
Salvation Army Library, Heritage Centre, Toronto
Spaced-Out Library, Toronto
Scott Library, York University, North York
National Library, Ottawa

In most cases, I asked to see every Canadian periodical held by each library that seemed likely to contain fiction. At the National Library, I looked only at those periodicals which (a) I knew contained fiction, and (b) had been only partially available in Toronto.

Some important periodicals had to be omitted from my coverage because they were not available at these libraries, notably *Western Producer* and the *Winnipeg Free Press Weekly*, and of course libraries are extremely reluctant to make periodicals available through inter-library loan. My application for a second year's grant to travel to western centres to see these periodicals was denied. The absence of regional and student magazines from outside Ontario is a regrettable but unavoidable feature of the bibliography.

Anthologies and story collections proved to be somewhat easier to find. I located them by searching library bookshelves and consulting sources like *Canadian Books in Print* and writers' survey responses. I found some textbooks in the library of the Ontario Institute for Studies in Education, but by and large I concentrated on general-interest anthologies and included textbook appearances of short stories only if I could find the textbook easily or if the information appeared in a survey response or other bibliographic source.

I wished to include more citations to radio broadcasts, and particularly wanted to update my records on "Anthology." Unfortunately, communications problems with the staff who replaced Robert Weaver at the CBC after his retirement led to my being denied access to the programme's files. The result is that while my records up to the end of 1980 remain fairly complete, those from 1981 onwards depend entirely on information gleaned from other sources. Sometimes authors cited stories in their survey responses as having been broadcast on "Anthology" during the 1954-1980 period, even though, according to my notes, no such reference appears in the programme's files. In such cases I have appended a question mark to the programme's title to indicate that the story may well have been broadcast on a different programme. I wrote to CBC regional headquarters throughout eastern and western Canada asking for records of local programmes that broadcast short stories, and received good responses from Edmonton ("Alberta Anthology") and Vancouver ("Hornby Collection").

The most controversial approach I took was the survey I conducted of Canadian writers. I endeavoured to make my work on this project as widely known as possible among published authors, using every avenue I could think of to "spread the word." The writers I contacted directly were those whose addresses I knew from my doctoral research, or who could be reached through their publishers. I asked writers to fill out forms listing all their short-story publications; as for authors whose works are well-documented in published studies and bibliographies, I asked simply that they tell me about stories such sources might not list. The bibliographic and biographical information I received from lesser-known writers proved to be invaluable, and in general the responses led me to publications I would certainly have missed. If I could not locate the book or periodical cited in the survey response, I used the author's information as part of the final listing accompanied by an annotation to that effect. To date, I have received story lists from about 160.

Most of the writers who responded to my direct requests for information or my advertisements were glad to help and pleased that the bibliography was being compiled. Some, however, objected, believing that I was conducting the survey *instead* of indexing publications. In fact, the survey was designed to *supplement* the bulk of my research work; I was actually reluctant to conduct the survey because of the inevitable unreliability of some of the responses, but felt I had no other way of finding stories in very obscure Canadian and foreign books and periodicals (which in some cases are not available in Canadian libraries). The responses cited broadcasts on radio programmes for which archival records are either nonexistent or unobtainable. Also, the responses led to the identification of pseudonymous publications. Information like that can come only from the authors themselves. I might point out that while famous writers leave their personal papers with repositories, which make them available – in a limited way – to researchers, virtually all of the writers I surveyed had no such publicly accessible papers. In sum, the survey proved to be an indispensable tool in my research, and I was willing to undergo the occasional abusive correspondence in the interests of making my bibliography as comprehensive as possible.

Published Sources

A bibliography like this provides the researcher with quite special problems, because of its sheer size and the unavailability of many sources. A researcher compiling a bibliography of a single author's works, as mentioned above, can use his or her papers to find records of publications and even copies of the books and magazines in which the works appear. Fortunately, most well-known Canadian writers have had bibliographies of their works published, and apart from one notable exception I depended on these bibliographies for a sizeable amount of my data on these authors. A list of the bibliographies consulted is appended.

The exception was Norman Levine, whose papers are available at York University's Archives. Using his business correspondence and the copies of books and periodicals containing his stories that formed part of the collection, I was able to compile a reasonably complete record of his short-story publications. I cannot vouch for the completeness of the listings under other well-known authors' names, however; that will depend on the quality of the bibliographies already published.

For domestic publications, I continued to use CPI as my basic source, and confirmed all the publications listed under the "Short Stories" heading that I could. For foreign publications I relied on such indexes as the *Reader's Guide to Periodical Literature* and the *American Humanities Index*. If an index listed short stories under a separate heading, I scanned the list for works by Canadian authors; I therefore waited until I was finished the bulk of my research to begin this stage, so that I would know as many names of Canadian authors as possible. If an index did not list stories under a separate heading – the *Reader's Guide*, for instance, which began the practice only in the late 1970s – I made a list of Canadian authors known or believed to have published outside the country and scanned the index for their names. In all cases, I attempted to find the magazines themselves to confirm each citation; if that proved impossible, I used the information supplied by the index and provided an appropriate annotation to my citation.

Many indexes give very little information in their citations; they do not include initial articles in their titles (that is, "The ..." and "A ..."), nor do they cite all the pages on which a work appears if there are many interruptions. In those cases where I could not see the story itself, I have made suggestions as to the story's full title and used the symbol [+?] to indicate that the story may extend beyond the pages cited by the index.

Few of the magazines I looked at published their own cumulative indexes, although some of course provided annual indexes that proved more or less helpful. Only one periodical published an index that covered issues I was not able to see myself: *Skylark*. Unfortunately, as is often the case, the *Skylark* index cites issue numbers and first pages without giving the dates of the issues indexed.

There is one other source for domestic publications that deserves consideration here. In 1981 Judith Miller completed a thesis at York University entitled, "The Canadian Short Story Database: Checklists and Searches." The title promises much more than the thesis delivers. For one thing, in general Miller's database contains information on story volumes – story collections and anthologies – without citing the individual stories contained therein. More importantly, Miller handled the problem of what constituted a "Canadian short story" by not bothering to consider it at all. Her list of "short-story volumes" includes essay collections, history books, and, incredibly, novels. The database is not entirely useless; many story collections and anthologies that do not appear in standard sources like *Canadian Books in Print* do appear in her list. But the lack of editorial selectivity requires a potential user to exercise extreme caution. In any case, the present location of the database is unknown, so prospective users must consult the printouts that form the bulk of Miller's thesis.

For Canadian stories in foreign anthologies I depended on the *Short Story Index*, which until recently limited its coverage to books. SSI covers many anthologies of popular and genre fiction (e.g. science fiction and detective stories) – books where one might not ordinarily look for Canadian short stories. I scanned each volume of SSI for the period searching for Canadian authors; once again, I depended entirely on the index's information only if I could not find the works themselves.

Definitions

The most fundamental decision made by a bibliographer is choosing what to include and what to exclude. To explain my editorial choices I will define the terms in my title; within the delimiters outlined below, I have been as inclusive as possible.

English The bibliography includes only those short stories first written and published in English. It does not include translations into English of stories originally written in another language, even if English was the language of first publication. On the other hand, translations from English into other languages are included, so as to provide more complete publishing histories of those stories.

Canadian This was the most difficult of all editorial problems to solve. An author is considered Canadian if he or she is (a) a Canadian citizen; (b) a landed immigrant; or (c) a permanent or apparently permanent resident as of 1983. Canadian citizens living abroad are also included. Naturally, information on the citizenship status of most authors was simply unobtainable, so I used the criteria that served for the original bibliography (see above). The authors fall into three classes:

1. Those known to be Canadian, as defined above.

2. Those known to be residents of Canada at the time they published their work. Such authors are most likely to be Canadian, but some may be foreign.

3. Those for whom no biographical information is available but who appear in magazines that publish primarily, if not exclusively, Canadian authors.[1]

Student magazines posed a special problem. If I had information that a student short-story writer met the criteria for "Canadian" described above, there was no difficulty. Since information was usually not provided, however, I decided to cite all who published in such magazines as "unknown." Virtually all these writers, certainly, live in Canada, but it cannot be known whether they are Canadian citizens or students from elsewhere. Their status is thus more uncertain than other Canadian residents, so I thought it best to indicate that uncertainty.

On the other hand, anonymous publications are assumed to be by Canadians; no further information on these authors is likely to emerge, and often the pieces are written by editors, who generally qualify as "Canadians." Of course, this rule applies only to anonymous publications in Canadian periodicals that publish primarily or exclusively Canadians.

Brian Moore and Malcolm Lowry are two authors whose status as Canadians has long been open to debate. I decided to include them, in keeping with my desire to select inclusiveness over exclusiveness whenever such a choice had to be made. Anyone who feels they are not Canadian authors may simply ignore the citations.

Most of the information used in determining whether an author was Canadian came from the usual reference guides and notes on contributors, as well as author surveys. In addition, I surveyed some magazine editors asking them to provide whatever information they could on the authors they had published.

---

1 One respondent to my survey of magazine editors, Michael Fox of *Queen's Quarterly*, expressed the bizarre notion that a "Canadian short story" is one in which something Canadian appears, like a Canadian setting, regardless of the nationality of the author. A Canadian short story, he writes, is one "projecting a Canadian sensibility." The question begged is a very large one. Even Mr. Fox seems uncertain about just what constitutes a "Canadian sensibility"; he cites Robin Mathews' "Florentine Letourneau" as a story that projects it, but then admits that he cannot "articulate exactly how." In fact, to say a story is Canadian because it includes references to snow or Mounties is absurd, and reduces Canadian fiction to a small and artistically limited canon indeed.

As expected, the survey was largely futile, since most editors, especially those of little magazines, have neither the time nor the facilities to keep detailed files on their contributors. Nevertheless, a few, like Eugene McNamara of *University of Windsor Review*, Lesley Choyce of *Pottersfield Portfolio*, and Bernice Lever of *Waves*, returned well-marked survey forms, and Fraser Sutherland has compiled a biographical guide to the authors who appeared in *Northern Journey*.[1]

Short In most cases, I had little trouble deciding whether a story was of an acceptable length to be considered "short." I have included stories of one paragraph in length, and some of thirty pages or more. For longer works, rather than impose an arbitrary upper length limit, I relied on authorial and editorial classifications. Thus, stories described as "novelettes" (common among science-fiction writers) and "novellas" are not included. Jack Hodgins and Mavis Gallant regularly write very long "short stories" which I have included to avoid an unjustified exclusion. The number of stories that may exceed "short story" length, however that is defined, is too small to be of much significance.

Story Second only to the problem of the Canadianness of authors was the definition of "story." I defined a "short *story*" as a fictional prose narrative. A prose poem, monologue, or dialogue may be "fictional," but without some narrative movement it cannot be considered a story. Similarly, an anecdote such as the kind written by Gregory Clark may be a story, but it is not fictional (or at least not essentially fictional, despite the probable addition of "colour"). The story must be original, too; transcribed myths and legends are not included. Whenever I was uncertain about a work's genre I included it, but suggest in the annotation that it may not be a short story by indicating what it might be and using a question mark. I omit the question mark when the work could stand as a short story or a work of humour, satire, etc.

I have endeavoured to include all the subgenres of short fiction: "literary," romance, detective, science fiction, and so on. It proved impossible, however, to do a reasonably complete job

---

1 [Available in the magazine's files at York University Archives.]

with genres like crime stories and science fiction, both of which are the subjects of research by other bibliographers, notably Michael Richardson and John Bell. Readers interested in these genres will need to wait for the results of their work.

The bibliography is limited to adult short stories; children's and young adult fiction are not included. I define "adult" fiction as that written by and intended for people eighteen years of age and over. If a slightly younger author succeeds in publishing a story in a magazine designed for adults, however, I have included it unless it is specifically designated a children's story.

My goal has been inclusiveness; if I had any doubt about a story's qualifications as an "English-Canadian short story" I chose to include it and annotate it to express that doubt. In all probability I have mistakenly accepted stories that do not belong in the bibliography, but I preferred the risk of including too much to that of including too little.

Structure

The bibliography is designed to provide the user with access to the publishing history of any story when its author and/or title is known. The bibliography is in three main parts: *Lists Of Cited Publications*, *Author Index*, and *Title Index*.

The lists provide complete records and bibliographical information on the Canadian periodicals, anthologies, and indexes cited in the author index. The periodicals list shows which periodicals were seen in their entirety, which were seen only partially, and which were consulted only when specific stories were known to have appeared in them. Any periodical titles that are abbreviated in the author index are accompanied by their abbreviations. The anthology list gives full title, name(s) of editor(s), and publication data for each anthology cited, and the basis for this information if I did not see the anthology myself. The third list gives the full titles and abbreviations of the indexes cited. Appended to the lists is a set of notes on individual authors who posed special editorial problems, or who have had bibliographies of their works published that I have cited. If my information on a story comes from such a bibliography, I have annotated the story by citing the name(s) of the bibliography's compiler(s).

Following the lists is the main section, the author index. Authors appear alphabetically, of course. Under each author's name is, first, a list of his or her published story collections, including any short story published as a separate volume, then the individual stories follow; both lists are organized alphabetically by title. I have included only the first edition of each story collection unless two editions of equal importance were published by separate presses (see Audrey Thomas' *Ten Green Bottles*); paperback reprints are not included. If an individual story appeared more than once, its various periodical and book appearances are listed chronologically under the story's title.

The title index is designed to aid readers who know the title of a given work but not its author. The stories are thus listed alphabetically together with their authors, so that users are referred back to the author index for fuller information on the stories.

Citations

Each story citation is designed to give full publication data on every appearance, omitting superfluous information so that the citation may be kept as concise as possible without being obscure.

Author The author's name as listed in the citation is his or her full name, unless a shortened form is the one by which he or she is best known. A pseudonym is so noted, and the user is directed to the author's real name, unless – as is the case with Ann Copeland, for instance – the pseudonym is used for all or virtually all publications. The name is followed by the author's date(s), as these are known. After the date(s) appears information on the author's Canadianness: no symbol means that he or she is known to be Canadian, a "†" indicates that he or she is known to be a resident, and a "‡" indicates that no information is available.

Title The story's full title is given, although, as already mentioned, when the full title could not be determined a suggestion is made as to what might be missing. Any variant titles are noted. Sometimes, editors of large-circulation magazines introduced stories by incorporating the title into a sentence of their own composition, leaving the actual title ambiguous. I have tried to determine what is the real title and what is editorial addition by referring to the table of contents and internal evidence. If the story was published under a title different from the one originally supplied by the author, the published title is the one cited. The files of "Anthology" occasionally omit the title of a short story broadcast on the programme, referring only to the name of the story's author. In such cases I have depended upon information gleaned from other sources, especially survey responses, or simply said "[title(s) unknown]." If a story is published pseudonymously, the title is followed by the pseudonym used.

Publication The more obscure Canadian periodicals, and all foreign periodicals except *Saturday Evening Post*, are named in full, except for abbreviations like *Q* for Quarterly, *J* for Journal, and *R* for Review. If a foreign periodical is particularly obscure and its title provides no clue as to its country of origin, or if it shares a title with a Canadian periodical (e.g. *Descant*), an abbreviated form of the country of origin appears in brackets after the periodical's title. In the interests of conciseness, better-known Canadian periodicals are abbreviated, unless the title is so short (e.g. *Grain*) as to render abbreviation pointless. Books – both story collections and anthologies – are given short titles where appropriate.

Periodical numbering Following are the principles used in the citation of volume and issue numbers of periodicals:

Newspapers: No volume or issue numbers are given.
Monthlies: If a periodical was consistently monthly or bi-monthly during its history, only the volume number is given. If its frequency was inconsistent, both volume and issue numbers are given.
Quarterlies: If each issue was paginated separately, both volume and issue numbers are given. If the periodical had continuous pagination throughout the annual volume, only the volume number is given.
Annuals: Volume and/or issue numbers are provided.

Any periodical that numbers all of its issues consecutively is cited using "No." followed by the whole number. A periodical that uses both volume/issue and whole numbers is cited using both systems; thus, the relevant issue can be found regardless of how the periodical is bound and numbered by the library. A colon separates volume and issue numbers. For example:

3:1 *means* volume 3, issue number 1
3 No. 7 *means* volume 3, whole number 7
3:1 No. 7 *means* volume 3, issue number 1; whole number 7

Double issues are cited using a "/": e.g. 3:1/2 *means* volume 3, issues 1 and 2

Some religious periodicals, like *Our Family* and *Companion of St. Francis and St. Anthony*, were very inconsistently numbered. Users should therefore concentrate on the dates rather than the volume numbers of such magazines.

Date Day and full date are given for newspaper citations, full date for weeklies and monthlies. In the case of quarterlies, seasons are given preference over months. Only the year of publication is given for quarterlies which paginate throughout the annual volume, annual periodicals, and books; book years appear in parentheses. If an anthology title includes the year of publication (e.g. *New Canadian Writing* 1968) the date is omitted. For undated publications, I have either guessed at the date or depended upon the library's estimate, using a question mark to indicate the uncertainty. Publications that defy any estimate are cited using [n.d.] for "no date." If a periodical was dated but I was unable to determine the date, I have said "[date unknown]."

Pagination Only essential information about the pagination of stories appearing in periodicals is given. In popular magazines short stories are frequently illustrated; in such cases, if the illustration appears on a page devoid of text, that page is not cited. On the other hand, if any portion of the text or title appear on that page, it is cited, regardless of how small the portion is. Also, if the illustration acts as a one-page interruption of an otherwise continuous text, I saw no reason to exclude it and lengthen the citation unnecessarily. Full-page advertisements and other material that interrupt the text are never included in the pagination. Again, the symbol [+?] is used whenever a story may extend beyond the pages cited. Some foreign periodicals paginate material differently in different editions, so the citations will not conform exactly to the holdings of all libraries.

Annotation I have annotated a story if I was uncertain about its qualifications for inclusion, or if I did not see the story itself and depended upon another bibliographic source, such as an author's survey response, for the citation. Translators and language of translation are given in the annotation where applicable. If the piece may be an excerpt from a longer work of fiction, I have used the annotation "Excerpt?"; if I use the word without a question mark, it refers to an excerpt from a short story. The annotations have been kept to a minimum and are designed to be self-explanatory.

I have given individual citations only to those short stories which were published from 1950 onwards. Story collections and anthologies may contain works first published before that date, but such stories are not listed separately.

Conclusion

I have been referring to my project as an effort to compile a "complete" bibliography, knowing full well that that was an impossible task. I reasoned that by striving for completeness I would achieve the greatest possible comprehensiveness. The result has been a bibliography that contains surprising inclusions and disappointing omissions. It is certainly not designed to be a substitute for bibliographies of individual writers, which can supply researchers with much more detail on the publishing histories of individual short stories, particularly translations. What it can do is provide a reasonably full record of the canon of the Canadian short story during the period covered, directing readers to authors and works hitherto unknown.

NOTICE

My bibliographic work has not yet ended. I ask that authors write to me if I have omitted their stories, or made errors in spelling their names or the titles of their stories, or if they can provide biographical information on themselves or other authors. A bibliography of this size is bound to contain numerous errors which evade all efforts to correct them. I will therefore continue to accept additions or modifications to the bibliography, and publish a revised edition should the number of revisions warrant one.

List of Common Abbreviations

ABC · Australian Broadcasting Corporation
ABCMA · Annotated Bibliography of Canada's Major Authors
AHI · American Humanities Index
Atl · Atlantic
Aust · Australia
BBC · British Broadcasting Corporation
BC · British Columbia
CBC · Canadian Broadcasting Corporation
CPI · Canadian Periodical Index
CPLI · Catholic Periodical and Literature Index
Edm · Edmonton
Fri · Friday
Ger · Germany
Hal · Halifax
ILM · Index to Little Magazines: 1950-1967
INZP · Index to New Zealand Periodicals: 1966-1984
J · Journal
Lit · Literary
Mag · Magazine
Man · Manitoba
Mon · Monday
Mont · Montreal
Neth · Netherlands
Nfld · Newfoundland
N.Z. · New Zealand
NZBC · New Zealand Broadcasting Corporation
Ont · Ontario
OSSTF · Ontario Secondary School Teachers Federation
Ott · Ottawa
PPI · Popular Periodical Index
Pub · Publications
Q · Quarterly
RGPL · Reader's Guide to Periodical Literature
R · Review
Reg · Regina
S Afr · South Africa
SABC · South African Broadcasting Corporation

Sat · Saturday
Scot · Scotland
Sun · Sunday
SSI · Short Story Index
SWG · Saskatchewan Writers' Guild
Switz · Switzerland
Tor · Toronto
Thu · Thursday
Tue · Tuesday
UC · University College
UCC · United Church of Canada
U.K. · United Kingdom
Univ · University
U.S. · United States
Van · Vancouver
Wed · Wednesday
Winn · Winnipeg
Yugo · Yugoslavia

List of Periodical Name Abbreviations

Acta Vic · Acta Victoriana
Alch · The Alchemist
Annals · Annals of Good Ste. Anne
Antig R · Antigonish Review
Art & Lit R · Art & Literary Review
Arts Man · Arts Manitoba
Atl Guardian · Atlantic Guardian
Atl Insight · Atlantic Insight
BC Lib Q · B.C. Library Quarterly
Br Out · Branching Out
BC Monthly · British Columbia Monthly
Can J Chron R · Canadian Jewish Chronicle Review
CF · Canadian Forum
CFM · Canadian Fiction Magazine
CHJ · Canadian Home Journal
CJO · Canadian Jewish Outlook
Can Lit R · The Canadian Literary Review
Can Messenger · Canadian Messenger of the Sacred Heart
Can R · Canadian Review
CSSM · Canadian Short Story Magazine
Cap R · Capilano Review
Chat · Chatelaine
Chel J · Chelsea Journal
Cop Toad · Copper Toadstool
CG · Country Guide
CCWQ · Cross-Canada Writers' Quarterly
Dal R · Dalhousie Review
FH · Family Herald and Weekly Star
Fid · Fiddlehead
Gas Rain · Gasoline Rainbow
Geo Str Writing · Georgia Straight Writing Supplement
Gram · The Grammateion
Har · Harrowsmith
Ice Can · The Icelandic Canadian
Imp · Impulse
Imp Oil R · Imperial Oil Review
JCF · Journal of Canadian Fiction

JD · Jewish Dialog
Laom R · Laomedon Review
Lib · Liberty
Lit R · The Literary Review
Lit Store News · The Literary Storefront Newsletter
MM · Maclean's Magazine
Mal R · Malahat Review
Mar Adv · Maritime Advocate and Busy East
McGill Lit J · McGill Literary Journal
Miss Chat · Miss Chatelaine
Mont · The Montrealer
Mont R · Montreal Review
Moose R · Moosehead Review
NF · New Frontiers
Nfld Q · Newfoundland Quarterly
NHM · National Home Monthly
NJ · Northern Journey
NMFG · No Money from the Government
NR · Northern Review
NwJ · Northward Journal
Ont Lib R · Ontario Library Review
Ont R · Ontario Review
OPT · Only Paper Today/OPT [+]
Per · Periodics
Pier Spr · Pierian Spring
Pot Port · The Pottersfield Portfolio
Prairie J of Can Lit · The Prairie Journal of Canadian Literature
Pres Record · The Presbyterian Record
Pulp · 3¢ Pulp [+]
QQ · Queen's Quarterly
Rain Chr · Raincoast Chronicles
Read Ch · Reader's Choice
Read Dig · Reader's Digest
Repos · Seven Persons Repository
Room · Room of One's Own
Scar Fair · Scarborough Fair
SN · Saturday Night
Squatch J · Squatchberry Journal
SW · Star Weekly
Tam R · Tamarack Review
TL · Toronto Life
Tor S Asian R · The Toronto South Asian Review
TUR · Trinity University Review
UC Gargoyle · The University College Gargoyle
UC Observer · United Church Observer
UCR · University College Review
Uk Can · The Ukrainian Canadian
UTR · University of Toronto Review

UWR · University of Windsor Review
Was R · Wascana Review
WCR · West Coast Review
WWR · White Wall Review

Part 1: Lists of Cited Publicatic

Canadian Periodicals

INTRODUCTION

Listed here are the Canadian periodicals cited in the bibliography. In most cases, I was able to see the periodicals myself, although frequently I was unable to ascertain whether I saw all the issues published. If I did see the entire run of a periodical for the period 1950-1983. I have attached no annotation to the periodical's title. If I know that I saw only some of the issues, I have used a "+" sign to indicate that fact. "+?" denotes uncertainty about whether I saw the periodical's full run; my sense in such cases is that I did, but, as usually happens with little magazines, there was never any formal announcement of suspension of publication.

If I depended in whole or in part on the "Short Stories" listings of the *Canadian Periodical Index* for a periodical's fictional contents, I have put the initials CPI after its title. My dependence on CPI for such periodicals ranged from minimal to complete, depending on the nature of the periodical. Sometimes, the only information I had came from authors' survey responses; for each such periodical I have followed the title with "survey." Similarly, if my information came solely from indexes, author bibliographies, or other published sources apart from CPI, I have noted the fact using the word "indexes."

The periodicals are listed alphabetically by the first title under which they were published. Subsequent titles, if any, appeared separated by a " / ". If an abbreviation has been used, the abbreviation appears beside the periodical's title although if the abbreviation consists simply of replacing *Journal* with *J*, *Review* with *R*, etc., I saw no reason to note that. Also, all

periodicals beginning with the word Canadian and not otherwise abbreviated are cited using "Can" as a short form of that word.

Sometimes, little magazines with the same title were published in different cities. Where this was the case I have supplied the name of the city of publication after the periodical's title here and (in abbreviated form) in the bibliography itself. On the other hand, if one periodical was much better-known than its obscure namesake, I have given the city of the latter only. I have also provided the place of publication for any periodical which shares the name of a well-known magazine not cited in the bibliography.

10:47 Magazine [+]
2 O'Clock Rap [+?]
20 Cents Magazine [+]
3¢ Pulp [+] · *Pulp*
Abegweit Review [+?]
Acanthus
Acta Victoriana · *Acta Vic*
The Adder [+?]
Afterthought [+?]
Aircraft [+ - CPI]
The Alchemist · *Alch*
Alive
Alpha [+?]
Alphabet [CPI]
Alternative to Alienation [+?]
Amaranth [+]
Amethyst
Anglican Outlook/Christian Outlook
Annals of Good Ste. Anne [survey] · *Annals*
Anthol [+?]
Anthos *see* Review Ottawa
Antigonish Review · *Antig R*
The Ant's Forefoot [+?]
Applegarth's Folly
Art & Literary Review [+?] · *Art & Lit R*
Arts Manitoba · *Arts Man*
ArtsAtlantic

Atlantic Advocate *see* Atlantic Guardian
Atlantic Guardian [+?] · *Atl Guardian*
Atlantic Guardian/Atlantic Advocate · *Atl Guardian/AA* [+? - CPI]
Atlantic Insight [CPI] · *Atl Insight*
Atlantis
Atropos [+?]
Auguries [+?]
Avenue [+]
Axiom
B.C. Library Quarterly [+ - CPI] · *BC Lib Q*
Bakka Magazine [+]
ballsout [+?]
Beaver [CPI]
Beaver Bites [+]
Beetle [+?]
Better Boating [+]
Beyond the Fields We Know
The Bibliofantasiac [survey]
Black Cat Mystery Magazine
Black Moss [+]
Black Walnut [+]
blewointmentpress [+]
Blind Windows
Blow Up [+]
Blue Buffalo
Bluenose Magazine [+?]
Body Politic [+?]
Boreal/Northward Journal · Nw J
Borealis
Branching Out · *Br Out*
British Columbia Monthly · *BC Monthly*
Bulletin de l'association canadienne des humanités [survey]
C.S.P. World News [survey]
Caledonian
Calgary Magazine
Campus Canada [+?]
The Camrose Review
Canada Month [+]
Canadan Viesti
Canadian Audubon [CPI]
Canadian Banker
Canadian Boating [+]

Canadian Boy [survey]

Canadian Business [CPI]

Canadian Commentator

Canadian Ethnic Studies [CPI]

Canadian Fandom [indexed by John Robert Colombo (available only at Spaced-Out Library)]

Canadian Fiction Magazine · *CFM*

Canadian Forum [CPI] · *CF*

Canadian Golden West *see* Golden West

Canadian Holmes [+]

Canadian Home Journal · *CHJ*

The Canadian Home Leaguer

The Canadian Horse [+]

Canadian Jewish Chronicle Review · *Can J Chron R*

The Canadian Jewish News [survey]

Canadian Jewish Outlook · *CJO*

Canadian Labour [CPI]

Canadian Landrace Magazine [survey]

Canadian Lawyer

Canadian Life

Canadian Lifetime Magazine *see* Lifetime Magazine

The Canadian Literary Review [+?] · *Can Lit R*

Canadian Messenger of the Sacred Heart · *Can Messenger*

Canadian National Railways Magazine

Canadian Nature [CPI]

Canadian Review · *Can R*

Canadian Short Story Magazine · *[CSSM]*

Canadian Skater [+]

Canadian Welfare [CPI]

Canadian Wings [+]

Canadian Writing [+?]

The Capilano Review · *Cap R*

Catalyst

Catalyst [Brantford] [+?]

The Cataraqui Review [+?]

The Challenge [+]

Charasee Press

Chatelaine · *Chat*

Chelsea Journal · *Chel J*

Chiaroscuro [+]

Chimo!

The Christian Home [+?]

Christian Outlook *see* Anglican Outlook

City Magazine [+]

Co Tinneh/Coutanie/Cottonahou [+?]

Communicator [+]

Companion of St. Francis and St. Anthony [+] · Companion

The Compass

Concept [University of British Columbia - +]

Connexion [+?]

Contact [Canadian Writers' Guild - +]

Contempo [+]

Continuous Learning [CPI]

Copper Toadstool · *Cop Toad*

Copperfield

Cottonahou *see* Co Tinneh

Country Guide · *CG*

Coutanie *see* Co Tinneh

Creative Campus [+]

The Crier [+?]

Cross-Canada Writers' Quarterly *see* New Writers' News

The Crossley Annual [+?]

Crowsnest [survey]

Cyclic [+?]

Da Vinci [+?]

Daily Planet [+]

Dalhousie Review [CPI] · *Dal R*

Dandelion · *Dand*

Dark Fantasy [+]

The Deaf Canadian Magazine

Delta

Descant · *Des*

Dime Bag [+?]

Dimensions [+]

Direction [York University - +?]

Diversions [+?]

DNA Tape Magazine [+]

Dragonbane

Dragonfields

Dreamweaver [+?]

Duel [+?]

Early Evening Pieces [+?]

Earth and You [+]

Echo/O [Toronto - +?]

Echo [Vancouver]

Echoes
Eclipse [+?]
Edge
The Edmonton Culture Vulture [+?]
Edmonton Journal [+]
Edmonton Magazine [+?]
Either/Or [+?]
Elbow Drums [+]
Elite [+]
Emeritus [+?]
English Quarterly
Entropy Negative [+]
Ethos
Evening Telegram [survey]
event
Evidence
Exchange [+?]
Exchange [United Church of Canada - +]
Exile
Existère [+]
The Family Herald and Weekly Star · *FH*
Fantarama [+?]
The Far Point
La Favilla [+]
Fiddlehead [CPI] · *Fid*
The Fifth Page [+]
File [+?]
Fireflower [+]
Fireweed
The First Encounter
Flare *see* Miss Chatelaine
Floorboards [+?]
Folio [University of Western Ontario - +]
Folklore [survey]
Forge [+?]
Form [+?]
Forum [Ontario Secondary School Teachers Federation]
Freelance [+]
From 231 [+?]
From an Island *see* Introductions from an Island
The Front/It Needs to Be Said [+?]
Gaillardia [+]

Gambit [+?]

Gamut

Ganglia [+]

Gasoline Rainbow [+?] · *Gas Rain*

Gay Tide [+?]

Generation [+]

Georgia Straight [survey]

Georgia Straight Writing Supplement/Georgia Writing Straight Writing [+?] · *Geo Str Writing*

Germination

Giant Canadian Poetry Annual [+?]

Goblin

Golden West/My Golden West/Canadian Golden West [+?]

Grain

The Grammateion · *Gram*

Green's Magazine

grOnk [+]

Grub [+]

Gut [+?]

The Halcyon [+]

Hamilton Magazine

Harbinger

Harrowsmith [CPI] · *Har*

Harvest

Healthsharing

Heartland Northern Digest [+?]

Herizons

Hibiscus Dawn [+?]

Humanist in Canada

Hyperbole

Hysteria

The Icelandic Canadian · *Ice Can*

Ichor

Identity [series of literary volumes (i.e. story collections, novels, etc.)]

Image Nation [+]

Images [+]

Images About Manitoba

Imago

Imperial Oil Review [CPI] · *Imp Oil R*

Impulse · *Imp*

In Store [+?]

Industrial Sabotage [+?]

Ingluvin

Inland Sea [survey]
Inner Space
Inprint [+?]
Inscape [+?]
Inside [+?]
Intercourse
Interface [+]
Interior Voice [+]
Intervales [+?]
Introductions from an Island/From an Island [+?]
Iron/Iron II [+]
Is [+?]
It Needs to Be Said *see* The Front
Jabberwocky [+?]
Jargon [+]
Jaw Breaker [+?]
Jewish Dialog · *JD*
Journal of Canadian Fiction · *JCF*
Journal of Our Time [+?]
Jubilee [+?]
Kaleidoscope [+]
Karaki
Katharsis [+?]
Kensington Magazine [+?]
Laomedon Review · *Laom R*
Legion/Legionary [+]
Leisureways [survey]
Liberté [CPI]
Liberty · *Lib*
Lifetime Magazine/Canadian Lifetime Magazine [+?]
Light [indexed by John Robert Colombo in *Years of Light* (see Leslie A. Crouch in *Notes on Individual Authors*)]
Like It Is [+]
Limbo [+?]
Link [+]
Liontayles [+?]
The Literary Review [+?] · *Lit R*
The Literary Storefront Newsletter [+?] · *Lit Store News*
The Living Message [+]
Lodgistiks [+?]
Loomings
Los [+?]
The Lunatic Gazette [+]

Maclean's Magazine [CPI] · *MM*
Magenta Frog [+?]
Makar [+?]
Makara
The Malahat Review · *Mal R*
Mamashee *see* Quest for a Common Denominator
Mandala [+]
March [+?]
Maritime Advocate and Busy East [+] · *Mar Adv*
Marooned [+?]
The Marxist Quarterly/Horizons
Masada [+]
Matrix
Mayfair [+?]
McGill Literary Journal [+?] · *McGill Lit J*
Media [+?]
Melmoth Vancouver/Vancouver Surrealist Newsletter [survey]
The Mennonite [survey]
Mennonite Brethern Herald [survey]
Migdal [+]
Mir [+?]
Miss Chatelaine/Flare · *Miss Chat*
Mission Magazine
Missionary Monthly
The Mitre/New Mitre [+]
Modicum [+]
Montreal Poems [+]
Montreal Review [+?] · *Mont R*
Montreal Writers' Forum
The Montrealer [+ - CPI] · *Mont*
Moongoose [+?]
Moosehead Review · *Moose R*
Mosaic [indexes]
Motion [+?]
Mouth [+?]
Mudpie [+]
Muse [+]
Musicworks [+]
Muskeg Review [+]
My Golden West *see* Golden West
The Mysterious East
National Home Monthly · *NHM*

Native People [CPI]
Nebula
New Breed [+]
New Frontiers · *NF*
New Literature and Ideology
New Mitre *see* The Mitre
The New Quarterly [+?]
New Thursday
New Writers' News/Cross-Canada Writers' Quarterly [+] · CCWQ
NeWest Review
Newfoundland Quarterly [CPI] · *Nfld Q*
Newfoundland Stories and Ballads [indexes]
Next Exit
Nightwinds [+]
Nimbus [+?]
NMFG - No Money from the Government [+]
North [+ - CPI]
Northern Journey · *NJ*
Northern Mosaic [+?]
Northern Review · *NR*
Northward Journal *see* Boreal
Nova Canada [+?]
Nowhere from Nowhere [+?]
O: Publication of the Arts *see* Echo [Toronto]
Ode [+?]
Old Nun Magazine [+?]
On the Bias
Onion [+?]
Only Paper Today/OPT [+] · *OPT*
Ontario Library Review [CPI] · *Ont Lib R*
Ontario Review · *Ont R*
Onward/Rapport
OPT *see* Only Paper Today
Origins
Orion
Ostara [+?]
Other Voices
Otherside [+?]
Our Family [+]
Our Times [+]
Outdoor Canada [+ - CPI]
The Outlook [+]

Oyster in the Ooze [+?]
Pacific Nation [+?]
Pacific Profile
The Panic Button [+]
Parallel
Parole [+?]
The Patriot [University of Alberta - survey]
The Pedestal [+?]
Pemmican Journal [+?]
Performing Arts [CPI]
Periodics · *Per*
Pierian Spring · *Pier Spr*
Pinch [+?]
Pluck [+?]
pm Magazine
Poesis - Anything on Rye [+]
Poetry WLU [+]
Pom Seed [+?]
Pop See Cul [+]
Popular Illusion [+?]
Porcepic
Portico [+?]
Potboiler Magazine
Potlatch [+?]
The Pottersfield Portfolio · *Pot Port*
Prairie Fire *see* Writers' News Manitoba
The Prairie Journal of Canadian Literature [+?] · *Prairie J of Can Lit*
The Presbyterian Record [+] · *Pres Record*
Prism International
Prism [Montreal - +?]
Probe [+]
The Probe [University of Toronto - +]
The Probe [University of Saskatchewan - survey]
Public Affairs [CPI]
Qolus [+?]
Quarry [+]
Queen's Quarterly [CPI] · *QQ*
Quest [CPI]
Quest for a Common Denominator/Mamashee · *Mam*
Quote Unquote [+?]
Radical Reviewer [+?]
Raincoast Chronicles [+?] · *Rain Chr*

Rampike [+?]
Random [+?]
Rapport *see* Onward
Raven [University of British Columbia - +?]
Raven [+?]
Re. Visions [+?]
Reader's Choice · *Read Ch*
Reader's Digest [CPI] · *Read Dig*
Reflections [+?]
Region [+]
Release [+?]
Report on Farming *see* Winnipeg Free Press Weekly
Return [+?]
Review Ottawa/Anthos [+?]
Revue 2/Revuenotes [+?]
Rikka [+?]
The Rivers Bend Review [+]
Rod & Gun [CPI]
Room of One's Own · *Room*
RPM [+?]
Rubicon
Rude [+]
Rune
Rustler [+]
Saelala [+]
Salt [+?]
Samisdat [+]
Sand Patterns [+?]
Sarnia Gazette [survey]
Saturday Night [CPI] · *SN*
Satyrday *see* Yorkville Yawn
Scan [+?]
Scarborough Fair · *Scar Fair*
Scarlet and Gold [+?]
Scrivener [+?]
Scruncheons [+?]
Seagull [+?]
Seasons [CPI]
Scraph [+]
Seven [+?]
Seven Persons Repository · *Repos*
The Sheet [+?]

Sift [+?]
Simcoe Review [+?]
Skylark [+]
Spear [+]
Split Level [+?]
Squatchberry Journal [+?] · *Squatch J*
Star Weekly · *SW*
Stardust [+?]
Stet [+]
Strange Faeces (No. 17, All-Canadian issue)
The Stump [+]
Take One [CPI]
Talon [+?]
Tamarack Review [CPI] · *Tam R*
Targya [+?]
Tawow [CPI]
This Magazine [CPI]
This - Media Free Times [+]
Thornhill Month [+]
Thumbprints [+?]
TickleAce
Tide [+?]
Tish
Tit Magazine [+]
Titmouse Review
Toronto Globe and Mail [survey]
Toronto Life [CPI] · *TL*
The Toronto South Asian Review · *Tor S Asian R*
The Toronto Star - Sunday Star Short Story Contest
Touchstone [+?]
The Towncrier Literary Magazine [+]
Toybox
Trial [+]
Tridentine [+]
Trinity University Review · *TUR*
True North/Down Under
Trup [+?]
Twelfth Key [+?]
Twelve Mile Creek [+]
The Twig [+?]
Tyro [+?]
The Ukrainian Canadian [+] · *Uk Can*

The Uncertified Human/The Human
Undergrad [+]
United Church Observer [+] · *UC Observer*
The University College Gargoyle [+] · *UC Gargoyle*
University College Review · *UCR*
University of Alberta Patriot *see* The Patriot
University of Manitoba Alumni Journal [survey]
University of Toronto Review · *UTR*
University of Windsor Review · *UWR*
Vagabond [+?]
Vancouver Magazine [+]
Vancouver Streets [+?]
Vancouver Surrealist Newsletter *see* Melmoth Vancouver
Vancouver Writers' Free Press - Revue · *VWFP/Revue*
Vane [+]
Vanguard [+]
The Varsity/Varsity Literary Issue [+]
Ventilator [+]
Versus [+?]
La Vie en Rose [+]
View from the Silver Bridge [+?]
Viewpoints
Volume 63 [+?]
War Cry [+]
Wascana Review · *Was R*
Waterloo Review [CPI]
Waves
Wee Giant [+?]
Weekend [CPI]
West Coast Review · *WCR*
Western People [+] · *West People*
Western Producer [+] · *West Producer*
White Wall Review · *WWR*
Why Magazine [+?]
Windows [+?]
The Womb [+?]
Word Loom [+?]
Wordjock [+]
Wot [+?]
Writ
Writers News Manitoba/Prairie Fire
Writing

Yes [+?]
York Literary Series [+?]
Yorkville Yawn/Saturday [+]
Zest

Anthology Series

INTRODUCTION

Anthology series fall somewhere between periodicals and books; they usually appear annually, and contain either new stories or reprints. I have listed below the anthology series I consulted - both Canadian and foreign - along with details of which issues I indexed or learned about through survey responses. As in the periodicals list, those series that may continue beyond the dates indexed are annotated using the symbol "+?." Arabic numerals have been substituted for Roman ones to maintain consistency.

Note: Short Story Index covered many of these series fully, so the bibliography contains partial data on Canadian stories appearing in issues I did not see.

Alberta Speaks/Alberta Writers Speak. Ed. Beatrice Clink. Words Unlimited Writers Groups. [1957], 1960, 1964, 1967, 1969, [+?]

Alberta Writers Speak see *Alberta Speaks.*

American Review see *New American Review.*

Anthology of Best Short Short Stories. New York: Frederick Fell. 7 (1959) [survey].

Aurora: New Canadian Writing. Ed. Morris Wolfe. Toronto: Doubleday. 1978-1980.

Best American Short Stories. Ed. Martha Foley et al. Boston: Houghton Mifflin. 1950-1983.

The Best from Galaxy. Various editors. New York: Ace. 4 (1976).

Best Detective Stories of the Year. Ed. Edward D. Hoch. New York: Elsevier-Dutton. 1981.

Best Little Magazine Fiction. Ed. Curt Johnson. New York: New York Univ Press. 1971.

Canadian Children's Annual. Ed. Robert F. Nielson. Hamilton: Potlatch. 1978 [survey].

Canadian Short Fiction Anthology. Various editors. Vancouver: Intermedia Press. [1] (1976), 2 (1982).

Canadian Short Stories. Ed. Robert Weaver. Toronto: Oxford Univ. Press. [First Series] (1960), Second Series (1968), Third Series (1978).

Chrysalis. Ed. Roy Torgeson [?]. New York: Doubleday. 1 [date unknown] [survey]. 10 (1983).

HEXA. Antwerp: Exa. 8 (1982) [survey].

Impressions. Ed. John Metcalf. Ottawa: Oberon Press. First (1980), Second (1981), Third (1982).

London Magazine Stories. London: London Magazine Editions. 1 (1969)-6 (1974); 8 (1976)-11 (1979). [+?]

Nebula Award Stories. Ed. Joe Haldeman. New York: Holt, Rinehart & Winston. 17 (1983).

Nebula Awards. Ed. Robert Silverberg. New York: Arbor House. 18 (1983).

New American Review/American Review. New York/Toronto: New American Library. 1 (1967)-10 (1970); 12 (1971)-20 (Apr 1974); 23 (Oct 1975)-26 (27 Nov 1975).

New Canadian Stories/Best Canadian Stories. Various editors. Ottawa: Oberon Press. 1972-1983.

New Campus Writing. Ed. Nolan Miller & Judson Jerome [?]. New York: Grove. 3 (1959) [survey].

New Canadian Writing. Toronto: Clarke Irwin. 1968, 1969.

New Stories. Various editors. London: Hutchison/British Arts Council. 1 (1976); 3 (1978), 4 (1979). [+?]

New World Writing. New York: New American Library. 1 (1952)-5 (1954). [+?]

New Writings in SF. Ed. John Carnell. London: Dennis Dobson/Corgi. 11 (1968); 20 (1972), 21 (1972; 1973). [+] New York: Bantam. 8 (1971).

Northern Ontario Anthology. Ed. Fred Manson. Cobalt: Highway Book Shop. 1 (1977), 2 (1978). [+?]

Outset. Ed. Abraham Ram. Montreal: Sir George Williams Univ. Press. 1973, 1974.

Pick of Today's Short Stories. Ed. John Pudney. London: Putnam. 6 (1955); 8 (1957), 9 (1958); 13 (1962).

Prize Stories of 19--: The O'Henry Awards. Various editors. New York: Doubleday. 1950; 1954; 1956-1958; 1960; 1962; 1964; 1966-1975; 1977; 1979-1983.

The Pushcart Prize: Best of the Small Presses. Ed. Bill Henderson. New York: Pushcart Press. 2 (1977)-5 (1980).

Rubaboo. Toronto: Gage. 2 (1963); 4 (1965) [survey].

Saskatachewan Writing. Regina: Saskatchewan Arts Board. 1 (1960), 2 (1963). [3?] (1965) [survey].

Shadows. Ed. Charles L. Grant. New York: Doubleday. 4 (1981).

Short Story & Poetry Yearbook. [Publication data unknown]. 1969 [survey].

Smoke Signals: A Collection of Prize-Winning Entries from the Saskatchewan Writers' Guild Literary Competition. Seven Persons: Repository Press. 1 (1974?) 2 [date unknown], 3 (1978), 4 [date unknown] - based on Saskatchewan Writers' Guild survey response.

The Story So Far. Various editors. Toronto: Coach House Press. 1 (1971)-5 (1978) (4 - The Story So Four).

Universe. Ed. Terry Carr. New York: Doubleday. 11 (1981).

Winter's Tales. Ed. A. D. Maclean. London: Macmillan. 6 (1960)-22 (1976).

Words from Inside Ed. David Helwig. n.p.: n.p. 1971- 1973+?

Writing Group Publications. Toronto: Univ. of Toronto Department of Education. 1970-1971, 1971-1972. Various anthologies: In Complete (1970-1971), Sowing [1972?], Pax [1969-1970], In Touch (1975).

Year's Best Fantasy Stories. Ed. Arthur W. Saha [?]. New York: Daw 8 (1982).

Year's Best Horror Stories. Various editors. New York: Daw. 3 (1975).

Anthologies

100% CRACKED WHEAT. Ed. Bob Currie, Gary Hyland, & Jim McLean. Moose Jaw: Coteau, 1983.

1955 ANTHOLOGY OF BEST ORIGINAL SHORT SHORTS. Ed. Robert Oberfirst. Ocean City, N.J.: Oberfirst, 1955. Based on SSI.

22 STORIES ABOUT HORSES AND MEN. Ed. Jack B. Creamer. New York: Coward-McCann, 1953. Based on SSI.

29 STORIES. Ed. Michael Timko. New York: Alfred A. Knopf, 1975.

ACROSS A CROWDED ROOM: AN ANTHOLOGY OF ROMANCE. Ed. Paul Dupont. London: Leslie Frewin, 1965.

AGAIN, DANGEROUS VISIONS. Ed. Harlan Ellison. New York: Doubleday, 1972.

AIR. Ed. Peter Carver. Toronto: Peter Martin, 1977.

THE ALBERTA DIAMOND JUBILEE ANTHOLOGY. Ed. John W. Chalmers. Edmonton: Hurtig, 1979.

THE ALBERTA GOLDEN JUBILEE ANTHOLOGY. Ed. W. G. Hardy. Toronto: McClelland & Stewart, 1955.

ALFRED HITCHCOCK'S TALES TO MAKE YOU QUAKE & QUIVER. Ed. Cathleen Jordan. New York: Dial Press/Davis, 1982.

ALIENATED MAN. [Editor unknown]. [Place unknown]: Hayden, 1972. Based on Hugh Garner, *Omnibus*.

ALL AGOG. [Editor unknown]. Toronto: Coach House Press, 1982. Based on Robert Sawyer survey response.

ALL MANNER OF MEN. Ed. Riley Hughes. New York: P. J. Kennedy & Sons, 1956. Based on SSI.

ANALOG ANNUAL. Ed. Ben Bova. New York: Pyramid, 1976. Based on science fiction indexes.

ANALOG YEARBOOK. Ed. Ben Bova. New York: Baronet, 1978. Based on science fiction indexes.

ANDROMEDA I: AN ORIGINAL SF ANTHOLOGY. Ed. Peter Weston. London: Dennis Dobson, 1979.

ANTHOLOGY: SASKATCHEWAN HOMECOMING '71: HOMESPUN STORIES AND RHYMES BY SASKATCHEWAN AUTHORS. Ed. Meredith B. Banting. Regina: Banting, 1971.

AN ANTHOLOGY OF CANADIAN LITERATURE IN ENGLISH 1/2. Ed. Russell Brown & Donna Bennett. Toronto: Oxford Univ Press, 1982; 1983.

APHRODISIAC: FICTION FROM CHRISTOPHER STREET. New York: Coward, McCann & Geoghegan, 1980.

ARGOSY BOOK OF SPORTS STORIES. Ed. Rogers Terrill. New York: A. S. Barnes, 1953. Based on SSI.

ARNUK UND ANDERE KANADISCHE ERZAHLUNGEN. Ed. Walter Riedel. Basel/Tubingen: Erdmann, 1976. Based on W. D. Valgardson survey response.

THE ARTIST IN CANADIAN LITERATURE. Ed. Lionel Wilson. Toronto: Macmillan, 1976.

THE ATLANTIC ADVOCATE'S HOLIDAY BOOK. Ed. D. Kermode Parr. Fredericton: Brunswick Press, 1961.

ATLANTIC ANTHOLOGY. Ed. Will R. Bird. Toronto: McClelland & Stewart, 1959.

BAFFLES OF WIND AND TIDE: AN ANTHOLOGY OF NEWFOUND-LAND POETRY, PROSE AND DRAMA. Portugal Cove: Breakwater, 1974.

BECKONING TRAILS. Ed. P. W. Diebel & Madeline Young. Toronto: Ryerson Press, 1962.

BENNETT CERF'S TAKE ALONG TREASURY. Ed. Leonora Hornblow & Bennett Cerf. New York: Doubleday, 1963. Based on SSI.

THE BERKLEY SHOWCASE: NEW WRITINGS IN SCIENCE FICTION AND FANTASY 4. Ed. Victoria Schochet & John Silbersack. New York: Berkley, 1981.

BEST CANADIAN SHORT STORIES. Ed. John Stevens. Toronto: McClelland & Stewart/Seal, 1981.

BEST FOR WINTER: A SELECTION FROM TWENTY-FIVE YEARS OF WINTER'S TALES. Ed. A. D. Maclean. London: Macmillan, 1979.

THE BEST MODERN CANADIAN SHORT STORIES. Ed. Ivon Owen and Morris Wolfe. Edmonton: Hurtig, 1978.

BEST MOUNTED POLICE STORIES. Ed. Dick Harrison. Edmonton: Univ of Alberta Press, 1978.

THE BEST OF GRAIN. Ed. Caroline Heath, Don Kerr, & Anne Szumigals-ki. [Regina?]: Saskatchewan Writers Guild, 1980.

BEST SPORTS STORIES. Ed. Paul Edwards. London: Faber & Faber, 1966.

BEST WEST INDIAN STORIES. Ed. Kenneth Ramchand. London: Nelson Caribbean, 1982. Based on "Samuel Selvon: A Preliminary Bibliography."

BEYOND TIME. Ed. Sandra Ley. New York: Pocket Books, 1976. Based on H. R. Percy survey response.

BIG TIME MYSTERIES. Ed. Brett Halliday. New York: Dodd, Mead, 1958. Based on SSI.

BLACK WATER: THE ANTHOLOGY OF FANTASTIC LITERATURE. Ed. Albert Manguel. Toronto: Lester & Orpen Denys, 1983.

THE BLASTY BOUGH. Ed. Clyde Rose. St. John's: Breakwater, 1976.

A BOOK OF CANADIAN STORIES. Ed. Desmond Pacey. Rev. ed.; Toronto: Ryerson Press, 1962.

BREAKTHROUGH FICTIONEERS. Ed. Richard Kostelanetz. West Glover, VT.: Something Else Press, 1973.

A BRIDLE OF GLASS. Saint John: La Société Anonyme de Poèsie, 1973.

BRITISH COLUMBIA. Ed. Reginald Eyre Watters. [Toronto]: McClelland & Stewart, 1958; rev. ed. 1961.

BRITISH COLUMBIA: A CELEBRATION. Ed. George Woodcock. Edmonton: Hurtig, 1983.

BRITISH MOTIFS. [Editor unknown]. Glenview, Ill.: Scott, Foresman, 1973. Based on Joyce Marshall survey response.

BY GREAT WATERS. Ed. Peter Neary & Patrick O'Flaherty. Toronto: Univ of Toronto Press, 1974.

CANADA IN US NOW. Ed. Harold Head. Toronto: nc Press, 1976.

CANADIAN ANTHOLOGY. Ed. Carl F. Klinck & Reginald E. Watters. 3rd. ed.; Toronto: Gage, 1974.

THE CANADIAN CENTURY: ENGLISH-CANADIAN WRITING SINCE CONFEDERATION. Ed. A.J.M. Smith. Toronto: Gage, 1973.

CANADIAN HUMOUR AND SATIRE. Ed. Theresa Ford. Toronto: Macmillan, 1976.

CANADIAN LITERATURE: TWO CENTURIES IN PROSE. Ed. Brita Mickleburgh. Toronto: McClelland & Stewart, 1973.

CANADIAN LITERATURE IN THE 70'S. Ed. Paul Denham & Mary Jane Edwards. Toronto: Holt, Rinehart & Winston, 1980.

CANADIAN MYTHS AND LEGENDS. Ed. Michael O. Nowlan. Toronto: Macmillan, 1977.

CANADIAN PROSE AND GRAMMAR EXERCISES. [Editor unknown]. [Publication data unknown]. Based on Hugh Garner, *Omnibus*.

CANADIAN SHORT STORIES. Ed. Robert Weaver & Helen James. Toronto: Oxford Univ Press, 1952.

THE CANADIAN SHORT STORY. Ed. Tony Kilgallin. Toronto: Holt, Rinehart & Winston, 1971.

CANADIAN STORIES OF ACTION AND ADVENTURE. Ed. John Stevens & Roger J. Smith. Toronto: Macmillan, 1978.

CANADIAN VIEWPOINTS: AN ANTHOLOGY OF CANADIAN WRITING. Ed. Allen Andrews, Diane Thompson, Douglas Cronk. Victoria: Prov of British Columbia, Ministry of Education, 1983. Based on Miriam Waddington volume of ABCMA.

CANADIAN WINTER'S TALES. Ed. Norman Levine. Toronto: Macmillan, 1968.

CANADIAN WRITING TODAY. Ed. Mordecai Richler. Harmondsworth: Penguin, 1970.

A CANADIAN YULETIDE TREASURY. Toronto: Clarke, Irwin, 1982.

CARIBBEAN ANTHOLOGY OF SHORT STORIES. Kingston: The Pioneer Press, 1953. Based on "Samuel Selvon: A Preliminary Bibliography."

CARIBBEAN PROSE. Ed. Andrew Salkey. London: Evans Brothers, 1967.

CARIBBEAN PROSE: AN ANTHOLOGY FOR SECONDARY SCHOOLS. Ed. Andrew Salkey. London: Evans, 1967. Based on "Samuel Selvon: A Preliminary Bibliography."

CARIBBEAN RHYTHMS: THE EMERGING ENGLISH LITERATURE OF THE WEST INDIES. Ed. James T. Livingston. New York: Washington Square Press, 1974.

CAROSELLO DI NARRATORI INGLESE. Ed. Aldo Martello. Milan: Aldo Martello, 1954. Based on *Malcolm Lowry: A Bibliography.*

CARRAY. Ed. James Lee Wah. London: Macmillan, 1977. Based on "Samuel Selvon: A Preliminary Bibliography."

CAT ENCOUNTERS: A CAT-LOVERS ANTHOLOGY. Ed. Seon Manley & Gogo Lewis. New York: Lothrop, Lee & Shepherd, 1979. Based on SSI.

CAVALCADE OF THE NORTH. Ed. George E. Nelson. New York: Double-day, 1958.

CHEZZETCOOK: AN ANTHOLOGY OF CONTEMPORARY POETRY AND FICTION FROM ATLANTIC CANADA. Ed. Lesley Choyce. Halifax: Wooden Anchor Press, 1977.

CHILDHOOD AND YOUTH IN CANADIAN LITERATURE. Ed. M. G. Hesse. Toronto: Macmillan, 1979.

CHOICE PARTS. Ed. Seymour Mayne. Oakville: Mosaic Press/Valley Editions, 1976.

COMING ATTRACTIONS: STORIES BY SHARON BUTALA, BONNIE BURNARD & SHARON SPARLING. Ed. David Helwig & Sandra Martin. Ottawa: Oberon Press, 1983.

COMMON GROUND. Ed. Marilyn Berge et al. Vancouver: Press Gang, 1980.

COMPASS. [Editor unknown]. [Glenview, Ill.]: Scott, Foresman, 1971. Based on Shirley Faessler survey response.

CONNECTIONS 1. [Editor unknown]. Toronto: Gage, 1981. Based on Anne Hart survey response.

CONNECTIONS 3. Ed. R. Danes & Glen Kirkland. Toronto: Gage, 1982. Based on W. D. Valgardson survey response.

CONTEMPORARY FICTION. [Editor unknown]. [City unknown], U.S.: [Publisher unknown], 1976. Based on Crad Kilodney survey response.

CONTEMPORARY SURREALIST PROSE. Ed. Dona Sturmanis & Edwin Varney. Vancouver: Intermedia Press, 1979.

CONTEMPORARY VOICES: THE SHORT STORY IN CANADA. Ed. Donald Stephens. Scarborough: Prentice-Hall, 1972.

CONTEXTS 1/2. Ed. Clayton Graves & Christine McClymont. Toronto: Nelson, 1981.

COPYRIGHT CANADA. Ed. A. Dawe. Toronto: Macmillan, 1978. Based on W. D. Valgardson survey response.

CORE: STORIES AND POEMS CELEBRATING THE LIVES OF ORDI-NARY PEOPLE WHO CALL TORONTO THEIR HOME. Ed. Ruth Johnson & Enid Lee. Toronto: Johnson & Lee, 1982.

CORNISH SHORT STORIES. Ed. Denys val Baker. London: Penguin, 1976. Based on David Watmough survey response.

COWBOYS, COWBOYS, COWBOYS. Ed. Phyllis Reid Fenner. New York: Franklin Watts, 1950. Based on SSI.

CREATION. Ed. Robert Kroetsch. Toronto: new press, 1970.

CROSSROADS 1: CANADIAN STORIES, POEMS AND SONGS. Ed. William Boswell, Betty Lamont & John Martyn. Toronto: Van Nostrand Reinhold, 1979.

CURRENT ASSETS: FICTION AND POETRY FROM THE WRITERS' CO-OPERATIVE. Montreal: Writers' Co-operative, 1973.

DE BESTE BUITENLANDSE VERHALEN VAN DE BEZIGE BIJ. Amsterdam: Uitgeverij de Besige Bij, 1978. Based on *Malcolm Lowry: A Bibliography.*

DEATH. Ed. Stuart David Schiff. New York: Playboy Paperbacks, 1982. Based on SSI.

DECEITS OF ECSTASY. Saint John: La Société Anonyme de Poèsie, 1971.

THE DEMANDING AGE. Ed. Ronald Side & Ralph Greenfield. Toronto: McGraw-Hill, 1970.

THE DEPRESSION IN CANADIAN LITERATURE. Ed. Alice K. Hale & Sheila A. Brooks. Toronto: Macmillan, 1976.

DIE KINDER-KULTUURU. [Editor unknown]. South Africa: [Publisher unknown]. Based on Hugh Garner, *Omnibus.*

DIE WEITE REISE: KANADISCHE ERZAHLUNGEN UND KURZGESHICHTEN. Ed. Ernst Bartsch. Berlin: Verlag Volk und Welt, 1974.

DOG SHOW. Ed. Wilhelmina Harper. Boston: Houghton, Mifflin, 1950. Based on SSI.

DON'T STEAL THIS BOOK. Ed. Ron Marken. Toronto: Green Tree, 1974.

DORYLOADS. Ed. Kevin Major. Portugal Cove: Breakwater, 1974.

DOUBLE VISION: AN ANTHOLOGY OF TWENTIETH-CENTURY STO-RIES IN ENGLISH. Ed. Rudy Wiebe. Toronto: Macmillan, 1976.

EARLY SEPTEMBER. Ed. James MacNeill. Toronto: Thomas Nelson, 1980. Based on Anne Hart survey response.

EARTH. Ed. Peter Carver. Toronto: Peter Martin, 1977.

EAST OF CANADA: AN ATLANTIC ANTHOLOGY. Ed. Raymond Fraser, Clyde Rose, & Jim Stewart. Portugal Cove: Breakwater, 1976.

EASTERLY: 60 ATLANTIC WRITERS. Ed. Blaine E. Hatt. Don Mills: Academic Press, 1983.

ECHOES 1. Ed. Peter Brennan & Harry Brown. Toronto: Oxford Univ Press, 1983.

EGTAJAK 1978-79: OT VILAGRESZ ELBESZELESEI. Ed. Laszlo Horvath. Budapest: Europa Konyvkiado, 1979. Trans. Klora Molnor.

ELBOW ROOM: A BOOK OF SHORT STORIES. Ed. Linda Field & Mary Beth Knechtel. Vancouver: Pulp Press, 1979.

ELLERY QUEEN'S GRAND SLAM. Ed. Ellery Queen. New York: World, 1970.

ELLERY QUEEN'S MAZE OF MYSTERIES. Ed. Ellery Queen. New York: Dial Press/Davis, 1982.

ELLERY QUEEN'S VEILS OF MYSTERY. Ed. Ellery Queen. New York: Dial Press/Davis, 1980. Based on SSI.

ELLERY QUEEN'S WINGS OF MYSTERY. Ed. Ellery Queen. New York: Dial Press/Davis, 1979.

THE EVOLUTION OF CANADIAN LITERATURE IN ENGLISH 1945-1970. Ed. Paul Denham. Toronto: Holt, Rinehart & Winston, 1973.

FACE TO FACE: ANTHOLOGY OF NEW BRUNSWICK WOMEN WRITERS. Ed. Alice Van Wart et al. Fredericton: Centennial Print & Litho, [1979?].

FAMILY PORTRAITS. Ed. Ian Underhill. Toronto: McClelland & Stewart, 1978.

FASCIST COURT. Ed. Bill Bissett. Vancouver: blewointmentpress, [1970].

FICTION OF CONTEMPORARY CANADA. Ed. George Bowering. Toronto: Coach House Press, 1980.

FIDDLEHEAD GREENS: STORIES FROM THE FIDDLEHEAD. Ed. Roger Ploude & Michael Taylor. Ottawa: Oberon Press, 1979.

FINE LINES: THE BEST OF MS. FICTION. Ed. Ruth Sullivan. New York: Charles Scribner's, 1981.

FIRE. edited by Peter Carver. Toronto: Peter Martin, 1978.

FOREIGN FICTIONS: 25 CONTEMPORARY STORIES FROM CANADA, EUROPE, LATIN AMERICA. Ed. John Biguenet. New York: Vantage, 1978.

FORUM: CANADIAN LIFE AND LETTERS 1920-70: SELECTIONS FROM THE CANADIAN FORUM. Ed. J. L. Granatstein & Peter Stevens. Toronto: Univ of Toronto Press, 1972.

FOUR HEMISPHERES: AN ANTHOLOGY OF ENGLISH SHORT STORIES FROM AROUND THE WORLD. Ed. W. H. New. Toronto: Copp Clark, 1971.

FOURTEEN STORIES HIGH. Ed. David Helwig & Tom Marshall. Ottawa: Oberon Press, 1971.

FREE FALL: AN ANTHOLOGY OF THE WRITING DIVISION, BANFF CENTRE. [Editor unknown]. [Banff: Banff Centre for the Arts?], 1975. Based on Martin Avery survey response.

THE FRENCH CANADIAN EXPERIENCE. Ed. Gaston Saint-Pierre. Toronto: Macmillan, 1979.

FRESH GREASE: NEW WRITINGS FROM THE MARITIMES. Ed. Bill Templeton, Elizabeth Zimmer, & Charlotte Townshend. Halifax: Straw Books, 1971.

FROM THE GREEN ANTILLES: WRITINGS OF THE CARIBBEAN. Ed. Barbara Howes. New York: Macmillan, 1966.

FROM THIS PLACE: A SELECTION OF WRITING BY WOMEN OF NEWFOUNDLAND AND LABRADOR. Ed. Bernice Morgan, Helen Porter, & Geraldine Rubia. St. John's: Jesperson Printing, 1977.

THE FRONTIER EXPERIENCE. Ed. Jack Hodgins. Toronto: Macmillan, 1975.

THE FRUITS OF EXPERIENCE. Ed. Arlene Cushman. n.p.: Emanation Press, 1978.

GETTING HERE. Ed. Rudy Wiebe. Edmonton: NeWest Press, 1977.

GREAT CANADIAN ADVENTURE STORIES. Ed. Muriel Whitaker. Edmonton: Hurtig, 1979.

GREAT CANADIAN ANIMAL STORIES. Ed. Muriel Whitaker. Edmonton: Hurtig, 1978.

GREAT CANADIAN SHORT STORIES. Ed. Alec Lucas. New York: Dell, 1971.

GREAT CANADIAN SPORTS STORIES. Ed. George Bowering. Ottawa: Oberon Press, 1979.

GREAT CANADIAN WRITING: A CENTURY OF IMAGINATION. Ed. Claude Bissell. Toronto: The Canadian Centennial, 1966.

GROWING UP CANADIAN: STORIES OF CHILDHOOD AND ADOLESCENCE IN CANADA. [Editor unknown]. Toronto: Gage, 1983. Based on Alistair MacLeod survey response.

HARVEST: ANTHOLOGY OF MENNONITE WRITING IN CANADA. Ed. William De Fehr et al. Altona, Man: Mennonite Historical Society of Manitoba, 1974.

HEARTLAND: AN ANTHOLOGY OF CANADIAN STORIES. Ed. Katheryn Maclean Broughton. Scarborough: Nelson, 1983.

HERE AND NOW: BEST CANADIAN STORIES. Ed. Clark Blaise & John Metcalf. Ottawa: Oberon Press, 1977.

HEROIC FANTASY. Ed. Gerald W. Page & Hank Reinhardt. New York: Daw, 1979.

HIGH FLIGHT. Ed. J. Ranton McIntosh, Franklin L. Barrett, & Claude E. Lewis. Toronto: Copp Clark, 1951.

HORIZON: WRITINGS OF THE CANADIAN PRAIRIE. Ed. Ken Mitchell. Toronto: Oxford Univ Press, 1977.

ILLUSION ONE/TWO: FABLES, FANTASIES AND METAFICTIONS. Ed. Geoff Hancock. Toronto: Aya Press, 1983.

THE IMMIGRANT EXPERIENCE. Ed. Leuba Bailey. Toronto: Macmillan, 1975.

IN COMPLETE see Anthology Series list under *Writing Group Publications.*

IN SEARCH OF OURSELVES. [Editor unknown]. [Toronto?]: [Publisher unknown], 1967. Based on Hugh Garner, *Omnibus.*

IN THE LOOKING GLASS: TWENTY-ONE MODERN SHORT STORIES BY WOMEN. Ed. Nancy Dean & Myra Stark. New York: G. P. Putnam's Sons/Capricorn, 1977.

IN TOUCH see Anthology Series list under *Writing Group Publications.*

IN YOUR OWN WORDS 1/2. edited by Joan M. Green & Ian W. Mills. Toronto: Holt, Rinehart & Winston, 1982.

INQUIRY INTO LITERATURE 1 /2 /3 /4. Ed. Bryant Fillion & Jim Henderson. Toronto: Collier Macmillan, 1980.

INTRODUCTION TO LITERATURE. Ed. Jack David & Robert Lecker. Toronto: Holt, Rinehart & Winston, 1982.

INVITATION TO SHORT STORIES. Ed. H. L. Willis & W. R. McGillivray. Toronto: Macmillan, 1958.

IRISH GHOST STORIES. Ed. Joseph Hone. [Place unknown]: Hamish Hamilton & Curtis Brown, 1977. Based on editorial note to Brian Moore, "The Sight" in *Black Water.*

ISLAND PROSE AND POETRY: AN ANTHOLOGY. Ed. Allan Graham. Charlottetown: Irwin Printing, 1973.

ISLAND VOICES: STORIES FROM THE WEST INDIES. Ed. Andrew Salkey. New York: Liveright, 1965. Originally entitled *Stories from the Caribbean.*

ISLAND WOMEN: OUR PROSE & POETRY. Ed. L. Brehaut et al. Charlottetown: Ragweed Press, 1982.

ISOLATION IN CANADIAN LITERATURE. Ed. David Arnason. Toronto: Macmillan, 1975.

IT DOESN'T HAVE TO BE LOUSY TO BE PRINTED. Ed. Douglas Kay Campbell. Toronto: Voltaire Press, 1974.

JOURNEYS 2. Ed. Jim French. Toronto: McClelland & Stewart, 1979.

KALEIDOSCOPE. Ed. John Metcalf. Toronto: Van Nostrand Reinhold, 1972.

KANADISCHE ERZAHLER DER GEGENWART. Ed. Armin Arnold & Walter Riedel. Zurich: Manesse Verlag, Conzett & Huber, 1967.

KLANAK ISLANDS. Ed. William McConnell. Vancouver: Klanak Press, 1959.

LANDMARKS. [Editor unknown]. [Glenview, Ill.]: Scott, Foresman, 1983. Based on Shirley Faessler survey response.

LATITUDE. [Editor unknown]. [Glenview, Ill.]: Scott, Foresman, 1974. Based on Shirley Faessler survey response.

LESBIAN FICTION: AN ANTHOLOGY. Ed. Elly Bulkin. Watertown, MA.: Persephone Press, 1981. Based on "Jane Rule: A Bibliography."

THE LESBIANS' HOME JOURNAL: STORIES FROM THE LADDER. Ed. Barbara Grier & Coletta Reid. Baltimore: Diana Press, 1976. Based on "Jane Rule: A Bibliography."

LISTENING COMPREHENSION. Ed. W. S. Fowler. London: Thomas Nelson & Sons, 1975.

LITERARY GLIMPSES OF THE COMMONWEALTH. Ed. James B. Bell. Toronto: Wiley, 1977. Based on "Samuel Selvon: A Preliminary Bibliography."

LITERATURE IN CANADA 2. Ed. Douglas Daymond & Leslie Monkman. Toronto: Gage, 1978.

LITERATURE OF THE WORLD. Ed. Thelma G. James et al. New York: McGraw Hill, 1963. Based on "Samuel Selvon: A Preliminary Bibliography."

LOVE STORIES. Ed. Martin Levin. New York: Quadrangle, 1975.

A MACLEAN'S READER. Ed. Ralph Allen [?]. Toronto: William Collins Sons, 1950.

MADDENED BY MYSTERY: A CASEBOOK OF CANADIAN DETECTIVE FICTION. Ed. Michael Richardson. Toronto: Lester & Orpen Denys, 1982.

MAE WEST IS DEAD: RECENT LESBIAN AND GAY FICTION. Ed. Adam Mars-Jones. London: Faber & Faber, 1983.

MAGIC REALISM. Ed. Geoff Hancock. Toronto: Aya Press, 1980.

MAN AND HIS WORLD: STUDIES IN PROSE. Ed. Malcolm Ross & John Stevens. Toronto: J. M. Dent & Sons, 1961.

MANY WINDOWS: 22 STORIES FROM AMERICAN REVIEW. New York: Harper, 1982.

THE MARITIME EXPERIENCE. Ed. Michael O. Nowlan. Toronto: Macmillan, 1975.

MATINEES DAILY. Ed. Terence Byrnes. Montreal: Quadrant Editions, 1981.

METAVISIONS. Ed. Geoff Hancock. Dunvegan: Quadrant Editions, 1983.

THE MINORITY EXPERIENCE. Ed. Michael Marland. London: Longman, 1978. Based on "Samuel Selvon: A Preliminary Bibliography."

MODERN CANADIAN STORIES. Ed. Giose Rimanelli & Roberto Ruberto. Toronto: McGraw-Hill Ryerson, 1966.

MODERN CANADIAN STORIES. Ed. John Stevens. Toronto/New York: Bantam, 1975.

MODERN STORIES IN ENGLISH. Ed. W. H. New & H. J. Rosengarten. New York: Thomas Y. Crowell, 1975.

MODERNE ERZAHLER DER WALT: KANADA. Ed. Walter Riedel. Türbingen/Basel: Erdmann Verlag, 1976.

MORAL FICTION: AN ANTHOLOGY. Ed. Joe David Bellamy. Canton, NY: Fiction International, 1980.

MORE STORIES FROM WESTERN CANADA. Ed. Rudy Wiebe & Aritha van Herk. Toronto: Macmillan, 1980.

MORE WANDERING STARS: AN ANTHOLOGY OF JEWISH FANTASY AND SCIENCE FICTION. Ed. Jack Dann. New York: Doubleday, 1981.

MOUNTAIN & PLAIN. Ed. Don Gutteridge. Toronto: McClelland & Stewart, 1978.

MULTIPLE CHOICES. Montreal: The Writers' Cooperative, 1975.

MUSICAL OXYGEN AND VEGETABLE TORSOS. Saint John: La Société Anonyme de Poèsie, 1970.

THE NARRATIVE VOICE. Ed. John Metcalf. Toronto: McGraw-Hill Ryerson, 1972.

NEARLY AN ISLAND: A NOVA SCOTIAN ANTHOLOGY. St. John's: Breakwater, 1979.

NEW BODIES. Ed. Lorne Gould, introd. n.p.: Emanation Press, 1981.

A NEW ENCOUNTER. Ed. Andy Wainwright. Ottawa: Oberon Press, 1969.

THE NEW ROMANS: CANDID CANADIAN OPINIONS OF THE U.S. Ed. A. W. Purdy. Edmonton: Hurtig, 1968.

NEW VOICES: CANADIAN UNIVERSITY WRITING OF 1956. Ed. Earle Birney et al. Toronto: J. M. Dent & Sons, 1956.

NEW VOICES 2. Ed. George R. R. Martin. New York: Harcourt, Brace Jovanovich, 1979.

NEW VOICES 2: AMERICAN WRITING TODAY. Ed. Don M. Wolfe. New York: Hendricks House, 1955.

NEW WORLDS: A CANADIAN COLLECTION OF STORIES. Ed. John Metcalf. Toronto: McGraw-Hill Ryerson, 1980.

THE NEWCOMERS: INHABITING A NEW LAND. Ed. Charle E. Israel. Toronto: McClelland & Stewart, 1979.

NORTHERN LIGHTS. Ed. George E. Nelson. Garden City, New York: Doubleday, 1960.

THE NORTON ANTHOLOGY OF SHORT FICTION. Ed. R. V. Cassill. New York: W. W. Norton, 1981.

NOT TO BE TAKEN AT NIGHT: THIRTEEN CLASSIC CANADIAN TALES OF MYSTERY AND THE SUPERNATURAL. Ed. John Robert Colombo & Michael Richardson. Toronto: Lester & Orpen Denys, 1981.

ON THE LINE: NEW GAY FICTION. Ed. Ian Young. Truemansburg, N.Y.: The Crossing Press, 1981.

ON THE LINE: READINGS IN THE SHORT FICTION OF CLARK BLAISE JOHN METCALF AND HUGH HOOD. Ed. Robert Lecker. Toronto: ECW Press, 1982.

ON THE ROAD. Ed. Gary Botting & Samir Mattar. n.p.: Univ of Alberta & Univ of Calgary Graduate Student Associations, 1972.

ONE OUT OF MANY: A COLLECTION OF WRITINGS BY 21 BLACK WOMEN IN ONTARIO. Ed. Liz Cromwell. Toronto: Wacacro Productions, 1975.

ONTARIO '67. [Editor unknown]. [Publication data unknown]. Based on Dave Godfrey, *Death Goes Better with Coca-Cola.*

THE ONTARIO EXPERIENCE. Ed. John Stevens. Toronto: Macmillan, 1976.

OPEN HIGHWAYS. [Editor unknown]. [Glenview, Ill.]: Scott, Foresman, 1968. Based on Victoria Branden survey response.

OTHER CANADAS: AN ANTHOLOGY OF SCIENCE FICTION AND FANTASY. Ed. John Robert Colombo. Toronto: McGraw-Hill Ryerson, 1979.

THE OTHER PERSUASION: SHORT FICTION ABOUT GAY MEN AND WOMEN. Ed. Seymour Kleinberg. New York: Vintage, 1977.

OUTLAWS. Ed. Erling Friis-Baastad. Guelph: Alive Press, 1974.

OVER THE HORIZON. New York: Duell, Sloan & Pearce, 1960. Based on SSI.

THE OXFORD ANTHOLOGY OF CANADIAN LITERATURE. Ed. Robert Weaver & William Toye. Toronto: Oxford Univ Press, 1973.

THE PAPERBACK CONSPIRACY. [Editor unknown]. [New York: National Lampoon?], 1974. Based on Crad Kilodney survey response.

PAX see Anthology Series list under *Writing Group Publications.*

THE PENGUIN BOOK OF CANADIAN SHORT STORIES. Ed. Wayne Grady. Markham/Harmondsworth: Penguin, 1980.

THE PENGUIN BOOK OF MODERN CANADIAN SHORT STORIES. Ed. Wayne Grady. Markham/Harmondsworth: Penguin, 1982.

PERCEPTIONS IN LITERATURE. [Editor unknown]. Boston: Houghton Mifflin, 1972. Based on "Henry Kreisel: A Canadian Exile Writer?"

PERSONAL FICTIONS: STORIES BY MUNRO, WIEBE, THOMAS, & BLAISE. Ed. Michael Ondaatje. Toronto: Oxford Univ Press, 1977.

THE PHOENIX TREE: AN ANTHOLOGY OF MYTH FANTASY. Ed. Robert H. Boyer & Kenneth J. Zahorski. New York: Avon, 1980.

THE PITS/GRIT. Ed. Barry McKinnon. n.p.: [Repository Press?, 1977].

PLAYBACK: CANADIAN SELECTIONS. Ed. Jack David & Michael Park. Toronto: McClelland & Stewart, 1978. Based on "Phyllis Gotlieb: A Checklist of Her SF."

THE PLAYBOY BOOK OF CRIME AND SUSPENSE. New York: Playboy Press, 1966.

THE PLEASURES OF FICTION. [Editor unknown]. [Don Mills]: Addison-Wesley, 1972. Based on Hugh Garner, *Omnibus.*

POLISHED PEBBLES: A BLUEWATER ANTHOLOGY. Sarnia: Seeker, 1974.

POSH: AN ANTHOLOGY OF STUDENT WRITING. Ed. Randy Katz & Roxanne Pressoir. Montreal: [Vanier College], n.d.

THE PRAIRIE EXPERIENCE. Ed. Terry Angus. Toronto: Macmillan, 1975.

PREJUDICE: 20 TALES OF OPPRESSION AND LIBERATION. Ed. Charles R. Larson. New York: New American Library/Mentor, 1971.

PROSE PAGEANT. [Editor unknown]. Toronto: Ryerson Press, 1963. Based on H. R. Percy survey response.

PROSE POLITICAL. [Editor unknown]. [City unknown], UK: [Publisher unknown], 1977. Based on Crad Kilodney survey response.

PROTEUS: VOICES FOR THE 80'S. Ed. Richard S. McEnroe. New York: Ace, 1981.

THE PULP MILL: A COLLECTION OF LOCAL SHORT STORIES. Ed. John Harris & Barry McKinnon. Prince George: Repository Press, 1977.

RAINSHADOW: STORIES FROM VANCOUVER ISLAND. Ed. Ron Smith & Stephen Guppy. Lantzville: Oolichan; Victoria: Sono Nis Press, 1982.

RED WINDSOR. [Editor unknown]. [City unknown], U.K.: [Publisher unknown], [1977?]. Based on Crad Kilodney survey response.

RESPONDING TO READING. Ed. Robert J. Ireland. Don Mills: Addison-Wesley, 1983. Based on Anne Hart survey response.

RITES OF PASSAGE. Ed. Don Gutteridge. Toronto: McClelland & Stewart, 1979.

THE ROLE OF WOMAN IN CANADIAN LITERATURE. Ed. Elizabeth McCullogh. Toronto: Macmillan, 1975.

ROOTHOG: CONTEMPORARY BRITISH COLUMBIA WRITING. Ed. John Harris. Prince George: Repository Press, 1981.

SASKATCHEWAN GOLD. Ed. Geoffrey Ursell. Moose Jaw: Coteau, 1982.

SATURDAY NIGHT AT THE FORUM. Ed. Steve Luxton. Montreal: Quadrant Editions, 1981.

SCENES FROM AMERICAN LIFE: CONTEMPORARY SHORT FICTION. Ed. Joyce Carol Oates. New York: Vanguard Press, 1973.

THE SEARCH FOR IDENTITY. Ed. James Foley. Toronto: Macmillan, 1976.

SEEING THROUGH SHUCK. Ed. Richard Kostelanetz. New York: Ballantine, 1972. Based on Ray Smith survey response.

SELECTIONS FROM MAJOR CANADIAN WRITERS. Ed. Desmond Pacey. Toronto: McGraw-Hill Ryerson, 1974.

SELECTIONS FROM THE C.F.U.W. WRITING PROJECT 78-79. n.p.: n.p., [1979?].

A SENSE OF PLACE. Ed. T. M. Ford. Edmonton: Alberta Education, 1979. Based on W. D. Valgardson survey response.

THE SEVEN DEADLY SINS OF SCIENCE FICTION. Ed. Isaac Asimov, Charles G. Waugh, & Martin H. Greenberg. New York: Fawcett Crest, 1980.

SF: INVENTING THE FUTURE. Ed. R. Duncan Appleford. Scarborough: Bellhaven House, 1972.

SHORT SHORT STORIES. Ed. Reingard M. Nischik. Paderborn, Ger: Ferdinand Schöningh, 1983. Based on Fraser Sutherland survey response.

SHORT STORY MAGIC. Ed. Beaulah Garland Swayze. Scarborough: McGraw-Hill, 1955. Based on CBIP.

UN SIECLE DE LITTERATURE CANADIENNE/A CENTURY OF CANADIAN LITERATURE. Ed. Guy Sylvestre & H. Gordon Green. Montreal: Editions HMH; Toronto: Ryerson Press, 1967.

SINGING. Ed. Bernice Lever et al. Cobalt: Highway Book Shop, 1980.

SINGING UNDER ICE. Ed. M. Grace Mersereau. Toronto: Macmillan, 1974.

SIXTEEN BY TWELVE: SHORT STORIES BY CANADIAN WRITERS. Ed. John Metcalf. Toronto: McGraw-Hill Ryerson, 1970.

SKOOKUM WAWA: WRITINGS OF THE CANADIAN NORTHWEST. Ed. Gary Geddes. Toronto: Oxford Univ Press, 1975.

SMALL WONDERS. Ed. Robert Weaver. Toronto: CBC Enterprises, 1982.

SNOWMOBILES FORBIDDEN. Ed. David Chenoweth & Charles Gurd. Montreal: [McGill Univ Press?], 1971.

SOMETIMES MAGIC: A COLLECTION OF OUTSTANDING STORIES FOR THE TEENAGE GIRL. Ed. Hallie Barnett. New York: Platt & Munk, 1966. Based on Mavis Gallant ABCMA volume.

SOWING see Anthology Series list under *Writing Group Publications.*

SPACESUITS & GUMSHOES: AN ANTHOLOGY OF SCIENCE FICTION AND CRIME STORIES. Ed. Richard Lunn. Toronto: Macmillan, 1972.

SPECULATIONS. Ed. Isaac Asimov & Alice Laurance. Boston: Houghton Mifflin, 1982.

THE SPICE BOX: AN ANTHOLOGY OF JEWISH CANADIAN WRITING. Ed. Gerri Sinclair & Morris Wolfe. Toronto: Lester & Orpen Denys, 1981.

SPLICES. Ed. Yves Lavigne. Oakville: Mosaic Press/Valley Editions, 1975.

STAGES: LITERATURE OF NEWFOUNDLAND AND LABRADOR 2. Ed. Eric Norman et al. St. John's: Breakwater, 1980. Based on Anne Hart survey response.

STATEMENTS 2: NEW FICTION. Ed. Jonathan Baumbach & Peter Spielberg. New York: Fiction Collective, 1977.

STORIES FROM ACROSS CANADA. Ed. Bernard L. McEvoy. Toronto: McClelland & Stewart, 1966.

STORIES FROM ATLANTIC CANADA. Ed. Kent Thompson. Toronto: Macmillan, 1973.

STORIES FROM CANADA: ERZAHLUNGEN AUS KANADA. Ed. Angela Uthe-Spencker. Ebenhausen: Langewiesche-Brandt, 1969. Trans. Angela Uthe-Spencker.

STORIES FROM ONTARIO. Ed. Germaine Warkentin. Toronto: Macmillan, 1974.

STORIES FROM PACIFIC & ARCTIC CANADA. Ed. Andreas Schroeder & Rudy Wiebe. Toronto: Macmillan, 1974.

STORIES FROM SEVEN COUNTRIES. [Editor unknown]. [City unknown], Africa: Juta & Co, 1972. Based on James Reaney survey response.

STORIES FROM THE CANADIAN NORTH. Ed. Muriel Whitaker. Edmonton: Hurtig, 1980.

STORIES FROM THE LITERARY REVIEW. Ed. Charles Angoff. Rutherford, N.J.: Fairleigh Dickinson Univ Press, 1969.

STORIES FROM THE NEW YORKER *1950-1960.* New York: Simon & Schuster, 1960.

STORIES FROM THE TRANSATLANTIC REVIEW. Ed. Joseph F. Mc-Crindle. New York: Holt, Rinehart & Winston, 1970.

STORIES FROM WESTERN CANADA. Ed. Rudy Wiebe. Toronto: Macmillan, 1972.

STORIES OF CHRISTIAN LIVING. Ed. John Edward Lantz. New York: Association Press, 1950. Based on SSI.

STORIES OF QUEBEC. Ed. Douglas Daymond & Leslie Monkman. Ottawa: Oberon Press, 1980.

STORIES OF THE MODERN SOUTH. Ed. Ben Forkner & Patrick Samway. New York: Bantam, 1978.

STORIES PLUS. Ed. John Metcalf. Toronto: McGraw-Hill Ryerson, 1979.

STORIES TO READ AGAIN. Ed. H. Gordon Green. Fredericton: Brunswick Press, 1965.

STORIES WITH JOHN DRAINIE. Ed. John Drainie. Toronto: Ryerson Press, 1963.

STORY AND STRUCTURE. Ed. [L.?] Perrine & [T. M.] Ford. Toronto: Academia Press, 1981. Based on Rudy Wiebe survey response.

THE STORY-MAKERS. Ed. Rudy Wiebe. Toronto: Macmillan, 1970.

STRANGERS IN THEIR OWN LAND. [Editor unknown]. Stuttgart: Ernst Klett Verlag, [date unknown]. Based on Hugh Garner, *Omnibus.*

STUBBORN STRENGTH: A NEW BRUNSWICK ANTHOLOGY. Ed. Michael O. Nowlan. Don Mills: Academic Press, 1983.

STUDENT ORACLE. Ed. Noel Hudson-Jones & Julian Ross. Nelson: D.T.U.C. Writing Programme, 1979.

SUNDOGS: STORIES FROM SASKATCHEWAN. Ed. Robert Kroetsch. Moose Jaw: Coteau, 1980.

SUNLIGHT & SHADOWS. Ed. James A. MacNeill & Glen A. Sorestad. Don Mills: Thomas Nelson & Sons, 1974.

THE SUN'S EYE: WEST INDIAN WRITING FOR YOUNG READERS. Ed. Anne Walmsley. London: Longman, 1968. Based on "Samuel Selvon: A Preliminary Bibliography."

SURVIVAL 2. [Editor unknown]. Toronto: House of Anansi Press, [date unknown]. Based on Hugh Garner, *Omnibus.*

TALES FROM THE SKIPPER. Ed. H. K. Rigg. Barre, MA.: Barre, 1968.

TELLING TALES. [Editor unknown]. [Place unknown]: [Publisher unknown], 1973. Based on Hugh Garner, *Omnibus.*

TEMPER OF THE TIMES: AN ANTHOLOGY OF ASSORTED CONTEMPORARY LITERATURE. Ed. Ralph Greenfield & Ronald Side. Toronto: McGraw-Hill, 1969.

TEN FOR WEDNESDAY NIGHT. Ed. Robert Weaver. Toronto: McClelland & Stewart, 1961.

THIS BOOK IS ABOUT COMMUNICATION. [Editor unknown]. Toronto: Ryerson Press, 1970. Based on Victoria Branden survey response.

THIS ISLAND PLACE. Ed. Robert Fraser. London: Harrap, 1981.

THREE TIMES FIVE: SHORT STORIES BY BEVERLY HARRIS GLORIA SAWAI FRED STENSON. Ed. Douglas Barbour. Edmonton: NeWest Press, 1983.

THURSDAY'S VOICES: STORIES FROM A WORKSHOP OF NEW WRITERS. Second ed.; Toronto: Childe Thursday, 1983.

TIGERS OF THE SNOW. Ed. James A. MacNeill & Glenn A. Sorestad. Don Mills: Thomas Nelson & Sons, 1973.

THE TIME GATHERERS: WRITINGS FROM PRISON. Ed. Gertrude Katz. Montreal: Harvest House, 1970.

THE TIME OF YOUR LIFE: AN ANTHOLOGY OF SHORT STORIES. Ed. James Henderson. Toronto: Macmillan, 1967.

TIME PIECES. Montreal: Montreal Writers' Co-operative, 1974.

TITLE UNKNOWN: WRITINGS BY ONTARIO WOMEN. Ed. Judith Merril, Lydia Burton, & Liz Cromwell. Toronto: n.p., 1975.

TOGETHER. [Editor unknown]. New York: Harcourt, Brace Jovanovich, 1975. Based on Alistair MacLeod survey response.

THE TORONTO BOOK: AN ANTHOLOGY OF WRITINGS PAST AND PRESENT. Ed. William Kilbourn. Toronto: Macmillan, 1976.

TORONTO SHORT STORIES. Ed. Morris Wolfe & Douglas Daymond. Toronto: Doubleday, 1977.

TRADITION - INTEGRATION - REZEPTION: ANNALEN ZWEITES SYMPOSIUM DEUTSCHKANADISCHE STUDIEN. Ed. Karin R. Gürttler & Herfried Scheer. Montreal: Université de Montréal. Based on ''Henry Kreisel: A Canadian Exile Writer?''

TRANSITIONS 2. Ed. Edward Peck. Vancouver: CommCept, 1978.

TREASURE CHEST OF SPORTS STORIES. Ed. Max John Herzberg. New York: Julian Messner, 1951. Based on SSI.

A TREASURY OF NEWFOUNDLAND PROSE AND VERSE SELECTED FROM BOOKS PUBLISHED BY HARRY CUFF PUBLICATIONS. Ed. Harry A. Cuff. St. John's: Harry Cuff, 1983.

TREELINE 2. Ed. Maidie Hilmo & Harry Morgan. Fort St. John/Dawson Creek: Treeline Press, 1983.

A TRUE LIKENESS: LESBIAN AND GAY WRITING TODAY. Ed. Felice Picano. New York: The Sea Horse Press, 1980. Based on ''Jane Rule: A Bibliography.''

TWELVE NEWFOUNDLAND SHORT STORIES. Ed. Percy Janes & Harry Cuff. St. John's: Harry Cuff, 1982.

THE URBAN EXPERIENCE. Ed. John Stevens. Toronto: Macmillan, 1975.

VARIATIONS ON A GULF BREEZE. Ed. Florence Roper & William J. Grant. [Charlottetown]: P.E.I. Centennial Commission, 1973.

VISIONS 2020: FIFTY CANADIANS IN SEARCH OF A FUTURE. Ed. Stephen Clarkson. Edmonton: Hurtig, 1970.

VISIONS FROM THE EDGE: AN ANTHOLOGY OF ATLANTIC CANADIAN SCIENCE FICTION AND FANTASY. Ed. John Bell & Lesley Choyce. Porter's Lake: Pottersfield Press, 1981.

VOGUE'S GALLERY. [London?]: [Vogue Magazine?], 1962. Based on Levine papers.

VOICE AND VISION. Ed. Jack Hodgins & William H. New. Toronto: McClelland & Stewart, 1972.

VOICES DOWN EAST. Ed. Donald Cameron. Halifax: The 4th Estate, [1973].

VOICES II. [Editor unknown]. [Publication data unknown]. Based on Hugh Garner, *Omnibus.*

THE VOICES OF KITIMAT 1967. [Kitimat]: Kitimat Writers' Club, 1967.

WATER. Ed. Peter Carver. Toronto: Peter Martin, n.d.

THE WEST COAST EXPERIENCE. Ed. Jack Hodgins. Toronto: Macmillan, 1976.

WEST INDIAN NARRATIVE: AN INTRODUCTORY ANTHOLOGY. Ed. Kenneth Ramchand. Rev. ed.; Surrey: Thomas Nelson & Sons, 1980.

WEST INDIAN STORIES. Ed. Andrew Salkey. London: Faber & Faber, 1960.

WEST INDIAN STORIES. Ed. John Wickham. London: Ward Lock Educational, 1981. Ward Lock Educational Short Stories No. 19.

WEST OF FICTION. Ed. Leah Flater, Aritha van Herk, & Rudy Wiebe. Edmonton: NeWest Press, 1983.

WHALES: A CELEBRATION. Ed. Greg Gatenby. Toronto: Prentice-Hall/Lester & Orpen Denys, 1983.

WILD ROSE COUNTRY: STORIES FROM ALBERTA. Ed. David Carpenter. Ottawa: Oberon Press, 1977.

WINNIPEG STORIES. Ed. Joan Parr. Winnipeg: Queenston House, 1974.

A WOMAN'S PLACE: AN ANTHOLOGY OF SHORT STORIES. Ed. L. M. Schulman. New York: Macmillan, 1974. Based on Mavis Gallant ABCMA volume and SSI.

WOMEN AND FICTION: SHORT STORIES BY AND ABOUT WOMEN. Ed. Susan Cahill. New York: New American Library, 1975.

WOMEN AND FICTION 2. Ed. Susan Cahill. New York: New American Library, 1978.

WOMEN IN CANADIAN LITERATURE. Ed. M. G. Hesse. Ottawa: Borealis Press, 1976.

WOMEN OF THE WEIRD: EERIE TALES BY THE GENTLE SEX. Ed. Seon Manley & Gogo Lewis. New York: Lothrop, 1976.

THE WORLD OUTSIDE. Ed. Ann Reit. New York: Four Winds, 1977. Based on SSI.

WORLD STORIES. [Editor unknown]. [Place unknown]: University of South Carolina Press, 1977. Based on Hugh Garner, *Omnibus.*

WRITERS AND WRITING. Ed. Patricia Thorvaldson. Toronto: TV Ontario Publications, 1981.

THE WRITERS' CIRCLE. Ed. Rose Cowan. Winnipeg: Univ of Winnipeg Press, 1974.

THE WRITER'S WORKSHOP. Ed. John Parker. Don Mills: Addison-Wesley, 1982. Based on W. D. Valgardson survey response.

ZADIRY. [Editor unknown]. Moscow: Molodaya Gvardije, 1983. Based on Alistair MacLeod survey response.

ZATERIANNAIA ULITSA: SOVREMENNAIA KANADSKAIA NOVELLA. Ed. N. Krolik. Moscow: Progress, 1971. Based on *Malcolm Lowry: A Bibliography.*

ZIEJEWEL. Amsterdam: Uitgeverij Bert Bakker, 1980. Based on ''Jane Rule: A Bibliography.''

Indexes

For each of the indexes listed below - unless otherwise noted - I looked at all of the relevant volumes covering the period, including 1984 volumes which included 1983 material. I have appended the abbreviations I used when citing the indexes in annotations. Following the main list is a supplementary list of science fiction indexes consulted; since they have virtually identical titles I have provided full publication data on them to indicate precisely which volumes I used.

American Humanities Index [AHI]

Canadian Periodical Index [CPI]

Catholic Periodical and Literature Index [CPLI]

Index to Little Magazines: 1950-1967 [ILM]

Index to New Zealand Periodicals: 1966-1984 [INZP]

Index to South African Periodicals

International Index to Periodicals: 1950-1965

Social Sciences and Humanities Index: 1965-1974

Humanities Index: 1974-1984

Miller, Judith Helen. "The Canadian Short Story Database: Checklists and Searches." Ph.D. York Univ., 1981.

Popular Periodical Index: 1973-1982 [PPI]

Reader's Guide to Periodical Literature [RGPL]

Short Story Index [SSI]

Index to the Science Fiction Magazines 1926-1950. Donald B. Day, comp. Boston: G. K. Hall, 1952; rev. ed. 1982.

Index to the Science-Fiction Magazines, 1951-1965. Erwin S. Strauss, comp. Cambridge, MA.: M.I.T. Science Fiction Society, 1965.

Index to the Science Fiction Magazines 1966-1970. West Hanover, MA.: New England Science Fiction Association, 1971.

Index to the Science Fiction Magazines. Cambridge, MA.: Twaci Press: 1977-1983.

Index to the Science Fiction Magazines. Cambridge, MA.: Twaci Press: 1977-1983.

Index to the Semi-Professional Fantasy Magazines. Cambridge, MA.: Twaci Press: 1982.

Notes on Individual Authors

The following notes deal with problems too involved to be covered in annotations, and supply information on published sources used for well-known authors. The most important such source for my bibliography is the *Annotated Bibliography of Canada's Major Authors* series (Toronto: ECW Press). Below, I give the name of the compiler, the volume number, and the year of publication for each bibliography from the series; in the annotations I have simply used the abbreviation ABCMA. While the bibliographies in the series are sometimes incomplete, they represent an invaluable source of information on writers' short-story publications in obscure and foreign publications. Other bibliographies consulted are cited giving full publication information, or as much as is known.

The notes also cover special editorial problems, especially involving those authors whose works do not fit neatly into the category of "short story," and those whose survey responses supplied ambiguous or incomplete data on publications and broadcasts. Since the CBC and its affiliates keep poorer records of broadcasts than do many writers, it is not likely that more detailed information on broadcasts will ever be obtained.

Margaret Atwood - ABCMA Vol. 1 (1979); Alan J. Horne, comp.

Don Austin's works straddle the line between fiction and prose poetry; I have appended the annotation "prose poem?" only to those works that are especially difficult to classify.

Don Bailey has left his papers at the Thomas Fisher Rare Book Library. Based on a cursory inspection, I believe that consulting them would not have contributed substantially if at all to the listings.

William Bankier - Cook, Michael L., comp. *Monthly Murders*. Westport, Conn.: Greenwood Press, 1982. Riley, John M. *Twentieth Century Crime and Mystery Writers*. New York: St. Martin's Press, 1985.

Victoria Branden returned a survey response in which broadcast stories are listed as having been broadcast on "Stories with John Drainie" or "Canadian Short Stories," but she could not recall which story appeared on which program. Sometimes, she could only supply the contract date, not the date of broadcast; in such cases I have estimated the latter. Also, she listed stories appearing in children's magazines and anthologies, which I have omitted unless the story appeared as well in an adult publication.

Michael Bullock's works could best be called "fictions"; I have included the ones he cited in his survey response and those that have a clear narrative thrust.

Eileen Cade-Edwards's stories are difficult to classify for quite a different reason: they are not definitely fictional or non-fictional. It appears that most of her stories are true, if somewhat embellished.

Leslie Croutch - Colombo, John Robert, ed. Bibliography. *Years of Light: A Celebration of Leslie A. Croutch*. Toronto: Hounslow Press, 1982.

Robertson Davies' stories were originally read aloud at the University of Toronto's Massey College Gaudy Nights.

Marian Engel - Wengle, Annette. "Marian Engel: A Select Bibliography." *Room*, 9:2 (1984), 92-9

Beatrice Fines listed articles and serials among her short stories in her very full survey response. When in doubt I relied on my own notes and the titles of works to determine whether they merited inclusion.

Mavis Gallant - ABCMA Vol. 5 (1984). Judith Skelton Grant and Douglas Malcolm, comp.

John Patrick Gillese's listings are somewhat incomplete. Gillese published widely and used many pseudonyms. On the other hand, most of his stories appeared before 1950; some of these may well be included in his listings.

Dave Godfrey's early stories (collected in *Death Goes Better with Coca-Cola*) initially appeared as part of *Saturday Night*'s "Outdoors" column.

Phyllis Gotlieb - Bell, John, comp. "Phyllis Gotlieb: A Checklist of Her SF." *ARC*, No. 14 (Spr 1985), 21-4.

Jack Hodgins - As already noted, all of his stories are included regardless of length.

Hugh Hood - ABCMA Vol. V (1984). J. R. (Tim) Struthers, comp.

W.P. Kinsella's listings are extremely incomplete. Ann Knight has published *W.P. Kinsella: A Partially-Annotated Checklist (1953-1983)*, but it is not widely available.

Henry Kreisel - Gurttler, Karin. Bibliography. "Henry Kreisel: A Canadian Exile Writer?" In *The Old World and the New: Literary Perspectives of German-Speaking Canadians*. Ed. Walter Riedel. Toronto: Univ. of Toronto Press, 1984, pp. 94-106.

Irving Layton - Mayne, Seymour. "Irving Layton: A Bibliography-in-Progress 1931-1971." *WCR*, 7:3 (Jan. 1973), 23-32.

Norman Levine recycled much of his autobiographical material for stories, articles, and novels. I have included whatever appears designed to stand on its own as a work of fiction. (Occasionally even magazine editors had difficulty classifying his work; in fact, one newspaper treated "A Canadian Upbringing" as non-fiction.)

Malcolm Lowry - Lowry wrote his stories well before 1950, but many were not published until much later. I have included those stories not published before 1950, although they do not really belong to the period.

See: Woolmer, J. Howard. *Malcolm Lowry: A Bibliography*. Revere, PN: Woolmer/Brotherson, 1983.

D.M. Morris - Her first name may be Doris or Dorothy; I have listed the two separately in case they are different authors.

Alice Munro - Because she calls it a novel I have omitted *Lives of Girls and Women*, which could easily be classified a story collection.

Dorothy O'Connell's Chiclet Gomez stories were originally broadcast on the CBC.

Howard O'Hagan - The first-publication dates of his stories have been difficult to determine, so I have included the stories I cannot definitely disqualify.

Desmond Pacey - Tierney, Frank M., ed. Bibliography. *Waken, Lords and Ladies Gay*. Ottawa: Univ. of Ottawa Press, 1974.

Helen Porter has read aloud and had broadcast numerous stories; the listings contain only those I could find in print.

Sam Ray - The stories originally appeared in the *Ottawa Evening Citizen Saturday Magazine* under "Question of the Week."

Brenda Riches's works are occasionally difficult to classify, and her survey response cites as "prose poems" works I initially considered fiction. Rather than remove such works from the listings I have kept and annotated them.

Mordecai Richler, like Norman Levine, uses the same autobiographical material in his sketches, short stories, and novels. I have included those works that seem most like short stories. ABCMA Vol. 1 (1979); Michael Darling, comp.

Spider Robinson - I have not included works designated "novelettes."

Leon Rooke - Struthers, J. R. (Tim), et al., comp. "A Preliminary Bibliography of Works by Leon Rooke." *CFM*, No. 38 (1981), 148-64.

Jane Rule - Allison, Ruth, and Ralph Crane, comp. "Jane Rule: A Bibliography: 1 November 1984." Unpublished; Rule sent a copy in her survey response.

Ted Russell's stories were originally broadcast.

Charles Saunders - Saunders, Charles, comp. "The Complete Imaro Checklist 1975-1979." *Dark Fantasy*, No. 18 (1978), 38-42.

Samuel Selvon - Nasta, Susheila. "Samuel Selvon: A Preliminary Bibliography." *J of Commonwealth Lit*, 18:1 (1983), 130-43.

Norman "Doc" Skinner is a self-professed "liar" whose stories usually begin as entries in "tall-tale" contests. I have included those that have been printed, since they are fiction, although they could just as easily be labelled humour.

Rhoda Elizabeth Playfair Stein returned a lengthy story list that mixes adult short stories in among juveniles and articles. I have selected those works known or suspected to be adult stories, in the process likely omitting some works that should have been included.

Gertrude Story's survey response provides the dates on which stories were purchased for radio broadcast rather than the broadcast dates themselves, so I have guessed at the approximate dates of broadcast.

Miriam Waddington - ABCMA Vol. 6 (1985); Laurie Ricou, comp.

David Watmough's stories were broadcast extensively on the CBC, both nationally and regionally in British Columbia. Watmough could not supply much information on these numerous broadcasts; I have listed only those for which I had records.

Ethel Wilson - ABCMA Vol. 5 (1984); Bonnie Martyn McComb, comp.

PART II: AUTHOR INDEX

A., A.
"Old Love" *Pacific Profile* 1:1 (Fall 1961), 25-6 [Originally published in *Transition*].

A.J.N. – *See* N., A.J.

A.N.P [pseudonym]
"The Evening Bells" *Prism* (Mont) No. 2 (1956), 61-3.

Aaron, Michael – *See* Conger, Lesley and Aaron, Michael.

Aass, Jane‡
"The Dancers" *Alpha* 5:2 (Win 1980), 18.

Abbey, Lloyd and Fearns, John
See also Abbey, Lloyd; Fearns, John.
THE ANTLERED BOY Fredericton: Fiddlehead, 1970.

Abbey, Lloyd
See also Abbey, Lloyd and Fearns, John.
"David" *Muse* 1966-67, 13-5.
"Stilts" *Grain* 8:1 [1980], 58-61.

Abbott, Douglas
"The Last Cowboy" *Outset* 1973, 1-7.

Abelsen, Terry‡
"Journey's End" *Words from Inside* 1976, 30-2.
"Out of Control" *Words from Inside* 1976, 28-9.

Ablack, Vera‡
"Whirlpool" *Driftwood* [No. 1] (Apr 1973), 39-43.

Ablett, Pauline†
"Pride Comes Before a Fall" *Origins* 12:1 (Apr 1982), 94-117.

Abnett, Eileen†
"Love Feast" *Pier Spr* 7:4 (Aut 1982), 14-22.
"A Private Sorrow" *Pier Spr* 8:3 (Sum 1983), 42-57.
"A Very Common Condition" *Heartland* No. 2 (Jan-Feb 1981), 14-6, 77-80.
"A Very Common Condition" *Pier Spr* 7:1 (Win 1982), 48-55.
"A View Before Nightfall" *Pier Spr* 8:2 (Spr 1983), 45-54.

Abramovitz, Beverley‡
"The Ring" *Outset* 1974, 1-4.

Abrams, Tevia‡

"Autumn Idyll" *Prism* (Mont) 1958, 29-33.

Acheson, Cavan‡

"Acquired Airs on Ailing High Street" *Liontayles* Win 1967, 49-61.

Acheson, James Dean‡

"Ordeal" *Simcoe R* No. 1 (Win 1976), 39-42.

Acks, Daniel

"Emulation" *Laom R* 2:1 (Mar 1976), 28-32.
"Journey" *Laom R* 1:1 (Dec-Jan 1975), 29-30.

Acland, Lois

"Change of Scene" *Chat* 50 (June 1977), 47, 81-2, 84, 86.

Acorn, Milton (1923-1986)

I'VE TASTED MY BLOOD Ed. Al Purdy. Toronto: Ryerson Press, 1969.
MORE POEMS FOR PEOPLE Toronto: nc Press, 1972.
"The Garbageman Is Drunk" *More Poems for People* (1972), 41-4 [Also entitled "The Man from Headless Valley" and "This Is What the Sign Says: The Garbageman Is Drunk"].
"The Legend of the Winged Dingus" *I've Tasted My Blood* (1969), 77-80.
"The Man from Headless Valley" *Copperfield* No. 1 (1969), 34-40 [Also entitled "This Is What the Sign Says: The Garbageman Is Drunk" and "The Garbageman Is Drunk"].
"The People Wrote It" *NF* 4:3 (Fall 1955), 19.
"The Red and Green Pony" *I've Tasted My Blood* (1969), 80-7.
"This Is What the Sign Says: The Garbageman Is Drunk" *Katharsis* 3:1 (Spr 1970), 16-8 [Also entitled "The Garbageman Is Drunk" and "The Man from Headless Valley"].

Adair, Victor‡

"Bombs Away" *Introductions from an Island* 1971, 30-4.

Adams, Ian (1937-)

"Drowning Gophers" *Repos* No. 12 (Fall 1974), 28-37.

Adams, Richard‡

"Romance of the Children" *Early Evening Pieces* No. 1 (Aug 1975), 15-6.

Adamson, Arthur†

"The Spell of the Ex" *Des* 11:4/12:1 Nos. 30/31 (1980-81), 57-61.

Adamson, Regmore†

"The Music Lesson" *Canadian Short Stories* (1952), 109-14.

Adby, Zara†

"The Bottle Depot" *Gas Rain* 2 (1978), 9-11.

Addario, Frank‡

"Five-Twenty" *Gram* 3:1 (Nov 1977), 4-7.

Addison, B.D.‡
"The Visitation" *AA* 67 (Apr 1977), 57-61.

Adelaide, Sister Mary‡
"Love Must Say 'No' " *Can Lifetime* 4 (May-June 1974), 22-6.
"The Smile" *Can Lifetime* 4 (July-Aug 1974), 14-7.

Ades, Terry‡
"The Inspiration of Gustave Morose" *VWFP/Revue* 1:5 (July 1975), 10-1.

Adler, Eric‡
"Observations of a Street Walker" *Outset* 1974, 5-8.

Adler, Naomi‡
"Dedication" *Amaranth* Spr 1981, [1 p].

Agazarian, Yvonne†
"Final Absolution" *CF* 31 (June 1951), 59, 61-2.
"Final Absolution" *pm* 1:1 (Nov 1951), 34-40.

Agetees, George†
"Letter to Time" *Mont Writers' Forum* 1:7 (Apr 1979), 8-14.
"She Broke Up with Him and Then I Broke Up with Him" *Mont Writers' Forum* 2:2 (Nov 1979), 7-13.
"Soft Places on the Main" *Mont Writers' Forum* 1:10 (July-Aug 1979), 14-7.

Ahmad, Iqbal†
"Grandma" *Literary R* (U.S.) 12 (1969), 445-53.
"The Kumbh Fair" *Fid* No. 80 (May-June-July 1969), 44-52.
"Time to Go" *CF* 46 (Apr 1966), 302-4.

Aho, S.†
"Sunshine for Frisky" *Pier Spr* 6:1 (Win 1981), 30-4.

Aihoshi, Susan M.†
"Nightmare in Retrospect" *Thursday's Voices* (1983), 13-7.

Aitken, W.E.‡
"Too Little! Too Late!" *UC Observer* 12 (1 Feb 1951), 29.

Ajzenstadt, Sam‡
[Untitled] *Jargon* [No. 4] (1961-62), 3-56.

Akenson, Donald Harmon (1941-)
"Farming: The Ontario Line Fences Act (1970)" *QQ* 90 (1983), 132-5.

Akerman, Eric‡
"Pete" *Can Life* 1:5 (Fall 1950), 6-7, 30-1.

Akerman, Jeremy (1942-)
"Wednesday's Child" *Pot Port* 2 (1980-81), 34-5.

Akins, Russell
"The Rock Man" *event* 8:1 (1979), 37-42.

Alaric, Harvey B.
"Night of the Golden Moon" *Black Cat* 1:3 (Hallowe'en 1981), 23-9.

Albatross [pseudonym]
"A Weaver of Dreams" *Nfld Q* 53:1 (Mar 1954), 46.

Albert, Maxine (1943?-)
"During the Fall" *Title Unknown* (1975), 32.

Albert, Nan – *See* Green, H. Gordon.

Aldridge, Mary-Catherine‡
"Perfidia" *Kaleidoscope* 1955-56, 14-7.

Alexander, Joan‡
"The Knife" *TUR* 96:2 (Spr 1983), 46-56.

Alexander, R.W.
"A Book of Birds" *FH* 12 Oct 1961, 54-5.
"The Coon" *FH* 20 Oct 1960, 32-3, 39.

Alexis, Andre†
"Impressions of Africa" *Des* 14:5 No. 43 (Win 1983-84), 93-7.

Alford, Edna (1947-)
A SLEEP FULL OF DREAMS Lantzville, B.C.: Oolichan, 1981.
"Barbed Wire and Balloons" *Sundogs* (1980), 1-14.
"The Birthmark" *Br Out* 6:3 (1979), 12-7.
"Communion" *Prism* 15:2/3 (Sum-Fall 1976), 4-10.
"Communion" *Sleep Full of Dreams* (1981), 57-65.
"Companionship" *Can Golden West* 14:1 [1979?], 20-7.
"Companionship" *Sleep Full of Dreams* (1981), 140-55.
"Fall Cleaning" *Sleep Full of Dreams* (1981), 83-93.
"Five to a Hand" *Dand* 8:1 (1981), 101-12.
"The Garden of Eloise Loon" *NeWest R* 7 (Sept 1981), 11-3.
"The Garden of Eloise Loon" *Saskatchewan Gold* (1982), 179-87.
"A Good Day for a Parade" *Dand* 1 (Sum 1975), 12-23 [Also entitled "Half-Past Eight"].
"Half-Past Eight" *Sleep Full of Dreams* (1981), 66-82 [Also entitled "A Good Day for a Parade"].
"Half-Past Eight" *100% Cracked Wheat* (1983), 331-52.
"Head" *Dand* 9:2 (1982), 39-42.
"The Hoyer" *Fid* No. 111 (Fall 1976), 89-100.
"The Hoyer" *Sleep Full of Dreams* (1981), 9-26.
"Mid-May's Eldest Child" *Sleep Full of Dreams* (1981), 27-40.
"Poll 101" *Sleep Full of Dreams* (1981), 94-107.
"Transfer" *Dand* 8:1 (1981), 8-21.
"Tuesday, Wednesday, Thursday" *JCF* Nos. 17/18 (1976), 8-16.
"Tuesday, Wednesday, Thursday" *Sleep Full of Dreams* (1981), 108-21.

"Under the I" *Sleep Full of Dreams* (1981), 122-39.
"Under the I" *West of Fiction* (1983), 304-18.
"The Visitor" *Sleep Full of Dreams* (1981), 41-56.

Alford, Norman (1929-)
"Allergy" *Mal R* No. 26 (Apr 1973), 57-62.
"Beyond Words" *JCF* 3:3 (1974), 5-8.
"Beyond Words" *Canadian Short Fiction Anthology* (1976), 1-8.
"The Bridge" *CFM* No. 14 (Sum 1974), 48-54.
"The Bungalow" *Mal R* No. 15 (July 1970), 102-8.
"One of Us" *JCF* No. 23 (July 1979), 5-18.
"The Party" *Versus* No. 1 (Sum 1976), 31-5.
"The Swept Place" *Nantucket R* 4 (May 1975), 23[+?] [Based on survey response].
"To the Uncharted Land" *Fid* No. 85 (May-June-July 1970), 93-7.
"To the Uncharted Land" *CBC [Van]* CBC [Van] [date unknown] [Based on survey response].
"The Way Back" *Mal R* No. 50 (Apr 1979), 147-54.

Allaby, Ian†
"Love and Ambrose" *Des* 11:4/12:1 Nos. 30/31 (1980-81), 53-6.

Allan, Ted (1917-)
"The Beating" *CBC "Anthology"* 17 Aug 1974.
"Big Boys Shouldn't Cry" *CBC "Anthology"* [date unknown] [Based on survey response].
"Birdie" *CBC "Anthology"* 1983 [Based on survey response].
"Crazy Joe" *CBC* [date unknown] [Based on survey response].
"For Whom the Horses Run" *Sunday Telegraph Mag* 1961 [Based on survey response].
"Lies My Father Told Me" *Canadian Short Stories* (1952), 41-7.
"Lies My Father Told Me" *Northern Lights* (1960), 531-5.
"Lies My Father Told Me" *CBC "Anthology"* 11 Oct 1975.
"Lies My Father Told Me" *Crossroads 2* (1979), 74-81.
"Lies My Father Told Me" *Inquiry into Literature 3* (1980), 280-6.
"Lies My Father Told Me" *Spice Box* (1981), 82-7.
"Looking for Bessie" *BBC "Monday Night at Home"* 1956 [Based on survey response].
"Love Is a Long Shot" *CBC "Anthology"* 20 Apr 1974.
"A Menace to Society" *CBC "Anthology"* 1983[?] [Based on survey response].
"The Moon to Play With" *CBC "Anthology"* [date unknown] [Based on survey response].
"My Father's Inventions" *CBC "Anthology"* [date unknown] [Based on survey response].
"Rags, Clothes, Bottles" *CJO* 19 (Jan 1981), 11-2.
"Squirrels and Summer Flowers" *CBC "Anthology"* 3 Apr 1971.
"Squirrels and Summer Flowers" *CBC "Anthology"* 1982.
"Two Sisters" *CBC "Anthology"* 198? [Based on survey response].
"What Am I Doing Christmas?" *CBC "Anthology"* 1982 [Based on survey response].
"When Everything Is Allowed" *CBC "Anthology"* 1981 [Based on survey

response].

"When My Uncle Was the Messiah" *CBC "Anthology"* 21 Sept 1974.

"Willie the Squowse" *London Times Saturday R* 1979 [Also anthologized and translated into eleven languages; based on survey response].

"The Woman Luli Sent Me" *BBC* "Monday Night at Home" 1957 [Based on survey response].

Allen, Dale‡

"Joseph" *CSSM* 1:3 (July 1975), 5-8.

Allen, Glen‡

"Been a Bad Winter" *Can Dimension* 8 (June 1972), 23-6.

"Noon Hour" *North* 11 (July-Aug 1964), 38-41.

Allen, Guy B.†

"October 30, 1946" *Repos* No. 6 (Spr 1973), 21-2.

Allen, Heather†

(1942-)

"Old Folks at Home" *Read Ch* 1:3 (Win 1982), 68-72.

"Stockpiling" *Read Ch* 1:1 (Spr 1982), 26-33.

Allen, M.E.†

"Homage" *Quarry* 32:4 (Aut 1983), 40-9.

Allen, Mary Stuart (1935-)

"The Last Summer" *Title Unknown* (1975), 10.

Allen, Peter‡

"Daedalus in the Underworld" *Acta Vic* 82:2 (Feb 1958), 35-6.

Allen, Robert (1946-)

"Bluto's Blues" *Moose R* No. 7 (1983), 19-24.

"from The Weary Chronicles" *Matrix* No. 17 (Fall 1983), 40-57.

"The Man Who Rebuilt Butterflies" *Saturday Night at the Forum* (1981), 66-9.

"The Skippers" *Quarry* 30:3 (Sum 1981), 56-65.

Allen, Robert Thomas (1911-)

"Evening without Clark Gable" *CHJ* Nov 1952, 10, 38, 40-2, 46-7, 50, 52.

"The Gas Bag" *MM* 71 (22 Nov 1958), 22-3, 62-4 [Magazine parody].

"Grassi Place" *MM* 71 (7 June 1958), 24-5, 45-6.

"It's a Woman's World" *Lib* 30 (Apr 1953), 20-1, 38-40.

Allingham, Aari†

"The Cow-Woman" *Ode* No. 3 [n.d.], [1 p].

Allison, Rosemary†

"Aunt Lil" *Writing* No. 2 (Win 1980-81), 11-2.

Allister, Will

"Hail to the Chief" *CBC [Van]* "Hornby Collection" 11 Oct 1980.

Almon, Bert (1943-)

"On an Airless Satellite" *Was R* 10:1 (Spr 1975), 32-7.

"Uncle Charlie Crosses the Tracks" *Fiction Texas* 1:1 (1978), 36-42 [Based on survey response].

Almond, Paul

"A Sheaf of Wheat" *FH* 14 Jan 1954, 24-5.

"A Sheaf of Wheat" *Stories to Read Again* (1965), 79-92.

Alopecia, Anna – *See* Smith, A.J.M.

Alsop, Wayne‡

"The Memory" *Mandala* 1970, 64-5.

Amernic, Jerry‡

"Edward VII" *Scar Fair* 2 (1974-75), [8 pp].

"The Seduction of Molly McGee" *Scar Fair* 1 (1973-74), 48-53.

Ames, Bill‡

"Boats Should Be Seen and Not Heard" *Better Boating* 11 (Sept 1975), 24-5.

"The Bosun and the Blonde" *Better Boating* 11 (Feb 1975), 28-9.

"Nuts to Knots" *Better Boating* 11 (June 1975), 40-1 [Humour].

"Welcome Aboard! Champagne, My Dear?" *Better Boating* 10 (Sept 1974), 8-10.

Amiel, Barbara (1940-)

"The Coloured Pencils" *Undergrad* Spr 1962, 30-4.

Ammeter, A.E.†

"The Cranberry Stain" *Images About Manitoba* 1:2 (Mar 1976), 4-6.

"The Quality of Mercy" *CSSM* 1:4 (Oct 1975), 42-4.

Amprimoz, Alexandre (1948-)

IN ROME Toronto: Three Trees Press, 1980.

SELECTED WRITINGS Winnipeg: Turnstone Press, 1982 [Based on CBIP].

"Biting the Dogs" *CFM* No. 16 (Win 1975), 92-8.

"Each Asparagus Is an Angel" *Exile* 3:3/4 (1976), 49-56.

"Early Impressions" *Beyond Baroque* (U.S.) 2:2 No. 712 (1972), 54-7.

"Escargots" *Fid* No. 108 (Win 1976), 43-50.

"Filming an Idea" *Grain* 10:2 (May 1982), 56-8.

"Forced Labour" *Was R* 10:1 (Spr 1975), 23-30.

"Good-bye Bibi" *Fid* No. 121 (Spr 1979), 97-107.

"The House" *CFM* No. 9 (Win 1973), 9-15.

"The House" *In Rome* (1980), 43-8.

"I Want My Mother" *Des* 11:4/12:1 Nos. 30/31 (1980-81), 82-96.

"In Praise of Professionals" *Wee Giant* 2:3 (Spr 1979), 30-1.

"The Last Struggle for Life" *Exile* 2:3/4 (1975), 121-31.

"Lazar Cat" *Quarry* 31:1 (Win 1982), 23-30.

"Nonno Liked to Sleep" *Rampike* 3:2 [1983?], 57.

"Not Only of Words" *Waves* 4:1 (Aut 1975), 64-5.

"Notes for an Impossible Fiction" *Was R* 13:1 (Spr 1978), 20-2.

"O.T. Necrapala" *Grain* 7:1 [1979], 39-44.

"Of Rats and Snakes (A University Legend)" *UWR* 10:2 (Spr-Sum 1975), 58-63.

"Preludes" *Was R* 8:2 (Fall 1973), 23-33.

"Preludes" *In Rome* (1980), 7-18.

"A Prophet with Hindsight" *Arts Man* 2:2 (Win 1983), 68.

"The Rattlesnake" *CFM* No. 10 (Spr 1973), 58-71.

"The Rattlesnake" *In Rome* (1980), 31-42.

"Repeating Dreams" *Des* 9:1/2 Nos. 20/21 (1978), 136-43.

"Seeds for the Sonata of Birds" *Prism* 12:2 (Fall 1972), 4-14.

"Seeds for the Sonata of Birds" *In Rome* (1980), 19-29.

"The Story I Never Heard" *Rubicon* No. 2 (Win 1983-84), 30-2.

"Street Plays in the Village of Black Houses" *Arts Man* 2:2 (Win 1983), 68-9.

"Street Plays in the Village of Black Houses" *Des* 14:4 No. 42 (Fall 1983), 129-30.

"Suicide Seeds" *Repos* No. 13 (Win 1975), 28-36.

"A Text" *Repos* Nos. 17/18 (Win-Spr 1976), 85-7.

"Thinking About One of His Stories" *Cap R* No. 10 (Fall 1976), 140-2.

[Title unknown] *Quarterly* 1974 [Based on survey response].

[Title unknown] *CSP. World News* 1975, [5 pp] [Based on survey response].

[Titles unknown] *Center* (1973; 1974) [Based on survey response].

[Titles unknown] *Orion* (U.S.) 1972; 1973 [Based on survey response].

[Titles unknown] *Slowglass* 1974 [Based on survey response].

[Titles unknown] *Wisconsin R* 1974 [Based on survey response].

[Titles unknown] *New York Cultural Review* 1974 [Based on survey response].

"When in Rome" *Grain* 7:1 [1979], 29-38.

"You Are a Bastard Mr. Death" *Quarry* 32:2 (Spr 1983), 50-2.

"The Yo-Yo Champ" *Des* 11:1/2 Nos. 27/28 (1980), 210-1.

Anastacio, Michael‡

"The Image Is Like That, It Started Out of a Simple Light" *Scar Fair* 9 (1982), 43-4 [Prose poem?].

Ancevich, Jon‡

"Fadeaway" *Varsity Lit Issue* Fri, 13 Dec 1963, 21-3.

"Graduation Day" *TUR* 75:2 (Jan 1962), 10-31.

"The Oil Baptists of the Indignants" *Jargon* 1961-62, 20-4.

"Pilgrimage" *TUR* 75:1 (Nov 1961), 24-7.

Anco, Rich‡

"A Midnight Clear" *Varsity* Fri, 12 Dec 1952, 2.

Anderson, Alberta†

"Late Bloom" *Fresh Grease* (1971), 42-8.

Anderson, Dagny†

"Shadows in the Snow Storm" *Treeline* 2 (1983), 26-7 [Non-fiction?].

Anderson, Evelyn‡

"The Latest 'Noos' from By-Pass Cove" *Atl Guardian* 7 (Oct 1950), 24-6.

Anderson, Fred‡

"Summer Course" *Outset* 1974, 9-23.

Anderson, G.S.†

"The Face of God" *Pres Record* 90 (Dec 1965), 18-20.

Anderson, Gwendolyn‡
"Solo" *Alpha* 4:2 (Win 1979), 14, 27, 34.

Anderson, Helen Weldon†
"Ethel and the Pink Lady's Slippers" *Can Messenger* 92 (May 1982), 8-9.
"Mrs. Miller Goes to Ottawa" *Can Messenger* 89 (May 1979), 8-9.
'The Triangle" *Can Messenger* 90 (Nov 1980), 8-9, 18.

Anderson, Jay‡
"Edie" *AA* 53 (June 1963), 77-9.

Anderson, Jim‡
"Athens" *TUR* 79:1 (Oct-Nov 1965), 22-6.
"Knock, Knock" *TUR* 79:4 (Apr 1966), 24-6.

Anderson, Mavis†
'I Knew Queen Victoria's Sister" *Earth and You* 4 Nos. 19/20 [n.d.], 5-10.

Anderson, Rod‡
'Think of a Number" *TUR* 68:5 (Sum 1956), 33-6.

Anderson, Thomas‡
'The Nature of the Beast" by Therion *TUR* 73:1 (Nov 1959), 12-5.

Anderson, Tonia‡
"Quietus" *Creative Campus* 1964, 9-11.

Andre-Czerniecki, Marion (1921-)
'The American Boots" *JD* Rosh Hashanah 1977, 44-7, 52-5, 60.
'The Gates" *Mont* 36 (Apr 1962), 46-9.
'The Gates" *CBC "Anthology"* 20 Apr 1962.
'The Gates" *JD* Passover 1975, 62-5.
'The Leave-Taking" *JD* Passover 1975, 40-3, 46-9, 52-7.
'The Leave-Taking" *JD* Rosh Hashanah 1976, 22-7, 30-3, 36-9.
'Maria B" *JD* Passover 1979, 2-6, 8, 10, 12, 14, 16, 18.
'The Saviour" *JD* Passover 1980, 26, 28, 30, 32.
'The Unique Case of Professor Talentire" *JD* Passover 1977, 14-20.

Andrews, Bill‡
"Smashing" *Katharsis* 1971, [8 pp].

Andrews, Donald‡
'Hunter's Death" *AA* 58 (Nov 1967), 40-1, 43.

Andrews, Jancis‡
"Claws" *CBC [Van] "Hornby Collection"* 8 Jan 1983 [Genre unspecified].

Andrews, Louise†
"Ascrololidan" *JD* Hanukah 1974, 38-9.
"Officer 19826" *JD* Passover 1974, 36-43.

Andrews, Marke†
'Home Life" *CFM* Nos. 2/3 (Spr-Sum 1971), 63-6.

Andrus, David A.

"As Young as She Felt" *JCF* No. 20 (1977), 68-82.

"Up North" *UTR* 6 (1982), 25-7.

Andrychuk, Krist

"From Suburbia" *Quarry* 21:3 (Sum 1972), 40-8.

Angus, Irist

"Henry's Birthday" *First Encounter* 1971, 8-11.

Annan, A.C.‡

"Blue" *Raven* No. 7 (Nov 1958), [6 pp].

Annand, Alan M.

"Able Baker One" *Antig R* No. 18 (Sum 1974), 59-66.

"A Bagful of Holes" *Antig R* No. 30 (Sum 1977), 11-4.

"Rosie Was a Good Old Dog" *Fid* No. 106 (Sum 1975), 31-7.

Annesley, Fred†

"Short Circuit" *Waves* 11:4 (Spr 1983), 29-38.

Annett, R. Ross (1895-)

See also Annett, R. Ross and Annett, William S.

"Babe and the Birds and Bees" *Sat Eve Post* 226 (26 June 1954), 31, 56-8, 60.

"Babe and the Bully" *Sat Eve Post* 229 (26 Jan 1957), 31, 46-8.

"Babe and the Cattle Thief" *Sat Eve Post* 227 (25 Dec 1954), 25, 76-7.

"Babe and the Hungry Soldier" *Sat Eve Post* 224 (15 Dec 1951), 31, 70-1, 73-4.

"Babe in Disgrace" *Sat Eve Post* 222 (29 Apr 1950), 35, 90, 92-3, 95-6.

"Babe Prays for a Miracle" *Sat Eve Post* 225 (13 Sept 1952), 30, 138, 140, 142-3, 145.

"Babe's Christmas Wish" *Sat Eve Post* 228 (17 Dec 1955), 31, 50, 54.

"Babe's New Dog" *Sat Eve Post* 229 (1 Sept 1956), 29, 65-7.

"Babe's Strange Illness" *Sat Eve Post* 228 (1 Oct 1955), 31, 102, 104-6.

"Babe's Surprise" *Sat Eve Post* 230 (7 June 1958), 36, 81, 84, 88-9.

"Big Joe's Alibi" *Sat Eve Post* 232 (18 June 1960), 34, 74. 76.

"Big Joe's Dilemma" *Sat Eve Post* 233 (6 Aug 1960), 31, 80-1.

"Blizzard Warning" *SW* 4 Apr 1953, II:10, 12.

"The Bridge" *SW* 9 Jan 1954, II:1, 12.

"Confidence Man" *Sat Eve Post* 224 (18 Aug 1951), 31, 42, 45-6, 49.

"A Couple of Dimes" *FH* 6 Aug 1959, 20-1.

"A Dream House" *FH* 15 Jan 1953, 24-5, 31.

"Gentle Like a Cyclone" *22 Stories About Horses and Men* (1953) [Pre-1950? Based on SSI].

"A Job with a Future" *SW* 12 Nov 1955, II:3, 12.

"Joe's Secret Plan" *Sat Eve Post* 231 (23 Aug 1958), 31, 79-82.

"The Land-Grabber" *Sat Eve Post* 226 (1 Aug 1953), 31, 79-81.

"Like with a Preacher" *SW* 25 Apr 1964, 8-9, 12, 16.

"Little Joe on the Spot" *Sat Eve Post* 231 (9 May 1959), 37, 59-60, 62.

"Little Joe on Trial" *Sat Eve Post* 232 (1 Aug 1959), 31, 44, 46, 48.

"Little Joe vs. the Blackmailer" *Sat Eve Post* 231 (13 Sept 1958), 37, 60, 64, 66.

"Little Joe's Revenge" *Sat Eve Post* 230 (8 Feb 1958), 31, 72, 74.

"The Pay-Off" *FH* 13 July 1953, 20-1, 48.

"Pop's Springtime Fancy" *Sat Eve Post* 229 (16 Mar 1957), 37, 128-32.
"A Promise to Babe" *Sat Eve Post* 228 (20 Aug 1955), 31, 87-90.
" 'Step' for Short" *SW* 23 Sept 1950, I:7, 13.
"Stolen Money" *Sat Eve Post* 224 (10 May 1952), 35, 146-8, 150-1.
"A Surprise for Babe" *Sat Eve Post* 225 (8 Nov 1952), 35, 115, 117-8, 121.
"The Suspicious Stranger" *Sat Eve Post* 223 (27 Jan 1951), 28, 139-43.
"A Wife for Pop" *Sat Eve Post* 226 (8 May 1954), 37, 140, 143-4, 146.

Annett, William S. (1928-)

See also Annett, R. Ross and Annett, William S.
"The Bad Weed" *CF* 30 (Oct 1950), 157, 159.
"The Death of the Coyote" *NR* 3:3 (Feb-Mar 1950), 23-6.
"Rebellion of Brill" *SW* 10 Sept 1955, I:1, 14.
"The Relic" *Canadian Short Stories* (1952), 76-87.

Annett, R. Ross and Annett, William S.

See also Annett, R. Ross; Annett, William S.
"A Guy Named Riley" *SW* 11 Feb 1956, II:3, 12.

Anonymous

"5 to 9" *Hysteria* 1:4 (Spr 1982), 12-4 [Listed as article].
"Barnyard Socialism" *Outlook* [1981], 16.
"Bath Oil" *JD* Sum 1972, 56-7.
"Beach" *On the Bias* 1 [n.d.], [2 pp].
"Better Have a Cigar, Judge!" *Scarlet & Gold* No. 40 (1958), 148 ["From an old issue of *The Quarterly*" (editorial note)].
"Billy the Bladge" *Scarlet and Gold* No. 46 (1964), 137.
"Brief Encounter" *Pulp* 2:17 (15 Nov 1974), [2 pp].
"Canada's Crucial Role in Europe" *Hyperbole* No. 3 (May 1962), [2 pp].
"Christmas Homecoming" *Nfld Q* 57:4 (Dec 1958), 4-5, 34-6, 45-6.
"The City of the Dead" *Iron* No. [10] (Spring Iron [1970?]), [2 pp] ["Hawilgate 1924" at end of story].
"The Club" *TUR* 84:3 (Sum 1971), 10-1.
"The Confessions of Santa Claus" *Onward* 24 Dec 1961, 3-4.
"The Confessions of Santa Claus" *Rapport* Dec 1968, 12-3.
"Danger in the Desert" *SW* 6 Apr 1957, 12-3, 28.
"A Day's Journey" *Writing* No. 1 (Sum 1980), 11-2.
"Dem Ole Mosquito Blues" *Hibiscus Dawn* No. 3 (16 Oct 1967), 1-2.
"The Demonstration" *New Literature & Ideology* No. 19 (Feb 1976), 88-106.
"The Devil Dance on Orleans" *Can Life* 1:4 (Spr 1950), 5.
"Dirty Face Pete" *Scarlet and Gold* No. 46 (1964), 137.
"The Eternal Prospector" *Scarlet & Gold* No. 47 (1965), 89.
"Fable One" *Gambit* No. 5 [n.d.], [1 p].
"Fact or Fiction or Whatever" *Outlook* [1981], [1 p].
"The Fire Mountain" *Magenta Frog* No. 2 (1972), [7 pp].
"Flight from Christmas" *SW* 14 Dec 1957, 18-9.
"For Your Own Good" *Harbinger* 7 Aug 1968, 12-3.
"Frisco ... " *Beetle* No. 2 (4 Jan 1971), 13.
"Grandpa" *Pulp* 3:9 (1 Jan 1976), [4].
"Grogery Pack Tells About the Real Compleat Angler" *Hyperbole* No. 3 (May 1962), [1 p] [Parody].

"Had Myself a Merry Little Christmas" *Pedestal* 4:1 (Jan 1972), 5.

"Headofficestuff" *Gambit* No. 5 [n.d.], [1 p].

"High Finance" *Scarlet & Gold* 35 (1953), 125, 127.

"I a Wino" *Afterthought* 1:1 (May 1970), 25.

"I Want to Be Free" *Flow* Win [1975?], [1 p].

"An Important Change in My Outlook on Life as a Result of Two Events That Took Place During My Childhood" *Magenta Frog* No. 2 (1972), [5 pp].

"Indian 'Cinderella' " *Elbow Drums* [Apr 1978?], [3 pp].

"Legend of the Cards" *Scarlet & Gold* No. 46 (1964), 145.

"A Lighter Shade of Green" *TUR* 81:2 (Win 1968), 18-20.

"The Lone Cabin Mystery" *Scarlet & Gold* No. 45 (1963), 41-4.

"Madame Bovary's Training Bra" *OPT* 7:4/5 (Sept-Oct 1980), 7 ["A Suppressed Episode by Gustav Flaubert and Derek Pell"].

"A Mother's Love" *Nfld Q* 57:2 (June 1958), 23, 25.

"Mrs Watchimacallit" *Pedestal* 3:7 (July 1971), 2.

"Night in the Big Swamp" *SW* 5 Jan 1957, 24-5, 32.

"NLG X-B " *Pinch* Nov 1965, 23.

"Offspring" *Prism* (Mont) No. 2 (1956), 36-8.

"On the Avenue" *Pinch* Nov 1965, 20-1.

"Operation Smoothie" *Time Gatherers* (1970), 59-61.

"Party" *TUR* 81:2 (Win 1968), 7-8.

"Paul" *Flow* Win [1975?], [2 pp].

"Philosophy of Design" *This – Media Free Times* 1:1 B [n.d.], [5 pp].

"Pink Garter for Prudence" *SW* 7 Mar 1964, 6-9.

"A Question" *JD* Sum 1975, 76-80.

"The Question" *Amethyst* 3:3 (Spr 1964), 25-6.

"Rags of a Saint" *Migdal* 2:2 [n.d.], 7.

"The Reason Why" *Onward* 6 Mar 1955, 146-7.

"School Days" *Outlook* Dec 1977, 30-1.

"Seamus and the Windy Day" *Magenta Frog* No. 2 (1972), [3 pp].

"A Selection from the Private Records of the Late Deceased Dr. O'Faolan Umna n'Atura, Humanist" *Jabberwocky* Feb 1966, [9 pp].

"The Shadow Fighter" *Magenta Frog* No. 2 (1972), [4 pp].

"A Short Visit to Heaven" *Magenta Frog* No. 2 (1972), [2 pp].

"Sottish Solomon" *Los* No. 5 (1977), 11.

"Temple and Car" *Blow Up* 1:4 (1980), [1 p].

"There's No Free Lunch" *Elbow Drums* Mar 1976, [2 pp].

"Ticket to Ride" *UC Gargoyle* 26:4 (2 Dec 1981), 6.

"Too Much Dough" *Uk Can* 6 (1 Mar 1952), 4 [Listed as "Humour and Satire"].

"A Touch of ... Larceny" *Scarlet & Gold* No. 48 (1966), 49-54.

"Tripper" *Pulp* 3:15 (15 Apr 1976), [2-4].

"Unknown Column #314 – A Totally Fictitious Allegory to Make with What You Will" *Daily Planet* 11 Jan 1969 [?], [1 p].

[Untitled] *Marooned* Feb 1967, [2 pp].

[Untitled] *blewointmentpress* 4:1 [1966?], [1 p].

"Warning: Walking Can Be Dangerous" *Outlook* Oct 1983, 18-21.

"Where My Cowboy Boots Have Been" *UC Gargoyle* 26:4 (2 Dec 1981), 7.

"You Gotta Stay Ahead" *Time Gatherers* (1970), 50-9.

"You're Their Mother" *Pedestal* 3:2 (Feb 1971), 15 [Non-fiction?].

"Yule Get Yours" *Varsity* Thu, 13 Dec 1956, 6.

Anthony, George‡
"Triplex" *Fifth Page* 1962, 29-32.

Antoniak, Jane
"The Unusual Marker" *Squatch J* No. 10 (Win-Spr 1979-80), 36-7.

Antoshewski, Anne-Marie†
"A Gift of Trust" *Northern Mosaic* 1 (Dec 1981), 13.

Appleby, Margaret A.‡
"The Death's Head" *AA* 52 (Jan 1962), 68.

Appleford, R. Duncan† (1938-)
"Origin Unknown" *SF: Inventing the Future* (1972), 86-94.
"Origin Unknown" *Read Ch* 1:1 (Spr 1982), 86-93.

Appleton, Hilary‡
"End of an Era" *Quote Unquote* 2:4 (Oct 1979), 11.

Arato, Rona†
"Meyer Kempel's Garden" *Read Ch* 2:1 (Spr 1983), 34-9.

Archer, Rodney‡
"Grendel Greene" *TUR* 74:2 (Mar 1961), 16-8 [Based on medieval romance].
"Grunda Mist" *TUR* 73:2 (Dec 1959), 4-5.

Arelio, Deanne‡
[Untitled] *Repos* No. 1 [1972], 15-27.

Argondezzi, Vincent‡
"The Talking Hearing Aid" *Deaf Can* 5:8/9 (Aug-Sept 1980), 31-3.

Ariano, David‡
"The Green Pickle" *Pier Spr* 1:2 (Spr 1977), 38 [Satire].

Ariano, Vera Nanson†
"Jimmy" *Pier Spr* Spr 1978, 30-2.

Armand, Dorothy‡
"A Woman in Love" *Raven* 2 [No. 4] (Spr 1957), 26-30.

Armour, Heather†
"It's Not What You Think" *Mont Writers' Forum* 2:5 (Feb 1980), 9-14.

Armstrong, Dorothy L.‡
"A Lion Skin" *AA* 54 (Sept 1963), 73, 75.

Armstrong, George‡
"Reinhardt" *Pier Spr* 1:1 (Aut 1976), 41-4.

Armstrong, Margaret†
"The Triangle" *From* 231 [1:1] (Spr 1972), 1-8.

Armstrong, Patricia (1913-)

"Almost All for Love" CBC [Reg] "Saskatchewan Short Stories" 1972 [Based on survey response].

"A-Walkin & A-Talkin" CBC [Reg] "Saskatchewan Short Stories" 15 Jan 1977 [Based on survey response].

"The Baking Powder Tin" West Producer 16 July 1959, 16 [Based on survey response].

"Bobby & the Fire Chief" CBC "Bernie Braden Reads a Story" 1954; 1955 [Based on survey response].

"The Bracelet" West Producer 2 May 1957, 16 [Based on survey response].

"Calamitous Courtship" CHJ Feb 1958, 27, 45-6, 52 [Also entitled "Rocky Road to Romance"].

"The Cellars of Buffalo Junction" CBC [Reg] "Saskatchewan Short Stories" 1974 [Based on survey response].

"Christmas Magic" CBC [Reg] "Saskatchewan Short Stories" 1974 [Based on survey response].

"The Cold Honeymoon Wind" West Producer 19 Nov 1959, 24 [Based on survey response].

"Contrary Katrina" SW 26 Apr 1958, 24-5, 46.

"The Councillor" West Producer 7 Aug 1958, 16 [Based on survey response].

"Day of Decision" Smoke Signals 3 (1978) [Based on SWG survey response].

"The Fairy Princess & the Feet of Clay" West Producer 14 July 1966, C3 [Based on survey response].

"The Feud and the Fire" FH 21 July 1966, 38-9.

"The Girl Above the Mantle" Woman's Illustrated Aug 1958 [Based on survey response].

"Grownups Get So Muddled" West Producer 13 Sept 1956, 16 [Based on survey response].

"The Hobo Tea" FH 19 Mar 1953, 28-9, 38-9.

"The Hobo Tea" Landrace Mag Nov 1957, 13[+?] [Based on survey response].

"Impossible Pupil" FH 14 Apr 1960, 24-5, 28.

"In Small Towns, Everybody Knows" CBC [Reg] "Saskatchewan Short Stories" 1974 [Based on survey response].

"It Wasn't Seemly" FH 19 June 1952, 24-5.

"The Lady and the Labourer" Read Ch 2:1 (Spr 1983), 74-80.

"The Lady Was a Horse Thief" FH 10 Nov 1965, 28-9.

"Letter from Home" West Producer 26 Apr 1973, C2 [Based on survey response].

"Lines Don't Lie" West Producer 30 Oct 1958, 16 [Based on survey response; may be entitled "Lines Never Lie"].

"Mail-Order Bride" CHJ Sept 1956, 19, 34, 36, 39-41.

"Mail-Order Bride" Woman's Illustrated (U.K.) 12 July 1958 [Based on survey response].

"Man from Nowhere" West Producer 23 Mar 1961, 19 [Based on survey response].

"The Man in the Elevator" West Producer 1957 [Based on survey response].

"Mr. Waverly and Slippery Jake" Skylark 17:2 (Win 1980), 16-20.

"My Father and the Book Agent" Smoke Signals 2 [Date unknown] [Based on SWG survey response].

"No Glamor in Glasses" West Producer 17 Apr 1958, 24 [Based on survey

response].

"No Thrill for Nancy" *West Producer* 14 Nov 1957 [Based on survey response].

"Nobody Ever Knew" *CBC [Reg] "Ambience"* 1981 [Based on survey response].

"Peanut Butter Hero" *CSSM* 2:1 (Jan 1976), 31-4.

"Rocky Road to Romance" *Woman's Illustrated* 24 May 1958 [Also entitled "Calamitous Courtship"; based on survey response].

"Rod's Pound of Flesh" *Report on Farming* Nov 1980, 31 [Based on survey response].

"A Romp with Comp" *Skylark* 2:1 (Oct 1965), 29 [Based on survey response].

"A Sensible Man" *FH* 24 Nov 1966, 32-3.

"The Showdown" *West Producer* 15 Aug 1957, 14 [Based on survey response].

"A Small Thing" *West Producer* 23 Feb 1961 [Based on survey response].

"The Story of Millicent" *Can Landrace Mag* 1958 [Based on survey response].

"That Sort of Day" *West Producer* 3 Nov 1960, 21 [Based on survey response].

"The Third Wish" *CBC [Reg] "Saskatchewan Short Stories"* 1973 [Based on survey response].

"The Visit" *CBC [Reg] "Ambience"* 18 Dec 1982 [Based on survey response].

"Was I You – I Wouldn't" *West Producer* 22 May 1958, 16 [Based on survey response].

"A Wife Runs Away" *Report on Farming* Sept 1982 [Based on survey response].

"Wilderness Wife" *FH* 28 Nov 1957, 24-5.

"You Can't Trust Farmers" *FH* 25 June 1953, 20-1.

Armstrong, Sean†

"Border Crossing" *This* 17:2 (June 1983), 29-33.

Arn, Robert (1942-)

"Not Again?" *Saskatchewan Writing* 2 (1963), 43-51.

Arnason, David (1940-)

FIFTY STORIES AND A PIECE OF ADVICE Winnipeg: Turnstone Press, 1982.

"Binary Lovers" *Story So Far* 5 (1978), 7-16.

"Binary Lovers" *Fifty Stories* (1982), 99-109.

"The Body" *Fifty Stories* (1982), 29-35.

"The Committee" *Prairie Fire* 4:4 (Mar-Apr 1983), 20-3.

"The Event" *Fifty Stories* (1982), 77-84.

"Fifty Stories and a Piece of Advice" *Fifty Stories* (1982), 1-16.

"A German Lunatic on Top of the CPR Building" *Fifty Stories* (1982), 193-8.

"The Indian, the Dancer and the Sailor" *Fifty Stories* (1982), 41-6.

"Lady in Waiting" *Fifty Stories* (1982), 123-5.

"A Letter to History Teachers" *Fifty Stories* (1982), 85-91.

"Morning Letter" *Arts Man* 1:3/4 (Win 1978), 93-6.

"Morning Letter" *Fifty Stories* (1982), 111-21.

"The Movie" *Fifty Stories* (1982), 145-9.

"Oli Andras" *Fifty Stories* (1982), 141-3.

"Over and Over" *Fifty Stories* (1982), 47-52.

"Owl on Cairn" *Fifty Stories* (1982), 37-40.

"Sleeping Jesus and the Scavengers" *Fifty Stories* (1982), 127-40.

"The Sunfish" *Fifty Stories* (1982), 61-75.

"They Went Berrypicking" *Fifty Stories* (1982), 53-9.
"The Unmarried Sister" *Arts Man* 2:1 (Fall 1982), 72.
"The Washing Machine" *Fifty Stories* (1982), 17-27.

Arnold, Ricky‡

"The Agreement" *Acta Vic* 79:[2] (Dec 1952), 18-9.
"The Tragic Tale of Old Burwash" *Acta Vic* 76:1 (Nov 1951), 17-8.

Arnott, Hope‡

"The Wedding" *Acta Vic* 74:3 (Jan 1950), 15-7.

Arrell, Leigh‡

"Nine to Five" *Muse* 60:2 (Dec 1950), 11-2.

Arrol, Ed†

" 'Interlude at Rainbow' " *Onward* 5 June 1955, 353-5, 366-7.
" 'Interlude at Rainbow' " *Onward* 6 June 1965, 3-4.
"Zou Zou and the Preacher" *Onward* 28 Oct 1956, 689-91, 703.
"Zou Zou and the Preacher" *Onward* 27 Spet 1964, 4-5, 10-1.

Arscott, David

ACROSS THE MARGIN AND OTHER STORIES Vancouver: n.p., 1970 ["Seven of these stories are essentially true. All are presented as fiction" (author's note)].
"Across the Margin" *Across the Margin* (1970), 1-32.
"Breakdown" *Across the Margin* (1970), 108-21.
"Committee Report" *Across the Margin* (1970), 61-77.
"Mountain" *Across the Margin* (1970), 78-83.
"Precision, Perception and an Oil Drum" *Across the Margin* (1970), 103-7.
"A Question of Outlook" *Across the Margin* (1970), 89-102.
"The Signal" *Across the Margin* (1970), 33-9.
"The Stallion" *Across the Margin* (1970), 40-9.
"A Twentieth Century Success" *Across the Margin* (1970), 84-8.
"Whiteout" *Across the Margin* (1970), 50-60.

Arthur, Harry‡

"Did He Who Made the Lamb Make Thee?" *Varsity Lit Issue* Tue, 1 Mar 1955, 4-5 [Excerpt].

Aselstyne, Lynn‡

"Dnoyeb Em" *Talon* [1:2 (1964?)], [1 p].

Ash, Fred

"Easter Morning on Tinker Island" *War Cry* 21 Apr 1973, 14-5 [Non-fiction?].

Ashcroft, Sheila†

"Cloe" *Miss Chat* 10 (Sum 1973), 73, 100-3.
"The Convert" *Miss Chat* 11 (3 Sept 1974), 76-81.
"Lovers" *Miss Chat* 12 (13 Nov 1975), 78, 92-4.
"The Mind's Eye" *Miss Chat* 11 ([Spr] 1974), 69-73.
"Reflections of Sartre" *New Mitre* No. 1 (1971), 48-50.
"Resurrection" *New Mitre* 1972, 31-2.

Ashford, Deborah†

"A Day in the Death of a Housewife" *CFM* No. 14 (Sum 1974), 74-86.

Aspler, Tony (1939-)

"The Parrot" *Contemporary R* 219 (Oct 1971), 201-4.
"The Teacher" *JCF* 3:4 (1975), 39-40.

Asplund, Susan†

"Murder of a Man" *Whetstone* Spr 1971, [2 pp].

Asquith, Glenn H.‡

"Christmas and Mr. Smith" *Pres Record* 99 (Dec 1975), 14-6.
"The Christmas Star" *Pres Record* 98 (Dec 1974), 2-3.

Assmann, Winny (1956-)

"Woolsey" *Amaranth* Spr 1981, [3 pp].

Astin, John – *See* MacKinnon, Donald.

Atchison, Michael‡

"Invasion of Privacy" *Adder* 1:2 [1961?], 11.

Atkinson, George‡

"Even Machines Break Down" *Undergrad* Spr 1953, 12-6.

Atkinson, Keith†

"The Idiot Lady" *Waves* 10:1/2 (Sum-Fall 1981), 26-9.

Atkinson, Steve‡

"A Long Way Home" *Alive* No. 43 [n.d.], 10.

Atman [pseudonym]

"Lament for a Writer" *Prism* (Mont) No. 3 (1957), 38-9.

Atwood, Joan-Mary‡

See also Atwood, Joan-Mary and Holt, Muriel.
"The Ball" *Acta Vic* 74:3 (Jan 1950), 7-9.
"Ciceronia Graduateth" *Acta Vic* 75:4 (Mar 1951), 19-20.
"Sladislavus Buyeth a House" *Acta Vic* 75:1 (Mar 1951), 19-20.

Atwood, Joan-Mary and Holt, Muriel‡

See also Atwood, Joan-Mary.
"Rebellion on Euclid Avenue" *Acta Vic* 74:3 (Jan 1950), 22.

Atwood, Margaret (1939-)

BLUEBEARD'S EGG Toronto: McClelland & Stewart, 1983.
DANCING GIRLS Toronto: McClelland & Stewart, 1977.
MURDER IN THE DARK: SHORT FICTIONS AND PROSE POEMS Toronto:
Coach House Press, 1983.
"The Afterlife of Ishmael" *Whales* (1983), 210.
"Betty" *Chat* 51 (Feb 1978), 41, 84, 86-8, 90, 92-4.
"Betty" *MS Mag* 9 (Oct 1980), 59, 61, 63-4, 81-2.
"Betty" *Fine Lines* (1981), 195-216.

"Betty" *Bluebeard's Egg* (1983), 111-32.
"Bluebeard's Egg" *Bluebeard's Egg* (1983), 133-66.
"Bluebeard's Egg" *Chat* 56 (Nov 1983), 79, 119-22, 124, 126, 130-2.
"Bread" *Iowa R* 12:2/3 (Spr-Sum 1981), 7-8.
"The Child Is Now" *Sheet* 1:1 (Jan 1960), 10-2.
"A Cliché for January" *Acta Vic* 83:4 (Feb 1959), 7-9.
"Dancing Girls" *Dancing Girls* (1977), 219-36.
"Encounters with the Element Man" *Imp* 1:2 (Win 1972), 24-31.
"Encounters with the Element Man" *Story So Far* 2 (1973), 9-16.
"Giving Birth" *Dancing Girls* (1977), 237-54.
"Giving Birth" *Chat* 51 (Mar 1978), 35-6 [Excerpt].
"The Glass Slippers" *Acta Vic* 82:3 (Mar 1958), 16-7.
"Going to Bed" *Evidence* No. 9 [1965?], 5-10.
"The Grave of the Famous Poet" *72: New Canadian Stories* 112-33.
"The Grave of the Famous Poet" *Modern Canadian Stories* (1975), 62-74.
"The Grave of the Famous Poet" *Dancing Girls* (1977), 85-98.
"Hair Jewellery" *MS Mag* 5 (Dec 1976), 53-4, 82-3, 85-8.
"Hair Jewellery" *Dancing Girls* (1977), 111-30.
"Happy Endings" *Murder in the Dark* (1983), 37-40.
"Horror Comics" *Murder in the Dark* (1983), 13 [Prose poem?].
"Hurricane Hazel" *Bluebeard's Egg* (1983), 31-59.
"Insula Insularum" *Acta Vic* [85:3] (Feb 1961), 6-11.
"Lives of the Poets" *Dancing Girls* (1977), 203-17.
"Lives of the Poets" *SN* 92 (Apr 1977), 38-43.
"Loulou; or, The Domestic Life of the Language" *Bluebeard's Egg* (1983), 61-81.
"Loulou; or, The Domestic Life of the Language" *SN* 98 (June 1983), 60-4, 66, 68-9.
"The Man from Mars" *Dancing Girls* (1977), 19-42.
"The Man from Mars" *Ont R* No. 6 (Spr-Sum 1977), 7-24.
"The Man from Mars" *Pushcart Prize 3* (1978), 490-509.
"The Man from Mars" *Penguin Book of Modern Canadian Short Stories* (1982), 297-316.
"Marrying the Hangman" *Cap R* No. 7 (Spr 1975), 17-9.
"Marrying the Hangman" *Fiction of Contemporary Canada* (1980), 41-3.
"The Pilgrimage" *Acta Vic* 83:2 (Dec 1958), 34-6.
"Polarities" *Tam R* No. 58 (1971), 3-25.
"Polarities" *Dancing Girls* (1977), 43-69.
"Polarities" *Wild Rose Country* (1977), 149-75.
"Polarities" *Best Modern Canadian Short Stories* (1978), 59-77.
"Polarities" *Canadian Short Stories 3* (1978), 1-29.
"Polarities" *Penguin Book of Canadian Short Stories* (1980), 397-418.
"The Porcupine Murders" *CBC "Anthology"* 7 June 1975.
"Rape Fantasies" *Fid* No. 104 (Win 1975), 3-11.
"Rape Fantasies" *Dancing Girls* (1977), 99-110.
"Rape Fantasies" *Toronto Short Stories* (1977), 1-11.
"Rape Fantasies" *TL* Apr 1977, 58-60, 109, 111-2.
"Rape Fantasies" *Fiddlehead Greens* (1979), 125-37.
"Rape Fantasies" *Canadian Literature in the 70's* (1980), 108-16.
"Raw Materials" *Murder in the Dark* (1983), 19-25.
"The Resplendant Quetzal" *Dancing Girls* (1977), 161-78.

"The Resplendant Quetzal" *Mal R* No. 41 (Jan 1977), 175-88.

"The Resplendant Quetzal" *CBC "Anthology"* 2 Apr 1977.

"The Resplendant Quetzal" *Short Story International* No. 41 [date unknown] [Based on SSI].

"The Resplendant Quetzal" *Anthology of Canadian Literature in English 2* (1983), 482-91.

"The Salt Garden" *Bluebeard's Egg* (1983), 203-29.

"Scarlet Ibis" *Bluebeard's Egg* (1983), 181-201.

"Significant Moments in the Life of My Mother" *Bluebeard's Egg* (1983), 11-29.

"Simmering" *Fireweed* No. 10 (Spr 1981), 66-8.

"Simmering" *Murder in the Dark* (1983), 31-3.

"Simmering" *Vie en rose* No. 13 (Sept-Oct 1983), 44-5 [As "A l'Étuvée"; trans. Françoise Guénette].

"The Sin Eater" *Small Wonders* (1982), 11-22.

"The Sin Eater" *CF* 62 (May 1982), 25-8.

"The Sin Eater" *Bluebeard's Egg* (1983), 231-44.

"Spring Song of the Frogs" *Bluebeard's Egg* (1983), 167-80.

"The Sunrise" *Bluebeard's Egg* (1983), 245-65.

"Testament Found in a Bureau Drawer" *Prism* 5:2 (Aut 1965), 58-65.

"Training" *Dancing Girls* (1977), 179-202.

"A Travel Piece" *SN* 90 (May 1975), 49-56.

"A Travel Piece" *Dancing Girls* (1977), 145-60.

"A Travel Piece" *Best Canadian Short Stories* (1981), 282-94.

"True Romances" *Exile* 7:3/4 (1981), 5-9.

"Uglypuss" *Bluebeard's Egg* (1983), 83-110.

"Under Glass" *Harper's* 244 (Feb 1972), 78-82.

"Under Glass" *Dancing Girls* (1977), 71-83.

"Unearthing Suite" *Bluebeard's Egg* (1983), 267-85.

"The War in the Bathroom" *Alphabet* No. 8 (June 1964), 63-72.

"The War in the Bathroom" *Dancing Girls* (1977), 7-18.

"When It Happens" *Chat* 48 (Sept 1975), 50-1, 93, 95-6, 98-9.

"When It Happens" *Dancing Girls* (1977), 131-43.

"When It Happens" *Redbook* 160 (Jan 1983), 58, 61, 63.

Auersperg, Ruth‡

"The Denial" *CBC "Anthology"* 26 Jan 1962.

Augustine, Wilma‡

"Snips and Snaps" *Acta Vic* 80:4 (Mar 1956), 14-5.

Austen, Doug‡

"Gnome's Dome" *Gut* No. 4 (Spr 1975), 12.

Austin, Don (1946-)

"After September" *OPT* 7:4/5 (Sept-Oct 1980), 1.

"Apartment Hunting in the East End" *Grain* 9:4 (Nov 1981), 41.

"The Artist" *Pulp* 4:6 (15 June 1977), [4].

"The Artist" *OPT* 4:6 (Sept 1977), 11.

"The Cat" *TickleAce* No. 7 (Fall 1983), 25.

"The Dictator" *Pulp* 3:4 (1 May 1977), [1, 4].

"Doctor" *BC Monthly* 5:3 (Apr 1981), 22-3.

"Empires of the Air" *BC Monthly* 5:3 (Apr 1981), 27 [Prose poem?].

"The Historian" *BC Monthly* 4:5 (July 1979), [1 p].

"i saw cortez in the streets of the city" *Pulp* 3:23 (1 Jan 1977), [2-3] [Prose poem?].

"I Wanted to Call You" *TickleAce* No. [5] (1980), 31.

"If I Were Einstein or Wittgenstein or Poe" *BC Monthly* 4:5 (July 1979), [1 p].

"Me" *OPT* 6:3 (Apr 1979), 3.

"The Neurotic's Handbook" *Elbow Room* (1979), 27-71 [Series of prose pieces].

"The Newspaper" *Ichor* No. 2 (1981), 35-6.

"Portable Cities" *Pulp* 4:9 (1 Sept 1977), [2-3] [Prose poem?].

"The Relaxed Anarchist" *BC Monthly* 4:5 (July 1979), [2 pp].

"The Sex Life of Accident Victims" *Popular Illusion* No. 3 (Jan 1978), [1 p].

"She Fell Asleep Sunbathing Outside Her Apartment Building" *Grain* 9:4 (Nov 1981), 42.

"A Starfish" *TickleAce* No. 7 (Fall 1983), 24.

"Things Not Occurring Rapidly" *Ichor* No. 2 (1981), 33.

"Victims" *Pulp* 3:24 (1 Feb 1977), [4].

"Winner Take Nothing" *BC Monthly* 4:5 (July 1979), [2 pp].

Austin, Jeremy‡

"Whiskeyjack" *Scruncheons* 1:2 (Sept 1973), 5-20.

Avery, Martin (1955-)

COTTAGE COUNTRY STORIES Toronto: A.S.P. Communications, 1981.

COTTAGE GOTHIC Ottawa: Oberon Press, 1982.

THE SINGING RABBI: NEW STORIES Ottawa: Oberon Press, 1983.

[TITLE UNKNOWN] [Toronto?]: A.S.P. Communications, 1982 [Based on survey response].

"The Canadian Diaspora" *Singing Rabbi* (1983), 5-17.

"Cat #400" *OPT* 4:7 (Oct 1977), 7.

"Cat #400" *Cottage Country Stories* (1981), 31.

"Chinese Gold" *80: Best Canadian Stories* 7-20.

"Chinese Gold" *Cottage Gothic* (1982), 5-17.

"The Circle of Love" *[Title unknown]* (1982) [Based on survey response].

"Cottage Gothic" *Cottage Gothic* (1982), 57-73.

"Filing" *Cottage Country Stories* (1981), 18-9.

"Four Kinds of Fantasy" *Cap R* No. 11 (1977), 24.

"Four Kinds of Fantasy" *First Impressions* (1980), 25-6.

"Green Ideas" *Cap R* No. 11 (1977), 22-3.

"Green Ideas" *First Impressions* (1980), 17-9.

"Hockey and the Bald-Headed Great Aunts" *Free Fall* (1975) [Based on survey response].

"Hockey Night in Canada Jr." *First Impressions* (1980), 26-8.

"Hockey Night in Canada Jr." *Cottage Gothic* (1982), 18-29.

"The Holocaust Remembrance Service" *Singing Rabbi* (1983), 74-84.

"I Have Died. She Lives" *[Title unknown]* (1982) [Based on survey response].

"Jerusalem & Home" *Singing Rabbi* (1983), 18-25.

"Just a Picosecond!" *Imp* 7:4 (Sum 1979), 47-8.

"The Komedy Kabaret" *Singing Rabbi* (1983), 85-92.

"Lives of the 400,000" *Grain* 7:2 [1979], 47-9.

"Lives of the 400,000" *First Impressions* (1980), 29-33.

"Mini-Marts" *English Q* 9:4 (Win 1976-77), 105-6.
"The Music on the Barge" *Cottage Country Stories* (1981), 5-17.
"The Muskokians" *Cottage Country Stories* (1981), 20-30.
"Nazis, Communists, Presbyterians & Jews in Norman Bethune's Hometown" *Singing Rabbi* (1983), 25-56.
"NBSS: The Ugly Brothers" *Cottage Gothic* (1982), 43-56.
"The O.H." *Cottage Country Stories* (1981), 3-4.
"Promised Land Newfoundland" *Singing Rabbi* (1983), 57-73.
"Round Trip Ticket" *Des* 11:3 No. 29 (1980), 116-22.
"The Rugger Look" *First Impressions* (1980), 38-51.
"The Rugger Look" *Writing* No. 1 (Sum 1980), 38-41.
"The Rugger Look" *Cottage Gothic* (1982), 30-42.
"Santa's Village" *Cottage Gothic* (1982), 86-94.
"Second Wind" *Cottage Country Stories* (1981), 49.
"See No Evil" *Boreal* No. 9 (1977), 59-61 [Also entitled "Wildlife Studies"].
"The Singing Rabbi" *Singing Rabbi* (1983), 93-104.
"Soviet Jewellery" *Singing Rabbi* (1983), 26-34.
"Telephones" *OPT* 4:7 (Oct 1977), 9.
"Telephones" *First Impressions* (1980), 33-8.
"Three Question" *[Title unknown]* (1982) [Based on survey response].
"When Fishermen Meet" *English Q* 9:4 (Win 1976-77), 91.
"Wildlife Studies" *Direction:* [No. 3] (Spr 1976), [4 pp] [Also entitled "See No Evil"].
"Wildlife Studies" *First Impressions* (1980), 19-24.
"Winter Carnival" *Cottage Gothic* (1982), 74-85.

Avison, Margaret (1918-)
"Listen Now" CBC "*Anthology*" 1 Dec 1966.
"Night Edition" *CF* 32 Feb 1953), 251-4.

Awde, Jonathan‡
"The Constructing of Lawrence 2" *TUR* 79:2 (Dec 1965), 22-4.

Aydelotte, Van – *See* Green, H. Gordon.

Aylen, John
"I Do, I Do or, The Energy for Bloodsport" *Quarry* 30:4 (Aut 1981), 117-21.
"Sense" *McGill Lit J* 3:1 (Win 1982), 42-7.

Ayre, John‡
"Harlequins of the Night" *Acta Vic* 93:4 (Apr 1969), 10-4.
"The Sons of Lear" *Acta Vic* 93:3 (Feb 1969), 33-7.
"Victims of the Temple" *Acta Vic* 94:3 (Feb 1970), 3-10.
"The Yellow Amelias" *Acta Vic* 94:4 (Apr 1970), 38-41.

Ayre, Robert H.
"John Womble's Second Dream" *MM* 70 (22 June 1957), 32-3, 54-6.
"Mr. Nicholson's Spendid Adventure in Bigamy" *MM* 69 (21 July 1956), 16-7, 49-51.
"P. Tidmus and the Fish" *MM* 68 (15 Oct 1955), 19, 66-8.

B., Jane
"Genesis Revisited" *Singing* (1980), 34-5.
"Night Caller" *Singing* (1980), 36-7.

Baar, Anita
"Cut!" *Outset* 1973, 8-12.

Babb, Audrey W.‡
"The Adjustment" *Can Lifetime* 4 (Jan-Feb 1974), 22-6.

Babic, Loranne†
"Andy" *CSSM* 1:1 (Jan 1975), 5, 7-8.

Babineau, Brian‡
"Fragments of a Bed/Ridden Man" *Jabberwocky* [No. 1 (1965?)], [4 pp].
"Snowflake, Snowflake" *Jabberwocky* Feb 1966, [5 pp].

Babstock, George‡
"The Gamble of Past Years" *Nfld Q* 71:3 (Jan 1975), 30-1.
"Sea in His Blood" *Nfld Q* 75:2 (Fall 1979), 12.
"This Is It" *Nfld Q* 72:1 (Dec 1975), 14.
" 'Twas a Bumper Trip" *Nfld Q* 77:4 (Win 1981-82), 14-5.
"Who Gets What?" *Nfld Q* 72:4 (Dec 1976), 12.

Bacchus, Noel
YOU'VE GOT TO SHOW ME AND OTHER STORIES Toronto: McClelland & Stewart, 1953 [Based on Miller].

Bach, Kathleen
"The Secret" *event* 3:3 [n.d.], 53-7.

Backmeyer, LaDonna Breidford†
"The Christmas Bird" *Ice Can* 39:2 (Win 1980), 10-4.

Bacque, James (1929-)
"An Allegory for Our Times" *Can Dimension* 8 (June 1971), 63-4.
"The Cookburning Woodstove" *Har* 3:3 No. 15 (1978), 93-4, 96-8.
"The Day the Queen Came to Minnicog" *Har* 2:6 No. 12 (1978), 72-83.
"Forbidden Words" *Chat* 52 (Oct 1979), 50, 106, 108, 112-3, 116, 118.
"The High Snow" *Creation* (1970), 67-72.
"A Small Film" *Creation* (1970), 73-80.
"Sun and Earth for a Dollar" *Creation* (1970), 81-7.
"Turkey Feathers" *Har* 3:4 No. 16 (1978), 87, 89-92, 94-5.

Baerstein, Tsigane
"How I Got Cured: A Testimonial" *Matrix* No. 14 (Win 1982), 49-56.
"How I Got Cured: A Testimonial" *Metavisions* (1983), 36-46.
"An Offer of Freedom" *Matrix* No. 10 (Fall-Win 1979-80), 1-14.
"Raising the Dead" *Antig R* No. 55 (Aut 1983), 109-19.
"Sacred Mushrooms of Canada" *Grain* 10:4 (Nov 1982), 41-6.
"Writer's Retreat" *Hysteria* 1:4 (Spr 1982), 11, 20-3.

Bailey, Arn‡

"Cool Water" *Acta Vic* 78:4 (Mar 1954), 30-2.
" 'Daddy' " *Acta Vic* 79:4 (Mar 1955), 19-21.

Bailey, Betty‡

"The Blue Stool" *Smoke Signals* [1974?], 46-53.

Bailey, Bill

THE WINDOW Prince George: Repository Press, 1977.
"Staying" *Window* (1977), [4 pp].

Bailey, Bruce†

"Duet for Solo Yang" *Des* No. 1 [1970], [4 pp].
"Satori (Reduced to Clear)" *Des* No. 2 (Spr 1971), [6 pp].
"A Scene by Anton Chekhov" *Des* No. 4 (Spr 1972), 43-8.

Bailey, Don (1942-)

IF YOU HUM ME A FEW BARS I MIGHT REMEMBER THE TUNE Ottawa:
Oberon Press, 1973.
MAKING UP Ottawa: Oberon Press, 1981.
REPLAY Ottawa: Oberon Press, 1975.
THE SORRY PAPERS Ottawa: Oberon Press, 1979.
"Abortion Just Ain't What It Used to Be" *Alive* 2:8 (July-Aug 1971), 24-7.
"After the Events of Caesar" *Making Up* (1981), 95-104.
"All Sales Final" *CBC "Anthology"* 5 Feb 1977.
"All Sales Final" *Sorry Papers* (1979), 53-66.
"A Bauble for Bernice" *72: New Canadian Stories* 45-56.
"A Bauble for Bernice" *If You Hum* (1973), 92-104.
"A Bauble for Bernice" *Moderne Erzühler der Walt: Kanada* (1976), 372-86 [As
"Eine Kleinigkeit für Bernice"; trans Walter Riedel].
"Because I Needed to Know" *Alive* No. 30 [1973], 15-6.
"The Border Crossing" *Making Up* (1981), 73-94.
"Bread and Jam" *Alive* No. 34 [1974], 19.
"Cut Me a Slice and Make It Thin" *Alive* [1:10] (Nov 1970), 19-25.
"Cut Me a Slice and Make It Thin" *If You Hum* (1973), 39-51.
"Dirty Laundry" *CBC "Anthology"* 19 Jan 1979.
"Dirty Laundry" *Making Up* (1981), 20-8.
"An Ending, a Beginning" *JCF* 3:3 (1974), 29-34.
"Eric the Red" *75: New Canadian Stories* 101-20.
"Eric the Red" *Sorry Papers* (1979), 33-52.
"A Few Notes for Orpheus" *Fourteen Stories High* (1971), 9-22.
"A Few Notes for Orpheus" *CBC "Anthology"* 12 June 1971.
"A Few Notes for Orpheus" *If You Hum* (1973), 77-91.
"A Few Notes for Orpheus" *Tigers of the Snow* (1973), 27-39.
"A Few Notes for Orpheus" *Modern Canadian Stories* (1975), 207-21.
"A Few Notes for Orpheus" *Replay* (1975), 136-49.
"A Few Notes for Orpheus" *Transitions 2* (1978), 3-14.
"A Few Notes for Orpheus" *Writers and Writing* (1981), 140-53.
"A Few Words in Private" *CFM* No. 5 (Win 1972), 53-64.
"A Few Words in Private" *If You Hum* (1973), 126-40.
"The Greta Script" *Quarry* 27:2 (Spr 1978), 12-28.

"The Greta Script" *Sorry Papers* (1979), 67-88.

"The Greta Script" CBC "*Anthology*" 24 Feb 1979.

"The Groundhog" *Alive* 2:4 (Mar 1971), 8-11.

"Hamburger Heaven" *WCR* 16:4 (Spr 1982), 3-8.

"Hamburger Heaven" *83: Best Canadian Stories* 82-91.

"If You Hum Me a Few Bars I Might Remember the Tune" *Quarry* 18:3 (Spr 1969), 4-12.

"If You Hum Me a Few Bars I Might Remember the Tune" CBC "*Anthology*" 4 Apr 1970.

"If You Hum Me a Few Bars I Might Remember the Tune" *If You Hum* (1973), 7-18.

"If You Hum Me a Few Bars I Might Remember the Tune" *Replay* (1975), 77-87.

"It Felt Like Christmas" *Quarry* 21:2 (Spr 1972), 17-24.

"Letter to Anne" *Alive* No. 40 [1974], 15-6.

"A Little to the Left of Centre" *If You Hum* (1973), 105-25.

"A Little to the Left of Centre" *CFM* No. 11 (Aut 1973), 45-62.

"Making Up" *Making Up* (1981), 105-19.

"My Brother" *CFM* No. 14 (Sum 1974), 17-21.

"Nothing Bothers Me" *event* 3:1 [1973], 6-13.

"Nothing Bothers Me" *If You Hum* (1973), 30-8.

"On Our Way to the Flea-Market" *Sorry Papers* (1979), 89-117.

"The Overhead" *Alive* 3:1 [1972?], 19-23.

"The Parking Lot Attendant" *Alive* 2:7 (June 1971), 33-9.

"A Poem Is a Sort of Subway Token" *Alive* 3:2 No. 21 [1972?], 32.

"Rain on the Roof" *Sorry Papers* (1979), 118-31.

"Recurrence" CBC "*Anthology*" 19 July 1980.

"Recurrence" *Making Up* (1981), 29-41.

"Recurrence" *Chat* 54 (July 1981), 38-9, 84, 86, 88, 90, 92.

"Ring Around the Rosie" CBC "*Anthology*" 4 Aug 1973.

"Ring Around the Rosie" *Replay* (1975), 5-20.

"Ring Around the Rosie" *Sorry Papers* (1979), 15-32.

"Shared Accommodation" *Making Up* (1981), 42-60.

"The Sorry Papers" *Sorry Papers* (1979), 5-14.

"The Sorry Papers" *CF* 59 (Apr 1979), 24-6.

"The Sorry Papers" CBC "*Anthology*" 15 Sept 1979.

[Title unknown] *If You Hum* (1973), 19-29.

[Title unknown] *If You Hum* (1973), 141-54.

"Tree House" *WCR* 5:3 (Jan 1971), 3-8.

"Tree House" CBC "*Anthology*" 22 Jan 1972.

"Tree House" *If You Hum* (1973), 66-76.

"Vignette: Photographs or Portrait Showing Only Head and Shoulders with Background Shaded Off" *Alive* No. 27 [1973], 31-7.

"The Walrus and the Carpenter" *If You Hum* (1973), 52-65.

"The Walrus and the Carpenter" *Replay* (1975), 21-33.

"The Walrus and the Carpenter" *Toronto Short Stories* (1977), 96-108.

"Why Do You Lie?" *Sorry Papers* (1979), 132-44.

"The Widow's Walk" *Making Up* (1981), 61-72.

"The Window People" *Chat* 53 (Feb 1980), 52-4, 56, 58, 60.

"The Window People" *Making Up* (1981), 5-19.

"The Woman Alone Thing" *Alive* 2:6 ([May] 1971), 35-9.

Baillie, Isabel
"Don't Put Your Heart on a Horse" *MM* 66 (1 Aug 1953), 18, 40-2.

Baillie, Janice‡
"Dave" *Mont R* No. 3 (Spr-Sum 1980), 42-3.

Baillie, John H.‡
"What Are You Babbling About, Jerry?" *Mandala* 1978, 31-3.

Bain, Dena‡
"Day Eight: Morning and Afternoon" *Stardust* 2:1 [n.d.], 7-22.
"Entropy, Atlas, and the Tortoise" *Stardust* 2:2 [n.d.], 31-4.
"Gloops" *Stardust* 1:4 [n.d.], 3-15.
"Tournament" *Stardust* 2:1 [n.d.], 26-35.
"Vision" *Stardust* 2:3 [n.d.], 40-9.

Baird, Irene†
"A Learning Situation" *North* 14 (Nov-Dec 1967), 10-6.

Baird, K.A.†
"Dr. Ed's Last Sleigh Ride" *Dal R* 43 (1963), 190-9.

Baker, Cynthia‡
"The Duchess" *Edmonton Journal* Fri, 7 Apr 1967, 54.
"Tempted, Tried, and True" *Edmonton Journal* Fri, 17 Feb 1967, 46.

Baker, Helen‡
"The Goat-Man" *Stump* 2:2 (Fall 1978), 20-8.

Baker, Kent‡
"Mildred" *CBC "Anthology"* 30 Sept 1978.

Baker, Mark‡
"The Zeal of Thine House" *AA* 67 (Dec 1976), 58-61.

Baker, Rita (1932-)
"The Brave Music of a Distant Drum" *Living Message* 86 (May 1975), 19-21.
"Clara" *Rapport* Feb 1969, 20.
"I Know Where I'm Going" *Rapport* Sept 1970, 24-5.
"I Know Where I'm Going" *Polished Pebbles* (1974), 15-7.
"A Lovely Day" *Rapport* Apr 1970, 8-9.
"A Lovely Day" *Living Message* 93 (Mar 1982), 19-20.
"Road to Nowhere" *Rapport* Sept 1969, 31.
"Road to Nowhere" *Living Message* 94 (Nov 1983), 27.
"Run Children" *Living Message* 88 (May 1977), 19-22.
"A Thing of Beauty" *Rapport* Apr 1969, 10-1.
"A Thing of Beauty" *Living Message* 84 (Jan 1973), 10-2.
"You Cant Trust Anyone These Days" *Can Messenger* 79 (Feb 1969), 12-3.

Baker, Steven‡
"Mile-High Lemon Meringue Pie" *Stump* Spr 1983, 14-21.

Baker-Pearce, Mike‡
"The Loved Ones Bit" *Alive* No. 34 [1974], 10.

Baldridge, Mary Humphrey†
"Coffee Break" *Grain* 4:1 [1976], 23-5.

Baldridge, Mary Humphrey (1937-)
"Build Me a Monument" *Mont* 36 (July 1962), 34-8.
"Ginny, and the Dog" *Dand* 8:2 (1981), 27-31.

Baldwin, Laura†
"Something Old, Something New" *Read Ch* 1:1 (Spr 1982), 34-9.

Baliozian, Ara
"The Greek Poetess" *JCF* 4:1 No. 13 (1975), 30-44.
"Medusa" *Fid* No. 102 (Sum 1974), 40-50.
"Organ Recital" *Fid* No. 102 (Sum 1974), 24-39.
"Organ Recital" *Canadian Short Fiction Anthology 2* (1982), 139-49.

Balk, Christianne‡
"Arboretum" *Canadian Short Fiction Anthology* (1976), 9-20.

Ball, John‡
"Cross the Road" *TUR* 95:1 (Jan 1982), 24-5.

Ball, Owen‡
"Legacy" *Generation* 1969, 33-5.
"Legacy" *Spear* 6 (Apr 1977), 35-6, 46.

Ballantine, Andrew Campbell†
"Lion-Taming for Beginners" *Stories with John Drainie* (1963), 118-23.

Ballantine, Emile†
"The Eagles Soar" *Pemmican J* Spr 1983, 44-6.

Balma, Donna†
"Strike" *BC Monthly* 5:3 (Apr 1981), 30-4.

Balon, Brett‡
"Dust of the Ages: A Hyperbolic Fabulist Essay" *Freelance* 10 (Feb 1981), 15-24.

Baltensperger, Peter (1938-)
"Collector's Items" *Alch* 2:3 No. 7 (Fall 1982), 21-6.
"The Fruit but Not the Tree" *Des* 10:3/4 Nos. 25/26 (1979), 134-9.
"Mosquito Story" *Northwoods J* (U.S.) 5:6 (Scorpio 1977), 18-20 [Based on survey response].
"Mosquito Story" *Chel J* 5 (July-Aug 1979), 167-9.
"Of Dreams and Other Fools" *event* 3:3 [1974?], 44-8.
"Parquette" *Antig R* No. 28 (Win 1977), 23-8.
"Reflections" *Limbo* 2:7/8 (Nov 1967), 42-3, 46-7.
"Shadows in the Sand" *Dal R* 52 (1972), 401-6.

"The Thing About Jenny" *Halcyon* No. 12 (Win 1966-67), 82-7.
"The Tower" *The Bibliofantasiac* No. 10 (Sept-Oct 1983), 9-10 [Based on survey response].

Baltensperger, Rita

"In Search of Perfection" *Halcyon* No. 12 (Win 1966-67), 72-3.
"Only a Child" *Halcyon* No. 12 (Win 1966-67), 71.

Bamford, Wendy (1966-)

"The Elsinor Squires; or, A Study in Danish; or, The Castle of Fear" *Can Holmes* 7:2 (Dec 1983), 11-6.

Bancroft, Marjory†

"A Study in Geometry" *Singing Under Ice* (1974), 22-9.

Bankier, William (1928-)

"A Bad Scene" *Ellery Queen* July 1973 [Based on Riley].
"The Big Bunco" *Ellery Queen* Nov 1974 [Based on Riley].
"The Big Bunco" *Ellery Queen's Wings of Mystery* (1979), 85-95.
"Breaking Free" *Ellery Queen* 81 (Mar 1983), 54-71.
"Brother, Can You Spare a Crime?" *Alfred Hitchcock* 26 (16 Sept 1981), 40-1.
"Brough, as in Rough" *Alfred Hitchcock* 21 May 1980 [Based on Riley].
"By the Neck Until Dead" *Ellery Queen* Jan 1974 [Based on Riley].
"Cattle Call" *Ellery Queen* Sept 1979 [Based on Riley].
"C'est Voulu" *Ellery Queen* Jan 1975 [Based on Riley].
"The Choirboy" *Alfred Hitchcock* 25 (15 Dec 1980) [Based on Cook].
"The Choirboy" *Best Detective Stories of the Year 1981* 88-102.
"Concerto for Violence and Orchestra" *Ellery Queen* 77 (17 June 1981), 120-8.
"The Confrontation Scene" *Alfred Hitchcock* 26 (24 June 1981), 4-17.
"Crazy Old Woman" *Alfred Hitchcock* 25 (19 Nov 1980), 4-18.
"Dangerous Enterprise" *Ellery Queen's Veils of Mystery* (1980) [Based on SSI].
"Dangerous Enterprise" *Ellery Queen* Sept 1975 [Based on Riley].
"Defensive Moves" *Alfred Hitchcock* 25 (13 Aug 1980), 5-20.
"Den of Thieves" *Alfred Hitchcock* Jan 1977 [Based on Riley].
"Devil's Advocate" *Ellery Queen* Feb 1979 [Based on Riley].
"Doors" *Ellery Queen* 80 (Oct 1982), 133-9.
"Dr. Temple Is Dead" *Ellery Queen* 75 (11 Feb 1980), 75-9.
"The Dream of Hopeless White" *Alfred Hitchcock* 23 (Dec 1978), 5-18.
"Duffy's Last Contract" *Alfred Hitchcock* 24 (Sept 1979), 17-25.
"Events at Headland Cottage" *Ellery Queen* 75 (30 June 1980), 47-56.
"The Eye of the Beholder" *Alfred Hitchcock* Apr 1978 [Based on Riley].
"Fall with the Rain" *Lib* 30 (Nov 1953), 26-9, 59-60.
"Fear and Trembling" *Alfred Hitchcock* June 1979 [Based on Riley].
"A Fierceness Deep Inside" *Ellery Queen* 78 (2 Dec 1981), 112-5.
"The Final Twist" *Ellery Queen* Jan 1977 [Based on Riley].
"The Final Twist" *Ellery Queen's Maze of Mysteries* (1982), 109-15.
"Funny Man" *Ellery Queen* 79 (27 Jan 1982), 53-67.
"A Funny Thing Happened" *Alfred Hitchcock* 24 (Nov 1979), 87-96.
"The Gag of the Century" *Ellery Queen* 45 (Feb 1965), 99-110.
"A Game of Errors" *Alfred Hitchcock* 23 (Sept 1978), 5-25.
"Girls, Like White Birds" *Ellery Queen* Apr 1979 [Based on Riley].

"Happiness You Can Count On" *Ellery Queen* 77 (1 Jan 1981), 111-23.
"A Hint of Danger" *Ellery Queen* Apr 1978 [Based on Riley].
"The Immortal Quest" *Alfred Hitchcock* 23 (Jan 1978), 92-9.
"The Impossible Scheme" *Alfred Hitchcock* Oct 1979 [Based on Riley].
"In the House Next Door" *Ellery Queen* Sept 1977 [Based on Riley].
"IOU One Life" *Ellery Queen* Sept 1976 [Based on Riley].
"Is There a Killer in the House?" *Alfred Hitchcock* 24 (Aug 1979), 103-20.
"The Last Act Was Deadly" *Alfred Hitchcock* 23 (June 1978), 4-19.
"The Last One to Know" *Alfred Hitchcock* 25 (26 Mar 1980), 107-21.
"Laughing Chaz" *Alfred Hitchcock* June 1977 [Based on Riley].
"Lorenzo the Inventor" *Alfred Hitchcock* 23 (May 1978), 47-55.
"Lost and Found" *Alfred Hitchcock* 23 (Nov 1978), 63-8.
"A Lovely Bottle of Wine" *Alfred Hitchcock* 22 (Apr 1977), 85-91.
"The Main Event" *Ellery Queen* Feb 1978 [Based on Riley].
"Making a Killing with Mama Cass" *Alfred Hitchcock* 25 (30 Jan 1980), 4-19.
"The Man of the Hour" *Alfred Hitchcock* 24 (July 1979), 31-46.
"Marti Roch" *Alfred Hitchcock* 26 (27 May 1981), 5-22.
"The Missing Missile" *Alfred Hitchcock* 27 Feb 1980 [Based on Riley].
"My Brother's Killer" *Ellery Queen* Apr 1973 [Based on Riley].
"My Name Is Lorenzo, Goodbye" *Alfred Hitchcock* 24 (Dec 1979), 99-106.
"The Mystery of the Missing Penelope" *Ellery Queen* Dec 1978 [Based on Riley].
"The Mystery of the Missing Guy" *Ellery Queen* Dec 1979 [Based on Riley].
"Nothing to Lose" *Alfred Hitchcock* 25 (23 Apr 1980), 5-15.
"One Clear Sweet Clue" *Ellery Queen's Headliners* (1971) [Based on Riley].
"Only If You Get Caught" *Ellery Queen* 78 (7 Oct 1981), 30-42.
"Paid in Advance" *Ellery Queen* 76 (6 Oct 1980), 99-107.
"The Piper's Caper" *Ellery Queen* Mar 1979 [Based on Riley].
"Play for the Lady" *Lib* 31 (July 1954), 22-3, 42-6.
"Policeman's Lot" *Ellery Queen* 62 (Oct 1973) [Based on Cook].
"Policeman's Lot" *Ellery Queen's Masks of Mystery* (1978) [Based on Riley].
"Rapunzel, Rapunzel" *Alfred Hitchcock* Mar 1977 [Based on Riley].
"The Rescue of Professor Parkindon" *Ellery Queen* Oct 1977 [Based on Riley].
"The Road without a Name" *Ellery Queen's Giants of Mystery* (1976) [Based on Riley].
"Rock's Last Role" *Alfred Hitchcock* 24 (Mar 1979), 65-73.
"The Solid-Gold Lie" *Alfred Hitchcock* 25 (1 Oct 1980), 70-4.
"To Kill an Angel" *Ellery Queen* Aug 1976 [Based on Riley].
"Traffic Violation" *Ellery Queen* 50 (Sept 1967), 144-52.
"The Trial of Judge Axminster" *Alfred Hitchcock* 24 (Apr 1979), 5-14.
"The Voice of Doreen Gray" *Ellery Queen* Aug 1977 [Based on Riley].
"What Happened in Act One" *Ellery Queen's Mystery Mix* (1964) [Based on Riley].
"What Really Happened?" *Ellery Queen* July 1976 [Based on Riley].
"Where Will It All End" *Ellery Queen* 80 (Sept 1982), 20-30.
"Who Steals My Face?" *Alfred Hitchcock* 23 (Feb 1978), 5-18.
"The Window" *Alfred Hitchcock's Tales to Take Your Breath Away* (1977), 347-81.
"The Woman in the Control Room" *Ellery Queen* July 1979 [Based on Riley].
"You Get What You Deserve" *Alfred Hitchcock* 16 July 1980 [Based on Riley].

Banky, Jake†
   "Unicorn" *Evidence* No. 4 (Win 1962), 7-12.

Bannerji, Himani
"Going Home" *Rikka* 7:1 (Spr 1980), 23-6.
"The Other Family" *Mudpie* 1:4 (Sept 1980), 8-9 [Children's?].
"The Story of a Birth" *Fireweed* No. 16 (Spr 1983), 123-33.

Banting, Meredith
"The Duplicate Cheque" *Onward* 15 Aug 1965, 10.

Bantjes, June†
"The Voice of Authority" *Antig R* No. 15 (Aut 1973), 9-13.

Barb, Michael†
"Long Distance Tragedies" *Nebula* No. 19 (1981), 28-33.

Barbeau, Malcolm
"An Everyday Morning" *Boreal* No. 6 (1976), 69-74.

Barbour, Sharon (1944-)
"Billy the Kid Is Dead" *Aurora* 1979 189-95.

Barbusse, Henri‡
"Jesus Exploited" *Alive* No. 55 (16 Oct 1975), 5.

Barclay, Byrna (1940-)
"After the Story" *Smoke Signals* 3 (1978) [Based on *SWG* survey response].
"Second Cousin Once Removed" *West Producer* 1974 [Based on survey response].
"Staying with the Dream" *Nw J* No. 17 (1980), 65-72.
"Testimony" *Sundogs* (1980), 15-28.
"Testimony" *NeWest R* 5 (Apr 1980), 8-9, 12, 14.
"The Woman Who Talks to Canada Geese" *Saskatchewan Gold* (1982), 245-53.

Bardsley, Alice
"The Boy in the Barn" *AA* 70 (Dec 1979), 41-2, 44.
"Journey to Light" *CG* 78 (Apr 1959), 76-8 [Children's?].

Barford, Grace L.
"Cobbler's Children" *Onward* 21 Nov 1965, 13-4 [Non-fiction?].
"Money Really Isn't Everything" *Onward* 18 Apr 1965, 12-3 [Non-fiction?].

Barker, Bessie M.
"The Advent of Gopher" *Onward* 27 May 1962, 6-7, 13-4.
"Anniversary Gift" *Onward* 9 May 1965, 3-4.
"Aunt Linnie's Lantern" *Onward* 15 Dec 1957, 792-5.
"Babies, Babies, Everywhere" *Onward* 28 June 1959, 404-5.
"The Battle of the Biscuits" *Saskatchewan Homecoming* (1971), 72-4.
"Bread and Butter" *Onward* 2 May 1954, 274-5, 286-7.
"The Cherry-Wood Chair" *Onward* 3 July 1955, 422-3, 427.
"A Closer Look" *Onward* 21 Feb 1953, 113-5.
"Drought" *Saskatchewan Homecoming* (1971), 171-3.
"Easter for Stephen Carley" *Onward* 29 Mar 1959, 200-2.
"An Echo for Frances" *Onward* 13 June 1954, 372-4.

"Ethelbert Comes to Call" *Onward* 23 Nov 1958, 744-5, 750-1.
"A Hint of Poochiness" *Rapport* June 1968, 38-9.
" 'I Reserve the Right ...' " *Onward* 15 Nov 1953, 721-3, 734-5.
"The Impractical Gift" *Onward* 62 (28 Dec 1952), 819-20.
"Ironstone Chalice" *Onward* Aug 1967, 22-3.
"The Listener" *Onward* 24 July 1960, 465-7, 478.
"Long View" *Onward* 24 May 1953, 326-7, 323.
"A Matter of Conviction" *Onward* 21 Aug 1966, 3-4, 7.
"The Message Garden" *Onward* 7 Feb 1953, 90-1, 95.
"New Associations" *Onward* 8 Mar 1953, 148-9, 153.
"New Citizens" *Onward* 21 June 1953, 385-7.
"New Love for Leopold" *Onward* 7 May 1961, 296-7, 300-1.
"One Christmas Star" *Onward* 11 Dec 1955, 786-8.
"One Easter Lily" *Onward* 26 Mar 1967, 5-6, 13.
"Over the Skyline" *Onward* 18 Oct 1953, 657-9.
"Period Piece" *Onward* 62 (7 Sept 1952), 561-3, 571.
"A Prairie Easter Lily" *Onward* 17 Apr 1960, 241-4, 247.
"Retribution" *Onward* 60 (18 June 1950), 385-8, 398-9.
"Saga of the Sow" *Saskatchewan Homecoming* (1971), 149-50.
"Shy Boy – Shy Girl" *Onward* 27 June 1965, 3-4, 13.
"Soap-and-Water Charity" *Onward* 1 Aug 1954, 481-3, 487.
"Square Nails" *Onward* 62 (2 Mar 1952), 129-31.
"The Stirring Mouse" *Onward* 17 Dec 1961, 3-5, 11.
"The Strawberry Man" *Onward* 24 Jan 1953, 54-5, 62-3.
"Three for the Price of One" *Onward* 18 June 1967, 6-7.
"Tickets for Mother's Day" *Onward* 9 May 1954, 289-91.
"The Travelling Lilies" *Onward* 6 Apr 1958, 216-9.
"Trees" *Onward* 29 Mar 1953, 198-9.
"The Untouchable Gifts" *Onward* 23 Dec 1956, 825-6.
"When the Power Failed" *Onward* 16 Dec 1962, 3-7.
"A Wider Window" *Onward* 60 (13 Aug 1950), 518-9, 527.
"The Women in His Life" *Onward* 2 Apr 1961, 209-11, 222.

Barker, H.T.†
"The Ice Road" *AA* 54 (Feb 1964), 49-52, 54.
"The Ice Road" *Stories from Across Canada* (1966), 79-92.

Barkhouse, Joyce C. (1913-)
"Without Glory" *Onward* 7 June 1959, 356-8.

Barnard, Leslie Gordon (1890-1961)
See also Barnard, Margaret E. and Barnard, Leslie Gordon.
"[A?] Friend of Beau's" *Extension* 45 (June 1950), 6-7[+?] [Based on CPLI].
"All Expenses Paid" *SW* 3 Sept 1955, II:3, 6.
"All-Expense Tour" *SW* 6 Nov 1954, I:1, 12.
"And a Sea Bird Calling" *Sign* 40 (May 1961), 36-40.
"[The?] Anniversary" *Extension* 51 (Apr 1957), 16-7[+?] [Based on CPLI].
"Anything You Want" *Sign* 33 (Dec 1953), 16-8[+?] [Based on CPLI].
"The Bargain" *SW* 18 May 1957, 20-1.
"Benny and the Mermaid" *CG* May 1957, 16, 57-8.
"Bucket of Roses" *FH* 25 Dec 1952, 14-5.

"Could Be I'm Romantic" *SW* 13 Sept 1952, II:6.
"Don't Let It Change Us" *FH* 17 July 1952, 20-1.
"Fool's Paradise" *SW* 17 Aug 1957, 24-5, 37.
"For Crying Out Loud" *Columbia* 37 (July 1957), 8[+?] [Based on CPLI].
"Four into One Goes Once" *Extension* 51 (Dec 1956), 18[+?] [Based on CPLI].
"Four Men and a Box" *Scholastic* 69 (4 Jan 1957), 20[+?] [Based on RGPL].
"A Friend of Beau's" *FH* 31 Aug 1950, 16-7, 22.
"The Girl on the Square" *SW* 19 Dec 1953, I:7.
"[The?] Great Man" *Extension* 47 (Mar 1953), 31[+?] [Based on CPLI].
"Green Leaves Falling" *CG* Apr 1952, 8, 71-2.
"Happy Birthday to You" *CG* Apr 1954, 15, 72-3.
"The Hard Way" *SW* 4 Aug 1956, I:6.
"The Harpoon" *SW* 23 June 1951, I:9.
"High Altitude" *SW* 24 July 1954, II:9.
"Holiday Eve" *CHJ* May 1955, 11, 70-2.
"Home Is the Sailor" *FH* 28 Feb 1952, 24-5, 30.
"Is a Good Thing" *Extension* 45 (Oct 1950), 18-9[+?] [Based on CPLI].
"It Won't Happen Again" *CG* Sept 1953, 14, 66-9.
"Journey Back to Love" *Chat* 28 (Apr 1956), 16-7, 56-64.
"A Lesson for Albert" *SW* 22 Sept 1956, I:9.
"The Little Green Hat" *FH* 29 Sept 1960, 24-5, 28.
"The Luck of the Kid" *FH* 21 June 1951, 18-9, 48.
"The Man Nance Married" *SW* 1 Dec 1956, 14-5, 25.
"The Man Who Worked for Joe the Barber" *CG* Sept 1952, 9, 76-8.
"Marriages Are Made" *Sign* 32 (June 1953), 40-4.
"Marriages Are Made" *FH* 10 June 1954, 24-5, 31.
"A Matter of Horse Sense" *CG* Apr 1956, 14, 57-8, 60.
"May the Best Man Win!" *Extension* 50 (Jan 1956), 18-20[+?] [Based on CPLI].
"May the Best Man Win!" *SW* 14 Apr 1956, I:7.
"Mr. Carew's Contract" *SW* 27 Sept 1958, 24-5, 44[?] [Last page(s) were not microfilmed].
"[The?] Murderer" *Sign* 33 (Aug 1953), 56-7[+?] [Based on CPLI].
"No Time to Talk" *Extension* 53 (Dec 1958), 23[+?] [Based on CPLI].
"None But the Lonely" *Extension* 51 (Jan 1957), 22[+?] [Based on CPLI].
"Not Quite New Shop" *SW* 2 Feb 1957, 16-7.
"Off-shore Wind" *SW* 16 July 1960, 10-3, 41.
"Okay, Mr. Z" *Ave Maria* 91 (16 Apr 1960), 21-2[+?] [Based on CPLI].
"Package Deal" *FH* 28 July 1960, 10-1, 24.
"People Talk Too Much" *FH* 30 Apr 1953, 20-1.
"Portrait of Cousin Dennis" *Mayfair* 27 (Oct 1953), 38-9. 54.
"The Posse" *Extension* 46 (May 1952), 8-9[+?] [Based on CPLI].
"The Posse" *SW* 9 May 1953, II:1, 12.
"The Quiet House" *Stories with John Drainie* (1963), 87-91.
"[The?] Revolving Door" *Sign* 30 (Mar 1951), 62-3[+?] [Based on CPLI].
"The Saboteur" *FH* 6 Jan 1955, 20.
"Short Cut for Mr. Poppin" *Weekend* 1 (24 Nov 1951), 18.
"So Much a Word" *Sign* 31 (Nov 1951), 52-3[+?] [Based on CPLI].
"So Much a Word" *FH* 15 May 1952, 28.
"So Small a Thing" *Extension* 46 (Apr 1952), 12-3[+?] [Based on CPLI].
"So Small a Thing" *SW* 31 Jan 1953, I:5.

"Some Day We'll Go" *Extension* 52 (June 1957), 23[+?] [Based on CPLI].

"Successor to Laura" *CHJ* June 1951, 16, 85-92.

"Such Bright Ideas" *Sign* 32 (Jan 1953), 16-8[+?] [Based on CPLI].

"This Is It" *Sign* 29 (Apr 1950), 40-3[+?] [Based on CPLI].

"This Is It" *FH* 25 Jan 1951, 22-3.

"This My Son" *Ave Maria* 90 (18 July 1959), 12[+?] [Based on CPLI].

"The Threatening Storm" *Chat* 27 (Oct 1954), 23, 60-1, 66-70.

"Time to Talk" *SW* 4 June 1960, 20-3.

"The Town Where Mary Lived" *CG* Nov 1952, 10, 65.

"Trip without Marge" *FH* 11 Aug 1955, 18-9.

"Trouble at Timothy's" *FH* 27 Jan 1955, 22-3.

"The Two Boats" *FH* 19 Apr 1950, 28-9.

"White Meadows" *Extension* 49 (Dec 1954), 11[+?] [Based on CPLI].

"Window Slammer" *FH* 7 June 1956, 26-7, 37.

"Windward Summer" *CHJ* Sept 1950, 22, 24, 30-1, 86-7, 89.

"[The?] Woodlot" *Sign* 36 (June 1957), 44-6[+?] [Based on CPLI].

"Written in the Sand" *FH* 13 May 1954, 32-3.

"You Get to Know People" *SW* 19 Feb 1955, II:4.

"You Never Heard?" *Extension* 54 (Sept 1959), 23[+?] [Based on CPLI].

"Young Man's Fancy" *FH* 5 Aug 1954, 16-7, 23.

Barnard, Margaret E.

See also Barnard, Margaret E. and Barnard, Leslie Gordon.

"Difficult Choice" *Extension* 50 (Dec 1955), 6[+?] [Based on CPLI].

"Go Away, Baby" *SW* 25 July 1953, I:3.

"Key to Rosemary" *CG* July 1954, 8, 39-42.

"Meat Balls Tomorrow" *SW* 19 Mar 1955, II:3, 12.

"Men Are Only People" *SW* 27 Mar 1954, I:3, 12.

"Nellie Went Away" *CG* Sept 1955, 62, 72-5.

"Reach for an Angel" *Sign* 32 (July 1953), 46-50.

"The Spencers" *Days of Grass* (1965) [Pre-1950? Based on SSI].

"The Wacky Bunch" *CHJ* Aug 1957, 31, 52-6.

"Young Man in a Hurry" *SW* 15 Mar 1958, 44-5.

Barnard, Margaret E. and Barnard, Leslie Gordon

"[A?] Chit of a Girl" *Extension* 47 (May 1953), 16-7[+?] [Based on CPLI].

"Christmas at Home" *Chat* 27 (Dec 1954), 21, 47-53, 56.

"Different Summer" *Extension* 50 (July 1955), 22[+?] [Based on CPLI].

"Fiddlers Three" *Ave Maria* 90 (1 Aug 1959), 8[+?] [Based on CPLI].

"Fiddlers Three" *FH* 27 Oct 1960, 26-7, 34.

"How Beautiful Is the Rain" *Extension* 46 (June 1951), 12-3[+?] [Based on CPLI].

"How Beautiful Is the Rain" *SW* 6 Sept 1952, II:8, 12.

"I've Got to Tell You, Darling" *CHJ* Feb 1950, 12-4, 16, 26-8.

"Last Day of All" *Ladies Home J* 67 (Aug 1950), 38-9, 128-31.

"Look Who's Laughing" *Weekend* 2 (31 May 1952), 18-9, 26.

"The Pinnacle" *SW* 28 Mar 1959, 28-9, 39.

"Roses for Mickey" *FH* 1 Mar 1950, 28-9, 37.

"See What Jeff Says" *Extension* 51 (Sept 1956), 10-1[+?] [Based on CPLI].

"So Wide the Sea" *CHJ* Apr 1953, 20-1, 84-7, 90-2.

"The Spell of the Snow Crater" *SW* 10 Jan 1959, [14-5?], 41 [First page(s) were not microfilmed].

"Try It On for Size" *Extension* 48 (Mar 1954), 14[+?] [Based on CPLI].
"Uncle Herbert's Silver Moon" *FH* 1 Mar 1956, 20-1, 32.
"You're Very Young" *Chat* 26 (Mar 1953), 18-9, 47-9, 55-8, 60-2.

Barnard, Murray‡
"The Idealist" *AA* 56 (Aug 1966), 25, 27, 29, 31-2.

Barnes, Bill [William J.?]‡
"The Necessary Evil" *TUR* 71:4 (Mar 1958), 21-3.

Barnes, Lilly
"There Must Be Others ... " *CF* 62 (Nov 1982), 24-8.
"Vacations in the Sun" *This* 16:3 (July 1982), 30-2.

Barnes, M.R.‡
"Living in a Personality" *Gram* 1:3 (Mar 1976), 11-2.

Barnett, S.M.‡
"Late Arrival" *Edmonton Journal* Thu, 6 June 1967, 6.

Barnhouse, D.P. (1914-)
"The Day Granddad Quit the Sea" *Tales from The Skipper* (1968), 104-12.
"Halfway to the Mountain" *CG* 83 (July 1964), 33-6.
"Knowing Anna" *Inquiry into Literature* 1 (1980), 70-6.
"Knowing Anna" *Echoes* 1 (1983), 322-7.
"The Rivals" *Alberta Diamond Jubilee Anthology* (1979), 292-5 [Non-fiction?].
"Social Leopard" *Edmonton Journal* Mon, 3 Dec 1962, 4 [Humour].
"A Walk through the Park" *Onward* 27 Oct 1963, 6-7.
"A Walk through the Park" *Onward* 11 June 1967, 12-3.

Barr, Allan†
"A Dream of Horses" *Grain* 7:2 [1979], 35-6.

Barr, Elinor‡
"White Otter Castle" *Squatch J* Nos. 14/15 (June 1983), 13-4.

Barreto-Rivera, Rafael (1944-)
"Leaves Leaving" *Story So Four* (1976), 10-1.

Barrett, Alan John†
"David" *Forge* Feb 1957, 36-8.
"Of Gardens ... " *Forge* Dec 1956, 5-7.

Barrett, Herb†
"The Port of No Return" *Origins* 11:1 (Mar 1981), 27-35.

Barrick, Geoffrey‡
"The Day I Saw God" CBC *"Alberta Anthology"* 4 Oct 1980.
"McCloskey's Plan" CBC *"Alberta Anthology"* 9 Oct 1982.

Barrick, Steve‡
"For Sunshine" *Dime Bag* No. 12 (Nov 1974), [1 p].
"Wings in the Night" *Alpha* 7:2 (Apr 1983), 23-5.

Barrington, John‡
"Citrus Flaked Sunshine" *Folio* 19:2 (Spr 1967), 6-8.

Barry, Lisa†
"Froba Fraxler" *Miss Chat* 11 (9 May 1974), 25, 83-4.

Barry, P.S.
"The Civilizing Influence" *Edge* No. 4 (Spr 1965), 52-4.

Barta, John‡
"Macaroni Lost (After Giovanni Miltonio)" *Varsity Lit Issue* Fri, 13 Dec 1963, 12-3.

Bartlett, Brian (1953-)
FINCHES FOR THE WAKE Fredericton: Fiddlehead, 1971.
"The Cure of the Lawyer's Wife" *Aurora* 1980 185-94.
"The Dummy Was Alive" *Quarry* 23:4 (Aut 1974), 25-32.
"From One Chair on the Hill" *Finches for the Wake* (1971), 24-8.
"Glimpses in the Fields" *Fid* No. 113 (Spr 1977), 51-64.
"Jay's Aviary" *AA* 62 (Dec 1971), 31-2, 34, 36.
"Jay's Aviary" *Stories from Atlantic Canada* (1973), 166-73.
"The Polar Passion" *Fid* No. 115 (Fall 1972), 14-31.
"Son" *78: Best Canadian Stories* 141-52.
"Son" *UWR* 14:1 (Fall-Win 1978), 30-8.
"Tent by the Sea" *Prism* 17:2 (Fall 1978), 10-22.
"Woman on Hill" *Fid* No. 103 (Fall 1976), 49-61.

Bartlette, Sandra – *See* Birdsell, Sandra.

Bartley, Allan‡
"Last Job" *Alive* 3:1 [1972?], 31.
"On Friday" *Alive* 3:2 No. 21 [1972?], 27-8.
"The Shoveller" *Alive* 3:4 No. 23 [1972], 29-31.

Bartley, Jim†
"Evening Out" *Body Politic* No. 93 (May 1983), 34-5.

Bartolini, D[onna]
"Blue Streams, Yellow Dandelion" *Existère* 1:1 (Oct 1980), 8.

Barton, Marie†
"Arni Laxdal" *Green's* 3:3 (Spr 1975), 43-51.

Bartram, Gerald†
"A Christmas Story" *Random* Dec [1968], 11-3.
"Jimmy Turner's Secret File" *Chel J* 1 (Sept-Oct 1975), 237-42.

Bass, Jack A.‡
"The Lion Sleeps" *Creative Campus* 1967, 26-7.

Bastow, E.
"The Sobering of Joshua, the Shuswap" *Was R* 7:1 (1972), 15-22.

Bates, Hilary‡
"A Shorte Tale Concerning a Woeful Warlock" *Folio* 18:2 (Spr 1966), 27-8.

Batten, Jack (1932-)
See also Batten, Jack and Bliss, Michael.
"Country Club" *MM* 84 (July 1971), 30, 53, 55-6, 58.

Batten, Jack and Bliss, Michael
See also Batten, Jack.
"The Adventure of the Annexationist Conspiracy" *Maddened by Mystery* (1982), 1-19 [Also entitled "Sherlock Holmes' Great Canadian Adventure"].
"Sherlock Holmes' Great Canadian Adventure" *Weekend* 27 (28 May 1977), 8-14 [Also entitled "The Adventure of the Annexationist Conspiracy"].

Battistuzzi, Richard‡
"Bill" *Alive* [1:7] (June [1970]), [2 pp].
"The Cathedral" *Alive* No. 30 [1973], 37-8.

Battley, Mark R.‡
"Smelts" *TUR* 96:2 (Spr 1983), 27-9.

Bauchman, Rosemary
"Change of Perspective" *FH* 18 Mar 1965, 78-9.
"Day of Mourning" *FH* 13 Oct 1966, 69-70.
"Dual Warning" *FH* 17 Mar 1966, 50-1.
"Flowers for the Teacher" *FH* 9 June 1966, 32-3, 36.

Bauer, Frances (1934-)
"The Birdlady" *Room* 8:3 (1983), 32-41.
"The Lady in the Schiaparelli Shoes" *Grain* 9:1 (Feb 1981), 34-41.

Bauer, George†
"A Northern Christmas Story" *North* 25 (Nov-Dec 1978), 24-9.

Bauer, Nancy (1936-)
FLORA, WRITE THIS DOWN Fredericton: Fiddlehead Books, 1982 [Connected stories; novel?].
"The Bad" *Flora, Write This Down* (1982), 61-3.
"Bad Hand" *Flora, Write This Down* (1982), 34-41.
"Benjamin" *Flora, Write This Down* (1982), 81-4.
"Boneset" *Flora, Write This Down* (1982), 7-14.
"Bonfire" *Flora, Write This Down* (1982), 15-20.
"Chronicles" *Flora, Write This Down* (1982), 102-7.
"Dance, Dance, Wherever You May Be" *CFM* No. 22 (Sum 1976), 74-80.
"Dance, Dance, Wherever You May Be" *Stubborn Strength* (1983), 110-8.
"Disorder" *Flora, Write This Down* (1982), 55-60.
"The Facts of Life" *Flora, Write This Down* (1982), 71-80.
"Feeling My Way Forward" *Flora, Write This Down* (1982), 113-5.
"The Foundation of This House" *Flora, Write This Down* (1982), 134-6.
"Incomprehensible Visiting" *Flora, Write This Down* (1982), 119-33.
"Is There a Balm in Gilead" *Flora, Write This Down* (1982), 26-33.
"Like a Curve in a Waterfall" *Flora, Write This Down* (1982), 21-5.

"A Pleroma of Cousins" *Flora, Write This Down* (1982), 48-52.
"Priscilla" *Flora, Write This Down* (1982), 97-101.
"Prologue" *CFM* No. 44 (1982), 6-12.
"Seeking Carefully with Tears" *Flora, Write This Down* (1982), 108-12.
"A Shout of Joy" *Flora, Write This Down* (1982), 89-93.
"Something Out There" *Flora, Write This Down* (1982), 85-8.
"Spikenard Root" *Flora, Write This Down* (1982), 42-7.
"Stranger and Pilgrim" *Flora, Write This Down* (1982), 64-70.
"The Weeping of the People" *Flora, Write This Down* (1982), 116-8.

Bauer, Walter (1904-)
"My Father's Tailor" *Shenandoah* 13:4 (Sum 1962), 5-10 [Based on ILM].
"There Has Never Been a Deluge" *NJ* No. 2 (1972-73), 60-4.

Bauer, William A. (1932-)
A FAMILY ALBUM Ottawa: Oberon Press, 1979.
"The Clairvoyant" *Family Album* (1979), 104-19.
"Fern" *Family Album* (1979), 79-103.
"The Hounds of Barkerville" *JD* Passover 1972, 22-33.
"The Hounds of Barkerville" *Family Album* (1979), 32-56.
"How Babies Are Made" *Family Album* (1979), 57-78.
"How the Hungry Are Fed" *Canadian Short Fiction Anthology* 2 (1982), 127-34.
"Never Bet on a Dead Horse" *CFM* No. 13 (Spr 1974), 28-34.
"Never Bet on a Dead Horse" *Magic Realism* (1980), 59-64.
"Pig-of-the-Wind: A Fragment from the Archives" *Fid* No. 78 (Jan-Feb 1969), 32-41.
"The Reading of Signs" *Antig R* No. 12 (Win 1973), 47-56.
"This Story Ends in a Pinegrove" *Family Album* (1979), 5-31.
"What Is Interred with Their Bones" *Fid* No. 116 (Win 1978), 53-67.
"What Is Interred with Their Bones" *Family Album* (1979), 120-50.
"What Is Interred with Their Bones" *Fiddlehead Greens* (1979), 25-49.
"A Woeful Pageant of the Seventh Age" *Fid* No. 123 (Fall 1979), 47-64.

Baum, Esther†
"Delinquent?" *Forge* Dec 1957, 21-2.

Baycroft, Perry‡
"How I Lost My Mind" *Repos* Nos. 23/24 (1977-78), 56.

Bayly, John†
"Sunday Morning After Chapel" *On the Bias* 1 [n.d.], [6 pp].

Bazley, Elizabeth‡
"The Forest" *Acta Vic* 78:1 (Nov 1953), 20.

Bazley, Walter‡
"The Rorqual" *TUR* 62:6 (Mar 1950), 31-5.

Beachey, Anne
"Cat's Best Friend" *Polished Pebbles* (1974), 37-40.
"If You Wish upon a Star" *Can Messenger* 82 (Sept 1972), 18-9.

Beadle, Gert†

"The Survivor" *Fireweed* No. 9 (Win 1981), 43-50.

Beal, Bill‡

"The Tilsley Thunderbolt" *Muse* 63:1 (Mar 1954), 12-3.

Beasley, B.J.‡

"Die Now and Live Later (An Adult Fairy Tale)" *Words from Inside* 1976, 33-4.
"Die Now and Live Later (An Adult Fairy Tale)" *Communicator* 8:3 [n.d.], [2 pp].

Beattie, Elizabeth‡

"Character Sketch" *Acta Vic* 78:2 (Dec 1953), 17-8.
"Professors and Professors and Professors" *Acta Vic* 78:3 (Feb 1954), 19.

Beattie, Jessie L. (1896-)

HASTEN THE DAY Toronto: United Church of Canada, 1961.
"Chrysanthemum Transplanted" *Hasten the Day* (1961), 82-94.
"Emile" *Hasten the Day* (1961), 70-80.
"Heard in the Echo" *Hasten the Day* (1961), 58-68.
"Into the Sunset" *Hasten the Day* (1961), 96-105.
"Jeanie" *Hasten the Day* (1961), viii-10.
"Out of the Storm" *Hasten the Day* (1961), 12-24.
"Outside the Structure" *Hasten the Day* (1961), 106-17.
"The Red Silk Dress" *Hasten the Day* (1961), 38-47.
"Second Harvest" *Hasten the Day* (1961), 26-36.
"Where Fades the Thin Line" *Hasten the Day* (1961), 48-56.

Beatty, D.J.‡

"Story" *Acta Vic* 89:2 (Spr 1965), 8-10.

Beaumont, Alison

"The Legacy" *Was R* 17:2 (Fall 1982), 37-45.

Beauvais, Ronald‡

"Bad Santa Claus" *Intercourse* Nos. 12/13 (Jan 1970), 6.
"Hidden Treasure" *Intercourse* Nos. 12/13 (Jan 1970), 5.
"The Meeting" *Intercourse* Nos. 12/13 (Jan 1970), 5.

Beck, J.P.‡

"Beyond a Destiny" *Rude* Prelim No. 3 [n.d.], [3 pp].
"The First Journey" *Rude* Prelim No. 3 [n.d.], [2 pp].

Beck, Norma Jean (1924?-)

"Christmas Is for Secrets" *CG* Dec 1958, 35-8.
"The Doctor's Busy Just Now" *Varsity* Tue, 21 Feb 1956, 1, 3-4.
"First Date" *Chat* 29 (June 1957), 17, 34-7.
"Forecast: Wet!" *CG* 79 (May 1960), 59-62.
"The Lovable Thief" *Chat* 32 (Jan 1959), 17, 54-6.
"The Saving Grace" *CG* 78 (Sept 1959), 47-51.
"Special Occasion" *Varsity* Tue, 21 Feb 1956, 5, 7-8.

Beck, Rosalie†
"The Bridesmaid" *Amethyst* 2:1 (Aut 1962), 9-11.

Beckett, Judith‡
"Chair by the Window" *Nw J* No. 24 (1981), 73-8.

Bedard, Fran‡
"Half-Breeds" *Muskeg R* 4 [1976], 58-60.

Bedard, Michael (1949-)
PIPE & PEARLS: A GATHERING OF TALES Toronto: Gardenshore Press, 1980.
WOODSEDGE AND OTHER TALES Toronto: Gardenshore Press, 1979.
"At the End of the Lane" *Pipe & Pearls* (1980), 68-75.
"The Book" *Woodsedge* (1979), 30-4.
"The Briar Way" *Woodsedge* (1979), 94-105.
"The Chalk Circle" *Pipe & Pearls* (1980), 105-24.
"The Day After Death" *WWR* 2:1 (1980), 76-81.
"The Dreadwood" *Woodsedge* (1979), 65-75.
"The Dream Master" *Pipe & Pearls* (1980), 125-34.
"The Dream Path" *Woodsedge* (1979), 22-9.
"The Gift of the Fairies" *Woodsedge* (1979), 76-81.
"In the Prison" *Pipe & Pearls* (1980), 39-67.
"The Lightning Bolt" *Woodsedge* (1979), 53-64.
"The Mask" *Pipe & Pearls* (1980), 76-90.
"Pipe & Pearls" *Pipe & Pearls* (1980), 1-22.
"The Playground" *Woodsedge* (1979), 91-3.
"Pool of Paradise" *Woodsedge* (1979), 12-21.
"The Steamer Trunk" *Pipe & Pearls* (1980), 91-104.
"The Turret Room" *Woodsedge* (1979), 82-90.
"The Two Hills" *Woodsedge* (1979), 35-44.
"Underground" *Pipe & Pearls* (1980), 23-38.
"The Witch Tree" *Woodsedge* (1979), 45-52.
"The Wizard of Danbury Wood" *Pipe & Pearls* (1980), 135-42.
"Woodsedge" *Woodsedge* (1979), 1-11.

Bedoya, Fausto – *See* Jirgins, Karl E.

Beech, Doreen
"Break-Up" *CSSM* 2:3 (Sum 1976), 20-3.

Beer, R.M.‡
"Gretel" *AA* 55 (Dec 1964), 25-7.

Begamudre, Ven†
"Apocalypse Later" *Smoke Signals* 4 [date unknown] [Based on *SWG* survey response].
"Holiday Father" *Saskatchewan Gold* (1982), 23-37.

Beghtol, Claire

"The Cheese Stands Alone" *Quarry* 24:4 (Aut 1975), 17-30.
"Family Ties" *CFM* No. 14 (Sum 1974), 4-16.
"Intersections" *WCR* 7:2 (Oct 1972), 35-8.
"There's Been a Death" *QQ* 76 (1969), 681-91.
"Under the Skin" *Fid* No. 112 (Win 1977), 60-8.

Behrens, Peter (1954-)

"Anarchy" *Stories of Quebec* (1980), 149-67.
"As We Are" *Second Impressions* (1981), 39-51.
"In Montreal" *78: Best Canadian Stories* 153-61.
"Morning, Valley of the Ten Peaks" *Prism* 17:1 (Sum 1978), 15-23.
"Music" *Matinees Daily* (1981), 70-81.
"Outremont" *79: Best Canadian Stories* 9-21.
"Passion" *Second Impressions* (1981), 15-38.
"We Are All Strangers Here" *Second Impressions* (1981), 52-74.

Beilin, Elaine‡

"A Midsummer's Nightmare or Like It or Lump It" *On the Bias* 2 (1968), [2 pp].
[Untitled] *On the Bias* 1 [n.d.], [1 p].
[Untitled] *On the Bias* 1969, [2 pp].

Beirnes, Peggy‡

"Minstrel Show" *NF* 4:4 (Win 1955), 2-6.

Beissel, Henry (1929-)

"The Sniper" *Aurora* 1978 60-6.

Belcourt, Lesley Tarrant‡

"Yesterday's Ship" *CBC [Edm] "Alberta Anthology"* 6 Sept 1980.

Belfry, Chris‡

"Plums Are Important Perhaps" *Dime Bag* [No. 18] Fiction Issue 1 (Mar 1977), 24-6.

Belinski, P.X.‡

"To Be a God" *Fascist Court* [1970], 44-5.

Belknap, Shane‡

"Best Left Unsaid" *Chiaroscuro* 13 (1969-70), 15-6 [Non-fiction?].

Bell, Don (1936-)

"The Adventures of Pocketman" *Blow Up* 1:10 (Dec-Jan 1980-81), [3 pp].
"The Autobiography of Mervyn Rose" *Viewpoints* 2:2 (Spr 1967), 22-7.
"The Car" *Viewpoints* 4:1 (1969), 58-62.
"C'est Drôle la Langue Anglaise" *Chimo!* 1:2 (1978), 35-7 [Humour].

Bell, Everett A.

THE THIRTEENTH HOUR Oakville: Humanity, 1976 [Based on CBIP].

Bell, Gay

" 'I'-grec Is Y: Autonomie" *Common Ground* (1980), 122-30.
" 'I'-grec Is Y: Autonomie" *Body Politic* No. 66 (Sept 1980), 26-8.

Bell, John (1952-)

"Crossroads" *Dark Fantasy* No. 23 (1980), 35-41.

"The Day Frank Schoonover Died" *Cop Toad* 1:4 (May 1978), 73-6 [Title based on survey response].

"The Echo of a Metronome" *Nebula* Nos. 21/22 (1982), 29-34.

"Face" *Quarry* 24:3 (Sum 1975), 25-31.

"A Fitting Place" *Dark Fantasy* No. 17 (Nov 1978) [Based on survey response].

"Walk" *Quarry* 22:2 (Spr 1973), 24-6.

"Window" *QQ* 84 (1977), 77-9.

Bell, John Leslie

"The Fall of the Ariadne" *Dand* 1 (Sum 1975), 34-47.

"The Last Run of the Ten-Twenty" *Can Lifetime* 4 (Sept-Oct 1974), 22-6.

"The Red Ball" *event* 5:2 [1976?], 41-8.

"The Temple of Their Gods" *QQ* 86 (1979), 58-67.

"Two Men from Alamein" *QQ* 83 (1976), 250-6.

Bell, Leslie†

"The Partisans" *CF* 53 (Mar 1974), 34-5.

Bell, Mackenzie‡

"Discovery" *Stardust* 2:2 [n.d.], 9-18.

"Leaves" *Stardust* 2:3 [n.d.], 25-7, 30-3.

"PFSD" *Stardust* 1:4 [n.d.], 29-53.

"The Wish" *Stardust* 3:1 [n.d.], 61-75.

Bell, Marion†

"Pyramidalis" *Read Ch* 1:3 (Win 1982), 3-14.

Bell, Michael‡

"Thursday Evening" *Forge* 1952, 38.

Bell, Roger†

"Party Below" *Quarry* 11 (Mar 1962), 18-9.

Bell, Wade

THE NORTH SASKATCHEWAN RIVER BOOK Toronto: Coach House Press, 1976.

"1912: The Bridge Beginning" *North Saskatchewan River Book* (1976), 13-6.

"1912: The Bridge Beginning" *Alberta Diamond Jubilee Anthology* (1979), 207-9.

"An Animal Tale" *Story So Far* 5 (1978), 19-28.

"The Conversion" *North Saskatchewan River Book* (1976), 66-83.

"Country Music" *North Saskatchewan River Book* (1976), 25-31.

"History of the Canadian West" *Matrix* 1:1 (Spr 1975), 8-10.

"History of the Canadian West" *North Saskatchewan River Book* (1976), 8-12.

"Judy & the Archivist" *North Saskatchewan River Book* (1976), 59-64.

"(a mellowdrama)" *North Saskatchewan River Book* (1976), 87-97.

"Mountains & Rivers & an Arctic Sea" *North Saskatchewan River Book* (1976), 50-7.

"Mountains & Rivers & an Arctic Sea" *More Stories from Western Canada* (1980), 25-32.

"Music for a Wet Afternoon" *Story So Far* 3 (1974), 127-30.

"Music for a Wet Afternoon" *North Saskatchewan River Book* (1976), 42-7.
"My Dear Dr. Pinkham" *North Saskatchewan River Book* (1976), 22-4.
"Phantoms" *North Saskatchewan River Book* (1976), 19-21.
"The Satie Church" *North Saskatchewan River Book* (1976), 37-9.
"Stupidity Has Come to the Plains" *North Saskatchewan River Book* (1976), 34-6.
"The Sturgeon" *North Saskatchewan River Book* (1976), 33.

Bellan, Matt‡
"The Visitor" *Mandala* 1972, 60-2.

Beller, Jacob†
"The Last Kiss" *AA* 56 (Nov 1965), 45-6, 48.
"Red Lights" *Viewpoints* 2:2 (Spr 1967), 45-8.

Belserene, Paul†
"Cups" *Grain* 8:3 (Nov 1980), 30-3.
"How I Came to Canada" *Canadian Short Fiction Anthology 2* (1982), 96-8.

Beltrano, Frank†
"Museum Piece" *Thursday's Voices* (1983), 67-74.

Belva, Dena‡
"The Bath" *Potlatch* No. 1 (Jan 1964), 1-4.

Bemisch, Milo‡
"The Companion" *Our Times* 1:5 (Nov 1982), 8.

Bemrose, John‡
"The Bell" *Acta Vic* 93:2 (Dec 1968), 20-2.
"Eve" *Acta Vic* 93:3 (Feb 1969), 3-8.

Bénéteau, Marcel (1951-)
"The Ants" *JCF* No. 22 (1978), 5-12.
"In the Woods" *Quarry* 30:1 (Win 1981), 10-4.
"The Reunion" *event* 7:2 (1978), 110-9.
"Three Visions of the Madonna" *Fid* No. 110 (Sum 1976), 61-71.

Benger, JoAnne‡
"Death and the Farmer" CBC "*Alberta Anthology*" 22 Nov 1980.
"Final Death" *West People* No. 130 (25 Mar 1982), 12.
"Garbage Man John" *West People* No. 122 (28 Jan 1982), 11.
"Sour Gas" *West People* No. 174 (3 Feb 1983), 15.

Bennett, A.‡
"If God Hadn't Intended Man to Fly, He Would Have Given Him Roots" *Acta Vic* 101:1 (Fall 1976), 21-2.

Bennett, Bill‡
"The View from the Hill" *Acta Vic* 81:2 (Dec 1956), 7-9.

Bennett, Jennifer (1947-)
"Sleepers" *Chat* 56 (Oct 1983), 87, 137-8, 140, 142.

Bennett, Katherine†
"An Understanding" *Can Messenger* 85 (Jan 1975), 18-9.

Bennett, Michael‡
"Gull" *Folio* 20:3 (Spr 1968), 21-2.

Bennett, Warren†
"The Long Journey" *Was R* 2:1 (1967), 21-30.

Benoit, Lee – *See* Green, H. Gordon.

Benstead, Steven‡
"The Card Player" *Pier Spr* 4 (Nov 1979), 11-7.
"The Weatherman" *Mandala* 1973, 39-46.

Bent, Foster†
"Not Yet ... Not Yet" *Amethyst* 2:1 (Aut 1962), 5-7.

Bentley, Allen‡
"The Image" *Acta Vic* 79:[2] (Dec 1954), 19-21.

Berenyi, Yulika†
"About an Old Man" *Forge* Mar 1958, 18-21.

Beresford-Howe, Constance (1922-)
"The China Shepherdess" *Chat* 54 (Feb 1981), 55, 66-8, 72, 76-7, 80-1.
"The Face of Innocence" *Chat* 29 (Nov 1957), 69-72.
"Jeanne" *Chat* 53 (Apr 1980), 50, 68, 70, 72, 74, 76, 78, 80.
"The Right Age" *Chat* 54 (Jan 1981), 41, 108, 110, 113-4, 116.
"The Second Mrs. Lindsay" *Chat* 52 (Nov 1979), 64-5, 93, 96, 98, 101, 105-6, 108.
"The Turning Tide" *CHJ* June 1954, 20-1, 29-30, 32, 81-2, 84, 86.

Bereshko-Hunter, Ludmilla [pseudonym]
"And with Two Such Husbands" *CBC* "Anthology" 28 June 1980.
"And with Two Such Husbands" *Saturday Night at the Forum* (1981), 70-80.
"The Only Place on Earth" *Matinees Daily* (1981), 33-49.

Bereska, Brigette‡
"The Bundle" *Stump* 5:1 (Fall-Win 1980), 18-9.

Berg, Sharon (1954-)
"The Marvelous Gift" *Quarry* 31:2 (Spr 1982), 56-9.

Berger, David‡
"The Difference Between Good and Evil" *Jargon* 1961-62, 47-54.

Berger, Harvey†
"Francesco" *Mont Writers' Forum* 2:3 (Dec 1979), 6-12.

Berger, Joanne‡
"Susan" *CSSM* 1:2 (Apr 1975), 62-3.

Bergman, Brian‡
"Lilith" *Gas Rain* [1] (Mar 1977), 4-8.

Bergren, Myrtle
A BOUGH OF NEEDLES: ELEVEN CANADIAN SHORT STORIES Toronto: Progress Books, 1964.
"Black Mountain" *Bough of Needles* (1964), 9-17.
"The Christening" *Bough of Needles* (1964), 81-7.
"The Cougar at Old Tie Camp" *Bough of Needles* (1964), 39-50.
"The Day God Died for Benny" *Bough of Needles* (1964), 28-38.
"The Flitting Bird" *Stump* 2:2 (Fall 1978), 4-8.
"A Hard Pull" *Bough of Needles* (1964), 58-66.
"Lonesome Bus" *Stump* 1:2 (Fall 1977), 27-34.
"One Day's Peace" *Bough of Needles* (1964), 51-7.
"A Simple Fellow" *Uk Can* 16 (1 Jan 1962), 10.
"The Simple Fellow" *Bough of Needles* (1964), 94-8.
"Smoke in the Hills" *Rain Chr* No. [8] [n.d.], 32-5.
"Some People's Luck" *Bough of Needles* (1964), 75-80.
"The Strangers" *Bough of Needles* (1964), 88-93.
"The Swedes Who Never Went Back" *Bough of Needles* (1964), 67-74.
"When I Was Seventeen" *Bough of Needles* (1964), 18-27.
"The Yellow Rose" *Stump* 1:1 (Spr 1977), 36-40.

Berketa, Raymond (? -1965)
"The Black Cross" *Uk Can* 20 (15 May 1966), 9-10.
"The Black Cross" *Uk Can* 33 (May 1981), 40-2.

Bermiller, Arthur‡
"Simplicity in Life or The Pastries" *J of Our Time* No. 3 (1982), 63-6.

Bernard, Anne – *See* Copeland, Ann.

Bernhardt, Peter‡
"Social Walls" *Fifth Page* 1961, 21-4.

Berry, David‡
"Alec" *Acta Vic* 94:4 (Apr 1970), 20-3.
"From the Taoist Parables" *Story So Far* 2 (1973), 66-71.
"Rodrigo's Dream" *Acta Vic* 96:2 [n.d.], 1-4.

Berry, Malcolm‡
"The Family" *Introductions from an Island* 1976, 26-9.

Berryman, J.‡
"Third Wind" *Outlook* Spr-Sum 1979, [2 pp].

Bettison, Margaret‡
"The Children" *CBC "Anthology"* 13 Apr 1962.
"Something in Common" *CBC "Anthology"* 30 Aug 1964.

Bevan, Alan
"Blood and the Northern Lights" *Dal R* 50 (1970), 344-9.
"Cul de Sac" *Fid* No. 57 (Sum 1963), 24-8.
"An Evening Out" *Evidence* No. 4 (Win 1962), 85-93.

Beveridge, Karl – *See* Conde, Carole and Beveridge, Karl.

Bhatia, June
"The Suicide Tower" *CBC "Alberta Anthology"* 31 Oct 1981.

Bialik, H.G.‡
"The Afternoon Holds Manifold Promises" *Forge* 1950, 37-9.

Biderman, Ruth‡
"No Special Reason" *Des* No. 16 (Win 1976-77), 43-8.
[Untitled] *UCR* Win 1983, 12-4.

Biel, Kent C.†
"There Was a Crooked Man" *Prism* 13:2 (Win 1973), 98-107.

Bigalow, Mary
"A Piping from the Sea" *Sand Patterns* No. 12 (1974), 6-13.
"The Sea Glass" *Variations on a Gulf Breeze* (1973), 86-96.

Biley, Bill‡
"Things to Say" *Uk Can* 6 (1 Jan 1952), 8.

Bilovus, Linda†
"Natura Finds a Husband" *Posh* [n.d.], [1 p].

Birch, David‡
"Remembered Forms" *Kensington* Dec 1972, [4 pp].

Birch, Frank‡
"Where the Devil Would Have His Horns" *Fifth Page* 1968, 28-35.

Birch, Paul†
"No More Than Disguise" *Raven* 1:3 (Spr 1956), 35-7.

Birch-Jones, Sonia (1921-)
A FIRST CLASS FUNERAL. Lantzville, B.C.: Oolichan Books, 1983.
"Auntie Minnie" *JD* Hanukah 1981, 12-6.
"Auntie Minnie and the Goy" *First Class Funeral* (1983), 108-22.
"A Buttercup for Uncle Lennie" by Sonia Croucher *JD* Sum 1980, 12-4.
"Chicken Soup" *JD* Passover 1982, 26-8, 30, 32, 34.
"Curtain Up" *by Sonia Croucher JD* Hanukah 1980, 31.
"Dilys O'Connor" by Sonia Croucher *JD* Rosh Hashanah 1978, 34-8.
"Dilys O'Connor" by Sonia Croucher *JD* Passover 1981, 40-2, 44, 46, 48.
"Dilys O'Connor" *First Class Funeral* (1983), 123-38.
"Don't Do God Any Favours" by Sonia Croucher *Introductions from an Island* (1975), 52-61.
"Don't Do God Any Favours" by Sonia Croucher *JD* Hanukah 1980, 18-20.
"Don't Do God Any Favours" *First Class Funeral* (1983), 9-18.

"The Dowry Man" *First Class Funeral* (1983), 65-78.

"The Dowry Man" *Mal R* No. 64 (Feb 1983), 8-19.

"A First Class Funeral" *Mal R* No. 50 (Apr 1979), 120-43.

"A First Class Funeral" by Sonia Croucher *JD* Sum 1980, 2-10.

"A First Class Funeral" *Rainshadow* (1982), 53-80.

"A First Class Funeral" *First Class Funeral* (1983), 79-107.

"Grandpa Saul" by Sonia Croucher *JD* Rosh Hashanah 1977, 76-8.

"Grandpa Saul" by Sonia Croucher *JD* Rosh Hashanah 1980, 20-2, 24.

"Grandpa Saul" *First Class Funeral* (1983), 29-38.

"Grandpa Saul" by Sonia Croucher *JD* Rosh Hashanah 1983, 22-4.

"It Pays to Have a Little Talk with God" by Sonia Croucher *JD* Rosh Hashanah 1980, 10-3.

"It Pays to Have a Little Talk with God" *First Class Funeral* (1983), 19-28.

"The Last Act" by Sonia Croucher *JD* Hanukah 1980, 42-3.

"Soap and Water" *Acanthus* 1 (Apr 1978), 40-6 [Excerpt].

"Soap and Water" by Sonia Croucher *JD* Passover 1981, 52-5.

"A Special Kind of Magic" *First Class Funeral* (1983), 39-54.

"Toffee Apples" by Sonia Croucher *Introductions from an Island* (1974), 50-8.

"Toffee Apples" by Sonia Croucher *JD* Hanukah 1980, 26-8.

"Toffee Apples" *First Class Funeral* (1983), 55-64.

"Tomorrow I'll Be Twenty-Eight and Old" *Mal R* No. 51 (July 1979), 5-18.

"Wicked Am I?" by Sonia Croucher *JD* Rosh Hashanah 1980, 2-8.

"Wicked Am I?" *First Class Funeral* (1983), 139-58.

Bird, Tom†

"For Pete's Sake" *Saskatchewan Homecoming* (1971), 100-1.

"Run Bertie Run!" *Saskatchewan Homecoming* (1971), 178-80 [Children's?].

Bird, Will R. (1891-1984)

ANGEL COVE Toronto: Macmillan, 1972.

"The Ambush" *FH* 8 Mar 1951, 28-9, 38.

"Bachelor Brother" *FH* 20 Sept 1951, 22-3, 49.

"The Cheat" *FH* 16 Aug 1951, 20-1.

"A Demon for a Decoy" *SW* 6 Jan 1951, I:1, 4.

"The Equivalent" *Angel Cove* (1972), 24-36.

"Fort Orders" *SW* 14 Apr 1951, I:1.

"Granny's Art" *Angel Cove* (1972), 63-74.

"The Green Far Hills" *SW* 22 Sept 1951, I:10-1.

"Helen Mary and the Stranger" *Angel Cove* (1972), 51-62.

"The Incredible German" *Weekend* 2 (23 Feb 1952), 18.

"The Last Trick" *Angel Cove* (1972), 214-27.

"Letters for Abel" *Angel Cove* (1972), 37-50.

"The Little Yorkie" *SW* 25 Feb 1950, II:3.

"The Love of Bride Crowdy" *Angel Cove* (1972), 149-58.

"The Making of a Man" *SW* 8 Nov 1952, I:1, 12.

"Ma's Easter Hat" *FH* 5 Apr 1950, 34-5.

"The Prisoner" *AA* 56 (Oct 1965), 45-7, 49-51, 53-5.

"Pro Tem" *Angel Cove* (1972), 1-23.

"Second Spring" *FH* 10 Sept 1953, 24-5.

"Stubborn Like His Pa" *Angel Cove* (1972), 170-84.

"Testing Time for Tiny Tim" *SW* 4 Mar 1950, II:3-4.

"An Upright People" *FH* 2 Nov 1950, 26-7, 35.
"The Weasel Skin" *Angel Cove* (1972), 200-13.
"The Weasel Skin" *Canadian Stories of Action and Adventure* (1978), 153-66.
"The Weasel Skin" *In Your Own Words* (1982), 99-110.
"Wedding on the Green" *FH* 11 May 1950, 24-5, 56.
"Witch's Power" *Angel Cove* (1972), 159-69.
"A Woman Can't Wait Too Long" *Angel Cove* (1972), 185-99.

Birdsell, Sandra (1942-)
NIGHT TRAVELLERS Winnipeg: Turnstone Press, 1982.
"Boundary Lines" *Night Travellers* (1982), 17-32.
"The Children Are Crying" *CA & B* 55:1 (Nov 1979), 13-5.
"Crystle's Tree" *Writers News Man* 3:1 (Mar 1981), [6 pp].
"The Day My Grandfather Died" *Night Travellers* (1982), 127-42.
"The Doll" *Chel J* 5 (May-June 1979), 120-1.
"Episode" *CBC [Winn]* 1978 [Based on survey response].
"Falling in Love" *Arts Man* 2:4 (Fall 1983), 52-7.
"The Flood" *Night Travellers* (1982), 1-16.
"Flowers for Weddings and Funerals" *NeWest R* 5 (Jan 1980), 8-9.
"Flowers for Weddings and Funerals" *Night Travellers* (1982), 91-8.
"I Ask Myself" *CBC* [1981?] [Based on survey response].
"Journey to the Lake" *Night Travellers* (1982), 143-58.
"Judgement" *Night Travellers* (1982), 99-111.
"My Blonde Tiger" *Images About Manitoba* 1:3 (Fall-Win 1976), 8-9.
"Night Travellers" *Night Travellers* (1982), 79-89.
"Pepra" *Grain* 4:3 [1976], 35-8.
"A Pink Granite Stone" *Origins* 8:4 (Dec 1978), 32-8.
"Pray for Sylvia" by Sandra Bartlette *Grain* 6:2 [1978], 6-13.
"Pray for Sylvia" *Best of Grain* (1980), 133-40.
"Pray for Sylvia" *More Stories from Western Canada* (1980), 215-27.
"The Rock Garden" *Night Travellers* (1982), 63-78.
"Safe in the Arms of Jesus" *Inland Sea* 1979, [12 pp] [Based on survey response].
"Short Story" by Sandra Bartlette *Cap R* No. 12 (1977), 5-7.
"Stones" *CBC* 1977 [Based on survey response].
"Stones" *Mandala* 1978, 5-6.
"Stones" *Night Travellers* (1982), 59-61.
"There Is No Shoreline" *Night Travellers* (1982), 159-82.
"Transposition" *CFM* No. [45] (1982-83), 35-51.
"Transposition" *Metavisions* (1983), 69-86.
"Truda" *Night Travellers* (1982), 33-43.
"Truda" *West of Fiction* (1983), 267-75.
"The Waiting Time" by Sandra Bartlette *Waves* 7:1 (Fall 1978), 8-12.
"The Wednesday Circle" *Grain* 9:3 (Aug 1981), 13-21.
"The Wednesday Circle" *Night Travellers* (1982), 45-57.
"The Wild Plum Tree" *Night Travellers* (1982), 113-26.
"The Wild Plum Tree" *NeWest R* 8 (Oct 1982), 8-10.

Birney, Earle (1904-)
BIG BIRD IN THE BUSH: SELECTED STORIES AND SKETCHES Oakville: Mosaic Press/Valley Editions, 1978.
"Enigma in Ebony" *MM* 66 (15 Oct 1953), 16-7, 104, 106-8 [Also entitled "Waiting for *Queen Emma*"].
"Waiting for *Queen Emma*" *Big Bird in the Bush* (1978), 9-19 [Also entitled "Enigma in Ebony"].
"What's This Agoosto?" *Montreal Standard* Sat, 29 July 1950, 14-5, 21 [Based on ABCMA].

Bishop, Terry‡
[Untitled] *Eclipse* No. 2 [n.d.], [2 pp].

Bissonnette, Larry‡
"Continuing Tales of the Little Fellow" *Deceits of Ecstasy* (1971), 3-8.

Bjarnason, Bogi†
"Her Boy" *Ice Can* 27:1 (Aut 1968), 49-53.
"My Pal" *Ice Can* 26:3 (Spr 1968), 38-9.
"The Purchased Letter" *Ice Can* 17:4 (Sum 1959), 33-9.
"A Rap at the Door" *Ice Can* 23:4 (Sum 1965), 41-3.
"The Tables Turned" *Ice Can* 25:2 (Win 1966), 34-5.
"The Tattered Lapel" *Ice Can* 19:2 (Win 1960), 65, 67.

Blacharczyk, Frank and Bissonnette, George†
DREAMS AND ASPIRATIONS: A SELECTION OF POEMS AND SHORT STORIES Kingston: privately printed, 1976 [Based on CBIP].

Black, Karen†
"Broken" *Miss Chat* 11 (14 Mar 1972), 35, 92-5.
"Just Friends" *Miss Chat* 13 (3 Aug 1976), 73, 89-91, 94-5.

Black, Lampman‡
"Midnight Special" *Portico* 3:2/3 [n.d.], 7-16.
"The Red Fox" *Portico* 2:3 (Spr 1978), 16-23, 34-41.

Black, Simon†
"King on a Rock" *CSSM* 2:1 (Jan 1976), 50-2.
"Nanuk ... the King!" *CSSM* 1:1 (Jan 1975), 17-20.

Blackburn, Robert (1919-)
"Between Me and the Dark" *QQ* 61 (1954), 63-70.
"The Clay Dish" *Canadian Short Stories* (1952), 228-36.

Blackwell, M.H.‡
"Not How You Play the Game" *Chiaroscuro* 8 (1964), 38-43.

Blackwell, Pearl – *See* Green, H. Gordon.

Blacock, Mary‡
"A Dartmoor Incident" *Acta Vic* 76:4 (Mar 1952), 19-20.
"Moods of Skye" *Acta Vic* 76:3 (Feb 1952), 29-30.

Blaine, Eric‡
"The Admission" *New Thursday* No. 1 (Spr 1974), 49-52.

Blaise, Clark L. (1940-)
A NORTH AMERICAN EDUCATION: A BOOK OF SHORT FICTION Toronto: Doubleday, 1973.
TRIBAL JUSTICE Toronto: Doubleday, 1974.
"Among the Dead" *American Review* No. 16 (Feb 1973), 213-21.
"Among the Dead" *Tribal Justice* (1974), 217-24.
"Among the Dead" *Double Vision* (1976), 324-31.
"At the Lake" *CBC "Anthology"* 7 July 1973.
"At the Lake" *Tribal Justice* (1974), 199-208.
"Before Sundown" *Carolina Q* 17:1 (Fall 1964), 31-41.
"The Bridge" *North American Education* (1973), 133-41.
"Broward Dowdy" *Shenandoah* 15:4 (Sum 1964), 33-43 [Based on ILM].
"Broward Dowdy" *Tribal Justice* (1974), 3-14.
"Broward Dowdy" *Stories Plus* (1979), 2-10.
"Burning Man" *Minnesota R* 7 (1967), 133-41.
"A Class of New Canadians" *Fid* No. 84 (Mar-Apr 1970), 26-33.
"A Class of New Canadians" *North American Education* (1973), 3-15.
"A Class of New Canadians" *Immigrant Experience* (1975), 94-102.
"A Class of New Canadians" *Best Modern Canadian Short Stories* (1978), 248-55.
"A Class of New Canadians" *Literature in Canada* (1978), 666-74.
"A Class of New Canadians" *Canadian Literature in the 70's* (1980), 121-9.
"Continent of Strangers" *North American Education* (1973), 84-129.
"Cut, Print" *SN* 90 (June 1975), 49-56.
"The Examination" *New Canadian Writing 1968* 106-20.
"Extractions and Contractions" *Student's Choice* (1970) [Based on SSI].
"Extractions and Contractions" *CBC "Anthology"* 14 Mar 1970.
"Extractions and Contractions" *Story So Far* (1971), 16-25.
"Extractions and Contractions" *North American Education* (1973), 41-58.
"Extractions and Contractions" *Personal Fictions* (1977), 186-96.
"Extractions and Contractions" *Stories of Quebec* (1980), 47-60.
"Eyes" *Fid* No. 91 (Fall 1971), 24-8.
"Eyes" *Narrative Voice* (1972), 17-21.
"Eyes" *North American Education* (1973), 16-24.
"Eyes" *Modern Stories in English* (1975), 26-31.
"Eyes" *Anthology of Canadian Literature in English 2* (1983), 543-7.
"The Fabulous Eddie Brewster" *New Canadian Writing 1968* 69-89 [Also entitled "The Mayor"].
"The Fabulous Eddie Brewster" *Tribal Justice* (1974), 27-46.
"The Fabulous Eddie Brewster" *Stories Plus* (1979), 11-26.
"Going to India" *North American Education* (1973), 59-83.
"Going to India" *Modern Canadian Stories* (1975), 21-39.
"Grids and Doglegs" *Tribal Justice* (1974), 47-61.
"He Raises Me Up" *CBC "Anthology"* 16 Sept 1972.
"He Raises Me Up" *Tribal Justice* (1974), 209-15.
"He Raises Me Up" *Personal Fictions* (1977), 218-23.
"How I Became a Jew" *New Canadian Writing 1968* 90-105.
"How I Became a Jew" *Tribal Justice* (1974), 105-19.
"Identity" *81: Best Canadian Stories* 7-19.

"I'm Dreaming of Rocket Richard" *Tribal Justice* (1974), 63-72.
"I'm Dreaming of Rocket Richard" CBC *"Anthology"* 24 Aug 1974.
"I'm Dreaming of Rocket Richard" *Personal Fictions* (1977), 197-205.
"I'm Dreaming of Rocket Richard" *Great Canadian Sports Stories* (1979), 9-19.
"Is Oakland Drowning?" *JCF* 1:2 (Spr 1972), 25-6.
"Man and His World" CBC *"Anthology"* 15 Mar 1980.
"Man and His World" *Fiction International* No. 12 (1980), 80-90.
"Man and His World" *Moral Fiction* (1980), 80-90.
"The Mayor" *Tam R* No. 42 (Win 1967), 14-32 [Also entitled "The Fabulous Eddie Brewster"].
"North" *Writing* No. 7 (Fall 1983), 11-2 [Excerpt].
"A North American Education" *Tam R* No. 56 (1971), 3-19.
"A North American Education" *Narrative Voice* (1972), 3-16.
"A North American Education" *North American Education* (1973), 162-84.
"A North American Education" *Double Vision* (1976), 307-23.
"Notes Beyond a History" *Shenandoah* 19:1 (Aut 1967), 3-15.
"Notes Beyond a History" *New Canadian Writing* 1968 121-34.
"Notes Beyond a History" *Great Canadian Short Stories* (1971), 312-24.
"Notes Beyond a History" *Tribal Justice* (1974), 91-104.
"Notes Beyond a History" *Personal Fictions* (1977), 206-17.
"Notes Beyond a History" *Canadian Short Stories 3* (1978), 31-46.
"Prying" *TL* Mar 1982, 38, 87-8, 91-2.
"Relief" *Shenandoah* 17:1 (Aut 1965), 82-92 [Based on ILM].
"Relief" *Tribal Justice* (1974), 15-26.
"The Salesman's Son Grows Older" *Shenandoah* 22:3 (Spr 1971), 39-52.
"The Salesman's Son Grows Older" *North American Education* (1973), 142-61.
"The Salesman's Son Grows Older" *Here and Now* (1977), 179-91.
"A Scholar's Work Speaks for Itself" *Colorado Q* 14 (Sum 1965), 41-7 [Based on ILM].
"The Seizure" *Tribal Justice* (1974), 75-89.
"The Sense of an Ending" *76: New Canadian Stories* 63-9.
"The Sense of an Ending" CBC *"Anthology"* 10 Apr 1976.
"South" *Small Wonders* (1982), 23-30.
"South" *CF* 62 (May 1982), 19-20, 37.
"Thibidault et Fils" *Prism* 5:3/4 (Win-Spr 1966), 26-42.
"Unmasking a Bourgeois" CBC *"Anthology"* 24 Jan 1976.
"The Voice of the Elephant" *JCF* 1:2 (Spr 1972), 26-7.
"Words for the Winter" *North American Education* (1973), 25-37.
"Words for the Winter" CBC *"Anthology"* 17 Mar 1973.
"Words for the Winter" *Personal Fictions* (1977), 177-85.

Blake, Dorothy‡

"Barancumbay" *Forge* Mar 1959, 6-10.
"Delia" *Forge* 22:1 (Spr 1960), 49-58.
"Delia" *Mont* 34 (May 1960), 39-45.

Blake, Ruth‡

"A Nova Scotia Jewellery Theft and It's Tragic Denouement" [sic] *Mar Adv* 41 (June 1951), 5-9 [Based on true story].

Blakeston, Oswell‡
"Don't Rock the Boat" *Onion* 5:5 (Nov 1981), 3.
"Ernest McCaudle" *Onion* 5:4 (Sept 1981), 5.
"The House Opposite" *Onion* 5:8 (July 1982), 1-2.
"In the Ingle Nook" *Onion* 5:5 (Nov 1981), 3.
"Let's All Go Round the Bend" *Onion* 5:2 (Mar 1981), 1.
"Sunday Afternoon" *Onion* 5:3 (June 1981), 1.
"Theodor's Wife" *Onion* 5:4 (Sept 1981), 5.

Blancher, Lew†
"The Bird" *WWR* 2:2 (1981), 67-70.

Blanchet, W. Wylie‡
"Henry Finds the Roar" *Rain Chr* No. 8 [n.d.], 45-52.

Blaylock, Susan†
"A Fear in the Night" *Forge* Mar 1958, 24-7.

Blenkin, Dorothy M.†
"The Silent Goose" *Edmonton Journal* Wed, 5 Feb 1964, 4.

Blesse, Landry‡
"International Incident" *AA* 52 (Jan 1962), 65-7.

Bliss, Michael (1941-) – *See* Batten, Jack and Bliss, Michael.

Blomquist, Sonia‡
"Unleavened Bread" *Muskeg R* 4 [1976], 40-3.

Blondal, Patricia (? -1959)
"Home for Christmas" *Chat* 32 (Dec 1959), 23, 90, 92, 95-6, 98, 102-5.

Bloom, Clement‡
"Aftermath of Revolution" *Prism* (Mont) No. 5 (Spr 1962), 54-64.

Bloom, David
"Busy Signal" *Canadian Short Fiction Anthology* (1976), 21-9.

Bloom, L.S.‡
"Party Discipline or Why I Flunked the Kantian Test" *Muse* 66 (1957), 19-21.

Bloomfield, W.M.‡
"In the Spell of Its Breathing" *AA* 55 (Jan 1965), 41-2, 44.

Blostein, David (1935-)
"The Cemetery Club" *Aurora* 1980 61-8.
"Die Happy" *Aurora* 1980 58-61.
"The Doulton Man" *Aurora* 1979 70-82.
"Little Deaths" *Aurora* 1980 68-70.
"Michael and All the Angels" *Aurora* 1980 54-8.
"Still Life of Lilac Blossoms" *New Voices* (1956), 98-101.

Blue, Janice† (1951?-)
"The Delicate Balance" *Chat* 46 (Oct 1973), 44, 72-4, 76.

Blue [pseudonym]
"The Oak Door" *Communicator* 10:2 [n.d.], [1 p].

Blum, Vicki‡
"Six Chicken Flight" *West People* No. 193 (16 June 1983), 2.

Blythe, Aleata E. (1931-)
A BIT OF YESTERDAY Winnipeg: Pemmican, 1982.
"Annie Gets Her House" *Bit of Yesterday* (1982), 50-2.
"Autumn Breezes" *Onward* Aug 1964, 13-4.
"Autumn Breezes" *Bit of Yesterday* (1982), 24-6.
"Blue Milk" *Bit of Yesterday* (1982), 79-82.
"Blue Milk" *Pemmican J* Win 1983, 38-9.
"Early Snow" *Bit of Yesterday* (1982), 32-5.
"Everyone a Loser" *Bit of Yesterday* (1982), 67-9.
"Everyone a Loser" *Pemmican J* Aut 1982, 43.
"The Failure" *Bit of Yesterday* (1982), 57-60.
"The Fancy Green Jacket" *Bit of Yesterday* (1982), 53-6.
"Forever a Secret" *Bit of Yesterday* (1982), 9-11.
"The Intruder" *West People* No. 136 (6 May 1982), 4-5.
"Man or Woman" *Bit of Yesterday* (1982), 30-1.
"Maybe Next Year" *Bit of Yesterday* (1982), 13-9.
"McCafferty's 100,000" *Pemmican J* Aut 1981, 30-2.
"McCafferty's 100,000" *Bit of Yesterday* (1982), 27-9.
"Minnie's Christmas Gift" *Bit of Yesterday* (1982), 41-4.
"Minnie's Gift" *Northern Mosaic* 1 (Dec 1981), 10.
"Nowhere But Yesterday" *Pier Spr* 6:3 (Sum 1981), 12-5.
"Old She" *Onward* 10 Sept 1967, 11-2 [Listed as article].
"Old She" *Bit of Yesterday* (1982), 1-4.
"Old She" *Northern Mosaic* 1 (Feb 1982), 12.
"Old Trevor" *Bit of Yesterday* (1982), 20-3.
"The Poker Game" *West People* No. 141 (10 June 1982), 12.
"The Road" *Bit of Yesterday* (1982), 45-9.
"The Silence" *Bit of Yesterday* (1982), 61-4.
"Thanks for Everything – Mother" *Can Lifetime* 4 (May-June 1974), 12-3.
"They Were Her Men" *Can Lifetime* 4 (Nov-Dec 1974), 10-1.
"They Were Her Men" *Northern Mosaic* 1 (Nov 1981), 12.
"Time for Thinking" *Rapport* May 1968, 28-30.
"Time for Thinking" *Bit of Yesterday* (1982), 71-7.
"Uncle Charlie's Prize" *Bit of Yesterday* (1982), 5-7.
"The Watch" *Bit of Yesterday* (1982), 37-40.

Boake, Mildred‡
"Mr. Lewis Saved My Soul (Five Times)" *UC Observer* 15 Sept 1969, 18-9.

Boas, Max‡

"Heir to the Land" *Prism* (Mont) No. 6 (Mar 1963), 53-9.

"O Sad, Lost, Gone and Never-to-Be-Found" *Prism* (Mont) No. 5 (Spr 1962), 3-32.

Boates, Bob‡

"Icicle" *Katharsis* 1971, [2 pp].

Bodie, Blake†

"So the Little Girl Knows" *Prism* 2:3 (Spr 1961), 8-21.

Boere, Theo‡

[Untitled] *Da Vinci* No. 2 (Spr 1974), 60-1.

Boghen, Radu D.†

"The Scribe" *Forge* Mar 1958, 28-30.

Boire, Gary†

"Stop Bath" *Quarry* 27:4 (Aut 1978), 51-4.

Boissonneau, Alice

"The Eye Clinic" by Alice Eedy *CBC "Anthology"* 27 Jan 1959.

"Green Lake and Moose Point" *CBC "Anthology"* 10 May 1975.

"John" *Alphabet* No. 14 (Dec 1967), 66-80.

"Lee Sang" by Alice Eedy *CF* 39 (July 1959), 89.

"The McCrimmons" by Alice Eedy *CF* 32 (Dec 1952), 202-3.

"The McCrimmons" *Stories from Ontario* (1974), 152-5.

"Mr. Jensen" by Alice Eedy *CF* 37 (Dec 1957), 203, 205-6.

"The Women" *Alphabet* No. 6 (1963), 18-23.

Boisvert, Michel†

"Trial by Chance" *Heartland* No. 1 (Nov-Dec 1980), 32-3, 72-4.

Bole, J. Sheridan†

"Betty's Empty Arms" *UC Observer* 15 Dec 1966, 18-9.

"The Farmer's Heart" *UC Observer* 15 Mar 1957, 13.

"For Maggie" *UC Observer* 1 May 1970, 30-1.

"Frank About Farming" *UC Observer* 15 Sept 1959, 11-2, 21.

"Just Two or Three" *UC Observer* 15 Nov 1965, 29-30.

"On a Snowy Sunday" *UC Observer* 1 Apr 1960, 7 [Non-fiction?].

"The Sparrow of Bethlehem" *UC Observer* 15 Dec 1965, 20-1.

Bolen, Dennis E.†

"The Fatality" *CFM* No. 17 (Spr 1975), 12-6.

"Toba Inlet" *Introductions from an Island* 1977, 47-50.

Boles, Rachel‡

"Inventory" *Scar Fair* 10 (1983), 52-5.

Bolger, William Neil‡

"Just a Moment" *Words from Inside* 1976, 4.
"Sidetrack" *Catalyst* (Brantford) 1:4 (1976), 60-2.
"Ward" *Catalyst* (Brantford) 1:3 (1975), 41.
"Ward" *Words from Inside* 1976, 1-3.
"Ward" *Communicator* 8:4 [n.d.], [3 pp].

Bolin, Janet†

"Carolina's Legacy" *Read Ch* 2:1 (Spr 1983), 40-8.
"Not Like This" *Harvest* No. 13 (June 1982), 13-8.
"Sassafras Tea" *Harvest* No. 10 (Sept 1981), 29-36.

Bond, E.H. *See* Walter, H. and Bond, E.H.

Bond, Eric Gary‡

"A Sure Footed Dream" *Fid* No. 83 (Jan-Feb 1970), 41-5.

Bond, F. Fraser‡

"Christmas Comes to Nor'East Tickle" *AA* 53 (Dec 1962), 16, 18-20.

Bondy, Roger‡

"Quidnunc" *Alpha* 5:1 (Fall 1980), 13, 25.

Bonellie, Janet‡

"The Freedom of the Cage" *CBC "Anthology"* 6 Aug 1968.
"Garden of the Sun" *CBC "Anthology"* 23 Sept 1972.
"Sundance" *CBC "Anthology"* 1 Nov 1969.
"There Are No Clocks in Eden" *CBC "Anthology"* 25 July 1970.

Bonneville, François A.†

"The Taste of Wyoming Sadness" *Des* 12:4/13:1/2 Nos. 34/35/36 (1981-82), 154-63.

Bontron, Frances†

"The Other Rock" *Can Messenger* 83 (Feb 1973), 14-5.

Booker, Jean‡

"The Birthday Gift" *Origins* 10:4 (Dec 1980), 4-7.
"Daisy" *Origins* 8:3 (Sept 1978), 25-7.
"The Final Insult" *Origins* 9:3 (Aut 1979), 22-3.
"The Lottery Ticket" *Origins* 9:1 (Mar 1979), 13-7.

Booker, Juliet‡

[Untitled] *UCR* Spr 1983, 12-3.

Boon, F.M.‡

"Coming Back Out" *First Encounter* 1968-69, [2 pp].

Boorman, Sylvia (1923-)

"Food for Poetry" *JCF* No. 21 (1977-78), 30-7.
"The Wholesome One" *Stories with John Drainie* (1963), 163-8.

Booth, Luella S.‡
"The Children" *QQ* 71 (1964), 76-84.
"It's Roses All the Way" CBC "*Anthology*" 15 Feb 1969.
"Man in the Mirror" *Fid* No. 66 (Fall 1965), 28-35.
"Man in the Mirror" CBC "*Anthology*" 22 Mar 1966.
"One of the Boys" *CF* 43 (Mar 1964), 276-8.

Borbas, Charles B.‡
"Don't Be Alone When It Happens to You" *Earth and You* 5 Nos. 25/26 [n.d.], 34-6.
"My Little Soldier" *Earth and You* 5 Nos. 29/30 [n.d.], 15-20 [Non-fiction?].

Borgese, Elizabeth Mann† (1918-)
"For Sale, Reasonable" *Visions from the Edge* (1981), 170-2.

Borkowski, Maria‡
"Talking Vagabond Blues" *Gram* 4:1 (Win 1979), 18-21.

Born, A.J.‡
"The Operator" *Mandala* 1971, 61-4.

Borovilos, John‡
"Important Work" *Forum* (OSSTF) 5 (Dec 1979), 229-30.

Borrell, Helen‡
"Judge Not" *Nfld Q* 66:3 (Sum 1968), 30-2.

Borsman, Carolyn‡
"The Director's Assistant" *Canadian Short Fiction Anthology* (1976), 31-4.

Boston, Stephen‡
"The Erosion of Privacy in the New Age or Caged on a Stage with No Place to Hide" *Prism* 17:2 (Fall 1978), 23-35.
"Family Reunion" *Fid* No. 124 (Win 1980), 72-86.

Boston, Stewart
"Betrayal" CBC "*Anthology*" 19 May 1973.
"The Candidate" CBC "*Anthology*" 16 June 1973.
"The Coming of the Wild Flowers" CBC "*Alberta Anthology*" 25 Sept 1982.
"The Least of My Brethren" CBC "*Anthology*" 5 Feb 1972.
"On His Majesty's Service" CBC "*Anthology*" 4 Mar 1972.
"The Rape of Maysie Weekend" *Stories from Atlantic Canada* (1973), 200-9.
"The Twain Shall Meet" CBC "*Anthology*" 12 Feb 1972.

Boszin, Andrew‡
"Artist Anonymous" *Earth and You* 2 No. 10 [n.d.], 9-11.
"Death of the Wild Goose" *Earth and You* 3 No. 11 [n.d.], 8-9.
"The Party" *Earth and You* 3 No. 16 [n.d.], 22-3.

Botting, Gary†
"The Alms" *On the Road* (1972), 5-10.

Bougie, Blaine†
"Phobia" *CFM* No. 4 (Aut 1971), 49.

Bourbonnais, Normand†
"The Tiger and the Zebra" *WWR* 2:1 (1980), 32-3.

Bourjeaurd, Jean†
"The Mixture as Before" *Contact* 2:11 (Fall 1973), 21-6.

Bourne, Stephen R.†
"Down on the Farm" *Pier Spr* 6:1 (Win 1981), 52-8.

Bouros, Lazare A.
"the pad" *Outset* 1973, 13-23.

Bouvette, Robin‡
"A Fairy" *Catalyst* (Brantford) 1:1 (1975), 15-6.

Bow, Jane
"A Screw Is Loosened" *Waves* 7:1 (Fall 1978), 12-7.
"A Tombstone or a Monument" *Nw J* No. 16 (1980), 41-6.
"Wild Harmony" *Boreal* No. 10 (1978), 62-6.

Bow, Patricia
"Post War" *Stardust* 3:2 (Spr 1981), 57-69.

Bowell, Don‡
"February" *Quarry* 15:1 (Sept 1965), 35-42.

Bowen, Robert O.‡
"Recognition" *Was R* 1:1 (1966), 15-22.

Bowen, Roger†
" 'One of the Lads ...' " *Makar* 1:2 (7 June 1967), 14-9.

Bowering, George (1935-)
FLYCATCHER AND OTHER STORIES Ottawa: Oberon Press, 1974.
A PLACE TO DIE Ottawa: Oberon Press, 1983.
PROTECTIVE FOOTWEAR Toronto: McClelland & Stewart, 1978.
"Apples" *Fourteen Stories High* (1971), 100-2.
"Apples" *Flycatcher* (1974), 112-4.
"Arbre de décision" *Illusion Two* (1983), 25-40.
"Arbre de décision" *Place to Die* (1983), 84-104.
"The Big Leagues" *Protective Footwear* (1978), 37-44.
"Carter Fell" *Cap R* No. 15 (1979), 69-85.
"Carter Fell" *Place to Die* (1983), 5-22.
"The Clam-Digger" *Place to Die* (1983), 105-17.
"Comparative Public Deaths" *Writing* No. 4 (Win 1981-82), 5-6.
"Comparative Public Deaths" *Place to Die* (1983), 47-51.
"Constantinople Boots" *CBC "Anthology"* 6 Dec 1969 [Title based on survey response].
"Constantinople Boots" *Antig R* No. 5 (Spr 1971), 21-6.
"Constantinople Boots" *Flycatcher* (1974), 90-5.

"The Creator Has a Master Plan" *Cap R* No. 11 (1977), 16-21.
"The Creator Has a Master Plan" *Protective Footwear* (1978), 147-53.
"The Deputy Sheriff" *Edge* No. 5 (Fall 1966), 68-9.
"Ebbe & Hattie" *Quarry* 19:1 (Fall 1969), 11-21.
"Ebbe & Hattie" *Flycatcher* (1974), 64-77.
"Ebbe's Roman Holiday" *Story So Far* 3 (1974), 39-47.
"Ebbe's Roman Holiday" *Protective Footwear* (1978), 134-46.
"The Elevator" *Tam R* No. 40 (Sum 1966), 21-9.
"The Elevator" *Flycatcher* (1974), 5-13.
"The Elevator" *Wild Rose Country* (1977), 139-48.
"Flycatcher" *Fid* No. 64 (Spr 1965), 30-6.
"Flycatcher" *Flycatcher* (1974), 29-37.
"Flycatcher" *Fiddlehead Greens* (1979), 176-85.
"Four California Deaths" *Prism* 21:2 (Dec 1982), 51-7.
"Four California Deaths" *Place to Die* (1983), 118-27.
"Four Jobs" CBC "Anthology" 14 Oct 1978.
"The Gamin on the Island Ferry" *QQ* 72 (1965), 347-54.
"Have You Seen Jesus?" *Talon* 4:4 [Win 1968?], 24-32.
"Have You Seen Jesus?" *Protective Footwear* (1978), 85-93.
"The Hayfield" *Dal R* 45 (1965), 182-8.
"The Hayfield" *Protective Footwear* (1978), 101-9.
"Highway Three" *event* 5:3 [n.d.], 10-4.
"Highway Three" *Protective Footwear* (1978), 120-5.
"The House on Tenth" *CF* 45 (Mar 1966), 275-8.
"The House on Tenth" *Forum* (1972), 386-91.
"The House on Tenth" *Protective Footwear* (1978), 23-36.
"How Delsing Met Frances & Started to Write a Novel" *Fid* No. 91 (Fall 1971), 78-83.
"How Delsing Met Frances & Started to Write a Novel" *Flycatcher* (1974), 96-103.
"The Lawnmower" *Wild Dog* (U.S.) 1:5 (30 Jan 1964), 18-23.
"The Lawnmower" *Protective Footwear* (1978), 55-61.
"Looking for Ebbe" *Fid* No. [73] (Sum 1967), 6-18.
"Looking for Ebbe" *Flycatcher* (1974), 14-28.
"Match-Boxes" *Place to Die* (1983), 36-46.
"No No No No No" *Gaillardia* [No. 5] (Mar 1966), 49-59.
"No No No No No" *Protective Footwear* (1978), 154-60.
"Old Bottles" *Place to Die* (1983), 52-64.
"Owning Up" *Protective Footwear* (1978), 110-9.
"The Promise of the Sky" *Evidence* No. 5 (1962), 5-10.
"Protective Footwear" *Black Moss* Ser 2 No. 2 (Fall 1976), 41-3.
"Protective Footwear" *Protective Footwear* (1978), 171-5.
"Quick Canada" *Center* (U.S.) 1 (Feb 1971) [Based on survey response].
"Re Union" *JCF* No. 16 (1976), 7-15.
"Re Union" *Protective Footwear* (1978), 9-22.
"The Representative" *Raven* No. 8 (Jan 1960), 10-5.
"The Representative" *Evidence* No. 8 [1964], 81-90.
"Ricardo and the Flower" *WCR* 2:3 (Win 1968), 12-21.
"Ricardo and the Flower" *Flycatcher* (1974), 38-53.
"Road Games" *Rampike* No. 2 (Spr 1981), 20 [Prose poem?].

"A Short Hagiography of Old Quebec" *Protective Footwear* (1978), 94-100.
"A Short Story" *Fiction of Contemporary Canada* (1980), 143-52.
"A Short Story" *Place to Die* (1983), 23-35.
"A Short Story" *West of Fiction* (1983), 330-9.
"Spans" *Des* No. 16 (Win 1976-77), 26-33.
"Spans" *Protective Footwear* (1978), 45-54.
"Student, Petty Thief, TV Star" *Place to Die* (1983), 65-83.
"Stuffed Horses" *Writing* No. 2 (Win 1980-81), 23.
"Summer: Vancouver" *Raven* No. 6 (Apr 1958), 27-8.
"A Tale Which Holdeth Children from Play" *Protective Footwear* (1978), 126-33.
"A Tale Which Holdeth Children from Play" *Mal R* No. 46 (Apr 1978), 77-83.
"Time and Again" *Quarry* 15:2 (Nov 1965), 7-14.
"Time and Again" *Modern Canadian Stories* (1966), 393-402.
"Time and Again" *Sixteen by Twelve* (1970), 158-65.
"Time and Again" *Flycatcher* (1974), 54-63.
"Time and Again" *Skookum Wawa* (1975), 288-95.
"To Be Dead" *Raven* No. 9 (Nov 1960), 32-4 [Listed as essay, and not included in survey response, but 'by' George Delsing (Bowering's fictional persona)].
"The Towers" *Edge* No. 5 (Fall 1966), 69-71.
"The Valley" *Parallel* 2:7 (June-July 1967), 42-5.
"The Wallet: An Exercise in Sixties West Coast Bourgeois Realism" *CF* 57 (Apr 1977), 31-4.
"The Wallet: An Exercise in Sixties West Coast Bourgeois Realism" *Protective Footwear* (1978), 161-70.
"The White Coffin" *Quarry* 17:1 (Fall 1967), 16-30.
"The White Coffin" *Protective Footwear* (1978), 62-80.
"Wild Grapes and Chlorine" *Story So Far* (1971), 28-37.
"Wild Grapes and Chlorine" *Flycatcher* (1974), 78-89.
"Wings" *Protective Footwear* (1978), 81-4.
"The Xalapa Handkerchief" *Flycatcher* (1974), 104-11.
"The Xalapa Handkerchief" *JCF* 3:1 (Win 1974), 21-3.

Bowering, Marilyn (1949-)
"The Garden" *CFM* No. 14 (Sum 1974), 87-91.

Bowerman, Pearson‡
"Giving Up the Ghost" *Legion* 56 (Jan 1982), 23-4.

Bowers, Rick†
"Yesterday and Forever" *New Q* 3:1 (Spr 1983), 37-42.

Bowes, Margaret†
"The Hand in the Dark" *Onward* 3 Nov 1963, 12-3.

Bowie, Douglas
"Cherries Jubilee" *CFM* No. 16 (Win 1975), 10-21.
"Dear Joanne" *Alive* 2:1 (Dec 1970), 23-6.
"Hiding Place" *CFM* No. 21 (Spr 1976), 16-29.
"Hiding Place" *CBC* "*Anthology*" 9 Dec 1978.

Bowman, Brian‡
"The Ice Dream Parlor" *Saskatchewan Gold* (1982), 70-85.

Bowman, Martin†

"Bird Shadow" *Versus* No. 1 (Sum 1976), 1-4.

Bowman, Russell‡

"The Peggy" *Evidence* No. 8 (1964), 101-10.

Bowser, Sara‡

"Goodnight Muse" *Panic Button* No. 16 (1964), 18.

Boyarsky, Abraham

A PYRAMID OF TIME Erin, Ont.: Porcupine's Quill, 1978.

"The Ball" *CFM* No. 10 (Spr 1973), 12-3.

"A Bird" *JD* Rosh Hashanah 1975, 56-7, 60-1, 64-5, 68-9, 72.

"A Birthday Party" *JD* Rosh Hashanah 1975, 76-8.

"A Birthday Party" *Pyramid of Time* (1978), 7-14 [Also entitled "My Birthday Party"].

"A Birthday Party" *Spice Box* (1981), 64-71.

"A Broken Game" *Strobe* 1973 [Based on survey response].

"A Broken Game" *JD* Sum 1975, 64-6.

"The Chair" *CFM* No. 10 (Spr 1973), 13-5.

"The Chair" *JD* Sum 1975, 5.

"A Hockey Game" *Pyramid of Time* (1978), 16-24.

"The Inspector" *CFM* No. 8 (Aut 1972), 14-27.

"A Letter from Jerusalem" *McGill Lit R* 1971 [Based on survey response].

"A Letter from Jerusalem" *JD* Sum 1975, 32-4.

"A Memorial Day" *JD* Hanukah 1977, 48-52.

"My Birthday Party" *JCF* 1:3 (Sum 1972), 19-22 [Also entitled "A Birthday Party"].

"My Fiancée" *Antig R* No. 16 (Win 1974), 65-70.

"My Fiancée" *JD* Sum 1975, 6-7.

"My Seven Daughters" *Antig R* No. 25 (Spr 1976), 25-34.

"The Philosopher of the People" *JD* Sum 1975, 27.

"The President" *Fid* No. 110 (Sum 1976), 44-59.

"The President" *JD* Hanukah 1976, 4-8.

"The President" *Pyramid of Time* (1978), 46-59.

"The Sabbath" *JD* Passover 1977, 82-6.

"The Sabbath" *Pyramid of Time* (1978), 63-74.

"The Scholar" *Sunday Evening Anthology* (1974) [Based on survey response].

"The Scholar" *JD* Sum 1975, 4.

"A Serbian Dance" *JD* Sum 1975, 40-3.

"A Serbian Dance" *Pyramid of Time* (1978), 36-44.

"The Sister" *JD* Sum 1975, 48-51.

"The Sister" *Pyramid of Time* (1978), 26-34.

"The Sister" *Fid* No. 95 (Fall 1982), 58-67.

"The Supplication" *JD* Sum 1975, 56-9.

"Three Boys" *CFM* No. 15 (Aut 1974), 62-5.

"Three Boys" *JD* Sum 1975, 35.

"Two Rooms" *JD* Sum 1975, 16-9.

"The Violinist" *JD* Sum 1975, 10-3.

"The Wheelchair Pusher" *Antig R* No. 14 (Sum 1973), 27-36.

"The Wheelchair Pusher" *JD* Sum 1975, 24-6.

Boyd, Josephine‡

"In Loco Parentis" *Acta Vic* 76:1 (Nov 1951), 25-8.
"On Being Left-Handed" *Acta Vic* 75:2 (Dec 1950), 18-9.
"Soufflés Need Support" *Acta Vic* 77:1 (Nov 1952), 22-3.

Boyd, June‡

"Few Are Chosen ... " *Edge* No. 2 (Spr 1964), 17-9 ["Satire"].

Boyd, Robert (1931-)

"The Last Journey" *Squatch J* No. 3 (June 1976), 23-9 [Semi-fictional].
"Noota and the Pilot" *Squatch J* No. 4 (Dec 1976), 57-64.
"A Wilderness Lesson" *Squatch J* No. 6 (Dec 1977), 42-6.

Boyer, Agnes‡

"The Deserter" *Prism* 12:3 (Spr 1973), 4-7.

Boyington, Lauren‡

"Magdalen" *UCR* 1982-83, 27.

Boyko, Elvina†

"Among the Ruins" *Room* 5:3 (1980), 31-43.
"Beloved" *Grain* 6:1 [1978], 9-14.
"Beloved" *More Stories from Western Canada* (1980), 239-47.
"The Myth of Serpentarius" *Story So Far* 5 (1978), 31-40.
"The Process" *Getting Here* (1977), 109-19.
"Tapestry" *Interface* 1 (1976) [Based on editorial note to "The Process"].

Boyle, Harry J. (1915-)

"Afternoon Shift" *FH* 8 Feb 1950, 28.
"And All His Wealth Was Wandering" *Beaver* 298 (Win 1967), 27-32.
"The Castle of Patrick O'Flynn" *FH* 1 Dec 1955, 24-5.
"A Christmas Eve in the Thirties" *CG* 85 (Dec 1966), 39-40.
"The Inheritance" *FH* 14 Dec 1950, 24.
"The Inheritance" *Stories to Read Again* (1965), 159-66.
"Jezebel Jessie" *Stories from Across Canada* (1966), 45-8.
"The Mailman on R.R. " *FH* 3 Jan 1952, 16.
"Present for Jimmy" *FH* 12 July 1951, 20.

Boyle, John‡

"In the Long Run" *Region* No. 8 (Sum 1966), [11 pp].

Boyle, John C.‡

"I'm Beginning to Lose My Humanity" *20 Cents* 3:10 (Dec 1969), [3 pp].
"I'm Still Losing My Humanity" *20 Cents* 4:1 (Jan 1970), [2 pp] [Prose poem?].

Boyle, Michael (1946-)

"The Front Table" *NJ* No. 4 (June 1974), 52-63.

Brackett, Dawnold‡

"Out of the Window" *Rampike* 3:2 [1983?], 36 [Prose poem?].

Bradbury, Esme

"Ground Level" *Ont R* No. 7 (Fall-Win 1977-78), 83-7.

Bradbury, Patricia†

"Mr. Lorda's Secret" *This* 17 (Dec 1983), 32-5.
"Someone with Such a Future" *This* 13 (Sept-Oct 1979), 10-3.

Bradford, Robert†

"The Digger" *Toronto Star* Sun, 10 Oct 1982, D5.

Bradley, Alan†

"The Assumption of Gilbert Penrose" *Smoke Signals 2* [date unknown] [Based on *SWG* survey response].
"Mrs. Plews" *Grain* 9:3 (Aut 1981), 41-3.

Bradley, Esme†

"The Guitar Lady" *Treeline 2* (1983), 143-53.

Bradshaw, Colleen†

"Family Ways" *Dal R* 61 (1981), 348-55.
"Impulses" *Antig R* No. 32 (Win 1978), 57-62.

Brady, Elizabeth‡

"Contrapposto: A Story" *Fireweed* Nos. 5/6 (Win-Spr 1979-80), 28-36.

Braithwaite, J. Ashton‡

"The Bad Trip" *Spear* 6 (Jan 1977), 28, 43.

Braitman, Stephen‡

"Art of Song" *Geo Str Writing* No. 7 (May 1971), 15.

Brand, Dionne†

[Untitled] *Fireweed* No. 17 (Sum-Fall 1983), 7-14.

Branden, Geoff – *See* Branden, Vicki.

Branden, Vicki

"Along the Snake-Fence Way" *CBC* [1964?] [Based on survey response].
"Along the Snake-Fence Way" *Rubaboo* 4 (1965) [Based on survey response].
"Along the Snake-Fence Way" *Open Highways* (1968) [Based on survey response].
"Ash-heels" *CBC* 28 May 1964 [Based on survey response].
"The Bears' Club Concert" *CBC* "*Stories with John Drainie*" 21 Oct 1963 [Based on survey response].
"The Bears' Club Concert" *CBC* "*Stories with John Drainie*" 29 Mar 1968 [Based on survey response].
"The Beechnut Eaters" *CBC* [1969?] [Based on survey response].
"The Beechnut Eaters" *CBC* "*Anthology*" [?] [Date unknown] [Survey response lists probable dates as 14 Feb 1969 and 30 July 1970].
"The Black Silk Dress" *CBC* 29 Nov 1968 [Based on survey response].
"The Chicken Who Thought He Was People" *CBC* 2 June 1969 [Based on survey response].
"The Chicken Who Thought He Was People" *Canadian Children's Annual* 1982 [Based on survey response].
"The Cleveland Fire" *CBC* 5 May 1970 [Based on survey response].

"The Day I Beat Up Mooneyes Cooper" *CBC* 16 Feb 1968 [Based on survey response].

"The Deer Slayer" *CBC* 5 Jan 1968 [Based on survey response].

"The Deer Slayer" *ABC* [Date unknown] [Survey response lists probable dates as Dec 1968 and Jan 1969].

"The Deer Slayer" by Geoff Branden *Canadian Boy* Mar-Apr 1969 [Based on survey response].

"The Deer Slayer" *This Book Is About Communication* (1970) [Based on survey response].

"The Diplomats" *CBC* 3 May 1963 [Based on survey response].

"The Diplomats" *CBC* 5 Feb 1965 [Based on survey response].

"The Diplomats" *CBC* 27 May 1968 [Based on survey response].

"The Easter Spirit" *CBC* [1966?] [Based on survey response].

"Et in Arcadia" *Cosmopolitan* (U.K.) 1979 [Based on survey response].

"Farming Scientific" *CBC* 19 May 1966 [Based on survey response].

"Farming Scientific" *CBC* 28 Mar 1967 [Based on survey response].

"Feet of Clay" *CBC* [1969?] [Based on survey response].

"The Fenians Are Coming" *CBC* [1966?] [Based on survey response].

"The Food of Love" *CBC* [1970?] [Based on survey response].

"Friend of My Youth" *CBC* [1969?] [Based on survey response].

"The Girls' Picnic" *CBC* 3 May 1966 [Based on survey response].

"The Heron Pool Fight" *CBC* 24 Feb 1969 [Based on survey response].

"his flashing eyes, his floating hair" *CBC* 13 Aug 1970 [Based on survey response].

"Home No More Home to Me" *CBC* [1967?] [Based on survey response].

"Home No More Home to Me" *CBC* [Date unknown] [Based on survey response].

"If Winter Comes" *CBC* 1 Feb 1966 [Based on survey response].

"Long Before Detroit" *CBC* [1966?] [Based on survey response].

"Next to Godliness" *CBC* 1 July 1965 [Based on survey response].

"Next to Godliness" *CBC* 26 Jan 1967 [Based on survey response].

"The Queen of Ireland" *CBC* 10 Dec 1965 [Based on survey response].

"The Queen of Ireland" *CBC* 24 June 1966 [Based on survey response].

"The Reluctant Genius" *CBC* "*Stories with John Drainie*" [1963?] [Based on survey response].

"The Reluctant Genius" *FH* 31 Mar 1966, 69, 71.

"The Reluctant Genius" *Century of Canadian Literature* (1967), 482-8.

"Shelter for Nelson" *Chat* 54 (Sept 1981), 62-3, 130, 132, 136, 139, 143.

"Sooner or Later" *CBC* 2 June 1961 [Based on survey response].

"Sooner or Later" *CBC* 4 Mar 1968 [Based on survey response].

"Sweet Babby" *CBC* 29 Sept 1971 [Based on survey response].

"Sweet Babby" *Canadian Children's Annual* 1978 [Based on survey response].

"Sweet Scent of Spring" *CBC* 13 Oct 1964 [Based on survey response].

"Sweet Scent of Spring" *CBC* 13 Mar 1967 [Based on survey response].

"The Teacher Wasn't Pretty" *CBC* 28 July 1965 [Based on survey response].

"The Trouble at Shelmerdines" *CBC* 25 Mar 1966 [Based on survey response].

"The Trouble at Shelmerdines" *NZBC* 15 Jan 1969 [Based on survey response].

"A Very Long Swim" *CBC* [1969?] [Based on survey response].

"The Waterloo of Alamawa Potessa" *CBC* 11 Dec 1968 [Based on survey response].

"When Old Age Shall This Generation Waste" *CBC* [1969?] [Based on survey response].

'The Wind Climber" *CG* 85 (Aug 1966), 31-2.

'The Wind Climber" *CBC* 26 Jan 1968 [Based on survey response].

Brandis, Marianne (1938-)

A SENSE OF DUST Carlisle: Brandstead Press, 1972.

"Ceremony of Innocence" *Muse* 1962, 10-6 [Based on survey response].

"The Christmas Candlestick" *Family Circle* 81 (Dec 1972), 26, 30, 32 [Based on survey response].

"Conte" *Muse* 1961, 28-9 [Based on survey response].

"Lonely as a Cloud" *Muse* 70 (1961), 13-5.

"Neptune's Way" *Muse* 1964, II:4-11.

'The Temple of the Unicorn" *Muse* 69 (1960), 18-23.

"Where Motley Is Worn" *Muse* 1963, 14-6.

Brandis, Maxine‡

"Adult Student" *AA* 52 (May 1962), 41-4, 46.

"A Call in the Fog" *AA* 49 (May 1959), 89-95.

'Foreigner in the Family" *AA* 51 (Aug 1961), 61, 63-4, 66.

'The Living Christmas Tree" *AA* 50 (Dec 1959), 27-8, 30-1, 33.

'To Grow into a Man" *AA* 54 (Nov 1963), 67-9.

Brasen, Terese

'Princess" *Getting Here* (1977), 67-84.

Brask, Per K.†

'The Sign" *NeWest R* 9 (Sept 1983), 16-7.

Brass, Peter‡

"Old Mattresses and New Coffins" *Loomings* 1:1 (1979), 37-50.

Bratton, Mark‡

'The Talks" *Alive* [1:7] (June [1970]), [3 pp].

Brauer, Joanna‡

'Put This Dream on My Charge Account" *Onion* 4:4 (Dec 1979), 2-3.

Braun, Lois (1949-)

'The Edge of the Cornfield" *Scrivener* 4:1 (Win 1983), 33-5.

'The Maltese Mistress" *Grain* 11:2 (May 1983), 42-8.

"A Population of Birds" *Antig R* No. 49 (Spr 1982), 97-103.

Braune, Elizabeth† (1957?-)

'The Avalanche" *Can Lifetime* 4 (Mar-Apr 1974), 3-5.

Braven, Luisa†

'Under the Crab-Apple Tree" *Room* 7:3 (1982), 53-60.

Brebner, John‡

"A Story" *Intercourse* No. 8 (Aug 1968), 13-6.

Breen, Melwyn† (1924?-)
"Scent of Magnolias" *NHM* 51 (June 1950), 12, 27-9.

Breidal, Bruce‡
"Don't Say Nothing" *From an Island* Feb 1979, 14-6.

Breingan, J.N.†
"Falling Stars" *Mont Writers' Forum* 1:9 (June 1979), 8-10.

Bremner, Lary
"A Signal at Crossings" *BC Monthly* 3:9 (June 1978), 43 [Prose poem?].
"Taking It from the Top" *BC Monthly* 3:9 (June 1978), 42 [Prose poem?].

Brenna, Dwayne†
"Playing Ball" *Grain* 5:3 [1977], 15-21.

Brennan, Anthony
"The Game of Love" *Chat* 48 (July 1975), 34, 59-64, 66.
"Ship to Shore" *Axiom* 1:3 (Win 1974-75), 24-9, 31.

Brennan, Frank‡
"The English Bobby in Canada" *Alive* No. 157 (20 Oct 1979), 14-5.
"Fighting to Win" *Alive* No. 108 (8 Apr 1978), 14-7.
"Night Shift" *Alive* No. 58 (6 Nov 1976), 4.

Brennan, Reg‡
"The Butternut Tree" *Qolus* [No. 1] (Mar 1967), 13-25.

Brennan, T. Casey‡
"Goddess" *Bakka* No. 5 (Spr-Sum 1977), 64-8.

Breslow, Maurice (1935-)
"Freddy Nothing" *QQ* 90 (1983), 1005-14.

Brewer, Hank – *See* Green, H. Gordon.

Brewer, Jackie‡
"That Summer in Auxerre" *AA* 55 (Sept 1964), 55-6, 58-62, 64.

Brewster, Elizabeth (1922-)
A HOUSE FULL OF WOMEN Ottawa: Oberon Press, 1983.
IT'S EASY TO FALL ON THE ICE Ottawa: Oberon Press, 1977.
"Aggie" *East of Canada* (1976), 1-7.
"Between the Fall and the Flood" *CF* 49 (June 199), 68-71.
"Comfort Me with Apples" *It's Easy to Fall on the Ice* (1977), 34-44.
"The Conversion" *Dal R* 56 (1976), 299-306.
"The Conversion" *It's Easy to Fall on the Ice* (1977), 14-23.
"The Escape" *It's Easy to Fall on the Ice* (1977), 24-33.
"Essence of Marigold" *Fid* No. 116 (Win 1978), 5-11.
"Essence of Marigold" *House Full of Women* (1983), 17-27.
"Farewell to Moss Lake" *CBC "Anthology"* 20 Feb 1971.
"Flower Girl" *It's Easy to Fall on the Ice* (1977), 96-112.
"Her First Apartment" *House Full of Women* (1983), 82-104.

"A House Full of Women" *Dal R* 59 (1979), 105-13.
"A House Full of Women" *House Full of Women* (1983), 5-16.
"Illusions of Young Men" *Br Out* 6:3 (1979), 28-9, 48.
"It's Easy to Fall on the Ice" *Quarry* 19:2 (Win 1970), 3-10.
"It's Easy to Fall on the Ice" *Stories from Atlantic Canada* (1973), 156-65.
"It's Easy to Fall on the Ice" *It's Easy to Fall on the Ice* (1977), 45-56.
"The Letters" *Fid* No. 121 (Spr 1979), 40-6.
"The Letters" *House Full of Women* (1983), 44-54.
"Moving to Moss Lake" *Fid* No. 78 (Jan-Feb 1969), 15-22.
"A Nest of Dolls" *House Full of Women* (1983), 55-64.
"A Perfect Setting" *Des* 10:2 No. 24 (1979), 95-105.
"A Question of Style" *SN* 95 (June 1980), 34-41.
"A Question of Style" *House Full of Women* (1983), 28-43.
"Shivaree" *Fid* No. 85 (May-June-July 1970), 7-13.
"Silent Movie" *It's Easy to Fall on the Ice* (1977), 57-66.
"Silent Movie" *More Stories from Western Canada* (1980), 13-21.
"Strangers" *Fid* No. 109 (Spr 1976), 78-93.
"Strangers" *It's Easy to Fall on the Ice* (1977), 67-86.
"Teeth" *Dand* 5 (Win-Spr 1979), 46-9.
"Understanding Eva" *It's Easy to Fall on the Ice* (1977), 113-27.
"Visiting Aunt Alix" *House Full of Women* (1983), 65-81.
"Visiting Hours" *CF* 45 (Aug 1965), 107-9.
"Visiting Hours" *It's Easy to Fall on the Ice* (1977), 5-13.
"Voyage Home" *It's Easy to Fall on the Ice* (1977), 87-95.
"Winter's Rains and Ruins" *QQ* 78 (1971), 394-403.
"The Year Vicki Came Home" *CBC "Anthology"* 21 Feb 1970.

Briar, Matthew‡

"4001: The Vice-Principal" *Forum* (OSSTF) 3 (Feb 1977), 33, 35-6.
"News" *Forum* (OSSTF) 2 (Oct 1976), 165-6.
"Open House" *Forum* (OSSTF) 3 (Mar 1977), 73-4 [Satire].

Bridger, Steve‡

"Entertaining" *Potlatch* No. 6 (Mar 1966), 1-9.

Brierly, Jim†

"Apricots" *Forge* Dec 1954, 29-30.
"The Bear" *Forge* 1954, 59.

Briffett, Isabel

"... And in the Morning" by Pearl Page *Onward* 11 Nov 1956, 721-3, 735.
"The Adopted Family" *Onward* 62 (13 July 1952), 433-5, 446-7.
"Afterglow" by Pearl Page *Onward* 27 Aug 1961, 548-50, 558.
"The Apple" *Onward* 24 Feb 1957, 16-7, 127.
"The Beachcomber" *Onward* 21 Nov 1954, 737-9, 750-1.
"The Bequest" by Pearl Page *Onward* 24 Mar 1968, 3, 12-3.
"The Boy Next Door" *Onward* 8 July 1962, 3-5, 10.
"The Bridge Builders" *Onward* 18 Oct 1959, 657-9, 670-1.
"The Brook" *Onward* 60 (3 Sept 1950), 561-4.
"The Bubble" by Pearl Page *Onward* 12 Aug 1956, 513-6, 526.
"The Changing of Enoch" *Onward* 7 Nov 1954, 708-10.

"The Cocoon" *Onward* 10 July 1955, 433-5, 447.

"The Courage Corsage" by Pearl Page *Onward* 5 July 1959, 424-6.

"The Crevasse" by Pearl Page *Onward* 2 Nov 1958, 689-90, 702-3.

"The Crystal Ball" *Onward* 29 July 1956, 484-5, 494-5.

"A Cup of Sugar" *Onward* 12 Apr 1953, 228-30.

"Dark River" *Onward* 15 Apr 1956, 241-3, 255.

"The Debt" by Pearl Page *Onward* 23 Sept 1956, 614-5, 623.

"Different Thanksgiving" *Onward* 11 Oct 1953, 641-3, 654-5.

"The Dilemma" *Onward* 26 Jan 1958, 49-50, 56-8.

"Dividends" *Onward* 60 (26 Nov 1950), 758-60.

"The Family Tree" *Onward* 21 June 1959, 385-8.

"The Fence" *Onward* 61 (16 Sept 1951), 582-4.

"A Game of Chess" by Pearl Page *Onward* 10 July 1960, 433-6.

"The Garden" by Pearl Page *Onward* 1 Mar 1959, 136-7, 142.

"Gold" *Onward* 61 (28 Jan 1951), 49-51.

"The Golden Goose" *Onward* 3 Nov 1957, 689-91, 702-3.

"The Good Samaritan" *Onward* 61 (1 July 1951), 401-3, 411.

"The Good Works Spirit" *Onward* 60 (29 Oct 1950), 694-5, 698-9.

"The Happiest Easter" *Onward* 61 (25 Mar 1951), 177-9, 190-1.

"The Hollow Tree" *Onward* 60 (10 Sept 1950), 582-4, 587.

"The Homemaker" *Onward* 18 Mar 1956, 182-3, 190-1.

"Island Saga" *Onward* 6 May 1956, 289-92.

"Jacob's Ladder" by Pearl Page *Onward* 11 June 1961, 370-2, 377.

"Jacob's Ladder" *Onward* 13 June 1965, 3-4, 13.

"Joy Ride" *Onward* 21 Aug 1960, 537-9, 541.

"Keep a Green Bough in the Heart, and the Singing Bird Will Come" *Onward* 12 Feb 1967, 4-5, 13 [Fictionalized reminiscence?].

"The King of Spain's Daughter" *Onward* 11 Dec 1960, 788-92.

"The Kite's Tale" by Pearl Page *Onward* 2 Mar 1958, 129-32, 142.

"Kitty's Kitchen" *Onward* 31 May 1953, 340-1, 350-1.

"Lamb in the Thicket" by Pearl Page *Onward* 29 July 1962, 4-5, 10-1.

"The Lantern" *Onward* 60 (2 Apr 1950), 214-6, 222.

"Leap-Year Birthday" *Onward* 26 Feb 1956, 134-5, 143.

"The Lemon Lily Town" *Onward* 13 July 1958, 433-6.

"The Limper" *Onward* 14 Mar 1954, 161-3, 171.

"Line of Steel" *Onward* 20 Feb 1955, 121-3, 127.

"The Little Lamp" *Onward* 8 Mar 1959, 145-7, 154-5.

"The Little Lamp" *Onward* 6 Mar 1966, 3-5, 12.

"The Little Mother" by Pearl Page *Onward* 1 May 1955, 277-9, 286.

"The Loaves and Fishes" *Onward* 23 Oct 1955, 673-5, 686-7.

"The Long Road Home" by Pearl Page *Onward* 6 Nov 1960, 708-10, 712.

"Loon's Landing" *Onward* 4 Feb 1962, 5-7.

"The Lost and Found Canary" by Pearl Page *Onward* 30 Mar 1958, 193-5, 202-3.

"The Lost-and-Found Home" *Onward* 26 Dec 1954, 822-4, 827.

"The Magic Carpet" *Onward* 6 Mar 1955, 148-51.

"The Magic Circle" *Onward* 62 (31 Aug 1952), 545-7, 559.

"The Man Who Found Himself" *Onward* 30 July 1961, 481-4, 493.

"Mark Brown's Moccasins" *Onward* 6 Feb 1955, 81-3, 94-5.

"Martin Gilmer's Hour" by Pearl Page *Onward* 22 Aug 1954, 529-31, 542-3.

"The Migrant Man" by Pearl Page *Onward* 5 Mar 1961, 148-9, 154.

"Mr. Jonathan's Suit" by Pearl Page *Onward* 17 Nov 1957, 729-30, 735.

"Mrs. Dolan's Ride" *Onward* 17 Mar 1957, 168-70.

"Much Ado" *Onward* 28 Apr 1957, 266-7, 270.

"The Neighbour Man" *Onward* 10 Sept 1961, 3-5, 15.

"A Newfoundland Christmas" by Pearl Page *Onward* 13 Dec 1953, 785-7, 798-9.

"Not in the News" by Pearl Page *Onward* 10 Mar 1957, 145-7, 159.

"The Octopus" *Onward* 60 (16 July 1950), 450-1, 453.

"Old Bull" *Onward* 25 Aug 1963, 3-5, 8.

"Old Harry and the Fourth Commandment" *Onward* 14 Oct 1962, 3-5, 10.

"The Old Man of the Sea" *Onward* 16 Mar 1958, 164-5, 174.

"One of the Family" *Onward* 61 (9 Sept 1951), 561-3, 575.

"The One Talent" *Onward* 62 (17 Feb 1952), 97-9, 107.

"The Open Door" *Onward* 12 June 1960, 376-8.

"The Outer Berth" *Onward* 1 Nov 1953, 692-3, 702-3.

"The Panther" *Onward* 31 July 1960, 484-5, 494.

"Park Benches" by Pearl Page *Onward* 22 Jan 1961, 49-51, 56-7.

"Parrot in a Pew" *Onward* 25 Apr 1965, 3-4, 13-4.

"The Partners" *Onward* 61 (7 Jan 1951), 10-1, 14-5.

"The Prism" *Onward* 62 (16 Mar 1952), 164-5, 171.

"The Prodigal" *Onward* 20 Sept 1953, 592-5, 599.

"A Rose for Johnny Dan" *Onward* 22 Sept 1957, 593-5, 607.

"The Round-About Will" by Pearl Page *Onward* 22 Nov 1959, 740-2, 747.

"The Run-Away Holiday" *Onward* 62 (3 Aug 1952), 481-3.

"The Sea and Mary Ellen" *Onward* 11 Sept 1955, 577-9, 585, 590.

"The Second Mile" *Onward* 6 Mar 1960, 145-8, 158.

"Shoe-String Playboy" by Pearl Page *Onward* 20 May 1956, 323-4, 330-1.

"The Sign That Never Changed" *Onward* 16 Sept 1956, 596-7, 606-7.

"Skipper Zeke Sets All Right" *Onward* 20 Oct 1963, 3-5, 14.

"The Slough" *Onward* 30 Aug 1959, 548-50, 559.

"Sparrows on a Roof" by Pearl Page *Onward* 14 Feb 1960, 97-100.

"The Square Peg" *Onward* 62 (25 May 1952), 325-6, 334-5.

"Standard of Living" *Onward* 62 (30 Nov 1952), 756-8, 766-7.

"The Stone" *Rapport* June 1969, 33-4.

"The Strong Man" *Onward* 61 (23 Sept 1951), 597-9, 606-7.

"The Third Safari" *Onward* 17 Apr 1955, 241-3, 254-5.

"The Three Graces" *Onward* 1 July 1956, 420-1, 430.

"Through a Glass Darkly" *Onward* 60 (2 July 1950), 422-3, 430-1.

"The Tiger Was a Cat" *Onward* 25 Mar 1962, 3-4, 14-5.

"Tim Garnet's Legacy" *Onward* 2 June 1957, 340-2, 351.

"Treasure Trove" *Onward* 15 May 1955, 305-7, 318.

"Treasure Trove" *Onward* 14 July 1957, 433-5, 438, 447.

"A Trip to Slocum's Creek" *Onward* 3 Mar 1968, 3-4, 14.

"Two Codes" *Onward* 60 (22 Jan 1950), 49-51.

"Two of a Kind" *Onward* 9 Aug 1959, 500-2, 507.

"The Unwilling Twig" *Onward* 28 Aug 1955, 545-7, 558-9.

"Warp & Woof" by Pearl Page *Onward* 1 Feb 1959, 72-5.

"A Watch and a Work-Out" *Onward* 11 Aug 1963, 8-11.

"The Way It Was" *Onward* 20 Aug 1961, 530-2, 543.

"Where the Wild Thyme Blows" *Onward* 10 Sept 1967, 3-5.

"The White Peacock" *Onward* 19 Feb 1961, 116-8, 123.
"The White Walrus" *Onward* 28 June 1964, 3-4, 13-4.
"The Young Chatelaine" by Pearl Page *Onward* 18 Aug 1957, 513-5, 526.

Bristow, Susan
"Blind Man's Bluff" *Chel J* 5 (Sept-Oct 1979), 215-7.
"In Silent Desperation" *AA* 69 (Nov 1978), 70-4.
"The Salt of Life" *event* 4:3 [1974?], 62-8.
"A Slow and Steady Decline" *Prism* 15:2/3 (Sum-Fall 1976), 54-61.

Broadfoot, J.B.†
"Whomsoever I Shall Kiss" *Earth and You* 3 No. 14 [n.d.], 6-11.

Brock, Paul†
"Mother's Hideaway" *Onward* 3 Jan 1965, 12-4.
"Plain Jane" *Onward* 28 Aug 1966, 4-5, 13.

Brockenshire, Frank‡
"The Stairs: A Parable" *Kaleidoscope* Mar 1960, 25-8.

Brockie, William†
"The Lone Cabin Mystery" *Beaver* 290 (Win 1959), 18-9.

Brockmann, Frieda‡
"Patsies for Purchases" *West People* No. 172 (20 Jan 1983), 10-1.

Brockway, R.W.
"Aradia" *Pier Spr* 1:2 (Spr 1977), 45-9.
"The Man Who Did Not Watch the Olympics" *CSSM* 2:4 (Fall 1976), 27, 29-30.

Brodie, Blake
"Somebody Has to Buy the New York Times" *Campus Canada* 1:1 (Feb 1953), 13, 51-2.

Brodsky, Myrtle† (1892?-)
"Tea-Room" *Rapport* June 1971, 30-1.

Brody, Leslie‡
"Gloria" *Pulp* 4:15 (15 Feb 1978), [1-2].

Brodzki, Marek‡
"Reflections onto a Golden Life" *Echo* (Tor) 2:1 (Fall 1970), [3 pp].

Bronson, A.A.‡
"A Tale with No Women" *Story So Far* 3 (1974), 77-80.

Brook, Kay†
"The Gift" *Alberta Golden Jubilee Anthology* (1955), 351-6.

Brooke, Lindsay‡
"Home" *Outset* 1973, 24-9.

Brooks, Eunice†

"Aphelion" *Canadian Short Fiction Anthology* 2 (1982), 15-20.
"Ortona Again" *Vancouver Mag* 12 (Mar 1979), 102-5, 107.
"Poetry Workshop" *Interior Voice* No. 4 (May 1983), 20-3.
"Seven Years Later" *Vancouver Mag* 11 (Aug 1978), 29, 31-2, 35.
"The Tie That Binds" *Interior Voice* No. 5 (July-Aug/Sum 1983), 22-5.

Brooks, Kathleen‡

"Sarah" *Stump* Spr 1983, 25-8.

Brown, Allan‡

"Where Two or Three Are Gathered Together" *Nebula* No. 9 (Feb 1979), 6-8.

Brown, Amy Hatchford (1945-)

"A Clean Blackness" *event* 2:2 [1972], 69-72.

Brown, Barbara A.†

"At Home" *Br Out* 4:5 (Dec 1977), 26-8.
"Morning-Afternoon-Infinity" *Br Out* 5:4 (1978), 15-9.

Brown, Betty‡

"The Long Fall" *J of Our Time* No. 3 (1982), 67-8.
"A Sense of Myself" *J of Our Time* No. 2 (1979), 27-8 [Non-fiction?].

Brown, Cassie

"Black Rock Sunker" *Nfld Q* 54:2 (June 1955), 38-45.

Brown, Crombie‡

"Jack O'Lantern" *Doryloads* (1974), 154-7.
"The Old Pauline" *Nfld Q* 68:1 (Spr 1971), 10-3.

Brown, Dorothy Howe‡

"The End of Summer" *My Golden West* 3 (Fall 1968), 19.
"Spooker" *Can Golden West* 7 (Sum 1971), 22-3 [Non-fiction?].

Brown, Gordon†

"Whispers" *Thursday's Voices* (1983), 33-43.

Brown, Horace

HORACE BROWN'S ENCORE Toronto: Voyageur Books, 1977.
"The Door to Ward B" *Lib* 27 (Jan 1951), 33, 61.
"Sun in His Eyes" *Encore* (1977), 22-3.
"The Taste of Ice Cream" *Encore* (1977), 60-6.
"Treadmill for a Lucky Man" *Encore* (1977), 41-3.

Brown, Isobel

"Seventy-Two Hours" *From This Place* (1977), 155-64.

Brown, Jean E.†

"Child" *Prism* 17:1 (Sum 1978), 39-42.

Brown, Jim‡

"The Hunters" *Geo Str Writing* No. 3 (1-8 Apr 1970), 6.

Brown, Joy

"Call Me Anytime" *NHM* Sept 1950, 29-31.
"The First Kiss" *FH* 31 Jan 1952, 20-1.
"The First Kiss" *Stories to Read Again* (1965), 99-108.
"The Girl Who Wore the Diamonds" *Weekend* 3 (28 Feb 1953), 30.

Brown, Joy and Davidson, John

See also Brown, Joy; Davidson, John.
"Not the Marrying Kind" *Weekend* 4 (21 Aug 1954), 18-20, 33.

Brown, Julia†

"The Swim" *Prism* 3:4 (Win 1963), 41-9.

Brown, Mae Hill

"Autumn Appointment" *Stump* 1:1 (Spr 1977), 5-7.
"Howie" *Stump* Spr 1981, 9-13.

Brown, Miranda‡

"A Christmas Story" *Missionary Monthly* 30 (Dec 1955), 484-5.

Brown, Paul

"Cornucopia" *CCWQ* 3:1 (Win 1981), 10-1.

Brown, Paul Cameron†

THE LAND OF LOOK BEHIND Toronto: Three Trees Press, 1979.
"Adua" *Land of Look Behind* (1979), 73-5.
"Automobile Soft Legs" *Land of Look Behind* (1979), 63-6.
"The Bloodfish" *Land of Look Behind* (1979), 53-4.
"Brébeuf" *Land of Look Behind* (1979), 59.
"City the Insects Invade" *Land of Look Behind* (1979), 60.
"Errands" *Land of Look Behind* (1979), 47-50.
"The Garden Patch" *Land of Look Behind* (1979), 55-6.
"The Hire" *Land of Look Behind* (1979), 21-5.
"Jaribu" *Land of Look Behind* (1979), 70-2.
"The Monarch" *Land of Look Behind* (1979), 57-8.
"The Nightlamp" *Land of Look Behind* (1979), 26-9.
"The Pelly, the Powder and the Snake" *Land of Look Behind* (1979), 67-9.
"Plaudits" *Land of Look Behind* (1979), 61.
"Ponchontas" *Land of Look Behind* (1979), 51-2.
"Rip" *Land of Look Behind* (1979), 76-9.
"The Sandpit" *Land of Look Behind* (1979), 36-40.
"Seaeggs" *Land of Look Behind* (1979), 16-20.
"The Strongbox" *Land of Look Behind* (1979), 30-5.
"To Cross the Bay" *Land of Look Behind* (1979), 9-13.
"Upturn the Rock" *Land of Look Behind* (1979), 14-5.
"The Wager" *Land of Look Behind* (1979), 41-6.

Brown, Randy‡

"Heil!" *Sowing* [1972?], 58-61.
"Heil!" *Modern Canadian Stories* (1975), 254-6.
"His Alone" *Writing Group Pub* 1971-72, 17-9.

"Madame Palanina" *In Complete* [1970-71], 64-6.
"Narcissus" *Sowing* [1972?], 87-9.
"Narcissus" *Acta Vic* Fall 1974, 26-7.

Brown, Robert†
"A Day at the Springs" *Grain* 7:2 [1979], 3-7.

Brown, Ron‡
"Interface" *Thumbprints* No. 2 (Spr 1975), [2 pp].

Browne, Colin‡
"He Said" *Roothog* (1981), 37.
"L'Arrivee" *Roothog* (1981), 35-6.
"The Movies" *Roothog* (1981), 33-4.
"Shower Parade" *Roothog* (1981), 40-3.
"The Telegram" *Roothog* (1981), 38-9.
"Whether Clarence Lowry Was Here" *Pulp* 4:23 (15 Nov 1978), [1-3].

Browne, Elisa Beth†
"Peaches" *event* 3:3 [n.d.], 13-6.

Browne, Linda‡
"The Tagger" *Folio* 13:2 (Spr 1961), 62-4.

Browne, Norman G.‡
"Pleasant Dreams" *Can Fandom* No. 26 (Sept 1955), 20-3.

Browne, Robert‡
"Einstellung" *Introductions from an Island* 1974, 40-6.

Browne, Tom†
"The Bargain" *Companion* 39 (Sept 1976), 26-8.
"Christmas Comes to Deer Lick Creek" *Can Lifetime* 4 (Nov-Dec 1974), 28-31.
"No Place to Hide" *Our Family* 26 (June 1974), 33-5.
"Trudging to the City" *Can Lifetime* 4 (Sept-Oct 1974), 11-2.

Brownell, Elizabeth‡
"Unless a Life Be ... " *TUR* 68:2 (Dec 1955), 9-13.

Broy, Evelyn J.‡
"The Small Black Hat" *Kaleidoscope* 1958, 14-7.

Bruce, Charles T. (1906-1971)
"Cadence" *AA* 47 (Dec 1956), 27-30.
"Inheritance" *AA* 48 (Jan 1958), 84-8.
"Jarvey and the Dolphin" *AA* 47 (May 1957), 94-7.
"The Letters" *Mont* 25 (Nov 1951), 58-9.
"Love Is the Surest Gamble" *Chat* 27 (June 1954), 22-3, 48-9, 54-7.
"A Matter for Spike" *AA* 47 (July 1957), 59-62.
"People from Away" *AA* 47 (Jan 1957), 57-61.
"People from Away" *Atlantic Advocate's Holiday Book* (1961), 5-16.
"The Pond Place" *AA* 49 (Dec 1958), 77-80.
"Sand" *AA* 47 (Sept 1956), 21-3.

"School House Hill" *Mont* [27] (Nov 1953), 37-9.
"The Sloop" *AA* 49 (Oct 1958), 40, 43-5, 47.
"South End Avenue" *JCF* 1:1 (Win 1972), 5-7.
"Surrender" *Lib* 30 (Mar 1953), 18-9, 68.
"Suspense" *Dal R* 32 (1952), 197-200.
"Tidewater Morning" *SW* 30 Apr 1955, I:7.
"Tidewater Morning" *AA* 49 (Nov 1958), 73-80.

Bruce, Hubert‡

"The Bluefish" *Modicum* 5:1 (Mar 1975), [2 pp].

Bruce, John‡

"A Certain Light" CBC "*Anthology*" 30 Apr 1977.
"The Colours of Summer" CBC "*Anthology*" 10 May 1980.

Bruchovsky, Olga‡

"The Poet with the Perfect Reputation" *Acta Vic* 77:4 (Mar 1953), 19-21.
"The Shoe and the Future" *Acta Vic* 75:3 (Feb 1951), 21-3.
"Stopover" *Varsity Lit Issue* Mon, 5 Mar 1951, 5.

Bruederlin, Barbara‡

"Through the Gates of Gethsemane" *Prairie Fire* 4:4 (Mar-Apr 1983), 25-9.

Brulotte, Gaetan‡

"The Sentinel" *Can Lit R* No. 1 (Fall-Win 1982), 31-40.

Bruneau, Bernard†

"Badla – Revenge!" *Can Messenger* 80 (July-Aug 1970), 18-9.
"The Bridge of Fear" *Can Messenger* 78 (Apr 1968), 12-3.
"God Doesn't Sleep" *Can Messenger* 90 (Feb 1980), 8-9.
"I Fled Him Down the Nights" *Can Messenger* 81 (Oct 1971), 18-9.
"The Moving Story of a Last Confession" *Can Messenger* 74 (June 1964), 12-4.
"Night Errand" *Can Messenger* 83 (Nov 1973), 12-3.
"The Night the Earth Opened" *Can Messenger* 93 (June 1983), 14-5.
"The Night the Mountains Crumbled" *Can Messenger* 80 (Mar 1970), 11-3.
"The Outcast" *Can Messenger* 91 (Sept 1981), 8-9, 15.
"The Price" *Can Messenger* 82 (Oct 1972), 16-7.
"The Pyx" *Can Messenger* 90 (July-Aug 1980), 8-9.
"The Search" *Can Messenger* 84 (June 1974), 12-3, 20.
"Terminal Case" *Can Messenger* 79 (July-Aug 1969), 12-3.
"Terror by Night" *Can Messenger* 88 (June 1978), 8-9.

Bruneau, H.‡

"A Club for Anyone" *Creative Campus* 1963, 9-12.
"Our Last Respects" *Creative Campus* 1963, 43-5.

Bruner, Arnold‡

"The Baby Needs a Pair of Shoes" *Undergrad* 1965, 24-30.

Bruns, Ina

"The Barclay House" *CG* Feb 1954, 8, 60, 62-3, 65-6.
"Bus Ride" *Edmonton Journal* Thu, 9 July 1964, 4 [Non-fiction?].
"The Buzz Barrett Story" *CG* Oct 1956, 10, 37-42.
"The Courtship of Cassie Barrett" *CG* June 1957, 13, 36-40.
"The Gift" *FH* 10 May 1962, 28, 31.
"Louise" *FH* 22 Jan 1953, 28-9.
"My First Canadian Christmas" *FH* 22 Dec 1966, 32, 34.
"Our Bull Barcelona" *CG* Oct 1952, 13, 52-3.
"A Stranger to Remember" *FH* 7 Sept 1961, 26-7.
"The Whispering Machine" *FH* 12 June 1952, 20-1.

Brunt, R.J.

"The Bare Facts" *North* 15 (Jan-Feb 1968), 4-7.
"The Child" *North* 16 (Jan-Feb 1969), 35-9.
"The Voice of the North" *North* 15 (July-Aug 1968), 24-8.
"The Voice of the North" *Stories from Pacific & Arctic Canada* (1974), 238-46.
"The Voice of the North" *Stories from the Canadian North* (1980), 171-9.
"The Wedding of Willi Auger" *North* 14 (July-Aug 1967), 16-20.
"The Yellowest Xmas Tree" *North* 14 (Nov-Dec 1967), 4-7.

Bruzzese, Salvatore (1953?-)

"The Window" *Grain* 2:2 [1974], 32-3.

Bryant, Alan J.‡

"Johnny" *TUR* 66:4 (Mar 1954), 7-10.
"Sea Scape" *TUR* 65:3 (Feb 1953), 10-3.

Bryant, Cullene‡

"1960" *Varsity Lit Issue* Fri, 18 Mar 1960, 12.
"Beyond the Rising Sun" *Acta Vic* 84:3 (Apr 1960), 18-21.
"Teen-Age Sixty" *Acta Vic* [85]:1 (Nov 1960), 8.

Bryden, John‡

"A Walk in the Dark" *Muse* 1964 Vol. 2, 2-7.

Bryden, Ronald‡

"The Golden Trees" *TUR* 62:6 (Mar 1950), 9-18.
"The Man in the Street" *Varsity Lit Issue* Fri, 3 Mar 1950, 3, 8.

Brydges, Stewart (1914-)

"The Big Lie That Won" *Squatch J* No. 1 (June 1975), 17.

Bryon, Judi

"Fanshawe Park" *Applegarth's Folly* No. 2 (1975), 98.

Bryson, David‡

"The Fallen Sheep" *Muse* 63:1 (Mar 1954), 16-7.

Bryson, Ruth‡

"The Art of the Late Essay" *Acta Vic* 80:4 (Mar 1956), 12-3.

Buchar, Frank†

"The Fall" *Northern Ontario Anthology* 1 (1977), 49-51.

Buckaway, Catherine M. (1919-)

"A Step into Courage" *Fireweed* No. 17 (Sum-Fall 1983), 81-8.

Buckie, Robert C.†

"Edinburgh Vellomaniacs" *Wee Giant* 2:3 (Spr 1979), 26-8.

Buckland, D.‡

"Pearl" *Canadian Short Fiction Anthology* (1976), 35-45.

Buckle, Daphne *See* Marlatt, Daphne.

Buckler, Ernest (1908-1984)

THE REBELLION OF YOUNG DAVID AND OTHER STORIES Ed. Robert D. Chambers Toronto: McClelland & Stewart, 1975.

"The Accident" *Chat* 33 (May 1960), 39, 117-8, 120-2, 124-6.

"Anything Can Happen at Christmas" *Chat* 29 (Dec 1957), 66-8.

"The Bars and the Bridge" *FH* 24 Apr 1958, 17.

"The Bars and the Bridge" *Stories with John Drainie* (1963), 42-7.

"The Bars and the Bridge" *Time of Your Life* (1967), 94-100.

"Blame It on the Snow" *SW* 21 Dec 1957, 22-3.

"By Any Other Name: A Holiday Romance" *AA* 47 (June 1957), 48, 79-80.

"By Any Other Name: A Holiday Romance" *Atlantic Advocate's Holiday Book* (1961), 59-68.

"Choose Your Partners" *AA* 52 (Aug 1962), 62-4, 66-7, 69.

"Cleft Rock, with Spring" *AA* 48 (Oct 1957), 89-90.

"Cleft Rock, with Spring" *Rebellion of Young David* (1975), 126-32.

"The Clumsy One" *MM* 63 (1 Aug 1950), 8-9, 28-30.

"The Clumsy One" *Rebellion of Young David* (1975), 53-64.

"The Concerto" *AA* 48 (Feb 1958), 65-7.

"The Darkest Time" *CHJ* May 1958, 31, 64-6.

"The Doctor and the Patient" *AA* 51 (July 1961), 65-6.

"The Dream and the Triumph" *Chat* 28 (Nov 1956), 12-3, 33-6, 38, 40-5.

"The Dream and the Triumph" *Rebellion of Young David* (1975), 67-81.

"The Echoing Hills" *AA* 48 (May 1958), 75-7.

"The Educated Couple" *Weekend* 2 (7 June 1952), 18-9, 29, 35, 37.

"The Eruption of Albert Wingate" *AA* 47 (Nov 1956), 27-9.

"Glance in the Mirror" *AA* 47 (Jan 1957), 53, 55.

"Glance in the Mirror" *Rebellion of Young David* (1975), 133-8.

"Goodbye Prince" *CHJ* Dec 1954, 16, 52-5, 59-60.

"Guilt on the Lily" *AA* 53 (Aug 1963), 61-9.

"The Harness" *Modern Canadian Stories* (1966), 137-47 [Also entitled "The Rebellion of Young David"].

"The Harness" *Family Portraits* (1978), 34-43.

"Humble Pie" *Weekend* 4 (25 Sept 1954), 28-9.

"In Case of Emergency" *AA* 47 (Aug 1957), 69-72.

"Last Delivery Before Christmas" *Chat* 26 (Dec 1953), 11, 30, 34-6, 38-42.

"Last Delivery Before Christmas" *Rebellion of Young David* (1975), 97-113.

"The Line Fence" *Better Farming* 125 (Feb 1955), 32-3 [Based on Willmott].

"Long, Long After School" *Rebellion of Young David* (1975), 122-6.

"Long, Long After School" *AA* 50 (Nov 1959), 42-4.

"Man and Snowman" *Voices Down East* [1973], 13-5, 17.

"Nettles into Orchids" *AA* 51 (Aug 1961), 70-1.

"One Sweet Day" *AA* 52 (Jan 1962), 51, 53.

"A Present for Miss Merriam" *Chat* 25 (Dec 1952), 8, 36-42, 44.

"A Present for Miss Merriam" *Rebellion of Young David* (1975), 81-97.

"A Present for Miss Merriam" *Canadian Yuletide Treasury* (1982), 126-42.

"The Rebellion of Young David" *MM* 64 (15 Nov 1951), 23, 36-8. [Also entitled "The Harness"].

"The Rebellion of Young David" *Rebellion of Young David* (1975), 7-17.

"The Rebellion of Young David" *Nearly an Island* (1979), 126-38.

"Should Auld Acquaintance" *FH* 23 Apr 1959, 28-9.

"A Sign of the Times" *NHM* 51 (July-Aug 1950), 11, 32.

"Summer Stock" *Weekend* 2 (9 Feb 1952), 30-1.

"The Wild Goose" *AA* 50 (Oct 1959), 91-5.

"The Wild Goose" *Stories from Across Canada* (1966), 70-8.

"The Wild Goose" *Rebellion of Young David* (1975), 115-21.

"The Wild Goose" *Canadian Stories of Action and Adventure* (1978), 65-72.

Buckler, Grant‡

"Dear Santa" *Alpha* [1:3] (Dec 1976), 9-11 [Reprinted from *Gaslight* (editorial note)].

Budra, Paul

"A Memory of the Conservatory" *UC Gargoyle* 2:3 (11 Nov 1978), 12 [Sketch?].

"Tiny Battles" *UCR* 1978-79, 48-53.

Buffoono [pseudonym]

"The Hat" *TUR* 64:4 (Mar 1952), 30-2.

Bullard, Jean‡

"Turnip-o-Lantern" *AA* 70 (Oct 1979), 90-1.

Buller, Betty‡

"Second Honeymoon" *Contact* 2:10 (Sum 1973), 4-8.

Buller, Herman

"Quebec: A Whimsical Speculation" *CJO* 7 (Oct 1969), 8-10.

Bullock, Michael (1918-)

GREEN BEGINNING/BLACK ENDING: FABLES Vancouver: Sono Nis Press, 1971.

RANDOLPH CRANSTONE AND THE PURSUING RIVER Vancouver: Rainbird Press, 1975.

SIXTEEN STORIES AS THEY HAPPENED Vancouver: Sono Nis Press, 1969.

"again noire" *Green Beginning/Black Ending* (1971), 119-34.

"anatomy of melancholy" *Randolph Cranstone* (1975), 119.

"the apple tree" *Randolph Cranstone* (1975), 102-3.

"the attic" *Randolph Cranstone* (1975), 180.

"the autobiographer" *Randolph Cranstone* (1975), 176.

"back to the tree" *Sixteen Stories* (1969), 90-3.

"the bald head" *Green Beginning/Black Ending* (1971), 66-7.

"the barber of seville bank" *Green Beginning/Black Ending* (1971), 68-9.

"biting the dust" *Randolph Cranstone* (1975), 153.

"the black engine" *Randolph Cranstone* (1975), 164.

"black horse, white horse" *Randolph Cranstone* (1975), 146-7.

"the black knight and the green woman" *Randolph Cranstone* (1975), 156.

"black lightning" *Green Beginning/Black Ending* (1971), 158-9.

"the blue bush" *Van Surrealist Newsletter* 1:1 (1980), 7 [?] [Based on survey response].

"the blue halo" *Sixteen Stories* (1969), 97-100.

"the boulder and the lake" *Green Beginning/Black Ending* (1971), 105-6.

"the bull" *Green Beginning/Black Ending* (1971), 137.

"the carcasses" *Green Beginning/Black Ending* (1971), 166-8.

"the carrot" *Green Beginning/Black Ending* (1971), 84-5.

"the cat" *Green Beginning/Black Ending* (1971), 107-10.

"the cattle" *Green Beginning/Black Ending* (1971), 39-40.

"the cavern" *Far Point* No. 2 (Spr-Sum 1969), 27-8.

"Cranstone enters the darkness" *Shearsman* (Malaysia) No. 5 (1982), 46-54 [Based on survey response].

"the crocodile and the serpent" *Kayak* (U.S.) No. 22 (1970), 39-40.

"the crocodile and the serpent" *Green Beginning/Black Ending* (1971), 95-6.

"the crossing" *Green Beginning/Black Ending* (1971), 60-2.

"the cry" *Tam R* No. 63 (Oct 1974), 72 [Listed as poem].

"the cry" *Randolph Cranstone* (1975), 131.

"the curtain" *Randolph Cranstone* (1975), 165.

"cycle" *CFM* No. 12 (Win 1974), 76-8.

"cycle" *Randolph Cranstone* (1975), 128-9.

"danger" *Van Surrealist Newsletter* 1:1 (1980), 6 [?] [Based on survey response].

"darkness" *Green Beginning/Black Ending* (1971), 73-4.

"darkness" *CFM* No. 39 (1981), 24.

"the diamond" *Kayak* (U.S.) No. 31 (1973), 39-40.

"the diamond" *Randolph Cranstone* (1975), 116-7.

"the dragonfly" *Randolph Cranstone* (1975), 190.

"dream life of the ant" *Shearsman* (Malaysia) No. 7 (1982), 80 [?] [Based on survey response].

"dreaming water" *Van Surrealist Newsletter* 1:1 (1980), 8 [?] [Based on survey response].

"dreaming water" *CFM* No. 39 (1981), 25.

"the duck" *Randolph Cranstone* (1975), 144-5.

"the eagle and its reflection" *Tam R* No. 63 (Oct 1974), 75 [Listed as poem].

"the eagle and its reflection" *Randolph Cranstone* (1975), 137.

"the eggshells" *Randolph Cranstone* (1975), 100-1.

"the elderly gentleman and the tattered hag" *Kayak* (U.S.) No. 22 (1970), 38-9.

"the elderly gentleman and the tattered hag" *Green Beginning/Black Ending* (1971), 82-3.

"the elderly gentleman and the young-old lady" *CFM* Nos. 24/25 (Spr-Sum 1977), 8-9.

"the expanding and contracting lake" *Sixteen Stories* (1969), 101-3.

"the face" *Randolph Cranstone* (1975), 167.

"falling tree" *CFM* No. 39 (1981), 24.

"the fields" *Randolph Cranstone* (1975), 109-11.

"figures in a landscape" *Melmoth Van* No. 1 (1981), 27-32 [Based on survey response].

"the firebird and the arrow" *Tam R* No. 63 (Oct 1974), 71 [Listed as poem].

"the firebird and the arrow" *Randolph Cranstone* (1975), 138.

"the fish" *Randolph Cranstone* (1975), 118.

"the flight" *Expression* No. 8 (1968), 26-7 [Based on survey response].

"the flight" *Sixteen Stories* (1969), 85-6.

"the flower that started the day" *Green Beginning/Black Ending* (1971), 47-8.

"the frogs" *Randolph Cranstone* (1975), 112-3.

"the genie" *Randolph Cranstone* (1975), 130.

"the giraffe who turned purple" *Randolph Cranstone* (1975), 141-2.

"the girl at the bus stop" *Green Beginning/Black Ending* (1971), 146-8.

"the girl at the bus stop" *CFM* Nos. 2/3 (Spr-Sum 1971), 16-7.

"the glass thimble" *Perspectives* (U.S.) Spr 1974, 13-20 [Based on survey response].

"the glass thimble" *Randolph Cranstone* (1975), 196-206.

"the golden emporer" *Randolph Cranstone* (1975), 139.

"the green girl" *Green Beginning/Black Ending* (1971), 15-36.

"the green girl" *CFM* No. 1 (Win 1971), 23-41.

"the hand" *Popular Illusion* No. 3 (Jan 1978), [1 p].

"the harbour" *Green Beginning/Black Ending* (1971), 97-100.

"the hat" *Shearsman* (Malaysia) No. 7 (1982), 81 [?] [Based on survey response].

"the head" *CFM* Nos. 24/25 (Spr-Sum 1977), 7-8.

"the head" *Canadian Short Fiction Anthology 2* (1982), 56-7.

"the houses" *Green Beginning/Black Ending* (1971), 41-2.

"the hunter and the flower" *Expression* No. 6 (1967), 25 [Based on survey response].

"the hydra" *Green Beginning/Black Ending* (1971), 113-4.

"in search of Noire" *Green Beginning/Black Ending* (1971), 177-85.

"in search of Noire" *CFM* Nos. 2/3 (Spr-Sum 1971), 10-5.

"in the log" *Randolph Cranstone* (1975), 169.

"the insect" *Randolph Cranstone* (1975), 191-2.

"the invulnerable ovoid aura: a first report on an epoch-making scientific experiment" *CFM* No. 21 (Spr 1976), 48-56.

"the invulnerable ovoid aura: a first report on an epoch-making scientific experiment" *Illusion One* (1983), 57-66.

"japanese roses" *Shearsman* (Malaysia) No. 7 (1982), 79 [?] [Based on survey response].

"journey in search of a shell" *Green Beginning/Black Ending* (1971), 138-45.

"journey in search of a shell" *CFM* Nos. 2/3 (Spr-Sum 1971), 19-25.

"kitten among the bulrushes" *Green Beginning/Black Ending* (1971), 70-3.

"the leaf" *Green Beginning/Black Ending* (1971), 54-7.

"the lost wind" *Randolph Cranstone* (1975), 182.

"a man, a girl and a door" *Prism* 8:1 (Sum 1968), 92-5.

"a man, a girl and a door" *Sixteen Stories* (1969), 15-9.

"a man and his dog" *Randolph Cranstone* (1975), 154.

"man on a bicycle" *BC Lib Q* 36:4 (Apr 1973), 21-2.

"man on a bicycle" *Randolph Cranstone* (1975), 155.
"the man who loved Rusty Iron" *Kayak* (U.S.) No. 55 (1981), 17.
"the man who loved trees" *Sixteen Stories* (1969), 79-81.
"the man with burning hair" *CFM* Nos. 24/25 (Spr-Sum 1977), 9.
"the manor house" *CFM* No. 39 (1981), 26-7.
"the message" *Randolph Cranstone* (1975), 166.
"the monolith" *Green Beginning/Black Ending* (1971), 162-3.
"my hand and the girl" *Green Beginning/Black Ending* (1971), 43-4.
"the net" *Sixteen Stories* (1969), 87-9.
"the net" *Prism* 8:3 (Spr 1969), 27-9.
"a new direction" *Green Beginning/Black Ending* (1971), 80-1.
"the nightmares" *Green Beginning/Black Ending* (1971), 175-6.
"Noire's dialogues" *Sixteen Stories* (1969), 20-54.
"Noire's eyes" *BC Lib Q* 36:4 (Apr 1973), 22-3.
"the obelisk" *Randolph Cranstone* (1975), 125.
"the open gate" *Sixteen Stories* (1969), 112-6.
"the path" *Green Beginning/Black Ending* (1971), 154-5.
"the path" *Kayak* (U.S.) No. 26 (1971), 10-1.
"the plough and the mice" *Madrona* (U.S.) 7 (1973), 44 [Based on survey response].
"the plough and the mice" *Randolph Cranstone* (1975), 185.
"the procession" *Green Beginning/Black Ending* (1971), 173-4.
"the pursuing river" *Tam R* No. 63 (Oct 1974), 74 [Listed as poem].
"the pursuing river" *Randolph Cranstone* (1975), 99.
"the pursuit" *Randolph Cranstone* (1975), 168.
"the railway station" *Expression* No. 10 (1968), 26-9 [Based on survey response].
"the railway station" *Sixteen Stories* (1969), 110-1.
"the railway track and the canal" *Green Beginning/Black Ending* (1971), 151-3.
"the railway track and the canal" *CFM* Nos. 2/3 (Spr-Sum 1971), 17-9.
"the rain" *CFM* No. 12 (Win 1974), 75-6.
"the rain" *Randolph Cranstone* (1975), 132-3.
"the rat" *Green Beginning/Black Ending* (1971), 164-5.
"raven and fir tree" *Kayak* (U.S.) No. 22 (1970), 39.
"raven and fir tree" *Grenn Beginning/Black Ending* (1971), 115.
"reality is" *Green Beginning/Black Ending* (1971), 186-9.
"Red Beard's quest" *Sixteen Stories* (1969), 67-9.
"the return of Noire" *Sixteen Stories* (1969), 55-64.
"the road and the rock" *Kayak* (U.S.) No. 31 (1973), 40-1.
"the road and the rock" *Randolph Cranstone* (1975), 126-7.
"the rock" *Green Beginning/Black Ending* (1971), 63-5.
"Roditi" *CFM* Nos. 32/33 (1979), 10-4.
"the rose" *Green Beginning/Black Ending* (1971), 172.
"the scarlet woman" *Green Beginning/Black Ending* (1971), 160-1.
"the scent of honey" *Green Beginning/Black Ending* (1971), 101-4.
"the seed filament" *Randolph Cranstone* (1975), 189.
"sera" *Green Beginning/Black Ending* (1971), 169-71.
"the shadows" *Randolph Cranstone* (1975), 172-3.
"Six daffodils" *Green Beginning/Black Ending* (1971), 52-3.
"the skipper" *Madrona* (U.S.) 7 (1973), 45 [Based on survey response].
"the skipper" *Randolph Cranstone* (1975), 186.

"the snake and the spring" *Randolph Cranstone* (1975), 143.

"the soap builders" *Green Beginning/Black Ending* (1971), 89.

"story" *Randolph Cranstone* (1975), 174-5.

"story of my life" *Randolph Cranstone* (1975), 193.

"the student and the lobster" *BC Lib Q* 36:4 (Apr 1973), 20-1.

"the student and the lobster" *Randolph Cranstone* (1975), 114-5.

"Sumiko" *Expression* No. 11 (1968), 22-3 [Based on survey response].

"sun" *CFM* No. 39 (1981), 24.

"symmetry" *CBC* "Anthology" [Based on survey response; probable dates: 27 July or 3 Aug 1974].

"symmetry" *CFM* No. 12 (Win 1974), 78-80.

"symmetry" *Randolph Cranstone* (1975), 122-4.

"three oranges" *Kayak* (U.S.) No. 55 (1981), 18.

"through the trees to the river" *Sixteen Stories* (1969), 70-3.

"the tiger" *Tam R* No. 63 (Oct 1974), 73 [Listed as poem].

"the tiger" *Randolph Cranstone* (1975), 136.

"tiger in the park" *Expression* No. 9 (1968), 28-9 [Based on survey response].

"tiger in the park" *Sixteen Stories* (1969), 107-9.

"the tigress" *CFM* No. 39 (1981), 27-9.

"the tiny people" *CFM* No. 11 (Aut 1973), 41-2.

[Titles unknown] *Expression* No. 2 (1966), 25-7 [Based on survey response].

"the tiny people" *Randolph Cranstone* (1975), 107-8.

"to the top of the tower" *Sixteen Stories* (1969), 74-6.

"the tomb" *Randolph Cranstone* (1975), 179.

"the traveller and his staff" *Perspectives* (U.S.) Spr 1974, 10-2 [Based on survey response].

"the traveller and his staff" *Randolph Cranstone* (1975), 150-2.

"the tree of the crows" *Randolph Cranstone* (1975), 140.

"the trees and the fish" *Green Beginning/Black Ending* (1971), 45-6.

"the trees and the fungi" *Green Beginning/Black Ending* (1971), 77-9.

"two girls and a man coming and going" *Prism* 7:1 (Sum 1967), 10-3.

"two girls and a man coming and going" *Sixteen Stories* (1969), 11-4.

"two men with knives" *CFM* Nos. 24/25 (Spr-Sum 1977), 10.

"two monsters" *Randolph Cranstone* (1975), 188.

"two moons" *Randolph Cranstone* (1975), 187.

"the ultimate poem" *Randolph Cranstone* (1975), 181.

"the unicorn" *CFM* No. 11 (Aut 1973), 43-4.

"the unicorn" *Randolph Cranstone* (1975), 105-6.

"the vampire" *Green Beginning/Black Ending* (1971), 111-2.

"the vanishing landscape" *Green Beginning/Black Ending* (1971), 49-51.

"vicissitudes of a couple" *Randolph Cranstone* (1975), 163.

"a walk in the dust" *Randolph Cranstone* (1975), 159-60.

"the walking country" *Green Beginning/Black Ending* (1971), 149-50.

"the walnut tree" *Randolph Cranstone* (1975), 104.

"watery room" *CFM* No. 39 (1981), 25-6.

"the well" *Green Beginning/Black Ending* (1971), 156-7.

"the well" *Popular Illusion* No. 3 (Jan 1978), [1 p].

"a whispering" *Randolph Cranstone* (1975), 161-2.

"white gloves" *CFM* Nos. 24/25 (Spr-Sum 1977), 9-10.

"the white sheet and the couple" *Kayak* (U.S.) No. 22 (1970), 40-1.

"the white sheet and the couple" *Green Beginning/Black Ending* (1971), 93-4.
"the windmill" *Green Beginning/Black Ending* (1971), 58-9.
"the woolen garment" *Randolph Cranstone* (1975), 177-8.

Bunner, Freda Newton
"Bungalo and the Python" *Onward* 15 Nov 1959, 727 [Non-fiction?].
"The Life of Riley" *Onward* 27 Nov 1966, 12-4.
"Wanted – Grandmothers with Attics" *CG* 78 (June 1959), 62.

Burch, Mark A.†
"The Hermit" *Pier Spr* 7:4 (Aut 1982), 43-59.

Burdick, Steven‡ (1945?-)
"Alexander's Letters, Continued" *Notes from Nowhere* No. 1 (1977), 9-18 [Non-fiction?].

Burgess, Helen
"The Homecoming" *FH* 8 Nov 1956, 38.
"The Ladies" *FH* 3 July 1952, 16.
"The Ladies" *Stories to Read Again* (1965), 25-30.

Burke, Brian†
"Just Another Guy Out for a Ride on His Bike" *New Q* 3:2 (Sum 1983), 47-55.

Burke, James
"I'm a Big Girl Now" *Weekend* 2 (21 June 1952), 32.
"Too Young" *Weekend* 2 (15 Mar 1952), 38.

Burke, Jim
"Willie" *Winnipeg Stories* (1974), 30-46.

Burke, Leah‡
"Lou – The Skating Butcher" *2 O'Clock Rap* 5 (1977), 14-5.

Burke, Mary‡
"Beware of the Dog" *20 Cents* 4:1 (1970), [1 p].

Burkman, Kay‡
"The Last Laugh" *Acta Vic* 93:2 (Dec 1968), 13-5.
"Sonny Boy" *Acta Vic* 91:3 (Apr 1967), 21-2.

Burles, Mary Jo
"A Carpet of Roses" *FH* 11 Feb 1960, 10-1, 24.
"A Carpet of Roses" *Stories to Read Again* (1965), 211-6.
"A Dress for a Dance" *FH* 2 June 1960, 10-1, 23.
"The Long, Long Mile" *FH* 27 Nov 1958, 14-5, 30.
"Pictures of an Old Maid's Family" *FH* 14 May 1959, 28-30.
"The Subtle Touch" *SW* 6 Feb 1960, 30-2.

Burley, Margaret F.‡
"Carpenters and Kings" *AA* 67 (Dec 1976), 9-10, 12.
"The Grandfather" *AA* 65 (Mar 1975), 32-4.

Burman, Jack†

"Sam & Anna" *Writ* No. 4 (Spr 1972), 62-4.

Burnard, Bonnie

"Crush" *NeWest R* 8:5 (Feb 1983), 8-9.
"Grizzly Mountain" *Coming Attractions* (1983), 59-67.
"Reflections" *Saskatchewan Gold* (1982), 269-81.
"Reflections" *Coming Attractions* (1983), 76-90.
"Windows" *Coming Attractions* (1983), 68-75.

Burnell, Ethel D.†

" 'Add to –' " *Home Leaguer* 7 (Mar 1960), 5.
"Alone!" *Home Leaguer* 5 (July 1957), 5.
"Blind Eyes to See" *Home Leaguer* 7 (Oct 1959), 5.
" 'The Blind Leading the Blind' " *Home Leaguer* 6 (July 1958), 5.
" 'Can We Help'?" *Home Leaguer* 5 (Mar 1958), 5 [Non-fiction?].
"The Doll" *Home Leaguer* 6 (Sept 1958), 5.
" 'Drop One, Pick One' " *Home Leaguer* 5 (Jan 1958), 5.
" 'Finding Peace of Mind' " *Home Leaguer* 6 (Oct 1958), 5.
"Gain Through Loss" *Home Leaguer* 5 (June 1957), 5.
" 'God Bless You' " *Home Leaguer* 5 (Oct 1957), 5.
"Granny Grant" *Home Leaguer* 7 (July-Aug 1959), 5.
" 'Happiness' " *Home Leaguer* 6 (Aug 1958), 5.
"Here Too – They Serve" *Home Leaguer* 5 (Feb 1958), 5.
"His Last Gift" *Home Leaguer* 5 (May 1958), 5.
"I Was Here First!" *Home Leaguer* 5 (Sept 1957), 5.
" 'I've Found the Friend' " *Home Leaguer* 6 (June 1958), 5.
" 'The Last Page' " *Home Leaguer* 3 (Oct 1955), 5.
" 'The Lord Used Me!' " *Home Leaguer* 6 (Apr 1959), 5.
"The Ministry of the League of Mercy" *Home Leaguer* 3 (Dec 1955), 10.
"A Modern Prodigal's Return" *Home Leaguer* 4 (Dec 1956), 5.
"Much in Little" *Home Leaguer* 6 (May 1959), 5.
" 'Over-Rated Do-Gooders!' " *Home Leaguer* 5 (Dec 1957), 5.
"A Sense of Wonder" *Home Leaguer* 7 (Nov 1959), 5.
"She Wanted to Hear the Bagpipes" *Home Leaguer* 5 (Nov 1957), 5.
" 'The Silver Lining' " *Home Leaguer* 6 (Feb 1959), 5.
[Untitled] *Home Leaguer* 3 (Feb 1956), 5.
[Untitled] *Home Leaguer* 3 (Mar 1956), 5.
[Untitled] *Home Leaguer* 3 (Apr 1956), 5.
[Untitled] *Home Leaguer* 4 (June 1956), 5.
[Untitled] *Home Leaguer* 4 (July 1956), 5.
[Untitled] *Home Leaguer* 4 (Aug 1956), 5.
[Untitled] *Home Leaguer* 4 (Sept 1956), 5.
[Untitled] *Home Leaguer* 4 (Oct 1956), 5.
[Untitled] *Home Leaguer* 4 (Nov 1956), 5.
[Untitled] *Home Leaguer* 4 (Apr 1957), 5, 12.
[Untitled] *Home Leaguer* 5 (Aug 1957), 5.
[Untitled] *Home Leaguer* 6 (Nov 1958), 5.
[Untitled] *Home Leaguer* 6 (Jan 1959), 5.
[Untitled] *Home Leaguer* 7 (Apr 1960), 5.

"We Need a Mother" *Home Leaguer* 4 (May 1957), 5.
"A Wonderful Day" *Home Leaguer* 7 (Sept 1959), 5.
"You'll Never Have to Take Me Home Again" *Home Leaguer* 4 (Mar 1957), 5.

Burnett, Eileen†
"And Gladly Teach ... " *Can Lifetime* 4 (Mar-Apr 1974), 22-3.
"Outfoxed" *West People* No. 201 (1 Sept 1983), 14.
"Sip into the Past" *CSSM* 2:1 (Jan 1976), 11-5.

Burnett, Virgil (1928-)
TOWERS AT THE EDGE OF A WORLD: TALES OF A MEDIEVAL TOWN
Toronto: Nelson, 1980.
"Actaeon" *Des* 13:4 No. 38 (Fall 1982), 61-4.
"Aleth" *Towers* (1980), 25-6.
"Constance" *Towers* (1980), 47-64.
"Djaa" *Towers* (1980), 89-118.
"Fausta" *Towers* (1980), 141-64.
"Gerardus" *Towers* (1980), 29-45.
"Gundegar" *Towers* (1980), 7-11.
"Hugues" *Towers* (1980), 13-23.
"Isabeau" *Towers* (1980), 83-6.
"Julie" *Towers* (1980), 177-88.
"King Folly" *Towers* (1980), 67-76.
"Malliardus" *Towers* (1980), 191-208.
"A Masked Ball" *CFM* Nos. 40/41 (1981), 63-71.
"Omphale" *Mal R* No. 54 (Apr 1980), 103-9.
"Picaroon" *TriQuarterly* No. 42 (Spr 1978), 41-51.
"Queen Constance" *TriQuarterly* No. 40 (Fall 1977), 260-75.
"Queen Constance" *Illusion One* (1983), 147-62.
"Queen Death" *Towers* (1980), 79-80.
"Rhys" *Towers* (1980), 167-75.
"Violette" *Towers* (1980), 129-38.
"Xavier" *Towers* (1980), 121-7.

Burnford, Sheila
"Poor Albert Floated When He Died ..." *Blackwood's Mag* 285 (May 1959), 416-20.
"Poor Albert Floated When He Died ... " *Women of the Weird* (1976), 28-35.

Burningham, Bradd‡
"The Girl with the Baby Arms" *Saskatchewan Gold* (1982), 140-64.

Burnley, John‡
"Larry the Lobster" *Alive* No. 66 (26 Feb 1977), 4.
"A Question of Class Solidarity" *Alive* No. 44 [n.d.], 9.
"Racism Is Not Debatable!" *Alive* No. 43 [n.d.], 13.
"The Shoe" *Alive* No. 44 [n.d.], 10-1.

Burns, Jim‡
"Julian" *Ant's Forefoot* No. 1 (Fall 1967), [1 p].

Burns, Mary†

"After Hours" *Nw J* No. 26 (1982), 52-60.
"The Circle" *UWR* 17:2 (Spr-Sum 1983), 54-9.
"Greta" *Nw J* No. 23 (1981), 69-75.
"Lady of the Ocean" *event* 9:2 (1980), 163-8.
"Links" *Harvest* No. 12 (Jan 1982), 5-12.

Burns, R.‡

"Ballygennon Revisited" *Stories with John Drainie* (1963), 212-20.

Burns, Richard M.‡

"Hobe" *CBC "Anthology"* 11 June 1977.

Burns, Robert A. McA.‡

"A Double Gin" *Forge* Mar 1959, 29-33.
"A Quiet Life" *Forge* 23:1 (Win 1960), 52-8.
"We Were All Going Home" *Forge* 23:2 (Dec 1961), 15-20.

Burrs, Mick

"Composition in Black and White" *Sundogs* (1980), 29-34.
"Composition in Black and White" *Smoke Signals* 4 [date unknown] [Based on *SWG* survey response].
"The Day They Threw Eggs at Ringo Starr" *JCF* 2:2 (Spr 1973), 18-24.

Burston, Daniel‡

"The Train Ride to Siberia: A Fable" *Alternative to Alienation* No. 1 (Mar-Apr 1974), 7.

Burton, Rosemary‡

"A Bit of Music" *UTR* 1:1 (Spr 1977), 32-5.

Burville, Victor‡

"Tale of a Mouse" *Muse* 60:1 (Nov 1950), 23-5.

Bury, J. Colbrook‡

"Strike Sketch" *TUR* 65:4 (Mar 1953), 8, 15-9.

Bush, Helen‡

"Molly and the Stone Beads" *Can Nature* 16 (Nov-Dec 1954), 168-70 [Based on CPI].
"Molly Goes on an Expedition" *Can Nature* 17 (Nov-Dec 1955), 167-9 [Based on CPI].

Bush, Pamela (1947-)

"Bedtime Story" *Face to Face* (1979), 7-16.
"The Rites of Spring" *Fid* No. 110 (Sum 1976), 86-97.

Bushell, Sidney

"After Many Days" *Onward* 61 (4 Nov 1951), 694-6.
"At the Organ" *Onward* 10 May 1953, 292-4, 303.
"At the Upper Pool" *Onward* 22 Feb 1953, 116-7, 126.
"An Axe-Handle" *Onward* 13 Mar 1955, 171.
"An Axe-Handle" *Onward* 24 Apr 1966, 3.

"Catalogue Christmas" *Onward* 61 (16 Dec 1951), 790-1, 795.
"Christmas Memories" *Onward* 61 (23 Dec 1951), 801-2, 814 [Non-fiction?].
"Down Tickle" *Onward* 18 Jan 1959, 47.
"Duck Blind" *Onward* 61 (21 Oct 1951), 657-9.
"The Flower Pot" *Onward* 20 July 1958, 449-51.
"Happy Is the Man" *Onward* 62 (12 Oct 1952), 641-3, 654-5.
"It's Christmas" *Onward* 62 (14 Dec 1952), 785-7.
"The Judge's Sermon" *Onward* 62 (6 Apr 1952), 214-6, 222-3.
"The Judge's Sermon" *Onward* 8 Apr 1962, 6-7, 11-2.
"The Judge's Sermon" *Onward* 20 Mar 1966, 3-5, 13.
"Late Blooming" *Onward* 22 July 1962, 3-5, 8.
"Mrs. Cobbett's Secret" *Onward* 62 (26 Oct 1952), 673-5, 683.
"Of Physical Culture" *Onward* 3 June 1962, 12-4 [Humour].
"Of Physical Culture" *Onward* 30 Jan 1966, 12-3.
"Quarantine Christmas" *Onward* 21 Dec 1958, 810-1, 814.
"Quarantine Christmas" *Onward* 27 Dec 1964, 4-6, 10.
"Remembered April" *Onward* 26 Sept 1954, 609-11, 622-3.
"The Ring: A Tale of Chedabucto Bay" *Onward* 61 (28 Oct 1951), 682-3, 686-7.
"The Social" *Onward* 9 Aug 1953, 497-9.
"A Sweet-Smelling Savour" *Onward* 29 Apr 1956, 273-5, 286.
"Thank You, God" *Onward* 13 Jan 1957, 25-7, 31.
"Till She Find It" *Onward* 11 Jan 1953, 20-2, 27.
"Unto One of the Least" *Onward* 60 (4 June 1950), 353-4.

Buswell, Shirley†
"Olivia: A Short Story" *Whetstone* Spr 1974, [3 pp].

Butala, Sharon (1940-)
"Arlene" *Saskatchewan Gold* (1982), 165-78.
"Belle in Winter" *NeWest R* 9 (Oct 1983), 12-4.
"Breaking Horses" *Coming Attractions* (1983), 10-21.
"Breaking Horses" *Grain* 11:1 (Feb 1983), 34-40.
"The Mission" *Coming Attractions* (1983), 37-50.
"O What Venerable & Reverend Creatures" *Coming Attractions* (1983), 22-36.

Butler, Douglas‡
"Heat of the Light" *TUR* 91:2 (Apr 1978), 29-34.

Butler, J.E.P.‡
"The Discovery of Canada" *AA* 48 (May 1958), 96-7.
"The Discovery of Canada" *Atlantic Advocate's Holiday Book* (1961), 97-101.

Butler, Juan
"A Great Whore" *Harbinger* 3:8 (8 July 1970), [2 pp].

Butler, Paula
"Festival du Poulet" *Fid* No. 134 (Oct 1982), 7-12.

Butt, Grace
"Mrs. Kollin" *From This Place* (1977), 170-2.
"The Time Skipper Joe Knocked Off Swearing" *Nfld Q* 67:2 (July 1969), 30-1.
"The Time Skipper Joe Knocked Off Swearing" *Baffles of Wind and Tide* (1974), 20-3.

Butterwick, Jessie‡
"Spring Manoeuvres" *Edmonton Journal* Wed, 3 Apr 1963, 4.

Butterworth, Judith†
"The Game" *New Q* 2:1 (Spr 1982), 29-31.
"The Visit" *New Q* 1:1 (Spr 1981), 23-5.

Butts, Allan Richard (1955-)
"The Game" *UTR* 4 (Spr 1980), 7-9.
"A Moment in the Life of Bonzo the Cat" *UTR* 5 (1981), 11.

Butts, Ed P. (1951-)
"The Challenge" *Like It Is* 1:2 (Spr 1975), 42-3 ["a fictionalized version of a real incident ... "(auther's note)].
"Dance of the Dolls" *New Q* 1:2 (Sum 1981), 5-9.
"Judgement" *Like It Is* 2:1 [n.d.], 38-9.
"A One Way Dialogue" *Can Messenger* 81 (Jan 1971), 12-3.
"The Rat Game" *New Q* 2:3 (Fall 1982), 35-42.
"Richard" *Like It Is* 1:4 [1975], 52-3.
"Rioter, Harbour Grace, Boxing Day, 1883" *Alive* No. 38 [1974], 16.
"Survival" *New Q* 1:1 (Spr 1981), 11-7.
"Thief, God, Thief" *Charasee Press* No. 10 [n.d.], 7, 12.
"Traps" *Like It Is* 2:5 (Spr 1977), 40-2.

Buyukmihci, Hope Sawyer‡
"Green Pastures" *AA* 61 (Nov 1970), 57, 59-60, 62-4.
"The Stump" *AA* 67 (June 1977), 49-53.
"The White Lilacs" *AA* 67 (Sept 1976), 32-4.

Byers, Valerie‡
"The Stranger" *Tyro* 1962, 45-9.
"Very Green, Very Rubbery" *Tyro* 1962, 9-12.

Byrnes, Slim†
"Muddy Waters" *Treeline 2* (1983), 31-4.

Byrnes, Terence (1948-)
WINTERING OVER Dunvegan, Ont.: Quadrant Editions, 1980.
"Aurora/Anna Marie" *Wintering Over* (1980), 7-11.
"A Better Life" *Wintering Over* (1980), 27-38.
"Coupal Street" *Wintering Over* (1980), 39-51.
"Food People" *Wintering Over* (1980), 96-110.
"Food People" *81: Best Canadian Stories* 20-35.
"Getting the Hang of It" *Prism* 17:2 (Fall 1978), 39-50.
"Getting the Hang of It" *79: Best Canadian Stories* 22-37.
"Getting the Hang of It" *Wintering Over* (1980), 12-26.

"Listening In" *Wintering Over* (1980), 52-66.
"A Member of the Department" *Wintering Over* (1980), 67-78.
"A Reasonable Man" *Wintering Over* (1980), 79-95.
"Wintering Over" *80: Best Canadian Stories* 21-31.
"Wintering Over" *Wintering Over* (1980), 111-20.

Byrne-Wood, Margaret‡
"Aunt Addie's Xmas Caper" *Sand Patterns* No. 19 (1976), [10 pp].

Byzewski, Julie
"A Story" *Squatch J* No. 2 (Jan 1976), 21-3.

C., J.H.
"Winter Hill" *TUR* 69:4 (Mar 1957), 14-9.

C., W.R.
"The Best Is Yet to Be" *TUR* 69:3 (Feb 1957), 25-8.

Cacchioni, Mark‡
"Just Baloney Story" *Geo Str Writing* No. 1 (29 Oct-5 Nov 1969), 31.

Cade-Edwards, Eileen
"Be a Listener" *Pres Record* 93 (Oct 1968), 18-9.
"A Dream Hat for Easter" *Can Lifetime* 2 (Mar-Apr 1972), 18-9.
"Give a Little Extra" *Pres Record* 95 (Feb 1971), 20-1 [Non-fiction?].
"How to Live with People" *Pres Record* 93 (June 1968), 14.
"I'm Sorry" *Pres Record* 96 (Oct 1972), 16 [Non-fiction?].
"It Could Have Been Me" *Pres Record* 95 (May 1971), 2.
"No Time for Listening" *Pres Record* 93 (Mar 1968), 2-3.
"Remember Woody" *Pres Record* 95 (Nov 1971), 17 [Non-fiction?].
"Where Lilies Bloom Free" *Can Lifetime* 3:2 (Mar-Apr 1973), 36-7.
"Why Don't We Ask First?" *Pres Record* 96 (Mar 1972), 13 [Non-fiction?].

Cadogan, Elda (1916-)
"But You *Can* Get a Man with a Gun" *MM* 66 (1 Aug 1953), 12-3, 45-6, 48.
"The Five Cent Piece" *CHJ* July 1957, 18, 47-8.
"Nothing but the Truth" *Chat* 29 (Apr 1957), 16-7, 76-83.
"Time and the Tide" *CHJ* Sept 1957, 51-2, 54, 57-8.
"When the Women Went on Strike" *MM* 67 (1 Dec 1954), 22, 66-9, 72-3.

Cady, Irving H.†
"A Piece of String" *Can National Mag* 42 (Dec 1956), 14-5.

Caesar, Floyd‡
"The Dream" *Muse* 65 (1956), 33.
"Eighteen" *Muse* 65 (1956), 18-9.

Cahil, Philip‡
"Don't Blow, Birdie!" *Motion* No. 3 (25 July 1962), [2-4].

Cahill, Brian‡
"*Idylls of the King*: A Newfoundland Version" *AA* 67 (Dec 1976), 34-5.
"My Cousin Ned and the Canadian Ethos" *Mont* 33 (Apr 1959), 24-5.
"The Romance of the Beekeeper" *Mont* 31 (Dec 1957), 36.

Cain, Tom‡
"Alkali Dust" *Acta Vic* 77:4 (Mar 1953), 23-5.

Cairncross, Larissa† (1955?-)
"A Record of Past Failures" *Title Unknown* (1975), 12.

Cairns, A.T.
"By the Sea" *Dand* 3 (Spr-Sum 1977), 15-21.
"Island" *Dal R* 58 (1978), 95-103.
"Visitant" *Dal R* 46 (1966), 348-55.

Cairns, John C.‡
"Mr. Day" *Folio* 4:2 [Apr 1950], [6 pp].
"Renaissance" *Folio* 4:1 [Jan 1950], [7 pp].

Cairns, Malcolm‡
"How to Punctuate a Date: For Better or for Worse" *Sand Patterns* No. [22] (Sum 1978), [2 pp].

Caldnell, Jack‡
"The Rain Guage" *Scarlet and Gold* No. 40 (1958), 20.

Caldwell, Cal‡
"Business" *Undergrad* Win 1953, 27-8.
"Compensation" *Undergrad* Spr 1954, 24-7.
"Message" *Undergrad* Spr 1954, 31-6.

Callaghan, Barry (1937-)
THE BLACK QUEEN STORIES Toronto: Lester & Orpen Denys, 1982.
"All the Lonely People" *Punch* [date unknown] [Based on *Black Queen Stories*].
"All the Lonely People" *SN* 96 (Dec 1981), 40-7.
"All the Lonely People" *Black Queen Stories* (1982), 88-106.
"And So to Bed" *Black Queen Stories* (1982), 129-38.
"Anybody Home?" *Black Queen Stories* (1982), 26-37.
"The Black Queen" *Punch* 276 (13 June 1979), 1041-2.
"The Black Queen" *Ont R* No. 13 (Fall-Win 1980-81), 58-60.
"The Black Queen" *Black Queen Stories* (1982), 58-62.
"The Cohen in Cowan" *Punch* 277 (28 Nov 1979), 1014-6.
"The Cohen in Cowan" *TL* Dec 1980, 64, 100-2, 106.
"The Cohen in Cowan" CBC "*Anthology*" 20 Dec 1980.
"The Cohen in Cowan" *Black Queen Stories* (1982), 47-57.
"Crow Jane's Blues" *Punch Book of Short Stories* 2 [date unknown] [Based on *Black Queen Stories*].
"Crow Jane's Blues" *Punch* 277 (15 Aug 1979), 249-50.
"Crow Jane's Blues" CBC "*Anthology*" 23 Aug 1980.
"Crow Jane's Blues" *Ont R* No. 14 (Spr-Sum 1981), 33-6.
"Crow Jane's Blues" *Black Queen Stories* (1982), 8-14.

"Dark Laughter" *Punch* 277 (7 Nov 1979), 840-1.
"Dark Laughter" *Black Queen Stories* (1982), 63-9.
"A Drawn Blind" *Punch Book of Short Stories* 3 [date unknown] [Based on *Black Queen Stories*].
"A Drawn Blind" *Punch* 278 (30 Jan 1980), 192-4.
"A Drawn Blind" *Black Queen Stories* (1982), 119-28.
"The End of Something" *SN* 98 (Aug 1983), 46-51.
"The Muscle" *Weekend* 28 (17 June 1978), 12-3.
"The Muscle" *Punch* 275 (27 Sept 1978), 504-5.
"The Muscle" *Black Queen Stories* (1982), 1-7.
"Night Prayers" *Otherside* No. 2 (Win 1960), 20-1.
"Poodles John" *Black Queen Stories* (1982), 70-87.
"Prowlers" *Black Queen Stories* (1982), 107-18.
"Silent Music" *Exile* 8:3/4 (1981), 15-33.
"Silent Music" *Black Queen Stories* (1982), 139-65.
"Spring Water" *Punch* 277 (12 Sept 1979), 406-7.
"Spring Water" *Black Queen Stories* (1982), 38-46.
"A Terrible Discontent" *Black Queen Stories* (1982), 15-25.

Callaghan, Mary C.†
"Star-Crossed" *CSSM* 1:2 (Apr 1975), 17-21.

Callaghan, Michael‡
"If Thine Eye Offend Thee" *Folio* 5:2 (Apr 1951), [3 pp].

Callaghan, Morley (1903-)
"The Bachelor's Dilemma" *Chat* 23 (Aug 1950), 3.
"The Bachelor's Dilemma" *MM* 63 (1 Aug 1950), 25.
"The Bachelor's Dilemma" *SN* 65 (1 Aug 1950), 18-9.
"The Bachelor's Dilemma" *Time* 56 (21 Aug 1950), 30-1.
"The Bachelor's Dilemma" *Toronto Star* Sat, 19 Dec 1959, 28.
"The Bachelor's Dilemma" *TL* Jan 1974, 46-7.
"The Bachelor's Dilemma" *Canadian Yuletide Treasury* (1982), 110-2.
"A Cap for Steve" *Esquire* 38 (July 1952), 34, 109-11.
"A Cap for Steve" *Westermanns Monatshefte* 94:3 (1953-54), 5-8 [As "Die blaue Kappe"; in German; trans. Hildegard Jany; based on ABCMA].
"A Cap for Steve" *Man and His World* (1961), 252-63.
"A Cap for Steve" *Singing Under Ice* (1974), 99-111.
"A Cap for Steve" *Great Canadian Sports Stories* (1979), 57-69.
"A Cap for Steve" *Journeys 2* (1979), 51-60.
"A Cap for Steve" *New Worlds* (1980), 74-83.
"A Cap for Steve" *Penguin Book of Canadian Short Stories* (1980), 127-36.
"The Doctor's Son" *Ten for Wednesday Night* (1961), 94-104.
"The Insult" *Weekend* 5 (2 Apr 1955), 20-1, 28, 34-5.
"Just Like Her Mother" *Chat* 29 (Oct 1957), 121-3.
"Keep Away from Laura" *MM* 65 (1 Nov 1952), 13, 35-7.
"The Lucky Lady" *Weekend* 4 (27 Nov 1954), 36, 39, 46, 51.
"Magic Hat" *Redbook* Dec 1951, 42-3, 70, 72-3 [Based on ABCMA].
"The Meterman, Caliban, and Then Mr. Jones" *Exile* 1:3 (1973), 124-57.
"On the Edge of a World" *Esquire* 35 (Jan 1951), 106.
"Santa Claus Jones" *Lib* 31 (Dec 1954), 17, 54, 59-61.

"Something for Nothing" *CHJ* May 1954, 18-9, 26-9.

"The Way It Ended" *CHJ* Sept 1953, 12-3, 34-5, 39.

"We Just Had to Be Alone" *MM* 68 (5 Mar 1955), 18-9, 59-61.

Callaghan, Will N., Jr.‡ (1947-1974)

"The Eye of God" *Quarry* 22:2 (Spr 1973), 27-33.

"The Zoo" *Quarry* 24:3 (Sum 1975), 56-69.

Callow, Sherry‡

"Base Born" *Eclipse* No. 4 (1977), 6.

Caloren, Fred‡

"The Plight of the Vociferous Clamour Unlimited" *Acta Vic* 80:2 (Dec 1955), 17-8.

Cameron, Anne (1938-)

"The Grandmother" by Cam Hubert and Betty Jane Jones *Room* 2:1 (1976), 48-58.

"Legends of the Copper Woman" *Fireweed* No. 8 (Fall 1980), 19-23.

"Nai-Nai" by Cam Hubert *Room* 2:1 (1976), 32-7.

"Nobody's Women" *Common Ground* (1980), 61-80.

"Sometimes Andy Mathison Has Some Great Ideas" *Fireweed* Nos. 3/4 (Sum 1979), 110-9.

[Untitled] *Fireweed* No. 13 (1982), 125-8.

"Working Wife and Mother" by Cam Hubert *Room* 2:1 (1976), 60-6.

Cameron, Donald (1937-)

"Batman and the Communist Party" *JCF* 1:4 (Fall 1972), 15-9.

"A Chippy Little Number" *Intercourse* No. 9 (Oct 1968), 15-8.

"Composition: Double Exposure" *76: New Canadian Stories* 30-7.

"Composition: Double Exposure" CBC "Anthology" 26 June 1976.

"Fungus" *Floorboards* No. 2 (Oct 1969), 27-33.

"Justice" *CF* 49 (July 1969), 93-5.

"Love by the Book" *Fid* No. 78 (Jan-Feb 1969), 54-63.

"Magic Realism" CBC "Anthology" 29 Nov 1975.

"The Philosophical Dodge" *QQ* 77 (1970), 211-6.

"Snapshot: The Third Drunk" *Atlantic Monthly* 233 (June 1974), 88-93.

"Snapshot: The Third Drunk" *East of Canada* (1976), 8-19.

"Snapshot: The Third Drunk" *Canadian Short Stories 3* (1978), 48-61.

"Summertime" *Fid* No. 90 (Sum 1971), 50-7.

"Tell Me, Would You Get Married Again?" *SN* 88 (Feb 1973), 21-4.

"Upon Grounds of Adultery" *NJ* Nos. 7/8 (1976), 42-52.

Cameron, Eric

"The Abyss" *QQ* 74 (1967), 701-6.

"The Abyss" *Demanding Age* (1970), 306-10.

"A Crust of Bread" *Living Message* 87 (June 1976), 28-9.

"Dark Mirror" *AA* 63 (July 1973), 26-7, 68.

"Darkness" *Our Family* 19 (Feb 1967), 22-4.

"A Day to Remember" *AA* 55 (Apr 1965), 49, 51-2, 54-6.

"Destroying Angel" *Was R* 8:1 (Spr 1973), 15-23.

"Destroying Angel" *Short Story International* 1 No. 1 [date unknown] [Based on editorial note to "The Turning Point" in *Short Story International*].

"A Fact of Life" *Companion* 33 (Oct 1970), 25-7.

"A Flying Visit" *Living Message* 86 (Feb 1975), 21-3.

"A Good Catch" *Living Message* 86 (June 1975), 19-21.

"Hello and Goodbye" *Short Story International* No. 40 [date unknown] [Based on SSI].

"Help Wanted" *AA* 64 (Jan 1974), 38-40.

"A Hitch in Time" *AA* 64 (Oct 1973), 23, 25.

"Horse Sense" *Our Family* 16 (Oct 1964), 22-4.

"Land of Heart's Desire" *Was R* 7:1 (1972), 55-66.

"The Legacy" *AA* 63 (Mar 1973), 21, 23.

"The Man Who Believed in Christmas" *AA* 71 (Dec 1980), 66-7, 69-70.

"One of These Days" *Companion* 36 (Nov 1973), 22-6.

"One Summer" *Short Story International* No. 34 [date unknown] [Based on SSI].

"One Summer" *QQ* 77 (1970), 395-403.

"The Question Mark" *Companion* 35 (Mar 1972), 23-5.

"The Red Bikini" *QQ* 76 (1969), 239-49.

"The Rival" *Short Story International* No. 27 [date unknown] [Based on SSI].

"The Rival" *Companion* 36 (May 1973), 25-7.

"The Sanctuary" *Living Message* 85 ([Mar] 1974), 21-3.

"Saturday Night" *event* 5:1 [n.d.], 26-31.

"So Much for Stukynamud" *Short Story International* No. 7 [date unknown] [Based on editorial note to "The Turning Point"].

"So Much for Stukynamud" *British Columbia* (1961), 249-55.

"Strange Music" *CF* 30 (Nov 1950), 184-6.

"Thorn in the Flesh" *QQ* 75 (1968), 476-81.

"The Turning Point" *QQ* 73 (1966), 398-420.

"The Turning Point" *Kanadische Erzähler der Gegenwart* (1967), 273-310 [As "Der Wendepunkt"; trans. Trudis Reber].

"The Turning Point" *Die Weite Reise* (1974), 230-58 [As "Der Wendepunkt"; trans. Peter Kleinhempel].

"The Turning Point" *Short Story International* 3 No. 16 (Oct 1979), 15-38.

"The Way Back" *Living Message* 85 (Sept 1974), 20-1.

Cameron, Jess [pseudonym] – *See* Jess, Cameron.

Cameron, John Cullen†

SHORT STORIES n.p.: privately printed, 1976.

"Doctor Symes' Daughter" *Short Stories* (1976), 36-41.

"Early Loves of Angus Gordon" *Short Stories* (1976), 25-36.

"Lady Craig" *Short Stories* (1976), 41-55.

"Paradise" *Short Stories* (1976), 12-25.

"Yvonne" *Short Stories* (1976), 5-12.

Cameron, Margaret†

"There Is a Time for Everything" *WWR* 2:4 No. 8 (1983), 84-9.

Cameron, Michael

"The Ottawa Valley" *Prism* 17:1 (Sum 1978), 43-4.

Cameron, Sandy‡
"The Clean Old Man" *Tridentine* 5 (Apr 1969), 24-5.

Cameron, William‡
"The Ascension" *Jargon* 1965, 20-5.

Cameron, Zita†
"The Mourner" *Can Messenger* 70 (Sept 1960), 10-2, 43.

Camp, Merle‡
"Clue to Retire" *Bakka* No. 7 (Fall 1977), 36-9, 42.

Campbell, Alphonsus P. (1912-)
"Blessed Are the Meek" *Can R* 2:2 (July-Aug 1975), 34-5.
"The Good Lieutenant" *Island Prose and Poetry* (1973), 166-9.
"Local Color" *Variations on a Gulf Breeze* (1973), 56-64.
"My Manuscript Discovery" *Katharsis* 2:1 (Spr 1969), 12-7.

Campbell, Angelena H.†
"The Farmer's Daughter or Theology in a Nutshell" *Onward* 29 June 1958, 401-2, 409-11.
"The Farmer's Daughter or Theology in a Nutshell" *Onward* 1 Nov 1964, 3-5, 14.
"Gather Them In" *Onward* 5 Jan 1958, 6-8.
"The Sinners of Shilone" *Onward* 22 May 1960, 321-3, 334-5.

Campbell, Anne†
"The Vocation" *Sundogs* (1980), 35-41.

Campbell, Betty‡
"The Beloved Dissenter" *Katharsis* 3:1 (Spr 1970), 53-6.
"The Search" *Sand Patterns* No. 16 (Win 1975), [4 pp].

Campbell, Craig†
"Glass Bodies" *Antig R* No. 29 (Spr 1977), 11-6.

Campbell, D.A.‡
"Rio" *March* 2 (1963), 31-7.

Campbell, Donald‡
"The Regulars and the Fisher King" *Stet* Mar 1961, 3-7.

Campbell, Maria‡
"La Beau Sha Sho" *Edmonton Mag* 1 (Jan 1980), 25-6.
"La Beau Sha Sho" *CBC "Alberta Anthology"* 8 Nov 1980.

Campbell, Marjorie‡
"The Ring" *Bluenose* 2:4 (Spr 1978), 20-1 [Based on true incident].
"Winter Morning Long Ago" *Bluenose* 1:3 (Win 1976-77), 16-7.

Campbell, Ronald† (1942?-)
"Happening on the Left" *Folio* 18:1 (Fall 1965), 9-12.
"Land of the Free" *Folio* 16:1 (1963-64), 9-15.

Campbell, Sheila
"The White Squirrel" *Room* 2:4 (1977), 29-39.

Campbell, Wanda Blynn
THE PROMISE Vancouver: Pulp Press, 1983.
"The Baby" *Tam R* No. 79 (Aut 1979), 13-8.
"The Baby" *Promise* (1983), 7-13.
"Birthday Party" *Promise* (1983), 39-45.
"Death Is Always Part of Dinner" *Promise* (1983), 66-9.
"The Favour" *Promise* (1983), 78-83.
"Headlights" *Promise* (1983), 32-8.
"In Season" *Promise* (1983), 14-24.
"Kisses" *Promise* (1983), 84-92.
"Moose" *Promise* (1983), 70-7.
"Of Generations" *Promise* (1983), 93-122.
"Rabbit" *Promise* (1983), 25-31.
"Socks" *Promise* (1983), 123-9 [Originally broadcast on BBC].
"The Thaw" *Promise* (1983), 46-65.

Campion, Bridget‡
"The Lane" *Gram* 1:1 (Dec 1975), 9-14.
"Spike the Spider" *Gram* 2:4 (Apr 1977), 1-5.

Canal, Selby‡
"Prologue" *Probe* 2:2 (Spr 1961), 25-6.

Capelovitch, Ed†
"Strange Honour" *Forge* 1953, 50-4.

Cappon, Cormac Gerald‡
"Halfway House" *Alpha* 5:1 (Fall 1980), 11, 15, 22.

Carew, Captain John
"Missing Person" *War Cry* 25 Mar 1967, 15, 18.
"Out of the Storm – A Bear" *War Cry* 22 Dec 1973, 14-5.
"Song in the Night" *War Cry* 25 Dec 1965, 6-7.

Carey, Barbara
"Conundrum" *Waves* 10:1/2 (Sum-Fall 1981), 18-25.
"The Last Cadenza" *Harvest* No. 10 (Apr 1981), 7-18.
"The Machinators" *UTR* 1:1 (Spr 1977), 26-7.
"Machinators" *Alpha* 4:2 (Win 1979), 10, 12, 24.
"On Summer Lawns" *Harvest* No. 13 (June 1982), 21-30.
"On Summer Lawns" *CA & B* 58:4 (Sum 1983), 19-21.
"A Place in This House" *CA & B* 56:2 (Win 1981), 19-21.
"Prisoner of Conscience" *CCWQ* 3:4 [n.d.], 13-5.
"Protection from the Past" *Read Ch* 1:3 (Win 1982), 73-80.
"Something Special" *Harvest* No. 8 (Dec 1979), 22-31.
"Wednesday's Child" *Living Message* 91 (Dec 1980), 19-21.

Carey, Paul‡
[Untitled] *Los* No. 1 (Jan 1975), [7 pp].

Carey, Pauline (1932-)

"The Game" *Onion* 3:8/9 (Aug-Sept 1978), 5-6.

"The Man Who Liked Women" *Onion* 3:2 (Feb 1978), 8.

"Mrs. Rose and the Waterfall" *Onion* 3:11/12 (Nov-Dec 1978), 12.

Carisbrooke, Stephen‡

"Buster" *Legion* 32 (Apr 1958), 33.

Carlisle, Eric‡

"Death in the Autumn" *Talon* [1:1 (n.d.)], [2 pp].

Carlsen, Johann – *See* Green, H. Gordon.

Carlson, Chuck

SCIENTIFIC WORKS, ETC. Vancouver: Vancouver Community Press, 1972.

"Astral Sonic" *Cap R* 1:1 (Spr 1972), 5-10.

"A Government Grant at Last" *Pulp* 4:6 (15 June 1977), [1].

"Out West with Lady Sutton-Smith" *Scientific Works* (1972), 43-8.

"Petra Goggin's Letter" *Story So Far* 2 (1973), 73-7.

"A Working Paper" *Pulp* 4:18 (1 May 1978), [1-2, 4].

Carlton, Edna P.†

"Bill's Bride" *Onward* 21 Sept 1958, 593-5.

"The Butchering" *Onward* 5 Oct 1958, 625-7.

"The Diamond" *Onward* 4 June 1961, 360-1, 366.

"Every Good Gift" *Onward* 8 Dec 1957, 771-3.

"It's So Peaceful in the Country" *Onward* 4 Aug 1957, 485-6, 494.

"Mightier Than the Sword" *Onward* 12 Apr 1959, 238-9.

"Please, Teacher" *Onward* 12 Jan 1958, 17-9, 25.

"Room with a View" *Onward* 7 Aug 1955, 505, 510.

"Summer Play" *Onward* 15 Feb 1959, 104-5, 110-1.

"The Talents" *Onward* 23 June 1963, 10-2.

"The Valiant Hearts" *Onward* 10 Nov 1957, 712-4.

"Workmen Not Ashamed" *Onward* 22 Nov 1964, 11.

Carlyle, Andrew‡

"The Snow Man" *Acta Vic* 102:1 (Fall 1977), 18-9.

Carney, Dora

"Exactly 1,000.00" *FH* 17 Dec 1953, 20-1.

Carney, Robert‡

"The Boy and the Mountain" *Kaleidoscope* 1954-55, 22-3.

Carpenter, David (1941-)

"The Father's Love" *Can Lit R* No. 2 (Sum 1983), 47-61.

"Getting the Word" *Fid* No. 132 (Apr 1982), 73-82.

"Getting the Word" *100% Cracked Wheat* (1983), 301-19.

"Making It" *Saskatchewan Gold* (1982), 117-39.

"Protection" *SN* 96 (Jan 1981), 42-8, 50.

Carr, Grace†
"The Last Coin" *CSSM* 2:1 (Jan 1976), 15-6.

Carr, Jo-Ann†
"A Little Child Shall Lead Them" *Onward* 30 Dec 1956, 840-1.
"Mike" *Intervales* No. 2 (1960), 43-6.

Carr, Roberta‡
See also Carr, Roberta, with William Grant and Joe Koegh.
"The Incomplete Messenger" *Can Fandom* No. 18 (Sept 1953), 8-9.

Carr, Roberta, with William Grant and Joe Koegh‡
See also Carr, Roberta.
"Spectacular" *Can Fandom* No. 30 (Sept 1956), 13-8.

Carrier, Jean-Guy (1945-)
MY FATHER'S HOUSE Ottawa: Oberon Press, 1974.
"Adieu Marie" *My Father's House* (1974), 12-7.
"The American" *Was R* 11:1 (Spr 1976), 49-52.
"The Days of Winter Yet to Come" *My Father's House* (1974), 61-6.
"Diamonds" *Imp* 3:1 (Fall 1973), 9-13.
"A Dream" *My Father's House* (1974), 55-60.
"En Ontario Batinge" *Was R* 7:2 (Fall 1972), 33-9.
"The Exorcism of Jean Matteau's Devil" *My Father's House* (1974), 67-79.
"He Had a Dog Once" *My Father's House* (1974), 18-21.
"He Had a Dog Once" *Modern Canadian Stories* (1975), 173-7.
"In Moonlight" *My Father's House* (1974), 51-4.
"Maniwaki Mon Amour" *Fid* No. 95 (Fall 1972), 90-1.
"No One's Fault" *CFM* No. 20 (Win 1976), 27-36.
"Nor Did Anyone Call After Him" *Prism* 12:2 (Fall 1972), 72-80.
"Nor Did Anyone Call After Him" *My Father's House* (1974), 80-9.
"Pat Hebert" *Can R* 3:2 (May 1976), 36-40.
"A Premonition" *Transitions* 2 (1978), 17-28.
"A Premonition" *Magic Realism* (1980), 89-100.
"The Purest Profit" *My Father's House* (1974), 5-11.
"Quiet Months and Years" *My Father's House* (1974), 33-5.
"Reveillon" *Other Voices* 8:3 (Nov 1972), [1 p] [Prose poem?].
"Seguin's Last Train" *My Father's House* (1974), 90-5.
"The Sermon on the Mount Redone" *My Father's House* (1974), 36-50.
"So Many Children" *CF* 52 (Feb 1973), 10-1.
"A Strangeness of Habit, a Twist of Mind" *Was R* 7:2 (Fall 1972), 29-32.
"A Strangeness of Habit, a Twist of Mind" *73: New Canadian Stories* 89-92.
"A Strangeness of Habit, a Twist of Mind" *My Father's House* (1974), 22-32.
"Thin Hands" *CFM* No. 27 (1977), 40-6.
"Whatsis Name" *CF* 52 (Feb 1973), 10-1.

Carriere, Marguerite
"Debut" *Weekend* 3 (6 June 1953), 12-3, 28.
"The First Millionaire" *Weekend* 3 (9 May 1953), 46.
"Fortune Lies Westward" *FH* 14 Sept 1950, 40-1, 64.
"A Long Journey Home" *Stories with John Drainie* (1963), 207-11.

"Love Story" *Weekend* 3 (7 Feb 1953), 16-7.
"Percheron Girl" *Weekend* 2 (16 Feb 1952), 20-1.
"Pickup at Twilight" *Weekend* 4 (13 Feb 1954), 24-5, 42, 44.
"The Runaway Bride" *Chat* 28 (Feb 1956), 12, 38-46.
"Transplanted" *Chat* 26 (Nov 1953), 17, 35-41.

Carriere, Monique and Rene
"A Matter of Stature" *FH* 29 Dec 1955, 18-9.

Carroll, Elizabeth‡
"The Concert" *Yes* 1:1 (Apr 1956), [7 pp].
"The Coquette" *New Voices* (1956), 79-85.
"The Fair" *Forge* Mar 1956, 25-8.
"The Family" *New Voices* (1956), 86-94.
"Suffer Little Children" *Forge* Feb 1957, 39-44.
"The Travellers" *Forge* Dec 1956, 10-7.

Carroll, Jean†
"Mr. Naseltoes and Mr. Lapidarius" *Prism* 14:2 (Sum 1975), 18-30.

Carson, Ann‡
"The Dangers of Travel for Young Females" *TUR* 63:3 (Feb 1951), 35-9.
"Protectors of the Race" *TUR* 62:5 (Feb 1950), 23-7.

Carson, Bryant†
"Anchovies" *Pulp* 2:9 (15 June 1974), [3 pp].
"The First Wall" *Prism* 10:1 (Sum 1970), 44-60.
"I Can't Figure Anything Out Anymore but Then I Never Could Am I Doing What I Ought to or Merely What I Should?" *Elbow Room* (1979), 174-83.
"Leaving Home Again" *Pulp* 5:11 (31 Jan 1981), [4 pp].
"The Old House Was Being Eaten" *Elbow Room* (1979), 165-73.
"Presents from the Sea" *Elbow Room* (1979), 153-64.
"The Quest Theme in Canadian Literature" *Pulp* 1:2 (1 Dec 1972), [1].
"The Saint" *Pulp* 1:2 (1 Dec 1972), [1].
"The Same Old Story" *Pulp* 2:2 (1 Feb 1973), [2 pp].
"The Story of How Doctor Dalton Solved the Mystery About Who Killed Old Sleezer: A Murder Mystery" *Pulp* 1:15 (15 June 1973), [1].

Carson, Jane‡
"The Settler" *TUR* 63:3 (Feb 1951), 5-8.

Carson, Susan
"Dear God! Eternity" *Forge* 25:1 (Feb 1963), 59-64.
"Thy Will Be Done" *Forge* [24]:1 (Feb 1962), 19-23.

Carstairs, B.‡
"A Story" *Pulp* 3:4 (15 Aug 1975), [4].

Carter, Dyson†
"The Man Who Remembered Inhumanity: A Space Age Tale" *Uk Can* 18 (1 Jan 1964), 9-10.

Carter, Len – *See* Green, H. Gordon.

Carter, Shane‡
"We'll Go Hunting When I Get Home" *Scar Fair* 10 (1983), 36-40.

Caruso, Barbara
"Song" *Volume 63* No. 3 (Sum 1965), 51-2.

Carver, Patricia‡
"A Peach Tree on Lincoln Street" *Origins* 10:4 (Dec 1980), 26-30.

Cary, Joseph‡
"Homunculus" *J of Our Time* No. 3 (1982), 49-55.

Case, Geraldine†
"Aunt Emily Tells a Story" *Nfld Q* 53:4 (Dec 1954), 30-5.

Case, James G.‡ (1930-)
"The Mayor" *Jargon* 1958-59, 30-6.

Casey, Billy Lee‡
"This Transparent Static" *UC Gargoyle* [13] (Win 1967), [1 p].

Cash, Gwen†
"Bright Flowers for Elsie" *Lib* 30 (Dec 1953), 31, 60-2.

Casper, Claudia‡
"Lima without Ears" *Harvest* No. 4 (June 1978), 18-26.

Casselman, Bill‡
"Bedlamb Pasture" *Chiaroscuro* 8 (1964), 53-60.

Cassidy, Sky
"The Last River" *BC Monthly* 3:9 (June 1978), 62.

Castillo, Charles†
"The 'Arctic Cat' " *CFM* No. 12 (Win 1974), 65-73.
"Snicker-Snack, Crying Wolf" *Was R* 11:1 (Spr 1976), 33-44.

Cates, Helen†
"Cry of the Heart" *Edmonton Journal* Tue, 11 June 1968, 5.

Cathcart, Graham‡
"False to Your Calling" *Anglican Outlook* 5:6 (Apr 1950), 9.

Cathcart, L.M.†
" 'Say Mom Know What Happened in School Today?' " *This* 2:3 (Sum 1968), 91-2.

Caulfield, Johanne
"The Last Rose" *CCWQ* 5:1 (1983), 4-6 [Excerpt?].
"One Way Ticket" *Mont Writers' Forum* 1:8 (May 1979), 6-10.

Cavajnaro, Jack†
[Untitled] *Pits/Grit* [1977], [7 pp].

Cave, Gladys M.‡
See also Cave, Gladys M. and Whiteway, Mary Mercer.
"The Admiral" *AA* 52 (June 1962), 27-8.

Cave, Gladys M. and Whiteway, Mary Mercer‡
See also Cave, Gladys M.
"Drummer's Rock" *AA* 53 (Jan 1963), 43-4, 46-7.

Caverhill, Austin‡
"The Choice" *Forge* 1952, 54-61.

Cederstrom, J.C.‡
[Untitled] *Halcyon* 12 (Win 1966-67), 25.

Chabot, Nikki‡
"Ookpik's Winter" *AA* 55 (July 1965), 53-5.

Chafe, Fred†
"Death at Thanksgiving" *Forge* 1950, 40-4.

Chaisson, Michael‡
"The Night Clerk" *Pulp* 1:3 (15 Dec 1972), [2].

Challers, Jeff – *See* Gillese, John Patrick.

Challis, John‡
"Preface" *Laom R* 4 (Apr 1978), 6-9.

Chalmers, John W.‡
"The Smile of the Mortician" *CBC* "*Alberta Anthology*" 29 Oct 1983.
"The Tunnel" *AA* 67 (Jan 1977), 24-5.

Chalmers, Penny – *See* Kemp, Penny.

Chambers, Doug‡
"In the Night Season" *TUR* 74:4 (Sum 1961), 20-4.

Chambers, John†
"Ace Up His Sleeve" *Kaleidoscope* 1958, 10-2.
"The Morning Mr. Spelina's Great-Great-Grandfather Danced All Night at the Ball" *This* 2:3 (Sum 1968), 56-62.

Chambers, Patrick‡
"Please! Help Me!" *AA* 67 (Jan 1977), 37-8.

Chamish, Barry†
"The Climb" *Laom R* 4 (Apr 1978), 60-4.
"Epistle to Cindy-Sue" *Strange Faeces* No. 17 (June 1975), 38-40.

'The Kind of Guy" *Green's* 3:3 (Spr 1975), 55-8.
'The Pilgrim and the Fisherman" *Green's* 5:2 (Win 1977), 47-9.
'The Right Market" *NJ* No. 6 (June 1976), 51-3.

Chanady, Amaryll B.†
'The One-Way Ticket" *Antig R* No. 55 (Aut 1983), 79-83.

Chaplan, Lucille Singer†
'The Smell of Green" *Can Life* 1:5 (Fall 1950), 15-6, 37.

Chapman, Marie‡
"Sighing: From the Diary of Jane Queale" *Rampike* 3:2 [1983?], 53.

Chapman, Sheila‡
'Job Experience: Telephone Soliciting" *Inprint* 2:3 [n.d.], 18 [Untitled] *Inprint* 3:1 [n.d.], 27.

Chappell, Constance.
CANADIANS TOGETHER Toronto: United Church of Canada, n.d.
"Charting a New Course" *Canadians Together* [n.d.], 22-7.
"From Quebec to Hongkong" *Canadians Together* [n.d.], 17-21.
"Getting to Know Rachel" *Canadians Together* [n.d.], 44-50.
'The Good Samartian of the Sea" *Canadians Together* [n.d.], 28-30.
"Healing Hands" *Canadians Together* [n.d.], 51-6.
"Matt's Great Day" *Canadians Together* [n.d], 38-43.
"Miriam's Quest" *Canadians Together* [n.d.], 31-7.
'Ted of All People's" *Canadians Together* [n.d.], 3-9.
'They Met the Test" *Canadians Together* [n.d.], 10-6.

Chappus, Peggy Rae‡
"Sasquatch" *Generation* Spr 1968, 20-2.

Chard, Jean Marie (1947-)
"Space Greens" *Visions from the Edge* (1981), 187-91.

Charles, Barry†
"Egotizm" *Story So Far* 2 (1973), 33-43.

Charles, F.
"Trail of the Scrimshaw" *Black Cat* No. 1 (1981), 30-45.

Charney, Anne (1940?-)
"A Gift of Stamps" *Chat* 55 (Oct 1982), 116-7, 202, 206, 208.

Charr, Wendy‡
'The Dolphins" *CBC [Van] "Hornby Collection"* 17 Feb 1979.

Chatterton, John†
"Lulu of the D'Isturbed: A Poor Woman" *Acta Vic* 89:1 [1964], 35-42.
'The Mariposa Hunting Excursion" *Acta Vic* 88:2 [1964], 41-6.

Chatupa, James†
"I Saw Them in Love, Peter and Sue" *CFM* No. 1 (Win 1971), 56-61.

Cheesbrough, E.†
"Concerning Bodily Exercise" *AA* 56 (Feb 1966), 63.
"Orbituary" *AA* 56 (Sept 1965), 120.
"Some Recent Developments in the High Cost of Government" *AA* 56 (Jan 1966), 74.

Chen, Jean‡
"Hot Day" *Intervales* [No. 3 (1963?)], 20-1.

Chertkoff, Gary‡
"Interlude" *Muse* 61:1 (Dec 1951), 26-7.

Cheshire, John‡
"Perhaps a Myth" *J of Our Time* No. 2 (1979), 33.

Chevraux, Sharleen‡
"A Bracelet and a Telegram" *Can Golden West* 11 (Fall 1975), 30-1, 36.

Chevreau, Jonathan†
"The Chess Player" *Alpha* [1:5] (Feb 1977), 21-2.

Child, Robin‡
"Abandoned Carnival" *Origins* 9:1 (Mar 1979), 38 [Prose poem?].

Childerhose, Robert‡
"We Got Trouble, Captain" *Imp Oil R* 47 (June 1963), [1 p].

Chin, Frank‡
"Yes, Young Daddy" *Rikka* 7:2 (Sum 1980), 37-44.

Chisholm, Bennett‡
"The Jewel Studded Comb" CBC *"Alberta Anthology"* 25 Sept 1982.

Chiu, Mabel‡ (1955?-)
"The Dance" *Canadian Short Fiction Anthology* (1976), 53-5.
"Roots" *Revue* 2 No. 1 (1976), 31-3.

Chometsky, Harvey†
"Anyone's Autobiography" *Roothog* (1981), 67-9.

Choy, Wayson S.†
"The Sound of Waves" *Prism* 2:4 (Sum 1961), 4-16.

Choyce, Lesley (1952-)
EASTERN SURE Halifax: Nimbus, 1980.
"Beaverbrook in Love" *Potboiler* 1:6 (Spr-Sum 1983), 56-9.
"Boylan Briggs Salutes the New Cause" *Lunatic Gazette* Ser 2 1:2 (Nov-Dec 1982), 13-5.
"Buddha at the Laundromat: A Parable" *New Q* 2:2 (Sum 1982), 6-9.
"Cement" *Eastern Sure* (1980), 39-46.
"Conventional Emotions" *Dal R* 60 (1980), 508-16.
"The Cure" *Eastern Sure* (1980), 99-111.
"The Cure" *Puckerbrush R* 4:2 (Win 1982), 19-25 [Based on survey response].

"Dancing the Night Away" *Fid* No. 136 (June 1983), 63-8.
"Finishing Touch" *Eastern Sure* (1980), 113-22.
"Hake Massacre" *Chezzetcook* (1977), 103-6.
"Half Truths" *Portico* 5:1/2 [n.d.], 38-45.
"Happily Ever After" *Eastern Sure* (1980), 69-78.
"Inheriting the Earth" *New Q* 3:1 (Spr 1983), 25-32.
"It All Comes Back Now" *Eastern Sure* (1980), 13-8.
"The Loneliness of the Long Distance Writer" *Orion* 1:2 (1982), 18-20.
"Ordeal of Jimmy Robicheau" *Eastern Sure* (1980), 31-7.
"Ordeal of Jimmy Robicheau" *CCWQ* 3:1 (Win 1981), 20-1.
"The Portable Forest" *Nebula* Nos. 21/22 (1982), 102-8.
"Privileged Information" *Pot Port* 4 (1982-83), 46-8.
"The Public Good" *Eastern Sure* (1980), 91-8.
"The Reconciliation of Calan McGinty" *UWR* 15:1/2 (Fall-Win/Spr-Sum 1979-80), 102-8.
"The Reconciliation of Calan McGinty" *Eastern Sure* (1980), 79-89.
"The Return of Hanford McDermid" *Eastern Sure* (1980), 57-68.
"The Return of Hanford McDermid" *Matrix* No. 12 (Win 1981), 23-9.
"Ruben" *Chezzetcook* (1977), 49-54.
"Rupert Preston's Bad Year" *Pot Port* 1 (1979-80), 16-8.
"Rupert Preston's Bad Year" *Eastern Sure* (1980), 19-29.
"Rupert Preston's Bad Year" CBC *"Audio Stage"* Spr 1981 [Based on survey response].
"Saving Grace" *Eastern Sure* (1980), 47-55.
"Touch of a Vanished Hand" *New Q* 2:1 (Spr 1982), 17-23.
"Unadvertised Specials" *Writing* No. 6 (Spr 1983), 57-9.

Christensen, Helen F. – *See* Green, H. Gordon.

Christie, Jack‡
"Man in a Cannon" *Image Nation* 1:7 (Sat, 21 June 1969), [1 p].

Christie, Michael
"George and Lisbeth" *Edge* No. 8 (Fall 1968), 35-40.
"Rolling Down the Bowling Green" *Prism* 4:4 (Spr 1965), 22-31.
"What Has Wings But Cannot Fly?" *Prism* 5:2 (Aut 1965), 4-11.

Christopherson, Claudia‡
"Triptych" *Des* 12:4/13:1/2 Nos. 34/35/36 (1981-82), 113-5.

Christy, Jim (1945-)
" '51 Studebaker" *Alive* No. 40 [1974], 10-2.
" 'Bo" *Outlaws* (1974), 15-48.
"College Street Turnaround" *Des* Nos. 11/12 (Spr-Sum 1975), 84-6.
"How I Became Champ" *Toronto Short Stories* (1977), 88-95.
"My Fate" *Aurora* 1979 36-45.
"New Living Quarters" *Aurora* 1978 140-9.
"Nickel and Dime" CBC *"Anthology"* 14 Apr 1979.
"To Hell with This Cockeyed World" *Aurora* 1980 78-90.
"Too Old to Quit" *North American R* 265:3 (Sept 1980), 38-41.

Chryssoulakis, Mary
"Paper Dolls" *Living Message* 84 (June 1973), 19-21.
"Summer Vacation" *Polished Pebbles* (1974), 29-34.

Chuley [pseudonym]
"Back Alley Lord" *Communicator* 4:6 (Nov-Dec 1975), 18-22.

Chushingura [pseudonym]
"L'Amour est fini" *Scar Fair* 2 (1974-75), [3 pp].

Cinquant, Peter‡
"Ours Is the Cause of All Mankind" *20 Cents* 4:5/6 (June 1970), [6 pp].
"Tom Swift and His Giant Spoofnik or Saved by My Pink Underwear" *20 Cents* 4:7 (Sept 1970), [8 pp].

Clamp, Murray‡
"A Ghost in the House" *Bluenose* 1:4 (Spr 1977), 15-6.

Claraseumyra [pseudonym]
"My Story" *UC Gargoyle* [13] (Win 1967), [4 pp].

Clare, Jim†
"Unaware They Served" *War Cry* 25 July 1964, 5.

Clare, John P.
"Along Came Love" *American Mag* 151 (Apr 1951), 26-7, 84-90.
"The Day That Was Wonderful" *Extension* 54 (July 1959), 12[+?] [Based on CPLI].
"Diamonds in the Sky" *Collier's* 132 (30 Oct 1953), 38-41, 46-7.
"Double Solitaire" *Collier's* 130 (11 Oct 1952), 42.
"Easy Come, Easy Go" *Woman's Home Companion* 79 (Jan 1952), 20-1[+?] [Based on RGPL].
"The House Where My Heart Lives" *Collier's* 128 (22 Sept 1951), 24, 70-2, 74.
"The Night Grandma Swam the Lake" *MM* 70 (31 Aug 1957), 16-7, 29-32, 34.
"Out of Sight Out of Love" *Cosmopolitan* 141 (Dec 1956), 46-9[+?] [Based on RGPL].
"Some Day I'll Love You" *Woman's Home Companion* 78 (Dec 1951), 24-5[+?] [Based on RGPL].
"The Strange Death of Sam Fletcher" *MM* 63 (1 Sept 1950), 20, 33, 35-7.
"There's This Girl" *Collier's* 128 (6 Oct 1951), 34.
"Time Enough Tomorrow" *American Mag* 154 (Sept 1952), 24, 116-8, 120-1.
"Weep with Me" *Collier's* 130 (15 Nov 1952), 44.

Clark, D.M. (1937-)
"Above Two Forks: Sunday, February 11, 1917" *Cap R* No. 21 (1982), 21-6.
"Dawn at the Sleepy-Dust Motel" *Grain* 10:2 (May 1982), 22-3.
"Going Away" *Was R* 10:2 (Fall [1975]), 30-5.
"St. Jose[p]h Asylum: Fall 1915" *UWR* 16:2 (Spr-Sum 1982), 78-82.
"That Was a Good Year" *CF* 56 (Mar 1977), 16-7.

Clark, Flora‡
"Baptism" *UTR* 2:1 (Spr 1978), 15-6.

Clark, Isabel†

"Eanna" *Antig R* No. 11 (Aut 1972), 25-9.

Clark, Jennifer‡

"Fat and Furry" *Front* No. 5 (Oct 1978), [2 pp].

Clark, Joan (1934-)

FROM A HIGH THIN WIRE Edmonton: NeWest Press, 1982.

"The Dogs" *Dand* 2 (Spr-Sum 1976), 10-7.

"From a High Thin Wire" *From a High Thin Wire* (1982), 139-50.

"From a High Thin Wire" CBC *[Edm]* "*Alberta Anthology*" 8 Oct 1983.

"God's Country" *JCF* Nos. 31/32 (1981), 112-23.

"God's Country" *From a High Thin Wire* (1982), 9-24.

"The Hand on My Breast" *Waves* 6:3 (Spr 1978), 8-14.

"Her Father's Daughter" *Fid* No. 129 (Spr 1981), 5-13.

"Her Father's Daughter" *From a High Thin Wire* (1982), 25-38.

"Her Salvation" *JCF* No. 24 [1979], 42-51 [Also entitled "Salvation"].

"Historical Fiction" *From a High Thin Wire* (1982), 39-53.

"The Holy Roller Empire" *Chat* 54 (Jan 1981), 34, 102, 104-5, 108.

"The Holy Roller Empire" *From a High Thin Wire* (1982), 125-38.

"Italian Spaghetti" *From a High Thin Wire* (1982), 83-96.

"Passage by Water" *Br Out* 7:2 (1980), 16-21.

"Passage by Water" *From a High Thin Wire* (1982), 55-68.

"Rose Coloured Glasses" *CFM* No. 17 (Spr 1975), 51-8.

"Salvation" *From a High Thin Wire* (1982), 97-108 [Also entitled "Her Salvation"].

"Saturday Night Dance" *Was R* 13:2 (Fall 1978), 69-76.

"The Stuff Dreams Are Made Of" *Dal R* 57 (1977-78), 697-708.

"The Tail of the Female" *From a High Thin Wire* (1982), 69-82.

"The Tail of the Female" *Chat* 55 (Apr 1982), 62, 160-2, 164, 166, 168.

"Territory" *From a High Thin Wire* (1982), 109-24.

"Trip" *JCF* 2:1 (Win 1973), 8-9.

"What Happened to Maudie" *JCF* 2:4 (Fall 1973), 23-5.

Clark, Matthew†

"I Should Explain About Sally" *CFM* No. 17 (Spr 1975), 17-9.

Clark, Ross‡

"Going Down" *Adder* 1:2 [1961?], 6.

Clarke, Andrew C.†

"Diamonds of Vengeance" *Green's* 2:4 (Sum 1974), 28-31.

Clarke, Austin C. (1934-)

WHEN HE WAS FREE AND YOUNG AND HE USED TO WEAR SILKS Toronto: House of Anansi Press, 1971.

"The Collector" *Transatlantic R* No. 24 (Spr 1967), 24-37.

"The Collector" *Stories from The Transatlantic Review* (1970), 62-74.

"The Collector" CBC "*Anthology*" 3 Feb 1973.

"Early Early Early One Morning" *Bim* 10 No. 38 (Jan-June 1964), 78-88 [Also entitled "An Easter Carol"].

"Early Early Early One Morning" *West Indian Stories* (1981), 33-47.

"An Easter Carol" *Mont* 38 (Apr 1964), 35-40. [Also entitled "Early Early Early One Morning"].

"An Easter Carol" *When He Was Free* (1971), 1-15.

"An Easter Carol" *Stories Plus* (1979), 32-43.

"An Easter Carol" CBC "*Anthology*" 5 Apr 1980.

"The Ending Up Is the Starting Out" *Bim* 9 No. 35 (July-Dec 1962), 181-3.

"Four Stations in His Circle" *SN* 80 (Dec 1965), 23-7.

"Four Stations in His Circle" *When He Was Free* (1971), 51-63.

"Give It a Shot" CBC "*Anthology*" 16 Aug 1980.

"Give It a Shot" *J of Caribbean Studies* 2 (1981), 39-50.

"Give It a Shot" CBC "*Anthology*" 1982 [Based on story collection *When Women Rule* (1985)].

"Give Us This Day: And Forgive Us" *Tam R* No. 38 (Win 1966), 21-34 [Excerpt?].

"Give Us This Day: And Forgive Us" *When He Was Free* (1971), 64-79.

"Griff!" *Tam R* No. 58 (1971), 34-50.

"Hammie and the Black Dean" *New American Review* 14 (1972), 219-47.

"Hammie and the Black Dean" *Many Windows* (1982), 253-79.

"I Hanging On, Praise God!" *Bim* 9 No. 36 (Jan-June 1963), 275-81.

"I Hanging On, Praise God!" *From the Green Antilles* (1966), 93-100.

"An Invitation to Join" *Lit R* 1:1 (1983), 46-53.

"Leaving This Island Place" *Bim* 10 No. 40 (Jan-June 1965), 240-9.

"Leaving This Island Place" *When He Was Free* (1971), 130-9.

"Leaving This Island Place" CBC "*Anthology*" 3 July 1971.

"Leaving This Island Place" *This Island Place* (1981), 3-11.

"The Motor Car" *When He Was Free* (1971), 90-111.

"The Motor Car" *Here and Now* (1977), 96-113.

"On One Leg" CBC "*Anthology*" 14 Aug 1971.

"The Rendezvous" CBC "*Anthology*" 15 July 1978.

"Short Story" *Evidence* No. 3 (Fall 1961), 31-4.

"They Heard a Ringing of Bells" *Evidence* No. 7 (Sum 1963), 5-18.

"They Heard a Ringing of Bells" CBC "*Anthology*" 16 Aug 1964.

"They Heard a Ringing of Bells" *When He Was Free* (1971), 16-29.

"They Heard a Ringing of Bells" *Stories from Ontario* (1974), 56-69.

"They Heard a Ringing of Bells" *Canada in Us Now* (1976), 48-58.

"They Heard a Ringing of Bells" *Toronto Short Stories* (1977), 74-87.

"They Heard a Ringing of Bells" *Literature in Canada* (1978), 505-15.

"This Black Woman Sure Has Problems Like Hell" CBC "*Anthology*" 26 Sept 1970

[Title unknown] *Liberté* 11 (mars-avril 1969), 93-105 [As "Un problème de cabinet"; trans. Hubert Aquin].

"Waiting for the Postman to Knock" *Bim* 10 No. 39 (July-Dec 1964), 159-70.

"Waiting for the Postman to Knock" *When He Was Free* (1971), 30-50.

"A Wedding in Toronto" *Tam R* No. 45 (Aut 1967), 54-8, 60, 62-4.

"A Wedding in Toronto" *Canadian Writing Today* (1970), 223-31.

"A Wedding in Toronto" *When He Was Free* (1971), 80-9.

"A Wedding in Toronto" *Immigrant Experience* (1975), 85-93.

"What Happened?" *Evergreen R* 14 No. 85 (Dec 1970), 21-2, 61-7.

"What Happened?" *Prejudice* (1971), 189-204.

"What Happened?" *When He Was Free* (1971), 112-29.

"When He Was Free and Young and He Used to Wear Silks" CBC "Anthology" 6 Mar 1971.

"When He Was Free and Young and He Used to Wear Silks" CF 51 (Oct 1971), 20-3, 58.

"When He Was Free and Young and He Used to Wear Silks" When He Was Free (1971), 140-51.

"When the Letter Came Back" Mont 39 (Jan 1965), 25-30.

"Why Didn't You Use a Plunger?" CBC "Anthology" 3 Oct 1967.

"Why Didn't You Use a Plunger?" Tam R No. 52 (1969), 51-7, 60-2.

"Why Didn't You Use a Plunger?" Yale Literary Mag 138:3 (Fall 1969), 26-30.

"Why Didn't You Use a Plunger?" CBC "Anthology" 19 Sept 1970.

"Why Didn't You Use a Plunger?" Toronto Book (1976), 166-76.

"The Woman with the BBC Voice" Tam R No. 29 (Aut 1963), 27-35.

"Words, Words, Words Is the Future" Bim 10 No. 37 (July-Dec 1963), 29-35.

Clarke, Bob†
"Not Quiet Cricket" Raven 1:1 (Dec 1955), 10-1.

Clarke, David‡
"The Disney Murder" Blow Up 1:6 (July-Aug 1980), [2 pp].

Clarke, Gwendoline P.
"Anniversary House" FH 20 Mar 1952, 28-9.
"Brown Coat" FH 6 Sept 1951, 22-3.

Clarke, H.D.‡
"The Cross Is Bent" Prism (Mont) No. 2 (1956), 26-31.

Clarke, James‡
"The Departure" Acta Vic 74:4 (Feb 1950), 26-30.
"The Dream" Acta Vic 75:2 (Dec 1950), 43-8.

Clarke, John J.†
"They Do Not Discriminate" Fifth Page 1962, 5-8.

Clarkson, Dave – See Green, H. Gordon.

Clarkson, Vi‡
"The Longest Hour" Edmonton Journal Fri, 1 Dec 1967, 39.

Claxton, Lillian†
IN HIGH SECURITY AND OTHER STORIES Kingston: Daily News Office, n.d [Non-fiction? Pre-1950? Based on Miller].

Clayton, Thomas‡
"The Chronicle of Alexandra Atherton" Deaf Can 4:8 (Aug-Sept 1979), 23-4.

Clegg, Robin‡
"Archie" Alive No. 26 [1973], 16.

Cleland, Elizabeth‡
"The Firmament of Time" TUR 66:4 (Mar 1954), 30-4.

Clemence, Esme†
"In Search of Graham Greene" *Fid* No. 97 (Spr 1973), 82-9.

Clement, Bill‡
"Mrs. Trudeau's Diary" *Trup* 1:1 [1971], 16-7.
"Spider" *Trup* 1:1 [1971], 13-4.
"What It's Like" *Trup* 1:1 [1971], 14.

Clement, John†
"The Boy in the Picture" *Quarry* 29:3 (Sum 1980), 55-6.
"Love, Lost and Found" *Des* 12:4/13:1/2 Nos. 34/35/36 (1981-82), 130-4.

Clement, Steve‡
"One Left Turn Too Many" *Cop Toad* 1:4 (May 1978), 85-92.

Clemmer, E.F.‡
"Ice Carnival" *West People* No. 177 (24 Feb 1983), 6-7.

Clifford, Wayne‡
"An Interruption" *Story So Far* 5 (1978), 43-7.
"Portrait of a Final Summer" *UC Gargoyle* [10] (Jan 1964), [2 pp].

Clifton, Merritt
"The Almost-Didn't" *Samisdat* 21:1 (1979), 61-7.
"Born Again" *Samisdat* 19:1 (1979), 77-83.
"Death's Head" *Samisdat* 22:3 (1979), 32-6.
"Incest" *Matrix* Nos. 6/7 (1978), 107-15.
"Of Truth and Shadows" *Matrix* No. 14 (Win 1982), 62-7.
"The Prince of Peace" *Samisdat* 17:1 (1978), 55-64.
"The Wind Blows Around" *Samisdat* 15:1 (1977), 56-68.
"Windows & She" *Samisdat* 21:2 (1979), 16-20.

Cline, Amanda‡
"Truck Start" *Writers News Man* 4:2 (Dec 1982), 15-20.

Clink, Beatrice†
"A Ride for Life" *Alberta Speaks* 1957, 29-33.

Clissold, Carol – *See* Green, H. Gordon.

Clovis, An‡
"Slave to Tradition" *Cop Toad* 1:4 (May 1978), 10-4.

Coates, Eleanor‡
"But Not for Keeps" *AA* 52 (June 1962), 37-40, 42, 44.

Cobban, William‡
"Hands" *Contact* 3:3 (Sum-Fall 1974), 2-7.

Coburn, Marion†
"Problem(s) in Paradise" *Selections from the C.F.U.W. Writing Project 1978-79*
13-7.

Cockell, Douglas‡
"Mordred" *Sowing* [1972?], 35-40.

Cockerill, A.W.†
"Angakok of Kiglapait" *North* 19 (Nov-Dec 1972), 28-31.

Cockrell, Patricia M.‡
"Sardine Sandwiches" *Scar Fair* 7 (1979-80), 16-8.

Coggon, Myrtle Amelia‡
"Morning for Ever" *AA* 51 (July 1961), 60, 62-4.

Cogswell, Fred (1917-)
"An Evening with Emily" *Trace* No. 61 (Sum 1966), 186-9.

Cohen, Annette‡
"The Spiritual Life of Sari Green" *CBC "Anthology"* 13 Feb 1968.

Cohen, David‡
"Mrs. Lumner" *Prism* (Mont) No. 7 (Mar 1964), 42-9.

Cohen, Leonard (1934-)
"Barbers and Lovers" *Ingluvin* No. 2 (Spr 1971), 10-9.
"Luggage Fire Sale" *Parallel* 1:2 (May-June 1966), 40-4.
"Luggage Fire Sale" *Partisan R* 36 (1969), 91-9.
"Trade" *Tam R* No. 20 (Sum 1961), 59-65.

Cohen, Matt (1942-)
CAFÉ LE DOG Toronto: McClelland & Stewart, 1983.
COLUMBUS AND THE FAT LADY AND OTHER STORIES Toronto: House of Anansi Press, 1972.
THE EXPATRIATE: COLLECTED SHORT STORIES Toronto: General, 1982.
NIGHT FLIGHTS Toronto: Doubleday, 1978.
TOO BAD GALAHAD (Toronto: Coach House Press, 1972).
"After Dinner Butterflies" *Columbus and the Fat Lady* (1972), 145-52.
"After Dinner Butterflies" *JD* Rosh Hashanah 1972, 12-3.
"After Dinner Butterflies" *Modern Canadian Stories* (1975), 263-9.
"After Dinner Butterflies" *Air* (1977), 103-5.
"After Dinner Butterflies" *Literature in Canada* (1978), 684-8.
"After Dinner Butterflies" *Expatriate* (1982), 83-8.
"Amazing Grace" *73: New Canadian Stories* 105-9.
"At the Empress Hotel" *Mal R* No. 59 (July 1981), 100-19.
"At the Empress Hotel" *Café Le Dog* (1983), 141-64.
"Brain Dust" *Night Flights* (1978), 167-80.
"Brain Dust" *Expatriate* (1982), 271-84.
"Brothers" *Night Flights* (1978), 17-27.
"Brothers" *Expatriate* (1982), 121-31.
"Café Le Dog" *Café Le Dog* (1983), 165-82.
"Christmas Lost and Found" *Weekend* 26 (25 Dec 1976), 4-6.
"The Colours of War" *CBC "Anthology"* 1 Oct 1977 [Excerpt?].
"Columbus and the Fat Lady" *Columbus and the Fat Lady* (1972), 197-213.
"Columbus and the Fat Lady" *Night Flights* (1978), 29-43.

"Columbus and the Fat Lady" *Penguin Book of Canadian Short Stories* (1980), 443-55.

"Columbus and the Fat Lady" *Expatriate* (1982), 285-98.

"Country Music" *Columbus and the Fat Lady* (1972), 69-80.

"Country Music" *Night Flights* (1978), 103-12.

"Country Music" *Expatriate* (1982), 227-36.

"The Cure" *Night Flights* (1978), 1-16.

"The Cure" *Expatriate* (1982), 143-58.

"Death of a Friend" *SN* 91 (July-Aug 1976), 52-7.

"Death of a Friend" *Toronto Short Stories* (1977), 176-90.

"Death of a Friend" *Night Flights* (1978), 145-59.

"Death of a Friend" *Expatriate* (1982), 249-63.

"Death of a Guppy" *Café Le Dog* (1983), 103-13.

"The Empty Room" *Columbus and the Fat Lady* (1972), 155-63.

"The Empty Room" *Imp* 2:1 (Aut 1972), 5-13.

"The Empty Room" *Fiction of Contemporary Canada* (1980), 155-60.

"The Empty Room" *Expatriate* (1982), 89-95.

"The End" CBC *"Anthology"* 6 Nov 1971.

"The End" *Imp* No. 1 (1971), 27-34.

"The End" *Columbus and the Fat Lady* (1972), 23-30.

"The End" CBC *"Anthology"* 26 Feb 1972.

"The End" *Expatriate* (1982), 29-34.

"The Expatriate" *Expatriate* (1982), 1-20.

"The Expatriate" *Penguin Book of Modern Canadian Short Stories* (1982), 529-46.

" 'Franz' " *CF* 56 (Feb 1977), 41-4.

"The Funeral" CBC *"Anthology"* 4 Sept 1971.

"Glass Eyes and Chickens" *Har* 1:4 (Nov-Dec 1976), 24-8.

"Glass Eyes and Chickens" *Night Flights* (1978), 93-102.

"Glass Eyes and Chickens" *Expatriate* (1982), 217-26.

"Golden Whore of the Heartland" *CFM* Nos. 45/46 (1982-83), 113-48.

"Golden Whore of the Heartland" *Café Le Dog* (1983), 9-60.

"The Hanged Man" *Har* 1:5 (Jan-Feb 1977), 60-3, 65-6.

"The Hanged Man" *Night Flights* (1978), 57-67.

"The Hanged Man" *Expatriate* (1982), 171-81.

"Heyfitz" *Night Flights* (1978), 135-44.

"Heyfitz" *Expatriate* (1982), 207-16.

"I Dreamed I Saw the Queen Last Night" *Per* Nos. 7/8 (Win 1981), 116.

"In Search of Inspiration" *Imp* 9:1 (Spr 1981), 17-21.

"Janice" CBC *"Anthology"* 2 Dec 1972.

"Janice" *Columbus and the Fat Lady* (1972), 83-93.

"Janice" *Night Flights* (1978), 83-91.

"Janice" *Expatriate* (1982), 197-205.

"Keeping Fit" *Columbus and the Fat Lady* (1972), 63-6.

"Keeping Fit" *JD* Rosh Hashanah 1972, 7.

"Keeping Fit" *Great Canadian Sports Stories* (1979), 122-4.

"Keeping Fit" *Expatriate* (1982), 57-8.

"Life on This Planet" *Café Le Dog* (1983), 61-75.

"A Literary History of Anton" *Story So Four* (1976), 97-101.

"A Literary History of Anton" *Night Flights* (1978), 161-6.

"A Literary History of Anton" *Expatriate* (1982), 265-70.

"Loose Change" *Story So Far* 3 (1974), 151-4.

"Loose Change" *CFM* No. 13 (Spr 1974), 4-8.

"A Love for the Infinite" *North American R* 265:2 (June 1980), 24-7.

"A Love for the Infinite" *Café Le Dog* (1983), 131-40.

"Nihilism or Insanity: The Strange Life of Ichabod Oise" *This* 1:4 (Aut 1967), 49-56.

"The Nurse from Outer Space" *Columbus and the Fat Lady* (1972), 49-60.

"The Nurse from Outer Space" *Expatriate* (1982), 47-55.

"Our Passion Lit the Night" *Columbus and the Fat Lady* (1972), 33-47.

"Our Passion Lit the Night" *Expatriate* (1982), 35-46.

"Pat Frank's Dream" *Aurora* 1978 199-206.

"The Secret" *74: New Canadian Stories* 125-32.

"The Secret" *Night Flights* (1978), 125-33.

"The Secret" *Expatriate* (1982), 133-41.

"Sentimental Meetings" *Café Le Dog* (1983), 114-30.

"The Sins of Tomas Benares" *CFM* No. 43 (1982), 14-32.

"The Sins of Tomas Benares" *Café Le Dog* (1983), 76-102.

"Spadina Time" *Columbus and the Fat Lady* (1972), 183-95.

"Spadina Time" *Story So Far* 2 (1973), 44-53.

"Spadina Time" *Expatriate* (1982), 111-20.

"Straight Poker" *Columbus and the Fat Lady* (1972), 129-43.

"Straight Poker" *CBC "Anthology"* 26 Aug 1972.

"Straight Poker" *Quarry* 22:4 (Aut 1973), 15-27.

"Straight Poker" *Expatriate* (1982), 69-81.

"Summer Crossings" *Sewanee R* 87 (1979), 55-72.

"Too Bad Galahad" *Columbus and the Fat Lady* (1972), 165-80.

"Too Bad Galahad" *Expatriate* (1982), 97-109.

"Too Sweet Sorrow" *CBC "Anthology"* 18 Oct 1969.

"The Toy Pilgrim" *Columbus and the Fat Lady* (1972), 95-115.

"The Toy Pilgrim" *Night Flights* (1978), 69-82.

"The Toy Pilgrim" *Expatriate* (1982), 183-96.

"Uncle Philbert and His Big Surprise" *Columbus and the Fat Lady* (1972), 117-27.

"Uncle Philbert and His Big Surprise" *Expatriate* (1982), 59-67.

"The Universal Miracle" *Night Flights* (1978), 113-23.

"The Universal Miracle" *Expatriate* (1982), 237-47.

"Vogel" *Night Flights* (1978), 45-55.

"Vogel" *CBC "Anthology"* 28 Jan 1978.

"Vogel" *TL* Mar 1978, 44, 113, 115, 117.

"Vogel" *Expatriate* (1982), 159-69.

"The Watchmaker" *Columbus and the Fat Lady* (1972), 11-20.

"The Watchmaker" *Spice Box* (1981), 72-8.

"The Watchmaker" *Expatriate* (1982), 21-8.

"A Week in New York" *SN* 95 (Dec 1980), 66-71.

Cohn, Judith‡

"Television" *VWFP/Revue* 1:2 (Apr 1975), 4, 12.

Cohn, Marlene‡

"Journeys" *UCR* 1977-78, 37-40.

"Not with a Bang" *CBC "Anthology"* 19 Nov 1977.

Colby, Elsie Wilson†
"Mission John" *Onward* 25 May 1958, 330-1, 335.

Cole, David
"The Last Resort" *Axiom* 2:3 (Feb-Mar 1976), 34-50.

Cole, Michael‡
"Sunday" *Fifth Page* 1967, 21-3.

Cole, Patricia‡
"Our Super-pet's About to Pop" *20 Cents* 4:7 (Sept 1970), [4 pp] [Prose poem?].

Cole, Pete – *See* Green, H. Gordon.

Coleman, Thelma†
"Wilderness Marriage" *QQ* 77 (1970), 89-98.

Coleman, Victor (1944-)
See also Coleman, Victor and Fones, Robert; Coleman, Victor and Young, David A.
"Old Man" *CF* 44 (Nov 1964), 183-4.
"Pulp" *Rampike* 3:1 (1983), 26-7.
"What's Been Happening to God's Kingdom Since 1914?" *Ant's Forefoot* No. 3 (Win 1969), 17.

Coleman, Victor and Fones, Robert
See also Coleman, Victor; Coleman, Victor and Young, David A.; Fones, Robert and Nations, Opal L.; Fones, Robert.
"The Polychromatic Murmurs" *Writ* No. 4 (Spr 1972), 71-3.

Coleman, Victor and Young, David A.
See also Coleman, Victor; Coleman, Victor and Fones, Robert; d'Or, Vic and Young, David; Young, David.
"De Z-shore" *Writ* No. 4 (Spr 1972), 68-70.
"Flying" *Cap R* No. 5 (Spr 1974), 57.
"History of Poets: Benny Goodman" *Cap R* No. 5 (Spr 1974), 58-60.
"Hitch Hype" *Cap R* No. 5 (Spr 1974), 58.

Collective, April
"The Ones We Never See" *Alive* No. 38 [1974], 12.
"Our Inheritance: Struggle Ever, Capitulation Never!" *Alive* No. 46 (Dec-Jan 1975-76), 10.

Colley, Kenneth – *See* Dyba, Kenneth.

Collicott, George‡
"Younger Days" *Dime Bag* [No. 18] Fiction Issue 1 (Mar 1977), 1-5.

Collier, Diana G.
"The Birth of My Father" *Fid* No. 94 (Sum 1972), 94-103.
"Catharsis" *JCF* 2:4 (Fall 1973), 30-6.
"The Collapse of Empires" *Inscape* 13:1 (Fall 1976), 41-57.
"A Good Time in the Old Town" *Prism* 13:2 (Win 1973), 20-8.

"Love Letter to a Friend" *Fid* No. 105 (Spr 1975), 26-37.
"Orchids After Midnight" *Was R* 11:1 (Spr 1976), 71-9.
"Prodigal Son" *Antig R* No. 30 (Sum 1977), 47-58.
"The Things You Do" *CBC "Anthology"* 2 Aug 1975.

Collings, Simon‡
"Death" *Des* 13:4 No. 38 (Fall 1982), 75-84.
"A Prodigal Tale" *Des* 14:2 No. 40 (Spr 1983), 99-110.

Collins, Anne (1952-)
"First Flight" *Aurora* 1979 20-32.
"Help Wanted" *Fireweed* No. 10 (Spr 1981), 23-6.
"Uncle Hoffer and the Hat" *West Producer* [1966?] [Based on survey response].

Collins, David M.
"Directions" *Writ* No. 3 (Win 1972), 93-103.
"Down Among the Wallabies" *Writ* No. 7 (Fall 1975), 5-9.
"Games" *Writ* No. 2 (Win-Spr 1971), 24-35.
"Home Country" *Writ* No. 1 (Spr 1970), 18-26.
"Notes for the Twelfth of May" *Writ* No. 4 (Spr 1972), 5-11.
"Strategies" *Story So Far* 2 (1973), 17-24.

Collins, Michael‡
"Fat Albert" *Contact* 4:1 (Spr 1975), 25-9.
"Lincoln – Man or Myth?" *VWFP/Revue* 1:6 (Aug 1975), 8.
"A Push for Cupid" *Contact* 3:4 (Win 1974), 14-8.

Collins, Pamela‡
"On Welsh and Names" *CBC "Alberta Anthology"* 20 Nov 1982.

Collins, R.G.†
"Appetites" *Was R* 17:1 (Spr 1982), 60-86.

Colonel Smith – *See* Smith, Colonel.

Colson, Theodore (1935-)
"The Black House" *Stubborn Strength* (1983), 130-3.
"The Dog Did It" *JCF* No. 24 [1979], 34-41.
"The Path to Haydon Pool" *AA* 70 (Jan 1980), 49, 51-2.
"The Pergola" *Antig R* No. 31 (Aut 1977), 21-32.
"The Saving of Sister Oothout" *JCF* No. 19 (1977), 31-7.
"Sunday Morning as a Kaleidoscope" *JCF* 4:3 No. 15 (1975), 22-6.
"The Valley of Achor" *Pot Port* 4 (1982-83), 4-7.

Colter, Rob‡
"Summer's Wind" *NJ* Nos. 7/8 (1976), 75-82.

Colton, Janice Holland†
"Requiem of a Passage" *Whetstone* Spr 1973, 20-2.

Colucci, Joseph‡
"The Worst Is Not" *Prism* (Mont) [No. 1] (1955), 59-62.

Colville, C.‡

"Always Look Back" *First Encounter* 1968-69, [5 pp].

Colwill, Elaine†

"The Pilgrim Express" *Waterloo R* No. 6 (Win 1961), 31-40.

Conard, Audrey‡

"Consideration" *Room* 5:3 (1980), 47-9.

Conde, Carole and Beveridge, Karl‡

"Standing Up" *Image Nation* No. 25 (Sum 1982), 30-5.

Coney, Michael G. (1932-)

"The Bridge on the Scraw" *Fantasy and Science Fiction* 45 (July 1973), 112-24.
"Catapult to the Stars" *Fantasy and Science Fiction* 52 (Apr 1977), 90-110.
"The Gateway to Now" *Fantasy and Science Fiction* 47 (July 1974), 76-89.
"The Hook, the Eye and the Whip" *Seven Deadly Sins of Science Fiction* (1980), 293-317.
"The Initiation of Akasa" *Fantasy and Science Fiction* 46 (Jan 1974), 145-58.
"The Manya" *Fantasy and Science Fiction* 44 (Mar 1973), 120-34.
"Penny on a Sky Horse" *Galileo* Nos. 11/12 (1979), 49-55.
"Sixth Sense" *Vision of Tomorrow* 1:1 (Aug 1969), 43-9.
"Starthinker 9" *Andromeda* 1 (1979), 25-35.
"Susanna, Susanna!" *Fantasy and Science Fiction* 43 (Nov 1972), 144-58.
"The Tertiary Justification" *New Writings in SF* 21 (1972; 1973), 147-89.
"Those Good Old Days of Liquid Fuel" *Fantasy and Science Fiction* 50 (Jan 1976), 63-82.
"Troubleshooter" *Worlds of If* 20 (May 1970), 27-37, 143-5.

Conger, Lesley

See also Conger, Lesley and Aaron, Michael.
"Another One" *Ladies Home J* 75 (July 1958), 56, 119.
"The Boy in the Dream" *Ladies Home J* 74 (May 1957), 71, 149-50.
"Daughter of Kings" *Ladies Home J* 74 (July 1957), 62, 84-6.
"[A?] Dream of the South Seas" *Cosmopolitan* 148 (Apr 1960), 91-3[+?] [Based on RGPL].
"Forever Young" *Woman's Home Companion* 79 (Aug 1952), 28-9[+?] [Based on RGPL].
"A Hat for Billy Jim" *MM* 64 (1 Feb 1951), 18-9, 30-1.
"Hayaqwas and the Cross" *Weekend* 1 (17 Nov 1951), 19, 32-3, 35.
"Hayaqwas and the Cross" *Stories with John Drainie* (1963), 30-5.
"Heart of the Family" *Good Housekeeping* 164 (Apr 1967), 106-7.
"[The?] Indispensable Woman" *Redbook* 119 (Aug 1962), 46-7[+?] [Based on RGPL].
"The Inside Window" *Ladies Home J* 76 (Jan 1959), 34, 91.
"It's Very Dark by Six" *Cosmopolitan* 150 (Jan 1961), 92-5[+?] [Based on RGPL].
"Let Me Cherish This Child" *Good Housekeeping* 155 (Sept 1962), 75, 127-8, 130, 133.
"Lies" *Weekend* 5 (11 June 1955), 33, 35.
"A Little World So Big" *Weekend* 3 (22 Aug 1953), 14-5.
"The Pest" *Weekend* 4 (12 June 1954), 24-5.

"The Summer Cabin" *Stories with John Drainie* (1963), 76-81.
"[The?] Third Party" *Cosmopolitan* 148 (Mar 1960), 87-9[+?] [Based on RGPL].
"They Never Tell Anyone" *Weekend* 2 (2 Feb 1952), 12-3, 25.
"The Voters Love a Happy Family" *CF* 36 (Sept 1956), 132, 134.
"When You Give Your Heart" *Good Housekeeping* 157 (July 1963), 59, 167-9.
"[A?] Whisper. A Kiss" *Redbook* 116 (Jan 1961), 48-9[+?] [Based on RGPL].
"The White Kitten" *FH* 20 Feb 1958, 28-9.

Conger, Lesley and Aaron, Michael
See also Conger, Lesley.
"Love in a Flash" *Weekend* 4 (29 May 1954), 36.
"The Watchers" *Weekend* 4 (16 Oct 1954), 11, 45, 53.
"The Wolf Pup" *Weekend* 4 (2 Oct 1954), 14, 47-8.

Conlon, Jim‡
"No Prophet Now" *Alive* 1:3 (Feb [1970]), [3 pp].

Conly, Susan†
"Amid the Glory" *Pres Record* 105 (Dec 1981), 2-3 [Non-fiction?].
"Celebration" *Pres Record* 106 (Apr 1982), 2-3.
"The Deep Treasure" *Pres Record* 104 (Mar 1980), 2-3 [Non-fiction?].
"What Is That in Your Hand?" *Pres Record* 104 (July-Aug 1980), 2-3.

Conn, Desmond‡
"Christmas Candle" *AA* 47 (Dec 1956), 43-5.

Conner, Orville†
"Last Tears of Boyhood" *JCF* Nos. 17/18 (1976), 43-9.

Connolly, Jacqueline
"A Fly Buzzing" *Variations on a Gulf Breeze* (1973), 45-8.
"Snowball" *Island Women* (1982), 24-6.

Connolly, Michael†
"The Resolution" *WWR* 1:3 (Spr 1978), 50-1.

Connor, Will
"African Violets" *CSSM* 3:2 (Spr 1977), 29-33.

Conroy, Tom‡
"Ride in the Night" *AA* 55 (Mar 1965), 48.

Conway, Jim‡
"To the Bay" *Gram* 1:4 (Apr 1976), 21-6.

Conway, Maggie‡
"Men Wanted" *Gram* 2:1 (31 Oct 1976), 1-7.

Cook, A.‡
"Morning" *Chiaroscuro* 8 (1964), 7.

Cook, David‡
"The Frozen Phoenix" *Targya* 1:1 [n.d.], [4 pp].

Cook, David R. Southwick†
"It Is Old and It Is Beautiful" *Laom R* 1:1 (Dec-Jan 1975), 53-5.

Cook, George†
"Doubles" *Laom R* 3:1 (Mar 1977), 60-4.
"Love for Learning: A Tale of Passion and Poetry" *UTR* 1:1 (Spr 1977), 22-4.

Cook, Gregory M.‡
"Bonfire on the Beach" *AA* 52 (July 1962), 60, 62-4.
"The Cigarette Pack" *Amethyst* 3:3 (Spr 1964), 34-9.
"City Date" *Amethyst* 3:3 (Spr 1964), 43-8.
"Mulatto Girl" *Amethyst* 3:3 (Spr 1964), 40-2.
"My Babysitter" *Amethyst* 1:1 (Spr 1962), 24-5.

Cook, Hilary‡
[Untitled] *Scar Fair* 10 (1983), 19.
[Untitled] *Scar Fair* 10 (1983), 66.

Cook, Hugh (1942-)
"A Canadian Education" *Des* 11:1/2 Nos. 27/28 (1980), 197-209.
"Clown" *Fid* No. 130 (Sum 1981), 39-50.
"Cracked Wheat – 1" *Antig R* No. 39 (Aut 1979), 13-23.
"Exodus" *Mal R* No. 51 (July 1979), 53-64.
"First Snow" *NeWest R* 5 (Oct 1979), 10-2.
"A Lesson in Dance" *Vanguard* 11:4 (July-Aug 1981), 6-7.
"The White Rabbit" *Was R* 13:1 (Spr 1978), 23-30.

Cook, Michael
"The Bunkhouse" *CBC "Anthology"* 20 May 1978.
"Old Charlie" *Voices Down East* [1973], 34-5.

Cooke, Ronald J.‡
"Beginner's Luck" *Atl Guardian* 7 (Aug 1950), 34-8.

Cooke, Walter†
"Brown Penny" *Tawow* 7:1 (1980), 37.

Coombes, Blaine†
"Negatives" *Cap R* No. 22 (1982), 5-10.
"Rough Sketch" *Cap R* No. 22 (1982), 11-8.

Coombs, Vera†
"No Humming of Wires" *Contact* 2:11 (Fall 1973), 9-11.

Cooper, Anne‡
"Sisters" *TUR* 91:1 (Nov 1977), 18-22.

Cooper, Audrey‡
"Honestly, It's Nothing" *Contact* 3:3 (Sum-Fall 1974), 14-6.
"A Tale from Life on the Danforth" *Contact* 4:1 (Spr 1975), 2-8.

Cooper, Bill‡
"Crawl of the Open Road" *Acta Vic* 76:2 (Dec 1951), 17-9.

Cooper, Bob‡

"Ada and the Raccoon" *UCR* Spr 1976, 43-51.

Cooper, Jas E.‡

"Hobby" *Origins* 10:4 (Dec 1980), 66.

"Skipping the Facts of Life" *Origins* 10:4 (Dec 1980), 65.

Cooper, Mel

"Beginnings" *Des* 12:2/3 Nos. 32/33 (1981), 109-15.

"A Change in Circumstances or Fanny's Courtship: A Romance" *Des* 10:3/4 Nos. 25/26 (1979), 172-89.

"The Glass Lampshade" *Des* 12:2/3 Nos. 32/33 (1981), 145-55.

"The Promised Land" *Des* Nos. 8/9 (Spr-Sum 1974), 57-61.

Cooperman, Stanley Roy

"Walk to the Station" *Playboy Book of Crime and Suspense* (1966), 65-70.

Copeland, Ann [pseudonym] (1932-)

AT PEACE Ottawa: Oberon Press, 1978.

THE BACK ROOM Ottawa: Oberon Press, 1979.

"At Peace" *CFM* No. 22 (Sum 1976), 81-99.

"At Peace" *77: Best Canadian Stories* 187-215.

"At Peace" *Best American Short Stories* 1977 43-65.

"At Peace" *At Peace* (1978), 138-64.

"At Peace" *Stories Plus* (1979), 48-68.

"At Peace" *Timely and Timeless* [1983?] [Based on survey response].

"The Back Room" *Back Room* (1979), 23-38.

"The Bear's Paw" *Back Room* (1979), 59-72.

"Beginning" *UWR* 14:1 (Fall-Win 1978), 42-56.

"Beginning" *Back Room* (1979), 5-22.

"Cassie" *Back Room* (1979), 103-21.

"Cloister" *Western Humanities R* 29 (1975), 269-82.

"Cloister" *At Peace* (1978), 93-108.

"Distance" *Pot Port* 3 (1981-82), 6-8.

"Distance" *Easterly* (1983), 40-8.

"Fame" *Fid* No. 133 (July 1982), 21-8.

"Fame" *83: Best Canadian Stories* 36-48.

"The Garage Sale" *TL* Oct 1979, 68, 139-46.

"Getting the Picture" *UWR* 17:1 (Fall-Win 1982), 72-80.

"The Golden Thread" *At Peace* (1978), 58-92.

"Higher Learning" *At Peace* (1978), 38-57.

"Hostess" *Pot Port* 5 (1983-84), 15-8.

"Jubilee" *At Peace* (1978), 109-37.

"The Lord's Supper" *Texas Q* 19:1 (Spr 1976), 50-60.

"The Lord's Supper" *At Peace* (1978), 23-37.

"The Magic Monastery" *Snapdragon* (U.S.) 7:1 (Fall 1983), 42-54 [Based on survey response].

"Meeting" *Ont R* No. 8 (Spr-Sum 1978), 5-11.

"Miscarriage" *Back Room* (1979), 39-58.

"Mission" *Black Fly R* No. 3 (Spr 1982), 29-41 [Based on survey response].

"My Father's House" *Back Room* (1979), 122-39.

"My Father's House" *Fid* No. 120 (Win 1979), 97-108.

"Return" *Back Room* (1979), 140-9.

"A Room" *Casements* (U.S.) 2:1 (Spr 1981), 22-6 [Based on survey response].

"Siblings" by Anne Bernard *CFM* No. 18 (Sum 1975), 26-39.

"Siblings" *At Peace* (1978), 5-22.

"Sisterhood" *Room* 7:1/2 (1982), 90-101 [Excerpt?].

"Will" *Long Story* (U.S.) [1983?] [Based on survey response].

"A Woman's Touch" *Back Room* (1979), 73-102.

Copeland, David‡

"Grotesques" *TUR* 95:1 (Jan 1982), 6-13.

"Mae" *TUR* 96:1 (Jan 1983), 6-17.

"Mae" *UTR* 7 (Spr 1983), 2-7.

Copeland, Violet‡

"Blue Jacket, Blue Jeans" *Smoke Signals* 3 (1978) [Based on *SWG* survey response].

Copithorne, Agnes‡

"The Ancient and Honorable Art of Wool-Gathering" *Legion 50 (June 1975), 16-7 [Non-fiction?]*.

Copithorne, Judith

"Sea Change" *blewointmentpress* 2:4 (Sept 1964), [7 pp].

Copland, Alfred

"Manuel" *North* 13 *(July-Aug 1966), 18-20*.

Copps, Robert‡

"Notes to a Novel" *Womb* [No. 1] (1967), 30-7.

Corbett, Edward Annand (1887-1964)

"Ever Build a House?" by T. H. Rombosis *CF* 31 (Apr 1951), 11-2

"Ever Build a House?" *Continuous Learning* 6:1 (Jan-Feb 1967), 17-20.

Corbett, Eva‡

"A Lonely Walk" CBC *"Alberta Anthology"* 14 Nov 1981.

Corbett, Isabel Scott‡

"As Loved Our Fathers" *Atl Guardian* 8 (June 1951), 15-6, 18, 21, 23-5.

"Hot Supper" *Atl Guardian* 7 (Feb 1950), 30-5.

Corbett, Lenore M.

"Gusto" *Northern Ontario Anthology* 2 (1978), 23 [Non-fiction?].

Cormack, Barbara Villy

"The Hair-Do" *Onward* 20 Sept 1959, 598-9, 606-7.

"Nine O'Clock Lift" *Alberta Golden Jubilee Anthology* (1955), 357-65.

"The Talents" *Onward* 26 Aug 1962, 3-4.

"The Talents" *Onward* 10 Mar 1968, 3-4.

"The Waiting Room" *Onward* 30 Apr 1961, 273-5, 287.

Cormier, Louis‡
"A Day in the Life of Jean-Jean Leblanc" *Mysterious East* Apr 1970, 24-5.

Corning, Emilia†
"Dance" *Prism* 17:1 (Sum 1978), 47-58.
"Venetian Glass" *Matrix* 2:1 (Spr 1976), 5-6.

Corps, Doreen†
"All He Needed" *Onward* 18 Mar 1962, 12-3 [Non-fiction?].
"Diplomacy" *Onward* 14 Oct 1962, 6-7 [Non-fiction?].
"Tortillas for Lunch" *Onward* 29 Apr 1962, 12-3.

Corrigall, Melodie† (1942-)
"Scarlet Ribbons" *This* 17:3 (Aug 1983), 27-30.

Corrigall, Melodie Joy†
"Gethin and Horace Go to Market" *Halcyon* 10 (1964), 24-5.
"The Period of Soon" *Canadian Short Fiction Anthology* (1976), 57-8.
"The Story of Gethin and Horace" *Halcyon* 10 (1964), 23-4.

Corse, Murray‡
"Sick Leave" *Edge* No. 5 (Fall 1966), 35-43.

Corwin, Phillip‡
"Happiness" *Titmouse R* No. 7 [n.d.], 8-10.

Cosier, Anthony (Tony)
"The Christmas Deer" *Simcoe R* No. 11 (Win 1981), 18-23.
"The Derrick" *Ichor* No. 2 (1981), 45-8.
"Ensemble" *Prism* 18:2 (Win 1979-80), 117-20.
"Jean Pierre Robichaud" *Origins* 10:4 (Dec 1980), 72-4.
"A Story of the Renaissance" *First Encounter* 12 (1981-82), 15.

Cosseboom, Ray‡
"Moo Moo" *Salt* No. 15 (Fall 1976), 10.
"Mrs. Pierson" *Was R* 10:2 (Fall [1975]), 27.
"Uncle: Building Something" *Salt* No. 15 (Fall 1976), 10.

Costello, Kevin†
"The Future of Little Banana" *event* 4:2 [1974?], 28-35.

Cote, Christine‡
"A Matter of Principle" *Los* No. 8 (Mar 1982), 16-9.

Cote, J. Richard‡
"The Search – A Sketch" *Inscape* No. 3 (Win 1959), 30-3.

Cottrell, Terence Lloyd‡
"Stay Me with Flagons" *Scar Fair* 1 (1973-74), 39-47.
"This Fell Sergeant" *Scar Fair* [3] (1975-76), 81-90.

Coughlan, Jack‡
"Last Armistice Day" *Folio* 5:1 [Jan 1951], [4 pp].

Coulbeck, Art G.‡
"The Chinese Lover" *UC Gargoyle* [10] (Jan 1964), [4 pp].
"Circle of Ashes" *Jargon* 1962-63, 9-14.
"The Tabasco Caper" *Undergrad* 1964, 3-6.
"Theme for Mother's Day" *Undergrad* Spr 1963, 11-5.

Coull, Barry†
"Faces" *Motion* No. 6 (25 Dec 1962), [1-4].

Coulton, Doris†
"Winds of Change" *Rapport* Mar 1969, 5-7.

Coultrey, Peter‡
"The Lesser Canada" *Creative Campus* 1957, 2-5.

Countryman, Glenn‡
"White Man's Everything" *Targya* 1:2 (Fall 1973), 11-2.

Courchesne, Peter‡
"Just a Simple Story" *Folio* 13:2 (Spr 1961), 36-40.
"The Pointillistic" *Folio* 14:2 (Spr 1962), 6-9.
"Puddin' and Pie" *Folio* 14:1 (Fall-Win 1961), 9-12.

Courrin, Elva†
"Old Miss Armstrong" *Stories with John Drainie* (1963), 149-54.

Covey, Eva Alice‡
"Remembering Annie" *West People* No. 194 (23 June 1983), 14-5.

Cowan, Andrew†
"1" *Pop See Cul* No. 6 (Aut 1967), 16-7.
[Untitled] *Pop See Cul* No. 8 (Sum 1968), 18-9.

Cowan, Connie†
"The Flowering of Miss Ellen" *Read Ch* 1:2 (Sum 1982), 49-55.

Cowan, Judith (1943-)
"Toronto Tragedy" *NJ* No. 6 (June 1976), 35-41.

Coward, Mary Ann†
"A Beginning and an Ending" *CBC* [date unknown] [Source unknown].

Cowasjee, Saros (1931-)
NUDE THERAPY Ottawa: Borealis Press, 1979.
STORIES AND SKETCHES Calcutta: Writers Workshop, 1970.
"A4" *Times of India* 5 May 1963 [Based on survey response].
"A4" *Stories and Sketches* (1970), 25-7.
"A4" *Nude Therapy* (1979), 67-70.
"Another Train to Pakistan" *Blitz* (India) 19 June 1965, 19 [Based on survey response].
"Another Train to Pakistan" *Stories and Sketches* (1970), 7-11.
"Another Train to Pakistan" *Nude Therapy* (1979), 30-6.
"The Beggar" *Blitz* (India) 15 Apr 1972, 27 [Based on survey response].

"Bharat Mata Ki Jai" *Illustrated Weekly of India* 2 Dec 1973, 37-41 [Based on survey response].

"Boarding a French Vessel" *Illustrated Weekly of India* 1 Jan 1961, 39 [Based on survey response].

"The Captain" *Nude Therapy* (1979), 110-9.

"The Chowkidar" *Thought* (India) 21 Jan 1961, 11-3 [Based on survey response].

"The Chowkidar" *Stories and Sketches* (1970), 17-24.

"The Chowkidar" *Nude Therapy* (1979), 45-55.

"The General Secretary" *Indian Literature* 12:1 (1969), 40-6 [Based on survey response].

"The General Secretary" *Stories and Sketches* (1970), 34-40.

"The General Secretary" *Nude Therapy* (1979), 79-88.

"His Father's Medals" *Illustrated Weekly of India* 24 July 1966, 25-7 [Based on survey response].

"His Father's Medals" *Stories and Sketches* (1970), 1-6.

"His Father's Medals" *Nude Therapy* (1979), 22-9.

"I Remember" *Illustrated Weekly of India* 19 Sept 1971, 27 [Based on survey response].

"The Meeting" *New Delhi* 15 Oct 1979 [Based on survey response].

"My Shikari's Wife" *Yojana* (India) 15 Dec 1957, 11-3 [Based on survey response].

"My Shikari's Wife" *Stories and Sketches* (1970), 50-4.

"My Shikari's Wife" *Nude Therapy* (1979), 102-9.

"Nude Therapy" *JCF* 3:3 (1974), 16-9.

"Nude Therapy" *Nude Therapy* (1979), 7-21.

"The Road to Stardom" *Filmfare* (India) [date unknown], 19 [Based on survey response].

"The Sentry" *Times of India* 6 May 1962 [Based on survey response].

"The Sentry" *Stories and Sketches* (1970), 28-33.

"The Sentry" *Nude Therapy* (1979), 71-8.

"A Short Story" *Stories and Sketches* (1970), 12-6.

"A Short Story" *CBC* Nov 1970 [Based on survey response].

"A Short Story" *Nude Therapy* (1979), 37-44.

"Staff Only" *Illustrated Weekly of India* 26 Mar 1961, 25-9 [Based on survey response].

"Staff Only" *Stories and Sketches* (1970), 41-9.

"Staff Only" *Nude Therapy* (1979), 89-101.

"Unfinished" *Times of India* 26 June 1966, 8 [Based on survey response].

"The Well of the Bluebull" *Nude Therapy* (1979), 56-66.

"What Price Bread" *Blitz* (India) 30 Oct 1971, 25 [Based on survey response].

"The Writer" *Times of India* 24 Apr 1965, 7 [Based on survey response].

Cowie, Marilyn†

"A Child, One Night" *Prism* 2:3 (Spr 1961), 24-7.

Coyne, John‡

"Writer-in-Residence" *Gaillardia* [No. 5?] (Mar 1966), 60-77.

Crabtree, Peter‡

"Summer Journey" *TUR* 64:4 (Mar 1952), 9-13.

"Two Afternoons: One World" *TUR* 65:3 (Feb 1953), 22-8.

Cragg, Patricia Perry†
  "Fringe" *CCWQ* 3:4 [n.d.], 17-20.

Craig, Cheryl Lynne†
  "The Fantasy" *Pier Spr* Spr 1978, 19-20.

Craig, Jean Carol†
  "A Rose Is a Rose" *Forge* Spr 1955, 28-32.
  "There Are No Single Causes" *New Voices* (1956), 65-76.
  "There Are No Single Causes" *Forge* Mar 1956, 11-9.

Craigie, Alexander
  "Dizzy Blonde" *Can Banker* 61:2 (Spr-Sum 1954), 112-5.
  "Hold-Up at Castleborough" *Can Banker* 62:1 (Spr 1955), 144-50.

Craig-James, Janet†
  "The Empty Room" *Can Messenger* 86 (Feb 1976), 12-3, 19.
  "Eyes on a New Home" *Can Messenger* 86 (Oct 1976), 14-5.
  "Kaleidoscope" *Onward* 19 Feb 1967, 3-5.
  "Spring Time" *Can Messenger* 86 (May 1976), 14-6.

Crandall, Kathy‡
  "Andante" *Amaranth* Spr 1981, [3 pp].

Cranton, Judy‡
  "A Flash of Pink" *AA* 68 (Mar 1978), 63-5.
  "Like Leading a Lamb" *AA* 65 (Aug 1975), 56-8.

Crawford, Joyce†
  "Elizabeth" *Waves* 1:2 (Aut 1972), 72.

Crawford, Terry†
  "Salvador the Serendipitous Seer" *Floorboards* No. 2 (Oct 1969), 3-8.
  "The Wolves of the Devil" *Alive* [2:2] (Jan 1971), 3-8.

Creal, Margaret
  THE MAN WHO SOLD PRAYERS Toronto: Lester & Orpen Denys, 1981.
  "At Sunnyside Villa" *Man Who Sold Prayers* (1981), 39-62.
  "Counterpoint" *Man Who Sold Prayers* (1981), 63-81.
  "Inland Beach" *Man Who Sold Prayers* (1981), 102-15.
  "The Man Who Sold Prayers" *Hudson R* 30 (1977), 53-78.
  "The Man Who Sold Prayers" *Man Who Sold Prayers* (1981), 1-38.
  "Prairie Spring" *Man Who Sold Prayers* (1981), 116-31.
  "Tales from a *Pensione*" *Man Who Sold Prayers* (1981), 82-101.
  "A Town without a Graveyard" *Man Who Sold Prayers* (1981), 154-98.
  "Two Women" *Man Who Sold Prayers* (1981), 132-53.

Creighton, Dave‡
  "Show Business" *Acta Vic* 77:4 (Mar 1953), 22-3.
  "Tale of a Modern Xmas, Neither Sentimentality nor Festive Tradition" *Varsity Fri*, 15 Dec 1961, 2.

Creighton, Norman†

"The Day of the Gaspereau" *CHJ* May 1954, 20-1, 29-32, 35.

"Katy and the Nest Egg" *Weekend* 2 (3 May 1952), 35.

Crerar, T.H.†

"A Chronicle" *Imp* 2:2 (Win 1973), 6-27.

Crerar, Tom‡

"An Afternoon" *TUR* 63:2 (Aut 1950), 8-13.

"The Saint" *TUR* 62:5 (Feb 1950), 9-17.

Crispin, Jane‡

"Akudlik: The Half-Way House" *TUR* 91:2 (Apr 1978), 35-6.

"The Wooden Woman" *TUR* 91:1 (Nov 1977), 38.

Croll, Mike†

"Mt. Currie Rodeo, Mt. Currie, B.C." *NJ* No. 5 (May 1975), 8-13.

Crompton, Susan‡

"Gods' Death" *Los* No. 6 (1980), 16-20.

Cromwell, Liz†

"Fairy Tale" *[Title Unknown]* (1975), 13-4.

Cronenberg, David (1943-)

"The Death of the Lute" *UC Gargoyle* Spr 1967, [1 p].

"A Difficult Birth" *Jargon* [No. 5] (1962-63), 28-33.

"You Haven't Really Lost a Daughter" *Undergrad* Spr 1963, 25-7.

Cropas, Nyna‡

"The Guitar Man" *First Encounter* 1969-70, 4-9.

"Shông: The Growing Upwards" *First Encounter* 1969-70, 26-31.

Cropps, Marjorie E.†

"Ghosts Are Old-Fashioned" *Onward* 25 Oct 1964, 12-3.

Crossley, Vicki‡

"Doris Parkinson's Solution" *Student Oracle* (1979), 19-30.

Croucher, Sonia – *See* Birch-Jones, Sonia.

Crouse, Paul‡

"Send Me Back Sunday" *Muse* 1966-67, 8-9.

Croutch, Leslie A. (1915-1969)

YEARS OF LIGHT: A CELEBRATION OF LESLIE A. CROUTCH Ed. John Robert Columbo Toronto: Hounslow Press, 1982.

"The Authentic Apologue, or The Maladroit Iconoclast Exposed" *Light* No. 64 (Dec 1956), 3-6.

"The Day the Bomb Fell" *Amazing Stories* 24 (Nov 1950), 100-7.

"The Day the Bomb Fell" *Years of Light* (1982), 18-25.

"The Immigrant" *Light* No. 44 (Feb 1950), 5-7.
"The Immigrant" *Years of Light* (1982), 5-9.
"Jason Crull" *Light* No. 68 (1961), 2-13.

Crow, S.‡
"Allegory" *Acta Vic* 92:2 (Dec 1967), 11.

Crowe, David‡
"The Apostate" *UC Gargoyle* [15] (Spr 1967), 35-9.

Crowe, Donald‡
"They Were All Very Nice About It" *Seven* [n.d.], [2 pp].

Crowe, Eleanor†
"Economics (or, Sex at Six)" *Iron II* No. 21 (1978), 8-9.
"Sticks" *Per* No. 2 (Fall 1977), 24-5.
"The Visitor" *Roothog* (1981), 19-23.

Crowe, Helen† (1955-)
"Common Ground" *Flare* 3 (Dec 1981), 55-6.

Crowe, Keith†
"Journey Before Spring" *North* 14 (Mar-Apr 1967), 7-10.

Crowell, Bill (1925-)
"Blind Trade" *AA* 73 (June 1983), 36-7.
"The Connoisseur" by Ross MacAndrew *Bluenose* 3:2 (Fall 1978), 38-9.
"The Frosted Bottle Affair" *AA* 71 (Oct 1980), 22-5.
"James Learns the Pipes" by Ross MacAndrew *Bluenose* 2:1 (Sum 1977), 4-7.
"Red Tarnation" by Ross MacAndrew *Bluenose* 1:2 (Fall 1976), 17-8, 20.

Crowell, Peter
"Fontanelle" *Fid* No. 116 (Win 1976), 12-23.
"Michael in Branches" *Fid* No. 111 (Fall 1976), 62-70.
"Ravioli" *Des* 10:3/4 Nos. 25/26 (1979), 42-62.
"Sugarpops and Razorblades" *Canadian Short Fiction Anthology* (1976), 59-64.
"Uncle Sammy and Me" *Antig R* No. 29 (Spr 1977), 59-68.
"When Your Mother Comes to Visit" *CFM* No. 21 (Spr 1976), 88-99.
"When Your Mother Comes to Visit" *Magic Realism* (1980), 45-57.

Crowshaw, Laurie‡
[Untitled] *Eclipse* [No. 1] [n.d.], 25-6.

Crowther, Joan‡
"In the Dark" *Lifetime* 3 (May-June 1973), 32-3.

Cruess, Jim‡
"Hemispheres" *Gram* 8:2 (Spr 1983), 29-34.

Cuevas, Ernesto (1923-)
"An Adult Education" *CFM* No. 7 (Sum 1972), 13-6.
'The Important Thing" *CFM* No. 9 (Win 1973), 42-50.
'The Important Thing" *CBC "Anthology"* 12 Oct 1974.
'Lock the Doors, Lock the Windows" *Canadian Short Stories* (1952), 191-203.
"Organization" *CF* 48 (Nov 1968), 188-90.
'The Progress of a Spy" *Quarry* 26:4 (Aut 1977), 10-6.
'The Wooden Indian" *CFM* No. 8 (Aut 1972), 9-11.

Cull, David
'The Boats" *Motion* No. 3 (25 July 1962), [6-8].
'The Clothes" *Motion* No. 5 (25 Oct 1962), [6-8].
'The Departure" *Motion* No. 2 (25 June 1962), [1-2].
'The Load" *Motion* No. 6 (25 Dec 1962), [9-10].
'The Load" *Campus Canada* 1:1 (Feb 1963), 53-4.
'Two Part Soliloquy from the House of Love" *Motion* No. 1 (25 May 1962), [2 pp] [Excerpt?].
'The Waves" *Motion* No. 4 (25 Aug 1962), 3-4.

Cullen, Burke†
'The Driller" *Treeline* 2 (1983), 66-9.

Cullen, Michael James (1948-)
HERITAGE OF THE SPECKLED BIRD Calgary: Westlands Book Express, 1982 [Based on CBIP].

Culliford, Clair†
'The Grates of Heaven" *Quote Unquote* 2:1 (Jan 1979), 11.

Cummer, Don
"Desmoulins among the Olive Groves" *Des* 8:3 No. 19 (1977), 91-102.
"Dreamland and Other Poems" *NeWest R* 5 (Apr 1980), 8-9.
'The Face of Georges Jacques Danton" *Quarry* 27:3 (Sum 1978), 7-12.
'Just Before the Bastille Fell" *Des* 9:1/2 Nos. 20/21 (1978), 126-35.
'When I Am King, Dilly Dilly" *Grain* 9:4 (Nov 1981), 26-32.

Cumming, Doug‡
[Untitled] *Pulp* 2:8 (15 May 1974), [3].

Cummins, Willis‡
'What Price Freedom" *Canada in Us Now* (1976), 66-9.

Cunningham, James‡
'The Little Boats" *TUR* 73:3 (Feb 1960), 10-20.
"Safety-Pin" *TUR* 70:1 (Nov 1957), 22-9.
'The Summer Afternoon" *TUR* 72:1 (Nov 1958), 9-23.

Cunningham, Louis Arthur (1900-1954)
"Be My Love Always" *NHM* 51 (Oct 1950), 47-9, 51.
"Corky" *Weekend* 2 (5 July 1952), 26-7.
'Dark Pursuit" *SW* 9 July 1955, II:5.
'The Enchanted Bookshop" *FH* 26 Mar 1953, 28-9, 38.

"Flower Piece" *NHM* 51 (Mar 1950), 6-7, 24-5.

"The Terrible Secret of M. Laroche" *MM* 63 (1 Nov 1950), 18-9, 32-3.

"The Voice of an Angel" *Weekend* 5 (8 Jan 1955), 12-3.

"The Way of the Strong" *Lib* 29 (Oct 1952), 20, 42, 44.

Cunningham, Shaun†

"The Axeman" *Grain* 9:4 (Nov 1981), 50-1.

Curran, Kitty

"Christmas on the Flats" *FH* 22 Dec 1955, 10-1.

"Homestead Honeymoon" *FH* 17 Jan 1952, 24-5.

"Lesson in Love" *FH* 25 Nov 1954, 32-4.

"Lonesome Summer" *FH* 13 Feb 1958, 32-4.

"Miss Higgins Goes to Summer School" *FH* 3 Feb 1955, 20-1, 26.

"The Smell of Dust" *FH* 1 Apr 1954, 24.

Currie, Doris M.

"And Be My Love" *FH* 9 Feb 1956, 20, 29, 33.

"And Be My Love" *Stories to Read Again* (1965), 55-60.

"The Carpet People" *FH* 24 Mar 1955, 22-3.

"Command Performance of Johnny" *FH* 13 Mar 1958, 16-7.

"January Slump" *FH* 22 Jan 1959, 26, 30.

"Love Has Its Reasons" *FH* 14 Aug 1958, 20-1.

"The Old Man and the Mountain" *FH* 4 Feb 1960, 20-1, 23.

"Phonsie, the Unfortunate Wooer" *FH* 8 Dec. 1960, 18-9, 25.

"Sampson and Delilah" *FH* 22 Mar 1956, 26-7, 41.

Currie, Robert (1937-)

NIGHT GAMES Moose Jaw: Coteau Books, 1983.

"All Kinds" *CBC* "*Saskatchewan Short Stories*" 1973 [Based on survey response; also entitled "That Kind"].

"Assembly Line" *CBC [Reg]* "*Saskatchewan Short Stories*" 1972 [Based on survey response].

"Beer Bottle Hill" *Night Games* (1983), 15-28.

"The Boat" *Night Games* (1983), 53-9.

"Frayed" *Grain* 1:1 (June 1973), 44-9.

"From the Shadows" *Night Games* (1983), 77-85.

"Geranium!" *Saskatchewan Gold* (1982), 51-9.

"Geranium!" *Night Games* (1983), 1-7.

"The Girl in the White Dress" *Skylark* 5:2 (Win/Jan 1969), 18-27.

"Guys, Drinking" *Night Games* (1983), 31-43.

"Hunting" *CBC [Reg]* "*Saskatchewan Short Stories*" 1977 [Based on survey response].

"I Know What I Like" *NeWest R* 4 (Feb 1979), 6-7.

"I Know What I Like" *Sundogs* (1980), 42-8.

"I Know What I Like" *Night Games* (1983), 86-92.

"Killing Time" *Night Games* (1983), 100-5.

"Like a Man" *CBC [Reg]* "*Saskatchewan Short Stories*" 1974 [Based on survey response].

"A Little Protection" *Night Games* (1983), 93-9.

"Night Games" *Smoke Signals* (1974), 9-16.

"Possibilities" *Night Games* (1983), 106-20.

"That Kind" *Creative Saskatchewan* (1972) [Also entitled "All Kinds"; based on survey response].

"The Trouble with Sex" *Night Games* (1983), 8-14.

"Victory Party" *Night Games* (1983), 44-52.

"The White Dress" *Night Games* (1983), 63-73.

Currie, Sheldon (1934-)

THE GLACE BAY MINER'S MUSEUM Ste. Anne de Bellevue: Deluge Press, 1979.

"The Accident" *CFM* No. 46 (1983), 120-31.

"Dic Mihi de Nostra, Quae Sentis, Vera Puella" *Antig R* No. 7 (Aut 1971), 13-8.

"Dic Mihi de Nostra, Quae Sentis, Vera Puella" *Glace Bay Miner's Museum* (1979), 59-64.

"The Glace Bay Miner's Museum" *Antig R* No. 24 (Win 1975), 35-53.

"The Glace Bay Miner's Museum" *Glace Bay Miner's Museum* (1979), 7-22.

"He Said, Parenthetically" *Antig R* 1:1 (Spr 1970), 100-2.

"He Said, Parenthetically" *Glace Bay Miner's Museum* (1979), 23-5.

"Her Wonders to Perform" *Glace Bay Miner's Museum* (1979), 72-88.

"Jesus Creep" *Antig R* No. 8 (Win 1972), 55-61.

"Jesus Creep" *Glace Bay Miner's Museum* (1979), 65-71.

"Lauchie and Liza and Rory" *Antig R* No. 47 (Aut 1981), 21-5.

"The Lovers" *Mont R* 1:1 (Spr-Sum 1979), 40-4.

"The Lovers" *Glace Bay Miner's Museum* (1979), 45-58.

"Mary" *Antig R* 1:2 (Sum 1970), 5-17.

"Mary" *Glace Bay Miner's Museum* (1979), 26-38.

"On Parle Par Coeur" *CA & B* 58:3 (Spr 1983), 19-21.

"The Path" *Antig R* No. 39 (Aut 1979), 59-66.

"Pomp and Circumstances" *Antig R* No. 28 (Win 1977), 33-64.

"Pomp and Circumstances" *Glace Bay Miner's Museum* (1979), 89-118.

"Sanabitur Anima Mea" *Glace Bay Miner's Museum* (1979), 39-44.

Currie, Suzanne‡

"The Escape" *Abegweit R* 3:1 (Spr 1980), 61-3.

Curry, John W.

"January 1983" *Industrial Sabotage* No. 14 [Mar 1983], [1 p].

Curry, Julia‡

"The Quilt" *Los* No. 8 (Mar 1982), 58-66.

Curtis, Margaret

"Everybody Else Is Running" *Chat* 45 (Nov 1972), 41, 88, 90-3.

Curtis, Mary‡

"Running Laughing" *Contact* 3:4 (Win 1974), 64-8 [Non-fiction?].

Cusack, Pauline†

"Louder Than Words" *Can Messenger* 91 (Apr 1981), 8-9.

Cushing, Daniel‡

"Almost Train Time" *Fifth Page* 1962, 13-7.

Cushing, Leo‡
"The Runner – A Satire" *Kaleidoscope* 1956-57, 5-7.
"The Walker – A Mood" *Kaleidoscope* 1956-57, 7-8.

Cuson, Tom‡
"Vision of the Burning Gate" *Titmouse R* No. 3 (Sum 1973), 55-6.

Cuthand, John‡
"An Enchanted Christmas" *New Breed* 13 (Dec 1982), 14-5, 23.

Cutt, Joanne E.
"Willows" *Variations on a Gulf Breeze* (1973), 67-70.

Cyr, Rita‡
"An Eavesdropper" *Intervales* [No. 3 (1963?)], 26-8.

Czeszak, Andrew – *See* Sherman, Tom.

Czojka, Christine†
"The Return" *CSSM* 1:3 (July 1975), 56-8.

D., G.
"after an anonymous french novelist" *UC Gargoyle* Spr 1967, [1 p].

D., L. – *See* Duncan, Leslie.

Dabydeen, Cyril (1945-)
STILL CLOSE TO THE ISLAND Ottawa: Commoner's, 1980.
THE GLASS FOREHEAD Cornwall: Vesta, 1983 [Based on CBIP].
"Across the River" *Tor S Asian R* 1:2 (Sum 1982), 11-8.
"All for Love" *Still Close to the Island* (1980), 36-42.
"Antics of the Insane" *Still Close to the Island* (1980), 20-6.
"At the Going Down of the Sun" *Was R* 16:2 (Fall 1981), 67-75.
"At Your Own Peril" *CA & B* 57:4 (Sum 1982), 15-8.
"Bitter Blood" *Fid* No. 113 (Spr 1977), 6-14.
"Bitter Blood" *Fiddlehead Greens* (1979), 115-24.
"Bitter Blood" *Still Close to the Island* (1980), 105-11.
"Canine Sun" *CF* 59 (Sept 1979), 26-7.
"Canine Sun" *Still Close to the Island* (1980), 27-9.
"A Car Is Just Like an Eating Baby" *Still Close to the Island* (1980), 51-6.
"Everlasting Love" *Antig R* 23 (Aut 1975), 53-5.
"A Far Place Home" *Rikka* 7:2 (Sum 1980), 25-8.
"Feud" *Nw J* No. 24 (1981), 55-60.
"Funny Ghosts" *Quarry* 30:2 (Spr 1981), 35-40.
"Go an' Play in the Traffic" *Still Close to the Island* (1980), 43-50.
"Go an' Play in the Traffic" *Nebula* No. 16 (1980), 48-54.
"A Kind of Feeling" *Antig R* No. 44 (Win 1980), 83-90.
"A Longer Life" *Still Close to the Island* (1980), 71-6.
"Mammita's Garden Cove" *Still Close to the Island* (1980), 84-91.
"Memphis" *Still Close to the Island* (1980), 77-83.

"A Mighty Vision" *CFM* Nos. 36/37 (1980), 136-41.
"Mother of Us All" *Still Close to the Island* (1980), 15-9.
"Mouthful" *Grain* 6:2 [1978], 26-32.
"Mouthful" *Still Close to the Island* (1980), 92-9.
"A Plan Is a Plan" *Dal R* 62 (1982-83), 659-67.
"Rain All Day" *Still Close to the Island* (1980), 57-63.
"A Ringer's Circle" *Still Close to the Island* (1980), 64-70.
"Still Close to the Island" *Waves* 7:2 (Win 1979), 11-5.
"Still Close to the Island" *Still Close to the Island* (1980), 100-4.
"A Vampire Life" *Still Close to the Island* (1980), 9-14.
"When It Rains in the Sunshine, a Witch Is Getting Married" *Still Close to the Island* (1980), 30-5.

Daem, Mary (1914-)

See also Daem, Mary and Deeder, Peg.
"The Battle" *Can Messenger* 63 (July 1953), 463-7.
"The Ghost Whose Name Was Change" *Weekend* 3 (14 Nov 1953), 12-3, 35.
"Give Me Love" *NHM* 51 (Nov 1950), 40-3.
"Nan Finds a Cure" *Can Messenger* 61 (Jan 1951), 39-43.
"The Planned Returning" *FH* 24 May 1951, 22-3.
"A Spot for Elizabeth" *Can Messenger* 62 (Aug 1952), 534-7.
"Willy" *CSSM* 1:3 (July 1975), 28-31.

Daem, Mary and Deeder, Peg

See also Daem, Mary.
"All the Room in the World" *FH* 2 Oct 1952, 24.
"The Blue Gown" *FH* 4 Sept 1952, 20.
"The Business of the Blinds" *Weekend* 2 (26 July 1952), 12-3.

Dafoe, Christopher‡

"Wings Over Dumottan" *CBC "Anthology"* 31 Oct 1970.

Dagg, Mel (1937-)

SAME TRUCK DIFFERENT DRIVER Calgary: Westlands, 1982.
"The Blue Heron" *Same Truck Different Driver* (1982), 107-16.
"End of Summer" *Grain* 3:2 [1975], 52-4.
"End of Summer" *Best of Grain* (1980), 10-2.
"End of Summer" *Same Truck Different Driver* (1982), 51-5.
"Fire Weed" *JCF* No. 20 (1977), 42-9.
"Fire Weed" *Same Truck Different Driver* (1982), 57-70.
"The Gift" *JCF* 3:4 (1975), 22-5.
"Have You Got a Rag" *JCF* 1:4 (Fall 1972), 20-2.
"Journey Inland" *CBC "Anthology"* 16 Apr 1977.
"Journey Inland" *JCF* Nos. 31/32 (1981), 84-91.
"Journey Inland" *Same Truck Different Driver* (1982), 93-106.
"The Mistake" *JCF* Nos. 28/29 (1980), 84-98.
"The Mistake" *Matinees Daily* (1981), 102-18.
"The Mistake" *Same Truck Different Driver* (1982), 71-92.
"The Museum of Man" *Fid* No. 107 (Fall 1975), 47-55.
"The Museum of Man" *Same Truck Different Driver* (1982), 27-40.
"Same Truck, Different Driver" *Same Truck Different Driver* (1982), 13-26.

"Sunday Evening on Axe Flats" *JCF* No. 19 (1977), 7-11.
"Sunday Evening on Axe Flats" *More Stories from Western Canada* (1980), 231-8.
"Sunday Evening on Axe Flats" *Same Truck Different Driver* (1982), 41-50.
"Ways of Going" *Same Truck Different Driver* (1982), 117-29.

Daigneault, Paul‡

"The Yellow Door" *Catalyst* (Brantford) 1:2 (1975), 32-3.

Dakin, Laurence

"The Djinn of Shubel's Mountain: A Maritime Tale" *Public Affairs* 15:1 (Aut 1952), 50-2.
"The Old Man of the Mountains" *Dal R* 31 (1952), 292-6.

Dale, Mark‡

"The Giant's Tomb" *TUR* 83:3 [n.d.], [2 pp].

Dales, Walter A.

"The Builders" *FH* 2 Sept 1965, 22, 32.
"The Cloud-Watcher" *Weekend* 2 (8 Nov 1952), 10-1.
"Cupid's Rifle" *Weekend* 2 (1 Mar 1952), 18-9.
"The Forgetful Bride" *Weekend* 4 (3 Apr 1954), 20-1.
"The Hired Man" *SW* 4 July 1953, II:6.
"Home on the Midnight" *Chat* 26 (Aug 1953), 19, 40, 43-5, 47.
"Love Story for Ma" *Weekend* 2 (12 Jan 1952), 10, 28-9.
"Mathematics for the Lonely" *Weekend* 3 (20 June 1953), 38.
"Meet My Lovely Daughter" *Weekend* 2 (9 Aug 1952), 14-6.
"A Special Girl for Him" *SW* 15 Nov 1952, I:9, 12.

D'Alfonso, Antonio

"Anticipation" *Alch* 1:3 (1976), [9 pp].

Dalrymple, A.J.‡

"Just for Fun" *Beaver* 291 (Win 1960), 42-3.

Dalton, Sheila

"Dreams of Freedom, Dreams of Need" *CCWQ* 3:2/3 [n.d.], 24-6.
"Feminist Blues" *Hysteria* 2:3 (Sum 1983), 5 [Non-fiction?].
"The Girl Who Turned into a Bird" *CCWQ* 2:4 (Fall 1980), 8-9.
"The Man Who Divorced His Wife Because She No Longer Looked Like Marilyn Monroe" *Des* 9:1/2 Nos. 20/21 (1978), 87-93.
"Monday Is a Bad Day" *Random* 3:5 (Mar [1969]), 24-5.
"An Old Witch Remembers" *Wee Giant* 3:3 (Fall 1980), 25-7.
"An Old-Fashioned Girl" *Rune* No. 7 (Win 1982), 42-57.
"Third Time Under" *Wee Giant* 4:1 (Win 1980-81), 28-32.
"Visiting the Grave" *Des* 10:1 Nos. 22/23 (1978-79), 49-52.

Daly, Michael E.†

"The Society of Jesus" *JCF* No. 22 (1978), 29-37.

Daly, Thomas‡

"Study in Self-Consciousness #2" *Undergrad* Win 1953, 25-6.

Damion, Jean-Paul‡
"Old Friends" *VWFP/Revue* 1:3 (May 1975), 8-9.

Dampf, Michael‡
"Another Season" *Writ* No. 10 (1978), 27.
"Between the Headboard and the Foot" *Writ* No. 10 (1978), 25.
"Kitchen Knives (Hashish)" *Writ* No. 10 (1978), 26.
"The Laundry Room" *Writ* No. 10 (1978), 24.
"A Lonely Woman Afraid of Mirrors" *Writ* No. 11 (Fall 1979), 22-5.
"Of Passion" *Writ* No. 8 (1976), 40-2.
"Optional Prefaces" *Writ* No. 10 (1978), 23.
"The Problem" *Writ* No. 11 (Fall 1979), 17-21.
"Triptych" *Writ* No. 8 (1976), 36-9
[Untitled] *Writ* No. 8 (1976), 30-5.

Danard, Joan‡
"Barbara Ramsden with a Fancy 'R' " *Fifth Page* 1967, 7-10.

Dance, James Michael† (1954?-)
"A Plague of Armadillos" *Canadian Short Fiction Anthology* (1976), 65-7.

Daniel, Michael‡
"The Circular Lady" *TUR* 90:3 (Apr 1977), 17-8.

Daniels, D.S.†
"Another Boy" *Can Writing* 1:1 (Win 1950), 32-4.
"The Canadian Road" *NF* 4:2 (Sum 1955), 40-2.

Danys, Ruth (1946-)
"Mystery at the Henderson Shipping Company" *Toronto Star* Sun, 14 Nov 1982, F5.

Daquano, R.‡
"Dialogue of Two Teachers" *Pedantics* 1966, 50.

Darling, Fran†
"Birthday Journey" *Hysteria* 2:1 (Win 1982-83), 13-7.

Darling, John‡
"Diamonds Threaded Yellow" *Raven* No. 5 (Dec 1957), 23-32.

D'Arrigo, Stephen‡
"Pythagoras" *Rude* Prelim No. 3 [n.d.], [3 pp].

Das, Satya†
"Bonds" *Grain* 7:1 [1979], 59-62.

Daunt, James‡
"The Trip to Detroit" *Region* No. 8 (Sum 1966), [6 pp].

Daurio, Beverley (1953-)

NEXT IN LINE Toronto: Prototype, 1982 [*viz.*, Identity 4 (Win 1982)].
"Marty Was Sitting Gracelessly in the Corner (Oblique[)]" *Onion* 4:4 (Dec 1979), 5.
"Reclining Nude" *Grain* 8:1 [1980], 36-7.
"Snippet" *Onion* 5:2 (Mar 1981), 4.
"Team Town" *OPT* 6:4/5 (May-June 1979), 24-5.
"A Temporary Obsession" *Ichor* No. 1 (Win 1980), 27-31.
"Three Months" *Onion* 5:7 (Mar 1982), 1-3 [Untitled] *Gram* 3:1 (Nov 1977), 12-5.

Davey, Frank (1940-)

"The Mural" *Fid* No. 69 (Sum 1966), 23-9.
"The River" *Motion* No. 2 (25 June 1962), [3-4].

David, Jack (1946-)

"joseph and t" *Canadian Short Fiction Anthology* (1976), 69-71.

Davidson, Bill†

"Gordie" *Folio* 4:2 [Apr 1950], [4 pp].

Davidson, Carol E.†

"Boys Will Be Boys" *Squatch J* No. 10 (Dec/Win-Spr 1979-80), 35-6.

Davidson, Craig‡

" 'How Beautifully Blue the Sky the Glass Is Rising Very High Continue Fine I Hope I May ...' " *Potlatch* No. 1 (Jan 1964), 7-12.
"Fresh Air and Westward Expansion" *Potlatch* No. 5 (Dec 1965), 34-43.
"The Third Grotesque" *Qolus* [No. 1] (Mar 1967), 31-4.

Davidson, Doug‡

"Oasis" *Acta Vic* 76:4 (Mar 1952), 13-7.

Davidson, John‡

"The Captain Wore His Scarf" *Weekend* 4 (23 Jan 1954), 30.

Davidson, John Hugh‡

'The Circle of a Jumper" *CBC "Anthology"* 3 July 1976.

Davies, Ann‡

"Dinner in Chile" *AA* 52 (Apr 1962), 16, 19.

Davies, Joanne H.†

'Techniques of Living" *Yes* 1:2 (Aug 1956), [2 pp].

Davies, P.

"Death of an Unknown Hamburgher" *Beaver Bites* 1:3 (20 May 1976), [1 p] [Humour?].

Davies, Robertson (1913-)

HIGH SPIRITS Markham/Harmondsworth: Penguin, 1982.
ONE HALF OF ROBERTSON DAVIES Toronto: Macmillan, 1977.
"Animal U" *One Half* (1977), 92-6.
"Animal U" *TL* Oct 1977, 54, 125.

"The Cat That Went to Trinity" *One Half* (1977), 97-106.
"The Cat That Went to Trinity" *Cat Encounters* (1979) [Based on SSI].
"The Cat That Went to Trinity" *Not to Be Taken at Night* (1981), 15-25.
"The Cat That Went to Trinity" *High Spirits* (1982), 93-102.
"The Charlottetown Banquet" *High Spirits* (1982), 43-52.
"Conversations with the Little Table" *High Spirits* (1982), 139-49.
"Dickens Digested" *One Half* (1977), 107-15.
"Dickens Digested" *High Spirits* (1982), 73-81.
"Einstein and the Little Lord" *High Spirits* (1982), 175-86.
"The Ghost Who Vanished by Degrees" *High Spirits* (1982), 13-21.
"The Great Queen Is Amused" *High Spirits* (1982), 23-32.
"The King Enjoys His Own Again" *High Spirits* (1982), 151-61.
"The Kiss of Krushchev" *High Spirits* (1982), 83-92.
"The Night of the Three Kings" *High Spirits* (1982), 33-41.
"Offer of Immortality" *High Spirits* (1982), 187-98.
"Offer of Immortality" *Twilight Zone* 2:4 (July 1982), 26-31.
"The Perils of the Double Sign" *High Spirits* (1982), 127-38.
"The Pit Whence Ye Are Digged" *High Spirits* (1982), 115-26.
"Refuge of Insulted Saints" *High Spirits* (1982), 63-72.
"Revelation from a Smoky Fire" *High Spirits* (1982), 7-12.
"The Ugly Spectre of Sexism" *High Spirits* (1982), 103-13.
"When Satan Goes Home for Christmas" *High Spirits* (1982), 53-61.
"The Xerox in the Lost Room" *High Spirits* (1982), 163-74.

Davies. Kevin†
"Melting" *Grain* 5:1 [1977], 3-4.

Davis, Frances
"Rosamunda" *Saturday Night at the Forum* (1981), 95-100.

Davis, Lois McLean‡
"Cypernetics at Home" *Edmonton Journal* Fri, 17 Sept 1965, 57.

Davis, Martha‡
"The Retirement Party" *TUR* 92:2 (Apr 1979), 41-5.

Davis, Pat‡
"The Swamp" *Undergrad* Mar 1957, 20-5.

Davis, R.‡
"The Evolution of Harry" *Ichor* No. 1 (Win 1980), 11-8.

Davis, Sheila‡
"Far Out, Man" *Driftwood* [No. 1] (Apr 1973), 25-35.
"Torrance" *Driftwood* [No. 1] (Apr 1973), 10-2.

Davison, Marion‡
"March Mo(u)rning" *Bluenose* 1:4 (Spr 1977), 38-9.

Davitt, F.G.‡
"Soliloquy of a Common Man" *Gram* 2:1 (31 Oct 1976), 12-4.

Dawe, Tom (1940-)
THE LOON IN THE DARK TIDE St. John's: Harry Cuff, 1981 [Based on advertisements].
"The Apple Tree" *East of Canada* (1976), 171-7.
"An Off-Shore Wind" *Baffles of Wind and Tide* (1980), 24-8.
"Sculpin" *Baffles of Wind and Tide* (1974), 3-7.
"Snow Fall" *Nfld Q* 69:2 (Oct 1972), 12-4.

Dawson, Fielding and Woods, Hanford
"Mystery in Marin" *Da Vinci* No. 6 (Aut 1979), 68-70.

Dawson, Virginia Douglas‡
"Miss French" *Stories with John Drainie* (1963), 135-42.

Day, Gene (1951-1982)
See also Day, Gene and Jack, Gale.
"By Power of Scalpel" by Howard E. Day *Cop Toad* 1:1 (Dec 1976), 2-6.
"The Fever Time" by Howard E. Day *Cop Toad* 1:2 (July 1977), 77-80.

Day, Gene and Jack, Gale
See also Day, Gene.
"Proxy" *Cop Toad* 1:2 (July 1977), 35-52.

Day, Howard E. – *See* Day, Gene.

Day, Peggy†
"The Blue Taffeta Dress" *Living Message* 87 (Apr 1976), 22-3.
"A Cry from the Heart" *Living Message* 87 (Oct 1976), 23-5.

Day, T.‡
"The Wolf Who Did" *Heartland* No. 1 (Nov-Dec 1980), 83.

de Barros, Paul
"Cut Off at the Broken Arms" *BC Monthly* 3:1 (Oct 1976), [1 p].
"The Day After They Shot the Bear" *Iron II* No. 1 (1975), 29-35.
"A Function of the Community" *Per* No. 4 (Fall 1978), 23-6.
"The Greatest Show on Earth" *Per* No. 1 (Spr 1977), 5-6.
"High Speed Interchange" *Repos* Nos. 23/24 (1977), 11.
"In a Draw" *Cap R* No. 18 (1980), 38-42.
"In a Draw" *Roothog* (1981), 7-11.
"A Rifle Can Shoot Far" *Repos* Nos. 19/20 (Sum-Fall 1976), 1-4.
"Some Evidence of Foxing" *BC Monthly* 3:3 (Dec 1976), [3 pp] [Prose poem?].
"A Writer's Eye" *Per* Nos. 7/8 (Win 1981), 88-9.

de Cointet, Guy‡
"Mrs. Newton" *File* 4:4 (Fall 1980), 49-54.

de Creszenzo, Marianne†
"The Crystal Rose Dream" *Pier Spr* 8:4 (Aut 1983), 7-15.

de la Roche, Mazo (1885-1961)

A BOY IN THE HOUSE AND OTHER STORIES Boston: Little, Brown, 1952 [Based on *Selected Stories*].

SELECTED STORIES OF MAZO DE LA ROCHE Ed. Douglas Daymond Ottawa: Univ.

of Ottawa Press, 1979.

"A Boy in the House" *Boy in the House* (1952) [Based on *Selected Stories*].

"The Celebration" *Boy in the House* (1952) [Based on *Selected Stories*].

"The Celebration" *Selected Stories* (1979), 175-90.

"A Fighting Chance" *Harper's Bazaar* [UK?] Mar 1954 [Based on Daymond].

de Lint, Charles

See also de Lint, Charles and Harris, MaryAnn.

A PATTERN OF SILVER STRINGS Ottawa: Triskell Press, 1981 [Based on survey response].

DE GRIJZE ROOS Antwerp: Een Eza Uitgave, 1983 [In Flemish; based on survey response].

GLASS EYES AND COTTON STRINGS Ottawa: Triskell Press, 1982 [Based on survey response].

IN MASK AND MOTLEY Ottawa: Triskell Press, 1983 [Based on survey response].

THE MOON IS A MEADOW Ottawa: Triskell Press, 1980 [Based on survey response].

THE OAK KING's DAUGHTER Ottawa: Triskell Press, 1979 [Based on survey response].

"Dennet & the Fiddler" *Night Voyages* No. 8 (1982) [Based on survey response].

"The Fair, the Foul & the Foolish" *Sorcerer's Apprentice* No. 2 (1979) [Based on survey response].

"The Fane of the Grey Rose" *De Grijze Roos* (1983) [As "De Tempel van de Grijze Roos"; trans. Clement Caremans; based on survey response].

"The Iron Stone" *Space and Time* No. 61 (1982), 4[+?] [Based on science fiction indexes].

"A Kingly Thing" *Beyond the Fields We Know* No. 1 (Aut 1978), 78-89.

"The Moon Is a Meadow" *HEXA 8* (Belgium) (1982) [As "Da Maan is een Weide"; in Flemish; trans. Tony Meesdom; based on survey response].

"My Ainsel' " *Cop Toad* Nos. 6/7 (1979), 27-9.

"Nareth the Questioner" *Valhalla* No. 1 (1979) [Based on survey response].

"The Night of the Valkings" *Space and Time* No. 49 (1978) [Based on survey response].

"The Oak King's Daughter" *De Grijze Roos* (1983) [As "De Dochter van de Eikkoning"; trans. Johan Vanhecke; based on survey response].

"Of the Temple in the City of the Burning Spire" *Valhalla* No. 1 (1979) [Based on survey response].

"A Pattern of Silver Strings" *Year's Best Fantasy Stories* 8 (1982), 129-50.

"A Pattern of Silver Strings" *De Grijze Roos* (1983) [As "Een Weefsel van Zilveren Snaren"; trans. Bob van Laerhoven; based on survey response].

"The Ring of Brodgar" *Space and Time* No. 58 (1980) [Based on survey response].

"Stormraven" *Sorcerer's Apprentice* No. 12 (1981) [Based on survey response].

"A Tale of Tangle Who Has Many Names" *Valhalla* No. 1 (1979) [Based on survey response].

"The Three That Came" *Cop Toad* 3:5 (Jan 1979), 9-12.
"Wings Over Antar" *Dragonbane* No. 1 (Spr 1978), 19-34 [Novelette?].
"Wizard's Bounty" *Dark Fantasy* No. 21 (Oct 1979), 26-44.
"Woods and Waters Wild" *SPWAO Showcase* No. 1 (1981) [Based on survey response].

de Lint, Charles and Harris, MaryAnn
See also de Lint, Charles.
"Humphrey's Christmas" *OSCAR* 10:4 (1981) [Based on survey response].

de Looze, L.‡
"Two Villages" *Ont R* No. 16 (Spr-Sum 1982), 75-9.

de Marco, Don‡
"The Blue Planet" *Uncertified Human* 1:3 (Aug 1973), 6.

de Meulles, Richard†
"Nero's Immortal Soul" *Read Ch* 1:2 (Sum 1982), 37-48.

de Santana, Hubert‡
"The O'Carroll Archipelago" *Aurora* 1979 123-30.

de Villiers, Marq‡
"The Golden Rule" *WWR* 1:2 (Win 1977), 43-7.

de Vries, Anne‡
"Autumn and Fear" *Edmonton Journal* Fri, 4 Mar 1966, 55.
"Bells Are Ringing" *Edmonton Journal* Fri, 18 Feb 1966, 51.

de Yoe, Judy‡
"Roger-Case 9807" *Stump* 5:1 (Fall-Win 1980), 21-3.

Deacove, James‡
"Homecoming" *Creative Campus* 1961, 21-5.
"Little Willie" *Creative Campus* 1961, 4-7.
"Synopados (He Who Follows Behind)" *Creative Campus* 1961, 44-50.

Deally, Margaret‡
"Joe Pynoo Sees It Through" *JCF* 3:3 (1974), 39-42.

Dean, Darryl‡
"Wot de Hell Ah Go Do?" *Canada in Us Now* (1976), 72-5.

Dean, Maureen‡
"Back Home" CBC *"Anthology"* 19 Mar 1957.

Deane, Christopher‡
"Fallen Leaves" *Writing Group Pub* 2 [1969-70], 23-7.
"In Touch" *In Touch* (1975), 4-11.
"The Other Half" *Writing Group Pub* 1970-71, 14-5.
"Our Father" *Pax* [1969-70], 54-60.
"Our Father" *Writing Group Pub* 2 [1969-70], 55-62.
"Remembrance Day" *Pax* [1969-70], 7-10.

Deane, James‡
"Nika, a Tale of the Surf" *AA* 51 (Sept 1960), 25-6, 28, 31-2, 34-5, 37-40.
"The Red Picket" *AA* 50 (Jan 1960), 81-7.
"The Worm That Lived" *AA* 53 (Nov 1962), 27-32, 34.

Dearborn, Dorothy E.
"The Village and the Old Man" *AA* 52 (Aug 1962), 77-8.
"Willie" *AA* 66 (July 1976), 14-6.
"Willie" *Stubborn Strength* (1983), 75-81.

d'Easum, Lille†
"Return to P'yongyang" *Raven* 1:1 (Sept 1955), 34-9.

DeBeck, Brian‡
"The Mill" *Geo Str Writing* No. 7 (May 1971), 14.

Deblois, Diane†
"Chez le Notaire" *Mont Writers' Forum* 1:4 (Jan 1979), 8-9.

DeCampo, Paul‡
"From Here to Where" *Simcoe R* No. 9 (Win 1980), 40-3.

Decker, Ken (1952-)
BACKYARD GENE POOL Dunvegan, Ont.: Quadrant Editions, 1982.
"AbsTRACTION" *Imp* 10:2 (Win 1982), 22-5.
"Earth Station" *Backyard Gene Pool* (1982), 73-82.
"ESCHAR" *Backyard Gene Pool* (1982), 109-14.
"ESCHAR" *Rampike* 2:3 (1982), 37.
"Hexagonal Throughput" *Saturday Night at the Forum* (1981), 33-5.
"Hexagonal Throughput" *Backyard Gene Pool* (1982), 31-6.
"Job Search" *Backyard Gene Pool* (1982), 83-6.
"Job Search" *Scrivener* 4:1 (Win 1983), 17.
"L'Ecole des Soupes" *Backyard Gene Pool* (1982), 87-103.
"Ligature and Competition" *Backyard Gene Pool* (1982), 115-31.
"Look Here!" *Backyard Gene Pool* (1982), 11-20.
"Mobile Homes" *Backyard Gene Pool* (1982), 37-64.
"Molecular-Clock-Evaluation" *Backyard Gene Pool* (1982), 105-7.
"Tony Chestnut Talking" *Imp* 8:4 (Fall-Win 1980), 29-31.
"Tony Chestnut Talking" *Backyard Gene Pool* (1982), 65-72.
"Where Seldom Is 'Herd' a Discouraging Word" *Backyard Gene Pool* (1982), 21-30.
"Where Seldom Is 'Herd' a Discouraging Word" *Imp* 9:3/4 (Spr 1982), 38-9.

Decoteau, L.†
"The Wolf" *Mont* 24 (Nov 1953), 56-7, 60-1.

Dedels, Dorothy M.†
"Mother's Pets Are Very Old" *Onward* 19 Sept 1965, 12-3 [Humour].

Deeder, Peg – *See* Daem, Mary and Deeder, Peg.

DeFaveri, Ivan†

"Maurice" *Raven* 1:1 (Sept 1955), 12-5.
"Wood Pile" *Raven* 1:3 (Spr 1956), 5-7.

Dehaas, David†

"Cabin at the Wolf" *Outdoor Can* 9 (May 1981), 29-30, 32-3, 35-6, 39.
"Ghost of Legend" *Outdoor Can* 10 (Jan-Feb 1982), 19-21, 23.
"The Last One" *Outdoor Can* [9] (Fishing Annual 1981), 81, 78.

Deindorfer, Gary‡

"Riders Incognito" *Panic Button* No. 12 (1963), 26-8.
"Visit to an Art House" *Panic Button* No. 14 (1963), 16-9 [Non-fiction?].

Dekker, Frieda‡

"Saplings" *Whetstone* Spr 1972, [3 pp].

Delahanty, C.E.‡

"Sima" *Driftwood* 1979, 11-4.

Delaney, John

"The Magic Words" *Alberta Writers Speak* 1964, 32-7.
"The Native Albertan" *Alberta Writers Speak* 1960, 59-66.
"The Prophecy" *Alberta Writers Speak* 1964, 78-88.
"The Vision" *Alberta Writers Speak* 1967, 100-10.

Delday, Elva‡

"Party Line" *West People* No. 204 (22 Sept 1983), 11.

Deluca, Steve‡

"The Painting" *Eclipse* No. 4 (1977), 14.

Delver, Emily‡

"My Children Bring the Sun" *Native People* 9 (16 Jan 1976), 12 [Based on CPI].

Dempsey, Ian†

"Going West" *Simcoe R* No. 11 (Win 1981), 40-8.
"A Honeymoon" *CA & B* 56:3 (Spr 1981), 33-5.
"A Sea Change" *Quarry* 31:2 (Spr 1982), 46-55.

Dempsey, Jane (1956?-)

"Goodbye, Pam" *Miss Chat* 14 (10 Mar 1977), 78-9, 105-6, 108, 110-1.
"The Real World of Peregrine Hull" *Chat* 52 (Nov 1979), 46, 80, 82, 84, 86, 91, 93.
"You Make Your Own Breaks" *Was R* 18:1 (Spr 1983), 29-34.

Dempster, Barry (1952-)

"The Advent" *Dal R* 58 (1978), 481-8.
"Barry's Bay" *Third Impressions* (1982), 58-82.
"The Burial" *Fid* No. 120 (Win 1979), 3-21.
"The Burial" *Third Impressions* (1982), 30-57.
"Dangerous Fish" *Dal R* 59 (1979), 519-26.
"Dangerous Fish" *Third Impressions* (1982), 19-29.
"The Exploitation of the Sun" *CJRY* (York Univ) 1980 [Based on survey

response].

"The Exploitation of the Sun" *Des* 11:1/2 Nos. 27/28 (1980), 177-94.
"Familiar Runner" *Waves* 6:2 (Win 1978), 13-9.
"Fast Miracles" *Harvest* Nos. 5/6 (Sept 1978), 15-24.
"Going on Alone" *UWR* 15:1/2 (Fall-Win/Spr-Sum 1979-80), 76-96.
"A Large K in Kill" *Prism* 17:2 (Fall 1978), 53-64.
"A Large K in Kill" *80: Best Canadian Stories* 32-46.
"The Man Who Met an Angel" *Quarry* 30:1 (Win 1981), 55-64.
"Pacific Tyranny" *event* 8:2 (1979), 33-43.
"Story That Saw Defeat" *UWR* 13:2 (Spr-Sum 1978), 51-64.

Denby, Netha K.†

"Familiar" *Hysteria* 2:3 (Sum 1983), 9-11 [Serial?].
"Listing" *Hysteria* 2:2 (Spr 1983), 6-8 [Serial?].

Deneau, Denis Phillippe (1934-)

"Clyde Langdon, In Word, Indeed" *Kaleidoscope* 1958, 20-1.
"Shadow in the Morning" *Kaleidoscope* 1956-57, 3-4.
'The Tender Leaf" *Kaleidoscope* 1955-56, 3-7.
'You Can't Get Out" *Kaleidoscope* 1958, 3-7.

Denisoff, Dennis†

"Amarie Can Camp" *Fid* No. 133 (July 1982), 71-4.
"Cat Women on Mars" *Writing* No. 3 (Sum 1981), 21-2.

Dennis, David E.‡

'The Day in a Life" *Stardust* 1:3 (1976), 56-71.

Dennis, Ian‡

"A Child's Story of the Hill" *UCR* Spr 1976, 38-40.
"Freeman's Cheesecake" *UCR* Spr 1975, 23-4.
"God Is a Plant" *UCR* Spr 1975, 30-2.
'The Romance of the Plastic Rose" *UCR* Spr 1975, 24-30.
'Twa Hornbills" *UCR* Spr 1977, 42-7.

Dennis, Michael†

'between monday and friday courage grows" *WWR* 2:2 (1981), 105-6 [Prose poem?].

Denny, A. de Courcy

SWINGS AND ROUNDABOUTS: A COLLECTION OF STORIES New York: Greenwich, 1959 [Based on Miller].

Denoon, Ann‡

"Harold and the Dragon" *Undergrad* Spr 1963, 7-10.

Dent, David‡

"Decision" *Halcyon* 13 (Win 1967-68), 47-56.

Derevanchuk, Gordon
"Bride of the Vodyanyk" *Cop Toad* 3:5 (Jan 1979), 87-94.
"Lord of Lightning" *Dark Fantasy* No. 12 (1979), 4-24.
"Perchance to Dream" by Gordon Derry *Dark Fantasy* No. 9 (1976), 14-23.

Derij, J.W. (1951-)
"In Transit" *Antig R* No. 43 (Aut 1980), 27-30.
"Postage Stamp" *Mal R* No. 62 (July 1982), 173-83.

Derksen, Jim‡
"All the Leaves Blow Around" *Mandala* 1970, 67-70.
"The Man and the Cat" *Mandala* 1971, 70-5.
"That Night and the Storm" *Mandala* 1970, 71-7.

Derry, Gordon – *See* Derevanchuk, Gordon.

Desjardins, Phil‡
"The Secrets of Jonathan Coates" *Alive* 2:9 [Sept 1971], 13-5 [Untitled] *Alive* 2:5 [Apr 1971], 31.

Devaney, Dan‡
"The Joining (I)" *Stump* 5:1 (Fall-Win 1980), 33-6.
"The Joining (II)" *Stump* 5:1 (Fall-Win 1980), 37-8.

Devereaux, Bob‡
"Jokers Are Wild" *Alive* 3:1 [1972?], 24-30.

Devlin, Ivan Hope‡
"No Raisins for Katrina" *West People* No. 186 (28 Apr 1983), 7.

Devore, Roy
"Johnny Skunk" *Alberta Writers Speak* 1960, 78-80.

Dewar, Andrew†
"The Star Wench" *WWR* 2:1 (1980), 58-62.

Dewar, Helen‡
"The Auction" *Northern Ontario Anthology* 2 (1978), 31-3.

Dewdney, Christopher (1951-)
"Case A-7" *Imp* 9:1 (Spr 1981), 6.
"Hand in Glove with an Old Hat" *Per* No. 1 (Spr 1977), 42-3.
"A Story" *OPT* 4:5 (July 1977), 15.

Dewdney, Keewatin
"The Mathematician" *Folio* 16:2 (Spr 1964), 30-6.
"The Slaughterhouse" *Alphabet* No. 9 (Nov 1964), 9-18.
"The Snowflake" *Folio* 14:2 (Spr 1962), 16-24.

DeWitt, Ed†
"The Suitcase Man" *Read Ch* 2:1 (Spr 1983), 25-33.

DeWitt, Ross‡
"Mrs. Pepper, O.B.E." *AA* 53 (Mar 1963), 65-8.

Dewsnap, David†
"Hitch-Hiking" *Either/Or* No. 6 (Spr 1968), 19-21.
"The New Bridge" *Either/Or* No. 9 (Win 1970), [4 pp].

Dexter, Laura M.†
"Salt, Bitter Sea" *Amethyst* 1:1 (Spr 1962), 7-9.

Dey, Myrna†
"Hospital Visit" *Read Ch* 1:2 (Sum 1982), 81-9.
"Peonies and Bleeding Hearts" *Was R* 13:1 (Spr 1978), 61-8.

di Michele, Mary (1949-)
"Out of the Doll's House" *Nebula* No. 9 (Feb 1979), 36-7.

Diadick, Cynthia‡
"Allison and the Visitor" *AA* 63 (Mar 1973), 63-4.

Diamond, Marc†
"Coach Onion" *Writ* No. 4 (Spr 1972), 90-111.
"Danny's Sister" *Moose R* 1:2 (1978), 7-11.
"The Prankster Finds Solitude" *Writ* No. 3 (Win 1972), 55-63.

Dick, George†
"The Hawk" *Quarry* 3 [1954?], 7-10.

Dick, Jane‡
"The Glass Door" *Mandala* 1971, 68-9.

Dickey, Len‡
"The Drunk" *Origins* 8:1 (Mar 1978), 12.

Dickie, Allan‡
"A Shakespearian Tragedy" *Fifth Page* 1961, 5-7.

Dickie, Francis‡
"An Authority on Racing" *Can Horse* 5 (June 1965), 17, 40-1.

Dickinson, Don (1947-)
"The Accident Business" *Fid* No. 128 (Win 1981), 77-84.
"Fighting the Upstream" *CFM* Nos. 30/31 (1979), 92-102.
"Fighting the Upstream" *Third Impressions* (1982), 85-100.
"Flying" *Grain* 5:3 [1977], 46-51.
"Kozicki & the Living Dog" *QQ* 84 (1977), 51-60.
"Kozicki & the Living Dog" *Third Impressions* (1982), 101-15.
"The Natural Man" *Was R* 8:2 (Fall 1973), 49-53.
"Novillero" *Mal R* No. 62 (July 1982), 160-7.
"Novillero" *Metavisions* (1983), 217-23.
"The Other War" *Was R* 15:1 (Spr 1980), 53-67.

"The Part He Sees His Country" *CFM* No. 39 (1981), 44-54.
"The Part He Sees His Country" *Third Impressions* (1982), 116-31.
"The Shepherd's Revolt" *JCF* No. 20 (1977), 21-41.

Dickinson, George†
"An Affair of Frogs" *Onward* 1 May 1966, 3-5.
"The Place Whereon Thou Standest" *Onward* 24 Dec 1967, 3 [Listed as article].
"Preacher for the Day" *Blackwood's Mag* 297 (Mar 1965), 256-60.
"Preacher for the Day" *Onward* 2 Jan 1966, 3-5, 13.

Dickinson, Jim‡
"The Snowman" *Varsity Lit Issue* Fri, 3 Mar 1950, 5-7.

Dickinson, Mary Lou (1937-)
"A Country Weekend" *UWR* 12:2 (Spr-Sum 1977), 21-34.
"A Country Weekend" *CBC "Anthology"* 15 Dec 1979.
"First She Killed Him ..." *Writ* No. 8 (1976), 71-85.
"For the Record" *NJ* No. 4 (June 1974), 8-14.
"Forester" *Grain* 2:1 [1974], 24-5.
"He Looked Around" *Writ* No. 8 (1976), 12-5.
"How's the Traffic on Bloor Street?" *Waves* 4:2 (Win 1976), 3-9.
"The Masquerade" *Des* Nos. 11/12 (Spr-Sum 1975), 110-3.
"Which One Are You?" *Imp* 6:4/7:1 (1978), 20.

Dickson, Barry‡
"Birth" *Chiaroscuro* 7 (1964), 9-10.
"How I Won the Medal in Vietnam or I Like Nuts in My Chocolate Bar" *Chiaroscuro* 9 (1956-66), 40-4.
"The Wake" *Chiaroscuro* 7 (1964), 11-2.
"We Have Always Been Heroes" *Chiaroscuro* 9 (1965-66), 27-8.

Dickson, Carlotta – *See* Green, H. Gordon.

Dickson, Doris‡
"The Gramaphone" *CBC "Anthology"* 30 Aug 1975.

Dienheim, Anthony [pseudonym] (1923-)
"The Queen" *JCF* 2:2 (Spr 1973), 30-2.
"Wolf Tracks" *Stories from Pacific & Arctic Canada* (1974), 213-20.

Dille, Carolyn‡
"I Called to My Mother" *Ichor* No. 1 (Win 1980), 21-4.

Dillon, Norma‡
"The Creative Crowd" *Repos* No. 7 (Sum 1973), 35-41.
"A House" *Freelance* 9:10 (July 1980), 24-5.

Dinn, Elizabeth
"The Scarlet Jacket and the Middy Blouse" *Atl Guardian* 10 (June 1953), 17-8, 20-4.

Dinniwell, Douglas‡
"The Coming Out" *CBC "Anthology"* 6 Apr 1962.
"A Dollar or Nothing" *CBC "Anthology"* 25 Nov 1960.
"An Old Bush Pilot Flies Again" *CBC "Anthology"* 19 Jan 1962.
"Practising" *CBC "Anthology"* 1 Nov 1975.

Dinsmore, Bob‡
"Don't Think About Elephants" *TUR* 74:3 (Apr 1961), 26-9.

Diotte, Robert†
"The Separation" *JCF* Nos. 17/18 (1976), 25-32.

Disher, I. Scott‡
"The Diary of Anna Stairs: Being the Real Life Observations of a Canadian Lady Living in Montreal a Century Ago" *Mont R* No. 12 (Dec-Jan 1981-82), 10 ["Fictional memoirs"].

Disturbed, Venus [pseudonym]
"The Romantic Idiot" *TUR* 63:3 (Feb 1951), 21-8.

Diver, Geraldine A.
"What Do Bakers Die Of" *Toronto Star* Sun, 4 Oct 1981, F6.

Dixon, J.†
"North by North West" *Nw J* No. 26 (1982), 71-3.
"Two – From There" *Nw J* No. 24 (1981), 68-70.

Dixon, Kevin‡
"Fred Gets the Point" *Simcoe R* No. 8 (Spr 1980), 3 [Untitled] *Simcoe R* No. 2 (Spr 1977), 34-5.

Dlugasz, Yosef D.†
"The Rock" *Waves* 1:2 (Aut 1972), 12-8.

Dnieper, Robert D.‡
"The Battleford Incident" *Undergrad* Spr 1951, 10-2.

Dobb, Ted (1935-)
"The Boy Who Roared Like a Man" *event* 3:2 [1973], 8-12.
"Citizens of That Country" *Prism* 13:1 (Sum 1973), 93-101.
"Goat's Grace" *CFM* No. 10 (Spr 1973), 51-7.
"The Jacket" *Was R* 8:2 (Fall 1973), 59-65.
"Juggler" *JCF* 3:1 (Win 1974), 24-6.
"Mana" *CFM* No. 6 (Spr 1972), 27-30.
"Mary Polowy" *Grain* 1:2 (Dec 1973), 19-23.
"Saturday Collection" *Folio* 11:1 (1959), 15 [Based on survey response; genre unspecified].

Dobbs, Bryan‡
"Ariadne's Sister" *Creative Campus* 1961, 34-8.

Dobbs, Kildare R.E. (1923-)
PRIDE AND FALL Toronto: Clarke, Irwin, 1981.
"A Christmas Story" *CF* 39 (Dec 1959), 206-8.
"Confessions of a Memsab" *Tam R* No. 3 (Spr 1957), 16-24 [Also entitled "A Memsahib's Confession"].
"The Dreamer" *Pride and Fall* (1981), 140-51.
"The Happiness Pill" *Mont* 35 (July 1961), 18-9.
"The Happy Warrior" *Pride and Fall* (1981), 104-16.
"The Legend of Solo the Hunter" *Mont* 35 (Nov 1961), 45-51.
"A Memsahib's Confession" *Pride and Fall* (1981), 129-39 [Also entitled "Confessions of a Memsab"].
"Mr. Elephant's Magnificent Moment" *SN* 75 (24 Dec 1960), 20-1, 23-4.
"Night Junction" *Mont* 35 (Apr 1961), 22-4.
"On the Sidewalk" *CF* 40 (Oct 1960), 155-7.
"A Question of Motive" *Pride and Fall* (1981), 117-28.
"Studies of the Ilanga District" *Tam R* No. 41 (Aut 1966), 22-41.
[Title unknown] *CBC "Anthology"* 22 Jan 1960.
[Title unknown] *CBC "Anthology"* 15 Mar 1969.
"Trial of a Lesser Magistrate" *London Mag* 5:6 (Sept 1965), 80-6.
"A Wedding" *Pride and Fall* (1981), 82-103.
"Yusuf and Maria" *Pride and Fall* (1981), 152-64.

Dobinson, George‡
"A Deal's a Deal" *AA* 59 (Sept 1968), 29, 31, 33-4.

Dobson, Sydney‡
"Getting Off on the Right Foot" *Legion* 48 (Sept 1973), 17, 46.

Dodd, Alan‡
"Critical Mess" *Panic Button* No. 14 (1963), 32-3.

Dodd, Barrie†
"Settin' on a Gold Mine" *Green's* 12:1 (Aut 1983), 5-9.

Dodd, Judith A.†
"The Gift" *Muskeg R* 5 [n.d.], 35-9.

Dodge, William†
"In the Dark Gymnasium of a Warm Spring Night" *Des* 12:4/ 13:1/2 Nos. 34/35/36 (1981-82), 146.

Doerksen, Gerald†
"The Three Friends" *Read Ch* 1:2 (Sum 1982), 72-80.

Dolan, Douglas (1955-)
"The Loon's Egg" *Quarry* 32:1 (Win 1983), 12-22.
"Transformations of the Knife" *Des* 11:1/2 Nos. 27/28 (1980), 169-76.

Dolman, Robert Hartley‡
"Vanessa" *Alive* No. 35 [1974], 13.

Dominskyj, Marianne†
"Camilla" *Pier Spr* 5:[3] (Sum 1980), 8-14.
"The Looking-Glass Child" *Pier Spr* [1:4] (Win 1978), 30-5.
"The Mirror" *Pier Spr* 5:2 (Spr 1980), 23-9.
"Robert: A Mirror Image" *Harvest* No. 3 (Mar 1978), 6-8.

Donaldson, Allan†
"The Death of Mr. Lee" *CBC "Anthology"* 29 May 1971.
"The Death of Mr. Lee" *Des* 11:3 No. 29 (1980), 70-9.
"Elegy for a Sergeant" *Fid* No. 134 (Oct 1982), 63-72.
"Home Front" *JCF* Nos. 28/29 (1980), 135-46.
"The Refugee" *Des* 12:2/3 Nos. 32/33 (1981), 159-74.

Donaldson, Andrew
"Afternoon on a Kettle Lake" *Northern Ontario Anthology* 2 (1978), 52-6.

Donaldson, Anne
"Long Long Ago" *Alberta Writers Speak* 1967, 18-24.

Donnell, David (1939-)
"Ezra Loomis and the Chinks" *CFM* Nos. 45/46 (1982-83), 60-2.
"Hadley and the First Child" *CFM* Nos. 45/46 (1982-83), 56-8.
"Jung and Freud in America" *CFM* Nos. 45/46 (1982-83), 58-60.
"Toronto/the War" *CFM* Nos. 45/46 (1982-83), 52-6.

Donnelly, John F.†
"Hop Sing" *QQ* 75 (1968), 330-7.
"The Oslund House" *Tam R* No. 26 (Win 1963), 40-7.
"A Promise of Silence" *Fid* No. [74] (Fall 1967), 18-27.

Donnelly, Maggie†
"Jake's Fortune" *CSSM* 2:1 (Jan 1976), 4-7.
"Jake's Fortune" *Northern Mosaic* 1 (Apr 1981), 10-1.
"Ye Olde Attic Gift Shoppe" *Northern Mosaic* 1 (Dec 1981), 6.

Donohue, Patrick
"The Interview" *Folio* 21:1 (Fall 1968), 29-32.
"Mrs. Malloy" *Ave Maria* 105 (18 Feb 1967), 26-7.
"Romance" *Quarry* 32:2 (Spr 1983), 4-8.

Donovan, Rita†
"Alarm Clock Dreams" *Dand* 10:2 (1983), 14-8.
"Parallel Lines" *NeWest R* 6 (June 1981), 13-4, 16.

Donovan, Robert E.†
"A Nip in the Air" *Outdoor Can* 11 (Feb 1983), 20-2.

Donovan, Terry‡
"Why Did 6 Old Friends Kill Themselves?" *Toronto Star* Sun, 31 Oct 1982, D5.

d'Or, Vic and Hutton, Bill
See also d'Or, Vic and Young, David; d'Or, Vic and Nations, Opal L.
"Snow Job" *BC Monthly* 2:2 (Feb 1974-77 [?]), [2 pp].

d'Or, Vic and Nations, Opal L.
    See also d'Or, Vic and Hutton, Bill; d'Or, Vic and Young, David; Fones, Robert and Nations, Opal L.; Gold, Artie and Nations, Opal L.; Kilodney, Crad and Nations, Opal L.; Nations, Opal L.
    "The Spectre of Art" *Strange Faeces* No. 17 (June 1975), 60-76.

d'Or, Vic and Young, David
    See also Coleman, Victor; Coleman, Victor and Young, David A.; d'Or, Vic and Hutton, Bill; d'Or, Vic and Nations, Opal L.; Young, David.
    "Stolen Moments" *Story So Far* 2 (1973), 83-109.

Doran, J.†
    "The Writer of a Fact of Life" *Quarry* 29:[2] (Spr 1980), 37-41.

Dorland, Keith R.†
    "The Greatest Thing" *Quarry* 17:2 (Win 1968), 24-7.

Dorman, Alexander‡
    "The 'shine Can" *Nfld Q* 66:1 (Sept-Nov 1967), 31-2.

Dorn, Ed‡
    "Of Eastern Newfoundland, Its Inns & Outs" *Geo Str Writing* No. 8 (27 July 1971), 10-2.

Dornan, Chris‡
    "Film Noir" *Unearth Mag* (U.S.) 1:4 (Fall 1977), 74-83.
    "Man in Vacuum" *Unearth Mag* (U.S.) 1:2 (Spr 1977), 2-8.
    "The Night the Arcturians Landed" *Stardust* 1:4 [n.d.], 17-23.
    "The Night the Arcturians Landed" *Unearth Mag* (U.S.) 1:1 (Win 1977), 74-9.
    "Skirmish at Crater Alphonsus" *Stardust* 2:1 [n.d.], 3-6.

Dorrington, D.R.‡
    "It Has Been Seven Years / It Has Been Seventy Years" *In Store* No. 1 (Apr 1969), 14-6.

Dorsey, Candas Jane (1952-)
    "Columbus Hits the Shoreline Rag" *Getting Here* (1977), 49-63.
    "The Dancing Master" *CBC [Edm] "Alberta Anthology"* 16 Oct 1982.
    "Sally Go 'Round the Roses" *Br Out* 2:1 (Jan-Feb 1975), 28-30.
    "You'll Remember Mercury" *NeWest R* 5 (Mar 1980), 8-9.

Dotto, Lydia‡
    "Fantasy Coming True" *Legion* 53 (Mar 1979), 21-4.

Doubt, Bryan†
    "The Nephew" *Versus* No. 1 (Sum 1976), 17-22.

Dougherty, Dan (1946?-)
    "Henry Smoot's Practical Joke" *Pulp* 3:4 (15 Aug 1975), [1-2] [Excerpt?].

Douglas, D.A.‡
    "Escape" *Edmonton Journal* Fri, 24 Sept 1965, 29.

Douglas, Gilean‡
"Ready for Everything" *AA* 55 (Sept 1964), 93-4.

Douglas, Molly†
"Alice" *CSSM* 2:1 (Jan 1976), 3-4.
"Let It Be" *Legion* 52 (July 1977), 25, 48-9.
"The Test" *CSSM* 1:4 (Oct 1975), 3-4.

Douglas, Will – *See* Green, H. Gordon.

Douma, Felix†
"Oil Barrel" *This* 12 (Dec 1978), 13-7.

Dow, David – *See* Green, H. Gordon.

Dow, John
"Brother Simon" *Onward* 28 Nov 1965, 3-4.
"John the Baptist" *Onward* 6 Feb 1966, 5, 14.
"Judas Iscariot as Seen by Simon, the Zealot" *Onward* 27 Feb 1966, 3-5.
"Matthew" *Onward* 26 Sept 1965, 6-7, 14.
"Nicodemus" *Onward* 7 Nov 1965, 3-5.
"Philip" *Onward* 9 Jan 1966, 3-5.

Dowbiggin, Bruce†
"It's Guilt That Makes the World Go Round" *Auguries* [No. 1 (1976)], 25-36.

Dowling, Tom‡
"The Lonely Quiet" *Deaf Can* 4:6 (June 1979), 3-5.

Downer, Don‡
"Silver Chief" *Nfld Q* 63:3 (Fall 1964), 19-22.

Downes, Gwladys V. (1915-)
"Aunt Di: A Tale of the Twenties" *CBC "Anthology"* 18 Dec 1976.
"Aunt Di: A Tale of the Twenties" *Mal R* No. 50 (Apr 1979), 245-57.

Downey, Fairfax‡
"The Reindeer Buyer" *AA* 49 (Dec 1958), 17.

Downie, Glen R.†
"Light" *Antig R* No. 51 (Aut 1982), 115-8.

Downie, Jill
"The Unreal Country" *Chat* 50 (Apr 1977), 51, 68, 70-1.

Downs, Tommy
"The Promise" *Skylark* 11:2 (Win 1975), 58-60.
"Two Peas in a Pod" *CSSM* 2:3 (Sum 1976), 25-7, 29.

Dowright, George Oliver‡
"Pete's Story – A Chronicle of Galactic Lust and High Drama" *Nightwinds* 1:1 (Sum 1979), 23-4.

Doyle, Bill‡
    "A Bear Escape" *Legion* 54 (Oct 1979), 24, 27-8 [Non-fiction?].
    "Eye to Glassy Eye" *Legion* 54 (June 1979), 16, 19.

Doyle, Dan
    "And Counting for the Knockdowns, George Bannon" *Matrix* 2:1 (Spr 1976), 13-9.
    "And the Legs All Dangling Down-O" *Alpha* 2:4 (Dec 1977), 5-14.
    "Clamtorts and Hippocrumps" *Alpha* Feb 1977, 3-6, 12.
    "Flim-Flam Man" *Alpha* 2:6 (Feb 1978), 25-6, 32.
    "One for the Master" *Review Ottawa* 1:1 (Aut 1977), 34-40.
    "A Plate of Spaghetti" *Matrix* 1:1 (Spr 1975), 22-4.
    "Undertow" *Chel J* 4 (July-Aug 1978), 176, 193.
    "Until We've Found the Center of the Circle" *Alpha* Apr 1977, 3-5.

Doyle, Donna (1950?-)
    "The Feast of Christ the King" *Pot Port* 4 (1982-83), 25.

Doyle, John‡
    "Cressida Got Nothing on This Kid" *Generation* Win 1967, 39.

Doyle, Judith
    "Elliott's Disorder" *OPT* 6:4/5 (May-June 1979), 14 [Prose poem?].
    "Envy" *Imp* 8:3 (Sum 1980), 41-3.
    "Fading" *Imp* 9:1 (Spr 1981), 43-4.
    "Flicker Vertigo" *OPT* 6:1 (Feb 1979), 10-2 [Prose poem?].
    "Rate of Descent" *Imp* 10:3 (Spr-Sum 1983), 35-7.
    "Test Patterns 1-3" *OPT* 4:9 (Dec 1977), 18.
    "Transcript" *Imp* 9:2 (Fall 1981), 4-6 [Excerpt?].

Doyle, Nancy
    "The Boy Who Was Lucky" *Uk Can* 6 (1 Feb 1952), 8.
    "The Buzzer" *Uk Can* 14 (15 Nov 1960), 9.
    "The Day the Computer Went Wild" *CJO* 10 (Feb 1972), 14-5.
    "A Day to Remember" *Uk Can* 7 (15 Apr 1953), 7-8.
    "A Day to Remember" *Alive* No. 43 [n.d.], 19-20.
    "Even as the Fortress Walls" *Uk Can* 8 (1 Sept 1954), 7, 11.
    "Even as the Fortress Walls" *Alive* No. 42 [1975], 16-7.
    "The Fate of Other People" *CJO* 8 (Sept-Oct 1970), 20, 22.
    "The Flowers You Did Not Bring Me" *CJO* 17 (Apr 1979), 13-4.
    "The Glory and the Grief" *Alive* No. 38 [1974], 10-1.
    "The House on the Top of the Hill" *Uk Can* 18 (15 Mar 1964), 9-10.
    "In the Bright of the Moon" *Uk Can* 11 (1 Feb 1957), 11, 16.
    "In the Bright of the Moon" *Alive* No. 40 [1974], 20.
    "Let Me Bury My Dead" *Uk Can* 17 (1 June 1963), 10.
    "The Menace" *CJO* 14 (Sept-Oct 1976), 11-2 ["An Episode"].
    "The Oath" *CJO* 5 (July-Aug 1967), 21-2.
    "Of the Fathers" *Alive* No. 46 (Dec-Jan 1975-76), 9.
    "The Refuge" *Uk Can* 8 (1 Mar 1954), 8-9.
    "The Right to Live" *NF* 1:4 (Win 1953), 21-4.
    "Suddenly Last Spring" *Uk Can* 19 (15 Jan 1965), 9-10.

"Suddenly Last Spring" *Alive* No. 48 (Apr 1976), 9-10.
"Taller Than His Tall Self" *CJO* 5 (Mar 1967), 12-3.
"The Thirteenth Juror" *Uk Can* 17 (15 Nov 1963), 9-10.
"To the Drug Store for Evale" *CJO* 12 (Sept 1974), 14-5.
"U-Turn on University" *CJO* 4 (Apr 1966), 12-3.
"Waiting for Mrs. O'Malley" *Uk Can* 7 (15 Nov 1953), 8-9.

Doyle, Terence E.†
"Aftermath" *Antig R* No. 46 (Sum 1981), 83-91.

Draayer, Ken‡
"Game" *Quarry* 23:3 (Sum 1974), 11-4.
"Game" *Communicator* Oct 1974, 46-7.
"Rainy Days" *Quarry* 18:4 (Sum 1969), 30-4.

Drache, Sharon (1943-)
" 'Boychick': A Fable" *JD* Passover 1983, 8-9.
" 'The Gingeriascope' " *JD* Sum 1981, 12-5.
"Jeremiah Proosky" *JD* Hanukah 1978, 4-6.
"A Kitel (for Solomon)" *JD* Passover 1981, 50-1.
"Let's Go Shopping" *JD* Passover 1983, 38-40, 42, 44, 46.
"Let's Make Music" *JD* Passover 1983, 16, 18-20, 22-4, 26.
"Little Boxes" *JD* Passover 1983, 2-6.
"Little Boxes" *Viewpoints* 12:5 (June-July 1983), 6-8.
"Lobster Soufflé" *JD* Passover 1983, 12-5.
"The Meeting" *JD* Passover 1983, 28-30, 32-4, 36.
"The Mikveh Man" *Quarry* 30:2 (Spr 1981), 51-62.
"The Pintele and the Mote" *JD* Hanukah 1979, 2-5.
"Sofer S'tm" *JD* Passover 1981, 28-30, 32, 34.

Drachman, Wolf‡
"The Cat Screamed" *CBC [Van] "Hornby Collection"* 16 Jan 1982.
"Dilemma" *CBC [Van] "Hornby Collection"* 6 Dec 1980.
"Petrified" *CBC [Van] "Hornby Collection"* 8 Jan 1983 [Genre unspecified].

Dragland, Stan (1942-)
"Alice Is" *Applegarth's Folly* No. 2 (1975), 30-1.
"Beth Gôlert" *Lit R* 1:1 (1983), 21.
"The Case Is Altered" *Writing* No. 1 (Sum 1980), 42.
"Journeys Through Bookland" *Lit R* 1:1 (1983), 21-4.
"Mercury" *Story So Four* (1976), 102.
"Penelope's Dog" *Writing* No. 4 (Win 1981-82), 11-2.

Drayton, Geoffrey† (1924-)
"Christopher" *Cataraqui R* 1:1 (Spr 1951), 36-44.

Drepaul, Joe‡
"Cheiron Came" *Chiaroscuro* 9 (1965-66), 29-36.
"Pan American Announces" *Chiaroscuro* 8 (1964), 27-9.
"Wear This for Me" *Chiaroscuro* 9 (1965-66), 49-55.

Dreschel, Andrew†
"The Hypocrite" *event* 4:2 [1974?], 64-81.

Drew, Mabel E.†
"A Quiet Weekend" *CA & B* 46:3 (Spr 1971), 7-8, 14-5.
"The Sand Banks" *Lib* 30 (June 1953), 38-9, 74-5.
"The Woman on the Bench" *Mam* 2:1 [n.d.], [6 pp].

Drew, Mary
GASTOWN STORIES Toronto: N Press, 1981 [Based on Miller].

Drew, N. John‡
"Come Down, Come Down: A Faery Fantasy" *Intervales* No. 2 (1960), 21-4.

Drew, Wayland (1932-)
"Arabesque" *Acta Vic* 81:3 (Mar 1957), 5-8.
"Beat No Drums for Him" *Tam R* No. 12 (Sum 1959), 29-53.
"Erratic" *Seasons* 20:4 (Win 1980), 30-6.
"Homage to Axel Hoeniger" *73: New Canadian Stories* 120-30.
"Miss Darby's Room" *CBC "Anthology"* 31 Aug 1974.
"The Terrible Fate of Joshua Sibbs" *Acta Vic* 81:1 (Nov 1956), 31-4.
"To Raise a Child" *Tam R* No. 4 (Sum 1957), 23-30.
"Widow's Walk" *CBC "Anthology"* 11 Dec 1971.
"Wood" *74: New Canadian Stories* 76-84.

Dronyk, Levi (1949-)
"Baxter Jack" *Prism* 17:2 (Fall 1978), 67-75.
"Circle of Confusion" *From an Island* 10:1 [n.d.], 32-5, 53.
"Green Felt Blues" *Introductions from an Island* 1976, 37-46.

Drummond, R. Jill†
"White Knight to King's Pawn" *Whetstone* Spr 1974, [2 pp].

Drylie, William
"Her Name Is Susan" *SW* 6 Nov 1954, II:7.
"Never Forge a Valentine" *SW* 12 Feb 1955, I:7.
"TV Sets a Trap" *SW* 17 Jan 1953, I:8.

Duclos, David‡
"Two Removes" *TUR* 92:2 (Apr 1979), 32-3 [Prose poem?].

Duffie, Archie†
"Where Is My Wandering Car Tonight?" *Can National Mag* 42 (Oct 1956), 8-9.

Duffin, Ken†
" 'Cyclone' Taylor and the Case of Armada Base III" *Nightwinds* 1:1 (Sum 1979), 21-2.
"Dead Centre" *Quote Unquote* 1:2 (Nov 1978), 4.
"A Meeting of Minds" *Quote Unquote* 2:1 (Jan 1979), 7.
"Moments of Most Madness" *Quote Unquote* 2:2 (Mar 1979), 7.
"The Night Is Black and Orange Fire" *Nightwinds* 1:1 (Sum 1979), 35-6.
"The Night Is Black and Orange Fire" *Quarry* 32:2 (Spr 1983), 32-3.

"A Place to Land" *Nightwinds* 1:1 (Sum 1979), 1-4.
"A Place to Land" *Portico* 3:2/3 [n.d.], 40-6.
"Stretching a Point" *Nightwinds* 2:1 (Spr 1980), 19.

Dufresne, John‡
'Two Students" *Dreamweaver* 2:2 [n.d.], 21-2.

Duggan, Edwin J.
"... loosers, weepers" [sic] *Black Walnut* 2 (1972), 1-6.

Duggan, Robert‡
'Boy on Fire" *Kaleidoscope* 1958, 22-6.

Duloff, Nick‡
"Believe and You Shall See" *Fifth Page* [1969?], 30-2.

Dumbrille, Dorothy‡
"Abram Came Out of a February Blizzard" *UC Observer* 15 Mar 1965, 17-8, 32.

Duncan, Chester
"Up and Down in the Depression" *Winnipeg Stories* (1974), 131-6.

Duncan, Frances (1942-)
"Change of Life" *CFM* No. 20 (Win 1976), 37-43.
"CompartMENTALization" *Room* 1:4 (Win 1976), 42-7.
"Flowers for the Dead" *Room* 1:2 (Sum 1975), 25-8.
"Flowers for the Dead" *Canadian Short Fiction Anthology 2* (1982), 53-5.
"Gallstones" *VWFP/Revue* 1:6 (Aug 1975), 11.
'The Gravel Pile" *Room* 3:3 (1977), 2-10.
'The Home Handyman" *NJ* Nos. 7/8 (1976), 33-5.
"Immolation" *CFM* No. 16 (Win 1975), 22-8.
"Magic Moments Moonglow" *Room* 1:2 (Sum 1975), 23-5.
"Merry-Go-Round" *Lit Store News* No. 30 (Nov 1980), 9.
"Modern Communication" *CFM* No. 17 (Spr 1975), 44-6.
"Once in a Quiet Neighbourhood" *Diversions* 5:1 (1975), 47-50.
'The Rain Forest" *Makara* 1:4 (June-July 1976), 17-20.
'The Return" *NJ* Nos. 7/8 (1976), 35-7.
'The Squirrel" *Common Ground* (1980), 43-51.
"Was That Malcolm Lowry" *Room* 6:3 (1981), 28-40.
'The West Coast Trail" *Room* 2:4 (1977), 2-10.
"Yvonne" *Room* 1:2 (Sum 1975), 20-2.

Duncan, Francis
"Turtles" *Pulp* 3:11 (1 Feb 1976), [3-4].

Duncan, George
'The Mourners" *Waves* 9:1 (Aut 1980), 20-3.

Duncan, Helen‡
"A Little Patience" CBC *"Anthology"* 17 Feb 1961.

Duncan, Kathy†
'The Lake" *Cap R* No. 4 (Fall-Win 1973), 27-31.

Duncan, Leslie
"A Case of Non-Involvement" *Beaver Bites* 1:1 (5 Mar 1975), [1 p].
"A Couple and a Cow" *Beaver Bites* 1:2 (15 Apr 1976), [1 p].
"The Funeral" *Beaver Bites* 2:1 (Jan 1977), 48-9.
"A Haven for the Aged" *Beaver Bites* 1:7 (Oct 1976), 30-1.
"My Case of Fleeting Fever Fame, or How I Stopped Worrying and Learned to Love Fatal Diseases" *Beaver Bites* 2:1 (Jan 1977), 46-7.

Duncan, M.M.
"Father Shannon's Nest Egg" *Can Messenger* 70 (Aug 1960), 10-2, 41.
"Hannibal the Great" *Alberta Writers Speak* 1960, 7-14.
"Minnie and the Moocher" *Alberta Writers Speak* 1969, 62-8.
"Papa and Angus" *Alberta Speaks* 1957, 23-8.
"Papa and Angus" *FH* 17 Jan 1957, 14-5.
"The Sunday Man" *Alberta Writers Speak* 1964, 68-76.

Duncan, W.T.‡
"Journey Home" *Stories with John Drainie* (1963), 129-34.
"Journey Home" *Tigers of the Snow* (1973), 153-7.

Dungey, Christopher‡
"Gap for the Circle" *Origins* 11:1 (Mar 1981), 52-8.

Dunham, Lynne† (1947-)
"The Red Leaf" *event* 2:3 [1973], 62-3.

Dunn, C.A.‡
"The Death of the Marionettes" *Muse* 1964 Vol. 2, 10-2.

Dunn, J.M.†
"Macedonia's Revenge" *Antig R* No. 55 (Aut 1983), 59-64.

Dunn, James†
"S/he" *Cap R* No. 26 (1983), 67-70.
"Sunday Afternoon on the Grande Jatte" *Waves* 10:3 (Win 1982), 14-5.

Dunn, Keller‡
"Mr. Prigg Inherits the Earth" *Alpha* 7:1 (Nov 1982), 9-12.

Dunn, Tim†
"Period Piece" *Can R* 2:1 (Feb 1975), 20-1, 23-4.

Durrie, Miles‡
"Paddy" *Stump* 2:2 (Fall 1978), 37-9.

Durvis, J.S.†
"Till Death ... " *Next Exit* 1:3 (Fall 1980), 5-6.

Dust, Julian†
"Insanity" *Stardust* 3:1 [n.d.], 47-60.
"Quest" *Stardust* 2:1 [n.d.], 37-53.
"Self-Portrait" *Stardust* 2:3 [n.d.], 3-14.
"Spencerville" *Stardust* 3:2 (Spr 1981), 27-35.

Dutton, Paul‡
"The Somnolent" *Writing* No. 4 (Win 1981-82), 41-2.
"Uncle Rebus Clean-Song" *Story So Four* (1976), 103-8.

Dworkin, Martin S.†
"The Rocket Guns" *Can Commentator* 5 (July-Aug 1961), 24-6.

Dyba, Kenneth
"Baseball Game" *Pier Spr* 7:1 (Win 1982), 6-19.
"Blaze" *Dand* 10:1 (1983), 26-34.
"Buster and the Blue Dahlia" *Rubicon* No. 1 (Spr 1983), 7-13.
"Cornucopia" *Lunatic Gazette* Ser 2 1:4 [date unknown], 13 [Based on survey response].
"Crimson Lake" *Origins* 12:3 (Win 1982), 38-63.
"Exam" *CCWQ* 3:2/3 [n.d.], 12-3.
"Foxtails" *Grain* 8:3 (Nov 1980), 44-9.
"Garden" *Pier Spr* 7:3 (Sum 1982), 9-13.
"Garden" *Grain* 10:4 (Nov 1982), 30-1.
"Kovack Bros." *Matrix* No. 12 (Win 1981), 59-63.
"Love Letter 37 Minos/Calgary" *Quarry* 30:1 (Win 1981), 35-7.
"Mumma" *Rune* No. 7 (Win 1982), 82-95.
"Nordegg" by Kenneth Colley *CF* 59 (June-July 1979), 23-5.
"Orange Cripple" *Mam* [6:3] (Sum 1983), [6 pp].
"Ruth" *event* 10:2 (1981), 77-86.
"Sandstone Animals" *Des* 12:4/13:1/2 Nos. 34/35/36 (1981-82), 139-45.
"The Tall Grass" *Grain* 9:2 (May 1981), 15-9.

Dybvig, Leslie (1930-)
SHORT STORIES ABOUT SASKATCHEWAN Regina: Privately printed, 1980.
"Aunt Aggie's Last Escapade" CBC *"Stories with John Drainie"* 1961; 1963 [Based on survey response].
"Aunt Aggie's Last Escapade" *Short Stories About Saskatchewan* (1980), 1-5.
"Betting Sam's Last Bet" CBC *"Stories with John Drainie"* 1962; 1963 [Also on Australian radio 1968; based on survey response].
"Betting Sam's Last Bet" *Short Stories About Saskatchewan* (1980), 7-11.
"The Bow Is Always Drawn" *Short Stories About Saskatchewan* (1980), 33-45.
"Cole Slaw" CBC *"Stories with John Drainie"* 1960 [Based on survey response].
"Day of Reckoning" *Newscene* (Nfld) 1971 [Based on survey response].
"Dirty Kid and Colonel Boogie" *West Producer* 1973 [Based on survey response].
"Dirty Kid and Colonel Boogie" *Short Stories About Saskatchewan* (1980), 65-70.
"The Great Intendant Plays St. Nick" *West Producer* 1957 [Based on survey response].
"The Great Intendant Plays St. Nick" CBC *"Stories with John Drainie"* 1961; 1962; 1967 [Based on survey response].
"The Hell Raising Church Raiser" *Short Stories About Saskatchewan* (1980), 13-7.
"The Kitchen Curtains" *Short Stories About Saskatchewan* (1980), 147-51.
"A Lesson in Sympathy" *Short Stories About Saskatchewan* (1980), 113-7.
"The Man in the Street Scene" *Short Stories About Saskatchewan* (1980), 103-6.
"The Meddlers" *West Producer* 1965 [Based on survey response].
"Mite Pitkin" *Short Stories About Saskatchewan* (1980), 53-7.

"Mite Pitkin" *CBC "Stories with John Drainie"* 1961 [Based on survey response].
"Near Miss" *Real Confessions* 1968 [Based on survey response].
"Nowhere Waving Back" *Columbia* (1976) [Based on survey response].
"Observant Night Man" *CBC "Stories with John Drainie"* [Based on survey response].
"Ole and the Fate of Man" *Short Stories About Saskatchewan* (1980), 141-5.
"Ole and the Irishman" *Short Stories About Saskatchewan* (1980), 129-34.
"Patrick O'Malley Sheds His Coat" *Short Stories About Saskatchewan* (1980), 85-9.
"The Pony" *Short Stories About Saskatchewan* (1980), 107-11.
"Pride to the Last Prune" *Short Stories About Saskatchewan* (1980), 97-101.
"The Quiet Conscience" *West Producer* 1966 [Based on survey response].
"The Quiet Conscience" *Short Stories About Saskatchewan* (1980), 91-6.
"The Redman's Burden" *Newscene* 1970 [Based on survey response].
"The Redman's Burden" *Short Stories About Saskatchewan* (1980), 59-64.
"Sean O'Leary and the Swede" *CBC "Stories with John Drainie"* 1964; 1965; 1967 [Based on survey response].
"Sean O'Leary and the Swede" *Short Stories About Saskatchewan* (1980), 135-40.

"The Splurge of Charlie Harris" *Short Stories About Saskatchewan* (1980), 19-26.
"Survival of the Fittest" *CBC "Stories with John Drainie"* 1962; 1963 [Based on survey response].
"The Trier" *Short Stories About Saskatchewan* (1980), 119-28.
"The Upsetting Man" *Short Stories About Saskatchewan* (1980), 47-51.
"Viscount Joshua" *West Producer* 1965 [Based on survey response].
"Viscount Joshua" *Short Stories About Saskatchewan* (1980), 71-6.
"Viscount Joshua Takes a Bride" *West Producer* 1965 [Based on survey response].
"Viscount Joshua Takes a Bride" *Short Stories About Saskatchewan* (1980), 77-83.
"The Wedding" *CBC "Stories with John Drainie"* [date unknown] [Based on survey response].
"The Wedding" *Short Stories About Saskatchewan* (1980), 27-31.

Dyce, Peter
"The Employee" *Writ* No. 10 (1978), 60-94.
"Metamorphosis – Six Years" *Prism* (Mont) No. 3 (1957), 45-9.
"Reflections on a Commuter" *Prism* (Mont) 1:2 (1956), 49-52.

Dyck, E.F.
[Title unknown] *CBC "Anthology"* 8 Oct 1977.
"Versions" *CFM* No. 13 (Spr 1974), 43-5.

Dyer, Evelyn†
"Hostility" *First Encounter* 1971, 32-3.

Dyke, Dave Hart‡
"His Nemesis" *WWR* 1:3 (Spr 1978), 21-30.

Dymant, Margaret†
"Never Seek to Destroy" *83: Best Canadian Stories* 116-25.

Dynan, Margaret†
"Miss Sullivan in Her Element" *Quarry* 23:4 (Aut 1974), 49-56.

Dyroff, Jan Michael‡
"Grass Burning" *Alive* No. 41 [1975], 32-3.

Eades, Murray‡
"The Royal Dirge" *Acta Vic* 78:3 (Feb 1954), 24.

Eames, David‡
"A Collector's Piece" *Stories with John Drainie* (1963), 59-63.

Earl, Cy – *See* Green, H. Gordon.

Earl, Lawrence‡
"The Lake That Didn't Like Us" *AA* 53 (May 1963), 33-40.
"Who Said There Ain't No Heaven" *AA* 55 (Aug 1965), 57, 59-61.

Earle, Kathleen†
"Gentle Rain" *Nw J* No. 23 (1981), 81-9.

Earle, Ruthven‡
"Scarlett's Web" *Acta Vic* 102:1 (Fall 1977), 7.

Easley, Shirley-Dale†
"If We Make It Through the Winter" *Des* 14:5 No. 43 (Win 1983-84), 125-9.

Easson, Bruce‡
"Grey Noon of Madness" *Acta Vic* 76:3 (Feb 1952), 25-8.

Eastman, Harriet‡
"The Wart" *UCR* 1980-81, 33-4.

Eastoe, Derek‡
"Laying on with Macduff" *Forum* (OSSTF) 6 (Dec 1980), 218-9 [Humour].

Easton, Alan
THE ADVENTURES OF CAPTAIN HAYLESTONE Toronto: McGraw-Hill Ryerson, 1975.
"The Barge" *Adventures of Captain Haylestone* (1975), 24-38.
"Cruising" *Adventures of Captain Haylestone* (1975), 39-55.
"The Foul Trophy" *Adventures of Captain Haylestone* (1975), 56-72.
"The Girl from the Maritimes" *Adventures of Captain Haylestone* (1975), 1-23.
"Loading Deep" *Adventures of Captain Haylestone* (1975), 127-43.
"Pandemonium in the Cockpit" *Adventures of Captain Haylestone* (1975), 109-26.
"Rum Compass" *Adventures of Captain Haylestone* (1975), 73-89.
"Scuttling" *Adventures of Captain Haylestone* (1975), 144-71.
"Special Cargo" *Adventures of Captain Haylestone* (1975), 90-108.

Eaton, Jean†
"With a Heart on Her Sleeve" *Chat* 26 (Sept 1953), 17, 94-100.

Eaton, John†

"Rice Pudding" *Was R* 11:1 (Spr 1976), 55-67.

Eaton, Lucy Ellen (1905-)

DEAR GOD! Castlegar: privately printed, 1981 [Based on CBIP].
"He Wanted Adventure" *CSSM* 1:3 (July 1975), 44-8.
"If You Ask for a Fish" *Saskatchewan Homecoming* (1971), 184-5.

An Eavesdropper [pseudonym]

"Through an Open Window" *UC Observer* 15 (1 Feb 1953), 5.

Ebbeson, Barbara†

"A Famous Egyptologist" *Makara* 1:5 (Aug-Sept 1976), 42-7.

Ebong, William Esap‡

"The Dilemma" *Fifth Page* 1968, 6-7.

Eby, Robert E.‡

"New Brunswick Mourning" *Communicator* Oct 1974, 30-1.
"New Brunswick Mourning" *Words from Inside* 1975, 23-4.
"Recognition" *Communicator* Aug [1974], 8-9.

Eccleston, K.‡

"Needle in a Grove" *Raven* 2 [No. 4] (Spr 1957), 18-21.

Edenson, Jerry‡

"The Process" *Seraph* [1965], [1 p].

Edgar, Keith

"Ode to a Poetess" *FH* 28 Aug 1952, 16-7, 23.

Edinborough, Arnold

"The Polymerised Woman" *Cataraqui R* 1:2 (Sum 1951), 45-7.

Edmonds, Edward L.‡

"Bearing Christmas Gifts" *Abegweit R* 1:1 (1974), 46-51.
"Generation Gap" *Sand Patterns* No. 2 (Nov 1972), [2 pp].

Edwards, Caterina†

"All Life from the Sea" *Br Out* 1:1 (Mar-Apr 1974), 18-20.
"Everlasting Life" *Getting Here* (1977), 87-106.
"Frost King" *Dand* 7:2 (1980), 72-9.
"Island of the Nightengales" *More Stories from Western Canada* (1980), 182-97.
"The Last Young Man" *JCF* 2:2 (Spr 1973), 25-8.
"Sarah" *New Thursday* No. 1 (Spr 1974), 15-37.

Edwards, David R.†

"With Palms and Scattered Garments" *Onward* 7 Apr 1963, 3, 11.
"With Palms and Scattered Garments" *Onward* 19 Mar 1967, 4-5.

Edwards, F.D.†

"The Man Who Got Sick" *Writ* No. 15 (1983), 39-43.

Edwards, Hope†
"Tears for Peace" *Read Ch* 1:1 (Spr 1982), 15-6.

Edwards, Lionel†
"In Retrospect: The Going" *Marxist Q* No. 18 (Sum 1966), 3-10.

Edwards, Mary Kay
"The Alabaster Box" *FH* 12 Apr 1951, 28-9.
"All Her Own" *FH* 20 Aug 1953, 20.
"Consider the Lilies" *FH* 10 Apr 1952, 24-5, 31.
"A Dollar's Worth of Santa Claus" *FH* 23 Dec 1954, 10-1, 26.
"Glad Eastertide" *FH* 3 Apr 1958, 26-7.
"Gum Chewing Angel" *FH* 20 Dec 1951, 22-3. 26.
"The Last Kiss" *FH* 1 Mar 1951, 22-3.
"The Last Kiss" *Stories to Read Again* (1965), 109-18.
"Sun in Her Face" *FH* 23 Oct 1952, 28-9, 35, 64.
"Whither Thou Goest ... " *FH* 26 July 1956, 18-9, 27.

Edwards, N.†
"Going Buggy" *Mam* 2:3 (Fall 1978), [5 pp].

Edwards, Reid F.‡
"Last Call" *Mandala* 1976, 19-21.

Edwards, W. Stewart‡
"What Has the Liquor Traffic Done for ... You! You! You!" *Can Life* 1:3 (Win 1949-50), 16, 37 [Listed as satire].

Edweirdo [pseudonym]
"The Cuish" *Communicator* Aug [1974], 66-7.

Eedy, Alice – *See* Boissonneau, Alice.

Egan, Patricia†
"The Trap" *CSSM* 1:4 (Oct 1975), 49-52.

Eglitis, Joseph† (195?-)
"Time in London" *Ichor* No. 2 (1981), 51-6.

Egner, Brian†
" 'Physician, Heal Thyself' " *Raven* 1:3 (Spr 1956), 30-1.

Egyedi, Bela (1913-1983)
"Co-Owner of Theoretical 'toutou' " *Delta* No. 20 (Feb 1963), 9-12.
"The Job-Haunt" *Antig R* No. 33 (Spr 1978), 65-73.
"Oldman's Last Ride" *Antig R* No. 17 (Spr 1974), 68-78.
"Open Air Haircut with a Fat Canada Goose" *Antig R* No. 14 (Sum 1973), 95-9.
"Trude's Homecoming" *Antig R* No. 22 (Sum 1975), 51-9.
"White Spot" *Antig R* No. 31 (Aut 1977), 77-83.

Ehrlich, Hilari†
"Burnt Umber" *Antig R* No. 44 (Win 1980), 11-6.

Eibel, Deborah†
"The Place of His Hiring" *Forge* Mar 1959, 24-6.

Eikenberry, Gary
"Angel" *Pot Port* 3 (1981-82), 42-3.
"Carving" *Antig R* No. 48 (Win 1982), 41-4.
"Mr. Deacon" *CCWQ* 5:1 (1983), 8-9, 28.
"Night Driving" *Matrix* No. 14 (Win 1982), 24-8.
"Street Scenes" *New Q* 2:2 (Sum 1982), 45-50.
"Survivors" *Pot Port* 2 (1980-81), 22-4.
"Time Rules" *Nebula* Nos. 21/22 (1982), 20-8.

Eirikson, Irene‡
"The Coffee Break" *Alive* No. 73 (16 Apr 1977), 1.

Eisenbichler, Konrad‡
"Heart-Aches Column Answered: Native Witchdoctor Performs Operation (A True Confession)" *Acta Vic* 104:1 (Spr 1980), 14.
"A Stranger in the House" *Acta Vic* 106:1 (Fall 1981), 4-5.

Eisler, Ken‡
"Graffito" *Pulp* 2:21 (1 Feb 1975), [2 pp].

Ekbaum, Salme (1912-)
"The Buried Letter" *[Title Unknown]* (1975), 21.

Eldredge, Kristy‡
"More Dolls Than Balls" *Inprint* 3:1 [n.d.], 24-5.

Eley, Bonita Bishop
"The Magician's Last Act" *Black Cat* 1:4 (Win 1981-82), 54-65.

Elflandsson, Galad
"The Basilisk" *Cop Toad* 3:5 (Jan 1979), 42-56.
"The Flat on Rue Chambord" *Dark Fantasy* No. 22 (1980), 4-23 [Novella?].
"The Hand of the King" *Dark Fantasy* No. 12 (1979), 34-48.
"How Darkness Came to Carcosa" *Dragonbane* No. 1 (Spr 1978), 35-45.
"Night Rider on a Pale Horse" *Phoenix Tree* (1980), 269-79.
"Nightfear" *Dark Fantasy* No. 15 (1978), 10-9.
"The Piper of Dray" *Cop Toad* 2:3 (Jan 1978), 41-51.
"A Tapestry of Dreams" *Beyond the Fields We Know* No. 1 (Aut 1978), 4-8.
"The Valley of the Sorrows" *Heroic Fantasy* (1979), 58-68.
"The Virgins of Po" *Cop Toad* 1:4 (May 1978), 35-44.
"The Way of Wizards" *Dragonfields* No. 3 (Sum 1980), 78-87.

Elford, Jean (1911-)
"Boiled Owl" *Polished Pebbles* (1974), 41-5 "Boiled Owl" *Deaf Can* 3:1 (Jan-Feb 1978), 4-6.
"Christmas Came to Pearl Street" *Can Messenger* 83 (Dec 1973), 18-9.
"Death Wore a Long Red Sock" *Catalyst* (Brantford) 1:5 [1976?], 73.
"The Giver without a Gift" *AA* [66] (Dec 1975), 29-31.

"Locked Out of Christmas" *Companion* 34 (Dec 1971), 25-8.
"Show and Tell" *Rapport* Oct 1970, 24-5.
"Tradition Bound" *Green's* 2:3 (Spr 1974), 18-24.

Elgaard, Elin (1950-)
"Cat in My Irises" *Antig R* No. 36 (Win 1979), 65-73.
"Dew" *Antig R* No. 24 (Win 1975), 17-20.
"Half a Worm" *Literary Half-Yearly* 15:1 (Jan 1974), 59-62 [Based on survey response].
"Half a Worm" *Confrontation* (U.S.) No. 12 (Spr-Sum 1976), 82-4 [Based on survey response].
"Impatience" *Antig R* No. 35 (Aut 1978), 37-46.
"Instant" *Grain* 10:4 (Nov 1982), 4-13.
"Marks" *Antig R* No. 19 (Aut 1974), 11-4.
"My Woman" *Antig R* No. 17 (Spr 1974), 19-22.
"Old Snoot" *Antig R* No. 12 (Win 1973), 17-21.
"Ring-a-Ring o' Roses" *JCF* Nos. 31/32 (1981), 66-83.
"Squashed Spruce" *Matrix* 2:2 (Win 1977), 26-30.
"Suddenly, Last Leaf" *Fid* No. 122 (Sum 1979), 68-86.
"Tidals" *Grain* 10:4 (Nov 1982), 47-54.

Elianna [pseudonym]
"The Christmas Carols' Annual Meeting" *UC Observer* 15 Dec 1964, 27.

Elliott, Alan†
"A Touch of Horse Flesh" *Fid* No. 133 (July 1982), 59-67.

Elliott, George (1923-)
THE KISSING MAN Toronto: Macmillan, 1962.
"An Act of Piety" *Kissing Man* (1962), 1-12.
"The Commonplace" *Kissing Man* (1962), 113-23.
"The Commonplace" *Tam R* No. 22 (Win 1962), 40-8.
"The Commonplace" *Story-Makers* (1970), 65-73.
"The Commonplace" *Voice and Vision* (1972), 20-5.
"Four Little Words" *76: New Canadian Stories* 53-62.
"The Kissing Man" *Kissing Man* (1962), 67-73.
"The Kissing Man" CBC *"Anthology"* 9 Mar 1962.
"The Kissing Man" *Ontario Experience* (1976), 94-9.
"A Leaf for Everything Good" *Kissing Man* (1962), 75-88.
"A Leaf for Everything Good" *Mountain & Plain* (1978), 48-57.
"The Listeners" *Kissing Man* (1962), 29-39.
"The Man Who Lived Out Loud" *Kissing Man* (1962), 89-100.
"A Room, a Light for Love" *Kissing Man* (1962), 49-66.
"The Way Back" *Kissing Man* (1962), 125-36.
"The Way Back" *Stories from Ontario* (1974), 205-14.
"What Do the Children Mean?" *Kissing Man* (1962), 101-11.
"When Jacob Fletcher Was a Boy" *Kissing Man* (1962), 13-27.
"You'll Get the Rest of Him Soon" *Kissing Man* (1962), 41-8.

Elliott, Larry‡
"Never Lonely" *Fifth Page* 1961, 13-6.

Elliott, Noreen‡

"The Flame of Faith" *Stump* 1:2 (Fall 1977), 40-6.

Elliott, W.M.

"The Two Witches" *FH* 26 Oct 1961, 54-5.

"The Two Witches" *Stories to Read Again* (1965), 137-45.

Ellis, A.‡

"Lines from a Judgement" *Ode* No. 1 [n.d.], 14-6.

Ellis, Harry†

"Communications Is a Many Splendor'd Thing" *Deaf Can* 4:8 (Aug-Sept 1979), 29-30.

"Communications Is a Many Splendor'd Thing" *Deaf Can* 5:11/12 (Nov-Dec 1980), 33-6.

"The Deaf Penalty" *Deaf Can* 4:1 (Jan 1979), 6-7.

"Deafiness & Daffiness" *Deaf Can* 3:3 (May-June 1978), 12-4.

"Granny Not!" *Deaf Can* 3:4 (July-Aug 1978), 24-5.

"Hauling Away a Lighter" *Deaf Can* 4:6 (June 1979), 8.

"How to Invent a Better Egg Timer" *Deaf Can* 5:4 (Apr 1980), 20-2.

"McDuff's Last Case" *Deaf Can* 6:7 (July 1981), 23-6.

"Miniature Color Television" *Deaf Can* 2:4 (July-Aug 1977), 23-4 [Humour?].

"Mission Improbable" *Deaf Can* 5:6 (June 1980), 14-7.

"A Phable of Phool's Paradise, or A Tale of Compassionate Phlim-Phlam" *Deaf Can* 5:8/9 (Aug-Sept 1980), 17, 20-2.

"Some Neighborhood!!" *Deaf Can* 2:5 (Sept-Oct 1977), 26-7.

"A Story or Something" *Deaf Can* 6:11 (Nov 1981), 22-7.

Ellis, Keith‡

"At the End of Summer" *Was R* 5:1 (1970), 45-53.

"Seeing and Touching" *Undergrad* Spr 1958, [5 pp].

Ellis, Patrick‡

"Mr. Hor. Brunose Considers Marriage" *Skylight* [No. 1] (1978), 25-8.

Ellison, Jack‡

"Solo" *Can Wings* 16 (Dec 1974), 18-9.

Ellison, Joanne†

"A Place Where There Is No Darkness" *event* 12:1 (1983), 18-26.

Emberly, Kenneth†

"At Night" *Antig R* No. 49 (Spr 1982), 15-20.

"Coming Up Clean" *Scrivener* 4:1 (Win 1983), 28-9.

"Still Life in Leather" *Prism* 19:3 (Spr 1981), 119-22.

Embleton, Rick‡

"The Trap" *Chiaroscuro* 8 (1964), 16-7.

Emkeit, Ron L.†

"In a Castle, in a Kingdom by the Sea" *Don't Steal This Book* (1974), 176-8.

"L.O.V.E." *Don't Steal This Book* (1974), 45-9.

"The Pet Mouse" *Catalyst* (Brantford) 1:5 (1976), 74.

"The Wall" *Catalyst* (Brantford) 1:5 (1976), 73.

Endres, Robin Belitsky

"Marion Fernleigh Takes a Walk" *Room* 6:4 (1981), 45-54.

Enemark, Brett†

"Delta" *Iron II* No. 4 (Nov 1976), 32-3.

"Descent" *Iron II* No. 21 (1978), 3-4.

"Weekend" *Pulp Mill* (1977), 79-87.

Eng, Rose‡

"The Tenant" *UTR* 2:1 (Spr 1978), 27-32.

Engel, Howard (1931-)

"The Corn Beef Madeleine" *JD* Hanukah 1972, 42-7.

"The Corn Beef Madeleine" *JD* Sum 1983, 36-8.

"The Last Friday of Every Month" *JD* Hanukah 1971, 52-3.

"My Vacation in the Numbers Racket" *JD* Passover 1976, 58-61.

"Quiet Chat" *CF* 57 (May 1977), 29-30.

"Thighbones" *Muse* 63:1 (Mar 1954), 10-1.

Engel, Marian (1933-1985)

INSIDE THE EASTER EGG Toronto: House of Anansi Press, 1975.

"Amaryllis" CBC *"Anthology"* 7 Mar 1970.

"Amaryllis" *Fourteen Stories High* (1971), 103-11.

"Amaryllis" *Inside the Easter Egg* (1975), 42-50.

"Anita's Dance" *Chat* 54 (Nov 1981), 66-7, 240, 242.

"Bicycle Story" *Inside the Easter Egg* (1975), 163-72 [also entitled "Moment of Youth"].

"Blue Glass and Flowers" *83: Best Canadian Stories* 59-68.

"The Book of Life, God's Album" CBC *"Anthology"* 30 Mar 1974 [also entitled "Marshallene at Work"].

"Break No Hearts This Christmas" *Inside the Easter Egg* (1975), 91-8.

"Crow Moon" by Marian Passmore *Muse* 63:1 (Mar 1954), 28-35.

"The Fall of the House That Jack Built" *Inside the Easter Egg* (1975), 133-40.

"Family Allowance" *Weekend* 28 (17 June 1978), 34-6.

"Father Instinct" *Chat* 52 (Aug 1979), 32-3, 48, 50, 52.

"Feet" *Quest* 10 (Dec 1981), 45-6, 48.

"Forbesy" *Chat* 50 (Sept 1977), 53, 76-8, 80-1.

"Girl in a Blue Shirtwaist" *Chat* 47 (Feb 1974), 35, 59-62 [also entitled "Inside the Easter Egg"].

"A Girl of Reputation" *Chat* 45 (Oct 1972), 52, 100-3.

"Home Thoughts from Abroad" *Inside the Easter Egg* (1975), 63-74 [also entitled "Ruth and Rosebud"].

"I See Something, It Sees Me" *Fid* No. 101 (Spr 1974), 3-5.

"I See Something, It Sees Me" *Inside the Easter Egg* (1975), 18-22.

"Inside the Easter Egg" *Inside the Easter Egg* (1975), 3-17 [also entitled "Girl in a

Blue Shirtwaist"].

"The Last Christmas" CBC "Anthology" 20 Dec 1975 [also entitled "Break No Hearts This Christmas"].

"The Last Happy Wife" Chat 50 (Mar 1977), 43, 64, 66.

"Madame Eglantine" CBC "Anthology" 18 June 1977.

"Madame Hortensia, Equilibriste" SN 92 (Sept 1977), 46-50.

"Marshallene at Work" Inside the Easter Egg (1975), 141-5 [also entitled "The Book of Life, God's Album"].

"Marshallene on Rape" Inside the Easter Egg (1975), 105-10.

"Meredith and the Lousy Latin Lover" Inside the Easter Egg (1975), 115-22.

"Meredith and the Lousy Latin Lover" Chat 49 (Jan 1976), 22, 71-4.

"Mina and Clare" Inside the Easter Egg (1975), 23-33.

"Moment of Truth" Chat 47 (July 1974), 22, 40-2 [also entitled "Bicycle Story"].

"Nationalism" CBC "Anthology" 18 Aug 1973.

"Nationalism" Inside the Easter Egg (1975), 99-104.

"An Olive Branch" CBC "Anthology" 23 Jan 1971.

"Only God, My Dear" Inside the Easter Egg (1975), 123-32 [also entitled "Too Many Parts"].

"Ruth" Inside the Easter Egg (1975), 157-62.

"Ruth and Rosebud" CBC "Anthology" 10 Feb 1973 [also entitled "Home Thoughts from Abroad"].

"The Salt Mines" Inside the Easter Egg (1975), 34-41.

"The Salt Mines" Ont R No. 3 (Fall-Win 1975-76), 5-11.

"The Santa Claus Syndrome" Chat 47 (Dec 1974), 36-7, 83-4.

"Say It with Food" CBC "Anthology" 26 Dec 1970.

"Sublet" Inside the Easter Egg (1975), 75-83.

"Taped" UWR 13:1 (Fall-Win 1977), 78-81.

"The Tattooed Woman" CBC "Anthology" 8 Nov 1975.

"Tents for the Gaudy-Dancers" CBC "Anthology" 19 Aug 1972.

"Tents for the Gaudy-Dancers" Inside the Easter Egg (1975), 146-56.

"There Is a Sweetness in Decay" CBC "Anthology" 11 July 1970.

"Too Many Parts" Chat 44 (Oct 1971), 44, 96, 98, 101-2 [also entitled "Only God, My Dear"].

"Transformations" Inside the Easter Egg (1975), 51-9.

"Transformations" Chat 48 (Oct 1975), 66-7, 115-8.

"Triolet" by Marian Passmore Muse 64:1 (1955), 9-11.

"The Vanishing Lakes" CBC "Anthology" 8 Mar 1980.

"What Do Lovers Do?" Inside the Easter Egg (1975), 84-90.

Engkent, Garry‡

"The Last Prisoner" Chiaroscuro 13 (1969-70), 32-8.

"When the Long Sheeps Gallop" Chiaroscuro 14 Part II (Apr 1971), 1.

English, L.E.F.

"The Emigrant – A Christmas Story" Nfld Q 54:4 (Dec 1955), 4-6, 40.

Enns, Robert‡

"A Leavetaking" Chiaroscuro 9 (1965-66), 17-8.

Ens, Alvin G.†

"The Englander and Our Hans" Harvest (1974), 27-31.

Enwright, William
"Bayonet" *Popular Illusion* No. 4 (1978), [4 pp].
"The Genius" *Waves* 6:1 (Aut 1977), 16-20.
"Phantase" *VWFP/Revue* 1:2 (Apr 1975), 1, 11-2.
[Untitled] *BC Monthly* 3:9 (June 1978), 63-4.

Epps, Bernard‡
"How Not to Buy a Horse" *Moose R* No. 8 (1983), 21-4.
"Rib of Eve" *Matrix* No. 11 (Sum 1980), 3-15.

Erian, Soraja†
"Through the Iron Gate" *Thursday's Voices* (1983), 45-55.

Eric, P.‡
"The Ninth of May" *Prism* (Mont) 1:2 (1956), 46-8.

Ericsson, Sue†
"The Murder That Saved a Marriage" *Magic Realism* (1980), 105-10.
"You're New Here, Eh?" *Toronto Star* Sun, 27 Aug 1978, A15.

Erkelenz, Michael‡
"The Letter" *TUR* 93:1 (Jan 1980), 22-5.

Erne, Andy‡
"Blue Mountain Majesty" *WWR* 1:1 (Spr 1976), 23-4.

Errat, M.†
"Reflections of Madeleine" *Makara* 2:3 [1977], 44-7.

Erskine, J.S.†
"The Devil Came to Trinidad" *Dal R* 38 (1958), 47-54.
"Galatea" *Dal R* 40 (1960), 187-205.
"The Little Siren" *Dal R* 46 (1966), 63-6.

Esdaille, Daphne‡
"The Forbidden Bay" *Spear* [3] (Aug 1973), 57.

L'Esperance, David‡
"The Door, the Woman and the Snake" *Forge* 1951, 10-1.

Estabrook, Barry†
"Belinda's Story" *CFM* No. 17 (Spr 1975), 38-43.
"Crossing" *Quarry* 24:4 (Aut 1975), 31-40.
"The Waiters" *CF* 54 (Oct 1974), 48-9.

Esterholm, Jeff‡
"Strom's Father" *Alpha* 7:1 (Nov 1982), 13-4.

Estill, Lyle‡
"Government, Farming, and Water Sports" *Lit R* 1:1 (1983), 5-9.

Etco, Mildred†
"The Remaining Years" *Viewpoints* 4:3 (1969), 60-4.

Etheridge, David
  "Supreme" *Fid* No. 135 (Jan 1983), 7-16.

Ettinger, John‡
  "Makin' Out: Sunday" *Communicator* 4:6 (Nov-Dec 1975), 8-9.

Euringer, Fred (1933-)
  A DREAM OF HORSES Ottawa: Oberon Press, 1975.
  "Centennial Portrait" *Dream of Horses* (1975), 68-97.
  "A Christmas Pageant" *Dream of Horses* (1975), 98-107.
  "A Dream of Horses" *Dream of Horses* (1975), 5-45.
  "Hades Revisited" *Acta Vic* 81:3 (Mar 1957), 23.
  "Homer's Door" *Dream of Horses* (1975), 108-25.
  "One More for the Practical Cats" *Tam R* No. 25 (Aut 1962), 87-97.
  "One More for the Practical Cats" *Dream of Horses* (1975), 46-59.
  'The Rat and the Goose" *74: New Canadian Stories* 9-15.
  'The Rat and the Goose" *Dream of Horses* (1975), 60-7.
  "Requiem" *Acta Vic* 80:1 (Nov 1955), 9.

Evanier, David (1940-)
  THE ONE-STAR JEW San Francisco: North Point Press [?].
  THE SWINGING HEADHUNTER Vancouver: November House, 1972.
  "8:30 to 10:00 P.M." *One-Star Jew* (1983), 178-82.
  'The Arrest" *One-Star Jew* (1983), 183-92.
  "Cancer of the Testicles" *Paris R* 16 No. 61 (Spr 1975), 142-58.
  "Cancer of the Testicles" *One-Star Jew* (1983), 15-31.
  'The Creator of the One-Fingered Lily" *Chelsea* (U.S.) No. 40 (1981), 28-37.
  'The Creator of the One-Fingered Lily" *One-Star Jew* (1983), 3-14.
  "Greenwich Village Blues" *event* 1:2 (Fall 1971), 77-86.
  "Greenwich Village Blues" *Swinging Headhunter* (1972), 56-66.
  "Guidance" *Swinging Headhunter* (1972), 33-55.
  'The Jewish Buddha" *Midstream* 19 (Apr 1973), 54-63.
  'The Jewish Buddha" *One-Star Jew* (1983), 48-61.
  "Jolson Sings Again" *One-Star Jew* (1983), 203-23.
  'The Light of My Father" *Swinging Headhunter* (1972), 1-7.
  'The Lost Pigeon of East Broadway" *One-Star Jew* (1983), 133-63.
  'The Man Who Refused to Watch the Academy Awards" *Commentary* 63 (Apr 1977), 53-9.
  'The Man Who Refused to Watch the Academy Awards" *One-Star Jew* (1983), 70-87.
  "My Rabbi, Ray Charles, and Singing Birds" *Moment* (U.S.) 4 (Nov 1978), 6-8.
  "My Rabbi, Ray Charles, and Singing Birds" *One-Star Jew* (1983), 62-9.
  'The One-Star Jew" *Paris R* 21 No. 76 (Fall 1979), 168-209.
  'The One-Star Jew" *Best American Short Stories* 1980 44-79.
  'The One-Star Jew" *One-Star Jew* (1983), 91-132.
  'The Princess" *One-Star Jew* (1983), 164-77.
  "Rockefeller Center" *Story Q* (U.S.) No. 13 (1981), 80-94.
  "A Safe Route on Eighty-Third Street" *Transatlantic R* No. 57 (Oct 1976), 114-5.
  "A Safe Route on Eighty-Third Street" *One-Star Jew* (1983), 88-90.
  "Selective Service" *Paris R* 17 No. 67 (Fall 1976), 85-101.
  "Selective Service" *One-Star Jew* (1983), 32-47.

"A Sense of Responsibility" *One-Star Jew* (1983), 193-202.
"The Swinging Headhunter" *Swinging Headhunter* (1972), 73-99.
"The Swinging Headhunter" *Tam R* No. 65 (Mar 1975), 5-29.
"What Is to Be Done?" *Swinging Headhunter* (1972), 8-32.
"What Time Is It?" *Swinging Headhunter* (1972), 67-72.
"What Time Is It?" *event* 1:3 (Win 1972), 83-7.

Evans, Allen Roy†

"The Everlasting Arms" *Onward* 6 Feb 1966, 3-4.
"Far-Off Event" *Onward* 22 Dec 1957, 814-5.
"The Lone Igloo" *Onward* 14 Mar 1965, 4-5.
"The Lone Igloo" *Rapport* Apr 1971, 32-4.
"Love Finds a Way" *Onward* 28 May 1961, 338-9.
"Love Finds a Way" *Onward* 1 Aug 1965, 3-4, 8.
"Sky Music" *Onward* 24 Nov 1957, 737-9.
"Then There Were None" *Onward* July 1964, 13-5.

Evans, Christopher Dudley

"Annieism & the American Way" *Campus Canada* Nov 1963, 57 [Humour].

Evans, D.G.†

"Kitsilano" *Folio* 18:2 (Spr 1966), 19-25.

Evans, Dorothy‡

"Billy and the Bears" *AA* 50 (Aug 1960), 67.

Evans, Hubert (1892-1986)

"Ghost Town Dog" *Dog Show* (1950) [Based on SSI].
"Ghost-Town Dog" *Best Book of Dog Stories* (1964) [Based on SSI].
"A Gift at Parting" *Onward* 24 Jan 1960, 49-51, 62.
"Heritage" *Onward* 19 Sept 1954, 593-5, 606-7.
"Home for Christmas" *Onward* 61 (23 Oct 1951), 803-5.
"Home for Christmas" *Onward* 23 Dec 1962, 6-7.
"Living Waters" *Onward* 1 Feb 1953, 65-8.
"Loyalty" *Onward* 20 Mar 1955, 182-3, 190-1.
"Night of Testing" *Onward* 31 Oct 1954, 689-93.
"River Reckoning" *Onward* 16 Nov 1958, 728-9, 735.
"Rocky" *Onward* 15 Aug 1954, 513-5.
"A Special Case" *Onward* 12 Dec 1954, 790-2, 798-9.
"Steveston 1926" CBC *[Van]* "Hornby Collection" 15 Nov 1980.
"Steveston 1926" *Mal R* No. 63 (Oct 1982), 139-40.

Evans, J.A.S. (1931-)

"The Amherst Ghost" *AA* 48 (Oct 1957), 75, 77.
"The Bear Walker" *CF* 39 (June 1959), 55-7.
"The First Vision" *Approach* No. 26 (Win 1958), 5-7.
"Fog" *AA* 52 (Jan 1962), 69-72.
"Galatea" *AA* 47 (Aug 1957), 74-5.
"One Hot Day" *Cyclic* 1:2 (Aut 1965), 8-10.
"The Portland Vase" *AA* 50 (Dec 1959), 69-70, 72.
"Sarah" *AA* 51 (Sept 1960), 105-6.
"The Serving of Mushrooms" *AA* 52 (Dec 1961), 53.

Evans, Lewis‡
"Hunting License" *Edmonton Journal* Fri, 2 Dec 1966, 63.

Evoy, Karen‡
"Abelard Aldo Farquhar" *Flow* Win [1975?], [2 pp].

Ewing, Betty Moore
"After Great Pain, a Formal Feeling" *UCR* 1978-79, 23-30.
"Margot: 1969" *Quarry* 29:4 (Aut 1980), 80-6.
"The Reunion" *Quarry* 24:3 (Sum 1975), 39-45.

Ewing, Eleanor‡
"Carolling When We Were Kids" *UC Observer* 15 Dec 1963, 27-8.

Ewing, Wain
"A Day by the Ocean, a Night on the Town" *Canadian Short Fiction Anthology* (1976), 73-6.
"Plant Light and Las Vegas" *Writ* No. 10 (1978), 9.

Ezrin, Bob‡
"Identity" *Marooned* Feb 1967, [1 p].

F., Katharine
"Time Is Not Soon Enough" *Singing* (1980), 38-40.

F.C.N [pseudonym]
"A Last Tribute" *Prism* (Mont) [No. 1] (1955), 57-8.

Faessler, Shirley (1921-)
"The Apple Doesn't Fall Far from the Tree" *SN* 98 (Feb 1983), 56-63.
"A Basket of Apples" *Atlantic Monthly* 223 (Jan 1969), 70-6.
"A Basket of Apples" *CBC "Anthology"* 8 Mar 1969.
"A Basket of Apples" *Sixteen by Twelve* (1970), 128-39.
"A Basket of Apples" *Stories from Ontario* (1974), 172-86.
"A Basket of Apples" *Women in Canadian Literature* (1976), 137-47.
"A Basket of Apples" *Spice Box* (1981), 97-109.
"Can I Count You In?" *Atlantic Monthly* 229 (Jan 1972), 63-9.
"Can I Count You In?" *CBC "Anthology"* 9 Sept 1972 [As "Can I Count on You?" [?]].
"Henye" *Tam R* No. 56 (1971), 50-72.
"Henye" *Narrative Voice* (1972), 28-47.
"Henye" *Toronto Short Stories* (1977), 50-73.
"Intercede for Us, Auntie Chayele" *Tam R* No. 46 (Win 1968), 53-72.
"Lucy and Minnie" *Atlantic Monthly* 231 (Mar 1973), 82-4, 87-9.
"Lucy and Minnie" *CBC "Anthology"* 6 Oct 1973.
"Maybe Later It Will Come Back to My Mind" *Atlantic Monthly* 219 (Apr 1967), 101-4, 107-10.
"Maybe Later It Will Come Back to My Mind" *Canadian Short Stories 2* (1968), 331-57.
"Maybe Later It Will Come Back to My Mind" *CBC "Anthology"* 14 June 1969.

"Maybe Later It Will Come Back to My Mind" *Narrative Voice* (1972), 47-63.

[Title unknown] *Compass* (1971) [Based on survey response].

[Title unknown] *Latitude* (1974) [Based on survey response].

[Title unknown] *Landmarks* (1983) [Based on survey response].

Fagan, Cary

"Billets Doux" *Des* 8:3 No. 19 (1977), 61-3.

"Bright Green Plants" *Waves* 9:1 (Aut 1980), 32-7.

"The Dream House" *Nimbus* 2:2 (Spr 1981), 18-22.

"Figuring Her Commission" *Wee Giant* 4:3 (1981), 26-31.

"The Grindstone Man" *Origins* 10:1 (Spr 1980), 10-7.

"The Holding Jar" *Harvest* No. 1 (Sum 1977), 10-7.

"Holiday's End" *Harvest* No. 2 (Fall 1977), 26-9.

"Image in the Shattered Mirror" *Portico* 2:1 (Win 1978), 19-23.

"In High Park" *Pier Spr* 6:3 (Sum 1981), 35-42.

"The Lesson" *UTR* 5 (Spr 1981), 31-2.

"A Mystery" *Harvest* No. 9 (June 1980), 10-4.

"Show Me the Feast" *Portico* 2:2 (Win-Spr 1978), 31-8.

"Somewhere My Love" *UCR* Spr 1980, 16-8.

"Under the Weather" *Mam* 1:4 [n.d.], [10 pp].

Fahlman, Jean‡

"The Masterpiece" *West People* No. 136 (6 May 1982), 4-5.

"Me Against the World" *Smoke Signals* 4 [date unknown] [Based on *SWG* survey response].

Faiers, Christopher (1948-)

"Tweedledee and Tweedledum" *Alive* No. 80 (11 June 1977), 10.

Fairley, Bruce†

"The Act of Creation" *event* 9:2 (1980), 154-62.

"Snow Hole" *CBC "Anthology"* 13 Oct 1979.

Faivre, Regine‡

"Parade Square" *Scrivener* 2:1 (Spr 1981), 11-4.

Falconer, Roger‡

"Suddenly Very Quiet" *Stump* 4:1/2 (Spr 1980), 40-2.

Falstaff, Jake‡

"Alice in Justiceland" *Uk Can* 7 (15 Nov 1953), 5 [Satire].

Farah, Nuruddin‡

"A Crooked Rib" *CBC "Anthology"* 18 Oct 1980.

Farmer, Bernard J.

"Great Aunt Selina" *FH* 29 Oct 1953, 20-1.

Farquhar, David‡

"A Moon Incident" *Poesis* 2 (Aut 1970), [2 pp].

Fasick, Laura‡

"The Farewell" *UC Gargoyle* 2 (Dec 1978), 6.

"Sobbing Through the Day: Part Two" *UC Gargoyle* 2 (Dec 1978), 16 [Parody].

Faulknor, Cliff (1913-)

"The Do-It-Yourself Murder" *AA* 54 (Nov 1963), 37-40.

"Maybe Next Year" *CG* 82 (Jan 1963), 35-8.

"Nobody Told the Fish" *CG* 79 (Sept 1960), 35-6, 38.

"Nobody Told the Fish" *Dand* 2 (Spr-Sum 1976), 47-53.

"The Outboard" *SW* 24 Dec 1966, 14-7.

"The Outboard" *CG* 86 (Dec 1967), 36-8, 40.

"The Settler from Stettler" *SW* 30 July 1960, 22-5.

"The Settler from Stettler" *CG* 82 (Sept 1963), 37-40.

"The Worry Wart" *CG* 87 (Feb 1968), 50, 54-5.

Fausett, J.C.‡

"The Coming of Night" *Undergrad* Spr 1958, [3 pp].

Fawcett, Brian (1944-)

MY CAREER WITH THE LEAFS & OTHER STORIES Vancouver: Talonbooks, 1982.

"Abel's Brother" *Roothog* (1981), 121-3.

"The Agent of Language" *Per* No. 2 (Fall 1977), 5-7.

"Bomb Shelters" *My Career with the Leafs* (1982), 18-22.

"Burial of the Dead" *Iron* No. 7 (1969), 17-8.

"Champions" *My Career with the Leafs* (1982), 83-91.

"Columbus Hotel" *Pulp Mill* (1977), 3-5.

"The Coming of the Barbarians" *My Career with the Leafs* (1982), 53-62.

"Drinking It Up" *My Career with the Leafs* (1982), 72-82.

"The Friend" *Pulp Mill* (1977), 9-13.

"The Friends" *Tish* No. 43 (1969), [3 pp].

"The Friends" *Geo Str Writing* No. 4 (6-13 May 1970), 10-1.

"The Friends" *Pulp Mill* (1977), 6-8.

"Friends" *Pulp Mill* (1977), 14-7 [Not the same as above].

"Gang Warfare: A Love Story" *My Career with the Leafs* (1982), 100-7.

"Giants" *My Career with the Leafs* (1982), 9-13.

"Golfing with the Old Man" *My Career with the Leafs* (1982), 23-7.

"Golfing with the Old Man" *Writing* No. 5 (Spr 1982), 23-2.

"An Interest in Bears" *My Career with the Leafs* (1982), 132-44.

"Johnny's Game" *My Career with the Leafs* (1982), 28-32.

"The Life of Robert Oomer" *Cap R* No. 14 (1978), 101-4.

"Losers" *My Career with the Leafs* (1982), 165-73.

"The Loss of the Marquess of Queensbury" *My Career with the Leafs* (1982), 63-71.

"Making Up the Distance" *My Career with the Leafs* (1982), 126-31.

"Mules" *My Career with the Leafs* (1982), 115-25.

"My Career with the Leafs" *Writing* No. 3 (Sum 1981), 3-7.

"My Career with the Leafs" *My Career with the Leafs* (1982), 174-90.

"One Story, Two Tales" *Iron II* No. 4 (Nov 1976), 36-7.

"Petals" *My Career with the Leafs* (1982), 33-41.

"Slug" *My Career with the Leafs* (1982), 145-53.

"Snotbox" *My Career with the Leafs* (1982), 159-64.
"Some Things Are True" *My Career with the Leafs* (1982), 108-14.
"Sunday Night" *My Career with the Leafs* (1982), 154-8.
"The Tennis Court Oath" *My Career with the Leafs* (1982), 42-52.
"Water Ballet" *My Career with the Leafs* (1982), 92-9.
"Wild Horses" *My Career with the Leafs* (1982), 14-7.

Fawcett, Heather†
"Letter to Nigeria" *Fid* No. 136 (June 1983), 7-10.

Fawcett, Patrick‡
"An Excellent Specimen" *Edmonton Journal* Fri, 6 Jan 1967, 29.
"Ozymandias" *Edmonton Journal* Fri, 9 Sept 1966, 53.

Fay, Michael†
"The Little Green Book" *Dand* 5 (Win-Spr 1979), 22-30.
"Puck Among the Tea Biscuits" *Can Golden West* 12a:1 (Christmas 1976), 33-42.
"The Whirlabout" *Can Golden West* 12a:[4] (Sum 1977), 51-4.

Fearns, John.
See also Abbey, Lloyd and Fearns, John.
"The Mother" *Antlered Boy* (1970), 41-5.

Fedorowicz, Jan‡
"The Decline and Fall of the Emergency World-Salvation and Conquest Club" *Echo* (Tor) 2:1 (Fall 1970), [5 pp].
"Florian's Apocalypse" *Echo* (Tor) 2:4 (Sum 1971), 10-2.

Feindel, Michael‡
"Morninglory Tears" *Pulp* 3:19 (15 Aug 1976), [1, 4].

Feinstein, Robert†
"George, the TXI Model" *CFM* No. 17 (Spr 1975), 34-7.

Fenerty, Ron‡
"The Hell of It All" *Inside* No. 3 [Dec 1964], 5-7.
"Some Will Never Quit" *Inside* 2:2 [n.d.], 13-4.

Fenton, Terry (1940-)
"October Monday" *Saskatchewan Writing* (1960), 7-17.

Ferguson, Graeme‡
"A Yellow Ceiling" *Acta Vic* 76:3 (Feb 1952), 11-2.

Ferguson, Rosemary†
"The Laughing Wood" *Nw J* No. 23 (1981), 90-101.

Fergusson, Anne (1912-)
"Bic the Bull" *CCWQ* 2:3 (Sum 1980), 9-10.
"C.N. – Northern Route" *Pier Spr* 8:4 (Aut 1983), 24-5.

Fernie, Lynne‡
"Some Essential Points About Fish" *Fireweed* No. 7 (Sum 1980), 101-3.

Ferns, John‡
"Maisie" *Folio* 19:2 (Spr 1967), 28-30.
"The Mother" *Folio* 18:2 (Spr 1966), 11-5.

Fernstrom, Ken†
"The Boy Who Insisted" *Canadian Short Fiction Anthology* (1976), 77-80.
"Snowman" *Echo* (Van) No. 2 (Fall 1976), 7-8.

Ferrie, R.‡
"Thou Shalt Not Kill" *Probe* 1:1 (1960), 6-7.

Ferrier, Ian†
"The Bridge" *Quarry* 27:3 (Sum 1978), 47-56.

Ferrier, Mary Jane‡
" 'Ducdame' " *Forge* 1951, 25-6.

Ferris, Harry T.‡
"The Hitch-Hiker" *AA* 54 (Aug 1964), 74.

Ferris, Thomas
"The Gun Closet" *74: New Canadian Writing* 52-61.

Fetherling, Doug (1947-)
"The Luckiest of Them All" *CBC "Anthology"* 12 July 1969.
[Title unknown] *CBC "Anthology"* 26 July 1969.
"Without Malice, the American Way" *CBC "Anthology"* 17 Oct 1970.
"Without Malice, the American Way" *Quarry* 20:4 (1971), 46-51.
"The Wow Sound of the Prairie" *CF* 49 (Mar 1970), 285-6.

Fidler, Vera
"A Present for a Baby" *Echoes* No. 209 (Christmas 1952), 29, 32.
"Roots" *FH* 10 Oct 1957, 28-9, 34.

Field, Ann‡
"The Gate" *Driftwood* 1979, 3-6.

Field, L.L.
"The Cut-Glass Pickle Dish" *Read Ch* 1:3 (Win 1982), 15-20.
"Distant Thunder" *WCR* 18:2 (Oct 1983), 12-7.
"The Effect of Narcissism on Form and Content" *Pulp* 5:11 (31 Jan 1980), [1 p].
"Pink Lady" *Common Ground* (1980), 94-102.
"Salty Dog" *Elbow Room* (1979), 3-25.
"Winnifred Longden's Commercial Crusade" *Mal R* No. 56 (Oct 1980), 128-37.

Field, Nancy‡
"My Friend Mrs. Wallis" *CJO* 11 (July 1973), 15-6.

Field, Roger‡
"Get into the Woods" *Pulp* 1:5 (15 Jan 1973), [3-4].

Fielden, Charlotte

"The Bauer-Hirsch Law of Survival or The Hazards of Living" *Tam R* No. 59 (1971), 3-25.

"Bubeh Meisse" *Imp* 3:1 (Fall 1973), 33-9.

Fielder, Martyn†

"Through Pools of Light" *Heartland* No. 2 (Jan-Feb 1981), 34-6 [Excerpt?].

Fielding, Cheryl†

"Friends Always" *Pier Spr* 6:3 (Sum 1981), 22-8.

Filip, Raymond (1950-)

"Allophone" *Mont R* 1:2 (Fall 1979), 23-30.

"The Best Ice in Quebec" *QQ* 85 (1978), 440-6.

"Chantal" CBC "Anthology" 11 Aug 1979.

"Chantal" CBC "Once More from the Top" 29 Oct 1979 [Based on survey response].

"Olympic Hawks and Doves" *Antig R* No. 34 (Sum 1978), 35-48.

"Rat Racist" *Matrix* No. 12 (Win 1981), 82-95.

"St. Patrick's Day Cabane à Sucre" *Germination* 4:1 (Win 1979), [5 pp].

"Walking on Cried Rivers" *Fid* No. 135 (Jan 1983), 47-56.

"Winter of Content" *Quarry* 27:4 (Aut 1978), 38-47.

Filipow, Bernard R.‡

"Tramonto" *Alpha* 4:1 (Fall 1979), 24, 33.

Filson, Bruce K.†

"The Keeper of Error" *New Q* 2:4 (Win 1983), 31-5.

"My Seventh Day at School" *Origins* 9:3 (Aut 1979), 13-5.

"We Are Three, Not Counting the Combine" *Ichor* No. 2 (1981), 59-64.

Filter, Reinhard†

"Absolutely Nothing" *Origins* 7:4 (Dec 1977), 11-4.

"Hhar'ani" *Origins* 8:1 (Mar 1978), 17-22.

"Protonics" *Origins* 11:3 (Win 1981), 82-91.

Findlay, David K. (1901-)

"Bait for Bachelors" *Sat Eve Post* 234 (17 June 1961), 26-7, 60-1.

"Big Spender from the West" *Sat Eve Post* 233 (8 Oct 1960), 24, 84, 87.

"Danger Canyon" *Sat Eve Post* 225 (19 July 1952), 24, 94-5.

"The Decoy for Ducks" *SW* 25 Nov 1950, I:8, 12.

"The Evidence" *Town* (U.K.) 8 (Jan 1967), 8, 70.

"The Girl Who Had Accidents" *Sat Eve Post* 230 (21 June 1958), 28, 54-6.

"Lady, Make Up Your Mind" *Sat Eve Post* 223 (7 Oct 1950), 39, 89, 92-3.

"Love Comes Home Again" *SW* 19 May 1951, II:3, 12.

"Love with Hammer and Nails" *SW* 7 Aug 1954, I:3, 6.

"Marriage Is a Dangerous Sport" *Collier's* 125 (21 Jan 1950), 22-3[+?] [Based on RGPL].

"Miss Hubbard Went to the Cupboard" *SW* 24 May 1952, I:1, 12.

"The Nesting Instinct" *Sat Eve Post* 231 (21 Mar 1959), 30, 114-5, 117.

"Never a Fire Bird" *SW* 29 Apr 1950, II:1.

"Star Performance" *SW* 7 Jan 1950, II:1.

"Su Chen" *The Saint Mag* (U.K.) Dec 1966 [Based on survey response].

"Substitute Groom" *Sat Eve Post* 223 (28 Apr 1951), 31, 62, 64, 66, 68.

"Suicide on Skis" *Sat Eve Post* 222 (29 Apr 1950), 30, 124, 127-8, 130.

"Suicide on Skis" *Treasure Chest of Sports Stories* (1951) [Based on SSI].

"Thunderbirds" *SW* 24 Oct 1953, II:3.

"Turn-About" *SW* 11 Feb 1956, II:5, 12.

"Vroom Vroom" *Ladies Home J* 78 (Mar 1961), 53, 107, 109.

Findley, Timothy (1930-)

"About Effie" *Tam R* No. 1 (Aut 1956), 48-60.

"The Book of Pins" *74: New Canadian Stories* 111-24.

"Daybreak at Pisa: 1945" *Tam R* No. 83/84 (Win 1982), 90-7 [Described by Findley as "a scene from a work-in-progress: a play ... " though in fictional form].

"E.R.A." *Cavalier* 20 (Apr 1970), 30-2, 74-7 [Based on survey response].

"Island" *Newcomers* (1979), 85-95.

"A Long Hard Walk" *Newcomers* (1979), 145-55.

"Losers, Finders: Strangers at the Door" *75: New Canadian Stories* 57-75.

"Out of the Silence" *Ethos* 1:1 (Sum 1983), 26-8.

"The People on the Shore" *CBC "Anthology"* 23 Feb 1974 [Title based on survey response].

"Sometime – Later – Not Now" *New Orleans R* 3 (1972), 13-20.

"The War" *CBC "Anthology"* 4 Mar 1958.

Fines, Beatrice E. (1917-)

"And None to Spare" *West Producer* Sept 1964 [Also entitled "Discovery"; based on survey response].

"A Bear for Punishment" *Winnipeg Free Press [Weekly?]* Jan 1966 [Based on survey response].

"Behind Every Successful Man" *Rapport* Oct 1968, 40-4.

"Books in the Bush" *CBC "Stories with John Drainie"* Mar 1962 [Based on survey response].

"Books in the Bush" *West Producer* Apr 1964 [Based on survey response].

"The Brocade Sofa" *Onward* 19 June 1966, 3-4.

"The Brocade Sofa" *CBC [Colin Jackson's programme]* July 1977 [Based on survey response].

"Carols for Miss Hedley" *Standard* (U.S.) Dec 1966 [Based on survey response].

"The China Teapot" *West People* Nov 1980 [Based on survey response].

"The China Teapot" *Short Story International: Student Series* Mar 1983 [Based on survey response].

"Crazy Dobbs" *Onward* 29 May 1966, 3-5, 14.

"The Crosswalk" *FH* 14 Apr 1966, 56-7.

"The Decision" *Our Family* 31 (Apr 1980), 34-5.

"Discovery" *Evangel* (U.S.) Mar 1965 [Also entitled "And None to Spare"; based on survey response].

"Discovery" *Standard* (U.S.) May 1966 [Based on survey response].

"Edge of the Circle" *Chat* 36 (Nov 1963), 33, 91-2, 94, 96 [Also entitled "In the Shadow of Her Sister"].

"Far Above Rubies" *Evangel* (U.S.) Sept 1962 [Based on survey response].

"Far Above Rubies" *Standard* (U.S.) Aug 1963 [Based on survey response].

"Forsaking All Others" *Onward* 18 Aug 1963; 25 Aug 1963, 3-4, 8; 6-8.

"Forsaking All Others" *Standard* (U.S.) July 1964 [Based on survey response].

"Forsaking All Others" *Sat Eve Post* 244 (Fall 1972), 84-5.

"Forsaking All Others" *Short Story International* No. 19 (1980), 29-39.

"Gift of Oranges" *Evangel* (U.S.) Dec 1962 [Based on survey response].

"Gift of Oranges" CBC *"Stories with John Drainie"* Mar 1972 [Based on survey response].

"Gift of Oranges" *Can Messenger* 85 (Dec 1975), 18-9.

"Harness of Memory" *West Producer* Apr 1960 [Based on survey response].

"Home Place" *West Producer* Jan 1960 [Based on survey response].

"In the Shadow of Her Sister" *Story World* (U.K.) Oct 1980 [Also entitled "Edge of the Circle"; based on survey response].

"In the Shadow of Her Sister" *Secrets* (U.K.) Feb 1981 [based on survey response].

"The Last of the Pioneers" *Chat* 44 (Nov 1971), 44, 54, 56, 60 [Also entitled "Welcome the New Pioneers"].

"Let the Fox Go Free" *CG* 86 (Feb 1967), 63-5.

"The Lie" *Rapport* Nov 1970, 25-8.

"Love Is a Growing Thing" *Can Messenger* 84 (Oct 1974), 12-3, 20.

"Man from the Past" *Winnipeg Free Press [Weekly?]* Feb 1961 [Based on survey response].

"A Matter of Trust" *Christian Home* 1972 [Based on survey response].

"A Matter of Trust" *Singing Under Ice* (1974), 126-35.

"The Measure of a Man" *Secrets* (U.K.) Feb 1981 [Based on survey response].

"Murchison's Moose" *FH* 28 June 1962, 26-7.

"Murchison's Moose" CBC *"Stories with John Drainie"* Oct 1965 [Based on survey response].

"Murchison's Moose" *Winnipeg Free Press [Weekly?]* July 1966 [Based on survey response].

"Murchison's Moose" *Sat Eve Post* 245 (Nov-Dec 1973), 79-81, 86.

"New Day Dawning" *Story World* (U.K.) Mar 1975 [Also entitled "The New Road"; based on survey response].

"The New Road" *Evangel* (U.S.) Aug 1964 [Also entitled "New Day Dawning"; based on survey response].

"No Flour in the Barrel" *FH* 7 Jan 1965, 28-9.

"No Flour in the Barrel" CBC *"Stories with John Drainie"* June 1967 [Based on survey response].

"No Flour in the Barrel" *Short Story International No.* 30 [Win 1982] [Based on survey response].

"No Flour in the Barrel" *Short Story International: Seedling Series* Dec 1982 [Based on survey response].

"The Reason Why" *Red Star* (U.K.) Jan 1978 [Based on survey response].

"Remember When" *Secrets* (U.K.) Aug 1981 [Based on survey response].

"A Second Chance" *Chat* 42 (Sept 1969), 34, 56, 58, 60, 62.

"A Second Chance" *Story World* (U.K.) Sept 1974 [Based on survey response].

"The Stoneboat and the Bride" *West People* July 1982 [Based on survey response].

"The Tamarack Tree" *West Producer* Mar 1961 [Based on survey response].

"The Tender View" *Onward* 13 Oct 1963, 3-5, 12.

"The Tender View" *Standard* (U.S.) May 1964 [Based on survey response].

"The Tender View" *Onward* 16 Apr 1967, 3-5, 7.

"The Tender View" *Our Family* 22 (Nov 1970), 26-8.
"The Water Witch" *West Producer* 3 June 1965 [Based on survey response].
"Welcome the New Pioneers" *Story World* (U.K.) Jan 1976 [Also entitled "The Last of the New Pioneers"; based on survey response].
"Western Encounter" *West Producer* Nov 1959 [Based on survey response].
"When Freddy Brought the Cream" *West People* No. 133 (15 Apr 1982), 2.
"Who's Afraid of the Planning Committee?" *Chat* 38 (July 1965), 21, 54, 56.
"Will You Love Me Tomorrow?" *Red Star* (U.K.) Jan 1975 [Based on survey response].

Finlay, Michael†
"The Cafe" *CFM* No. 1 (Win 1971), 18-20.

Finnigan, Joan (1925-)
"Command Performance" *Fid* Nov-Dec 1970, 1-31 [Novelette? Published as separate volume].
"A Flight to Montreal" *Fid* No. 61 (Sum 1964), 28-38.
"A Flight to Montreal" *Fiddlehead Greens* (1979), 102-14.
"In a Brown Cottage" CBC "*Anthology*" 14 June 1969.
"May Day Rounds: Renfrew County" CBC "*Anthology*" 2 Nov 1968.
"The Miracle Drug" *Fid* No. 57 (Sum 1963), 44-50.
"Mirror Images" *Chat* 53 (May 1980), 44, 193-4, 196.
" 'Some of the Street in' " *Literary R* (U.S.) 8 (1965), 456-67.

Fipps, Mohammed Ulysses‡
"The Ruse" *Outlook* Feb-Mar 1978, 7-8.

Firestone, Catherine†
"Kazabazua" *NJ* No. 5 (May 1975), 33-41.

Fischer, Gretl Kraus‡
"Driftwood of the Pacific" *CF* 36 (Oct 1956), 153-5.

Fisher, Chris‡
"The Enlightenment of Mrs. Simpson" *100% Cracked Wheat* (1983), 274-90.

Fisher, Gale
"Black to Checkmate" *New Voices* (1956), 15-24.
"Romance" *New Voices* (1956), 25-9.

Fisher, Jennifer†
"The Edge of Friday Night" *Flare* 3 (Nov 1981), 120-1, 118, 128, 130, 132.

Fisher, Mary†
"Moose Story" *Squatch J* No. 8 (Dec 1978), 4-7 [Non-fiction?].
"Tragedy at McLeod Beach" *Squatch J* No. 7 (June 1978), 56-8 [Non-fiction?].

Fisher, Michael J.‡
"A Bohemian in the Underworld" *Alive* No. 36 [1974], 22 [Sketch?].
"Toronto Evening" *Alive* No. 30 [1973], 50.

Fisher, Paul‡
"Ahbrose C. Friendly and the Free World" *Prism* (Mont) Fall 1965, 11-5.

Fisher, Peter†
"The Coffee Shop" *Lit R* 1:1 (1983), 35-6.

Fitchette, James†
"Ocean of Flies" *Waves* 9:2 (Win 1981), 22-32.

Fitzgerald, Judith
"First Person Regular" *BC Monthly* No. 29 (Apr 1982), 56-61.

Fitzpatrick, Brenda†
"Creature at Night" *Mam* [6:3] (Sum 1983), [2 pp].

Fitzpatrick, Eva†
"Hoofbeats in the Night" *Black Cat* No. 6 (1982), 3-6.

Fitzpatrick, Helen‡
"Did You Ever Want to Raise Bees ... ?" *Edmonton Journal* Fri, 14 Oct 1966, 59.
"Love Is the Reason" *Companion* 35 (Apr 1972), 25-6.
"The Reason Is Love" *Edmonton Journal* Thu, 7 Apr 1966, 50.
"The Sounding Brass" *Edmonton Journal* Fri, 10 June 1966, 55.
"Suzie Baby!" *Edmonton Journal* Fri, 21 July 1967, 25.
"Susie Baby!" *Can Messenger* 77 (Oct 1967), 9.
"What Could I Do?" *Edmonton Journal* Fri, 3 Nov 1967, 34.
"What Could I Have Done?" *Can Messenger* 78 (Mar 1968), 12-3 [also entitled "What Could I Do?"].

FitzSimmons, Edward Peter‡
"Suppose Your Mother" *Forge* 1952, 35-7.
"Works and Days" *Forge* 1953, 55-64.

Flannigan, Rod‡
"Survivors" *RPM* No. 1 (Apr 1980), 27-31.

Flatt, Mary‡
"Elmer" *Muse* 62:1 (Spr 1953), 3-5.
"Fog" *Muse* 60:3 (Feb 1951), 16 [Prose poem?].
"The Higher Things" *Muse* 62:1 (Spr 1953), 22-4.
"Light" *Muse* 60:3 (Feb 1951), 16-8.
"Sidewalk Blues: A Great Canadian Tragedy" *Muse* 61:1 (Dec 1951), 11-2.
"Willie" *Muse* 63:1 (Mar 1954), 5-7.

Flatt, Olive Augusta
GRANDMA'S STORIES Hamilton: Davis Lisson, 1951 [Based on Miller].

Flechtman, Wilfred†
"Saviours" *Matrix* 1:1 (Spr 1975), 5-7.

Fleming, Morag‡
"Jonah II" *Forge* 1966, 33-6.

Fletcher, Peggy (1930-)

WHEN THE MOON IS FULL Cornwall: Vesta, 1977.

"The Beautiful Tide" *When the Moon Is Full* (1977), 88-96.

"The Doll Lady" *When the Moon Is Full* (1977), 107-13.

"Indian Givers" *When the Moon Is Full* (1977), 23-31.

"Jenny and the Witnesses" *When the Moon Is Full* (1977), 14-22.

"The Kites" *Living Message* 83 (Mar 1972), 20-1.

"The Kites" *When the Moon Is Full* (1977), 51-6.

"Lords of the Night" *Companion* 34 (July-Aug 1971), 16-9.

"Lords of the Night" *When the Moon Is Full* (1977), 32-6.

"Miss Jane's Other World" *When the Moon Is Full* (1977), 97-106.

"Miss Poke's Search for Love" *Companion* 33 (Nov 1970), 26-8.

"Miss Poke's Search for Love" *Polished Pebbles* (1974), 23-6.

"Miss Poke's Search for Love" *When the Moon Is Full* (1977), 37-41.

"The Night of the Big Gale" *Antig R* No. 43 (Aut 1980), 11-20.

"No Time for Christmas" *When the Moon Is Full* (1977), 76-80.

"Old Friends" *Mam* 6:2 (Win 1983), [8 pp].

"Parade" *When the Moon Is Full* (1977), 69-75.

"Room 101" *When the Moon Is Full* (1977), 64-8.

"Someone Who Understands" *Chat* 44 (June 1971), 24, 46, 48-50.

"The Threshold" *When the Moon Is Full* (1977), 81-7.

"A Touch of Gentle Sorrow" *Rapport* Oct 1969, 28-9.

"A Visit from Uncle" *When the Moon Is Full* (1977), 57-63.

"Visiting Rights" *Br Out* 1:5 (Nov-Dec 1974), 36-8, 44.

"Visiting Rights" *When the Moon Is Full* (1977), 42-50.

"When the Moon Is Full" *When the Moon Is Full* (1977), 5-13.

Fleury, Val [pseudonym]

"House of Ice" *Chel J* 1 (Jan-Feb 1975), 21-36.

Flives, Ivack‡

"Christmas Story" *UC Gargoyle* 27 (7 Dec 1982), 4.

[Untitled] *UC Gargoyle* 27 (6 Apr 1983), 7.

Flood, Cynthia (1940-)

"Beatrice" *JCF* No. 24 [1979], 67-77.

"Bill" *Makara* 1:3 (Apr-May 1976), 38-40, 44-7.

"Contradictions Among the People" *Room* 6:3 (1981), 55-77.

"Imperatives" *Matrix* No. 13 (Spr-Sum 1981), 45-53.

"Night Feeding" *Makara* 3:3 (Fall 1978), 36-9.

"On California Street" *Was R* 3:2 (1968), 5-25.

"On the Point" *Fireweed* No. 14 (Fall 1982), 41-9.

"On the Point" *CBC* "Anthology" 5 Feb 1983 [Based on survey response].

"Porridge and Silver" *QQ* 88 (1981), 708-17.

"The Road to the Graveyard" *Quarry* 29:4 (Aut 1980), 113-20.

"Roses Are Red" *Common Ground* (1980), 131-47.

"Summer's Lease" *Atlantis* 7:1 (Fall 1981), 77-90.

Flood, Robert J.

"Land without Mills" *Outset* 1974, 65-70.

Floras, John‡
    "Him" *TUR* 86:2 (Mar 1973), [4 pp].

Flury, Kay
    "It Might Happen Here" *Echoes* No. 232 (Aut 1958), 8, 20.
    "Let's Have a Function" *Echoes* No. 238 (Spr 1960), 24-5.
    "The Stained Glass Window" *Onward* 25 Nov 1962, 4-5, 10-1.
    "The Stained Glass Window" *Onward* 20 Feb 1966, 3-5, 12.

Flynn, Nore‡
    "The Mutation" *Varsity Lit Issue* Mon, 22 Feb 1954, 3, 8.
    "The Peril of Two Carat" *Acta Vic* 78:1 (Nov 1953), 20-1.

Fodor, T.C.‡
    "Museum Piece" *Front* No. 6 (May 1979), 19-27.
    [Untitled] *New Mitre* 85 (1980), 29-30.

Foley, Brendan‡
    "The Man Who Thought of Everything" *Earth and You* 12 Nos. 47/48 [n.d.], 31-6.

Foley, James (Jim)
    "Like a Roe or a Young Hart" *Fifth Page* 1963, 3-6.
    "Like a Roe or a Young Hart" *Campus Canada* 1:1 (Feb 1963), 54-5

Foley, Mark‡
    "Ice-Elation" *Dime Bag* [No. 18] Fiction Issue 1 (Mar 1977), 5-7.
    "The Story Teller" *Dime Bag* No. 13 (Mar 1975), [1 p].

Foley, Sheila†
    "Mechanical Therapy" *CFM* No. 14 (Sum 1974), 28-35.

Folkes. David‡
    "The Crack" *UCR* Spr 1976, 33-7.

Fones, Robert
    See also Coleman, Victor and Fones, Robert; Fones, Robert and Nations, Opal L.
    "The Ballad of Al Shadow" *Writing* No. 1 (Sum 1980), 6-7.
    "The Blank-Faced People of Iden Moor" *20 Cents* 3:1/2 (Apr 1969), [3 pp].
    "The Flying Cat" *Writing* No. 1 (Sum 1980), 3.
    "Heteronyms" *Writing* No. 1 (Sum 1980), 6.
    "The Turtle" *Writing* No. 1 (Sum 1980), 4-5.

Fones, Robert and Nations, Opal L.
    See also Fones, Robert; Nations, Opal L.
    " 'Here Comes the Canada Council' " *OPT* 4:7 (Oct 1977), 4.

Fontaine, Patricia†
    "Cause for Alarm" *Images About Manitoba* 1:3 (Fall-Win 1976), 18-9.
    "In Sickness and in Health ... " *Companion* 34 (July-Aug 1971), 27-9.
    "Rings and Things" *Pier Spr* 4:4 (Aut 1979), 12-21.

Foord, Isabelle‡
"Jennifer Jane" *Inside* 2:4 [n.d.], 18-9.

Foran, Charles‡
"In the Pocket" *Gram* 1980-81, 29-31.
"Sarsfield Bridge" *Gram* 8:1 (Fall 1982), 7-16.
"Whitecaps" *Gram* 8:2 (Spr 1983), 9-15.

Forbell, Fraser‡
"A Long Time Ago" *Harvest* No. 3 (Mar 1978), 30-2.

Forbes, Greg†
"At the Burning Ghat" *Nebula* No. 14 (1980), 28-33.
"The Coke Machine" *Matrix* 3:1 (Sum 1977), 22-4.
"Lives of Maple Sugar/La Vie du sucre d'érable" *Matrix* 1:2 (Fall 1975), 37-40.
"On the Dharmsala Road" *Quarry* 28:1 (Win 1979), 3-8.

Forbes, Joyce T.‡
"The Tears of Things" *Art & Lit R* 1:1 (Fall 1972), 15-21.

Ford, Bernard‡
"A Day in the Life ... " *Can Skater* 7:3 (June-July 1980), 32-4.

Ford, Cathy (1952-)
"Ambulance Blues Note" *Cap R* No. 10 (Fall 1976), 162-7.
"Bird Hitch-Hiking" *Br Out* 3:3 (July-Aug 1976), 29-31.
"Conversations" *Canadian Short Fiction Anthology* 2 (1982), 80-4.
"Cut Flowers: A Rape Story" *Cap R* No. 10 (Fall 1976), 160-1.
"The Kind of Story Your Mother Would Love" *Waves* 8:1 (Fall 1979), 4-7.
"The Sweet Smell of Flowers" *Quarry* 29:4 (Aut 1980), 99-105.

Ford, Frederic C.†
"The World's Fastest Flying Tuba" *Thursday's Voices* (1983), 5-11.

Ford, James‡
"Reflections" *Writ* No. 1 (Spr 1970), 85-93.

Forer, Anne‡ (1945?-)
"The Adventure of the French Bathroom" *Room* 8:3 (1983), 13-6.

Forer, Mort
"The Lucky Coins" *Stories with John Drainie* (1963), 14-21.
"My Uncle's Black-Iron Arm" *Winnipeg Stories* (1974), 23-9.
"My Uncle's Black-Iron Arm" *Fire* (1978), 91-3.

Forest, Alan‡
"Blackout" *Raven* No. 6 (Apr 1958), 24-5.
"The Gay Tragedy" *Raven* No. 7 (Nov 1958), [1 p].

Forgie, Diane‡
"The Mistake" *Smoke Signals* 2 [date unknown] [Based on *SWG* survey response].

Foros, Adam†
"The Only Place on Earth" *CA & B* 56:4 (Sum 1981), 22-5.

Forrest, Bob‡
"The Harder the Worse" *Folio* 18:2 (Spr 1966), 5-8.

Fortier, Mark†
"The Tower" *Des* 11:1/2 Nos. 27/28 (1980), 129-31.
"Woman with Corpse: Study for Fiction No. 1" *Antig R* No. 25 (Spr 1976), 17-9.

Foster, Chris‡
"A Ship in the Night" *Why* 2:1 (1960), 37-41.

Foster, David‡
"The Specialist" *Forum* (OSSTF) 5 (Feb 1979), 17-8.

Foster, Dennis (1940-)
"Colt Headstone" *Short Story International* 3 No. 15 (Aug 1979), 9-11.

Foster, Graeme
"Catching Hell" *Cap R* No. 4 (Fall-Win 1973), 16-9.

Foster, John H.‡
"Three for All" *Alive* No. 42 [1975], 40-1.

Foster, Malcolm (1931-)
"The Color of My True Love's Hair" *Story* 36:4 No. 141 (July-Aug 1963), 17-25.

Foster, Thelma H.
"The Arab Steed" *CSSM* 2:4 (Fall 1976), 43-5, 47.
"The Queen Who Walked on Stilts" *CSSM* 3:1 (Win 1977), 45-8.

Foster, W.B.
"Young Dr. Trail" *AA* 58 (Jan 1968), 36-7, 39, 41.

Fothergill, Robert J.
"Grand Performance" *Weekend* 4 (26 June 1954), 14-5, 39, 41.
"One Frog Held Out" *Weekend* 4 (18 Sept 1954), 12, 35, 40.
"Train Blues" *Weekend* 3 (24 Jan 1953), 26.

Fountain, Eileen‡
"'Arry, 'Arry, Quite Contrary" *Edmonton Journal* Fri, 18 Mar 1966, 37.
"First Flight" *Edmonton Journal* Fri, 19 Mar 1965, 4.
"Mrs. Mary 'awkins Takes Her Winnin's" *Edmonton Journal* Fri, 4 Feb 1966, 48.

Fowke, H. Shirley
"The Accolade" *Stories with John Drainie* (1963), 82-6.
"The Faithful Goose" *AA* 47 (June 1957), 27-30 ["based on truth and the essentials are correct" (author's note)].
"The Metamorphosis of Mr. Thims: A Modern Fable" *AA* 50 (Sept 1959), 106-11.
"The Metamorphosis of Mr. Thims: A Modern Fable" *Atlantic Advocate's*

Holiday Book (1961), 101-8.
"The Salvation of Paddy O'Flynn" *Stories with John Drainie* (1963), 112-7.
"Vanity of Vanities" *AA* 54 (Mar 1964), 57, 59-68.

Fowlie, Barry‡
"Red" *Alive* No. 47 (Feb-Mar 1976), 1, 16-8.

Fox, C.M.†
"The Secret Mission" *Grain* 6:3 [1978], 36-8.

Fox, Gail (1942-)
"The Cause for War" *JCF* 1:1 (Win 1972), 14-6.
"The Family Meal" *JCF* 2:4 (Fall 1973), 16-7.
"The Man Who Killed Hemingway" *72: New Canadian Stories* 102-11.
"The Man Who Killed Hemingway" *Miss Chat* 10 ([Win] 1973), 102-6.

Fox, James J.‡
"Two Old Fools" *AA* 50 (May 1960), 16-20, 22, 24, 26-33.

Fox, Joseph‡
"Release" *Prism* (Mont) No. 2 (1956), 32-5.

Fox, Marion
MIDGET STORIES FOR BUSY PEOPLE: NUMBER 1 Saint John: Barnes
Hopkins, 1954 [Based on Miller].

Foxcroft, Wm.‡
"Maynard's Mistake" *Introductions from an Island* 1977, 51-6.

Francisci, L.‡
"To the Colour Green" *Gram* 8:1 (Fall 1982), 36-9.

Frank, Bernhard
"Time and Tennis" *Des* Nos. 11/12 (Spr-Sum 1975), 91-4.

Frankel, Vera†
"Tomorrow I'll Be TEN" *Forge* 22:1 (Spr 1960), 59-66.
"The Unfortunate Demise of Miss Pilk" *Forge* 23:2 (Dec 1961), 46-62.

Fraser, Catharine†
"Any Shepherds for Tea?" *Chat* 23 (Dec 1950), 9, 66, 68-70.

Fraser, D.M. (1946-1985)
CLASS WARFARE Vancouver: Pulp Press, 1974.
THE VOICE OF EMMA SACHS Vancouver: Arsenal Editions, 1983.
"Class Warfare" *Class Warfare* (1974), 67-90.
"Dumbo Nelson" *Voice of Emma Sachs* (1983), 95-123.
"Elephantiasis" *Pulp* 3:2 (15 June 1975), [2 pp].
"Elephantiasis" *Voice of Emma Sachs* (1983), 36-41.
"Eschatology" *Voice of Emma Sachs* (1983), 42-59.
"The Examination" *Class Warfare* (1974), 27-31 [also entitled "Too Much
Nothing"].
"The Jardine Exhibition" *Voice of Emma Sachs* (1983), 67-91.

"The Letters" *Class Warfare* (1974), 52-7.
"The Letters" *Pulp* 2:5 (14 Mar 1974), [2 pp].
"Marching to Praetoria" *Class Warfare* (1974), 13-9.
"Marie Tyrell" *Class Warfare* (1974), 34-51.
"Masterpiece Avenue" *Pulp* 1:4 (1 Jan 1973), [2-3].
"Masterpiece Avenue" *Class Warfare* (1974), 20-6.
"Prelude and Theme" *Voice of Emma Sachs* (1983), 11-21.
"Santa Claus" *Class Warfare* (1974), 32-3.
"Send Not to Know" *Voice of Emma Sachs* (1983), 60-3.
"Seredonia" *Pulp* 5:11 (31 Jan 1980), [3 pp].
"The Sweetness of Life" *Pulp* 1:23 (15 Oct 1973), [2 pp].
"The Sweetness of Life" *Class Warfare* (1974), 58-63.
"Too Much Nothing" *Pulp* 1:11 (1 May 1973), [1] [Also entitled "The Examination"].
"The Voice of Emma Sachs" *Voice of Emma Sachs* (1983), 127-32.
"War and Peace" *Pulp* 2:23 (15 Mar 1975), [4 pp].
"War and Peace" *Voice of Emma Sachs* (1983), 25-35.

Fraser, Jim‡

"Little Red Riding Hood" *Acta Vic* 77:1 (Nov 1952), 20-1.

Fraser, Keath (1944-)

TAKING COVER Ottawa: Oberon Press, 1982.
"The Emerald City" *Mal R* No. 65 (July 1983), 24-50.
"Healing" *Taking Cover* (1982), 39-55.
"Healing" *Mal R* No. 62 (July 1982), 108-21.
"Le Mal de l'Air" *82: Best Canadian Stories* 12-42.
"Le Mal de l'Air" *Taking Cover* (1982), 8-38.
"Mother and Father Talk of Going South" *Taking Cover* (1982), 56-67.
"Mother and Father Talk of Going South" *Cap R* No. 23 (1982), 7-17.
"Nation, Nation" *Taking Cover* (1982), 85-96.
"Nation, Nation" *Fid* No. 133 (July 1982), 7-13.
"Roget's Thesaurus" *Taking Cover* (1982), 5-7.
"Sigiri: Palace in the Sky" *Mal R* No. 21 (Jan 1972), 50-9.
"Taking Cover" *Nebula* Nos. 21/22 (1982), 7-13.
"Taking Cover" *Taking Cover* (1982), 128-38.
"This Is What You Were Born For" *CFM* Nos. 40/41 (1981), 155-75.
"This Is What You Were Born For" *Taking Cover* (1982), 97-127.
"The Violin" *Taking Cover* (1982), 68-84.

Fraser, Peter D.†

"A Possible Title" *Voices Down East* [1973], 38-41.

Fraser, Raymond

THE BLACK HORSE TAVERN Montreal: Ingluvin, 1972.
"The Actor" *Black Horse Tavern* (1972), 171-7.
"Bertha and Bill" *Black Horse Tavern* (1972), 179-87.
"Captive" *Fid* No. 54 (Fall 1962), 24-6.
"Chatham's Flying Saucer" *Fid* No. 79 (Mar-Apr 1969), 23-33 [also entitled "The Newbridge Sighting"].
"A Cold Frosty Morning" *Black Horse Tavern* (1972), 127-39.

"College Town Restaurant" *Black Horse Tavern* (1972), 141-4.

"Cookie" *JCF* 3:2 (1974), 36-40.

"Cookie" *Toronto Short Stories* (1977), 164-75.

"Cookie" *CBC "Anthology"* 22 Jan 1977.

"During Mass" *CFM* No. 14 (Sum 1974), 36-47.

"Getting to Sleep" *Intercourse* No. 5 (Win 1967), 5, 7.

"The Janitor's Wife" *Black Horse Tavern* (1972), 145-70.

"The Newbridge Sighting" *Black Horse Tavern* (1972), 89-100 [Also entitled "Chatham's Flying Saucer"].

"On the Bus" *Black Horse Tavern* (1972), 101-13.

"The Quebec Prison" *Black Horse Tavern* (1972), 21-88.

"The Quebec Prison" *Tam R* No. 61 (Nov 1973), 34-48.

"The Quebec Prison" *Stories of Quebec* (1980), 110-36.

"Renting a TV" *CF* 48 (Nov 1968), 191.

"Spanish Jack" *Black Horse Tavern* (1972), 115-25.

"They Come Here to Die" *Black Horse Tavern* (1972), 5-20.

"They Come Here to Die" *JCF* 1:2 (Spr 1972), 7-12.

"They Come Here to Die" *East of Canada* (1976), 20-33.

"The Warm Wind Goes" *Fid* No. 51 (Win 1962), 20-4.

"Wolf Poses as Grandmother – He Attacks, Rapes Young Redhead" *Intercourse* No. 11 (Apr 1969), 16-8.

Fraser, Ross‡

"The Haircut" *Co Tinneh* No. 1 [n.d.], 13-6.

Free Park [pseudonym]

"Trains West" *Popular Illusion* No. 3 (Jan 1978), [1 p].

Freeman, Jonathan‡

"Locus of Control" *Acta Vic* 108:1 (Fall 1983), 14-5.

Freeman, Michael†

"Ceramic Meanderings" *WWR* 1:1 (Spr 1976), 61-5.

"two-four" *WWR* 1:4 (Fall 1979), 28-30.

Freeman, T.J.‡

"A Pirate Called the 'Sea Owl' " *Nfld Q* 52:2 (June 1953), 36, 38 [Non-fiction?].

Freeman, Victoria‡

"Connection" *Hysteria* 1:1 (Spr 1980), 12-4.

Freethy, Dyved‡

"The Atheist" *Stump* 1:1 (Spr 1977), 16-8.

Freiberg, Stanley

NIGHTMARE TALES Ottawa: Borealis Press, 1980.

"Apple Autumn" *Nightmare Tales* (1980), 8-20.

"The Building of the Ship" *Nightmare Tales* (1980), 72-83.

"The Building of the Wall" *Nightmare Tales* (1980), 54-64.

"Death and Dr. Landrin" *Nightmare Tales* (1980), 84-93.

"The Gospel Woods" *Nightmare Tales* (1980), 65-71.

"The Ice House" *Nightmare Tales* (1980), 33-40.

"The Junk Dealer" *Nightmare Tales* (1980), 41-6.
"The Legacy" *Nightmare Tales* (1980), 47-53.
"Old Man of the Cape" *Nightmare Tales* (1980), 1-7.
"The Swamp" *Nightmare Tales* (1980), 21-32.

Fremlin, Gerald†
"An Ear to a Knot Hole" *Folio* 4:2 [Apr 1950], [2 pp].

French, Doris
"The Burning Crusade of Andrew McNorran" *MM* 68 (20 Aug 1955), 16-7, 27-8, 30-3.
"Take Care of Linda" *CHJ* Sept 1951, 22-3, 41-4, 46-7.

French, Richard†
"Memoirs of a Gunfighter" *Waves* 2:3 (Spr 1974), 14-5.
"Though Nothing Shows" *Waves* 2:1 (Aut 1973), 72-5.

Frew, Glenn‡
"Privates" *Rampike* 3:1 (1983), 44.

Frey, Cecelia
"The Rooming House" *CBC "Anthology"* 31 Mar 1979.
"The Rooming House" *Dand* 9:1 (1982), 37-47.
"The Rose Garden" *CBC "Alberta Anthology"* 10 Sept 1983.
"Soft Shell" *Wee Giant* 4:2 (1981), 17-9.
"Sunday Driving" *Blue Buffalo* 1:2 (Spr 1983), [1 p].
"Tamar Ferouin Amongst the Savages" *Dal R* 62 (1982), 460-72.

Frey, Lilly†
"The Hunter" *Treeline* 2 (1983), 60-2.

Friday, Jo‡
"Story" *Acta Vic* 89:2 (Spr 1965), 24-6.

Friedman, Irena (1944-)
"Circus" *CF* 53 (Apr 1973), 24-5.
"Dimitri: An Unfinished Portrait" *Aurora* 1978 26-34.
"The Easy Child" *Redbook* 152 (Dec 1978), 52-3.
"Explosions" *CFM* No. 14 (Sum 1974), 59-63.
"Have You Ever Killed a Spider?" *WCR* 10:2 (Oct 1975), 10-2.
"A Hungarian Rhapsody" *Flare* 1:4 (Dec 1979), 51-2, 84, 86, 88.
"L'avenir degagé, l'avenir engagé" *SN* 90 (Sept 1975), 49-56.
"Mushrooms for a Stroganoff" *Quarry* 20:2 (Sum 1971), 34-7.
"The Neilson Chocolate Factory" *Toronto Short Stories* (1977), 149-63.
"The Neilson Chocolate Factory" *Canadian Short Stories 3* (1978), 63-80.
"Night Train" *Antig R* No. 13 (Spr 1973), 9-13.
"Night Train" *CBC "Anthology"* 1 Sept 1973.
"A Photograph, in Black and White" *Prism* 15:1 (Spr 1976), 75-81.
"Pigeons" *Prism* 13:2 (Win 1973), 141-7.
"Rain" *Matrix* No. 17 (Fall 1983), 10-8.
"Sabras" *CBC "Anthology"* 7 Aug 1976.
"Saturday Night Game" *NJ* Nos. 7/8 (1976), 69-74.

"Spring Comes to Ksirocambi" *CBC "Anthology"* 1 Nov 1980.
"Strays" *Tam R* No. 76 (Win 1979), 54-80.
"Sunday in the Park" *Tam R* No. 67 (Oct 1975), 81-6.
"Visions" *CBC "Anthology"* 2 Aug 1980.
"Willie" *CBC "Anthology"* 25 Aug 1979.
"A Woman Crossing the Street" *CBC "Anthology"* 17 May 1975.
"Yellow Curtains" *Prism* 14:1 (Aut 1974), 4-9.

Friedman, Peter‡
"The One-Eyed Rabbit and the Fistulated Dog" *Panic Button* No. 15 (1963), 12-4.

Friedman, Tom‡
"Running" *Alpha* 2:6 (Feb 1978), 11.

Friend, David‡
"The Thief" *TUR* 91:2 (Apr 1978), 43-4.

Friesen, Josephine
"The Harvest" *Island Women* (1982), 38-43.

Friesen, Victor Carl (1933-)
"Brief Candle" *Can R* 3:6 (Dec 1976), 20-2.
"Fence" *CF* 49 (Dec 1969), 214-5.
"Fence" *CBC "Anthology"* 10 Jan 1970.
"My Summer of '42" *CBC "Anthology"* 30 Nov 1974.
"My Summer of '42" *Canadian Children's Annual* 1979 (1978), 65-71.
"My Summer of '42" *West People* No. 193 (16 June 1983), 14-5 [Based on survey response].
"Neighbors" *CSSM* 1:4 (Oct 1975), 38-41.
"Old Mrs. Dirks" *QQ* 78 (1971), 443-8.
"Old Mrs. Dirks" *Stories from Western Canada* (1972), 167-75.
"Old Mrs. Dirks" *Harvest* (1974), 71-7.
"The Two Sisters" *Fid* No. 94 (Sum 1972), 37-44.
"Yesterday's Child" *Folklore* 3:3 (Sum 1982), 23-6 [Based on survey response].

Friesen, Zara†
"Inner Circle" *NeWest R* 6 (Dec 1980), 7-9.

Frith, Alex‡
"The Night Is Long" *Prism* (Mont) 1:2 (1956), 53-7.

Frog, Simon (1943-)
"The Remembered Lake" *Tawow* 6:2 (1978), 32-3.

Fromhold, J.†
"Child of Fury" *CSSM* 1:3 (July 1975), 8-9.

Frost, Bean‡
"Our Club" *TUR* 92:2 (Apr 1979), 5-7.
"A Very Lame Man" *TUR* 92:1 (Jan 1979), 32-4.

Fuchs, Terry‡

"November, Georgian Bay" *Alive* No. 31 [1973], 23.
"Sharp Rock Inlet" *Boreal* No. 7 (1977), 109-11.
"Two Episodes in the Life" *Alive* No. 32 [1973], 47.

Fuhringer, Sandy†

"Is Anyone Out There Working" *Wee Giant* 4:3 (1981), 32-4 [Listed as non-fiction].

Fulford, Robert

"The Good Wife" *Chat* 49 (Nov 1976), 44, 76, 78-80, 84, 86.
"The Good Wife" *Toronto Short Stories* (1977), 203-14.

Fulford, Robin

"At Dusk the Sound: The Story of a Boy and a Dog" *Toronto Star* Sun, 21 Sept 1980, D5.
"The Unpredictable Point" *Acanthus* 2 (Apr 1979), 47-53.

Fulford, Susan

"Saturday Matinee and Me" *TUR* 83:3 [n.d.], [1 p] [Prose poem?].

Fuller, Arthur†

"Coming Out Is a Long Time" *CF* 55 (Aug 1975), 26-30.
"Life on a Gram Scale" *CF* 59 (Aug 1979), 25-7.

Fullerton, Barbara‡

"Sarah & Wellington" *Alpha* [1:5] (Feb 1977), 17.

Funke, Carl‡

"The End of the Road" *Pedantics* 1965, 73-4.

Furberg, Jon†

"Ye Gods & Little Fishes" *Pulp* 3:20 (1 Sept 1976), [1-2].

Furcha, Edward J. (1935-)

"Waiting for the Return of the Prodigal" *UC Observer* Sept 1978, 18-9.

Furey, L.J.†

"In the Final Sounds of Play" *Antig R* No. 27 (Aut 1976), 65-9.
"A Kind of Joy" *Antig R* No. 23 (Aut 1975), 41-3.
"Merely Modern" *Antig R* No. 22 (Sum 1975), 41-4.
"Merry-Go-Round" *Antig R* No. 23 (Aut 1975), 37-9.

Furlong, Harry‡

"Red Scarf for Christmas" *Folio* 4:1 [Jan 1950], [8 pp].

Futhey, John F.†

"A Rose By Any Other Name" *Chat* 52 (Oct 1979), 53, 172, 174, 176, 178.

G.D. – *See* D., G.

Gabel, Miriam (1922-)
"The Drowsy Shopper" *[Title Unknown]* (1975), 15-6.

Gabori, Susan‡
"The Dreams of Harry S" *Fruits of Experience* (1978), 27-42.

Gabrielli, John†
"At the Insanity Factory" *Tam R* No. 67 (Oct 1975), 95-103.

Gabris, Linda†
" ... Smell a Fool" *BC Monthly* 5:3 (Apr 1981), 20-1.

Gaddes, Sara†
"Monologue" *From an Island* 10:1 [n.d.], 48.

Gaetz, Jamie (1954-)
"Rain, Rain, Rain" *CBC "Alberta Anthology"* 3 Sept 1983.

Gagnon, Christine‡
"Mother's Day Visit" *West People* No. 136 (6 May 1982), 6.

Gaitskill, Mary†
"Something Better Than This" *Br Out* 5:1 (1978), 18-21.

Galbraith, Mary†
"The Last Trip" *Polished Pebbles* (1974), 9-13.

Gale, Jack – *See* Day, Gene and Jack, Gale.

Gale, Kay‡
"Take Two Aspirins ... " *Forum* (OSSTF) 6 (Mar 1980), 81.

Galemba, Ronald S.‡
"Metamorphosis" *Liontayles* Win 1967, 11.

Gall, Glendy (1957-)
"Train to Lausanne" *Mal R* No. 51 (July 1979), 77-91.

Gallant, Cathy‡
"Cajolery" *Katharsis* 1:1 (Apr 1967), 34-5.

Gallant, Donna (1948-)
"What's a Fella Gonna Do?" *Island Prose and Poetry* (1973), 201-2.
"What's a Fella Gonna Do?" *Maritime Experience* (1975), 89-91.

Gallant, Jimmy‡
"Maelstrom of Madness" *Outlook* June-July 1983, 28-9.

Gallant, Mavis (1922-)
THE END OF THE WORLD AND OTHER STORIES Toronto: McClelland & Stewart, 1974.
FROM THE FIFTEENTH DISTRICT New York: Random House, 1979.
HOME TRUTHS: SELECTED CANADIAN STORIES Toronto: Macmillan, 1981.

MY HEART IS BROKEN New York: Random House, 1964.
THE OTHER PARIS Boston: Houghton Mifflin, 1956.
THE PEGNITZ JUNCTION New York: Random House, 1973.
"About Geneva" *End of the World* (1974), 46-51.
"About Geneva" *Anthology of Canadian Literature in English 2* (1983), 76-81.
"Acceptance of Their Ways" *New Yorker* 35 (30 Jan 1960), 25-8.
"Acceptance of Their Ways" *My Heart Is Broken* (1964), 3-13.
"Acceptance of Their Ways" *Great Canadian Short Stories* (1971), 203-11.
"Acceptance of Their Ways" *End of the World* (1974), 52-9.
"Acceptance of Their Ways" *Women and Fiction* 2 (1978), 287-95.
"The Accident" *New Yorker* 43 (28 Oct 1967), 55-9.
"The Accident" *CBC "Anthology"* 13 Dec 1969.
"The Accident" *Canadian Writing Today* (1970), 260-72.
"The Accident" *End of the World* (1974), 95-105.
"The Accident" *CBC "Anthology"* 7 Sept 1974.
"The Accident" *Modern Canadian Stories* (1975), 126-40.
"An Alien Flower" *New Yorker* 48 (7 Oct 1972), 34-44.
"An Alien Flower" *Pegnitz Junction* (1973), 167-93.
"April Fish" *New Yorker* 43 (10 Feb 1968), 27-8.
"The Assembly" *Harper's* 260 (May 1980), 75-8.
"The Assembly" *81: Best Canadian Stories* 36-44.
"The Assembly" *Best American Short Stories* 1981, 150-7.
"August" *Best American Short Stories* 1960 64-101.
"An Autobiography" *Pegnitz Junction* (1973), 101-29.
"An Autobiography" *Here and Now* (1977), 19-38.
"Autumn Day" *New Yorker* 31 (29 Oct 1955), 31-8.
"Autumn Day" *Other Paris* (1956), 31-53.
"Baum, Gabriel, 1935-( )" *From the Fifteenth District* (1979), 139-61.
"Baum, Gabriel, 1935-( )" *New Yorker* 54 (12 Feb 1979), 30-40, 43-4.
"Bebe's Place" *Mont* 32 (Apr 1958), 52-7.
"Bernadette" *New Yorker* 32 (12 Jan 1957), 24-34.
"Bernadette" *Stories from The New Yorker 1950-1960* (1960), 96-118.
"Bernadette" *My Heart Is Broken* (1964), 14-41.
"Bernadette" *Canadian Short Stories 2* (1968), 60-93.
"Bernadette" *Die Weite Reisse* (1974), 70-102 [Trans. Peter Kleinhempel].
"Bernadette" *Penguin Book of Canadian Short Stories* (1980), 207-29.
"Better Times" *New Yorker* 36 (3 Dec 1960), 59-65.
"Between Zero and One" *New Yorker* 51 (8 Dec 1975), 38-47.
"Between Zero and One" *Legion* 51 (Dec 1976), 17-9.
"Between Zero and One" *Home Truths* (1981), 238-60.
"Bonaventure" *Home Truths* (1981), 135-72.
"The Burgundy Weekend" *Tam R* No. 76 (Win 1979), 3-39.
"By the Sea" *New Yorker* 30 (17 July 1954), 27-30.
"The Captive Niece" *New Yorker* 44 (4 Jan 1969), 28-32.
"Careless Talk" *New Yorker* 39 (28 Sept 1963), 41-7.
"The Circus" *New Yorker* 40 (20 June 1964), 38-40.
"The Colonel's Child" *New Yorker* 59 (10 Oct 1983), 44-7.
"The Cost of Living" *My Heart Is Broken* (1964), 157-93.
"Crossing France" *Critic* (U.S.) 19:3 (Dec 1960-Jan 1961), 15-8.
"A Day Like Any Other" *New Yorker* 29 (7 Nov 1953), 37-44.

"The Deceptions of Marie-Blanche" *Other Paris* (1956), 122-40.

"Dido Flute, Spouse to Europe (Addenda to a Major Biography)" *New Yorker* 56 (12 May 1980), 37 [Humour?].

"The Doctor" *New Yorker* 53 (20 June 1977), 33-42.

"The Doctor" *Home Truths* (1981), 295-316.

"An Emergency Case" *New Yorker* 32 (16 Feb 1957), 34-6.

"The End of the World" *New Yorker* 43 (10 June 1967), 36-9.

"The End of the World" *Canadian Winter's Tales* (1968), 103-13.

"The End of the World" *End of the World* (1974), 88-94.

"The End of the World" *Best Canadian Short Stories* (1981), 225-32.

"Ernst in Civilian Clothes" *New Yorker* 39 (16 Nov 1963), 54-8.

"Ernst in Civilian Clothes" *Pegnitz Junction* (1973), 131-47.

"Europe by Satellite" *New Yorker* 56 (3 Nov 1980), 47.

"The Flowers of Spring" *NR* 3:5 (June-July 1950), 31-9.

"A Flying Start" *New Yorker* 58 (13 Sept 1982), 39-44.

"The Four Seasons" *New Yorker* 51 (16 June 1975), 32-40, 43-6, 49.

"The Four Seasons" *From the Fifteenth District* (1979), 3-35.

"French Crenellation" *New Yorker* 56 (9 Feb 1981), 33.

"From Gamut to Yalta" *New Yorker* 56 (15 Sept 1980), 40-1.

"From Sunrise to Daybreak (A Year in the Life of an Émigré Review)" *New Yorker* 56 (17 Mar 1980), 34-6 [Humour?].

"From the Fifteenth District" *New Yorker* 54 (30 Oct 1978), 36-8.

"From the Fifteenth District" *From the Fifteenth District* (1979), 162-8.

"From the Fifteenth District" *Harper's & Queen* Mar 1980, 66, 68, 70 [Based on ABCMA].

"Going Ashore" *Other Paris* (1956), 69-103.

"Good Deed" *New Yorker* 45 (22 Feb 1969), 35-41.

"Grippes and Poche" *New Yorker* 58 (29 Nov 1982), 42-50.

"His Mother" *New Yorker* 49 (13 Aug 1973), 28-33.

"His Mother" *From the Fifteenth District* (1979), 213-24.

"His Mother" *Montreal Star* Sat, 15 Sept 1979, H1, H4 [Based on ABCMA].

"The Hunter's Waking Thoughts" *New Yorker* 38 (29 Sept 1962), 34-5.

"The Ice Wagon Going Down the Street" *My Heart Is Broken* (1964), 246-73.

"The Ice Wagon Going Down the Street" *Home Truths* (1981), 107-34.

"The Ice Wagon Going Down the Street" *Penguin Book of Modern Canadian Short Stories* (1982), 267-89.

"The Ice Wagon Going Down the Street" *Anthology of Canadian Literature in English 2* (1983), 81-96.

"In Italy" *New Yorker* 32 (25 Feb 1956), 32-6.

"In the Tunnel" *New Yorker* 47 (18 Sept 1971), 34-47.

"In the Tunnel" *End of the World* (1974), 142-67.

"In the Tunnel" *Home Truths* (1981), 72-106.

"In Transit" *New Yorker* 41 (14 Aug 1965), 24-5.

"In Youth Is Pleasure" *New Yorker* 51 (24 Nov 1975), 46-54.

"In Youth Is Pleasure" *Home Truths* (1981), 218-37.

"In Youth Is Pleasure" *Writers and Writing* (1981), 68-84.

"In Youth Is Pleasure" *Penguin Book of Modern Canadian Short Stories* (1982), 319-34.

"Irina" *New Yorker* 50 (2 Dec 1974), 44-52.

"Irina" *Canadian Short Stories 3* (1978), 82-104.

"Irina" *From the Fifteenth District* (1979), 225-43.
"Its Image on the Mirror" *Legion* 51 (Dec 1976), 14-5.
"Jeux d'Ete" *New Yorker* 33 (27 July 1957), 30-4.
"Jorinda and Jorindel" *New Yorker* 35 (19 Sept 1959), 38-42.
"Jorinda and Jorindel" *Home Truths* (1981), 17-28.
"Larry" *New Yorker* 57 (16 Nov 1981), 50-2.
"The Latehomecomer" *New Yorker* 50 (8 July 1974), 31-40.
"The Latehomecomer" *From the Fifteenth District* (1979), 117-39.
"The Legacy" *New Yorker* 30 (26 June 1954), 22-9.
"The Legacy" *Other Paris* (1956), 152-72.
"Lena" *New Yorker* 59 (30 Oct 1983), 40-5.
"Madeline's Birthday" *New Yorker* 27 (1 Sept 1951), 20-4.
"Malcolm and Bea" *New Yorker* 44 (23 Mar 1968), 35-43.
"Malcolm and Bea" *End of the World* (1974), 106-19.
"Mau to Lew: The Maurice Ravel – Lewis Carroll Friendship" *Exile* 7:3/4 (1981), 220-30.
"Mau to Lew: The Maurice Ravel – Lewis Carroll Friendship" *Illusion One* (1983), 13-23.
"The Moabitess" *New Yorker* 33 (2 Nov 1957), 42-6.
"The Moabitess" *My Heart Is Broken* (1964), 42-54.
"The Moslem Wife" *New Yorker* 52 (23 Aug 1976), 28-42, 44-5.
"The Moslem Wife" *From the Fifteenth District* (1979), 36-74.
"Mousse" *New Yorker* 56 (22 Dec 1980), 31.
"My Heart Is Broken" *New Yorker* 37 (12 Aug 1961), 32-4.
"My Heart Is Broken" *My Heart Is Broken* (1964), 194-202.
"My Heart Is Broken" *Canadian Short Stories 2* (1968), 94-104.
"My Heart Is Broken" *CBC "Anthology"* 24 May 1969.
"My Heart Is Broken" *Four Hemispheres* (1971), 162-8.
"My Heart Is Broken" *Contemporary Voices* (1972), 8-13.
"My Heart Is Broken" *Evolution of Canadian Literature in English* (1973), 134-8.
"My Heart Is Broken" *End of the World* (1974), 60-6.
"New Year's Eve" *New Yorker* 45 (10 Jan 1970), 25-30.
"New Year's Eve" *End of the World* (1974), 130-41.
"Night and Day" *New Yorker* 38 (17 Mar 1962), 48-50.
"O Lasting Peace" *New Yorker* 47 (8 Jan 1972), 34-40.
"O Lasting Peace" *Pegnitz Junction* (1973), 149-66.
"The Old Friends" *New Yorker* 45 (30 Aug 1969), 27-30.
"The Old Friends" *Pegnitz Junction* (1973), 89-99.
"The Old Place" *Texas Q* 1:2 (Spr 1958), 66-80.
"On with the New in France" *New Yorker* 57 (10 Aug 1981), 31 [Humour?].
"One Aspect of a Rainy Day" *New Yorker* 38 (14 Apr 1962), 38-9.
"One Morning in June" *New Yorker* 28 (7 June 1952), 27-31.
"One Morning in June" *Sometimes Magic* (1966), 3-17 [Based on ABCMA].
"Orphans' Progress" *New Yorker* 41 (3 Apr 1965), 49-51.
"Orphans' Progress" *Home Truths* (1981), 56-62.
"The Other Paris" *New Yorker* 29 (11 Apr 1953), 27-36.
"The Other Paris" *Other Paris* (1956), 1-30.
"The Other Paris" *End of the World* (1974), 15-33.
"A Painful Affair" *New Yorker* 57 (16 Mar 1981), 39-43.
"Paolo and Renata" *Southern R* NS 1 (1965), 199-209.

"The Picnic" *New Yorker* 28 (9 Aug 1952), 23-8.
"The Picnic" *Other Paris* (1956), 104-21.
"The Picnic" *End of the World* (1974), 34-45.
"Poor Franzi" *Other Paris* (1956), 54-68.
"Potter" *From the Fifteenth District* (1979), 169-212.
"The Prodigal Parent" *New Yorker* 45 (7 June 1969), 42-4.
"The Prodigal Parent" *End of the World* (1974), 120-5.
"The Prodigal Parent" *Home Truths* (1981), 63-70.
"Questions and Answers" *New Yorker* 42 (28 May 1966), 33-8.
"A Recollection" *New Yorker* 59 (22 Aug 1983), 28-32.
"The Rejection" *New Yorker* 45 (12 Apr 1969), 42-4.
"The Remission" *From the Fifteenth District* (1979), 75-116.
"The Remission" *Best American Short Stories* 1980 80-118.
"A Report" *New Yorker* 42 (3 Dec 1966), 62-5.
"Rose" *New Yorker* 36 (17 Dec 1960), 34-7.
"Rue de Lille" *New Yorker* 59 (19 Sept 1983), 43-4.
"Saturday" *New Yorker* 44 (8 June 1968), 32-40.
"Saturday" *Stories of Quebec* (1980), 80-100.
"Saturday" *Home Truths* (1981), 29-48.
"Señor Pinedo" *New Yorker* 29 (9 Jan 1954), 23-8.
"A Short Love Story" *Mont* 31 (June 1957), 48, 60, 62.
"Siegfried's Memoirs" *New Yorker* 58 (5 Apr 1982), 42-3.
"Speck's Idea" *80: Best Canadian Stories* 47-98.
"Speck's Idea" *Best American Short Stories* 1980 119-58.
"The Statues Taken Down" *New Yorker* 41 (9 Oct 1965), 53-6.
"The Sunday After Christmas" *New Yorker* 43 (30 Dec 1967), 35-6.
"Sunday Afternoon" *New Yorker* 38 (24 Nov 1962), 52-8.
"Sunday Afternoon" *My Heart Is Broken* (1964), 203-17.
"Sunday Afternoon" *Woman's Place* (1974), 42-59 [Based on ABCMA].
"Thank You for the Lovely Tea" *New Yorker* 32 (9 June 1956), 36-40, 42, 44, 47-8.
"Thank You for the Lovely Tea" *Home Truths* (1981), 2-16.
"This Space" *New Yorker* 57 (6 July 1981), 35 [Humour?].
"Treading Water" *New Yorker* 58 (24 May 1982), 33.
"Two Questions" *New Yorker* 37 (10 June 1961), 30-6.
"An Unmarried Man's Summer" *My Heart Is Broken* (1964), 218-45.
"An Unmarried Man's Summer" *End of the World* (1974), 67-87.
"Up North" *New Yorker* 35 (21 Nov 1959), 46-8.
"Up North" *Home Truths* (1981), 49-55.
"Vacances Pax" *New Yorker* 42 (16 July 1966), 26-9.
"Varieties of Exile" *New Yorker* 51 (19 Jan 1976), 26-35.
"Varieties of Exile" *Home Truths* (1981), 261-81.
"La Vie Parisienne" *New Yorker* 57 (19 Oct 1981), 41 [Humour?].
"Virus X" *Home Truths* (1981), 173-216.
"Voices Lost in Snow" *New Yorker* 52 (5 Apr 1976), 38-43.
"Voices Lost in Snow" *Home Truths* (1981), 282-94.
"The Wedding Ring" *New Yorker* 45 (28 June 1969), 41-2.
"The Wedding Ring" *End of the World* (1974), 126-9.
"When We Were Nearly Young" *New Yorker* 36 (15 Oct 1960), 38-42.
"Willi" *New Yorker* 38 (5 Jan 1963), 29-31.
"Wing's Chips" *New Yorker* 30 (17 Apr 1954), 35-8.

"Wing's Chips" *Other Paris* (1956), 141-51.
"With a Capital T" *CFM* No. 28 (1978), 8-17.
"With a Capital T" *79: Best Canadian Stories* 38-51.
"With a Capital T" *Home Truths* (1981), 317-30.

Galloway, David R.†

'The Scent of Cedars" *AA* 47 (Mar 1957), 46, 48-9.
'The Scythe" *Dal R* 30 (1950), 128-32.
'The Vacation" *QQ* 65 (1958), 476-8.

Galloway, Priscilla (1930-)

"Act of Apostacy: (The Boy Next Door)" by Anne Peebles *CBC "Anthology"* 11 Dec 1976.
"Act of Apostacy: (The Boy Next Door)" by Anne Peebles *Chat* 50 (Apr 1977), 50, 104-9.
'The Days of Youth Are Long" *Forum* (OSSTF) 8 (Dec 1982), 208-10.
"Deja Vu" *Waves* 11:1 (Fall 1982), 27-9.

Galt, George‡

'This Is the Grim Season" *Quarry* 23:3 (Sum 1974), 20-8.

Gane, Margaret Drury (1926-)

" 'Til He Takes a Wife" *Chat* 45 (May 1972), 27, 58, 60, 62, 64.
"A Day Off in the Life of Connie Rime" *Chat* 47 (May 1974), 45, 62, 64, 66-8.
"A Few Words Before Dinner" *SN* 90 (Dec 1975), 44-50.
"Joyful Christmas" *Chat* 44 (Dec 1971), 21, 56-9.
"Nothing at Face Value" *Chat* 46 (June 1973), 41, 52, 54, 56, 58-9.
'The Perfect Catch" *Chat* 46 (Jan 1973), 28, 44-6.
'The Purpose of the Exercise" *Chat* 49 (Sept 1976), 45, 89-90, 92, 94-6.
'The Rich Girls of Rosedale" *Chat* 47 (Sept 1974), 45, 60-2, 64, 66, 68.
'Turning Point" *Chat* 49 (Aug 1976), 35, 52, 54-6, 58.

Gant, Eric W.†

'The Broken Hand" *Repos* No. 16 (Aut 1975), 10-2.
'The Evil Man" *Canadian Short Fiction Anthology* (1976), 91-4.
'The Exterminator" *Grain* 4:2 [1976], 45-6.

Garber, Daniel†

'Thirty White Horses" *Writ* No. 13 (1981), 12-5.

Garber, Lawrence (1937-)

"Four Walls" *Jargon* No. 2 (Spr 1961), 26-31.
"In Pursuit of the Maraschino" *Varsity Lit Issue* Fri, 13 Dec 1963, 7-8.
'The Mind's Eye" *Otherside* No. 3 (Mar 1961), 8, 29.
'The Mind's Eye" *Undergrad* Spr 1961, 24-7.
"Myth and Mistake" *Undergrad* Spr 1961, 1-3.
"Old Red" *Otherside* No. 1 (Aut 1959), 16-7.
'The Pit" *UC Gargoyle* 22 Mar 1961, [2-3].
"Portrait of Vernon" *Undergrad* Spr 1960, 7-8.
'Tales from the Quarter" *Varsity* Fri, 6 Dec 1963, 10.

"Tales from the Quarter" *Varsity* Fri, 13 Dec 1963, 17.
"Visions Before Midnight" *Penguin Book of Canadian Short Stories* (1980), 343-57.
"Writ on Water" *Otherside* No. 1 (Aut 1959), 12-5.

Gardner, Jigs†

"The Fox" *Voices Down East* [1973], 22-5.

Gardner, W.W.

"The Affair of Gormley's Cow" *Nfld Q* 57:3 (Sept 1958), 9, 44-6, 48.
"Bound by Gold Chains" *FH* 11 Jan 1951, 18-9, 26.
"The Deadhead" *Nfld Q* 56:4 (Dec 1957), 5, 46-7.
"Let Not the Sun Go Down" *FH* 5 May 1960, 24-5, 29.
"Many Are the Brave" *Stories of Christian Living* (1950) [Based on SSI].
"Phantom Hill" *Atl Guardian* 8 (Nov 1951), 21-2, 24-5.
"These Men See" *FH* 12 Sept 1963, 68-9, 71.
"The Waters of Marah" *FH* 31 May 1951, 18-9, 27.
"The Wicked Fleeth" *AA* 48 (June 1958), 85, 87-8.

Gardner, William‡

"The Closet Society" *Humanist in Can* 15:3 (Aut 1982), 31 [Originally published in *The Churchman*].

Garen, Robert

"The Forces" *UWR* 1:2 (Spr 1965), 236-8.
"The Old Woman" *Kaleidoscope* 1963, 16-8.
"The Old Woman" *UWR* 3:2 (Spr 1968), 30-2.

Garneau, Kay – *See* Green, H. Gordon.

Garner, Hugh (1913-1979)

A HUGH GARNER OMNIBUS Toronto: McGraw-Hill Ryerson, 1978 [Contains detailed information on the publishing histories of short stories included].
HUGH GARNER'S BEST STORIES Toronto: Ryerson Press, 1963.
THE LEGS OF THE LAME AND OTHER STORIES Ottawa: Borealis Press, 1976.
MEN AND WOMEN New York: Simon and Schuster, 1973.
VIOLATION OF THE VIRGINS Toronto: McGraw-Hill Ryerson, 1971.
THE YELLOW SWEATER AND OTHER STORIES Toronto: Collins, 1952.
"Act of a Hero" *Violation of the Virgins* (1971), 35-9.
"Act of a Hero" *Inquiry into Literature* 2 (1980), 49-53.
"All the Gay Days" *CHJ* Mar 1957, 29, 70-2.
"All the Gay Days" *Men and Women* (1973), 51-8.
"All the Gay Days" *Women in Canadian Literature* (1976), 164-8.
"Another Day, Another Dollar" *CBC "Anthology"* 22 Mar 1966.
"Another Day, Another Dollar" *Men and Women* (1973), 106-14.
"Another Time, Another Place, Another Me" *Violation of the Virgins* (1971), 1-7.
"Another Time, Another Place, Another Me" *Canadian Anthology* (1974), 410-4.
"Artsy-Craftsy" *Temper of the Times* (1969), 37-48.
"Artsy-Craftsy" *CBC "Anthology"* 25 Apr 1970.
"Artsy-Craftsy" *Men and Women* (1973), 213-27.
"Artsy-Craftsy" *Omnibus* (1978), 453-67.
"Black and White and Red All Over" *CBC "Sunday Night"* 25 Oct 1964 [Based

on *Omnibus*].

"Black and White and Red All Over" *Temper of the Times* (1969), 136-45.

"Black and White and Red All Over" CBC *"Anthology"* 20 Mar 1971.

"Black and White and Red All Over" *Men and Women* (1973), 1-12.

"Black and White and Red All Over" *Omnibus* (1978), 584-95.

"Brightest Star in the Dipper" *Violation of the Virgins* (1971), 144-79.

"Captain Rafferty" *Lib* 28 (May 1951), 26-7, 60, 62-6.

"Captain Rafferty" *Yellow Sweater* (1952), 212-20.

"Captain Rafferty" *Men and Women* (1973), 144-51.

"Coming Out Party" *Chat* 23 (Sept 1950), 16-7, 26-8, 30.

"Coming Out Party" *Yellow Sweater* (1952), 179-84.

"Coming Out Party" *Men and Women* (1973), 129-43.

"The Compromise" *CHJ* Sept 1952, 14-5, 75, 78, 82.

"The Conversion of Willie Heaps" *NR* 4:3 (Feb 1951), 2-10.

"The Conversion of Willie Heaps" *Yellow Sweater* (1952), 46-57.

"The Conversion of Willie Heaps" *Best American Short Stories* 1952 151-9.

"The Conversion of Willie Heaps" *Best Stories* (1963), 1-11.

"The Conversion of Willie Heaps" CBC *"Anthology"* *[?]* 1965 [Based on *Omnibus*].

"The Conversion of Willie Heaps" *Omnibus* (1978), 417-27.

"The Conversion of Willie Heaps" CBC *"Anthology"* 3 Mar 1979.

"A Couple of Quiet Young Guys" *CF* 31 (July 1951), 82-3, 85.

"A Couple of Quiet Young Guys" *Yellow Sweater* (1952), 39-45.

"A Couple of Quiet Young Guys" *Best Stories* (1963), 24-9.

"The Customer Is Always Right" *Legs of the Lame* (1976), 95-100.

"The Decision" CBC *"Anthology"* 10 Apr 1959.

"The Decision" *Men and Women* (1973), 172-82.

"The Decision" *Women in Canadian Literature* (1976), 169-76.

"Desire" *Lib* 31 (Nov 1954), 20-1, 50, 52-3, 55-6, 58, 60.

"Don't Ever Leave Me" CBC *"Anthology"* 24 Jan 1956.

"Don't Ever Leave Me" *Men and Women* (1973), 96-105.

"Dwell in Heaven, Die on Earth" CBC *"Anthology"* 1 Sept 1966.

"Dwell in Heaven, Die on Earth" *Men and Women* (1973), 76-89.

"E Equals MC Squared" CBC *"Stories with John Drainie"* [date unknown] [Based on *Omnibus*].

"E Equals MC Squared" CBC *"Wednesday Night"* 29 Aug 1962 [Based on *Omnibus*].

"E Equals MC Squared" *Best Stories* (1963), 224-35.

"E Equals MC Squared" *Canadian Short Stories 2* (1968), 44-59.

"E Equals MC Squared" CBC *"Anthology"* 23 Aug 1969.

"E Equals MC Squared" CBC *"Anthology"* 27 May 1972.

"E Equals MC Squared" *Canadian Literature* (1973), 273-82.

"E Equals MC Squared" *Omnibus* (1978), 596-607.

"The Expatriates" *Best Stories* (1963), 70-4.

"The Fall Guy" *Lib* 28 (July 1951), 34-5, 68.

"The Fall Guy" *Yellow Sweater* (1952), 172-8.

"The Fall Guy" *Men and Women* (1973), 90-5.

"The Father" by Jarvis Warwick *CHJ* Feb 1958, 14-5, 36, 38-40.

"The Father" *Best Stories* (1963), 12-23.

"The Father" CBC *"Anthology"* 27 Apr 1967.

"The Father" *CBC "Anthology"* 13 Sept 1969.

"The Father" *CBC "Anthology"* 10 June 1972.

"Final Decree" by Jarvis Warwick *CHJ* Apr 1957, 19, 50-2.

"The Happiest Man in the World" [?] *CBC "Anthology"* 8 Feb 1968 [As "The Happiest Man in Town" [?]].

"The Happiest Man in the World" *Fourteen Stories High* (1971), 35-50.

"The Happiest Man in the World" *Violation of the Virgins* (1971), 92-108.

"The Happiest Man in the World" *Urban Experience* (1975), 3-19.

"Homecoming" *CBC "Anthology"* 22 Feb 1975.

"An Hour to Wait" *Violation of the Virgins* (1971), 60-72.

"How I Became an Englishman" *Best Stories* (1963), 236-42.

"Hunky" *CBC "Wednesday Night"* 11 May 1960 [Based on *Omnibus*].

"Hunky" *Ten for Wednesday Night* (1961), 122-39.

"Hunky" *Best Stories* (1963), 166-81.

"Hunky" *Canadian Short Stories 2* (1968), 23-43.

"Hunky" *CBC "Anthology"* 2 Aug 1969.

"Hunky" *CBC "Anthology"* 22 Apr 1972.

"Hunky" *Oxford Anthology of Canadian Literature* (1973), 149-61.

"Hunky" *CBC "Stories with John Drainie"* [date unknown] [Based on *Omnibus*].

"I'll Never Let You Go" *Chat* 25 (Aug 1952), 19, 27-30.

"I'll See You Again" by Jarvis Warwick *Lib* 30 (June 1953), 22-3, 52-3, 55.

"Interlude in Black and White" *Yellow Sweater* (1952), 34-8.

"Interlude in Black and White" *Best Stories* (1963), 182-5.

"It's Been a Long Time" *Chat* [34] (Feb 1961), 29, 55-8, 60-1.

"It's Been a Long Time" *Violation of the Virgins* (1971), 180-93.

"Jacks or Better, Jokers Wild" *CF* 54 (Feb 1975), 24-8.

"Jacks or Better, Jokers Wild" *Legs of the Lame* (1976), 83-94.

"Jacks or Better, Jokers Wild" *CBC "Anthology"* 29 Jan 1977.

"The Legs of the Lame" *CBC "Anthology"* 11 May 1974.

"The Legs of the Lame" *Tam R* No. 64 (Nov 1974), 55-70.

"The Legs of the Lame" *Legs of the Lame* (1976), 1-16.

"The Legs of the Lame" *Canadian Short Stories 3* (1978), 106-25.

"The Legs of the Lame" *Penguin Book of Canadian Short Stories* (1980), 191-205.

"The Londonderry Air" *Yellow Sweater* (1952), 195-211.

"The Londonderry Air" *Men and Women* (1973), 183-97.

"Losers Weepers" *CBC "Anthology"* 6 Jan 1973.

"Losers Weepers" *Men and Women* (1973), 13-26.

"Losers Weepers" *73: New Canadian Stories* 60-73.

"Losers Weepers" *Legs of the Lame* (1976), 67-78.

"Lucy" *CHJ* Apr 1952, 10-1, 63-5, 69, 72-3.

"Lucy" *Best Stories* (1963), 30-43.

"The Magnet" *Best Stories* (1963), 135-47.

"The Magnet" *CBC "Anthology"* 26 July 1969.

"The Magnet" *CBC "Anthology"* 24 June 1972.

"Make Mine Vanilla" *Best Stories* (1963), 55-61.

"Mama Says to Tell You She's Out" *Men and Women* (1973), 27-40.

"The Man with the Musical Tooth" *Yellow Sweater* (1952), 141-56.

"The Man with the Musical Tooth" *Quarry* 24:3 (Sum 1975), 12-24.

"The Man with the Musical Tooth" *Legs of the Lame* (1976), 55-66.

"The Man with the Musical Tooth" *CBC "Anthology"* 3 Dec 1977.

"A Manly Heart" *CHJ* June 1955, 32, 34, 36, 38-9 [As "The Manly Heart"].

"A Manly Heart" *Best Stories* (1963), 195-205.

"A Manly Heart" CBC *"Mid-Week Theatre"* 10 Nov 1965 [Based on *Omnibus*].

"A Manly Heart" *Time of Your Life* (1967), 15-28.

"A Manly Heart" CBC *"Anthology"* 6 Sept 1969. [As "The Manly Heart"].

"A Manly Heart" *Voices 2* (1976) [Based on *Omnibus*].

"A Manly Heart" *Omnibus* (1978), 555-65.

"A Manly Heart" *Rites of Passage* (1979), 19-27.

"A Manly Heart" *Core* (1982), 103-8.

"The Moose and the Sparrow" CBC *"Anthology"* 4 Dec 1971.

"The Moose and the Sparrow" *Kaleidoscope* (1972), 106-15.

"The Moose and the Sparrow" *Men and Women* (1973), 41-50.

"The Moose and the Sparrow" *Singing Under Ice* (1974), 1-10.

"The Moose and the Sparrow" *Best Canadian Short Stories* (1981), 125-32.

"The Moose and the Sparrow" *In Your Own Words* (1982), 227-33.

"Moving Day" *Legs of the Lame* (1976), 23-38.

"A Night on the Town" CBC *"Anthology"* 28 Feb 1970.

"A Night on the Town" *Violation of the Virgins* (1971), 128-43.

"No More Songs About The Suwanee" *Best Stories* (1963), 117-22.

"Not That I Care" *Chat* 28 (Feb 1956), 11, 55-9.

"Not That I Care" *Men and Women* (1973), 152-62.

"The Nun in Nylon Stockings" *Best Stories* (1963), 186-94.

"The Old Man's Laughter" *Yellow Sweater* (1952), 71-7.

"The Old Man's Laughter" *Legs of the Lame* (1976), 121-6.

"One, Two, Three Little Indians" [Broadcast 19 May 1950; published in Romania 1964; based on *Omnibus*].

"One, Two, Three Little Indians" *Lib* 27 (Dec 1950), 19, 45-51.

"One, Two, Three Little Indians" *Canadian Short Stories* (1952), 116-27.

"One, Two, Three Little Indians" *Yellow Sweater* (1952), 225-38.

"One, Two, Three Little Indians" CBC *"Wednesday Night"* 1954 [Based on *Omnibus*].

"One, Two, Three Little Indians" CBC *"Stories with John Drainie"* 1955 [Based on *Omnibus*].

"One, Two, Three Little Indians" CBC *"Stories with John Drainie"* 1956 [Based on *Omnibus*].

"One, Two, Three Little Indians" *Book of Canadian Stories* (1962), 261-72.

"One, Two, Three Little Indians" *Best Stories* (1963), 243-54.

"One, Two, Three Little Indians" *Modern Canadian Stories* (1966), 228-38.

"One, Two, Three Little Indians" *In Search of Ourselves* (1967) [Based on *Omnibus*].

"One, Two, Three Little Indians" *Kanadische Erzühler der Gegenwart* (1967), 229-45 [As "Ein, zwei, drei kleine Indianer"; trans. Walter Riedel].

"One, Two, Three Little Indians" *Stories from Canada* (1969), 76-103.

"One, Two, Three Little Indians" CBC *"Anthology"* 27 Sept 1969.

"One, Two, Three Little Indians" CBC International Service Nov 1969 [Based on *Omnibus*].

"One, Two, Three Little Indians" *Survival 2* [Based on *Omnibus*].

"One, Two, Three Little Indians" *Strangers in Their Own Land* [Date unknown] [Based on *Omnibus*].

"One, Two, Three Little Indians" CBC *"Anthology"* 18 Apr 1970.

"One, Two, Three Little Indians" CBC "To See Ourselves" 21 Oct 1971 [Based on *Omnibus*].

"One, Two, Three Little Indians" *Alienated Man* (1972) [Based on *Omnibus*].

"One, Two, Three Little Indians" *Pleasures of Fiction* (1972) [Based on *Omnibus*].

"One, Two, Three Little Indians" CBC "*Anthology*" 20 May 1972.

"One, Two, Three Little Indians" *Canadian Century* (1973), 351-60.

"One, Two, Three Little Indians" *Evolution of Canadian Literature in English* (1973), 73-80.

"One, Two, Three Little Indians" *Die Weite Reise* (1974), 44-57 [As "Ein, zwei, drei kleine Indianer"; trans. Peter Kleinhempel].

"One, Two, Three Little Indians" *Stories from Ontario* (1974), 130-41.

"One, Two, Three Little Indians" *Canadian Prose and Related Grammar Exercises* (1976) [Based on *Omnibus*].

"One, Two, Three Little Indians" *Ontario Experience* (1976), 70-81.

"One, Two, Three Little Indians" *Omnibus* (1978), 428-40.

"One for the Road" *QQ* 82 (1975), 249-57.

"One for the Road" *Legs of the Lame* (1976), 141-51.

"One Mile of Ice" CBC "Stories with John Drainie" [date unknown] [Based on *Omnibus*].

"One Mile of Ice" CBC 26 Jan 1951 [Based on *Omnibus*].

"One Mile of Ice" *Canadian Short Stories* (1952), 1-12.

"One Mile of Ice" *Yellow Sweater* (1952), 157-71.

"One Mile of Ice" *Best Stories* (1963), 123-34.

"One Mile of Ice" *CBC International Service* June 1968 [Based on *Omnibus*].

"One Mile of Ice" CBC "*Anthology*" 19 July 1969.

"One Mile of Ice" CBC "*Anthology*" 3 June 1972.

"One Mile of Ice" *Telling Tales* (1973) [Based on *Omnibus*].

"One Mile of Ice" *Crossroads 2* (1979), 150-63.

"One Mile of Ice" *Journeys 2* (1979), 14-24.

"One Mile of Ice" *Inquiry into Literature 1* (1980), 81-93.

"One Mile of Ice" *Die Kinder-Kultuuru* [date unknown] [Afrikaans translation; based on *Omnibus*].

"Our Neighbours the Nuns" *NR* 4:6 (Aug-Sept 1951), 27-33.

"Our Neighbors the Nuns" *Yellow Sweater* (1952), 24-33.

"Our Neighbours the Nuns" *Best Stories* (1963), 62-9.

"A Pair of Deuces" CBC "*Anthology*" 15 Apr 1978.

"The Premeditated Death of Samuel Glover" *Yellow Sweater* (1952), 221-4.

"The Premeditated Death of Samuel Glover" *Legs of the Lame* (1976), 79-81.

"The Premeditated Death of Samuel Glover" *Toronto Short Stories* (1977), 12-5.

"The Premeditated Death of Samuel Glover" *Not to Be Taken at Night* (1981), 44-8.

"Red Racer" *NHM* 51 (Sept 1950), 85-9.

"Red Racer" *Yellow Sweater* (1952), 108-22.

"Red Racer" *Best Stories* (1963), 75-87.

"Red Racer" CBC "*Anthology*" 6 May 1972.

"Red Racer" *Contemporary Voices* (1972), 14-22.

"Red Racer" *Canadian Stories of Action and Adventure* (1978), 124-52.

"Saskatchewan Hero" *Lib* 32 (Oct 1955), 20-1.

"See You in September" CBC "*Anthology*" 14 Sept 1974.

"See You in September" *CFM* No. 18 (Sum 1975), 73-86.

"See You in September" *Legs of the Lame* (1976), 39-53.

"A Shelter from the Rain" CBC "Anthology" 23 Jan 1968.

"A Shelter from the Rain" *QQ* 78 (1971), 227-39.

"A Shelter from the Rain" *Violation of the Virgins* (1971), 73-91.

"A Short Walk Home" *JCF* 3:1 (Win 1974), 44-9.

"A Short Walk Home" CBC "*Anthology*" 16 Feb 1974.

"A Short Walk Home" *Miss Chat* 12 (8 May 1975), 40-1, 89-90, 94-6.

"A Short Walk Home" *Legs of the Lame* (1976), 153-67.

"A Short Walk Home" *Omnibus* (1978), 468-83.

"Some Are So Lucky" *Yellow Sweater* (1952), 78-98.

"Some Are So Lucky" *Cavalcade of the North* (1958), 595-607.

"Some Are So Lucky" *Best Stories* (1963), 148-65.

"Some Are So Lucky" CBC "*Anthology*" 12 July 1969.

"The Sound of Hollyhocks" CBC "*Anthology*" 12 Dec 1967.

"The Sound of Hollyhocks" *Liberté* 11 (mars-avril 1969), 107-25 [As "Les secrets des roses trémières"; trans. Hubert Aquin].

"The Sound of Hollyhocks" *Tam R* No. 52 (1969), 5-18.

"The Sound of Hollyhocks" *Violation of the Virgins* (1971), 20-34.

"The Sound of Hollyhocks" *Tigers of the Snow* (1973), 7-19.

"Spill of Guilt" CBC "*Anthology*" 21 July 1979.

"The Spinster" *CHJ* Apr 1958, 21, 60-1, 64-5.

"The Spinster" *Men and Women* (1973), 115-28.

"Station Break" *JCF* No. 13 (Spr 1974), 45-59.

"Station Break" *Legs of the Lame* (1976), 101-19.

"Station Break" CBC "*Anthology*" 26 Mar 1977.

"Step-'n-a-half" CBC "*Anthology*" 10 Oct 1970.

"Step-'n-a-half" CBC "*Anthology*" 12 Dec 1970.

"Step-'n-a-half" *Tam R* No. 59 (1971), 32-48.

"Step-'n-a-half" *Violation of the Virgins* (1971), 40-59.

"Step-'n-a-half" *Omnibus* (1978), 484-502.

"Stood-Up Date" *Lib* 37 (July 1960), 49, 60, 62, 65.

"The Stretcher Bearers" *Yellow Sweater* (1952), 99-107.

"The Stretcher Bearers" *Best Stories* (1963), 206-12.

"Stumblebum" *Men and Women* (1973), 59-64.

"Stumblebum" *Great Canadian Sports Stories* (1979), 34-40.

"Tea with Miss Mayberry" *Chat* 28 (June 1956), 14, 50-9.

"Tea with Miss Mayberry" *Best Stories* (1963), 88-101.

"Tea with Miss Mayberry" CBC "*Anthology*" 30 Aug 1969.

"Tea with Miss Mayberry" CBC "*Anthology*" 17 June 1972.

"A Trip for Mrs. Taylor" *Chat* 24 (Oct 1951), 21, 36, 38, 40-1.

"A Trip for Mrs. Taylor" *Women's World* (U.K.) 1952 [Based on *Omnibus*].

"A Trip for Mrs. Taylor" *Yellow Sweater* (1952), 58-70.

"A Trip for Mrs. Taylor" *Invitation to Short Stories* (1958), 86-100.

"A Trip for Mrs. Taylor" *Chat* 31 (July 1958), 56-7.

"A Trip for Mrs. Taylor" *Northern Lights* (1960), 251-8.

"A Trip for Mrs. Taylor" *Best Stories* (1963), 213-23.

"A Trip for Mrs. Taylor" CBC "Anthology" 6 Aug 1969.
"A Trip for Mrs. Taylor" *Compass* (1971) [Based on *Omnibus*].
"A Trip for Mrs. Taylor" *Great Canadian Short Stories* (1971), 149-59.
"A Trip for Mrs. Taylor" CBC "Anthology" 29 Apr 1972.
"A Trip for Mrs. Taylor" *Latitude* (1974) [Based on *Omnibus*].
"A Trip for Mrs. Taylor" *Women in Canadian Literature* (1976), 263-70.
"A Trip for Mrs. Taylor" *World Stories* (1977) [Based on Omnibus].
"A Trip for Mrs. Taylor" *Omnibus* (1978), 441-52.
"A Trip for Mrs. Taylor" *New Worlds* (1980), 23-31.
"A Trip for Mrs. Taylor" CBC "Schools and Youth" [date unknown] [Based on *Omnibus*].
"Twelve Miles of Asphalt" *Violation of the Virgins* (1971), 109-27.
"Twelve Miles of Asphalt" CBC "Anthology" 24 July 1971.
"Twelve Miles of Asphalt" *Omnibus* (1978), 566-83.
"A Visit with Robert" *Yellow Sweater* (1952), 123-40.
"A Visit with Robert" *Best Stories* (1963), 102-16.
"A Visit with Robert" CBC "Anthology" 16 Aug 1969.
"Wait Until You're Asked" *Catalyst* (Brantford) 1:4 (1975), 57.
"Wait Until You're Asked" *Legs of the Lame* (1976), 17-22.
"Wait Until You're Asked" CBC "Anthology" 27 Oct 1979.
"Waiting for Charley" *Imp Oil R* 49 (Dec 1965), 15-8.
"Waiting for Charley" *Men and Women* (1973), 163-71.
"A Walk on Y Street" *Men and Women* (1973), 198-212.
"A Walk on Y Street" CBC "Anthology" 20 Oct 1973.
"A Walk on Y Street" *Legs of the Lame* (1976), 127-40.
"The Wasted Years" *Chat* 32 (Sept 1959), 33, 118, 120-5, 127.
"What a Way to Make a Living" *Violation of the Virgins* (1971), 8-19.
"What a Way to Make a Living" *Quarry* 20:3 (Aut 1971), 3-15.
"The Yellow Sweater" *Chat* 24 (Mar 1951), 16, 41, 46, 48, 50.
"The Yellow Sweater" *Yellow Sweater* (1952), 11-23.
"The Yellow Sweater" *Best Stories* (1963), 44-54.
"The Yellow Sweater" *Modern Canadian Stories* (1966), 217-27.
"The Yellow Sweater" CBC "Anthology" 20 Sept 1969.
"The Yellow Sweater" *Sixteen by Twelve* (1970), 24-32.
"The Yellow Sweater" CBC "Anthology" 13 May 1972.
"The Yellow Sweater" *Modern Canadian Stories* (1975), 147-58.
"The Yellow Sweater" *Moderne Erzühler der Walt: Kanada* (1976), 190-201 [As "Der gelbe Pullover"; trans. Walter Riedel].
"You Never Ast Me Before" *Tam R* No. 35 (Spr 1965), 3-12.
"You Never Ast Me Before" *Men and Women* (1973), 65-75.

Garner, Kay – *See* Green, H. Gordon.

Garnet, Eldon (1946-)
"Bones Blues" *Story So Four* (1976), 109-34.
"Escapism" *Imp* 8:4 (Fall-Win 1980), 18-9.
"The First of Further Adventures of John J. McCary" *Acta Vic* 92:2 (Dec 1967), 18.
[Untitled] *OPT* 2:5 (Feb 1975), [1].

Garratt, James (1954-)

"The Millyard" *Squatch J* No. 13 (June 1982), 22-3.

"Miskwabia Lake" *Squatch J* Nos. 14/15 (June 1983), 63-4.

"Northern Chimera" *Nw J* No. 24 (1981), 65-7.

Garrow, Barb‡

"Through a Dark Wood" *Folio* 17:2 (Spr 1965), 5-10.

Garside, Allan E.‡

"Heritage" *AA* 69 (May 1979), 61-3.

Garth, Richard‡

"The Killers" *Forge* Mar 1959, 34-6.

Garvie, Peter‡

"The Rocks" *CBC "Anthology"* 28 Jan 1958.

"Tea with Relations" *CBC "Anthology"* 29 Apr 1960.

Garvin, Guy C.‡

"The Rainstorm" *AA* 54 (May 1964), 37-9.

"The Whistle Blows at Five" *Trial* 1966, [4 pp].

Garwood, Lana

"The Strap" *CSSM* 3:1 (Win 1977), 28-30.

Gasgoyne, R.†

"The Robbery" *CSSM* 2:3 (Sum 1976), 60-3.

Gasparini, Len (1941-)

"Nightfall" *event* 5:2 [1975], 22-37.

"Nightfall" *CBC "Anthology"* 15 May 1976.

"See the Dark" *Matrix* 1:2 (Fall 1975), 25-32.

"See the Dark" *Nebula* No. 3 (1976), 75-84.

"Tilt" *CBC "Anthology"* 13 Nov 1976.

"Trucks: The Fifth Wheel" *CBC "Anthology"* 26 Nov 1977.

Gaston, Bill†

"Angel" *Prism* 17:1 (Sum 1978), 92-102.

"Maria's Older Brother" *Fid* No. 123 (Fall 1979), 7-14.

Gaston, Clifford†

"The Nigger-Jack Tree" *Outset* 1973, 30-41.

Gatchell, Constance‡

"The Power" *Dreamweaver* 2:2 [n.d.], 16-7.

Gaul, Avery‡

"The Chinese Madonna" *AA* 51 (Dec 1960), 67, 69-71.

"The Fire-Proof Doors" *AA* 51 (Aug 1961), 41, 43, 45-51.

"The Woman at Bore Light" *AA* 50 (June 1960), 99-102.

Gault, Connie†

"at dusk / just when / the Light is filled with birds" Grain 9:4 (Nov 1981), 19-24.

"at dusk / just when / the Light is filled with birds" *Saskatchewan Gold* (1982), 226-34.

"Why Fade These Children of the Spring" *Grain* 11:1 (Feb 1983), 4-6.

Gaunt, Laura‡

"Blackie" *Undergrad* Spr 1956, 38-40.

"Metamorphosis" *Writing Group Pub* 1970-71, 16-20.

Gauthier, Guy‡

"Dreams for Doctor Freud" *Creative Campus* 1965, 65-8.

Gauvreau, Gil‡

"Lemmy and Guido in Wonderlands" *Generation* Spr 1968, 42-3.

Gaysek, Fred

THE YOUNG MAN AND THE DOG Toronto: Prototype, 1981 [*viz., Identity 1*].

Gazey, Marilyn‡

"Another Drunken Indian" *WWR* 1:1 (Spr 1976), 55-9.

Geauch, Agnes‡

"Tea-Time" *Edmonton Culture Vulture* 1:2 (Fri, 24 Oct 1975), 9-10.

Geddes, Gary

"The Pickling of Guingin" *Aurora* 1979 217-28.

"The Unsettling of the West" *Moose R* 1:2 (1978), 24-40.

"The White Flag" *Gas Rain* 1 (Mar 1977), 9-11.

Gehl, John‡ (1937-)

"Mr. Dimmler" *Jargon* 1958-59, 11-6.

Geitzler, Fran†

"Beginner's Luck" *Amethyst* 1:1 (Spr 1962), 3-5.

"Men and the Moon" *Amethyst* 2:3 (Spr 1963), 21-4.

"Old Man" *Amethyst* 3:2 (Win 1964), 38-46.

"The Printed Word" *Amethyst* 3:1 (Fall 1963), [3 pp].

"The Rock" *Amethyst* 2:1 (Aut 1962), 3-4.

General Idea [pseudonym].

See also Bronson, A.A.

"Vis à Vis" *File* 3:1 (Fall 1975), 54-9 [Excerpt?].

Gentleman, Dorothy Corbett†

"Gene and the Horses" *Pier Spr* 5:2 (Spr 1980), 43-6.

Gentleman, Kirstie‡

"Holydays" *Halcyon* 10:1 (1964), 19-22.

"Wedding Review" *Halcyon* 10:1 (1964), 12-3 [Attribution unclear].

George, Thomas‡
"The Braggart" *Atl Guardian* 7 (Apr 1950), 55-8.

Gerard, Lance (1948-)
"Annie d'Entremont's Dream" *Was R* 8:1 (Spr 1973), 35-8.

Gerrond, Mike†
"The Squirrel Tale" *WWR* 1:3 (Spr 1978), 5-6.

Gershenovitz, N. David‡
"About Norad and Santa" *Varsity* Fri, 14 Dec 1962, 2.

Gerstenberger, Donna‡
"A Matter of Survival" *QQ* 68 (1961), 273-9.

Gesner, Claribel
"The Innkeeper's Wife" *AA* 55 (Dec 1964), 45, 47, 49.
"Which Christmas Was He Most Dear?" *AA* 62 (Dec 1971), 21.

Ghan, Linda
"The Conversion" *Chat* 52 (Oct 1979), 52, 164, 166, 172.

Giambagno, Domenica†
RISVEGLIOE TRIONFO/WAKING UP AND TRIUMPH Weston: privately printed, 1976 [Based on CBIP].

Gibb, Alice M.
"The Settlement" *Polished Pebbles* (1974), 73-7.

Gibb, Jardine† (1948-)
"In Case of Accident" *Room* 3:1 (1977), 64-9.
"Portrait" *event* 4:3 [1974?], 79-88.
"We Have Gone to Find a Merry-Go-Round" *Mam* 1:2 [n.d.], [5 pp].

Gibbons, Maurice
"Amid the Alien Corn" *New Voices* (1956), 157-63.

Gibbs, Betty‡
"Hallowe'en" *Edmonton Journal* Thu, 29 Oct 1964, 4.

Gibbs, Robert (1930-)
I'VE ALWAYS FELT SORRY FOR DECIMALS Ottawa: Oberon Press, 1978.
"Across the Threshold of the Dark Night" *ArtsAtlantic* 2:4 (Sum 1980), 39.
"Catholics, Catholics, Ring the Bell" *Fid* No. 115 (Fall 1977), 92-105.
"Catholics, Catholics, Ring the Bell" *I've Always Felt Sorry for Decimals* (1978), 87-109.
"Come On and Play War" *I've Always Felt Sorry for Decimals* (1978), 128-47.
"Get on Board, Sinners" *JCF* No. 21 (1977-78), 15-29.
"Get on Board, Sinners" *I've Always Felt Sorry for Decimals* (1978), 62-86.
"I Always Knew There Was a Lord" *JCF* 1:3 (Sum 1972), 16-8.
"I Always Knew There Was a Lord" *Stories from Atlantic Canada* (1973), 104-12.
"I've Always Felt Sorry for Decimals" *I've Always Felt Sorry for Decimals* (1978), 110-27.

"I've Always Felt Sorry for Decimals" *Stories Plus* (1979), 73-84.

"Oh, Think of the Home Over There" *JCF* 4:1 No. 13 (1975), 6-21.

"A Villain Rare" *Pot Port* 3 (1981-82), 22-5.

"Way Out on Life's Stormy Raging Sea" *JCF* 2:1 (Win 1973), 33-42.

"Way Out on Life's Stormy Raging Sea" *I've Always Felt Sorry for Decimals* (1978), 5-42.

"You Know What Thought Did" *75: New Canadian Stories* 76-93.

"You Know What Thought Did" *I've Always Felt Sorry for Decimals* (1978), 43-61.

Gibson, Margaret (1948-)

THE BUTTERFLY WARD Ottawa: Oberon Press, 1976.

CONSIDERING HER CONDITION Toronto: Gage, 1978.

"Ada" by Margaret Gibson Gilboord *74: New Canadian Stories* 16-35.

"Ada" *Butterfly Ward* (1976), 5-27.

"Ada" *Best Modern Canadian Short Stories* (1978), 180-94.

"All Over Now" *Considering Her Condition* (1978), 53-67.

"All Over Now" *Writers and Writing* (1981), 92-103.

"Brian Tattoo: His Life and Times" *Considering Her Condition* (1978), 29-51.

"Brian Tattoo: His Life and Times" *Miss Chat* 15 (Apr 1978), 80-1, 84, 91-3, 96.

"The Butterfly Ward" *Butterfly Ward* (1976), 119-33.

"The Butterfly Ward" *Toronto Short Stories* (1977), 121-33.

"The Butterfly Ward" *Heartland* (1983), 94-105.

"Considering Her Condition" *Butterfly Ward* (1976), 51-78.

"Dark Angel, Pale Fire" *Considering Her Condition* (1978), 1-28.

"Goldfish and Other Summer Days" *Considering Her Condition* (1978), 101-7.

"Making It" by Margaret Gibson Gilboord *75: New Canadian Stories* 170-92.

"Making It" *Butterfly Ward* (1976), 96-118.

"Making It" *Canadian Literature in the 70's* (1980), 181-97.

"Mother's Milk" *Considering Her Condition* (1978), 69-82.

"The Phase" *Butterfly Ward* (1976), 28-50.

"Still Life" *Considering Her Condition* (1978), 83-100.

"A Trip to the Casbah" *Butterfly Ward* (1976), 79-95.

"The Water Fairy" *Considering Her Condition* (1978), 109-20.

Gibson, Shirley Mann

"Stone-Cutter" *SN* 93 (June 1978), 40-3.

"Stone-Cutter" *79: Best Canadian Stories* 52-8.

Gibson, William‡

"Burning Chrome" *Omni* 4 (July 1982), 72-7, 102, 104, 106-7.

"Burning Chrome" *Nebula Awards* 18 (1983), 106-30.

"Fragments of a Hologram Rose" *Unearth Mag* (U.S.) 1:3 (Sum 1977), 72-7.

"The Gernsback Continuum" *Universe* 11 (1981), 81-90.

"Johnny Mnemonic" *Nebula Award Stories* 17 (1983), 88-108.

"Margaret" *Gram* 3:1 (Nov 1977), 24.

Giddings, Alice‡

"The Skylark and the Nightengale" *Emeritus* 2 (Spr 1966), 4-5.

Giesbrecht, Vern
"Double Fault" *CSSM* 2:4 (Fall 1976), 9-12.
"The Suitcase" *Diversions* 5:1 (1975), 24-8.

Giffin, David A.‡
"Death" *Amethyst* 3:1 (Fall 1963), [6 pp].

Gifford [pseudonym]
"Journey ... " *Alpha* 3:1 (Fall 1978), 26-8.

Gilbert, Anne‡
"The Ladadantée" *Eclipse* No. 4 (1977), 8-11.

Gilbert, Gerry.
See also Itter, Carole and Gilbert, Gerry.
"Canada's National Magazine" *OPT* 6:4/5 (May-June 1979), 1.
"The (C)old Grey Blue" *BC Monthly* 5:2 (Apr 1980), [2 pp].
"Daddy's Gone a-Hunting" *Per* No. 2 (Fall 1977), 20-1.
"Fourteen Stories" *Story So Far* 3 (1974), 9-17.
"The Old Grey Blues" *BC Monthly* 5:2 (Apr 1980), [2 pp].
"Writing Time" *OPT* 6:8 (Oct 1979), 1.

Gilbert, Lara
"The Ant's Dream" *BC Monthly* No. 29 (Apr 1982), 24.

Gilbert, Michael A.†
"Heaven-57" *Nebula* Nos. 21/22 (1982), 53-62.
"Interview on an April Afternoon" *Matrix* No. 16 (Spr 1983), 12-7.

Gill, Stephen (1932-)
LIFE'S VAGARIES (FOURTEEN SHORT STORIES) Cornwall: Vesta, 1974.
"Another Trap" *Life's Vagaries* (1974), 76-81.
"Aunt Disappears" *Life's Vagaries* (1974), 18-21.
"A Contemporary Poet" *Life's Vagaries* (1974), 95-9.
"Death of a Dream" *Life's Vagaries* (1974), 82-7.
"Determination" *Life's Vagaries* (1974), 56-60.
"Enigma" *Life's Vagaries* (1974), 66-70.
"The Eternal Mystery" *Life's Vagaries* (1974), 88-94.
"Fate or Coincidence" *Life's Vagaries* (1974), 61-5.
"London to Ottawa" *Life's Vagaries* (1974), 13-7.
"A Pathan Soldier" *Life's Vagaries* (1974), 22-6.
"Toys" *Life's Vagaries* (1974), 71-5.
"Two Votaries" *Life's Vagaries* (1974), 27-32.
"What a Mistake!" *Life's Vagaries* (1974), 33-48.
"The Younger Brother" *Life's Vagaries* (1974), 49-55.

Gillatt, Susan†
"Exits" *Writing* No. 3 (Sum 1981), 42-4.

Gillen, Beth
"Tammie's Shoe Box" *FH* 6 Nov 1952, 24-5, 33.

Gillen, Kathleen Mollie

"The Forty Dollar Plan" *FH* 21 Aug 1952, 20-1, 26.

Gillese, John Patrick (1920-)

See also Wilson, Betty and Gillese, John Patrick.

KIRBY'S GANDER Toronto: Ryerson Press, 1957.

"The $100 Bill" *Our Family* 16 (Apr 1964), 22-5.

"Altar of Faith" *Our Family* 18 (Sept 1966), 22-4.

"Bandit of the Marsh" *CG* Apr 1955, 11, 67-70.

"Bandit of the Marsh" *Kirby's Gander* (1957), 70-89.

"The Bargain Ox" *Collier's* 129 (12 Apr 1952), 26[+?] [Based on RGPL].

"The Bargain Ox" *CG* May 1958, 17, 60-4.

"The Bargain Ox" *Singing Under Ice* (1974), 188-203.

"The Bargain Ox" *Our Family* 34 (Oct 1983), 22-7.

"Because of a Dream" *Ave Maria* 83 (12 May 1956), 14-7 [Based on CPLI].

"Big Mike" *FH* 4 Feb 1954, 24-5.

"[The?] Big Orphan Boy" *Catholic Home J* 52 (Dec 1952), 14-5[+?] [Based on CPLI].

"Broken Horn" *FH* 7 Feb 1952, 28-9, 35.

"Broken Horn" *Kirby's Gander* (1957), 90-108.

"Bushwhacker's Christmas" *FH* 24 Dec 1953, 14-5.

"Coldpaw's Country" *CG* Nov 1953, 8, 47-55.

"Coldpaw's Country" *Kirby's Gander* (1957), 170-200.

"[The?] Crossroads" *Extension* 45 (Nov 1950), 18-9[+?] [Based on CPLI].

"Cupid and the Carefree Lady" *CG* June 1954, 9, 51-3.

"Destiny's Child" *Weekend* 2 (6 Sept 1952), 20-1.

"Destiny's Child" *Kirby's Gander* (1957), 22-33.

"Devil Dog!" *FH* 17 May 1956, 30-1, 47.

"Dynamite Duggan's Courtship" *Our Family* 16 (Jan 1964), 22-5.

"Escape Money" *Catholic Home J* 54 (Apr 1954), 17[+?] [Based on CPLI].

"Especially Worthy" *FH* 19 May 1955, 28-9, 44.

"Especially Worthy" *Alberta Diamond Jubilee Anthology* (1979), 43-52.

"Farewell, Little Flying Squirrel" *Our Family* 34 (July-Aug 1983), 34-6.

"A Farewell for Mr. Moran" *CG* 84 (Oct 1965), 43-4, 47-8.

"A Farewell for Mr. Moran" *Our Family* 18 (Oct 1966), 21-4 [As "Farewell to Mr. Moran"].

"Father Came from Boston" *FH* 3 May 1962, 24-5.

"[The?] First Garden" *Ave Maria* 71 (18 Feb 1950), 213-6 [Based on CPLI].

"Flame's Family" *CG* Mar 1952, 83-8.

"Forever Too Late" *CG* 84 (Mar 1965), 75-7.

"A Fox Is Where You Find Him" *Kirby's Gander* (1957), 161-9.

"The Friendly Ones" *Kirby's Gander* (1957), 201-12.

"[The?] Front Page Story" *Ave Maria* 76 (16 Aug 1952), 203-7 [Based on CPLI].

"[A?] Girl in Lilac Time" *Catholic Home J* 52 (Apr 1952), 16-9[+?] [Based on CPLI].

"[The?] Good-bye Gift" *Ave Maria* 76 (22 Nov 1952), 655-60 [Based on CPLI].

"The Great Man" *FH* 12 Jan 1961, 16-7.

"Her Last Visit Home" *FH* 23 Aug 1956, 18-9, 27.

"Homestead" *FH* 4 June 1953, 20-1.

"Jack High" by Jeff Challers *Our Family* 18 (Feb 1966), 22-4.

"Kirby's Gander" *Alberta Golden Jubilee Anthology* (1955), 376-88.

"Kirby's Gander" *FH* 15 Nov 1956, 14-5, 30-1.
"Kirby's Gander" *Kirby's Gander* (1957), 1-21.
"The Kittlings" *CG* 85 (Feb 1966), 59-60.
"Lady of Windigo Hills" *Kirby's Gander* (1957), 53-69.
"The Last Gamble" *SW* 9 Aug 1958, 20, 38.
"The Last Hunt" *SW* 16 July 1955, I:5.
"The Last Hunt" *Kirby's Gander* (1957), 122-32.
"The Letter" *Catholic Home J* 53 (Oct 1953), 14-5[+?] [Based on CPLI].
"Lonely Monarch" *FH* 1 Nov 1951, 24-5, 49.
"Lonely Monarch" *Kirby's Gander* (1957), 34-52.
"The Love Gods" *CG* July 1958, 15, 39-42.
"The Love Letter" *Apostle* 42 (July 1964), 18-20[+?] [Based on CPLI].
"A Man Is Born" *CG* 71 (Jan 1960), 35-8.
"A Memory of Gideon" *Our Family* 19 (July-Aug 1967), 20-4.
"A Memory of Judith Waring" *FH* 15 Jan 1959, 24-6, 30.
"Night with No Moon" *CG* Jan 1956, 12, 47-50.
"Nothing New Under the Sun" *Ave Maria* 76 (27 Dec 1952), 820-2 [Non-fiction? Based on CPLI].
"Old Johnstone's Exit" *Ave Maria* 73 (31 Mar 1951), 399-400 [Based on CPLI].
"Only the Dead Are Neutral" *Extension* 55 (Nov 1960), 24-5[+?] [Based on CPLI].
"Only the Dead Are Neutral" *Apostle* 42 (Oct 1964), 20-3[+?] [Based on CPLI].
"Our Home Was a Haven" *Ave Maria* 72 (26 Aug 1950), 270-4 [Based on CPLI].
"Pain Killer" *CG* Nov 1955, 10, 44-8.
"Perspective" *Ave Maria* 78 (26 Sept 1953), 12-5 [Based on CPLI].
"Portrait of a Father" *FH* 27 Oct 1955, 28-9.
"[The?] Price of a Hat" *Ave Maria* 77 (17 Jan 1953), 83-8 [Based on CPLI].
"The Price of a Piano" *FH* 23 Dec 1954, 22-3, 26.
"Refugee on the River" *SW* 31 Mar 1956, II:5.
"Return to Redvale" *SW* 27 Aug 1955, I:9.
"[The?] Riches of Charity" *Ave Maria* 78 (12 Dec 1953), 19-22. [Non-fiction? Based on CPLI].
"The Right Wife for George" *CHJ* July 1957, 21, 41-3.
"[A?] Riverful of Stars" *Ave Maria* 76 (2 Aug 1952), 139-44 [Based on CPLI].
"Saga of a Strange Valley" *CG* Sept 1954, 12, 43-5.
"The Saga of Susie" *CG* May 1953, 12, 80.
"The Saga of Susie" *Kirby's Gander* (1957), 151-60.
"The Saplings" *FH* 26 Nov 1953, 28-9, 36.
"Self Made Man" *FH* 29 Sept 1950, 20-1.
"[The?] Sign of the Swami" *Catholic Home J* 51 (Sept 1951), 16-8[+?] [Based on CPLI].
"That Day in Spring" *Ave Maria* 75 (14 June 1952), 749-52 [Based on CPLI].
"This Man Called Joe" *Can Messenger* 75 (Nov 1965), 8-10 [Reminiscence?].
"Tho' Me and My True Love" *Our Family* 19 (May 1967), 21-4.
"The Typewriter" *CG* June 1955, 12, 50-3.
"The Typewriter" *All Manner of Men* (1956).
"The Typewriter" *Our Family* 34 (Sept 1983), 40-4.
"A Walk in the Park" *Our Family* 20 (Sept 1968), 22-4.
"Wanderer of the Waters" *FH* 9 Dec 1954, 20-1.
"Wanderer of the Waters" *Kirby's Gander* (1957), 109-21.

"Wanderer of the Waters" *Our Family* 18 (May 1966), 20-3.
"A Way with Women" *Our Family* 16 (May 1964), 23-4.
"Wheat Over the Hill" *CG* Sept 1958, 16, 44, 46-50.
"When a Man Follows a Dream" *Ave Maria* 71 (11 Feb 1950), 175-80 [Based on CPLI].
"Where the Irish Are" *Ave Maria* 72 (21 Oct 1950), 531-5 [Based on CPLI].
"Where the Irish Are" *FH* 15 Mar 1951, 26-7.
"Wildcat 13" *CG* Aug 1953, 8, 39-43.
"Wildcat 13" *Apostle* 42 (Sept 1964), 22-6[+?] [Based on CPLI].
"Wise One of Windigo Hills" *CG* Sept 1951, 8-9, 41.
"Wolf King's Mate" *Kirby's Gander* (1957), 133-50.
"Woman Alone" *CG* 81 (Feb 1962), 50-2.
"Woman Alone" *Our Family* 18 (Apr 1966), 21-4.
"[A?] Writer Remembers" *Ave Maria* 77 (20 June 1953), 19-22 [Non-fiction? Based on CPLI].
"You Never Walk Alone" *CG* 82 (Feb 1963), 39-40, 42-3.

Gillespie, G.J.‡
"Jerome" *AA* 48 (June 1958), 69, 71-2.

Gillespie, Joan†
"The Christmas-Cake Doll" *Campus Canada* 1:1 (Feb 1963), 56-8.

Gillespie, William D. (1958-)
"Wooden Ships" *event* 9:2 (1980), 148-53.

Gillette, Agnes
KALADAR AND OTHER STORIES Deseronto: privately printed, 1977.
"Battle in the Swamp" *Kaladar* (1977), 18-25.
"Kaladar" *Kaladar* (1977), 1-17.
"Mui" *Kaladar* (1977), 25-35.
"Trapped" *Kaladar* (1977), 35-8.

Gilliam, John‡
"Bee Cause" *Alive* No. 157 (20 Oct 1979), 17.
"Changes" *Alive* No. 172 (3 Oct 1981), 9-10.
"Hand to Hand" *Alive* No. 152 (15 Sept 1979), 13-5.
"Preparing the Foundations" *Alive* No. 139 (16 June 1979), 8-12.
"Team Play" *Alive* No. 138 (9 June 1979), 16.

Gillies, Glory‡
"Mr. Tilton Comes Through" *Acta Vic* 78:4 (Mar 1954), 24-6.
"The Old House" *Acta Vic* 79:3 (Feb 1955), 25-6.
"Terror" *Acta Vic* 78:3 (Feb 1954), 23-4.

Gillis, Susan†
"Fragments" *Antig R* No. 31 (Aut 1977), 11-4.

Gilmore, R.V.‡
"The Nun" *Creative Campus* 1965, 59-62.

Gilson, Michael†
"The Wager" *Orion* No. 1 (Sum 1981), 14-5.

Giovinazzo, William A., Jr.‡
"The Way 'tings' Go" *Nightwinds* 2:1 (Spr 1980), 44.

Givner, Joan†
"The Lost Sheep" *Was R* 18:2 (Fall 1983), 21-9.

G[ladstone], J[ames]‡
"Bedtime Story" *Pinch* Nov 1965, 22.

Glassco, Hugh†
"Lost" *Nw J* No. 23 (1981), 79-81.

Glassco, John (1909-1981)
"Countess Isobel and the Torturer" *JD* Sum 1972, 32-41.
"Mr. Noad" *CF* 32 (Mar 1953), 277-80.
"The Pigtail Man" *JD* Hanukah 1973, 47-57.
"A Season in Limbo" by Silas N. Gooch *Tam R* No. 23 (Spr 1972), 55-84.
"A Season in Limbo" *Canadian Century* (1973), 413-40.

Glay, George Albert.
See also Murray, Rona and Glay, George Albert.
"The Window" *CHJ* Dec 1953, 22, 55-9.

Gledhill, Robert†
"Gone Home" *From 231* 2:1 (Sept 1973), 6-11.

Gleeson, Sean†
"Solipsist" *Words from Inside* 1971, [2 pp].

Glen, John‡
"Cooling" *Forge* 1950, 32-6.
"The Victim" *Forge* 1950, 9-13.

Glendenning, Donald‡
"The Dumb Writer" *Acta Vic* [95:3] (Spr 1971), 24-9.
"A Polished Boo-or-Two" *Acta Vic* 96:2 [n.d.], 48-52 [Untitled] *Acta Vic* 96:1 [n.d.], 16-22.

Glennon, Lorraine
"Borges and I" *Cap R* No. 14 (1978), 39-48.

Glover, Douglas H. (1948-)
THE MAD RIVER AND OTHER STORIES Windsor: Black Moss Press, 1981.
"Between the Kisses and the Wine" *Mad River* (1981), 83-99.
"Cats Have Kittens" *Pier Spr* 4:4 (Aut 1979), 35-48.
"The Destiny of Man" *Pier Spr* [1:4] (Win 1978), 6-22.
"Floater" *NJ* No. 5 (May 1975), 55-9.
"Hail" *Tam R* No. 62 (1974), 49-55.
"Hail" *Mad River* (1981), 29-37.
"Horse" *Fid* No. 104 (Win 1975), 95-104.

"Horse" *Mad River* (1981), 38-49.

"The Mad River Blues Song" *JCF* No. 22 (1978), 44-57.

"The Mad River Blues Song" *Mad River* (1981), 9-28 [As "The Mad River"].

"Panther" *Mad River* (1981), 100-10.

"Pender's Visions" *NJ* Nos. 7/8 (1976), 9-19.

"Pender's Visions" *Mad River* (1981), 50-63.

"There Might Be Angels" *Mal R* No. 59 (July 1981), 48-59.

"Ursula" *Fid* No. 136 (June 1983), 29-37.

"Wild Horses" *Fid* No. 117 (Spr 1978), 33-44.

"Wild Horses" *Mad River* (1981), 64-82.

Glucksman, Trevor‡

"The Master Approach" *pm* 1:3 (Feb [1952]), 21-5 [Non-fiction?].

Glunna, J.C.‡

"Santa Snatched" *Varsity* Thu, 13 Dec 1956, 10.

Gnarowski, Michael (1934-)

"the old priest hailed me stay" *Yes* 1:2 (Aug 1956), [4 pp].

Gnonscentz, Phulloph [pseudonym]

"Little Orville Andy" *Liontayles* Win 1967, 4.

Godfrey, Dave (1938-)

DARK MUST YIELD Toronto: Press Porcepic, 1978.

DEATH GOES BETTER WITH COCA-COLA Toronto: House of Anansi Press, 1967.

"The Big Game Fisherman in Florida" *SN* 82 (May 1967), 49-50 [Also entitled "Flying Fish"].

"Binary Dysfunction" *Dark Must Yield* (1978), 151-8.

"CP 59" *Dark Must Yield* (1978), 159-66.

"Elephant He Go Come Here Plenty" *SN* 82 (Feb 1967), 55, 57 [Also entitled "Fulfilling Our Foray"].

"Escape from My Winter Pent House" *SN* 82 (Apr 1967), 44, 47 [Non-fiction?].

"The First Encountering of Mr. Basa-Basa and His Excellency, Ling Huo" *Tam R* No. 41 (Aut 1966), 113-8.

"Flying Fish" *Death Goes Better* (1967), 59-61 [Also entitled "The Big Game Fisherman in Florida"].

"Flying Fish" *Great Canadian Sports Stories* (1979), 97-9.

"Fragment" *CF* 39 (Jan 1960), 228-30.

"Fulfilling Our Foray" *Death Goes Better* (1967), 63-7 [Also entitled "Elephant He Go Come Here Plenty"].

"The Generation of Hunters" *Death Goes Better* (1967), 11-4.

"The Generation of Hunters" *New Romans* (1968), 112-5.

"Gossip: The Birds That Flew, the Birds That Fell" *Tam R* No. 30 (Win 1964), 3-32.

"Gossip: The Birds That Flew, the Birds That Fell" *New Canadian Writing* 1968 141-63.

"Gossip: The Birds That Flew, the Birds That Fell" *Dark Must Yield* (1978), 49-67.

"Gossip: The Birds That Flew, the Birds That Fell" *Penguin Book of Canadian*

Short Stories (1980), 359-77.

"The Hard-Headed Collector" *Tam R* No. 40 (Sum 1966), 3-14.

"The Hard-Headed Collector" *Death Goes Better* (1967), 103-15.

"The Hard-Headed Collector" *Story-Makers* (1970), 293-304.

"The Hard-Headed Collector" *Four Hemispheres* (1971), 389-98.

"The Hard-Headed Collector" *Great Canadian Short Stories* (1971), 289-300.

"The Hard-Headed Collector" *Canadian Century* (1973), 617-26.

"The Hard-Headed Collector" *Dark Must Yield* (1978), 13-23.

"I'd Bale It" *Dark Must Yield* (1978), 44-8.

"Images. From a Moving Railway Car" *Genesis West* No. 7 (Win 1965), 51-66 [Based on ILM].

"In the Distant Singing Guts of the Moment" *Death Goes Better* (1967), 25-38.

"Kwame Bird Lady Day" *New Canadian Writing* 1968 175-200.

"Kwame Bird Lady Day" *Contemporary Voices* (1972), 23-39.

"Mud Lake: If Any" *Death Goes Better* (1967), 69-72 [Also entitled "Of Ducks and Death"].

"A New Year's Morning on Bloor Street" *CBC "Anthology"* 24 Mar 1973.

"A New Year's Morning on Bloor Street" *Imp* 2:3/4 (1973), 71-89.

"A New Year's Morning on Bloor Street" *Dark Must Yield* (1978), 131-42.

"A New Year's Morning on Bloor Street" *Fiction of Contemporary Canada* (1980), 107-17.

"Newfoundland Night" *Tam R* No. 23 (Spr 1962), 43-51.

"Newfoundland Night" *Best American Short Stories* 1963 166-74.

"Newfoundland Night" *Canadian Short Stories 2* (1968), 318-30.

"Newfoundland Night" *Dark Must Yield* (1978), 24-32.

"Night Tripper" *Death Goes Better* (1967), 39-44.

"Night Tripper" *Canadian Anthology* (1974), 552-5.

"Noise and No Victory" *TUR* 74:3 (Apr 1961), 4-13.

"Of Ducks and Death" *SN* 82 (Jan 1967), 42, 44 [Also entitled "Mud Lake, If Any"].

"On the River" *Death Goes Better* (1967), 81-92.

"On the River" *New Canadian Writing* 1968 164-74.

"On the River" *Literature in Canada* (1978), 596-604.

"On the River" *Best Modern Canadian Short Stories* (1978), 136-43.

"An Opening Day" *Death Goes Better* (1967), 15-9 [Also entitled "Pheasants in the Corn"].

"An Opening Day" *Here and Now* (1977), 147-50.

"Out in Chinguacousy" *Death Goes Better* (1967), 73-9.

"Out in Chinguacousy" *Stories from Ontario* (1974), 260-6.

"Pheasants in the Corn" *SN* 82 (Aug 1967), 33, 35 [Also entitled "An Opening Day"].

"A Pier for Danny" *TUR* 70:2 (Dec 1957), 23-7.

"A Python of the Gaspé" *SN* 81 (Nov 1966), 76.

"River Two Blind Jacks" *Tam R* No. 19 (Spr 1961), 3-14.

"River Two Blind Jacks" *Canadian Short Stories 2* (1968), 301-17.

"River Two Blind Jacks" *Frontier Experience* (1975), 56-69.

"River Two Blind Jacks" *Moderne Erzähler der Welt: Kanada* (1976), 331-45 [As "Flü der blinden Holzfüller"; trans. Manfred Kuxdorf].

"River Two Blind Jacks" *Dark Must Yield* (1978), 33-43.

"Side Effects" *Rampike* 3:2 [1983?], 18-21.

"This Bureaucrat Loves the Limbo" *Dark Must Yield* (1978), 143-50.
"Three Nights" *TUR* 70:3 (Feb 1958), 9-16.
"Two Smiths" *Death Goes Better* (1967), 45-52.
"Two Smiths" *Modern Stories in English* (1975), 93-9.
"Up in the Rainforest" *Death Goes Better* (1967), 53-8.
"Up in the Rainforest" *SN* 82 (Nov 1967), 81-2.
"The Way We Do It Here" *Death Goes Better* (1967), 93-102.
"The Way We Do It Here" *Ontario '67* [Based on *Death Goes Better with Coca-Cola*].
"The Winter Stiffs" *Death Goes Better* (1967), 21-4.
"The Woman Whose Child Fell from the Tower" *Dark Must Yield* (1978), 167-90.

Godsell, Philip H.†
"The Scarlet Trail" *Scarlet and Gold* No. 33 (1951), 13, 15-21.

Goebel, Ulf‡
"Uniformities" *Alch* 1:4 (1979), 27-37.

Goede, William†
"Five Fingers, No Thumb" *UWR* 7:2 (Spr 1972), 54-61.
"That's Entertainment!" *Grain* 10:4 (Nov 1982), 32-8.

Gold, Artie and Nations, Opal L.
See also Nations, Opal L.
"A Race for Freedom" *Da Vinci* No. 6 (Aut 1979), 44-61 [Second part was to have appeared in the next issue (never published?)].

Goldberg, Harvey (1949-)
"Settling a Score" *Outset* 1973, 42-4.

Goldie, Olive
"A Sense of Remembrance" *FH* 10 Mar 1960, 24-5.

Goldman, Alvin (1927-)
"Almost Like Dead" *Canadian Short Stories* (1952), 216-27.

Goldman, Hazel†
"Just One Room" *CF* 48 (Nov 1968), 190.

Goldman, Marlene‡
[Untitled] *Images* 4:2 (Nov 1982), 8.

Goldstein, Allan‡
"Diary of the Pilot" *New Bodies* (1981), 97-111.

Goldstein, Ethel‡
"Mercy Killing" *Forge* 1951, 12-3.

Gollan, Don†
"Out for Lunch" *Quarry* 4 (Spr 1955), 5-6.

Gomery, Percy
"The Ingenuity of Trapper Jim" *Can Banker* 68:1 (Spr 1961), 134-6 [Non-fiction?].
"Manoeuvre of Trapper Jim" *Can Banker* 67:3 (Win 1960), 119-21 [Non-fiction?].
"Trapper Jim" *Can Banker* 67:1 (Spr 1960), 139-41 [Non-fiction?].

Goodale, Don‡
"Lost and Found" *Muse* 60:4 (Apr 1951), 11.

Goodall, Ray‡
"The University That Never Was (A Modern Parable)" *Whetstone* Spr 1971, [3 pp].

Goodchild, Peter‡
"Spiritus Mundu" *CBC [Van] "Hornby Collection"* 20 Oct 1979.

Goodeve, Patrick R.‡
"Marsha" *Bakka* No. 5 (Spr-Sum 1977), 38-41.

Goodman, Arnold†
"Old Friends" *Writ* No. 15 (1983), 44-51.

Goodman, Lynn†
"A Journey of Love" *CSSM* 2:2 (Spr 1976), 15-8.

Goodwin, Debi Awde†
"The Bargain Boat" *WWR* 2:2 (1981), 18-22.

Goodwin, Irene Lloyd‡
"Wings Over Pigeboogwek" *Bluenose* 2:2 (Fall 1977), 8-12.

Goodwin, Mary (? -1983)
"Mrs. Martin's Day" *Pot Port* 4 (1982-83), 11-2.

Goodyear, Cyril‡
"Metik" *Atl Guardian* 7 (Mar 1950), 64-6.

Gool, Reshard‡
"The Child" *Voices Down East* [1973], 44-5.
"Operation Cordelia" *Tor S Asian R* 1:3 (Fall-Win 1982-83), 35-43.

Gordon, Betty (1921-)
"The Big-Time Spender" *Anthology of Best Short Stories* 7 (1959), 188-91 [Based on survey response].
"The Big-Time Spender" *Edmonton Journal* Fri, 17 Mar 1967, 58.
"Just a Whim" *Edmonton Journal* Fri, 11 Aug 1967, 30.

Gordon, George‡
"The Ceremony of Innocence" *Muse* 64:1 (1955), 22-6.

Gordon, Jaimy‡
"A Short Fair History of a Family" *Inscape* 7:2 (Sum 1969), 1-19.

Gordon, Janet
"The Soft Summer Air" *Atl Guardian* 10 (May 1953), 26-31.

Gordon, Joanna†
"Toro!" *New Voices* (1956), 55-61.
"Toro!" *Raven* 1:3 (Spr 1956), 16-20.

Gordon, John‡
"A Swallow Bellies Turn" *Talon* [2:3] (Spr 1965), 11 [Sketch?].

Gordon, Robert
MINES AND BLAZING PINES Cobalt: Highway Book Shop, 1979 [Based on CBIP].

Gore, Anita†
"A Short Story" *Fireweed* No. 16 (Spr 1983), 91-7.

Gormann, Adele M.‡
"Green Goddess" *Stardust* 1:1 (1975), 2-17.

Gormley, Nancy K.†
"Looking Up" *Face to Face* (1979), 59-64.
"Looking Up" *AA* 67 (Dec 1976), 16-7.

Gosselin, Madeleine‡
"Qu'Appelle Christmas 1885" *New Breed* Dec 1979, 27.

Gostlin, Kermit‡
"The End of It" *Fifth Page* 1967, 29-30.

Gotlieb, Phyllis (1926-)
SON OF THE MORNING AND OTHER STORIES New York: Ace Books, 1983.
"Blue Apes" *Berkley Showcase: New Writings in Science Fiction and Fantasy* 4 (1981), 147-81 [Novelette?].
"A Bone to Pick" *Fantastic Stories* 9 (Oct 1960), 48-71.
"Gingerbread Boy" *If/Worlds of If* 10 (Jan 1961), 90-103.
"Gingerbread Boy" *Space Suits and Gumshoes* (1972), 128-47.
"Gingerbread Boy" *Best Canadian Short Stories* (1981), 188-201.
"Gingerbread Boy" *Son of the Morning* (1983), 80-94.
"A Grain of Manhood" *Fantastic Stories* 8 (Sept 1959), 76-88.
"A Grain of Manhood" *Great Science Fiction Magazine* 2 Nov 1966, 85[+?] [Based on science fiction indexes].
"A Grain of Manhood" *Tigers of the Snow* (1973), 199-210.
"A Grain of Manhood" *Son of the Morning* (1983), 148-59.
"Item: One Bed, Two Cups Sack" *Can Life* 1:4 (Spr 1950), 24.
"The Military Hospital" *Fourteen Stories High* (1971), 84-99.
"The Military Hospital" CBC "Anthology" 2 Oct 1971.
"The Military Hospital" *SF: Inventing the Future* (1972), 160-74.
"The Military Hospital" *Fantasy and Science Fiction* 46 (May 1974), 44-57.
"The Military Hospital" *Modern Canadian Stories* (1975), 179-95.
"The Military Hospital" *Other Canadas* (1979), 185-97.
"The Military Hospital" *Son of the Morning* (1983), 65-79.

"The Newest Profession" *Speculations* (1982), 167-90.
"Phantom Foot" *Amazing Stories* 33 (Dec 1959), 7-20.
"Phantom Foot" *Most Thrilling Science Fiction Ever Told* No. 3 (1966), 45-58.
"Phantom Foot" *Stardust* 3:2 (Spr 1981), 3-16.
"Phantom Foot" *Son of the Morning* (1983), 131-47.
"Score/Score" *Visions 2020* (1970), 211-21.
"Score/Score" *Playback* (1978) [Based on Bell].
"Sunday's Child" *Cosmos* 1:3 (Sept 1977), 57-64, 66-71.
"Tauf Aleph" *More Wandering Stars* (1981), 1-18.
"Tauf Aleph" *Son of the Morning* (1983), 1-21.
"Valedictory" *Amazing Stories* 38 (Aug 1964), 46-52.
"Yeshua X" *JD* Hanukah 1972, 4-5.

Goto, Edy
"The Dream" *WCR* 16:1 (Sum 1981), 5-8.

Gottlieb, Paul‡
"Fatigue" *Prism* (Mont) 4 (1961), 6-11.

Goudie, Elizabeth†
"Aunt Annie and Uncle Bert" *East of Canada* (1976), 178-81.

Gough, Bruce‡
"A Chance Encounter" *Alive* No. 36 [1974], 22.

Gould, Florence†
"The Blue Blouse" *Mal R* No. 49 (Jan 1979), 39-46.

Gould, Jan
THE BOATHOUSE QUESTION Sidney, BC: Gray's, 1978.
"The Boathouse Question" *Boathouse Question* (1978), 1-27.
"Crab Traps" *Boathouse Question* (1978), 29-42.
"An Early Morning Message" *Boathouse Question* (1978), 151-70.
"The Glories of Greece" *Introductions from an Island* 1975, 39-51.
"The Glories of Greece" *Boathouse Question* (1978), 75-94.
"Gumphy" *Edmonton Journal* Wed, 11 Mar 1964, 4.
"The Lady" *My Golden West* 4 (Fall 1969), 30-1, 34.
"The Latest Island News" *Boathouse Question* (1978), 123-49.
"Northern Lights and Other Local Phenomena" *CBC* "*Anthology*" 27 May 1978.
"Oh, That Virgin Hair" *Boathouse Question* (1978), 95-121.
"Print on the Wall" *Edmonton Journal* Thu, 10 Oct 1963, 4 [Non-fiction?].
"Smile for the Crying Basket" *Boathouse Question* (1978), 43-74.
"The Snake in the Wall" *CBC* "*Anthology*" 31 Jan 1970.
"The Stop Sign" *Edmonton Journal* Thu, 5 Mar 1964, 4.
"A Temporary Arrangement" *Boathouse Question* (1978), 171-205.
"What I Could Tell Them" *Fireweed* Nos. 3/4 (Sum 1979), 41-51.

Gould, Maria‡
"The Consultation" *New Mitre* 85 (1980), 35.

Gould, Terry (1949?-)

"A Comparatively Nice View" *Waves* 6:3 (Spr 1978), 15-24.

"Jews Are Women" *Repos* Nos. 19/20 (Sum-Fall 1976), 64-70 ["an aged Montrealer's recollection, translated from the Yiddish-Canadian" (author's note)].

"Organic Living" *Waves* 7:3 (Spr 1979), 22-5.

'The Payment of Little Debts" *Mal R* No. 56 (Oct 1980), 139-53.

'The Routine" *event* 6:1 [1977], 26-37.

"So It's My Fault?" *Mal R* No. 55 (July 1980), 11-23.

Goulden, Alban†

IN THE WILDERNESS: STORIES Seven Persons: Repository Press, 1973.

'The Accident" *In the Wilderness* (1973), 20-3.

"Child Language" *In the Wilderness* (1973), 17-9.

'The Clearing" *In the Wilderness* (1973), 80.

'The Forest" *In the Wilderness* (1973), 33-41.

'In the Wilderness" *Iron* [No. 11] Bottom Iron (1971), [7 pp].

'In the Wilderness" *In the Wilderness* (1973), 74-83.

'The Mountain" *In the Wilderness* (1973), 7-12.

'The Others" *Iron* Nos. 8/9 (1970), 35-7.

'The Others" *In the Wilderness* (1973), 42-4.

'Parts of the Story" *Iron* [No. 10] Spring Iron [n.d.], [4 pp].

'Parts of the Story" *In the Wilderness* (1973), 24-8.

'Prison Essays" *In the Wilderness* (1973), 29-32.

'The Ride" *In the Wilderness* (1973), 1-6.

'The Sheepherder" *In the Wilderness* (1973), 13-5.

'The Snake" *Repos* No. 7 (Sum 1973), 13-22.

Goulden, Ron‡

'The Boat Ride" *Repos* No. 7 (Sum 1973), 46-52.

'The Hole – Thing" *Repos* No. 6 (Spr 1973), 39-40.

Gourlay, Elizabeth†

'The Brink of Destruction" *Fid* No. 41 (Sum 1959), 36-43.

"Crow" *UWR* 17:1 (Fall-Win 1982), 32-43.

"Sons and Mothers" *CBC [Van] "Hornby Collection"* 20 Feb 1982.

"Still Life with Flowers" *Room* 1:4 (Win 1976), 60-5.

Govan, Margaret

" 'And There Came Wise Men ...' " *Onward* 3 Jan 1960, 1-4, 14-5.

" 'And There Came Wise Men ...' " *Onward* 3 Jan 1965, 4-6, 10-1.

"Atonement" *Rapport* Apr 1969, 35-7.

'The Boy and the Girl" *Onward* 13 Feb 1966, 3-4.

"Cheering Section" *Onward* 1 Nov 1964, 6-7.

"Christmas Presents" *Onward* 12 Dec 1965, 3-5.

'The Debunker" *Onward* 14 Nov 1965, 3-5.

'The Empty Tomb" *Onward* 6 Apr 1958, 209-11, 222-3.

'The Empty Tomb" *Onward* 18 Apr 1965, 5-6, 9-10.

'The Fragile Surpriser" *Onward* 27 Mar 1966, 3-5, 14.

'The Image" *Rapport* May 1968, 16-20.

'The Insignificant Young Man" *Onward* 2 Oct 1966, 3-4, 13.

"It Doth Not Yet Appear What We Shall Be" *Onward* 14 Apr 1963, 11-2.
"The King's Gift" *Onward* 26 Feb 1967, 3-4.
"The King's Justice" *Onward* 16 Jan 1966, 3-4, 14.
"Little Boy Lost" *Onward* 9 Dec 1956, 785-7, 794-5.
"The Major Advance" *Onward* 3 Oct 1965, 3-4.
"Miracle" *Onward* 26 Nov 1967, 3-4, 10.
"Miracle Refused" *Onward* 3 Dec 1967, 3-5.
"The Rich Young Ruler" *Onward* 8 Jan 1967, 3-4.
"The Search for Christmas" *Rapport* Dec 1968, 32-6.
"The Secret" *Onward* 27 Sept 1964, 6-7.
"The Story of a Nurse" *Onward* 62 (18 May 1952), 310-1.
"The Submarine" *Rapport* Sept 1968, 12-7.
"The Sudden Door" *Onward* 8 Oct 1967, 3-4, 7.
"Tragic Planet" *Onward* 11 Dec 1966, 3-4.
"Witness in a Lesson" *Onward* 29 Nov 1964, 6-7.

Govier, Katharine (1948-)
"According to Your Cloth" *Des* Nos. 11/12 (Spr-Sum 1975), 95-9.
"Cuiseine Français" [sic] *CBC "Anthology"* 2 Feb 1980.
"The Dancer" *More Stories from Western Canada* (1980), 165-76 [Also entitled "Fables IV: The Dancer"].
"The Dragon" *Des* 11:4/12:1 Nos. 30/31 (1980-81), 30-9.
"The Dragon" *81: Best Canadian Stories* 45-57.
"Fables I: The Garden" *CF* 55 (Sept 1975), 53-6.
"Fables IV: The Dancer" *CF* 57 (Feb 1978), 25-8 [Also entitled "The Dancer"].
"The Independent Woman" *Flare* 2 (June-July 1980), 86-7, 96, 98, 100, 102.
"Marie" *Des* No. 10 (Win 1974), 46-52.
"Monday of the Sixth Week" *Miss Chat* 12 (28 Aug 1975), 56, 71-3, 76.
"Monologue by a Photographer" *Des* No. 16 (Win 1976-77), 38-41.
"The Morning" *Grain* 2:1 [1974], 16-20.
"A New Start" *Chat* 55 (July 1982), 30, 48, 50.
"Pas de Deux" *Miss Chat* 11 (9 May 1974), 26, 85-7.
"Rona's Complaint" *Weekend* 28 (18 Nov 1978), 8-10.
"The Thief" *CBC "Anthology"* 18 Mar 1978 [Also entitled "The Thief – Fables III"].
"The Thief – Fables III" *Prism* 17:1 (Sum 1978), 105-16 [Also entitled "The Thief"].

Gower, Richard†
"The Batter Was Scratched" *Pier Spr* 6:2 (Spr 1981), 23-30.
"The Day the Boys Wore Ties" *Pier Spr* 7:2 (Spr 1982), 27-30.
"The Man Who Loved Cadillacs" *Pier Spr* 5:[3] (Sum 1980), 38-41.
"Romeo MacClean and the Dishwasher" *Pier Spr* 5:[4] (Fall 1980), 42-6.

Grabowski, Simon†
"From the Sargasso Diary" *CFM* No. 4 (Aut 1971), 29-40.

Grace, Gregory‡
"Calaban's Last Journey" *Mandala* 1970, 55-7.
"In Defence of Calaban" *Mandala* 1970, 58-60.

Grace, Peter‡
"A Miss Is as Good as a Mile" *Rivers Bend R* 1:9 (May 1974), 40-1, 43-4.

Grady, Wayne
"Fugue" *SN* 97 (Dec 1982), 48-50, 52-4, 56, 58, 60.

Graham, Ferne
"Camp Daze" *Rapport* June 1968, 17-23.
"Dear Baby" *Onward* 23 Oct 1966, 3-4, 11.
"Golden Anniversary" *Onward* 10 Jan 1965, 6-7 [Fictional letter; not a story?].
"Hippies' Child" *Rapport* Jan 1969, 38-41.
"Land of the Dying" *Onward* 8 Oct 1967, 5-6 [Listed as article].
"Move Over, Shepherds" *Onward* 25 Dec 1966, 4-5, 13.
"Whither Thou Goest" *Onward* 5 June 1966, 3-5, 14.

Graham, Gary‡
"Place" *Scruncheons* 1:2 (Sept 1973), 58-62.
"Sense of Place" *Pulp* 1:9 (1 Apr 1973), [2].

Graham, Hugh†
"Beautiful Bev Caldwell" *Quarry* 27:1 (Win 1978), 51-64.

Graham, Kathleen†
"River People" *Quarry* 29:4 (Aut 1980), 121-8.

Graham, Michael R.‡
"The Out Islands" *AA* 54 (Jan 1964), 55-8.

Graham, Peter William‡
"Justice" *Creative Campus* 1963, 53-62.

Graham, Robert‡
"How Much Do You Pay for the Sun" *Acta Vic* 87:2 [1963], 33-5.
"The Jew Boy" *Acta Vic* 87:3 [1963], 19-26.
"Ptarmigan" *Acta Vic* 90:1 (Nov 1965), 7-12.
"The Sniper" *Acta Vic* 90:2 (Dec 1965), 8-14.

Graham, T.‡
"The Execution of the Infant Mary" *Alive* No. 45 (Nov 1975), 11.
"The Originator" *Alive* No 57 (30 Oct 1976), 2.

Graham, Tammy†
"Ben" *Folio* 17:2 (Spr 1965), 23-31.
"Gatsby and Oranges" *Folio* 16:2 (Spr 1964), 3-4.
"The Girl on the Shore" *Folio* 17:1 (Fall 1964), 18-22.
"The Stoker" *Folio* 16:2 (Spr 1964), 19-21.

Grainger, Louise‡
"Same Old Stories" *West People* No. 177 (24 Feb 1983), 13.

Grainger, Thomas†
"Not for Zenocrate Alone" *Prism* 2:1 (Fall 1960), 15-22.

Granewall, Christine†
"The Crayfish Festival" *From an Island* 13:1 (Spr 1981), 67-72.

Grant, Diane‡
"The Intellectual" *Raven* No. 8 (Jan 1960), 3-5.

Grant, Dorothy‡
"The Orange Tree" *Alive* No. 42 [n.d.], 18.

Grant, John‡
"The Born Salesman" *Acta Vic* 81:1 (Nov 1956), 35-6.

Grant, June†
"The Day of Abbie's Great Decision" *Chat* 29 (Apr 1957), 19, 86-91.

Grant, Katharine‡
"The Ruby" *AA* 71 (Apr 1981), 57-8, 60.

Grant, Leslie H.‡
"The Last Bridge" *Words from Inside* 1972, 17-9.

Grant, Lois†
"The Taxi" *Blue Buffalo* 1:2 (Spr 1983), [5 pp].

Grant, Peter‡
"Memo to Nobody" *Acta Vic* 77:2 (Dec 1952), 20-1.

Grant, Ralph‡
"Painfully Plain" *Katharsis* 1:1 (Apr 1967), 36.

Grant, William – *See* Carr, Roberta, with William Grant and Joe Koegh.

Grant, William J.
"An Encounter" *Sand Patterns* No. 13 (Spr 1975), [10 pp].
"Marbles of the Dancing Floor" *Sand Patterns* No. 20 (Win 1977), [12 pp] [Reprint [?]].
"The Swimmer" *Abegweit R* 2:2 (Fall 1975), 129-37.
"The Trash Collector" *Variations on a Gulf Breeze* (1973), 73-85.

Grantmyre, Barbara
A ROSE FOR MINNIE MULLET Fredericton: Brunswick Press, 1964.
"Ah! May the Red Rose" *AA* 49 (Sept 1958), 89-96.
"And Ice ... Mast High ... " *AA* 48 (Jan 1958), 68-73.
"Aria for Araby" *AA* 54 (Sept 1963), 60, 62-3.
"A Bit of Butter" *Rose for Minnie Mullet* (1964), 44-60.
"The Chipmunk" *FH* 31 Mar 1955, 18-9.
"Christmas Goose" *Stories with John Drainie* (1963), 155-62.
"The Dollar Knife" *Rose for Minnie Mullet* (1964), 71-83.
"Eight Prunes ... or Three?" *AA* 47 (Sept 1956), 72-7.
"Eight Prunes ... or Three?" *Atlantic Advocate's Holiday Book* (1961), 25-35.
" 'Erbert Winch" *Rose for Minnie Mullet* (1964), 95-102.
"Happy Birthday, an April Caprice" *AA* 47 (Apr 1957), 11-2.
"Is Oft Interred" *AA* 50 (Feb 1960), 35-6, 38-40.

"The Kindness" *Rose for Minnie Mullet* (1964), 84-90.
"Lady with a Cold" *AA* 53 (Feb 1963), 34, 36.
"Lem's New Suit" *Weekend* 3 (21 Mar 1953), 28-9.
"Lem's New Suit" *Rose for Minnie Mullet* (1964), 61-70.
"The Magnolia Tree" *Weekend* 4 (8 May 1954), 28-9, 46, 51.
"The Magnolia Tree" *Atlantic Anthology* (1959), 248-54.
"A Matter of Transportation" *Weekend* 4 (20 Mar 1954), 24-5, 42-3.
"Melody on a Ferry" *AA* 47 (June 1957), 51-3.
"Mrs. George" *AA* 53 (Aug 1963), 36-8.
"Music, When Soft Voices Die" *Weekend* 2 (1 Nov 1952), 18-9.
"The Only Woman Who Ever Puzzled Me" *MM* 68 (29 Oct 1955), 19, 28, 30-2, 34-6.
"The Only Woman Who Ever Puzzled Me" *Rose for Minnie Mullet* (1964), 138-57.
"Papa's Girl" *Rose for Minnie Mullet* (1964), 103-13.
"The Prisoner" *AA* 53 (Oct 1962), 39.
"A Rose for Minnie Mullet" *Weekend* 4 (28 Aug 1954), 10-1, 23.
"A Rose for Minnie Mullet" *Rose for Minnie Mullet* (1964), 9-18.
"The Royal Oak" AA 47 (Oct 1956), 39-46.
"Sawdust Mama" *Weekend* 2 (5 Jan 1952), 16-7.
"Sawdust Mama" *Rose for Minnie Mullet* (1964), 114-9.
"Sawkey and the Status Symbol" *FH* 4 Aug 1966, 38.
"Sawkey Mullet Collects a Debt" *Weekend* 5 (23 Apr 1955), 6-7, 30.
"Sawkey Mullet Collects a Debt" *Rose for Minnie Mullet* (1964), 34-43.
"The Scissors" *AA* 53 (June 1963), 33, 35.
"Strictly for the Birds" *Rose for Minnie Mullet* (1964), 120-37.
"The Walk Home" *Rose for Minnie Mullet* (1964), 91-4.
"Widow's Aid" *Weekend* 3 (12 Dec 1953), 10-1, 29.
"Widow's Aid" *Rose for Minnie Mullet* (1964), 19-33.

Gration, Gwen†
"The Queen's Marys" *CFM* No. 17 (Spr 1975), 27-33.

Graves, Phil‡
"May Sleep Be with You" *Rampike* 3:2 [1983?], 58.

Graves, Warren
"Welcome Home" *CBC "Alberta Anthology"* 10 Sept 1983.

Grawbarger, Josephine
"Andrew and Mr. Cat" *Squatch J* No. 7 (June 1978), 44-8.
"The Grey Goose" *Squatch J* No. 5 (June 1977), 51-4.

Gray, Betty‡
"Sunday Morning" *CBC "Anthology"* 17 Jan 1976.

Gray, Charles‡
"The Fishermen That Walk Upon the Beach" *AA* 58 (Mar 1968), 46-52, 54, 56.
"Target 2124" *AA* 57 (Aug 1967), 28-9, 31-5, 37-9.

Gray, Hal‡
"Groceries" *Canadian Short Fiction Anthology* (1976), 95-100.

Gray, John
"The Bottomless Purse" *MM* 72 (5 Dec 1959), 19, 44, 46, 50, 52.
"How Bamford-Gordon Abolished the Income Tax" *MM* 70 (27 Apr 1957), 22-3, 46, 50, 52.
"The Man Who Conquered Davy Crockett" *MM* 68 (24 Dec 1955), 9, 26, 28-30.
"Subject: Centaur" *MM* 66 (15 Apr 1953), 22-3, 48, 51-4.
"Who Was the Woman of the Glove?" *MM* 67 (15 Aug 1954), 12, 60-1.

Gray, Kitty†
"Auntie Bones Becomes a Canadian" *Voices of Kitimat 1967* 20-5.

Gray, Lillian Collier
"Journey for Abner" *FH* 17 Apr 1952, 28-9.
"The Watch" *FH* 3 Aug 1950, 14.

Gray, Roberta B.‡
"The Great Fall Supper" *UC Observer* 15 Oct 1968, 20-1 [Non-fiction?].

Green, Galen‡
"A Brief Discourse on Human Affections" *WCR* 8:1 (June 1973), 49-50.

Green, H. Gordon (1912-)
"An Affair of the Heart" by Will Merton *FH* 5 July 1962, 52-3.
"The Age of Insolence" *FH* 28 Mar 1957, 16-7, 38.
"The Alibi" by Lee Benoit *FH* 20 Nov 1958, 28-9.
"All Is Not Gold" by Nina Horner *FH* 24 Nov 1955, 28-9.
"Almost a War" *FH* 30 Aug 1956, 18.
"Almost a War" *Stories to Read Again* (1965), 131-5.
"... And the Greatest of These" *FH* 2 Apr 1953, 24-5.
"Another Sunrise" *Onward* 11 Apr 1954, 225-7, 238-9.
"The Artist Who Went to Heaven" by Art Maguire *FH* 22 Nov 1956, 16-7, 38.
"As Others See Us" by R. H. Morrison *FH* 16 Aug 1956, 20.
"A Bargain with Fate" *Farm J* (U.S.) 77 (July 1953), 33, 60, 62.
"The Battle of the Budget" by Kay Garneau *FH* 2 Oct 1958, 24-5.
"A Bear Named Sue" by Art Magill *FH* 19 July 1956, 18-9.
"Beast of Prey" *Weekend* 3 (23 May 1953), 30-2, 34.
"Beast of Prey" *FH* 8 Dec 1964, 31-3.
"The Beautiful Lie" *FH* 13 Oct 1955, 22-3.
"Before I Go" by Carol Clissold *FH* 27 June 1957, 23.
"Big Newf" by Len Carter *FH* 25 Apr 1963, 70-1.
"Black Sheep! Black Sheep!" *FH* 17 Feb 1966, 68-9, 71.
"Le Bon Dieu of Jacques Hillaire" by Kay Garneau *FH* 23 Feb 1961, 54-5.
"The Boy Who Went on Strike" *SW* 5 Apr 1952, I:4, 10.
"The Boy Who Went on Strike" *FH* 28 June 1956, 20-1, 29.
"The Boy Who Wouldn't Give Up" *FH* 20 Dec 1956, 12-4.
"The Boy Who Wouldn't Learn" *Onward* 21 Mar 1954, 186-7, 190-1.
"[The?] Boy with the Big Tongue" 1955 Anthology of Best Original Short Shorts [Based on SSI].
"Boy with a Wicked Tongue" *FH* 22 July 1954, 16.
"The Bread That Didn't Return" *FH* 7 Apr 1955, 28-9, 37.
"The Bugler of Nippombara" by Len Carter *FH* 2 Feb 1967, 47.

"Bull Loose" by Ken Ledoux *FH* 1 June 1961, 39.

"The Case of the Stiff-Necked Saints" *FH* 4 Mar 1965, 36-7, 63.

"The Cat with a Woman's Eyes" *FH* 11 Feb 1954, 28-9.

"The Cheque" *FH* 2 Jan 1958, 20-1, 25.

"Chip on the Shoulder" *FH* 8 Sept 1955, 24-5.

"The Christening at Dhu Varren" *FH* 29 Mar 1962, 28.

"Christmas Is an Uproar" *FH* 23 Dec 1954, 24-5.

"Christmas Is the Spirit" *FH* 19 Dec 1957, 6-7.

"The Christmas of Donegan's Brawl" *SW* 12 Dec 1964, 8-10, 19.

"The Christmas of the Last Partridge" *FH* 21 Dec 1961, 16-7.

"The Christmas Story I Tell My Children" *Farm J* (U.S.) 84 (Dec 1960), 32, 41-2.

"The Chub" by Carlotta Dickson *FH* 2 Apr 1959, 22-3, 27.

"Church Going Down" *Chat* 23 (May 1950), 26-7, 56-9, 63-4.

"The Clock That Will Never Leave Home" by David Dow *FH* 6 June 1963, 45, 55.

"Cobra" *FH* 4 Feb 1965, 42, 46.

"Contract for the Great Novel" *FH* 14 Sept 1961, 22, 26.

"The Crime of Fergus McKim" by R. H. Morrison *FH* 30 Jan 1958, 24, 26.

"The Crowing Hen" by Helen F. Christensen *FH* 25 Jan 1968, 35.

"Cupid Wears No Halo" by Kay Garneau *FH* 30 Mar 1961, 22-3.

"The Cure" *FH* 30 Nov 1950, 22-3, 32.

"The Curious Holdup at Longhorn Creek" by Cy Earl *FH* 17 Sept 1959, 28-31.

"The Dangerous Age" *FH* 6 Feb 1958, 24-5.

"The Darkest Day" by R. H. Morrison *FH* 4 Dec 1958, 20-1.

"Dead Man's Coppers" by R. H. Morrison *FH* 13 Sept 1956, 26-7.

"A Decent Man" *FH* 22 Apr 1954, 28-9, 36.

"The Delicate Situation" *FH* 5 Nov 1964, 32-3.

"The Devil's Treasure" by Newt Herd *FH* 31 Oct 1957, 24.

"Dinner with an Old Man" by Lillian Jolliffe *FH* 13 Dec 1956, 14-5.

"Do I Look So Old?" by Kay Garneau *FH* 5 June 1958, 21.

"The Drain Commissioner's Christmas" *FH* 20 Dec 1951, 14-5.

"The Drunk" *FH* 4 Aug 1955, 18-9.

"The End of the Rope" *SW* 11 Oct 1958, 32-3, 48.

"Evening in Brussels" by Cy Earl *FH* 19 Feb 1959, 28-9, 36.

"Evesham" by Len Carter *FH* 8 Feb 1968, 35-6.

"Excuse My Dust" *FH* 22 Oct 1953, 28.

"The Face of Crime" by R. H. Morrison *FH* 7 Apr 1960, 26-7, 31.

"Farewell, Beatles" by Len Carter *FH* 11 Jan 1968, 28-9.

"Fate Smiled the Other Way" by R. H. Morrison *FH* 4 May 1961, 39.

"Father and the Schoolteacher" *FH* 15 Dec 1960, 16-7.

"Father Was a Fancier" *FH* 19 Jan 1956, 22-3, 33.

"Final Message" *FH* 29 Apr 1965, 62-3.

"First Day at School" by Carlotta Dickson *FH* 3 Sept 1959, 20-1, 25.

"The First Stone" *FH* 26 Sept 1963, 68-70.

"The Five Wills of Rory McTavish" by R. H. Morrison *FH* 12 Mar 1959, 16-7.

"Flight from Courage" by R. H. Morrison *FH* 24 Sept 1953, 24-5, 33.

"Footloose and Fiancee Free" by Lillian Jolliffe *FH* 3 Nov 1955, 30-1.

"For the Love of Marcy" *SW* 1 Nov 1952, I:10, 12.

"For the Love of Marcy" *Onward* 17 Oct 1954, 657-9, 670-1.

"For the Love of Marcy" *FH* 25 Oct 1956, 14-6.

"Funeral for a Horse" *FH* 27 Mar 1952, 28-9, 37.

"The Gas Saver" by Kay Garneau *FH* 30 Oct 1958, 28-9.

"The Gift" *FH* 22 Oct 1959, 26-7, 30-1.

"Gift for a Stubborn Son" *FH* 20 Dec 1962, 27, 29.

"Girl from Peace River" *FH* 19 July 1951, 16-7.

"The Girl I Left Behind" by Nick Peterson *FH* 23 Feb 1956, 24-5, 39.

"The Girl Who Understood" by Nan Albert *FH* 5 Nov 1953, 24-5, 33.

"God's Rooster" *FH* 4 May 1950, 26-7.

"The Gold Brick" by Johann Carlsen *FH* 11 Nov 1954, 24.

"The Golden Wedding" *FH* 8 May 1958, 28-9.

"The Greatest of These" *Onward* 16 Aug 1953, 513-6, 527.

"Gypsy Fiddler" *Challenge* 19 (8 Oct 1950), 3-8, 10-1.

"The Hateful Suitor" by Newt Herd *FH* 2 May 1957, 24-5.

"Having Eyes to See" *FH* 7 Oct 1964, 28, 30.

"Head in the Clouds" by Jim Walker *FH* 3 June 1954, 20-1.

"The Height of a Boy" *Farm J* (U.S.) 80 (Nov 1956), 81-2. 87-8, 90, 92 [Also entitled "The Height of a Lad"].

"The Height of a Lad" *FH* 12 Sept 1957, 26-7, 30-1 [Also entitled "The Height of a Boy"].

"Her Dear Deluded Daughter" *FH* 29 May 1952, 24-5, 33.

"The Hero Who Was Scared of Cows" by Cy Earl *FH* 28 May 1959, 24-6.

"Home the Warrior" by R. H. Morrison *FH* 16 Apr 1959, 18-9.

"Hooray for No System" by R. H. Morrison *FH* 24 Aug 1961, 20-1.

"How a Man Ought to Die" by Milt Wallace *FH* 23 July 1959, 18-9.

"How Much a Pound?" *Weekend* 2 (30 Aug 1952), 24-5.

"How Much a Pound" *Onward* 3 May 1953, 273-5.

"How Much a Pound?" *FH* 13 June 1957, 24-5.

"The Hunt" by Johann Carlsen *FH* 27 Aug 1953, 20-1.

"I Remember Buckshot" by R. H. Morrison *FH* 24 Nov 1960, 12-3, 30.

"Ignorance Is Not Bliss" by Dave Clarkson *FH* 26 Jan 1956, 20-1, 29.

"The Independent One" by Nick Peterson *FH* 30 June 1955, 18-9.

"The Inevitable Decision" *FH* 18 Jan 1951, 24-5.

"Jeff Was a Mind Reader" *Farm J* (U.S.) 81 (Jan 1957), 30-1, 68-70.

"The Jinx" by Eddy M. Liddell *FH* 10 Feb 1955, 24-5.

"John Gilder's Argument" *FH* 17 Aug 1950, 18-9.

"John K. Sugarue's First Million" *FH* 18 Feb 1965, 43, 61.

"The King Who Had No Tongue" *SW* 20 Oct 1956, I:6.

"The Lass from Cape Breton" *SW* 12 Sept 1953, I:1, 12.

"The Last Present" *Onward* 12 Sept 1954, 577-9, 590-1.

"The Lawyer's Letter" *SW* 19 Oct 1957, 8-9, 34.

"Legend of Stonyhill" by Will Martin *FH* 3 Sept 1953, 20-1.

"A Lesson for the Teacher" *Challenge* 19 (23 Apr 1950), 5-6, 10.

"A Lesson in Character" *FH* 20 Jan 1955, 24-5, 30.

"Lesson in Humiliation" by Johann Carlsen *FH* 9 Jan 1958, 22-3.

"Let Love Come After" by Carlotta Dickson *FH* 10 Dec 1959, 20-1.

"Letter to My Father" *FH* 9 Oct 1958, 22-3.

"Little Girls Giggling" *FH* 29 Sept 1955, 22-3.

"The Little War of the Roses" by Carlotta Dickson *FH* 16 Mar 1961, 10-1.

"Little White Lie" by R. H. Morrison *FH* 14 Aug 1952, 20-1, 26.

"The Littlest Sinner" *FH* 5 Nov 1959, 22-3, 27.

"The Long Lost Love" by Eddy M. Liddell *FH* 21 Oct 1954, 28-9, 36.

"Love Is Always an Accident" by Milton Wallace *FH* 8 Dec 1955, 18-9.

"The Love of Limpy Joe" *FH* 18 Oct 1951, 26-7.

"Lover Come Back" by Carlotta Dickson *FH* 18 Sept 1958, 28-30.

"Lumberman's Brawl" by Art Maguire *FH* 14 June 1956, 20-3.

"Madman's Logic" *FH* 22 Mar 1951, 26-7, 36.

"The Man in the Marsh" by Nick Peterson *FH* 15 Sept 1955, 26-7.

"Man of Steel" by Kay Garneau *FH* 16 May 1957, 14-5.

"The Man Who Couldn't Forgive" *SW* 24 Dec 1960, 8-9, 30.

"The Man Who Hated Children" *FH* 31 Mar 1960, 20-1, 27.

"The Man Who Lost His Credit" by Bill Wheatley *FH* 3 Dec 1959, 18-9.

"The Man Who Waved the Flag" *Stories of Christian Living* (1950) [Based on SSI].

"The Man Who Waved the Flag" *FH* 25 June 1959, 20-1, 25.

"The Man Who Went Before" by Kay Garneau *FH* 12 Nov 1959, 20-1.

"The Man with the Many Barns" *FH* 23 June 1955, 24-5, 47.

"A Man's Integrity" *FH* 8 Mar 1950, 28-9, 64.

"Master's Degree" by Bud Lamp *FH* [date unknown], 24-5, 32.

"Midnight in the Afternoon" *FH* 18 July 1963, 34-5.

"Moment of Glory" by Kay Garneau *FH* 14 Jan 1960, 18, 23.

"Moment of Impulse" by Lillian Jolliffe *FH* 10 Aug 1961, 22.

"Moonlight Becomes You" by Carlotta Dickson *FH* 13 Aug 1959, 12-3.

"Moose Roast for Dinner" *SW* 9 Nov 1963, 10-2.

"Mother and the Ice Storm" by Will Merton *FH* 14 Mar 1963, 78.

"The Mother-in-Law" by Kay Garneau *FH* 29 Aug 1957, 23.

"Mr. Atkinson's Bats" by Leo Petrant *FH* 17 Aug 1961, 23.

"Mr. Monahan's Revenge" *FH* 22 Dec 1955, 24-5, 29.

"My Friend Gossip" by Kay Garneau *FH* 29 Oct 1959, 24-6.

"My Papa's Feud with the Tax Men" by Kay Garneau *FH* 20 Apr 1961, 54-5.

"Mysterious Orphanage" *Onward* 5 July 1953, 420-2, 430-1.

"Mysterious Orphanage" *FH* 11 Sept 1958, 12-3, 28-9.

"Mystery on the Collection Plate" by Will Merton *FH* 6 Dec 1962, 28-9.

"Nature Woman" by Art Maguire *FH* 21 Jan 1960, 24-5.

"Next Table Over" by David Dow *FH* 31 May 1962, 18.

"The Night McLeish Went Dry" by R. H. Morrison *FH* 26 Sept 1957, 24, 28.

"The Night of the Decree" by Carol Clissold *FH* 3 Oct 1957, 25-6.

"The Night of the Thunder Pump" *FH* 1 Aug 1963, 34-5.

"Night Watch" *SW* 11 Feb 1950, I:9-10.

"Night Watch" *FH* 12 Feb 1958, 28-30.

"No Apology Needed" by R. H. Morrison *FH* 31 May 1959, 36-7.

"No Band for Aunt Polly" by Lillian Jolliffe *FH* 27 Apr 1961, 27, 47.

"No Bargain Today" by Newt Herd *FH* 8 Aug 1957, 23.

"No Love Required" by Nan Albert *FH* 15 Dec 1955, 20-1, 32.

"No Photos Please" by Kay Garner *FH* 16 Dec 1954, 16-8.

"No Room for Sentiment" by Milton Wallace *FH* 30 Dec 1954, 16-7.

"The Nobleman" by Kay Garneau *FH* 25 Aug 1960, 16-7.

"Not Much in the Pulpit" by Lillian Jolliffe *FH* 26 Mar 1959, 16-7.

"Not the Marrying Kind" by Kay Garneau *FH* 10 Apr 1958, 16-7, 35.

"Old Flame" by Lillian Jolliffe *FH* 1 Oct 1959, 24-5.

"Old Maid's Children" *FH* 11 Dec 1952, 24-5, 56.

"Stubborn As They Come" *FH* 28 Oct 1954, 20-1, 26.

"Stubborn's No Name" by R. H. Morrison *FH* 21 Aug 1958, 22-3.

"Swan Song for Sir Craigie" *FH* 3 Feb 1966, 54.

"Synopsis of an Irishman's Love Affair" *SW* 14 Nov 1964, 24-5, 28, 34.

"Tears for Father's Day" *SW* 18 June 1955, I:7.

"Tears for Father's Day" *FH* 18 June 1959, 20, 24.

"The Temptation of Ian" *Onward* 31 Jan 1953, 65-7.

"Thanksgiving Surprise" *Onward* 14 Oct 1956, 662-3, 670-1.

"That Boy! That Boy!" *SW* 31 July 1954, I:1, 7.

"That Which Was Lost" by Lillian Jolliffe *FH* 15 Apr 1954, 28-9, 37.

"A Thief in the House" by Jim Salter *FH* 31 Aug 1961, 20.

"This I Will Keep" by Lillian Jolliffe *FH* 28 Jan 1960, 20-1, 26.

"Three Bells for the Steeple" *FH* 22 Dec 1960, 8-9.

"Till the Right One Comes Along" by Ken Ledoux *FH* 23 June 1966, 33.

"Time and Tide" *FH* 12 Oct 1950, 26-7, 58.

"A Time to Remember" by Van Aydelotte *FH* 13 Jan 1955, 20-1.

"To Meet the Family" by Lillian Jolliffe *FH* 4 July 1963, 36-7, 47.

"To My Daughter in Love" *CHJ* Aug 1951, 9, 38-9, 49-52, 54.

"To the Stars" by Art Maguire *FH* 3 Jan 1957, 18.

"Too Much Fun for Nothing" by Kay Garneau *FH* 16 Jan 1958, 24.

"Too Sweet to Speak" by R. H. Morrison *FH* 13 June 1958, 17.

"Tough Boy" *FH* 14 July 1960, 20-1, 24.

"Trial by Night" *Onward* 18 Jan 1953, 33-6, 46-7.

"The Unclouded Eyes" *Onward* 62 (4 May 1952), 273-6, 286-7.

"The Unclouded Eyes" *FH* 11 June 1953, 24-5, 33.

"Unexpected Emergency" by Lillian Jolliffe *FH* 21 Apr 1960, 28-9, 34.

"The Unexpected Valentine" by Lillian Jolliffe *FH* 9 Feb 1961, 18-9.

"The Unforgiveable Sin" by Will Martin *FH* 5 Mar 1953, 28-9, 39.

"The Unseen" by Pete Cole *FH* 13 Nov 1958, 26-7.

"The Vision" by Jim Salter *FH* 17 Mar 1960, 14-5, 33.

"Voice from the Past" by R. H. Morrison *FH* 2 July 1953, 16-7, 23.

"The Vote" by Jim Salter *FH* 8 Sept 1960, 26-7.

"The Way It Ought to Be" *FH* 3 Dec 1953, 28-9.

"The Way of the Transgressor" *FH* 24 May 1962, 26.

"The Weed" by Madeleine Thornton *FH* 1 Nov 1956, 15.

"Were You the Hero?" *FH* 23 Sept 1954, 24-5.

"When Father Couldn't Say Grace" *FH* 22 Aug 1957, 23-4.

"When Father Couldn't Say Grace" *Reader's Choice Treasury* (1964) [Based on SSI].

"When Hamish Hung Up His Kilt" by R. H. Morrison *FH* 7 Aug 1958, 18-9.

"When the Roll Is Called Up Yonder" *Onward* 60 (26 Feb 1950), 129-31, 142-3.

"Why I Never Went to University" by R. H. Morrison *FH* 18 July 1957, 23.

"Wife Beater" by Art Maguire *FH* 31 July 1958, 23, 32.

"The Wife Who Was Really a Slave" by Carlotta Dickson *FH* 8 Jan 1959, 20-1.

"Will You Show Me a Light, Lad" *FH* 11 Nov 1965, 36-7, 42.

"Witness for the Crown" by R. H. Morrison *FH* 15 Sept 1960, 12-3.

"The Woman Who Wanted No Love" *SW* 26 Aug 1950, II:1, 4.

"The Woman Who Wanted No Love" *FH* 30 Apr 1959, 12-3, 24.

Green, Robert
"The Best of Enemies" *Stories with John Drainie* (1963), 143-8.
"Cupboard Love" *Mont* 38 (Sept 1964), 16-7.
"The Day Travers Lost His Pills" *Mont* 40 (Mar 1966), 50-1.
"Go, Go, Go!" *Mont* 38 (Apr 1964), 20-2.
"Peculiar Inspector Carstairs" *Stories with John Drainie* (1963), 48-53.
"The Peeping Dog" *Mont* 39 (July 1965), 17-8.
"The Peeping Game" *Mont* 38 (July 1964), 23-4.
"The Tupper Toupee Man" *Mont* 37 (June 1963), 20-1.

Green, Robin†
"Suckers" *Thursday's Voices* (1983), 57-66.

Green, Shane‡
"A Good Heart Dies" *Communicator* 6:1 [n.d.], 24-6.

Green, Taylor‡
[Untitled] *UCR* Win 1983, 7.
[Untitled] *UCR* Win 1983, 26-8.

Green, Terence M.
"Of Children in the Foliage" *Aurora* 1979 102-8.
"The Rites of Spring" *Forum* (OSSTF) 7 (Apr 1981), 71-3.
"Susie Q²" *Isaac Asimov's Science Fiction Mag* 7:8 No. 66 (Aug 1983), 104-20.
"Till Death Do Us Part" *Fantasy and Science Fiction* 61 (Dec 1981), 92-103.

Greenbaum, Jonathan‡
"A Will to Fail" *Viewpoints* 12:2 (Fall 1982), 50-5.

Greene, Anna‡
"Gone Is My Fear of Sailing" *Better Boating* 11 (Sept 1975), 56-9.
"Half a Bass Is Better Than No Love at All" *Better Boating* 10 (July-Aug 1974), 40-2.
"Love on a 22-Footer" *Better Boating* 11 (Mar 1975), 16-8.

Greene, Elizabeth†
"Let Me Always Love" *Catalyst* 1:1 (Aut 1967), 22-8.
"A Matter of Directions" *Catalyst* 2:1 (Fall 1968), 10-5.
"Riconoscenza" *Catalyst* No. 2 (Spr 1968), 10-4.

Greenstone, Gerry‡
"A Man and an Older Man" *Jaw Breaker* No. 3 (Feb 1972), 12-3.

Greenwald, Roger‡
"File for an Exposé: by Dawson F. Tillbury" *Writ* No. 4 (Spr 1972), 27-51.

Greenway, Eric‡
"The Mourning Dead" *Repos* No. 4 (Fall 1972), 26-49.
"The Pond" *Repos* No. 1 [1972], 5-8.
"The Sickness" *Repos* No. 2 [1972], 4-11.

Greenway, Rex‡

"Crowgull" *CBC "Anthology"* 23 Mar 1974.
"Dunn's Wife" *CBC "Anthology"* 28 July 1973.
"The Ghost Dancers" *CBC "Anthology"* 12 Jan 1974.
"A Night Out" *CBC "Anthology"* 19 Mar 1977.
"We'll Wait Until Dusk" *CBC "Anthology"* 19 May 1978.
"The Wrong Track" *CBC "Anthology"* 8 Sept 1973.

Greenwood, Gail‡

"Hippopotamus" *CBC "Alberta Anthology"* 18 Sept 1982.

Greenwood, Joan‡

"A Horse Called Bill" *AA* 50 (June 1960), 58-9.
"Kamloops Baby" *British Columbia* (1961), 354-9.

Greer, David† (1946-)

"A Sentimental Journey" *Mal R* No. 64 (Feb 1983), 52-63.

Gregg, John†

"Smashing Capital" *View from the Silver Bridge* 2:3 (June 1973), 14-27.

Grenfell, Wilfred T.

"When Christmas Came to Cape St. Anthony" *FH* 19 Dec 1963, 22-3.

Grennan, William‡

"Horse Thieves" *Scarlet and Gold* No. 35 (1953), 33-5.
"A Prairie Fire Tragedy" *Scarlet & Gold* No. 36 (1954), 30-1.

Grenon, Joan‡

"A New Dress for Maggie" *Edmonton Culture Vulture* 1:1 (Fri, 26 Sept 1975), 12-3, 20-2.

Gridly, Verity‡

"The Point" *Windows* [1969?], [2 pp].

Grier, Dave†

"Go with Gladness" *Forge* 1953, 42-5.

Grieveson, Brian†

"Chemical Row" *Charasee Press* No. 9 (1972), 8, 12, 21.
"Fantasy Child" *Charasee Press* No. 8 (Feb 1972), 8. 11. 19.
"Hasta La Vista" *Charasee Press* No. 3 (Sept 1971), 8-9.
"Midnight Sun" *Charasee Press* No. 4 (Oct 1971), 7, 10.
"Moroccan Exports" *Charasee Press* No. 7 (Jan 1972), 9. 12, 15, 18.
"The Prisoner" *Charasee Press* No. 5 (Oct 1971), 8, 12.
"Thessalon" *Charasee Press* No. 6 (Dec [1971]), 7, 10.
"Under Control" *Stardust* 1:2 (1976), 53-60.

Griffin, George‡

"An Accident" *TUR* 69:1 (Nov 1956), 29-31.
"The Fiery Chariot" *TUR* 70:2 (Dec 1957), 8-16.
"Quinsey Pursues a Butterfly" *TUR* 69:3 (Feb 1957), 32-4.
"Young Men Will Do It" *TUR* 69:5 (Sum 1957), 38-41.

Griffin, Harold†

"The Leaving" *Inscape* 3:2 (Spr 1964), 1-8.

Griggs, Terry (1951-)

"Harrier" *CF* 62 (Sept 1982), 21, 24-5, 36.
"India" *Mal R* No. 66 (Oct 1983), 7-12.

Grills, Barry W.†

"Death by Seniority" *Quarry* 25:2 (Spr 1976), 25-32.
"A Game with Adonis" *Quarry* 26:1 (Win 1977), 40-8.
"A Game with Adonis" *78: Best Canadian Stories* 58-69.
"A Game with Adonis" *Great Canadian Sports Stories* (1979), 100-11.
"A Long Labor" *Grain* 5:2 [1977], 31-7.
"Talent" *Quarry* 22:4 (Aut 1973), 35-44.

Grimster, Ellen†

"A Change of Heart" *Can Lifetime* 2 (July-Aug 1972), 14-5.
"A Skink in My Jewel Box" *Edmonton Journal* Fri, 12 May 1967, 64 [Humour?].
"A Skink in My Jewel Box" *Can Lifetime* 2 (May-June 1972), 9-10.
"A Skink in My Jewel Box" *Legion* 52 (June 1977), 11.
"The Tree" *CSSM* 1:4 (Oct 1975), 16-9.
"Where There's a Will" *Can Lifetime* 2 (Mar-Apr 1972), 9-11.
"Where There's a Will" *CSSM* 1:3 (July 1975), 1-3.

Grisak, Garry†

"The Game" *CSSM* 1:2 (Apr 1975), 9-13.
" 'Hemo' " *CSSM* 2:4 (Fall 1976), 31-4.

Groome, B.W.‡

"The Fall" *Stump* 1:2 (Fall 1977), 21-5.

Grossman, Rita‡

"Blues for Tommy" *Can Fandom* No. 28 (Feb 1956), 16-24.

Grouchey, Margaret†

"Journey Home" *Nfld Q* 56:2 (June 1957), 19-20, 31, 33-5.

Grube, John (1930-)

"Southern Exposure" *Gut* 4:1 (Aug-Sept 1978), 13-7.

Grushko, Brenda‡

"And So It Goes" *Mandala* 1972, 49-50.

Guareschi, Giovanni

"A Baptism" *Beaver Bites* 1:7 (Oct 1976), 32-3.

Gubins, Indra‡

"An Autumn Day" *Acta Vic* 86:2 (Spr 1962), 9-12.
"For a Piece of Bread" *Acta Vic* 87:2 [1963], 19-26.

Guderian, Evelyn‡

"Christmas and White Roses" *From 231* 1:2 (Dec 1972), 1-4.

Gudjonson, Eric†

"Canoe Trip" *Prism* 2:3 (Spr 1961), 44-6.

"The Dappled Mares" *Prism* 2:3 (Spr 1961), 38-41.

Guertin, John‡

"An Old Woman Raging in the Face of Extinction" *Laom R* 4 (Apr 1978), 47-9.

Gueulette, Sue‡

"The Intruder" *Stump* 4:1/2 (Spr 1980), 5-6.

Gugeler, Fritz‡

"Immortality" *Connexion* 1:1 (Dec 1968), [4 pp].

Guillet, Valerie‡

" 'Careless Memories' " *Los* No. 8 (Mar 1982), 44-6.

Gunn, Genni†

"The Assertion of Jordan Lemke" *Read Ch* 2:1 (Spr 1983), 64-73.

Gunn, Walter‡

"The Journey" *Varsity* Wed, 14 Dec 1960, 10.

Gunn, William [pseudonym]

"Open for Business" *NeWest R* 9 (Nov 1983), 10-2.

Gunnars, Kristjana (1948-)

THE AXE'S EDGE Victoria: Press Porcepic, 1983.

"Asa Sigmundsson: Holiday" *Axe's Edge* (1983), 85-93.

"Epistle of Wilderness" *Nw J* No. 21 (1982), 26-47.

"Fridrik Sveinsson: Mice" *CF* 59 (Nov 1979), 20-2.

"Fridrik Sveinsson: Mice" *Axe's Edge* (1983), 29-36.

"Gudfinna, Bells" *Axe's Edge* (1983), 7-15.

"Halfdán Sigmundsson, Guest" *CFM* Nos. 36/37 (1980), 39-45 ["Translated from the Icelandic by the author" (editorial note)].

"Halfdán Sigmundsson: Guest" *Axe's Edge* (1983), 37-45.

"Halldor Thorgilsson: Crossroads" *Axe's Edge* (1983), 47-59.

"Holiday, My Bone" *Lögberg-Heimskringla* 96 (3 Dec 1982) [Based on survey response].

"Kolla, Ticks" *NeWest R* 5 (Feb 1980), 8-9.

"Kolla, Ticks" *Sundogs* (1980), 49-54.

"Kolla, Ticks" *Axe's Edge* (1983), 69-75.

"Páll Thorláksson: Bloodletter" *Axe's Edge* (1983), 23-8.

"Pètur Arnason, Roundup" *Lögberg-Heimskringla* 95 (9 Oct 1981) [Based on survey response].

"Pétur Arnason, Roundup" *Axe's Edge* (1983), 17-22.

"The Song of the Reindeer" *Icelandic Writing Today* (Sept 1982) [Based on survey response].

"Sveinborg Sigfúsdòttir, Grasses" *Lögberg-Heimskringla* 95 (14 May 1982) [Based on survey response].

"Sveinborg Sigfúsdòttir: Grasses" *Axe's Edge* (1983), 61-8.

"Tómas Jónasson, Jazz" *Arts Man* 3:1 (Win/Nov 1983), 65-9.

"Tómas Jónasson, Jazz" *Axe's Edge* (1983), 77-83.

Gunnery, Sylvia C.†

"Daughters" *Grain* 8:1 [1980], 50-6.

"Fantasy and Circumstance" *CFM* Nos. 30/31 (1979), 103-7.

Gunning, Robert M.‡

"Rio" *Generation* Win 1967, 26-30.

Guppy, Steve (1951-)

ANOTHER SAD DAY AT THE EDGE OF THE EMPIRE Lantzville: Oolichan Books, 1983 [Based on CBIP].

"Another Sad Day at the Edge of the Empire" *CFM* Nos. 45/46 (1982-83), 25-34.

"The Catch" *Mal R* No. 50 (Apr 1979), 96-113.

"Flying Things" *Introductions from an Island* 1975, 34-8.

"A Portrait of Helena Leafly, with Bees" *CFM* No. 46 (1983), 15-23.

"Silence" *Mal R* No. 46 (Apr 1978), 133-6.

"The Tale of the Ratcatcher's Daughter" *Rainshadow* (1982), 170-8.

Guss, Joseph‡

"A Grand View of the Dog" *Deceits of Ecstacy* (1971), 27-8.

Gustafson, Pat‡

"The Old Man" *CBC "Alberta Anthology"* 6 Sept 1980.

Gustafson, Ralph B. (1909-)

THE BRAZEN TOWER Toronto: Roger Ascham Press, 1974.

THE VIVID AIR: COLLECTED STORIES Victoria: Sono Nis Press, 1980.

"Classical Portrait" *Dal R* 32 (1952), 131-5.

"Classical Portrait" *Vivid Air* (1980), 56-9.

"Heaven Help Us" *JCF* 1:1 (Win 1972), 16-8.

"Helen" *New Mexico Q R* 20 (1950), 549[+?] [Based on ILM].

"Helen" *Vivid Air* (1980), 73-81.

"In Point of Fact" *QQ* 60 (1953), 344-54.

"In Point of Fact" *Vivid Air* (1980), 82-90.

"The Paper-Spike" *NR* 5:5 (June-July 1952), 34-8.

"The Paper Spike" *Brazen Tower* (1974), 89-95.

"The Paper-Spike" *Vivid Air* (1980), 69-72.

"Shower of Gold" *CF* 39 (Nov 1959), 177-9.

"Shower of Gold" *Brazen Tower* (1974), 111-20.

"Shower of Gold" *Vivid Air* (1980), 91-6.

"The Tangles of Neaera's Hair" *Prism* 4:3 (Win 1965), 25-9.

"The Tangles of Neaera's Hair" *Brazen Tower* (1974), 125-33.

"The Tangles of Neaera's Hair" *Vivid Air* (1980), 111-5.

"The Vivid Air" *Tam R* No. 10 (Win 1959), 8-19.

"The Vivid Air" *Vivid Air* (1980), 101-10.

Guthro, Lisa‡

"The Guest" *TUR* 93:1 (Jan 1980), 16-9.

"A Night to Remember" *Acta Vic* 106:1 (Fall 1981), 30-9.

Guy, Ray

"Midsummer Gladness" *East of Canada* (1976), 182-5.

Gzowski, Peter J. (1934-)
"Wider and Deeper" *Undergrad* Spr 1956, 9-11.

H.M.M. – *See* M., H.M.

Haas, Diana‡
"The Ducks" *Undergrad* Aut-Win 1952, 9-11.

Haas, Maara
"A Way Out of the Forest" *Winnipeg Stories* (1974), 119-24.

Hadzipetros, Emmanuel J.†
"War of the Worlds Revisited" *Bakka* No. 6 (Fall 1977), 19-21.

Hadzipetros, Sophia‡
"Macaronia, Moussaka and Baklava and a Little Bit of Retsina Too" *Dime Bag* [No. 18] Fiction Issue 1 (Mar 1977), 14-6.

Haensel, Regine G.
"Goldenrod" *NeWest R* 7 (Apr 1982), 14-5.
"Pine Trees and Snow" *Grain* 9:1 (Feb 1981), 41-3.

Hagan, Derek [pseudonym]
"Fragment" *Acta Vic* 90:3 (Feb 1966), 9-11.

Hager, Carl‡
"The Sentence" *Alive* [1:7] (June [1970]), [3 pp].

Hagey, Mary†
"The Long Way Home" *Prism* 21:1 (Sept 1982), 20-9.

Haggerty, Joan (1940-)
"Dancehall" *CBC "Anthology"* 29 Apr 1978.
"Jake" *McCall's Working Mother* Sept 1980 [Based on survey response].
"Jake" *CBC "Anthology"* 19 Apr 1980.

Haig-Brown, Roderick (1908-)
WOODS AND RIVER TALES Ed. Valerie Haig-Brown Toronto: McClelland & Stewart, 1980 ["I have no doubt that most, if not all, are true stories, and, in many cases, personal experiences" (editorial note)].
"Best Partner a Man Ever Had" *Woods and River Tales* (1980), 121-9.
"Black Fisherman" *Woods and River Tales* (1980), 166-74.
"Buster" *Woods and River Tales* (1980), 31-6.
"The Cabin" *Woods and River Tales* (1980), 21-30.
"Christmas Patrol" *Mayfair* 27 (Dec 1953), 32, 81.
"Gun Law: The Judgment of Billy's Partner" *Woods and River Tales* (1980), 37-43.
"Gun Law: The Red-Headed Woman's Judgment" *Woods and River Tales* (1980), 44-55.
"Hold Your Tongue" *Woods and River Tales* (1980), 83-9.
"The Homestead" *Woods and River Tales* (1980), 63-9.

"The Man with the Briefcase" *Woods and River Tales* (1980), 157-65.
"New Blood" *Woods and River Tales* (1980), 145-56.
"Night of the Wolves" *Read Dig* 119 (July 1981), 30-2.
"The Passing of a Primitive" *Woods and River Tales* (1980), 56-62.
"A Reputation" *Woods and River Tales* (1980), 107-11.
"The Searcher" *Woods and River Tales* (1980), 112-20.
"Spearheads" *Woods and River Tales* (1980), 90-106.
"The Sweep" *Woods and River Tales* (1980), 175-82.
"Three Men Against the Sea" *High Flight* (1951), 453-65.
"Uncle Reg" *Woods and River Tales* (1980), 183-9.
"The Vigil" *Woods and River Tales* (1980), 70-82.
"A Walk to Derek's Landing – January 1935" *Woods and River Tales* (1980), 130-6.
"The Wharf" *New Yorker* 26 (23 Sept 1950), 98-102.
"The Wharf" *Woods and River Tales* (1980), 137-44.

Hails, Anna
"Sally" *Outset* 1973, 45-7.

Haiven, Larry‡
"Bingo the Oh-Shit Game" *Random* Dec [1968], 15-6.

Hajes, A.J.†
"He Speaks to Me of Alphonse" *Pier Spr* 7:4 (Aut 1982), 29-31.

Halbus, Frank W.‡
"A Soldier Returns" *Contact* 3:2 (Spr 1974), 23-6.

Halbus, Mary‡
"Recuperation at Nantucket" *Contact* 3:2 (Spr 1974), 8-12.

Hale, Barrie (?-1986)
"Come on Back to the Party" *Raven* No. 6 (Apr 1958), 10-1.
"An In Between Time" *Raven* No. 9 (Nov 1960), 14-26.
"The Parents of Pop" *TL* Nov 1979, 60, 156-8, 160.
"Premature Departures" *TL* Sept 1978, 36-7, 164, 166.

Haley, J.H.‡
"One Afternoon" *Amethyst* 4:1 (Aut 1964), 23-5.

Haley, Peter‡
"An Ode to the Night" *10:47* 1:3 (1967), 39-41.

Halfpenny, Tonia†
"The Monster" *Scrivener* 1:1 (Spr 1980), 5-9.

Hall, Christopher W.†
"Aftermath" *Stardust* 3:1 [n.d.], 27-37.
"Probably Over Thirty" *Stardust* 1:2 (1976), 27-45.
"Tailfeather" *Stardust* 1:1 (1975), 22-51.

Hall, Edwin‡
"Karelia Suite" *Scruncheons* 1:1 (1972), 51-4.

Hall, Elaine D.‡

"On Living Alone" *Images About Manitoba* 1:3 (Fall-Win 1976), 9-14.

Hallawell, Nancy‡

"For True Harmony" *Pedantics* 1965, 93-4.

Hallett, Susan‡

"The End of the Summer" *Portico* 1:2 [n.d.], 4-7.

Halliday, David (1948-)

THE BLACK BIRD Erin: Porcupine's Quill, 1982.

"Aaron" *DeKalb Literary Arts J* [date unknown] [Based on survey response].

"The Artist" *Split Level* 2:1 (1975), [2 pp].

"The Artist" *deKalb Literary Arts J* (U.S.) [date unknown] [Based on survey response].

"Breaking" *Stardancer* (U.S.) [date unknown] [Based on survey response].

"The Clown" CBC "Anthology" 24 Sept 1977.

"The Departed" *Harvest* Nos. 5/6 (Sept 1978), 52-4.

"End of the Road" *Whetstone* [date unknown] [Based on survey response].

"The End of the Romance" *Harvest* Nos. 5/6 (Sept 1978), 50-1.

"escape" *Van Streets* 1:1 (Spr 1982), [2 pp].

"Excerpts from Bogart's Diary" *Waves* 9:2 (Win 1981), 18-21.

"Excerpts from Bogart's Diary" *Black Bird* (1982), 7-8; 26-7; 43-4; 62-3; 89.

"Final Excerpt from Bogart's Diary" *Otherthan R* [date unknown] [Based on survey response].

"The Gunfight" *Waves* 10:3 (Win 1982), 32-48.

"Hooker" *Origins* 11:1 (Mar 1981), 67-8.

"the husband" *Repos* No. 33 (Spr 1981), 20-2.

"interlude" *Mam* 5:2/3 (Fall-Win 1981-82), [2 pp] [Listed as poem; survey response lists as story].

"Interview: Humphrey Bogart (After His Death)" *Acanthus* 3 (Apr 1980), 40-55.

"Interview: Humphrey Bogart (After His Death)" *Moose R* No. 6 (1982), 33-45.

"Interview: Humphrey Bogart (After His Death)" *Black Bird* (1982), 93-105.

"Interview: Humphrey Bogart (After His Death)" *Metavisions* (1983), 11-21.

"Jack's Dream" *Matrix* 2:2 (Win 1977), 14-5.

"The Last Fix" *Exile* 8:3/4 (1981), 132-3.

"Lower Than the Angels" *Stardancer* (U.S.) [date unknown] [Based on survey response].

"Mirror, Mirror" *Waves* 11:1 (Fall 1982), 30-42.

"Murder of a Candidate for a Post-Doctorate Degree" *Origins* [date unknown] [Based on survey response].

"Notes from a Diary " *Earth and You* [date unknown] [Based on survey response].

"On Reading the Rockies/Reaching Susan Musgrave" *Origins* 9:4 (Dec 1979), 8-13.

"On Reading the Rockies/Reaching Susan Musgrave" *Earth and You* 9 Nos. 39/40 [n.d.], 186-9.

"The Prince" *Whetstone* [date unknown] [Based on survey response].

"Seduction" *Stardancer* (U.S.) [date unknown] [Based on survey response].

"Suicide" *Stardancer* (U.S.) [date unknown] [Based on survey response].

"The Tenant" *Harvest* Nos. 5/6 (Sept 1978), 46-9.

'The Tenant" *Waves* 7:3 (Spr 1979), 19-21.
'The Tenant" *Maker* [date unknown] [Based on survey response].
'The Village" *CCWQ* 4:4 (1982), 8-10.
'The Village Contracts 4" *Mam* 6:1 (Sum 1982), [3 pp].
'The Village The Apartment 3" *Wot* 4:2 (Fall 1982), 16-23.
"A Walk" *New Writers' News* 2:1/2 (Win-Spr 1979-80), 25-6.
'War" *JCF* 4:3 No. 15 (1975), 27-43.
"the wedding" *Repos* No. 33 (Spr 1981), 15-20.
"the wedding" *Van Streets* 1:1 (Spr 1982), [4 pp].
'The Wife" *Exile* 8:3/4 (1981), 122-4.
'Yonge Street" *Earth and You* [date unknown] [Based on survey response].

Halonen, H.‡
'The Christmas Tree" *NF* 3:4 (Win 1954), 43-4.

Halstead, P.G.†
'Here Be Dragons" *Our Family* 26 (Dec 1974), 18-21.

Ham, R.K.‡
'The Unhappy Medium" *Varsity Lit Issue* Fri, 1 Feb 1952, 4.

Hambling, Jack (1927-)
"One Up for the Tories" *TickleAce* No. 2 (Apr 1978), 36-40.

Hamill, Tom‡
'Equality" *Driftwood* 1979, 7-8.

Hamilton, D.E.‡
'The Card in the Window" *AA* 54 (Mar 1964), 83.

Hamilton, Harry‡
'Pappa Falconi" *Contact* 3:4 (Win 1974), 3-9.

Hamilton, John‡
'The Forest and the Man" *UCR* Spr 1983, 23-7.
'Return to Eden" *UCR* 1981-82, 47-50.
'The Wasp" *UCR* 1982-83, 29.

Hamilton, Patricia‡
"Fishface's Leg" *West People* No. 200 (25 Aug 1983), 10-1.
"Leaves Must Fall" *Edmonton Journal* Fri, 3 Sept 1965, 31.

Hamilton, Susan
'Forward" *Body Politic* No. 54 (July 1979), 28-9.

Hamm, Mark‡
"Secrets" *Writing* No. 5 (Spr 1982), 32-4.

Hammarlow, Catherine‡
"Uncle Otto's Weighty Problem" *Beaver* 300 (Win 1969), 60-2.

Hammell, Steven Dale†

"Armagma Polareddon" *Cop Toad* 1:2 (July 1978), 18-33, 53-6.

"The Black Swans of the Loch Lothlomond" *Cop Toad* 1:1 (Dec 1976), 8-14, 17-28 [Novelette?].

"Mongrel and the Bear" *Dark Fantasy* No. 19 (1979), 4-13.

"Summer of Monsters" *Twilight Zone* 2:7 (Oct 1982), 20-6.

Hammond, Arthur

"When He Arrived Home" CBC "*Anthology*" 21 Jan 1958.

"When He Arrived Home" *Waterloo R* No. 5 (Sum 1960), 20-6.

Hancock, Anthony‡

"Seas to Armageddon ... and Beyond" *Forge* 27:1 (Feb 1965), 29-36.

Hancock, Ronald Lee

THE MAN SITTING IN PLACE PIGALLE AND OTHER SHORT SHORT STORIES Calgary: Chinook, 1973.

"An Affair in Yemen" *Man Sitting in Place Pigalle* (1973), 12-4.

"The Battle" *Man Sitting in Place Pigalle* (1973), 42-3.

"Behind the Wall" *Man Sitting in Place Pigalle* (1973), 37.

"The Day for a Fish" *Man Sitting in Place Pigalle* (1973), 5-7.

"El Toro" *Man Sitting in Place Pigalle* (1973), 26-7.

"George Twospot" *Man Sitting in Place Pigalle* (1973), 48-50.

"A Glass of Cognac" *Man Sitting in Place Pigalle* (1973), 9-11.

"The Great Bear Expedition" *Man Sitting in Place Pigalle* (1973), 45-7.

"The House" *Man Sitting in Place Pigalle* (1973), 33.

"The Making of a President" *Man Sitting in Place Pigalle* (1973), 38-9.

"The Mallorcan Concerto" *Man Sitting in Place Pigalle* (1973), 17-8.

"The Man Sitting in Place Pigalle" *Man Sitting in Place Pigalle* (1973), 1-2.

"The Model Boat" *Man Sitting in Place Pigalle* (1973), 22-3.

"On a Moroccan Roof" *Man Sitting in Place Pigalle* (1973), 24-5.

"Padre Martina" *Man Sitting in Place Pigalle* (1973), 29-30.

"The Physicist and the Poet" *Man Sitting in Place Pigalle* (1973), 19-21.

"A Sketch of a Junk Pile" *Man Sitting in Place Pigalle* (1973), 34-5.

"The Student" *Man Sitting in Place Pigalle* (1973), 40-1.

"Vera Cruz" *Man Sitting in Place Pigalle* (1973), 52-5.

"Waiting for the 6:40" *Man Sitting in Place Pigalle* (1973), 15-6.

"The Witch in the Woods" *Man Sitting in Place Pigalle* (1973), 56-7.

Handler, Denyse‡

"A Little Folk Tale for Pro-Lifers" *Uncertified Human* 5:9 (Feb 1978), 22-3.

Hanley, Kathleen‡

"The Tom" *Acta Vic* 103:1 (Spr 1979), 42-5.

Hannaford, Nigel†

"The Last Hour of Irena Baronovitch" *Treeline* 2 (1983), 94-102.

Hannam, Appleton‡

"Satire on Sanity" *Either/Or* No. 9 (win 1970), [4 pp].

Hannant, Larry†
"The Butchers" *Alive* No. 42 [1975], 19.
"Light Traveller" *New Q* 1:2 (Sum 1981), 58-63.

Hansen, Frances E.‡
"For Better or for Worse" *Amethyst* 1:1 (Spr 1962), 9-15.

Hansen, Laurence†
"The Wonder of Light" *War Cry* 20 Dec 1958, 6, 18.

Hanson, Esther Schneider‡
"Image without Flaw" *AA* 58 (Feb 1968), 45-6, 48-9.
"A Keg of Herring for Linnea" *AA* 55 (Sept 1964), 43, 45-7, 50.
"The Night of Farbror Pelle's Ghost" *AA* 54 (Oct 1963), 59-64.

Hanson, Hart‡
"A Day at the Zoo" *UCR* Spr 1980, 28-9.
"Never Go to Dinner" *UC Gargoyle* 25 (5 Nov 1980), 9.

Hanson, R.D.‡
"Winter Day" *Industrial Sabotage* No. 14 [Mar 1983], [3 pp].

Hara, John T.‡
"The Problem of the Woman's Point of View" *Can Business* 24 (Feb 1951), 44-5, 88.

Harasym, Sally†
"The Anniversary" *Antig R* No. 46 (Sum 1981), 37-8.

Harasymiw, Bohdan‡
"Another Fable" *Inside* No. 2 [Nov 1964], 9 [Satire].
"A Fable" *Inside* No. 2 [Nov 1964], 8 [Satire].

Hardin, Herschel
"The Devil and the Disciple" *Tam R* No. 24 (Sum 1962), 34-45.

Harding, Cy†
"Coffee for the Bailiff" *NF* 2:1 (Spr 1953), 15-7.

Harding, John†
"A Carriage Affair" *CBC "Anthology"* 26 July 1980.
"The Fishes Hornpipe" *Wot* 1:1 [n.d.], 13-9.
"His Eyes in the Storm" *Repos* No. 25 (Spr 1979), 9-17.
"The Joy of Elevated Thoughts" *Nebula* No. 8 (1978), 3-31.
"A Terminal Report" *CBC "Anthology"* 26 May 1979.

Harding, Mark‡
"Olivia's Disappointment" *Scar Fair* 7 (1980), 7-9.

Hardy, W.G. (1895-)
"The Czech Dog" *Can Golden West* 8 (Sum 1972), 30-1.
"I'm But a Stranger Here" *CHJ* Feb 1951, 22-4, 27-9, 40-1, 44.
"The Philistine" *MM* 63 (15 Nov 1950), 12, 46, 48-9, 52, 54.

Harestad, J.B.‡
    "The Gifts" *Stump* 1:2 (Fall 1977), 66-70.

Hargreaves, H.A. (1928-)
    NORTH BY 2000 Toronto: Peter Martin, 1975.
    "Brothers" *Newest R* 4 (May 1979), 8-9.
    "CAIN[n]" *New Writings in SF* 20 (1975), 83-133.
    "CAIN[n]" *North by 2000* (1975), 57-99.
    "Dead to the World" *New Writings in SF* 11 (1968), 139-56.
    "Dead to the World" *New Writings in SF* 8 (1971), 125-41.
    "Dead to the World" *North by 2000* (1975), 1-15.
    "Dead to the World" *Heartland* (1983), 45-58.
    "In His Moccasins" *Calgary Mag* 1 (Aug 1979), 36-8, 40-2, 61.
    "In His Moccasins" *Edmonton Mag* 1 (Aug 1979), 32-4, 36, 38-9.
    "Infinite Variation" *Other Canadas* (1979), 214-9.
    "More Things in Heaven and Earth" *New Writings in SF* 17 (1970), 11-66 [Novella?].
    "More Things in Heaven and Earth" *North by 2000* (1975), 115-60.
    "Protected Environment" *North by 2000* (1975), 43-55.
    "Protected Environment" *Alberta Diamond Jubilee Anthology* (1979), 176-85.
    "Requiem for a Bookman" *CBC [Edm] "Alberta Anthology"* 4 Sept 1982.
    "Tangled Web" *New Writings in SF* 21 (1972; 1973), 117-46.
    "Tangled Web" *North by 2000* (1975), 17-41.
    "Tee Vee Man" *New Worlds* 46 (Dec 1963), 60-71.
    "Tee Vee Man" *Lambda I and Other Stories* (1965), 57-70 [Based on *North by 2000*].
    "Tee Vee Man" *Lambda I y otros relatos* (1967), 61-77 [As "El Hombre de la television"; based on *North by 2000*].
    "Tee Vee Man" *North by 2000* (1975), 101-13.
    "Tee Vee Man" *Air* (1977), 54-60.

Harington, C.R.
    "Death at Bridport Inlet" *Golden West* Jan-Feb 1966, 20.

Harley, Jorda Anne†
    "Petruniach" *Matrix* 1:1 (Spr 1975), 11-4.

Harley, Peter
    "Good Citizen" *Twelve Newfoundland Short Stories* (1982), 14-8.
    "Used Stars" *Antig R* No. 52 (Win 1983), 43-51.

Harlow, Robert (1923-)
    "Heroes" *Matinees Daily* (1981), 89-101.
    "The Sound of a Horn" *Klanak Islands* (1959), 21-33.

Harnden, John‡
    "The Visit" *Muskeg R* 5 [n.d.], 24-5.

Harper, A.W.J.‡
    "The Right to Life" *Origins* 10:4 (Dec 1980), 70-1.

Harper, Mandy‡
   "Only the Children" *Portico* 3:4 (1979), 5-7.
   "This Is Blue" *Portico* 2:3 (Spr 1978), 13-5.

Harper, Richard C.†
   "Cry 'Warlock' Softly Angel" *WCR* 1:2 (Fall 1966), 17-9.

Harrington, Michael F.
   "Carcajou" *Stories from Pacific & Arctic Canada* (1974), 108-18.
   "The Great Debate at Squid Tickle" *Weekend* 3 (10 Jan 1953), 26.
   "Lukey's Boat" *MM* 64 (15 Nov 1951), 43.
   "The Schemer" *Weekend* 4 (9 Oct 1954), 32-3, 42, 53.

Harris, Beverly
   "The Day They Set Out" *Three Times Five* (1983), 25-33.
   "Light" *Three Times Five* (1983), 17-24.
   "Oh, Sylvia" *Three Times Five* (1983), 34-41.
   "Queenie" *Three Times Five* (1983), 11-6.
   "The Soma Building" *Three Times Five* (1983), 42-52.

Harris, Bob‡
   "The Telephone Call" *Alive* No. 118 (24 June 1978), 7-9.

Harris, C.K.‡
   "The Heiress" *Origins* 9:2 (June 1979), 30-2.

Harris, Christopher‡
   "A Sentimental Love-Story" *TUR* 92:2 (Apr 1979), 11-3.

Harris, Fredie Steve‡
   "The History Lesson" *Can Month* Mar 1963, 20-1 [Satire].
   "Tyrannosaurus Rex" *Can Month* 2:3 (Mar 1962), 38-9 [Satire].

Harris, Janice†
   "The Caprice Hotel" *Cap R* No. 5 (Spr 1974), 29-32.

Harris, John (1942-)
   "Cowboy" *Per* No. 6 (Fall 1979), 53-7.
   "Dean Pretty and the Dragon" *Caledonian* 4:2 (Jan 1976), 16-23.
   "A Dialogue Concerning the Moon" *Caledonian* 7:1 (Oct 1977), 22-32.
   "The Giant" *Pulp Mill* (1977), 45-51.
   "Leaves" *Repos* No. 5 (Jan 1973), 30-6.
   "Local Initiatives" *Cap R* No. 26 (1983), 56-66.
   "Making Light of the Love in the Moon" *Writing* No. 7 (Fall 1983), 23-6.
   "The Man with the Bad Bladder" *Pulp Mill* (1977), 52-9.
   "Man's Best Friend" *Repos* No. 3 [1972], 20-45.
   "Mr. Image" *Cap R* 1:4 (Fall-Win 1973), 20-4.
   "The Quarry" *Repos* No. 8 (Fall 1973), 46-50.
   "The Quarry" *Pulp Mill* (1977), 43-4.
   "Root Hog" *Roothog* (1981), 55-6.
   "Rose and the Red Stallion" *Caledonian* 6:2 (Nov 1976), 8-12.
   "The Wealth of Nations" *Per* Nos. 7/8 (Win 1981), 76-81.

Harris, John Norman (1915-)

"The Best Years of Their Live" *MM* 71 (1 Mar 1958), 25, 30, 32-5.

"The Bolshevik and the Wicked Witch" *MM* 66 (1 Apr 1953), 18-9, 58, 60, 62, 64, 66.

"It Takes a Woman to Run a Railroad" *MM* 69 (18 Aug 1956), 22-3, 30-3.

"Mail" *MM* 63 (15 Dec 1950), 13, 47-9.

"Porky Proctor's Downfall" *MM* 68 (19 Mar 1955), 24-5, 45-52.

"Postcard from Abdul" *Weekend* 3 (5 Sept 1953), 8-9.

"The Stowaway" *MM* 71 (18 Jan 1958), 22-3, 32-6.

Harris, Marcia‡

"Barriers" *Raven* 2 [No. 4] (Spr 1957), 33-40.

Harris, Paula†

[Untitled] *Waves* 5:2/3 (Spr 1977), 32-4.

Harris, Walter†

"The Day Auntie Became a Zombie" *Lib* 31 (Oct 1954), 33, 52, 54, 56-8, 60-1.

"The Embrace of Death" *Lib* 31 (Dec 1954), 28, 70, 72-3, 76.

"The Experiment" *Lib* 31 (Sept 1954), 26, 60-2.

"The Great Banff Mountain Climbing Scandal" *Lib* 36 (Apr 1959), 30, 68-70.

"The Great Rosedale Beauty Contest" *Lib* 38 (May 1961), 22, 40, 42-3.

"How My Auntie Became Prime Minister" *Lib* 35 (May 1958), 37, 48-50.

"How My Auntie Communed with the Ghost of Mackenzie King" *Lib* 36 (Nov 1959), 35, 42, 48-9.

"Mix a Little Murder in the Wine, Dear" *Lib* 35 (Nov 1958), 25, 74.

"My Auntie's Christmas Flight to the Moon" *Lib* 35 (Dec 1958), 30, 60, 63-4.

"The Schoolmistress and the Sheik of Ontario" *Lib* 35 (Apr 1958), 28, 62.

Harrison, A.S.A.†

"Ada's Desire" *Cap R* Nos. 8/9 (Fall-Spr 1975-76), 13-21.

"Ada's Desire" *Miss Chat* 14 (2 Aug 1977), 80, 90, 92, 94-5, 99.

"The Mechanic" *Imp* 9:2 (Fall 1981), 49-51.

"Nellie's Mistake" *Imp* 8:2 (Spr 1980), 45-6.

"A Walk in the Park" *Story So Far* 3 (1974), 29-31.

Harrison, D.B.‡

"Tommy Arrives" *Anglican Outlook* 11:5 (Mar 1956), 16-7 [Non-fiction?].

Harrison, Devin

"Even Dying Takes a Long Time" *Mal R* No. 44 (Oct 1977), 124-38.

Harrison, E.W.‡

"Accident-Prone" *Stories with John Drainie* (1963), 192-7.

Harrison, Edelmera†

"A Ghost's Sense of Humour" *Outset* 1973, 48-56.

Harrison, Elizabeth‡

"Canadiaiana" *TUR* 72:4 (Mar 1959), 10-6 [Satire].

"Diary from France" *TUR* 69:4 (Mar 1957), 26-30.

Harrison, John Kent (1946-)
"Drugstore Cowboy" *Weekend* 29 (4 Aug 1979), 6-9.

Harrison, June‡
"My Uncle – The Engineer" *Stump* 4:1/2 (Spr 1980), 29-33.

Harrison, Kim‡
"Deep Inside Woodwards" *Grain* 7:3 [1979], 42-5.

Harrop, Gerry
THE THREE LOVES OF MONICA BLAKE AND OTHER STORIES Hantsport,
N.S.: Lancelot Press, 1981.
"The Maiden" *Three Loves of Monica Blake* (1981), 42-61.
"Space" *Three Loves of Monica Blake* (1981), 30-41.
"The Three Loves of Monica Blake" *Three Loves of Monica Blake* (1981), 7-29.

Harrow, K.J.†
"The Search by 'Jorge Luis Borges' " *Antig R* No. 13 (Spr 1973), 53-9.

Hart, Anne
"The Friday Everything Changed" *Chat* 49 (Apr 1976), 42, 100, 103-4 [Also
entitled "Next Week This Time"].
"The Friday Everything Changed" *Crossroads* 2 (1979), 12-21.
"The Friday Everything Changed" *Early September* (1980) [Based on survey
response].
"The Friday Everything Changed" *Contexts* 2 (1981), 3-9.
"The Friday Everything Changed" *Connections* 1 (1981) [Based on survey
response].
"The Friday Everything Changed" *In Your Own Words* (1982), 234-40.
"The Friday Everything Changed" *Responding to Reading* (1983) [Based on
survey response].
"Help Me, Hepplewhite" *Blasty Bough* (1976), 61-9.
"Help Me, Hepplewhite" *CBC [Hal] "Radio Noon Three"* 1978 [Based on survey
response].
"Help Me, Hepplewhite" *CBC [Hal] "Audio Stage"* 1979.
"Help Me, Hepplewhite" *Easterly* (1983), 64-71.
"A Lovely Place to Visit" *Chat* 46 (Mar 1973), 34, 56, 60-2.
"Next Week This Time" *From This Place* (1977), 143-51 [Also entitled 'The
Friday Everything Changed"; based on survey response].
"Next Week This Time" *Stages* 2 (1980).

Hart, Don‡
"Selected Works" *Laom R* 2:1 (Mar 1976), 15-7.
[Untitled] *Laom R* 2:1 (Mar 1976), 156.

Hart, Kathy†
"Lin" *Intervales* No. 2 (1960), 17-9.
"Shawnigan" *Intervales* [No. 1] (1959), 11-4.

Hart, Michael‡
"Play It Again, Eddy" *CBC "Alberta Anthology"* 18 Oct 1980.

Hart, William‡

"The Stigmata" *Forge* 25:1 (Feb 1963), 67-83.

Hartman, Matt†

"Renee" *Prism* 14:1 (Aut 1974), 65-75.

Harvey, Jennifer A. Becks†

"The Acorn" *Onward* 2 Oct 1960, 630-1.

"Acorn" *Onward* 12 Mar 1961, 170-1, 175.

"Bricks, Boards and Books" *Onward* 24 Apr 1960, 266-7.

"The Cat-Hater" *Onward* 8 Jan 1961, 26-7, 30-1.

"Chez Nous" *Onward* 7 Jan 1962, 12-3, 15.

"Country Style" *Onward* 19 June 1960, 394-5, 398.

"Culinary Confusion" *Onward* 5 Apr 1959, 218-9.

"Danger – Girl at Work" *Onward* 27 Jan 1959, 56-8.

"Debut" *Onward* 11 Feb 1962, 12-5.

"The Disruptors" *Onward* 1 Mar 1959, 134-5, 141.

"Girl on the Beach" *Onward* 14 Aug 1960, 513-5.

"A Glimpse of Eden" *Onward* 10 Oct 1965, 12-3.

"Holiday for Mum" *Onward* 24 Aug 1958, 529-30.

"Horrid Upheavals" *Onward* 10 May 1959, 294-5.

"The Horticulturalist" *Onward* 27 Feb 1966, 12-4.

"The Invalid" *Onward* 6 Jan 1963, 12-3.

"The Invalid" *Onward* Apr 1968, 34-6.

"A King's Daughter" *Onward* 6 Jan 1957, 6-8.

"The Letter" *Onward* 20 Nov 1955, 737-9.

" 'Letters without Ending' " *Onward* 27 July 1958, 468-70.

"Lived in Full" *Onward* 23 Apr 1961, 266-7, 270.

"Lost for Words" *Onward* 11 Jan 1959, 26-7.

"The Mink Jacket" *Onward* 15 Sept 1957, 581-2.

"The Mink Jacket" *Onward* 13 Mar 1966, 5, 13.

"The Mix-Up" *Onward* 25 Dec 1955, 823.

"Moving In" *Onward* 5 Feb 1961, 90-1, 95.

"Mr. Ling and the Petunias" *Onward* 13 May 1962, 3-4.

"Mr. Ling and the Petunias" *Onward* 28 Jan 1968, 3-4.

"Mr. Willis and the Heavenly Twins" *Onward* 17 June 1956, 389, 398-9.

"Nothing to It" *Onward* 20 Nov 1960, 742-3.

"The Outsider" *Onward* 27 Sept 1959, 611-2.

"Pink Clouds" *Onward* 6 Dec 1959, 778-9.

"Reprieve for Signor Scagnetti" *Onward* 6 Sept 1959, 570-1.

"Secret Admirer" *Onward* 22 Sept 1963, 4-6.

"Six of One" *Onward* 18 Sept 1960, 602-3, 606-7.

"Speakez-vous the Engleesho?" *Onward* 13 Oct 1957, 644-5, 651.

"Surprise for Maria" *Onward* 18 May 1958, 305-6, 314-5.

"There in Spirit" *Onward* 21 May 1961, 332-5.

"Thick and Thin" *Onward* 7 July 1957, 424-6.

"The Tip" *Onward* 7 Dec 1958, 776-7, 783.

"To Chase a Cowboy Hat" *Onward* 9 Apr 1961, 228-30.

"A Touch of Magic" *Onward* 9 Mar 1958, 148-9.

"The Treasure Chest" *Onward* 5 Oct 1958, 629-30, 634.

"The True Measure" *Onward* 25 Feb 1962, 3-4, 13.

"Ups and Downs" *Onward* 29 Oct 1961, 12-5.
"Water Babies" *Onward* 19 May 1957, 308-9.
"We Did It Ourselves" *Onward* 7 Oct 1956, 641-3.
"Wedding Bells" *Onward* 1 Feb 1959, 70-1, 75.
"A Woman to Pity" *Onward* 10 Dec 1961, 4-6.

Harvey, Kay L.†
"Henrietta the Porcupine" *Onward* 12 June 1966, 12-3 [Non-fiction?].
"I'll Never Forget Miss Lemon" *Rapport* June 1970, 30-1.

Harvey-Jellie, Nora
"Return of the Shepherd" *FH* 20 July 1950, 16-7, 19.

Harvor, Beth (1936-)
WOMEN AND CHILDREN Ottawa: Oberon Press, 1973.
"Countries" *73: New Canadian Stories* 131-43.
"Countries" *Women and Children* (1973), 97-111.
"A Day at the Front, a Day at the Border" *Fid* No. 91 (Fall 1971), 85-97.
"A Day at the Front, a Day at the Border" *Women and Children* (1973), 112-29.
"The Enchantment" *TL* Nov 1981, 49, 170-2, 175-8, 180, 183.
"Foreigners" *Penguin Book of Canadian Short Stories* (1980), 319-37.
"Heart Trouble" *New Yorker* 55 (12 Mar 1979), 38-47.
"Heart Trouble" *Penguin Book of Modern Canadian Short Stories* (1982), 483-501.
"The Hudson River" *Fid* No. 88 (Win 1971), 67-83 [Also entitled "Small Mercies"].
"The Hudson River" *Women and Children* (1973), 130-52.
"Lapsang and Oolong" *SN* 90 (Nov 1975), 51-8.
"Lies in Search of the Truth" *UWR* 7:1 (Fall 1971), 13-26.
"Lies in Search of the Truth" *Women and Children* (1973), 33-51.
"Magicians" *72: New Canadian Stories* 64-74.
"Magicians" *Women and Children* (1973), 75-86.
"Magicians" *Modern Canadian Stories* (1975), 269-79.
"Monster Baby" *Women and Children* (1973), 5-13.
"More Like Birds Than Birds" *Women and Children* (1973), 70-4.
"The Needle's Eye" *Women and Children* (1973), 87-96.
"Our Lady of All the Distances" *Women and Children* (1973), 153-64.
"Our Lady of All the Distances" *Women in Canadian Literature* (1976), 178-84.
"Pain Was My Portion" *Hudson R* 23 (1970), 495-509.
"Pain Was My Portion" *Best American Short Stories* 1971 118-33.
"Pain Was My Portion" *Stories from Atlantic Canada* (1973), 117-33.
"Pain Was My Portion" *Women and Children* (1973), 14-32.
"The Paraphernalia of Consolation" *Media* No. 1 (1966), 34-9.
"Small Mercies" *Miss Chat* 13 (11 Nov 1976), 94-6, 98-106 [Also entitled "The Hudson River"].
"Stars, Moons" *JCF* 4:3 No. 15 (1975), 52-61 [Also entitled "Travelling On"].
"Summer Mournings, 1959" *Women and Children* (1973), 52-69.
"Sun After the War" CBC "*Anthology*" 15 Oct 1977.
"Tea with Katherine Mansfield's Sister" *QQ* 80 (1973), 213-8.
"Travelling On" *77: Best Canadian Stories* 37-63 [Also entitled "Stars, Moons"].

Harwood, Mary‡
"Loyalty" *Muse* 59:4 (Apr 1950), 15.

Haskins, David†
"The Final Solution" *Viewpoints* 10:1 (Spr 1979), 50-6 [Based on real incident].
"Getting Ready" *Fruits of Experience* (1978), 43-52.
"The Room" *Fid* No. 117 (Spr 1978), 45-51.
"Thirteen Steps" *JCF* Nos. 28/29 (1980), 5-10.

Hassan, Ray‡
"The Autobiography of Pax Balanski" *Rude* Prelim No. 3 [n.d.], [4 pp].

Hauser, Gwen‡
"Isis Returns" *Strange Faeces* No. 17 (June 1975), 54-5.

Havelock, Ray‡
"The Case of the 7 Note Song" *Bakka* No. 7 (Fall 1977), 50-61.

Hawkes, Mark S.†
"The Bannard Stone" *Read Ch* 2:1 (Spr 1983), 81-94.

Hawkins, David Geoffrey (1929-)
"Dangerous Mission" *Saskatchewan Writing* 1960 40-5.

Hawkins, Susan C.†
"The Labour" *Scrivener* 2:2 (Fall 1981), 13-4.

Hawkins, William‡
"they who stood on guard" *Inscape* No. 4 (Win 1960), 24-6 [Prose poem?].

Hawrelko, John†
"The Beggar at Bedford" *CBC [Edm] "Alberta Anthology"* 13 Nov 1982.
"The Machine" *CBC [Edm] "Alberta Anthology"* 27 Sept 1980.
"Two Chained Jack" *NeWest R* 4 (Jan 1979), 11-2.

Hawryluk, Paul
"Just for the Sport" *Companion* 39 (July-Aug 1976), 27-30.
"Second Thoughts" *Companion* 42 (Feb 1979), 26-7.
"Time to Live" *Companion* 38 (May 1975), 18-22.

Hawson, Joan‡
"A Man in the Park" *TUR* 75.2 (Jan 1962), 49-53.

Hawthorn, Margaret‡
"Chad: Its Rise, Its Age, Its Fall" *Raven* No. 5 (Dec 1957), 11-4.

Hay, Eldon R.‡
"Truro/Summer/'73" *Sand Patterns* No. 14 (Sum 1975), [6 pp].

Hay, Elizabeth†
"Nights" *Raven* No. 2 (Spr 1981), [4 pp].
"Stan" *Per* Nos. 7/8 (Win 1981), 29-30.
"Yellowknife" *Per* No. 4 (Fall 1978), 43-5.

Hayes, Ada†
"Hook Line and Mrs. Sinclair" *Voices of Kitimat 1967* 127-30.

Hayes, Anne‡
"The First Mate Takes Over" *Better Boating* 11 (Mar 1975), 30-1.

Hayes, Diana†
"The Birds and the Bells in Bobby's Tower – A Parable" *event* 12:2 (1983), 108-15.

Haynes, D. (1949?-)
"Two Sundays" *event* 5:1 [n.d.], 48-55.

Hayward, Colin J. (1943?-)
"The Captain" *Folio* 17:1 (Fall 1964), 11-3.
"Echoes from Gethsemane" *Folio* 16:2 (Spr 1964), 40-2.

Hazell, Mary
"The Blockade Runners" *Chat* 43 (Mar 1970), 26, 85-8, 90, 92.
"Border of Deceit" *Chat* 44 (Apr 1971), 28-9, 90-4, 96.
"Checkpoint" *Chat* 41 (Feb 1968), 30-1, 58, 60-2.
"Escape by Night" *Chat* 47 (Feb 1974), 38, 48, 50, 52-3.
"Scent of Gold" *Chat* 45 (July 1972), 27, 51-4, 56.

Heal, Jeanne‡
"In Broad Daylight" *West People* No. 202 (8 Sept 1983), 14-5.

Heard, F.E.
"The Reconcilement" *Living Message* 86 (Mar 1975), 19-20.
"Water Under the Bridge" *Living Message* 85 (Feb 1974), 22-3.
"Water Under the Bridge" *Companion* 38 (Oct 1975), 24-6.

Heath, Jean†
"My Grandmother" *Pier Spr* 4:2 (Spr 1979), 20-5.

Heath, Martin‡
"Gotta See That Man" *NF* 1:1 (Win 1952), 9-10.

Heath, Terence (1936-)
"the aunt" *the truth* (1972), 34.
"the aunt" *Stories Plus* (1979), 96.
"the balloons" *the truth* (1972), 23.
"the basement" *the truth* (1972), 8.
"the basement" *Stories Plus* (1979), 92-3.
"the basement" *New Worlds* (1980), 136.
"the bicycle" *the truth* (1972), 40-2.
"the brown dog" *the truth* (1972), 4-5.
"the brown dog" *Stories Plus* (1979), 91-2.
"the caretaker" *the truth* (1972), 39.
"the chinaman" *the truth* (1972), 12-3.
"the coach" *the truth* (1972), 64-5.
"the collection" *the truth* (1972), 24-5.

"the collection" *Stories Plus* (1979), 94-5.
"the collection" *New Worlds* (1980), 137-8.
"the dogfight" *the truth* (1972), 43.
"the erection" *the truth* (1972), 14.
"the fart" *the truth* (1972), 48.
"the father" *the truth* (1972), 35-7.
"the father" *Stories Plus* (1979), 96-7.
"the feel" *the truth* (1972), 69.
"the fight" *the truth* (1972), 52-3.
"the filling" *the truth* (1972), 32-3.
"the frogs" *the truth* (1972), 1-2.
"the frogs" *Story So Far 2* (1973), 115-6.
"the hard" *the truth* (1972), 27-8.
"the honeywagon" *the truth* (1972), 61-3.
"the hunters" *the truth* (1972), 21-2.
"the icehouse" *the truth* (1972), 31.
"the ink" *the truth* (1972), 66.
"the knock-out" *the truth* (1972), 9-10.
"the mother" *the truth* (1972), 3.
"the mother" *Stories Plus* (1979), 91.
"the mountie" *the truth* (1972), 50-1.
"the mountie" *Stories Plus* (1979), 98-9.
"the police" *the truth* (1972), 58.
"the police" *New Worlds* (1980), 138-9.
"the post" *the truth* (1972), 15.
"a proper burial" *CFM* No. 11 (Aut 1973), 4-15.
"a proper burial" *Sundogs* (1980), 55-8.
"the psalmist" *Story So Far 3* (1974), 49-55.
"the rinkhut" *the truth* (1972), 38.
"the shingle arrow gun" *the truth* (1972), 19-20.
"the soldier" *the truth* (1972), 44-5.
"the soldier" *Stories Plus* (1979), 97-8.
"the strap" *the truth* (1972), 16-7.
"the strap" *Story So Far 2* (1973), 114-5.
"the strap" *Stories Plus* (1979), 93-4.
"the strap" *New Worlds* (1980), 140-1.
"the strawberries" *the truth* (1972), 49.
"the strawberries" *New Worlds* (1980), 139.
"the strip" *the truth* (1972), 6-7.
"the sunday school lesson" *the truth* (1972), 46.
"the sunday school lesson" *Story So Far 2* (1973), 117.
"the swimming trunks" *the truth* (1972), 29-30.
"the tail" *the truth* (1972), 54-5.
"the tail" *Stories Plus* (1979), 98-100.
"the tail" *New Worlds* (1980), 141.
"the team" *the truth* (1972), 67-8.
"the theologue" *the truth* (1972), 59-60.
"the tongue" *the truth* (1972), 11.
"the tongue" *Stories Plus* (1979), 93.
"the truants" *the truth* (1972), 47.

"the truth" *the truth* (1972), 56-7.
"the truth" *Story So Far* 2 (1973), 112-3.
"the truth" *Stories Plus* (1979), 100-1.
"the voice" *the truth* (1972), 26.
"the witch" *the truth* (1972), 18.

Heather [pseudonym]

"The Watchers" *Selections from the CFUW Writing Project* 1978-79 [1979], 22-7.

Heather, H.M.†

"Man Against Machine" *Atl Guardian* 10 (July 1953), 12-5.
"Troubled Waters" *Atl Guardian* 9 (Sept 1952), 29-33.

Heatley, Marney†

"Megan's Vampire" *New Q* 3:1 (Spr 1983), 15-24.
"Tiger and Me" *Toronto Star* Sun, 5 Oct 1980, D5.

Heavisides, Martin†

"The First Ever Use of the Comparison Test in Advertising History" *Targya* 1:2 (Fall 1973), 38-43.
"Slice of Life" *Rampike* 3:2 [1983?], 55.

Hebb, Marian‡

"The Poetry of Politics" *Acta Vic* 82:2 (Feb 1958), 5-7.

Hebert, Robbie‡

[Untitled] *Communicator* Oct 1974, 42.

Heble, Ajay

THE BURGER JOINT WAS CLOSED THE BURGER JOINT WAS CLOSED Toronto: Rheta Press, 1983.
"Confidence of the Balcony Phantoms" *UCR* 1981-82, 41-3.
"Confidence of the Balcony Phantoms" *Burger Joint Was Closed* (1983), [3 pp].
"Construction in the Fog" *UCR* 1982-83, 9-11.
"Construction in the Fog" *Burger Joint Was Closed* (1983), [3 pp] [Monologue?].
"Dry Spots" *Burger Joint Was Closed* (1983), [4 pp].
"Pitcher Has a Rubber Nose" *Burger Joint Was Closed* (1983), [2 pp].
"Slingshot" *Burger Joint Was Closed* (1983), [2 pp].
"Slipping on the Same Step Twice" *Burger Joint Was Closed* (1983), [1 p].
"Starring the Giraffe" *UCR* Win 1983, 19-20.
"Unbalanced Diet" *Burger Joint Was Closed* (1983), [2 pp].

Heckbert, Steve†

"Mir"michi Squash" *First Encounter* 7 (1975-77), 10-1.
"Stroke of Twelve" *First Encounter* 8 (1977-78), 20-1.

Hedges, Doris

"The Engagement Book" *CHJ* Apr 1951, 9, 42, 44, 48, 50-1, 54, 56.
"Masquerade" *CHJ* Mar 1957, 31, 74-7.

Hedley, Leslie‡

"The Tallest Jewish Basketball Player in the World" *WCR* 6:2 (Oct 1971), 40-3.

Hedley, Peter‡
"The Frog" *Nova Canada* 1:1 (May 1969), 15-7.

Hedlin, Ralph
"The Outlaw Hounds" *FH* 5 Sept 1957, 24-5, 29.
"Papa Passes Judgment" *FH* 19 Aug 1954, 24-5, 31.
"The Perambulating Pastor" *FH* 2 Aug 1956, 18-9.

Heide, Christopher (1951-)
"Driving Home in the Rain" *Alch* 1:3 (1976), [7 pp].
"In a Shopkeeper's Window" *Karaki* No. 5 (Dec 1975), 38-40.
"The Last Day Before My Father's Holiday" *Chel J* 3 (Nov-Dec 1977), 287-90.
"Letter from Matt Arthur's Fishpond" *CFM* No. 18 (Sum 1975), 40-9.
"A Photograph of Man" *Nebula* No. 3 (1976), 66-8.
"Ted Slaumwhite's Garden" *Alpha* 2:2 (Oct 1977), 5-6, 9, 23.

Heide, Reg‡
"Goddamned War" *Nightwinds* 2:1 (Spr 1980), 17-9.

Heine, Henrich‡
"A Passover Eve" *CJO* 21 (Apr 1983), 9-10.

Hekkanen, Ernest (1947-)
"All Night Gas Bar" *event* 11:1 (1982), 124-9.
"Antique Gertie Laughed" *Literary R* (U.S.) 14 (1970-71), 168-76.
"The Bather" *event* 9:2 (1980), 50-6.
"The Black Tom" *Waves* 8:3 (Spr 1980), 15-7.
"Bring Back the Bands, Please" *Fid* No. 129 (Spr 1981), 15-30.
"Cadillacs and Chevies Don't Mix" *Waves* 5:2/3 (Spr 1977), 10-22.
"Cadillacs and Chevies Don't Mix" *Second Impressions* (1981), 77-92.
"Chasing After Carnivals" *Fid* No. 120 (Win 1979), 48-59.
"Chasing After Carnivals" *Second Impressions* (1981), 93-110.
"The Confession" *Chel J* 5 (Nov-Dec 1979), 263-5.
"The Day After" *Pier Spr* Aut 1978, 10-7.
"The Disarrayed" *Literary R* (U.S.) 12 (1969), 477-84.
"A Faithful Friend" *Des* 9:1/2 Nos. 20/21 (1978), 72-9.
"The Fatal Error" *Mal R* No. 55 (July 1980), 124-30.
"Have a Little Decency" *Quarry* 27:1 (Win 1978), 23-30.
"Have a Little Decency" *Second Impressions* (1981), 122-31.
"I Work in the City" *Prism* 15:2/3 (Sum-Fall 1976), 79-84.
"In the New World" *Nw J* Nos. 18/19 (1980), 110-5.
"Plut's Discovery" *Chel J* 4 (Mar-Apr 1978), 77-80.
"The Rite" *CFM* Nos. 32/33 (1979), 15-21.
"The Rite" *Second Impressions* (1981), 111-21.
"The Successor" *Mal R* No. 62 (July 1982), 129-43.
"The Taking of Lake Shutney" *event* 12:2 (1983), 48-64.

Heller, Sheryl‡
"The Wheel" *Pom Seed* 1982, 40-1.

Helman, Cecil‡

"The Three Disguised Invasions of Earth" *Titmouse R* No. 6 (Sum-Fall 1976), 19-21.

Helwig, David (1938-)

THE STREETS OF SUMMER Ottawa: Oberon Press, 1969.

"An Act of Love" *CBC "Anthology"* 25 Oct 1969.

"Adam on the Art of Dying" *QQ* 85 (1978-79), 608-14.

"After School" *Quarry* 15:2 (Nov 1965), 27-9.

"Among the Trees of the Park" *CF* 48 (May 1968), 42-4.

"Among the Trees of the Park" *Streets of Summer* (1969), 138-43.

"Aria da Capo" *80: Best Canadian Stories* 99-114.

"A Christmas Mouse" *UC Gargoyle* 19 Dec 1958, 2-3.

"The Colonel" *QQ* 70 (1963), 233-6.

"The Colonel" *Streets of Summer* (1969), 124-7.

"Deerslayer" *Varsity Lit Issue* Fri, 18 Mar 1960, 6.

"Deerslayer" *CF* 42 (Sept 1962), 134.

"Deerslayer" *Streets of Summer* (1969), 111-4.

"Deerslayer" *Canadian Anthology* (1974), 558-9.

"Dogfight" *Undergrad* Spr 1958, [3 pp].

"Dogfight" *UTR* 1 (1958), 21-2.

"The Fall of a Sparrow" *Undergrad* Spr 1958, [3 pp].

"The Harrying of Bokalewski" *Exchange* 2:3 (Feb-Mar 1962), 55-60.

"The Heat of Summer" *CF* 39 (Apr 1959), 8-10.

"The Heat of Summer" *CBC "Anthology"* 2 June 1961.

"Heather from Swanage" *Streets of Summer* (1969), 128-34.

"A Hook into the Rough" *Quarry* 15:4 (Aug 1966), 24-30.

"A Hook into the Rough" *Streets of Summer* (1969), 115-23.

"A Hook into the Rough" *Great Canadian Sports Stories* (1979), 112-21.

"A Hundred Things Forgotten" *Streets of Summer* (1969), 144-50.

"In Exile" *Streets of Summer* (1969), 173-80.

"In Exile" *Fid* No. 80 (May-June-July 1969), 64-70.

"In Exile" *Stories from Ontario* (1974), 70-6.

"In Exile" *Transitions 2* (1978), 133-8.

"The Lost World" *Undergrad* Spr 1960, -9.

"The Magic Carnival" *Undergrad* Aut 1958, 22-4.

"A Note from Jimmy" *Streets of Summer* (1969), 135-7.

"One Evening" *Streets of Summer* (1969), 13-20.

"One Evening" *Sixteen by Twelve* (1970), 171-6.

"One Evening" *In Your Own Words* (1982), 173-7.

"Presences" *CBC "Anthology"* 5 June 1971.

"Presences" *Narrative Voice* (1972), 70-5.

"Prophecies for April" *CFM* No. 7 (Sum 1972), 38-41.

"Red Barn, Interior" *JCF* 1:4 (Fall 1972), 35-41.

"A Road through Summer Fields" *Quarry* 16:4 (Sum 1967), 21-8.

"A Room High Over the City" *Nebula* No. 14 (1980), 10-9.

"A Room with Flowers" *Undergrad* Spr 1959, 19-30.

"A Room with Flowers" *Mont* 34 (Dec 1960), 34-9.

"The Small Rain" *Quarry* 17:3 (Spr 1968), 16-20.

"The Small Rain" *Streets of Summer* (1969), 181-7.

"Something for Olivia's Scrapbook I Guess" *SN* 83 (Mar 1968), 33-8.

"Something for Olivia's Scrapbook I Guess" *Canadian Short Stories* 2 (1968), 358-78.

"Something for Olivia's Scrapbook I Guess" *Streets of Summer* (1969), 151-66.

"Something for Olivia's Scrapbook I Guess" *Canadian Short Story* (1971), 35-49.

"Something for Olivia's Scrapbook I Guess" *Contemporary Voices* (1972), 40-50.

"Something for Olivia's Scrapbook I Guess" *Die Weite Reise* (1974), 347-66 [As "Wieder etwas für Olivia Sammlung"; trans. Peter Kleinhempel].

"Something for Olivia's Scrapbook I Guess" *Toronto Short Stories* (1977), 215-30.

"Streetcar, Streetcar, Wait for Me" *Streets of Summer* (1969), 9-12.

"Streetcar, Streetcar, Wait for Me" *Kaleidoscope* (1972), 26-30.

"Streetcar, Streetcar, Wait for Me" *Writers and Writing* (1981), 184-7.

"Swimming Out, Swimming Back" *WCR* 6:1 (June 1971), 21-2.

"Things That Happened Before You Were Born" *Narrative Voice* (1972), 75-9.

"The Way Things Are" *CF* 40 (Jan 1961), 228.

"The Widower Bird" *JCF* 1:1 (Win 1972), 8-10.

"Winners and Losers" *CFM* No. 6 (Spr 1972), 37-47.

"The Winter of the Daffodils" *CF* 42 (Nov 1962), 181-2.

"The Winter of the Daffodils" *Streets of Summer* (1969), 167-72.

"The Winter of the Daffodils" *Forum* (1972), 351-4.

Hembrow, J.A.†
"Swamp Wise" *CSSM* 2:3 (Sum 1976), 3-7.

Hemingway, Grace Elton†
"These Are My Neighbours" *Onward* 24 Sept 1961, 3-4, 7 [Non-fiction?].

Henderson, Catherine†
"The Bridgeman" *Origins* 12:1 (Apr 1982), 66-70.

"Remember Neelie" *Origins* 10:4 (Dec 1980), 36-44.

Henderson, Charles, Jr.‡
"Rear Them Right" *Alive* No. 26 [1973], 16.

Henderson, Dorothy‡
"The Reluctant Mousekeeper" *UC Observer* July 1973, 18-9 [Monologue].

Henderson, Hugh B.†
"The Sanctuary" *Intervales* No. 2 (1960), 25-9.

Henderson, Jeff‡
"An Unknown Hero" *Simcoe R* No. 8 (Spr 1980), 10-2.

Henderson, Keith†
"After May 20th" *Quarry* 31:2 (Spr 1982), 14-21.

"A Game or Three" *Forge* 26:1 (Feb 1964), 66-79.

"Less and Less Human" *Quarry* 31:2 (Spr 1982), 9-13.

Henderson, Margaret S.‡
"As I Lay Dying: Faulkner Revisited" *Scar Fair* 9 (1982), 36.

Hendrickson, Magda†
"Centennial Comes to Purple Hill" *Edmonton Journal* Thu, 8 June 1967, 8.

Hendrie-Quinn, J.†
"I Shot an Arrow in the Air" *Fresh Grease* (1971), 49-53.

Hendry, Peter
"Aya-oo" *CG* Nov 1956, 12, 38-40.
"The Little Hunter" *CG* Apr 1957, 58, 70.
"Old Chris" *CG* Oct 1957, 15, 35-8.
"Once a Rebel" *CG* Oct 1955, 8, 40-2.
"Option to Sell" *FH* 15 Oct 1959, 16-7, 39.
"Othello's Affair with the Civil Service" *FH* 29 May 1958, 24-6.
"The Sportsman" *CG* Nov 1958, 41-4.

Hendry, Thomas‡
[Title unknown] *CBC "Anthology"* 19 Nov 1957.

Henighan, Stephen
"Adrian and Oliver" *Pier Spr* 5:[4] (Fall 1980), 32-7.
"The Sun of Coricancha" *Des* 13:4 No. 38 (Fall 1982), 39-41.

Henighan, Tom
"At Approximately Three P.M... . " *Can Lit R* No. 1 (Fall-Win 1982), 13-5.
"The Explorers" *Antig R* No. 47 (Aut 1981), 47-60.
"The House" *UWR* 17:1 (Fall-Win 1982), 57-71.

Henley, Patricia†
"Let Me Call You Sweetheart" *CCWQ* 4:1 (Win 1982), 12-3.

Hennessey, Michael
"The Hunters" *Katharsis* 1:1 (Apr 1967), 24-8.
"The New and Wonderful Land (1846)" *JCF* No. 20 (1977), 50-67.
"The Patriot Game" *Katharsis* 2:1 (Spr 1969), 58-68.
"Wolf's Day in Court" *Abegweit R* 4:1 (Spr 1983), 85-103.

Henriques, Alexandra‡
"A Case of Innocence" *Scar Fair* 6 (1979), 55-7.
"Fairy Tale" *Scar Fair* 7 (1979-80), 25-6.

Henry, Ann Maude
"The Dance of the Bells" *MM* 70 (28 Sept 1957), 20, 46, 48, 50, 52.
"The Magic Life" *MM* 68 (17 Sept 1955), 16-7, 36, 38, 40, 43-4, 46-8.
"The Park" *CBC "Anthology"* 6 July 1974.

Henry, Brian‡
"Tiger's Tale" *UC Gargoyle* 2 (Apr 1979), 6.

Henry, Cam
"Love Is an Active Verb" *Folio* 4:2 [Apr 1950], [5 pp].

Hepworth, Brian (? -1986)
"Sailing to Istanbul" *Waves* 2:3 (Spr 1974), 48-52.

Herbart, Elizabeth†
"The Black Dog" *Antig R* No. 38 (Sum 1979), 11-4.

Herbert, John
"Bad Girl" *Onion* 5 (Sept 1981), 3-4.
"Be Good" *Onion* 5 (Nov 1981), 5.
"Meeting Mr. Camp" *Onion* 3 (Aug-Sept 1978), 6-7.
"The Most Beautiful Shoulders" *Onion* 5 (Dec-Jan 1982), 1-3.
"Torments of the Neoflight Trauma Critic" *Onion* 3 (Nov-Dec 1978), 12.

Herd, Newt – *See* Green, H. Gordon.

Heriteau, Jacqui
"The Devil and the Steeple Builder" *Weekend* 3 (28 Nov 1953), 28-9, 48, 50.
"Portrait of Libby" *Chat* 26 (Oct 1953), 15, 104-7.

Hershorn, Ruth
"Broadway Matinée" *Flare* 4 (Dec 1982), 46-8.

Hertz, Kenneth V.
"The Last Canadian Dreidel Maker" *CJO* 19 (Nov-Dec 1981), 9-12.

Hertzman, Judy‡
"The Old Man" *Los* No. 7 (Mar 1981), 45-9.
"The Visitor" *Los* No. 6 (1980), 29-36.

Hetherington, Laurie‡
"The Loneliest Man" *Eclipse* [No. 1] [n.d.], 8-9.

Heuchert, T.M.†
"Collector's Choice" *CSSM* 2:3 (Sum 1976), 30-3.

Hewitt, Molly‡
"Bard Sinister" *Acta Vic* 80:3 (Feb 1956), 22-5.

Hewko, Kati‡
"Dimitri" *Story So Far* 3 (1974), 95.

Heyd, Ruth‡
"An Inner Parlour" *Kaleidoscope* 1954-55, 10-4.

Heyward, Helen‡
"Annie" *Pedantics* 1965, 58.

Heywood, Rosalie
"The Plight of Ellen" *Free Press Weekly* 1 June 1955 [Based on *Singing Under Ice*].
"The Plight of Ellen" *Singing Under Ice* (1974), 94-7.
"What Price Glory?" CBC *"Canadian Short Stories"* [date unknown] [Based on *CSSM*].
"What Price Glory?" *CSSM* 3:2 (Spr 1977), 61-2, 69-71.

Hibberd, Dale‡
"Bubble Bath for Two" *Forge* 1950, 51-4.

Hickman, Tom†
"The Saga of Joe Sable" *Tam R* No. 60 (Oct 1973), 32-44.

Hicks, John V.
"The Chord That Was Lost" *CF* 31 (Sept 1951), 128-9.
"The Fable Frogs of Seigo Slough" *Saskatchewan Gold* (1982), 111-6.
"Melody for a Bull" *Contexts* 1 (1981), 250-3 [Children's?].
"The Rivers Run to the Sea" *Smoke Signals* 2 [date unknown] [Based on *SWG* survey response].
"The Rivers Run to the Sea" *Sundogs* (1980), 59-64.

Hiebert, Susan†
"Page 51" *West People* No. 186 (28 Apr 1983), 10-1.
"The Way of Knowledge" *Onward* 3 July 1966, 3-4.
"Without the Trimmings" *Living Message* 83 (Dec 1972), 4-5.

Higgins, D.W.‡
"The Pork-Pie Hat" *Rain Chr* No. 9 [n.d.], 12-5.

Higham, C.M.M.‡
"The Bridge Builder" *AA* 65 (Apr 1975), 17-8.

Higham, John†
"Bill Grant Goes West" *Antig R* No. 44 (Win 1980), 65-72.
"When Morning Came" *Scar Fair* 10 (1983), 11-4.

Higo, T.K.
"Egg Whites and Yolks" *WCR* 16:1 (Sum 1981), 69-72.

Hildebrandt, Gloria‡
"Danny Fire" *TUR* 93:2 (Apr 1980), 18-23.
"The Last Easter" *TUR* 92:2 (Apr 1979), 17-8.
"Rebecca" *TUR* 91:1 (Nov 1977), 39-42.
"The Stone Room" *TUR* 93:1 (Jan 1980), 5-9.
"The Tournament" *TUR* 90:2 (Dec [1976]), 10-5.

Hill, D.R.‡
"Time Is No Boundary" *TUR* 68:1 (Nov 1955), 17-25.

Hill, David‡
"100% Healthy" *Karaki* No. 5 (Dec 1975), 16-8.

Hill, Deborah‡
"Fragmentation" *TUR* 83:1 (Fall 1969), 23.

Hill, Doug‡
"The Circle" *TUR* 66:1 (Nov 1953), 22-9.
"The Eyes Had It" *Forum* (OSSTF) 7 (May-June 1981), 131-3.
"Melinda" *TUR* 66:4 (Mar 1954), 17-9.

Hill, Edward†
"Young Blood Must Have Its Course, Lad and Every Dog His Day" *Quarry* 31:3 (Sum 1982), 49-62.

Hill, Elizabeth†
"The Undertaker's Tale" *Stories with John Drainie* (1963), 175-80.

Hill, Gerald†
"Tommy Douglas Avenue" *Writing* No. 5 (Spr 1982), 43-4.

Hill, Jerry‡
"The Rebirth" *Halcyon* 12 (Win 1966-67), 101-2.

Hill, Jocelyn Rennie‡
"Spring" *TUR* 63:3 (Feb 1951), 32-3.

Hill, Kathy (1956?-)
"The Days Are Longer" *JCF* No. 19 (1977), 40-4.

Hill, Kay‡
"The Flitting of the *Nancy Gay*" *AA* 62 (June 1972), 16-7.

Hill, Larry
"My Side of the Fence" *Des* 11:4/12:1 Nos. 30/31 (1980-81), 69-78.
"Richard de la Bonnevoie's Pet Monkeys" *Des* 12:2/3 Nos. 32/33 (1981), 184-202.

Hill, O. Mary‡
"John Grant Becomes a Minister" *Pres Record* Nov 1950, 320, 329 [Non-fiction?].

Hill, Romie‡
"What Colour Is Love?" *AA* 59 (July 1969), 62-4.

Hillhouse, Gordon‡
"Now It Can Be Told" *Legion* 27 (Oct 1952), 13.
"Now It Can Be Told" *Legion* 33 (July 1958), 48.

Hinatsu, Connie (1957?-)
"The Telegram" *Title Unknown* (1975), 20.

Hindmarch, Gladys (1940-)
BOAT STORIES Vancouver: Talonbooks, 1975 [Based on CBIP].
"After Birth Sketches" *Iron II* No. 1 (1975), 1-9.
"Fair Harbour My Eye" *Cap R* No. 12 (1977), 57-64.
"The Fifth Peter Story" *Imago* No. 20 (1974), 81-4.
"The Fifth Peter Story" *Skookum Wawa* (1975), 265-8.
"The Fifth Peter Story" *Fiction of Contemporary Canada* (1978), 137-41.
"Had a Wife" *Prism* 3:2 (Win 1962), 50-2.
"Had Another" *Motion* No. 4 (25 Aug 1962), 4-7.
"How It Feels" *Story So Far* (1971), 109-12.
"How It Feels" *Stories from Pacific & Arctic Canada* (1974), 139-43.
"I Gotta Get Outta Here" *Iron II* No. 4 (Nov 1976), 5-7.
"Just Because These Words" *Cap R* No. 11 (1977), 76-80 [As "A Boat Story,"; title based on survey response].
"No Cheese" *NMFG* No. 4 (May 1976), [4 pp].
"Nothing Is Simple" *Geo Str Writing* No. 9 (3 Sept 1971), 10-1.
"Nothing Is Simple" *Writing* No. 6 (Spr 1983), 21-3.
"The Old Woman Who Lived in a Boathouse" *Tish* No. 27 (Nov 1964), 6-7.
"Other Men Make the" [sic] *Geo Str Writing* No. 5 (30 Sept-6 Oct 1970), 12.

"Other Men Make the" *Story So Far* (1971), 11-5.
"The Peter Stories" CBC *"Anthology"* 13 Jan 1979.
"A Short Short Story" *Motion* No. 6 (25 Dec 1962), [11].
"A Single Scrambled" *Geo Str Writing* No. 5 (30 Sept-6 Oct 1970), 13.
"A Single Scrambled" *Return* No. 3 (May 1973), 8-9.
"Some Trip This Is Going to Be" *Geo Str Writing* No. 7 (May 1971), 2-3.
"Something's Going On" *Cap R* No. 4 (Fall-Win 1973), 5-7.
"Such As It Is" *Geo Str Writing* No. 1 (29 Oct-5 Nov 1969), 26-7.
"They Know What They're Doing" *Iron* No. 3 (1967), 18-23.
"They Know What They're Doing" *Geo Str Writing* No. 3 (1-8 Apr 1970), 15.
"This Job's Been Good to Me" *Per* No. 2 (Fall 1977), 8-12.
"To Be Here" *Per* Nos. 7/8 (Win 1981), 35-9.
"Tulips" *Georgia Straight* [1970?] [Based on survey response].
"Where They Are" *Pacific Nation* No. 2 (Feb 1969), 6-10.
"Where They Are" *Geo Str Writing* No. 1 (29 Oct-5 Nov 1969), 26.
"Which Way to Go" *Iron* Nos. 8/9 (1970), 39-42.
"The Wrong Place" *Iron* No. 5 (1969), 37-46.
"You Wouldn't Want To" *Cap R* No. 15 (1979), 128-34.
"Zeballos, B.C." *Cap R* No. 4 (Fall-Win 1973), 8-15.

Hirsch, John
"Monologue" *NR* 5:6 (Feb-Mar 1953), 37-43.

Hiscock, Reid‡
"The Old Man" *Scar Fair* 10 (1983), 69-75.
"The Pea Patch" *Scar Fair* 9 (1982), 47-54.

Hivon, Gerard‡
"La Justice" *Potlatch* No. 4 (Jan 1965), 35-40.

Hjorteland, Elaine‡
"Until Proven Innocent" *West People* No. 178 (3 Mar 1983), 11-2.

Hladzuk, Veronica‡
"A Simple Story" *Kaleidoscope* 1963, 24.

Hlookoff, Peter
"Conversations with My Mind" *BC Monthly* 3:1 (Oct 1976), [3 pp] [Prose poem?].

Hlynsky, David
SALVAGE Toronto: Coach House Press, 1981.
"Boy Scouts on Luau" *OPT* 4:7 (Oct 1977), 10.
"Boy Scouts on Luau" *Salvage* (1981), [8 pp].
"Chinchilla for a Hot Afternoon" *Salvage* (1981), [11 pp].
"The Day Time Stopped Standing Still" *Imp* 8:4 (Fall-Win 1980), 36-8.
"The Day Time Stopped Standing Still" *Salvage* (1981), [7 pp].
"Dead Ted Snuff ... Puff Piece" *Salvage* (1981), [7 pp].
"The Only Albino at the Bus Stop" *Salvage* (1981), [15 pp].

Hoaken, Gail‡
"Golden Windows" *Acta Vic* 82:3 (Mar 1958), 32-3.
"Miss Cork" *Acta Vic* 82:1 (Nov 1957), 7-8.

Hobart, Virginia‡
"Guests and Fish" *CBC "Alberta Anthology"* 1 Oct 1983.

Hobbs, Gillian‡
"Memories of Love and War" *AA* [66] (Nov 1975), 51.
"Not with a Bang" *CBC "Anthology"* 10 July 1976.
"A Story for All Hallows Eve" *AA* 68 (Oct 1977), 45-6.
"The Wedding Dress" *AA* 71 (Mar 1981), 72-3.

Hockin, Louise
"Paper Hangover" *Pacific Profile* 1:1 (Fall 1961), 29-31 [Non-fiction?].

Hocking, Beverly
"Catch" *Waves* 8:1 (Fall 1979), 18-20.
"Her Uncle" *Matrix* No. 10 (Fall-Win 1979-80), 72-6.
"November 1, 1979" *Room* 5:4 (1980), 48-53.
"A Rowboat, a Submarine" *Student Oracle* (1979), 79-89.
"The Trap" *Grain* 8:2 [1980], 29-35.

Hockley, Vernon
"The Best Fishing Hole in B.C." *MM* 71 (12 Apr 1958), 20-1, 32, 34, 36.
"The Iron Mikado" *Mont* 33 (June 1959), 20-4.
"The Race for the Love of Mizpah Jenkins" *MM* 69 (23 June 1956), 26-7, 48-50.
"The Search for Strangler Sweeney" *MM* 70 (20 July 1957), 24-5, 34, 36-7.
"The Truth About the Sasquatch" *MM* 71 (10 May 1958), 34, 67-8, 70, 72.
"What Would Carrie Nation Do?" *MM* 69 (1 Sept 1956), 24-6, 28.

Hodder, Uda‡
"Good People" *First Encounter* 13 (1983), 44-6.

Hodes, Barbara Thal†
"Bonded" *Room* 7:4 (1982), 48-56.

Hodgins, Jack (1938-)
SPIT DELANEY'S ISLAND Toronto: Macmillan, 1976.
THE BARCLAY FAMILY THEATRE Toronto: Macmillan, 1981.
"After the Season" *Was R* 6:2 (1972), 55-69.
"After the Season" *Stories from Pacific & Arctic Canada* (1974), 69-88.
"After the Season" *Skookum Wawa* (1975), 47-61.
"After the Season" *Spit Delaney's Island* (1976), 152-69.
"At the Foot of the Hill, Birdie's School" *CFM* No. 12 (Win 1974), 81-94.
"At the Foot of the Hill, Birdie's School" *Spit Delaney's Island* (1976), 137-51.
"By the River" *Cap R* 1:3 (Spr-Sum 1973), 5-12.
"By the River" *Spit Delaney's Island* (1976), 115-22.
"By the River" *British Columbia: A Celebration* (1983), 194-6.
"By the River" *Water* [n.d.], 101-4.
"Change of Scenery" *CF* 62 (June-July 1982), 23-6.
"Change of Scenery" *Rainshadow* (1982), 92-104.

"Change of Scenery" *Small Wonders* (1982), 31-43.

'The Concert Stages of Europe" *SN* 93 (July-Aug 1978), 36-49.

'The Concert Stages of Europe" *New Worlds* (1980), 84-100.

'The Concert Stages of Europe" *Barclay Family Theatre* (1981), 1-23.

"Edna Pike, on the Day of the Prime Minister's Wedding" *event* 2:1 [1972], 26-33.

"Every Day of His Life" *Spit Delaney's Island* (1976), 86-97.

"Every Day of His Life" *Best Canadian Short Stories* (1981), 46-57.

"Great Blue Heron" *Prism* 14:2 (Sum 1975), 38-43.

'The Importance of Patsy McLean" *JCF* 2:1 (Win 1973), 5-7.

'The Importance of Patsy McLean" *Isolation in Canadian Literature* (1975), 77-84.

'In the Museum of Evil" *JCF* 3:1 (Win 1974), 5-10.

'Invasions '79" *Barclay Family Theatre* (1981), 24-67.

'Ladies and Gentlemen, the Fabulous Barclay Sisters!" *Barclay Family Theatre* (1981), 280-99 [Also entitled "Those Fabulous Barclay Sisters"].

'The Lepers' Squint" *Story So Far* 5 (1978), 49-65.

'The Lepers' Squint" *Penguin Book of Canadian Short Stories* (1980), 379-95.

'The Lepers' Squint" *Barclay Family Theatre* (1981), 160-80.

'The Lepers' Squint" *Anthology of Canadian Literature in English 2* (1983), 440-53.

"A Matter of Necessity" *CF* 49 (Jan 1970), 245-7.

'More Than Conquerors" *JCF* No. 16 (1976), 49-88 [Novella?].

'More Than Conquerors" *77: Best Canadian Stories* 64-129 [Novella?].

'More Than Conquerors" *Barclay Family Theatre* (1981), 101-59.

'More Than Conquerors" *Penguin Book of Modern Canadian Short Stories* (1982), 361-411.

'Mr. Pernouski's Dream" *Barclay Family Theatre* (1981), 68-100.

"Open Line" *Antig R* No. 9 (Spr 1972), 11-7.

"Other People's Troubles" *Spit Delaney's Island* (1976), 123-33.

'The Plague Children" *Weekend* 29 (4 Aug 1979), 10-3.

'The Plague Children" *Magic Realism* (1980), 17-28.

'The Plague Children" *Barclay Family Theatre* (1981), 262-79.

'The Plague Children" *West of Fiction* (1983), 110-24.

'Promise of Peace" *North American R* NS 6:4 OS No. 254 (Win 1969), 27-32.

'The Religion of the Country" *Spit Delaney's Island* (1976), 98-114.

'The Religion of the Country" *Stories Plus* (1979), 106-20.

'Separating" *Spit Delaney's Island* (1976), 3-23.

'Separating" *Canadian Short Stories 3* (1978), 127-52.

'Silverthorn" *Fire* (1978), 98-101.

'Spit Delaney's Island" *Spit Delaney's Island* (1976), 170-99.

'The Sumo Revisions" *Barclay Family Theatre* (1981), 181-261 [Novella?].

'The Sumo Revisions" *Interface* 4:8 (Sept 1981), 30-4 [As "Victims of the Masquerade"; excerpt].

'Those Fabulous Barclay Sisters" *TL* Jan 1981, 54-5, 89-95 [Also entitled "Ladies and Gentlemen, the Fabulous Barclay Sisters!"].

'Three Women of the Country" *JCF* 1:3 (Sum 1972), 22-38.

'Three Women of the Country" *Spit Delaney's Island* (1976), 24-69.

'Three Women of the Country" *Transitions 2* (1978), 31-70.

'The Trench Dwellers" *Cap R* No. 5 (Spr 1974), 11-24.

"The Trench Dwellers" *Spit Delaney's Island* (1976), 73-85.
"The Trench Dwellers" *West Coast Experience* (1976), 90-103.
"Witness" *Alphabet* Nos. 18/19 (June 1971), 67-73.

Hodgins, Norris
THE PARSLEYS AND THE SAGE Toronto: Ryerson Press, 1952.
"Attention" *Parsleys and the Sage* (1952), 57-61.
"Ballast" *Parsleys and the Sage* (1952), 147-50.
"Beds" *Parsleys and the Sage* (1952), 117-20.
"Bread-Making" *Parsleys and the Sage* (1952), 113-6.
"Budgets" *Parsleys and the Sage* (1952), 134-7.
"Calves" *Parsleys and the Sage* (1952), 18-22.
"Cherries" *Parsleys and the Sage* (1952), 45-8.
"Chickens" *Parsleys and the Sage* (1952), 82-5.
"Colds" *Parsleys and the Sage* (1952), 129-33.
"Concrete" *Parsleys and the Sage* (1952), 66-8.
"Cutworms" *Parsleys and the Sage* (1952), 32-5.
"Dark" *Parsleys and the Sage* (1953), 49-52.
"Direction" *Parsleys and the Sage* (1952), 27-31.
"Dust" *Parsleys and the Sage* (1952), 143-6.
"Eggs" *Parsleys and the Sage* (1952), 108-12.
"Floors" *Parsleys and the Sage* (1952), 69-73.
"Glass-Blowing" *Parsleys and the Sage* (1952), 14-7.
"Habits" *Parsleys and the Sage* (1952), 5-8.
"Husbands" *Parsleys and the Sage* (1952), 41-4.
" 'I'll Be Seeing You!' " *Parsleys and the Sage* (1952), 151-3.
"Inertia" *Parsleys and the Sage* (1952), 103-7.
"Ladders" *Parsleys and the Sage* (1952), 74-7.
"November" *Parsleys and the Sage* (1952), 99-102.
"Painting" *Parsleys and the Sage* (1952), 138-42.
"Paper" *Parsleys and the Sage* (1952), 23-6.
"Pickles" *Parsleys and the Sage* (1952), 86-90.
"Purring" *Parsleys and the Sage* (1952), 125-8.
"Robins" *Parsleys and the Sage* (1952), 9-13.
"Rumination" *Parsleys and the Sage* (1952), 53-6.
"Shower Baths" *Parsleys and the Sage* (1952), 95-8.
"Sleep" *Parsleys and the Sage* (1952), 91-4.
"Snoring" *Parsleys and the Sage* (1952), 1-4.
"Swimming" *Parsleys and the Sage* (1952), 78-81.
"Swim-Suits" *Parsleys and the Sage* (1952), 36-40.
"Vacation-Packing" *Parsleys and the Sage* (1952), 62-5.
"Windows" *Parsleys and the Sage* (1952), 121-4.

Hofbauer, Pat‡
"In the Darkness of the Light" *Scar Fair* 2 (1974-75), [1 p] [Prose poem?].

Hoffer, Fannie†
"Diamond Solitaire" *CF* 30 (Feb 1951), 251-2.

Hoffer, Sorryl
"Arrivederci, Evelyn" *Chat* 49 (Mar 1976), 34-5, 76, 78, 80-2.
"The Italian Lesson" *Outset* 1974, 71-84.
"Stones" *Fid* No. 103 (Fall 1974), 29-35.
"They're Asking for You, Bettina" *Chat* 47 (June 1974), 26-7, 38, 40-2.

Hoffman, Edith‡
"At Spring Melt" *Quarry* 29:3 (Sum 1980), 31-7.
"Help!" *CSSM* 2:3 (Sum 1976), 11, 13-5.
"Pictures" *UCR* Spr 1977, 31-6.
"Promises" *UTR* 1:1 (Spr 1977), 9-12.
"The Roofer's Guarantee" *UTR* 2:1 (Spr 1978), 6-9.

Hoffman, Michael‡
"Mad Adventure in a Hotel in Bangkok" *JCF* 3:4 (1975), 14-21.

Hoffos, Signe†
"Maria Rising" *Miss Chat* 9 (16 Nov 1972), 26, 74.

Hofmann, Greta – *See* Nemiroff, Greta Hofmann.

Hofsess, John‡
"Of Happiness and Despair, We Have No Measure" *Muse* 1965-66 No. 2, 16-23.

Hogan, Robert†
"Events Leading to My Departure" *WCR* 8:3 (Jan 1974), 26-8.
"Thirteen Other Ways of Looking at a Blackbird" *WCR* 8:1 (June 1973), 24-7.

Hogan, Robert† (1941-)
"At the Edge" *Des* 10:1 Nos. 22/23 (1978-79), 104-15.
"People Die" *SN* 96 (Feb 1981), 46-9.
"Scenes of the Alhambra" *event* 8:2 (1979), 13-32.

Hogg, Bob (1942-)
"After Not Having Quite Enough" *Motion* No. 1 (25 May 1962), [1 p] [Prose poem?].
"The Miss" *Motion* No. 6 (25 Dec 1962), [5-9].
"Smalltown" *Motion* No. 2 (25 June 1962), [5-7].
"The Trip" *Motion* No. 5 (25 Oct 1962), [1-6].

Hogg, Brian
"The Warrior" *CBC "Anthology"* 14 Nov 1970.

Holberg, Darlyne‡
"The Elevator Man" *West People* No. 208 (20 Oct 1983), 10-1.

Holden, Helene F.
"Arnold" *Room* 4:1/2 (1978), 152-9.
" 'Emovora' " *Br Out* 6:3 (1979), 18-22.
"Mornings, or I Don't Want to Go to the Country" *event* 4:3 [1974?], 32-9.
"The Partner" *Chat* 55 (June 1982), 54-5, 143-4.

Holden-Lawrence, Monica‡
"A Biography" *Story So Far* 3 (1974), 87-9.

Holdstock, P.J.
"Going Back" *event* 12:1 (1983), 73-9.

Holland, James [pseudonym]
"The Perfect Segment: An Allegory of Undergraduate Life" *Acta Vic* 90:3 (Feb 1966), 13-20.

Holland, Kerry†
"Break-In" *Communicator* 8:5 (Dec 1979), 28-9.

Holland, Marjorie‡
"Winds of Despair" CBC *"Alberta Anthology"* 8 Nov 1980.

Holley, Melvin (1955-)
"Birthright" *Pot Port* 2 (1980-81), 14-8.

Holley, T.M. (1955-)
"Bukowski Sunrise" *Chezzetcook* (1977), 75-86.
"Declining Westward: A Romantic Outline" *Chezzetcook* (1977), 40-1.

Hollingshead, Archie†
"A Pioneer Stopping Place" *Alberta Speaks* 1957, 12-4.
"Shangri-la on the Peace" *Alberta Writers Speak* 1964, 22-5.
"Wrong Way Trail" *Alberta Writers Speak* 1960, 16-20.

Hollingshead, Greg (1947-)
FAMOUS PLAYERS Toronto: Coach House Press, 1982.
"Bedtime" *UWR* 14:2 (Spr-Sum 1979), 60-8.
"Cooper" *Matrix* No. 10 (Fall-Win 1979-80), 58-61.
"Cooper" *Famous Players* (1982), 119-24.
"Famous Players" *CFM* Nos. 40/41 (1981), 141-54.
"Famous Players" *Famous Players* (1982), 125-46.
"Harry the Dream" *Story So Far* 5 (1978), 67-75.
"I Love Dragon Lady" *Gas Rain* [1] (Mar 1977), 12-3.
"I Love Dragon Lady" *Pulp* 4:23 (15 Nov 1978), [3-4].
"IGA Days" *Aurora* 1980 95-104.
"IGA Days" *Famous Players* (1982), 29-38.
"Kingbird" *JCF* Nos. 31/32 (1981), 98-111.
"Last Days" *Dal R* 58 (1978-79), 674-81.
"Last Days" *Famous Players* (1982), 55-65.
"Life with the Prime Minister" *CF* 58 (Apr 1978), 24-7.
"Life with the Prime Minister" *Famous Players* (1982), 9-20.
"Mary Duncan" *Cap R* No. 11 (1977), 87-91.
"Mary Duncan" *Alberta Diamond Jubilee Anthology* (1979), 228-31.
"My Father, with Both Hands" *Writ* No. 9 (1977), 78-88.
"My Father, with Both Hands" *Famous Players* (1982), 39-49.
"My Jogger" *Gas Rain* 3 (1979), 8-11.
"My Jogger" *Writ* No. 12 (1980), 5-14.
"My Jogger" *Famous Players* (1982), 110-8.

"Out the Mirror" *Camrose R* No. 4 [n.d.], 38-43.
"Red Muffins" *Story Q* (U.S.) No. 13 (1981), 7-20.
"Red Muffins" *Famous Players* (1982), 77-97.
"The Return of Harry the Dream" *Famous Players* (1982), 98-109.
"The Revenge of Eddie Reeser" *Des* No. 15 (Fall 1976), 16-9.
"The Revenge of Eddie Reeser" *Famous Players* (1982), 50-4.
"Seabright" *Cap R* No. 14 (1977), 5-10.
"The Sound" *Aurora* 1978 110-20.
"The Story of Alton Finney" *Fid* No. 119 (Fall 1978), 46-52.
"The Story of Alton Finney" *79: Best Canadian Stories* 59-68.
"Story Story" *Quarry* 30:4 (Aut 1981), 94-101.
"Strange Cargo" *Famous Players* (1982), 66-76.
"Strange Cargo" *Matrix* No. 15 (Spr-Sum 1982), 34-40.
"Tuktoyaktuk" *Des* 9:1/2 Nos. 20/21 (1978), 80-6.
"Tuktoyaktuk" *Gas Rain* 2 (1978), 4-7.
"Tuktoyaktuk" *Famous Players* (1982), 21-8.
"Watches" *Per* 7/8 (Win 1981), 42-50.
"Why Don't You Love Me" *event* 7:1 (1978), 26-36.
"You Never Know" *Cap R* No. 11 (1977), 81-6.

Hollingshead, Rosemary‡
"I'm Free! I'm Free!" *Pulp* 1:2 (1 Dec 1972), [2].
"Story" *Pulp* 2:6 (15 Apr 1974), [2 pp].

Hollingsworth, Margaret (1939-)
"Tulips" *83: Best Canadian Stories* 25-35.

Holloway, Robin‡
"The Last Monday" *In Complete* [1970-71], 82-7.
"The Machine Age" *Sowing* [1972?], 75-80.
"Out of the Forest" *Writing Group Pub* 1971-72, 6-7.

Hollyer, Cameron (1926-)
"Murk IV Meets Watson the Benedict" *Can Holmes* 7:1 (Aut 1983), 5-7.

Holman, Lloyd†
"The Cross and the Shopping Bag" *Companion* 46 (Sept 1983), 14-6.
"The Day the Cow Ate Cake" *West People* No. 204 (22 Sept 1983), 14.

Holmes, Ken†
"Flat-Mate (The Disappearance of Mrs Mabel Maganickle)" *Mam* 6:1 (Sum 1982), [1 p].
"Klee" *Mam* 3:3 (Fall 1979), [3 pp].

Holmes, Nancy
"The Obstetrical Eye" *Dand* 10:2 (1983), 60-9.

Holmes, Rex‡
"Nor Cake, Either" *CA & B* 46:1 (Fall 1970), 5, 19-20.

Holt, Maria†
"Something Mysterious Has Arrived" *Pier Spr* 6:2 (Spr 1981), 36-7.

Holt, Muriel – *See* Atwood, Joan-Mary and Holt, Muriel.

Holt, Patricia‡
"Jed" *Communicator* 10:1 [n.d.], [1 p].

Holterman, Anne‡
See Steffler, George and Holterman, Anne.

Holz, Cynthia†
"In the New House" *event* 11:1 (1982), 109-23.
"Rabbit-Skinning" *Waves* 8:3 (Spr 1980), 8-14.
"Simon" *Quarry* 31:2 (Spr 1982), 37-45.
"Whyntcha Write Happy Stories?" *Fid* No. 124 (Win 1980), 3-11.

Home, Elizabeth†
"Paradise Mislaid" *New Voices* (1956), 152-5.

Homer, Daniel Scott†
"Play and Pay" *Pemmican J* Sum 1982, 40-3.

Honsinger, Robert‡
"Rain at Night" *10:47* 1:3 (1967), 37-8.

Hood, Esther‡
"A Cricket Match in Grenada" *Spear* Nov 1971, 34, 43.

Hood, Hugh (1928-)
AROUND THE MOUNTAIN: SCENES FROM MONTREAL LIFE Toronto: Peter Martin, 1967.
DARK GLASSES Ottawa: Oberon Press, 1976.
FLYING A RED KITE Toronto: Ryerson Press, 1962.
THE FRUIT MAN, THE MEAT MAN, AND THE MANAGER Ottawa: Oberon Press, 1971.
NONE GENUINE WITHOUT THIS SIGNATURE Toronto: ECW Press, 1980.
SELECTED STORIES Ottawa: Oberon Press, 1978.
"After the Sirens" *Flying a Red Kite* (1962), 124-35.
"After the Sirens" *Contemporary Voices* (1972), 51-8.
"After the Sirens" *Kaleidoscope* (1972), 59-70.
"After the Sirens" *Tigers of the Snow* (1973), 159-69.
"After the Sirens" *Frontier Experience* (1975), 94-105.
"After the Sirens" *Other Canadas* (1979), 151-60.
"An Allegory of Man's Fate" *JCF* 3:1 (Win 1974), 50-4.
"An Allegory of Man's Fate" *Dark Glasses* (1976), 130-43.
"An Allegory of Man's Fate" *Selected Stories* (1978), 219-32.
"Around Theatres" *Parallel* 1:3 (July-Aug 1966), 47-50.
"Around Theatres" *Around the Mountain* (1967), 49-64.
"August Nights" *CF* 61 (Aug 1981), 20-5.
"Bicultural Angela" *Around the Mountain* (1967), 35-48 [Also entitled "Scenes from Montreal Life III: Bicultural Angela"].
"Boots" *Narrative Voice* (1972), 90-4.
"Boots" *Dark Glasses* (1976), 29-35.
"Breaking Off" *None Genuine without This Signature* (1980), 12-29.

"Brother André, Père Lamarche, and My Grandmother Eugenie Blagdon" *Alphabet* No. 13 (June 1967), 34-49.

"Brother André, Père Lamarche, and My Grandmother Eugenie Blagdon" *Fruit Man* (1971), 55-71.

"The Changeling" *CF* 41 (Mar 1962), 274-80.

"The Chess Match" *Fid* No. 53 (Sum 1962), 38-47.

"The Chess Match" *Dark Glasses* (1976), 76-86.

"The Chess Match" *Fiddlehead Greens* (1979), 138-50.

"A Childhood Incident" *Salt* No. 12 (Win 1974-75), 12-6.

"A Childhood Incident" *None Genuine without This Signature* (1980), 57-64.

"Crosby" *SN* 93 (Jan-Feb 1978), 45, 49-51, 53.

"Crosby" *None Genuine without This Signature* (1980), 30-43.

"Cura Pastoralis" *Contact* (U.S.) 3:3 No. 11 (1962), 56-61.

"Cura Pastoralis" *Fruit Man* (1971), 173-87.

"Dark Glasses" *73: New Canadian Stories* 110-9.

"Dark Glasses" *CBC "Anthology"* 20 Jan 1973.

"Dark Glasses" *Dark Glasses* (1976), 119-29.

"Dark Glasses" *Selected Stories* (1978), 208-18.

"The Dog Explosion" *Fruit Man* (1971), 143-52.

"The Dog Explosion" *Modern Stories in English* (1975), 120-7.

"Doubles" *Fid* No. 118 (Sum 1978), 5-22.

"Doubles" *None Genuine without This Signature* (1980), 167-89.

"Educating Mary" *Mont* 39 (Sept 1965), 24-31.

"The End of It" *Flying a Red Kite* (1962), 218-39.

"The End of It" *Tam R* No. 24 (Sum 1962), 3-22.

"The End of It" *Canadian Winter's Tales* (1968), 54-78.

"The End of It" *Canadian Century* (1973), 362-79.

"The End of It" *Selected Stories* (1978), 65-86.

"Every Piece Different" *Waves* 11:2/3 (Win 1983), 5-14.

"The Fable of the Ant and the Grasshopper" *Yes* No. 13 (Dec 1964), [6 pp].

"Fallings from Us, Vanishings" *Flying a Red Kite* (1962), 1-17.

"Fallings from Us, Vanishings" *Mont* 36 (May 1962), 22-6.

"Fallings from Us, Vanishings" *Selected Stories* (1978), 7-23.

"February Mama" *None Genuine without This Signature* (1980), 118-33.

"February Mama" *Des* 11:4/12:1 Nos. 30/31 (1980-81), 17-29.

"Flying a Red Kite" *Flying a Red Kite* (1962), 176-88.

"Flying a Red Kite" *Prism* 3:3 (Spr 1962), 4-13.

"Flying a Red Kite" *Modern Canadian Stories* (1966), 302-13.

"Flying a Red Kite" *Canadian Short Stories 2* (1968), 199-214.

"Flying a Red Kite" *Canadian Short Story* (1971), 22-32.

"Flying a Red Kite" *Evolution of Canadian Literature in English* (1973), 192-9.

"Flying a Red Kite" *Selections from Major Canadian Writers* (1974), 224-31.

"Flying a Red Kite" *Die Weite Reise* (1974), 135-49 [As "Der rote Drachen"; trans. Peter Kleinhempel].

"Flying a Red Kite" *Modern Canadian Stories* (1975), 195-207.

"Flying a Red Kite" *Urban Experience* (1975), 23-35.

"Flying a Red Kite" *Air* (1977), 23-7.

"Flying a Red Kite" *Anthology of Canadian Literature in English 2* (1983), 251-9.

"Friends and Relations" *Repos* No. 6 (Spr 1973), 1-9.

"The Fruit Man, the Meat Man, and the Manager" *CF* 48 (Aug 1968), 104-6.

"The Fruit Man, the Meat Man, and the Manager" CBC "Anthology" 25 Jan 1969.

"The Fruit Man, the Meat Man, and the Manager" *Fruit Man* (1971), 188-97.

"The Fruit Man, the Meat Man and the Manager" *Literature in Canada* (1978), 448-55.

"The Fruit Man, the Meat Man & the Manager" *Selected Stories* (1978), 159-68.

"A Game of Touch" *Tam R* Nos. 50/51 (1969), 73-83.

"Getting to Williamstown" *Tam R* No. 34 (Win 1965), 3-14.

"Getting to Williamstown" *Best American Short Stories* 1966 113-24.

"Getting to Williamstown" *Canadian Short Stories* 2 (1968), 215-30.

"Getting to Williamstown" *Sixteen by Twelve* (1970), 76-85.

"Getting to Williamstown" *Fruit Man* (1971), 9-21.

"Getting to Williamstown" *Akzente* (Ger) 23 (June 1976), 230-40 [As "Unterwegs nach Williamstown"; trans. Walter Pache; based on ABCMA].

"Ghosts at Jarry" *78: Best Canadian Stories* 43-57.

"Ghosts at Jarry" *None Genuine without This Signature* (1980), 44-56.

"God Has Manifested Himself unto Us as Canadian Tire" *76: New Canadian Stories* 18-29.

"God Has Manifested Himself unto Us As Canadian Tire" CBC "Anthology" 20 Aug 1977.

"God Has Manifested Himself unto Us As Canadian Tire" *None Genuine without This Signature* (1980), 1-11.

"God Has Manifested Himself unto Us as Canadian Tire" *Whig-Standard Mag* (Kingston) 16 Aug 1980, 8-9 [Based on ABCMA].

"Going Out as a Ghost" *Fid* No. 101 (Spr 1974), 61-73.

"Going Out as a Ghost" CBC "Anthology" 20 July 1974.

"Going Out as a Ghost" *Dark Glasses* (1976), 7-21.

"Going Out as a Ghost" *Selected Stories* (1978), 180-94.

"Gone Three Days" *None Genuine without This Signature* (1980), 98-117.

"The Good Listener" *None Genuine without This Signature* (1980), 134-44.

"The Good Tenor Man" *Encore* No. 3 (Oct 1963), 4-5, 15-7 [Based on ABCMA].

"The Good Tenor Man" *Colorado Q* 12 (1964), 274-87 [Based on ABCMA].

"The Good Tenor Man" *Fruit Man* (1971), 72-87.

"Le Grand Déménagement" *Around the Mountain* (1967), 65-79.

"The Granite Club" *JCF* 1:1 (Win 1972), 10-4.

"A Green Child" *Around the Mountain* (1967), 127-39.

"A Green Child" *Selected Stories* (1978), 110-20.

"Harley Talking" *Fruit Man* (1971), 133-42.

"Harley Talking" *Quarry* 20:3 (Aut 1971), 16-26.

"He Just Adores Her" *Flying a Red Kite* (1962), 136-57.

"He Just Adores Her" *Mont* 36 (Jan 1962), 24-30.

"The Hole" *CFM* No. 7 (Sum 1972), 20-5.

"The Hole" *Canadian Anthology* (1974), 506-11.

"The Hole" *Dark Glasses* (1976), 110-8.

"The Holy Man" *Tam R* No. 37 (Aut 1965), 3-18.

"The Holy Man" *Fruit Man* (1971), 102-18.

"Hugh Hood's Version of 'Diddle Diddle Dumpling' " *Imp* 3:1 (Fall 1973), 19-21.

"I'm Not Desparate" [sic] *Exchange* 1:1 (Nov 1961), 64-6.

"Incendiaries" *Grain* 2:1 [1974], 32-7.

"Incendiaries" *Dark Glasses* (1976), 53-62.

"Incendiaries" *Best of Grain* (1980), 122-8.

"The Isolation Booth" *Tam R* No. 9 (Aut 1958), 5-12.

"It's a Small World" *Tam R* No. 46 (Win 1968), 101-8.

"Light Shining Out of Darkness" *Around the Mountain* (1967), 21-33.

"Light Shining Out of Darkness" *Selected Stories* (1978), 87-97 [Also entitled "Montreal Evening, with Gypsies: Light Shining Out of Darkness"].

"Looking Down from Above" *Around the Mountain* (1967), 81-94 [Also entitled "Scenes from Montreal Life VI: Looking Down from Above"].

"Looking Down from Above" *Selected Stories* (1978), 98-109.

"Looking Down from Above" *Stories of Quebec* (1980), 168-79.

"Looking Down from Above" *On the Line* (1982), 121-30.

"Montreal Evening, with Gypsies: Light Shining Out of Darkness" *SN* 81 (Apr 1966), 30-2 [Also entitled "Light Shining Out of Darkness"].

"A Near Miss" *Fid* No. 94 (Sum 1972), 3-15.

"A Near Miss" *Dark Glasses* (1976), 36-52.

"New Country" *None Genuine without This Signature* (1980), 65-76.

"Nobody's Going Anywhere!" *Flying a Red Kite* (1962), 158-75.

"Nobody's Going Anywhere!" *Selected Stories* (1978), 47-64.

"None Genuine without This Signature or Peaches in the Bathtub" *None Genuine without This Signature* (1980), 145-66.

"O Happy Melodist!" *Flying a Red Kite* (1962), 18-39.

"One Owner, Low Mileage" *CBC "Anthology"* 21 Nov 1967.

"One Owner, Low Mileage" *Liberté* 11 (mars-avril 1969), 127-42 [As "D'Occasion, comme neuve"; trans. Hubert Aquin].

"One Owner, Low Mileage" *Fruit Man* (1971), 119-32.

"One Way North and South" *Tam R* No. 41 (Aut 1966), 82-94.

"One Way North and South" *Around the Mountain* (1967), 95-111.

"Paradise Retained" *Fruit Man* (1971), 153-61.

"The Perfect Night" *Story* 36:4 No. 141 (July-Aug 1963), 101-7.

"The Pitcher" *CF* 43 (Apr 1963), 12-5.

"The Pitcher" *Dark Glasses* (1976), 97-109.

"The Pitcher" *Great Canadian Sports Stories* (1979), 20-33.

"Places I've Never Been" *Visions 2020* (1970), 101-14.

"Places I've Never Been" *Fruit Man* (1971), 88-101.

"Places I've Never Been" *Selected Stories* (1978), 145-58.

"Predictions of Ice" *Around the Mountain* (1967), 155-66.

"Recollections of the Works Department" *Flying a Red Kite* (1962), 63-98.

"Recollections of the Works Department" *Canadian Writing Today* (1970), 67-80.

"Recollections of the Works Department" *Oxford Anthology of Canadian Literature* (1973), 215-24.

"Recollections of the Works Department" *Toronto Book* (1976), 134-66.

"Recollections of the Works Department" *Toronto Short Stories* (1977), 16-49.

"The River Behind Things" *Around the Mountain* (1967), 167-75.

"The River Behind Things" *Selected Stories* (1978), 121-8.

"Scenes from Montreal Life III: Bicultural Angela" *CF* 46 (Aug 1966), 106-9 [Also entitled "Bicultural Angela"].

"Scenes from Montreal Life VI: Looking Down from Above" *Prism* 6:2 (Aut 1966), 4-13 [Also entitled "Looking Down from Above"].

"A Season of Calm Weather" *QQ* 70 (1963), 76-93.

"A Sherbrooke Street Man" *Parallel* 1:5 (Christmas 1966), 50-4.
"Silver Bugles, Cymbals, Golden Silks" *Flying a Red Kite* (1962), 40-62.
"Silver Bugles, Cymbals, Golden Silks" *Selected Stories* (1978), 24-46.
'The Singapore Hotel" *Fid* No. 84 (Mar-Apr 1970), 9-16.
'The Singapore Hotel" CBC *"Anthology"* 30 May 1970.
'The Singapore Hotel" *Fruit Man* (1971), 162-72.
'The Singapore Hotel" *Fiddlehead Greens* (1979), 151-62.
'The Small Birds" *82: Best Canadian Stories* 43-56.
"Socks" *Narrative Voice* (1972), 85-9.
"Socks" *Dark Glasses* (1976), 22-8.
"A Solitary Ewe" *Literary R* (U.S.) 8 (1965), 468-93.
"A Solitary Ewe" *Fruit Man* (1971), 38-54.
'The Sportive Center of Saint Vincent de Paul" *Around the Mountain* (1967), 1-20.
"Starting Again on Sherbrooke Street" *Around the Mountain* (1967), 141-54.
"Suites and Single Rooms, with Bath" CBC *"Anthology"* 18 May 1962.
"Suites and Single Rooms, with Bath" *QQ* 79 (1972), 366-73.
'Thanksgiving: Between Junetown and Caintown" *CFM* No. 18 (Sum 1975), 16-25.
'Thanksgiving: Between Junetown and Caintown" *Dark Glasses* (1976), 63-75.
'Thanksgiving: Between Junetown and Caintown" *Selected Stories* (1978), 195-207.
'Three Halves of a House" *Tam R* No. 20 (Sum 1961), 5-26.
'Three Halves of a House" *Flying a Red Kite* (1962), 99-123.
'Three Halves of a House" *Great Canadian Writing* (1966), 20-1 [Excerpt].
'Three Halves of a House" *Great Canadian Short Stories* (1971), 241-62.
'Three Halves of a House" *Best Modern Canadian Short Stories* (1978), 195-211.
'Three Halves of a House" *Penguin Book of Canadian Short Stories* (1980), 259-78.
'The Tolstoy Pitch" *Fid* No. 79 (Mar-Apr 1969), 44-59.
'The Tolstoy Pitch" *Fruit Man* (1971), 22-37.
'The Tolstoy Pitch" *Selected Stories* (1978), 129-44.
'The Village Inside" *Around the Mountain* (1967), 113-26.
'The Village Inside" *Here and Now* (1977), 61-9.
"We Outnumber the Dead" *Prism* 21:3 (Apr 1983), 67-76.
"Where the Myth Touches Us" *Flying a Red Kite* (1962), 189-217.
"Where the Myth Touches Us" *QQ* 69 (1962), 211-36.
"Where the Myth Touches Us" *Stories from Ontario* (1974), 215-40.
"Where the Myth Touches Us" *Penguin Book of Modern Canadian Short Stories* (1982), 231-53.
'Whos Paying for This Call" *Fruit Man* (1971), 198-207.
'Whos Paying for This Call" *Canadian Anthology* (1974), 500-6.
'Whos Paying for This Call" *Selected Stories* (1978), 169-79.
'The Winner" *Jubilee* No. 3 [n.d.], 4-21.
'The Woodcutter's Third Son" *None Genuine without This Signature* (1980), 77-97.
'The Woodcutter's Third Son" *Anthology of Canadian Literature in English 2* (1983), 259-73.
'Worst Thing Ever" *Intercourse* Nos. 12/13 (Jan 1970), 13-8.
'Worst Thing Ever" *Dark Glasses* (1976), 87-96.

Hoogstraten, Vinia

"Afternoon of Love" *Chat* 25 (Sept 1952), 7, 55-7.
"Alienation of Affection" *McCall's* 85 (Apr 1958), 44-5[+?] [Based on RGPL].
"Henbane and a Tablespoon of Violets" *Echoes* No. 239 (Sum 1960), 8-9.
"The Long View" *CHJ* Jan 1954, 15, 67-8, 70.
"The Lost Cowhand" *Chat* 25 (Mar 1952), 19, 40-3.
"Lucky Sign" *Onward* 18 Sept 1955, 598-600, 606.
"Methuselah to Disaster in One Hour" *Echoes* No. 210 (Spr 1953), 9, 25-6.
"Moment of Decision" *CHJ* July 1956, 10, 49-50.
"Prelude to a Big Night" *Echoes* No. 218 (Spr 1955), 6-7, 29.
"A Present from an Angel" *Good Housekeeping* 141 (Nov 1955), 72-3, 184, 187-8.
"Those Who Wait" *CHJ* Dec 1952, 24, 26-9.

Hoolboom, Michael‡

"Last Journal" *Des* 12:2/3 Nos. 32/33 (1981), 116-24.

Hooper, Mollie

"Escape" *CSSM* 3:2 (Spr 1977), 18-9, 33-7.

Hopson, Brett†

"Life Is a Three and Two Changeup" *Pits/Grit* [1977], [9 pp].

Hopwood, V.G.†

"Nadya Visits Washington" *NF* 1:1 (Win 1952), 31-5.

Horan, Robert‡

"It Happens Every Year" *Communicator* Feb 1975, 40-4.

Hornborg, Sten‡

"Love Among the Bookstacks" *Alpha* 2:2 (Oct 1977), 21, 28.

Horne, Lewis B. (1932-)

"And Mae Flowered" *Ball State Univ Forum* 15:1 (Win 1974), 71-7.
"Coming Home" *Smoke Signals* [1] [1974?], 29-35.
"Coming Home" *riverSedge* 3 (Win 1980), 100-5 [Based on survey response].
"A Doting Walk" *CFM* No. 21 (Spr 1976), 65-71.
"Dream-Visions" *Ohio R* 13:2 (Win 1972), 86-93.
"The Ending of Journeys" *Was R* 16:1 (Spr 1981), 40-54.
"Exposure" *Gramercy R* 3 (Spr 1979), 14-21 [Based on survey response].
"The Father" *CutBank* 9 (Fall-Win 1977), 19-27 [Based on survey response].
"The Fear" *Coe R* 4 (Spr 1974), 57-66 [Based on survey response].
"Flood Time" *Descant* (U.S.) 18 (Win 1974), 21-9 [Based on survey response].
"Her Father's Daughter" *riverSedge* 4 (1982), 30-6 [Based on survey response].
"How a Birthday Was Passed and a Sorrow Set" *Chariton R* 3 (Fall 1977), 42-53 [Based on survey response].
"The Illness" *Mississippi R* 4:1 (1975), 92-105.
"Interim" *Cimarron R* (U.S.) 27 (Apr 1974), 19-28 [Based on survey response].
"A Kind Husband" *Twigs* 12 (Fall 1975), 7-14 [Based on survey response].
"The Last Dancer" *Quartet* 6 Nos. 45/46 (Win-Spr 1974), 9-19.
"Mansion, Magic, and Miracle" *Colorado Q* 22 (1973), 189-202.
"Mansion, Magic, and Miracle" *Best American Short Stories* 1974 52-66.
"Mergers" *Oyez R* 7 (1979), 61-80 [Based on survey response].

"Peggy and the Olivers" *Descant* (U.S.) 13 (Fall 1978), 2-15 [Based on survey response].

"The People Who Were Not There" *Kansas Q* 5 (Sum 1973), 27-37 [Based on survey response].

"The Red Iris" *Ont R* No. 3 (Fall-Win 1975-76), 77-91.

"Roadshow" *Chariton R* 7:1 (Spr 1981), 55-64.

"Run, Run, as Fast as You Can" *Chariton R* 9:1 (Spr 1983), 65-75 [Based on AHI and survey response].

"The Runaway" *Literary R* (U.S.) 23 (1979), 89-101.

"The Sad Beauty of Children" *Quartet* (U.S.) 8 Nos. 57/58 (Win-Spr 1977), 12-5.

"Seeing Strangers" *Descant* (U.S.) 17 (Fall 1972), 20-38 [Based on survey response].

"The Short Visit Home" *Florida Q* 4:1 (Spr 1971), 1-10.

"A Small Tone" *Four Quarters* (U.S.) 28:1 (Aut 1978), 20-6 [Based on AHI and survey response].

"Stereo" *Four Quarters* (U.S.) 31:1 (Aut 1981), 13-20 [Based on AHI and survey response].

"The Stroke" *San Jose Studies* 7:2 (May 1981), 51-7 [Based on AHI and survey response].

"A Summer to Sing – A Summer to Cry" *Prairie Schooner* 44 (1970), 95-120.

"The Swimmer" *Ball State Univ Forum* 18:4 (Aut 1977), 29-37 [Based on AHI and survey response].

"Thor Thorsen's Book of Days" *Cimarron R* (U.S.) 12 (Sum 1970), 67-79 [Based on survey response].

"The Walk Away" *Prism* 22:1 (Oct 1983), 7-16.

"What Do Ducks Do in the Winter?" *Saskatchewan Gold* (1982), 254-68.

"What Do Ducks Do in the Winter?" *Ascent* 1 [n.d.], 33-44 [Based on survey response].

"When Dry Summers End" *Discourse* (U.S.) 12 (1969), 42-53.

"Widow's Sanctuary" *Des* 12:2/3 Nos. 32/33 (1981), 125-30.

"Wives, New Wives, and Mothers" *On Campus* (Univ of Saskatchewan) 18 May 1979, 6-7 [Based on survey response].

"Wives, New Wives, and Mothers" *Descant* (U.S.) 23:2 (Win 1979), 22-4.

"Zina's Version" *Dialogue: A Journal of Mormon Thought* 11 (Spr 1978), 77-83 [Based on survey response].

Horne, Marcel

"Hastings Jungle Vancouver" *Outlaws* (1974), 75-6.

"Roll-Downs & Pin-Heads" *Outlaws* (1974), 81-7.

Horne, N. – *See* Kalman, Judy.

Horne, N.R.‡

"When We Saw a Sign" *Edmonton Journal* Wed, 18 Mar 1964, 4.

Horner, Bill (1940?-)

"Goodbye, Northwest" *Read Ch* 1:2 (Sum 1982), 31-6.

Horner, Nina – *See* Green, H. Gordon.

Horodezky, Zeporah†

"Daniel" *Des* 11:3 No. 29 (1980), 67-9.

"Notes on Singer Isle" *Quarry* 29:2 (Spr 1980), 46-51.

Horse, Benjamin [pseudonym]

"The Marble King" *Grain* 5:3 [1977], 3-8.

"Radio Cafe" *Grain* 5:2 [1977], 41-5.

"A Room Full of Research Assistants" *Grain* 4:2 [1976], 21-5.

Horst, Roger†

"I Am a Poet" *Chiaroscuro* 13 (1969-70), 29-30.

"In and Out of the Park" *CBC "Anthology"* 16 June 1979.

"Pete" *Quarry* 25:1 (Win 1976), 52-5.

"Sanders" *Grain* 5:3 [1977], 29-38.

"Virgil" *Quarry* 25:1 (Win 1976), 55-9.

Horwood, Harold (1923-)

ONLY THE GODS SPEAK [St. John's]: Breakwater Books, 1979.

"The Acid is Shitty in Vancouver" *Voices Down East* [1973], 30-3 [Also entitled "The Acid is Lousy in Vancouver"].

"The Acid Is Lousy in Vancouver" *Only the Gods Speak* (1979), 118-27 [Also entitled "The Acid Is Shitty in Vancouver"].

"Among the Sharks" *Only the Gods Speak* (1979), 55-62.

"A Chant for One Voice" *Only the Gods Speak* (1979), 128-30.

"Coming to an End" *74: New Canadian Stories* 85-96.

"Coming to an End" *Only the Gods Speak* (1979), 70-9.

"Descent of Woman" *Only the Gods Speak* (1979), 45-54.

"Every Morning Is Christmas" *Evening Telegram* 23 Dec 1968, 10[+?] [Based on survey response].

"Iniquities of the Fathers" *Only the Gods Speak* (1979), 94-101.

"Island of the Innocents" *Only the Gods Speak* (1979), 22-8.

"The Lady Who Fought at the Siege of Jerusalem" *QQ* 81 (1974), 412-8.

"The Lady Who Fought at the Siege of Jerusalem" *Only the Gods Speak* (1979), 15-21.

"Look Man, I Love You" *Scruncheons* 1:2 (Sept 1973), 82-6.

"Look Man, I Love You" *Blasty Bough* (1976), 113-7.

"Look Man, I Love You" *Only the Gods Speak* (1979), 114-7.

"Love in a Very Cold Climate" *Only the Gods Speak* (1979), 87-93.

"Manuel's Shark" *Only the Gods Speak* (1979), 29-34.

"Men Like Summer Snow" *Stories from Pacific & Arctic Canada* (1974), 230-7.

"Men Like Summer Snow" *Only the Gods Speak* (1979), 81-6.

"The Raven's Nest" *AA* 57 (July 1967), 41-3.

"The Shell Collector" *73: New Canadian Stories* 93-104.

"The Shell Collector" *Only the Gods Speak* (1979), 35-44.

"Some of His Best Friends" *Only the Gods Speak* (1979), 63-9.

"Some of His Best Friends" *Best Canadian Short Stories* (1981), 144-50.

"The Sound of Thunder" *JCF* 4:3 No. 15 (1975), 73-80.

"The Sound of Thunder" *Only the Gods Speak* (1979), 1-8.

"Through Dreaming Towns" *Only the Gods Speak* (1979), 9-14.

Hosein, Clyde (1940-)

THE KILLING OF NELSON JOHN AND OTHER STORIES London: London Magazine Editions, 1980.

"Bianca" *Killing of Nelson John* (1980), 61-71.

"The Bookkeeper's Wife" *Tor S Asian R* 1:3 (Fall-Win 1982-83), 72-5.

"Crow" *Killing of Nelson John* (1980), 24-31.

"Curtains" *Killing of Nelson John* (1980), 72-80.

"Her House" *Killing of Nelson John* (1980), 52-60.

"I'm a Presbyterian, Mr. Kramer" *Killing of Nelson John* (1980), 42-51.

"I'm a Presbyterian, Mr. Kramer" *This Island Place* (1981), 106-15.

"The Jeweller" *Killing of Nelson John* (1980), 16-23.

"The Killing of Nelson John" *Killing of Nelson John* (1980), 96-102.

"Mahal" *London Magazine Stories* 11 (1979), 46-9.

"Mahal" *Killing of Nelson John* (1980), 11-5.

"Morris; Bhaiya" *Killing of Nelson John* (1980), 114-28.

"Morris; Bhaiya" *Tor S Asian R* 2:2 (Sum 1983), 80-90.

"Partners" *Killing of Nelson John* (1980), 81-95.

"Shoes" *Killing of Nelson John* (1980), 103-13.

"The Signature" *London Magazine Stories* 11 (1979), 43-6.

"The Signature" *Killing of Nelson John* (1980), 7-10.

"The Sword" *Killing of Nelson John* (1980), 32-41.

Hosmar, Berta

STORIES BY THE FIRESIDE Whitby: A. Hosmar, 1976 [Based on CBIP].

Hospital, Janette Turner (1942-)

"After the Fall" *QQ* 88 (1981), 67-73.

"Ashes to Ashes" *Encounter* 60 (May 1983), 3-8.

"The Baroque Ensemble" *QQ* 89 (1982), 505-13.

"The Dark Wood" *Dal R* 59 (1979-80), 696-704.

"A Dream of Isfahan" *Chat* 53 (July 1980), 31, 42, 44, 48, 50.

"From the Time of King Solomon's Ships" *CBC* "Anthology" 29 Dec 1979.

"Golden Girl" *Mademoiselle* 87 (Oct 1981), 104, 106, 112, 240, 242, 244.

"The Inside Story" *CF* 60 (Apr 1980), 28-31.

"Our Little Chamber Concerts" *SN* 97 (June 1982), 46-8, 50-3.

"The Owl-Bander" *CFM* Nos. 45/46 (1982-83), 173-80.

"Some Have Called Thee Mighty and Dreadful" *North American R* 264:2 (Sum 1979), 33-6.

"Waiting" *Atlantic Monthly* 241 (Mar 1978), 110-4, 116.

"Walking on Water" *Chat* 55 (Nov 1982), 64-5, 112, 116, 118.

"You Gave Me Hyacinths" *Mal R* No. 46 (Apr 1978), 137-43.

Hossick, Hugh and Wiley, Tom‡

"Hoss and the Yuk-Chick-toes" *Anthos* 2:1/2 (1980), 94-9.

Host, Fred‡

"A Long Story" *Varsity* Fri, 18 Mar 1960, 7-8.

Hough, N.C. (1951-)

"Matherstruck" by George Twelftree *Repos* No. 12 (Fall 1974), 43-5.

"A Plain Story" by George Twelftree *Repos* No. 15 (Sum 1975), 21-2.

Houghton, Norman‡

"Three-Ring Businessman" *Performing Arts* 7:3 (1970), 44-6.

House, Patricia – *See* Vicari, Patricia.

Houser, Gwenyth‡

"Water in the Dust-Bowl" *Inside* No. 4 [Jan 1965], 5 ["Metamyth"].

Hovey, Joan Hall‡

"The Dreamer" *AA* 70 (Apr 1980), 15-6, 18, 20.

Howard, Blanche M.

"When Every Woman Looked Like Regina Lee" *MM* 69 (7 July 1956), 21, 42, 44-6.

Howard, Dorothy

"Quicksilver" *Lib* 30 (July 1953), 24-5, 69.

Howard, Randy

"Annie's Apple" *Acta Vic* 81:2 (Dec 1962), 3-6.
"Annie's Apple" *Campus Canada* Nov 1963, 26-7, 54.
"Bug-Bearing for Fun and Profit" *Acta Vic* [85]:2 (Jan 1961), 8-9.
"Charmaine and the Wizard" *Varsity Lit Issue* Fri, 13 Dec 1963, 15-6.
"Ends and Means" *Acta Vic* 84:3 (Apr 1960), 3-5.
"Evening and Night" *Acta Vic* 84:2 (Mar 1960), 14-6.
"Golgotha by the Sea" *Acta Vic* 86:1 (Aut 1961), 15-6.
"Overheard" *Acta Vic* 87:1 [1962], 11-2.
"P.T." *Acta Vic* 86:1 (Aut 1961), 4-10.

Howard, Richard‡

"The Broken Reed" *TUR* 74:2 (Mar 1961), 6-8.
"The Counterfeiter" *TUR* 75:1 (Nov 1961), 12-5.
"Here Is No Water" *TUR* 73:2 (Dec 1959), 24-6.
"In the Moon's Sphere" *TUR* 74:1 (Dec 1960), 14-6.
"There Are Damons at the Bottom of My Garden ... or, The Pythias Legend Revisited" *TUR* 74:3 (Apr 1961), 16-7.

Howard, William‡

"Variations" *Abegweit R* 1:2 (Fall 1974), 12-22.

Howarth, Jean

"The Novitiate" *Canadian Short Stories* (1952), 146-50.

Howarth, Jessmin‡

"Wise Woman" *J of Our Time* No. 2 (1979), 29-31.

Howe, Thomas C.†

"Night in Gethsemanie" *CFM* No. 4 (Aut 1971), 3-5.

Howell, Bill†

"Looking for a Girl in an Orange Flower Dress" *Either/Or* No. 5 (Fall 1967), 20-2.

"The View from Uncle Dave's Window" *Either/Or* No. 6 (Spr 1968), 1-3.

"The Wickedness of Rubin Broome" *Either/Or* No. 7 (Win 1968), [2 pp].

Howell, Wayne‡

"The Final Instalment" *Legion* 56 (Feb 1982), 24.

Hrynkiw, Oreste‡

"A Dialogue" *TUR* 75:2 (Jan 1962), 44-7.

"Pipistrello" *TUR* 76:3 (Jan 1963), 28-32.

Hubbard, Dexter

"Dingo Hunter" *Can Messenger* 71 (May 1961), 16-9, 46, 48.

"Discrimination" *Mont* 34 (Mar 1960), 41-2.

"Duel in the Smokehouse" *Can Messenger* 68 (Aug 1958), 495-8.

"Father Moran's Trick" *Can Messenger* 71 (Sept 1961), 14-6.

"Love, a Lunenberger, and Rappie Pie" *Bluenose* 2:1 (Sum 1977), 28-31.

"Memorial for Old Doc" *FH* 26 Jan 1961, 23.

"Monkey in the Cockpit" *Can Messenger* 68 (Jan 1958), 17-21.

"The Moon Toucher" *Axiom* 2:5 (July 1976), 26-9, 60.

"The Nagger" *Can Messenger* 69 (May 1959), 24-6, 47.

"A Present for My Mother" *FH* 7 May 1959, 24-5, 27.

"Roses for Mother's Day" *FH* 11 May 1961, 22.

"Saga of the Sauerkraut Juice" *FH* 13 Feb 1964, 62-3.

"Uncle Dud and the Runaway Automobile" *Can Messenger* 68 (Oct 1958), 633-7.

"Uncle Dud Goes Bear Hunting" *Can Messenger* 70 (Apr 1960), 42-5, 47.

"A Wife for Antonio" *Can Messenger* 68 (Mar 1958), 155-9.

Hubert, Cam – *See* Cameron, Anne.

Hubert, Cam and Jones, Betty Jane.

See also Cameron, Anne.

"The Grandmother" *Room* 2:1 (1976), 48-58.

Hudson, Noel†

"Late Lunch in Car 19" *Writing* No. 4 (Win 1981-82), 46.

"The Moment Prior" *Zest* No. 16 (Nov 1983), 22-3.

"Old Pangburn & the Walking Crayfish" *Writing* No. 3 (Sum 1981), 33.

"Salmon" *Writing* No. 2 (Win 1980-81), 31.

"The Woman Who Bred Them for War" *Interior Voice* No. 2 (June-July/Spr-Sum 1982), 14-5.

Huggan, Isabel (1943-)

"Bridges" *event* 7:2 (1978), 102-9.

"Bus 7" *Quarry* 29:4 (Aut 1980), 4-7.

"Celia Behind Me" *Grain* 4:3 [1976], 3-8.

"Celia Behind Me" *Best of Grain* (1980), 39-44.

"Celia Behind Me" *First Impressions* (1980), 54-63.

"Jack of Hearts" *First Impressions* (1980), 82-105.

"Sawdust" *First Impressions* (1980), 64-81.

"Sorrows of the Flesh" *CHEZ-FM (Ott)* "*Rhyme and Reason*" June 1982 [Based on survey response].
"Sorrows of the Flesh" *83: Best Canadian Stories* 186-214.
"Up and Down, Round and Round" *Quarry* 26:3 (Sum 1977), 38-43.
"The Violation" *Har* 4:4 No. 24 (Dec 1979), 99-100, 102-3.

Hughes, Charles‡
"A Very Minor Tragedy" *Pier Spr* [No. 3] (Win 1978), 14-5.

Hughes, Gail
"The Head" *Edge* No. 8 (Fall 1968), 111-6.

Hughes, J. McK.†
"The Elves" *Alberta Speaks* 1957, 15-6.

Hughes, Ora Wayne†
"To the Gods Below" *New Q* 2:3 (Fall 1982), 47-55.
"Triangle" *New Q* 2:1 (Spr 1982), 37-47.

Hughes, Philip
"The Hero Despite Himself" *Origins* 10:1 (Spr 1980), 30-2.
"Pie in the Sty" *Alpha* 4:1 (Fall 1979), 12.

Hughes, Philip B. (1905-)
"Another Christ" *SN* 81 (Dec 1966), 29-31.
"Catherine and the Winter Wheat" *MM* 67 (1 July 1954), 21, 38-9.
"Catherine and the Winter Wheat" *Scholastic* (U.S.) 65 (6 Oct 1954), 19[+?] [Based on RGPL].
"Catherine and the Winter Wheat" *Scholastic* (U.S.) 69 (25 Oct 1956), 38-9[+?] [Based on RGPL].
"Catherine and the Winter Wheat" *Our Family* 24 (Apr 1972), 26-8.
"Cold Christmas in Kent County" *Varsity* Fri, 9 Dec 1955, 3.
"For Love of Denise" *Sat Eve Post* 232 (31 Oct 1959), 30, 82-4.
"A Gift of Ivory" *Chat* 28 (Dec 1956), 15, 59-61.
"Is Stealing a Girl Really Stealing?" *MM* 67 (1 Nov 1954), 23, 40, 42.
"The Non-Taxable Loves of Mrs. Ollenberger" *MM* 71 (15 Mar 1958), 21, 30, 32, 36-7.
"Of Laws and Compasses" *Varsity* Thu, 13 Dec 1956, 6.
"Put Away Your Bugle, Soldier" *MM* 72 (7 Nov 1959), 39, 46-7, 50.

Hughes, Robert†
"Christmas at Sulpher for the Lonely Brigade" *UC Observer* 12 (15 Dec 1950), 9, 43-5.

Hulet, William†
"The Glass" *Quote Unquote* 2:2 (Mar 1979), 12.

Hull, Lynn†
"The Circus" *Pulp Mill* (1977), 71-5.

Hull, Raymond
"Play, Fellow" *Klanak Islands* (1959), 17-20.

Hulse, Louise‡

"Knit for Tatt – the Tale of a Snail (A Fairy Tale for Adults)" *Diversions* 2:1 (19 Apr 1970), 5-7.

Hultch, U. (1945-)

"Watch the Birdie" *Bakka* No. 5 (Spr-Sum 1977), 112-4.

Humble, Jacquelyn†

"Ominous Stranger" *Chat* 42 (May 1969), 28, 46-8, 50-1.

Hummell, Steven‡

"The Gift of the Bear" *Legion* 54 (Dec 1979), 20-3.
"West Lounge" *Legion* 55 (July 1980), 12-4, 27.

Hummer, Pietsche Mae‡

"A Moonlit Night Is a Woman's Business Office" *OPT* 3:3 (Jan-Feb 1976), 14-5.

Humphreys, David C.†

"Guido" *Newcomers* (1979), 205-15.

Humphries, David‡

"Thunder in Autumn" *Undergrad* Spr 1960, 27-33.

Humphries, Tom†

"Arbiter of Spring" *Edmonton Journal* Wed, 25 Mar 1964, 4 [Humour].
"A Child's Flower" *Edmonton Journal* Thu, 29 Apr 1965, 4.
"Diaper Talk" *Edmonton Journal* Fri, 19 Nov 1965, 61 [Humour].
"Elegy in Ice" *Edmonton Journal* Thu, 12 Mar 1964, 4 [Non-fiction?].
"The Homestead" *Edmonton Journal* Thu, 27 May 1965, 4.
"House of Glass" *Edmonton Journal* Wed, 24 Mar 1965, 4.
"Johnny" *Edmonton Journal* Wed, 24 Feb 1965, 4.
"Livability Test" *Edmonton Journal* Wed, 4 Dec 1963, 4 [Non-fiction?].
"Man Against Mouse" *Edmonton Journal* Thu, 19 Mar 1964, 4.
"Next Year Country" *Edmonton Journal* Wed, 22 Apr 1964, 4.
"Once Upon a Time" *Edmonton Journal* Thu, 21 Jan 1965, 4 [Non-fiction?].
"Songs Beyond Recall" *Edmonton Journal* Fri, 15 Oct 1965, 60.
"You Don't Understand" *Edmonton Journal* Thu, 13 Feb 1964, 4.
"You Don't Understand" *BC Lib Q* 34:2/3 (Oct-Jan 1970-71), 19-21.

Hunking, Diane‡

"The Colt" *Can Horse* 12 (July 1972), 30-1.

Hunt, Edward‡

"Tears in the Afternoon" *Gram* 2:4 (Apr 1977), 10.

Hunt, Reg†

"The Price of a Cup of Coffee" *Versus* No. 3 (Spr 1977), 57-65.

Hunter, Beth L.‡

"The Funny Man" *Muskeg R* 4 [1976], 3-6.

Hunter, Brad‡

"The Diary Fragments of Joseph Ahlmahn" *Acta Vic* 96:1 [n.d.], 4-9.

Hunter, Bruce†
"Command Performance" *Raven* No. 10 (Mar 1962), 26-8.
"Private Property" *Dand* 6 [n.d.], 8-13.

Hunter, Mary Alice‡
"Christmas Revisited" *Varsity* Fri, 10 Dec 1954, 12.
"Help! Murder!" *TUR* 66:2 (Christmas 1953), 10-1.

Huntington, Terry†
"The English Lesson" *English Q* 16:3 (Fall 1983), 66-8 [Sketch?].

Hurlbut, Eric‡
"Journeyman" *Nightwinds* 1:1 (Sum 1979), 9-12.

Hurley, Gillian†
"The Shipwreck" *Outset* 1973, 57-62.

Hurley, Joan Mason
"Salad Days" *Room* 4:3 (1979), 16-27.

Hurley, Richard A.‡
"Call Ruby" *Origins* 9:3 (Aut 1979), 31-4.

Hurly, Paul‡
"Tichara, A ndi to Ziba!" *Acta Vic* 98:1 (Dec 1973), 33-40.

Huser, Glen†
"Dance" *Prism* 16:2 (Fall 1977), 35-45.
"The Recital" *Dand* 9:1 (1982), 63-73.

Hushlak, Mary Ann (1949-)
"Just Jessica" *Mal R* No. 62 (July 1982), 199-201.

Hutchins, Hazel J.‡
"All the Queen's Horses" CBC *"Alberta Anthology"* 3 Sept 1983.
"Snowbound" CBC *"Alberta Anthology"* 29 Nov 1980.

Hutchinson, Alice‡
"Paper Doom" CBC *"Alberta Anthology"* 13 Nov 1982.

Hutchinson, Bobby† (1941?-)
"The Gyro Effect" *Chat* 56 (Mar 1983), 63, 105-6, 110, 112, 114.
"Pheidippides Was Not a Family Man" *Chat* 54 (Oct 1981), 74, 146-7, 150, 156, 160, 162.

Hutchinson, Rosemary‡
"The Coal-Oil Kids" *Legion* 57 (Jan 1983), 21, 45-6 [Non-fiction?].
"Cruising on the Queen E" *Legion* 56 (Feb 1982), 9-10 [Non-fiction?].
"Garbage Run" *Legion* 56 (May 1982), 17-8.

Hutchison, Bruce (1901-)
UNCLE PERCY'S WONDERFUL TOWN Vancouver: Douglas & McIntyre, 1981.
"A Canadian Parable" *Free Press Weekly* 26 Aug 1978 [Based on *Reader's Digest*].
"A Canadian Parable" *Read Dig* 119 (Aug 1981), 110-1 [Condensed].
"The Canadian Saga" *Uncle Percy's Wonderful Town* (1981), 71-83.
"The Epic of Petit Trudeau" *Uncle Percy's Wonderful Town* (1981), 59-68.
"A Great Day" *Uncle Percy's Wonderful Town* (1981), 97-109.
"Half-Breed" *Uncle Percy's Wonderful Town* (1981), 143-58.
"Homecoming" *Uncle Percy's Wonderful Town* (1981), 197-203.
"The Love Affair" *Uncle Percy's Wonderful Town* (1981), 85-95.
"Men of Genius" *Uncle Percy's Wonderful Town* (1981), 111-27.
"A Mighty Echo" *Uncle Percy's Wonderful Town* (1981), 11-24.
"A Mighty Echo" *Read Dig* 121 (Oct 1982), 80-5.
"The Old Man's Seeds" *Golden West* May-June 1966, 12-3 [Originally in *Vancouver Sun*].
"The Scientific Method" *Uncle Percy's Wonderful Town* (1981), 129-41.
"Sir John's Bed" *Uncle Percy's Wonderful Town* (1981), 27-38.
"Three Fishers" *Uncle Percy's Wonderful Town* (1981), 161-77.
"Whisky Jack" *Uncle Percy's Wonderful Town* (1981), 179-95.
"Without Fear or Favor" *Uncle Percy's Wonderful Town* (1981), 41-56.

Hutchison, David‡
"Class Extinction" *Liontayles* Win 1967, 38-40.
"Waiting" *Liontayles* Win 1967, 37-8.

Huth, Robin‡
"Don't I Know You?" *Edmonton Journal* Fri, 19 Jan 1968, 29.

Hutton, Bill.
See also d'Or, Vic and Hutton, Bill.
"The Declaration of Independence" *Is* No. 4 [n.d.], [1 p] [Prose poem?].
"The Eisenhower Years" *Ant's Forefoot* No. 1 (Fall 1967), [1 p].
"The Indians of the Southwest" *Ant's Forefoot* No. 1 (Fall 1967), [1 p].
"The Kid Who Got Pushed Around All His Life" *Is* No. 5 (1968), [2 pp].
"Who's Your Pal?" *Image Nation* 1:6 (6 June [1969]), [3 pp].

Hutton, William Finlay‡
"Brothers by the Wall" *Words from Inside* 1976, 18.
"Gregor Strassen" *Words from Inside* 1972, 12-3.
"The Predators" *Words from Inside* 1976, 38.

Huxley, Brenda‡
"The Adventures of Brenda Lady Coal-Sampler" *Pedestal* 2:6 (July-Aug 1970), 13.

Hyatt, Murray‡
"Momma Will Hear You" *Forge* 1952, 45-6.

Hyatt, Paul‡
"Sylvan Hart" *Womb* [No. 1] (1967), 17-24.

Hyde, Glen‡
  [Untitled] *TUR* 85:3 (Apr 1972), 7 [Prose poem?].

Hyland, Gary‡
  "The Kill Man" *Salt* No. 12 (Win 1974-75), 12-6.

I.F.V. – *See* V., I.F.

Ibbitson, John‡
  "Customer Service" *TUR* 91:2 (Apr 1978), 37-41.

Ibsen, Norman‡
  "The Samaritan" *Folio* 4:1 [Jan 1950], [5 pp].
  "Search" *Folio* 5:2 (Apr 1951), [5 pp].
  "Southern Exposure" *Folio* 5:1 [Jan 1951], [6 pp].

Illidge, Paul‡
  "Asylum" *Alive* No. 36 [1974], 19.
  "The Fighter" *Alive* No. 26 [1973], 39-41.
  "Something to Eat" *Alive* No. 31 [1973], 36-7.

Inglis, George‡
  "An Irish Chip" *Edmonton Journal* Wed, 3 Mar 1965, 4.
  "An Irish Chip" *North* 15 (May-June 1968), 44-5.

Inglis, Jean
  "And the Green Hills Laugh" *CF* 35 (Aug 1955), 105-7, 109.
  "And the Green Hills Laugh" *Forum* (1972), 294-8.
  "The Gentle Wind" *CF* 31 (Oct 1951), 153-5, 157.
  "The Sacrifice" *Acta Vic* 74:4 (Feb 1950), 12-5.

Inglis, Patricia†
  "father lamonte" *Contact* 2:11 (Fall 1974), 28.
  "Possession" *Contact* 3:2 (Spr 1974), 20-2.

Inkster, Tim (1949-)
  "Ray Bradley" *Random* 3:4 (Jan [1969]), 23 [Non-fiction?].

Inman, P.‡
  "Number 1" *Titmouse R* No. 5 (Win 1974-75), 43-5.

Innis, Mary Quayle (1899-)
  "From Where I Sit" *UC Observer* 1 Aug 1966, 24.
  "The Lived-In Look" *Stories with John Drainie* (1963), 187-91.

Ipellie, Alootook
  "Old Man Carver" *Beaver* 311:1 (Sum 1980), 49-52.

Ireland, Ann (1954-)

"At the End of the Line" *BC Monthly* 3:1 (Oct 1976), [1 p].
"The Blood Is on the Cup" *event* 6:1 [1977], 47 [Prose poem?].
"Field Felt" *event* 6:1 [1977], 48 [Prose poem?].
"The Great Speckled Bird" *BC Monthly* 3:1 (Oct 1976), [2 pp].
"The Journals" *Canadian Short Fiction Anthology* (1976), 101.
"Queen Street 3 Soundings" *Per* No. 3 (Spr 1978), 30-1.

Irvine, Connie†

"The Fool" *Prism* 7:1 (Sum 1967), 83-94.
"Requiem" *Raven* No. 10 (Mar 1962), 14-9.

Irvine, R.B.

"The Bed" *CHJ* Apr 1956, 10, 63-6.
"Daughter of Tantaley" *Prism* 1:3 (Spr 1960), 28-31.
"The Mermaid on His Stomach" *MM* 66 (15 May 1953), 18-9, 50-4, 56.
"Plumbers Can Dish It Out Too" *Weekend* 5 (20 Aug 1955), 16-7, 26.
"Why Raymond Joined the Navy" *Weekend* 5 (14 May 1955), 31-2, 38-9, 44-5.

Iserman, Jenny†

"Friends" *Toronto Star* Sun, 30 Oct 1983, C10.

Ison, Olivine†

"Little Arrow" *Alberta Writers Speak* 1967, 77-84.
"Miracle at Ram River" *Alberta Writers Speak* 1969, 19-26.

Israel, Charles E.

"The Succession" *Newcomers* (1979), 25-35.

Israel, Inge

"The Mars Bar" *CBC [Edm] "Alberta Anthology"* 22 Oct 1983.
"The Red Painting" *CBC [Edm] "Alberta Anthology"* 6 Nov 1982.

Itani, Frances (1942-)

"Anna" *Quarry* 32:2 (Spr 1983), 64-8.
"An August Wind" *Fid* No. 124 (Win 1980), 36-9.
"An August Wind" *Contexts* 2 (1981), 274-7.
"Black Eyes Almond Skin ... " *Rikka* 5:4 (Win 1978), 9-10 [Second part of three-part short story entitled "The Thickness of One Sheet of Paper"].
"Burst of a Birdheart" *CBC "Anthology"* 9 Mar 1974.
"Clayton" *CBC "Anthology"* 13 Feb 1982 [Based on survey response].
"Did You Ever Eat a Sheep's Nose?" *Fid* No. 118 (Sum 1978), 61-4.
"Drawing the Pillow" *Antig R* No. 45 (Spr 1981), 11-8.
"Dream Island" *Antig R* No. 39 (Aut 1979), 37-43.
"Dream Island" *CBC "Audio Stage"* 12 Jan 1980 [Based on survey response].
"Grandmother" *QQ* 89 (1982), 710-21.
"His Family" *Br Out* 6:3 (1979), 30-2, 47.
"Iron Wheels" *NeWest R* 2 (Mar 1977), 6-7.
"Megan" *QQ* 87 (1980), 672-8.
"Privacies" *CBC "Anthology"* 3 May 1980.
"Privacies" *Fid* No. 130 (Sum 1981), 62-72.
"P'tit Village" *QQ* 84 (1977), 218-26.

"Separation" *UWR* 16:2 (Spr-Sum 1982), 56-71.
"A Tangle of Voices" *NeWest R* 3:1 (Sept 1977), 6-7.
"A Tangle of Voices" *CBC "Anthology"* 12 Aug 1978.
"Truths or Lies A Writer's Diary" *Room* 8:3 (1983), 68-77.
"A Very Modern Person" *CF* 58 (Mar 1979), 24-6.

Itter, Carole
See also Itter, Carole and Gilbert, Gerry.
"The Chicken Story Part V" *Twelfth Key* No. 0 (West Coast Works) (1977), [2 pp] [Excerpt?].
"Clearing" *Per* No. 4 (Fall 1978), 5-8.
"Excerpts from Journal" *Return* No. 3 (May 1973), 1-3 [Poetry?].
"The Outing" *Cap R* Nos. 8/9 (Fall-Spr 1975-76), 22-5.
"Ten Sketches" *Room* 1:3 (Fall 1975), 54-63.
"Whistle, Daughter, Whistle" *Per* Nos. 7/8 (Win 1981), 147-60.

Itter, Carole and Gilbert, Gerry
See also Gilbert, Gerry; Itter, Carole.
"A Sad Story" *Twelfth Key* No. 0 (West Coast Works) (1977), [2 pp] [Poem?].

Itwaru, Arnold
"The Attendant" *Rikka* 6:1 (Spr 1979), 22-4.

Izzard, Douglas M.‡
"And Bells Did Ring" *Driftwood* No. 2 (1974), 37-40.

J.H.C. – *See* C., J.H.

J.S.O [pseudonym]
"From the Perimeter" *Pulp* 3:17 (15 June 1976), [1, 3-4].

Jaboll, Stan‡
"A Post Christmas Carol" *Pulp* 3:23 (1 Jan 1977), [1-2].

Jackson, Carl‡
"I Hear a Tambourine" *Imp* 3:2 [n.d.], 19-24.

Jackson, Eloise‡
"My Literary Career" *Stump* Spr 1981, 22-6.

Jackson, J. Graham (1949-)
GARDENS Scarborough: Catalyst, 1976.
"Andanta, Ma Non Troppo" *Gardens* (1976), 61-7.
"Another Time, Another Place" *Gardens* (1976), 15-21.
"Another Time, Another Place" *On the Line* (1981), 201-6.
"Charm" *Gardens* (1976), 39-44.
"The Death of a Loving Man" *Gardens* (1976), 23-9.
"Excerpts from Gérarde's Diary" *Acta Vic* 96:1 [n.d.], 30-2.
"Gardens" *Gardens* (1976), 9-13.
"Henrietta & and the Green Man" *Gardens* (1976), 69-77.
"I Am Dying, Dying" *Gardens* (1976), 53-8.

"Mr & Mrs Cassandra Brown" *Gardens* (1976), 47-51.
"Peter & John: Two Cameos" *Acta Vic* 94:1 (Nov 1969), 21-3.
"Prairie Dreams" *Gardens* (1976), 33-7.
"The Shirt Off My Back" *Gardens* (1976), 87-94.
"Le Temps des Citrouilles: A Story for Michael" *Body Politic* No. 31 (Mar 1977), 12-3.
"Terminus: A New Beginning" *Acta Vic* 94:4 (Apr 1970), 43-9.
"The Verlaine Symposium" *Onion* Oct 1979, 1-2.
"Vichyssoise" *Gardens* (1976), 79-84.

Jackson, Lee‡
"What Happened to Johnny?" *CBC "Alberta Anthology"* 13 Sept 1980.

Jackson, Marni‡
"A Social Disease, So to Speak" *Acta Vic* 90:1 (Nov 1965), 35-7.

Jackson, Pat‡
"Bunkhouse Betty" *Rain Chr* No. 10 [n.d.], 35-7.

Jackson, Philip
"The Instrument of Death" *New Bodies* (1981), 11-23.

Jacob, John‡
"Investigation" *Pulp* 2:14 (15 Sept 1974), [1 p].
"One of Our Agents Is Missing" *Pulp* 2:14 (15 Sept 1974), [1 p].

Jacobs, M. Culross‡
"Red Light, Green Light" *Alpha* 5:1 (Fall 1980), 7-8, 16, 18, 27.

Jacobs, William†
"Last Night on Lombard Street" *JD* Hanukah 1971, 10-1, 13, 15, 17, 19, 21, 23.
"Last Night on Lombard Street" *JD* Rosh Hashanah 1978, 2-9.

Jaffe, Sherrill‡
"For Leather or Worse" *Titmouse R* No. 7 [n.d.], 33-4.
"The Lost Key" *Titmouse R* No. 7 [n.d.], 32.
"Nobody's Business" *Titmouse R* No. 6 (Sum-Fall 1976), 24-5.

Jake [pseudonym]
"Glass of Beer" *Dime Bag* No. 12 (Nov 1974), [1 p].

Jakob, Conrad – *See* Reinl, Constance and Jakob, Conrad.

Jakober, Marie
"The Children of Pan" *Edmonton Journal* Tue, 21 June 1966, 5, 8.
"Find the Sun" *Writing* No. 5 (Spr 1982), 45-7.
"The Gift" *QQ* 83 (1976), 85-92.
"The Inheritance" *Interface* 3:5 (Sum 1980), 20-2, 92.
"Love at Trevor Station" *JCF* No. 22 (1978), 19-28.

Jalava, Jarmo‡
"Harold" *Alpha* 5:1 (Fall 1980), 5, 31.

James, Janet Craig
  "The Four Letter Word" *Northern Ontario Anthology* 2 (1978), 81-2.

James, Jean‡
  "Amen, Charlie's Harvest" *CBC "Alberta Anthology"* 13 Sept 1980.

James, Richard
  "A Red Letter Day" *Waves* 103 (Win 1982), 4-13.

Jameson, Hazel (1914-)
  "The Passing" *Was R* 13:1 (Spr 1978), 33-40.

Jamie [pseudonym]
  "A Barbed Hook" *TUR* 64:3 (Jan 1952), 45.

Jamieson, Kevin‡
  "The Puppet People" *New Bodies* (1981), 91-5.

Janes, Percy (1922-)
  "Captain Stephen Hawco" *Twelve Newfoundland Stories* (1982), 19-24.
  "Curtains" *Nfld Q* 74:3 (Fall 1978), 3-4.
  "Dandy" *Nfld Q* 77:1 (Spr 1981), 38-40.
  "The Private Executioner" *Nfld Q* 76:3 (Fall 1980), 17-9.
  "The Streetcomber" *Nfld Q* 75:3 (Dec 1979), 3-4.
  "The Streetcomber" *Treasury of Newfoundland Prose and Verse* (1983), 74-7.

Janoff, Douglas†
  "The Twilight of Her Youth" *Word Loom* No. 1 (Win 1981-82), 14-23.

Jansen, Dagmar‡
  "Gimmie Shelter" *Fantarama* 3:3 (Mar 1979), 29.

Jardine, Paula†
  "Crane" *Gas Rain* 2 (1978), 12-7.

Jarman, Mark†
  "Nowadays Clancy Can't Even Sing" *Fid* No. 130 (Sum 1981), 5-13.

Jarvis, Allen‡
  "The Too Old Man" *Re. Visions* 1:2 (1970), 9-10.

Jarvis, June N.†
  "An April Hour" Onward 8 Apr 1962, 13-4 [Non-fiction?].
  "An April Hour" *Onward* 30 Apr 1967, 13-4.
  "As We Forgive" *Onward* 8 Nov 1964, 6-7.
  "A Day for Remembering" *Onward* 10 Nov 1963, 4-5.
  "I Remember Aunt Linda" *Onward* 18 Nov 1962, 12-3 [Reminiscence?].

Jasiura, Barbara†
  "The Best Man" *Fid* No. 118 (Sum 1978), 55-60.

Jasper, Lori†

" ... on Thursday in autumn like today and that's the truth" *Motion* No. 3 (25 July 1962), [1-2].

'The Children and the Pedant" *Motion* No. 4 (25 Aug 1962), [1-3].

"Fragment of a Single Mind" *Motion* No. 1 (25 May 1962), [2 pp] [Prose poem?].

Jeffels, Ronald R.

"Autumn Episode" *Lib* 29 (Nov 1952), 29, 36-40.

"A Fall of Birds" *MM* 74 (4 Nov 1961), 21, 47, 49-51.

"Male Guest" *Lib* 29 (Sept 1952), 18-9, 44-6.

"Of Times Past: A Wine Warp" *Can Lawyer* 4 (Nov-Dec 1980), 30-1.

Jeffrey, Carole-Lynn‡

'The Waiting Game" *Intervales* [No. 3 (1963?)], 7-9.

Jeffrey, David L.†

"Mother Is the Necessity of Invention" *Antig R* No. 53 (Spr 1983), 19-35.

Jeffrey, Neil†

"Second Person" *Waves* 4:3 (Spr-Sum 1976), 29-31.

Jeffries, Pat†

'The First of November" *Miss Chat* 9 (16 Mar 1972), 78, 107.

"A Strange Day" *Miss Chat* 8 (10 Aug 1971), 144-5, 147-9.

Jeggerings, Ronald† (1941?-)

'The Empty Gun" *Green's* 5:4 (Sum 1977), 38-44.

Jelinek, Vera‡

'Beyond the Horizon" *Varsity Lit Issue* Mon, 5 Mar 1951, 7.

'I Became a Ghost" *Acta Vic* 77:3 (Feb 1953), 26-8.

'The Red Horses" *Varsity Lit Issue* Wed, 11 Feb 1953, 6.

'The Swamp Pool" *Acta Vic* 76:4 (Mar 1952), 23-6.

Jelliffe, Vaughn†

"Cabines Sur Mer" *Room* 8:3 (1983), 62-7.

Jenoff, Marvyne

'Boots" *Waves* 8:2 (Win 1980), 5-6.

'The Occasional Rise and Fall of Mitch Moley" *Creative Campus* 1964, 70-85.

'The Singular Sisters" *Nimbus* 1:2 (Fall 1979), 27-9.

"Skin" *Matrix* No. 8 (Win 1979), 10-1.

Jensen, Kevin‡

'Hunters Lost" *West People* No. 203 (15 Sept 1983), 12.

Jensen, Leif‡

"A Victory" *Outlook* Spr 1980, 23-4.

Jensen, LeRoy‡

"Noah's Ark (1961)" *Why* 1:2 (1960), 50-2.

Jensen, Phyllis†
"Not a Medical Emergency" *Healthsharing* 4:2 (Spr 1983), 12-6.

Jenson, Carole‡
"The Long Walk Home" *Pedantics* 1965, 89-90.

Jess, Cameron†
"If Thy Brother Offend Thee ... " *Amethyst* 4:1 (Aut 1964), 5-8.
"The Joyride" *JCF* 4:1 No. 13 (1975), 22-9.
"The Lock" by Jess Cameron *Amethyst* 3:3 (Spr 1964), 2-5.
"The Overlap" by Jess Cameron *Amethyst* 3:2 (Win 1964), 8-11.
"The Patriot" by Jess Cameron *Amethyst* 3:3 (Spr 1964), 12-6.
"The Stand-Off" by Jess Cameron *Amethyst* 3:3 (Spr 1964), 6-11.

Jiles, Paulette
"Indian Princess" *SN* 92 (Dec 1977), 82-7.

Jim – *See* Paul & Jim.

Jirgins, Karl E. (1952-)
"The Achilles' Truth" *Writing* No. 4 (Win 1981-82), 39-40.
"A Bedtime Story" *Imp* 9:3/4 (Spr 1982), 47.
"Culture Shock: Yesterday's Dreams, Tomorrow's Nightmares" by Fausto Bedoya *OPT* 6:1 (Feb 1979), 16.
"Early Morning Exile (Maalox and Rye)" *Writing* No. 2 (Win 1980-81), 20-2.
"Highway 69 Is Disappearing" *Rampike* 2:3 (1982), 63.
"Subterranean Cognizance (The Torpedo Strikes)" *OPT* 6:1 (Feb 1979), 1.
"Typewriter" *Rampike* 2:1/2 (1982), 33.

Job, Pat‡
"Diary of an Executive" *Scar Fair* 1 (1973-74), 17-20.

Joe [pseudonym]
"Mary Poppins Took a Trip" *Satyrday* No. 4 (1966), 6.

Joffre, Jeffrey†
"The Slaughterhouse" *Viewpoints* 2:4 (1967), 61-4.

Johannson, Robert D.‡
"The Paperboy" *Creative Campus* 1963, 25-32.

Johansen, John†
"The Case of the Shattered Eggshell" *Whetstone* Spr 1972, [2 pp].

John, Beno
"Duet for Two Lovers and an Abandoned Suite" *Gas Rain* 2 (1978), 34-41.
"For Galois, Linda, Pam and Me" *NeWest R* 6:9 (May 1981), 11-2, 14.
"Hero" *Gas Rain* [1] (Mar 1977), 14-8.
"Necessity Is the *Pimp* of Invention" *Gas Rain* 3 (1979), 21-30.

Johns, Ted‡
"Three Fraud Stories" *Twelve Mile Creek* No. 2 [n.d.], 12-4.

Johnsen, Hank†
"Between the Pillars" *Versus* No. 3 (Spr 1977), 37-46.

Johnson, A.L.†
'The Endurance Test" *Can Lifetime* 4 (Mar-Apr 1974), 20-1 [Non-fiction?].

Johnson, C.D. Paisley‡
"Black Jack Taylor" *Nfld Q* 61:1 (Spr 1962), 13 [Pre-1950?].

Johnson, Carol‡
"The Blessed Virgin" *Raven* No. 8 (Jan 1960), 6-9.
"The Star-Cross" *Motion* No. 5 (25 Oct 1962), [8-9].
"Strange Fruit" *Motion* No. 3 (25 July 1962), [4-6].

Johnson, Chris†
"Game Over Lightly" *Stardust* 3:2 (Spr 1981), 37-8.

Johnson, Eric (1949?-)
"Behind the Eight Ball Again" *Outset* 1973, 63-9.

Johnson, G. Bertha
"Catskinners Paradise" *Ice Can* [33:3] (Spr 1975), 36-42.
"The Curse of the Manitou Wapow" *CG* Dec 1953, 8, 28-30.
"Frescoed with Angels" *Ice Can* 28:2 (Win 1969), 30-2.
"The Game of Chance" *Ice Can* 13:3 (Spr 1955), 34-9.
"The Great Dog Race" *Ice Can* 39:2 (Win 1980), 28-32.
"The Letter" *CSSM* 2:2 (Spr 1976), 3-7.
"On the Hoof" *Ice Can* 8:3 (Spr 1950), 18-21.
"The Promised Land" *CSSM* 3:1 (Win 1977), 3-7, 67-8.
"The Promised Land" *Ice Can* 37:1 (Aut 1978), 8-12.
"Winds of Wrath" *Ice Can* 24:2 (Win 1965), 41, 43, 45, 47, 49, 51, 53.

Johnson, Janet†
"Mrs. Quinton, Your Son ... " *Rapport* May 1971, 16-8.

Johnson, L.P.V. (1905-)
'The Hamper" *Edmonton Journal* Wed, 19 Dec 1962, 4.

Johnson, Linda Wikene (1950-)
"Bleeding" *Repos* Nos. 17/18 (Win-Spr 1976), 133-9.
"Bleeding" *Pulp Mill* (1977), 113-26.
"Canyon" *Was R* 8:1 (Spr 1973), 30-1.
"Coyote" *event* 8:1 (1979), 31-6.
'The Illustrator" *CFM* No. 5 (Win 1972), 12-46.
'The White Jeep" *Prism* 12:2 (Fall 1972), 36-9.

Johnson, Margaret Coleman†
'Profile at Four" *Alberta Golden Jubilee Anthology* (1955), 403-8.

Johnson, Myron‡
"A Boy, a Girl and a Sunday" *Edge* No. 6 (Spr 1967), 67-72.

Johnson, Ruth†

"His Move" *Can Messenger* 83 (Jan 1973), 14-5.

Johnson, S.‡

"Glenda and the Painter" *Muskeg R* 4 [1976], 49-50.
"Overlapping of the Pale" *Muskeg R* 4 [1976], 12-3.

Johnson, Terry‡

"The Room" *From an Island* Feb 1979, 32-3.

Johnson, Vera D. (1920?-)

"Black 6 on Red 7" *MM* 64 (15 Jan 1951), 9, 32, 34, 39-40.
"Death in the Toy Parade" *MM* 66 (1 Dec 1953), 28, 73, 75-8.
"He Married for Murder" *SW* 1 Aug 1959, 24, 43.
"The Huckemeyer Story" *Northern Lights* (1960), 543-53 [Also entitled "A Man's Got to Lie Once in a While"].
"The Long Night" *MM* 66 (15 Apr 1953), 15, 55-8, 60.
"A Man's Got to Lie Once in a While" *MM* 66 (1 Feb 1953), 20, 39-42 [Also entitled "The Huckemeyer Story"].
"The Pilgrimage" *CF* 38 (Feb 1959), 257-8.
"The Silent Star of Stratford" *MM* 66 (15 Aug 1953), 12-3, 57-61.
"Vigil on the Rock" *MM* 68 (10 Dec 1955), 38, 58, 60, 62, 64.
"The Way Is Hard and Weary" *CF* 33 (Apr 1953), 14-7.

Johnston, Alexander‡

"A Christmas Story" *Acta Vic* 83:2 (Dec 1958), 5-7.

Johnston, Basil H.†

"The Grandchildren" *Boreal* No. 2 (1975), 21-5.
"The Kiss and the Moonshine" *Tawow* 4:4 (1974), 21.
"The Miracle" *Tawow* 4:4 (1974), 18-9.
"Yellow Cloud's Battle with the Car" *Tawow* 4:4 (1974), 22-3.

Johnston, D. Maureen‡

"The Well" *Can Lifetime* 2 (May-June 1972), 12-3.

Johnston, Doris M.†

"Well" *CSSM* 1:3 (July 1975), 16-9.

Johnston, George (1913-)

"Astypalaian Knife" *Cosmopolitan* 139 (Dec 1955), 18-25 [Based on RGPL].
"Brotherly Love" *Atlantic Monthly* 196 (Oct 1955), 68-71.
"A Good Trick on Hens" *Alphabet* No. 5 (Dec 1962), 18-34.
"Moose Meat" *Alphabet* No. 4 (June 1962), 45-52.

Johnston, J.D.‡

"The Night of the Longest Day" *UC Observer* Nov 1971, 14-5 [Non-fiction?].

Johnston, Nandy

"Bella Cleans the Closets" *UC Observer* 1 June 1964, 25.

"No One Ever Told Me" *Onward* 1 Oct 1967, 12-3 [Listed as article; fictional letter?].

"Nobody Walks Nowadays" *UC Observer* 1 Dec 1965, 21.

Johnston, Stella†

"Baseball at Renfrew" *Alberta Writers Speak* 1960, 15-6.

"Return of the Buffalo" *Alberta Writers Speak* 1969, 46-50.

"There's Always Room for Two More" *Alberta Diamond Jubilee Anthology* (1979), 197-8 [Originally published in *West Producer*].

"The Way Things Happen" *Alberta Writers Speak* 1964, 47-51.

Johnstone, Rick†

"nunc dimitus" *Quarry* 15:3 (Mar 1966), 31-2.

"Rum Sky Rum Sun" *Quarry* 13 (1963-64), 35-6.

"Two Pages from a Journal" *Quarry* 14 (1964-65), 27-8.

Jolliffe, Lillian – *See* Green, H. Gordon.

Jolowski, Wendy‡

"Arnold and Fonzie" *Titmouse R* No. 7 [n.d.], 3.

Jonas, George (1935-)

"The Iguana" *Tam R* No. 70 (Win 1977), 42-6.

"The King" *FH* 24 June 1965, 34.

Jones, Barbara†

"At the Count of Ten" *Mam* 6:4 (Win 1983-84), [3 pp].

"The Western Shirt" *Mam* [6:3] (Sum 1983), [4 pp].

Jones, Betty Jane – *See* Hubert, Cam and Jones, Betty Jane.

Jones, Clive†

"Parkdale Farm" *Waves* 11:2/3 (Win 1983), 31-4.

Jones, Donald G.

"Clay for Moulding" *Forge* 1952, 52-3.

"The Excretion" *NR* 5:6 (Feb-Mar 1953), 31-5.

"The Letter" *Forge* 1951, 42-7.

Jones, G.H.J.‡

"Home from the Hill" *Rod & Gun* 71 (Oct 1969), 6-8.

Jones, Gerald†

"Grandfather's House" *Nfld Q* 69:2 (Dec 1972), 10-2.

"Revenge" *Nfld Q* 69:4 (Mar 1973), 39-40.

Jones, Grania

"Cunard" *Catalyst* 2:2 (Win 1968-69), 22-4.

Jones, Kim

"Christmas Eve" *Forge* 1952, 39-44.

Jones, Michael‡
"Sanford" *Chiaroscuro* 9 (1965-66), 14-5.

Jones, Miriam‡
"Scenario" *Acta Vic* 107:1 (Fall 1982), 12-5.

Jones, Paul‡
"Mrs. Magennis" *Mitre* 2 (1970), 46-50.

Jones, R.J.†
"Amputations" *Quarry* 27:1 (Win 1978), 7-9.

Jones, R[ichard].
"Sagitta" *Pier Spr* 1:1 (Aut 1976), 22-8.
"Washington Valley" *Pier Spr* Spr 1978, 44-9.

Jones, Sandra‡
"The Ugly Frog" CBC *"Alberta Anthology"* 2 Oct 1982.

Jordan, Godfrey‡
"Crud Story" *Mouth* 2:4 [n.d.], 2.

Jordan, Kimberley‡
"Requiescat" *Scar Fair* [3] (1975-76), 37-45.

Jordan, Marjorie
"Miss Minnie" *NHM* 51 (May 1950), 12-3, 38-40.

Jordan, Zoe†
"The Girl Who Loved Children" *Evidence* No. 4 (Win 1962), 37-41.

Joseph, Alexander Callow
THE ROVIN' PIGEON Toronto: n.p., 1950 [Based on Miller].

Joslyn, Linda‡
"Mrs. Mills' Morning" *Can Writing* 1:1 (Win 1950), 18-21.
"Oh, My Lovely Kimi" *Can Writing* 1:2 (Sum 1951), 28-38.

Joyce, F.N.‡
"Peter's Boat" *Nfld Q* 72:3 (July 1976), 34, 36-7.

Jubb, D.E.‡
"Step Off into Darkness" *Tyro* 1962, 14-8.

Judy, Stephanie†
"Narrative " *Canadian Short Fiction Anthology* (1976), 103.

Julian, Marilyn (1944-)
"Blue Ring" *Prism* 15:2/3 (Sum-Fall 1976), 92-6.
"Business" *CF* 54 (Jan 1975), 30-2.
"Cycloids: Two Wheels" *Fid* No. 104 (Win 1975), 55-73.
"House of Cards" *Chat* 49 (Feb 1976), 35, 90, 92-3.
" 'It Happens All the Time' " *JCF* 4:3 No. 15 (1976), 62-72.

"Mary Ellen" *Grain* 1:2 (Dec 1973), 8-15.
"A Season for Sharks" *Br Out* 3:2 (Apr-June 1976), 25-9, 48.
"SIN: A Parable" *Fireweed* No. 5/6 (Win-Spr 1979-80), 89-93.
"Thanksgiving Monday: 1960" *Grain* 2:1 [1974], 45-52.
"Umbrella" *Br Out* 4:2 (May-June 1977), 18-21.
"The Wife Sawed in Half" *Fid* No. 98 (Sum 1973), 57-64.

Julien, Florence†
"An Ecumenical Challenge" *Onward* 23 Apr 1967, 3-4, 11 [Non-fiction?].
"Misfit and Miracle" *Onward* 13 Nov 1966, 12-4.

Jupiter, Lord – *See* Lord Jupiter.

K.E [pseudonym]
" 'We Like Hugs!' " *Pulp* 4:7 (1 July 1977), [1, 4].

Kaal, Hans†
"Augustin's Wife" *Forge* Dec 1956, 7-10.
"Born of Lemmon" *Yes* 1:1 (Apr 1956), [6 pp].
"The Judgment of Paris" *Forge* Mar 1956, 6-10.
"A Rendezvous in the Bathtub" *Forge* Dec 1957, 24-30.

Kadey, Carroll
"Abigail" *Sand Patterns* No. 15 (Fall 1975), 2.
"The Academician" *Sand Patterns* No. 9 (1974), 28-9.
"The Chiseler" *Sand Patterns* No. 13 (Spr 1975), [5 pp].
"The Irritant" *Sand Patterns* No. 10 (1974), 17-9.
"The Mesmerizing Artist" *Variations on a Gulf Breeze* (1973), 22-3.
"The Mob" *Sand Patterns* No. 7 (Sept 1973), [3 pp].
"The Purple Garters" *Sand Patterns* No. 11 (1974), 4-7.
"Sergeant Froissart" *Island Prose and Poetry* (1973), 5-8.
"Sergeant Froissart" *Variations on a Gulf Breeze* (1973), 5-8.
"Short Story" *Sand Patterns* No. 3 (Jan 1973), [3 pp].
"Somnambulism" *Variations on a Gulf Breeze* (1973), 50.
"The Supplicant" *Variations on a Gulf Breeze* (1973), 99-100.
"Thirteen O'Clock" *Variations on a Gulf Breeze* (1973), 53 [Untitled] *Sand Patterns*
No. 3 (Jan 1973), [2 pp].

Kaey, Arden
"Fare Well, a Long Farewell" *Moderne Erzühler der Walt: Kanada* (1976), 202-12
[As "Fahre wohl, ein langes Fahrewohl"; trans. Walter Bauer].

Kafka, Pat†
"The Lesson" *Outset* 1973, 70-6.

Kahn, Charles R.‡
"Portrait" *Varsity* Fri, 10 Mar 1967, 6.

Kaiser, Terry‡
"John" *In Store* No. 1 (Apr 1969), 24-5.
"Rosie" *In Store* No. 1 (Apr 1969), 26-7.
"Tuesday" *In Store* No. 1 (Apr 1969), 23.

Kalb, Sandra†
"Mother Goose Acres – 1973" *Outset* 1973, 77-82.

Kalman, Judy
"Free Associations" *Camrose R* No. 5 [n.d.], 32-6.
"Is This All You Think About?" *Per* Nos. 7/8 (Win 1981), 102-7.
"Michael's Story" *Origins* 12:2 (Sum 1982), 103-17.
"Quality Stock" *UWR* 14:2 (Spr-Sum 1979), 36-46.
"Words and Hands" by N. Horne *Mont Writers' Forum* 1:5 (Feb 1979), 6-13.

Kaminsky, Helen
'The Gates of Hell" *Varsity* Fri, 10 Mar 1967, 7.
'The Shape of the White Waves" *Catalyst* 2:2 (Win 1968-69), 35-9.

Kanitz, Walter (? -1986)
'The Bridge" *Can Life* 2:2 (Nov-Dec 1951), 18-20.
'Infants, Dogs and Teachers" *Can Life* 2:1 (Spr 1951), 23, 29.

Kanner, Alexis‡
"Mr. Mendel and the Other Side" *Forge* Mar 1959, 53-9.

Kanurkas, Irene
'The Intellectual" *Scar Fair* 7 (1979-80), 19-21.

Kardok, Butch‡
'The Autobiography of an Ocean Fucker" *Nebula* No. 15 (1980), 40-3.

Kari, Briar‡
"Around About Midnight" *Stump* 5:1 (Fall-Win 1980), 26-9.
'Exile" *Stump* Fall-Win 1982, 27-8.

Karkut, Tadeusz [Ted]
'The Pipe" *Echo* (Tor) 4:1 (Sept-Oct 1972), 16.
"A Short Story" *Echo* (Tor) 4:6 (Aug-Sept 1973), 24-5.

Katherine, Sister St. Joan‡
"Saturday" *Pedantics* 1965, 84.

Katz, Barry‡
"Sure Wish Somehow" *Anthol* No. 3 (Spr 1974), 16-7.

Katz, Bernard‡
"April Is the Cruelest Month ... " *Seraph* 1964, 17-8.

Katz, Bruce (1951-)
"2406 Royal Street" *Outset* 1973, 83-9.

"The Freedom of Slaves" *Outset* 1974, 85-94.
"The Freedom of Slaves" *event* 7:2 (1978), 7-19.
"The Nicest Neighbour" *Thumbprints* [No. 1] (Win 1975), [4 pp].

Kaufman, Pat‡
"Sneakers" *Nebula* Nos. 21/22 (1982), 119-21.

Kaufmann, F. [pseudonym]
"The Game" *Prism* 8:2 (Aut 1968), 33-7.

Kavanagh, Patrick
"Orion" *Chicago R* 31:4 (Spr 1980), 161-8.

Kavaner, Mar‡
"Piece of String" *In Store* No. 1 (Apr 1969), 20-1.

Kawai, Haruo†
"Waiting" *Duel* No. 1 (Win 1969), 70-5.

Kawalilak, Ron A.
"The Girl Who Sweeps the Porch" *Harvest* Nos. 5/6 (Sept 1978), 32-3.
"A Novel" *Writ* No. 10 (1978), 15-22.
"The Sickness" *Grain* 7:3 [1979], 50-9.
"Suffer the Little Children" *Pulp* 4:13 (30 Nov 1977), [1-2].
"Suffer the Little Children" *Elbow Room* (1979), 117-50.
"The Wrong People" *Grain* 9:2 (May 1981), 20-5.
"The Wrong People" *CBC [Van]* "Hornby Collection" 4 Dec 1982.

Kawano, Roland†
"After the Ceremony" *Rikka* 6:4 (Win 1979), 39-44.
"The Next Day" *Rikka* 7:2 (Sum 1980), 30-5.

Kay, Margaret B.†
"Everyone Is Someone" *CSSM* 1:4 (Oct 1975), 11-4.
"My Friend Andrew" *CSSM* 2:2 (Spr 1976), 23-5, 27-8.

Kay, Steve†
"Tower People" *Musicworks* No. 24 (Sum 1983), 16.

Kaye, Aaron S.‡
"At the Threshold of the Known" *It Doesn't Have to Be Lousy* (1974), 15-6.
"On the Life of a Bull" *It Doesn't Have to Be Lousy* (1974), 16-7.

Kaye, Marcia†
"Travel: Cyprus" *WWR* 1:3 (Spr 1978), 12-7.

Kean, Alex‡
"Lost in the Rain Forest" *Rain Chr* No. 6 [n.d.], 18-21.

Keane, Mary†
"Corny McCarthy's Culture Shock" *Toronto Star* Sun, 2 Sept 1979, A15.

Kearns, Lionel (1937-)

"Enterprise" *Imago* No. 7 [n.d.], 6-8.

"Enterprise" *Prism* 7:1 (Sum 1967), 98-9.

"The Parable of the Seventh Seal" *New Romans* (1968), 99-102 [Untitled] *Tish* No. 28 (Jan 1965), 3-5.

Kee, Kathy‡

"Paradise Lost?" *Simcoe R* No. 8 (Spr 1980), 6-7.

Keefe, K.B.‡

"How Three Little Pigs Were Baptized" *Anglican Outlook* 5:4 (Feb 1950), 19 [Satire].

Keefer, Janice Kulyk

"Mrs. Mucharski and Her Princess" *Atlantis* 9:1 (Fall 1983), 79-85, 87-8.

"The Starry Night Sky" *Des* 12:4/13:1/2 Nos. 34/35/36 (1981-82), 168-78.

Keel, Joan†

"The Annulment" *Stump* Aut 1981, 9-13.

"Death Ray" *Hysteria* 2:1 (Win 1982-83), 20-1.

Keeler, Judy‡

"The Interview" *Rune* 1:1 (Spr 1974), 47-55.

"The Life of a Poet" *TUR* 91:1 (Nov 1977), 45.

"The Story of a Film" *Da Vinci* 2:1 No. 4 (Aut 1975), 64-8.

"Stumps" *TUR* 85:2 (Feb 1972), 11.

Keeling, Nora (1933-)

THE DRIVER Ottawa: Oberon Press, 1982.

"Agathe" *Fourteen Stories High* (1971), 51-9.

"Armand's Rabbit" *Driver* (1982), 40-56.

"The Bird-Winged Truck Driver" *Driver* (1982), 15-21.

"The Driver" *QQ* 80 (1973), 41-7.

"The Driver" *Driver* (1982), 5-14.

"Green Blades of Grass" *Driver* (1982), 57-67.

"Himmler, Hotshot and Dandy" *Driver* (1982), 22-39.

"Mary's Mother" *Quarry* 22:2 (Spr 1973), 51-3.

"Memoir: To Guy" *Driver* (1982), 68-109 [Novella?].

"Rhoda & Julia" *CFM* No. 8 (Aut 1972), 28-32.

"The Year" *72: New Canadian Stories* 92-5.

Keene, Peggy†

"Me Name?" *Cap R* 1:2 (Fall 1972), 5-8.

Keerma, Michael‡

"Discovery" *Acta Vic* 97:1 [n.d.], 15-22.

Kehler, Terry‡

"The Conversation" *Stump* 4:1/2 (Spr 1980), 21-2.

Keith, Allen†

"On a Quiet Winter's Morn" *Kitimat Voices* 1967 146-8.

Keith, John†

"Dénouement" *CFM* No. 12 (Win 1974), 4-8.

Keith, Sarah†

"An Indian Hand" *Can Messenger* 79 (Oct 1969), 12-3.

Kellenhauser, John T.‡

"14" *Nebula* No. 7 (1978), 44.

Kelley, Brian†

"Skye Hill" *Forge* 1953, 46-9.

Kelley, Paul†

"Theory of the Novel" *Cap R* No. 28 (1983), 75-81.

Kelly, Dermot†

"The Day Elvis Presley Died" *Scrivener* 1:1 (Spr 1980), 2-4, 26-8.
"Double-Riding, Robbing the Chapel and Singing in the Cemetery" *Scrivener* 2:1 (Spr 1981), 25-6.
"The Family Rock Star" *Scrivener* 2:2 (Fall 1981), 3-5, 28-9.
"The Girl to Kill For" *Scrivener* 2:1 (Spr 1981), 23-4.
"A Punk Christmas" *McGill Lit J* 3:1 (Win 1982), 33-7.

Kelly, Gary‡

"A Chinese Fable" *Acta Vic* 89:1 [1964], 14-5.
"Story" *Acta Vic* 88:2 (1964), 5-6.

Kelly, Joy‡

"Boundary Line" *Choice Parts* (1976), 18-25.

Kelly, M.T. (Terry) (1947-)

THE MORE LOVING ONE Windsor: Black Moss Press, 1980.
"The Bird" *Grain* 4:1 [1976], 20-1.
"Darling I Have Found Myself in You" *event* 7:2 (1978), 37-41.
"Darling I Have Found Myself in You" *More Loving One* (1980), 123-7.
"The Death of Tom McGuire" *Waves* 8:2 (Win 1980), 3-4.
"Eloise" *More Loving One* (1980), 101-9.
"The First Trip Up" *Des* 10:1 Nos. 22/23 (1978-79), 60-78.
"Grief" *Link* No. 13 (9 Oct 1977), 1-10.
"Grief" *More Loving One* (1980), 111-22.
"My Vegetable Love" *NJ* No. 4 (June 1974), 75-80 ["a short story based on an excerpt from a novel of the same name" (author's note)].
"Oliver Loon" *Northern Ontario Anthology* 1 (1977), 52-7.
"Unbodied Souls" *TL* June 1983, 40-1, 94, 96-8.
[Untitled] *Dime Bag* No. 4 (Nov 1971), [2 pp].
"The Victim's Joy" *Fid* No. 108 (Win 1976), 91-105.

Kelly, Marjorie‡

"An Account of Clara's Passing" *Driftwood* 1979, 15-6.
"Consuming Passion" *Driftwood* 1979, 23-6.
"Harvest Blessed" *Driftwood* 1979, 17-8.

Kellythorne, Walt

"Booze and Music" *event* 5:1 [n.d.], 56-61.

"The Hidden Eye" *Wot* 3:1 (Spr 1981), 38-41.

"Houses" *Grain* 10:3 (Aug 1982), 20-1.

"The Last Long Summer" *Grain* 8:1 [1980], 6-13.

"The Man Who Knew Everything" *JCF* 4:3 No. 15 (1975), 44-51.

"Old Friends" *event* 6:1 [1977], 38-46.

"Saturday Night in Yugoslavia" *Grain* 4:2 [1976], 3-10.

"Saturday Night in Yugoslavia" *Best of Grain* (1980), 152-9.

"Study" *Grain* 103 (Aug 1982), 22-3.

"The Witness" *Grain* 3:1 [1975]? 66-72.

Kelsey, Robin‡

"Just Like Li Po" *Prism* 11:3 (Spr 1972), 4-7.

"Kotzko Was a Writer Who Did Not Write" *Quarry* 17:3 (Spr 1968), 32-3.

"Norman's Chinese Junk" *Imp* 1:2 (Win 1972), 35-7.

Kelsey, Sheila‡

"The Tiles" *Either/Or* No. 4 (Fall 1966), 20-2.

Kemeny, Eva‡

"Bushy: Tale of a Squirrel" *Varsity* Fri, 12 Dec 1952, 3.

Kemp, Penny (1944-)

"Coffins" *Room* 3:4 (1978), 20-5.

"Forms and Fragments" *Makara* 3:2 [n.d.], 42-3.

"Gargoyle" by Penny Chalmers *BC Monthly* 3:3 (Dec 1976), [3 pp].

"Good Morning" by Penny Chalmers *Per* No. 1 (Spr 1977), 59.

"Meditation in an Emergency" by Penny Chalmers *Canadian Short Fiction Anthology* (1976), 47-51.

"Monarchs" *Story So Far* 5 (1978), 77-87.

"No End to Winter" *Waves* 9:3 (Spr 1981), 34-8.

Kendall, Wallis‡

"Encounter" *Edmonton Journal* Thu, 14 Jan 1965, 4.

"Wealth – Shared" *Edmonton Journal* Mon, 8 June 1964, 6-7.

Kendrick, N.H.†

"Birth of a Legend" *CSSM* 1:2 (Apr 1975), 53-6.

Kennedy, Brian‡

"Lazarus" *Prism* (Mont) No. 7 (Mar 1964), 15-33.

Kennedy, Cliff F.‡

"Diamonds and Coaldust" *Bluenose* 4:2 (Oct 1979), 14-6.

Kennedy, Daniel‡

"Tell Me What You See" *Prism* 10:2 (Aut 1970), 15-22.

Kennedy, F.M.†

"Smallboatmen" *Atl Guardian* 9 (July 1952), 29-37.

Kennedy, John‡
[Untitled] *Scar Fair* 2 (1974-75), [1 p].
[Untitled] *Scar Fair* 6 (1979), 53-4.

Kennedy, Sheila‡
"A, to Zeee" *Spear* 2 (Apr 1973), 14-5.

Kennedy, Thomas†
"Shadow Fruit" *Nebula* Nos. 21/22 (1982), 125-33.

Kennon, Janie†
"The Apprentice" *Prism* 8:3 (Spr 1969), 104-9.
"Don Quixote's Horse" *Prism* 8:3 (Spr 1969), 102-4.
"Letters from Another Country" *Prism* 10:2 (Aut 1970), 42-4.
"Story of a Poor Man" *Prism* 8:3 (Spr 1969), 100-1.

Kenny, George (1952-)
INDIANS DON'T CRY Toronto: Chimo, 1977.
"The Drowning" *Indians Don't Cry* (1977), 30-4.
"Indians Don't Cry" *Indians Don't Cry* (1977), 7-10.
"Just Another Bureaucrat" *Indians Don't Cry* (1977), 36-8.
"Lost Friendship" *Indians Don't Cry* (1977), 11-7.
"On the Shooting of a Beaver" *Indians Don't Cry* (1977), 19-23.
"Summer Dawn on Loon Lake" *Indians Don't Cry* (1977), 40-5.
"Track Star" *Indians Don't Cry* (1977), 47-67.
"Welcome" *Indians Don't Cry* (1977), 25-8.

Kenny, Wade†
"Outside the Window" *Pot Port* 2 (1980-81), 48-9.
"A Telephone Booth" *Death* (1982) [Based on SSI].

Kent, Armoral‡
"The Sandman of Goville" *AA* 56 (Sept 1965), 98, 100, 102, 104.

Kent, Christopher‡
"A Pledge for Bobby Ellis" *Legion* 54 (Dec 1979), 18-9, 42 [Non-fiction?].

Kent, Duncan†
"The Survivor" *CFM* No. 8 (Aut 1972), 90-2.

Kent, Peter‡
"Dodger's Place" *Quarry* 29:1 (Win 1980), 18-26.
"Ruin" *Story So Far* 5 (1978), 89-92.

Kent, Valerie (1947-)
WHEELCHAIR SONATA Toronto: Coach House Press, 1974.
"By the Light of the Heliotrope Barbell" *Wheelchair Sonata* (1974), 59-64.
"The Cathedral" *CFM* No. 8 (Aut 1972), 87-9.
"A Day of the Spanish Civil War" *Wheelchair Sonata* (1974), 53-8.
"Dialogue" *Wheelchair Sonata* (1974), 17-20.
"Fade Out" *Yes* No. 18 (Dec 1969), [5 pp].
"Fade Out" *Wheelchair Sonata* (1974), 71-7.

"Katydid" *CFM* No. 9 (Win 1973), 63-6.
"Little Green Flowers" *Wheelchair Sonata* (1974), 11-6.
"Lunch Under Cover" *Imp* 1:2 (Win 1972), 18-21.
"Lunch Under Cover" *Wheelchair Sonata* (1974), 65-9.
"The Magician" *O* No. 26 (Win 1976), 23-5.
"Oh Sunny California" *Wheelchair Sonata* (1974), 35-42.
"The Other Woman" *CF* 54 (May-June 1974), 70-1.
"The Other Woman" *Wheelchair Sonata* (1974), 27-33.
"The Party" *Outset* 1973, 90-4.
"Polly Wants a Cracker" *Story So Far* (1971), 58-64, 81.
"Polly Wants a Cracker" *Wheelchair Sonata* (1974), 43-51.
"PoP PoP" *Story So Far* 2 (1973), 118-25.
"PoP PoP" *Wheelchair Sonata* (1974), 79-86.
"Wheelchair Sonata" *Wheelchair Sonata* (1974), 21-5.
"Why the Devil – Mule?" *Outset* 1973, 95-9.

Kent, Winona†
"Tower of Power" *Flare* 4 (Sept 1982), 48-50, 53-4, 58.

Kent-Barber, Rosemary‡
"The Little Girl and the Moth" *Raven* 1:2 (Dec 1955), 18-9.
"The Test" *Raven* No. 5 (Dec 1957), 15-6.

Kenyon, Linda (1956-)
"A Life in Laundry" *New Q* 3:3 (Fall 1983), 63-6.
"Waiting for Rain" *Hysteria* 2:2 (Spr 1983), 12-5.

Kenyon, Michael‡
"Train" *Prism* 20:4 (Sum 1982), 7-13.
"Train" *Metavisions* (1983), 62-8.
"Twenty Nights in Northeast Africa" *Quarry* 32:2 (Spr 1983), 9-15.

Kenyon, Nancy†
"The Knight and the Maiden" *Acta Vic* 81:3 (Mar 1957), 34-7.
"Mr. Smith and Incredible Grace" *Acta Vic* 81:1 (Nov 1956), 7-8.

Ker, H.†
"Chinese Freemasons and the Dart Coon Club" *WWR* 2:3 No. 7 (1982), 21-2.

Kerlikowske, Elizabeth‡
"Hiding" *Choice Parts* (1976), 28-31.

Kernaghan, Eileen
"The Atavists" *Diversions* 2:1 (19 Apr 1970), 19-22.
"Thieras" *Room* 6:1/2 (1981), 63-91.
"Vanishing Act" *Diversions* Sept 1969, 9-11.

Kero, Melvin†
"The Compartment" *Prism* 1:3 (Spr 1960), 37-45.

Kerpneck, Harvey (1932-)
"Home Again" *Undergrad* Spr 1955, 35-6.

Kerr, Elizabeth†

"The Blizzard" *Nfld Q* 59:3 (Fall 1960), 36-9.

Kerslake, Susan (1943-)

"Did You Ever Think ... " *Antig R* No. 51 (Aut 1982), 75-85.

"Hebel" *CFM* Nos. 32/33 (1979), 111-8.

"Mirror Mirror Off the Wall" *New Q* 3:2 (Sum 1983), 15-24.

"Push-me Pull-you" *Room* 7:3 (1982), 61-78.

"The Rules" *Pot Port* 1 (1979-80), 30-3.

"Skye" *CFM* Nos. 40/41 (1981), 120-33 [As "from *The Book of Fears*"; title based on survey response].

"Sweet Grass" *Grain* 10:2 (May 1982), 51-2.

Kesterton, Mike‡

"A Few Words from Barney" *Stardust* 2:2 [n.d.], 3-7.

Ketchen, Susan†

"Faith and the Blind Man's Symphony" *Miss Chat* 10 (Sum 1973), 72, 112-4.

"The Home Waltz" *Miss Chat* 10:3 (1973), 93, 102, 104-5.

Ketcheson, Doug‡

"Longboat" *Mandala* 1972, 57-9.

Kevin, George‡

"Sometimes I Forget" *Can Writing* 1:2 (Sum 1951), 18-22.

"The Tourists" *Can Writing* 1:1 (Win 1950), 5-10.

Keyes, John (1936-)

"Broken Field" *Quarry* 30:2 (Spr 1981), 20-7.

"Notes on a Blemish" *Edge* No. 4 (Spr 1965), 87-92.

"The Robert Wagner Chorale and the Three Wise Men" *Prism* 4:2 (Aut 1964), 6-22.

"Shooting It" *CFM* Nos. 40/41 (1981), 13-25.

"Shooting It" *Metavisions* (1983), 187-200.

Khankhoje, Maya‡

"The Transistor Radio" *Los* No. 7 (Mar 1981), 11-6.

Kidd, Roberta‡

"The Lesson" *Eclipse* No. 4 (1977), 15-8.

Kidder, John‡

"Sinister Isn't Always Left" *Talon* [1:3] (Feb 1964), 5-7.

Kidney, Dorothy Boone‡

"Call Me Merrydell" *AA* 58 (Aug 1968), 39, 41-4.

Kilbourne, Frances†

"The Legacy" *Lifetime* 3 (May-June 1973), 4.

Kilodney, Crad (1948-)

GAINFULLY EMPLOYED IN LIMBO Toronto: privately printed, 1980.

LIGHTNING STRUCK MY DICK Toronto: Virgo Press, 1980.

WORLD UNDER ANAESTHESIA Toronto: Charnel House, 1979.

"Advanced Oboe Problems" *Lightning Struck My Dick* (1980), 115-21.

"Agriculture" *Poetry Q* (U.K.) Nos. 20/21/22 [n.d.], 26-31 [Based on survey response].

"Agriculture" *Lightning Struck My Dick* (1980), 57-62.

"Annuit Coeptis and Doorknobs in My Ear Generally" *Split Level* 1:1 (1974), [5 pp].

"Annuit Coeptis and Doorknobs in My Ear Generally" *Lightning Struck My Dick* (1980), 9-14.

"The Applicant" *Iron* (U.K.) No. 30 (Oct-Dec 1980), 13-7 [Based on survey response].

"Bakery Boys" *Cosmic Circus* (U.S.) No. 4 (1977), 17 [Based on survey response].

"Bakery Boys" *Krox* (U.K.) No. 10 (1977), 5-6 [Based on survey response].

"Beans & Binoculars" *Aspect* (U.S.) Nos. 72/73 (July-Dec 1977), 68-70.

"A Beaver Tale" *OPT* 5:3 (Apr 1978), 1.

"The Book That I Wrote While I Lived" *Smoke* (U.K.) No. 8 (Mar 1978), 20-1 [Based on survey response].

"A Canadian Custom" *Elite* 3:4 (Dec 1977), 44-6, 70 [Based on survey response].

"The Cesar Franck Story" *Fiction* (U.S.) 1:3 (Aug-Sept 1972), 19-23 [Based on survey response].

"The Cesar Franck Story" *Lightning Struck My Dick* (1980), 15-24.

"Conference Call" *OPT* 6:9 (Nov 1979), 21.

"Conference Call" *Joe Soap's Canoe* (U.K.) No. 4 (Jan 1980), 18-9 [Based on survey response].

"Convincing Professor Brindle About Flying Saucers" *Fiction* (U.S.) No. 7 (1974), 51-3, 63 [Based on survey response].

"Convincing Professor Brindle About Flying Saucers" *Lightning Struck My Dick* (1980), 47-56.

"The Country Doctor" *Before and After Science ...* No. 1 (1982), 11-3 [Based on survey response].

"Dark Intruder" *Prose Political* (1977), 8-12 [Based on survey response].

"The Day Saturn Crashed into the Earth" *National Lampoon* 1 (Aug 1970), 77-9 [Based on survey response].

"The Day Saturn Crashed into the Earth" *Paperback Conspiracy* (1974), 32-41 [Based on survey response].

"Death of a Canadian Writer" *Alpha* 2:5 (Jan 1978), 5, 33.

"The Discovery of Bismuth" by Louis Trifon *Des* No. 15 (Fall 1976), 32-8.

"Duh" *Junction* (U.S.) 2:1 (Fall-Win 1973-74), 9-13 [Based on survey response].

"Excerpts from My Autobiography" *Gainfully Employed in Limbo* (1980), 32-8.

"The Extremely Sane Postal Workers of Yellowknife" *Portico* 4:1 (1980), 33-4, 53-60.

"Filling Orders in Albania" *Gainfully Employed in Limbo* (1980), 20-1.

"Filling Orders in Albania" *Chock* (U.K.) No. 4 [n.d.], 18-9 [Based on survey response].

"Forget That Grapefruit; Here Come the Midgets" *Prism* 12:3 (Spr 1973), 43-6.

"Forget That Grapefruit; Here Come the Midgets" *World Under Anaesthesia* (1979), 21-4.

"Gainfully Employed in Canada" *Gainfully Employed in Limbo* (1980), 5-7.

"Glox, Equaling Honeycoo" *New Voices* (U.S.) Spr 1974, 183-90 [Based on survey response].

"The Hard-Working Garbage Men of Cleveland" *Da Vinci* No. 6 (Aut 1979), 29-35.

"The Hard-Working Garbage Men of Cleveland" *Lightning Struck My Dick* (1980), 107-14.

"The Hard-Working Garbage Men of Cleveland" *World Under Anaesthesia* (1980), 25-30.

"The History of the World" *World Under Anaesthesia* (1979), 15-20.

"Hot Line" *Bogg* (U.K.) No. 36 [n.d.], 13-4 [Based on survey response].

"Hot Line" *Alpha* 3:1 (Fall 1978), 10.

"In the Culture Warehouse" *Skylight* [No. 1] (1978), 41-4 [As "In the Cultural Warehouse].

"In the Culture Warehouse" *Lightning Struck My Dick* (1980), 28-32.

"It Came from Beneath the Slush Pile or the Mountain Elephants of Delaware" *CFM* No. 12 (Win 1974), 57-60.

"It Came from Beneath the Slush Pile or the Mountain Elephants of Delaware" *Lightning Struck My Dick* (1980), 89-93.

"Janitors & Kitchen Staff" *OPT* 7:4/5 (Sept-Oct 1980), 8-9.

"The Krazy World of Crad Kilodney" *Dreamweaver* 1:3 [n.d.], 19-21.

"The Last Interview with Crad Kilodney" *OPT* 7:6/7 (Jan-Feb 1981), 14-7.

"The Last Secrets of Omega" *Crow's Nest* (U.S.) No. 3 (1977), 66-74 [Based on survey response].

"The Last Secrets of Omega" *Iron (U.K.)* No. 16 (Mar-May 1977), 4-8 [Based on survey response].

"The Last Secrets of Omega" *Lightning Struck My Dick* (1980), 79-88.

"Lightning Struck My Dick" *Lightning Struck My Dick* (1980), 3-8 [Also entitled "Nuts and Bolts"].

"A Likely Story" *Firelands Arts R* (U.S.) 1973, 26-9 [Based on survey response].

"Logic" *Contemporary Fiction* (1976), 133-41 [Based on survey response].

"Logic" *Lowlands R* (U.S.) No. 4 (1977), 25-31 [Based on survey response].

"Logic" *Lightning Struck My Dick* (1980), 33-40.

"The Mentally Disturbed Astronomers of Cincinnati" *Lightning Struck My Dick* (1980), 63-78.

"Midnight Trousers" *Iron* (U.K.) No. 20 (Mar-May 1978), 7-10 [Based on survey response].

"Midnight Trousers" *World Under Anaesthesia* (1979), 7-14.

"Midnight Trousers" *Nebula* No. 9 (Feb 1979), 24-33.

"Midnight Trousers" *Lightning Struck My Dick* (1980), 94-103.

"My Posthumous Fame" *Canadian Short Fiction Anthology 2* (1982), 48.

"My Re-creation of the World" *Lightning Struck My Dick* (1980), 25-7.

"My Work as a Hole" *Ludd's Mill* (U.K.) Nos. 16/17 [n.d.], 10 [Based on survey response].

"My Work as a Hole" *Foothill Q* (U.S.) 3:2 (1979), 25-7 [Based on survey response].

"My Work as a Hole" *World Under Anaesthesia* (1979), 34-6.

"Nuts and Bolts" *Junction* (U.S.) 1:3 (Spr 1973), 141-4 [Also entitled "Lightning Struck My Dick"; based on survey response].

"Obligatory Tit Time" *Zest* No. 10 (Nov 1982), 18-9 [Based on survey response].

"Office Worker's Dreams" *Iron* (U.K.) No. 24 (Mar-May 1979), 34-7 [Based on survey response].

"Office Worker's Dreams" *New Kent Q* (U.S.) 4:1 (Win 1979), 48-56 [Based on survey response].

"Office Worker's Dreams" *Gainfully Employed in Limbo* (1980), 8-13.

"Pork College" *Split Level* 1:2 [n.d.], [5 pp].

"Pork College Heroes" *Nebula* No. 3 (1976), 54-7.

"Pork College Lethargy" *Titmouse R* No. 7 [n.d.], 17-21.

"Pork College Mystery" *Strange Faeces* No. 17 (June 1975), 32-4.

"Return to Pork College" *OPT* 7:4/5 (Sept-Oct 1980), 3-6.

"Scenarios" *Mine* (U.S.) Oct 1979 [Excerpt; based on *Gainfully Employed in Limbo*].

"Scenarios" *Gainfully Employed in Limbo* (1980), 22-7.

"Tainted Data" *Gainfully Employed in Limbo* (1980), 28-31.

"Teleological – With Chicken Meat" *Carolina Q* [23]:3 (Fall 1971), 81-8.

"The True Story of My Dentist, Dr. Mark Litvack" *OPT* 6:9 (Nov 1979), 16.

"The True Story of My Dentist, Dr. Mark Litvack" *Lightning Struck My Dick* (1980), 41-6.

"Waiting for Halley's Comet" *Nicotine Soup* (U.S.) 2:2 (Oct 1978), 5 [Based on survey response].

"Waiting for Halley's Comet" *World Under Anaesthesia* (1979), 31-3.

"Warehouse Worker's Dreams" *Iron* (U.K.) No. 24 (Mar-May 1979), 30-4 [Based on survey response].

"Warehouse Worker's Dreams" *Gainfully Employed in Limbo* (1980), 14-9.

"Warehouse Worker's Dreams" *Writing* No. 4 (Win 1981-82), 3-4.

"A Well-Adjusted Man" *Rustler* 1:5 [1979], 56-60, 62.

"What the Arrival of New York State Onions Meant to Me" *Not Guilty!* (U.S.) Nos. 5/6 (1980), 100-1 [Based on survey response].

"When Polyhistoricism Receded" *Lowlands R* (U.S.) No. 8 (1979), 10-1 [Based on survey response].

"When Polyhistoricism Receded" *Trends* (U.K.) 2:4 (1979), 28-30 [Based on survey response].

"When Polyhistoricism Receded" *Lightning Struck My Dick* (1980), 104-6.

"The Window" *Deep Earth Revue* (U.K.) No. 2 (Jan 1979), 3 [Based on survey response].

"The Window" *OPT* 6:3 (Apr 1979), 4.

"The Window" *Gainfully Employed in Limbo* (1980), 39-40.

"The Window" *Lowlands R* (U.S.) No. 10 (1981), 17-8 [Based on survey response].

"The World's Dullest Story" *Red Windsor* [1977?], 16-8 [Based on survey response].

Kilodney, Crad and Nations, Opal L.
See also Kilodney, Crad; Nations, Opal L.
"Shoot-Out at Dead Dog Gulch" *OPT* 6:8 (Oct 1979), 8-10.

Kimmett, Deborah†
"The First Kiss" *Freelance* Nov 1979, 12-3.

King, Carol†
"Wintering Place" *Prairie Fire* 4:5 (July-Aug 1983), 20-4.

King, Earl‡

"Hitler Argentine Journal" *Pulp* 3:16 (15 May 1976), [1-2].

"Three in One" *Pulp* 2:19 (1 Jan 1975), [1 p].

King, Florence†

"How Fame Was Thrust Upon Me" *Alberta Speaks* 1957, 45-6.

King, John Michael†

"A Rebirth" *Pier Spr* Spr 1978, 50 [Non-fiction?].

King, Tom‡

"Fugitive Til New Year's" *Can Horse* 7 (Dec 1967), 53-6, 58-9.

Kingsbury, Donald

"The Ghost Town" *Astounding* 49 (June 1952), 58-81.

Kingsley, F [pseudonym]

"A Most Unusual Winter" *Grain* 1:2 (Dec 1973), 47-51.

Kinsella, W.P. (1935-)

THE BALLAD OF THE PUBLIC TRUSTEE Vancouver: William Hoffer Standard Editions, 1982 [Based on CBIP].

BORN INDIAN Ottawa: Oberon Press, 1981.

DANCE ME OUTSIDE Ottawa: Oberon Press, 1977.

THE MOCCASIN TELEGRAPH AND OTHER STORIES Markham & Harmondsworth: Penguin, 1983.

SCARS Ottawa: Oberon Press, 1978.

SHOELESS JOE JACKSON COMES TO IOWA Ottawa: Oberon Press, 1980.

"The Alligator Report – with Questions for Discussion" *Ethos* 1:1 (Sum 1983), 14-8.

"The Ballad of the Public Trustee" *Matrix* No. 13 (Spr-Sum 1981), 59-65.

"The Ballad of the Public Trustee" *Moccasin Telegraph* (1983), 69-78.

"Between" *Dance Me Outside* (1977), 131-9.

"Between" *Axiom* 3:4 (July-Aug 1977), 43-5, 52.

"Black Wampum" *Des* 9:1/2 Nos. 20/21 (1978), 62-71.

"Black Wampum" *Scars* (1978), 102-111.

"The Blacksmith Shop Caper" *Shoeless Joe* (1980), 123-32.

"Bones" *Scars* (1978), 15-21.

"Born Indian" *CFM* Nos. 32/33 (1979), 22-5.

"Born Indian" *Born Indian* (1981), 5-11.

"The Bottle Queen" *CA & B* 57:3 (Spr 1982), 21-3.

"The Bottle Queen" *Moccasin Telegraph* (1983), 1-9.

"Buffalo Jump" *Born Indian* (1981), 50-61.

"Buffalo Jump" *Moose R* 3:1 (1981), 28-36.

"Butterflies" *Dance Me Outside* (1977), 41-8.

"Canadian Culture" *Story So Far* 5 (1978), 95-105.

"Canadian Culture" *Scars* (1978), 30-42.

"Caraway" *Dance Me Outside* (1977), 60-8.

"Caraway" *Prism* 16:1 (Spr 1977), 101-7.

"Caraway" *The Spirit That Moves Us* 3:1/2 (Fall-Win 1977-78), 22-9.

"Caraway" *Rites of Passage* (1979), 28-34.

"Caraway" *The Spirit That Moves Us* 6:2/3 (1982), 54-61.

"The Chicken Dancer" *NeWest R* 4 (Apr 1979), 8-9.
"The Chicken Dancer" *Born Indian* (1981), 71-81.
"The College" *Moccasin Telegraph* (1983), 105-17.
"Dance Me Outside" *Des* No. 15 (Fall 1976), 6-11.
"Dance Me Outside" *Dance Me Outside* (1977), 21-8.
"Does Anybody Know How They Make Campaign Buttons?" *Karaki* No. 4 (Jan 1973), 21-2.
"Dr. Don" *Moccasin Telegraph* (1983), 95-103.
"Dreams" *Scars* (1978), 43-51.
"Driving Toward the Moon" *NeWest R* 8 (Apr 1983), 9-14.
"Electrico Utensilo" *Introductions from an Island* (1976), 17-8.
"The Elevator" *CFM* Nos. 40/41 (1981), 6-12.
"Fata Morgana" *JCF* No. 24 [1979], 26-33 [Also entitled "Green Candles"].
"The Fawn" *NeWest R* 3:6 (Feb 1978), 6-7.
"The Fawn" *Scars* (1978), 139-44.
"Feathers" *Dance Me Outside* (1977), 121-30.
"Fiona the First" *Mal R* No. 50 (Apr 1979), 161-76.
"Fiona the First" *Shoeless Joe* (1980), 5-25.
"First Names and Empty Pockets" *Des* 11:3 No. 29 (1980), 80-94.
"First Names and Empty Pockets" *Shoeless Joe* (1980), 133-53.
"First Names and Empty Pockets" *81: Best Canadian Stories* 58-78.
"First Names and Empty Pockets" *Anthology of Canadian Literature in English 2* (1983), 386-97.
"For Zoltan, Who Sings" *CBC [Edm] "Alberta Anthology"* 7 Nov 1981.
"The Forest" *Waves* 6:1 (Aut 1977), 4-8.
"The Forest" *Scars* (1978), 95-101.
"The Four-Sky-Thunder Bundle" *Scars* (1978), 123-38.
"Fugitives" *Moccasin Telegraph* (1983), 177-96.
"Goldie" *Born Indian* (1981), 62-70.
"Goldie" *Quarry* 30:1 (Win 1981), 21-7.
"Gooch" *Dance Me Outside* (1977), 149-58.
"Goose Moon" *Scars* (1978), 112-22.
"The Grecian Urn" *Mal R* No. 46 (Apr 1978), 110-23.
"The Grecian Urn" *Shoeless Joe* (1980), 74-92.
"The Grecian Urn" *Best Canadian Short Stories* (1981), 239-53.
"Green Candles" *Moccasin Telegraph* (1983), 33-43 [Also entitled "Fata Morgana"].
"Hopfstadt's Cabin" *View from the Silver Bridge* 2:1 (May 1972), 8-12.
"Horse Collars" *Dance Me Outside* (1977), 29-33.
"I Remember Horses" *Born Indian* (1981), 117-31.
"I Was a Teen-Age Slumlord" *Edmonton Journal* Fri, 27 May 1966, 56.
"Illiana Comes Home" *CFM* No. 20 (Win 1976), 7-16.
"Illiana Comes Home" *Dance Me Outside* (1977), 5-20.
"Illiana Comes Home" *77: Best Canadian Stories* 7-22.
"The Inaugural Meeting" *Dance Me Outside* (1977), 107-13.
"Indian Struck" *Dand* No. 5 (Win-Spr 1979), 5-11.
"Indian Struck" *Born Indian* (1981), 12-21.
"Intermediaries" *Scrivener* 3:1 (Spr 1982), 5-6, 16.
"The Jackhammer" *Edmonton Journal* Fri, 24 June 1966, 29.
"The Job" *Blue Buffalo* 1:1 (Oct 1982), 19-21.

"John Cat" *Scars* (1978), 52-60.

"John Cat" *Tam R* No. 73 (Win 1978), 63-9.

"Jokemaker" *Born Indian* (1981), 39-49.

"The Kid in the Stove" *Matrix* 2:1 (Spr 1976), 3-4.

"The Kid in the Stove" *Dance Me Outside* (1977), 81-5.

"The Kid in the Stove" *Fire* (1978), 62-4.

"The Kid in the Stove" *More Stories from Western Canada* (1980), 56-60.

"The Kidnapper" *Scars* (1978), 61-6.

"The Killing of Colin Moosefeathers" CBC "*Anthology*" 31 May 1980.

"The Killing of Colin Moosefeathers" *Born Indian* (1981), 82-94.

"Lark Song" *Repos* Nos. 19/20 (Sum-Fall 1976), 45-52.

"Lark Song" *Air* (1977), 31-4.

"Lark Song" *Dance Me Outside* (1977), 114-20.

"Linda Star" *Fid* No. 109 (Spr 1976), 4-13.

"Linda Star" *Dance Me Outside* (1977), 69-80.

"Longhouse" *Was R* 11:1 (Spr 1976), 17-22.

"Longhouse" *Dance Me Outside* (1977), 140-8.

"Manitou Motors" *Scars* (1978), 84-94.

"Manitou Motors" *West of Fiction* (1983), 69-77.

"Mankiewitz Won't Be Bowling Tuesday Nights Anymore" *Shoeless Joe* (1980), 93-103.

"Marco in Paradise" *Rain Chr* No. 10 [n.d.], 53.

"The McGuffin" *Dance Me Outside* (1977), 49-59.

"The Moccasin Telegraph" *Moccasin Telegraph* (1983), 21-31.

"Mother Tucker's Yellow Duck" *Prism* 20:4 (Sum 1982), 32-42.

"Mother Tucker's Yellow Duck" *Rainshadow* (1982), 146-59.

"The Mother's Dance" *Moccasin Telegraph* (1983), 155-66.

"Mr. Whitey" *Scars* (1978), 5-14.

"Mr. Whitey" *UWR* 13:2 (Spr-Sum 1978), 84-92.

"Nests" *Iowa R* 13:3/4 (Spr 1982), 185-93.

"Nests" *Moccasin Telegraph* (1983), 119-30.

"The Night Manny Mota Tied the Record" *Small Wonders* (1982), 45-58.

"A Page from the Marriage Manual for Songhees Brides" *CSSM* 1:4 (Oct 1975), 41-4.

"Panache" *Dance Me Outside* (1977), 34-40.

"Panache" *Alberta Diamond Jubilee Anthology* (1979), 214-8.

"Parts of the Eagle" *Moccasin Telegraph* (1983), 45-57.

"Penance" *QQ* 83 (1976), 443-7.

"Penance" *Dance Me Outside* (1977), 100-6.

"A Picture of the Virgin" *Shoeless Joe* (1980), 104-22.

"Pit Lamping" *Scars* (1978), 22-9.

"Pius Blindman Is Coming Home" *Moccasin Telegraph* (1983), 167-75.

"Pretend Dinners" *Pushcart Prize 5* (1980), 424-31.

"Pretend Dinners" *Born Indian* (1981), 139-48.

"The Queen's Hat" *Moccasin Telegraph* (1983), 141-53.

"The Queen's Hat" *CF* 62 (Feb 1983), 18-21, 37.

"A Quite Incredible Dance" *Shoeless Joe* (1980), 26-37.

"The Rattlesnake Express" *Scars* (1978), 77-83.

"The Rattlesnake Express" *This* 12:3 (July-Aug 1978), 26-7.

"The Runner" *Edmonton Mag* 2 (Aug 1980), 32-5.

"The Runner" *Born Indian* (1981), 95-104.

"Scars" *Scars* (1978), 145-54.

"Scars" *New Worlds* (1980), 67-73.

"The Sense She Was Born With" *Matrix* Nos. 6/7 (1978), 51-7.

"The Sense She Was Born With" *Moccasin Telegraph* (1983), 59-68.

"Shoeless Joe" *Edmonton Mag* 4 (Sept 1982), 25-8, 61-3 [Excerpt from novel and story collection].

"Shoeless Joe Jackson Comes to Iowa" *Aurora* 1979 5-18.

"Shoeless Joe Jackson Comes to Iowa" *Shoeless Joe* (1980), 38-54.

"Shoeless Joe Jackson Comes to Iowa" *Penguin Book of Modern Canadian Short Stories* (1982), 427-39.

"Shoeless Joe Jackson Comes to Iowa" *Illusion Two* (1983), 11-23.

"Sister Ann of the Cornfields" *Shoeless Joe* (1980), 68-73.

"The Sisters" *Born Indian* (1981), 22-38.

"Slaves" *Scars* (1978), 67-76.

"Something Evil This Way Comes" *Edmonton Journal* Fri, 16 Sept 1966, 52.

"Something to Think About" *SN* 96 (May 1981), 46-51.

"Strings" *Release* No. 3 (Sum 1980), 25-6.

"Strings" *Moccasin Telegraph* (1983), 11-20.

"Suits" *Born Indian* (1981), 132-8.

"Suits" *Canadian Short Fiction Anthology 2* (1982), 21-5.

"Syzygy" *Wee Giant* 4:1 (Win 1980-81), 33-5.

"Three of a Kind" *CCWQ* 4:2/3 (1982), 34-5.

"Ups and Downs" *Dance Me Outside* (1977), 86-99.

"Vows" *Moccasin Telegraph* (1983), 131-9.

"Voyeur" *Karaki* No. 5 (Dec 1975), 21-3.

"Waiting for the Call" *Shoeless Joe* (1980), 55-67.

"Weasels and Ermines" *Aurora* 1980 225-37.

"Weasels and Ermines" *Born Indian* (1981), 149-63.

"Where the Wild Things Are" *Moccasin Telegraph* (1983), 79-94.

"White Running Shoes" *View from the Silver Bridge* 2:1 (May 1972), 1-7.

"Yellow Scarf" *Born Indian* (1981), 105-16.

Kinsley, William

"The Hole" *New Voices* (1956), 144-51.

Kiperchuk, Helen‡

"Dear Daria" *Alive* [1:9] (Oct 1970), 28-9.

Kirby, Ilona‡

"The Grange" *Pedantics* 1965, 83.

Kirchmier, Wolf‡

"A Fairy Tale" *Forum* (OSSTF) 3 (Mar 1977), 57, 59.

"Schooltime Soon" *Forum* (OSSTF) 5 (Mar 1979), 87-8.

Kirk, Donald‡

"Cherries" *Raven* No. 7 (Nov 1958), [1 p].

Kirk, Heather†

"Oswiecim" *Word Loom* No. 2 (1983), 41.

Kirkwood, Hilda‡

"Aunt Marion's House" *CF* 39 (Dec 1959), 202-3.

"The Ice Floes" *CF* 41 (Oct 1961), 159-61.

"A Kind of Education" *CBC "Anthology"* 9 June 1979.

"Mother and Mrs. O'Reilly" *CF* 40 (Dec 1960), 205-7.

Kischuck, Michael‡

"Conventional Hypocrisy" *Scar Fair* 8 (1981), 84-5.

Kishibe, Kaye‡

"The Jellyfish: An Old Story Retold" *Folio* 14:2 (Spr 1962), 30-4.

Kishkan, Theresa (Terry) (1955-)

"The Brand" *From an Island* 13:1 (Spr 1981), 9-14.

"Clo-oose" *Repos* No. 28 (Win 1979), 14-5.

"Love-Song to Palinurus" *Mal R* No. 50 (Apr 1979), 156-60.

"Middens" *Repos* No. 28 (Win 1979), 12-3.

"Mid-Winter" *Fid* No. 121 (Spr 1979), 64-5.

"Sketches for a Story" *Fid* No. 121 (Spr 1979), 63-4.

"Stephen" *Mal R* No. 53 (Jan 1980), 101-6.

Kitcher, W.H.C.†

"Sucking In: A Fable" *Rubicon* No. 1 (Spr 1983), 106-8.

"Time for a Smoke" *Antig R* No. 55 (Aut 1983), 93-6.

Kizik, Andy‡

"The Cross of David" *Kaleidoscope* Mar 1960, 28-31.

Klebeck, William J.

"Background of Blowing Topsail" *New Q* 3:3 (Fall 1983), 5-14.

"Hair on My Chest" *NeWest R* 8 (Dec 1982), 8-9.

"Pieces" *Sundogs* (1980), 65-7.

"Sting" *Prism* 21:1 (Sept 1982), 7-15.

"Sting" *Saskatchewan Gold* (1982), 202-13.

"White Rabbits" *Cap R* No. 21 (1982), 27-9.

Kleiman, Edward (1932-)

THE IMMORTALS Edmonton: NeWest Press, 1980.

"The Bicyclist" *Arts Man* 1:3/4 (Win 1978), 41-4.

"The Bicyclist" *Immortals* (1980), 137-45.

"Crystal Pillow" *Alphabet* No. 1 (Sept 1960), 59-68.

"Feldman vs. Buchalter: A New World Parable" *NeWest R* 4 (Mar 1979), 8-9, 12.

"Feldman vs. Buchalter: A New World Parable" *Immortals* (1980), 37-47.

"Greenspan's Studio" *Immortals* (1980), 147-54.

"The Handicap" *JCF* 3:2 (1974), 5-13.

"The Handicap" *Childhood and Youth in Canadian Literature* (1979), 96-107 [Excerpt].

"The Handicap" *Immortals* (1980), 79-97.

"Harry the Starman" *Immortals* (91980), 119-27.

"The Heart Surgeon" *Antig R* No. 38 (Sum 1979), 77-87.

"The Heart Surgeon" *Immortals* (1980), 111-8.

"The Immortals" *JCF* Nos. 17/18 (1976), 33-42.

"The Immortals" *Immortals* (1980), 49-60.
"The Immortals" *More Stories from Western Canada* (1980), 40-55.
"The Immortals" *West of Fiction* (1983), 96-108.
"My Mercurial Aunt" *Fid* No. 119 (Fall 1978), 82-93.
"My Mercurial Aunt" *Immortals* (1980), 99-110.
"A New-Found Ecstasy" *Des* 10:2 No. 24 (1979), 113-26.
"North End Faust" *Immortals* (1980), 129-36.
"A Red Haired Girl on a White Horse" *Immortals* (1980), 61-77.
"The Sea Shell" *Immortals* (1980), 33-6 [Also entitled "The Shell"].
"The Shell" *CF* 33 (Sept 1953), 133-4 [Also entitled "The Sea Shell"].
"A Summer Afternoon with the North End Buccaneers" *Immortals* (1980), 13-23.
[Title unknown] *CBC "Anthology"* 27 Dec 1955.
"Watch Out for Ronnie" *Creative Campus* 1962, 19-30.
"Watch Out for Ronnie" *Immortals* (1980), 25-31.
"Westward O Pioneers!" *Winnipeg Stories* (1974), 101-18.

Klein, Jack
"Death and the Maiden" *Forge* 26:1 (Feb 1964), 9-16.
"Nobody, but Nobody, Underhells Gimbel's" [sic] *Forge* 25:1 (Feb 1963), 12-6.

Klemm, Joachim‡
"The Wanderer" *Existère* 1:1 (Oct 1980), 2.

Kletke, Glenn‡
"The Departure" *Creative Campus* 1961, 10-4.

Knapp, G.L.†
"Artistic Artifice" *Can Lifetime* 1 (Nov-Dec 1971), 13-4.
"Cool-Calm-and Collected" *Can Lifetime* 3 (Nov-Dec 1973), 14-6.
"The Lady and the Cop" *Can Lifetime* 2 (Sept-Oct 1972), 14-5.

Knapton, Lucy†
"A Fish Out of Water" *Writers News Man* Nos. 8/9 (Aug 1979), [4 pp].

Knechtel, Mary Beth†
"Acts of Love" *OPT* 5:1 (Feb 1978), 16.
"Blow Job" *Pulp* 5:8 (15 July 1979), [2-3].
"Bobby's Story" *Pulp* 5:11 (31 Jan 1980), [2 pp].

Knight, Ann†
"Shock Treatments" *Scrivener* 2:2 (Fall 1981), 19-21.

Knight, David‡
"A Kind of Mordent" *CF* 60 (Oct 1980), 24-6.

Knowles, Rebecca (1899-)
"The Passenger" *Title Unknown* (1975), 3, 34-40.

Knox, Claire Neville
   See also Knox, Claire Neville and Lûsse, Georgina.
   "A Fish for Mr. Waddington" *Weekend* 3 (14 Feb 1953), 38.
   "The Party" *Weekend* 2 (22 Nov 1952), 28-9.

Knox, Claire Neville and Lûsse, Georgina
   See also Knox, Claire Neville; Lûsse, Georgina.
   "Annie's Daughter" *CHJ* Oct 1953, 13, 66, 68, 72-3, 76.

Knox, Gary†
   "A Statue" *Antig R* No. 43 (Aut 1980), 35-7.

Knox, Olive
   "Brave Harvest" *SW* 28 Sept 1957, 24-5, 41.
   "Bush Angel" *SW* 11 June 1955, I:9.
   "Chief Mahnomen" *Echoes* No. 212 (Aut 1953), 11, 32 [Listed as article but clearly fiction].
   "The Evening Star" *CG* Dec 1954, 9, 30-4.
   "No Divorce" *Lib* 34 (Nov 1957), 31, 73-4.
   "No Place for a Woman" *SW* 6 Mar 1954, I:5.
   "When Love Is Forever ... " *SW* 14 July 1956, II:1, 12.

Knudsen, Joyce
   "The Red Living Room" *Onward* 25 Oct 1959, 675-6.
   "The Strange Boy" *Onward* 7 Feb 1960, 94-5 [Nonfiction?].
   "Uneasy Companions" *Onward* 10 Jan 1960, 19 [Nonfiction?].

Koegh, Joe – *See* Carr, Roberta, with William Grant and Joe Koegh.

Koerte, Helen
   CHINESE MUSIC BOX & OTHER STORIES Guelph: Alive Press, 1971.
   "Across Symphony Hall" *Chinese Music Box* (1971), 30-40.
   "Across Symphony Hall" *Alive* 2:6 No. 16 ([May] 1971), 23-9.
   "Chinese Music Box" *Fid* No. 85 (May-June-July 1970), 54-9.
   "Chinese Music Box" *Chinese Music Box* (1971), 9-16.
   "Easter Sunday" *Chinese Music Box* (1971), 66-9.
   "Ecstasy of Clara Hobson" *Chinese Music Box* (1971), 22-9.
   "Ego Game" *Chinese Music Box* (1971), 55-65.
   "Encounter" *Chinese Music Box* (1971), 49-54.
   "Nicholas Bratzlavet" *Creative Campus* 1967, 42-50.
   "Nicholas Bratzlavet" *Chinese Music Box* (1971), 41-8.
   "The Story of Joe Canoe" *CF* 48 (Feb 1969), 252-3.
   "The Story of Joe Canoe" *Chinese Music Box* (1971), 17-21.

Kofman, Anni‡
   "Lonesome Canary" *West People* No. 207 (13 Oct 1983), 7.

Kogawa, Joy (1935-)
   "Are There Any Shoes in Heaven?" *FH* 18 Feb 1965, 44-5, 47.
   "The Hamster Cage" *FH* 30 Mar 1967, 34-5.
   "Obasan" *Rikka* 4:1 (Spr 1977), 36-40.
   "Obasan" *CBC "Anthology"* 16 Dec 1978.

Kohane, Jack‡
"Amory Was Released Today" *Alive* 3:2 No. 21 [1972?], 29-30.

Kohut, Michael†
"The Green Fox" *Moongoose* No. 4 (Nov 1972), [1 p].

Kolding, Sigrid†
"The Relic" *Mitre* 2 (1970), 25-8.

Kollonay. Georgina‡
"The Housewife's Dilemma" *Pedestal* 2:3 (Apr 1970), 6.

Kome, Penney†
"Preponderance of the Great" *Miss Chat* 11 (1 Aug 1974), 92-8.
"The Tale of the Illicit Ape" *New Bodies* (1981), 43-8.

Kon, Louis‡
"Plitochny Chay" *NF* 4:3 (Fall 1955), 13-5.

Koncel, Mary Aleta‡
"The Bird and the Boulder" *Titmouse R* No. 7 [n.d.], 44.
"Love That Hair" *Titmouse R* No. 7 [n.d.], 45.
"The Visitor" *Titmouse R* No. 7 [n.d.], 44.

Konoval, Karin‡
"The Blind Beggar" *CBC [Edm] "Alberta Anthology"* 18 Sept 1982.
"Deirdre Dickens" *CBC [Edm] "Alberta Anthology"* 28 Nov 1981.

Korber, Freda†
"The Bulldogs All Have Rubber Teeth" *Sundogs* (1980), 68-74.
"When the Boys Come Home" *Saskatchewan Gold* (1982), 214-25.

Korowiakowski, Eugeniuz
"Christmas Blues" *JCF* No. 24 [1979], 5-14.
"Los Machos/The He-Men" *JCF* Nos. 28/29 (1980), 35-46.

Kosacky, Helen†
"Just in Memory" *Time Pieces* (1974), 40-50.
"Midnight Moons" *Time Pieces* (1974), 15-24.
"Mountain in No Zone and Friends" *Time Pieces* (1974), 93-101.

Kosar, Rochell‡
"Daydreamers" *Smoke Signals* 2 [date unknown] [Based on *SWG* survey response].

Kostash, Myrna (1944-)
"Istanbul" *Des* No. 6 (Spr 1973), 52-8.
"Love Letters: A Docu-Drama of the Sixties" *Des* Nos. 8/9 (Spr-Sum 1974), 66-78.
"Right Back Where I Started From" *This* 16 (Dec-Jan 1982-83), 30-4.
"Right Back Where I Started From" *Camrose R* No. 3 [n.d.], 3-12.
"Showdown" *Getting Here* (1977), 33-45.

Kouhi, Elizabeth‡
"A Canadian Story" *Nw J* Nos. 18/19 (1980), 104-10.

Kowal, Victor†
"The Horse Buster" *Fid* No. 95 (Fall 1972), 49-50.
"My Silver Boots" *Prism* 10:1 (Sum 1970), 81-2.

Kozak, Roman‡
"Penance" *Mandala* 1973, 48-54.

Krachun, Peggy†
"The Family Reunion" *Twelve Newfoundland Short Stories* (1982), 25-38.

Krahn, Ruth‡
"Still Life" CBC *"Alberta Anthology"* 15 Oct 1983.

Kraintz, Dona† (1956?-)
"The Butterfly" *Miss Chat* 12 (6 Feb 1975), 52, 76-81.

Krakovsky, Shel‡
"Black Is White" *Varsity* Fri, 12 Feb 1965, Review 3.

Kratis, Diana†
"A Puff of Smoke" *WWR* 1:3 (Spr 1978), 42-6.

Krause, Pat†
FRESHIE Hamilton: Potlatch, 1981 [Connected stories].
"Campaigns" *Freshie* (1981), 62-9.
"Day One" *Freshie* (1981), 7-11.
"Finals" *Freshie* (1981), 90-5.
"The Freshie Frolic" *Freshie* (1981), 19-25.
"Licence to Live" *Freshie* (1981), 54-61.
"The Lookout Stone" *Saskatchewan Gold* (1982), 1-12.
"Playboy" *Smoke Signals* 3 (1978) [Based on *SWG* survey response].
"Playboy" *Sundogs* (1980), 75-82.
"Playboy" *100% Cracked Wheat* (1983), 92-103.
"Roll Call" *Freshie* (1981), 12-8.
"Salvage Drive" *Freshie* (1981), 26-34.
"Scheduled Meetings" *Freshie* (1981), 36-44.
"Sign Posts" *Freshie* (1981), 71-81.
"Spring Tournaments" *Freshie* (1981), 45-53.
"Sudden Squalls" *Smoke Signals* 4 [date unknown] [Based on *SWG* survey response].
"Swing Session" *Freshie* (1981), 96-101.
"The Water Ballet" *100% Cracked Wheat* (1983), 20-33.
"Yearbook Day" *Freshie* (1981), 82-9.

Kreiner, Philip (1952-)
PEOPLE LIKE US IN A PLACE LIKE THIS Ottawa: Oberon Press, 1983.
"Flying Fish (Ocho Rios: 1975)" *CF* 60 (June-July 1980), 20-4.
"The Gadfly Stung Me" CBC *"Anthology"* 13 Dec 1980.
"Rupertsland" *Tam R* No. 79 (Aut 1979), 50-2.

"That Year My Father Died" *CF 59* (Oct 1979), 20-2.
"That Year My Father Died" *People Like Us* (1983), 72-9.
"We Collide in Our Dreams" *JCF* No. 30 (1980), 65-78.
"We Collide in Our Dreams" *People Like Us* (1983), 51-71.

Kreisel, Henry (1922-)
THE ALMOST MEETING Edmonton: NeWest Press, 1981.
"The Almost Meeting" *CBC [Edm] "Alberta Anthology"* 4 Oct 1980.
"The Almost Meeting" *CBC "Anthology"* 15 Nov 1980.
"The Almost Meeting" *Almost Meeting* (1981), 11-21.
"The Almost Meeting" *NeWest R* 7 (Sum 1982), 6-7.
"Annerl" Prism 2:4 (Sum 1961), 35-40.
"Annerl" *Almost Meeting* (1981), 81-8.
"Annerl" *Interface* 4:3 (Apr 1981), 51-3.
"An Anonymous Letter" *CBC "Anthology"* 25 Nov 1958.
"An Anonymous Letter" *Wild Rose Country* (1977), 115-28.
"An Anonymous Letter" *Almost Meeting* (1981), 91-103.
"The Broken Globe" *Alberta Golden Jubilee Anthology* (1955), 409-19.
"The Broken Globe" *Literary R* (U.S.) 8 (1965), 484-95.
"The Broken Globe" *Best American Short Stories* 1966 155-65.
"The Broken Globe" *Stories from The Literary Review* (1969), 20-34.
"The Broken Globe" *Perceptions in Literature* (1972), 98-106 [Based on Gürttler].
"The Broken Globe" *Stories from Western Canada* (1972), 92-103.
"The Broken Globe" *Moderne Erzühler der Walt: Kanada* (1976), 252-64 [As "Der verbeulte Globus"; trans. Walter Riedel].
"The Broken Globe" *Best Modern Canadian Short Stories* (1978), 50-8.
"The Broken Globe" *Alberta Diamond Jubilee Anthology* (1979), 92-101.
"The Broken Globe" *Almost Meeting* (1981), 135-47.
"The Broken Globe" *Anthology of Canadian Literature in English II* (1983), 98-105.
"The Broken Globe" [Also translated into Swedish and Italian (not seen)].
"Chassidic Song" *Tam R* No. 75 (Fall 1978), 78-87.
"Chassidic Song" *CBC "Anthology"* 6 Oct 1979.
"Chassidic Song" *Almost Meeting* (1981), 25-35.
"An Evening with Sholom Aleichem" *CBC [Edm] "Alberta Anthology"* 11 Sept 1982.
"An Evening with Sholom Aleichem" *Prism* 21:3 (Apr 1983), 7-18.
"Homecoming: A Memory of Europe After the Holocaust" *CBC "Anthology"* 16 Apr 1957.
"Homecoming: A Memory of Europe After the Holocaust" *Klanak Islands* (1959), 7-15.
"Homecoming: A Memory of Europe After the Holocaust" *Almost Meeting* (1981), 39-77.
"The Travelling Nude" *Prism* 1:1 (Sept 1959), 7-17.
"The Travelling Nude" *More Stories from Western Canada* (1980), 73-86.
"The Travelling Nude" *Almost Meeting* (1981), 107-20.
"The Travelling Nude" *West of Fiction* (1983), 157-68.
"Two Sisters in Geneva" *QQ* 67 (1960), 67-75.
"Two Sisters in Geneva" *Neue Zürcher Zeitung* 8 Jan 1961 [As "Zwei Schwestern in Genf"; based on Gürttler].
"Two Sisters in Geneva" *Book of Canadian Stories* (1962), 294-303.
"Two Sisters in Geneva" *Modern Canadian Stories* (1966), 262-70.

"Two Sisters in Geneva" *Kanadische Erzühler der Gegenwart* (1967), 377-90 [As "Zwei Schwestern in Genf"; trans. Armin Arnold].

"Two Sisters in Geneva" *Tradition-Integration-Rezeption* (1979), 132-9 [Based on Gürttler].

"Two Sisters in Geneva" *Almost Meeting* (1981), 123-32.

Kremberg, Rudy‡
"The Method" *Alternative to Alienation* No. 7 (Mar-Apr 1976), 15.
"Run Like the Devil" *Acta Vic* 102:2 (Fall 1978), 37-9.

Krenz, Reynold
"Riding the Rails" *Grain* 4:1 [1976], 42-5.

Kristen, Marti‡
"One Foot Before Moscow" *AA* 56 (Mar 1966), 49-51, 53, 55.

Kritsch, Holly‡
"Ward C" *Driftwood* 1979, 31-4.

Kroeker, Ben‡
"Regeneration" *Creative Campus* 1965, 10-1.

Kroetsch, Robert (1927-)
"The Blue Guitar" *CF* 37 (Feb 1958), 250-1.
"Defy the Night" *Univ of Kansas City R* 26:3 (Spr 1960), 229-33 [Also entitled "Earth Moving"].
"Earth Moving" *Stories from Western Canada* (1972), 134-40 [Also entitled "Defy the Night"].
"The Harvester" *MM* 69 (29 Sept 1956), 22-3, 36, 38, 42-3.
"Mrs. Brennan's Secret" *MM* 70 (14 Sept 1957), 36-7, 94-8.
"Old Man Stories" *Grain* 1:1 (June 1973), 1-6 [Poetry?].
"The Stragglers" *Mont* 24 (Apr 1950) [Based on survey response].
"That Yellow Prairie Sky" *MM* 68 (30 Apr 1955), 28-9, 48-50.
"That Yellow Prairie Sky" *Creation* (1970), 16-25.
"That Yellow Prairie Sky" *Modern Canadian Stories* (1975), 106-15.
"That Yellow Prairie Sky" *Air* (1977), 108-11.
"That Yellow Prairie Sky" *Literature in Canada* (1978), 435-41.
"That Yellow Prairie Sky" *Best Modern Canadian Short Stories* (1978), 96-102.
"The Toughest Mile" *Mont* 24 (Nov 1950), 38.
"Who Would Marry a Riverman?" *MM* 69 (4 Feb 1956), 18-9, 28-9, 32, 34.

Kropp, Josefa (1944-)
"The White Wolf" *This* 15 (May-June 1981), 26-8.

Kropp, Paul‡
"On Sheep" *Forum* (OSSTF) 9 (Oct-Nov 1983), 119 [Satire].

Krotz, Larry†
"A Travel Piece" *Arts Man* 2:3 (Sum 1983), 33-4.

Kruberg, Galina‡
"Severing the Ties" *Muse* 65 (1956), 10, 36.

Krueger, Lesley
"Conversations with Chairman Mao" *Tam R* No. 75 (Fall 1978), 55-66.
"Going to See the Baba" *QQ* 89 (1982), 356-67.
"Growing Up Rosie" *Tam R* Nos. 81/82 (Win 1981), 74-90.
"The Invasion of Don Mills by Enemy Forces" *Little Mag* 13:3/4 (1982), 109-25.
"The Killdeer Nest" *Des* 12:4/13:1/2 Nos. 34/35/36 (1980-81), 208-23.

Kruger, Earl†
"Veritas, a Morality" *Forge* 1950, 66-8.

Krzeczunowicz, Sarah‡
"Pearls Before Swine" *Pigs* (1981), 64-71.

Kubicek, Tom†
"The Sun in the Evening" *Duel* No. 1 (Win 1969), 81-9.

Kudrick, Sylvia†
"The Facts of the Matter" *Treeline* 2 (1983), 111-2.

Kuipers, Jelte‡
"The Suicide" *Muse* 1964-65 Vol. 2, 23-6.

Kunnas, Susan‡
"Hair Grows Half an Inch Every Month" *UCR* Spr 1983, 11 [Prose poem?].

Kurtz, Jean‡
"Portrait" *In Touch* (1975), 21.

Kuschinski, Charles‡
"Sweet Hell" *Nebula* No. 15 (1980), 30-2.

Kushmelyn, Christina (1957-)
"Despair of Nothing" *Title Unknown* (1975), 24.

Kushner, Donn (1927-)
THE WITNESSES AND OTHER STORIES Ottawa: Borealis Press, 1980.
"Baldur's Death" *Antig R* No. 37 (Spr 1979), 77-84.
"Baldur's Death" *Witnesses* (1980), 26-31.
"The Librarians" *Bullétin de l'Association canadienne des humanités* 1965 [Based on survey response].
"The Librarians" *Witnesses* (1980), 38-48.
"A Matter of Luck" *Fid* No. 68 (Spr 1966), 42-8.
"A Matter of Luck" *Witnesses* (1980), 12-7.
"Miami" *Witnesses* (1980), 59-65.
"Paying the Piper" *Fid* No. 83 (Jan-Feb 1970), 57-65.
"Paying the Piper" *Witnesses* (1980), 18-25.
"The Peeping Tom" *CF* 37 (Apr 1957), 17-8.
"A Ruined Maid" *Inscape* 9:2 (Aut 1971), 40-8.
"A Ruined Maid" *Witnesses* (1980), 49-58.
"The Scientist's Wife" *Fid* No. 121 (Spr 1979), 67-79.
"The Scientist's Wife" *Witnesses* (1980), 66-77.
"Two Europeans" *Alphabet* No. 10 (July 1965), 32-9.

"Two Europeans" *Witnesses* (1980), 32-7.
"The Witnesses" *Fid* No. [77] (Sum 1968), 4-19.
"The Witnesses" *Witnesses* (1980), 1-11.
"Writing Jewish Stories" *Viewpoints* 12:1 (Feb 1983), 6-8.

Kuti, John‡
"The Messiah" *Chiaroscuro* 9 (1965-66), 9-12.

Kutlesa, Joso
THE SUNRISE OF JOY AND LOVE Toronto: Mystic Press, 1973.
"The Agony of Being Alive" *Sunrise of Joy and Love* (1973), 41-8.
"Aliya" *Sunrise of Joy and Love* (1973), 23-9.
"Anita in Love" *Sunrise of Joy and Love* (1973), 77-84.
"The Crack-Up" *Sunrise of Joy and Love* (1973), 67-75.
"A Discovery of Canada" *Sunrise of Joy and Love* (1973), 49-56.
"The Exotic Encounters" *Sunrise of Joy and Love* (1973), 109-15.
"Expectations" *Sunrise of Joy and Love* (1973), 99-108.
"The Heart-Broken Lady" *Sunrise of Joy and Love* (1973), 57-65.
"A Kind, Beautiful, Understanding Mother" *Sunrise of Joy and Love* (1973), 7-13.
"The Mystic Adventurer" *Sunrise of Joy and Love* (1973), 85-91.
"Secrets of the Human Heart" *Sunrise of Joy and Love* (1973), 15-21.
"Silvana and Eliot" *Sunrise of Joy and Love* (1973), 117-24.
"The Sunrise and the Lovers" *Sunrise of Joy and Love* (1973), 1-6.
"The Surprise" *Sunrise of Joy and Love* (1973), 93-8.
"The Tender Moment in Life" *Sunrise of Joy and Love* (1973), 31-9.

Kwasny, Barbara J.‡
"A Gem of a Day" *Edmonton Culture Vulture* 1:1 (Fri, 26 Sept 1975), 14-5, 18-9.

Kyte, Ernest C.‡
"The Death of a Dog" *Can Life* 1:3 (Win 1949-50), 6-7, 36.

L.D. – *See* Duncan, Leslie.

La Haye, Marguerite
"Peeling Labels" *Mam* 5:2/3 (Fall-Win 1981-82), [6 pp].
"The Preacher's Kid" *Mam* 3:3 (Fall 1979), [10 pp].
"The Summer the Wind Fell" *Northern Ontario Anthology* 2 (1978), 63-6.
"A Tournament with Truth" *CSSM* 2:4 (Fall 1976), 23, 25-6.
"Victoria" *Origins* 10:3 (Sept 1980), 48-53.

Laba, Mark
See also Ross, Stuart and Laba, Mark.
"It Was a Slight Misunderstanding" *Images* 2:6 (Mar 1981), 11.
[Untitled] *Industrial Sabotage* No. 14 [Mar 1983], [1 p] [Sketch?].
[Untitled] *Toybox* No. 1 (15 Oct 1982), [1 p].

L'Abbé-Jones, Pauline
"The Blue Door" *Outset* 1974, 95-8.

Labonte, Ron (1953-)
"Museum" *CFM* No. 7 (Sum 1972), 17-9.

Lacy, Ed
"Death-Bed Gamble" *AA* 55 (Oct 1964), 47-9, 54-5.

Ladoo, Harold Sonny (1945-1973)
"The Quiet Peasant" *Imp* 2:3/4 (1973), 11-7.
"The Quiet Peasant" *CBC "Anthology"* 4 May 1974.
"The Quiet Peasant" *Canada in Us Now* (1976), 90-3.

Laflamme, Guy
"The Archaeologist on the Anatolian Plateau" *CFM* No. 15 (Aut 1974), 79-86.
"Kiki" *Alch* 1:2 [1975], 21-8.
"Me and MacCracken" *Quarry* 25:1 (Win 1976), 36-45.

Laforme, George‡
"[A?] Day on the Trapline" *BC Outdoors* 38 (Dec-Jan 1982-83), 53-4[+?] [Based on CPI].

Lagnado, Robert†
"No Black Envy" *Quarry* 5 (Spr 1956), 21-5.

Laidlaw, Alice – *See* Munro, Alice.

Lake, Rhody†
"The Father" *My Golden West* 4 (Sum 1969), 28-9.

Lalonde, Wendy‡
"Victory Dance" *Alpha* 7:2 (Apr 1983), 17-9.

Lalor, George T.‡
"A Chat with God" *Images About Manitoba* 1:2 (Mar 1976), 18-21.

Lamb, Ken‡
"The Axe" *Raven* No. 6 (Apr 1958), 5-9.

Lamb, Marcia‡
"Just to Be Content" *Mandala* 1972, 51-5.

Lamb, Murray‡
"If He Hollers Let Him Go" *Los* No. 4 (Jan 1977), [22 pp].
"Tale of a Kinsman" *Mont Writers' Forum* 1:2 (Nov 1978), 8-12.

Lambert, Barbara
"Bedtime Story" *Stories with John Drainie* (1963), 64-70.
"Renascence" *Raven* 2 No. 4 (Spr 1957), 2-11.

Lambert, Claudia
"On the Corner" *WCR* 18:2 (Oct 1983), 3-7.

Lambert, Elizabeth M. (Betty) (1933-)
"Guilt" *WCR* 13:2 (Oct 1978), 3-15.
"The Last Dinner" *Elbow Room* (1979), 187-225.
"The Man Who Found Happiness: A Fable" *QQ* 64 (1957), 56-63.
"The Pony" *New Voices* (1956), 33-42.

Lambert, Rick†
"Evening Scrub Football in Greece" *Des* No. 4 (Spr 1972), 16-7.
"The Moon Dancers" *Des* No. 3 (Fall 1971), 17-20.
"Sometimes I Feel Like Going Down" *Waves* 1:1 (Spr 1972), 65-74.

Lamont, Margo‡
"Tommy, Are You with Us?" *Alpha* 2:1 (Sept 1977), 23-4.

Lamp, Bud – *See* Green, H. Gordon.

Lampert, Gerald (192?-1978)
"The Joshua Levine Cassettes: Numbers 1, 4, 11, 14, 18, 23" *Story So Four* (1976), 154-8.
"Sarah's Cod Liver Oil" *JD Passover* 1972, 35-9.

Landis, Scott†
"The Fever" *Har* 7:3 No. 45 (Oct-Nov 1982), 59-62, 99.

Landreth, Tomas‡
"Solitary Stroll" *CBC "Alberta Anthology"* 22 Oct 1983.

Landsberg, Michele
"Short Story" *Undergrad* Spr 1961, 5-9.

Landy, Francis‡
"My Zaida and Aunt Ellen" *Waves* 5:2/3 (Spr 1977), 38-9.

Lane, John‡
"Journey to Nowhere" *Repos* Nos. 21/22 (Win-Spr 1977), 49-52.

Lane, Pat (1939-)
"What Does Not Change" *Outlaws* (1974), 91-5 [Prose poem?].

Lane, William†
"The Cookie Crumbles" *Story So Far* 2 (1973), 154-7.

Lang, Frances‡
[Untitled] *Writ* No. 10 (1978), 5-8.

Langan, Vernabea‡
"Return" *Tyro* 1962, 22-4.

Lange, Gerald‡
"Crossing" *Titmouse R* No. 5 (Win 1974-75), 6.

Langer, Howie‡
"The Sabbath After" *Masada* 5:2 (Feb 1974), 11-2.

Langevin, John‡
"A Christmas Fantasy" *Varsity* Fri, 14 Dec 1962, 7.
'The Cloud of Unknowing" *Varsity Lit Issue* Fri, 13 Dec 1963, 2-3.

Langford, Ernest
'The Poker Game" *event* 9:1 (1980), 74-81.
'The Potlatch" *Tam R* Nos. 50/51 (1969), 20-35.

Langhout, Mary†
"Roll Over, Beethoven" *Twelve Newfoundland Short Stories* (1982), 39-42.
'We Two Are Now One" *From This Place* (1977), 152-4.

Langille, Gord‡
"Escape" *Acta Vic* 78:3 (Feb 1954), 20-2.

Langille, Mary‡
"Once Upon a Time" *TUR* 96:1 (Jan 1983), 24-5.
[Untitled] *TUR* 96:1 (Jan 1983), 39-48.

Langlais, Richard
"Dead Flies" *Posh* [n.d.], [2 pp].
'From the Root Cellar" *Posh* [n.d.], [3 pp].

Langston, Corrine‡
'The Drive" *CBC "Anthology"* 7 Nov 1970.

Lapp, Eula C.‡
"After the Darkness – The Dawn" *Missionary Monthly* 28 (Apr 1953), 149-51.

Lappin, Ben
'The Holdup" *MM* 71 (8 Nov 1958), 25, 40, 42, 44-5.
"Ottawa's First (and Last) Sidewalk Cafe" *MM* 68 (9 July 1955), 18-9, 35-7.

Larmour, Anne‡
"And Nothing Was Left" *Acta Vic* 77:3 (Feb 1953), 24-5.
"A 'Black Cat' Crossed Their Path" *Acta Vic* 78:3 (Feb 1954), 25-6.
'The Dream" *Acta Vic* 77:1 (Nov 1952), 21-2.
'It's a Cinch" *Acta Vic* 77:2 (Dec 1952), 17-8.

Larsen, Carl‡
'The Bear Went Over the Mountain" *Yes* 2:3 (Feb 1958), [3 pp].
'Pages from the Life and Times of Solomon Ander" *Yes* 2:1 (Apr 1957), [4 pp].

Lasby, Brian‡
'The Confinement of Time" *Nightwinds* 1:1 (Sum 1979), 29-30.

Lash, Timothy‡
"Dream Sequence" *TUR* 80:4 (Mar 1967), 12-3.

Lassen, Judy‡
"But in a Fiction, in a Dream of Passion ... " *Prism* 17:1 (Sum 1978), 137-9.

Latimer, Hugh‡
"Nada, Nada y Nada" *Prism* (Mont) 1958, 20-3.

Latta, William†
"Jerome" *Was R* 7:1 (1972), 27-38.

Laturnus, Ted†
"A Brief His-Story of Mental Health" *Diversions* 4:1 (1973), 18-23.

Laub, Marshall‡
"A Matter of Logic" *Edge* No. 8 (Fall 1968), 91.
"The Negotiator" *Inside* 2:4 [n.d.], 13-4.
"The Playmate" *Pluck* 1:2 (Spr 1968), 21-6.

Lauder, Scott†
"Opened in Error. Please Forward" *Des* No. 16 (Win 1976-77), 24-5.

Laudon, H.V.†
"In Plain Words" *Antig R* No. 46 (Sum 1981), 59-61.
"In Plain Words" *Body Politic* No. 81 (Mar 1982), 32.

Laufer, Judith (1955-)
"Rose" *From an Island* 10:1 [n.d.], 21-2.

Laurence, Elsie Fry
"The Phoenix" *Stories with John Drainie* (1963), 92-8.
"The Poor Moriartys" *CHJ* Apr 1950, 20, 48, 50, 52-3, 55-7.

Laurence, Margaret (1926-)
A BIRD IN THE HOUSE Toronto: McClelland & Stewart, 1970.
THE TOMORROW-TAMER AND OTHER STORIES London: Macmillan, 1963.
"A Bird in the House" *Atlantic Monthly* 214 (Nov 1964), 64-71.
"A Bird in the House" *Canadian Winter's Tales* (1968), 79-102.
"A Bird in the House" *Bird in the House* (1970), 89-113.
"A Bird in the House" *Sixteen by Twelve* (1970), 55-70.
"A Bird in the House" *Moderne Erzühler der Walt: Kanada* (1976), 284-305 [As "Ein Vogel im Haus"; trans. Walter Riedel].
"A Bird in the House" *Women and Fiction* 2 (1978), 304-21.
"A Bird in the House" *West of Fiction* (1983), 186-202.
"The Calling of the Loons" CBC *"Anthology"* 2 Feb 1964 [Also entitled "The Crying of the Loons" and "The Loons"].
"The Crying of the Loons" *AA* 56 (Mar 1966), 34-8 [Also entitled "The Calling of the Loons" and "The Loons"].
"The Drummer of All the World" *QQ* 62 (1956), 487-504.
"The Drummer of All the World" *Tomorrow-Tamer* (1963), 1-19.
"The Drummer of All the World" *Evolution of Canadian Literature in English* (1973), 160-70.
"The Exiles" *Sat Eve Post* 234 (3 June 1961), 28-9, 44-5, 50-1 [Also entitled "The Perfume Sea"].
"The Exiles" *Saturday Evening Post Stories* 1962 [Based on SSI].
"A Fetish for Love" *Tomorrow-Tamer* (1963), 161-81.
"Godman's Master" *Prism* 1:3 (Spr 1960), 46-64.

"Godman's Master" *Tomorrow-Tamer* (1963), 134-60.

"A Gourdful of Glory" *Tam R* No. 17 (Aut 1960), 5-20.

"A Gourdful of Glory" *Tomorrow-Tamer* (1963), 225-44.

"A Gourdful of Glory" *Canadian Short Stories 2* (1968), 127-49.

"A Gourdful of Glory" *Great Canadian Short Stories* (1971), 225-40.

"A Gourdful of Glory" *Double Vision* (1976), 201-16.

"A Gourdful of Glory" *World Outside* (1977) [Based on SSI].

"A Gourdful of Glory" *Best Modern Canadian Short Stories* (1978), 123-35.

"A Gourdful of Glory" *Penguin Book of Modern Canadian Short Stories* (1982), 105-19.

"The Half-Husky" CBC *"Anthology"* 10 Oct 1967 [Also entitled "Nanuk"].

"The Half-Husky" *Liberté* 11 (mars-avr 1969), 143-61 [As "Le bætard"; trans. Jean Paré].

"The Half-Husky" *Bird in the House* (1970), 155-72.

"The Half-Husky" *Inquiry into Literature* 3 (1980), 14-26.

"Horses of the Night" *Chat* 40 (July 1967), 47, 70, 72, 74-7.

"Horses of the Night" *Winter's Tales* 15 (1969), 33-57.

"Horses of the Night" *Bird in the House* (1970), 128-54.

"Horses of the Night" *Contemporary Voices* (1972), 59-73.

"Horses of the Night" *Stories from Western Canada* (1972), 218-39.

"Horses of the Night" *Depression in Canadian Literature* (1976), 38-60.

"Horses of the Night" *Rites of Passage* (1979), 56-74.

"Jericho's Brick Battlements" *Bird in the House* (1970), 173-207.

"The Loons" *Bird in the House* (1970), 114-27 [Also entitled "The Calling of the Loons" and "The Crying of the Loons"].

"The Loons" *Narrative Voice* (1972), 104-12.

"The Loons" *Selections from Major Canadian Writers* (1974), 216-22.

"The Loons" *Die Weite Reise* (1974), 259-72 [As "Die Seetaucher"; trans. Karl Heinrich].

"The Loons" *Prairie Experience* (1975), 85-96.

"The Loons" *Double Vision* (1976), 217-27.

"The Loons" *Horizon* (1977), 193-201.

"The Loons" *Mountain & Plain* (1978), 18-27.

"The Loons" *Transitions 2* (1978), 81-90.

"The Loons" *Best Canadian Short Stories* (1981), 272-81.

"The Loons" *Heartland* (1983), 33-43.

"Mask of Beaten Gold" *Tam R* No. 29 (Aut 1963), 3-21.

"Mask of Beaten Gold" *JCF* No. 27 (1980), 23-40.

"The Mask of the Bear" *Chat* 38 (Feb 1965), 27, 54-9.

"The Mask of the Bear" *Winter's Tales* 2 (1965), 37-61.

"The Mask of the Bear" *Bird in the House* (1970), 60-88.

"The Mask of the Bear" *Canadian Anthology* (1974), 479-92.

"The Merchant of Heaven" *Prism* 1:1 (Sept 1959), 52-74.

"The Merchant of Heaven" *Tomorrow-Tamer* (1963), 50-77.

"The Merchant of Heaven" *Modern Stories in English* (1975), 173-93.

"Nanuk" *Argosy* Nov 1967 [Also entitled "The Half-Husky"; based on ABC-MA].

"The Perfume Sea" *Winter's Tales* 6 (1960), 83-120 [Also entitled "The Exiles"].

"The Perfume Sea" *Tomorrow-Tamer* (1963), 20-49.

"The Perfume Sea" *Four Hemispheres* (1971), 276-95.

"The Perfume Sea" *Here and Now* (1977), 39-60.
"The Pure Diamond Man" *Tomorrow-Tamer* (1963), 182-204.
"The Pure Diamond Man" *Tam R* No. 26 (Win 1963), 3-21.
"A Queen in Thebes" *Tam R* No. 32 (Sum 1964), 25-37.
"A Queen in Thebes" *Canadian Century* (1973), 583-94.
"A Queen in Thebes" *Canadian Stories of Action and Adventure* (1978), 84-97.
"A Queen in Thebes" *Other Canadas* (1979), 160-71.
"A Queen in Thebes" *JCF* No. 27 (1980), 41-51.
"The Rain Child" *Winter's Tales* 8 (1962), 105-42.
"The Rain Child" *Tomorrow-Tamer* (1963), 105-33.
"The Sound of the Singing" *Winter's Tales* 9 (1963), 62-104.
"The Sound of the Singing" *Bird in the House* (1970), 3-38.
"The Spell of the Distant Drum" *Sat Eve Post* 235 (5 May 1962), 24-5, 76, 78, 80-2
[Also entitled "The Voices of Adamo"].
"A Time of Waiting" *Chat* 43 (Feb 1970), 34, 53, 55-60.
"To Set Our House in Order" *Ladies Home J* 81 (Mar 1964), 81-2, 127-8, 130-1.
"To Set Our House in Order" *Modern Canadian Stories* (1966), 247-61.
"To Set Our House in Order" *Bird in the House* (1970), 39-59.
"To Set Our House in Order" *Kaleidoscope* (1972), 10-25.
"To Set Our House in Order" *Narrative Voice* (1972), 113-25.
"To Set Our House in Order" *Modern Canadian Stories* (1975), 158-73.
"To Set Our House in Order" *Role of Woman in Canadian Literature* (1975), 36-51.
"To Set Our House in Order" *Literature in Canada* (1978), 410-22.
"To Set Our House in Order" *Penguin Book of Canadian Short Stories* (1980), 243-57.
"To Set Our House in Order" *Anthology of Canadian Literature in English 2* (1983), 154-64.
"The Tomorrow-Tamer" *Prism* 3:1 (Fall 1961), 36-54.
"The Tomorrow-Tamer" *Tomorrow-Tamer* (1963), 78-104.
"The Tomorrow-Tamer" *Sixteen by Twelve* (1970), 38-55.
"The Tomorrow-Tamer" *Anthology of Canadian Literature in English 2* (1983), 139-53.
"Uncertain Flowering" *Story* No. 4 (1953), 9-34.
"The Voices of Adamo" *Tomorrow-Tamer* (1963), 205-24 [Also entitled "The Spell of the Distant Drum"].
"The Voices of Adamo" *Canadian Short Stories 2* (1968), 105-26.

Laurent, Lucien‡
"The House on the Island" *Undergrad* Aut 1950, 18-22.

Laver, Sue†
"Listen to This Train" *Cap R* No. 27 (1983), 74-86.

Laverne, Samuel‡
"The Professor" *Muse* 67 (1958), 22-7.

Lavigne, Jean-Luc‡
"The Graveyard Shift" *Choice Parts* (1976), 34-9.

Laviolette, Emily A.
THE OYSTER & THE MERMAID AND OTHER ISLAND STORIES Fernwood, P.E.I.: Elaine Harrison, 1975 [Based on CBIP].

Lavoie, Edgar (1940-)
"The Destruction of Main Street" *Squatch J* No. 4 (Dec 1976), 5-11 [Satire].
"The Foundering of Squatchberry" *Squatch J* No. 3 (June 1976), 5-10 [Satire].
"The Great Sanitary Landfill Debate" *Squatch J* No. 1 (June 1975), 4-10.
"The Hunting of the Snerk" *Squatch J* No. 2 (Jan 1976), 5-10.

Lavoie, Stephanie‡
"Second Sight" *AA* 67 (Aug 1977), 61-2.

Law, Charles‡
"Arthur and the Labrat" *Introductions from an Island* 1972, 26-30.

Lawrence, Charles M.‡
"The Ladder" *TUR* 65:2 (Jan 1953), 9-17.

Lawrence, Dorothy Elderkin‡
"Gaily Comes My Love" *AA* 49 (June 1959), 57, 59.

Lawrence, S.A.M.
"The Damnation of Jed Staley" *Pacific Profile* 1:1 (Fall 1961), 32-41.

Lawrence, Scott‡
"Convergence" *New Mitre* 85 (1980), 17-20.

Lawson, David†
"Rusty at McClintock's" *Saturday Night at the Forum* (1981), 101-23.
"The Stray Cats of District Saint-Louis" *NJ* No. 6 (June 1976), 43-50.

Lawson, Eric‡
"The Museum" *Pom Seed* 1982, 45-8.

Layer, Ethel‡
"Too Late to Liberate" *Stump* 1:2 (Fall 1977), 62-5 [Non-fiction?].

Layman, Annemarie‡
"A Piece of Love" *Images About Manitoba* 1:3 (Fall-Win 1976), 23-5.

Layton, Boschka (1918-)
THE PRODIGAL SUN: POEMS, STORIES AND DRAWINGS Oakville: Mosaic Press/Valley Editions, 1982.
"Guardian Angel" *Prodigal Sun* (1982), 47-51.
"Love in the Attic" *Prodigal Sun* (1982), 53-8.
"Musical Hell" *Prodigal Sun* (1982), 59-63.
"Thanksgiving Dinner" *Prodigal Sun* (1982), 65-71.

Layton, Irving (1912-)
ENGAGEMENTS: THE PROSE OF IRVING LAYTON Toronto: McClelland & Stewart, 1972.
THE SWINGING FLESH Toronto: McClelland & Stewart, 1961.

"Mrs Polinov" *Origin* (U.S.) 17 (Fall-Win 1956), 25-40 [Based on Mayne].
"Mrs Polinov" *Swinging Flesh* (1961), 71-87.
"Mrs Polinov" *Engagements* (1972), 269-84.
"Osmeck" *Swinging Flesh* (1961), 128-38.
"Osmeck" *CF* 40 (Feb 1961), 249-52.
"Osmeck" *Engagements* (1972), 323-32.
"A Plausible Story" *Origin* (U.S.) 14 (Aut 1954), 91-104 [Based on Mayne].
"A Plausible Story" *Swinging Flesh* (1961), 32-46.
"A Plausible Story" *Book of Canadian Stories* (1962), 244-59.
"A Plausible Story" *Engagements* (1972), 233-46.
"Unemployed" *Swinging Flesh* (1961), 106-15.
"Unemployed" *Great Canadian Short Stories* (1971), 140-8.
"Unemployed" *Engagements* (1972), 302-10.

Layton, Max
"Mandi" *Des* 14:3 No. 41 (Sum 1983), 40-7.
"My Yarmulka" *Antig R* No. 53 (Spr 1983), 57-66.
'The Myth of Joel Ickerman" *Des* 13:3 No. 37 (Sum 1982), 85-102.

Lazarus, Emma [pseudonym]
"Headway" *Body Politic* No. 60 (Feb 1980), 27-8.

Lazarus, John (1947-)
'The Goblin and the Student" *CBC [Van] "Hornby Collection"* 24 Nov 1979 ["Fairy tale"].

Lazier, Ann‡
"Next to the Raspberries" *TUR* 67:2 (Dec 1954), 26-8.

Lea, Irene Barbara
"One Saturday in June" *Mal R* No. 59 (July 1981), 11-9.

Lea, Joseph William‡
'The Poetry Reading" *Alive* No. 48 (Apr 1976), 11.

Lebel, John‡
"About Stars" *Kaleidoscope* 1956-57, 16-7.

LeBourdais, Isabel
'But for the Grace of God" *CHJ* June 1950, 18-9, 24, 26-8, 32, 52.
"Second Wife" *CHJ* Mar 1950, 21, 54-8, 60-4.

Leckie, Keith‡
'Post-Dated" *Matrix* 2:2 (Win 1977), 22-3.

Leclair, Elizabeth†
"Murder on the Northumberland Ferry" *Black Cat* No. 5 [n.d.], 28-39.

LeCorre, Kathryn (Kathy) (1950-)
"Cakes, Piles and Pianos" *Mal R* No. 58 (Apr 1981), 120-2.
"Wood-Worms and Walnuts" *Mal R* No. 64 (Feb 1983), 143-7.

LeDain, Gerald‡

"On the Way Home" *Anglican Outlook* 6:9 (July 1951), 9-8.
"Peter Smiley's Influence" *Anglican Outlook* 6:7 (May 1951), 12-3.

Ledbetter, Ken (1931-)

"An Act of God" *Quarry* 25:1 (Win 1976), 9-21.
"Eyes That Went Away" *UWR* 11:1 (Fall-Win 1975), 30-6.
"Idiots" *CFM* No. 17 (Spr 1975), 92-101.
"Idiots" *Magic Realism* (1980), 79-88.

Leddy, Joseph‡

"God Bless You" *Kaleidoscope* 1955-56, 11-3.

Ledoux, Ken – *See* Green, H. Gordon.

Leduc, Gäetane

"When No One Was Watching" *Alive* 2:9 [Sept 1971], 8-12.

Ledwell, Frank J.

"DJ" *Abegweit R* 4:1 (Spr 1983), 43-9.

Lee, Arthur†

"Sweet Potatoes" *Dal R* 37 (1957), 85-8.

Lee, Bibi‡

"Scab" *Fireweed* No. 14 (Fall 1982), 101-4.

Lee, Carroll H.†

"An Improbable Evangelist" *UC Observer* 15 June 1968, 31 [Non-fiction?].
"Influential Citizen" *Rapport* Sept 1968, 36-7 [Non-fiction?].
"The Long Road to Christmas" *UC Observer* 15 Dec 1968, 18-9, 46.
"More Blessed to Give" *UC Observer* Oct 1973, 24-5 [Non-fiction?].
"The Parable of Sourdough" *UC Observer* 15 Nov 1967, 47.
"The Parable of the Rutted Road" *UC Observer* 1 Sept 1965, 23-5, 46.
"Saved by the Bells" *Pres Record* 97 (Feb 1973), 2-3.
"Sorry, My Wife Doesn't Live Here" *UC Observer* 15 Oct 1967, 22-3.
"A Time for Decision" *War Cry* 2 Aug 1974, 10-1.
"The Web Spinners" *Pres Record* 107 (Sept 1983), 14-6 [Non-fiction?].

Lee, David‡

"The Art of Walking by Car" *Acta Vic* 80:3 (Feb 1956), 14.

Lee, Dennis

"The Present" *Acta Vic* 83:3 (Jan 1959), 5-6.

Lee, Jennifer‡

"The House" *Simcoe R* No. 9 (Win 1980), 20-3.

Lee, Kim‡

"Trio" *Outset* 1974, 99-102.

Lee, Pamela†

"Dead Meat" *CF* 30 (Jan 1951), 232-3.

Lee, Ron‡
"A Tactical Exigency" *Kaleidoscope* 1955-56, 8-10.

Lee, Ronald†
"It Won't Be Long Now" *Cyclic* 1:1 (June 1965), 12 [Sketch?].

Lee, Sky
"Broken Teeth" *WCR* 16:1 (Sum 1981), 20-3.

Lee, Thirza M.†
"He Was Almost My Baby" *UC Observer* 15 May 1968, 22-3, 45-6.
"Swinging Doors" *Onward* July 1967, 14-5, 25.
"That Romantic Cake" *Onward* 26 June 1966, 12-3 [Humour?].
"There's Always a Christmas" *Onward* 19 Dec 1965, 12-3 [Non-fiction?].

Lees, Gene (1928?-)
"A Big Hand for Danny" *CHJ* Sept 1952, 18-9, 40-6.

Lees, Margaret†
"All Our Tomorrows" *West People* No. 200 (25 Aug 1983), 11.
"The Loaf of Bread" *Saskatchewan Homecoming* (1971), 51-2.

Legate, John‡
"The Friendly Fog" *Crier* 1:3 (Oct 1964), 33-6.
"The Top of the Pine Tree" *AA* 51 (Aug 1961), 85-6.

Legault, Donald
"The Great Garbage Strike" *Cop Toad* 1:4 (May 1978), 22-4.
"Setting Traps" *Cop Toad* 2:3 (Jan 1978), 12-4.

Leggett, Catharine† (1951-)
"Brandywine" *event* 11:1 (1982), 92-103.
"Snowstorm" *event* 9:1 (1980), 105-11.
"Snowstorm" *CBC [Van] "Hornby Collection"* 18 Dec 1982.

Lehman, Paul R.
"He Who Laughs" *Alpha* 4:2 (Win 1979), 5, 22, 30.

Leibowitz, Fred‡
"Smoke Gets in Your Eyes" *TUR* 82:3 (Sum 1969), 6-9.

Leigh, Mary‡
"Our Father" *Forge* 27:1 (Feb 1965), 49-53.

Leigh, Mildred†
"Days of Innocence and Truth" *Saskatchewan Homecoming* (1971), 111-3.

Leitao, Lino (1930-)
COLLECTED SHORT TALES New York: Carlton Press, 1972.
GOAN TALES Cornwall: Vesta, 1977.
SIX TALES Cornwall: Vesta, 1980.
"Armando Rodrigues" *Goan Tales* (1977), 54-70.
"The Colonial Bishop's Visit" *Tor S Asian R* 2:2 (Sum 1983), 52-4.

"The Curse" *Collected Short Tales* (1977), 49-60.
"The Curse" *Tor S Asian R* 1:1 (Win 1982), 1-10.
"Dona Amalio Quadros" *Pacific Moana Q* 6:3/4 (July-Oct 1981), 242-53.
"The Ghost" *Six Tales* (1980), 23-32.
"The Hidden Truth" *Six Tales* (1980), 7-22.
"The Hindu Goan" *Six Tales* (1980), 48-63.
"Jaffer's Chicken" *Collected Short Tales* (1972), 7-36.
"The Mad Woman" *Goan Tales* (1977), 71-91.
"The Marriage" *Collected Short Tales* (1977), 61-93.
"The Miracle" *Goan Tales* (1977), 9-29.
"Mr. Saldanha" *Six Tales* (1980), 33-47.
"The Portuguese Governor" *Collected Short Tales* (1977), 37-48.
"The Slap" *Goan Tales* (1977), 92-113.
"The Son" *Goan Tales* (1977), 30-53.
"The Son" *J of South Asian Lit* 18:1 (Win-Spr 1983), 131-43.
"Summary" *Six Tales* (1980), 64-7.
"Summary" *Goa Today* (India) [date unknown] [Based on survey response].
"Thanks to Goa Bus System!" *Six Tales* (1980), 68-82.

Leitch, Adelaide (1921-)

MAINSTREAM Toronto: Canadian Council of Churches, 1966 [Based on CBIP].
"The Lady on the Limb" *SW* 25 June 1955, II:5-6.
"The Lonely One" *SW* 16 Apr 1955, I:6.
"Operation Oliver" *SW* 19 Aug 1950, II:3.
"The Voice of Cape des Loups" *SW* 12 May 1956, II:5, 12.

LeMay, Bonnie

"The Best Dog That Ever Was" *CBC [Edm] "Alberta Anthology"* 7 Nov 1981.
"Mr. Woodford's Legacy" *NeWest R* 5 (Dec 1979), 8-9.

Lemelin, Roger

"The Plouffes Visit Toronto" *MM* 72 (9 May 1959), 30, 57-8, 60.

Lemm, Richard

"Border Incident" *JCF* No. 19 (1977), 45-64.
"Internal Combustion" *CFM* No. 21 (Spr 1976), 30-41.
"Meteors of Wishing, with Long Tails of Guilt" *VWFP/Revue* 1:2 (Apr 1975), 1, 8-9.
"Street Musician" *Karaki* No. 6 (June 1977), 56-62.
"Swede" *event* 6:2 [1977], 45-50.

Lemna, D.F.‡

"Horse Power" *West People* No. 128 (11 Mar 1982), 6-7.

Lemond, Edward†

"The Recruit" *Quarry* 20:4 (1971), 32-45.
"The Toy That Had to Be Returned" *CFM* No. 7 (Sum 1972), 34-7.

Lenardson, Paula†

"Girls' Talk" *Origins* 11:2 (June 1981), 29-33.

Lennick, D.‡
"East End" *Muskeg R* 3 (1975), 31-6.

Lennon, Pauline‡
"May Wine" *Flare* 4 (Aug 1982), 38, 40, 42.

Lennox, Gary†
"In This Day and Age" *Des* 11:4/12:1 (1980-81), 79-81.

Lennox, Kathy
"Old Crow" *Nw J* No. 23 (1981), 75-8.

Lenoir-Arcand, Christine (1946-)
SHADOWS Cornwall: Vesta, 1978.
"Back in the Alley" *Outset* 1974, 24-7.
"Back in the Alley" *Shadows* (1978), 55-61.
"A Child Bride Grows Up" *Shadows* (1978), 27-32.
"Jumping Jackie" *Shadows* (1978), 71-81.
"Memoirs of a Girl" *Shadows* (1978), 62-70.
"New Year's Eve" *Shadows* (1978), 15-26.
"No Choice" *Shadows* (1978), 82-90.
"Of Saints, Hags, and Martyrs" *Shadows* (1978), 45-54.
"Prelude to New Year's Eve" *Quarry* 29:3 (Sum 1980), 14-22.
"Snake Charmer" *Shadows* (1978), 91-113.
"Tom-All-Alone" *Shadows* (1978), 5-14.
"Zoomates" *Shadows* (1978), 33-44.

Leon, John A.†
"The Closet Creature Reinterpreted" *Fid* No. 85 (May-June-July 1970), 38-41.
"Some Notes on Three Mongoloid Configurations" *Edge* No. 9 (Sum 1969), 119-23.

Leonard, J. Benjamin‡
"Claude's Christmas" *Writing Group Pub* 1971-72, 38-40.

Leone, Nicole†
"Family Sacraments" *event* 11:2 (1982), 73-91.

Leonhardt, Richard A.†
"The Plan" *From 231* [1:1] (Spr 1972), 1-8.

Lepage, Ramon‡
"Studying Causes Schizophrenia" *Forge* 1967, 25-9.

Lerman, Arlene‡
"The Monkey's Uncle" *Writing Group Pub* 2 [1969-70], 39-41.

LeVay, John‡
"No Man's Land" *Portico* 3:1 [n.d.], 8-12.

Lever, Bernice (1936-)
"The Creative Affair" *Contact* 4:2 (Fall 1975), 15-6.
"Tell Me" *Waves* 2:2 (Win 1974), 42-9.

Leveson, E.R.†
"Goosefeathers" *Pier Spr* 5:1 (Win 1980), 4-13.

Levesque, Anne
"The Loggers" *Squatch J* No. 12 (1981), 50-3.
"The Snake" *Squatch J* No. 7 (June 1978), 3-7.

Levin, Malcolm A.†
DILEMMA [with John A. Eisenberg] Toronto: Holt, Rinehard and Winston, 1971 [School textbook with stories designed to illustrate moral questions].
"Jeremy's Choice" *Dilemma* (1971), 13-9.
"Mayor Boswell's Campaign" *Dilemma* (1971), 1-8.
"The Raid" *Dilemma* (1971), 21-5.

Levin, Morry†
"The Dream" *Entropy Negative* No. 5 (1972), [1 p].

Levine, Norman (1924-)
I DON'T WANT TO KNOW ANYONE TOO WELL AND OTHER STORIES Toronto: Macmillan, 1971.
IN LOWER TOWN Ottawa: Commoners', 1977.
EIN KLEINES STUCKCHEN BLAU Hamburg/Dusseldorf: Claassen Verlag, 1971 [Trans. Annemarie and Heinrich Böll and Reinhard Wagner].
DER MANN MIT DEM NOTIZBUCH Leipzig: Verlag Philipp Reclam, 1975.
DER MANN MIT DEM NOTIZBUCH Leipzig: Verlag Philipp Reclam, 1979 [Trans. Gabriele Bock, Annemarie and Heinrich Böll, and Reinhard Wagner].
ONE WAY TICKET London: Martin Secker & Warburg, 1961.
SELECTED STORIES Ottawa: Oberon Press, 1975.
THIN ICE Ottawa: Deneau and Greenberg, 1979.
"Because of the War" *82: Best Canadian Stories* 57-73.
"Because of the War" *Penguin Book of Modern Canadian Short Stories* (1982), 515-27.
"Boiled Chicken" *Spectator* 211 (20 Dec 1963), 817-8 [Sketch?].
"By a Frozen River" *CBC "Anthology"* 17 Aug 1974.
"By a Frozen River" *QQ* 82 (1975), 215-23.
"By a Frozen River" *New Lugano R* (Switz) Nos. 11/12 (1976), 30-3.
"By a Frozen River" *New Stories* 1 (1976), 233-41.
"By a Frozen River" *SN* 91 (Dec 1976), 49-52.
"By a Frozen River" *Canadian Short Stories 3* (1978), 154-66.
"By a Frozen River" *Thin Ice* (1979), 1-12.
"By a Frozen River" *BBC "Morning Story"* 2 Jan 1979.
"By a Frozen River" *BBC "Morning Story"* 12 Sept 1979.
"By a Frozen River" *Penguin Book of Canadian Short Stories* (1980), 231-40.
"By a Frozen River" *BBC "Short Story"* 5 Feb 1980.
"By a Frozen River" *Toronto Star* Sun, 21 Aug 1983, D5.
"By the Richelieu" *I Don't Want to Know* (1971), 55-68 [Also entitled "The Cocks Are Crowing"].
"By the Richelieu" *Here and Now* (1977), 9-18.
"By the Richelieu" *Woman's Journal* (U.K.) July 1977, 98, 100-1, 103-4.
"By the Richelieu" *Stories Plus* (1979), 126-35.
"By the Richelieu" *Der Mann mit dem Notizbuch* (1979), 183-95 [As "Am

Richelieu"; trans. Reinhard Wagner].

"By the Richelieu" *Stories of Quebec* (1980), 137-48.

"Canada Made Me" *Bananas* (U.K.) No. 8 (Sum 1977), 32-3.

"A Canadian Upbringing" *Vogue* (U.K.) 119 (1 Sept 1962), 100-1, 133 [Also entitled "Getting Away from Home"].

"A Canadian Upbringing" *AA* 56 (May 1966), 29-31.

"A Canadian Upbringing" *CBC [Fredericton]* 1968? [Based on papers].

"A Canadian Upbringing" *Mont* 42 (Apr 1968), 42-5, 48.

"A Canadian Upbringing" *Neue Zurcher Zeitung* (Switz) No. 269 (Sonntag 14 Juni 1970), 50 [As "Eine kanadische Jugend"; in German].

"A Canadian Upbringing" *Ein kleines Stückchen Blau* (1971), 225-34 [As "Eine kanadische Jugend"].

"A Canadian Upbringing" *I Don't Want to Know* (1971), 111-9.

"A Canadian Upbringing" *Montreal Star* Sat, 24 Apr 1971, 29.

"A Canadian Upbringing" *Cornhill Mag* No. 1068 (Sum 1971), 457-63.

"A Canadian Upbringing" *Pointer* (U.K.) 9:3 (Sum 1974), 18-9, 22.

"A Canadian Upbringing" *Elegance* (Neth) 32 (Apr 1975), 77-9 [As "Een Canadese opvoeding"].

"A Canadian Upbringing" *Der Mann mit dem Notizbuch* (1975), 5-12 [As "Eine kanadische Jugend"; trans. Annemarie and Heinrich Böll].

"A Canadian Upbringing" *Ottawa Journal* Fri, 24 Dec 1976, 7.

"A Canadian Upbringing" *Best Modern Canadian Stories* (1978), 212-7.

"A Canadian Upbringing" *Égtájak* 1978-79 (Hung) (1979), 364-71 [As "Kanadai Neveltetés"; in Hungarian; trans. Klára Molnár].

"A Canadian Upbringing" *Der Mann mit dem Notizbuch* (1979), 35-42 [As "Eine kanadische Jugend"; trans. Annemarie and Heinrich Böll].

"A Canadian Upbringing" *Magyar Elet* 33 (Karacsony [Christmas] 1980), 7 [As "Kanadai Neveltetés"; in Hungarian; trans. Klára Molnár].

"A Canadian Upbringing" *Writers and Writing* (1981), 27-33.

"Champagne Barn" *CBC "Anthology"* 19 Apr 1975.

"Champagne Barn" *New Lugano R* (Switz) 3:3/4 (Sept-Oct 1977), 48-51.

"Champagne Barn" *New Stories* 3 (1978), 251-63.

"Champagne Barn" *Tam R* No. 75 (Fall 1978), 30-41.

"Champagne Barn" *Thin Ice* (1979), 60-72.

"Champagne Barn" *BBC "Morning Story"* 12 Feb 1979.

"Champagne Barn" *CBC "Tuesday Night"* [date unknown] [Based on papers].

"Class of 1948" *CBC "Anthology"* 27 Oct 1973 [Also entitled "Class of 1949"].

"Class of 1948" *QQ* 81 (1974), 377-89.

"Class of 1948" *Winter's Tales* 20 (1974), 58-77.

"Class of 1949" *BBC* 28 July 1977 [?] [Based on papers] [Also entitled "Class of 1948"].

"Class of 1949" *Art International* (Switz) 22:2 (Feb 1978), 62-6.

"Class of 1949" *BBC* 13 Apr 1979.

"Class of 1949" *BBC* 30 Sept 1979.

"Class of 1949" *Thin Ice* (1979), 13-29.

"Class of 1949" *CBC "Anthology"* 12 Jan 1980.

"The Cocks Are Crowing" *Mont* 33 (July 1959), 27-36, 38 [Also entitled "By the Richelieu"].

"The Cocks Are Crowing" *Harper's Bazaar* (U.K.) 63 (Feb 1961), 80, 92-4.

"The Cocks Are Crowing" *CBC "Anthology"* 27 Oct 1961.

"The Cocks Are Crowing" *One Way Ticket* (1961), 107-22.

"The Cocks Are Crowing" *AA* 56 (Nov 1965), 55-6, 58-9.

"The Cocks Are Crowing" *Mont* 43 (Apr 1969), 16-7, 22, 28, 38, 44, 47, 52-3.

"The Cocks Are Crowing" *Ein kleines Stückchen Blau* (1971), 93-108 [As "Wenn die Hùhne krùhen"].

"The Cocks Are Crowing" *Selections from Major Canadian Writers* (1974), 208-14.

"The Cocks Are Crowing" *Bulletin* (Neth) No. 43 (Feb 1977), 14-8 [As "De Hanen Kraaien"; trans. James Brockway].

"Continuity" *CBC "Anthology"* 22 May 1976.

"Continuity" *CF* 60 (Dec-Jan 1980-81), 18-21.

"Continuity" *81: Best Canadian Stories* 79-92.

"The Dilletantes" *Mont* 33 (Mar 1959), 20-2.

"The Dilletantes" *Harper's Bazaar* (U.K.) 62 (Sept 1960), 96, 99-100, 102.

"The Dilettantes" *One Way Ticket* (1961), 147-57.

"The Dilettantes" *Ein kleines Stückchen Blau* (1971), 109-19 [As "Die Dilettanten"].

"The Dilettantes" *Der Mann mit dem Notizbuch* (1975), 56-64 [As "Die Dilettanten"; trans. Annemarie and Heinrich Böll].

"The Dilettantes" *Der Mann mit dem Notizbuch* (1979), 175-82 [As "Die Delettanten"; trans. Annemarie and Heinrich Böll].

"English for Foreigners" *Spectator* 207 (22 Sept 1961), 377.

"English for Foreigners" *I Don't Want to Know* (1971), 107-10.

"The English Girl" *Across a Crowded Room* (1965), 1-5 [Also entitled "First Encounters with the Opposite Sex"].

"The English Girl" *Harper's Bazaar* (U.K.) 72 (Apr 1965), 92, 94, 134.

"The English Girl" *AA* 57 (May 1967), 45-8.

"The English Girl" *Woman's Home Journal* Sept 1968, 31, 83-4.

"The English Girl" *Femina and Woman's Life* (S Afr) 23 Jan 1969, 20, 22, 24-5.

"The English Girl" *Ein kleines Stückchen Blau* (1971), 153-61 [As "Das englische Mùdchen"].

"The English Girl" *I Don't Want to Know* (1971), 69-76.

"The English Girl" *ER das Herrenmagazin* (Ger) 2 (Feb 1971), 78-80 [As "Das englische Madchen"; trans. Heinrich and Annemarie Böll].

"The English Girl" *Chat* 44 (Nov 1971), 38-9, 62, 64.

"The English Girl" *Genossenschaft* (Switz) 2:10; 2:11 (Mar 1972), [1 p]; [1 p].

"The English Girl" *Der Mann mit dem Notizbuch* (1975), 49-55 [As "Das englische Mùdchen"; trans. Reinhard Wagner].

"The English Girl" *Selected Stories* (1975), 28-35.

"The English Girl" *Der Mann mit dem Notizbuch* (1979), 196-202 [As "Das englische Mùdchen"; trans. Reinhard Wagner].

"The English Girl" *BBC* [date unknown] [Based on papers].

"Every Time I Write a Story, Someone Dies ..." *London Evening Standard* Sat, 3 June 1961, 7 [Non-fiction?].

"A Father" *Adam International R* 32 (1967), 32-6.

"A Father" *I Don't Want to Know* (1971), 147-53.

"A Father" *Selected Stories* (1975), 5-11.

"A Father" *Der Mann mit dem Notizbuch* (1979), 16-21 [As "Ein Vater"; trans. Gabriele Bock].

"A Father" *Ottawa Citizen* Fri, 24 Dec 1982, 27 [Also entitled "My Uncle" [?]].

"Feast Days and Others" *One Way Ticket* (1961), 159-71.

"Feast Days and Others" *I Don't Want to Know* (1971), 95-106.

"Feast Days and Others" *Ein Kleines Stückchen Blau* (1971), 121-33 [As "Festtage – und andere"].

"First Encounters with the Opposite Sex" *Vogue* (U.K.) 121 (1 Mar 1964), 136-7 [Also entitled "The English Girl"].

"For Auld Lang Syne" *Spectator* 209 (28 Dec 1962), 987-8.

"For Auld Lang Syne" *Pick of Today's Short Stories* 14 [1963?] [Based on papers].

"For Auld Lang Syne" *Mont* 39 (Dec 1965), 23-4.

"From a Seaside Town" *Winter's Tales* 11 (1965), 62-82 [Also entitled "Why Do You Live So Far Away?"].

"From a Seaside Town" *Listening Comprehension* (1975), 24-5 [Excerpt].

"From a Seaside Town" *CBC* "Sunday Night" [date unknown] [Based on papers].

"Getting Away from Home" *Globe Mag* 7 Mar 1970, 6-7 [Also entitled "A Canadian Upbringing"].

"Gifts: 'It's Only Money' " *Quest* 11 (Dec 1982), 44-7, 50, 52, 54-5.

"The Girl Next Door" *Thin Ice* (1979), 106-13.

"The Girl Next Door" *Chat* 52 (Feb 1979), 40, 61-2.

"The Girl Next Door" *BBC* "Morning Story" 6 Nov 1979 [?].

"The Girl Next Door" *CBC* "Anthology" 8 Nov 1980.

"The Girl Next Door" *Ottawa Citizen* Sat, 24 Dec 1983, 33.

"Grace & Faigel" *Thin Ice* (1979), 89-105.

"Hello, Mrs. Newman" *CBC* 5 Mar 1977 [?] [Based on papers].

"Hello, Mrs. Newman" *CBC* "Anthology" 13 Aug 1977.

"Hello, Mrs. Newman" *Avenue* (Neth) Apr 1978, 183-4 [As "Hallo, Mrs. Newman"; in Dutch; trans. Jos Knipscheer].

"Hello, Mrs. Newman" *Thin Ice* (1979), 80-8.

"I Don't Want to Know Anyone Too Well" *Town* (U.K.) 4 (July 1963), 62-3, 70, 73.

"I Don't Want to Know Anyone Too Well" *Mont* 37 (Dec 1963), 33-7.

"I Don't Want to Know Anyone Too Well" *AA* 56 (Jan 1966), 47-50, 52.

"I Don't Want to Know Anyone Too Well" *London Hilton Mag* (U.K.) 3:11 (Apr 1966), 36-7, 39-40.

"I Don't Want to Know Anyone Too Well" *I Don't Want to Know* (1971), 132-46.

"I Don't Want to Know Anyone Too Well" *Ein kleines Stückchen Blau* (1971), 163-78 [As "Ich möchte keinen Menschen zu gut kennen"].

"I Don't Want to Know Anyone Too Well" *Der Mann mit dem Notizbuch* (1975), 65-77 [As "Ich mochte keinen Menschen zu gut kennen"; trans. Reinhard Wagner].

"I Don't Want to Know Anyone Too Well" *Der Mann mit dem Notizbuch* (1979), 22-34 [As "Ich möchte keinem Meschen zu gut kennen"; trans. Reinhard Wagner].

"I Don't Want to Know Anyone Too Well" *BBC* "Morning Story" 19 Mar 1979.

"I Don't Want to Know Anyone Too Well" *CBC* "Wednesday Night" [date unknown] [Based on papers].

"I Like Chekhov" *Mont* 39 (Mar 1965), 17-9 [Also entitled "It's Nice to Be on the Move"].

"I Like Chekhov" *I Don't Want to Know* (1971), 77-83.

"I Like Chekhov" *Daily Telegraph Mag* No. 370 (26 Nov 1971), 75-6.

"I Like Chekhov" *Der Mann mit dem Notizbuch* (1979), 65-70 [As "Ich mag

Tschechow"; trans. Gabriele Bock].

"I'll Bring You Back Something Nice" CBC "Anthology" 16 July 1968 [Also entitled "For Auld Lang Syne"].

"I'll Bring You Back Something Nice" Canadian Winter's Tales (1968), 131-49.

"I'll Bring You Back Something Nice" Ein kleines Stückchen Blau (1971), 235-57 [As "Ich Bring dir etwas Schönes mit"].

"I'll Bring You Back Something Nice" Genossenschaft (Switz) Nos. 14/15-No. 18 (30 Mar-27 Apr 1972), [4 pp] [As "Ich bring dir etwas Schönes mit"; in German; trans. Annemarie and Heinrich Böll; in four parts].

"I'll Bring You Back Something Nice" Der Mann mit dem Notizbuch (1975), 78-96 [As "Ich bring dir etwas Schönes mit"; trans. Annemarie and Heinrich Böll].

"I'll Bring You Back Something Nice" Selected Stories (1975), 61-81.

"I'll Bring You Back Something Nice" Der Mann mit dem Notizbuch (1979), 137-54 [As "Ich bring dir etwas Schönes mit"; trans. Annemarie and Heinrich Böll].

"In a Jewish Cemetery" Jewish Chronicle (U.K.) 25 Mar 1983, 45-6, 48.

"In Lower Town" CBC "Anthology" 11 Nov 1972.

"In Lower Town" Encounter 40 (Apr 1973), 11-4.

"In Lower Town" Selected Stories (1975), 107-16.

"In Lower Town" Sunday Times Mag 10 Oct 1976, 94 [As "First Fruit"; excerpt].

"In Lower Town" CBC "Anthology" 10 Dec 1977.

"In Lower Town" CBC "Anthology" 8 July 1978.

"In Lower Town" Art International (Switz) 22:7 (Nov-Dec 1978), 9-10.

"In Lower Town" BBC "Morning Story" 5 Dec 1978 [?].

"In Lower Town" Der Mann mit dem Notizbuch (1979), 7-15 [Trans. Gabriele Bock].

"In Lower Town" New Stories 4 (1979), 88-95.

"In Lower Town" Thin Ice (1979), 30-7.

"In Lower Town" BBC "Short Story" 6 Feb 1980.

"In Quebec City" CBC "Anthology" 20 Aug 1968.

"In Quebec City" Argosy (U.K.) 30 (Nov 1969), 23-33.

"In Quebec City" Fourteen Stories High (1971), 141-52.

"In Quebec City" I Don't Want to Know (1971), 7-22.

"In Quebec City" Selected Stories (1975), 12-27.

"In Quebec City" Elegance (Neth) 32:4 (Apr 1975), 79-82 [As "In de stad Quebec"].

"In Quebec City" Can R 3:1 (Feb 1976), 12-5.

"In Quebec City" BBC 25 July 1976.

"In Quebec City" BBC 26 Nov 1976 [?].

"In Quebec City" BBC "Morning Story" 22 Jan 1979.

"In Quebec City" BBC "Morning Story" 11 Sept 1979.

"In Quebec City" Spice Box (1981), 166-76.

"It's Nice to Be on the Move" Town (U.K.) 8 (Apr 1967), 45, 60 [Also entitled "I Like Chekhov"].

"A Kind of Miracle" Woman's Journal (U.K.) Dec 1964, 41, 131-2 [Abridged version of "Feast Days and Others"].

"The Lady and the Servant" NR 3:4 (Apr-May 1950), 14-8.

"The Lady and the Servant" CBC "Wednesday Night" ca. 1962.

"The Lesson" One Way Ticket (1961), 141-6.

"The Lesson" CBC "Stories with John Drainie" ca. 1962.

"Living in England" *CBC* "*Anthology*" 28 Oct 1960.

"The Man with the Notebook" *Norseman* 13:3 (May-June 1955), 201-? [Pages missing from copy in Levine papers].

"The Man with the Notebook" *Harper's Bazaar* (U.K.) 66 (June 1962), 84, 94, 97, 106.

"The Man with the Notebook" *Mont* 36 (Aug 1962), 21-4.

"The Man with the Notebook" *BBC* "*Morning Story*" 19 Aug 1964.

"The Man with the Notebook" *AA* 60 (Apr 1970), 32-3, 35-6.

"The Man with the Notebook" *I Don't Want to Know* (1971), 120-31.

"The Man with the Notebook" *Ein kleines Stüchchen Blau* (1971), 185-98 [As "Der Mann mit dem Notizbuch"].

"The Man with the Notebook" *Der Mann mit dem Notizbuch* (1975), 97-107 [As "Der Mann mit dem Notizbuch"; trans. Reinhard Wagner].

"The Man with the Notebook" *BBC* "*Morning Story*" 2 Mar 1979 [?].

"The Man with the Notebook" *Der Mann mit dem Notizbuch* (1979), 52-64 [As "Der Mann mit dem Notizbuch"; trans. Reinhard Wagner].

"The Man with the Notebook" *Elegance* (Neth) 37 (Oct 1980), 161, 163, 165, 167 [As "De Man Met Het Notitie-boekje"].

"A Memory of Ottawa" *Jewish Chronicle* 30 Sept 1960, 21, 33.

"A Memory of Ottawa" *Can Jewish News* Wed, 12 Oct 1960, 2, 8.

"A Memory of Ottawa" *One Way Ticket* (1961), 173-90.

"A Memory of Ottawa" *Ottawa Journal* Sat, 30 Sept 1961, 36.

"A Memory of Ottawa" *Ein Kleines Stückchen Blau* (1971), 135-52 [As "Enrinnung an Ottawa"].

"A Memory of Ottawa" *Der Mann mit dem Notizbuch* (1975), 13-27 [As "Enrinnerung an Ottawa"; trans. Reinhard Wagner].

"A Memory of Ottawa" *Der Mann mit dem Notizbuch* (1979), 155-68 [As "Enrinnerung an Ottawa"; trans. Reinhard Wagner].

"My Karsh Picture" *Harper's Bazaar* (U.K.) 67 (Jan 1963), 52, 74.

"My Karsh Picture" *Für Sie* (Ger) 14 (26 June 1970), 74, 76-7 [As "Man lùt sich von Karsh fotografieren"; in German; trans. Heinrich Böll].

"My Karsh Picture" *I Don't Want to Know* (1971), 49-54.

"My Karsh Picture" *Ein kleines Stückchen Blau* (1971), 179-84 [As "Foto Karsh"].

"My Karsh Picture" *Encounter* 37:3 (Sept 1971), 39-40.

"My Karsh Picture" *Pointer* (U.K.) 9:1 (Aut 1973), 18-9.

"My Karsh Picture" *Avenue* (Neth) Mar 1975, 151-2 [As "Mijn 'Karsh-Foto' "; trans. James Brockway].

"My Karsh Picture" *Der Mann mit dem Notizbuch* (1975), 28-32 [As "Foto Karsh"; trans. Reinhard Wagner].

"My Karsh Picture" *Ottawa Citizen* Sat, 20 Dec 1975, 45.

"My Karsh Picture" *Der Mann mit dem Notizbuch* (1979), 169-74 [As "Foto Karsh"; trans. Reinhard Wagner].

"My Karsh Picture" *New Worlds* (1980), 133-6.

"My Wife Has Left Me" *I Don't Want to Know* (1971), 84-94.

"My Wife Has Left Me" *Daily Telegraph Mag* No. 332 (5 Mar 1971), 41-2, 44, 46.

"My Wife Has Left Me" *Selected Stories* (1975), 42-52.

"My Wife Has Left Me" *Elegance* (Neth) 32:4 (Apr 1975), 75-7 [As "Mijn vrouw heeft mij verlaten"].

"My Wife Has Left Me" *Der Mann mit dem Notizbuch* (1979), 203-12 [As "Meine Frau hat mich verlassen"; trans.

Gabriele Bock].

"Oh! To Be an Expatriate" *Mont* 35 (Aug 1961), 22-4.

"Oh! To Be an Expatriate" *AA* 55 (May 1965), 26-7, 29-30, 32.

"A Particular Journey" *Pick of Today's Short Stories* 7 (1956) [Based on archives].

"A Particular Journey" *Mont* 34 (Sept 1960), 23-5, 41 [Also entitled "A Small Piece of Blue"].

"Pilchard Driving" *Norseman* 14:2 (Mar-Apr 1956), 104-6 [?] [Pages torn out in Levine papers copy].

"Ringa-Ringa-Rosie" *Mont* 34 (May 1960), 18-9.

"Ringa-Ringa-Rosie" *One Way Ticket* (1961), 77-85.

"Ringa-Ringa-Rosie" *Vogue* (U.K.) 117 (Aug 1961), 60-1, 109.

"Ringa-Ringa-Rosie" *Vogue's Gallery* (1962) [Based on archives].

"Ringa-Ringa-Rosie" *BBC "Morning Story"* 18 Jan 1965 [?].

"Ringa-Ringa-Rosie" *Selected Stories* (1975), 53-60.

"A Sabbath Walk" *Norseman* 10:5 (Sept-Oct 1952), 334-41 [?] [Pages torn out in Levine papers copy]; [also entitled "A Sunday Walk"]

"A Sabbath Walk" *Bottegho Oscure Quaderno* (Italy) No. 18 (Aut 1956), 129-41.

"A Sabbath Walk" *One Way Ticket* (1961), 123-39.

"A Sabbath Walk" *AA* 55 (Aug 1965), 69-73.

"A Small Piece of Blue" *One Way Ticket* (1961), 87-105.

"A Small Piece of Blue" *I Don't Want to Know* (1971), 23-39.

"A Small Piece of Blue" *Ein kleines Stückchen Blau* (1971), 73-92 [As "Ein kleines Stückchen Blau"].

"A Small Piece of Blue" *Die Weite Reise* (1974), 118-34 [As "Ein kleines Stückchen Blau"; trans. Annemarie and Heinrich Böll].

"A Small Piece of Blue" *Der Mann mit dem Notizbuch* (1975), 33-48 [As "Eine kleines Stückchen Blau"; trans. Annemarie and Heinrich Böll].

"A Small Piece of Blue" *Der Mann mit dem Notizbuch* (1979), 122-36 [As "En kleines Stückchen Blau"; trans. Annemarie and Heinrich Böll].

"A Small Piece of Blue" *Stories Plus* (1979), 135-45 [Also entitled "A Particular Journey"].

"Something Happened Here" *Small Wonders* (1982), 59-72.

"Something Happened Here" *CF* 62 (May 1982), 12-5, 36.

"Sometimes English, Sometimes French" *Norseman* 13:5 (Sept-Oct 1955), 347-53.

"South of Montreal" *I Don't Want to Know* (1971), 154-9.

"South of Montreal" *Selected Stories* (1975), 36-41.

"A Sunday Walk" *NR* 4:5 (June-July 1951), 29-38 [Also entitled "A Sabbath Walk"].

"Thin Ice" *CBC "Anthology"* 10 June 1978.

"Thin Ice" *BBC* 19 July 1978 [?].

"Thin Ice" *BBC "Morning Story"* 10 Oct 1978.

"Thin Ice" *Thin Ice* (1979), 114-24.

"Thin Ice" *BBC "Morning Story"* 10 Sept 1979.

"To Blisland" *Thin Ice* (1979), 73-9.

"To Blisland" *CBC "Anthology"* 18 Aug 1979.

"To Blisland" *BBC "Short Story"* 5 Dec 1979.

"A True Story" *CBC "Anthology"* 27 Feb 1968.

"A True Story" *AA* 61 (Feb 1971), 67-8, 70-2.

"A True Story" *CBC [Fredericton]* 1971.

"A True Story" *I Don't Want to Know* (1971), 40-8.

"A True Story" *Contemporary Voices* (1972), 74-8.

"A True Story" *Der Mann mit dem Notizbuch* (1979), 43-51 [As "Ein wahre Geschichte"; trans. Gabriele Bock].

"The Up and Downers" *Norseman* 11:2 (Mar-Apr 1953), 123-9 [?] [Pages torn out of Levine papers copy].

"A Visit" *CBC "Anthology"* 17 Feb 1973.

"A Visit" *Thin Ice* (1979), 48-59.

"A Visit" *Chat* 52 (June 1979), 47, 128, 130, 134, 138, 140.

"Waiting for the Storm" *Harper's Bazaar* (U.K.) 68 (Sept 1963), 117-8, 123 [Also published in Canada [?]].

"We All Begin in a Little Magazine" *CBC "Anthology"* 13 Nov 1971.

"We All Begin in a Little Magazine" *Encounter* 39:4 (Oct 1972), 13-7.

"We All Begin in a Little Magazine" *76: New Canadian Stories* 7-17.

"We All Begin in a Little Magazine" *Can R* 3:3 (July 1976), 26-9.

"We All Begin in a Little Magazine" *BBC "Morning Story"* 29 Nov 1978.

"We All Begin in a Little Magazine" *Thin Ice* (1979), 38-47.

"We All Begin in a Little Magazine" *BBC "Morning Story"* 24 Apr 1979.

"We All Begin in a Little Magazine" *BBC "Short Story"* 4 Feb 1980.

"We All Begin in a Little Magazine" *CBC "Anthology"* 24 May 1980.

"Why Do You Live So Far Away?" *CBC "Anthology"* 15 Mar 1966 [Also entitled "From a Seaside Town"].

"Why Do You Live So Far Away?" *Town* (U.K.) 8 (Jan 1967), 67-8, 73.

"Why Do You Live So Far Away?" *Ein Kleines Stückchen Blau* (1971), 199-224 [As "Warum Wohnst Du So Weit Weg"].

"Why Do You Live So Far Away?" *Selected Stories* (1975), 82-106.

"Why Do You Live So Far Away?" *Can R* 2:4 (Christmas 1975), 33-5, 37-40.

"A Writer's Story" *CBC "Anthology"* 22 June 1974.

"A Writer's Story" *New Lugano R* (Italy) No. 1 (1979), 29-35, 62.

"A Writer's Story" *Thin Ice* (1979), 125-37.

"A Writer's Story" *CBC "Anthology"* 17 Feb 1979.

Levson, Elliott H.‡

"Steam Room" *Raven* No. 6 (Apr 1958), 21-3.

Levy, David H.‡

"The Three Wise Men and the Christmas Star" *Thumbprints* No. 2 (Spr 1975), [2 pp].

Lewis, Alix‡

"It's a Phase" *Forge* 1950, 28-31.

Lewis, Brian Wyndham‡

"Avita" *North* 12 (Mar-Apr 1965), 28-31.

Lewis, David E.

A LOVER NEEDS A GUITAR AND OTHER STORIES Toronto: McClelland & Stewart, 1973.

"The Ben Hur Chariot Race" *A Lover Needs a Guitar* (1973), 49-55.

"Cleopatra's Asp" *A Lover Needs a Guitar* (1973), 105-7.

"The Day the Magician Came to Town" *A Lover Needs a Guitar* (1973), 99-104.

"Ed Wheeling" *A Lover Needs a Guitar* (1973), 88-98.

"Harriet" *A Lover Needs a Guitar* (1973), 117-23.
"I Remember Miss Jean Murdock" *A Lover Needs a Guitar* (1973), 21-8.
"A Lover Needs a Guitar" *A Lover Needs a Guitar* (1973), 56-62.
"Martin McGuire's Vomitorium" *A Lover Needs a Guitar* (1973), 63-72.
"Miss Hansell" *A Lover Needs a Guitar* (1973), 144-52.
"My Early Musical Career" *A Lover Needs a Guitar* (1973), 29-36.
"The Night Diefenbaker Stood on Guard" *A Lover Needs a Guitar* (1973), 153-60.
"A Night on the Town" *A Lover Needs a Guitar* (1973), 73-9.
"A Night on the Town" *MM* 86 (Apr 1973), 46, 52-4.
"The Night We Swished the Barrel" *A Lover Needs a Guitar* (1973), 124-32.
"Nine Is a Desperate Age" *A Lover Needs a Guitar* (1973), 11-20.
"Post Office" *A Lover Needs a Guitar* (1973), 37-42.
"The Richest Man in Canada" *MM* 85 (Dec 1972), 46-7, 50, 54, 56, 58, 60.
"The Richest Man in Canada" *A Lover Needs a Guitar* (1973), 133-43.
"Sally's Misadventures and Mine" *MM* 87 (Feb 1974), 38-9, 52.
"A School Concert" *A Lover Needs a Guitar* (1973), 43-7.
"Smoked Oysters" *A Lover Needs a Guitar* (1973), 108-16.
"The Time I Gave Jane the Diary" *A Lover Needs a Guitar* (1973), 80-7.

Lewis, Jennifer‡
"Coasting" *CBC "Alberta Anthology"* 15 Nov 1980.
"The Dress" *CBC "Alberta Anthology"* 2 Oct 1982.
"A Pot of Parsley" *NeWest R* 6 (Apr 1981), 5-6, 14.

Lewis, Leda M. (192?-)
"Lake of Spirits" *Contact* 2:10 (Sum 1973), 13-5.
"My Child, My Son, MY!" *Contact* 3:2 (Spr 1974), 27-8.

Lewis, Murray (1957-)
"Eolin" *Los* No. 7 (Mar 1981), 32-6.

Lewis, Ruth C.‡
"A Voice for Timothy Newton" *Jubilee* No. 3 (n.d.], 48-67.

Lewko, Judy†
"The Happy Smile" *Miss Chat* 6 (14 Aug 1969), 32, 116, 123.

Leyden, Douglas†
"Images for the Horsemen" *Quarry* 31:2 (Spr 1982), 60-8.

Leyerle, John
"The Wolf, the Fox and the Fishmonger" *Des* No. 6 (Spr 1973), 59-62.

Leyland, M.†
"Opportunity" *event* 12:1 (1983), 27-34.

Leznoff, Glenda
"Single and Available" *Mal R* No. 56 (Oct 1980), 108-17.
"Single and Available" *Flare* 2 (Dec 1980), 60-1, 65-6, 70.

Liddell, Eddy M. – *See* Green, H. Gordon.

Life [pseudonym]

"Sheltered Life" *Scar Fair* 1 (1973-74), 15-6.

Lifeso, E.L.†

"Buckshot for Strays" *Northern Mosaic* 1 (Jan 1982), 11.

"Stove Pipes" *CSSM* 1:4 (Oct 1975), 6-8.

Liggett, C.J.‡

"A Christmas Carol" *Random* 2:5 (18 Dec 1967), 1, 4.

Lil [pseudonym]

"Ave Atque Vale: A Malediction" *Acta Vic* 79:4 (Mar 1955), 22.

Lill, Wendy

"A Woman Is Sleeping by the Lake with Her Small Son and Baby" *Squatch J* No. 8 (Dec 1978), 26-9.

Lilla, Peter J.‡

"Bitter Is Our Loss" *Forge* 1950, 15-6.

Lillard, Charles

"Memoranda for an Illuminated Manuscript" *CFM* Nos. 2/3 (Spr-Sum 1971), 3-6.

Lima, Paul†

"There Was an Old Man" *Origins* 11:3 (Win 1981), 17-26.

Liman, Claude‡

"The House of Make-Believe" *Des* 14:2 No. 40 (Spr 1983), 87-98.

Linder, Norma West (1928-)

"Another Spring, Another Dream" *Chat* 48 (May 1975), 45, 60, 62-4.

"Boxes" *Pier Spr* 7:2 (Spr 1982), 7-9.

"Christmas on Manitoulin" *Sarnia Gazette* 20 Dec 1972 [Based on survey response].

"The Cornfield" *Origins* 8:2 (June 1978), 18-20.

"The End of the Game" *Our Family* 22 (Jan 1970), 22-3.

"Flowers in Haunted Castles" *Green's* 1:1 (Fall 1972), 32-8.

"Haggerty and the Big One" *CBC "Canadian Short Stories"* 13 Mar 1965 [Based on survey response].

"Haggerty Serves His Special" *Winnipeg Free Press [Weekly?]* 6 Aug 1966 [Based on survey response].

"Hester and the Special Fund" *Winnipeg Free Press [Weekly?]* 3 Sept 1966 [Based on survey response].

"Hester and the Special Fund" *CBC "Canadian Short Stories"* 1966 [Based on survey response].

"King of the Castle" *Companion* 29 (Jan 1966), 26-9.

"The Last Sweet Summer" *FH* 17 Feb 1966, 70-1.

"Martin Berman and Son" *CBC "Canadian Short Stories"* 1966 [Based on survey response].

"Martin Berman and Son" *Sarnia Gazette* 29 June 1967 [Based on survey response].

"Memories of Mervyn" *CBC "Canadian Short Stories"* [?] [Based on survey response].

"Memories of Mervyn" *Sarnia Gazette* 14 Oct 1970 [Based on survey response].

"Miracle at Malcolm's Cove" *AA* 57 (July 1967), 105, 107.

"A Mystery of Roses" *Chat* 39 (Nov 1966), 43, 56, 60, 64, 67.

"The Night Visitor" *Polished Pebbles* (1974), 3-7.

"Omnia Vincit Amor" *Living Message* 83 (Apr 1972), 27-8.

"Paddy and Pops" *CBC* ca. 1966 [Based on survey response].

"Paddy and Pops" *Catalyst* (Brantford) 1:4 (1975), 65.

"Pumpkin Lady" *Origins* 10:2 (June 1980), 40-7.

"Saturation Point" *Pier* Spr 8:2 (Spr 1983), 9-14.

"Saturday Afternoon" *Companion* 29 (Feb 1966), 22-5.

"Seven Words' Worth" *Pier* Spr 6:1 (Win 1981), 7-12.

"Something Close to Joy" *Report on Farming* Dec 1980 [Based on survey response].

"Sweet Comic Valentine" *Origins* 11:2 (June 1981), 18-21.

"The Two-Gun Kid" *Our Family* 18 (July-Aug 1966), 22-4.

"Winner's Circle" *Singing Under Ice* (1974), 183-6.

Lindsey, Robert‡

"Somer-Sault" *UCR* 1980-81, 18-23.

Lingenfelter, Veronica

"Reunion" *Saskatchewan Writing* 2 (1963), 36-42.

Linkovich, Stanley

"Belts" *Uk Can* 14 (1 Dec 1960), 9.

"Night Out" *Uk Can* 12 (1 Dec 1958), 9-10.

"Salvation on Queen Street" *Uk Can* 15 (1 Feb 1961), 9-10.

Linton, Laura‡

"Across the River" *AA* 52 (Mar 1962), 41, 43-4, 47.

Linttell, Anne‡

"Up Until Now" *Driftwood* [No. 1] (Apr 1973), 13-6.

Liontos, Demitri

"One Like Her" *Outset* 1974, 103-8.

Lipman, Robert‡

"Napoleon's Member" *Alch* 2:2 No. 6 (1981), 17-27.

Lippert, Laura‡

"The Darkroom" *Quarry* 27:1 (Win 1978), 34-9.

"A Sad Story" *This – Media Free Times* 2:1 (Win 1975), [1 p].

"The Fruits of Fertility" *event* 5:2 [1975], 5-14.

[Untitled] *Pulp* 4:11 (15 Oct 1977), [2-3].

"You" *Room* 4:4 (1979), 56-61.

Lippert, Lora – *See* Lippert, Laura.

Lisle, Glenn†
"A Stitch in Time" *Cop Toad* Nos. 6/7 (1979), 65-8.

Litman, Jane‡
"Casablanca Revisited" *Poetry WLU* Spr 1983, 30-3.

Little, C.H.†
"To Run a Big Boat" *Atlantic Advocate's Holiday Book* (1961), 36.

Little, Eden‡
"The Sparrow" *Fifth Page* 1964, 15-8.

Little, Jean
"The Saving Grace" *Acta Vic* 78:1 (Nov 1953), 17-9.

Littlejohn, Helen‡
"The Buttonhole" *AA* 55 (Sept 1964), 27, 29-31.
"The Rain Check" *Our Family* 16 (Feb 1965), 22-4.

Liu, Ron‡
"Action" *RPM* No. 1 (Apr 1980), 21-4.

Livesay, Dorothy (1909-)
A WINNIPEG CHILDHOOD Winnipeg: Peguis, 1973.
"Anna" *Winnipeg Childhood* (1973), 45-51 [Also entitled "An Immigrant"].
"Canadian Writers in Bulgaria" *JCF* No. 19 (1977), 38-9.
"Christmas" *Winnipeg Childhood* (1973), 39-44.
"The End of a War" *Winnipeg Childhood* (1973), 85-9.
"Father's Boy" *Winnipeg Childhood* (1973), 69-76.
"The First Crocus" *CF* 31 (Mar 1952), 276.
"First Trials" *Winnipeg Childhood* (1973), 53-9.
"The Glass House" *NR* 3:5 (June-July 1950), 1-10.
"The Glass House" *Best American Short Stories* 1951 218-27.
"The Guardian Angel" *Winnipeg Childhood* (1973), 29-32.
"An Immigrant" *Literary Half-Yearly* 13:2 (July 1972), 103-10 [Also entitled "Anna"].
"The Last Climb" *NR* 4:6 (Aug-Sept 1951), 2-8.
"The Last of the Czars" *Canadian Short Fiction Anthology* 2 (1982), 135-8.
"Matt" *CF* 32 (Jan 1953), 227, 229-30.
"Matt" *Forum* (1972), 283-5.
"Matt" *Winnipeg Childhood* (1973), 11-5.
"Matt" *Inquiry into Literature* 4 (1980), 79-83.
"The Mother-in-Law" *Br Out* Preview Issue (Dec 1973), 16-9 [Also entitled "The Wedding"].
"Mrs. Spy" *Winnipeg Childhood* (1973), 25-7.
"The Other Side of the Street" *Literary Half-Yearly* 13:2 (July 1972), 96-103.
"The Other Side of the Street" *Winnipeg Childhood* (1973), 77-83.
"The Party" *Winnipeg Childhood* (1973), 61-9.
"Preludes" *Mosaic* 3:3 (Spr 1970), 85-92 [As "A Prairie Sampler"; excerpt and revised].
"Preludes" *Winnipeg Childhood* (1973), 1-10.
"Preludes" *Inquiry into Literature* 2 (1980), 272-4.

"The Sparrows" *JCF* 1:1 (Win 1972), 25-7.
"The Sparrows" *Winnipeg Childhood* (1973), 33-8.
"The Two Willies" *JCF* 1:1 (Win 1972), 27-30.
"The Two Willies" *Winnipeg Childhood* (1973), 17-23.
"The Uprooting" *Winnipeg Childhood* (1973), 101-5.
"The Wedding" *Wild Rose Country* (1977), 129-38 [Also entitled "The Mother-in-Law"].
"A Week in the Country" *Stories from Western Canada* (1972), 148-57.
"A Week in the Country" *Winnipeg Childhood* (1973), 91-100.

Livesey, Margot
"The Dance" *Waves* 7:1 (Fall 1978), 3-8.
"Famous Cases of Defenestration" *Matrix* No. 14 (Win 1982), 13-21.
"The Garden at Louveciennes" *Waves* 8:2 (Win 1980), 17-23.
"Night" *Fireweed* No. 2 (Spr 1979), 63-5.
"Obituary" *Prism* 20:2 (Win 1982), 24-33.
"Reflections" *CCWQ* 5:4 (1983), 13-5.
"Secret Places" *Was R* 18:2 (Fall 1983), 63-71.
"Someone Else's" *Prism* 15:2/3 (Sum-Fall 1976), 113-7.
"The Umbrellas" *Fid* No. 133 (July 1982), 43-51.

Livingston, Marilyn
"The Garden" *Pot Port* 1 (1979-80), 30-3.

Lloy, Murph
"In Mother's Name" *Writers' Circle* (1974), 65-79.

Lloyd, Susan†
"Sparrow" *Miss Chat* 11 (14 Mar 1972), 36, 96-9, 104, 110.

Lockau, Kevin†
"Rebirth" *Read Ch* 1:3 (Win 1982), 60-7.

Lockhart, Laurie‡
"Death by Fetish" *WWR* 1:1 (Spr 1976), 11-5.
"Ears to Hear" *Harvest* No. 3 (Mar 1978), 16-22.
"Talk of Life" *WWR* 1:2 (Win 1977), 6-10.

Loewy, Ilse†
"The Sandals" *Rapport* Apr 1971, 19.

Loftus, Peggy‡
"The Grateful Tree" *Thornhill Month* 4 (Dec 1982), 38-9.

Logan, Dorothy E.
"The Miracle of the Piebald Nightie" *Onward* 17 Oct 1965, 3-4, 14.
"A Slice of Bread" *Onward* Aug 1964, 3.

Logan, Gloria‡
"The Visionary" *AA* 49 (June 1959), 67-70.

Loggie, Margaret L.†
"Red Ribbons" *New Voices* (1956), 118-24.

Loisier, Mary Jane‡
   "The Child Who Was Free" *Axiom* 2:3 (Feb-Mar 1976), 38, 49, 52, 55.

Long, Charles†
   "Out of Order" *Har* 5:7 No. 35 (Apr-May 1981), 86-8, 90-4.

Long, Haniel‡
   "How Pittsburgh Returned to the Jungle" *Image Nation* 1:6 (6 June [1969]), [1 p].

Longfield, Kevin (1950-)
   "A Long Night's Journey into Day" *CBC [Winn] "Manitoba Anthology"* 2 Oct 1982 [Based on survey response].

Longley, David‡
   "Fifty Miles from Chapleau" *Scar Fair* 1 (1973-74), 21-6.

Longstaff, Bill†
   "The Death of Charlie Bender" *CF* 54 (Aug 1974), 30-1.
   "The House of Jimmy Yee" *Fid* No. 127 (Fall 1980), 19-25.
   "The Thinker" *event* 8:2 (1979), 5-12.

Lonneberg, Lyle R.
   "I've Got a Secret" *event* 1:1 (Spr 1971), 83-7.
   "The Jump" *Prism* 10:3 (Spr 1971), 110-3.
   "Locomotive" *event* 2:3 [1973], 64-7.
   "Yo-Ho Yo-Ho" *event* 1:2 (Fall 1971), 60-6.

Loomer, Frank†
   "The Day the Dog Bit Jimmy Sadler" *AA* 58 (Sept 1967), 40, 43-4.
   "Porridge and Tears" *AA* 55 (Mar 1955), 24-8, 30.

Loomer, L.S.†
   "A Curious Toast" *AA* 48 (Dec 1957), 67-72.
   "A Curious Toast" *Atlantic Advocate's Holiday Book* (1961), 71-84.
   "Father Murphy's Dilemma" *AA* 68 (Dec 1977), 12-5.
   "The Village Dragon" *AA* 48 (Oct 1957), 61-3, 65.

Lord, Barry‡
   "Puritan" *Muse* 69 (1960), 30-1.
   "Rush Hour" *Muse* 68 (1959), 25-7.

Lord, J. Barry†
   "Howard" *Dal R* 44 (1964), 180-8.

Lord, Peter‡
   "The Continuing Journal of the Farm and Margaret, Parts 1 and 2" *Quarry* 20:2 (Sum 1971), 3-11.
   "True Romance" *Quarry* 23:1 (Win 1974), 42-8.

Lord, Peter (1947?-)‡
   "friday night at the project and tenuous relationships reaching to long island" *Duel* No. 1 (Win 1969), 5-9.

Lord Jupiter [pseudonym]
"The Early Life of King Lionfeather" *Gronk* Ser 7 No. 2 (Nov 1970), 3-4.

Loring, Frances Woolaver‡
"The New Enemy" *AA* 71 (Nov 1980), 30-1, 33.

Lovell, R.G.†
"Autobiography of a Poppy" *Legion* 28 (Sept 1953), 22-3.

Lovering, Virginia (1958-)
"Lisa's Tale" *Can Lit R* No. 2 (Sum 1983), 9-15.

Loverso, Caterina
"Full Moon" *Story So Far* 5 (1978), 107-15.

Lownsbrough, John‡
"Cal Teck's Last Stand" *Random* 2:2 (Nov 1967), 21-3.

Lowry, Malcolm (1909-1957)
AT A PANAMAN. ELEFANT ÉS KOLOSSZEUM. A FORRASHOZ VEZETÖ ERDEI OSVÉNY Budapest: Europa Konyvkiado, 1974 [Trans. Arpád Göncz; based on Woolmer].
CHINA AND KRISTBJORG'S STORY IN THE BLACK HILLS New York: Aloe Editions, 1974.
ESUCHANOS, OH SEÑOR, DESDE EL CIELO, TU MORADA Caracas: Editorial Tiempo Nuevo, 1971 [Trans. Eva Iribarne Dietrich; based on Woolmer].
HEAR US O LORD FROM HEAVEN THY DWELLING PLACE New York & Philadelphia: Lippincott, 1961.
HEAR US O LORD FROM HEAVEN THY DWELLING PLACE *Les lettres nouvelles* (France) Juillet-Aout 1962 [In French; trans. Clarisse Francillon & Georges Belmont; based on Woolmer].
HEAR US O LORD FROM HEAVEN THY DWELLING PLACE Milan: Feltrinelli, 1969 [In Italian; trans. Attilio Veraldi; based on Woolmer].
HORS UNS, O HERR, DER DU IM HIMMEL WOHNST Hamburg: Rowohlt, 1965 [Trans. Susanne Rademacher; based on Woolmer].
OUVE – NOS SENHOR DO CEU QUE E A TUA MORADA / ATRAVES DO CANAL DO PANAMA Lisbon: Iniciativas Editorials, 1977 [Trans. Ana Hatherly; based on Woolmer].
POR EL CANAL DE PANAMA Mexico City: Ediciones Era, 1969 [Trans. Salvador Elizondo].
PSALMS AND SONGS Ed. Marjorie Lowry New York: New American Library, 1975.
"The Bravest Boat" *Les lettres nouvelles* (France) nov 1953, 1067 [As "Brave petit bateau"; trans. Georges Belmont; based on Woolmer].
"The Bravest Boat" *Partisan R* 21 (1954), 275-88.
"The Bravest Boat" *British Columbia* (1961), 185-97.
"The Bravest Boat" *Hear Us O Lord* (1961), 13-27.
"The Bravest Boat" *Bennett Cerf's Take Along Treasury* (1963) [Based on SSI].
"The Bravest Boat" *Trio* (1965) [Based on SSI].
"The Bravest Boat" *Great Canadian Writing* (1966), 27-8 [Excerpt].
"The Bravest Boat" *Zateriannaia Ulitsa* (1971), 125 [As "Samaia khrabraia lodka"; in Russian; trans. N. Krolik; based on Woolmer].

"The Bravest Boat" *Stories from Pacific & Arctic Canada* (1974), 1-16.

"Bulls of the Resurrection" *Prism* 5:1 (Sum 1965), 4-11.

"China" *China* (1974), [8 pp].

"China" *Psalms and Songs* (1975), 49-54.

"China" *BC Monthly* 3:1 (Oct 1976), [7 pp].

"The Element Follows You Around, Sir!" *Show Mag* (U.K.) 4 (Mar 1964), 45 [Based on Woolmer].

"The Element Follows You Around, Sir!" *Les lettres nouvelles* (France) nov-dec 1964, 5 [As "Le feu de ciel vous suit à la trace, Monsieur!"; trans. Clarisse Francillon & Genevieve Serreau; based on Woolmer].

"The Element Follows You Around, Sir!" *Winter's Tales* 11 (1965), 83-119.

"The Element Follows You Around, Sir!" *Best for Winter* (1979), 178-201.

"Elephant and Colosseum" *Quaderni Milanesi* (Italy) Aut 1960, 37 [As "Elefante e colosseo"; trans. Giorgio Monicelli; based on Woolmer].

"Enter One in Sumptuous Armor" *Psalms and Songs* (1975), 228-49.

"Ghostkeeper" *American Review* No. 17 (May 1973), 1-34.

"Ghostkeeper" *Modern Canadian Stories* (1975), 75-106.

"Ghostkeeper" *Psalms and Songs* (1975), 202-27.

"Ghostkeeper" *Penguin Book of Canadian Short Stories* (1980), 139-65.

"Gin and Goldenrod" *Hear Us O Lord* (1963), 201-14.

"Gin and Goldenrod" *Story-Makers* (1970), 95-109.

"June the 30th, 1934" *Psalms and Songs* (1975), 36-48.

"Kristbjorg's Story in the Black Hills" *BC Monthly* 1:5 (Mar 1973), 1.

"Kristbjorg's Story in the Black Hills" *China* (1974), [4 pp].

"Kristbjorg's Story in the Black Hills" *Psalms and Songs* (1975), 250-3.

"Present State of Pompeii" *Partisan R* 26 (1959), 175-99.

"Present State of Pompeii" *Les lettres nouvelles* (France) juillet-aout 1960, 26 [As "Pompei, aujourd'hui"; trans. Clarisse Francillon; based on Woolmer].

"Present State of Pompeii" *Hear Us O Lord* (1961), 175-200.

"Present State of Pompeii" *Canadian Literature* (1973), 155-76.

"Present State of Pompeii" *De beste buitenlandse verhalen van de Bezige Bij* (1978), 127 [As "De juidige staat van Pompeji"; in Dutch; trans. Jan Gerhard Toonder; based on Woolmer].

"Strange Comfort Afforded by the Profession" *New World Writing* 3 (1953), 331-44.

"Strange Comfort Afforded by the Profession" *Carosello di narratori Inglese* (1954), 273 [As "I vanteggi del mestiere"; trans. Giorgio Monicelli; based on Woolmer].

"Strange Comfort Afforded by the Profession" *Les lettres nouvelles* (France) sept 1955, 193 [As "Étrange réconfort"; trans. Roger Giroux; based on Woolmer].

"Strange Comfort Afforded by the Profession" *Hear Us O Lord* (1961), 99-113.

"Strange Comfort Afforded by the Profession" *Canadian Short Story* (1971), 85-99.

"Strange Comfort Afforded by the Profession" *Canadian Anthology* (1974), 360-9.

"Strange Comfort Afforded by the Profession" *Modern Stories in English* (1975), 225-37.

"Through the Panama" *Les lettres nouvelles* (France) juillet-aout 1960, 109 [As "La traversée du Panama"; trans. Clarisse Francillon; based on Woolmer].

"Through the Panama" *Bonniers Litterata Magasin* (Swed) No. 31 (1962), 285 [As

"Genom Panama"; trans. Sonja Bergvall; based on Woolmer].
"Through the Panama" *Great Canadian Writing* (1966), 100 [Excerpt].
"Through the Panama" *Canadian Century* (1973), 527-50.
"Under the Volcano" *Prairie Schooner* 37 (1963-64), 284-300.
"Under the Volcano" *Canadian Winter's Tales* (1968), 1-21.
"Under the Volcano" *Great Canadian Short Stories* (1971), 116-32.
"Under the Volcano" *Canadian Anthology* (1974), 370-80.
"Under the Volcano" *Psalms and Songs* (1975), 187-201.

Lowther, Pat
"The Perfect Game" *Prism* 5:3/4 (Win-Spr 1966), 52-61.

Lucas, Victor‡
"Absolutely, Absolutely" *Quarry* 21:3 (Sum 1972), 3-10.

Luce-Kapler, Rebecca‡
"The Rawleigh Man" *CBC "Alberta Anthology"* 17 Sept 1983.

Luchsinger, Gabriel†
"Saror, House of Gold" *Wee Giant* 2:1 (Aut 1978), 34-5.
[Untitled] *Wee Giant* 2:1 (Aut 1978), 33.

Luckevich, Rosanne‡
"Jodi in a Life Not Hers" *Laom R* 4 (Apr 1978), 17-25.

Luckhurst, Elizabeth†
"The Colour of Crowd" *Prism* 1:4 (Sum 1960), 27.
"Gal Souzy" *Prism* 1:4 (Sum 1960), 27.

Luckhurst, Margaret†
"Father to the Rescue" *UC Observer* Nov 1970, 14-5 [Non-fiction?].
"It Happened Every Sunday" *UC Observer* July 1969, 18-9 [Non-fiction?].
"My Mother and the Starving Armenians" *UC Observer* 1 Mar 1970, 29-30 [Non-fiction?].

Ludwig, Jack (1922-)
REQUIEM FOR BIBUL Agincourt, Ont.: Book Society of Canada, 1967 [Based on CBIP].
"Celebration on East Houston Street" *Tam R* No. 27 (Spr 1963), 20-8.
"A Death of One's Own" *Tam R* No. 46 (Win 1968), 79-84.
"Death Was the Glass" *Midstream* 7:1 (Win 1961), 37-41.
"Death Was the Glass" *Catalyst* (Scarb) 2:1 (Fall 1968), 22-7.
"Einstein and This Admirer" *London Mag* 5:6 (Sept 1965), 65-74.
"Einstein and This Admirer" *Canadian Writing Today* (1970), 248-59.
"Marriage a-la-mode Orlick Miller" *Mont* 33 (Oct 1959), 41-6.
"Meesh" *Tam R* No. 21 (Aut 1961), 3-19.
"Requiem for Bibul" *Atlantic Monthly* 206 (Sept 1960), 58-63.
"Requiem for Bibul" *Ten for Wednesday Night* (1961), 106-20.
"Requiem for Bibul" *Book of Canadian Stories* (1962), 304-17.
"Requiem for Bibul" *Great Canadian Short Stories* (1971), 212-24.
"Requiem for Bibul" *Canadian Century* (1973), 464-74.
"Requiem for Bibul" *Urban Experience* (1975), 87-99.

"Requiem for Bibul" *Moderne Erzühler der Walt: Kanada* (1976), 266-83 [As "Requiem auf Bibul"; trans. Armin Arnold].
"Requiem for Bibul" *Horizon* (1977), 216-25.
"Shirley" *Tam R* Nos. 50/51 (1969), 52-68.
"A Woman of Her Age" *Tam R* No. 12 (Sum 1959), 6-25.
"A Woman of Her Age" *Quarterly Review of Literature* 12 (1963), 196-218.
"A Woman of Her Age" *Contemporary American Short Stories* (1967) [Based on SSI].
"A Woman of Her Age" *Canadian Short Stories 2* (1968), 231-58.
"A Woman of Her Age" *Stories of Quebec* (1980), 23-46.
"A Woman of Her Age" *Spice Box* (1981), 192-210.

Luider, Lyanda†
"From the Book of Angels" *Dand* 1 (Sum 1975), 50-2.
"Sanctuary" *Dand* 4 (Win 1978), 49-51.

Lukiv, Dan†
"Run for Your Life" *Mam* 6:2 (Win 1983), [4 pp].
"The Tractor and the Holiday" *Alpha* 7:1 (Nov 1982), 24-6.

Lum, Leslie†
"Old Age Gold" *Canadian Short Fiction Anthology 2* (1982), 99-107.

Lund, Mary (1940-)†
"Could We Visit Grace" *Face to Face* (1979), 24-36.

Lunn, Richard (1926-)
"Jungle Station" by Bill Richards *SW* 16 Mar 1963, 4-7.
"The Relic" *NR* 5:6 (Feb-Mar 1953), 14-6.

Lush, Richard M.
"Rejections" *Cap R* No. 23 (1982), 62.

Lûsse, Georgina
See also Knox, Claire Neville and Lûsse, Georginna.
"Bim" *FH* 20 Dec 1951, 10-1.
"The Luck of Miss Tina" *Weekend* 2 (15 Mar 1952), 10-1, 35, 37.
"Never a Cross Word" *FH* 26 Apr 1951, 22-3.

Lutely, A.B.‡
"Once Bitten, Twice Shy" *Legion* 58 (Aug 1983), 15, 21 [Non-fiction?].

Luxton, Stephen
"A Diptera Chronicle" *Matrix* 3:1 (Sum 1977), 13.
"A Fall of Sparrows" *Random* 3:4 (Jan [1969]), 12-5.
"Fat Lady" *Matrix* 3:1 (Sum 1977), 13.

Lyman, Katharine†
"The Circle Unbroken" *Scrivener* 1:1 (Spr 1980), 12.

Lyn, Dennis‡
"Castles" *Laom R* 1:1 (Dec-Jan 1975), 7-12.

Lynch, Gerald

"Auf Wiedersehen Sweetheart" *Wee Giant* 5:1 (1982), 20-34.
"Getting Your Goat" *Fid* No. 127 (Fall 1980), 61-81.
"The Misogge Parler" *Waves* 9:1 (Aut 1980), 4-15.
"A Pack of Clowns" *New Q* 2:2 (Sum 1982), 33-41.
"Present Tense Floating" *Matrix* No. 16 (Spr 1983), 21-7.
"Rita Maguire's Vermilion Dress" *Waves* 10:1/2 (Sum-Fall 1981), 6-17.
"Rounded with a Sleep" *Waves* 11:1 (Fall 1982), 17-25.
"Seamus and the Crow" *Cap R* No. 23 (1982), 69-82.
"Spice-Cake" *UWR* 17:1 (Fall-Win 1982), 44-56.
"When It Rains" *Fid* No. 117 (Spr 1978), 81-8.

Lynch, John‡

"The Contract" *Alive* [1:9] (Oct 1970), 10-1.
"The Teacher" *Alive* [1:8] (Sept-Oct 1970), 14.

Lyngseth, Joan

"Skin Deep" *Common Ground* (1980), 11-22.
"The Waste Sad Time" *Halcyon* 12 (Win 1966-67), 51-61.

Lynn, Eunice†

"Caraway Seed Cake" *Echoes* No. 198 (Spr 1950), 16, 43.

Lypchuk, D.‡

"Baby Snooky Comes Back" *Imp* 8:3 (Sum 1980), 6-8.

M., C.R.

"letter from the country" *Pulp* 5:9 (1 Sept 1979), [4].
"love and the mist" *Pulp* 4:16 (1 Mar 1978), [2].

M., H.M.

"Lunch and Native Wit and ... " *Rapport* Feb 1971, 18.

M., M.

"Making a Living" *Uk Can* 8 (15 July 1954), 2.

M [pseudonym]

"Marry Anger: An Unfinished Satire" *Raven* 1:2 (Dec 1955), 17.

Maag, Trudy†

"The Sweater" *Intervales* No. 2 (1960), 31-5.

Maar, John Zeljko‡

"So Close" *Northern Ontario Anthology* 2 (1978), 4-7.

MacAndrew, Ross – *See* Crowell, Bill.

MacArthur, F.H. (1896-)

"Darby McGee's Fairy: A Subject for Ridicule" *Sand Patterns* No. 7 (Sept 1973), [3 pp].

"Granddad's Futile Trip" *AA* 57 (Sept 1966), 41-3, 46.
"Granddad's Futile Trip" *Variations on a Gulf Breeze* (1973), 33-43.
"The Ring That Held a Curse" *Sand Patterns* No. 12 (1974), 28-9 [Non-fiction?].

MacCallum, Russell†
"Aunt Violet and the Rain and the Dead Flowers" *Mont* 35 (July 1961), 27-32.
"Gathen a Balka" *Mont* 36 (Nov 1962), 25-8.
"Mr. Mole" *Mont* 38 (Jan 1964), 26-31.
"Permanent" *Mont* 36 (Apr 1962), 21-2.

MacCormack, Terrance
"Bisexual Man" *Nebula* No. 3 (1976), 27 [Monologue].
"The Blonde and the Fifteen Little Girls" *Room* 1:4 (Win 1976), 51-7.
"Flight" *Inscape* 13:2 (Win 1976-77), 26-7.
"Give Me Back My Rags" *NJ* No. 3 (1973), 77-89.
"Harry" *NJ* No. 2 (1972-73), 38-53.
"Mona Lisa" *Inscape* 13:2 (Win 1976-77), 25.
"The Pleasures of Competition" *Nebula* No. 3 (1976), 26.
"Secrets" *Antig R* No. 30 (Sum 1977), 19-24.
"A Writer in the Family" *Nebula* No. 3 (1976), 26-7.
"The Writer's Nose" *Inscape* 13:2 (Win 1976-77), 28.

MacCrimmon, Harriett M.†
THIS IS MY COUNTRY AND OTHER STORIES Ilfracombe, U.K.: Arthur H. Stockwell, 1952.
"Prairie Angel" *This Is My Country* (1952), 18-23 [Non-fiction?].
"This Is My Country" *This Is My Country* (1952), 3-13.

MacDonald, Andy‡
" 'Thank God for Wicka!' " *Bluenose* 2:4 (Spr 1978), 28-30.

MacDonald, Bill‡
"The Time of the Spring Sun" *Creative Campus* 1958, 6-7.

Macdonald, Carmel†
"Breaking Point" *Camrose R* No. 4 [n.d.], 25-7.

MacDonald, D. Lorne‡
"The True Lover" *Gram* 1:4 (Apr 1976), 9-12.

MacDonald, D.G.†
"Of Young and Cold Nights" *CSSM* 2:1 (Jan 1976), 42-5.

MacDonald, David
"Bluenose in Toronto" *MM* 65 (1 July 1952), 10-1, 43.
"French Baseball" *JCF* 3:4 (1975), 5-11.
"Moving to the Country" *NJ* No. 3 (1973), 93-5.
"Rory Peter's Last Run" *MM* 66 (15 Jan 1953), 18, 28, 30, 32-4.
"Sticklebacks" *78: Best Canadian Stories* 101-16.

MacDonald, Deborah‡
"Horses Make Me Sad" *Sand Patterns* No. 5 (May 1973), [6 pp].

MacDonald, Dorothy†

"Annabelle and the Doctor" *CSSM* 2:4 (Fall 1976), 48-51.

Macdonald, Elizabeth‡

"Precious Amber" *AA* 62 (July 1972), 57.
"The Sunday Visit" *AA* 62 (Mar 1972), 56-8.

Macdonald, H.J.

"The Detachment Man" *MM* [85] (July 1972), 24, 50, 52, 54, 56 [Semi-fictional].
"The Detachment Man" *Best Mounted Police Stories* (1978), 248-58.

Macdonald, Helen†

"The Picnic" *Antig R* No. 20 (Win 1974), 48-60.

Macdonald, Jack‡

"Two Yellow Pails" *Des* 10:3/4 Nos. 25/26 (1979), 90-9.

MacDonald, Jake (1949-)

"Becoming" *NeWest R* 7:6 (Feb 1982), 12-6.
"Becoming" *West of Fiction* (1983), 277-90.
"Two Yellow Pails" *Heartland* No. 1 (Nov-Dec 1980), 17-8, 62-7.

MacDonald, John E.C.

"Junk" *Pot Port* 2 (1980-81), 29-31.

Macdonald, John Geddie‡

"Jo Portugais" *AA* 48 (Nov 1957), 86-8.

Macdonald, Lynne†

"Listen" *Grain* 11:3 (Aug 1983), 47-9.

MacDonald, Margaret‡

"The Leopard" *Des* 10:2 No. 24 (1979), 106-12.
"Still Waters" *Laom R* 1:1 (Dec-Jan 1975), 99-101.

Macdonald, Mary (1929-)

"The Obituary" *Mal R* No. 61 (Feb 1982), 168-82.

MacDonald, Odysseus†

"Three Sorts of Pity" *Chel J* 2 (Jan-Feb 1976), 24-5.

MacDonald, Ray‡

"The Mist" *Either/Or* No. 5 (Fall 1967), 2-5.

MacDonald, William J.†

"Weaf in the Garden" *Alphabet* No 2 (July 1961), 13-20.

MacEwen, Gwendolyn (1941-)

NOMAN Ottawa: Oberon Press, 1972.
"Athens: The Knitting Party" *QQ* 81 (1974), 551-60.
"Day of the Twelve Princes" *Tam R* No. 54 (1970), 5-23.
"Day of the Twelve Princes" *Noman* (1972), 26-46.
"Fire" *Noman* (1972), 18-25.

"Fire" *Miss Chat* 10 ([Win] 1973), 40, 112-3, 120.

"House of the Whale" *CBC "Anthology"* 11 Jan 1969.

"House of the Whale" *Fourteen Stories High* (1971), 23-34.

"House of the Whale" *Noman* (1972), 5-17.

"House of the Whale" *Toronto Short Stories* (1977), 191-202.

"House of the Whale" *Best Modern Canadian Short Stories* (1978), 166-74.

"Kingsmere" *Noman* (1972), 52-4.

'The Man in the Moore" *CFM* No. 46 (1983), 43-8.

'Mystras: The Search for the Great White Horse" *CBC "Anthology"* 13 Jan 1973.

'Mystras: The Search for the Great White Horse" *Mal R* No. 46 (Apr 1978), 95-104.

'Noman" *Noman* (1972), 81-120.

'The Oarsman and the Seamstress" *CBC "Anthology"* 25 Sept 1971.

'The Oarsman and the Seamstress" *Noman* (1972), 47-51.

"Olympia: The Runners" *QQ* 83 (1976), 41-6.

'The Second Coming of Julian the Magician" *Prism* 9:3 (Spr 1970), 104-22.

'The Second Coming of Julian the Magician" *Noman* (1972), 55-75.

'The Second Coming of Julian the Magician" *Fiction of Contemporary Canada* (1980), 119-35.

"Snow" *CBC "Anthology"* 17 July 1971.

"Snow" *Noman* (1972), 76-80.

"Snow" *Miss Chat* 10 ([Win] 1973), 40, 107, 112.

"Snow" *Canadian Anthology* (1974), 576-8.

"Snow" *Sunlight & Shadows* (1974), 160-3.

"Snow" *In Your Own Words* (1982), 116-9.

MacEwen, John A.†

"Four Sisters" *CF* 31 (Jan 1952), 228-9.

'The Sandcastle" *CF* 33 (July 1953), 83, 85.

Macey, Anne Louise‡

"Encounter" *Alive* [2:2] (Jan 1971), 19-23.

'Justice" *Alive* 2:9 [Sept 1971], 26-30.

MacFadden, Patrick‡

" ... And What's More, My Visitors Have Scaly Tails" *Pop See Cul* No. 4 [n.d.], 10-3.

"Descent to a Temperate Valley" *Forge* 1966, 65-72.

"An Evening with Reynard Rhomboid" *Forge* 26:1 (Feb 1964), 57-60, 63-5.

MacFarlane, David‡

"Morning at a Summer House Now Burnt Down" *Dime Bag* [No. 18] Fiction Issue 1 (Mar 1977), 21-3.

MacFarlane, Duncan‡

"China Bay" *TUR* 73:2 (Dec 1959), 6-13.

MacFarlane, John L.‡

'The Binoculars" *Amethyst* 2:3 (Spr 1963), 45-7.

MacGregor, Tony‡

"And It Came to Pass" *Fifth Page* 1968, 21-4.

Machniak, Carol‡
"Remember Love" *Smoke Signals* [1974?], 37-44.

MacInnes, Ron‡
"Monologue for Three" *Fifth Page* [1969?], 10-6.

MacIntosh, Keitha K. (1942-)
THE CROW SITS HIGH IN THE LILAC TREE AND OTHER STORIES Huntingdon, P.Q.: Kateri Press, 1982.
SHATTERED GLASS AND OTHER FRAGMENTS Dewittville, P.Q.: Sunken Forum Press, 1976.
"Any Dumb Bunny" *Rapport* Dec 1970, 20-1.
"The Crow Sits High in the Lilac Tree" *Crow Sits High* (1982), 29-37.
"Death Is a Bus That Can't Slow Down" *Shattered Glass* (1976), 22-4.
"The Devil Lives in a Grey Stone House" *Crow Sits High* (1982), 22-8.
"Five Times a Father" *FH* 7 Jan 1960, 12-3.
"For the Love of Yackie Sculler" *FH* 15 May 1958, 28-9.
"From Paris with Love" *FH* 9 Mar 1961, 54-5.
"Gift of Prometheus" *Mont Poems* No. 4 (Win 1978), 19-23.
"Great Aunt Harriett and the Red Ribbon Bull" *FH* 26 Feb 1959, 34-5.
"The Hippy Summer" *Outset* 1974, 109-16 [Also entitled "Owl"].
"The Little Red Hat" *FH* 2 July 1959, 20-1.
"The Magic Root" *Crow Sits High* (1982), 1-21.
"The Most Beautiful Skates in the World" *FH* 25 Dec 1958, 8-9.
"Owl" *Saturday Night at the Forum* (1981), 124-34 [Also entitled "The Hippy Summer"].
"A Place to Belong" *FH* 28 Sept 1961, 18-9.
"Reading, Writing and Two Red Braids" *FH* 27 Mar 1958, 28-9.
"Shoo, Flu, Don't Bother Me" *FH* 16 Oct 1958, 16-7, 34.

MacIntyre, Rod‡
"To the Warden, So You'll Know" *Oyster in the Ooze* 1:1 (Mar 1972), [2 pp].

MacIntyre, Wendy†
"For Elaine" *UWR* 17:2 (Spr-Sum 1983), 30-41.
"The Initiate" *Ichor* No. 2 (1981), 13-20.

Mack, Dorothy‡
"The Gingerbread House" *CSSM* 2:1 (Jan 1976), 25-7.

Mackay, Claire (1930-)
"Important Message: Please Read" *Toronto Star* Sun, 14 Sept 1980, D5.

MacKay, H.B.
"Those Who Go Down" *AA* 57 (Dec 1966), 45-8.

MacKay, Jed‡
"City Dreams" *TUR* 82:2 [n.d.], [1 p].

Mackenzie, Alan†
"Checkers" *Antig R* No. 24 (Win 1975), 67-71.
"Intersection" *Antig R* No. 21 (Spr 1975), 53-4.
"A Ruler of Mind" *Prism* 12:3 (Spr 1973), 8-12.

MacKenzie, Blake†
"Kru and the Mammoth" *Alberta Golden Jubilee Anthology* (1955), 420-9.

MacKenzie, Brenda (1952-)
"Mr. Arc-En-Ciel" *Mal R* No. 61 (Feb 1982), 192-207.

MacKenzie, Eric‡
"The Fallen Dust" *Fifth Page* 1964, 27-33.

Mackenzie, Laura Hunter†
"Fuente Vaqueros" *CF* 33.(May 1953), 37-8.

Mackenzie, Sophie†
"A Miracle for Christmas" *Alberta Speaks* 1957, 7-10.

MacKenzie, Wayne O.‡
"The Church and the Union" *UC Observer* 1 Sept 1968, 47.

Mackie, Dan‡
"The Anniversary" *Toronto Star* Sun, 7 Nov 1982, D5.

MacKinnon, Bernard (1932?-)
"Mario" *AA* 56 (June 1966), 50-8.
"Thanks Pal" *AA* 56 (Sept 1965), 69-70, 73-4, 76, 79.

MacKinnon, Brian†
"Premonition" *Laom R* 1:2 (Apr 1975), 85-7.

MacKinnon, Donald†
"Another Form of the Riddle" by John Astin *WCR* 4:3 (Jan 1970), 14-7.

MacKinnon, Lilian Vaux‡
"Cape Breton Picnic" *QQ* 74 (1967), 248-54.
"The Christmas Hat" *UC Observer* 14 (1 Dec 1952), 6.
"In Homage to Christmas" *UC Observer* 12 (15 Dec 1950), 8-9.
" 'Quiet! Please' " *UC Observer* 15 (15 Dec 1953), 10-1.
"Taking Hamish by Surprise" *UC Observer* 13 (15 Dec 1951), 8, 40-1.
"Thirty Years On" *UC Observer* 14 (1 Oct 1952), 19-20.

MacKinnon, Malcolm‡
"The Price of Peace" *Acta Vic* 76:4 (Mar 1952), 27-8.

Mackintosh, James‡
"Magic Words" *WCR* 14:1 (June 1979), 4.
"Smudge" *WCR* 14:1 (June 1979), 3.

MacKrow, Jack†

"Bears Aren't So Dumb" *Forge* 1950, 14.

"The Most Unforgettable Character I Have Met" *Forge* 1950, 64-5.

MacLaurin, Douglas†

RIFFS Toronto: McGraw-Hill Ryerson, 1982.

"999 in the Good Old Days" *Riffs* (1982), 95-107.

"Amitville Rip-Off" *Riffs* (1982), 62-5.

"B. Greenwood" *Riffs* (1982), 85-7.

"Big Bo" *Riffs* (1982), 28-37.

"Bikers Are Hard on the Digestion" *Riffs* (1982), 132-5.

"The Bouncer/Bus-Driving Therapy Man" *Riffs* (1982), 88-94.

"The Caddy Pervert" *Riffs* (1982), 108-11.

"Cash-Flow Cameron" *Riffs* (1982), 66-72.

"The Concert as Country as Cowshit" *Riffs* (1982), 117-24.

"The Conductor" *Riffs* (1982), 15-23.

"Coyote" *Riffs* (1982), 73-5.

"Hell, No! We Won't Go" *Riffs* (1982), 112-6.

"Justice" *Riffs* (1982), 125-31.

"Killer" *Riffs* (1982), 141-4.

"Lady T" *Riffs* (1982), 50-61.

"The Laird of Skid Row" *Riffs* (1982), 76-84.

"The Last Supper" *Riffs* (1982), 9-14.

"Old Rounders Never Die, They Just Steal Away" *Riffs* (1982), 38-44.

"The Suicide-Proof Leprechaun" *Riffs* (1982), 136-40.

"Want-Ad Lovers" *Riffs* (1982), 45-9.

"The White-Cane Wreck 'Em Derby" *Riffs* (1982), 24-7.

MacLean, James F.‡

"Fables of Faubus" *Adder* 2:1 ([1962?], 10-1.

"The Light" *Adder* 1:1 [1961?], 11-2.

MacLean, James S.‡

"The Sailboats" *Salt* No. 16 (Sum 1977), 17-21.

MacLean, Kenneth‡

"Afternoon Men" *Acta Vic* 81:1 (Nov 1956), 9-11.

"The Counter Earth" *Acta Vic* 97:2 (Apr 1973), 26-33.

"The Glassy Essence" *Acta Vic* 96:2 [n.d.], 37-9.

"This Beautiful Star" *Acta Vic* 98:2 (Apr 1974), 6-7.

Maclean, Muriel†

"A Baby for Rosanne" *Read Ch* 2:1 (Spr 1983), 8-12.

"Like Sisters" *Read Ch* 1:3 (Win 1982), 36-9.

"Like Sisters" CBC *"Canadian Short Stories"* [date unknown] [Based on *Reader's Choice*].

Maclean, Peter

"Things Were Simpler Then – Or Were They?" *Can Banker* 82:6 (1975), 30-1 [humour].

MacLean, Robert‡

"Ice Fishing" *JCF* 3:1 (Win 1974), 27-9.
"Steel Man" *Des* 14:3 No. 41 (Sum 1983), 48-60.

MacLennan, Hugh (1907-)

"My Last Colonel" *Mont* 33 (May 1959), 26-8.
"An Orange from Portugal" *Chat* 31 (July 1958), 54-5.
"An Orange from Portugal" *Modern Canadian Stories* (1966), 96-105.
"Remembrance Day, 2010 A.D." *Man and His World* (1961), 16-25.
"Remembrance Day, 2010 A.D." *Visions from the Edge* (1981), 162-8.

MacLennan, Toby

SINGING THE STARS Toronto: Coach House Press, 1983.
'The Absence of a Hole" *Singing the Stars* (1983), [6 pp].
'The Book of the Architects" *Singing the Stars* (1983), [11 pp].
"Cave of the Mother of the Moon" *Singing the Stars* (1983), [23 pp].
'The Limits of the Natural World" *Singing the Stars* (1983), [13 pp].
'The Periodic Stranger's Hand" *Singing the Stars* (1983), [10 pp].
'The Restaurant" *Strange Faeces* No. 17 (June 1975), 4-5.
[Untitled] *Titmouse R* No. 5 (Win 1974-75), 5.

MacLeod, Alistair (1936-)

THE LOST SALT GIFT OF BLOOD Toronto: McClelland & Stewart, 1976.
'The Boat" *Massachusetts R* 9:2 (Spr 1968), 247-66.
'The Boat" *Best American Short Stories* 1969 99-116.
'The Boat" *Scenes from American Life* (1973), 26-41.
'The Boat" *Stories from Atlantic Canada* (1973), 84-103.
'The Boat" *Together* (1975) [Based on survey response].
'The Boat" *Lost Salt Gift of Blood* (1976), 129-51.
'The Boat" *Best Modern Canadian Short Stories* (1978), 286-300.
'The Boat" *Transitions 2* (1978), 209-24.
'The Boat" *Canadian Viewpoints* (1981) [Based on survey response].
'The Boat" *Introduction to Literature* (1981) [Based on survey response].
'The Boat" *Growing Up Canadian* (1983) [Based on survey response].
'The Closing Down of Summer" *Fid* No. 111 (Fall 1976), 16-32.
'The Closing Down of Summer" CBC "Anthology" 7 July 1979.
'The Closing Down of Summer" CBC "Once More from the Top" 27 Sept 1979 [Based on survey response].
'The Closing Down of Summer" *Fiddlehead Greens* (1979), 61-88.
'The Golden Gift of Grey" *Twigs* 7 (Spr 1971) [Based on survey response].
'The Golden Gift of Grey" *Lost Salt Gift of Blood* (1976), 109-26.
'The Greater Good" *Intervales* Spr 1961 [Based on survey response].
'In the Fall" *Tam R* No. 60 (Oct 1973), 11-25.
'In the Fall" *Lost Salt Gift of Blood* (1976), 13-30.
'In the Fall" CBC "Atlantic Airwaves" 24 Sept 1983 [Based on survey response].
'The Lost Salt Gift of Blood" *Southern R* 10 (1974), 181-98.
'The Lost Salt Gift of Blood" CBC "Anthology" 9 Nov 1974.
'The Lost Salt Gift of Blood" *Best American Short Stories* 1975 144-61.
'The Lost Salt Gift of Blood" *Lost Salt Gift of Blood* (1976), 65-86.
'The Lost Salt Gift of Blood" *Canadian Short Stories III* (1978), 168-90.
'The Lost Salt Gift of Blood" *Best Canadian Short Stories* (1981), 208-24.

"The Lost Salt Gift of Blood" *Anthology of Canadian Literature in English* 2 (1983), 414-26.

"The Lost Salt Gift of Blood" *Heartland* (1983), 131-47.

"The Return" *AA* 62 (Nov 1971), 54-6, 58, 61, 63-4.

"The Return" CBC *"Anthology"* 10 Nov 1973.

"The Return" *Lost Salt Gift of Blood* (1976), 89-105.

"The Return" *Canadian Myths and Legends* (1977), 94-109.

"The Return" *Nearly an Island* (1979), 12-27.

"The Return" *Stories Plus* (1979), 150-61.

"The Return" CBC *[Hal]* Fall 1979 [Based on survey response].

"The Return" *In Your Own Words* (1982), 208-18.

"The Road to Rankin's Point" *Lost Salt Gift of Blood* (1976), 155-87.

"The Road to Rankin's Point" *Tam R* No. 68 (Spr 1976), 7-32.

"Second Spring" *CFM* Nos. 34/35 (1980), 28-45.

"To Every Thing There Is a Season" *Toronto Globe and Mail* Sat, 24 Dec 1977, 7 [Listed as fiction in survey response].

"The Vastness of the Dark" *Fid* No. 88 (Win 1971), 2-23.

"The Vastness of the Dark" *Lost Salt Gift of Blood* (1976), 33-62.

"The Vastness of the Dark" *Zadiry* [date unknown] [In Russian; based on survey response].

"Winter Dog" *CFM* Nos. 40/41 (1981), 50-62.

MacLeod, Gladys M.
"Ellen Denby's Husband" *Bluenose* 1:3 (Win 1976-77), 11-3.

MacLeod, Mildred‡
"Letter of Rejection" *Stump* 1:2 (Fall 1977), 10-6.

MacLeod, Robert‡
"Two Notes (from Under the Floorboards of a UBC Army Hut)" *Alive* 3:2 [1973], 23-5.

MacLure, Millar
"Homecoming" *Dal R* 43 (1963), 483-9.

"Homecoming" *Des* No. 1 [1970], [6 pp].

MacMann, Samuel Lavalliere
"The Death of a Precocious Poet" *Alpha* [1:3] (Dec 1976), 12-3.

"A Moment as Dionysus" *Alpha* 1:1 (Oct 1976), 7.

"A Vision of Death" *Alpha* [1:4] (Jan 1977), 14.

"A Woman of Some Beauty" *Alpha* 1:2 (Nov 1976), 13-4.

MacMaster, Rowland‡
"Countercheck" *Undergrad* Spr 1952, 15-22.

"The Scaffold" *Undergrad* Mar 1950, 17-21.

"Sic Transit Gloria Mundi" *Undergrad* Spr 1953, 7-10.

MacMillan, Alex‡
"Foster and His Dummy" *Parole* No. 1 [1981?], [2 pp] [Non-fiction?].

MacMillan, Angus‡

"City of Angus" *TUR* 64:1 (Nov 1951), 38-40.

"Pigs" *TUR* 63:3 (Feb 1951), 10-3.

MacMillan, Beatrice†

"Face into the Wind" *Our Family* 26 (Apr 1974), 30-2.

MacMillan, Gail

"An Act of Love" *Living Message* 87 (Sept 1976), 26-7.

"As It Should Be" *Can Messenger* 90 (Dec 1980), 8, 18.

"The Boy Who Didn't Play Baseball" *Can Messenger* 90 (Sept 1980), 8-9.

"The Boy Who Didn't Play Baseball" *Living Message* 92 (Apr 1981), 21-3.

" 'But ... ' " *Can Messenger* 85 (May 1975), 12-3.

"The End of the Tunnel" *Can Messenger* 86 (Mar 1976), 12-3.

"Faith of Our Fathers" *Living Message* 91 (Jan 1980), 23-5.

"The Geraniums" *Companion* 42 (May 1979), 13-4.

"How Was Your Day?" *Companion* 38 (Nov 1975), 22-5.

"A Lilly of the Fields" *Living Message* 88 (Mar 1977), 22-3.

"Listen, Oh Listen!" *Can Messenger* 85 (Oct 1975), 15.

"Listen, Oh Listen!" *Living Message* 88 (Dec 1977), 21-2.

"The Rose" *Living Message* 87 (Feb 1976), 28-9.

"Stranger in My House" *Companion* 38 (Feb 1975), 24-8.

"The Tulips" *Can Messenger* 84 (Mar 1974), 18-9.

"Whatever Became of Becky?" *Can Messenger* 85 (Feb 1975), 12-3.

"Whatever Became of Becky?" *AA* 65 (Aug 1975), 29-30.

"Whatever Became of Becky?" *Living Message* 88 (June 1977), 19-21.

MacMillan, Ian†

"Melvin" *NJ* No. 3 (1973), 24-5.

"The Parable of the Three Brothers" *WCR* 8:3 (Jan 1974), 21.

"A Suicide Note" *WCR* 8:3 (Jan 1974), 22-3.

"The Writer" *WCR* 8:3 (Jan 1974), 21-2.

MacMillan, William‡

"The Nanook in the Stone" *North* 14 (Sept-Oct 1967), 51-3.

MacNair, Janet†

"Hormone Pills" *Intervales* [No. 1] (1959), 19-22.

MacNeil, Mike‡

"Teachers" *Origins* 10:2 (June 1980), 55-8.

MacNeill, James A. (1933-)

UNDER THE SWEETGRASS SKY Saskatoon: Western Extension College, 1978.

"After Batoche" *Under the Sweetgrass Sky* (1978), 91-100.

"Germ Warfare" *Under the Sweetgrass Sky* (1978), 1-7.

"The Lady and the Doctor" *Under the Sweetgrass Sky* (1978), 9-15.

"Langston, Ladycloud, and the Horse That Swam Side-Stroke" *Under the Sweetgrass Sky* (1978), 101-8.

"The Medicine Line" *Under the Sweetgrass Sky* (1978), 17-25.

"No Time for Jerry" *Saskatchewan Writing* 1960 22-33.

"Octoberfire" *Under the Sweetgrass Sky* (1978), 37-44.

"Oh, Dear, What Can the Matter Be?" *Under the Sweetgrass Sky* (1978), 69-76.
"The Otherside Incident" *Under the Sweetgrass Sky* (1978), 27-35.
"The Peacemaker" *Under the Sweetgrass Sky* (1978), 77-90.
"Retrieval" *Under the Sweetgrass Sky* (1978), 45-52.
"Stage Struck" *Under the Sweetgrass Sky* (1978), 59-67.
"Voice in the Wilderness" *Under the Sweetgrass Sky* (1978), 53-8.
"Wintergreen – Evergreen" *Under the Sweetgrass Sky* (1978), 109-14.

MacNintch, John E.‡
"Old Mossback" *AA* 56 (July 1966), 48-52.

MacPherson, Carol†
"Pink Cotton Candy" *Intervales* No. 2 (1960), 5-11.

MacRae, Allan‡
"Streetcars, School and Sunday Matinees" *CBC "Alberta Anthology"* 30 Oct 1982.

MacRae, Jacquelyn‡
"Burnt Roses" *Folio* 17:1 (Fall 1964), 36-7.

MacSween, R.J.
THE BURNT FOREST AND OTHER STORIES Antigonish: Antigonish Press, 1975.
"Another Desperate Cry" *Burnt Forest* (1975), 88-92.
"Broken Glasses" *Antig R* No. 27 (Aut 1976), 23-9.
"The Burnt Forest" *Antig R* No. 18 (Sum 1974), 9-18.
"The Burnt Forest" *Burnt Forest* (1975), 5-14.
"The City of Eyes" *Burnt Forest* (1975), 137-41.
"The Dead Sun" *Burnt Forest* (1975), 122-6.
"The Eagle's Eye" *Antig R* No. 34 (Sum 1978), 21-8.
"The Face of Death" *Burnt Forest* (1975), 74-9.
"In the Park" *Burnt Forest* (1975), 53-62.
"A Jaundiced Liver" *Burnt Forest* (1975), 132-6.
"An Old Secret" *Burnt Forest* (1975), 127-31.
"Past Forgotten" *Antig R* No. 39 (Aut 1979), 75-82.
"The Play's the Thing" *Burnt Forest* (1975), 68-73.
"The Portrait" *Antig R* No. 11 (Aut 1972), 13-20.
"The Portrait" *Burnt Forest* (1975), 39-46.
"The Privy Council" *Burnt Forest* (1975), 47-52.
"The Privy Council" *Antig R* No. 21 (Spr 1975), 29-34.
"The Scream" *Burnt Forest* (1975), 113-21.
"Secrecy" *Burnt Forest* (1975), 109-12.
"Till Death" *Antig R* No. 15 (Aut 1973), 29-38.
"Till Death" *Burnt Forest* (1975), 15-25.
"The Touch of a Bird's Wing" *Antig R* No. 35 (Aut 1978), 11-7.
"The Treasure" *Burnt Forest* (1975), 80-7.
"The Treasure" *Antig R* No. 22 (Sum 1975), 19-26.
"The Two Portraits" *Burnt Forest* (1975), 93-7.
"The Vegetarian" *Antig R* 1:4 (Win 1971), 76-80.
"The Vegetarian" *Burnt Forest* (1975), 63-7.

"Weariness" *Burnt Forest* (1975), 104-8.
"When the Foundations Shake" *Burnt Forest* (1975), 98-103.
"The White Eye" *Antig R* No. 19 (Aut 1974), 21-6.
"The White Eye" *Burnt Forest* (1975), 26-31.
"Witch Doctor" *Burnt Forest* (1975), 32-8.
"Witch Doctor" *Antig R* No. 23 (Aut 1975), 17-22.

MacTavish, Grant†
"Creeps" *Treeline* 2 (1983), 137-9.

Madden, Peter
"Bad Day at the Bank" *Fid* No. 97 (Spr 1973), 50-61.
"A Closed Account" *Quarry* 22:3 (Sum 1973), 64-6.
"One for the Road" *Anthol* No. 3 (Spr 1974), 34-48.
"Taking a Chance" *Anthol* No. 2 (Win 1972-73), 37-40.
"The Way Back" *Anthol* [No. 1] (Spr 1972), 18-20.

Madison, Grant†
"Brave New Year" *Green's* 4:2 (Win 1976), 3-4.
"But Always April" *Onward* 3 Apr 1966, 11-2.
"The Secret" *Rapport* May 1970, 22-3.
"Young Moment" *Rapport* Sept 1970, 9.

Madott, Darlene (1952-)
"Bottled Roses" *Aurora* 1978 83-103.
"The First Day of June: I Turn Seventeen" *Dand* 9:2 (1982), 69-83.
"Fragments from a Photo Album" *Waves* 5:2/3 (Spr 1977), 51-6.
"Instructing the Young" *CF* 63 (Apr 1983), 20-1, 25-7.
"Letter to a Friend" *Antig R* No. 31 (Aut 1977), 53-61.
"The Namesake" *Can Ethnic Studies* 14:1 (1982), 111-8.
"Passengers" *event* 8:1 (1979), 100-2.
"A Promise to Norma Miller" *Grain* 4:3 [1976], 20-6.
"When John Brown and I Were Young" *Quarry* 28:2 (Spr 1979), 38-44.

Madsen, Margaret‡
"In the Shadows" *West Producer* 45 (6 June 1968), C2.

Maeers, Esther‡
"Georgie" *Acta Vic* 81:2 (Dec 1956), 15-6.
"A Little Child Shall Lead Them" *Acta Vic* 80:2 (Dec 1955), 22-3.

M[agalis]., E[laine].†
"Diana Betrayed" *Raven* No. 6 (Apr 1958), 15-20.

Magill, Art – *See* Green, H. Gordon.

Magnusson, K.‡
"Stony's Elfin Visitors" *Ice Can* 35:2 (Win 1976), 33-4, 41 [Non-fiction?].

Maguire, Art – *See* Green, H. Gordon.

Maher, Paul‡
"Joe Kennedy's Dream" *Atl Guardian* 9 (Mar 1952), 18-20.
"A Matter of Climate" *Atl Guardian* 8 (Sept 1951), 27-8.
"Remembering Newfoundland" *CBC "Anthology"* 28 Aug 1976.
"Restful Soul" *CBC "Anthology"* 20 Nov 1976.
"The Strange Case of Rev. Mr. Gow" *Atl Guardian* 8 (July 1951), 21-2.

Mahoney, Owen‡
"Fred as Told by Friend of Fred" *Alive* [1:10] (Nov 1970), 28.

Mahoney, Tracy†
"The Chinook" *CSSM* 2:2 (Spr 1976), 50-3.

Mahood, Maurice†
"The Last Moment" *CSSM* 3:1 (Win 1977), 58-62.

Maika, Patricia‡
"Fictional Tale of a Life Thus Far" *Radical Reviewer* No. 6 (Spr 1982), 20-1.

Main, Michael M.‡
"The Conscientious Conscience" *AA* 62 (Feb 1972), 23, 36.

Mairghread [pseudonym]
"Midwinter Night's Dream" *Varsity* Fri, 14 Dec 1951, 2.

Major, Kevin‡
"Buying a Watch for Billy's Christmas" *AA* 64 (Dec 1973), 48-9, 55.

Makdator, Walt‡
"Portrait of a Cross" *Fifth Page* 1961, 27-32.

Malag, Oonagh‡
"The Fabric of a Dream" *AA* 48 (June 1958), 65-7.

Malcolm, Susan†
" 'Some Enchanted Evening' " *Echoes* No. 237 (Christmas 1959), 5, 9.

Malcolmson, Bob‡
"One Morning" *Acta Vic* 88:1 [1963], 18.

Malik, Cynthia†
"Lamentation" *Antig R* No. 34 (Sum 1978), 63-70.
"You Never Told Me You'd Been to Mexico" *SN* 93 (Sept 1978), 40-7.

Malley, Michael‡
"Christmas Grace" *Grub* 2:5 (June 1971), 6.

Malloch, Bruce
"A Saturday Night Out in the Country" *Los* No. 7 (Mar 1981), 23-5.

Mallon, Jane‡
"The Incident" *Eclipse* No. 4 (1977), 19-21.

Malone, Doreen‡
"Her Story" *Abegweit R* 3:1 (Spr 1977), 75-7.

Maloney, Elizabeth†
"The Peeper" *Mont Writers' Forum* 1:3 (Dec 1978), 8-10.

Malt, Rick‡
"An Evening Walk" *Quarry* 12 (1962-63), 17-9.
"Neuton's Law" *Quarry* 14 (1964-65), 34-6 [Humour?].
"Trains" *Quarry* 12 (1962-63), 23.

Maltman, Kim‡
"Conscience" *Nw J* No. 20 (1981), 64.
"Hail" *Nw J* No. 20 (1981), 64.

Mandrake, Jill†
"The Dawn of the Gothic Period" *Prism* 14:3 (Win 1975), 46-50.
"The Latest Advance" *Canadian Short Fiction Anthology* (1976), 129-33.
"Maybe Tomorrow I'll See It All from Heaven" *Prism* 16:2 (Fall 1977), 74-82.
"Shore of Desire" *VWFP/Revue* 1:3 (May 1975), 16, 19.

Mandryk, Ted (1935?-1952)
"A Fishing Trip" *Uk Can* 7 (1 Aug 1953), 8.
"Gregory" *Uk Can* 7 (15 Apr 1953), 7.
"Hailing a Cab" *Uk Can* 7 (15 Aug 1953), 6.

Mandy, Margot†
"Metamorphosis" *Alpha* 1:1 (Oct 1976), 10.

Manicom, David [pseudonym]
"Leaves" *Acta Vic* 107:2 (Spr 1983), 10-2.
"Spring Gale" *Acta Vic* 107:1 (Fall 1982), 54-7.

Manion, Melanie‡
"The Cure" *Br Out* 2:6 (Nov-Dec 1975), 28-30.

Mann, Judy†
"Friday at the Travelodge" *Quarry* 29:4 (Aut 1980), 47-53.
"The Ground Rod" *Quarry* 29:4 (Aut 1980), 54-61.

Mann, Kay†
"A Boy's Castle" *Can Messenger* 86 (July-Aug 1976), 12-4.
"The Legend of the Locket" *Can Messenger* 87 (Nov 1977), 12-3.

Mann, Ted
"Pyrotechnic" *Pulp* 1:1 (15 Nov 1972), [1-2].
[Untitled] *Pulp* 1:3 (15 Dec 1972), [4].

Mannard, W.G.
"An Unrestricted View" *Outset* 1974, 123-8.

Manne, Michael C.†
"Exit Etc. Etc. Etc." *Sheet* 1:1 (Jan 1960), 4-6.

Manning, Dorothy
"The Search for the New Child" *Quarry* 27:1 (Win 1978), 11-6.

Manns, Stephanie‡
"Short Story" *Simcoe R* No. 8 (Spr 1980), 22-6.

Manos, Peter†
"Lenkowski's Diary" *Scrivener* 2:1 (Spr 1981), 3-5.

Manson, Sharon‡
"Chasers" *VWFP/Revue* 1:4 (June 1975), 8-9, 20.

Manzer, Ronald†
"One Mile Run" *Fid* No. 42 (Fall 1959), 53-6.
"One Mile Run" *Intervales* No. 2 (1960), 13-6.
"Walter" *Intervales* [No. 1] (1959), 39-46.

Marcellin, Philip
"Anna, Unpretty" *Alive* 2:6 No. 16 [May] 1971), 10-7.
"Don't Tread on Me" *Alive* No. 35 [1974], 16.
"In the Lazaretto" *Alive* 2:8 (July-Aug 1971), 40-5.
"Phoenix" *Alive* No. 29 [1973], 33-6.
"Three Days Out" *Alive* No. 32 [1973], 49.
"The World of Men" *Alive* No. 31 [1973], 47-9.

Marchaelle, Ilona
"Black Cockerel" *Matrix* No. 16 (Spr 1983), 36-44.
"Pigpens Can Be Reasonable Places" *Grain* 10:4 (Nov 1982), 40.

Marchand, Philip‡
"Father Malleus" *Random* 2:2 (Nov 1967), 18-20.

Marcuse, Katherine
"The Fearful Heart" *Chat* 26 (Feb 1953), 21, 48, 50, 52-3, 55.
"What Other Love?" *Chat* 42 (Mar 1969), 26-7, 83-4, 86, 88.

Mardon, Caroline‡
"Last Days" *UCR* 1978-79, 39-40.

Margeson, John (1920-)
"Spider Road" *QQ* 74 (1967), 429-36.

Margoshes, Dave (1941-)
"Afternoon in a Different Place" *Chelsea* (U.S.) No. 15 (June 1964), 47-59.
"The Caller" *Des* 8:3 No. 19 (1977), 84-90.
"The Cat Came Back" *UWR* 16:2 (Spr-Sum 1982), 83-8.
"The Cat Came Back" *Metavisions* (1983), 144-8.
"A Change of Life" *Mal R* No. 49 (Jan 1979), 77-90.
"A Change of Life" *Third Impressions* (1982), 158-76.
"Cross-Word" *BC Monthly* No. 32 (Sept 1983), [3 pp] [Listed as fiction in survey response].
"Death Came and Whispered in My Ear: Live" *Trace* No. 54 (May 1964), 277-83.
"The Dogs" *Pulp* 5:7 (1 June 1979), [1-2].

"A False Moustache" *Prism* 22:1 (Oct 1983), 47-58.
"The First Son, and the Second" *Nomad* (U.S.) No. 9 (Sum 1961), 34-8 [Based on survey response].
"Goodbye to All That" *Des* No. 15 (Fall 1976), 39-50.
"The Grass" *Dand* 7:1 (1980), 28-9.
"I Must Be Going" *North Stone R* (U.S.) No. 1 (Spr 1971), 51-3 [Based on survey response].
"Ladies Always Carry" *Trace* No. 71 (May 1970), 336-40.
"Lady of the Lake" *Dal R* 60 (1980), 38-48.
"Oh, Beautiful" *Blue Buffalo* 2:1 (Fall 1983), [2 pp].
"On an April Morning" *Quixote* (U.S.) 4:9 [1970?], 44-50 [Based on survey response].
"One Too Many Mornings" *Des* 10:2 No. 24 (1979), 89-94.
"The Pride of Man" *Grande Ronde R* No. 13 (Aug 1971), [n.p.] [Based on survey response].
"Rabbit Done Run, Seymour Went Away and Rosacoke's Got the Blues" *Des* 12:2/3 Nos. 32/33 (1981), 102-8.
"Rabbit Done Run, Seymour Went Away and Rosacoke's Got the Blues" *Third Impressions* (1982), 150-7.
"The Same Thing" *Dal R* 61 (1981), 559-68.
"Saturn Is My Home" *Mam* 6:1 (Sum 1982), [3 pp].
"Sunflowers" *Prism* 13:2 (Win 1973), 112-7.
"Those of Us Still Living" *Intrepid* (U.S.) Nos. 23/24 (Sum-Fall 1972), 33-6 [Based on survey response].
"Trespassers Will Be Violated" *Des* 9:1/2 Nos. 20/21 (1978), 111-25.
"Truckee Your Blues Away" *Dal R* 57 (1977), 119-29.
"Truckee Your Blues Away" *Third Impressions* (1982), 135-49.
"Well, Well, Well: Three Very Deep Subjects" *Consumption* No. 2 (Win 1968), 22-9 [Based on survey response].
"Where's Charlie?" *Exile* 4:1 (1976), 105-6.

Mark, Norm‡
"Deflowered & Debauched" *Panic Button* No. 13 (1963), 22-7.
"The Demonstration" *Panic Button* No. 16 (1964), 25.

Marks, Arlene F.
"Freddy Makes It Snow" *In Touch* (1975), 49-53.

Marlatt, Daphne (1942-)
"2-Night (Isla Mujères" [sic] *Per* No. 1 (Spr 1977), 49-51.
"In the Beginning" *Story So Far* 5 (1978), 117-9.
"Listen" *Raven* No. 1 (Fall 1979), [2 pp].
"Mokelumne Hill" *Story So Far* (1971), 48-51.
"No-Movement" by Daphne Buckle. *Evidence* No. 9 [n.d.], 50-9.
"Progreso" *Iron II* No. 4 (Nov 1976), 9-16.
"Progreso" *Fiction of Contemporary Canada* (1980), 95-104.
"The Sea-Haven" by Daphne Buckle. *Evidence* No. 6 [n.d.], 23-69 [Novella?].
"The Sea-Haven" by Daphne Buckle. *Modern Canadian Stories* (1966), 332-72.
"The Sprout" by Daphne Buckle. *Concept* No. 2 (Mar 1963), 43-8.
"Winter. Moving Just Inside the Door" *Story So Far* 3 (1974), 137-40.

Marlyn, John (1912-)
"Anna" *CBC "Anthology"* 7 Feb 1976.
"The Courtship of Uncle Janos" *CBC "Anthology"* 29 Sept 1966.
"The Courtship of Uncle Janos" *NeWest R* 8 (Nov 1982), 4-5.
"Good for You, Mrs. Feldesh" *CBC "Anthology"* 14 Feb 1976.
"Good for You, Mrs. Feldesh" *Dal R* 60 (1980-81), 670-84.
"A Member of the Family" *CBC "Anthology"* 21 June 1964.
"A Member of the Family" *CBC "Anthology"* 27 Aug 1968.
"Nail, Nail on the Wall" *CBC "Anthology"* 5 Nov 1957.
"Onkle Janos" *QQ* 61 (1955), 482-9.
"Onkle Janos" *CBC "Anthology"* 8 Mar 1955.

Marquis, Helen†
"Indian Christmas Carol" *CG* [80] (Dec 1961), 29-32.

Marriott, J. Anne (1913-)
"Better Off Dead" *CG* 87 (Jan 1968), 51-3.
"The Carillon" *CBC* [date unknown] [Based on survey response].
"The City Cousin" *CBC* 27 Oct 1950 [Based on survey response].
"The City Cousin" *CF* 34 (Nov 1954), 182-4.
"The Date" *Weekend* 3 (8 Aug 1953), 12, 20, 23.
"A Day Like Spring" *CBC "Anthology"* 7 May 1968.
"A Day Like Spring" *Fid* No. 82 (Nov-Dec 1969), 48-51.
"The Death of the Cat" *CBC* 6 Dec 1953 [Based on survey response].
"The Death of the Cat" *Aurora* 1979 85-95.
"A Dream of Blood" *CA & B* 55:4/56:1 (Sum-Fall 1980), 31-4.
"The Garden" *West Producer* 1970 [?] [Based on survey response].
"The Ice Forest" *CF* 30 (Mar 1951), 279-81.
"The Ice Forest" *CBC* 7 Mar 1951 [?] [Based on survey response].
"Institutions" *JCF* 3:2 (1974), 14-8.
"It's All Right, Mr. Khan" *Fid* No. 137 (Oct 1983), 41-9.
"The Ladder" *CBC "Canadian Short Stories"* 1969 [Based on survey response].
"The Ladies" *CBC "Anthology"* [?] 1957 [Based on survey response].
"The Ladies" *Fid* No. 91 (Fall 1971), 12-22.
"A Matter of Luck" *CG* 83 (Nov 1964), 33-5.
"Mrs. Absalom" *NR* 6:3 (Aug-Sept 1953), 28-39.
"Mrs. Absalom" *CBC "Anthology"* 9 Nov 1954.
"Mrs. Absalom" *British Columbia* (1961), 369-79.
"Never So Happy" *FH* 27 June 1968, 45-6.
"On a Sunday Afternoon" *QQ* 78 (1971), 553-8.
"On a Sunday Afternoon" *CBC "Anthology"* 8 July 1972.
"On a Sunday Afternoon" *Stories from Pacific & Arctic Canada* (1974), 49-56.
"On a Sunday Afternoon" *Die Weite Reise* (1974), 387-96 [As "An Einem Sonntagnachmittag"; trans. Gerhard Bottcher].
"The Party" *CBC* 1951 [Based on survey response].
"The Ride" *CBC* "Anthology" 1 May 1971.
"The Ride" *Prism* 11:2 (Aut 1971), 43-54.
"The Skinflint" *Weekend* 4 (31 July 1954), 10, 23, 29.
"Star Bright" *CBC "Stories with John Drainie"* 7 Dec 1964 [Based on survey response].
"Star Bright" *CBC "Stories with John Drainie"* 14 June 1965 [Based on survey

response].
"Stella" *Winter's Tales* 18 (1972), 235-50.
"Stella" *CBC "Anthology"* 26 Oct 1974.
"Stopover" *Tam R* No. 63 (Oct 1974), 44-56.
"Suitable Employment" *CBC "Anthology"* 31 Jan 1976.
"To the Castle" *CFM* No. 6 (Spr 1972), 64-9.

Mars, Jan‡

"Biking in Foreign Countries" *Portico* 3:1 [n.d.], 15-8, 38-41.

Marseillin, Philip†

'The Insect" *Tide* Nos. 5/6 (Spr-Sum [1971]), [5 pp].
'Plucked" *Quarry* 23:3 (Sum 1974), 44-5.

Marsh, Audrey‡

'The Beguiled [A Gentle Ghost Story]" *Bluenose* 2:2 (Fall 1977), 19-20.
"Lo Fat Speaks" *Vancouver Mag* 12 (Feb 1979), 70, 72-3.

Marsh, Wade‡

"As the Twig Is Bent" *NF* 1:2 (Spr 1952), 16-21.
'Not a Through Street" *NF* 2:1 (Spr 1953), 5-7.
"Saturday Afternoon" *NF* 3:3 (Aut 1954), 4-10.

Marshall, Carolyn‡

'Red Ribbon" *Fid* No. 46 (Aut 1960), 1-4.

Marshall, Christina‡

"Swan Song" *Stump* Spr 1983, 1-4.

Marshall, Douglas

"A Piece of Rope" *Otherside* No. 1 (Aut 1959), 22-4

Marshall, Joyce (1913-)

A PRIVATE PLACE Ottawa: Oberon Press, 1975.
'The Accident" *CBC "Anthology"* 13 Dec 1975.
'The Accident" *Fid* No. 108 (Win 1976), 62-9.
'The Accident" *Canadian Short Stories* 3 (1978), 192-203.
"All in the Winter's Cold" *CBC "Canadian Short Stories"* 16 June 1950 [Based on survey response].
"All in the Winter's Cold" *CBC International Service* July 1950 [Based on survey response].
"Among the Lost" *CBC "Bernie Braden Reads a Story"* 21 Mar 1950 [Based on survey response].
"Any Time at All" *Private Place* (1975), 118-35 [Mistitled "So Many Have Died" in first printing of collection].
"Avis de Vente" *CBC "Anthology"* 1983 [Based on survey response].
'Belgium Avenue" *CBC "Canadian Short Stories"* 25 Aug 1950 [Based on survey response].
'The Bicycle" *CBC "Canadian Short Stories"* 30 May 1953 [Based on survey response].
'The Box of Fudge" *CBC "Canadian Short Stories"* 27 Jan 1950 [Based on survey response].

"The Case of Cassandra Dop" *Small Wonders* (1982), 73-83.

"The Case of Cassandra Dop" CBC *"Anthology"* 22 May 1982 [Based on survey response].

"Copenhagen" CBC *"Anthology"* 12 Nov 1977.

"The Enemy" *Private Place* (1975), 22-34 [Also entitled "Ruin and Wrack"].

"The Enemy" *Anthology of Canadian Literature in English 1* (1982), 645-51.

"The Escape" CBC *"Anthology"* 14 May 1977.

"The Escape" *Aurora* 1978 123-33.

"The Escape" *CBC International Service* 1979 [Based on survey response].

"The Gradual Day" *CFM* No. 20 (Win 1976), 84-9.

"In the Midst of Life" *Mont* 33 (Apr 1959), 20-3.

"Learn It Early" *Seventeen* Aug 1950 [Based on survey response].

"The Little White Girl" CBC *"Anthology"* 25 May 1974.

"The Little White Girl" *Private Place* (1975), 65-76.

"The Little White Girl" *Stories of Quebec* (1980), 11-22.

"My Refugee" CBC *"Anthology"* 11 Sept 1982 [Based on survey response].

"My Refugee" *83: Best Canadian Stories* 146-59.

"Oh Jocelyn, My Friend" *CHJ* Mar 1953, 72, 74-80.

"The Old Woman" CBC *"Canadian Short Stories"* 12 May 1950 [Based on survey response].

"The Old Woman" *Canadian Short Stories* (1952), 48-60.

"The Old Woman" *Northern Lights* (1960), 727-36.

"The Old Woman" *British Motifs* (1973), 185-98 [Based on survey response].

"The Old Woman" *Private Place* (1975), 77-91.

"The Old Woman" *Writers and Writing* (1981), 162-74.

"The Old Woman" CBC *"Stories with John Drainie"* [date unknown] [Based on survey response].

"The One Who Asked" CBC *"Canadian Short Stories"* 8 Feb 1954 [Based on survey response].

"The Pair of Gloves" CBC *"Bernie Braden Reads a Story"* 11 Aug 1950 [Based on survey response].

"Paul and Phyllis" *Tam R* No. 72 (Fall 1977), 28-53.

"A Private Place" CBC *"Anthology"* 14 July 1973.

"A Private Place" *73: New Canadian Stories* 45-59.

"A Private Place" *Private Place* (1975), 5-21.

"A Question of Numbers" CBC *"Canadian Short Stories"* 1 Feb 1952 [Based on survey response].

"The Ride Home" *Mont* 32 (Oct 1958), 28, 30, 32.

"The Ride Home" CBC *"Anthology"* 18 Nov 1958.

"Rightly Call the Nymph" *Mont* 37 (May 1963), 30-5.

"Ruin and Wrack" CBC *"Anthology"* 15 July 1972 [Also entitled "The Enemy"].

"Salvage" *Private Place* (1975), 35-64.

"The Screaming Silence" *Lib* 30 (Oct 1953), 29, 48-50.

"Snow on Flat Top" *Mont* 34 (Dec 1960), 24-6.

"Snow on Flat Top" CBC *"Anthology"* 23 Dec 1960.

"So Many Have Died" *Tam R* No. 62 (1974), 9-30.

"So Many Have Died" *Private Place* (1975), 92-117 [Mistitled "Any Time at All" in first printing of collection].

"So Many Have Died" *Best Modern Canadian Short Stories* (1978), 218-35.

"Summer" CBC *"Anthology"* 13 July 1974.

"Summer" *75: New Canadian Stories* 42-56.
"Wait for Me" CBC *"Canadian Short Stories"* 21 Feb 1953 [Based on survey response].
"Windows" *CFM* No. 27 (1977), 102-12.
"The World Again" CBC *"Canadian Short Stories"* 16 Feb 1951 [Based on survey response].

Marshall, Linda‡
"My Testimony for the Lord" *Grub* 2:4 (Mar 1971), 6-12.
"Le plaidoyer d'une folle hommage à strindberg" *Grub* 1:5 (Apr 1970), 9-11.

Marshall, Lloyd‡
"Nostalgia" *Fifth Page* 1967, 14-6.

Marshall, Rand D.‡
"Ol' Biggy" *Was R* 16:2 (Fall 1981), 23-37.

Marshall, Tom
"An Evening in the Life of Harold Brunt" *Story So Far* 5 (1978), 121-8.
"The Man Who Loved Elizabeth Taylor" *JCF* No. 22 (1978), 38-43.
"Robert and Nancy (1968)" *Aurora* 1980 205-17.
[Untitled] *Ingluvin* No. 2 (Spr 1971), 63-4.

Marshalore [pseudonym]
"The Lady Lamp and the Fisherman" *Da Vinci* 2:1 No. 4 (Aut 1975), 94.

Marshman, Paul‡
"Northern Light" *Portico* 4:4 (1980), 21-5.

Marston, Tom‡
"An Old Soldier" *Chiaroscuro* 8 (1964), 31-3.
"The Traveller" *Chiaroscuro* 7 (1964), 33-8.

Marten, Anna‡
"The Songs" *Prism* 17:2 (Fall 1978), 88-96.

Martens, Debra‡
"A Blue Day" *Harvest* No. 13 (June 1982), 19-21.
"The Box" *Acta Vic* 105:1 (Fall 1980), 42-3.
"Natalia, Lady of Culture" *Des* 12:4/13:1/2 Nos. 34/35/36 (1981-82), 192-202.

Martijn, Charles A.†
"Pilgrim's Protest" *Forge* Dec 1956, 23-30.

Martin, Carl‡
"Much Is Forgiven" *Echo* (Tor) 5:1 (Oct-Jan 1973-74), 8-11.

Martin, Eric‡
"Trouble on Happy Lane" *Blow Up* 1:9 (Dec 1980), [2 pp].

Martin, Finley G.‡
"Scratch" *Inscape* 10:3 (Spr 1972 [?]), 19-26.

Martin, Gwyn‡
"Foxblood" *JCF* Nos. 28/29 (1980), 47-52.

Martin, J.L.
"A Lonesome Pine" *Can Audubon* 21 (Jan-Feb 1959), 25-7.

Martin, Morgan†
"West to the City of Lights" *Fid* No. 112 (Win 1977), 69-75.

Martin, Peter G.†
"If Winter Come" *Undergrad* Mar 1957, 12-6.
"The Moth" *Undergrad* Spr 1955, 15-9.

Martin, Rob‡
"The Life in a Day" *TUR* 82:2 [n.d.], [3 pp].

Martin, Sheila‡
"The Last Bus" *Acta Vic* 86:2 (Spr 1962), 7-8.

Martin, Tyndale‡
"It Hurts, Inside" *Forge* 1966, 21-3.

Martin, Will – *See* Green, H. Gordon.

Martineau, Barbara Halpern
"Spaces" *Room* 4:4 (1979), 8-15.

Martini, Clem‡
"Apologia for the LRT" *CBC "Alberta Anthology"* 11 Sept 1982.

Martinich, Aloysius‡
"Summer in Cleveland" *Generation* Jan 1966, 14-6 [Non-fiction?].
"Toy Boat" *Today* 19:9 (June 1964) [Based on *Generation*].
"Toy Boat" *Generation* Apr 1965, 18-23.
"Who Jew You" *Generation* Dec 1964, 17-20.

Martinson, Dorothy M.†
"The Fox" *CA & B* 57:2 (Win 1982), 14-5.

Marty, Sid (1944-)
"The Dude, the Warden and the Marvel Lake Kid" *Calgary Mag* 1 (Dec 1978), 34-7, 39-40, 77.

Maslowski, Alina†
"The Perfect Widow" *Green's* 3:4 (Sum 1975), 55-60.

Mason, Harriet†
"Cocoons" *Read Ch* 1:2 (Sum 1982), 56-63.

Mason, Kim
"The Seagull" *Voices of Kitimat* 1967 130-4.

Mason, Mike (1953-)

"All I Know About Incest" *CFM* Nos. 40-1 (1981), 34-49.

"All I Know About Incest" *83: Best Canadian Stories* 160-85.

"The Ballroom" *First Impressions* (1980), 138-40.

"Clouds for Sale" *Writers' News Man* 2:3 (May 1980), [2 pp].

"Connection" *First Impressions* (1980), 113-5.

"Dervish" *Grain* 6:2 [1978], 60-2.

"George Comes Down" *First Impressions* (1980), 121-3.

"Hills Are Like Blue Eyes" *First Impressions* (1980), 106-7.

"In the Boot" *Waves* 6:2 (Win 1978), 20-1.

"Laundromat Devotions" *Writers' News Man* No. 5 (Feb 1979), [1 p].

"Laundromat Devotions" *First Impressions* (1980), 110.

"Mondrian Skin" *First Impressions* (1980), 117-9.

"Morning Glory Jag" *First Impressions* (1980), 132-5.

"The Mountain" *First Impressions* (1980), 135-8.

"November Nose Job" *First Impressions* (1980), 123-8.

"The Only Decent Light" *78: Best Canadian Stories* 162-74.

"The Orange Bridge" *First Impressions* (1980), 108.

"Parchment" *Writers' News Man* Nos. 8/9 (Aug 1979), [2 pp].

"Parchment" *First Impressions* (1980), 116-7.

"Spring Cleaning" *First Impressions* (1980), 108-9.

"Stud" *First Impressions* (1980), 119-21.

"Sunday Afternoon" *First Impressions* (1980), 128-32.

"Tonsilitis" *First Impressions* (1980), 110-3.

"The Van" *Prism* 17:1 (Sum 1978), 146-53.

"The Van" *79: Best Canadian Stories* 84-94.

Massel, Dona Paul

"The Glass of Water" *New Q* 3:2 (Sum 1983), 31-8.

Massey, G. Merrin‡

"Green Ghosts" *AA* 66 (Sept 1975), 36-7.

Masters, Ian‡

"Nocturne" *TUR* 77:2 (Nov 1963), 29-30.

Masterton, Richard‡

"A Word Problem" *Scruncheons* 1:2 (Sept 1973), 71-4.

Matas, Carol‡

"What Is Work?" *Herizons* 1:6 (Aug 1983), 37.

Matas, Margaret Dwyer‡

"A Slice" *Prairie Fire* 4:5 (July-Aug 1983), 13-20.

Matcham, Linda†

"The Middletown Begonias" *Miss Chat* 16 (June-July 1979), 47, 88-94.

Mather, Barry

"Up-to-Date Nursery Stories" *MM* 69 (21 July 1956), 26.

Matheson, Graeme‡

"A Reading from Whitman" *Potlatch* No. 1 (Jan 1964), 20-3.

Matheson, Shirlee Smith†

"Willis" *Grain* 11:3 (Aug 1983), 37-40.

Matheson, Shirlee Smith

"The Wolves and the Heathens" *Treeline* 2 (1983), 88-92.

Mathews, Lawrence (1944-)

"Animal Noises" *Quarry* 29:1 (Win 1980), 62-8.
"The Border" *Quarry* 23:1 (Win 1974), 32-41.
"A Death in October" *Evidence* No. 8 (1964), 5-13.
"The Death of Arthur Rimbaud" *CFM* No. 17 (Spr 1975), 4-11.
"The Death of Arthur Rimbaud" *Magic Realism* (1980), 29-36.
"The Death of Arthur Rimbaud" *Not to Be Taken at Night* (1981), 144-54.
"A Fairy Tale" *Edge* No. 3 (Aut 1964), 30-4.
"Food" *CFM* No. 27 (Sum 1977), 28-33.
"Mars" *CF* 44 (Sept 1964), 135-6.
"O'Leary's Crack" *Quarry* 31:3 (Sum 1982), 20-7.

Mathews, Robin D. (1931-)

"Anniversary" *CF* 47 (July 1967), 81-4.
"The Biggest Bridge in the World" *Tam R* No. 43 (Spr 1967), 41-54.
"Climber" *QQ* 73 (1966), 235-43.
"Florentine Letourneau" *QQ* 90 (1983), 788-800.
"The Londoner" *QQ* 70 (1964), 551-8.
"My Brother, My Keeper" *Mont* 37 (Nov 1963), 28-30.
"Paris: April" *CF* 44 (Mar 1965), 277-8.
"The Strawberry Field" *Des* 14:5 No. 43 (Win 1983-84), 115-24.

Mathieson, Ken‡

" 'Edmonton, I Said,' I Said, Repeating What I Said" *New Mitre* No. 1 (1970), 42 [Dialogue].

Matson, Marshall†

"Daydreams" *Grub* 3:2 (June 1975), [2 pp].

Matsumura, Fumio‡

"Departure" *Folio* 13:2 (Spr 1961), 46-9.

Matta, John†

"Gills" *Scrivener* 4:1 (Win 1983), 38-9.

Matthews, Sandy‡

"Holiday 'Ad Lib' " *TUR* 77:1 (Oct 1963), 15-28.

Matthews, William‡

"The Case of the Trout in the Milk" *Moose R* 1:1 (1977), 11-2.

Matyas, Cathy (1957-)
"Ahead the Road Is" *Writ* No. 11 (Fall 1979), 55-60.
"Communion" *Grain* 7:3 [1979], 13-6.
"It's Too Late" *Des* 8:3 No. 19 (1977), 64-7.
"Push" *Writ* No. 9 (1977), 46-9.
"Theory of Forms" *UTR* 3 (Spr 1979), 6-7.

Maude, P.O.‡
"Harry" *Varsity Lit Issue* Fri, 13 Dec 1963, 18-20.
"A Reply from Darkest Dixie" *Varsity Lit Issue* Fri, 13 Dec 1963, 9.

Maude, Phil‡
'The Pitchman" *Acta Vic* 85:1 (Nov 1960), 14-5.

Mawhinney, Hal‡
'The Last Shall Be First??" *Windows* [1969?], [2 pp].

Mawson, Anthony R.‡
"Everything Will Be Wonderful" *Forge* 25:1 (Feb 1963), 75-80.

Maxted, Randolph
"Wrinkled Desert" *Grain* 10:4 (Nov 1982), 58-61.

Maxwell, Ward‡
"Acme Art & Sailboat Company / 'Tell Them Fetch' " *Inprint* 3:1 [n.d.], 27.

Maycock, Marjorie
'The Artist" *AA* 52 (July 1962), 21, 23-4.
'The Artist" *Stories with John Drainie* (1963), 106-11.

Mayer, Natalia‡
"Avoidance Coping" *Stardust* 2:2 [n.d.], 40-51.

Maynard, Fredelle Bruser
'The Red Dress" *Sat Eve Post* 240 (17 June 1967), 59-62.
'That Sensual Music" *Winnipeg Stories* (1974), 154-69.
"Worm in the Apple" *Lib* 41 (15 July 1964), 29.

Maynard, Rona
'The Grooviest Thing" *Catalyst* 2:2 (Win 1968-69), 9-15.

Mayne, Lise Guyanne‡
'The Season of Perfect Works" CBC "*Alberta Anthology*" 16 Oct 1982.

Mayoff, Steven†
"Glasgow" *Mam* [6:3] (Sum 1983), [3 pp].

Mays, John Bentley
'The Glorious Life and Death of Don Fernando de Soto" *Story So Four* (1976), 164-70.
'The Sewn Picture" *Cap R* Nos. 8/9 (Fall-Spr 1975-76), 49-68.
'The Victims' Ball" *Imp* 10:1 (Sum 1982), 48-50.

Mayse, Arthur

"The Beast That Couldn't Be" *Sat Eve Post* 227 (3 July 1954), 31, 74-6.
"Blood on His Hands" *Sat Eve Post* 230 (22 Mar 1958), 37, 46-7, 50, 52, 56.
"Boy on His Conscience" *Sat Eve Post* 228 (5 May 1956), 43, 126, 128, 130-1, 133.
"Bully on the Beach" *Sat Eve Post* 234 (22 Apr 1961), 24, 51-3, 62.
"Dead Man's Run" *Sat Eve Post* 228 (3 Sept 1955), 26, 56-7, 60-1.
"The Devil Was Aboard" *Sat Eve Post* 222 (17 June 1950), 30, 69, 71-2, 77-8, 80.
"Drag the Man Down!" *Sat Eve Post* 222 (4 Mar 1950), 24, 68-70, 72.
"The Finny Monster" *Blackwood's Mag* 293 (Feb 1963), 160-9.
"The Forbidden Island" *Sat Eve Post* 229 (23 Mar 1957), 35, 120, 122-3.
"Girl Stealer" *Sat Eve Post* 231 (5 July 1958), 27, 76-8.
"Girl with a Grudge" *Sat Eve Post* 229 (8 Dec 1956), 27, 126, 128-30.
"The Good Thief" *Sat Eve Post* 228 (2 July 1955), 34, 81-3.
"Good-by in Silence" *Sat Eve Post* 235 (3 Feb 1962), 22-3, 40-1.
"The Guilty Stain" *Sat Eve Post* 226 (15 May 1954), 30, 162-4, 167.
"The Haunted Dancers" *Sat Eve Post* 234 (8 July 1961), 20, 79-80.
"The Haunted Dancers" *Saturday Evening Post Stories* 1962 [Based on SSI].
"Haunted Ship" *Sat Eve Post* 226 (17 Apr 1954), 35, 68, 72, 75, 77, 79.
"The Hex-Man of Croaker's Hole" *MM* 64 (15 Mar 1951), 12, 40-3.
"The Lamp" *Lib* 28 (Jan 1952), 16-7, 34-8, 40.
"Midnight Mike" *Sat Eve Post* 226 (29 Aug 1953), 20, 52-3, 55.
"Midnight Mike" *Saturday Evening Post Stories* 1953 199-212.
"The Mountain of Death" *Sat Eve Post* 226 (7 Nov 1953), 24, 90, 93-4.
"A Name to Remember" *SW* 15 Feb 1964, 10-2.
"Outlaw Dog" *Sat Eve Post* 230 (27 July 1957), 31, 51, 54-5, 58-9.
"The Pirates of Copper River" *Sat Eve Post* 226 (25 July 1953), 34-5, 65-6, 69.
"Runaway Orphan" *Sat Eve Post* 227 (23 Oct 1954), 24, 42, 44, 49-50, 52.
"Sea Gypsy" *Sat Eve Post* 223 (30 June 1951), 26, 79-80, 83-5.
"Sea Gypsy" *Saturday Evening Post Stories* 1951 [Based on SSI].
"Second Chance" *Lib* 27 (June 1950), 57-63.
"Second Chance" *Rod & Gun* 66 (Sept 1964), 18-9, 22-6, 32.
"The Ship That Was Late" *SW* 21 Nov 1964, 26-9.
"Stolen Christmas" *Sat Eve Post* 225 (20 Dec 1952), 17, 81-3.
"The Terrible Temper of Kathy O'Mara" *Sat Eve Post* 226 (19 Dec 1953), 29, 68, 77.
"The Valley of Terror" *Sat Eve Post* 229 (19 Jan 1957), 34, 93-4, 96.
"The Widow's Kid" *Sat Eve Post* 230 (3 May 1958), 30, 93-5, 98.
"The Wildness in Her" *Sat Eve Post* 235 (24 Mar 1962), 48-9, 52-3, 56.
"Yesterday's Tomboy" *Sat Eve Post* 234 (7 Jan 1961), 39, 72, 76-7.

Mazei, Stephen‡

"Special" *Pinch* Oct 1965, 17.

McAiney, Phil‡

"And on My Left" *Generation* 1969, 7-9.
"Once Upon a Train" *Generation* 1970, [3 pp].
"What Do You Call Something Like This – Part Two" *Generation* 1969, 26-7 [Excerpt?].

McAllister, Clare

"Old Soldiers Also Die" *Can Welfare* 36 (15 Mar 1960), 70-1.
"Signing the 'A' Form" *Can Welfare* 36 (15 Jan 1960), 19-21.

McAllister, Lesley.

NO HABLA ESPANOL! Toronto: Prototype, 1982 [*viz.*, Identity 5 (Win 1982)].
"The Arrival" *Onion* 5:2 (Mar 1981), 2.
"Dr John H Watson: The Dead-Headed League" *OPT* 6:1 (Feb 1979), 4-5.
"Flight" *OPT* 7:6/7 (Jan-Feb 1981), 38-9.
"Jane" *OPT* 6:8 (Oct 1979), 6.
"The Land of Un" *JD* Hanukah 1974, 10-6.
"No Habla Espanol" *OPT* 7:4/5 (Sept-Oct 1980), 24-5.
"The Pool" *Quarry* 30:2 (Spr 1981), 28-34.
"The Trick" *Ichor* No. 1 (Win 1980), 45-51.

McAlpine, Mary†

"Mrs. Rankin" *CBC "Anthology"* 7 Dec 1954.
"Mrs. Rankin" *Tam R* No. 6 (Win 1958), 33-40.

McArthur, Dennis‡

"Tricking the Devil" *Outlook* Oct 1983, 6-11.

McAuliffe, Edward‡

"Fire in the Jungle" *Kaleidoscope* 1963, 21-3.

McCadden, Mike (1950-)

"The Boy and Annharrod" *Mal R* No. 57 (Jan 1981), 89-106.

McCaffery, Steve

"The Fall" *Story So Far* 3 (1974), 133.
"The Murder of Agatha Christie" *Story So Far* 5 (1978), 138-44.
"Sunday Funnies" *Story So Far* 5 (1978), 131-7.
[Untitled] *Imp* 4:4/5:1 (1976), [4 pp].

McCallum, Gary†

"The Chocolate Easter Rabbit" *event* 9:2 (1980), 64-78.

McCallum-Morash, Gordon†

"The Light at the End of the Cave" *Grain* 7:2 [1979], 17-21.
"Lions" *Grain* 6:1 [1978], 35-8.

McCarthy, Anne‡

"Be Thyself" *Driftwood* [No. 1] (Apr 1973), 45-6.
"Come Fly with Me" *Driftwood* [No. 1] (Apr 1973), 47-8.
"Together Again" *Driftwood* [No. 1] (Apr 1973), 44-5.

McCarthy, Dermot

"Totem" *Laom R* 1:1 (Dec-Jan 1975), 96-8.

McCarthy, Len‡

"The Case of the Yellow Corpse" *Legion* 48 (Mar 1974), 38-9.
"One Way to Skin a Cat" *Legion* 47 (May 1973), 47-8.

McCaughna, David†
"Marilyn Monroe Didn't Have a Date One Saturday Night" *First Encounter* 1971, 57-62.

McCauley, Glenn‡
'The Buried Life" *Acta Vic* 91:1 (Nov 1966), 3-5.

McClintock, Norah†
"Looking for Love" *Read Ch* 1:3 (Win 1982), 81-90.

McClung, Nellie (1929-)
'The Butterfly Ball" *Canadian Short Fiction Anthology* (1976), 105-6.

McClure, Mary†
"A Miner's Victory" *War Cry* 20 May 1961, 11.

McCluskey, John‡
'That Great Canadian Novel" *Grub* 4:2 (Mar 1977), [1 p].

McClusky, Ian†
"A Story" *Des* No. 13 (Win 1975), 74-9.

McColl, Earla-Kim‡
"Kristen" *Stump* 1:2 (Fall 1977), 36-7.

McColl, Len†
'Waiting for Mr. Big" *Toronto Star* Sun, 16 Oct 1983, D5.

McColl, William E.‡
'Becoming" *Tyro* 1962, 39-44.

McConnell, Alice (1913-1982)
"Aaron's Rod" *QQ* 62 (1955), 213-8.
'The Apricot Story" *Klanak Islands* (1959), 35-9.
'The Chalice of the Lord's Supper" *CBC "Anthology"* 18 Dec 1959.
"Child in Love" *Fid* No. 48 (Spr 1961), 29-38.
'The Feeble Virtue" *CBC "Anthology"* 10 May 1955.
"Goodbye Grannie" *CBC "Anthology"* 12 Mar 1957.
"In Sickness and in Health" *CBC "Anthology"* 1 Dec 1961.
'Participation" *Adelphi* (U.K.) 26 (Apr-June 1950), 230-2.
'Profile: Maria Madame des Salles Myself" *Prism* 1:2 (Win 1959), 36-49.
'The Thin Edge" *QQ* 65 (1958), 234-8.

McConnell, Gail A. (1939-)
"An Epitaph for Mrs. Parker" *Jargon* No. 2 (Spr 1961), 35-8.

McConnell, Shane‡
"Hunters in the Night" *Raven* No. 5 (Dec 1957), 4-7.
'The Hydrophobia Stunt" *Raven* No. 6 (Apr 1958), 29-33.

McConnell, William C. (1917-)

"The Catalyst" *pm* 1:2 (Dec-Jan [1951-52]), 35-45.

"Love in the Park" *Klanak Islands* (1959), 71-6.

"Love in the Park" *Great Canadian Short Stories* (1971), 178-83.

"Our Ballast Is Old Wine" *CF* 42 (July 1962), 85-7.

"Shale and Rock" *CBC "Anthology"* 20 Mar 1956.

[Title unknown] *CBC "Anthology"* 16 Dec 1980.

"Totem" *Canadian Short Stories* (1952), 137-45.

McCormack, Eric (1938-)

"Captain Joe" *New Q* 1:2 (Sum 1981), 49-53.

"Edward and Georgina" *New Q* 3:1 (Spr 1983), 5-11.

"The Fugue" *WCR* 17:4 (Apr 1983), 6-8.

"The Hobby" *Gamut* No. 2 [1983], 41-4.

"Lusawort's Meditation" *Gamut* No. 3 (May 1983), 25-7.

"No Country for Old Men" *Prism* 20:4 (Sum 1982), 19-20.

"The Temper" *Was R* 15:1 (Spr 1980), 37-44.

"Twins" *Mal R* No. 65 (July 1983), 117-21.

McCormack, Marilyn‡

"Random Error" *Introductions from an Island* 1974, 8-11.

McCormick, Frances

"The Countess Asked Us to Tea" *Chat* 40 (Feb 1967), 26, 89-91.

"Sunday Night Service at the Old Orange Hall" *Pres Record* 92 (Jan 1967), 3.

McCourt, Edward A. (1907-1972)

"Birth of a Hero" *FH* 4 July 1953, 16-7.

"Cranes Fly South" *Weekend* 5 (9 Apr 1955), 42-3.

"Cranes Fly South" *Stories from Western Canada* (1972), 141-5.

"Cranes Fly South" *Childhood and Youth in Canadian Literature* (1979), 27-31.

"Cranes Fly South" *Crossroads 1* (1979), 131-5.

"Cranes Fly South" *Inquiry into Literature* 1 (1980), 56-60.

"Cranes Fly South" *Read Dig* 117 (Sept 1980), 84-7 [Condensed].

"Cranes Fly South" *Contexts 2* (1981), 26-9.

"Cranes Fly South" *In Your Own Words* (1982), 10-4.

"Dance for the Devil" *Sat Eve Post* 225 (18 Oct 1952), 26-7, 55, 57-8, 60, 62.

"Dance for the Devil" *Saturday Evening Post Stories* 1952 229-43.

"Dance for the Devil" *Tigers of the Snow* (1973), 121-33.

"Dance for the Devil" *Moderne Erzühler der Walt: Kanada* (1976), 130-45 [As "Teufelstanz"; trans. Walter Riedel].

"Every Night Is Boat Race Night" *Mont* 37 (Mar 1963), 20-2 [Non-fiction?].

"The Hired Man" *QQ* 78 (1971), 60-9.

"The King Over the Water" *NR* 6:2 (June-July 1953), 25-34.

"The Locked Door" *NR* 3:6 (Aug-Sept 1950), 2-11.

"The Maltese Piano" *Mont* 37 (June 1963), 29-31.

"A Man for the Drink" *Mont* 35 (Dec 1961), 36-42.

"The Medicine Woman" *QQ* 73 (1966), 75-84.

"Night Patrol" *FH* 11 Mar 1954, 24-5, 31.

"Our Man on Everest" *Mont* 35 (Mar 1961), 24-7.

"Romance for Vivienne" *Weekend* 2 (24 May 1952), 20-1, 27.

"A Rope to Hang a Man" *SW* 31 Oct 1953, II:1, 12.
'The Trumpet Shall Sound" *FH* 6 Nov 1958, 16-7.
'The Uprooting" *FH* 25 Sept 1952, 24-5.
"Walk Through the Valley" *Weekend* 3 (3 Jan 1953), 22.
"Where There's a Will" *FH* 30 Aug 1951, 20-1.
'The White Mustang" *Canadian Short Stories* (1952), 14-26.
'The White Mustang" *Cavalcade of the North* (1958), 625-32.
'The White Mustang" *Wild Rose Country* (1977), 31-44.
'The White Mustang" *Inquiry into Literature* 1 (1980), 275-87.
"Who Walked with Kings" *FH* 29 June 1950, 18.

McCoy, Noddy
"Diving" *Story So Far* 3 (1974), 83-4.

McCoy, Sarah‡
'The Dark Ages" *Story So Four* (1976), 180-7.

McCracken, Melinda†
"And They Lived Happily Ever After" *Chat* 47 (Jan 1974), 29, 52-5.
'The Dainties" *Chat* 43 (Mar 1970), 32-3, 58, 60-2.
'Real Stars" *Miss Chat* 8 (9 Feb 1971), 82-8, 91.
"You Have to Learn to Fly" *Miss Chat* 7 (11 Aug 1970), 96, 150, 152, 155, 157.

McCubbin, Terrence‡
"Cabbagetown Overkill: The Story of One Man's Search for a Scene of the Ultimate Crime" *OPT* 6:1 (Feb 1979), 13.
"Editing Job in a Fake Park" *Rampike* 3:2 [1983?], 54.
'Remus Where Are You?" *Rampike* No. 1 [n.d.], 7-9.
"A Short History of Prophylactics" *Rampike* No. 2 (Spr 1981), 64-5.

McCutcheon, Kent‡
"Om" *Mouth* 2:1 [n.d.], 4.

McDermid, Doug‡
"Insignificant Invasion" *Acta Vic* 83:1 (Nov 1958), 23-5.

McDonald, Donna‡
"Dimitrios the Greek" *Take One* 1:7 (1967), 7-9 [Non-fiction?].

McDonald, I. Graham‡
"Waiting" *Gram* 1:2 (Feb [1976]), 9.

McDonald, Lynn‡
'The Wedding" *UCR* 1980-81, 54-9.

McDonald, Ruth†
" ... As Other Men Are" *Rapport* Jan 1969, 42.
"Day of Revelation" *Christian Home* 1 (Sept 1960), 21-4.
"Harvest of Love" *Onward* 29 Dec 1963, 6-7, 11.
"Lady for a Day" *Onward* 11 May 1958, 291-2, 302.
'The Lie" *Christian Home* 2 (Nov 1961), 26-8.
"Second Best" *Onward* 18 Mar 1962, 6-7, 14.

"Semi-Private" *Onward* 23 July 1961, 474-5.
"So Foolish Was I" *Onward* 60 (7 May 1950), 290-1, 303.
"The Tape Recorder" *Onward* 8 July 1956, 433-6.
"The Uninvited" *Onward* 8 May 1960, 295-7.

McDougall, Bill‡

"Escrebiscortion" *Other Voices* 4:3 (Nov 1968), 26-8.
"School Daze" *Other Voices* 5:2 (Aug 1969), [1 p].

McDougall, Colin M.

"Cardboard Soldier" *MM* 64 (15 July 1951), 13, 44-7.
"The Firing Squad" *MM* 66 (1 Jan 1953), 6, 28-33.
"The Firing Squad" *Northern Lights* (1960), 259-73.
"The Firing Squad" *Tigers of the Snow* (1973), 69-87.
"The Firing Squad" *Canadian Stories of Action and Adventure* (1978), 187-207.
"Let It Be Ellen" *Lib* 30 (May 1953), 36-7.
"Love Is for the Birds" *MM* 66 (15 July 1953), 14, 31-5.

McDougall, Joseph Easton‡

"Equimeat: A Three-Year Run to the Wire" *Can Business* 24 (Sept 1951), 32-3, 88, 90.
"I Prefer Dogs ... " *Can Business* 23 (Jan 1950), 52, 72, 74.
"Mr. Vertigo Tackles Inflation" *Can Business* 24 (July 1951), 36-7.

McElroy, Gil†

"AcroLat" *Nebula* No. 15 (1980), 17-20.

McElwee, Janie‡

[Untitled] *Talon* [2:1] (Aut 1964), 20.

McEwan, Lily†

"The Guest" *Can Messenger* 93 (Dec 1983), 8, 20-1, 23.
"Lead Kindly Light" *Can Messenger* 92 (Nov 1982), 8-9 [Non-fiction?].

McEwan, Tom†

"Paul Bunyan" *NF* 1:2 (Spr 1952), 1-7.
"Paul Bunyan" *Uk Can* 12 (15 Apr 1958), 9-10.

McEwen, Maud†

"High Walls" *Alberta Writers Speak* 1960, 24-7.

McFadden, David (1940-)

ANIMAL SPIRITS Toronto: Coach House Press, 1983.
THREE STORIES AND TEN POEMS Toronto: Prototype, 1982 [*viz., Identity* No. 2].
"The Christmas Card Hustler" *Harbinger* 3:5 (8 May 1970), 10.
"The Christmas Card Hustler" *Is* No. 8 (Spr 1970), [3 pp].
"The Christmas Card Hustler" *Animal Spirits* (1983), 129-50.
"The CN Tower" *Rampike* 3:1 (1983), 29.
"Drapes" *Quarry* 19:3 (Spr 1970), 22-8.
"Drapes" *Story So Far* (1971), 41-7.
"Drapes" *Animal Spirits* (1983), 201-24.

"Dying Metaphors" *Three Stories* (1982), [6 pp].

"Eckankar" *Three Stories* (1982), [2 pp].

"Everyday Life in the Twentieth Century" *Animal Spirits* (1983), 11-45.

"Free Samples" *Story So Far* 3 (1974), 148.

"Here Are Some More Snaps" *Fid* No. 87 (Nov-Dec 1970), 6-14.

"Hiroko Writes a Story" *Interface* 5:1 (Jan 1982), 75-7.

"Hiroko Writes a Story" *83: Best Canadian Stories* 69-81.

"The Iroquois Hotel" *Story So Far* 3 (1974), 143-8.

"The Iroquois Hotel" *Animal Spirits* (1983), 93-109.

"The List of Dreams" *Animal Spirits* (1983), 177-99.

"The Mysterious Moon Men of Canada" *Animal Spirits* (1983), 81-90.

"An Old Book of Poems Authored by My Brother" *Rampike* 3:2 [1983?], 22.

"The Pleasures of Love" *74: New Canadian Stories* 36-42.

"The Pleasures of Love" *Animal Spirits* (1983), 111-27.

"Queen Elizabeth II, Seduced" *Atropos* 1:1 (Spr 1978), 47 [Also entitled "The Seduction of Queen Elizabeth II"].

"The Rocks at the Bottom of the Lake" *Per* No. 3 (Spr 1978), 9-16.

"The Rocks at the Bottom of the Lake" *Animal Spirits* (1983), 227-43.

"The Seduction of Queen Elizabeth II" *Rampike* 3:1 (1983), 28 [Also entitled "Queen Elizabeth II, Seduced"].

"Seven Seas" *Three Stories* (1982), [4 pp].

"The Story of Anne" *Rampike* 2:1/2 (1982), 37.

"The Tremendous Spasm of Pain" *Animal Spirits* (1983), 69-79.

"Who Can Avoid a Place?" *72: New Canadian Stories* 112-21.

"Who Can Avoid a Place?" *Animal Spirits* (1983), 153-75.

"A Woman and Her Dog" *Animal Spirits* (1983), 47-66.

McFadden, Isobel (1907-)

"After These Years!" *Missionary Monthly* 34 (June 1959), 5-7.

"Bharta" *Onward* 28 Dec 1958, 820-1, 830.

"Complications" *Missionary Monthly* 34 (Feb 1959), 10-1.

"Endings and Beginnings" *Missionary Monthly* 33 (Oct 1958), 437-8.

"Hard Decision" *Missionary Monthly* 35 (Mar 1960), 16-9.

"Into His Own Country" *Missionary Monthly* 36 (Dec 1961), 19-21, 28-9.

"It Matters in Trinidad Too" *Missionary Monthly* 33 (Nov 1958), 483-4.

"Neighbors and Peculiar Sheep" *Missionary Monthly* 33 (Dec 1958), 531-2.

"Stories without Ending" *Missionary Monthly* 34 (Jan 1959), 3-4.

McFarlane, Beverley‡

"A Time for Sharing" *Spear* 6 (Dec 1976), 35-6, 45.

McFarlane, Greg†

"Digestive System" *Mam* 6:2 (Win 1983), [3 pp].

McFarlane, Lucy‡

"They Said He Was Simple" *Nfld Q* 77:2/3 (Sum-Fall 1981), 56-7.

McFee, Oonah.

"Song of Araby" *Texas Q* 14:1 (Spr 1971), 27-35.

"Song of Araby" *CBC "Anthology"* 29 Sept 1973.

McGillicutty, Jean-Luc – *See* Yates, J. Michael.

McGillivary, Judy
"Leaps" *Prism* 12:3 (Spr 1973), 20-2.
"The Picture" *CFM* No. 4 (Aut 1971), 50-2.

McGoogan, Kenneth
"Claudette" *Repos* Nos. 19/20 (Sum-Fall 1976), 75-81.
"Doing It" *Writ* No. 6 (Fall 1974), 25-30.
"Gazette Boy" *Quarry* 31:2 (Spr 1982), 30-6.
"The Incorrigible McGillicutty" *Alive* 3:6 No. 25 [1973?], 37-8.
"Oscar" *Canadian Short Fiction Anthology* (1976), 107-11.
"Thibideau" *Repos* Nos. 19/20 (Sum-Fall 1976), 71-4.

McGorman, Don (1947-)
"The Event" *Quarry* 31:1 (Win 1982), 40-8.
"Just Like the Orient Express" *JCF* Nos. 28/29 (1980), 11-30.
"Miss Banister and the Horseman" *Was R* 16:1 (Spr 1981), 19-28.

McGrath, Jerry
"Fog" *Waves* 10:4 (Spr 1982), 24-5.

McGrath, Patrick†
"The Efficient Intellectual" *Writ* No. 12 (1980), 26.
"The End of the Line" *New Bodies* (1981), 83-9.
"Tickets" *Writ* No. 12 (1980), 27-8.
"Writer's Block" *Writ* No. 12 (1980), 29-30.

McGrath, Robin
"The Parish House" *Flare* 5 (Mar 1983), 69-70, 72-5.

McGregor, Lee‡
"Lee 'N' Me" *Repos* No. 1 [1972], 10-1.

McHardy, Vincent (1955-)
"Better Than the Streets" *New Q* 2:3 (Fall 1982), 61-3.
"Keepsake" *Quarry* 32:2 (Spr 1983), 25-31.
"The Miracle Worker" *Poor Man's Press: Wealth/Poverty* (1983), 3 [Based on survey response].
"Sweet Trick" *Horror Show* (U.S.) Fall 1983, 34 [Based on survey response].
"Through a Chestnut Clearly" *Read Ch* 1:1 (Spr 1982), 47-70.
"When Evergreens Brown" *Read Ch* 1:3 (Win 1982), 31-5.

McIlroy, Kimball
"Hockey Etiquette" *SW* 14 Apr 1951, I:8, 12.
"Hockey Wife" *SW* 18 Feb 1956, I:3.
"Lucky Guy" *SW* 12 Mar 1955, II:6.
"Patrol" *NHM* 51 (Sept 1950), 72-4.
"Rookie Centre" *Weekend* 5 (26 Feb 1955), 12-3, 31, 43.
"The Secret Pitch" *SW* 23 Oct 1954, II:4.
"Southern Style" *SW* 7 Nov 1953, I:10, 12.
"Walter Simpson's Satellite" *SW* 7 Jan 1956, I:1.

McIntosh, Dave‡
"Remembrance" *Legion* 32 (Nov 1957), 14-5.

McIntosh, Don‡
"Malta" *NeWest R* 6:5 (Jan 1981), 5-6, 12.
"Mrs. T. and Her Boarder" *Gas Rain* [1] (Mar 1977), 23-6.

McIntosh, Robin‡
"NO MORE MESSAGES PLEASE stop" *Stump* Aut 1981, 25-8.

McIver, Emily Hollis†
"*Für Elise* Before the War" *Antig R* No. 40 (Win 1980), 53-64.

McKay, Fortesque
"The Indian Giver" *North* 13 (July-Aug 1966), 16-7.
"An Indian Tale of Birch Bark, Musk-Rat Tails & Rabbits Ears" *North* 13 (Nov-Dec 1966), 14-7.

McKay, Jacqueline‡
"Canada – The Land of Golden Opportunity" *Scar Fair* 8 (1981), 49-51.

McKay, Jean (1943-)
"June" *Camrose R* No. 1 [1981], 25-6.
"Old Photographs" *Grain* 2:2 [1974], 5-6.
"Storm" *Story So Four* (1976), 188-9.
"The White Tornado" *Imp* 4:2 (Spr 1975), [6 pp].

McKay, Muriel Saint
"The Birthday Present" *Weekend* 3 (14 Feb 1953), 10-1, 30.
"The Covenant" *Chat* 27 (Aug 1954), 16-7, 52, 54.
"Deep Roots" *Atl Guardian* 9 (Jan 1952), 36-9.
"The Exile" *Atl Guardian* 8 (July 1951), 49, 51-2, 55-6.
"The Hero" *Weekend* 5 (7 May 1955), 40, 44.
"The Hero" *FH* 8 Feb 1962, 23.
"I'll Take Archie" *Weekend* 2 (4 Oct 1952), 30.
"The Red Dory" *Weekend* 1 (29 Sept 1953), 34, 49, 51-2.
"Testing Ground" *SW* 7 May 1955, I:9.
"Uncle Samuel and the Crackie" *Atl Guardian* 10 (Sept 1953), 22-6.
"Uncle Samuel's Lady Love" *Weekend* 4 (6 Nov 1954), 37-8.
"The Way of the Sea" *Atl Guardian* 8 (Oct 1951), 38-41.

McKechnie, Ann
THE SATURDAY PARTY Toronto: Clarke, Irwin, 1973 [Based on CBIP].

McKee, Barbara‡
"The Old Corn Broom" *Contact* 3:3 (Fall 1974), 27-30.

McKeever, Harry Paul‡
"Escape!" *Rod & Gun* 61 (May 1960), 14 [Based on CPI].

McKellar, Iain‡
"Old Hunter" *Halcyon* 12 (Win 1966-67), 15-6.

McKenna, Brian J.‡
"Piano Blues" *Sand Patterns* No. [22] (Sum 1978), [2 pp].

McKenna, Colin‡
"From the Bridge" *Connexion* 1:1 (Dec 1968), [1 p] [Sketch?].

McKenzie, Earl†
"The Man and the Four-Eyed Dog" *Prism* 16:2 (Fall 1977), 66-73.

McKevitt, Garry (1947-)
"The Steps" *Mal R* No. 50 (Apr 1979), 178-91.
"The Steps" *Illusion Two* (1983), 73-86.

McKibbon, Mollie Pearce‡
"Petits Fours" *Driftwood* [No. 1] (Apr 1973), 22-4.

McKie, Florence‡
"For a New Life" *Edmonton Journal* Fri, 19 Feb 1962, 4.

McKim, Audrey (1909-)
"Heaven to Betsy" *CG* 78 (Apr 1959), 53-6, 58.
"Summer Storm" *CG* June 1956, 12, 44, 46-8.

McKim, Eleanor†
"The Indian Amulet" *Nfld Q* 55:2 (June 1956), 21-3, 25-6, 28.

McKinley, Philip‡
"Chapperwell's Secret" *Alpha* 5:2 (Win 1980), 5, 22, 30.

McKinnon, Barry†
"Lust Lodge" *Pulp Mill* (1977), 92-110.

McKinnon, Wayne Francis‡
"Maybe Tomorrow" *Sand Patterns* No. 18 (1976), [5 pp].

McLachlin, Stella†
"Then There Was This Character Mona Something or Other" *Canadian Short Fiction Anthology* (1976), 113-8.

McLaren, Floris (1904-)
"The Accordian" *Mayfair* 28 (Feb 1954), 32-3, 61-2.
"Chance Meeting in an Elevator" *Story So Far* 3 (1974), 149.
"A Date with Dora" *Canadian Short Stories* (1952), 61-7.
"A Day on the Trail" *CBC "Anthology"* 16 Aug 1975.
"The Man Who Saw the Sea-Serpent" *British Columbia* (1961), 221-31.
"The Story of Jenny" *CBC "Anthology"* 17 Jan 1956.
"The Story of Jenny" *Mont* 33 (Dec 1959), 51-3.

McLaughlin, Hilary‡
"Parasites of the Wasteland" *Random* [3:1] (Sept [1968]), 4-8 [Non-fiction?].

McLaughlin, Jeffrey‡
"A Search for More Than a Strawberry Sister" *Generation* 1971, [3 pp].

McLaughlin, Lorrie (? -1971?)

"The Easter-Egg House" *SW* 31 Mar 1956, I:7.

"The Girl That Men Forgot" *CHJ* Oct 1956, 31, 34, 36-7.

"Goodbye John" *CHJ* Nov 1957, 32, 43-4.

"Just Like Sisters" *Can Messenger* 78 (July-Aug 1968), 12-3.

"Love Is a Funny Thing" *CHJ* Mar 1956, 15, 57-9.

"Most Beautiful Night" *CHJ* Aug 1957, 23, 42, 44-5.

"My Name Is Ginny Martin" *Can Messenger* 77 (Nov 1967), 12-3.

"Oh Rupert, Dear, We Love You" *Can Messenger* 77 (July-Aug 1967), 16-7.

"One of Those Days" *Grail* Nov 1956, 34-41 [Based on CPLI].

"September Wedding" *AA* 48 (Sept 1957), 37-8.

"Sister of the Bride" *SW* 1 Nov 1958, 26-8.

"The Strictly Private Secretary" *CHJ* Jan 1957, 14, 60.

"What About Maggie?" *FH* 28 June 1951, 18-9, 27.

McLaughlin, Paul‡

"Henry" *Vane* No. 4 [n.d.], [4 pp].

McLaughlin, Peter‡

"Behind Every Successful Pope" *Des* No. 6 (Spr 1973), 49-50.

"Creation Story" *Des* Nos. 8/9 (Spr-Sum 1974), 62.

"Fourmidable" *Des* Nos. 8/9 (Spr-Sum 1974), 62-3.

"A Gathering of Riddles" *Des* No. 13 (Win 1975), 63.

"I Got Your Card About the Chickadees" *Story So Four* (1976), 192-4.

"The Maidservant" *Des* No. 6 (Spr 1973), 48-9.

"Night Thoughts" *Des* Nos. 8/9 (Spr-Sum 1974), 64.

"On Going" *Des* Nos. 8/9 (Spr-Sum 1974), 64-5.

"Paudeen's Riddle" *Des* No. 7 (Fall 1973), 56.

"The Queen" *Des* No. 7 (Fall 1973), 55.

"The Stool" *Des* No. 7 (Fall 1973), 57.

"This Actually Happened to a Friend of Mine" *Story So Four* (1976), 195-7.

McLean, Anne

"Black Chute" *Room* 4:3 (1979), 54-62.

"Black Falls" *Outset* 1973, 105-12.

"Changing for the Worse" *Fireweed* No. 10 (Spr 1981), 8-19.

"Confessions of Lucille Robillard, Accomplice" *Saturday Night at the Forum* (1981), 26-32.

"A Journal of Mona" *CF* 58 (Jan-Feb 1979), 27-30.

"Life on the Roof" *Cap R* No. 29 (1983), 60-70.

"Mallardville Monologues" *Fireweed* Nos. 5/6 (Win-Spr 1979-80), 54-7.

"Nineteen Seventy Five" *Cap R* No. 29 (1983), 48-59.

"Story" *Wee Giant* 1:3 (Spr 1978), 40-1.

McLean, D.A.‡

"Thoughtful Hunger: A Very Short Story" *Pom Seed* 1982, 55-6.

McLean, Rachel†

"Brian the Bull" *One Out of Many* (1975), 55-6.

"The Christmas Gift" *One Out of Many* (1975), 51-4.

"Harry the Hound Goes to Town" *One Out of Many* (1975), 46-50.

McLellan, Helen‡

"Sufficient unto the Day" *Stories with John Drainie* (1963), 8-13.

McLellan, Pat‡

"Let Us Remember" *Alive* No. 59 (13 Nov 1976), 4.
"One Enemy" *Alive* No. 68 (12 Mar 1977), 6-7.
"Wildcat" *Alive* No. 105 (18 Mar 1978); No. 106 (25 Mar 1978), 17-20; 14-6 [Listed as short story].
"The Wrench" *Alive* No. 57 (30 Oct 1976), 7.

McLeod, E. Vessie (1918-)

"The Difference" CBC "*Stories with John Drainie*" [1963-64?] [Based on survey response].
"The Difference" *QQ* 72 (1965), 542-8.
"The Difference" *Argosy* (U.K.) May 1967 [Based on survey response].
"The Difference" *SABC* [1971?] [Based on survey response].
"Long Ago and Far Away" CBC "*Stories with John Drainie*" 2 June 1966 [Based on survey response].
"Long Ago and Far Away" *FH* 29 Sept 1966, 45, 55.
"Reflections" *Woman's Outlook* (U.K.) [1965?] [Based on survey response].
"So Many 'If's' " *Family Star* (U.K.) 25 Feb 1967 [Based on survey response].
"Sound of Christmas" *Family Star* (U.K.) 1966 [Based on survey response].

McLeod, Joseph†

"Once There Was an Ordinary Boy" *Antig R* No. 37 (Spr 1979), 33-8.

McLeod, Kellsie – *See* McLeod, E. Vessie.

McLeod, Murdoch

POEMS AND STORIES FROM RAMBLES AROUND BRITISH COLUMBIA FOR B.C. CENTENNIAL YEAR 1958 Vancouver: privately printed, 1958.
"The Bear Story" *Rambles Around British Columbia* (1958), 42-5.
"Crows Nest" *Rambles Around British Columbia* (1958), 60-1.
"The Gardner Canal Goat" *Rambles Around British Columbia* (1958), 34-6, 38, 41.
"Lover's Leap" *Rambles Around British Columbia* (1958), 1-10.
"On the Crow's Nest Pass" *Rambles Around British Columbia* (1958), 59-60.
"Running the Rapids" *Rambles Around British Columbia* (1958), 66-8.
"Slocan Days" *Rambles Around British Columbia*" (1958), 50-5.

McLure, Bruce†

"The Big Bird Theory" *Prism* 18:1 (Spr-Sum 1979), 77-8.

McNamara, Eugene (1930-)

SALT Delta, B.C.: Sono Nis Press, 1975.
THE SEARCH FOR SARAH GRACE Windsor: Black Moss Press, 1977.
"After the Ball" *CHEZ-FM* (Ott) 19 June 1983 [Based on survey response].
"The Art of the Novel" *Chicago Mag* 28 (Nov 1979), 189[+?] [Based on PPI and survey response].
"The Art of the Novel" CBC "*Anthology*" Mar 1981 [Based on survey response].
"At the Going Down of the Sun and in the Morning" *SN* 96 (Mar 1981), 42-7.
"Beautiful Country, Burn Again" *CFM* No. 6 (Spr 1972), 57-63.
"Beautiful Country, Burn Again" *Salt* (1975), 70-8.

"Between" *QQ* 88 (1981), 264-72.

"The Big Moonlight Dance Cruise" *Quartet* (U.S.) 4 Nos. 30/31 (Spr 1970), 11-6.

"Bright, Agile, Impassable and Subtle" *SN* 94 (June 1979), 32-6, 38.

"A Change of Scene" *UWR* 4:2 (Spr 1969), 54-8.

"A Change of Scene" *Search for Sarah Grace* (1977), 50-5.

"Changes" *CFM* No. 17 (Spr 1975), 81-91.

"Changes" *CBC "Anthology"* 18 Sept 1976.

"Changes" *Search for Sarah Grace* (1977), 107-19.

"Convention" *First Encounter* 1969-70, 43-5.

"The Death of Buddy Holly" *Prism* 13:2 (Win 1973), 120-6.

"The Death of Buddy Holly" *Salt* (1975), 79-85.

"The Distance Between" *Evidence* No. 8 (1964), 20-31.

"The Distances" *Salt* (1975), 11-28.

"Down at the Point" *US Catholic* 31 (July 1965), 45-9.

"Down the Road" *Mal R* No. 16 (Oct 1970), 5-12.

"Down the Road" *Salt* (1975), 86-93.

"The Drowned Girl" *Western Humanities R* 24 (1970), 261-70.

"The Drowned Girl" *Salt* (1975), 101-12.

"Entropy" *CFM* No. 43 (1982), 65-73.

"Entropy" *Illusion Two* (1983), 63-72.

"The Ethics of Survival" *Denver Q* 4:1 (Spr 1969), 66-73.

"The Ethics of Survival" *Salt* (1975), 94-100.

"Fathers and Daughters" *Denver Q* 7:1 (Spr 1972), 46-62.

"Fathers and Daughters" *Search for Sarah Grace* (1977), 28-41.

"The Home Front" *Nebula* No. 3 (1976), 50-2.

"The Howard Parker Montcrief Hoax" *CFM* No. 12 (Win 1974), 39-54.

"The Howard Parker Montcrief Hoax" *Best American Short Stories* 1975 178-96.

"The Howard Parker Montcrief Hoax" *Search for Sarah Grace* (1977), 67-86.

"In the Museum" *December* (U.S.) 12:1/2 (1970), 39-41.

"Jamboree" *Copperfield* 2 (Spr 1970), 22-7.

"Jamboree" *Salt* (1975), 53-6.

"Just for the Night" *Quarry* 32:2 (Spr 1983), 53-63.

"Last Summer of Youth" *St. Jude Mag* Mar 1963 [Based on survey response].

"Made in Canada" *QQ* 75 (1968), 597-612.

"Made in Canada" *Demanding Age* (1970), 59-72.

"Made in Canada" *Die Weite Reise* (1974), 305-25 [Trans. Karl Heinrich].

"Made in Canada" *Stime der DDR* 6 June 1974 [Radio broadcast; based on survey response].

"Made in Canada" *Salt* (1975), 38-52.

"Made in Canada" *Transitions 2* (1978), 173-86.

"The May Irwin-John C. Rice Kiss" *Salt* (1975), 57-69.

"The May Irwin-John C. Rice Kiss" *Mal R* No. 36 (Oct 1975), 120-32.

"Midwinter" *Ont R* No. 8 (Spr-Sum 1978), 43-54.

"Midwinter" *CBC "Anthology"* 10 Feb 1979.

"Nineteen-Eleven" *CFM* Nos. 40/41 (1981), 108-19.

"Nineteen-Eleven" *Metavisions* (1983), 149-60.

"A Note on the Academic Life" *Texas Q* 9:1 (Spr 1966), 168-70.

"A Note on the Academic Life" *Search for Sarah Grace* (1977), 56-60.

"On One Side of Silence" *Quartet* (U.S.) 3 No. 24 (Fall 1968), 13-5.

"Pushing Fifty" *CFM* No. 27 (1977), 113-22.

"Pushing Fifty" *79: Best Canadian Stories* 69-83.
"The Search for Sarah Grace" *CFM* No. 21 (Spr 1976), 72-87.
"The Search for Sarah Grace" *Search for Sarah Grace* (1977), 96-101.
"The Terrible Trap" *Ave Maria* 103 (23 Apr 1966), 26-9.
"The Terrible Trap" *Search for Sarah Grace* (1977), 26-9.
"Three Women" *Quarry* 27:2 (Sum 1978), 53-60.
"To Burn" *CF* 47 (Jan 1968), 230-1.
"To Burn" *Forum* (1972), 406-8.
"To Burn" *Search for Sarah Grace* (1977), 102-6.
"The Unprotected Border" *Mal R* No. 26 (Apr 1973), 9-17.
"The Unprotected Border" *Salt* (1975), 29-37.
"Visitation" *CFM* Nos. 2/3 (Spr-Sum 1971), 31-8.
"Visitation" *Search for Sarah Grace* (1977), 42-9.
"A Walk to the Paradise Garden" *Evidence* No. 10 (1967), 161-7.
"A Walk to the Paradise Garden" *Search for Sarah Grace* (1977), 87-96.
"The Way to Concord" *Quartet* (U.S.) 3 No. 19 (Sum 1967), 9-14.
"The Way to Concord" *Search for Sarah Grace* (1977), 61-6.
"What More Will the Bones Allow?" *Edge* No. 8 (Fall 1968), 99-106.
"You Can't Get There from Here" *WCR* 4:3 (Jan 1970), 29-33.
"You Can't Get There from Here" *Salt* (1975), 113-21.

McNamee, James (1904-)

"Are People Monkeys?" *MM* 67 (1 Mar 1954), 22-3, 30, 32.
"Atlas Carries the Heavy Load" *CBC* "*Anthology*" 20 Dec 1955.
"G. Truehart, Man's Best Friend" *Over the Horizon* (1960) [Based on SSI].
"Give the Bride a Kiss, George" *MM* 66 (15 Sept 1953), 16, 66-9.
"How to Handle Women" *MM* 68 (1 Oct 1955), 16-7, 48, 50, 52-3.
"The Richest Woman in Town" *MM* 67 (1 Oct 1954), 16, 67-8, 70-1.
"The Shameless Wooing of Clarence Patterson" *MM* 68 (2 Apr 1955), 26-7, 42, 44, 46.
"Two Ways to Hook a Sucker" *MM* 66 (15 Aug 1953), 18-9, 30-1.

McNeil, Beatrice‡

"The Pyramid" *Fruits of Experience* (1978), 83-92.

McNichol, Philip‡

"Along a Dusty Road" *Chiaroscuro* 9 (1965-66), 19-24.
"A Verb: To Love" *Chiaroscuro* 9 (1965-66), 57-68.

McPhee, Brian‡

"Deux Croissants" *AA* 53 (June 1963), 55-60.

McQueen, Andrew‡

"Divided Chestnut Sleep" *First Encounter* 13 (1983), 22-3.

McQueen-Darcie, Margaret†

"The Race" *Mont Writers' Forum* [2:9] (Sept-Oct 1980), 13-6.

McQuillan, Pat‡

"The Kid" *Outset* 1973, 113-9.

McQuinn, Maureen‡

"Counterpart" *Bridle of Glass* (1973), 44.

McRae, Garfield (1938-)

"Millie, 'Ears,' and the Supreme Test" *Winnipeg Stories* (1974), 47-57.

"Millie, 'Ears,' and the Supreme Test" *Univ of Manitoba Alumni J* 34:3 (May 1974), 4-8.

"Miriam" *West Producer* 30 Apr 1970, C2 [Based on survey response].

"Miriam" *CBC [Winn] "Manitoba Short Stories"* 1977 [Based on survey response].

"The Old Bread Truck" *Images About Manitoba* 1:1 (Nov 1975), 5.

"A Summer's Ending" *West Producer* 10 Oct 1974, C2 [Based on survey response].

McRae, Robert†

"Slide" *QQ* 89 (1982), 89-99.

McRobbie, Genevieve

"Our Mysterious Neighbour" *Onward* 27 Dec 1959, 820-1, 824.

"The Reluctant Dog Catcher" *Onward* 19 July 1959, 458-9.

McWhinnie, Jill‡

"Dust to Dust" *Scar Fair* 1 (1973-74), 27-37.

"Pipe Dreams" *Scar Fair* 2 (1974-75), [10 pp].

McWhirter, George (1939-)

BODYWORKS Ottawa: Oberon Press, 1974.

COMING TO GRIPS WITH LUCY Ottawa: Oberon Press, 1982.

GOD'S EYE Ottawa: Oberon Press, 1981.

"Amigo" *God's Eye* (1981), 17-33.

"Another Friend for Mr. Duck" *God's Eye* (1981), 121-31.

"Another Friend for Mr. Duck" *Shearsman* (Malaysia) 3 [date unknown], 78-84 [Based on survey response].

"The Assassins of Don Chucho" *CFM* Nos. 40/41 (1981), 99-107.

"The Assassins of Don Chucho" *God's Eye* (1981), 34-47.

"The Burn" *Bodyworks* (1974), 134-41.

"The Cicada and the Cockroach" *God's Eye* (1981), 60-8.

"Coming to Grips with Lucy" *CFM* Nos. 40/41 (1981), 90-8.

"Coming to Grips with Lucy" *Coming to Grips with Lucy* (1982), 32-46.

"The Country" *CBC "Anthology"* Feb 1980 [Based on survey response].

"The Country" *God's Eye* (1981), 5-16.

"Cromac's Charabanc" *Bodyworks* (1974), 107-9.

"The Entertainment" *Ann Arbor R* No. 7 (1969) [Based on survey response].

"The Entertainment" *Bodyworks* (1974), 102-6.

"An Exchange of Skins" *CFM* No. 6 (Spr 1972), 52-6.

"An Exchange of Skins" *Bodyworks* (1974), 113-9.

"The Extinction of 'H' " *Prism* 8:3 (Spr 1969), 83-93.

"The Extinction of 'H' " *Bodyworks* (1974), 53-63.

"The Extinction of 'H' " *Stories from Pacific & Arctic Canada* (1974), 119-30.

"Firstie" *Coming to Grips with Lucy* (1982), 5-16.

"The Flags" *Coming to Grips with Lucy* (1982), 128-40.

"The Flags" CBC "Anthology" Nov 1982 [Based on survey response].

"The Followers (or Babes in the Field)" *Coming to Grips with Lucy* (1982), 62-78.

"A French Girl to Stay" *God's Eye* (1981), 93-102.

"From the Perimeters of Sarne" *Bodyworks* (1974), 78-9.

"A Good Swift Kick" *Coming to Grips with Lucy* (1982), 79-88.

"The Harbinger" *72: New Canadian Stories* 57-63.

"The Harbinger" *Bodyworks* (1974), 127-33.

"Heresy for Carnivores and Golfers" *Bodyworks* (1974), 80-90.

"A Horse Ride" *God's Eye* (1981), 69-79.

"An Imitation of Two Men" *Coming to Grips with Lucy* (1982), 47-61.

"The Man Who Wanted to Be a Spaniard" *Coming to Grips with Lucy* (1982), 105-16.

"Marinade" *Bodyworks* (1974), 33-43.

"Montage" *DNA* Nos. 5/6 [date unknown] [Based on survey response].

"Montage" *Bodyworks* (1974), 120-6.

"Moses to the Waterwork" *Bodyworks* (1974), 66-77.

"Museum Piece" *CFM* No. 1 (Win 1971), 42-55.

"Museum Piece" *Bodyworks* (1974), 19-27.

"The Necessity of Billy" *Coming to Grips with Lucy* (1982), 117-27.

"Nobody's Notebook" *CFM* Nos. 40/41 (1981), 81-9.

"Nobody's Notebook" *God's Eye* (1981), 80-92.

"Quarantine" *CFM* Nos. 32/33 (1979), 140-9.

"Quarantine" *Illusion Two* (1983), 51-61.

"Raising the Cougar" *Coming to Grips with Lucy* (1982), 17-31.

"The Sarnean: A Definition" *Bodyworks* (1974), 64-5.

"A School for Entertainers" *Bodyworks* (1974), 12-8.

"A School for Entertainers" CBC "Anthology" 6 May 1978.

"A Sea Change" CBC "Anthology" [Based on survey response; probable dates: 21 or 27 Mar 1970].

"A Sea Change" *Bodyworks* (1974), 9-11.

"Something to Grin At" *God's Eye* (1981), 103-20.

"The Song of Sarne" *Bodyworks* (1974), 47-52.

"The Sphincter" *DNA* Nos. 5/6 [date unknown] [Based on survey response].

"The Sphincter" *Bodyworks* (1974), 91-101.

"Strangulation" *Coming to Grips with Lucy* (1982), 89-104.

"Two Travellers" *God's Eye* (1981), 48-59.

"Why No Familiar Tune?" *Bodyworks* (1974), 142-51.

"Why No Familiar Tune?" *Carolina Q* 26:2 (Spr 1974), 92-100.

"Without Prefix" *Bodyworks* (1974), 28-32.

Meade, Ed†

"The Return" *View from the Silver Bridge* [1:2] [n.d.], 14-8.

Meadow, Barry‡

"King Andy" *Can Horse* 7 (Aug 1967), 31, 61.

Meckler, Frances†

"An Unexpected Prairie Blizzard" *Saskatchewan Homecoming* (1971), 193-4.

Medovoy, George

"The Man Who Came and Went" *JD* 1:1 (Spr 1970), 7.

Mehren, Kay Gullickson – *See* Mehren, Peter and Mehren, Kay Gullickson.

Mehren, Peter and Mehren, Kay Gullickson‡
"Metric Patrol" *Scar Fair* 7 (1979-80), 23-4.

Melamet, Max†
"The Adventures of Chaim Pferd" *Can J Chron R* June 1970, 6-7.
"Everybody Wants to Be a President" *Can J Chron R* Sept 1970, 8-9, 50.

Meldrum, Vernon‡
"Sauerkraut Please" *AA* 62 (Jan 1972), 31, 60, 66.

Melen, Terrance‡
"Far Thunder" *CF* 46 (Dec 1966), 209-11.
"Friday Night and Saturday Morning" *CF* 46 (June 1966), 63-5.

Melfi, Mary (1951-)
"The Dinner Party" *Des* 12:2/3 Nos. 32/33 (1981), 156-8.
"Forward" *CV 2* 4:1 (Win 1979), 2-3 [Satire].
"In the Crowd's Image" *Mam* 2:3 (Fall 1978), [4 pp].
"The Match" *It Needs to Be Said* Ser II, No. 2 (Fall 1976), 14 [Sketch or prose poem?].
"The Spool of Wire" *Antig R* No. 42 (Sum 1980), 23-5.
"The Thumb" *Blow Up* 1:7 (Sept 1980), [1 p].
"The X-Ray's Terrible Sting" *Nebula* No. 3 (1976), 14-5.

Melmer, J.R.†
"First, They Got Luke" *Diversions* 4:1 (1973), 8-16.

Meltzer, Edmund S.‡
"Into the Daylight" *Bakka* No. 6 (Fall 1977), 63-6.

Mencher, M.B.‡
"Mademoiselle Paul" *Compass* No. 8 (Win 1980), 105-11.
"Parkin-Jewell" *Compass* No. 5 (Win 1979), 63-78.

Mercer, Michael‡
"A Sense of Awareness" *Prism* (Mont) No. 8 (1965), 33-9.

Mercer, P.F.‡
"The Hitch Hiker" *Alive* [2:2] (Jan 1971), 26-7.

Meredith, Rita‡
"Recruiting" *Amethyst* 4:1 (Aut 1964), 34-6.
"The Water of Life" *Crier* 1:4 (Nov 1964), 26-7.

Merrow, Adin‡
"Quiet Hour" *Forge* 1951, 35-6.

Merton, Will – *See* Green, H. Gordon.

Merz, Sandra (1941-)
"The Picture" *event* 4:3 [1974?], 22-3.
"The Picture" *Water* [n.d.], 106.

Metcalf, Donald‡
"Monument" *Chiaroscuro* 9 (1965-66), 37-8.

Metcalf, John (1939-)
THE LADY WHO SOLD FURNITURE Toronto: Clarke, Irwin, 1970.
SELECTED STORIES Toronto: McClelland & Stewart, 1982.
THE TEETH OF MY FATHER Ottawa: Oberon Press, 1975.
"A Bag of Cherries" *Sixteen by Twelve* (1970), 180-5.
"A Bag of Cherries" *CBC "Anthology"* 19 Dec 1970.
"The Beef Curry" *Prism* 4:1 (Sum 1964), 14-9.
"Beryl" *CFM* No. 13 (Spr 1974), 14-27.
"Beryl" *CBC "Anthology"* 2 Nov 1974.
"Beryl" *Teeth of My Father* (1975), 113-30.
"Beryl" *Selected Stories* (1982), 213-28.
"The Children Green and Golden" *Was R* 3:1 (1968), 25-38.
"The Children Green and Golden" *New Canadian Writing* 1969 3-20.
"The Children Green and Golden" *Narrative Voice* (1972), 132-45.
"The Children Green and Golden" *CBC "Anthology"* 12 May 1973.
"The Children Green and Golden" *Die Weite Reise* (1974), 326-46 [As "Lasset die Kindlein zu mir kommen"; trans. Gerhard Bottcher].
"The Children Green and Golden" *Selected Stories* (1982), 119-35.
"Consequences" *Prism* 4:2 (Aut 1964), 41-3.
"Dandelions" *Lady Who Sold Furniture* (1970), 143-50.
"Dandelions" *Selected Stories* (1982), 112-8.
"Early Morning Rabbits" *Prism* 4:1 (Sum 1964), 7-13.
"Early Morning Rabbits" *Lady Who Sold Furniture* (1970), 103-10.
"Early Morning Rabbits" *Kaleidoscope* (1972), 34-41.
"The Eastmill Reception Centre" *Fid* No. 128 (Win 1981), 59-76.
"The Estuary" *CBC "Anthology"* 22 June 1967.
"The Estuary" *WCR* 3:1 (Spr 1968), 13-21.
"The Estuary" *New Canadian Writing* 1969 49-63.
"The Estuary" *Sixteen by Twelve* (1970), 186-97.
"The Estuary" *Moderne Erzühler der Walt: Kanada* (1976), 346-62 [As "Die Meeresbucht"; trans. Walter Riedel].
"The Estuary" *Selected Stories* (1982), 136-50.
"Flowers That Bloom in the Spring" *Teeth of My Father* (1975), 131-46 [Originally chapter from novel *Going Down Slow*].
"Gentle as Flowers Make the Stones" *QQ* 81 (1974), 221-37.
"Gentle as Flowers Make the Stones" *Teeth of My Father* (1975), 22-45.
"Gentle as Flowers Make the Stones" *Here and Now* (1977), 151-69.
"Gentle as Flowers Make the Stones" *Selected Stories* (1982), 229-49.
"Geography of the House" *Prism* 4:2 (Aut 1964), 34-5.
"The Happiest Days" *Prism* 4:2 (Aut 1964), 28-33.
"The Happiest Days" *Modern Canadian Stories* (1966), 324-7.
"The Happiest Days" *Canadian Short Story* (1971), 53-6.
"The Happiest Days" *Transitions 2* (1978), 203-6.
"I've Got It Made" *CF* 45 (Apr 1965), 12-3.

"Just Two Old Men" *Prism* 4:1 (Sum 1964), 20-5.
"Keys and Watercress" *Tam R* No. 45 (Aut 1967), 10-20.
"Keys and Watercress" *Canadian Writing Today* (1970), 297-307.
"Keys and Watercress" *Lady Who Sold Furniture* (1970), 118-29.
"Keys and Watercress" *Great Canadian Short Stories* (1971), 301-11.
"Keys and Watercress" *Writers and Writing* (1981), 6-16.
"Keys and Watercress" *Selected Stories* (1982), 101-11.
"One for Cupid" *Edge* No. 6 (Spr 1967), 19-24.
"Our Mr. Benson" *New Canadian Writing* 1969 41-8.
"Playground" *QQ* 85 (1978), 17-31.
"Playground" *CBC "Anthology"* 24 June 1978.
"The Practice of the Craft" *Fid* No. 100 (Win 1974), 43-53.
"The Practice of the Craft" *Teeth of My Father* (1975), 46-57.
"The Practice of the Craft" *Fiddlehead Greens* (1979), 89-101.
"Pretty Boy" *Lady Who Sold Furniture* (1970), 130-42.
"A Process of Time" *Modern Canadian Stories* (1966), 328-31.
"A Process of Time" *Prism* 4:1 (Sum 1974), 26-30.
"Robert, Standing" *CBC "Anthology"* 18 Jan 1969.
"Robert, Standing" *Fid* No. 82 (Nov-Dec 1969), 29-36.
"Robert, Standing" *New Canadian Writing* 1969 30-40.
"Robert, Standing" *Narrative Voice* (1972), 145-53.
"Robert, Standing" *Selected Stories* (1982), 151-60.
"Single Gents Only" *Mal R* No. 62 (July 1982), 73-88.
"Single Gents Only" *Metavisions* (1983), 172-86.
"The Strange Aberration of Mr. Ken Smythe" *73: New Canadian Stories* 9-22.
"The Strange Aberration of Mr. Ken Smythe" *CBC "Anthology"* 15 June 1974.
"The Strange Aberration of Mr. Ken Smythe" *Teeth of My Father* (1975), 7-21.
"The Strange Aberration of Mr. Ken Smythe" *Selected Stories* (1982), 161-73.
"The Teeth of My Father" *JCF* 3:1 (Win 1974), 11-7.
"The Teeth of My Father" *Teeth of My Father* (1975), 58-79.
"The Teeth of My Father" *Selected Stories* (1982), 174-93.
"A Thing They Wear" *Seven* [n.d.], [4 pp].
"A Thing They Wear" *Fid* No. 88 (Win 1971), 47-54.
"A Thing They Wear" *Teeth of My Father* (1975), 102-12.
"The Tide Line" *Lady Who Sold Furniture* (1970), 111-7.
"A Toy Called Peter Dog" *Prism* 4:2 (Aut 1964), 36-40.
"Walking Round the City" *New Canadian Writing* 1969 21-9.
"Walking Round the City" *CBC "Anthology"* 21 June 1969.
"The Years in Exile" *Teeth of My Father* (1975), 80-101.
"The Years in Exile" *Tam R* No. 67 (Oct 1975), 17-34.
"The Years in Exile" *Canadian Short Stories 3* (1978), 205-26.
"The Years in Exile" *Selected Stories* (1982), 194-212.

Metcalfe, B[rian]. R.

"Edward Allen Falls in Love" *TUR* 75:1 (Nov 1961), 28-32.
"Last Writing of an Unknown Officer of N-th Regiment Found Dead Near Aachen, May 3, 1945" *TUR* 76:2 (Nov 1962), 19-21.
"The Morning After" *TUR* 75:3 (Mar 1962), 49-52.
"Passage" *TUR* 74:2 (Mar 1961), 20-3.

Metcalfe, William‡
"Loon Lake" *Edge* No. 9 (Sum 1969), 39-40.

Meyers, Leonard W.
"The Brilliant Mr. Budge" *CSSM* 2:4 (Fall 1976), 57-9, 61-2.

Mezei, Stephen‡
"Beastly Story" *Onion* 5:4 (Sept 1981), 5-6.
"The Devastating Effect of the Toronto Transit Strike on the Artistic Development of Canada and Probably the Western World" *Onion* 4:1/2 (Feb 1979).
"Inner Beauty" *Onion* 5:1 (Oct 1979), 3.
"Love Letters" *Onion* 5:2 (Mar 1981), 3.
"Making Love to Pulu" *Onion* 3:5 (May 1978), 10.
"Pop Psychology" *Onion* 3:7 (July 1978), 3.
"The Resolution" *Onion* 5:6 (Dec-Jan [1981]-82), 5.
"Summer Loves" *Onion* 5:5 (Nov 1981), 1-2.

Michaels, Edward L.†
"Goldtooth Jimmy's Last Cup of Tea" *Heartland* No. 1 (Nov-Dec 1980), 25-7, 68-71.
"The Truant" *Heartland* No. 2 (Jan-Feb 1981), 22-5 [Excerpt?].

Michaels, Evelyne (1953-)
"Truck Stop" *Outset* 1974, 129-35.

Michaelson, Dave‡
"Did Dolly Say 'Mama'?" *Uk Can* 8 (1 Feb 1954), 6 [Listed under "Humour and Satire"].

Michaluk, Gary†
"Belladonna" *WWR* 2:3 No. 7 (1982), 91-5.

Michel, Robert‡
"2 Fridays" *Either/Or* No. 3 (Spr 1966), 4-5.

Michener, Wendy‡
"Out of the Cradle Endlessly Rocking" *TUR* 67:4 (Mar 1955), 10-6.

Michie, Maureen and Reynolds, Debbie‡
"Though I Walked Through the Valley of Darkness ... " *Scar Fair* 2 (1974-75), [3 pp].

Miciak, Ernie‡
"Buddies" *Gas Rain* 2 (1978), 25-8.

Micros, Marianne
"No Man's Castle" *event* 9:2 (1980), 24-31.
"The Sacrifice" *event* 9:2 (1980), 19-23.

Mikolasch, Andrew†
"Mind Trip" *Satyrday* No. 2 (1967), 10-1.
"Skipper the Sniffer" *Satyrday* No. 5 (Dec 1966), 7-9.

Milander, Mary Ellen†

"Bobrowski" *Flare* 3 (Aug 1981), 36, 90, 92, 94, 97-8.
"Tulips and a Hotdog" *Antig R* No. 50 (Sum 1982), 81-4.

Miles, Christine‡

"Cabin Fever" *Bluenose* 1:4 (Spr 1977), 36-7.

Millard, Peter T. (1932-)†

'The Diamond" *Mal R* No. 66 (Oct 1983), 107-20.
'The End of Braycourt" *Forge* Mar 1959, 17-21.
'The Green Light" *Forge* Mar 1958, 4-6.

Miller, Angela†

"God and Grandfather" *Room* 1:3 (Fall 1975), 64-5.

Miller, Glenn

"Souvenir" *Outset* 1973, 120-4.

Miller, Ivie‡

"Ebony Blueprint" *Edmonton Journal* Fri, 28 July 1967, 26.

Miller, J. Kit†

GODS BODYGUARDS Toronto: Permanent Press, 1979.
"All the Time in the World" *New Bodies* (1981), 113-45.
"Ghosts in Garter Belts" *Gods Bodyguards* (1979), 10-20.
'Jimmy Came Flying In" *Gods Bodyguards* (1979), 22-34.
"Loose Shoes" *OPT* 7:4/5 (Sept-Oct 1980), 26-7.
"Out to Lunch" *Gods Bodyguards* (1979), 36-40.
'Pale Beneath His Tan" *Gods Bodyguards* (1979), 2-8.
'Pale Beneath His Tan" *OPT* 6:3 (Apr 1979), 6.
'The Pueget Sound" *Gods Bodyguards* (1979), 42-62.
"Velvet Apes" *Gods Bodyguards* (1979), 64-76.

Miller, John G.‡

'The Pride of Horsechester" *Folio* 17:2 (Spr 1965), 15-7.

Miller, Kathleen D. (1951-)†

"A Certain Age" *Cap R* No. 23 (1982), 63-8.
'Now Voyager" *Flare* 3 (May 1981), 52-3, 108, 120-1, 126.

Miller, Malcolm‡

'The Journeys of Eugene" *Forge* Spr 1955, 35-9.
'The Monkey" *Forge* Dec 1954, 34-9.

Miller, Robert‡

'The Enactment" *Amaranth* No. 18 (Dec 1977), [4 pp].

Miller, Samuel (1956-)

'The Story of Max" *Flow* (Win [1975?]), [2 pp].
'The Wheel Chair Pusher" *Scrivener* 1:1 (Spr 1980), 19-25.

Miller, Stephen†

'Bay Bridge" *CFM* Nos. 2/3 (Spr-Sum 1971), 73-7.

Millet, Aynes‡
"Straw Flowers" *JCF* 3:1 (Win 1974), 18-20.

Millette, Richard
"For October" *NJ* No. 6 (June 1976), 56-60.

Milligan, Doris (1937?-)
"The Diary" *Island Women* (1982), 81-2.

Milligan, Jim‡
"No Individual" *Chiaroscuro* 7 (1964), 20-4.

Milliken, Ross‡
"Beneath the Smoking Lady" *UTR* 7 (Spr 1983), 14-5.

Millikin, Brenda‡
"Excerpt from a Letter to a Friend" *TUR* 85:3 (Apr 1972), 9-10.
[Untitled] *TUR* 84:2 (Win 1971), 5 [Prose poem?].

Millisor, Guy‡
"Forever Clouds" *Inside* No. 2 [Nov 1964], 11-4.

Millons, John†
"Vignette – A Summer Evening" *Prism* (Mont) [No. 1] (1955), 49-51.

Mills, Elizabeth†
"The Character and I" *Onward* 3 Sept 1961, 8-10.
"The Character and I" *Onward* 25 Sept 1966, 5-6.
"Little Unknown" *Onward* 15 Dec 1963, 6-7.
"The Mark" *Onward* 30 June 1963, 3-4.
"Mrs. Popsovitch, the Pig, and the Paragon" *Onward* 26 Feb 1961, 140-2.
"The Retributive Justice" *Onward* 26 Nov 1961, 4-6.
"The Retributive Justice" *Onward* 22 Oct 1967, 3-5.
"The Silver Bit of Potential" *Onward* 20 Mar 1960, 177-9, 188.
"Youth and Innovations" *Onward* 28 Jan 1962, 2-4.

Mills, John (1930-)
"Arms and the Poltroon" *QQ* 84 (1977), 186-202.
"At Station Melville" *JCF* Nos. 28/29 (1980), 99-134.
"The Colander" *Edge* No. 2 (Spr 1964), 45-9.
"Heronwood" *WCR* 5:1 (June 1970), 17-24.
"Joust in Eight Rounds" *Evidence* No. 9 [n.d.], 72-97.
"The Maltese Cross" *Evidence* No. 3 (Fall 1961), 9-14.
"The Road Runner" *Evidence* No. 10 (1967), 17-44.

Mills, Margaret (1923-)
"The Present" *Klanak Islands* (1959), 41-8.
"Three Lousy Poems and Something Else" *CBC "Anthology"* 5 Jan 1962.

Mills, Sparling
"Heroes" *WWR* 2:4 (1983), 49-50.

Millson, Larry‡
"I Just Don't Know" *Fifth Page* 1964, 24-7.

Milne, J.G.‡
"No Hope" *Stump* 5:1 (Fall-Win 1980), 8-10.

Milne, Lucie†
"Shadows" *Read Ch* 1:3 (Win 1982), 21-30.

Milne, Lynda‡
"A New Beginning" *Stump* Spr 1981, 29-31.

Milne, Sonny†
"The Wall" *Blue Buffalo* 1:2 (Spr 1983), [1 p].

Milner, Philip†
"Coming Up for Air" *Anthos* 2:1/2 (1980), 160-3.
"Kitty" *Read Ch* 1:1 (Spr 1982), 3-5.
"The Man Who Loved Mrs. Norman Torque" *Fid* No. 126 (Sum 1980), 45-9.

Minions, Stephen‡
"A Blood Named Charcoal" *Can Golden West* 13:4 [1978?], 28-31.
"Resolution" *Can Golden West* 12a (Fall 1977), 37-40.

Minni, C.D.
"Details from the Canadian Mosaic" *New Worlds* (1980), 106-10 [Excerpt?].
"Details from the Canadian Mosaic" *In Your Own Words* (1982), 140-4.
"El Dorado" *QQ* 89 (1982), 829-38.
"Gaps" *CFM* No. 20 (Win 1976), 187-93.
"He & I" *Waves* 12:1 (Fall 1983), 28-35.
"The Hunter" *AA* 55 (Nov 1964), 61-4.
"A Michelangelo Among Tailors" *QQ* 79 (1972), 93-6.
"Roots" *JCF* 3:2 (1974), 19-23.
"Roots" *Search for Identity* (1976), 104-15.

Minor, Junius [pseudonym]
"Utopia Embassey Moves!" *Uk Can* 6 (15 Oct 1952), 5 [Listed under "Humour and Satire"].

Minsos, Susan‡
"Kate" CBC *"Alberta Anthology"* 23 Oct 1982.

Mintz, Chavah†
"A Long Time Dying" *Fireweed* No. 13 (1982), 69-72.

Mintz, Helen‡
"Reason Enough" *CBC [Van] "Hornby Collection"* 20 Feb 1982.

Miraglia, Anne Marie‡
"The Letter I Would Have Written You" *UCR* 1977-78, 45-8.

Mirolla, Michael
"The Architect" *Quarry* 20:2 (Sum 1971), 25-8.
"Ernestine" *Prism* 10:3 (Spr 1971), 63-5.
"Exorcism" *WCR* 6:1 (June 1971), 24-6.
"Feud" *Prism* 10:3 (Spr 1971), 65-9.
"Kafka's Ghosts" *CFM* No. 1 (Win 1971), 73-4.
"The News Vendor" *Northwest R* 17:1 (1978), 70-102.
"Was Socrates the First Absurdist" *JCF* 2:1 (Win 1973), 19-21.

Misfeldt, James‡
"Across the River" *Nw J* No. 17 (1980), 63-5.
"The Soldier" *Grain* 4:3 [1976], 51-4.
"Then Came the Night" *Grain* 7:2 [1979], 38-42.
"Those Blue Hills" *Grain* 3:2 [1975], 39-40.
"Those Blue Hills" *Best of Grain* (1980), 37-8.
"A Time to Lose" *Grain* 5:3 [1977], 41-3.

Missio, Aldo G.‡
"Home and Native Land" *Scar Fair* 9 (1982), 68-73.

Mitcham, Peter†
"Equal Opportunities" *Fid* No. 92 (Win 1971), 23-35.
"For Their Sport" *UWR* 9:1 (Fall 1973), 49-60.

Mitchell, Beverly.
"Letter from Sakaye" *Fid* No. 99 (Fall 1973), 2-14.
"Letter from Sakaye" *Best American Short Stories* 1974 179-93.
"Letter from Sakaye" *Stories from Pacific & Arctic Canada* (1974), 17-33.
"Letter from Sakaye" CBC *"Anthology"* 19 Oct 1974.
"Letter from Sakaye" *Skookum Wawa* (1975), 218-30.
"Letter from Sakaye" *Inquiry into Literature* 2 (1980), 284-5 [Excerpt].

Mitchell, Chris‡
"One Day at Ponds" *Alive* No. 56 (23 Oct 1976), 7.

Mitchell, Donald M.‡
"A Rainy Afternoon in a French Port" *Can R* 1:2 (Apr 1974), 10.

Mitchell, Edith
"The First Day of Summer" *Nfld Q* 76:2 (Sum 1980), 25-7.

Mitchell, Ethel Golden†
"The Inkwell" *Lifetime* 4 (Mar-Apr 1974), 10-1.

Mitchell, Jeanine†
"Dialogue with Egomaniacal Man" *Pedestal* 6:3 [n.d.], 8-9.
"Letter from Mrs. H. Watkins" *Room* 1:3 (Fall 1975), 12-6.
"Tender Island" *Makara* 1:3 (Apr-May 1976), 24-5.

Mitchell, Ken (1940-)

EVERYBODY GETS SOMETHING HERE Toronto: Macmillan, 1977.

"The Bubble Gum King" *Salt* No. 13/14 (Win 1975-76), 4-8.

"The Bubble Gum King" *Everybody Gets Something Here* (1977), 7-14.

"A Contract Is a Contract" *JCF* 2:4 (Fall 1973), 26-9.

"A Contract Is a Contract" *Everybody Gets Something Here* (1977), 97-106.

"The Dangerfields" *Saskatchewan Gold* (1982), 102-10.

"Everybody Gets Something Here" *Was R* 1:1 (1966), 46-51.

"Everybody Gets Something Here" *Everybody Gets Something Here* (1977), 1-6.

"A Field of Slugs" *Writing* No. 1 (Sum 1980), 43-6.

"Garden of Earthly Delights" *Scottish R* Aug 1980 [Based on survey response].

"Give Me Your Answer, Do" *Everybody Gets Something Here* (1977), 62-70.

"Great Big Boffs They Are" *Saskatchewan Writing* 1965 [Based on survey response].

"Great Big Boffs They Are" *CBC [Winn]* June 1966 [Based on survey response].

"Great Big Boffs They Are" *CBC* 9 Nov 1968 [Based on survey response].

"Great Big Boffs They Are" *Everybody Gets Something Here* (1977), 71-7.

"The Great Electrical Revolution" *Prism* 9:3 (Spr 1970), 4-12.

"The Great Electrical Revolution" *Stories from Western Canada* (1972), 81-91.

"The Great Electrical Revolution" *Modern Canadian Stories* (1975), 115-26.

"The Great Electrical Revolution" *Urban Experience* (1975), 57-67.

"The Great Electrical Revolution" *Everybody Gets Something Here* (1977), 78-87.

"The Great Electrical Revolution" *Canadian Short Stories 3* (1978), 228-39.

"The Great Electrical Revolution" *BBC* (Scot) Feb 1981 [Based on survey response].

"The Great Electrical Revolution" *Writers and Writing* (1981), 121-30.

"The Great Electrical Revolution" *CBC* 24 Dec 1981 [Based on survey response].

"The Great Electrical Revolution" *West of Fiction* (1983), 37-45.

"The Great Electrical Revolution" *Huaxi (China)* [date unknown] [In Chinese; based on survey response].

"In Old Mexico" *Fid* No. 106 (Sum 1975), 89-104.

"In Old Mexico" *Everybody Gets Something Here* (1977), 15-28.

"Loose Ruck" *Sundogs* (1980), 83-92.

"Luck" *CBC [Reg]* Mar 1967 [Based on survey response].

"Luck" *CBC* 22 Mar 1968 [Based on survey response].

"Luck" *Everybody Gets Something Here* (1977), 45-53.

"The Masked Buddha" *Everybody Gets Something Here* (1977), 114-22.

"Pavlochenko's" *Cencrastus* (U.K.) Spr 1980 [Based on survey response].

"Stolen Roans" *Grain* 3:1 [1975], 28-34.

"Stolen Roans" *Everybody Gets Something Here* (1977), 29-37.

"Teachers" *CFM* No. 10 (Spr 1973), 4-11.

"Teachers" *Everybody Gets Something Here* (1977), 38-44.

"A Time to Sow" *Everybody Gets Something Here* (1982), 88-96.

"Truckin' " *Prism* 12:1 (Sum 1972), 105-11.

"Truckin' " *CBC "Anthology"* 15 Jan 1977 [Title based on survey response].

"Truckin' " *Everybody Gets Something Here* (1977), 54-61.

"Truckin' " *100% Cracked Wheat* (1983), 140-50.

"William" *CBC [Reg]* 1967 [Based on survey response].

"You Better Not Pout" *Smoke Signals* 2 [date unknown] [Based on *SWG* survey

response].

"You Better Not Pout" *CBC* 1975 [Based on survey response].

"You Better Not Pout" *NeWest R* 2 (Dec 1976), 6, 12.

"You Better Not Pout" *Everybody Gets Something Here* (1977), 107-13.

"You Better Not Pout" *More Stories from Western Canada* (1980), 33-9.

Mitchell, M.J.†

"Two Lonely People" *Can Messenger* 80 (June 1970), 12-3.

Mitchell, Marsha†

"Fragments of a Treaty Forever" *Room* 1:3 (Fall 1975), 2-8.

Mitchell, Mary‡

"Lament" *TUR* 68:3 (Feb 1956), 24-7.

Mitchell, Nick†

"The Captive" *Writ* No. 15 (1983), 17-27.

Mitchell, Sirjy‡

"King Kong and the Mouse" *Alive* No. 32 [1973], 26.

Mitchell, Sylvia Elizabeth Fisher

PRAIRIE ADVENTURES Regina: privately printed, 1958.

"A Dilly of a Job" *AA* 57 (Apr 1967), 30.

"The Hole in the Hill" *Prairie Adventures* (1958), 43-50 [Semi-fictional].

"Meet Mr. Santa Claus" *Prairie Adventures* (1958), 57-61 [Semi-fictional].

"Pipes" *Prairie Adventures* (1958), 26-8.

"The Shoes" *CG* 85 (Jan 1966), 45-6 [Same author?].

"Snow Trail" *Prairie Adventures* (1958), 9-10.

"The Star Shines Down" *Prairie Adventures* (1958), 57-61.

"The Straw Stack Room" *Prairie Adventures* (1958), 51-3 [Semi-fictional].

Mitchell, W.O. (1914-)

JAKE AND THE KID Toronto: Macmillan, 1961.

"Crocus at the Coronation" *MM* 66 (1 June 1953), 18-9, 46-8, 50, 52-3.

"The Day I Spoke for Mister Lincoln" *Imp Oil R* 46 (June 1962), 19-22 [Humour].

"The Golden Jubilee Citizen" *MM* 68 (25 June 1955), 33-4, 36, 38, 40.

"The Golden Jubilee Citizen" *Jake and the Kid* (1961), 172-84.

"The Golden Jubilee Citizen" *Time of Your Life* (1967), 102-17.

"How Crocus Got Its Seaway" *MM* 72 (20 June 1959), 16-7, 55-6, 58-60.

"Melvin Arbuckle's First Course in Shock Therapy" *MM* 76 (5 Oct 1963), 38, 40-1, 44-6.

"Melvin Arbuckle's First Course in Shock Therapy" *Singing Under Ice* (1974), 46-56.

"Patterns" *Ten for Wednesday Night* (1961), 58-71.

"Patterns" *Wild Rose Country* (1977), 91-103.

"The Princess and the Wild Ones" *MM* 65 (15 Mar 1952), 12-3, 25-6, 28-9.

"The Princess and the Wild Ones" *Cavalcade of the North* (1958), 430-8.

"The Princess and the Wild Ones" *Jake and the Kid* (1961), 158-71.

Mitton, M. Anne (1940-)
"Credit" *Pot Port* 5 (1983-84), 35.
"Foxes" *Antig R* No. 49 (Spr 1982), 115-6.
"Motherhood" *AA* 69 (Jan 1979), 39-40.
"The Music Festival" *AA* 70 (Apr 1980), 74, 76, 78.
"The Taste of the Earth" *Scrivener* 4:2 (Sum 1983), 11-3.
"The Tea" *Fid* No. 122 (Sum 1979), 40-6.
"Threads" *Fid* No. 129 (Spr 1981), 54-71.
"The Tree" *AA* 70 (Dec 1979), 31-2, 34.

Mitton, Roger‡
"Hitch-Hiker" *Driftwood* [No. 1] (Apr 1973), 49-56.

Mobley, Carla†
"The Separation" *Antig R* No. 54 (Sum 1983), 73-7.

Moelaert, John‡
"The Jogger" *Diversions* 5:1 (1975), 40-5.

Moen, Arlo M.†
"Alpha" *Alpha* 1:1 (Oct 1976), 5.

Moes, Peter‡
"The Last Time I Saw Paris" *Muse* 61:1 (Dec 1951), 17-8.

Moffat, Allan‡
"One Christmas Eve" *Muskeg R* 4 [1976], 34-7.

Moffatt, Greg‡
"Self-Portrait: The Welcome" *Acta Vic* 105:2 (Spr 1981), 37.

Mofina, R.H.‡
"I Remember You" *AA* 69 (Nov 1978), 83-5.
"A Native Son" *AA* 71 (Jan 1981), 77-9.

Mogelon, Alex†
"Oh, Bury Me Next to Sol Kosslitsky" *Viewpoints* 2:1 (Win 1967), 35-8.

Moldofsky, Mitch‡
"The Box" *Images* 1:2 (Nov 1979), 8.

Mole, Elsie Hadden†
"Finchley's Folly" *CSSM* 3:1 (Win 1977), 51.

Molinaro, Ursula‡
"Hatred Needs a Friend" *Edge* No. 4 (Spr 1965), 38-44.

Moller, Margaret†
"Summer Tempest" *Saskatchewan Homecoming* (1971), 173-8.

Molnar, Anne†
"All That Long Summer" *Quarry* 15:3 (Mar 1966), 15-9.

Mombourquette, Michael‡
"Mah-sei-nahe-gun (The Letter)" *Boreal* No. 9 (1977), 61-6.

Momson, G. Robert†
"The Peachstone" *Antig R* No. 41 (Spr 1980), 27-32.

Monckton, M.E.†
"His First Hard Knock" *Can Messenger* 79 (July-Aug 1969), 16-7.

Moncrieff, Charles‡
"Encounter with a Fool" *TUR* 67:1 (Nov 1954), 8-9.

Mondiale [pseudonym]
"Nietzsche, No. 69" *NeWest R* 3 (June 1978), 9-10.

Monk, Douglas†
"The Applicant" *Prism* 13:1 (Sum 1973), 109-15.

Monserrate, Angela†
"The New Lords" *Matinees Daily* (1981), 82-8.

Montagnes, Anne†
"Bare Ruined Choirs" *CBC "Anthology"* 8 Sept 1966.

Montague, Art‡
"Prologue" *Targya* 1:2 (Fall 1973), 16-9.

Montgomery, Peter‡
"The Puritan" *Inside* 2:4 [n.d.], 4-6.

Montour, Enos T.
"Little Mo 'Gets Religion' " *UC Observer* 1 Sept 1959, 15, 28.
"Too Big for Santa Claus" *Onward* 2 Feb 1958, 74-5 [Children's?].

Mooers, Vernon (1951-)
"The Unforgettable David" *Des* 11:1/2 Nos. 27/28 (1980), 158-62.

Moogk, Margeurite E.‡
"Midsummer Night's Dream" *Undergrad* Spr 1955, 24-5.

Moon, Bryan
"Dark Armies" *Fid* No. 131 (Jan 1982), 45-54.
"The Student Prince" *More Stories from Western Canada* (1980), 106-29.

Moore, Brenda‡
"Mikla-Sakan" *Acta Vic* 84:2 (Mar 1960), 2-4.

Moore, Brian (1921-)
TWO STORIES [place unknown]: Santa Susana Press, 1978 [based on *Penguin Book of Modern Canadian Stories*].
"The Apartment Hunter" *Best American Short Stories* 1967 175-85.
"Big Elephants Are No Longer Relevant" *CBC "Anthology"* 27 May 1960.
"Confession Four" *Weekend* 3 (14 Mar 1953), 28-9.

"The Confidence Man" *Weekend* 4 (13 Mar 1954), 12-3, 39.
"Dreamboat" *Weekend* 3 (28 Feb 1953), 10-1, 29.
"Enemies of the People" *Bluebook* 97 (May 1953), 13-7.
"A Friend of Mine" *Weekend* 3 (26 Dec 1953), 20.
"The Gift" *Weekend* 4 (13 Nov 1954), 36.
"Grieve for the Dear Departed" *Atlantic Monthly* 204 (Aug 1959), 43-6.
"Grieve for the Dear Departed" *CBC "Anthology"* 7 Oct 1960.
"Hearts and Flowers" *CBC "Anthology"* 22 Dec 1961.
"Holdup!" *American Mag* 155 (June 1953), 143 [Based on RGPL].
"The Incredible Carollers" *Weekend* 2 (13 Dec 1952), 38.
"The Lamp of El Azimair" *Weekend* 2 (23 Aug 1952), 12-3, 24.
"Lion of the Afternoon" *Atlantic Monthly* 200 (Nov 1957), 79-83.
"Lion of the Afternoon" *CBC "Anthology"* 3 Dec 1957.
"Lion of the Afternoon" *Cornhill Mag* 170 (1958), 149-58.
"Lion of the Afternoon" *Book of Canadian Stories* (1962), 283-93.
"Margaret's Baby" *Weekend* 3 (26 Sept 1953), 8-9.
"Mr. Hammamacher and the Evil Eye" *Weekend* 2 (16 Feb 1952), 28-9.
"Next Thing Was Kansas City" *Atlantic Monthly* 203 (Feb 1959), 77-9.
"Next Thing Was Kansas City" *CBC "Anthology"* 10 Mar 1959.
"Off the Track" *Ten for Wednesday Night* (1961), 158-67.
"Off the Track" *Modern Canadian Stories* (1966), 239-46.
"Off the Track" *Kaleidoscope* (1972), 83-91.
"Power Is Not Arithmetic" *Weekend* 2 (26 Jan 1952), 25.
"Preliminary Pages for a Work of Revenge" *CBC "Anthology"* 26 May 1961.
"Preliminary Pages for a Work of Revenge" *Mont* 35 (Dec 1961), 27-9.
"Preliminary Pages for a Work of Revenge" *Midstream* 7:1 (Win 1961), 57-61.
"Preliminary Pages for a Work of Revenge" *Canadian Writing Today* (1970), 139-45.
"Preliminary Pages for a Work of Revenge" *Critic* (U.K.) 35:1 (Fall 1976), 49-53.
"A Question of Command" *Weekend* 1 (3 Nov 1951), 18, 43.
"Reward" *Weekend* 3 (24 Oct 1953), 10.
"The Ridiculous Proposal" *Bluebook* 98 (Jan 1954), 51-4.
"Sassenach" *Atlantic Monthly* 199 (Mar 1957), 47-9.
"The Sight" *Irish Ghost Stories* (1977) [Based on *Black Water*].
"The Sight" *Not to Be Taken at Night* (1981), 82-102.
"The Sight" *Black Water* (1983), 652-9.
"Someone They Know" *Weekend* 4 (20 Feb 1954), 20.
"Uncle T" *Canadian Winter's Tales* (1968), 22-45.
"Uncle T" *Great Canadian Short Stories* (1971), 184-202.
"Uncle T" *29 Stories* (1975) [Based on SSI].
"Uncle T" *Two Stories* (1978) [Based on *Penguin Book of Modern Canadian Stories*].
"Uncle T" *Penguin Book of Modern Canadian Short Stories* (1982), 85-102.
"You Never Give Me Flowers" *Weekend* 1 (29 Sept 1951), 21.

Moore, Charlotte†

"Don't Cry, Little Girl" *Chat* 26 (May 1953), 11, 37-9, 43.
"Encore for Strings" *Echoes* No. 223 (Sum 1956), 6, 21-2.

Moore, Elwin‡

"The Amusement Centre" *Quarry* 28:1 (Win 1979), 49-54.

"Failure" *Was R* 12:2 (Fall 1977), 25-30.

"The Pulwharskie Dragon" *Was R* 10:2 (Fall [1975]), 68-78.

Moore, J.P.‡

"Boys at Play" *Gram* 8:1 (Fall 1982), 23-5.

Moore, Noel†

"The Script Conference" *Take One* 1:2 (Nov-Dec 1966), 18-20.

Moore, Peter (1934-)

"Four Loves" *QQ* 79 (1972), 515-7.

"Going Home" *TUR* 81:2 (Win 1968), 23.

"Summercamp" *TUR* 81:3 (Spr 1968), 7-8.

"Time Lost" *TUR* 82:1 (Fall 1968), 4-5.

Moore, Robert‡

"London Walk" *Forge* 23:2 (Dec 1961), 24-6.

Moore, Thomas‡

"I Meet the Major" *Doryloads* (1974), 138-41.

"The Summer My Mother Died" *Nfld Q* 72:1 (Dec 1975), 27-31.

Moorhouse, Eliza‡

"Dinner with Gordon Blue" *West People* No. 132 (8 Apr 1982), 12.

Moorman, Eliza‡

"School Bus" CBC *"Anthology"* 28 Nov 1970.

Moose, Martin H.†

"Travellers" *Canadian Short Fiction Anthology 2* (1982), 117-21.

Morash, Gordon‡

"Lions" *Best of Grain* (1980), 52-5.

Morgan, Caroline‡

"A Boy Went Out One Evening" *Random* 3:5 (Mar [1969]), 9.

Morgan. Bernice

"Martha Gets an Outing" *Blasty Bough* (1976), 70-6.

"Miranda" *From This Place* (1977), 165-9.

"Pictures" *Twelve Newfoundland Short Stories* (1982), 43-7.

"A Responsible Relative" *Nfld Q* 65:4 (June 1967), 30-2.

"Windows" *From This Place* (1977), 180-7.

Morison, Scott‡

"Gilman's Last Joke" CBC *"Alberta Anthology"* 27 Nov 1982.

Moritz, Janet†

"A Box of July" *WWR* 2:4 No. 8 (1983), 15-8.

Morley, Patricia (1929-)
"The Wrong Way" *Title Unknown* (1975), 22-3.

Morrell, Dave†
"Cicero's Disease" *Jabberwocky* Apr 1966, [4 pp].
"The Dance" *Jabberwocky* Feb 1966, [5 pp].
"Recherches" *Jabberwocky* [No. 1 (1965?)], [1 p].

Morrice, Hugh†
"Manifesto" *CFM* No. 1 (Win 1971), 72.

Morris, Cathy†
"Ghosts in the Alley" *Quote Unquote* 2:2 (Mar 1979), 13.

Morris, Doris M.†
"The Bear in the Blueberries" *Companion* 31 (Nov 1956), 6-9.
"Brother Jim and the Case of the Vanishing Ham" *Companion* 37 (Mar 1962), 16-20.
"The Cow's in the Corn" *Companion* 30 (July-Aug 1955), 7-11.
"Day of Judgment" *Companion* [39] (Mar 1964), 19-24.
"The Day Old Henry Decided to Forget" *Companion* [38] (June 1963), 16-21.
"Everyone Agreed Miss Prue Was a Sharp Old Gal" *Companion* [38] (Jan 1963), 16-21.
"God and Doc Murphy" *Companion* [38] (Feb 1963), 24-8.
" 'He's a Stubborn Man' " *Companion* 31 (July-Aug 1956), 12-5.
"The Perfectionist" *Rapport* June 1969, 18-20.
"The Return of Corny O'Shea" *Companion* [39] (Oct 1964), 22-6.
" 'Rover St. Patrick Murphy' " *Companion* 31 (Sept 1956), 6-8.
"Space in the Heart" Companion 37 (Oct 1962), 18-22.
"St. Joseph's Marvellous Boilers" *Companion* 30 (Nov 1955), 20-5.
"That First Million " *Companion* [39] (Jan 1964), 24-9.
"What an Awful Child!" *Companion* 30 (Sept 1955), 6-8.

Morris, Dorothy M.
"The Land of the Free" *Variations on a Gulf Breeze* (1973), 10-20.
"The Suffering" *Island Women* (1982), 86-8.

Morris, Flip‡
"Grandpa Salem Talks Sail" *Better Boating* 12 (June 1976), 30-2.
"Hello Boating! Goodbye Arnold" *Better Boating* 10 (Oct 1974), 13-5.

Morris, Neil K.‡
"Cold Duty Watch" *Legion* 47 (Dec 1972), 11, 41-2.

Morris, Richard‡
"The Disciple" *CBC "Alberta Anthology"* 9 Oct 1982.

Morris, Roberta‡
"An Occasion" *UCR* Spr 1975, 37.

Morrison, Harold R.W.
"The Farnsworth Collection" *WWR* 2:2 (1981), 43-50.
"Myself a Hero" *Mont* 41 (July 1967), 37, 39-41.
"Notes from a Suicide Diary" *Dal R* 39 (1959), 349-57.
"The Parade Square" *Dal R* 55 (1975), 505-10.
"The Patient Will Recover" *QQ* 65 (1959), 586-94.
"Questions" *QQ* 76 (1969), 319-35.

Morrison, Margaret‡
"Intersection" *Edmonton Journal* Fri, 1 Oct 1965, 58.
"The Misunderstood" *Onward* 7 May 1961, 302-3.
"The Pink Hat" *Onward* 18 Jan 1959, 38 [Humour].
"The Widow's Dilemma" *Can Lifetime* 1 (Sept-Oct 1971), 18-23.

Morrison, R.H. – *See* Green, H. Gordon.

Morrison, Robert (1939-)
"A Day on Someone's Island" *Anthol* No. 2 (Win 1972-73), 54-6.
"Flight" *Forge* 22:1 (Spr 1960), 12-6.

Morrissette, George (1938-)
"Dancing with Cuckoo-Gee" *Arts Man* 2:3 (Sum 1983), 26-8.
"War Baby" *NeWest R* 3 (Oct 1977), 6-7.

Morrissey, Philip†
"Encore" *Prism* 13:1 (Sum 1973), 12-8.

Morritt, Hope (1930-)
"Backlash in the Oil Patch" *Our Family* 19 (Mar 1968), 22-4.
"Christmas Lay Away" *Can Messenger* 76 (Dec 1966), 10-3.
"The Double Four Poster Bed" *Mam* 6:4 (Win 1983-84), [5 pp].
"Older Than Methuselah" *Alberta Writers Speak* 1960, 69-77.
"Run Son, Run" *Companion* 34 (Mar 1971), 21-4.
"Run Son, Run" *Polished Pebbles* (1974), 47-51.
"Sometimes Revenge Comes Quickly" *Can Messenger* 79 (Sept 1969), 12-3.
"The Sweet Taste of Revenge" *CBC* 15 June 1970 [Based on survey response].
" 'When I Put Out to Sea' " *Companion* 33 (Jan 1970), 16-9.

Morron, Glen [pseudonym]
"We Took a Scooter Holiday Through the Matto Grosso" *Hyperbole* No. 3 (May 1962), [2 pp].

Morrow, Dave‡
"Unto Death" *Muse* 1965-66 No. 1, 22-7.

Morrow, Mark‡
"The Handicap Was Blackmail" *Can Horse* 6 (Sept-Oct 1966), 34, 46-8.
"Sure Things Are for the Birds" *Can Horse* 7 (May 1967), 24-5, 32-4.
"Two Men on a Horse" *Can Horse* 7 (Sept 1967), 30-1, 54-5.

Mortenson, Constance†
"The Nino's Eyes" *Pulp Mill* (1977), 27-8.

Morton, Alex‡
"Harold in Heaven" *Either/Or* No. 4 (Fall 1966), 4-7.

Morton, Colin (1948-)
"The Butterfly" *JCF* No. 33 (1981-82), 27-44.
"The End" *Repos* No. 14 (Spr 1975), 62-7.
"England" *Repos* No. 5 (Jan 1973), 4-7.
"Moonlighting" *Grain* 6:1 [1978], 23-7.
"Musical Ride" *Grain* 3:1 [1975], 4-7.
"Not Who She Was What She Did" *Gas Rain* 3 (1979), 4-5.
"The Queen's Scout" *Gas Rain* 2 (1978), 42-3.
"What the Hell" *NeWest R* 3 (Jan 1978), 6-7.

Morton, Lionel
"The Complete Stranger" *Mal R* No. 48 (Oct 1978), 97-109.
"The Jacket" *Creative Campus* 1965, 20-7.
"My Biographer" *JCF* No. 19 (1977), 12-30.
"Old Man" *Body Politic* No. 89 (Dec 1982), 30-1.
"Pepper" *Mal R* No. 55 (July 1980), 28-45.
"A Place to Stay" *JCF* No. 21 (1977-78), 38-52.
"The Sailboat" *Creative Campus* 1964, 45-55.
[Untitled] *Creative Campus* 1966, 23-7.

Morton, Mark (1963-)
"Michlias" *Was R* 18:1 (Spr 1983), 19-23.

Morton, Murray‡
"Preface to His Memoirs" *Acta Vic* 82:1 (Nov 1957), 22-4.

Moser, Marie (1948-)
"The Long Gravel Road" CBC "*Alberta Anthology*" 24 Sept 1983.
"Scarlet, Scarlet" *Gas Rain* 3 (1979), 16-20.
"The Storm: Killarney Lake, Alberta, 1915" *NeWest R* 8:1 (Sept 1982), 12-4.

Moses, Daniel†
"A Mime with Two Sounds" *Prism* 16:2 (Fall 1977), 89-90.

Mosher, Edith (1910-)
FARM TALES Windsor, N.S.: Lancelot Press, 1976 ["Parts of this book are true, parts are fiction" (author's note)].
HAUNTED: TALES OF THE UNEXPLAINED Hantsport, N.S.: Lancelot, 1982 [Based on CBIP].
"The Bridge" *CG* 84 (Nov 1965), 36-7.
"Dear Mum, How're You Doing?" *Farm Tales* (1976), 46-72 [Mostly fictional].
"Horse Tales" *Farm Tales* (1976), 21-3.
"The Horse That Left His Mark" *Farm Tales* (1976), 24-9.
"A House with a Past" *Farm Tales* (1976), 42-5 [Non-fiction?].
"Lamplight and Rocking Chairs" *Farm Tales* (1976), 7-12.
"The Long Feud" *Farm Tales* (1976), 16-20.
"Maggie Was Game" *Farm Tales* (1976), 13-5.
"Masked Bandit in the Henhouse" *FH* 17 Nov 1960, 14-5, 31.
"The Night I Played Chicken with Eddy" *AA* 56 (Sept 1965), 110-2.

" 'There Ain't Nobody Loves Me' " *AA* 53 (Jan 1963), 55-60.
"Unsteady Eddie" *Farm Tales* (1976), 35-41.
"The Whopper" *CG* [80] (Aug 1961), 34-6.
"Wish on a Star, Silas" *Farm Tales* (1976), 30-4.

Mottadelli, Irene‡
"Winter Vacation" *JCF* No. 33 (1981-82), 59-78.

Moulton, Donna‡
"Splurge" *Atlantis* 1:1 (Fall 1975), 21-3.

Mounie, Ruth†
"Tea Party" *Outset* 1973, 125-7.

Mountford, Charles‡
"Second Life" *Jubilee* No. 2 [n.d.], 48-53.

Mouré, Erin (1955-)
"Taking Her Shot" *Waves* 10:4 (Spr 1982), 33-6.

Mouré, Ken
"Watching Mother" *Dand* 3 (Spr-Sum 1977), 35-9.

Mowat, Farley (1921-)
THE SNOW WALKER Toronto: McClelland & Stewart, 1975.
"Arnuk" *Moderne Erzühler der Walt: Kanada* (1976), 233-51 [Trans. Walter Riedel].
"The Blinding of André Maloche" *Sat Eve Post* 225 (15 Nov 1952), 38-9, 146-50.
"The Blinding of André Maloche" *Saturday Evening Post Stories* 1952 164-79.
"The Blinding of André Maloche" *Snow Walker* (1975), 19-42.
"Blizzard in the Banana Belt" *MM* 65 (1 Feb 1952), 13, 45-8.
"The Blood in Their Veins" *Snow Walker* (1975), 95-114.
"Dark Odyssey of Soosie" *Snow Walker* (1975), 183-222.
"The Desperate People" *Sat Eve Post* 223 (29 July 1950), 31, 42, 44, 46, 48.
"The Iron Men" *Snow Walker* (1975), 61-77.
"The Iron Men" *Best Canadian Short Stories* (1981), 151-63.
"The Last Husky" *Sat Eve Post* 227 (2 Apr 1955), 24, 58-9, 63-4.
"The Last Husky" *Saturday Evening Post Stories* 1955 178-92.
"The Last Husky" *Tigers of the Snow* (1973), 171-85.
"Lost in the Barren Lands" *Sat Eve Post* 224 (27 Oct 1951), 28-9, 106, 108, 110-2.
"Lost in the Barren Lands" *Saturday Evening Post Stories* 1951 [Based on SSI].
"The Riddle of the Viking Bow" *MM* 64 (1 Sept 1951), 12-3, 37-41.
"Snow" *Snow Walker* (1975), 9-18.
"The Snow Walker" *Snow Walker* (1975), 131-42.
"Stranger in Taransay" *Snow Walker* (1975), 43-59.
"Stranger in Taransay" *Inquiry into Literature* 3 (1980), 57 [Excerpt].
"Stranger in Taransay" *Contexts* 2 (1981), 232-43.
"Stranger in Taransay" *Canadian Stories of Action and Adventure* (1982), 98-111.
"Two Who Were One" *Snow Walker* (1975), 79-94.
"Walk Well, My Brother" *Snow Walker* (1975), 143-60.
"Walk Well, My Brother" *Journeys* 2 (1979), 34-45.
"Walk Well, My Brother" *Stories from the Canadian North* (1980), 67-81.

"Walk Well, My Brother" *West of Fiction* (1983), 47-58.
"The White Canoe" *Snow Walker* (1975), 161-82.
"The Woman and the Wolf" *Snow Walker* (1975), 115-30.
"The Woman He Left to Die" *Sat Eve Post* 225 (31 Jan 1953), 31, 98-102.
"The Woman He Left to Die" *Saturday Evening Post Stories* 1953 154-67.

Moyer, Carolyn
"Beer and Skittles" *Read Ch* 2:1 (Spr 1983), 13-7.
"Solace Stone" *Room* 1:2 (Sum 1975), 43-5.
"'Tis the Season to Be Jolly" *West Producer* 19 Dec 1974, C3 [Based on survey response].

Moyer, Kenneth A. (1913-)†
THE OLD CANOE Elmira: privately printed, 1977 [Based on CBIP].
PREACHER ON THE ROOF Elmira: privately printed, 1976 [Based on CBIP].

Moyle, Frank F.‡
"Caribou" *West People* No. 176 (17 Feb 1983), 10-1.

Moynihan, Robert†
"Party" *Antig R* No. 50 (Sum 1982), 105-7.

Mozel, Howard B.†
"People of the Twilight" *Portico* 3:2/3 [n.d.], 18-22, 29-39.

Muir, John Dapray‡
"Dry Graves" *Forge* Spr 1955, 33-4.

Mukherjee, Bharati (1942-)
"Debate on a Rainy Afternoon" *Massachusetts R* 7 (1966), 257-70.
"Isolated Incidents" *SN* 95 (Oct 1980), 52-4, 56, 59-60.

Mulkin, Grace‡
"Betty Earns a Nickname" *Can Nature* 12 (May-June 1950), 90-2 [Children's? Based on CPI].
"Bufo, a Grandmother Toad" *Can Nature* 12 (Jan-Feb 1950), 31-2 [Children's? Based on CPI].

Muller, Rita†
"The Door" *WCR* 3:3 (Win 1969), 42-4.

Multamaki, Ellen‡
"The Good Old Days" *Muskeg R* 4 [1976], 26-32.

Mundwiler, Leslie‡
"Truck Stop" *JCF* 3:4 (1975), 26-30.

Mundy, Bill‡
"In This Sign Conquer" *TUR* 63:2 (Aut 1950), 26-8.

Munro, Alice (1931-)
DANCE OF THE HAPPY SHADES Toronto: Macmillan, 1968.
LA DANSE DES OMBRES trans. Colette Tonge Montreal: Québec/Amerique, 1979.
THE MOONS OF JUPITER Toronto: Macmillan, 1982.
POUR QUI TE PRENDS-TU? trans. Colette Tonge Montreal: Québec/Amerique, 1981.
SOMETHING I'VE BEEN MEANING TO TELL YOU Toronto: McGraw-Hill Ryerson, 1974.
WHO DO YOU THINK YOU ARE? Toronto: Macmillan, 1978.
"Accident" *TL* (Nov 1977), 61, 87-8, 90-5, 149-50, 153-6, 159-60, 162-5, 167, 169-73.
"Accident" *Moons of Jupiter* (1980), 77-109.
"At the Other Place" by Alice Laidlaw *CF* 35 (Sept 1955), 131-3.
"Bardon Bus" *Moons of Jupiter* (1982), 110-28.
"Basket of Strawberries" *Mayfair* 27 (Nov 1953), 32-3, 78-80, 82.
"The Beggar Maid" *78: Best Canadian Stories* 9-42.
"The Beggar Maid" *Who Do You Think You Are?* (1978), 65-97.
"The Beggar Maid" *Best Canadian Short Stories* (1981), 96-121.
"The Beggar Maid" *Pour qui te prends-tu?* (1981), 97-142 [As "La jeune mendiante"].
"A Better Place Than Home" *Newcomers* (1979), 113-24.
"Boys and Girls" *Mont* 38 (Dec 1964), 25-34.
"Boys and Girls" *Dance of the Happy Shades* (1968), 111-27.
"Boys and Girls" *Sixteen by Twelve* (1970), 112-24.
"Boys and Girls" *Four Hemispheres* (1971), 89-101.
"Boys and Girls" *Die Weite Reise* (1974), 285-304 [As "Jungen und Mùdchen"; trans. Karl Heinrich].
"Boys and Girls" *Women in Canadian Literature* (1976), 11-21.
"Boys and Girls" *La danse des ombres* (1979), 143-62 [As "Garçons et filles"].
"Boys and Girls" *New Worlds* (1980), 120-32.
"Chaddeleys and Flemings: 1. Connection" *Moons of Jupiter* (1982), 1-18 [Also entitled "Connection"].
"Chaddeleys and Flemings: 2. The Stone in the Field" *Moons of Jupiter* (1982), 19-35 [Also entitled "The Stone in the Field"].
"Characters" *Ploughshares* (U.S.) 4:3 (1978), 72-82.
"Connection" *Chat* 51 (Nov 1978), 66-7, 97-8, 101, 104, 106 [Also entitled "Chaddeleys and Flemings: 1. Connection"].
"Dance of the Happy Shades" *Mont* 35 (Feb 1961), 22-6.
"Dance of the Happy Shades" *Canadian Short Stories II* (1968), 285-300.
"Dance of the Happy Shades" *Dance of the Happy Shades* (1968), 211-24.
"Dance of the Happy Shades" *Narrative Voice* (1972), 171-80.
"Dance of the Happy Shades" *Canadian Century* (1973), 491-501.
"Dance of the Happy Shades" *Here and Now* (1977), 85-95.
"Dance of the Happy Shades" *Toronto Short Stories* (1977), 260-72.
"Dance of the Happy Shades" *La danse des ombres* (1979), 259-73 [As "La danse des ombres"].
"The Dangerous One" *Chat* 29 (July 1957), 49-51.
"Day of the Butterfly" *Dance of the Happy Shades* (1968), 100-10.
"Day of the Butterfly" *Kaleidoscope* (1972), 92-102.

"Day of the Butterfly" *Ontario Experience* (1976), 102-12.
"Day of the Butterfly" *Crossroads* 2 (1979), 52-63.
"Day of the Butterfly" *La danse des ombres* (1979), 129-42 [As "Le jour du papillon"].
"Day of the Butterfly" *Inquiry into Literature* 4 (1980), 54-63.
"The Dimensions of a Shadow" by Alice Laidlaw *Folio* 4:2 [Apr 1950], [7 pp].
"Dulse" *Moons of Jupiter* (1982), 36-59.
"Dulse" *Penguin Book of Modern Canadian Short Stories* (1982), 463-81.
"The Edge of Town" *QQ* 62 (1955), 368-80.
"Executioners" *Something* (1974), 138-55.
"Forgiveness in Families" *CBC "Anthology"* 10 Mar 1973.
"Forgiveness in Families" *Something* (1974), 93-105.
"Forgiveness in Families" *West Coast Experience* (1976), 32-44.
"Forgiveness in Families" *Heartland* (1983), 107-17.
"Forgiveness in Families" *West of Fiction* (1983), 220-30.
"The Found Boat" *Something* (1974), 125-37.
"The Found Boat" *CBC "Anthology"* 6 Apr 1974.
"The Found Boat" *Role of Woman in Canadian Literature* (1975), 70-81.
"Good-by Myra" *Chat* 28 (July 1956), 17, 55-8.
"Half a Grapefruit" *Who Do You Think You Are?* (1978), 38-54.
"Half a Grapefruit" *Pour qui te prends-tu?* (1981), 61-82 [As "Un demi-pample-mousse"].
"Hard-Luck Stories" *Moons of Jupiter* (1982), 181-97.
"Home" *74: New Canadian Stories* 133-53.
"How Could I Do That?" *Chat* 28 (Mar 1956), 16, 65-70.
"How I Met My Husband" *Something* (1974), 45-66.
"How I Met My Husband" *Modern Canadian Stories* (1975), 1-20.
"How I Met My Husband" *Personal Fictions* (1977), 21-37.
"The Idyllic Summer" *CF* 34 (Aug 1954), 106-7, 109-10.
"Images" *Dance of the Happy Shades* (1968), 30-43.
"Images" *Narrative Voice* (1972), 161-71.
"Images" *Double Vision* (1976), 229-41.
"Images" *Personal Fictions* (1977), 9-20.
"Images" *La danse des ombres* (1979), 45-61.
"Labor Day Dinner" *Moons of Jupiter* (1982), 134-59.
"Marrakesh" *Something* (1974), 156-74.
"Material" *Tam R* No. 61 (Nov 1973), 7-25.
"Material" *Something* (1974), 24-44.
"Material" *Double Vision* (1976), 242-59.
"Material" *Personal Fictions* (1977), 55-71.
"Material" *Best Modern Canadian Short Stories* (1978), 24-38.
"Material" *Canadian Short Stories* 3 (1978), 241-63.
"Memorial" *Something* (1974), 207-26.
"Mischief" *Who Do You Think You Are?* (1978), 98-132.
"Mischief" *Pour qui te prends-tu?* (1981), 143-92 [As "Bôtises"].
"The Moons of Jupiter" *Moons of Jupiter* (1982), 217-33.
"The Moons of Jupiter" *Anthology of Canadian Literature in English* 2 (1983), 314-26.
"Mrs. Cross and Mrs. Kidd" *Moons of Jupiter* (1982), 160-80.
"Mrs. Cross and Mrs. Kidd" *Tam R* Nos. 83/84 (Win 1982), 5-24.

"The Office" *Mont* 36 (Sept 1962), 18-23.

"The Office" *Dance of the Happy Shades* (1968), 59-74.

"The Office" *Great Canadian Short Stories* (1971), 263-75.

"The Office" *Women and Fiction* (1975), 301-13.

"The Office" *Transitions 2* (1978), 141-52.

"The Office" *La danse des ombres* (1979), 81-98 [As "Le bureau"].

"The Ottawa Valley" *Something* (1974), 227-46.

"An Ounce of Cure" *Mont* 35 (May 1961), 26-30.

"An Ounce of Cure" *Dance of the Happy Shades* (1968), 75-88.

"An Ounce of Cure" *Sixteen by Twelve* (1970), 103-12.

"An Ounce of Cure" *Singing Under Ice* (1974), 147-60.

"An Ounce of Cure" *Sunlight & Shadows* (1974), 51-62.

"An Ounce of Cure" *Canadian Humour and Satire* (1976), 99-111.

"An Ounce of Cure" *Canadian Stories of Action and Adventure* (1978), 51-64.

"An Ounce of Cure" *La danse des ombres* (1979), 99-114 [As "Un rem de radical"].

"The Peace of Utrecht" *Tam R* No. 15 (Spr 1960), 5-21.

"The Peace of Utrecht" *Canadian Short Stories 2* (1968), 259-84.

"The Peace of Utrecht" *Dance of the Happy Shades* (1968), 190-210.

"The Peace of Utrecht" *Stories from Ontario* (1974), 241-59.

"The Peace of Utrecht" *Personal Fictions* (1977), 38-54.

"The Peace of Utrecht" *La danse des ombres* (1979), 235-58 [As "Le traité d'Utrecht"].

"The Photographer" *Artist in Canadian Literature* (1976), 93-104.

"Postcard" *Tam R* No. 47 (Spr 1968), 23-31, 33-9.

"Postcard" *Dance of the Happy Shades* (1968), 128-46.

"Postcard" *La danse des ombres* (1979), 163-84 [As "La carte postale"].

"Privilege" *Tam R* No. 70 (Win 1977), 14-28.

"Privilege" *Who Do You Think You Are?* (1978), 23-37.

"Privilege" *Pour qui te prends-tu?* (1981), 39-59 [As "Privil ge"].

"Providence" CBC "*Anthology*" 9 Apr 1977.

"Providence" *Who Do You Think You Are?* (1978), 133-51.

"Providence" *Pour qui te prends-tu?* (1981), 193-219.

"Prue" *New Yorker* 57 (30 Mar 1981), 34-5.

"Prue" *82: Best Canadian Stories* 74-9.

"Prue" *Moons of Jupiter* (1982), 129-33.

"Red Dress – 1946" *Mont* 39 (May 1965), 28-34.

"Red Dress – 1946" *Dance of the Happy Shades* (1968), 147-60.

"Red Dress – 1946" *In the Looking Glass* (1977), 199-211.

"Red Dress – 1946" *Childhood and Youth in Canadian Literature* (1979), 74-86.

"Red Dress – 1946" *La danse des ombres* (1979), 185-200 [As "La robe rouge – 1946"].

"Red Dress – 1946" *Rites of Passage* (1979), 8-19.

"Royal Beatings" *Who Do You Think You Are?* (1978), 1-22.

"Royal Beatings" *Norton Anthology of Short Fiction* (1981), 473-91.

"Royal Beatings" *Pour qui te prends-tu?* (1981), 9-38 [As "Royale raclées"].

"The Shining Houses" *Dance of the Happy Shades* (1968), 19-29.

"The Shining Houses" *Canadian Anthology* (1974), 520-6.

"The Shining Houses" *La danse des ombres* (1979), 31-43 [As "Le quartier neuf"].

"Simon's Luck" *Who Do You Think You Are?* (1978), 152-73.

"Simon's Luck" *Pour qui te prends-tu?* (1981), 221-51 [As "La chance de Simon"].

"Something I've Been Meaning to Tell You" *Something* (1974), 1-23.

"Something I've Been Meaning to Tell You" *Canadian Literature in the 70's* (1980), 19-35.

"Something I've Been Meaning to Tell You" *Anthology of Canadian Literature in English 2* (1983), 301-14.

"The Spanish Lady" *Something* (1974), 175-91.

"Spelling" *Who Do You Think You Are?* (1978), 174-88.

"Spelling" *Weekend* 28 (17 June 1978), 24-7.

"Spelling" *Best American Short Stories* 1979 150-6.

"Spelling" *Pour qui te prends-tu?* (1981), 253-72 [As "Le don d'épeler"].

"The Stone in the Field" *SN* 94 (Apr 1979), 40-5 [Also entitled "Chaddeleys and Flemings: 2. The Stone in the Field"].

"The Stone in the Field" *80: Best Canadian Stories* 115-31.

"The Stone in the Field" *Inquiry into Literature* 2 (1980), 182-3 [Excerpt].

"Story for Sunday" by Alice Laidlaw *Folio* 5:1 [Jan 1951], [5 pp].

"Sunday Afternoon" *CF* 37 (Sept 1957), 127-30.

"Sunday Afternoon" *Book of Canadian Stories* (1962), 327-36.

"Sunday Afternoon" *Dance of the Happy Shades* (1968), 161-71.

"Sunday Afternoon" *Selections from Major Canadian Writers* (1974), 244-9.

"Sunday Afternoon" *La danse des ombres* (1979), 201-12 [As "Un dimanche après-midi"].

"Tell Me Yes or No" *Chat* 47 (Mar 1974), 35, 54, 56-60, 62.

"Tell Me Yes or No" *Something* (1974), 106-24.

"Thanks for the Ride" *Tam R* No. 2 (Win 1957), 25-37.

"Thanks for the Ride" *Dance of the Happy Shades* (1968), 44-58.

"Thanks for the Ride" *Story-Makers* (1970), 47-60.

"Thanks for the Ride" *Modern Stories in English* (1975), 273-84.

"Thanks for the Ride" *La danse des ombres* (1979), 63-79 [As "Merci pour la balade"].

"Thanks for the Ride" *Penguin Book of Modern Canadian Short Stories* (1982), 71-82.

"The Time of Death" by Alice Laidlaw *CF* 36 (June 1956), 63-6.

"The Time of Death" *Modern Canadian Stories* (1966), 314-23.

"The Time of Death" *Dance of the Happy Shades* (1968), 89-99.

"The Time of Death" *Contemporary Voices* (1972), 128-34.

"The Time of Death" *La danse des ombres* (1979), 115-27 [As "L'heure de la mort"].

"A Trip to the Coast" *Ten for Wednesday Night* (1961), 74-92 [As "The Trip to the Coast"].

"A Trip to the Coast" *Dance of the Happy Shades* (1968), 172-89.

"A Trip to the Coast" *Evolution of Canadian Literature in English* (1973), 201-11.

"A Trip to the Coast" *La danse des ombres* (1979), 213-33 [As "Voyage à la côte"].

"The Turkey Season" *Moons of Jupiter* (1982), 60-76.

"Visitors" *Atlantic Monthly* 249 (Apr 1982), 91-8.

"Visitors" *Moons of Jupiter* (1982), 198-216.

"Walker Brothers Cowboy" *Dance of the Happy Shades* (1968), 1-18.

"Walker Brothers Cowboy" *Canadian Writing Today* (1970), 105-20.

"Walker Brothers Cowboy" *Oxford Anthology of Canadian Literature* (1973), 348-61.

"Walker Brothers Cowboy" *Stories from Ontario* (1974), 156-71.

"Walker Brothers Cowboy" *Depression in Canadian Literature* (1976), 92-109.

"Walker Brothers Cowboy" *La danse des ombres* (1979), 9-29 [As "Le cow-boy colporteur"].

"Walking on Water" *Something* (1974), 67-92.

"Who Do You Think You Are?" *Who Do You Think You Are?* (1978), 189-206.

"Who Do You Think You Are?" *Penguin Book of Canadian Short Stories* (1980), 299-316.

"Who Do You Think You Are?" *Pour qui te prends-tu?* (1981), 273-97 [As "Pour qui te prends-tu?"].

"The Widower" by Alice Laidlaw *Folio* 5:2 (Apr 1951), [5 pp].

"Wild Swans" *Who Do You Think You Are?* (1978), 55-64.

"Wild Swans" *TL* Apr 1978, 53, 124-5.

"Wild Swans" *Pour qui te prends-tu* (1981), 83-96 [As "Les cynes sauvages"].

"Winter Wind" *Something* (1974), 192-206.

"Winter Wind" *Family Portraits* (1978), 57-67.

"Winter Wind" *Literature in Canada* (1978), 477-87.

"Wood" *81: Best Canadian Stories* 93-110.

"Wood" *Best American Short Stories* 1981 241-54.

"The Yellow Afternoon" CBC "*Anthology*" 22 Feb 1955.

Munro, Jane‡

"Crow Takes the M's" *Makara* 3:3 (Fall 1978), 45-7 [Children's?].

Munro, Kate

"Bella" *Our Family* 19 (Jan 1968), 20-2.

Munroe, Rolf‡

"Why the Big Computer Broke Down Processing Census Returns from the Parish of St. Marys, York County, N.B." *AA* 61 (July 1971), 57, 59-60.

Murdie, Donna Haggarty (1948-)

"Dark Places" *CFM* No. 14 (Sum 1974), 64-73.

"The Time of Earth" *event* 4:3 [1974?], 51-7.

Murdoch, Benedict Joseph (1886-)

THE MURPHYS COME IN Fredericton: Brunswick Press, 1965.

"All Through the Night" *Murphys Come In* (1965), 87-97.

"Backhanded Inducement" *Murphys Come In* (1965), 175-88.

"The Bee Teasers" *Murphys Come In* (1965), 99-104.

"Days Before Tomorrow" *Ave Maria* 89 (10 Jan 1959), 20[+?] [Based on CPLI].

"Different Perspectives" *Ave Maria* 86 (10 Aug 1957), 18-21.

"Different Perspectives" *Murphys Come In* (1965), 77-86.

"Hard to Bear" *Murphys Come In* (1965), 237-45.

"It Is – They Will" *Murphys Come In* (1965), 189-95.

"The Manipulators" *AA* 52 (Oct 1961), 48-9, 51, 53-5.

"The Manipulators" *Murphys Come In* (1965), 127-40.
"More Here Than There" *AA* 52 (June 1962), 74-5.
"More Here Than There" *Murphys Come In* (1965), 57-62.
"The Murphy Touch" *Ave Maria* 82 (6 Aug 1955), 12-5.
"The Murphy Touch" *AA* 54 (July 1964), 69-70, 72-4.
"The Murphy Touch" *Murphys Come In* (1965), 63-75.
"The Murphys Don't Stay Licked" *Ave Maria* 81 (21 May 1955), 11-4.
"The Murphys Don't Stay Licked" *Murphys Come In* (1965), 23-34.
"No Challenge Needed" *Murphys Come In* (1965), 117-26.
"No Place for Basking" *AA* 54 (June 1964), 37-9.
"No Place for Basking" *Murphys Come In* (1965), 35-42.
"Old Enough to Quit?" *AA* 48 (Apr 1958), 57-63.
"Old Enough to Quit?" *Murphys Come In* (1965), 213-25.
"Pat Murphy Faces Up to It" *Murphys Come In* (1965), 247-55.
"Pat Murphy Takes Command" *AA* 55 (Sept 1964), 71-3, 75.
"Pat Murphy Takes Command" *Murphys Come In* (1965), 105-16.
"Pat Murphy Tries Psychology" *AA* 53 (July 1963), 57-9.
"Pat Murphy Tries Psychology" *Murphys Come In* (1965), 197-204.
"The Pinch Hitter" *Murphys Come In* (1965), 157-68.
"Progress Breaks Through the Hinterland" *Murphys Come In* (1965), 141-56.
"A Rugged Knight" *Murphys Come In* (1965), 227-35.
"Standing Up to It" *Murphys Come In* (1965), 43-55.
"There's a Lot in a Name" *Murphys Come In* (1965), 205-12.
"The Third Nugget" *Murphys Come In* (1965), 169-74.
"Waiting" *AA* 47 (Mar 1957), 81-3, 85-7.
"Waiting" *Murphys Come In* (1965), 9-22.

Murdoch, Nancy Clegg‡
"First Winter" *Edmonton Journal* Mon, 15 July 1963, 19.

Murphy, Aralt‡
"The Conjurer: A Canada Day Fable" *Legion* 53 (June 1978), 11, 20-1.
"Rum Along the Imjin" *Legion* 53 (Feb 1979), 11, 22-3.

Murphy, Bruce†
"October" *Gas Rain* 3 (1979), 31-3.

Murphy, Capt. Leo C.‡
"The Boat That Never Sailed" *Nfld Q* 57:2 (June 1958), 26-7.
"The Newfoundland Boat That Never Sailed" *Mar Adv* 45 (Nov 1954), 25-6 [Based on legend?].

Murphy, D.T. (Pat)‡
"Stop the Press" *Axiom* 2:1 (Aug-Sept 1975), 14-5.
"Tube Head" *Axiom* 1:4 (Spr 1975), 14-5, 30.

Murphy, Jeremiah‡
"The Wake" *Axiom* 3:2 (Feb-Mar 1977), 38-9.

Murphy, Kathleen‡
"The Wait" *Abegweit R* 3:1 (Spr 1980), 35-41.

Murphy, Marylynn†
"All for the Children" *From This Place* (1977), 173-4.

Murphy, Phil
"The Honeymoon" *SN* 97 (May 1982), 46-52.
"Prophet Still, If Bird or Devil" *SN* 82 (Dec 1967), 25-30.

Murphy, Sarah†
"A Comic Book Heroine" *NeWest R* 9 (Dec 1983), 13-6.

Murray, Aase‡
"Mail Order" *Edmonton Journal* Fri, 19 Apr 1968, 54.

Murray, David†
"A La Recherche d'Arbuthnot" *Quarry* 28:1 (Win 1979), 57-70.

Murray, Don
"The Bowl of Fruit" *Lib* 29 (Jan 1953), 14-5, 44-5.

Murray, Glenn†
"The Reprieve" *Antig R* No. 25 (Spr 1976), 9-12.

Murray, Heather†
"Driftwood Notes" *Room* 1:4 (Win 1976), 17-21.

Murray, Joan
"Anne in the Meadows" *CBC "Anthology"* 8 June 1967.
"The Girl That Ran Away" *Undergrad* 1964, 17-22.
"A Jazz Story" *Jargon* 1962-63, 17-25.
"The Kiss" *Des* 12:2/3 Nos. 32O/33 (1981), 175-82.
"Lizzie's Curator" *Des* 13:3 No. 37 (Sum 1982), 76-84.
"Lydia Growing Up" *CBC "Anthology"* 9 July 1968.
"Mary" *Undergrad* 1965, 3-5.
"Mrs. MacLean and the Governor-General" *Undergrad* Spr 1963, 21-4.
"Picker" *Des* 11:4/12:1 Nos. 30/31 (1980-81), 40-7.
"Sketch" *Undergrad* Spr 1962, 1-2.
" 'When the Saints Come Marching In' " *Undergrad* Spr 1962, 25-6.
"The White Nicotine" *CBC "Anthology"* 31 May 1969.

Murray, Rona (1924-)
See also Murray, Rona and Glay, George Albert.
"The Firing" *event* 10:1 (1981), 93-100.
"Homecoming" *Prism* 21:1 (Sept 1982), 63-71.
"Homecoming" *Metavisions* (1983), 53-61.
"Marina Island" *Room* 5:4 (1980), 2-14.
"Nana" *Mal R* No. 45 (Jan 1978), 299-307.
"New Year's Day" *Des* 12:4/13:1/2 Nos. 34/35/36 (1981-82), 179-91.
"New Year's Day" *83: Best Canadian Stories* 7-24.
"Night World" *Mal R* No. 50 (Apr 1979), 215-25.
"Night World" *Rainshadow* (1982), 179-90.

"The Officer and the Woman" *WCR* 18:1 (June 1983), 10-7.
"An Old Tale" *CBC* [Van] "Hornby Collection" 16 Jan 1982.
"Remembering" *Mal R* No. 62 (July 1982), 191-8.

Murray, Rona and Glay, George Albert
See also Glay, George Albert; Murray, Rona.
"Miracle at the Andovers" *CHJ* Oct 1953, 18, 25, 27, 46-8, 49, 54-5, 59.

Murray, Walter†
"The Great Atlantis Lotto" *UC Observer* Feb 1979, 37-8.

Musgrave, Susan
"The Night the French Chef Came to Dinner" *Vancouver Mag* Mar 1983, 118, 121-5.

Myers, Martin (1927-)
"Fragments" *JD* Sum 1972, 10-6.

Myers, Robert‡
"1111" *Story So Four* (1976), 198-9.
"Tradewinds" *Writ* No. 4 (Spr 1972), 74-5.

Myles, Roderick.
THE SHANTY BOY North Bay: privately printed, 1982 [Based on CBIP].

N., A.J.
"August Heat" *Undergrad* Win 1955, 14-6.

Nadia [pseudonym]
"A Man and His Dream" *Muse* 60:4 (Apr 1951), 16.

Nagal, Peter†
"The Ark" *CSSM* 2:1 (Jan 1976), 39-41.
"Without Sound" *CSSM* 1:2 (Apr 1975), 41, 43-5.

Naglin, Nancy†
"Felix's Pheasant" *Snowmobiles Forbidden* (1971), 80-96.
"Felix's Pheasant" *Miss Chat* 9 (8 Feb 1972), 66, 70-2, 78.

Nagorsen, Ross (1951-)
"Fool's Errand" *Nw J* No. 26 (1982), 45-51.
"A Story from the Polar Bear Capital" *Squatch J* No. 13 (June 1982), 12-8.

Najovits, Simson R.
"The Wailing Western Wall" *WCR* 4:1 (Spr 1969), 1-7.

Napier, Noel Marie‡
"Confessions of a Crazy Man" *Scar Fair* 9 (1982), 19-21.

Narvey, Fred

"Buddies" *CJO* 21 (Oct 1983), 7.
"Choosing a Second Career" *CJO* 18 (Apr 1980), 7.
"Frosty Friday" *CJO* 18 (Oct 1980), 7.
"Kildonan Park" *CJO* 18 (Feb 1980), 7.
"My Introduction to Culture" *CJO* 17 (Nov-Dec 1979), 15-6.
"A Tale without a Donkey" *CJO* 21 (July-Aug 1983), 15-6.
"Two for the Road" *CJO* 20 (Feb 1982), 7-9.

Nason, Colleen‡

"Liddle Black Boy" *New Thursday* No. 2 (1975), 44-5.
"The Ritual" *New Thursday* No. 2 (1975), 50-1.

Natale, C.†

"The Leaving" *York Lit Series* No. 3 (Win 1971), 9-10.

Nathans, Elyeh‡

"Beanut and the Seder" *CJO* 2 (Apr 1964), 14-5.

Nations, Opal L. (1941-)

See also Fones, Robert and Nations, Opal L.; Gold, Artie and Nations, Opal L.; Kilodney, Crad and Nations, Opal L.
THE STRANGE CASE OF INSPECTOR LOOPHOLE Montreal: Vehicule Press, 1977.
"Billy Haskell's Hanging" *Titmouse R* No. 4 (Spr 1974), 51-2.
"Bluebeard" *Canadian Short Fiction Anthology* 2 (1982), 76-9.
"Clove" *Titmouse R* No. 3 (Sum 1973), 13-7.
"The Etiquette of Invisible Eating" *Fruits of Experience* (1978), 125-32.
"God, Burgers and French Fries to Go" *Atropos* 1:1 (Spr 1978), 74-7.
"Juan Fortune" *New Worlds* (U.K.) No. 186 (Jan 1969), 34-5.
"Little Red Riding Hood" *The Smith* No. 20 (June 1978), 41-3.
"Lot's Wife" *Atropos* 1:1 (Spr 1978), 73.
"The Man and His Wife" *BC Monthly* 3:3 (Dec 1976), [1 p].
"Man and Lightning" *Atropos* 1:1 (Spr 1978), 73.
"The Man and the Vulture" *Atropos* 1:1 (Spr 1978), 73.
"More Testimonials By Recipients of Artificial Limbs" *Canadian Short Fiction Anthology* (1976), 135-6.
"Mr. Smudge Takes a Dip" *Da Vinci* 2:1 No. 4 (Aut 1975), 40-3.
"The New Pair of Shoes" *BC Monthly* 3:3 (Dec 1976), [1 p].
"Once Upon a Time in a City" *Titmouse R* No. 3 (Sum 1973), 20-4.
"The U.S. Chinese Immigrant's Book of the Art of Sex" *Pushcart Prize* 2 (1977), 310-6.
[Untitled] *Is* No. 11 (1972), [2 pp] [Prose poem?].
"The Wager" *BC Monthly* 3:3 (Dec 1976), [1 p].
"The Woman Beautiful" *X-1* (U.S.) (1976), 143-6.

Naylor, C. David

"Marilyn" *Des* 9:1/2 Nos. 20/21 (1978), 144-7.
"The Woodworker or, The Man Who Refinished His Wife" *Des* 11:1/2 Nos. 27/28 (1980), 126-8.

Neal, Ellen
"Fallen Rock" *CSSM* 3:2 (Spr 1977), 47-8.

Nebbs, Margaret
"The Florentine Table" *Black Cat* 1:2 (July-Aug 1981), 44-8.

Needles, K. Reed‡
"october thursday inattention" *TUR* 90:2 (Dec [1976]), 47-9.

Neil, Al
SLAMMER Vancouver: Pulp Press, 1981.
"7 Rue Nesle" *Slammer* (1981), 60-73.
"The Eyes of Ninotchka Raginsky" *Slammer* (1981), 19-31.
"Keizersgracht 69" *Slammer* (1981), 74-102.
"Laughter on 3rd Street" *Slammer* (1981), 54-9.
"October Days on the Alouette" *BC Monthly* 3:6/7 (Apr-May 1977), [16 pp] [Non-fiction?].
"October Days on the Alouette" *Slammer* (1981), 32-53.
"The Peashooter" *BC Monthly* 3:6/7 (Apr-May 1977), [7 pp].
"The Peashooter" *Slammer* (1981), 9-18.
"Slammer" *Slammer* (1981), 103-19.

Nella [pseudonym]
"Fresh Air" *Pulp* 2:11 (1 Aug 1974), [1 p].
"Peter Rabbit" *Pulp* 2:10 (15 July 1974), [2 pp].

Nelson, Bert‡
"Creeping Vine" *CBC [Van] "Hornby Collection"* 10 June 1978.

Nelson, Elizabeth‡
"Belinda" *West People* No. 122 (28 Jan 1982), 10.
"The Magic Ingredient" *West People* No. 174 (3 Feb 1983), 14-5.

Nelson, Harold‡
"Beauty Like a Rose" *Acta Vic* 77:2 (Dec 1952), 21-2.
"One Easy Lesson" *Acta Vic* 77:3 (Feb 1953), 21-3.

Nelson, Joanne L.†
"Till Human Voices Wake Us" *Room* 6:1/2 (1981), 11-22.

Nemiroff, Greta Hofmann (1937-)
"About Bert Israel" *Forge* Dec 1957, 33-6.
"Architects of the Youth" *CBC "Anthology"* [?] 1966 [Based on survey response].
"The Bird-Healer" by Greta Hofmann *New Voices* (1956), 164-8.
"Chez Sergei" *Room* 6:3 (1981), 3-22.
"The Day the War Ended" *CBC "Anthology"* 24 Jan 1970.
"The Day the War Ended" *Current Assets* (1973), 19-31.
"Mothers, Daughters: Barriers, Borders" *Room* 8:3 (1983), 17-31.
"Parable of Paragraphs" *Room* 6:4 (1981), 55-68.
"Rosi-ka's Ankles" *Fireweed* No. 10 (Spr 1981), 53-61.

"The Snow Man" by Greta Ellen Hofmann *Forge* Dec 1956, 17-23.
"We Are in a Car Going Somewhere" *Matrix* No. 16 (Spr 1983), 47-54.
"Wunderkind" *Current Assets* (1973), 69-74.

Nemiroff, Michael‡
"A Stranger in Paradise" *Prism* (Mont) No. 8 (1965), 15-6.

Nepszy, Geraldine†
"When Morning Comes" *Green's* 8:2A (Win 1980), 59-64.

Neufeld, Bob‡
"Diary of an Executioner" *Simcoe R* No. 1 (Win 1976), 38.
"The Prospector" *Simcoe R* No. 1 (Win 1976), 37.

Neufeld, K. Gordon†
"Parker's Elect" *Canadian Short Fiction Anthology* (1976), 137-49.

Neufeld, Susanne‡
"In My Own Magic" *Introductions from an Island* 1971, 35-6.

Neurosurgery – *See* Zonko.

Nevitt, Brian‡
"The Story of Icarus, the Boy Who Wanted to Fly; or a Portrait of the Artist as a Young Bird" *Forge* 26:1 (Feb 1964), 17-8.

Newberry, Sterling‡
"A New Volunteer" *Alive* No. 44 [n.d.], 19.

Newlove, John (1938-)
"The Egg" *event* 6:2 [1977], 24-31.
"The Sen-Sen Kid Dreams of Heaven" *Quarry* 25:3 (Sum 1976), 57-62.
"The Sen-Sen Kid Dreams of Heaven" *Saskatchewan Gold* (1982), 96-101.
"So Soft, So White" *Quarry* 22:4 (Aut 1973), 28-34.
"The Story of a Cat" *72: New Canadian Stories* 38-44.
"The Story of a Cat" *Fiction of Contemporary Canada* (1980), 33-8.

Newman, C.J. (1935-)
"An Arab Up North" *Tam R* No. 47 (Spr 1968), 45-53, 55-65, 67-70.
"An Arab Up North" *New Canadian Writing* 1969 126-52.
"An Arab Up North" *Spice Box* (1981), 144-65.
"The Best Lay I Ever Had" *JCF* 3:3 (1974), 35-8.
"Dreams of Men and Women" *JCF* No. 16 (1976), 33-8.
"Everything Must Be Sold" *New Canadian Writing* 1969 119-25.
"The Game of Limping" *Prairie Schooner* 48 (1974-75), 334-47.
"The Game of Limping" CBC "*Anthology*" 23 Aug 1975.
"*Untermensch* and *Kluger Kind*" *Mal R* No. 39 (July 1976), 81-4.
"The Last Beginning. The Last! The Last!" *CFM* No. 16 (Win 1975), 40-3.
"My Brother Solomon, the Bible, and the Bicycle" *Tam R* No. 43 (Spr 1967), 22-35.
"San Francisco – Hong Kong" *Prism* 11:3 (Spr 1972), 98-101.
"That Old David Copperfield Kind of Crap" *CFM* No. 9 (Win 1973), 20-31.

"The Tour-Guide Instructor" *CBC "Anthology"* 9 July 1977.
"Words of Glass" *Prism* (Mont) 1958, 15-8.
"Yenteh" *New Canadian Writing* 1969 105-18.
"You Are Very Much on My Mind" *Quarry* 24:1 (Win 1975), 19-23.
"Your Green Coat" *Mal R* No. 31 (July 1974), 77-82.

Newman, Frank†

"A Birthday Cake Forever" *Toronto Star* Sun, 7 Sept 1980, D5.

Newman, P.N.†

"To Write" *WWR* 2:4 No. 8 (1983), 95.

Newman, Peter C. (1929-)

"We Are Many" *Acta Vic* 74:3 (Jan 1950), 10-1.

Newman, Sol‡

"Jewboy!" *Was R* 6:1 (1971), 41-52.

Newton, Marion‡

"Thursday Afternoon" *AA* 57 (June 1967), 22, 24.

Nichol, bp (1944-)

CRAFT DINNER: STORIES & TEXTS 1966-76 Toronto: Aya Press, 1978.
THE TRUE EVENTUAL STORY OF BILLY THE KID Toronto: Weed/Flower Press, 1970 [Based on *Craft Dinner*].
"Early April" *Craft Dinner* (1978), [4 pp].
"Gorg: A Detective Story" *Story So Far* 3 (1974), 135.
"Gorg: A Detective Story" *Craft Dinner* (1978), [2 pp].
"The Long Weekend of Louis Riel" *Craft Dinner* (1978), [4 pp].
"Story" *Story So Far* (1971), 38-40.
"The True Eventual Story of Billy the Kid" *Craft Dinner* (1978), [4 pp].
"Twins – A History" *Story So Far* 2 (1973), 64-5.
"Twins – A History" *Craft Dinner* (1978), [3 pp].
"Twins – A History" *Fiction of Contemporary Canada* (1980), 171-2.
"Two Heroes" *Story So Four* (1976), 200-4.
"Two Heroes" *Craft Dinner* (1978), [6 pp].

Nichols, Don‡

"Shelley the Sensitive Plant" *Writ* No. 12 (1980), 65-7.

Nichols, Janet‡

"Summer Hunting Grounds" *J of Our Time* No. 1 (1977), 35-9 [Non-fiction?].

Nichols, Mark‡

"Homecoming" *Varsity* Tue, 16 Dec 1958, 8-9.

Nicholson, Maureen

"A Desire to Dance" *WCR* 17:2 (Oct 1982), 3-8.

Nicks, W. Frederick†

"Bullets Are for Catching" *Alive* 3:2 No. 21 [1972?], 30-1.
"The Partners" *Alive* 2:4 (Mar 1971), 29-36.
"The Road to Oblivion" *Alive* 2:9 [Sept 1971], 34-6.

Nicol, Eric (1919-)

"A Christmas Carol Update" *Chimo!* 4 (Dec 1981), 45-6.

"We Won't Talk About It" *Uk Can* 8 (1 June 1954), 5 [Originally published in *Vancouver Province (editorial note); humour?].*

Nicol, John†

"Nightmare" *Folio* 18:2 (Fall 1965), 4-5.

Nielsen, Angela F.‡

"Daft Davie" *Thornhill Month* 4 (Nov 1982), 50-2.

"Harry, the Businessman, Meets a Bag Lady" *Toronto Star* Sun, 17 Oct 1982, D5.

"Summertime" *Thornhill Month* 3 (July 1982), 20-1.

Nielson, Dorise†

"The Dance" *NF* 1:4 (Win 1953), 1-6.

Niffenson, Harvey‡

"Story in Force" *Prism* (Mont) 4 (1961), 26-31.

Nightengale, Christine‡

"Ondine" *Quarry* 26:3 (Sum 1977), 7-11.

Nimchuk, Michael John

"Dialogue" *Varsity Lit Issue* Tue, 1 Mar 1955, 1, 8.

"The Gift Box" *Undergrad* Spr 1956, 23-5.

"How Casey Lost His Girl" *Fid* No. 43 (Win 1960), 2-7.

"How Casey Lost His Girl" *Otherside* No. 2 (Win 1960), 12-4.

"The Hunter" *Varsity Lit Issue* Mon, 22 Feb 1954, 1.

"The Hunter" *CF* 39 (Dec 1959), 204-5.

"Lover Bounce High" *Undergrad* Spr 1955, 20-2.

"Pigeon" *Fid* No. 54 (Fall 1962), 43-50.

"Teddy Bear and the Pregnant Parallel" *CF* 40 (June 1960), 56-8.

"Teddy Bear and the Pregnant Parallel" *Otherside* No. 3 (Mar 1961), 22-4.

Nipp, Dora

"Window-Pane" *Fireweed* No. 16 (Spr 1983), 109-12.

Nishihata, Jesse†

"Wands Across Dark Rooms" *Prism* (Mont) No. 3 (1957), 50-3.

Nishimura, Wendy‡

"Smote Plums" *Whetstone* Spr 1971, [3 pp].

Noble, Charles

"The Moon" *Grain* 10:4 (Nov 1982), 16-8.

Noble, Dennis E.

"The Dragon and the Flower" *Writers' Circle* (1974), 1-7.

Nolan, Gladys†

"Brief Love Affair" *Lifetime* 2 (Jan-Feb 1972), 18-9.

"The New Source" *Lifetime* 2 (Sept-Oct 1972), 16-8.

"A Trip North" *Can Lifetime* 4 (July-Aug 1974), 4-7.

Noonan, Gerald
"The All-Star Game" *New Q* 1:1 (Spr 1981), 41-7.
"Lessons in Geometry" *New Q* 1:2 (Sum 1981), 14-21.
"Things You Couldn't Tell" *New Q* 2:3 (Fall 1982), 21-30.

Norman, Colin†
"A Matter of Indifference" *Quarry* 9 (Mar 1960), 13-6.
"A Matter of Small Importance" *Prism* 2:3 (Spr 1961), 4-7.
"The Meaning of Meaning" *Quarry* 7 (Mar 1958), [2 pp].
"So Much for That" *QQ* 83 (1976), 278-81.

North, Phil‡
"Grandpa Loved His Muzzle Loader" *Forest & Outdoors* 50 (Jan 1954), 12, 29.

Notar, Stephen†
"Enemies of the State" *New Q* 1:2 (Sum 1981), 26-34.
"Willow, Weep for Me" *Cyclic* 1:2 (Aut 1965), 3-6.

Novack, Deborah‡
"Why Should I Have Been There?" *Flow* Win [1975?], [3 pp].

Novak, Barbara (1951-)
"Christmas Under a Pale Green Sky" *Who & Why* Dec 1983 [Children's? Based on survey response].
"Courtship" *Waves* 11:1 (Fall 1982), 44-51.
"If Gauthier Should Read This" *Canadian Short Fiction Anthology* 2 (1982), 113-6.
"The Secret" *JD* Sum 1980, 26-8, 30, 32, 34.
"Solo Dive" *Br Out* 7:1 (1980), 28-31.
"The Victim" *Miss Chat* 13 (5 Oct 1976), 68-9, 85-6.

Nowlan, Alden (1933-1983)
MIRACLE AT INDIAN RIVER Toronto: Clarke, Irwin, 1968.
VARIOUS PERSONS NAMED KEVIN O'BRIEN: A FICTIONAL MEMOIR Toronto/Vancouver: Clarke, Irwin, 1973.
"About Memorials" *Fid* No. 137 (Oct 1983), 21-9.
"An Act of Contrition" *event* 2:2 [1972], 9-15.
"An Act of Contrition" *Various Persons* (1973), 97-105.
"Anointed with Oils" *Fid* No. 56 (Spr 1963), 40-7.
"Anointed with Oils" *Miracle at Indian River* (1968), 43-51.
"Anointed with Oils" *Selections from Major Canadian Writers* (1974), 251-5.
"Anointed with Oils" *Isolation in Canadian Literature* (1975), 66-73.
"Anointed with Oils" *New Worlds* (1980), 47-53.
"As Others See Us" *Dand* 3 (Spr-Sum 1977), 6-8.
"At the Edge of the Woods" *Prism* 2:2 (Sum 1961), 21-3.
"At the Edge of the Woods" *Miracle at Indian River* (1968), 25-8.
"At the Edge of the Woods" *Story So Far* (1971), 52-4.
"The Bear in the Orchard" *AA* 53 (Nov 1962), 14-5.
"Before His Very Eyes" *Pot Port* 1 (1979-80), 24-5.
"The Cage" *AA* 55 (Mar 1965), 43-5.
"A Call in December" *QQ* 68 (1961), 482-5.
"A Call in December" *Miracle at Indian River* (1968), 29-32.
"A Call in December" *Stories from Atlantic Canada* (1973), 70-3.

"A Call in December" *Mountain & Plain* (1978), 27-9.

"The Coming of Age" *Fourteen Stories High* (1971), 122-31.

"The Coming of Age" *Various Persons* (1973), 85-96.

"Cynthia Loves You" CF 41 (Aug 1961), 110-2.

"A Day's Work" *Edge* No. 3 (Aut 1964), 54-60.

"A Day's Work" *Miracle at Indian River* (1968), 97-106.

"Documentary: The Execution of Clemmie Lake" *Fid* No. 45 (Sum 1960), 7-9.

"Documentary: The Execution of Clemmie Lake" *Miracle at Indian River* (1968), 91-6.

"The Fall of a City" *AA* 53 (Sept 1962), 53, 55, 57.

"The Fall of a City" *Tigers of the Snow* (1973), 41-6.

"The Fall of a City" *Moderne Erzühler der Walt: Kanada* (1976), 313-8 [As "Die Vernichtung einer Stadt"; trans. Walter Riedel].

"The Fall of a City" *Childhood and Youth in Canadian Literature* (1979), 32-7.

"The Foreigner" CF 44 (Nov 1964), 182-3.

"The Foreigner" *Miracle at Indian River* (1968), 107-12.

"A Friend for Margaret" *Fid* No. 40 (Spr 1959), 1-5.

"The Girl Who Went to Mexico" *Miracle at Indian River* (1968), 78-90.

"The Girl Who Went to Mexico" *Sixteen by Twelve* (1970), 144-52.

"The Girl Who Went to Mexico" *Transitions 2* (1978), 123-31.

"The Girl Who Went to Mexico" *Best Canadian Short Stories* (1981), 26-35.

"The Glass Roses" *QQ* 69 (1962), 398-406.

"The Glass Roses" *Miracle at Indian River* (1968), 52-62.

"The Glass Roses" *Stories from Atlantic Canada* (1973), 74-83.

"Good Sir, Take My Advice and Do Not Die" CBC "Anthology" 27 Jan 1973.

"The Guide" CF 45 (Apr 1965), 11-2.

"The Guide" *Modern Canadian Stories* (1966), 389-92.

"The Guide" *Miracle at Indian River* (1968), 113-7.

"The Gunfighter" *Miracle at Indian River* (1968), 128-32.

"The Gunfighter" *Sunlight & Shadows* (1974), 105-9.

"Hainesville Is Not the World" *Fid* No. 52 (Spr 1962), 39-42.

"Hainesville Is Not the World" *Fiddlehead Greens* (1979), 7-11.

"The Heatherington Murder Case" *JD* Rosh Hashanah 1972, 43-8.

"Hello, Out There" *JCF* 1:1 (Win 1972), 30-2.

"The Hetherington Murder Case" *Various Persons* (1973), 117-27.

"His Native Place" *Fid* No. 81 (Aug-Sept-Oct 1969), 28-40.

"His Native Place" *Various Persons* (1973), 129-43.

"How to Sell Insurance" *Antig R* No. 46 (Sum 1981), 11-4.

"Humbly, for Fyodor" *Prism* 7:2 (Aut 1967), 88-91.

"Hurt" *QQ* 66 (1959), 473-6.

"Hurt" *Miracle at Indian River* (1968), 12-7.

"Hurt" *Canadian Anthology* (1974), 536-9.

"Hurt" *Nearly an Island* (1979), 168-72.

"The Imaginary Soldier" *JD* Passover 1972, 14-5, 17-20.

"The Imaginary Soldier" *Various Persons* (1973), 23-35.

"In Hiding" *Alphabet* No. 3 (Dec 1961), 15-23.

"In the Finland Woods" *Family Portraits* (1978), 28-34.

"Infidelity" *Waves* 6:2 (Win 1978), 4-12.

"The Innermost One" *Miracle at Indian River* (1968), 123-7.

"The Innermost One" *Edge* No. 8 (Fall 1968), 92-4.

"A Jukebox in the Kitchen" *Pluck* 1:2 (Spr 1968), 9-14.

"Kevin and Stephanie" *Tam R* No. 54 (1970), 24-31.

"Kevin and Stephanie" *Various Persons* (1973), 65-75.

"The Kneeling of the Cattle" *Various Persons* (1973), 77-83.

"The Last of Her Sons" *Dal R* 42 (1962), 50-4.

"Life and Times" *Fid* No. 89 (Spr 1971), 19-27.

"Life and Times" *Various Persons* (1973), 37-50.

"Life and Times" *Fiddlehead Greens* (1979), 12-24.

"Lonnie Comes Home" *Dal R* 41 (1961), 49-51.

"Lonnie Comes Home" *Miracle at Indian River* (1968), 74-7.

"Love Letter" *Amethyst* 2:4 (Sum 1963), 26-33.

"Love Letter" *Miracle at Indian River* (1968), 63-73.

"Miracle at Indian River" *Miracle at Indian River* (1968), 3-11.

"Miracle at Indian River" *Fid* No. [76] (Spr 1968), 5-13.

"Miracle at Indian River" *Modern Stories in English* (1975), 293-9.

"Monique" *Atl Insight* 1:5 (Aug 1979), 62-3.

"Morning Flight to Red Deer" *Prism* 21:2 (Dec 1982), 31-6.

"My Father the Fiddler" *AA* 51 (Nov 1960), 73.

"Night Watch" *UWR* 6:1 (Fall 1970), 28-32.

"Night Watch" *Various Persons* (1973), 107-15.

"Nightmare" *Fid* No. 48 (Spr 1961), 4-8.

"A Note on Gallows Humour" *Intercourse* No. 4 (Indian Summer [1966]), 6-7.

"Notes Toward a Plot for an Unwritten Short Story" *CF* 46 (Feb 1967), 254-5.

"Notes Toward a Plot for an Unwritten Short Story" *Miracle at Indian River* (1968), 118-22.

"One Cold Bright Afternoon" *JCF* 1:4 (Fall 1972), 10-1.

"One September Afternoon" *QQ* 81 (1974), 81-3.

"The Opening of a Door" *AA* 56 (Mar 1966), 20-2.

"A Rinky Dinky Do" *CF* 40 (Jan 1961), 228-9.

"Rumours of War" *WCR* 4:2 (Fall 1969), 1-9.

"Rumours of War" *Various Persons* (1973), 3-22.

"A Sick Call" *Miracle at Indian River* (1968), 18-24.

"A Sick Call" *New Worlds* (1980), 101-5.

"The Small Hours" *AA* 60 (Mar 1970), 42-4.

"There Was an Old Woman from Wexford" *Prism* 9:2 (Aut 1969), 30-9.

"There Was an Old Woman from Wexford" *AA* 61 (Mar 1971), 42-7.

"There Was an Old Woman from Wexford" *Contemporary Voices* (1972), 135-42.

"There Was an Old Woman from Wexford" *Various Persons* (1973), 51-64.

"The Thin Red Line" *Fid* No. 78 (Jan-Feb 1969), 87-91 [Titles unknown] *CBC "Anthology"* 25 Sept 1971.

"True Confession" *Book of Canadian Stories* (1962), 337-40.

"True Confession" *Fid* No. 52 (Spr 1962), 36-8.

"True Confession" *Maritime Experience* (1975), 74-7.

"The Unnatural Son" *CF* 48 (Apr 1968), 16-7.

"The Unnatural Son" *Forum* (1972), 408-11.

"Who Was the Greatest Writer Who Ever Lived?" *Adam International R* 32 Nos. 313/314/315 (1967), 57-64.

"Will Ye Let the Mummers In?" *CBC "Anthology"* 4 June 1977.

"Will Ye Let the Mummers In?" *CFM* Nos. 30/31 (1979), 184-95.

"The Year of the Revolution" *Small Wonders* (1982), 85-96.

Nowlan, Michael O. (1937-)
"A Christmas for Grandmother" *AA* 70 (Dec 1979), 80, 82, 84.
'The Last Bell" *AA* 68 (Dec 1977), 20-3.
"One Special Present" *AA* 74 (Dec 1983), 41-2.
'This Is Our Willie" *AA* 73 (Dec 1982), 41-3.

Nugent, Olive‡
"Arlene in One Day Land" *Diversions* 3:1 (1971), 13-4.

Nunn, Robert
'Inside the Square: A Fragment" *Catalyst* 1:1 (Aut 1967), 10-4.

Nuss, Joseph R.‡
"Masquerade" *Forge* Mar 1958, 8-9.

Nutting, Leslie‡
'The Prophet" *Grain* 5:2 [1977], 51-4.

Nyberg, Wayne‡
"Lord Newmountain's Love" *Potlatch* No. 5 (Dec 1965), 25-30.
"Selected Episodes from an Empty Diary" *Potlatch* No. 16 (Mar 1966), 39-46.

Oakey, Shaun†
'The Lost Man's Tale" *Dand* 8:2 (1981), 70-3.
"Until the Petals Fall Off" *Pier Spr* 6:4 (Aut 1981), 10-7.

Ober, Harold‡
'Real Roger" *Prism* 12:1 (Sum 1972), 123-32.
"Strange Fruit" *Prism* 13:3 (Spr 1974), 77-84.

Oborne, Louise Margaret†
'The Letter" *Antig R* No. 50 (Sum 1981), 91-5.

O'Brien, Bill T. (1943-)
'The Escape Artist" *Prism* 8:2 (Aut 1968), 13-8.
'Happy Birthday Little Anarchist" *event* 1:3 (Win 1972), 7-20.

O'Brien, Olive‡
"Musings of an Old Lady" *Sand Patterns* No. 11 (1974), 20-1.

O'Brien, Peter
'The Second Car" *Pot Port* 4 (1982-83), 31-2.

O'Brien, Richard‡
'I Remember El Stomacho" *Alive* No. 26 [1973], 45-9.
'It Should Happen to a Dog" *Alive* No. 31 [1973], 37.

Observer [pseudonym]
"Easter Passage" *Edmonton Journal* Thu, 8 Apr 1965, 4.

O'Connell, David‡
    "Strawberries and Marshmallows" *Katharsis* 3:1 (Spr 1970), 74-5.

O'Connell, Dorothy.
    CHICLET GOMEZ Ottawa: Deneau & Greenberg, [1977].
    COCK-EYED OPTIMISTS Ottawa: Deneau & Greenberg, 1980.
    "Aluminum Pots" *Cock-Eyed Optimists* (1980), 31-8.
    "Among My Souvenirs" *Chiclet Gomez* [1977], 8-15.
    "Authority Figures" *Cock-Eyed Optimists* (1980), 55-62.
    "Better Homes and Gardens" *Chiclet Gomez* [1977], 121-4.
    "The Big Time" *Chiclet Gomez* [1977], 65-71.
    "Birth and Death and the Whole Damn Thing" *Cock-Eyed Optimists* (1980), 180-5.
    "Bruno" *Chiclet Gomez* [1977], 135-8.
    "Bunk Beds" *Cock-Eyed Optimists* (1980), 21-5.
    "Camp Chiclet" *Chiclet Gomez* [1977], 105-10.
    "Cock-Eyed Optimists" *Cock-Eyed Optimists* (1980), 135-41.
    "Coming Home" *Cock-Eyed Optimists* (1980), 186-91.
    "Crucifixions" *Cock-Eyed Optimists* (1980), 101-8.
    "Crying at the Kitchen Table" *Cock-Eyed Optimists* (1980), 97-100.
    "Discoveries" *Chiclet Gomez* [1977], 98-104.
    "The Dumb Look" *Chiclet Gomez* [1977], 116-20.
    "Economists and Eggs" *Cock-Eyed Optimists* (1980), 160-5.
    "Fancy Yancy" *Cock-Eyed Optimists* (1980), 63-72.
    "Fangus" *Cock-Eyed Optimists* (1980), 109-15.
    "The Fat Farm Fiasco" *Chiclet Gomez* [1977], 1-7.
    "Foggy" *Cock-Eyed Optimists* (1980), 128-34.
    "Foot-in-Mouth" *Chiclet Gomez* [1977], 61-4.
    "Fred" *Cock-Eyed Optimists* (1980), 1-5.
    "Go Gomez!" *Cock-Eyed Optimists* (1980), 46-54.
    "The Grant Game" *Chiclet Gomez* [1977], 129-34.
    "Great Escapes" *Cock-Eyed Optimists* (1980), 155-9.
    "Green Thumbs" *Chiclet Gomez* [1977], 57-60.
    "Have I Got a Picture for You" *Chiclet Gomez* [1977], 89-93.
    "In Search of a Portfolio" *Chiclet Gomez* [1977], 84-8.
    "In the Spotlight" *Cock-Eyed Optimists* (1980), 173-9.
    "Inspections" *Chiclet Gomez* [1977], 52-6.
    "A Kick at the Couch" *Cock-Eyed Optimists* (1980), 39-45.
    "The Kid Network" *Cock-Eyed Optimists* (1980), 149-54.
    "The Lonely Blues" *Chiclet Gomez* [1977], 125-8.
    "The Long March" *Chiclet Gomez* [1977], 48-51.
    "The Mad Snickerer" *Chiclet Gomez* [1977], 72-8.
    "Mortality" *Cock-Eyed Optimists* (1980), 26-30.
    "Negotiations" *Cock-Eyed Optimists* (1980), 123-7.
    "Next Door Neighbours" *Chiclet Gomez* [1977], 111-5.
    "Of Agonizing and Organizing" *Chiclet Gomez* [1977], 16-22.
    "Options" *Herizons* 1:5 (July 1983), 35-7.
    "Our American" *Cock-Eyed Optimists* (1980), 142-8.
    "A Perfect Stranger" *Chiclet Gomez* [1977], 145-50.
    "Poor Is Powerful" *Cock-Eyed Optimists* (1980), 80-5.
    "The Poor People's Bugle" *Cock-Eyed Optimists* (1980), 166-72.

"The Pot Belly Pilferer, or The Heist at the Co-op" *Chiclet Gomez* [1977], 139-44.
"Pretty Plumbing" *Chiclet Gomez* [1977], 33-8.
"A Real Lady" *Chiclet Gomez* [1977], 23-8.
"Return of the Perfect Stranger" *Cock-Eyed Optimists* (1980), 73-9.
"The Secret Weapon" *Cock-Eyed Optimists* (1980), 6-12.
"Sneaker Week" *Chiclet Gomez* [1977], 39-42.
"Sneaker Week" *Dimensions* 8:1 (Jan-Feb 1980), 30-1.
"Some People Have No Sense of Humour" *Chiclet Gomez* [1977], 79-83.
"A Sow's Ear" *Cock-Eyed Optimists* (1980), 91-6.
"The Swell Party" *Chiclet Gomez* [1977], 43-7.
"Teeth" *Chiclet Gomez* [1977], 29-32.
"This Way to the Egress" *Cock-Eyed Optimists* (1980), 86-90.
"TV or Not TV" *Cock-Eyed Optimists* (1980), 116-22.
"Unleased Passion" *Chiclet Gomez* [1977], 94-7.
"Urban Renewal" *Cock-Eyed Optimists* (1980), 13-20.

O'Connor, John‡

"Patent Applied For" *Los* No. 7 (Mar 1981), 55-8.

Odell, Elizabeth

"The Hostess" *Gas Rain* 3 (1979), 43-6.

O'Donnell, Al‡

"The Old Farmhouse" *AA* 61 (Dec 1970), 24-5.

O'Fadlain, Sean

"Persecution Mania" *Beaver Bites* 1:7 (Oct 1976), 48-9.

Ogle, Robert Joseph (1928-)

WHEN THE SNAKE BITES THE SUN Saskatoon: Texchuck Enterprises, 1977 ["Half of them are fiction, half of them are non-fiction" (author's note)].
"Baggage" *When the Snake* (1977), 1-15.
"Bus Trip to Almora" *When the Snake* (1977), 51-61.
"The Dam" *When the Snake* (1977), 192-204.
"Did You Ever Think?" *When the Snake* (1977), 40-50.
"Flight 272" *When the Snake* (1977), 62-72.
"Good Dirt" *When the Snake* (1977), 108-19.
"Heart Attack ... Quien Sabe?" *When the Snake* (1977), 94-107.
"Holidays" *When the Snake* (1977), 179-91.
"Is That All There Is?" *When the Snake* (1977), 16-28.
"The Living Link" *When the Snake* (1977), 86-93.
"Mail" *When the Snake* (1977), 120-30.
"Parliament Hill" *When the Snake* (1977), 131-45.
" 'So Nice of You to Come' " *When the Snake* (1977), 164-78.
"The Swami" *When the Snake* (1977), 73-85.
"The Village" *When the Snake* (1977), 146-63.
"When the Snake Bites the Sun" *When the Snake* (1977), 29-39.

O'Hagan, Denis†

"Home" *CFM* No. 5 (Win 1972), 65-70.

O'Hagan, Howard.

THE WOMAN WHO GOT ON AT JASPER STATION AND OTHER STORIES
1963; rpt. Vancouver: Talonbooks, 1977.

"The Bride's Crossing" *Woman Who Got On* (1977), 67-77.

"The Bride's Crossing" *Best Canadian Short Stories* (1981), 36-45.

"The Fabulous Journey" *Weekend* 4 (13 Mar 1954), 34.

"Her Father's Daughter" *Weekend* 5 (29 Jan 1955), 8, 18, 22, 30.

"The Knife" CBC *"Anthology"* 25 May 1962.

"The Love Story of Mr. Alfred Wimple" *Woman Who Got On* (1977), 109-23.

"A Mountain Journey" CBC *"Anthology"* 11 Mar 1958.

"The Promised Land" *Woman Who Got On* (1977), 99-107.

"The Stranger" CBC *"Anthology"* 30 Oct 1956.

"The Tepee" *Stories from Western Canada* (1972), 25-34.

"The Tepee" *Moderne Erzähler der Walt: Kanada* (1976), 146-56 [As "Die Indianerzelt"; trans. Walter Riedel].

"The Tepee" *Woman Who Got On* (1977), 9-18.

"Trees Are Lonely Company" CBC *"Anthology"* 24 Apr 1956.

"Trees Are Lonely Company" *Tam R* No. 9 (Aut 1958), 29-38, 40-5.

"Trees Are Lonely Company" CBC *"Anthology"* 20 Oct 1961.

"Trees Are Lonely Company" *Woman Who Got On* (1977), 19-34.

"Trees Are Lonely Company" *Great Canadian Adventure Stories* (1979), 151-67.

"Ursus" *Mal R* No. 50 (Apr 1979), 49-64.

"Ursus" *Illusion One* (1983), 99-109.

"The Warning" *Weekend* 3 (21 Nov 1953), 18-9.

"The Warning" *Woman Who Got On* (1977), 35-9.

"The White Horse" *Skookum Wawa* (1975), 3-11.

"The Woman Who Got On at Jasper Station" *Woman Who Got On* (1977), 125-32 [Pre-1950?].

"The Woman Who Got On at Jasper Station" *Alberta Diamond Jubilee Anthology* (1979), 75-81.

O'Hearn, Audrey†

"Renovations" *Read Ch* 1:1 (Spr 1982), 6-13.

Ohm, Vibeke‡

"The Better Part of Surprise" *Was R* 12:2 (Fall 1977), 52-8.

"Fat Cat" *Was R* 9:2 (Fall 1974), 44-50.

"Lucilla: A Fable" *Room* 1:1 (Spr 1975), 52-6.

"Three Wheel Drive" *Br Out* 1:[4] (Sept-Oct 1974), 26-8.

Ohodbok, Ted‡

"The Dig" *Alpha* 2:6 (Feb 1978), 5, 13.

Ohs, Darrel‡

"Boom" *Eclipse* No. 4 (1977), 12-3.

Oikawa, Dulce‡

"Are You What You Are?" *Driftwood* No. 2 (1974), 45-9.

"A Matter of Propriety" *Driftwood* No. 2 (1974), 15-22.

Oja, Janis†

"Recognition" *Miss Chat* 6 (14 Nov 1969), 52, 62, 65-6.

Oki, Henry‡

"The Red Velvet Dress" *Varsity Lit Issue* Wed, 11 Feb 1953, 4-5.

Okun, Nicole†

"Patterns of Change" *Room* 3:3 (1977), 66-9.

Oldham, Robert†

"The Case of the Infrequent Visitor" *Hamilton Mag* 2 (Nov 1979), 25-7, 51-4.
"The Case of the Royal Arctic Theatrical" *Hamilton Mag* 3 (May 1980), 31-2, 34-5, 38-9, 46-8.
"Man About Hobbiton" *Mam* 2:2 [n.d.], [2 pp].

O'Leary, Denyse‡

"Marriage" *Repos* Nos. 17/18 (Win-Spr 1976), 3-48.

Oliver, Michael Brian (1946-)

"Getting Up" *Chezzetcook* (1977), 13-22.
"Grasshopper, Grasshopper" *AA* 59 (Mar 1969), 41-4.
"Haute Couture" *Fid* No. 84 (Mar-Apr 1970), 84-8.
"Like Superman or the Shadow" *event* 6:2 [1977], 32-44.
"The Morning Glory" *Copperfield* 3 (Nov 1970), 15-23.
"A Summer Afternoon Boat Ride" *AA* 58 (May 1968), 50-1, 53.
"They Don't Even Know My Name" *Chezzetcook* (1977), 62-8.
"They Don't Even Know My Name" *Axiom* 3:5 (Sept-Oct 1977), 40-4.

Olsen, Hank‡

"As Fair Flowers Fade" *Prism* 6:2 (Aut 1966), 51-7.
"Starscape" *Prism* 6:2 (Aut 1966), 97-107.

Olsen, Jimmy [pseudonym]

"Sunshine Superman" *Diversions* 4:1 (1973), 42-4.

Olsen, Starr‡

"The Auction" *Rivers Bend R* 1:7 (Jan-Feb 1974), 20-1.

Olson, Corinne‡

[Untitled] *Tide* 2:1 (Jan 1969), [1 p].

Olson, Ruth†

"A Case of Sour Grapes" *Northern Ontario Anthology* 2 (1978), 18-20.

Olson, Sheree-Lee†

"How Does a Barn Fall Down?" *Antig R* No. 42 (Sum 1980), 33-40.

O'Mahoney, Bob†

"Am I My Brother's Keeper?" *Can Messenger* 88 (July-Aug 1978), 8-9, 19.

O'Mahoney, W.†

"The Inheritance" *Prism* (Mont) 1967, 13-5.

Oman, Alan‡

"The Day They Took Our Town Away" *CBC [Van] "Hornby Collection"* 10 June 1978.

Ondaatje, Michael (1943-)

"Austin" *Per* No. 1 (Spr 1977), 44-6.
"The Barn" *Story So Far* (1971), 26-7.
"Lunch Conversation" *Per* No. 5 (Spr 1979), 29-31.

O'Neil, Ernie

"Double Happiness" *Companion* 36 (Oct 1973), 27-9.
"How Can I Lose, Doc?" *Companion* 37 (Sept 1974), 25-7.

O'Neil, Mary Jean Ritchie‡

"The Room" *Bridle of Glass* (1973), 37-40.

O'Neill, N.‡

"It's All a Question of Believing" *Scar Fair* 6 (1979), 11.

O'Neill, Paul

"The Mulberry Bush" *Twelve Newfoundland Short Stories* (1982), 48-59.

Orbeliani, Andre†

"The King's Jester" *Mir* No. 16 (May 1978), 45, 34.

Ord, Douglas‡

"First Love" *OPT* 4:7 (Oct 1977), 12-3.
"Five Dialogues on the Subject of Contemporary Literature" *OPT* 3:5 (May-June 1976), 12-3.
"Pastoral Romance" *Waves* 5:2/3 (Spr 1977), 23-4, 26-8.
"An Unbidden Monologue" *OPT* 4:3 ([Jan-Feb?] 1977), 13 [Non-fiction?].

O'Reilly, Patrick‡

"Channel of Violence" *CF* 47 (Jan 1968), 231-2.
"The Toy Piano" *Kaleidoscope* 1956-57, 9-12.

Orenstein, Brent‡

"Gerard Markle" *Acta Vic* 93:3 (Feb 1969), 10-1.

Orford, Mena†

"Rite of Passage" *Fid* No. 137 (Oct 1983), 7-11.
"Rite of Passage" CBC "*Alberta Anthology*" 29 Oct 1983.

O'Rourke, David‡

"Lady" *New Mitre* Spr 1978, 27-8.
"Phonecall" *New Mitre* No. 1 (1970), 37.
"Thaddeus" *New Mitre* No. 1 (1970), 29-31.

Orr, Edward‡

"Too Early to Rise" *Diversions* Sept 1969, 18-9.

Orrell, Herbert M.‡

"The Patriot" *QQ* 69 (1963), 568-73.

Orser, Forrest D.†

"Assorted Mooseheads" *Antig R* No. 18 (Sum 1974), 31-43.

Osborne, J.T.

'Billiards" *Pulp* 5:7 (1 June 1979), [2-3].

"A Dicker to Spare" *Elbow Room* (1979), 75-115.

'The End of Canada Week /78" *Pulp* 4:21 (15 July 1978), [1-3].

'Inside the Glass Hospital" *Pulp* 3:3 (1 July 1975), [1-3] [Same author?].

Osman, R.B.‡

'The Man Who Had a Clear Conscience" *Folio* 19:2 (Spr 1967), 12.

Osser, Harry†

'The Personality Box" *Quarry* 4 (Spr 1955), 36-8.

'The Tobacco Jar" *Quarry* 5 (Spr 1956), 17-20.

Ostenso, Martha (1900-1963)

'Journey in Darkness" *SW* 2 May 1953, I:9-10.

'Prairie Romance" *SW* 26 June 1954, II:4.

Ostrow, Joanna‡

"An American Dressage Rider" *CBC "Anthology"* 8 Sept 1979.

Oszeusko, Cornelia‡

"On My Return from Hell" *Earth and You* 7 Nos. 31/32 [n.d.], 10-1.

O'Toole, John R.‡

'The Old Man and the Tree" *Scar Fair* 9 (1982), 28-33.

Oudecek, Madia‡

"A Poet and a Star" *Alpha* 3:1 (Fall 1978), 12.

'The Story About a Sculptor" *Alpha* 3:1 (Fall 1978), 23.

"A Young Artist's Dreams" *Alpha* 3:1 (Fall 1978), 25.

Oughton, John (1948-)

"Cosmic Strip" *Waves* 5:2/3 (Spr 1977), 29-31.

'The Toothpick (for Al Capone)" *Rampike* No. 2 (Spr 1981), 49.

Owen, D.M.‡

"Last Call" *Gamut* No. 4 (Sept 1983), 59-62.

Owen, George

'Bitter with the Sweet" *Weekend* 3 (24 Jan 1953), 14-5.

"Cream of the Crop" *Weekend* 2 (6 Dec 1952), 24-5.

"Honeysuckle and Snickadoodles" *Weekend* 1 (20 Oct 1951), 14-5, 44-7.

'I'm Annoyed with Freud" *Weekend* 5 (2 Apr 1955), 11.

'The Lady Loved Music" *Weekend* 3 (12 Sept 1953), 36-8, 42.

'What Type Type of a Type Are You?" *Weekend* 1 (3 Nov 1951), 24-5.

'Words Are for the Birds" *Weekend* 4 (24 July 1954), 8, 21, 26.

Owens, Rhonda‡

'Tree of Life" *Stump* 4:1/2 (Spr 1980), 9-10.

Pacey, Desmond (1917-1975)

THE PICNIC AND OTHER STORIES Toronto: Ryerson Press, 1958.

WAKEN, LORDS AND LADIES GAY Ed. Frank M. Tierney Ottawa: Univ. of Ottawa Press, 1974.

"The Black House" *Picnic* (1958), 33-9.

"The Blue Souwester" *JCF* 4:3 No. 15 (1976), 9-14.

"The Boat" *Picnic* (1958), 10-9 [Also entitled "The Good Hope"].

"The Boat" *Book of Canadian Stories* (1962), 273-81.

"The Boat" *Waken, Lords and Ladies Gay* (1974), 37-44.

"The Boat" *Easterly* (1983), 123-9.

"The Boat" *Stubborn Strength* (1983), 52-9.

"The Boat" [Also published in German in Switzerland and Germany; see Tierney].

"The Brothers" *AA* 51 (May 1961), 69-73.

"The Candidate" *AA* 53 (Mar 1963), 78-83.

"A Fellow of Christhouse" *AA* 57 (Sept 1966), 65-6, 68-72.

"The Ghost of Reddleman Lane" *AA* 48 (Dec 1957), 45, 47-8.

"The Ghost of Reddleman Lane" *Picnic* (1958), 127-33.

"The Ghost of Reddleman Lane" *Beckoning Trails* (1962), 396-401.

"The Ghost of Reddleman Lane" *Waken, Lords and Ladies Gay* (1974), 95-100.

"The Ghost of Reddleman Lane" *Visions from the Edge* (1981), 150-3.

"The Good Hope" *QQ* 57 (1950), 325-34 [Also entitled "The Boat"].

"The Life and Death of Morning Star" *AA* 54 (Apr 1964), 33, 35-6, 38.

"The Lost Girl" *Picnic* (1958), 134-43.

"The Lost Girl" *AA* 49 (Sept 1958), 79-82.

"The Lost Girl" *Atlantic Anthology* (1959), 236-42.

"The Lost Girl" *Waken, Lords and Ladies Gay* (1974), 101-8.

"The Mirror" *Dal R* 34 (1954), 155-9.

"The Mirror" *Picnic* (1958), 26-32.

"The Mirror" *Waken, Lords and Ladies Gay* (1974), 75-80.

"The Misses York" *Picnic* (1958), 52-8.

"The Misses York" CBC "Canadian Short Stories" [Based on Tierney].

"A Moment of Love" *AA* 48 (Apr 1958), 80-1.

"The Odour of Incense" *CF* 37 (May 1957), 42-4.

"The Odour of Incense" *Picnic* (1958), 117-26.

"The Odour of Incense" *Stories with John Drainie* (1963), 198-206.

"On the Roman Road" *AA* 60 (May 1970), 35-7.

"On the Roman Road" *Waken, Lords and Ladies Gay* (1974), 57-64.

"The Picnic" *NR* 4:1 (Oct-Nov 1950), 36-41.

"The Picnic" *Neue Illustrierte* (Switz) 23 June 1956 [In German; based on Tierney].

"The Picnic" *National Zeitung* (Switz) 9 Sept 1956 [In German; based on Tierney].

"The Picnic" *Du* (Switz) Oct 1956 [In German; based on Tierney].

"The Picnic" *Picnic* (1958), 1-9.

"The Picnic" *Rhein-Neckar-Zeitung [Ger?]* 1971 [In German; based on Tierney].

"The Picnic" *Waken, Lords and Ladies Gay* (1974), 29-35.

"A Summer Afternoon" *AA* 62 (Aug 1972), 28-31.

"The Test" *Picnic* (1958), 40-51.

"The Test" *Waken, Lords and Ladies Gay* (1974), 65-73.

"That Day in the Bush" *CF* 34 (Jan 1955), 226-7.
"That Day in the Bush" *Picnic* (1958), 20-5.
"That Day in the Bush" *Waken, Lords and Ladies Gay* (1974), 45-9.
"The Trespasser" *Picnic* (1958), 89-96 [Also entitled "The Visit"].
"The Trespasser" *Waken, Lords and Ladies Gay* (1974), 81-6.
"The Visit" *AA* 50 (Feb 1960), 82-5 [Also entitled "The Trespasser"].
"Waken, Lords and Ladies Gay" *AA* 62 (Apr 1972), 18-20, 22.
"Waken, Lords and Ladies Gay" *Waken, Lords and Ladies Gay* (1974), 17-28.
"The Weasel" *CF* 39 (Feb 1960), 260-1.
"When She Comes Over" *Fid* No. 53 (Sum 1962), 21-6.
"When She Comes Over" *Waken, Lords and Ladies Gay* (1974), 51-6.

Pacey, Patricia‡
"Red Ribbon" *AA* 58 (July 1968), 33, 35-6.

Packer, Miriam†
"The Helper" *Matinees Daily* (1981), 24-32.
"Jeannine" *Viewpoints* 12:4 (May 1983), 4-6.

Pacznowsky, Mike†
"14 October 1966" *CFM* No. 1 (Win 1971), 89-93.

Page, P.K. (1916-)
"Unless the Eye Catch Fire ... " *Mal R* No. 50 (Apr 1979), 65-86
"Unless the Eye Catch Fire ... " *Metavisions* (1983), 123-44.
"Victoria" *Tam R* No. 69 (Sum 1976), 50-3.

Page, Pearl – *See* Briffett, Isabel.

Page, William‡
"Routine" *Alive* 3:2 No. 21 [1972?], 28-9.

Palmer, John
"The Man Behind the News" *CF* 53 (Feb 1974), 17-20.

Palomba, Laura†
"Light Through the Leaves" *Waves* 1:2 (Aut 1972), 17-26.
"Twilight Time" *Waves* 3:3 (Spr 1975), 69-73.
"Twilight Time" *CBC "Anthology"* 12 June 1976.
"Winter Friday" *Waves* 1:3 (Win 1973), 42-51.

Palsson, Gestur‡
"Sigurdur the Fisherman" *Vagabond* 1:1 (May 1951), 1-3, 56-71.

Paluk, William
"Back Door" *Smoke Signals* [1974?], 137-53.

Paolielo, Carlo‡
"The Tiger Lily" *Fruits of Experience* (1978), 99-112.

Paragot [pseudonym]
"Germ" *TUR* 66:3 (Feb 1954), 9-15.

Paratte, Henri Dominique†
"Evolution, Fox, and Associates" *Alpha* 2:3 (Nov 1977), 17-8.
"How Cuchulainn Went on the Glooscap Trail" *Alpha* [1:3] (Dec 1976), 3-6.
"Jason and the Swan" *Alpha* [1:4] (Jan 1977), 6-7, 11.

Pardy, Maryn‡
"A Little Girl in a Pink Dress" *Echoes* No. 245 (Win 1961), 4-5, 24-5.
"A Valentine for Martha" *Onward* 10 Feb 1957, 88-90.

Paris, Anne Porter
"The Fat Lady" *Br Out* 5:3 (1978), 18-21.

Parissi, N. James‡
"Repulsion" *Acta Vic* 102:2 (Fall 1978), 49.

Park, Bob‡
"The Versatile Group" *Gas Rain* [1] (Mar 1977), 27-30.

Park, Free – *See* Free Park.

Park, John†
"A House by the Sea" *Entropy Negative* No. 5 (1972), [3 pp].

Park, Lisa†
"The Audition" *CFM* No. 9 (Win 1973), 67-73.

Parker, Rick‡
"Time Meant That" *First Encounter* 5 (1973), 43.

Parker, W.A.†
"Home" *Fresh Grease* (1971), 54-8.

Parks, F.M.‡
"Road to Victory" *Undergrad* Spr 1952, 22-6.

Parks, Milton‡
"High Button Shoes" *Undergrad* Aut 1951, 12-3.

Parley, Kay‡
"Kleckner" *Prism* 5:2 (Aut 1965), 20-9.

Parr, D. Kermode
"The Gift of Fire" *Mar Adv* 40 (Mar 1950), 5, 7-9.
"Hard Tack for Mr. Calder" *AA* 56 (July 1966), 54-8.
"The Health Bootleggers" *Mar Adv* 40 (Jan 1950), 8-11.
"Murder at Eight Bells" *AA* 51 (June 1961), 71-6.

Parr, James‡
"While Shepherds Watched" *CBC* "*Anthology*" 24 Dec 1977.

Parr, John (1928-)
"Ah Youth, Ah Joy!" *Alphabet* No. 10 (July 1965), 17-31.
"The Escape" *Cyclic* 1:2 (Aut 1965), 11-6.
"A Golden Land of Summer Enchantment" *Fid* No. [75] (Win 1968), 42-74.
"Like Father, Like Son" *Cyclic* 1:3 (1966), 11-4, 16.
"Matt Dillon, Inspector Erskine and Joe Mannix Go to College" *JCF* 1:4 (Fall 1972), 23-9.
"Miss Mellowes" *Quarto* (U.S.) 6:21 (1954) [Based on survey response].
"New Star in the Heavens" *JCF* 3:3 (1974), 9-11.
"Vince Willys Strikes Again" *Plaintiff* (U.S.) 6:1 (1969), 4-12 [Based on survey response].
"White Land, Blue Toe" *Winnipeg Stories* (1974), 185-219.

Parris, Paula‡
"Wanting Picture" *First Encounter* 13 (1983), 38-9.

Parry, Carrietta†
"In a Couple of Hours the Rain May Stop" *Current Assets* (1973), 1-7.
"Watermelon's Funeral Oration" *Current Assets* (1973), 48-55.

Parsons, Fay
'The Unlikely Matchmakers" *CSSM* 3:2 (Spr 1977), 20-3, 56-60.

Parsons, Sandra‡
"Discovery" *Either/Or* No. 6 (Spr 1968), 14-5 [Prose poem?].

Parsons, W.B.‡
"Learning the Hard Way" *CBC "Alberta Anthology"* 23 Oct 1980.

Partington, David‡
"Bank Holiday" *Portico* 4:1 (1980), 5-11.
"Man of Destiny" *Portico* 2:1 (Win 1978), 4-9, 28-32.
'The Mighty Mr. Grundy: A Cautionary Tale for Little People (of All Ages)" *Portico* 2:2 (Win-Spr 1978), 12-8.
'The Wrath of Zeus" *Portico* 4:1 (1980), 48-9.

Partridge, Basil‡
"Below the Bridge" *AA* 54 (Apr 1964), 56-8.

Partridge, Shirley
"The Happy Wife" *Sand Patterns* No. 2 (Nov 1972), [3 pp].
'The Roommates" *Sand Patterns* No. 1 [n.d.], [3 pp].
'The Wharf" *Katharsis* 3:1 (Spr 1970), 35-6
'The Wharf" *Island Prose and Poetry* (1973), 183-4.

Passmore, Marian – *See* Engel, Marian.

Pastachuk, Pauline A.
'The Daffodils" *Alive* No. 26 [1973], 36-7.
"Of Tongue or Pen" *CA & B* 47:2 (Win 1971), 5, 21.
'Peace on Earth!" *Can Messenger* 87 (Jan 1977), 12-3, 18.

Pat, Al – *See* Joseph, Alexander Callow.

Pat [pseudonym]

"I, Myself" *Time Gatherers* (1970), 33-42.

"I, Myself" *Humanist in Can* 11:3 No. 46 (Aug 1978), 9, 38-9.

Paterson, Katherine†

"The Nurse" *Forge* 1952, 62-4.

Paterson, O.P.

"And I But a Poor Mermaiden" *Weekend* 3 (16 May 1953), 24-5, 40.

"Coronation Extra" *Weekend* 3 (30 May 1953), 10-1, 29, 37.

"First Catch Your Crook" *Weekend* 2 (29 Nov 1952), 30-1, 36.

"Grandfer's Deepfreeze" *Weekend* 2 (29 Mar 1952), 20-1.

"The Miracle at Saint Xavier" *Weekend* 2 (5 Apr 1952), 20-1, 36.

"Nice White Ones" *Weekend* 2 (27 Sept 1952), 22-3.

"A Vote for Sir Thomas" *Weekend* 3 (11 Apr 1953), 20-1, 26.

Patterson, Anne

"A Stray Cat at the Window" *Singing Under Ice* (1974), 113-5.

Patterson, Jayne†

"The Man Dynasty" *Waves* 9:2 (Win 1981), 14-6.

Patterson, Phyllis†

"Marble Halls" *Blue Buffalo* 1:2 (Spr 1983), [4 pp].

Paul & Jim‡

"Heads, Tails, or the Coin" *Alive* No. 26 [1973], 27.

Paust, J.‡

"The Old Man" *Probe* Fri, 5 Feb 1960, 2 [Non-fiction?].

Pauwels, Germaine†

"The Mannequin" *From an Island* 10:1 [n.d.], 36-9, 52-3.

Paxton, Maureen

"Wolf at the Door" *Common Ground* (1980), 103-21.

Payerle, George (1945-)

"Charlotte" *Mal R* No. 64 (Feb 1983), 77-82.

"The Dialogues of Fane" *CFM* Nos. 2/3 (Spr-Sum 1971), 67-72.

"The Dying" *CFM* No. 6 (Spr 1972), 33-6.

"The Dying" *Story So Far* 2 (1973), 27-32.

"Fane" *Mal R* No. 50 (Apr 1979), 115-8.

"Fane" *Illusion One* (1983), 53-5.

"The Historian" *Stories from Pacific & Arctic Canada* (1974), 195-9.

"In Winter – In Writing" *Story So Far* 2 (1973), 25-6.

"The Labyrinthine Investigations of Fane" *CFM* No. 1 (Win 1971), 13-7.

"The Nightwalk" *CFM* No. 11 (Aut 1973), 16-8.

"Patrol" *CFM* No. 6 (Spr 1972), 31-2.

"Wolfbane Fane" *Pushcart Prize 3* (1978), 318-31.

"Wolfbane Fane" *event* 3:3 [n.d.], 28-40.

Peabody, George
"A Day's Work" *Pot Port* 4 (1982-83), 14-5.

Pearcey, Lillian‡
"Mind and Matter" *Prism* (Mont) 1958, 26-7.

Pearson, Ailsa†
"The Happening" *Rapport* Feb 1971, 7.

Pearson, Glen
"The Party" *BC Monthly* 5:2 (Apr 1980), [2 pp].

Pearson, Phyllis†
"The Day That Young Man Came to Tea" *Onward* 5 Nov 1961, 4-6.
"The Day That Young Man Came to Tea" *Onward* 21 Mar 1965, 3-4.
"The Innkeeper" *Onward* 1 Apr 1962, 3-4, 11-2.
"The Innkeeper" *Onward* 23 Jan 1966, 3-5, 11.
"Love Casts Out Fear" *Onward* 19 Mar 1961, 184-5, 188-9.

Pederson, Steven
"A Fistful of Love" *New Voices* (1956), 171-8.

Peebles, Anne – *See* Galloway, Priscilla.

Peel, Harry‡
"Leaves for My Children" *Acta Vic* 92:3 (Feb 1968), 3-10.

Pegis, Jessica (1954?-)†
"Bernard Goes to a Party" *Title Unknown* (1975), 25-6.

Pegler, Arthur†
"Fred's Resurrection" *Rapport* Mar 1970, 4-5.
"Fred's Resurrection" *Exchange* (UCC) 2:2 (Win-Spr 1978), 20-1.

Pelargos, Anna‡
"The Horseman and the Red Columns" *Acta Vic* 107:1 (Fall 1982), 58-79 [Non-fiction?].

Pelland, Jim‡
"Fight or Die" *Outlook* Aug-Sept 1982, 11-3.

Peloquin, George‡
"A Peculiar Botanical Deficiency" *Fifth Page* 1963, 14-8.

Pelz, Bud‡
"Der Traum" *Muse* 1963, 6-7.

Pemberton, Prim
"89 Cent Wine" CBC "*Anthology*" 18 Oct 1975.
"I Don't Want You Back" *Chat* 51 (Oct 1978), 66-7, 80, 84, 88-9, 92, 95-6.
"Tell Me the Jokes I Know" CBC "*Anthology*" 2 Dec 1978.
"The Things You Understand" *Chat* 51 (Jan 1978), 24, 48, 50-4.
"Third Floor Back" *Chat* 53 (Oct 1980), 53, 85, 87, 90, 94-5.

Pendle, Walter Henry.
POEMS, SHORT TALES, PHANTASIES Vancouver: [publisher unknown], 1951 [Based on Miller].

Penfold, Russ‡
"The Kid and the Stick" *Alive* No. 29 [1973], 43-4.

Pengelley, M.B.‡
"The Great Film Night" *UC Observer* 1 Feb 1959, 6-7, 20.

Penman, Margaret‡
"Knife" *Undergrad* Win 1955, 7-10.
"Mrs. Morgan" *Undergrad* Spr 1956, 12-5.

Penner, Judith (1945-)
"Cuixmala" *77: Best Canadian Stories* 169-86.

Penney, Lloyd‡
"Death on Rewind" *WWR* 2:3 No. 7 (1982), 85-7.
"The Time Dilator" *WWR* 2:1 (1980), 6-11.
"The Wrong Number" *WWR* 2:1 (1980), 26-8.

Pepper, Leila
"The Heart Has Its Reasoning" *Lib* 29 (Feb 1953), 24-5.

Percy, Carol‡
"A Pretentious Tale" *UCR* 1981-82, 45-6.

Percy, H.R. (1920-)
THE TIMELESS ISLAND AND OTHER STORIES Toronto: Ryerson Press, 1960.
"Afterglow" *Quarry* 21:4 (Aut 1972), 12-9.
"Clay" *Pot Port* 1 (1979-80), 13-4.
"Don't Bring Lennie" *Short Story & Poetry Year Book* 1969 (U.K.) 7-19 [Based on survey response].
"Don't Bring Lennie" *Was R* 6:2 (1972), 29-37.
"Falling for Mavis" *75: New Canadian Stories* 131-52.
"A Gift of Wishes" *Nova Scotia Times* Dec 1975, 17-20 [Also entitled "A Wonder of Wishes"; based on survey response].
"Haliburton" *Crowsnest* 10 (Dec 1957), 17-9.
"Haliburton" *Timeless Island* (1960), 14-22.
"Happy's Christmas" *Legion* 46 (Dec 1971), 14.
"Hope" *Timeless Island* (1960), 47-55.
"An Inglorious Affair" *QQ* 79 (1972), 171-82.
"An Inglorious Affair" *CBC "Anthology"* 21 Apr 1973.
"An Inglorious Affair" *Short Story International* No. 29 (1981), 9-20 [Based on survey response].
"Its Own Reward" *Timeless Island* (1960), 65-74.
"Letter from America" *Beyond Time* (1976), 188-99 [Based on survey response].
"Letter from America" *Visions from the Edge* (1981), 179-85.
"Like Heaven" *Prism* 19:1 (Spr 1980), 54-62.
"La Manivelle" *Fair Lady* (S Afr) 1981 [Based on survey response].

"Mankipoo" *QQ* 76 (1969), 454-65.

"Mankipoo" *Canadian Short Fiction Anthology* 2 (1982), 150-8.

"A Model Lover" *New Q* 2:1 (Spr 1982), 5-15 [Also entitled "My Father's Fancy"].

"The Mountain" *Timeless Island* (1960), 148-63.

"My Father's Fancy" CBC "Anthology" 1 Apr 1978 [Also entitled "A Model Lover"].

"The Party Dress" *Timeless Island* (1960), 84-95.

"A Passable Likeness" *Pot Port* 2 (1980-81), 43-6.

"Reflections" *QQ* 81 (1974), 258-62.

"The Rendezvous" *Timeless Island* (1960), 124-35.

"The Sailor and the Snow Princess" *Timeless Island* (1960), 32-46.

"Sailor in the Chair" *Crowsnest* 6 (Mar 1954), 17-8, 28.

"Scar Tissue" *76: New Canadian Stories* 115-37.

"Scar Tissue" *Short Story International* No. 32 (1982), 17-36 [Based on survey response].

"The Scorpion Man" *Crowsnest* 7 (Mar 1955), 13-4.

"The Scorpion Man" *AA* 52 (Feb 1962), 49-51.

"The Scorpion Man" CBC [Ott] Feb 1965 [Based on survey response].

"Shadows" *Voices Down East* (1976) [Based on survey response].

"A Spirited Encounter" *Timeless Island* (1960), 96-103.

"Tearin' Her Down" CBC "Anthology" 26 Jan 1980.

"Tearin' Her Down" *CFM* No. 43 (1982), 41-8.

"The Timeless Island" *Vanity Fair* (U.K.) Fall 1950, 24-7, 59-63 [Based on survey response].

"The Timeless Island" *Timeless Island* (1960), 104-23.

"The Timeless Island" *Prose Pageant* (1963) [Based on survey response].

"The Timeless Island" *Not to Be Taken at Night* (1981), 26-43.

"Tinsel" *Timeless Island* (1960), 56-64.

"Waldo and Willie" *NJ* No. 5 (May 1975), 22-9.

"Waldo and Willie" *East of Canada* (1976), 43-56.

"The Walking Tree" *Timeless Island* (1960), 1-13.

"The Wastelander" *Timeless Island* (1960), 136-47.

"The Wedding Party" *Timeless Island* (1960), 75-83.

"A Wonder of Wishes" *Nearly an Island* (1979), 157-61 [Also entitled "A Gift of Wishes"].

Pereira, Anil‡

"Vive le Quebec Libre" *Stump* 5:1 (Fall-Win 1980), 48-50.

Pereira, Helen

"An Awfully Mature Person" by Helen Gowans *CF* 46 (Aug 1966), 100-2.

"An Awfully Mature Person" by Helen Gowans *Forum* (1972), 400-4.

"A Bouquet of Roses" *Word Loom* No. 2 (1983), 51-4.

"The Ride Home" *Lunatic Gazette* Feb 1983 [Based on survey response].

"Sour Notes from the Portuguese" *Lunatic Gazette* 1983 [Based on survey response].

Perkin, Darlene†

"Hector" *Pier Spr* Spr 1978, 5-7.
"Sensible Susan" *Pier Spr* [No. 3] (Win 1978), 15-20.
"Yesterday" *Pier Spr* 1:2 (Spr 1977), 35-6.

Perkins, Ralph A. (1956-)

"The Man on the Mountain" *Mal R* No. 59 (July 1981), 34-41.

Perkins, Vincent

"Dark of the Storm" *Fantastic Stories* 22 (Dec 1972), 60-5, 71.

Perks, Megan†

"Brothers" *New Q* 2:2 (Sum 1982), 24-9.

Peroff, Donya‡

"May I Have This Dance?" *TL* Mar 1979, 52, 121-4.

Perozak, Helen Irene‡

"Night and Day" *Muse* 60:4 (Apr 1951), 13-4.
"Somewhere Over the Rainbow" *Muse* 59:4 (Apr 1950), 5-10.

Perrault, Ernest G. (1922-)

"The Cure" *pm* 1:3 (Feb [1952]), 36-40.
"The Cure" *Stories from Pacific & Arctic Canada* (1974), 167-73.
"The Cure" *Modern Canadian Stories* (1975), 257-63.
"The Cure" *Transitions 2* (1978), 73-8.
"The End of the City" *Mont* 30 (Dec 1956), 23-5.
"Family Man" *Mont* 31 (Feb 1957), 14-7.
"The Reforming of McGregor" *CG* 84 (Dec 1965), 31-2.
"The Silver King" *Canadian Short Stories* (1952), 165-76.

Perry, Cecil†

"Even I Will Carry" *Rapport* Oct 1968, 14-5.
"Fill the Water Pots with Water" *Onward* 25 June 1967, 3-4.

Persky, Stan (1941-)

"A Bibliography for Gordon Lockhead" *NMFG* No. 4 (May 1976), [5 pp].
"The Finger" *Iron* No. 7 (1969), 5-7.
"The Finger" *Story So Far* (1971), 55-7.
"Notebook Entries" *Cap R* No. 5 (Spr 1974), 110-3.
"The Osoyoos Indians Picket Highway 97 at OK Falls and Then Decide to Take the Government to Court (A Film Scenario)" *Imago* No. 20 (1974), 67-9.
"Writings" *Cap R* No. 7 (Spr 1975), 150-61.

Person, A.D [pseudonym]

"Pravlijica (A Fairy Tale)" *CF* 61 (Feb 1982), 49-50.

Person, Lloyd‡

"The Alec" *Was R* 14:2 (Fall 1979), 34-44.
"A Tantrum Is a Tantrum Is a Tantrum" *Smoke Signals* 3 (1978) [Based on *SWG* survey response].

Peter, John D. (1921-)

VALLOR Toronto: York, 1978.

"All the Fun of the Fair" *MM* 65 (15 Oct 1952), 14-5, 28, 30, 32, 34, 36.

"From a Death to a View" *Vallor* (1978), 51-68.

"The Fun of the Fair" *Vallor* (1978), 119-30.

"Innocence" *Vallor* (1978), 71-4.

"Japonica" *Vallor* (1978), 107-18.

"Long Ago, Far Away" *Chat* 43 (Oct 1970), 36-7, 64, 66, 68-70.

"Lots of Room in Hell" CBC "*Anthology*" 18 Nov 1960.

"Lots of Room in Hell" *Vallor* (1978), 75-84.

"The Luck" *Vallor* (1978), 131-5.

"Make a Joyful Noise" *Mal R* No. 31 (July 1974), 21-64 [Novella?].

"Nothing Happened to Matt" *Weekend* 3 (2 May 1953), 10-1.

"Paleface Potlatch" *Vallor* (1978), 85-95.

"Snake-Eyes" *Vallor* (1978), 97-106.

"Tom's A-Cold" *Tam R* No. 23 (Spr 1962), 19-38.

Peters, A.W.M.‡

"Frontiers of Art" *TUR* 78:1 (Oct 1964), 19-20.

"It's God Again" *TUR* 78:2 (Nov-Dec 1964), 19-24.

"Love Those Lenses" *TUR* 79:4 (Apr 1966), 22-4.

"Us" *TUR* 78:1 (Oct 1964), 32.

Peters, C.M.‡

"On the Edge of the Knife" *VWFP/Revue* 1:4 (June 1975), 12, 20.

Peters, Cliff‡

"The Bus" *Generation* Apr 1965, 3-10.

"Tiger Under the Palm Tree" *Kaleidoscope* 1963, 8-10.

Peters, Evan [pseudonym]

"The Bear" *Can R* 3:4 (Sept 1976), 18-20.

Peters, Gregory J.‡

"A Different Cup of Tea" *Saelala* 1966, 14-6 [Non-fiction?].

Peters, Mac‡

"Air Vent" *TUR* 76:1 (Oct 1962), 9-15.

"The Beggar" *TUR* 78:3 (Jan-Feb 1965), 16-8 [Monologue].

"Mannequin's Love" *TUR* 79:1 (Oct-Nov 1965), 30-4.

"Tibs Baits Mr. Sibinoff" *TUR* 76:2 (Nov 1962), 42-50.

"Tibs' First Communion" *TUR* 77:1 (Oct 1963), 7-12.

Petersen, Olive MacKay (1907-)

"The Grand Day" by Olive M. MacKay *Can Messenger* 73 (Jan 1963), 12-4 [Same author?].

"One Angry Man" *CSSM* 2:2 (Spr 1976), 53, 55-6.

"One Blue Velvet Dress" *Onward* 24 (Dec 1967), 10-3.

"What Is a Good Time?" *Companion* 41 (Apr 1978), 11-3.

Peterson, Barry†

"Andromeda's Child" *event* 7:2 (1978), 136-42.
"Harvest" *Grain* 4:1 [1976], 40-1.
"The Swan" *event* 4:2 [1974?], 40-50.
"Tropisms" *event* 5:1 [n.d.], 40-3.

Peterson, Nick – *See* Green, H. Gordon.

Peterson, Phyllis Lee

"The Christmas House" *Ladies Home J* 75 (Dec 1958), 44, 117, 119.
"The Constant Lover" *Weekend* 3 (17 Oct 1953), 46.
"[A?] Dream So Real" *American Mag* 160 (July 1955), 32-3[+?] [Based on RGPL].
"The Facts of Life" *Weekend* 2 (23 Feb 1952), 10-1.
"Farewell, Dear Lady" *Chat* 34 (June 1961), 36-7, 70-6.
"The Finest Hour" *Weekend* 4 (9 Oct 1954), 14.
"In Memory of a Boy Named Johnny" *Chat* 25 (Apr 1952), 20, 48-50, 52, 54-5.
"The Last Door" *Chat* 27 (Apr 1954), 21, 54, 56-8.
"Last Spring" *Collier's* 126 (9 Sept 1950), 36 [Based on RGPL].
"Last Spring" *Chat* 31 (July 1958), 58-60.
"Martha" *Chat* 32 (Apr 1959), 33, 51-4, 56, 58-61.
"Monsieur Pantouffles" *Weekend* 2 (29 Mar 1952), 36.
"Mr. Cohen's Leprechaun" *Chat* 27 (Jan 1954), 17, 51-4.
"Pete's Rubbers" *Weekend* 2 (9 Feb 1952), 12.
"The Runaway" *Chat* 28 (Feb 1955), 14-5, 36-40, 42-3.
"Scandal in the Village" *Sat Eve Post* 228 (16 July 1955), 31, 46, 48, 50.
"The Summerhouse" *Chat* 48 (June 1975), 30, 78-85.
"That Pagan Charm" *Sat Eve Post* 225 (21 Feb 1953), 26, 53, 55, 58, 60, 62.
"The Undertaker of Ste Angele" *MM* 63 (15 May 1950), 19, 39-40, 42, 44, 46.
"White Is for Brides" *SW* 20 Oct 1956, I:1, 4.
"The Wonderful Years" *Chat* 49 Oct 1976, 55, 74, 76, 78, 80, 82, 84.
"Wooden Wings of Ste. Angele" *FH* 27 Dec 1951, 16-7, 22.
"You Went Away" *Sat Eve Post* 227 (19 Mar 1955), 24, 80, 82, 86-7.

Petkus, Donald‡

"The Conversation" *Generation* Mar 1964, 24-6.

Petrant, Leo – *See* Green, H. Gordon.

Petrie, Graham (1941?-)

"Herman" *Fantasy and Science Fiction* 45 (Aug 1973), 90-100.
"The Locust Keeper" *Paris R* 16 No. 64 (Win 1975), 187-92.
"Moving On" *Ont R* No. 10 (Spr-Sum 1979), 57-74.
"Night Exercise" *Texas Q* 18:4 (Win 1975), 32-41.
"Village Theatre" *Not to Be Taken at Night (1981)*, 63-9.

Petrie, Heather†

"The Birthday" *Miss Chat* 9 (10 Aug 1972), 102, 107-8.

Petrie, M. Ann

"A Feed of July Herring and New Potatoes" *CF* 55 (July 1975), 28-31.

Petro, Paul‡
[Untitled] *Amaranth* Spr 1981, [3 pp].

Pettijohn, Constance‡
"The Widow" *Can Lifetime* 4 (Nov-Dec 1974), 14-5.

Petty, Chris
"Earl Schapiro Sends His Best Regards" *Chat* 53 (Oct 1980), 52, 176, 180, 182, 186.

Pflug, Ursula‡
"Judy" *This* 17:4 (Oct 1983), 27-9.
"Memory Lapse at the Waterfront" *New Bodies* (1981), 35-41.

Philipovich, Marion†
"The Kite" *Uk Can* 13 (1 Dec 1959), 9-10.
"No Mail Today" *Uk Can* 13 (15 Jan 1959), 9.

Philipp, Rowland‡
"Cream in My Coffee" *Forge* Dec 1957, 4-7.
"The Long Corridor" *Forge* Dec 1957, 38-41.
"Quest" *Forge* Feb 1957, 34-5.
"When Winter Comes ... " *Forge* Mar 1959, 42-5.

Phillips, Alan (1917-)
"The Impossible Picture" *NR* 3:6 (Aug-Sept 1950), 37-43.
"The Presence in the Grove" *Canadian Short Stories* (1952), 27-40.
"Saturday Swim" *NR* 3:6 (Aug-Sept 1950), 31-7.

Phillips, Bluebell Stewart (1904-)
"Daniel O'Keefe and Jo" *Public Affairs* 13:4 (Sum 1951), 37-43.
"From Gabrielle Street to Mountain Heights" *Laom R* 1:1 (Dec-Jan [1974]-75), 56-65.
"A Girl Called Monday Morning" *FH* 22 Dec 1955, 22-3.
"The Line" *Public Affairs* 15:1 (Aut 1952), 34-40.
"Old Dan" *FH* 1 May 1952, 24-5, 30-1.
"Portrait of Margaret" *FH* 26 Apr 1950, 26-7.
"Portrait of Margaret" *Stories to Read Again* (1965), 43-53.
"Sidonia" *FH* 26 Dec 1957, 20-1, 25.
"Storm at Flatlands" *FH* 25 Dec 1958, 10-1.
"The Tinsel Gift" *FH* 23 Dec 1954, 16-7, 26.

Phillips, Edward O. (1931-)
"Classified: Personals" *UWR* 16:1 (Fall-Win 1981), 79-91.
"Matthew and Chauncey" *SN* 97 (Aug 1982), 46-8, 50, 52, 54, 56.
"Matthew and Chauncey" *83: Best Canadian Stories* 97-115.
"Mr. Greene" *Quarry* 30:2 (Spr 1981), 4-14.
"Music Festival" *Alpha* 4:3 (Spr 1980), 17, 24.

Phillips, Fred H.†
"The Justice of the Red Queen" *AA* 49 (Sept 1958), 76-8.
"The Justice of the Red Queen" *Atlantic Advocate's Holiday Book* (1961), 117-22.
"Murder After the Matinée" *AA* 59 (Oct 1968), 25-9.
"The Pawn Ticket" *AA* 49 (July 1959), 74.
"A Shot in the Arm" *AA* 48 (May 1958), 92-3.
"Two Days Leave" *AA* 50 (Nov 1959), 79, 81, 83.

Phillips, Jack H.
"Dog Trouble" *Alberta Speaks* 1957, 36-41.
"R-Day" *Alberta Writers Speak* 1960, 38-43.

Phillips, Linda‡
"A Time & a Place" *Alive* [1:7] (June [1970]), [1 p].
"Time Waits for No One" *Alive* [1:8] (Sept-Oct 1970), 24.

Phillips, Neal‡
"Tangiers February" *Ant's Forefoot* No. 8 (Spr 1971), 56-7.

Phillips, R.A.J.‡
"I Love People" *North* 7 (Mar-Apr 1960), 43-4.
"Uncertain Sounds" *North* 8 (May-June 1961), 38-9.

Phillips, Sharon P.‡
"A Very Special Day" *Rivers Bend R* 1:7 (Jan-Feb 1974), 39-42.

Phills, O.‡
"MM 80" *Blow Up* [1:3] (1980), [2 pp].

Phinney, Richard‡
"Partying" *TUR* 92:1 (Jan 1979), 21-6.
"The Wave" *TUR* 91:1 (Nov 1977), 6-8.

Pickard, Joan†
"To Everything There Is a Season" *From 231* [1:1] (Spr 1972), 1-10.

Pickersgill, Alan G.†
"The Armchair Revolutionary" *Alive* [2:2] (Jan 1971), 12-4.
"Not Even Silence" *Alive* No. 34 [1974], 16-7.
"Nowhere to Come From" *Alive* 2:3 (Feb 1971), 23-5.
"The Two Hitchhikers" *Alive* 1:4 (Mar [1970]), 3.

Pickersgill, Edward†
"The Boy and the Wolf" *Alive* No. 55 (16 Oct 1975), 8, 1.
"Mert Strikes Back" *Alive* No. 36 [1974], 11.
"The Yellow Light Road" *Alive* [1:8] (Sept-Oct 1970), 17-23.

Pickersgill, Ron†
"Story" *Alive* 1:6 (May [1970]), 10.

Pickett, Libby‡
"About Old Ladies" *Seraph* 1964, 12-3.

Pierterse, Cecilia‡
"The Sparrow" *Gram* 1:1 (Dec 1975), 23-6.

Pillar, Mabel‡
"The Best Gift of All" *Deaf Can* 2:6 (Nov-Dec 1977), 22-3.

Pilowsky-Santos, Judith†
"Silver Streams" *Fireweed* No. 16 (Spr 1983), 74-6.

Pils [pseudonym]
"Free for a While" *Outlook* Aug-Sept 1983, 16-8.

Pinay, Donna†
"The Government Man and the Indian or Is a Little Bit Really Better Than Nothing at All?" *New Breed* June 1978, 12-3.

Pinder, Leslie Hall†
"Olives Under the Table" *CFM* No. 8 (Aut 1972), 83-6.

Pineo, Mari‡
"Blues for Some Gamblers" *CBC "Anthology"* 2 June 1979.
"The Convent" *Prism* 3:3 (Spr 1962), 24-9 [Originally broadcast on CBC].

Pinsent, John C.‡
"Friday, the 13th" *Nfld Q* 67:1 (Christmas 1968), 29.

Pitcher, Arthur
"Easter Legacy" *War Cry* 9 Apr 1966, 14-5.
"Outport Homecoming" *War Cry* 19 Dec 1964, 4-5.

Pitman, Teresa†
"Barefoot" *Toronto Star* Sun, 9 Oct 1983, D5.

Pitsch, Terry‡
"The Humour and the Frustration" *Mandala* 1973, 35-8.

Pitt-Brooke, Linda†
"White and Other Colours" *CFM* No. 4 (Aut 1971), 24.

Pittman, Al (1940-)
"Beyond the Foothills" *Intercourse* No. 7 (Dec-Win 1967-68), 13-8.
"Bottles" *Floorboards* No. 1 [n.d.], 11-3.
"The Boughwolfen" *Fid* No. 135 (Jan 1983), 85-7.
"Consommé and Coca Cola" *Fid* No. 83 (Jan-Feb 1970), 12-4.
"Consommé and Coca Cola" *Stories from Atlantic Canada* (1973), 113-6.
"Consommé and Coca Cola" *Doryloads* (1974), 178-81.
"Consommé and Coca Cola" *Air* (1977), 78-9.
"Consommé and Coca Cola" *Inquiry into Literature* 3 (1980), 93-6.

Place, Rosalind†
"Night Thoughts" *Writ* No. 11 (Fall 1979), 13-6.

Plant, R.C.†

"Green Christmas" *Onward* 62 (28 Dec 1952), 821-2.

Plantos, Ted (1943-)

THE UNIVERSE ENDS AT SHERBOURNE & QUEEN Toronto: Steel Rail, 1977.

"Cashing a Cheque in Cabbagetown" *Can Poe Annual* 1976, 66-8 [Humour?].

"Cashing a Cheque in Cabbagetown" *Universe Ends at Sherbourne & Queen* (1977), 108-11.

"Normy Chalks His Cue" *Universe Ends at Sherbourne & Queen* (1977), 103-5.

"The Senator" *Universe Ends at Sherbourne & Queen* (1977), 42-3.

"So Long, Cabbagetown" *Universe Ends at Sherbourne & Queen* (1977), 98-100.

"So Long, Cabbagetown" *Core* (1982), 28-31.

"A Special Occasion" *Universe Ends at Sherbourne & Queen* (1977), 117-23.

"Stan's Complaint" *Universe Ends at Sherbourne & Queen* (1977), 77-8.

"Too Bad He Went Crazy" *Universe Ends at Sherbourne & Queen* (1977), 25-7.

"Too Bad He Went Crazy" *Quarry* 26:2 (Spr 1977), 32-4.

Plaskett, John‡

"The Cabin" *Acta Vic* 100:2 (Spr 1976), 18-9.

"Roll Call" *CF* 55 (Nov 1975), 28-31.

Plaut, W. Gunther (1912-)

HANGING THREADS Toronto: Lester & Orpen, 1978 [Also published as *The Man in the Blue Vest* New York: Toplinger, 1980].

"The Amulet" *Hanging Threads* (1978), 111-24.

"Enrique" *Hanging Threads* (1978), 11-21.

"M.C." *Hanging Threads* (1978), 147-55.

"The Man in the Blue Vest" *Hanging Threads* (1978), 73-95.

"The Manila Folder" *Viewpoints* 12:2 (Mar 1983), 6-7.

"The Match" *Hanging Threads* (1978), 137-45.

"Passport" *Hanging Threads* (1978), 97-109.

"The Petek" *Hanging Threads* (1978), 45-57.

"Reunion" *Hanging Threads* (1978), 59-71.

"Suicide" *Hanging Threads* (1978), 125-36.

"Train Ride" *Hanging Threads* (1978), 23-44.

Pletz, Joan†

"A Change of Air" *Grain* 11:3 (Aug 1983), 32-7.

"Natalie Said" *Antig R* No. 51 (Aut 1982), 95-105.

Plexman, A. Constance†

"Marriages Are Made in Heaven" *Northern Ontario Anthology* 2 (1978), 76-9.

Plimbley, Pat†

"In Spite of the War" *Whetstone* Spr 1973, 6-7.

Plourde, Marc (1951-)

THE SPARK PLUG THIEF Lasalle, P.Q.: New Delta Press, 1976.

THE WHITE MAGNET Montreal: D.C. Books, 1973.

"The Beekeeper and His Wife" *Spark Plug Thief* (1976), 86-97.

"The Beekeeper and His Wife" *Quarry* 26:4 (Aut 1977), 19-29.

"The Bookworm" *Grain* 2:2 [1974], 40-6.
"The Bookworm" *Spark Plug Thief* (1976), 9-18.
"The Bookworm" *Best of Grain* (1980), 63-9.
"The Farmer Element" *White Magnet* (1973), 51-7.
"The Farmer Element" *Quarry* 22:3 (Sum 1973), 22-8.
"First Thursday of the Month" *White Magnet* (1973), 58-63.
"First Thursday of the Month" *Spark Plug Thief* (1976), 72-7.
"First Thursday of the Month" *Earth* (1977), 16-20.
"First Thursday of the Month" *Mont Poems* No. 5 (1981), 64-7.
"The Flies in the Glass" *JD* Rosh Hashanah 1972, 26-7.
"The Flies in the Glass" *Spark Plug Thief* (1976), 50-3.
"Francis Wiper's Ailment" *Spark Plug Thief* (1976), 54-62.
"Francis Wiper's Ailment" *NJ* Nos. 7/8 (1976), 59-67.
"Freddy's Sister" *Spark Plug Thief* (1976), 29-38.
"General Dahl" *Grain* 2:2 [1974], 47-53.
"General Dahl" *Spark Plug Thief* (1976), 19-28.
"Incident with a Racoon" *QQ* 79 (1972), 340-4.
"Incident with a Racoon" *White Magnet* (1973), 45-50.
"Mister Whitford One Sunday Evening" *Writ* No. 11 (Fall 1979), 77-95.
"Out of the Blue" CBC "*Anthology*" 23 Nov 1974.
"The Spark Plug Thief" *Spark Plug Thief* (1976), 39-49.
"Tony B. in the Black Cat" *Spark Plug Thief* (1976), 63-71.
"The Windmill" *Grain* 4:2 [1976], 67-72.
"The Windmill" *Spark Plug Thief* (1976), 78-85.

Poelman, Leah†
"Party Line" *CSSM* 1:2 (Apr 1975), 60-2.
"Prohibition Paddy" *CSSM* 1:1 (Jan 1975), 1-4.

Poesiat, Bart‡
"Into the Future Life" *UC Gargoyle* [15] (Spr 1967), 28-34.

Pogue, Lucille†
"He Wished He Could Be Real" *Whetstone* Spr 1971, [2 pp].

Poirier, R.A.
"My Name Me" *Tam R* No. 64 (Nov 1974), 77-80.

Pollett, Ron (1900-1955)
"The Cat with the Yaller Face" *Doryloads* (1974), 128-34.
"The Garden on the Point" *Atl Guardian* 9 (Oct 1952), 37-9, 41-3, 45.
"Johnny the Pear" *Atl Guardian* 8 (Feb 1951), 18-32.
"The Matchmaker" *Atl Guardian* 13 (Feb 1956), 5-11, 29-32.
"Rum in the Pudding" *Atl Guardian* 7 (Dec 1950), 20-30.
"Ship Ahoy!" *Atl Guardian* 7 (Sept 1950), 20-30.
"Spring Is for the Lambs" *Atl Guardian* 9 (Apr 1952), 25-6, 31-4.
"The Tongue That Never Told a Lie" *Doryloads* (1974), 142-7.

Pollman, Olaf
"Rooms" *Edge* No. 7 (Win 1967-68), 39-42.

Pollock, Chris‡
[Untitled] *Alive* No. 31 [1973], 35.

Pollock, Sharon
"How Things Are" *Fid* No. 96 (Win 1973), 81-4.

Pomeroy, Elsie‡
"The Strange Awakening" *Mar Adv* 44 (Sept 1953), 25.

Pomeroy, Graham‡
"Natasha Rombova" *Choice Parts* (1976), 45-57.

Pomroy, Christopher‡
"The Helmet" *Driftwood* No. 2 (1974), 7-10.

P[onomarenko]., F[rancis].‡
"The Christened" *Prism* (Mont) No. 8 (1965), 24-5.

Pooley, Richard‡
"The Golden Ant" *Harbinger* 2:3 (2 May 1969), 5.
"How the Earth Gave Birth to Fire" *Harbinger* 2:4 (26 May 1969), 8.

Pope, Dan†
"The Ice Cream Man" *Scrivener* 3:1 (Spr 1982), 21-2.
"The Keeper of the Vineyard" *McGill Lit J* 3:2 (Sum 1982), 23-32.
"Night Creatures" *Scrivener* 2:2 (Fall 1981), 23-4.
"Nights" *Rampike* 3:1 (1983), 52.
"Nights and Mornings" *Scrivener* 3:1 (Spr 1982), 11.

Pope, Elizabeth‡
"Outside" *Can Fandom* No. 21 (June 1954), 5-7.

Pope, Helen Hofmann
"Granny Wins Canada" *Onward* 60 (20 Aug 1950), 529-31, 539, 542-3.

Pope, Pat‡
"Berty Simpson" *Stump* 4:1/2 (Spr 1980), 43-6.

Pope, Sandra†
"A Sharp Curve" *CSSM* 2:2 (Spr 1976), 47, 49.

Pope, Suzanne‡
"Labour of Love" *TUR* 95:2 (Spr 1982), 5-8.

Popkin-Clurman, Esther†
"Summer of '42 Retold" *event* 12:1 (1983), 66-72.

Porkolab, Gyorgy†
"Brief" *CFM* No. 1 (Win 1971), 21-2.

Porter, Eugene Gordon‡
"The Chancers" *March* [1] (Spr 1962), 33-65.

Porter, Helen

"Eva" *Voices Down East* [1973], 8-12.

"For Every Man an Island" *Nfld Q* 65:3 (Feb 1967), 34-40.

"A Long and Lonely Ride" *Antig R* No. 33 (Spr 1978), 31-43.

"Mainly Because of the Meat" *Nfld Q* 77:2/3 (Sum-Fall 1981), 22-5.

"Moving Day" *Baffles of Wind and Tide* (1974), 17-9.

"O Take Me as I Am" *Twelve Newfoundland Stories* (1982), 60-70.

"One Saturday" *Pot Port* 5 (1983-84), 28-31.

"The Plan" *Stories from Atlantic Canada* (1973), 174-89.

"The Smell of Wintergreen" *Nfld Q* 69:2 (Oct 1972), 27-8.

"Unravelling" *Nfld Q* 72:1 (Dec 1975), 9-11.

Porter, Ian‡

"Think of This When You Smoke Tobacco" *Varsity* Fri, 25 Sept 1964, 17.

Porter, John (1959?-)†

"What Will Harry Tell the Boss?" *Axiom* 2:4 (May 1976), 22-3.

Porter, Loraine†

"The First Canadian" *Echoes* No. 225 (Christmas 1956), 5, 21.

Portras, Daniel R.†

"Michael" *Skylark* 7:3 (Spr 1971), 59-63.

Portz, Wyatt†

"The Bear" *Writ* No. 2 (Win-Spr 1971), 88-103.

Potrebenko, Helen (1940-)

A FLIGHT OF AVERAGE PERSONS: STORIES AND OTHER WRITINGS Vancouver: New Star, 1979.

"And Always the Same Story" *Makara* 1:2 (Feb-Mar 1976), 40-7.

"And Always the Same Story" *Flight of Average Persons* (1979), 140-59.

"The Bird" *Metavisions* (1983), 103-29.

"The Bird" *Room* 8:1 (1983), 5-38.

"The Cab Business" *Repos* No. 12 (Fall 1974), 46-51.

"The Cab Business" *Flight of Average Persons* (1979), 110-5.

"February Morning" *Atlantis* 1:2 (Spr 1976), 94-7.

"February Morning" *Flight of Average Persons* (1979), 171-5.

"The Fifth Bundle" *Flight of Average Persons* (1979), 206-10.

"Gonna Come and Get You in a Taxi, Honey" *Room* 1:4 (Win 1976), 2-13.

"Gonna Come and Get You in a Taxi, Honey" *Flight of Average Persons* (1979), 122-34.

"A Good Job – For a Girl" *Flight of Average Persons* (1979), 9-24 [Also entitled "Lab Technician"].

"Have a Nice Day" *Prism* 16:1 (Spr 1977), 119-27.

"Have a Nice Day" *Flight of Average Persons* (1979), 176-86.

"Lab Technician" *Br Out* 1:3 (Aug 1974), 12-5, 38-9 [Also entitled "A Good Job – For a Girl"].

"A Late Socialization" *Flight of Average Persons* (1979), 72-82.

"New Girl" *Flight of Average Persons* (1979), 187-92.

"The Other Woman" *Canadian Short Fiction Anthology 2* (1982), 88-91.

"The Queer" *Prism* 12:2 (Fall 1972), 123-32.

"The Room Dweller" *Flight of Average Persons* (1979), 41-3.
"Stewart's Time" *Flight of Average Persons* (1979), 211-9.
"Taxi Drivers Don't Cry" *Grape* 4-17 July 1973 [Based on survey response].
"Taxi Drivers Don't Cry" *Flight of Average Persons* (1979), 116-21.
"When Winter Came" *Common Ground* (1980), 31-42.
"Willie" *Grain* 2:2 [1974], 66-8.
"Willie" *Flight of Average Persons* (1979), 44-8.

Potter, Chris‡
"Your Witness" *Diversions* 3:1 (1971), 6-8.

Potter, Esther Holm‡
"Remember Sappho" CBC *"Alberta Anthology"* 27 Aug 1983.

Poulakakis, Matt‡
"Raindrops" *Simcoe R* No. 2 (Spr 1977), 11.

Powell, Derek Reid†
"Cautionary Fable" *JCF* 2:4 (Fall 1973), 37-8.
"Fifth Horseman" *Alive* No. 27 [1973], 42.
"The Revenge" *Can R* 2:4 (Christmas 1975), 22-4.

Powell, Dorothy M. (1918-)
"Anemone" *Singing Under Ice* (1974), 37-45.
"At the Top of the Cliff" *Chat* 37 (Aug 1964), 16, 51-4.
"Davey, Dear" *Rapport* Feb 1969, 38-41.
"The Delicate Balance" *FH* 23 Dec 1965, 28-9.
"The Dress" *Chat* 37 (May 1964), 30, 44-6.
"The Dress" *Sat Eve Post* 246 (Dec 1974), 48-9, 80, 82.
"Dud's Place" *Onward* Apr 1968, 3-4, 10-3.
"Headlights in the Rain" *CG* 78 (Oct 1959), 51-4.
"Hello Bobbins" *CG* 82 (June 1963), 37-9.
"Kirsty" *FH* 28 Oct 1965, 54-5.
"Lion in the Lane" *CG* 84 (Feb 1965), 51-3.
"Love Is for Christmas" *CG* 87 (Dec 1968), 39-41.
"Love Is the Best Gift" *Chat* 37 (Dec 1964), 22-3, 40-3.
"Make-Believe Mother" *CG* 90 (Dec 1971), 35, 38.
"The Nearness of Grace" *FH* 13 Apr 1967, 58-60.
"Pinky" *FH* 16 Sept 1965, 32-3.
"Sand Castle" *Rapport* Mar 1971, 10-1.
"Sand Castle" *Our Family* 24 (Oct 1972), 26-8.
"Strangers on a Lonely Journey" *Chat* 44 (Mar 1971), 26, 52-4, 56.
"Wings in the Wind" *CG* Oct 1958, 15, 38-40.
"Winter Wedding" *FH* 22 Nov 1962, 32, 35.
"With Every Child" *Extension* 54 (Sept 1959), 10[+?] [Based on CPLI].
"With Every Child" *CG* 81 (June 1962), 33-4, 36.

Powell, Evelyn Jones‡
"Mrs. Thomas and the Pink Straw Hat" *UC Observer* 15 Apr 1965, 26-7.

Powell, Marilyn (1939-)

"But Thou Go By" *Undergrad* Spr 1958, [2 pp].

"Home Grown in the East End" *Toronto Short Stories* (1977), 140-8.

"A Psychological Story" *Aurora* 1980 110-6.

Powell, Rob‡

"The Sea" *Quarry* 25:2 (Spr 1976), 46-50.

Powell, Robert‡

"The Iron Age" *Anthos* 1:2 (Win 1978), 22-4.

Power, John

"The Anatomy of a Muskicide" *Can Boating* 53 (Sept 1977), 37-40.

"Bagging Bunnies" *Legion* 57 (Mar 1983), 20-1.

"Blind Justice" *Legion* 55 (Aug 1980), 22-4.

"The Coon Caper" *Legion* 58 (Oct 1983), 38, 42.

"Eating Crow" *Legion* 53 (Oct 1978), 23, 56.

"Fish That Go Bump in the Night" *Legion* 57 (Aug 1982), 22-4.

"Fox Fever" *Legion* 54 (Feb 1980), 20, 48-9.

"Going to Ground" *Legion* 53 (Feb 1979), 14-5.

"Hard to Swallow" *Legion* 54 (July 1979), 24-5, 43.

"A Hare-Raisin' Experience" *Legion* 55 (Feb 1981), 23-4.

"Just Pooling Around" *Legion* 57 (June 1982), 19-20, 37.

"The Moose That Roared" *Legion* 54 (Sept 1979), 25, 50-2.

"Mooseberry or Bust" *Legion* 54 (Apr 1980), 26-8.

"Muskie Madness" *Legion* 55 (Oct 1980), 30-2.

"Ol' Buck and the Buckpassers" *Legion* 52 (Sept 1977), 9, 58-9.

"Poaching" *Legion* 55 (June 1980), 30-2.

"A Premier Preserve" *Legion* 53 (Apr 1979), 24-5.

"Ruffed Up" *Legion* 56 (July 1981), 15-6.

"Sufferin' Steelheads" *Legion* 55 (Apr 1981), 28, 30.

"Swan Song" *Legion* 57 (Oct 1982), 22, 24, 26.

"Winning the Whitefish of the Weekend" *Legion* 52 (Feb 1978), 11, 20-1.

Powning, Beth (1949-)

"Aliens" *Was R* 12:2 (Fall 1977), 43-8.

"Amory Hawkes" *CBC [Hal] "Audio Stage"* Jan 1979 [Based on survey response].

"Benny" *Tam R* No. 69 (Sum 1976), 58-75.

"Immigrants at the Dump" *CFM* No. 16 (Win 1975), 84-8.

"Limbo" *Quarry* 25:2 (Spr 1976), 33-8.

"Limbo" *Face to Face* (1979), 69-75.

"The Mirror" *Quarry* 30:4 (Aut 1981), 24-9.

"Monkey Tricks" *Antig R* No. 18 (Sum 1974), 81-3.

"Mothers" *Prism* 17:2 (Fall 1978), 99-106.

"That Good Night" *Fid* No. 107 (Fall 1975), 6-16.

"That Good Night" *CBC "Anthology"* 14 Oct 1978 [Based on survey response].

Poy, Adrienne‡
"All in a Day" *TUR* 72:2 (Dec 1958), 24-42.
"The Bridge" *TUR* 73:4 (Mar 1960), 3-6.
"The Knowing Moment" *TUR* 70:2 (Dec 1957), 33-5.
"There Stands a Lady" *TUR* 70:3 (Feb 1958), 21-33.
"There Stands a Lady" *UTR* 1 (Spr 1958), 3-13.

Pratt, Terry‡
"How I Became a Vampire" *TUR* 75:3 (Mar 1962), 40-2.
"The Poker Game" *TUR* 78:2 (Nov-Dec 1964), 8-11.
"A Rooted Sorrow" *TUR* 76:1 (Oct 1962), 22-5.

Presant, Joan‡
"Excelsior" *Undergrad* Aut 1950, 16-8.

Price, Anna Mae‡
"Fire with Fire" *Northern Ontario Anthology* 1 (1977), 38-44.

Price, C.B.
"Cree Boy" *FH* 12 Apr 1956, 30-1.
"His Weakness" *FH* 5 Feb 1953, 28-9.
"Ma Kwet's Present" *FH* 19 Dec 1957, 8-9.
"No Fuss!" *FH* 27 Nov 1952, 28-9.
"No Fuss!" *FH* 10 Sept 1964, 26, 33.
"No Fuss!" *Stories to Read Again* (1965), 71-8.
"The Rabbit Hunt" *FH* 24 May 1956, 28-9.
"Squaw Fish Story" *FH* 6 Dec 1956, 27-8.
"The Strikem Flag" *FH* 7 May 1953, 24-5, 32.
"Tillicum Baby" *FH* 24 Dec 1953, 24-5.
"Timber Wolf" *FH* 20 Sept 1956, 24-5, 38.

Price, Flo‡
"Pigeons of Peace" *Nw J* Nos. 18/19 (1980), 100-4.
"Shorts Story" *Read Ch* 1:1 (Spr 1982), 17-24.

Price, Lorie‡
"The Wrong Man" *Crier* 1:1 (July 1964), 30-1, 33.

Price, Ray‡
"Two Worlds" *Edmonton Journal* Wed, 21 Oct 1964, 4.
"Why Did It Happen to Me?" *UC Observer* 15 Feb 1969, 28-9 [Non-fiction?].

Priest, Paul B.†
"Shadows" *Quarry* 27:3 (Sum 1978), 61-6.

Priest, Robert (1951-)
"Candles" *Waves* 8:1 (Fall 1979), 20.
"The Star Heart" *New Bodies* (1983), 25-33.

Primrose, Olive Clare‡
"The Morning at Harrods" *Stories with John Drainie* (1963), 181-6.

Primrose, Tom
   "The Old Skinner" *Golden West* Christmas 1965, 20.

Pritchard, Allan E.
   "A Helping Hand" *Kitimat Voices 1967* 137-40.

Proctor, Alan‡
   "The Climax" *Undergrad* Spr 1958, [4 pp].

Procunier, Peter†
   "Passage to Infinity" *Crossley Annual* 1965, 55-9.

Prokopchuk, Ivan‡
   "Marjorie" *Fifth Page* 1967, 36-40.

Proulx, Annie†
   "On the Antler" *Har* 7:4 No. 46 (Dec-Jan 1982-83), 51-3, 81-2, 84-7.

Puddester, John‡
   "Uncle Henry's Ghoster" *Atl Guardian* 9 (May 1952), 43-4, 46.

Puff [pseudonym]
   "Patata Frita" *Potlatch* No. 5 (Dec 1965), 10-22.

Pugsley, Edmund E.
   " 'Any Kind of Agent' " *SW* 6 Aug 1955, II:5.
   "Family Trait" *Onward* 27 Apr 1958, 257-8, 266-7.
   "God's Lake Voice" *SW* 2 Feb 1952, II:5, 12.
   "The Jellybean" *SW* 28 Mar 1953, II:4, 12.
   "A Man of His Word" *Onward* 12 July 1959, 433-5, 443.
   "Mud Digger" *SW* 10 Mar 1951, II:3-4.
   "No Excitement" *SW* 12 Feb 1955, II:6.
   "No Nerve to Lose" *SW* 3 Mar 1951, II:3-4.
   "A Solemn Deal" *SW* 27 Sept 1952, II:4.
   "Straight Talk" *Onward* 3 July 1960, 420-2.
   "Two Tickets to Muskeago" *SW* 10 Sept 1955, I:7.
   "Unsealed Memo" *SW* 6 Feb 1954, I:7.

Pugsley, Judith‡
   "The Empty Lot" *Existère* 1:1 (Oct 1980), 10.
   "On Seeing 'A Clockwork Orange' " *Existère* 1:1 (Oct 1980), 4.

Pullen, Charles‡
   "My Book" *Undergrad* Spr 1954, 20-3.
   "Old Comrades" *Acta Vic* 78:4 (Mar 1954), 26-8.

Pumphrey, Ron‡
   "Present for Mary" *Atl Guardian* 8 (Dec 1951), 25, 27-8.

Purdy, Al (1917-)
"At Home on McGill Street" *Mont* 38 (Mar 1964), 24-6.
"My Friend Julio" *Tam R* No. 33 (Aut 1964), 40-8.
'The Undertaker" *CF* 43 (Oct 1963), 156-9.
'The Undertaker" *Forum* (1972), 363-8.
'The Undertaker" *Not to Be Taken at Night* (1981), 70-81.

Purdy, Brian (1948-)
INTERLOPER Toronto: Three Trees Press, 1977.
TALE LIGHTS Toronto: Missing Link, 1976 [Based on CBIP].
"All the World's Crazies" *Interloper* (1977), 47-52.
'The Barking of Dogs" *Interloper* (1977), 69-77.
"A Brush with Manet" *Interloper* (1977), 53-60.
'The Fix" *Interloper* (1977), 29-32.
"A Great Night for Hospitals" *Interloper* (1977), 21-7.
"Miss Thames and Miss Findlay" *Interloper* (1977), 61-7.
'The Night Walk" *Interloper* (1977), 87-92.
"Obits for Picasso" *Interloper* (1977), 17-20.
"Old Magora" *Interloper* (1977), 9-15.
"Or Take a Tramp Steamer" *Portico* 2:2 (Win-Spr 1978), 5-8.
'Rent Please" *Interloper* (1977), 33-9.
"Small World" *Interloper* (1977), 79-85.
'Tell It to J. Edgar Hoover" *Interloper* (1977), 41-6.

Purdy, Debra M.†
" 'A Dancer's Foot' " *Read Ch* 1:3 (Win 1982), 49-59.

Putman, Alan‡
'Day of the Cyclops" *Forum* (OSSTF) 4 (Dec 1978), 209-10.

Pyper, C.B.
"One Thing After Another" *Can Life* 2:1 (Spr 1951), 9 [Excerpt?].

Quaadri, Muhammad‡
"Mr. Hetherington's Patrons" *TUR* 96:2 (Spr 1983), 16-20.

Quaggin, Alison‡
'The Clown Doll" *TUR* 93:2 (Apr 1980), 11-4.
'The Minister and the Murderess" *TUR* 92:1 (Jan 1979), 38-41.

Quain, Hamilton‡
"For Sale – One Pair of Golf Clubs" *Forge* 1950, 24-7.

Quarrington, Paul (1953-)
"Astronomy" *Writing* No. 2 (Win 1980-81), 41-3.

Quast, Jeanette†
'You'll Never Make It, Phillip" *CSSM* 3:1 (Win 1977), 62-5.

Quayle, Marjorie‡
"Discord" *Forge* 1950, 55-63.

Quin, Mike‡
   "Oscar Wants to Know" *Uk Can* 7 (1 Oct 1953), 5.
   "The Two Philosophers" *Uk Can* 7 (15 Dec 1953), 8.

Quinlan, Judith‡
   "The Bellatrix Report" *Stardust* 3:2 (Spr 1981), 21-6.
   "Write of Passage" *Stardust* 3:1 [n.d.], 79-88.

Quinton, Maurice‡
   "An Affair of Honour" *Scarlett and Gold* No. 44 (1962), 141, 143, 145, 147, 149, 151, 153.

Rabinovitch, Marvin
   "Year of the Eggroll" *Forge* 25:1 (Feb 1963), 31-9.

Rackham, Ruth‡
   "Why Should I?" *Acta Vic* 74:3 (Jan 1950), 29.

Raddall, Thomas H. (1903-)
   " 'The Credit Shall Be Yours' " *Weekend* 4 (9 Oct 1954), 2-4, 37.
   "The Dreamers" *Weekend* 5 (30 July 1955), 3-4.

Radigan, Mark‡
   "The Photograph" *Stump* 4:1/2 (Spr 1980), 13-6.

Radu, Kenneth
   "Baba" *Fid* No. 120 (Win 1979), 40-7.
   "The King" *Can R* 4:2 (Mar 1977), 15-7.
   "The Man Who Stopped Talking" *Mal R* No. 59 (July 1981), 93-9.
   "Nursery Tale" *Quarry* 27:4 (Aut 1978), 17-21.
   "One Hundred Dollars" *Waves* 7:2 (Win 1979), 4-10.
   "A Point of View" *Waves* 10:1/2 (Sum-Fall 1981), 43-67.
   "State Visit" *CFM* Nos. 32/33 (1979), 26-32.
   "Sundays" *Chel J* 6 (May-June 1980), 103-4, 137-8.
   "Tableau" *Quarry* 30:2 (Spr 1981), 42-50.
   "The Yellow Dress" *Waves* 9:2 (Win 1981), 5-13.

Rae, Angela‡
   "A Tie Game" *Poetry WLU* Spr 1983, 16-8.

Rae, Donna†
   "The Fraser River" *Br Out* 2:5 (Sept-Oct 1975), 32-5, 47.
   "Old-Fashioned" *Flare* 2 (Oct 1980), 77-8, 128, 134, 136-7.
   "Violent Spirit" *Grain* 7:1 [1979], 5-12.
   "The White Ravine" *Br Out* 7:2 (1980), 34-41.

Rae, George Menendez
   "Dear Mom" *FH* 24 July 1952, 16.
   "Score Settled" *FH* 9 Aug 1951, 20.

Raelo, Juan†
"The Piccolo" *McGill Lit J* 2:1 (Spr 1980), 55-64.

Raglon, Rebecca†
"You" *Antig R* No. 36 (Win 1979), 81-8.

The Rajah – *See* Phillips, R.A.J.

Rajkumar, Ken‡
"The John Brown" *Forge* 1967, 13-5.

Rakosy, Susan‡
"The Image and the Girl" *Kaleidoscope* 1954-55, 5-9.

Ramsden, Doug‡
"Slave October" *In Complete* [1970-71], 38-42.

Ramsden, J.D.‡
"Jeremy" *Laom R* 2:1 (Mar 1976), 89-92.

Ramshaw, Walter‡
"The Warrior" *Forge* 1951, 6-8.

Randall, Elizabeth‡
"Debbie" *Lunatic Gazette* Ser 2 1:2 (Nov-Dec 1982), 9.

Randall, Margaret‡
"Action: Smile. Promise a Real Letter Next Time. Really Do" *Writing* No. 3 (Sum 1981), 39-40.

Randall, Nora Delahunt†
"The Bulldozer That Went Away" *Makara* 2:4 [1977], 23-6.
"Can You Wear Earrings in the Woods?" *Makara* 1:1 (Dec 1975), 9-12.

Ranger, Ruth†
"Night Sweepers" *CSSM* 1:1 (Jan 1975), 22-4.

Rankin, Joyce‡
"The Last of the Dodos" *Alpha* 4:3 (Spr 1980), 11.

Ransom, Else‡
"Some Never Know" *AA* 59 (Feb 1969), 25-8.

Ranson, Dave‡
"Imagination's Wings" *Scar Fair* 10 (1983), 25-32.

Rapicano, Marianne‡
"Consummate Passion: A Gourmet's Delight" *Toronto Star* Sun, 28 Sept 1980, D5.

Rapoport, Janis
"Honeymoonland" *CFM* Nos. 40/41 (1981), 26-33.

Rapoport, Nessa (1953-)
"Katy" *Chat* 55 (Oct 1982), 118, 180, 182, 186, 188.

Rashley, R.E.†
"Drought" *JCF* 3:2 (1974), 41-2.

Rasmussen, Anita‡
'The Honourable Man" *Muskeg R* 4 [1976], 16-22.

Rasmussen, Daryl†
"Cloisons (Partitions)" *Cap R* No. 10 (Fall 1976), 143-59.

Ratcliffe, Bill‡
'Donahoe's Thumb" *Can Golden West* 12a:3 (Spr 1977), 32-7.

Raum, Elizabeth‡
"Goofy's Tits" *Smoke Signals* 4 [date unknown] [Based on *SWG* survey response].

Ravel, Aviva (1938?-)
"About Face" *CF* 47 (Oct 1967), 151-4.
'The Aluminum Tub" *Viewpoints* 6:3 (Fall 1971), 51-61.
'The Battered Tome" *JCF* Nos. 31/32 (1981), 92-7.
'Bereft" *CBC "Anthology"* 29 June 1967.
'The Donor Dinner" *Viewpoints* 8:3 (1974), 53-63.
"A Double Thread" *JCF* No. 16 (1976), 39-47.
'The Escape" *Viewpoints* 12:2 (Fall 1981), 34-43 [Excerpt?].
"Evening Courses" *Chat* 52 (Mar 1979), 41, 44, 118, 120, 122, 124, 126.
'The Gramaphone" *Viewpoints* 7:2 (1972), 22-8.
'Milestone" *Viewpoints* 3:3 (Sum 1968), 52-9.
'My Sister's Keeper" *Viewpoints* 5:2 (1970), 34-42.
'Not Everybody Can Live in Israel" *Viewpoints* 12:6 (Aug-Sept 1983), 5-6.
'Paper Roses" *Viewpoints* 9:3 (1976), 35-43.
"Smoked Out" *Chat* 52 (May 1979), 46-7, 69-70, 72, 74, 77.
"Success Story" *Moment* (U.S.) 5 (June 1980), 49-54.
'The Visit" *Viewpoints* 7:1 (1972), 37-49.

Rawdon, Michael
"Foxfire and Paradox" *Quarry* 31:4 (Aut 1982), 61-71.
"Gathering In" *WCR* 8:2 (Oct 1973), 13-8.
'In This Illumined Large, the Veritable Small" *Islands* (N.Z.) 7 (1978), 156-65.
'Transitions" *Landfall* (N.Z.) 34 (1980), 162-70.

Ray, Sam – *See* Hodgins, Norris.

Raycroft, R.G.‡
"5 Roses" *Forum* (OSSTF) 2 (Oct 1976), 169-71.

Rayson, Ruth‡
'Runaway Reindeer" *Varsity* Fri, 12 Dec 1952, 3.

Razzolini, Dante
"On Directness of Statement in the Bush" *Rod & Gun* 70 (Mar 1968), 25.

Rea, Charles‡
"The Decision" *Varsity Lit Issue* Fri, 3 Mar 1950, 6.
"The Weekend" *Varsity Lit Issue* Mon, 5 Mar 1951, 4.

Read, Bob‡
"From Frank's Diary" *Acta Vic* 93:2 (Dec 1968), 9-10.
"The Page's Song" *Acta Vic* 93:3 (Feb 1969), 22.

Read, David†
"Agatha and Homer" *Time Gatherers* (1970), 95-8.
"Mr. Stanley P. U. Smart" *Time Gatherers* (1970), 70-91.

Read, Elfreida‡
"Jade" CBC "*Anthology*" 22 Sept 1979.

Read, Mary‡
"The Rhinestone Cow" *Stump* Aut 1981, 1-4.

Read, Ranee R.‡
"Sybille at Twenty" *Lit R* 1:1 (1983), 37-8.

Ready, William B.‡
"The Bomb" CBC "*Anthology*" 22 July 1972.
"A Pair of Peacocks" CBC "*Anthology*" 18 Mar 1972.

Reambeault, Mary†
"Kaleidoscope" *Diversions* 5:1 (1975), 37-8.
"A Lonely Time of Day" *Diversions* 4:1 (1973), 3-5.

Reaney, James (1926-)
"The Bully" *Canadian Short Stories* (1952), 204-15.
"The Bully" *Stories from Seven Countries* (1972) [Based on survey response].
"Dear Metronome" *CF* 32 (Sept 1952), 134-7.
"The Dress" *Can Life* 1:4 (Spr 1950), 9, 37.

Rebel, Hermann‡
"A Jury Has to Eat" *Undergrad* 1964, 11-3.

Rebus, Philip†
"Cat Call" *Splices* (1975), 48-51.

Records, Sally‡
"The Coffee Shop" *Alpha* 5:2 (Win 1980), 9, 25, 27.
"Local Minister Goes Berserk – Sings, Tap Dances at Altar" *Alpha* 5:2 (Win 1980), 13.

Redant, Julia†
"The Business Manager" *Chel J* 5 (Mar-Apr 1979), 71-4.

Redant, Philip D.†
"Charlotte" *Pier* Spr Sum 1978, 38-40 [Non-fiction?].
"Dwight Makes Right" *Green's* 11:4 (Sum 1983), 27-33.

"The Festival" *Saskatchewan Homecoming* (1971), 158-62.
"The 'Non-Returned' Man" *Alpha* 5:1 (Fall 1980), 20, 32.
"Revival Preacher" *Green's* 10:4 (Sum 1982), 65-73.

Redbourne, Ray [probable pseudonym]
"Fauna Free Press" *Communicator* 9:2 [n.d.], [3 pp].

Reddick, Adrian‡
"Snow" *UC Gargoyle* 25 (16 Dec 1980), 9.

Redl-Hlus, Carolyn D.‡
"Three Women" *CBC "Alberta Anthology"* 23 Oct 1980.

Redmond, Chris†
"The Gargoyle" *CSSM* 2:1 (Jan 1976), 18-20.
"Preparations" *Canadian Short Fiction Anthology* 2 (1982), 109-12.

Redmond, Mary‡
"That Lazy Neighbour Family!" *Pres Record* 98 (Apr 1974), 15.

Redmond, Tess†
"Horses of the Sun" *Atlantis* 1:2 (Spr 1976), 54-66.

Reeve, Phyllis†
"A Pair of White Buck Shoes" *Lib* 36 (July 1959), 26, 42.

Regimbald, Therese†
"What About Billy-Boy?" *Blue Buffalo* 2:1 (Fall 1983), [3 pp].

Rehlinger, Oliver‡
"His Story" *Introductions from an Island* 1976, 7-10.

Reid, Dennis†
"The Elephant-Shaped Perfume Bottle" *Antig R* No. 45 (Spr 1981), 61-8.
"Plaza Del Loma" *Cap R* No. 22 (1982), 19-20.
"River" *Matrix* 3:1 (Sum 1977), 1.
"The Wedding" *Matrix* No. 10 (Fall-Win 1979-80), 28-32.

Reid, Dorothy M.
"Nanabozho and the Song: A New Northern 'Legend' " *Ont Lib R* 45 (Nov 1961), 227.

Reid, Helen B.‡
"The Harvesters" *Diversions* 3:1 (1971), 10-1.
"Something Special" *Diversions* 3:1 (1971), 4.

Reid, Iris R.
"How She Go, Johnny?" *Northern Ontario Anthology* 2 (1978), 24-6.

Reid, James†
"The Birds" *Motion* No. 1 (25 May 1962), [4 pp].

Reid, Jeffrey†
"Last Tuesday, Valkeria" *Waves* 9:2 (Win 1981), 33-6.

Reid, John (1916?-1985)
"Putting It Together" *CBC "Anthology"* 24 May 1975.
"A Sailboat in the Sky" *CBC "Anthology"* 15 Dec 1973.

Reid, Peter†
"Prince Sam and Princess Spray-Me-Not" *Writ* No. 3 (Win 1972), 41-5.
"The Sorcerer" *Writ* No. 3 (Win 1972), 37-8.

Reid, Robert W.‡
"The Banquet" *Acta Vic* 80:4 (Mar 1956), 9.
"Une Bonne Fôte de Noël" *Acta Vic* 80:2 (Dec 1955), 14.
"The Demon" *Acta Vic* 82:2 (Feb 1958), 18-9.
"The Envoys" *Acta Vic* 80:1 (Nov 1955), 20-1.
"The Retreat" *Acta Vic* 80:2 (Dec 1955), 16-7.
"The Warlord" *Acta Vic* 80:3 (Feb 1956), 21-2.

Reigo, Ants†
"Allan" *Fid* No. 106 (Sum 1975), 56-61.

Reinart, Ustun
"Lunch Counter" *Can Dimension* 16 (Jan 1983), 54.

Reinhard – *See* Walz, Reinhard.

Reinhardt, Jean†
"A Break for Lester" *West People* No. 181 (24 Mar 1983), 11.
"For Better or Worse" *Read Ch* 1:2 (Sum 1982), 90-2.
"Neighbor" *West People* No. 203 (15 Sept 1983), 14.
"Never the Loser" *CSSM* 2:2 (Spr 1976), 34-6.
"To Each Her Own" *Green's* 12:1 (Aut 1983), 53-7.

Reinhartz, Henia†
"Job of the Ghetto" *Contact* 2:11 (Fall 1973), 29-32.
"The Wedding" *Contact* 3:3 (Sum-Fall 1974), 9-13.

Reinl, Constance and Jakob, Conrad†
"Combination" *Stardust* 1:3 (1976), 4-35.

Reiter, David Phillip†
"The Man Had a Wife" *Fid* No. 96 (Win 1973), 18-32.

Renaud, Denise‡
"All in a Days' Work" *JCF* Nos. 28/29 (1980), 76-83.

Renner, Vivian (1943?-)
"Look What They're Doing" *Quarry* 22:3 (Sum 1973), 37-43.

Rensby, Harry†
"Descriptions" *CSSM* 2:1 (Jan 1976), 54-5.
"People Remaining" *Laom R* 1:1 (Dec-Jan 1975), 91-2.
"Sometimes a Draw Will Do" *Current Assets* (1973), 117-8.
"Tomorrow Will Be the Same" *Laom R* 1:1 (Dec-Jan 1975), 92-3.

Rentz, Kenneth G.‡
"A Leak in the Roof" *UC Observer* Nov 1975, 16-7.
"The Man Who Found God Through Suffering" *UC Observer* Feb 1971, 30-1.

Repka, William‡
"The Scrapper" *Scan* 5:1 (Feb-Mar 1969), 12-4.

Resnick, Rae‡
"Ugly Can Be Beautiful" *Miss Chat* 7 (19 Nov 1970), 72, 78, 80.

Reyes, R. Ivanov‡
"Vigil" *Nebula* No. 7 (1978), 60-7.

Reykdal, Art†
"Bringing Home the Bacon" *Ice Can* 29:3 (Spr 1971), 46-7.
"Shooting the Bull: The Need of Change" *Vagabond* 1:1 (May 1951), 8-9, 40-2.
"Three Muskrat Skins" *Vagabond* 1:1 (May 1951), 12-5.

Reynolds, Allan B.‡
"Once More into the Breach" *Legion* 53 (Apr 1979), 16-7, 59.

Reynolds, Debbie – *See* Michie, Maureen and Reynolds, Debbie.

Reynolds, Dickson – *See* Reynolds, Helen Mary Greenwood Campbell.

Reynolds, Helen Mary Greenwood Campbell
"Across Country" *High Flight* (1951), 38-48 [Children's?].
"Chuck Covered the Churches" by Dickson Reynolds *Onward* 17 May 1953, 305-7.
"A Sailor from Holland" by Dickson Reynolds *Onward* 60 (25 June 1950), 401-3.
"Six Feet of Frayed Rope" by Dickson Reynolds *Onward* 8 Feb 1953, 81-3, 95.

Reynolds, Norman†
"Drive" *Writ* No. 13 (1981), 5-11.

Reyto, Martin‡
"The Junebugs" *Random* 3:5 (Mar [1969]), 15-8.
"Mozy" *Random* 4:1 [n.d.], [9 pp].

Rice, Greg‡
"The Courage of Catherine Schubert" *West People* No. 130 (25 Mar 1982), 11.

Richards, Bill – *See* Lunn, Richard.

Richards, David Adams (1950-)
DANCERS AT NIGHT Ottawa: Oberon Press, 1978.
"Charlie" *Floorboards* No. 3 (Spr 1970), 13-4.
"The Child and the Boy" *AA* 62 (Dec 1971), 23, 46.
"Dancers at Night" *Dancers at Night* (1978), 132-49.
"The Fire" *Fid* No. 95 (Fall 1972), 92-109.
"The Fire" *Stories from Atlantic Canada* (1973), 134-55.
"Husband and Wife Gratten (1927)" *Prism* 17:2 (Fall 1978), 108-17.
"In This Age of Chess" *JCF* 2:1 (Win 1973), 24-8.
"Kopochus 1825" *Dancers at Night* (1978), 52-78.
"The Promise" *Antig R* No. 9 (Spr 1972), 47-51.
"The Promise" *Copperfield* 4 (Oct 1972), 27-31.
"Ramsey Taylor" *East of Canada* (1976), 57-79.
"Ramsey Taylor" *Dancers at Night* (1978), 29-51.
"A Rural Place" *Dancers at Night* (1978), 5-28.
"A Rural Place" *Canadian Literature in the 70's* (1980), 217-36.
"Safe in the Arms" *Fid* No. 113 (Spr 1977), 81-121.
"Safe in the Arms" *Dancers at Night* (1978), 91-131.
"We, Who Have Never Suffered" *Dancers at Night* (1975), 79-90.

Richards, Helen (1913-)
"The Mists Are Rising" *event* 1:3 (Win 1972), 67-8.

Richards, John†
"Fishing for the Bottom of the Lake" *Mont Writers' Forum* 2:8 (Aug 1980), 7-12.

Richards, Mabel
"The Sour Apple Tree" *Saskatchewan Writing* 2 (1963), 13-9.

Richardson, Eamon‡
"David's Wall Dream" *Random* 3:5 (Mar [1969]), 23.

Richardson, Peter‡
"In the Warm-Up Hut – A View of Mirabel Airport" *CCWQ* 3:2/3 [n.d.], 16-9.
"Offload on TAP" *Interior Voice* No. 1 (Win 1981-82), 12-5.

Riches, Brenda (1942-)
"Ararat" *Cap R* No. 12 (1977), 12-3.
"Clara Smiling" *event* 10:2 (1981), 73-6.
"Clara Smiling" *Saskatchewan Gold* (1982), 282-5.
"Cloth" *Cap R* No. 11 (1977), 5-9.
"Demeter's Daughter" *event* 6:1 [1977], 7-10.
"Demeter's Daughter" *Canadian Short Fiction Anthology* 2 (1982), 72-5.
"Dry Media" *Cap R* No. 14 (1978), 19-22.
"Fall" *Cap R* No. 14 (1978), 23-5.
From "Adam Never Had One" *Dand* 6 (n.d.], 49-52 [Excerpt?].
"Gall" *Cap R* No. 14 (1978), 14-8.
"Gall" *More Stories from Western Canada* (1980), 177-81.
"Gall" *West of Fiction* (1983), 215-8.
"Leavings" *event* 7:2 (1978), 124-5 [Listed as poem in survey response].
"Musician" *Cap R* No. 12 (1977), 15 [Listed as poem in survey response].
"Persimmon" *Cap R* No. 11 (1977), 10-3.

"Preserves" *event* 7:2 (1978), 133-5.
"Rites" *event* 7:2 (1978), 126-32.
"Rites" *Sundogs* (1980), 93-9.
"Some mornings" *Cap R* No. 23 (1982), 5-6 [Listed as poem in survey response].
"Stone" *Cap R* No. 12 (1977), 8-11.
"Strings" *Grain* 5:1 [1977], 42-6.
"Strings" *Best of Grain* (1980), 115-9.
"Styx" *Story So Far* 5 (1978), 159.
[Untitled] *Cap R* No. 12 (1977), 14 [Listed as poem in survey response].
[Untitled] *Cap R* No. 14 (1978), 12-3 [Listed as poem in survey response].
"Vanity" *Grain* 6:1 [1978], 17-8.

Richler, Mordecai (1931-)

THE STREET Toronto: McClelland & Stewart, 1969.
"The Art of Kissing" *Modern Canadian Stories* (1975), 140-7.
"The Balloon" *Mont* 32 (May 1958), 24-8.
"Bambinger" *AA* 56 (Dec 1965), 30-1, 33 [Also entitled "It's Harder to be Anybody"].
"Bambinger" *Street* (1969), 71-7.
"Bambinger" *Sixteen by Twelve* (1970), 90-4.
"Bambinger" *Singing Under Ice* (1974), 218-24.
"Bambinger" *Immigrant Experience* (1975), 52-7.
"Bambinger" *Moderne Erzähler der Walt: Kanada* (1976), 306-12 [Trans. Walter Riedel].
"Bambinger" *Transitions 2* (1978), 155-60.
"Bambinger" *In Your Own Words* (1982), 250-4.
"Benny, the War in Europe, and Myerson's Daughter Bella" *Mont* 30 (Oct 1956), 23-5.
"Benny, the War in Europe, and Myerson's Daughter Bella" *Book of Canadian Stories* (1962), 318-26.
"Benny, the War in Europe, and Myerson's Daughter Bella" *Street* (1969), 77-83.
"Benny, the War in Europe, and Myerson's Daughter Bella" *Oxford Anthology of Canadian Literature* (1973), 420-5.
"Benny, the War in Europe, and Myerson's Daughter Bella" *Penguin Book of Canadian Short Stories* (1980), 291-6.
"Benny, the War in Europe, and Myerson's Daughter Bella" *Best Canadian Short Stories* (1981), 182-7.
"The First Time I Left Home" *CBC "Anthology"* 4 Nov 1960.
"It's Harder to Be Anybody" *Mont* 35 (June 1961), 20-2 [Also entitled "Bambinger"; an excerpt from *Cocksure* (1968) appeared in *MM* 74 (7 Oct 1961) under the same title].
"IZZY" *CBC "Anthology"* 23 Feb 1980.
"Job Hunting" *Mont* 31 (Apr 1957), 47-9, 51, 53.
"A Liberal Education" *Paris R* 11 No. 42 (Win-Spr 1968), 55-65 [Re characters from *Cocksure*].
"Mortimer Griffin, Shalinsky, and How They Settled the Jewish Question" *Tam R* No. 7 (Spr 1958), 30-43 [Basis for Cocksure].
"Mortimer Griffin, Shalinsky, and How they Settled the Jewish Question" *Mont* 32 (Aug 1958), 16-20 [As "Griffin, and Shalinsky, and How They Settled the Jewish Question"].
"Mortimer Griffin, Shalinsky, and How They Settled the Jewish Question"

Town (U.K.) Nov 1963, 77-9, 91, 93 [Based on ABCMA].
"Mortimer Griffin, Shalinsky, and How They Settled the Jewish Question" *Jewish Life* Aug 1965, 12-7 [Based on ABCMA].
"Mortimer Griffin, Shalinsky, and How They Settled the Jewish Question" *Canadian Century* (1973), 477-89.
"Mortimer Griffin, Shalinsky, and How They Settled the Jewish Question" *Selections from Major Canadian Writers* (1974), 233-42.
"Mortimer Griffin, Shalinsky, and How They Settled the Jewish Question" *Best Modern Canadian Short Stories* (1978), 236-47.
"Mortimer Griffin, Shalinsky, and How They Settled the Jewish Question" *Spice Box* (1981), 211-23.
"Mr. Soon" *CBC* "Anthology" 11 May 1962.
"Mr. Soon" *AA* 56 (Apr 1966), 34-5.
"The Other Beach" *Stories of Quebec* (1980), 101-9.
"The Passing of Issy Hersh" *Tam R* No. 57 (1971), 5-29.
"Pinky's Squealer" *Street* (1969), 62-70 [Excerpt].
"Pinky's Squealer" *Kaleidoscope* (1972), 74-82.
"Pinky's Squealer" *Canadian Humour and Satire* (1976), 68-75 [As "The St. Urbain Street Heroes"].
"Playing Ball on Hampstead Heath" *Gentlemen's Mag* Aug 1966, 90, 140, 142-8 [Based on ABCMA].
"Playing Ball on Hampstead Heath" *Running Man* 1:2 (July-Aug 1968), 22-8 [Based on ABCMA].
"Playing Ball on Hampstead Heath" *Canadian Winter's Tales* (1968), 114-30.
"Playing Ball on Hampstead Heath" *Great Canadian Short Stories* (1971), 276-88.
"Playing Ball on Hampstead Heath" *Great Canadian Sports Stories* (1979), 41-56.
"Preparing for the Worst" *Running Man* 1:1 (May-June 1968), 52-3 [Based on ABCMA].
"Red Menace" *New Statesman* 62 (22 Sept 1961), 380-2.
"Red Menace" *Street* (1969), 46-52 [Excerpt].
"The Secret of the Kugel" *CBC* "Anthology" 19 Oct 1954.
"The Secret of the Kugel" *New Statesman* 15 Sept 1956, 305-6 [Based on ABCMA].
"The Secret of the Kugel" *Magasinet Tillaeg Til Politiken* 31 Aug 1957, 1-2 [As "Tante Fanny's Hemmelighed"; trans. Elisabeth Rasmussen; based on ABCMA].
"The Secret of the Kugel" *Mont* 31 (Oct 1957), 22-3.
"The Secret of the Kugel" *Pick of Today's Short Stories* 8 (1957), 179-83.
"The Secret of the Kugel" *SW* 13 Sept 1958, 20-1, 54.
"Seymour" *Playboy* 27 (June 1980), 125-6, 134, 213.
"Shooting the Breeze on St. Urbain" *CBC* "Anthology" 16 Feb 1962.
"Some Grist for Mervyn's Mill" *Kenyon R* 24 (1962), 80-105.
"Some Grist for Mervyn's Mill" *Town* (U.K.) Apr 1962, 60-3, 78, 80, 82, 84 [Based on ABCMA].
"Some Grist for Mervyn's Mill" *Mont* 36 (June 1962), 24-31.
"Some Grist for Mervyn's Mill" *Best American Short Stories* 1963 246-68.
"Some Grist for Mervyn's Mill" *Canadian Short Stories* 2 (1968), 150-82.
"Some Grist for Mervyn's Mill" *Street* (1969), 91-117.
"Some Grist for Mervyn's Mill" *Canadian Short Story* (1971), 59-81.
"Some Grist for Mervyn's Mill" *Die Weite Reise* (1974), 150-80 [As "Wasser auf

Mervyns Mähle"; trans. Peter Kleinhempel].

"The St. Urbain Street Heroes" – See "Pinky's Squeaker".

"The Summer My Grandmother Was Supposed to Die" *Ten for Wednesday Night* (1961), 24-41.

"The Summer My Grandmother Was Supposed to Die" *Modern Canadian Stories* (1966), 287-301.

"The Summer My Grandmother Was Supposed to Die" *Street* (1969), 33-46.

"The Summer My Grandmother Was Supposed to Die" *Literature in Canada* (1978), 487-99.

"The Summer My Grandmother Was Supposed to Die" *Anthology of Canadian Literature in English 2* (1983), 327-36.

"This Year at the Arabian Nights Hotel" *CBC "Anthology"* 17 Oct 1967.

"This Year at the Arabian Nights Hotel" *Tam R* No. 47 (Spr 1968), 9-18.

"This Year at the Arabian Nights Hotel" *Canadian Short Stories 2* (1968), 183-98.

"This Year at the Arabian Nights Hotel" *Liberté* 11 (mars-avril 1969), 163-79 [As "Cette année, à l'hôtel des mille et une nuits"; trans. Pierre Villon].

"This Year at the Arabian Nights Hotel" *Contemporary Voices* (1972), 143-51.

[Title unknown] *CBC "Anthology"* 15 June 1955.

"You Wouldn't Talk Like That If You Were Dead" *Mont* 32 (Dec 1958), 49-50, 52-3, 55-7.

Richman, Sharon Lea†

"The Gayo and the Leeofite Tree" *Alphabet* No. 3 (Dec 1961), 9-14.

"Saboo" *March* 2 (1963), 11-4.

Richmond, Jack‡

"Vacuum" *Generation* Mar 1964, 17-20.

Riddell, Bill‡

"Here We Go Round the Prickly Pear" *Acta Vic* 80:4 (Mar 1956), 16.

Riddell, John (1942-)

CRISS-CROSS Toronto: Coach House Press, 1977.

"The Block" *Criss-Cross* (1977), [10 pp].

"The Bottle" *Des* No. 10 (Win 1974), 52-5.

"The Bottle" *Criss-Cross* (1977), [6 pp].

"A Gift" *Criss-Cross* (1977), [5 pp].

"letterset" *Criss-Cross* (1977), [7 pp].

"Nightmare Hotel" *Des* No. 15 (Fall 1976), 20-31.

"The Novel" *Criss-Cross* (1977), [9 pp].

"October Leaves" *Folio* 19:2 (Spr 1967), 15-8.

"Process '76" *Criss-Cross* (1977), [12 pp].

"The Ramp" *Criss-Cross* (1977), [38 pp] [Novella?].

"Real Estate" *Des* No. 13 (Win 1975), 65-9.

"The Smugglers" *81: Best Canadian Stories* 111-27.

"The Speaker" *Des* 11:1/2 Nos. 27/28 (1980), 132-4.

Riddington, Bruce‡

"Evellyn" *Prism* (Mont) No. 5 (Spr 1962), 65-71.

"Lutist" *Prism* (Mont) No. 6 (Mar 1963), 25-31.

Rifka, Ruth
"Gauze" *Room* 2:2/3 (1976), 45-50 [Excerpt?].
"Maureen O'Hara with Pimples" *Br Out* 4:1 (Mar-Apr 1977), 21-2.
"Prologues to the Monkey Kid" *Contact* 3:4 (Win 1974), 54-5.
"Stewed Chicken Night" *Fid* No. 113 (Spr 1977), 16-22.

Rigby, Carle A.
"As You Would Have Them Do unto You" *Bluenose* 4:6 (June-July 1980), 11 [Also entitled "Retribution"].
"Marked by Fire" *Bluenose* 4:4 (Feb 1980), 12.
"Retribution" *Bluenose* 4:2 (Oct 1979), 31 [Also entitled "As You Would Have Them Do unto You"].
"Victoria Day" *Bluenose* 4:5 (Apr-May 1980), 8-9 [Non-fiction?].
"The Whip Smuggler" *Bluenose* 4:3 (Dec 1979), 15 [Non-fiction?].

Rigelhof, T.F. (1944-)
"At Hunter River" *Des* 13:3 No. 37 (1982), 64-75.
"A Few in the Hill" *Waves* 11:2/3 (Win 1983), 15-20.
"Great Escapes" *Des* 12:4/13:1/2 Nos. 34/35/36 (1981-82), 203-7.
"In the Gatineaus" *Compass* No. 9 (Spr 1980), 49-74.
"Master Bo-Lu at Rest" *JCF* No. 30 (1980), 45-64.
"Out of the Woods" *Compass* No. 7 (Aut 1979), 59-68.
"Retirements" *Mont R* No. 3 (Spr-Sum 1980), 39-42.

Rigutto, William‡
"Joe" *Flow* Win [1975?], [2 pp].

Riis, Sharon (1947-)
"Drinking Bitter" CBC "*Alberta Anthology*" 22 Nov 1980.
"Drinking Bitter" *Camrose R* No. 1 [1981], 31-3.
"Fear of Miracles" *NeWest R* 4 (June 1979), 8-9.
"Something I Do" *Per* No. 6 (Fall 1979), 5-10.

Rikely, Dan†
"The Captain's Son" *Origins* 9:4 (Dec 1979), 36-41.
"Fulton House" *CA & B* 57:1 (Fall 1981), 26-8.
"Harry" *Origins* 11:2 (June 1981), 53-6.
"Leece-oh" *Mam* 4:1 [1980], [6 pp].

Rikki [Erica Ducornet] (1943-)
THE BUTCHER'S TALES Toronto: Aya Press, 1980.
"Abracadabra" *CFM* Nos. 30/31 (1979), 152-4.
"Abracadabra" *Contemporary Surrealist Prose* (1979), 69-73.
"Abracadabra" *Butcher's Tales* (1980), 73-5.
"Aunt Rose and Uncle Freidle" *CFM* No. 6 (Spr 1972), 76-7.
"Aunt Rose and Uncle Freidle" *Butcher's Tales* (1980), 67-8.
"La Chincha (The Bed Bug)" *Butcher's Tales* (1980), 50-1.
"Clean" *CFM* No. 9 (Win 1973), 56-7.
"Clean" *Butcher's Tales* (1980), 77.
"Cream. Or: The Holy Trinity in the Kingdom of Heaven" *Butcher's Tales* (1980), 26-7.
"Desire" *Butcher's Tales* (1980), 37-8.

"The Double" *Butcher's Tales* (1980), 23.
"Electric Rose" *Butcher's Tales* (1980), 33.
"The Exorcist" *Butcher's Tales* (1980), 11-3.
"F*A*I*R*Y F*I*N*G*E*R" Butcher's Tales (1980), 47.
"The Folding Bed" *CFM* No. 16 (Win 1975), 89-90.
"The Folding Bed" *Butcher's Tales* (1980), 28-9.
"Foxes" *Butcher's Tales* (1980), 96-9.
"Friendship" *CFM* No. 6 (Spr 1972), 77-9.
"Fyodor's Bears" *CFM* Nos. 30/31 (1979), 151-2.
"Fyodor's Bears" *Butcher's Tales* (1980), 24-5.
"The Genius" *CFM* No. 13 (Spr 1974), 35-8.
"The Genius" *Contemporary Surrealist Prose* (1979), 78-83.
"The Genius" *Butcher's Tales* (1980), 89-92.
"Grace" *Butcher's Tales* (1980), 39-40.
"Harriet" *Butcher's Tales* (1980), 52-3.
"Hofritz" *Butcher's Tales* (1980), 14-5.
"I Will Never Forget You Ernie Frigmaster" *Butcher's Tales* (1980), 41-2.
"The Jade Planet" *Butcher's Tales* (1980), 93-5.
"Jungle" *CFM* No. 16 (Win 1975), 90-1.
"Jungle" *Butcher's Tales* (1980), 49.
"Luggage" *Grain* 2:2 [1974], 18-20.
"Luggage" *Butcher's Tales* (1980), 30-2.
"Lunch" *CFM* No. 9 (Win 1973), 57-8.
"Missy" *Iowa R* 10:4 (Fall 1979), 55-9.
"Missy" *Butcher's Tales* (1980), 85-8.
"The Monkey Lover" *Butcher's Tales* (1980), 64-6.
"Natural History" *TriQuarterly* 35:1 (Win 1976), 107-8.
"The Nipple" *Butcher's Tales* (1980), 54-7.
"Parasites (The Grocer's Wife)" *Contemporary Surrealist Prose* (1979), 66-8.
"Parasites (The Grocer's Wife)" *Butcher's Tales* (1980), 79-80.
"Pearl" *Grain* 4:3 [1976], 27-9.
"Pearl" *Contemporary Surrealist Prose* (1979), 84-8.
"Pearl" *Butcher's Tales* (1980), 61-3.
"Perfect" *Illusion One* (1983), 111-8.
"The Radiant Twinnie" *Butcher's Tales* (1980), 81-3.
"Sleep" *Grain* 4:2 [1976], 63-5.
"Sleep" *Mundus Artium* 9:1 (1976), 110-2.
"Sleep" *Butcher's Tales* (1980), 16-8.
"Spanish Oranges" *CFM* No. 20 (Win 1976), 4-6.
"Spanish Oranges" *Butcher's Tales* (1980), 19-21.
"Spanish Oranges" *Magic Realism* (1980), 101-3.
"Surfaces or Remembering" *Butcher's Tales* (1980), 58-9.
"Voyage to Ultima Azul" *Contemporary Surrealist Prose* (1979), 74-7.
"Voyage to Ultima Azul Chapter 79" *Butcher's Tales* (1980), 43-5.

Riley, Wilma L.†

"Fowl Supper" *Smoke Signals* 3 (1978) [Based on *SWG* survey response].
"Molly's New Hat" *jcf* No. 21 (1977-78), 53-60.
"Pies" *Sundogs* (1980), 100-9.
"Pies" *100% Cracked Wheat* (1983), 200-14.

Rilsky, Nika‡

"No Room" *Halcyon* 11 (Win 1965-66), 16-8.

Riman, Arthur†

"Shirley's Workaday Witness" *War Cry* 10 June 1961, 14.

Ringland, Mary†

"Angel in a Red Dress" *Onward* 31 Dec 1961, 6-7, 10-1.

"Flight at Freeze-Up" *Onward* 6 May 1962, 3-4.

"Flight at Freeze-Up" *Onward* 22 Aug 1965, 3-4.

"Friend of the Family" *Onward* 1 Sept 1963, 4-7 [Non-fiction?].

"The Nightengale Touch" *Onward* 22 Oct 1961, 4-5.

"The Stranger" *Onward* 23 Dec 1962, 12-3.

Ringland, Ruth R.†

"Old Jim Spenders" *Whetstone* Spr 1973, 48-51.

Ringwood, Gwen Pharis (1910-)

"Home Base" *FH* 27 Sept 1962, 62-3.

"The Last Fifteen Minutes" *Stories with John Drainie* (1963), 36-41.

"The Little Ghost" *Canadian Short Stories* (1952), 68-75.

"The Little Ghost" *Cavalcade of the North* (1958), 579-83.

"Little Joe and the Mounties" *FH* 14 Apr 1966, 78-9.

"Some People's Grandfathers Give them Cigarettes to Smoke" *FH* 31 Jan 1963, 44, 46.

"Some People's Grandfathers Give Them Cigarettes to Smoke" *Stories from Across Canada* (1966), 9-14.

"Some People's Grandfathers Give Them Cigarettes to Smoke" *Inquiry into Literature* 2 (1980), 118-23.

Riordan, Michael†

"Ali" *CBC "Anthology"* 10 Jan 1976.

"Blessed Are the Deviates: A Post-Therapy Check-Up on My Ex-Psychiatrist" *Body Politic* No. 21 (Dec 1975), 10-1 ["Sequel" to "Capital Punishment: Notes of a Willing Victim" (editorial note)].

"Capital Punishment: Notes of a Willing Victim" *Body Politic* No. 17 (Jan-Feb 1975), 14-21.

"The Lioness" *CBC "Anthology"* 6 Dec 1976.

"Romance" *Body Politic* No. 33 (May 1977), 19-21.

Ripley, Beth†

"The Moose Calf" *Treeline* 2 (1983), 41-3.

Ripley, John†

"On Honey Dew Hath Fed" *Intervales* [No. 1] (1959), 5-7.

Ripley, Richard‡

"One Day in March" *Folio* 19:1 (Fall 1966), 13-20.

Riskin, Mary W. (1950?-)
"The Gift of Maggie" CBC "*Alberta Anthology*" 6 Sept 1980.
"Last Respects" *Grain* 9:1 (Feb 1981), 53-7.
"The Perfect Parent" *Chat* 55 (Aug 1982), 51, 88, 90-1.

Ristich, David‡
"The Oracle" *Ganglia* No. 3 (1966), [3 pp].
"The Story of Jimmy Wracker" *Iron* No. 1 [Nov 1966], [3 pp].

Ritchie, Ian†
"Cornfield with Crows" *Des* 10:3/4 Nos. 25/26 (1979), 118-23.
"The Flood" *Waves* 8:1 (Fall 1979), 14-7.
"Rooftop and Below" *Waves* 10:3 (Win 1982), 24-30.

Ritchie, Rod‡
"Requiem for a Heavyweight" *Varsity* Fri, 18 Nov 1966, Review 7.

Ritter, Erika (1948-)
"Catcher in the Wry" *TL* Sept 1982, 58, 77-9, 81.
"A Quiet Little Dinner" *Fid* No. 111 (Fall 1976), 48-6.
"Secret Places" *Fid* No. 116 (Win 1978), 99-110.
"Summer Soldiers" *SN* 96 (June 1981), 62-8.
"Too Long at the Fair" *Chat* 49 (June 1976), 42, 56, 58, 60, 62, 64, 66.
"What Are Neighbours For?" *CFM* No. 16 (Win 1975), 57-83.
"What Are Neighbours For?" *Magic Realism* (1980), 173-200.
"You're a Taker" *SN* 94 (Dec 1979), 42-3, 45-9.

Ritter, Judy
"The Effects of Drought" *Makara* 3:3 (Fall 1978), 15-7 [Non-fiction?].
"Interstice" *Br Out* 2:4 (July-Aug 1975), 28, 43.

Ritts, Mort‡
"An Afternoon at the Zoo" *Acta Vic* 93:2 (Dec 1968), 3-5.
"Marcel" *Acta Vic* 92:4 (Apr 1968), 10-2.

Rivard, Ken‡
"Arnold's Secrets" *Alive* No. 42 [1975], 39.
"For a Few Beers" *Alive* No. 44 [n.d.], 19.

Rivers, J. Scott‡
"Jack and 'Whiskey Jack' " *Forge* 1951, 29-32.

Rivest, Phil‡
"Adrift" *Generation* Win 1967, 4-5.

Robb, Frank‡
"Double Role" *Legion* 30 (Jan 1956), 28-9.

Roberts, Dorothy (1906-)
"Corinna" *CF* 35 (May 1955), 32-5.
"Hunger" *NR* 4:4 (Apr-May 1951), 21-4.
"Hunger" *CBS* [i.e. CBC?] [date unknown] [Based on survey response].
"The Menace of Mr. Samson" *Chat* 27 (May 1954), 16, 86-9, 92.

"Mostly Sunny Today" *CF* 36 (July 1956), 82-3.
"A Patriotic Ballad" *NR* 5:5 (June-July 1952), 8-11.
"The Two Bedrooms" *Fid* No. 47 (Win 1961), 30-3.
"The Wanted" *NR* 6:2 (June-July 1953), 10-4.

Roberts, E.A.K.‡
[Untitled] *Makar* No. 3 (June 1968), 16-24.

Roberts, Joy‡
"Nameless Age" *Edmonton Journal* Thu, 16 Jan 1964, 4.

Roberts, Kevin (1940-)
FLASH HARRY & THE DAUGHTERS OF DIVINE LIGHT AND OTHER
STORIES Madeira Park, B.C.: Harbour, 1982.
TREE Madeira Park, B.C.: Harbour, 1980 [Based on CBIP].
"A Band Aid Kite" *Flash Harry* (1982), 56-60.
"Camping Trip" *Flash Harry* (1982), 15-24.
"Dance" *Fid* No. 124 (Win 1980), 12-4.
"Dance" *Flash Harry* (1982), 33-6.
"Dispensation" *Flash Harry* (1982), 71-84.
"Flash Harry & the Daughters of Divine Light" *Des* 11:3 No. 29 (1980), 95-100.
"Flash Harry & the Daughters of Divine Light" *Flash Harry* (1982), 8-14.
"Flight" *Sound/Vision* (radio, Aust) Mar 1983 [Based on survey response].
"The Merry Maid & Miss Chance" *Des* 11:1/2 Nos. 27/28 (1980), 212-8.
"The Merry Maid & Miss Chance" *Flash Harry* (1982), 1-7.
"A Nice Cold Beer" *Flash Harry* (1982), 39-48.
"No One Is Bigger" *Flash Harry* (1982), 49-55.
"The Pure Wound" *Des* 14:2 No. 40 (Spr 1983), 117-21 [Listed as "Prose"].
"Ride" *Flash Harry* (1982), 25-32.
"Royal Visit" *Flash Harry* (1982), 85-94.
"Royal Visit" *Radio SUV* (Aust) 10 Mar 1983 [Based on survey response].
"Salmon Run" *event* 2:1 [1972], 43-5.
"Taxi" *Matrix* No. 11 (Sum 1980), 80-3.
"Taxi" *Flash Harry* (1982), 61-6.
"Tree" *event* 6:2 [1977], 5-8.
"Tree" *Flash Harry* (1982), 67-70.
"Tree" *Rainshadow* (1982), 105-8.
"Walk" *Flash Harry* (1982), 37-8.
"Walk" *Moose R* No. 6 (1982), 46-7.

Roberts, Nancy†
"Visiting Miss M." *Antig R* No. 52 (Win 1983), 93-9.

Roberts, Terence†
"Image 1" *Imp* 2:1 (Aut 1972), 38-40.
"Image 2" *Imp* 2:1 (Aut 1972), 41-3.

Roberts, Theodore Goodridge (1877-1953)
"Kelpie Rapids" *FH* 6 July 1950, 20-1, 27, 42.
"Stranger on Pistol Creek" *NHM* 51 (Dec 1950), 37, 115-26.

Roberts, Tom
"All But My Ninth Birthday" *Per* No. 4 (Fall 1978), 19-22.
"Beached" *BC Monthly* 3:9 (June 1978), 36-7.
"An Intimate Letter" *Nw J* No. 24 (1981), 70-3.

Robertson, Brian‡
"From the Notebooks/Journals of Dwight Ripley" *Alpha* 4:1 (Fall 1979), 9.

Robertson, Don†
"One Sixty-Six Dash Two" *CSSM* 3:2 (Spr 1977), 11-4, 16-7.

Robertson, E.†
"In the Country" *Antig R* No. 33 (Spr 1978), 11-24.

Robertson, Ellison†
"The Clients" *Chezzetcook* (1977), 90-6.

Robertson, G. Ross‡
"The Year the Meadowlark Health Club Won the City Handball Championship" *CBC "Anthology"* 14 Dec 1974.

Robertson, Marjorie†
"The Predators" *Room* 1:3 (Fall 1975), 20-32.

Robertson, Strowan
"The Days of 1963, '64, '65 ... " *JCF* No. 30 (1980), 7-36.
"Gods Must Yield" *New Yorker* 50 (25 Mar 1974), 34-9.
"Her Highness" *Mal R* No. 51 (July 1979), 123-32.
"Vida" *Mal R* No. 20 (Oct 1971), 48-56.

Robin, Donald M.†
"Retirement" *CSSM* 3:1 (Win 1977), 31-3, 35, 72-4.

Robin, Max‡
"Don't Scratch Even If It Itches – Don't Cry Even If It Hurts" *Can J Chron R* Oct 1970, 93-6.

Robinson, Brad
"Let Sleeping Dogs Lie: A Barney Messerschmidt Mystery by Dachshund Hamster" *BC Monthly* 4:3 (Dec 1978), [21 pp] [Parody].
"Sospiri" *View from the Silver Bridge* 3:1 (Aug 1975), 22-9.

Robinson, C.R.
"Off the Prairie" *Winnipeg Stories* (1974), 170-84.

Robinson, Gail
"Emma" *Des* 11:3 No. 29 (1980), 101-12.
"Emma" *Grain* 8:2 [1980], 60-2.

Robinson, Gillian†
"Uncle / Heber" *Fireweed* No. 12 (1981), 60-1.

Robinson, Joan‡
"The Date" *UC Observer* 14 (1 Oct 1952), 19.
"House Proud" *UC Observer* 14 (1 Jan 1953), 15.

Robinson, Peter‡
"Why We Killed Mackee" *Spear* Mar 1973, 13-5, 17, 34-5.

Robinson, Rudy O.†
"A Free Country" *Prism* 1:4 (Sum 1960), 7-21.

Robinson, Spider (1948-)
ANTIMONY New York: Dell, 1980.
CALLAHAN'S CROSSTIME SALOON New York: Ace, 1977.
TIME TRAVELLERS STRICTLY CASH New York: Ace, 1981.
"Apogee" *Borealis* 1:1 (Sum 1978), 8-9.
"Apogee" *Antinomy* (1980), 232-5.
"The Centipede's Dilemma" *Callahan's Crosstime Saloon* (1977), 47-52.
"Chronic Offender" *Twilight Zone* 1:2 (May 1981), 36-45.
"Common Sense" *Pot Port* 1 (1979-80), 45-6.
"Dog Day Evening" *Time Travelers Strictly Cash* (1977), 57-69.
"Dog Day Evening" *Analog* 97 (Oct 1977), 137-46.
"Fivesight" *Omni* 1 (July 1979), 50-3, 108-10, 112.
"Fivesight" *Time Travelers Strictly Cash* (1981), 6-25.
"God Is an Iron" *Omni* 1 (May 1979), 66-8, 107-12.
"God Is an Iron" *Time Travelers Strictly Cash* (1981), 72-92.
"The Guy with the Eyes" *Analog* 90 (Feb 1973), 67-79.
"The Guy with the Eyes" *Callahan's Crosstime Saloon* (1977), 1-16.
"Half an Oaf" *Analog Annual* (1976), 195[+?] [Based on science fiction indexes].
"Half an Oaf" *Antinomy* (1980), 51-78.
"High Fidelity" *Oui* (U.S.) Apr 1983 [Based on science fiction indexes].
"Involuntary Man's Laughter" *Analog* 103 (Dec 1983), 83-94.
"It's a Sunny Day" *Galaxy* 37 (Jan 1976), 61-72.
"It's a Sunny Day" *Axiom* 3:6 (Nov-Dec 1977), 42-5, 49-51, 57-8.
"It's a Sunny Day" *Visions from the Edge* (1981), 193-202.
"Just Dessert" *Callahan's Crosstime Saloon* (1977), 102-7.
"Local Champ" *Time Travelers Strictly Cash* (1981), 146-51.
"The Magnificent Conspiracy" *Chrysalis* 1 [Based on *Antimony*].
"The Magnificent Conspiracy" *Antinomy* (1980), 280-307.
"Melancholy Elephants" *Analog* 102 (June 1982), 133-44.
"Mirror/rorriM, Off the Wall" *Analog* 98 (Nov 1977), 129-42, 144-6.
"Mirror/rorriM, Off the Wall" *Time Travelers Strictly Cash* (1981), 161-82.
"No Renewal" *Galaxy* 38 (Mar 1977), 151-5.
"No Renewal" *Other Canadas* (1979), 220-4.
"No Renewal" *Antinomy* (1980), 240-5.
"No Renewal" *In Your Own Words* (1982), 163-8.
"Not Fade Away" *Isaac Asimov's Science Fiction Mag* 6 (Aug 1982), 41-8.
"Overdose" *Galaxy* 36 (Sept 1975), 140-8.
"Overdose" *Best from Galaxy* 4 (1976), 124-36.
"Overdose" *Antinomy* (1980), 251-61.
"Pyotr's Story" *Analog* 101 (12 Oct 1981), 66-92.
"Satan's Children" *New Voices* 2 (1979), 231-80.

"Satan's Children" *Antinomy* (1980), 188-228.
"Serpents' Teeth" *Time Travelers Strictly Cash* (1981), 184-97.
"Serpents' Teeth" *Omni* 3 (Mar 1981), 66-70, 112.
"Soul Search" *Omni* 2 (Dec 1979), 67-70, 72, 136.
"Soul Search" *Time Travelers Strictly Cash* (1981), 27-39.
"Tin Ear" *Cosmos* 1:2 (July 1977), 23-7.
"Tin Ear" *Antinomy* (1980), 268-76.
"Too Soon We Grow Old" *Analog Yearbook* (1978), 66[+?] [Based on science fiction indexes].
"Too Soon We Grow Old" *Antinomy* (1980), 81-97.
"Two Heads Are Better Than One" *Analog* 95 (May 1975), 151-68.
"Two Heads Are Better Than One" *Callahan's Crosstime Saloon* (1977), 53-76.
"A Voice Is Heard in Ramah ... " *Analog* 95 (Nov 1975), 153-68.
"A Voice Is Heard in Ramah ... " *Callahan's Crosstime Saloon* (1977), 107-28.
"The Wonderful Conspiracy" *Callahan's Crosstime Saloon* (1977), 162-70.

Robison, Ruth†
"Quoth the Raven" *Kitimat Voices 1967* 141-4.

Robison, Wendy‡
"A Vision of Godliness" *Repos* No. 11 (Sum 1974), [8 pp].

Robson, Merrilee (1954?-)†
"Bull and Tulip" *Flare* 2 (Nov 1980), 111-2, 130, 132.
"Grace in the Bar" *Waves* 8:2 (Win 1980), 7-11.

Robson, Nora‡
"Searching for the Blue Heron" *CA & B* 58:1 (Fall 1982), 13-5.

Rockman, Arnold‡
"Each Man Is an Island" *Undergrad* Spr 1956, 28-34.

Rockwell, Vance‡
"Spring Song" *AA* 65 (May 1975), 44-6.

Roddan, Samuel
"The Bell-Ringers" *British Columbia* (1961), 546-55.
"The Blue Heron" *Rapport* Dec 1969, 9-11.
"Call of the Sea" CBC *"Anthology"* 13 Nov 1956.
"The Last Lesson" *Skylark* 1:2 [date unknown], 44 [Based on index].
"My Cup Runneth Over" *Rapport* Jan 1971, 12-4.
"A Sunday Picnic" *CF* 34 (Sept 1954), 131, 133.
"A Sunday Picnic" CBC *"Anthology"* 30 Nov 1954.
"The Way It Was in the Summer of '31" CBC *"Anthology"* 25 Aug 1973.
"The Wonderful Dreams of My Saintly Father" *Rapport* Nov 1968, 14-6.

Roddy, William‡
"At the Cottage" *Kaleidoscope* 1963, 19.
"Up Ahead" *Kaleidoscope* Apr 1961, 18-21.

Rodger, Oxford‡
"Third Grade Smart" *Prism* (Mont) Fall 1965, 21-2.

Rodgers, Bob‡
"About a Small Town and a Girl" *Creative Campus* 1957, 8-13.

Rodgers, Gordon (1952-)
"The Gold Dust Dancing Through the Flame" *Twelve Newfoundland Short Stories* (1982), 71-8.
"I Think They Were Laughing at Me" *TickleAce* No. 3 (Sum 1978), 4-5.

Rodgers, Joan
"The Fisherman" *Quarry* 24:2 (Spr 1975), 21-4.

Rodman, Hyman‡
"King of Spades" CBC "*Anthology*" 5 Mar 1957.
"The Time Is Green" *Forge* 1952, 47-51.

Rodriguez, Juan†
"Through No Other Door" *Pop See Cul* No. 8 (Sum 1968), 21-2.

Roedde, W.A.†
"Two Gals and a Guy" *Cataraqui R* 1:2 (Sum 1951), 35-8.

Rofihe, Rick (1950-)
"Mellie's Poem" *Voices Down East* [1973], 29.

Rogal, Stan
"Nailing Down Pornography" *WCR* 10:2 (Oct 1975), 25.
"The Prisoner's Dilemma" *Interior Voice* No. 2 (June-July/Spr-Sum 1982), 25-9.
"The Retreat" *Nimbus* 2:3/4 (Sum-Fall 1981), 15-8.

Roger, Robin‡
"The Plague" *UCR* Spr 1975, 33-6.

Rogers, Allan‡
"Magette" *TUR* 64:1 (Nov 1951), 33-7.

Rogers, Ann‡
"A Story" *Stump* Spr 1983, 43-5.

Rogers, Beth†
"Snowmoon" *Makara* 1:1 (Dec 1975), 40-5.

Rogers, Jeanne†
"The Last Summer" *Nfld Q* 70:2 (Nov 1973), 33-5.

Rogers, Linda‡
"Sunday" *Stump* Spr 1982, 1-4.

Roitner, Joseph
"Was Life Supposed to Be That Way" *Wee Giant* 2:2 (Win 1978-79), 31-5.

Rolheiser, Kenneth†
"No Broken Stones" *Our Family* 24 (Nov 1972), 20-1.

Rolheiser, Ronald†

"Flowers in His Eyes" *Our Family* 28 (May 1976), 24-6.
"Youthful Friendship" *Our Family* 24 (May 1972), 26-8.

Rollins, D.S.‡

"The Same Old Bridge" *Prism* (Mont) No. 8 (1965), 28-9.

Rombosis, T.H. – *See* Corbett, Edward Annand.

Romuld, Conrad†

"Me and Charlie and the Concentrated Ground" *Skylark* 3:3 [date unknown], 65 [Based on index].
"Me and Charlie and the Concentrated Ground" *Was R* 1:2 (1966), 16-25.

Ronald, George‡

"Battle of the Atlantic" *AA* 60 (June 1970), 73.

Rooke, Constance (1942-)

"Edvard and Katrina" *Southern R* 16 (1980), 675-93.
"Gatsby's Smile" *Antig R* No. 27 (Aut 1976), 11-6.
"Glenda Working" *Des* 13:4 No. 38 (Fall 1982), 42-6.
"Home Movies" *Quarry* 31:1 (Win 1982), 4-9.
"Mama Goose" *Grain* 4:3 [1976], 10-3.
"Sea Gifts" *Room* 1:4 (Win 1976), 68-7.
"The Sheffield Candlesticks" *Quarry* 28:2 (Spr 1979), 14-22.
"Snapshot" *Was R* 11:1 (Spr 1976), 47-8.

Rooke, Leon (1934-)

THE BIRTH CONTROL KING OF UPPER VOLTA Toronto: ECW Press, 1982.
THE BROAD BACK OF THE ANGEL New York: Fiction Collective, 1977.
CRY EVIL Ottawa: Oberon Press, 1980.
DEATH SUITE Toronto: ECW Press, 1981.
LAST ONE HOME SLEEPS IN THE YELLOW BED Baton Rouge: Louisiana State Univ. Press, 1968.
THE LOVE PARLOUR Ed. John Metcalf. Ottawa: Oberon Press, 1977.
VAULT: A STORY IN THREE PARTS Northwood Narrows, NH: Lillabulero, 1973 [Based on Struthers].
"Addressing the Assassins" *Prism* 18:2 (Win 1979-80), 22-5.
"Adolpho's Disappeared and We Haven't a Clue Where to Find Him" *Mal R* No. 50 (Apr 1979), 193-213.
"Adolpho's Disappeared and We Haven't a Clue Where to Find Him" *Cry Evil* (1980), 132-57.
"Agnes and the Cobwebs" *True North/Down Under* No. 1 (1983), 17-25.
"The Alamo Plaza" *Red Clay Reader* [1] (1964), 15-22 [Based on Struthers].
"The Alamo Plaza" *Last One Home* (1968), 36-56.
"Ancistrodon Priscivorus: Albion Gunther Jones and the Water Viper/Number Five in a Series of River Stories" *Carolina Q* 21:2 (Spr 1969), 4-16. [Based on Struthers].
"The Beggar in the Bulrush" *Reflections* (U.S.) 2:1 (Fall 1962), 40-56 [Based on Struthers].
"Beloved in the Bath, This Is My Beloved" *New Q* 3:3 (Fall 1983), 43-7.
"Biographical Notes" *CFM* Nos. 30/31 (1979), 53-75.

"Biographical Notes" *Cry Evil* (1980), 97-131.

"The Birth Control King of Upper Volta" *Birth Control King* (1982), 7-38.

"The Birth Control King of Upper Volta" *Antaeus* Nos. 49/50 (Spr-Sum 1983), 226-45.

"Break and Enter" *Vault* (1973), 25-37 [Based on Struthers].

"The Broad Back of the Angel" *Broad Back of the Angel* (1977), 184-201.

"The Broad Back of the Angel" *Statements* 2 (1977), 182-94.

"Building a Fire Under Peterson" *Antig R* No. 38 (Sum 1979), 21-6.

"Call Me Belladonna" *Love Parlour* (1977), 65-80 [Also entitled "The Love Parlor" and "Dangerous Women"].

"The Cat Killer" *Antioch R* 41 (1983), 421-9.

"A Christmas Fable" *The Tomahawk* 25 Dec 1958, 6-7 [Based on Struthers].

"Civilities" *Ion* No. 1 (Spr 1979), 10-6.

"Conjugal Precepts" *event* 3:2 [1973?], 61-72.

"The Continuing Adventures and Life Trials of Aunt Hattie" *North Carolina Anvil* 15 Apr 1967, 7-8 [Based on Struthers].

"Conversations with Ruth" *Was R* 10:1 (Spr 1975), 60-6.

"Conversations with Ruth: The Farmer's Tale" *CF* 60 (Feb 1981), 20-1.

"Dangerous Women" *Broad Back of the Angel* (1977), 169-83 [Also entitled "Call Me Belladonna" and "From the Love Parlor"].

"The Day Begins" *The Young Writer at Chapel Hill* No. 3 (Apr 1964), 5-13 [Based on Struthers].

"The Deacon's Tale" *Cry Evil* (1980), 5-23 [Also entitled "Oral History: The Deacon's Tale"].

"Deer Trails in Tzityonyana" *CF* 60 (Sept 1980), 25-8.

"Dear Trails in Tzityonyana" *Death Suite* (1981), 99-111.

"Deer Trails in Tzityonyana" *West of Fiction* (1983), 292-302.

"Devious Strangers" *see* "Sixteen Year-Old- Susan March Confesses to the Innocent Murder of All the Devious Strangers Who Would Drage Her Down".

"Dinner with the Swardians" *CFM* No. 11 (Aut 1973), 19-32.

"Dinner with the Swardians" *Magic Realism* (1980), 111-24.

"The Doorstep Syndrome or Nineteen-Year-Old Susan March Confesses to the Wanton Humiliation and Willful Destruction of All Her Numerous Parents" *Dand* 8:2 (1981), 15-22.

"The End of the Revolution and Other Stories" *Crazy Horse* (U.S.) No. 19 (Fall 1979), 73-90 [Based on Struthers].

"The End of the Revolution and Other Stories" *Cry Evil* (1980), 47-70.

"Field Service Four Hundred Forty-Nine from the Five Hundred Field Songs of the Daughters of the Vieux Carré" *Lillabulero* 1:4 (Fall 1967), 15-29 [Based on Struthers].

"Field Service Four Hundred Forty-Nine from the Five Hundred Field Songs of the Daughters of the Vieux Carré" *Last One Home* (1968), 72-94.

"Fine Water for a Sloop" *Antig R* No. 17 (Spr 1974), 47-59.

"The First Day of the World" *Mal R* No. 31 (July 1974), 104-24.

"First Publication 'Lost' Kafka Manuscript" *North Carolina Anvil* 5 Oct 1968, 5 [Based on Struthers].

"Five Oral Reports on the Death of a Friend" *Quarry* 23:1 (Win 1974), 49-54.

"Flux" *event* 12:2 (1983), 31-4.

"Foot-in-Field Story" *Rubicon* No. 2 (Win 1983-84), 64-8.

"For Love of Eleanor" *Southern R* 10 (1974), 631-55.

"For Love of Eleanor" *Here and Now* (1977), 114-34.

"For Love of Eleanor" *Love Parlour* (1977), 99-126.

"For Love of Gómez" *Love Parlour* (1977), 127-57.

"For Love of Gómez" *Southern R* 15 (1977), 370-91.

"For Love of Madeline" *Southern R* 8 (1972), 919-34.

"For Love of Madeline" *Love Parlour* (1977), 81-98.

"Friendship and Libation" *Broad Back of the Angel* (1977), 74-85.

"Friendship and Property" *79: Best Canadian Stories* 95-121.

"Friendship and Property" *Cry Evil* (1980), 71-96.

"Friendship and Rejuvenation" *Broad Back of the Angel* (1977), 86-93.

"Friendship and Rejuvenation" *CFM* Nos. 24/25 (Spr-Sum 1977), 103-8.

"From the Love Parlor" *Antig R* No. 26 (Sum 1976), 55-70 [Also entitled "Dangerous Women" and "Call Me Belladonna"].

"Fromm Investigations" *Cry Evil* (1980), 24-46.

"Further Adventures of a Cross Country Man" *Carolina Q* 19:2 (Spr 1967), 105-14 [Based on Struthers].

"Gin and Tonic" *Birth Control King* (1982), 131-48.

"A Girl and a Dummy and the Dummy's Best Friend" *Antig R* No. 21 (Spr 1975), 11-23.

"The Girl Who Collected Husbands" *North Carolina R* Sum 1976, 34-56 [Based on Struthers].

"The Girl Who Made Time" *Grain* 1:2 (Dec 1973), 32-46.

"The Girl Who Made Time" *Best of Grain* (1980), 93-109.

"Going for Broke" *Scrivener* 4:1 (Win 1983), 24.

"Hanging Out with the Magi" *CFM* No. 38 (1981), 60-73.

"Hanging Out with the Magi" *Death Suite* (1981), 137-55.

"Hanging Out with the Magi" *Illusion One* (1983), 67-82.

"Harry the Tiger Enters His Fiftieth Year" *Fid* No. 96 (Win 1973), 49-65.

"Hat Pandowdy" *Birth Control King* (1982), 101-18.

"The Hatted Mannequins of 54th Street" *Carolina Q* 21:2 (Spr 1969), 65-82 [Based on Struthers].

"The History of England, Part Four" *CFM* No. 46 (1983), 30-42.

"Hitting the Charts" *CFM* No. 38 (1981), 5-12.

"Hitting the Charts" *Birth Control King* (1982), 119-30.

"How the Raiders Are Doing" *Antig R* No. 16 (Win 1974), 17-30.

"How the Woman's Generation Movement Freed Heleda Bang from Her Tortures and Brought Midnight Oil to the Old Folks on Oak Bay Avenue and a Raging Sunshine Oh Yes to My Heart" *Western Humanities R* 26 (1972), 127-38.

"Ibena" *Quarry* 30:2 (Spr 1981), 15-9.

"The Ice House Gang" *Carolina Q* 18:3 (Fall 1966), 5-9 [Based on Struthers].

"The Ice House Gang" *Last One Home* (1968), 3-9.

"If Lost Return to the Swiss Arms" *Carolina Q* 16:1 (Win 1963), 18-32 [Based on Struthers].

"If Lost Return to the Swiss Arms" *Prize Stories: O'Henry Awards* 1965 [Based on SSI].

"If Lost Return to the Swiss Arms" *Love Parlour* (1977), 5-23.

"If Lost Return to the Swiss Arms" *Stories Plus* (1979), 167-80.

"If You Love Me Meet Me There" *UWR* 9:2 (Spr 1974), 41-7.

"If You Love Me Meet Me There" *Love Parlour* (1977), 42-50.

"If You Went to the River Why Were You Not Baptized?" *Carolina Q* 15:3 (Sum

1963), 7-15 [Based on Struthers].

"In the Garden" *Antaeus* No. 48 (Win 1983), 124-38.

"Iron Woman" *Broad Back of the Angel* (1977), 144-68.

"Jettatura" *Ohio R* 17:1 (Fall 1975), 89-103 [Based on Struthers].

"Jones' End" *Reflections* (U.S.) 3:1 (Spr 1964), 10-20 [Based on Struthers].

"Kiss the Devil Goodbye" *Fid* No. 105 (Spr 1975), 88-104.

"Lady Godiva's Horse" *Prism* 18:2 (Win 1979-80), 7-21.

"Lady Godiva's Horse" *Death Suite* (1981), 73-92.

"Last One Home Sleeps in the Yellow Bed" *Last One Home* (1968), 57-71.

"Leave Running" *Epoch* 24 (1974), 82-93 [Based on Struthers].

"Leave Running" *Love Parlour* (1977), 24-41.

"Licking Up Honey" *Scrivener* 4:1 (Win 1983), 23.

"Load Every Rift with Ore" *Carolina Q* 20:2 (Fall 1968), 7-47 [Based on Struthers].

"Mama Tuddi Done Over" *Des* 10:3/4 Nos. 25/26 (1979), 7-40.

"Mama Tuddi Done Over" *Best American Short Stories* 1980 272-301.

"Mama Tuddi Done Over" *Death Suite* (1981), 9-42.

"Manifesto A" *CFM* No. 18 (Sum 1975), 93-100.

"Memoirs of a Cross-Country Man" *Prism* 11:1 (Spr 1972), 64-74.

"Memoirs of a Cross-Country Man" *Love Parlour* (1977), 51-64.

"Murder Mystery (Do Something)" *CFM* No. 38 (1981), 55-9.

"Murder Mystery (Do Something)" *Death Suite* (1981), 93-8.

"Murder Mystery (The Rocker Operation)" *Antig R* No. 37 (Spr 1979), 11-5.

"Murder Mystery (The Rocker Operation)" *Death Suite* (1981), 54-8.

"Murder Mystery (The Strip)" *Death Suite* (1981), 129-36.

"Narcissus Consulted" *Mal R* No. 61 (Feb 1982), 132-42.

"Never but Once the White Tadpole" *New Campus Writing* 3 (1959), 184-95 [Based on Struthers].

"A New Strike Out Record for Every Day" *Carolina Q* 15:3 (Sum 1963), 70-83 [Based on Struthers].

"A Nicer Story by the 'B' Road" *Birth Control King* (1982), 71-83.

"A Nicer Story by the 'B' Road" *Fid* No. 134 (Oct 1982), 41-8.

"No Whistle Slow" *Broad Back of the Angel* (1977), 24-41.

"Not Far from the Borders of the Indian Ocean" *Carolina Q* 15:2 (Spr 1963), 39-63 [Based on Struthers].

"Numbers One Through Thirty of One Thousand Notes While Passing Between the Silent Borders of Your Country and Mine" *CFM* No. 4 (Fall 1971), 6-23.

"The Olive Eaters" *Carolina Q* 16:2 (Spr 1964), 5-12 [Based on Struthers].

"Oral History: The Deacon's Tale" *Fid* No. 121 (Spr 1979), 27-39 [Also entitled "The Deacon's Tale"].

"The Pope's Emissary" *Scrivener* 4:1 (Win 1983), 24.

"The Problem Shop" *CFM* No. 38 (1981), 29-43.

"The Problem Shop" *Death Suite* (1981), 156-75.

"Quiet Enough My Life of Late" *Fid* No. 92 (Win 1972), 59-65.

"Return of the Magician (in Love)" *Des* 13:4 No. 38 (Fall 1982), 85-91.

"The Selling of Heaven: A Folktale" *Scratchgravel Hills* (U.S.) No. 3 (1980), 18-22 [Based on Struthers].

"Shoe Fly Pie" *Birth Control King* (1982), 93-9.

"A Short Story Celebrating the Day of Public School Integration, New Orleans, La.: or, A Song by Gov. Jimmy Davis, Entitled: 'You Are My Sunshine' " *North Carolina Anvil* 19 Sept 1969 [Based on Struthers].

"Sing Me No Love Songs, I'll Say You No Prayers" *Epoch* 15 (Win 1966), 111-31 [Based on Struthers].

"Sing Me No Love Songs, I'll Say You No Prayers" *Birth Control King* (1982), 39-70.

"Sing Me No Love Songs, I'll Say You No Prayers" *Rainshadow* (1982), 23-52.

"Sisyphus in Winter" *CFM* No. 38 (1981), 44-54.

"Sixteen-Year-Old Susan March Confesses to the Innocent Murder of All the Devious Strangers Who Would Drag Her Down" *Was R* 13:2 (Fall 1978), 57-65 [Also entitled "Devious Strangers"].

"Sixteen-Year-Old Susan March Confesses to the Innocent Murder of All the Devious Strangers Who Would Drag Her Down " *80: Best Canadian Stories* 149-61 [Also entitled "Devious Strangers"].

"Sixteen-Year-Old Susan March Confesses to the Innocent Murder of All the Devious Strangers Who Would Drag Her Down" *Death Suite* (1981), 59-72.

"Sixteen-Year-Old Susan March Confesses to the Innocent Murder of All the Devious Strangers Who Would Drag Her Down" *CBC [Van] "Hornby Collection"* 16 Jan 1982.

"Sixteen-Year-Old Susan March Confesses to the Innocent Murder of All the Devious Strangers Who Would Drag Her Down" *Canadian Short Fiction Anthology* 2 (1982), 58-65.

"Sixteen-Year-Old Susan March Confesses to the Innocent Murder of All the Devious Strangers Who Would Drag Her Down" *Anthology of Canadian Literature in English* 2 (1983), 355-63.

"Some People Will Tell You the Situation at Henny Penny Nursery Is Getting Intolerable" *Matrix* No. 17 (Fall 1983), 2-6.

"Stalled" *CBC [Van] "Hornby Collection"* 29 Dec 1979 [Listed as monologue].

"Stalled" *CBC "Anthology"* 11 Oct 1980.

"Standing in for Nita" *Fid* No. 126 (Sum 1980), 3-15.

"Standing in for Nita" *Death Suite* (1981), 112-28.

"The Strange Affair of Reno Brown and Mama Tuddi" *Epoch* 14 (Fall 1964), 3-20 [Based on Struthers].

"The Third Floor" *Was R* 8:2 (Fall 1973), 39-44.

"The Third Floor" *Broad Back of the Angel* (1977), 137-43.

"Those Days Around the Tree-Town Corner Now" *Carolina Q* 14:3 (Sum 1962), 45-50 [Based on Struthers].

"The Walrus Feeders" *Carolina Q* 14:3 (Sum 1962), 52-6 [Based on Struthers].

"When Swimmers on the Beach Have All Gone Home" *Louisiana R* 2:1 (Sept-Oct 1967), 19-25 [Based on Struthers].

"When Swimmers on the Beach Have All Gone Home" *Last One Home* (1968), 10-35.

"When Swimmers on the Beach Have All Gone Home" *Transitions 2* (1978), 101-20.

"Why a Judaeo-Christian Philosophy That Knows So Much About the Nature of God Knows So Little About the Nature of Jack B. Woodcraft, III" *Western Humanities R* 28 (1974), 149-64.

"Why Agnes Left" *event* 10:1 (1981), 5-10.

"Why Agnes Left" *Birth Control King* (1982), 85-91.
"Why I Am Here Where I Am Talking to You Like This" *Epoch* 21 (1972), 313-26 [Based on Struthers].
"Winter Has a Lovely Face but Isn't Summer Hell" *New England R* No. [1?] (Spr 1962), 10-3 [Same as below? Based on Struthers].
"Winter Is Lovely, Isn't Summer Hell" *CFM* No. 38 (1981), 13-20.
"Winter Is Lovely, Isn't Summer Hell" *Death Suite* (1981), 43-53.
"Wintering in Victoria" *CFM* No. 15 (Fall 1974), 66-78.
"Wintering in Victoria" *76: New Canadian Stories* 99-114.
"Wintering in Victoria" *Broad Back of the Angel* (1977), 9-23.
"The Woman from Columbia" *Carolina Q* 17:1 (Fall 1964), 43-8 [Based on Struthers].
"Working Blind" *Writ* No. 15 (1983), 52-60.

Rooke, Leon and Constance
"85 Reasons Why I'm in the Fix I'm In" *Des* 12:2/3 Nos. 32/33 (1981), 132-43.
"No Whistle Slow" *Southern R* 12 (1976), 482-95.

Rooke, Richard‡
"The Intolerable Statue" *Chiaroscuro* 8 (1964), 19-24.

Rooney, Frances‡
"Evening at Home" *Common Ground* (1980), 52-60.

Root, Thomas A.‡
"Essex North's First and Last Rock 'N' Roll Star" *Generation* Mar 1964, 38-40.

Roper, Florence‡
"The Little White Cloud" *Sand Patterns* No. 15 (Fall 1975), [3 pp].

Rorke, Michael J.‡
"Eulogy for Don" *Alive* 2:7 No. 17 (June 1971), 18-20.

Rose, Bob
"Hopkins" *BC Monthly* 3:3 (Dec 1976), [3 pp].
"Kirkwood, Missouri" *Iron II* No. 4 (Nov 1976), 38-43.
"Smart Pig" *NMFG* No. 5 (June 1976), [2 pp].

Rose, Ellen‡
"One Fish, Two Fish" *Stump* 1:2 (Fall 1977), 1-8.

Rose, Ian‡
"The Dream" *CBC [Van] "Hornby Collection"* 24 Nov 1979.

Rose, Mildred A.
"Down in the Valley" *Skylark* 5:2 (Win/Jan 1969), 36-45.
"In the Forests of the Night" *CSSM* 3:2 (Spr 1977), 25-8.
"Shattered Idol" *CSSM* 2:1 (Jan 1976), 22-5.
"With Love, Father" *CSSM* 3:1 (Win 1977), 17-20.

Roseborough, Ron‡
"Bandit" *Outlook* 1:3 (Jan 1976), 25-7.

Rosenberg, Elsa†

"Abraham Muscovitch's Michael" *SN* 81 (Mar 1966), 32-6.
"Journey Around My Skull" *Viewpoints* 5:4 (1970-71), 47-51.
"Merry Christmas, Mrs. Cohen" *Viewpoints* 3:4 (Fall 1968), 57-63.

Rosenberg, Flash†

"Encounter of an Emotional Kind" *Antig R* No. 50 (Sum 1982), 55-9.
"Inside Out" *Antig R* No. 45 (Spr 1981), 75-83.

Rosenblatt, Joe (1933-)

"The Egg Poems Were Conceived ... " *Towncrier* Sept-Oct 1971, 2-3, 8, 13-4.
"Mandrillo" *ballsout* 1:2 (Sum 1969), [6 pp].
"With Love, Father" *CSSM* 3:1 (Win 1977), 17-20.

Rosenfeld, Rita

"All Kinds of People" *Northwoods J* (U.S.) 8:3 (Fall 1979) [Based on survey response].
"The Bubbe; the Zayde" *JD* Rosh Hashanah 1976, 54-8.
"By the Eyes You Can Always Tell" *Was R* 12:2 (Fall 1977), 33-40.
"Chicken Peddlar" *JD* Rosh Hashanah 1976, 6-10.
"Chrysalid" *Des* 10:3/4 Nos. 25/26 (1979), 125-32.
"Forever Dreaming" *Mam* 1:3 [n.d.], [5 pp].
"Friends of a Friend" *Waves* 8:3 (Spr 1980), 4-7.
"Gone Home" *Mam* 4:4 (Win-Spr 1981), [8 pp].
"The Honolulu Sun" *Antig R* No. 29 (Spr 1977), 39-51.
"I'd Have Kicked Her Out" *Fid* No. 123 (Fall 1979), 17-25.
"The Innocence of Rasputin" *Samisdat* 19:1 (1979), 55-60.
"Insect Collecting" *Antig R* No. 38 (Sum 1979), 33-43.
"Leonara's Passion" *Origins* 10:2 (June 1980), 23-9.
"The Letter Writer" *JD* Hanukah 1975, 20-1, 24.
"Life's a Ball" *Mam* 2:2 [n.d.], [8 pp].
"Michael Rode His Dream Aboard" *Prism* 18:1 (Spr-Sum 1979), 97-106.
"Moving with the Times" *Antig R* No. 40 (Win 1980), 33-45.
"My Sister's Keeper" *Des* 9:1/2 Nos. 20/21 (1978), 101-10.
"Old Friends" *This* 14 (Mar-Apr 1980), 15-7.
"Relations" *Origins* 10:2 (June 1980), 17-22.
"The Stars at Night" *Origins* 9:4 (Dec 1979), 19-30.
"That Special Day" *Antig R* No. 44 (Win 1980), 47-57.
"To Pass Through Honey" *Waves* 6:1 (Aut 1977), 9-16.
"Transplants" *CJO* 19 (Mar 1981), 11-2.
"The Whistler" *JD* Hanukah 1975, 6-8.

Rosenman, John B.‡

"The Human Factor" *Art & Lit R* 1:1 (Fall 1972), 34-8.

Rosenthal, Peter (1941-)

"At the Symphony" *QQ* 88 (1981), 485-9.
"Compensation Neurosis" *Quarry* 29:1 (Win 1980), 43-8.

Roskies, Ruth†

"David in Gath" *Forge* Feb 1957, 49-51.
"Quebec on a Sunday" *Forge* Mar 1956, 20.

Rosqui, Carolyn†

"A Curiosity" *QQ* 80 (1973), 74-8.

"A Fresh Tale" *Quarry* 24:1 (Win 1975), 24-9.

Ross, Brian†

"Jinja" *Thursday's Voices* (1983), 23-31.

Ross, Edeet (1955-)†

"Man at the Window" *Saturday Night at the Forum* (1981), 56-65.

"Shortly After the Incident on the Haifa-Tel Aviv Road" *Matinees Daily* (1981), 66-9.

Ross, Gary (1949?-)

"Before the Fall" *TL* Aug 1979, 58, 74-9.

"Blueberries" *SN* 95 (Sept 1980), 44-9.

"The Camp Director's Wife" *Weekend* 28 (17 June 1978), 36-9.

"Off-Season" *SN* 91 (June 1976), 59-66.

"Open Heart" *Chat* 54 (Oct 1981), 77, 167-8, 170-2, 176, 178.

"Tuesday" *Quarry* 21:1 (Win 1972), 31-6.

Ross, J.D.‡

"Just Between Two Worlds" *Acta Vic* 78:2 (Dec 1953), 18-20.

Ross, James (1943-)

"A.E. Levine, Retired" *JD* Sum 1973, 26-9.

"Arny Was Always Talking, See" *CF* 50 (June 1970), 140-1.

"Clean" *Carleton Miscellany* 17:1 (Win 1977-78), 54-60.

"A House for Señora Lopez" *New Orleans R* 6 (1979), 114-9.

"Jack Ronald Told the Lord" *Fid* No. 115 (Fall 1977), 60-4.

"Jackson, Doing His Rounds" *Prism* 13:1 (Sum 1973), 130-6.

"Jerry" *CSSM* 1:3 (July 1975), 40-4.

"Main Mast" *Axiom* 2:1 (Aug-Sept 1975), 20-3, 33-4, 41.

"Mythical Beasts" *CFM* No. 26 (Aut 1977), 24-31.

"Mythical Beasts" *Illusion Two* (1983), 41-50.

"Phoenix, Phoenix, Light & Fire" *CFM* No. 11 (Aut 1973), 63-71.

"Phoenix, Phoenix, Light & Fire" *Magic Realism* (1980), 125-33.

"A Rage for Order" *Des* 10:1 Nos. 22/23 (1978-79), 145-54.

Ross, Julian†

"The Wave" *Waves* 9:2 (Win 1981), 16.

Ross, June Marie†

"The Legend of F/O Stokely (Rtd.)" *Aircraft* 20 (Feb 1958), 27-8.

Ross, Mary Lowrey

"Free Speech" *CHJ* Sept 1955, 26, 28, 31-2, 40-1.

Ross, Nick – *See* Rousanoff, Nicholas.

Ross, Sinclair (1908-)

THE LAMP AT NOON AND OTHER STORIES Toronto: McClelland & Stewart, 1968.

THE RACE AND OTHER STORIES Ed. Lorraine McMullen Ottawa: Univ of Ottawa Press, 1982.

"The Flowers That Killed Him" *JCF* 1:3 (Sum 1972), 5-10.

"The Flowers That Killed Him" *More Stories from Western Canada* (1980), 248-66.

"The Flowers That Killed Him" *Race* (1982), 119-34.

"Jug and Bottle" *QQ* 56 (1949-50), 500-21.

"Jug and Bottle" *Race* (1982), 69-85.

"The Outlaw" *QQ* 57 (1950), 198-210.

"The Outlaw" *Canadian Short Stories* (1952), 237-47.

"The Outlaw" *Lamp at Noon* (1968), 24-34.

"The Outlaw" *Canadian Stories of Action and Adventure* (1978), 2-13.

"The Outlaw" *Great Canadian Adventure Stories* (1979), 16-27.

"The Runaway" *QQ* 59 (1952), 323-42.

"The Runaway" *Lamp at Noon* (1968), 83-98.

"Saturday Night" *QQ* 58 (1951), 387-400.

"Saturday Night" *Race* (1982), 87-97.

"Spike" *CBC "Anthology"* 19 Dec 1967.

"Spike" *Liberté* 11 (mar-avr 1969), 181-97 [In French; trans. Pierre Villon].

"Spike" *Race* (1982), 99-110.

Ross, Stuart (1959-)

See also Ross, Stuart and Laba, Mark.

BAD GLAMOUR: STORIES & POEMS 1975-1980 Toronto: Proper Tales Press, 1980 [Based on CBIP].

WHEN ELECTRICAL SOCKETS WALKED LIKE MEN Toronto: Proper Tales Press, 1981.

"The Boy Who Smiled" *When Electrical Sockets Walked Like Men* (1981), [2 pp].

"Captain Earmuff and His Little Party" *When Electrical Sockets Walked Like Men* (1981), [2 pp].

"Champion Takes Inventory" *When Electrical Sockets Walked Like Men* (1981), [2 pp].

"The Flout What Kilt Foster" *Musicworks* 1:5 (Fall 1978), 7.

"In the Lobby of the Phaedra" *When Electrical Sockets Walked Like Men* (1981), [2 pp].

"The Murder" *OPT* 6:1 (Feb 1979), 8.

"The Music" *When Electrical Sockets Walked Like Men* (1981), [2 pp].

"The Music" *OPT* 7:6/7 (Jan-Feb 1981), 40.

" 'No, Jerry, Don't Do It' " *When Electrical Sockets Walked Like Men* (1981), [1 p].

"Revenge Sequence" *When Electrical Sockets Walked Like Men* (1981), [1 p].

"Revenge Sequence" *Images* 2:6 (Mar 1981), 11.

"Tigermen with Spears" *When Electrical Sockets Walked Like Men* (1981), [2 pp].

Ross, Stuart and Laba, Mark

See also Laba, Mark; Ross, Stuart.

"The Fall Guy" *OPT* 6:1 (Feb 1979), 9.

Ross, Veronica (1946-)

DARK SECRETS Ottawa: Oberon Press, 1983.

GOODBYE SUMMER Ottawa: Oberon Press, 1980.

"Accounting" *Goodbye Summer* (1980), 110-28.

"Anna" *Atlantis* 8:2 (Spr 1983), 113-8.

"Between Lives" *Goodbye Summer* (1980), 80-93.

"Clayton the Fisherman" *Atl Insight* 5 (Apr 1983), 33-7.

"Dark Secrets" *Chat* 53 (Nov 1980), 50, 90, 92, 97-8.

"Dark Secrets" *Dark Secrets* (1983), 91-101.

"Dreams & Sleep" *Atl Insight* 3 (May 1981), 66-8, 70, 73.

"Dreams & Sleep" *Dark Secrets* (1983), 5-13.

"Getting Married, Just Like Everyone Else" *Redbook* 145 (Aug 1975), 71-3.

"Gifts" *Bluenose* 3:3 (Win 1978-79), 4-6.

"The Girls" *Chat* 53 (Aug 1980), 38, 56, 58, 60, 62, 64.

"The Girls" *Dark Secrets* (1983), 75-90.

"Homecoming" *Atl Insight* 2 (Sept 1980), 64, 66-71, 73-6.

"Hunters" *Dark Secrets* (1983), 14-26.

"I'm Still Here" *Goodbye Summer* (1980), 45-61.

"I'm Still Here" *Heartland* (1983), 193-204.

"Images" *Antig R* No. 49 (Spr 1982), 55-65.

"Images" *Metavisions* (1983), 87-96.

"In Leicester County" *Waves* 12:1 (Fall 1983), 21-5.

"In Transit" *Br Out* 4:4 (Sept-Oct 1977), 28-31.

"Island Funeral" *Dal R* 56 (1976-77), 687-96.

"A Light in the Night" *Chat* 49 (Aug 1976), 34, 62-7.

"Magdalena" *Goodbye Summer* (1980), 5-24.

"The Old Charm" *AA* 67 (Feb 1977), 32-4.

"An Old Man" *Antig R* No. 55 (Aut 1983), 13-9.

"On the Road" *Goodbye Summer* (1980), 94-109.

"Once He Started Looking" *Goodbye Summer* (1980), 25-44.

"Payday" *Pot Port* 4 (1982-83), 36-9.

"Persia Awakening" *Goodbye Summer* (1980), 129-43.

"Picnic" *Goodbye Summer* (1980), 62-79.

"Saturday Night, Bean Night" *Alpha* 2:3 (Nov 1977), 5-7, 24-5.

"Thanksgiving" *Dark Secrets* (1983), 37-49.

"That Summer" *New Q* 1:1 (Spr 1981), 31-9.

"That Summer" *Dark Secrets* (1983), 50-60.

"Ties" *Axiom* 2:2 (Oct-Nov 1976), 30-3, 45, 50-1.

"An Understated Look" *Dark Secrets* (1983), 61-74.

"A Visit to Her Son" *AA* 70 (June 1980), 76, 78-80.

"Where Are You Susanna Brown" *Axiom* 3:1 (Dec 1976), 26-7, 29-31, 46, 60, 62.

"Whistling" *Atl Insight* 1 (Sept 1979), 76-8.

"Whistling" *Atl Insight* 4 (Dec 1982), 60-2.

"Whistling" *Dark Secrets* (1983), 27-36.

"White Silence" *Har* 4:4 No. 26 (Mar 1980), 83, 85, 106.

Ross, W.E. Dan

See also Ross, W.E. Dan and Ross, Charlotte.

"Always a Motive" *With Malice Toward All* (1968) [Based on SSI].

"Always a Motive" *Tigers of the Snow* (1973), 107-12.

"And Susie Makes Three" *Companion* 30 (Oct 1967), 16-9.

"A Birthday in Reverse" *Companion* [38] (Apr 1963), 7-12.
"The Bottleneck" *Companion* 29 (Mar 1966), 25-8.
"The Case of the Silent Witness" *Can Messenger* 74 (Feb 1964), 8-10.
"Casebook" *AA* 71 (June 1981), 66-8.
"Castle in the Snow" *Can Messenger* 74 (Dec 1964), 8-11.
"Christmas Eve Decision" *Companion* [40] (Dec 1965), 25-8.
"The Common Touch" *Companion* 29 (May 1966), 23-6.
"The Deadly Whispers" *Companion* 33 (Feb 1970), 26-8.
"The Embroidery of Chao Li" *Can Messenger* 73 (July-Aug 1963), 10-3, 17.
"End of Summer" *Companion* 29 (Sept 1966), 26-9.
"Everyone Knows That!" *Companion* 34 (Jan 1971), 23-5.
"Find a Friend" *Companion* [39] (Apr 1964), 26-9.
"Four Words" *AA* 67 (Apr 1977), 47-8, 50.
"George Hurd's Problem" *AA* 70 (Feb 1980), 66, 68-70.
"The Girl Suddenly Found Luck" *Companion* [40] (May 1965), 24-6.
"Good Value" *AA* 66 (May 1976), 45-7.
"Good Value" *Stubborn Strength* (1983), 71-5.
"The Hitch-Hiker" *Macabre* [UK?] No. 2 (Win 1957), 20[+?] [Based on science fiction indexes].
"Impractical Joker" *AA* 71 (Sept 1980), 62, 64-5.
"Just Too Careless" *AA* 58 (Apr 1968), 24-7.
"A Lesson for Miss Randell" *Ave Maria* 86 (7 Sept 1957), 21-2, 28.
"A Little Lesson in Honesty" *Companion* 29 (July-Aug 1966), 26-8.
"Long Journey Home" *AA* 68 (May 1978), 61-3.
"Losers Sometimes Win" *Can Messenger* 74 (May 1964), 8-11.
"A Matter of Taste" *AA* 69 (Mar 1979), 44, 46-7.
"Matter of the Heart" *Companion* [40] (Nov 1965), 23-6.
"Moment of Revelation" *Companion* [40] (Feb 1965), 26-9.
"The Pearls of Li Pong" *Alfred Hitchcock's Tales to Make You Quake & Quiver* (1982), 343-8.
"The Quality of Courage" *Companion* 31 (Nov 1968), 22-6.
"The Quiet Town" *Companion* 30 (June 1967), 26-30.
"Road to True Worth" *Can Messenger* 80 (Nov 1970), 16-7.
"A Shudder of Wings" *AA* 69 (June 1979), 22, 24.
"SOS from Mei Wong" *Can Messenger* 75 (July-Aug 1965), 28-30.
"A Special Madonna" *Companion* 29 (Dec 1966), 22-5.
"A Special Madonna" *AA* 71 (Dec 1980), 59-60, 62.
"The Stranger Who Made His Mark" *Companion* 31 (Jan 1968), 8-11.
"The Tallest Tree" *AA* 55 (Dec 1964), 65, 67, 69-70.
"That Certain Moment" *AA* 70 (Sept 1979), 64, 66-7.
"The Tired Heart" *Onward* 7 July 1957, 421-2, 430-1.
"Trouble with the Sly Pastry Chef" *Companion* [39] (Sept 1964), 24-8.
"Vacation Romance" *AA* 72 (July 1982), 46-7.
"The Visit" *Companion* 32 (Apr 1969), 26-8.

Ross, [W.E.] Dan and Ross, Charlotte.

See also Ross, W.E. Dan.

"Betty's Big Moment" *Companion* [39] (Nov 1964), 12-5.
"Blinded by Selfishness" *Companion* [39] (Feb 1964), 20-4.
"Christmas Problem for Ruff" *Companion* [39] (Dec 1964), 23-6.
"Emergency Call" *Big Time Mysteries* (1958) [Based on SSI].

"The Girl from Gault Road" *Companion* [38] (Sept 1963), 19-22.
"Home for Christmas" *AA* 50 (Dec 1959), 81-5.
"The Problem Sister" *Companion* 36 (July-Aug 1961), 7-11.
"The Trophies" *Companion* [38] (Mar 1963), 11-5.
"Unknown Visitor" *Companion* 35 (Mar 1960), 19-21.

Rosser, Kent‡
"Duck Story" *Portico* 3:4 (1979), 39 [Humour?].

Rosta, Helen J.
"Belinda's Seal" *CBC [Edm] "Alberta Anthology"* 15 Oct 1983.
"Best Friend" *Grain* 2:2 [1974], 15-7.
"Bye Baby Bunting" *Br Out* 2:2 (Mar-Apr 1975), 30, 42-3.
"George" *Fid* No. 96 (Win 1973), 85-92.
"Going Home" *CBC [Edm] "Alberta Anthology"* 21 Nov 1981.
"Hunting Season" *Getting Here* (1977), 17-28.
"Hunting Season" *NeWest R* 2 (Feb 1977), 6-7, 12.
"In the Blood" *Room* 7:4 (1982), 6-11.
"Living Room" *Des* 12:4/13:1/2 Nos. 34/35/36 (1981-82), 116-29.
"Magpie" *Wild Rose Country* (1977), 70-8.
"Mail" *Prism* 13:2 (Win 1973), 4-8.
"The Maze" *Grain* 4:2 [1976], 39-42.
"Midsummer Feast" *More Stories from Western Canada* (1980), 267-76.
"Midsummer Feast" *West of Fiction* (1983), 320-8.
"One Goose" *JCF* 2:2 (Spr 1973), 29.
"The Sandpile" *Edmonton Mag* 2 (May 1980), 58-60, 70, 72, 77.
"Snow and Solitaire" *Quarry* 24:2 (Spr 1975), 43-7.
"This House" *Flare* 2 (May 1980), 84-5, 113-4, 116, 118.
"When the Bough Breaks" *Des* Nos. 11/12 (Spr-Sum 1975), 104-9.

Rother, James†
"As Long as It's the Truth" *Forge* 25:1 (Feb 1963), 51-[6?] [Page missing].
"The Deliverance of Armand" *Forge* Mar 1959, 27-8.

Rothoehler, Tamara‡
"The Unexpected Ending" *Stump* 5:1 (Fall-Win 1980), 52-4.

Rothschild, Robert P.‡
"Burgled" *Driftwood* No. 2 (1974), 11-4 [Non-fiction?].

Rousanoff, Nicholas‡
"The Accident" by Nick Ross" *UC Gargoyle* Tue, 28 Jan 1963, [2 pp].
"The Substitute" *Pedantics* 1966, 45-6.

Rowat, R.A.
"Entropy" *Outset* 1973, 128-31.

Rowdon, Larry†
"And the Lawns All Glistening" *Quarry* 26:4 (Aut 1977), 42-9.
"Keeper of the Legend" *event* 8:1 (1979), 8-30.
"Mary, Go Call the Cattle Home" *Fid* No. 128 (Win 1981), 36-50.

"Shake the Green Leaf off the Tree" *Fid* No. 118 (Sum 1978), 88-112.
"When the Lamp Is Shattered" *UWR* 15:1/2 (Fall-Win/Spr-Sum 1979-80), 29-37.

Rowell, Carolyn†
"Winter's End" *Matrix* 2:2 (Win 1977), 1-5.

Rowland, Jon‡
"The Corporate Secretary" *Acta Vic* 106:1 (Fall 1981), 46-51.
"Messages" *TUR* 94:1 (Jan 1981), 25-7.

Rowland, Judith†
"The Lynx and the Wolves" *Posh* [n.d.], [2 pp].
"The Three Fish" *Posh* [n.d.], [2 pp].

Royston, Carol†
"A Change of Season" *WWR* 2:2 (1981), 3-5.

(R)rose, Barbara [sic]‡
"The Love Bug" *Story So Far* 3 (1974), 111-3.

Ruberto, Roberto
"The Long Winter" *Prism* 1:4 (Sum 1960), 35-54.

Rubia, Geraldine
"The Blue Lamp" *Twelve Newfoundland Short Stories* (1982), 79-84.
"Shoes for Dancing" *Baffles of Wind and Tide* (1974), 11-6.
"The Taste of Wool" *Scruncheons* 1:1 (1972), 32-5.
"Verena" *From This Place* (1977), 175-9.

Rule, Jane (1931-)
OUTLANDER Iowa City: Naiad Press, 1981.
THEME FOR DIVERSE INSTRUMENTS Vancouver: Talonbooks, 1975.
"Anyone Will Do" *Redbook* 133 (Oct 1969), 108-9.
"The Bosom of the Family" *75: New Canadian Stories* 153-69.
"Brother and Sister" *72: New Canadian Stories* 30-7.
"Brother and Sister" *Theme for Diverse Instruments* (1975), 53-62.
"The Day I Don't Remember" *rara avis* No. 5 (Sum-Fall 1981), 25-9 [Based on Allison & Crane].
"The Day I Don't Remember" *Outlander* (1981), 15-9.
"The Day I Don't Remember" *Mae West Is Dead* (1983), 231-5.
"The Delicate Balance" *Chat* 49 (Dec 1976), 35, 58, 60, 62, 66.
"Dina Pyros" *Lesbians' Home Journal* (1976), 23-40 [Based on Allison & Crane].
"First Love/Last Love" *Christopher Street* 5:2 (1980), 34-6 [Based on Allison & Crane].
"First Love/Last Love" *Outlander* (1981), 107-12.
"The Furniture of Home" *Theme for Diverse Instruments* (1975), 97-107.
"Home Movie" *Sinister Wisdom* No. 14 (1980), 28-35 [Based on Allison & Crane].
"Home Movie" *Outlander* (1981), 3-14.
"House" *Theme for Diverse Instruments* (1975), 63-75.
"House Guest" *Ladder* 13 (Dec-Jan 1968-69), 23-30.

"Housekeeper" *Ladder* 15 (Apr-May 1971), 9-13.
"Housekeeper" *Theme for Diverse Instruments* (1975), 109-21.
"If There Is No Gate" *San Francisco R* 1:6 (Sept 1960), 30-4.
"If There Is No Gate" *CBC "Anthology"* 2 Feb 1962.
"If There Is No Gate" *Stories from Pacific & Arctic Canada* (1974), 89-94.
"If There Is No Gate" *Theme for Diverse Instruments* (1975), 133-9.
"In the Attic of the House" *Christopher Street* 3:12 (1979), 68-74 [Based on Allison & Crane].
"In the Attic of the House" *Aphrodisiac* (1980), 79-92.
"In the Attic of the House" *Lesbian Fiction* (1981), 23-31 [Based on Allison & Crane].
"In the Attic of the House" *Outlander* (1981), 95-105.
"In the Basement of the House" *Ladder* 16 (Apr-May 1972), 8-11.
"In the Basement of the House" *Theme for Diverse Instruments* (1975), 123-31.
"In the Basement of the House" *In the Looking Glass* (1977), 233-40.
"In the Basement of the House" *Ziejewel* (1980), 245-51 [As "In het souterrain"; based on Allison & Crane].
"Invention for Shelagh" *Theme for Diverse Instruments* (1975), 171-85.
"Joy" *Chat* 50 (Aug 1977), 31, 46, 48, 50-2.
"The Killer Dyke and the Lady" *Outlander* (1981), 81-7.
"Lilian" *Conditions* 1:2 (1977), 89-93 [Based on Allison & Crane].
"Lilian" *Outlander* (1981), 89-93.
"The List" *Chat* 42 (Apr 1969), 31, 94, 96, 98-9.
"Middle Children" *Ladder* 14 (Aug-Sept 1970), 9-12.
"Middle Children" *Theme for Diverse Instruments* (1975), 141-8.
"Middle Children" *Other Persuasion* (1977), 340-5.
"Middle Children" *True Likeness* (1980), 21-7 [Based on Allison & Crane].
"A Migrant Christmas" *Chat* 52 (Dec 1979), 39, 58, 60, 64, 66, 68-9, 71.
"Miss Wistan's Promise" *Christopher Street* 5:5 (1981), 40-5 [Based on Allison & Crane].
"Miss Wistan's Promise" *Outlander* (1981), 57-66.
"Moving On" *Redbook* 131 (June 1968), 86-7.
"My Country Wrong" *Ladder* 12 (Aug 1968), 8-18.
"My Country Wrong" *Theme for Diverse Instruments* (1975), 149-69.
"My Country Wrong" *Lesbians' Home Journal* (1976), 165-85 [Based on Allison & Crane].
"My Country Wrong" *Here and Now* (1977), 70-84.
"My Father's House" *Ladder* 15 (DecJan 1970-71), 10-5.
"My Father's House" *Theme for Diverse Instruments* (1975), 39-52.
"My Father's House" *Canadian Short Stories* (1978), 265-78.
"Night Call" *Outlander* (1981), 135-45.
"No More Bargains" *Redbook* 121 (Sept 1963), 68-9 [Based on Allison & Crane].
"Not an Ordinary Wife" *Redbook* 133 (Aug 1969), 70-1, 136-7.
"On the Way" *CBC "Anthology"* 10 Feb 1959.
"Outlander" *CFM* No. 23 (Aut 1976), 9-30.
"Outlander" *Outlander* (1981), 33-55.
"A Perfectly Nice Man" *Outlander* (1981), 125-33.
"A Perfectly Nice Man" *Mae West Is Dead* (1983), 146-55.
"Pictures" *Body Politic* No. 29 (DecJan 1976-77), 12-4.
"Pictures" *Outlander* (1981), 67-80.

"The Puppet Show" *Outlander* (1981), 21-32.

"The Sandwich Generation" CBC "*Anthology*" 24 Apr 1982 [Based on Allison & Crane].

"The Sandwich Generation" *Small Wonders* (1982), 97-107.

"Seaweed & Song" *Chat* 54 (May 1981), 52-3, 193-4, 196, 198.

"The Secretary Bird" *Chat* 45 (Aug 1972), 22, 50-2, 54.

"Sightseers in Death Valley" *Outlander* (1981), 113-23.

"Sightseers in Death Valley" CBC "*Anthology*" 7 Feb 1981 [Based on Allison & Crane].

"A Television Drama" *Theme for Diverse Instruments* (1975), 77-83.

"A Television Drama" *Literature in Canada* (1978), 500-4.

"A Television Drama" *West of Fiction* (1983), 245-9.

"Theme for Diverse Instruments" *Contemporary Voices* (1972), 152-67.

"Theme for Diverse Instruments" *Theme for Diverse Instruments* (1975), 9-37.

"Three Letters to a Poet" *Ladder 12* (MayJune 1968), 5-7.

"A Walk by Himself" *Klanak Islands* (1959), 59-69.

"A Walk by Himself" *Theme for Diverse Instruments* (1975), 85-96.

"Woorden Op Een Vensterbank" *Margriet [Neth?]* No. 43 (Oct 1968), 40-7, 53 [Based on Allison & Crane].

"You Cannot Judge a Pumpkin's Happiness by the Smile Upon His Face" CBC "*Anthology*" 30 Oct 1982 [Genre unspecified; based on Allison & Crane].

"Your Father and I" *Housewife* (U.K.) 23:8 (1961), 26-7, 77-81 [Based on Allison & Crane].

Rummel, Erika†

"Blackbird and the Poet" *Writ* No. 13 (1981), 44-56.

"Dreams in the Marketplace" *Quarry* 29:4 (Aut 1980), 28-35.

Rushton, Alfred (1942-)

MIND MAPS Toronto: Poseidon Press, 1970.

"The Bare Facts" *Gut* 1:2 (Nov 1973), 8, 15-6.

"The Feeder" *Mind Maps* (1970), 71-83.

"Haynes, the Machine, and Maud" *Story So Far* 2 (1973), 58-63.

"Laura Secord – Canadian Author Interview" *Gut* No. 6 (Win 1977), 14.

"The Life Preserve" *Mind Maps* (1970), 38-63.

"The Phoner" *Mind Maps* (1970), 15-26.

"The Synns" *Mind Maps* (1970), 84-94.

"The Temple Visitor" *Mind Maps* (1970), 1-14.

Rushton, Bethany K.†

"Gooseberry Twist" *Pier Spr* Sum 1978, 28.

Russell, G.E.‡

"The Bank Clerk" *Creative Campus 1967*, 12-20.

Russell, Lawrence (1941-)

"The Confession" *Prism* 19:3 (Spr 1981), 135-41.

"The Flight of the Flying Coffins" *JCF* No. 23 (1979), 48-75.

"Geometry & Dream" *CFM* No. 12 (Win 1974), 35-8.

"Magic Juice" *CFM* Nos. 2/3 (SprSum 1971), 78-87.
"The Rise of the Poet" *Karaki* No. 2 (Feb 1972), 17-24.
"Snow-Shadow Man" *CFM* No. 6 (Spr 1972), 70-5.

Russell, Nancy Ellen‡
"Tenth Medal" *West People* No. 211 (10 Nov 1983), 8-9.

Russell, Sheila MacKay (1920-)
"Abbie Was a Mudder" *Alberta Golden Jubilee Anthology* (1955), 444-56.
"All That I Can Give" *Chat* 42 (May 1969), 32, 65-6, 70-2.
"And All the Forbidden Tomorrows" *Chat* 35 (Oct 1962), 38-9, 101-2, 105-8.
"Behind the Nightengale Smile" *Chat* 37 (Feb 1964), 22-3, 53-61.
"Bitter Harvest" *Chat* 32 (Feb 1959), 29-31, 62, 64-5, 68-70.
"The Boy Nobody Wanted" *Chat* 38 (Aug 1965), 24, 49-52.
"A Case of Conflict" *Chat* 40 (Sept 1967), 40, 91-2, 94, 96, 100, 102, 104.
"Christmas Crisis" *Chat* 43 (Dec 1970), 23, 66-71.
"Confession" *Chat* 35 (May 1962), 32-3, 106-10.
"The Crisis Summer" *Chat* 38 (June 1965), 30-1, 56, 58-62.
"A Cry of Love" *Chat* 44 (Sept 1971), 43, 75-9.
"Deadline for Love" *Chat* 44 (Jan 1971), 27, 46-50.
"The Decision" *Chat* 36 (Feb 1963), 20, 68-72, 74-6.
"End of Loneliness" *Chat* 45 (Mar 1972), 30, 52, 54-6, 58-9.
"The Endless Ripples" *Chat* 39 (Apr 1966), 53, 108, 113-4, 116, 118-20.
"A Fact of Life" *Chat* 43 (Oct 1970), 33, 88-92.
"First Love" *Chat* 34 (May 1961), 39, 116, 118, 120, 122, 124.
"The Girl Who Made Good" *Chat* 36 (Aug 1963), 22-3, 38, 40, 42.
"The Glass Wall" *Chat* 37 (Oct 1964), 26, 67-73.
"Happiness Is Not a Home" *Chat* 40 (Oct 1967), 37, 118, 120-1, 124, 126.
"The Has-Been" *Chat* 36 (Apr 1963), 30, 81-5.
"Have Gun, Will Shoot" *Chat* 33 (Sept 1960), 34, 107-8, 110, 112, 116-20.
"Her Moment of Fulfillment" *Chat* 43 (Apr 1970), 37, 66, 68, 70, 72-3.
"His Mother's Son" *Chat* 35 (Feb 1962), 37, 52, 54-6, 58-9.
"The Hutterites" *Chat* 39 (Sept 1966), 40-1, 128, 130, 132, 134, 136-7.
"Kristy" *Chat* 36 (Dec 1963), 21, 51-6.
"Let Me Love You" *Chat* 33 (Apr 1960), 36, 68, 70, 72, 76-7, 82.
"Like the Earth and the Rain" *Chat* 37 (May 1964), 26, 53-8.
"The Little Mademoiselle" *Chat* 38 (Apr 1965), 26-7, 54-6, 58-60.
"The Marriage Breaker" *Chat* 41 (Mar 1968), 31, 52-6, 58.
"Marriage Is a Lonely Game" *Chat* 46 (May 1973), 35, 57-8, 60, 64, 66, 68.
"Marriage Makes Three" *Chat* 40 (Feb 1967), 23, 82-4, 86-8.
"A Moment of Truth" *Chat* 35 (Dec 1962), 33, 76-80.
"A Moment of Truth" *Chat* 42 (Feb 1969), 25, 51-5.
"Mr. Nightengale" *Chat* 41 (Jan 1968), 25, 49-52.
"My Husband, My Enemy" *Chat* 32 (June 1959), 29, 54, 56-60, 62, 64, 66.
"Now There Was Today" *Chat* 38 (Feb 1965), 23, 42-6.
"Of Fear and Love" *Chat* 39 (Oct 1966), 35, 66, 68, 73-4.
"One Shining Moment" *Chat* 40 (May 1967), 41, 68, 70, 72, 74, 76.
"Party Crowd" *Chat* 42 (July 1969), 18-9, 34-8.
"Past ... Incomplete" *Chat* 39 (July 1966), 23, 54, 56, 58-9.
"The Playgirl" *Chat* 37 (June 1964), 29, 56-61.
"Sari in the Kitchen" *Chat* 35 (Sept 1962), 37, 99-102, 104, 107-8.

"The Showdown" *Chat* 33 (June 1960), 31, 64-71.
"The Sisters" *Chat* 33 (Nov 1960), 41, 105-13.
"Spring Comes" *Chat* 46 (Feb 1973), 37, 54-8.
"Storm Centre" *Chat* 45 (Sept 1972), 47, 88-90, 92-4, 96.
"The Ten-Year Gap" *Chat* 46 (July 1973), 36-7, 66, 68-70.
"A Time of Testing" *Chat* 38 (Oct 1965), 40-1, 70-2, 74, 76.
"A Touching of Lives" *Chat* 41 (June 1968), 26, 48, 50, 52, 54.
"The Understanding Heart" *Chat* 39 (Feb 1966), 28, 50-4.
"The Victory" *Chat* 34 (Oct 1961), 40, 56, 58, 60, 62, 64-5.

Russell, Ted (1904-1977)

THE BEST OF TED RUSSELL 1 Ed. Elizabeth Russell Miller St. John's: Harry Cuff, 1982.

THE CHRONICLES OF UNCLE MOSE Ed. Elizabeth Russell Miller Portugal Cove: Breakwater Books, 1975.

TALES FROM PIGEON INLET Ed. Elizabeth Russell Miller St. John's: Breakwater Books, 1977.

"Airplanes" *Tales from Pigeon Inlet* (1977), 127-9.
"Alcoholic Liquor" *Best of Ted Russell* 1 (1982), 18-9.
"Algebra Slippers" *Tales from Pigeon Inlet* (1977), 32-4.
"All the Local News" *Tales from Pigeon Inlet* (1977), 155-6.
"Arguments" *Chronicles of Uncle Mose* (1975), 53-4.
"Arguments" *Tales from Pigeon Inlet* (1977), 60-2.
"Aunt Sophy" *Tales from Pigeon Inlet* (1977), 19-22.
"Aunt Sophy's Predicament" *Chronicles of Uncle Mose* (1975), 50-2.
"Aunt Sophy's Return" *Tales from Pigeon Inlet* (1977), 104-6.
"Babysittin' " *Chronicles of Uncle Mose* (1975), 83-6.
"Babysittin' " *East of Canada* (1976), 206-8.
"Bartle's Brook" *Tales from Pigeon Inlet* (1977), 93-4.
"Black Currants" *Tales from Pigeon Inlet* (1977), 161-4.
"Bravery" *Tales from Pigeon Inlet* (1977), 45-7.
"The Bull Moose (1)" *Chronicles of Uncle Mose* (1975), 103-5.
"The Bull Moose (2)" *Chronicles of Uncle Mose* (1975), 106-7.
"Business" *Chronicles of Uncle Mose* (1975), 65-7.
"Churchgoin' " *Chronicles of Uncle Mose* (1975), 74-6.
"Cold Weather" *Chronicles of Uncle Mose* (1975), 87-9.
"Comic Books" *Tales from Pigeon Inlet* (1977), 118-23.
"Crime Wave in Pigeon Inlet" *Best of Ted Russell* 1 (1982), 20-2.
"Crime Wave in Pigeon Inlet" *Treasury of Newfoundland Prose and Verse* (1983), 82-4.
"Cuban Heels" *Chronicles of Uncle Mose* (1975), 96-9.
"Curling" *Chronicles of Uncle Mose* (1975), 100-2.
"The Cynic" *Tales from Pigeon Inlet* (1977), 95-8.
"Dictionaries" *Chronicles of Uncle Mose* (1975), 68-70.
"The District Nurse" *Chronicles of Uncle Mose* (1975), 4-6.
"The District Nurse" *Earth* (1977), 42-3.
"Dogs" *Best of Ted Russell* 1 (1982), 28-30.
"The Drama Festival" *Tales from Pigeon Inlet* (1977), 137-9.
"Dressmakin' " *Chronicles of Uncle Mose* (1975), 58-61.
"Education" *Tales from Pigeon Inlet* (1977), 143-5.
"Education" *Best of Ted Russell* 1 (1982), 26-7.

"Eelskins" *Chronicles of Uncle Mose* (1975), 90-2.
"Football" *Tales from Pigeon Inlet* (1977), 113-5.
"Geese" *Chronicles of Uncle Mose* (1975), 110-2.
"Goin' Home" *Tales from Pigeon Inlet* (1977), 66-7.
"Grampa's Mistakes" *Chronicles of Uncle Mose* (1975), 55-7.
"Grampa's Only Sickness" *Chronicles of Uncle Mose* (1975), 12-4.
"The Grub Box" *Atl Guardian* 9 (June 1952), 32-5.
"The Grub Box" *Best of Ted Russell* 1 (1982), 14-6.
"Ice and 'Baccy" *Tales from Pigeon Inlet* (1977), 83-5.
"Ice and Ducks" *Tales from Pigeon Inlet* (1977), 110-2.
"Isolation" *Chronicles of Uncle Mose* (1975), 93-5.
"Jethro Noddy" *Chronicles of Uncle Mose* (1975), 7-8.
"John Cabot" *Chronicles of Uncle Mose* (1975), 47-9.
"King David" *Chronicles of Uncle Mose* (1975), 9-11.
"King David" *Best of Ted Russell* 1 (1982), 40-2.
"King David and Jethro" *Tales from Pigeon Inlet* (1977), 58-9.
"King David's Family Allowance" *Chronicles of Uncle Mose* (1975), 28-30.
"King David's Winter Outfit" *Chronicles of Uncle Mose* (1975), 34-6.
"Letter to Aunt Sophy" *Tales from Pigeon Inlet* (1977), 68-72.
"Loggin' " *Tales from Pigeon Inlet* (1977), 26-8.
"Louella and Grandma" *Best of Ted Russell* 1 (1982), 31-2.
"Men's Rights" *Chronicles of Uncle Mose* (1975), 77-9.
"Muldoon's Cove" *Tales from Pigeon Inlet* (1977), 157-60.
"My Brother Ki" *Tales from Pigeon Inlet* (1977), 37-8.
"New Year's Resolutions" *Chronicles of Uncle Mose* (1975), 62-4.
"Old-Fashioned Games" *Tales from Pigeon Inlet* (1977), 124-6.
"On the Halves" *Chronicles of Uncle Mose* (1975), 80-2.
"Our Natural Resources" *Best of Ted Russell* 1 (1982), 33-5.
"Outports" *Tales from Pigeon Inlet* (1977), 146-8.
"Paddy Muldoon" *Chronicles of Uncle Mose* (1975), 31-3.
"The Pilgarlic" *Tales from Pigeon Inlet* (1977), 165-71.
"Poppin' the Question" *Tales from Pigeon Inlet* (1977), 149-51.
"The Posse (1)" *Chronicles of Uncle Mose* (1975), 41-3.
"The Posse (2)" *Chronicles of Uncle Mose* (1975), 44-6.
"Potatoes" *Chronicles of Uncle Mose* (1975), 18-21.
"Property and the Law" *Tales from Pigeon Inlet* (1977), 35-6.
"Rabbits" *Tales from Pigeon Inlet* (1977), 140-2.
"Robinson Crusoe" *Tales from Pigeon Inlet* (1977), 86-8.
"Romancin' " *Tales from Pigeon Inlet* (1977), 152-4.
"Rumbly Cove" *Nfld Q* 67:2 (July 1969), 3-4.
"Salmon and Trout" *Tales from Pigeon Inlet* (1977), 73-5.
"Santa Claus" *Tales from Pigeon Inlet* (1977), 52-4.
"Sarah Skimple" *Doryloads* (1974), 110-1 [Pre-1950?].
"The Second Round (1)" *Chronicles of Uncle Mose* (1975), 22-4.
"The Second Round (2)" *Chronicles of Uncle Mose* (1975), 25-7.
"The Show Off" *Tales from Pigeon Inlet* (1977), 48-51.
"Singin' Carols" *Tales from Pigeon Inlet* (1977), 133-6.
"Skipper Joe's Trip to St. John's" *Tales from Pigeon Inlet* (1977), 39-41.
"Snakes" *Tales from Pigeon Inlet* (1977), 80-2.
"Stealin' the Holes" *Tales from Pigeon Inlet* (1977), 107-9.

"Swiles" *Tales from Pigeon Inlet* (1977), 23-5.
"T.V." *Tales from Pigeon Inlet* (1977), 63-5.
"Teachers" *Tales from Pigeon Inlet* (1977), 77-9.
"Thinkin' in Circles" *Tales from Pigeon Inlet* (1977), 130-2.
"Those New Ideas" *Tales from Pigeon Inlet* (1977), 116-7.
"Tourists" *Tales from Pigeon Inlet* (1977), 89-92.
"Toutens" *Chronicles of Uncle Mose* (1975), 71-3.
"Troutin' " *Best of Ted Russell* 1 (1982), 36-9.
"Uncle Mose Begins His Chronicles" *By Great Waters* (1974), 243-7.
"Under the Mistletoe" *Tales from Pigeon Inlet* (1977), 55-7.
"United Nations" *Tales from Pigeon Inlet* (1977), 29-31.
"University Opening" *Best of Ted Russell* 1 (1982), 24-5.
"The Value of King David" *Tales from Pigeon Inlet* (1977), 42-4.
"Weddin's" *Tales from Pigeon Inlet* (1977), 99-103.
"Whorts" *Chronicles of Uncle Mose* (1975), 108-9.
"Yes, Aunt Sophy, There Is" *Chronicles of Uncle Mose* (1975), 15-7.
"Youngsters" *Doryloads* (1974), 136-7.
"Youngsters" *Chronicles of Uncle Mose* (1975), 37-40.
"Youngsters" *Earth* (1977), 31-2.

Russo, Leonard
FIVE STORIES Westmount, P.Q.: Jaw Breaker Press, 1971.
"Charlie" *Five Stories* (1971), 27-[32].
"George" *Five Stories* (1971), 15-27.
"Luck" *Jaw Breaker* No. 1 (June 1971), 8-10.
"Something to Go On" *Five Stories* (1971), 8-14.
"Tags" *Five Stories* (1971), 4-7.
"This World We Live: Introduction" *Five Stories* (1971), 2-4.

Rutkis, S.‡
"The Stream" *Scar Fair* 4 (1976-77), 9.

Rutland, R.B.‡
" 'I Have a Letter for Mr. Frenchman ... ' " *TUR* 67:5 (Sum 1955), 32-41.

Rutledge, Leo†
"Night on the Mountain" *Treeline* 2 (1983), 11-7.

Rutt, Edwin
"The Cleverest Pickpocket in Quebec" *Lib* 33 (July 1956), 44-5.
"Freddy Rules the Waves" *Lib* 27 (June 1950), 30-5.
"Tallyho Toronto" *MM* 63 (15 Jan 1950), 10-1, 48-50.
"Tallyho Toronto" *Maclean's Reader* (1950), 123-33.

Rutty, Lorimer‡
"Summer Night" *Muse* 64:1 (1955), 14-6.

Ryan, E. Anne‡
"Euphoria" *AA* 52 (Mar 1962), 33-4, 36.
"The Yellow Gate" *AA* 47 (Apr 1957), 63-5, 67.

Ryan, Josephine

"C'mon, Get That Hair Cut!" *Companion* 29 (Oct 1966), 10-3.

"The Day Maggie and Mike Found the Real Meaning of Life and Love" *Companion* 31 (May 1968), 8-13.

"Edge of Innocence" *Chat* 43 (May 1970), 30, 71-2, 74.

"He Couldn't Argue with a Conscience" *Companion* 32 (Dec 1969), 19-21.

"Husbands Are for Keeping" *Green's* 3:2 (Win 1975), 22-34.

"It's My Uncle Barrett" *Companion* 32 (June 1969), 22-5.

"Jo Cancel Half a Line" *SW* 1 Oct 1966, 17-9.

"Joseph's Dilemma" *SW* 21 Jan 1967, 14-6.

"Journey's End" *Polished Pebbles* (1974), 85-8.

"Rebel Mother" *Chat* 42 (Nov 1969), 44, 54-6, 58, 60, 62, 64.

"The Waters Close Over" *Mam* 3:4 (Win 1980), [11 pp].

Ryan, Maxwell

"Blow Your Horn" *War Cry* 22 Dec 1979, 16-7.

"A Time to Remember" *Home Leaguer* 14 (Mar 1967), 5.

Ryan, Patricia‡

"The Cardinal's Levee" *Winnipeg Stories* (1974), 68-76.

Ryder, Huia†

"A Mantle for Maria" *Echoes* No. 222 (Spr 1956), 7, 26.

Ryga, George

"Betrothal" CBC "*Anthology*" 17 Nov 1961.

"Beyond a Crimson Morning" *Aurora* 1978 210-26.

"Black Is the Colour" *AA* 57 (Jan 1967), 25-9.

"Hope" *Uk Can* 5 (1 Oct 1951), 5.

"Old Sam" *Uk Can* 11 (15 Feb 1957), 9.

"Visit from the Pension Lady" *Newcomers* (1979), 177-88.

Rymer, John E.‡

"Man Versus Machine" *West People* No. 185 (21 Apr 1983), 12.

S., W.

"A Terrible Tragedy" *Undergrad* Mar 1957, 10-1.

Saari, Oliver E.‡

"The After-Life" *Can Fandom* No. 33 (Feb 1957), 14-7.

"The After-Life" *Can Fandom* No. 33a (Feb 1957), 96-9.

Sagaris, Lake

"Sue Solomon" *Room* 2:4 (1977), 44-8.

Saible, Janet†

"Visitation Street" *Br Out* 6:2 (1979), 14-8.

Sakamoto, Kerrit
"Autumn" *UCR* Spr 1983, 43-5.
"Blending" *UTR* 6 (1982), 2-3.
"The Coat" *Fireweed* No. 16 (Spr 1983), 32-5.
"Death in an Evacuation Camp of One Who Never Saw Japan" *UTR* 6 (1982), 17.

Sakhuja, Minnie A.‡
"Loving Carbon" *Scar Fair* 7 (1979-80), 18.

Sale, Peter
"A Matter of Principle" *Green's* 10:2 (Win 1982), 29-36.

Sallows, Roy‡
"Summer" CBC "*Alberta Anthology*" 1 Oct 1983.

Salminiw, Stephen†
"The Bishop" *Harvest* No. 2 (Fall 1977), 6-17.
"Last Scene Fishing" *Alpha* 2:[7] (Mar-Apr 1978), 5-6.
"An Underlying Sex Tragedy Written Especially for Television" *Alpha* 7:2 (Apr 1983), 33-5.
"Winthrop into the Flesh of Piano" *Inscape* 13:2 (Win 1976-77), 29-34.

Salter, C.R.B.‡
"The Breed" *Varsity Lit Issue* Fri, 3 Mar 1950, 1-2, 4.

Salter, Geoff‡
"Reciprocal" *Stardust* 3:1 [n.d.], 39-40.

Salter, Jim – *See* Green, H. Gordon.

Saltern, Margaret†
"The Piece of Green" *Prism* 2:2 (Win 1961), 42-7.

Saltzburg, Joan
"The Flower Pot" *CSSM* 2:3 (Sum 1976), 51-3.

Samotie, Bill‡
"Catch a Nigger by the Toe" *Fifth Page* 1964, 11-5.

Sample, Maureen†
"The Taming of Mrs. O'Leary" *Dand* 2 (Spr-Sum 1976), 36-42.

Samuel, George†
"Saint George the Lucky Dragon" *Dal R* 62 (1982), 223-6.

Sandbrook, Betty M.‡
"The Ebb Tide of Peader O'Meara" *QQ* 65 (1958), 263-9.

Sanderson, Helen (? -1962)†
"The Baby-Sitter" *Onward* 9 Nov 1958, 705-6, 718-9.
"How It Happens" *Onward* 17 Mar 1963, 12-3.

Sanderson, James‡
"The Healer" *Scar Fair* 5 (1977-78), 21-7.
"Hide and Seek" *Scar Fair* 4 (1976-77), 10-5.
"A Story for Jane" *UTR* 2:1 (Spr 1978), 21-2.

Sanderson, Vi‡
"Women in Battle" *New Breed* July 1982, 25-7.

Sandler, Robert†
"Betta Splendor" *Writ* No. 1 (Spr 1970), 50-8.

Sandman, John (1949-)
"Herb Cook's Breakfast" *CBC "Anthology"* 1 June 1974.
"One for the Road" *72: New Canadian Stories* 75-91.
"The Real Mrs. Hunter" *74: New Canadian Stories* 62-75.
"The Real Mrs. Hunter" *CBC "Anthology"* 12 Apr 1975.
"Running Back to Saskatoon" *CBC "Anthology"* 21 Aug 1976.

Sandor, Karl†
"About the Brown Paper Bags" *CFM* Nos. 2/3 (Spr-Sum 1971), 7-9.
"Fingers, Fingers" *CBC "Anthology"* 11 Jan 1975.
"Message to the Architect of the Revolution" *CFM* No. 27 (1977), 34-9.
"A Parable on a Parable" *Echo* (Van) No. 3 (1977), 15-8.
" 'Where Is Harvey Now?' " *Echo* (Van) No. 1 (Fall 1975), 26-7.
"Without Her" *CBC "Anthology"* 17 May 1975.

Sandor-Lofft, Suzanne‡
"Victim" *Aurora* 1980 124-9.

Sands, E.
"Temporarily Yours" *Makara* 1:3 (Apr-May 1976), 14-5.

Sanford, Claire†
"August Not Over" *Raven* No. 7 (Nov 1958), [5 pp].
"August Not Over" *Prism* 1:2 (Win 1959), 60-5.

Sangster, Allan
"Like in a Book" *CHJ* Jan 1950, 5, 23, 28-34.

Sangster, Hazel‡
"The Boy Next Door" *CBC "Alberta Anthology"* 1 Oct 1983.

Sangwine, Jean
"Barney" *Onward* 30 Oct 1960, 692-3.
"Hunting Season" *Getting Here* (1977), 17-28.
"Hunting Season" *NeWest R* 2 (Feb 1977), 6-7, 12.
"The Way of Wise Men" *Onward* 30 Dec 1962, 3-4, 13.
"The Way of Wise Men" *Onward* 31 Dec 1967, 3-5.

Sapergia, Barbara (1943-)

"Matty and Rose" *Saskatchewan Gold* (1982), 60-9.

"Matty and Rose" *This* 17 (Mar 1983), 30-4.

"Orest Kulak's Wonderful New Wheat" *100% Cracked Wheat* (1983), 162-89.

"Sun" *Sundogs* (1980), 110-9.

Sappol, Michael‡

"Text of a Lecture On:" *Titmouse R* No. 7 [n.d.], 24-5.

Sarah, Robyn (1949-)

"Furniture" *QQ* 90 (1983), 1126-33.

"Heading into Winter" *CFM* No. 44 (1982), 85-97.

"Heading into Winter" *Metavisions* (1983), 130-43.

"How Well We Filled the Wilderness" *Antig R* No. 36 (Win 1979), 11-4.

"Purgatory" *Mal R* No. 62 (July 1982), 184-90.

"Things That Don't Happen" *Antig R* No. 20 (Win 1974), 9-16.

"Traces" *Fid* No. 105 (Spr 1975), 25 [Listed as prose sketch].

"Wrong Number" *Fid* No. 105 (Spr 1975), 22-4 [Listed as prose sketch].

Sarna, Lazar

"How to Compile a Dictionary" *CFM* No. 4 (Aut 1971), 43-6.

"Towers" *Forge* 1967, 39-48.

Sarrazin, Jo-Ann‡

"What Feeling Was He Wearing That Day?" *SN* 85 (Sept 1970), 43-4, 46, 49.

Sasse, Joyce (1940?-) **and Dow, Janet**

"The Right to Be Socially Responsible" *Mission Mag* 2:2 (Dec 1978), 3-6.

Sather, Lily G.‡

"The Pilgrimage" *Can Lifetime* 4 (Jan-Feb 1974), 5-7.

Saunders, Charles R. (1946-)

"Amma" *Beyond the Fields We Know* No. 1 (Aut 1978), 22-34.

"Bwala Li Mwesu (The Moon Pool)" *Dark Fantasy* No. 8 (1976), 18-41.

"The Curse of the Bana-Gui" *Fantasy Crossroads* No. 14 (Fall 1978) [Based on Saunders].

"Death in Jukun" *Heroic Fantasy* (1979), 153-68.

"Horror in the Black Hills" *Dark Fantasy* No. 14 (1977), 26-46.

"Imaro and the Giant Kings" *Phantasy Digest* No. 4 (Sum 1978) [Based on Saunders].

"Jeroboam Henley's Debt" *Potboiler* 1:4 (Feb 1982), 45-9.

"Kibanda Ya Kufa (The Hut of Death)" *Dark Fantasy* No. 7 (Sept 1975), 18-26.

"Mai-Kulala" *Space and Time* No. 45 (Win 1977) [Based on Saunders].

"N'tu-Nusu Ya Chikanda (The Half-Men of Chikanda)" *Fantasy Crossroads* No. 9 (Aug/Sum 1976), 7-14.

"The Place of Stones" *Phantasy Digest* No. 1 (Fall 1976) [Based on Saunders].

"The Singing Drum" *Windhaven* (U.S.) 2 (1977), 9-12.

"The Skeleton Coast" *Dark Fantasy* No. 18 (1978), 4-37.

"Turkhana Knives" *Dragonbane* No. 1 (Spr 1978), 52-64.

Saunders, Dave‡

[Untitled] *Folio* 20:3 (Apr 1972), [1 p].

Saunders, Gary L.

"Flowers from the Sky" *AA* 66 (Oct 1975), 21-2.
"A Meal of Flippers" *Blasty Bough* (1976), 118-30.

Saunders, Les‡

"Good Times – Bad Times" *Lifetime* 2 (Jan-Feb 1972), 14-6.

Sawai, Gloria (1932-)

"3 Poems = 1 Story" *Three Times Five* (1983), 155-63.
"The Day I Sat with Jesus on the Sun Deck and a Wind Came up and Blew My Kimono Open and He Saw My Breasts" *Grain* 9:2 (May 1981), 5-14.
"The Day I Sat with Jesus on the Sun Deck and a Wind Came up and Blew My Kimono Open and He Saw My Breasts" *82: Best Canadian Stories* 80-96.
"The Day I Sat with Jesus on the Sun Deck and a Wind Came Up and Blew My Kimono Open and He Saw My Breasts" *Three Times Five* (1983), 143-54.
"Hang Out Your Washing on the Siegfried Line" *Three Times Five* (1983), 111-23.
"Memorial" *Three Times Five* (1983), 124-42.
"Mother's Day" *Aurora* 1978 180-92.
"Mother's Day" *Three Times Five* (1983), 99-110.

Sawyer, Constance‡

"Grand Finale" *CF* 60 (Nov 1980), 25-6.

Sawyer, Robert (1960-)

"Caught in the Web" *WWR* 2:3 (1982), 41-2.
"The Contest" *WWR* 2:1 (1980), 45-6.
"If I'm Here, Imagine Where They Sent My Luggage" *Village Voice* 14 Jan 1981 [Based on survey response].
"Ours to Discover" *Leisureways* Nov 1982 [Based on survey response].
"Pun-Dit" *All Agog* (1982) [Based on survey response].

Sayer, Frank‡

"Snowbound Christmas Train" *AA* 63 (Dec 1972), 36-7, 43.

Scammell, A.R. (Art)

MY NEWFOUNDLAND: STORIES, POEMS, SONGS Montreal: Harvest House, 1966.
"Confirmation Prelude" *My Newfoundland* (1966), 93-6 [Non-fiction?].
"Confirmation Prelude" *Baffles of Wind and Tide* (1974), 8-10.
"The Culler" *My Newfoundland* (1966), 81-9.
"The Culling Board" *Nfld Q* 56:3 (Sept 1957), 4-6, 49-50.
"Fish and Brewis" *Atl Guardian* 8:1 (Jan 1951), 20-6.
"Fish and Brewis" *My Newfoundland* (1966), 21-9.
"Fish and Brewis" *Doryloads* (1974), 93-102.
"Hard Cash" *By Great Waters* (1974), 213-8.
"Mail Day for Amelia" *My Newfoundland* (1966), 46-50.
"My Political Career" *My Newfoundland* (1966), 70-5.
"Night School" *My Newfoundland* (1966), 51-7.

"The Outdoor Motor" *My Newfoundland* (1966), 67-9.
"Render unto Caesar ... " *My Newfoundland* (1966), 62-6.
"Sea Fever" *My Newfoundland* (1966), 76-80.
"A Shot to Remember" *My Newfoundland* (1966), 58-61 [Non-fiction?].
"Trap Berth" *FH* 22 Sept 1955, 24-5, 39.
"Trap Berth" *My Newfoundland* (1966), 35-42.
"The Whale" *My Newfoundland* (1966), 90-2.

Scanlon, Margaret†
"Story One" *Waves* 7:3 (Spr 1979), 17-8.

Scarfe, Eunice†.
"Five O'Clock Train" CBC *"Alberta Anthology"* 17 Sept 1983.
"The Five O'Clock Train" *Mal R* No. 66 (Oct 1983), 26-31.

Schaire, Jeffrey†
"An Improvisation: Mysteries of Christianity" *Prism* 16:2 (Fall 1977), 107-11.

Schartner, Adelaide‡
"Waiting for Charly" CBC *"Alberta Anthology"* 20 Sept 1980.
"Written Evidence" *Edmonton Journal* Fri, 13 May 1966, 68.

Schaub, Michael
"Harbinger: A Romantic Tale" *Catalyst* 2:2 (Win 1968-69), 45-55.

Scheider-Livesley, Richard
"Galatic-Toc" *Outset* 1974, 136-9.

Schell, Winston G.†
"Goldfish and Other Elements" *Applegarth's Folly* No. 1 (Sum 1973), [2 pp].

Schendlinger, Mary
"If Jill Hadn't Taken" *Pulp* 5:11 (31 Jan 1980), [2 pp].
"School" *Common Ground* (1980), 23-30.
"The Sickbed" *Body Politic* No. 52 (May 1979), 21-4.

Schermbrucker, Bill (1938-)
CHAMELEON AND OTHER STORIES Vancouver: Talonbooks, 1983.
"Afterbirth" *Interface* 4 (Dec 1981), 21-4.
"Afterbirth" *Chameleon* (1983), 139-52.
"Aga Dawn" CBC *"Anthology"* [date unknown] [Based on Chameleon].
"Aga Dawn" *Roothog* (1981), 101-11.
"Aga Dawn" *Chameleon* (1983), 15-26.
"Another Movie" *Des* 11:3 No. 29 (1980), 136-56.
"Another Movie" *Chameleon* (1983), 73-94.
"Chameleon" *JCF* No. 24 [1979], 15-25.
"Chameleon" *Chameleon* (1983), 111-24.
"A Couple of Guys" *Repos* No. 8 (Fall 1973), 1-18.
"Esther: A Spring Sketch" *Grain* 7:3 [1979], 60-2.
"The Grave by the Fig" *JCF* Nos. 17/18 (1976), 57-67.
" 'Like a Hinge on a Gate' " *Cap R* No. 28 (1983), 36-56.
"Mile Eighteen" *JCF* Nos. 28/29 (1980), 53-75.

"Mile Eighteen" *Chameleon* (1983), 27-52.
"Mooching with Runcey" *Repos* No. 13 (Win 1975), 1-7.
"Muriuki's Mother" *Chameleon* (1983), 125-38.
"Roger Ash or The Year We Built the Golf Course" *Chameleon* (1983), 53-72.
"The Soul Thirsts" *Repos* Nos. 19/20 (Sum-Fall 1976), 11-7.
"Versions" *Cap R* No. 28 (1983), 57-73.
"Versions" *Chameleon* (1983), 95-110.
"Written in Cars: A Preface" *Grain* 10:4 (Nov 1982), 14-5.

Schilling, Rita‡

"Country Mouse and City Mouse" *Smoke Signals* [1974?], 55-9.

Schleich, David†

"The Burning" *JCF* 2:2 (Spr 1973), 33-6.
"A Measure of Rooms" *White Pelican* 3:2 (Spr 1973), 21-3.

Schmekel, Suzan‡

"Eve's Child" *Inscape* 3:1 (Fall 1963), 17-9.

Schoemperlen, Diane (1954-)

"Alone in the Empire" *CFM* No. 18 (Sum 1975), 66-72.
"Body No. 15" *Des* No. 14 (Sum 1976), 39-46.
"Bright Wire" *Nebula* No. 8 (1978), 44-53.
"The Climb" *CFM* No. 20 (Win 1976), 17-26.
"The Dance" *Room* 4:4 (1979), 68-75.
"An Evening in Two Voices" *Nebula* No. 8 (1978), 54-65.
"An Experiment in Point of View: The Edge" *CSSM* 2:1 (Jan 1976), 47-50.
"Frogs" *Quarry* 32:1 (Win 1983), 52-62.
"Future Tense" *Muskeg R* 4 [1976], 51-6.
"The Gate" *CA & B* 58:2 (Win 1983), 12-4.
"Histories" *Matrix* No. 12 (Win 1981), 33-43.
"The Journal of Glory Maxwell" *Muskeg R* 3 (1975), 13-21.
"Losing Ground" *event* 10:2 (1981), 19-34.
"Our Town" *NeWest R* 6 (Feb 1981), 8-9.
"Prophecies" *Harvest* No. 8 (Dec 1979), 6-12.
"Settings for a Love Poem" *UWR* 12:2 (Spr-Sum 1977), 80-3.
"Summer Scene" *Squatch J* No. 3 (June 1976), 44.
"This Music to Love" *CSSM* 1:3 (July 1975), 52-4.
"To Whom It May Concern" *Br Out* 3:4 (Sept-Oct 1976), 26-30.
"Waiting" *Quarry* 28:2 (Spr 1979), 51-60.

Schoen, Frank N.‡

"Daze in the Life of Jimmy D" *Mandala* 1968, 69-76.

Schole, Kevin†

"Super Alice Fornari" *Gas Rain* 3 (1979), 12-5.

Schonfeld, Marcia†

"Canary Bird" *Dal R* 54 (1974), 48-64.

Schoutsen, John (1956-)
"Bicycles Swings Baseball Cards" *Matrix* No. 15 (Spr-Sum 1982), 70-1.
'The Broken Hole" *Grain* 11:2 (May 1983), 38-42.
"Ghosts" *Matrix* No. 14 (Win 1982), 3-8.
'Thursday Morning Mothers" *Mal R* No. 62 (July 1982), 168-72.

Schreiber, H.E. (1929-)
"The Arlberg Adventure" *Outset* 1973, 136-41.
"White Wail" *Outset* 1974, 140-2.

Schroeder, Andreas (1946-)
THE LATE MAN Vancouver: Sono Nis Press, 1972.
"Breakfast at Minnie's Pit" *Canadian Short Fiction Anthology 2* (1982), 26-39.
"The Cage" *Late Man* (1972), 113-8.
"The Connection" *Late Man* (1972), 53-9.
"The Connection" *Sunlight & Shadows* (1974), 177-82.
"The Connection" *Inquiry into Literature* 3 (1980), 244-9.
"The Freeway" *Late Man* (1972), 61-92.
"The Late Man" *Fourteen Stories High* (1971), 132-40.
"The Late Man" *WCR* 5:3 (Jan 1971), 9-14.
"The Late Man" *Late Man* (1972), 11-21.
"The Late Man" *Tigers of the Snow* (1973), 98-105.
"The Late Man" *West Coast Experience* (1976), 48-57.
"The Late Man" *Not to Be Taken at Night* (1981), 155-64.
"The Meeting" *CFM* Nos. 2/3 (Spr-Sum 1971), 57-62.
"The Meeting" *Late Man* (1972), 93-100.
"The Mill" *72: New Canadian Stories* 96-101.
"One Tide Over" *76: New Canadian Stories* 138-54.
"One Tide Over" *CFM* No. 20 (Win 1976), 90-100.
"One Tide Over" *Magic Realism* (1980), 135-47.
"The Painter" *Late Man* (1972), 33-8.
"The Past People" *Late Man* (1972), 101-5.
"The Pub" *Fid* No. 87 (Nov-Dec 1970), 53-5.
"The Pub" *Late Man* (1972), 29-32.
"The Roller Rink" *Late Man* (1972), 43-52.
"The Roller Rink" *Stories from Pacific & Arctic Canada* (1974), 131-8.
"The Roller Rink" *Transitions 2* (1978), 93-9.
"The Roller Rink" *Great Canadian Sports Stories* (1979), 70-8.
"The Roller Rink" *Fiction of Contemporary Canada* (1980), 75-83.
"The Roller Rink" *Heartland* (1983), 167-74.
"The Theft" *Late Man* (1972), 39-42.
"The Train" *UWR* 6:2 (Spr 1971), 22-6.
"The Train" *Late Man* (1972), 107-12.
"The Tree" *Cave* (N.Z.) No. 1 (Apr 1972), 40-2 [Based on INZP].
"The Tree" *Late Man* (1972), 23-7.

Schroeder, Elizabeth G.‡
"Buffalo and Fish Pie" *Origins* 10:4 (Dec 1980), 14-7.

Schryver, Frank‡
"A Perfect Fit" *Gas Rain* [1] (Mar 1977), 39-40.

Schull, Christiane
"Glass Appetite" *Gamut* No. 3 (May 1983), 59-64.

Schull, Joseph J.
"Bay Rum" *Weekend* 2 (9 Aug 1952), 24.
"Everybody Comes in Handy" *Weekend* 3 (10 Jan 1953), 10-1, 16.
"For 3 Nights Only" *MM* 65 (1 May 1952), 18, 44-8.
"I Am for the Birds" *Weekend* 3 (4 Apr 1953), 38-9.
"The Jinker" *MM* 64 (15 Apr 1951), 20-1, 34-7.
"Last Mission" *Weekend* 5 (3 Sept 1955), 16-7, 32.
"qwertyuiop" *Weekend* 3 (7 Nov 1953), 10-1, 33.

Schutzman, Steve‡
"Momentous Prospects: A Myth" *Titmouse R* No. 7 [n.d.], 40.

Schwartz, Alvin†
"The Girl on the Olive Oil Can" *Current Assets* (1973), 32-47.

Schwartz, Judith†
"The Family" *Prism* 6:3 (Spr 1967), 13-24.
"The Living Quarter" *Potlatch* No. 6 (Mar 1966), 26-35.
"Mr Eugenides' Geometrical Dog Bone" *Potlatch* No. 3 (Nov 1964), 19-25.

Schwartzman, Victor‡
"Visions of Christ in a Wheelchair" *Image Nation* 1:5 (8 May 1969), 8-9.

Schweers, Gordon
"The Assassin" *Boreal* No. 7 (1977), 99-108.

Schweiger, Karol‡
"The Great Mouser of Wright Street" *AA* 69 (Aug 1979), 48-9, 51.

Scobie, Stephen (1943-)
"Deputy Bell" *Aurora* 1978 158-72.
"The Free Man" *SN* 93 (Apr 1978), 36-7, 40-7.
"Gunfight" *Story So Far* 5 (1978), 161.
"Mirror, Alberta" *Wild Rose Country* (1977), 104-14.
"The Philosopher's Stone" *Grain* 1:1 (June 1973), 7-25.
"The Philosopher's Stone" *Other Canadas* (1979), 225-39.
"Postscript" *JCF* 2:2 (Spr 1973), 37-8.
"Streak Mosaic" *Stories from Western Canada* (1972), 158-66.
"Streak Mosaic" *Horizon* (1977), 260-6.
"The White Sky" *CBC "Anthology"* 3 Oct 1970.
"The White Sky" *Fourteen Stories High* (1971), 153-70.

Scott, Anne†
"The Schism" *Forge* 1954, 60-5.

Scott, Chris†
"From the Asylum" *CBC "Anthology"* 15 Jan 1972.

Scott, Gail.
> SPARE PARTS Toronto: Coach House Press, 1981.
> "Climbing the Coiled Oak" *Room* 4:1/2 (1978), 129-43.
> "Climbing the Coiled Oak" *Spare Parts* (1981), 9-25.
> "Elisabeth Rides Again" *JCF* No. 30 (1980), 89-105.
> "Ottawa" *Spare Parts* (1981), 27-38.
> "Petty Thievery" *Spare Parts* (1981), 55-62.
> "Tall Cowboys and True" *Spare Parts* (1981), 47-54.
> "Withdrawal Sym-phonies" *Spare Parts* (1981), 39-46.

Scott, John†
> "At the Birdbath" *CBC "Anthology"* 26 Oct 1968.

Scott, Lynn†
> "Sometimes You Choose[–]Win or Lose" *Alpha* [1:4] (Jan 1977), 3-5.

Scott, Margerie
> "All a Star Should Be" *Brittania and Eve* (U.K.) Oct 1955 [Based on editorial note to "George and the Lonely Hearts"].
> "All My Loves" *CHJ* June 1957, 16, 33-4, 36.
> "Congenial Correspondent" *AA* 50 (Sept 1959), 85, 87, 89-90.
> "George and the Lonely Hearts" *Echoes* No. 221 (Christmas 1955), 5, 13.
> "Grand'mere" *FH* 4 June 1959, 24-5, 27.
> "Love Is for Everyone" *Echoes* No. 226 (Spr 1957), 37-8 [Under "Young Echoes" section; children's?].
> "Mees and L'Amour" *Mont* 31 (Mar 1957), 32, 34, 37.
> "Mme. Petitpas and the German Invaders" *Mont* 30 (June 1956), 42-3.
> "My Belgian Straw Hat" *Mont* 30 (Aug 1956), 58-9 [Non-fiction?].
> "The Prodigal Heart" *CHJ* Mar 1950, 22, 30-2, 46-8.
> "A State of Mind" *Mont* 32 (Jan 1958), 22-3.
> "To Kill a Ghost" *CHJ* Oct 1951, 10, 98-102, 104.

Scott, Moira‡
> "Waiting Up for Santa" *AA* 55 (Dec 1964), 62-4.

Scott, Orme‡
> "The Contract" *CBC [Van] "Hornby Collection"* 27 Jan 1979.

Scream, Jeanine – *See* Mitchell, Jeanine.

Scully, Greg‡
> "A State of Mind" *UTR* 6 (1982), 9-10.

Scupham, Peter‡
> "Symphonies That Sing" *Forge* [24]:1 (Feb 1962), 25-8.

Seajay [pseudonym]
> "Everyman's Uncle Fred" *Alive* [1:10] (Nov 1970), 14-5.

Sealey, Kelvin‡
> "The War" *Scar Fair* 8 (1981), 76-7.

Seaman, Kathleen†

"Happy Landing" *Voices of Kitimat 1967* 121-5.

Seamon, Roger†

[Untitled] *Geo Str Writing* No. 4 (6-13 May 1970), 15.

Sears, Dennis T. Patrick (1925-1976)

"The Bullying Ones" *Ave Maria* 103 (26 Mar 1966), 18-9.
"The Horse Wrangler" *FH* 26 Sept 1968, 45.
"The Swiss Bell Ringers" *SN* 91 (Apr 1976), 56-64.

Sears, Janet†

"The First Snow" *Antig R* No. 50 (Sum 1982), 37-43.

Seaton, Jean Q.†

"Discoveries" *Chel J* 4 (May-June 1978), 129-33.

Seay, Karen‡

"Mene Mene Tekel Upharsin" *New Mitre* No. 1 (1970), 17-9.

Sebastian, John‡

"Localized Peculiarities" *TUR* 82:2 [n.d.], [2 pp].

Seifert, Keith A.†

"Trophies" *Pier Spr* 6:2 (Spr 1981), 43-56.

Sellers, Peter‡

"Somebody Owes Me Money" *Dime Bag* [No. 18] Fiction Issue 1 (Mar 1977), 7-14.

Sellick, Lester (1913-)

"Abegweit Bound" *Island Prose and Poetry* (1973), 172-5.

Selvon, Samuel†

WAYS OF SUNLIGHT London: MacGibbon and Kee, 1957.
"As Time Goes By" *Bim* 3 No. 12 (June 1950), 322-4.
"As Time Goes By" *Caribbean Prose* (1967), 22-7.
"Basement Lullaby" *Ways of Sunlight* (1957), 175-80.
"Basement Lullaby" *New Statesman* 54 (17 Aug 1957), 196-8.
"Behind the Humming Bird" *Bim* 6 No. 23 (Dec 1955), 165-71.
"Brackley and the Bed" *Ways of Sunlight* (1957), 151-5.
"Brackley and the Bed" *West Indian Narrative* (1966), 100-5 [Based on Nasta].
"Brackley and the Bed" *Carray* (1977), 104-8 [Based on Nasta].
"Brackley and the Bed" *West Indian Narrative* (1980), 116-21.
"Brackley and the Bed" CBC "Anthology" 12 July 1980.
"Calypso in London" *Ways of Sunlight* (1957), 125-31.
"Calypso in London" *New Statesman* 53 (5 Jan 1957), 10-1.
"Calypsonian" *Bim* 5 No. 17 (Dec 1952), 40-7 [Also entitled "Song of Sixpence"].
"Calypsonian" *West Indian Stories* (1960), 106-17.
"Calypsonian" *Caribbean Literature: An Anthology* (1966), 72-83 [Based on Nasta].

"Calypsonian" *Four Hemispheres* (1971), 246-55.

"Calypsonian" *Caribbean Rhythms* (1974), 86-98.

"Calypsonian" *Literary Glimpses of the Commonwealth* (1977), 173-88 [Based on Nasta].

"Cane Is Bitter" *Bim* 4 No. 13 (Dec 1950), 59-66.

"Cane Is Bitter" *Caribbean Anthology of Short Stories* (1953), 56-8 [Based on Nasta].

"Cane Is Bitter" *Ways of Sunlight* (1957), 59-73.

"Cane Is Bitter" *London Mag* 5 (Jan 1958), 14-24.

"Cane Is Bitter" *Island Voices* (1965), 84-94.

"Cane Is Bitter" *From the Green Antilles* (1966), 125-37.

"Cane Is Bitter" *J of Caribbean Studies* 2 (1981), 150-60.

"Cane Is Bitter" *Best West Indian Stories* (1982), 117-27 [Based on Nasta].

"Cane Is Bitter" *Tor S Asian R* 1:3 (Fall-Win 1982-83), 1-11.

"Come Back to Grenada" *London Mag* 3 (Sept 1956), 25-32.

"Come Back to Grenada" *Tam R* No. 14 (Win 1960), 15-26.

'The Cricket Match" *Ways of Sunlight* (1957), 161-6.

'The Cricket Match" *Best Sports Stories* (1966), 82-7.

'The Cultivated Carib" *Bim* 7 No. 28 (Jan-June 1959), 224-30 ["An Extract"].

'Down the Main" *Ways of Sunlight* (1957), 38-49.

'Down the Main" *CBC "Anthology"* 28 Apr 1979.

"A Drink of Water" *Ways of Sunlight* (1957), 112-21.

"A Drink of Water" *Inquiry into Literature* 2 (1980), 234-5 [Excerpt].

"A Drink of Water" *Inquiry into Literature* 3 (1980), 271-8.

"Eraser's Dilemma" *Ways of Sunlight* (1957), 146-50.

"Eraser's Dilemma" *Literature of the World* (1963), 347-50 [Based on Nasta].

"Gussy and the Boss" *Bim* 6 No. 22 (June 1955), 68-71.

"Gussy and the Boss" *Ways of Sunlight* (1957), 104-11.

"Gussy and the Boss" *Island Voices* (1965), 78-83.

"Gussy and the Boss" *West Indian Stories* (1981), 58-65.

"Her Achilles Heel" *Words* 10 (1980), 51-4 [Based on Nasta].

"Her Achilles Heel" *Ambit* 91 (1982), 4-8 [Based on Nasta].

"Holiday in Five Rivers" *Ways of Sunlight* (1957), 50-8.

'If Winter Comes" *Ways of Sunlight* (1957), 156-60.

'Johnson and the Cascadura" *Ways of Sunlight* (1957), 11-37.

'Knock on Wood" *Evergreen R* 3:9 (Sum 1959), 25-33.

'Knock on Wood" *West Indian Stories* (1960), 88-97.

'The Little Men" *Bim* 6 No. 21 (Dec 1954), 56-8.

'Man, in England, You've Just Got to Love Animals" *Island Voices* (1965), 70-4.

'The Mango Tree" *Ways of Sunlight* (1957), 94-103.

'My Girl and the City" *Ways of Sunlight* (1957), 181-8.

'My Girl and the City" *Bim* 7 No. 25 (July-Dec 1957), 2-6.

'My Girl and the City" *West Indian Stories* (1960), 98-105.

'My Girl and the City" *From the Green Antilles* (1966), 138-44.

'My Girl and the City" *Caliban* 11:1 (1976), 35-41 [Based on AHI].

'My Girl and the City" *Best West Indian Stories* (1982), 180-5 [Based on Nasta].

"Obeah in the Grove" *Ways of Sunlight* (1957), 167-74.

"Obeah in the Grove" *Minority Experience* (1978), 114-21 [Based on Nasta].

"Obeah in the Grove" *This Island Place* (1981), 76-82.

"Ralphie at the Races" *CBC [Edm] "Alberta Anthology"* 23 Oct 1980.

"Song of Sixpence" *London Mag* 7 (Aug 1960), 35-44 [Also entitled "Calypsonian"].

"Talk" *Bim* 4 No. 15 (Dec 1951), 151-3.

[Title unknown] *Caribbean Narrative* (1966), 225-34 [Based on Nasta].

"The Village Washer" *New World Writing* 2 (1952), 125-30.

"The Village Washer" *Ways of Sunlight* (1957), 74-81.

"The Village Washer" *Sun's Eye* (1968), 52-9 [Based on Nasta].

"Waiting for Aunty to Cough" *Ways of Sunlight* (1957), 139-45.

"Waiting for Aunty to Cough" *West Indian Stories* (1960), 118-24.

"Waiting for Aunty to Cough" CBC "Anthology" 30 Aug 1980.

"Wartime Activities" *Ways of Sunlight* (1957), 82-93.

"When Greek Meets Greek" *Island Voices* (1965), 75-7.

"Working the Transport" *Ways of Sunlight* (1957), 132-8.

"Zeppi's Machine" CBC "Anthology" 26 Apr 1980.

Sengmueller, Fred‡
"Pompadex" *Gram* 1980-81, 17-8.

Senzer, David‡
"Fifteen Cents" *Quarry* 20:4 (1971), 25-31.

Serwylo, Ray†
"Baba" *Pier Spr* 6:2 (Spr 1981), 15-8.

Sessford, Ken‡
"Rannulf Robertson" *Skylark* 4:2 [date unknown], 37 [Based on index].

Setkowicz, Libby‡
"Bus Trapping in Ottawa" *Lunatic Gazette* Ser 2 1:2 (Nov-Dec 1982), 8.

Setton, Ruth Knafo
"Travelling" *JCF* No. 30 (1980), 37-44.

Sewell, John (1940-)
"Letter" *Acta Vic* 85:2 (Jan 1961), 11-2.

"Running Along" *Varsity Lit Issue* Fri, 13 Dec 1963, 9, 11.

"Story" *Acta Vic* 89:1 [1964], 5-11.

Sexton, J.D.†
"The Death of Justin Thatcher" *Laom R* 3:1 (Mar 1977), 13-5.

Sexton, Siobhan†
"Running Out of Breath" *WWR* 2:3 No. 7 (1982), 75-6.

Shainblum, Mark (1963-)
"Pharma" *Orion* No. 1 (Sum 1981), 33-5.

Shannon, Norman‡
"The Spectator" *Legion* 36 (Nov 1961), 8-9, 32.

Shannon, William G.‡
"Three Fish" *Folio* 14:2 (Spr 1962), 39-41.

Shantz, Brenda‡
"The Book Maker" *Muskeg R* 4 [1976], 46-7.
"Habeus Corpus" *Muskeg R* 4 [1976], 8-11.

Shapiro, David†
"The Closet" *Writ* No. 7 (Fall 1975), 81-94.
"The Competitor" *Writ* No. 6 (Fall 1974), 5-24.
"Ron" *Writ* No. 4 (Spr 1972), 12-21.

Shapiro, Frederic‡
"The Kilmarnovian Revolution" *Reflections* 1964, 77-82.

Sharara, Yacoub (1923-)
"The Patriot" *Outset* 1974, 143-9.

Sharma, D.T.‡
"Lawbreaker" *New Bodies* (1981), 147-50.

Sharman, Vincent (1928-)†
"Any Game You Want" *Prism* 2:2 (Win 1961), 54-75.
"Before the Sun Goes Down" *Tam R* No. 12 (Sum 1959), 57-71.

Sharp, Daryl‡
"The Flying Saucers Have Taken Off" *Can Fandom* No. 23 (Dec 1954), 9-13.

Sharp, Dorothy‡
"Raindrops Kept Falling on Their Heads" *Can Skater* 2 (Nov-Dec 1975), 1-3
[Fictionalized true story?].

Sharp, Edith Lambert†
"Strong Fences" *Stories with John Drainie* (1963), 71-5.

Sharp, [Mrs.] Bryce‡
"Margaret MacWilliams" *Abegweit R* 3:1 (Spr 1980), 19-23.

Sharpe, David (1951-)
"The Bikers" *CFM* No. 39 (1981), 81-6.
"In Another Light" *Prism* 17:2 (Fall 1978), 121-5.
"Niagara Fall" *CFM* Nos. 30/31 (1979), 165-77.
"Niagara Fall" *Illusion One* (1983), 37-51.
"Northern Light" *CFM* Nos. 24/25 (Spr-Sum 1977), 11-9.
"Overnight" *event* 10:1 (1981), 101-6.
"The Reincarnation Pool" *CA & B* 59:1 (Fall 1983), 17-9.
"The Semi-Omnipotent Engine" *CFM* Nos. 45/46 (1982-83), 162-72.
"Shadow Box" *New Q* 2:4 (Win 1983), 15-28.
"Stopped" *Tam R* No. 79 (Aut 1979), 61-6.
"Valley of the Shadow" *CFM* No. 43 (1982), 115-24.
"Valley of the Shadow" *Metavisions* (1983), 161-71.

Shaw, Hugh‡
"One Master" *Undergrad* Mar 1950, 6-8.

Shaw, Irene†
"Dear Earth" *Echoes* No. 224 (Aut 1956), 44-5.

Shaw, Joan Fern
"Asparagus" *Waves* 10:3 (Win 1982), 16-23.
"Cemetery" *New Q* 2:3 (Fall 1982), 13-7.
"Elah" *Grain* 10:2 (May 1982), 43-8.
"Men in My Life" *Read Ch* 1:2 (Sum 1982), 8-15.
"The Outhouse" *Fid* No. 122 (Sum 1979), 47-52.
"Raspberry Vinegar" *QQ* 90 (1983), 397-405.
"Red Sequins on Markham Street" *Matrix* No. 16 (Spr 1983), 2-10.
"Transfer" *Prism* 21:3 (Apr 1983), 58-61.

Shaw, Paul G.‡
"The Drummer" *Ventilator* 2:3 (Jan 1967), 8-12.
"Spring" *Ventilator* 3:2 (Dec 1967), 2-5.

Shaw, Stewart‡
"The Shipwreck" *Fruits of Experience* (1978), 113-21.

Shaw, Stuart†
"Montreal Receives Solly Krakowitz" *Alphabet* No. [11] (Dec-Mar 1965-66), 8-16.

Shea, Dorothy J.‡
"Josef and the Jellybean" *West People* No. 132 (8 Apr 1982), 7.

Sheard, Sarah
"Baby Face" *Writing* No. 1 (Sum 1980), 23.
"Closet-Play" *Per* No. 4 (Fall 1978), 9-14.
"The Conductor" *This* 15 (July-Aug 1981), 25-6.
"Fear Continued" *Writing* No. 2 (Win 1980-81), 19.
"Grande Prairie" *Per* Nos. 7/8 (Win 1981), 96-101.
"I Just Heard from Helen Again" *Per* No. 5 (Spr 1979), 19-20.

Sheils, Terry‡
"Analytica Number Two" *Acta Vic* 79:[2] (Dec 1954), 22-4.
" 'Encore' " *Acta Vic* 79:3 (Feb 1955), 23-4.
"The Gyroscope" *Acta Vic* 79:1 (Nov 1954), 21-2.
"Traffic" *Acta Vic* 78:2 (Dec 1953), 20-2.
"Two for the Money" *Acta Vic* 80:2 (Dec 1955), 8-13.

Shein, Brian
"Cowboy" *UC Gargoyle* [15] (Spr 1969), 14-8.
"Cowboy" CBC *"Anthology"* 15 Nov 1969.
"The Littlest Rubby" *Pulp* 2:19 (1 Jan 1975), [3 pp].
"The Obelisk" *Prism* 8:1 (Sum 1968), 100-2.
"On Being Mental" *CF* 60 (Apr 1981), 41-2.
"Rex Morgan, M.D." *Prism* 10:3 (Spr 1971), 29-30.
"The Special" by B. Sheinsky *Pulp* 3:1 (1 June 1975), [1-3] [Same author?].
"The Tower" *Antig R* No. 9 (Spr 1972), 59-66.
"Will You Go Hunt, My Lord?" *Prism* 7:2 (Aut 1967), 72-80.

Sheldon, Michael (1918-)

"A Campaign for Mr. Arrowman" *QQ* 67 (1960), 462-70.

"Chance Meeting" *Chat* 29 (Feb 1957), 19, 54-8.

"Delegate's Outing" *Weekend* 4 (28 Aug 1954), 30.

"The Flirtatious Phantom of Montreal" *MM* 68 (1 Feb 1955), 22-3, 30-1, 35-8.

"The Magic Brain of Sigismund Gantzoff" *MM* 69 (26 May 1956), 18-9, 47-52.

"Solution: Rob a Bank" *MM* 67 (1 Sept 1954), 12-3, 40-2.

"The Spirit of the Bank of Lower Canada" *MM* 68 (3 Sept 1955), 14-5, 39-40, 42-3.

"These Are the Bonnie Babes of the Bank of Lower Canada" *MM* 70 (21 Dec 1957), 22-3, 41-4.

"The Two Millionth Customer of the Bank of Lower Canada" *MM* 66 (1 Sept 1953), 18-9, 55-8.

Shepanski C[arl]. L.‡

"Ah Love! Ah Fraternity Life" *Probe* 3:1 (Nov 1961), 38-9.

"Rocky and the Philosopher" *Probe* 3:2 (Apr 1962), 35-7.

Shepherd, Harvey L.‡

"God Works in a Mysterious Way" *Varsity* Fri, 18 Mar 1960, 7, 10.

"Incident in the Place d'Armes" *Undergrad* Aut 1958, 5-7.

Shepherd, Helen†

"The Last Rose" *Contact* 2:11 (Fall 1973), 4-5.

Shepherd, R.W.‡

"Celina" *Varsity Lit Issue* Fri, 1 Feb 1952, 1, 7.

"Five Cents" *Varsity Lit Issue* Mon, 5 Mar 1951, 6, 8.

"Harold Winters" *Varsity Lit Issue* Mon, 5 Mar 1951, 1-2, 7-8.

"Shell Out" *Varsity Lit Issue* Fri, 1 Feb 1952, 5.

Sheppard, John‡

"The Dreamer" *WWR* 1:2 (Win 1977), 61-5.

Sheps, David

"I Found a Thing to Do" *Creative Campus* 1958, 24-6.

Sherman, Elizabeth

"The River" *Saskatchewan Writing* 2 (1963), 25-33.

Sherman, Joseph (1945-)

"Form Notes Toward a Jewish Poem" *JD* Rosh Hashanah 1972, 8-11, 14-7.

Sherman, Kenneth (1950-)

THE COST OF LIVING Oakville: Mosaic Press/Valley Editions, 1981.

"Achziv" *Waves* 1:2 (Aut 1972), 3-6.

"The Cost of Living" *Cost of Living* (1981), 23-4.

"History" *JD* Passover 1977, 52-3.

"Not a Word" *Waves* 2:1 (Aut 1973), 76-7.

"Soberman's Release" *Waves* 5:2/3 (Spr 1977), 40-5.

Sherman, Tom‡

3 DEATH STORIES Toronto: Art Metropole, 1977.

ANIMAL MAGNETISM OPT 4:10 (Jan 1978) [Issue as story collection [?]].

"Detroit Poison" *3 Death Stories* (1977), [4 pp].

"The End of the Spiral" *3 Death Stories* (1977), [12 pp].

"How to Watch Television" *Imp* 8:4 (Fall-Win 1980), 46-50.

"Is Scientific Thought Outrunning Common Sense" *OPT* 4:7 (Oct 1977), 14.

"The Kitchen Window View" *OPT* 4:10 (Jan 1978), 6-7.

"The Monitor, in the Voice of I" *OPT* 4:10 (Jan 1978), 8-11.

"Once Living in a Healthy State of Paranoia" *Imp* 8:1 (Fall 1979), 20-1.

"Red and Green Make Brown" 3 Death Stories (1977), [9 pp].

"A Representational Approach" *OPT* 4:10 (Jan 1978), 4-5.

"A Statement from Inside the Cultural Industrial Compound" *Imp* 9:2 (Fall 1981), 7-9.

"TBDF: Transborder Data Flow" *Imp* 10:1 (Sum 1982), 25-7 [Non-fiction?].

"They Introduced Me to My Homunculus" *OPT* 4:7 (Oct 1977), 15.

Sherrin, Robert G. (1951-)

"Best Falling Dead" *Prism* 17:2 (Fall 1978), 127-31.

"The Complete Field Commander" *CFM* No. 7 (Sum 1972), 4-7.

"Dream Three Hundred" *Cap R* No. 13 (1978), 8-12.

"Expresso" *CFM* No. 1 (Win 1971), 10-1.

"Forced Out" *Cap R* No. 13 (1978), 13-7.

"Incidents on a Trolley That Didn't Make the Newspapers the Following Day" *CFM* No. 1 (Win 1971), 11-2.

"Inside Passage" *Cap R* No. 18 (1980), 93-9.

"Intersection" *CFM* No. 4 (Aut 1971), 41-2.

"Man in the Black Magic Box" *Des* 14:5 No. 43 (Win 1983-84), 106-14.

"North by North by North" *Cap R* No. 18 (1980), 83-92.

"Schadenfroh" *Cap R* Nos. 8/9 (Fall-Spr 1975-76), 26-35.

"This Boy in His Narrow Bed" *Cap R* No. 18 (1980), 100-14.

Sherwood, Roland H.

"The 'First Christmas' " *Bluenose Mag* 2:3 (Win 1977-78), 8-12 [Non-fiction?].

Shewchun, Joan†

"The Perfect Couple" *Selections from the C.F.U.W. Writing Project* 1978-79 13-7.

Shiach, Allan‡

"Jean-Marc" *Forge* 23:1 (Win 1960), 30-5.

"The Watcher" *Forge* 23:2 (Dec 1961), 68-73.

Shields, Bill (1907-)

"The Actress and the Bishop" *FH* 24 Feb 1955, 22-4 [Same author?].

"The Crooked Knife" *FH* 8 Apr 1954, 28-30, 36.

Shields, Carol (1935-)†

"Accidents" *Mal R* No. 65 (July 1983), 105-11.

"Dolls, Dolls, Dolls, Dolls" *Aurora* 1980 16-29.

"Fragility" *SN* 98 (Apr 1983), 52-6.

Shields, Roy

"The Coyote Hunter" *FH* 21 Jan 1954, 24.

"The Man Who Loved a Pig" *FH* 5 July 1956, 18-9.

"The Man Who Loved a Pig" *Stories to Read Again* (1965), 119-30.

Shier, James‡

"The Quick" *Alive* 3:1 [1972?], 18.

Shifrin, Len

"A Tale of Two Chalahs" *Jargon* [No. 5] (1962-63), 35-6.

Shilvock, Margaret‡

"A Gentle Shove" *West People* No. 201 (1 Sept 1983), 15.

Shipley, Nan

"Beacon on the Beach" *Weekend* 4 (29 May 1954), 10-1, 46, 53.

"Border Bride" *SW* 25 Oct 1952, I:3.

"Captain of the Comet" *SW* 17 Oct 1953, I:3.

"Johnny Swanson's Debt" *SW* 17 Mar 1951, II:1, 4.

"Key to the House" *SW* 29 Apr 1950, I:3-4.

"The Lighted Windows" *SW* 27 Jan 1951, I:11.

"Linda's Brush with the Lake" *SW* 30 Sept 1950, II:3, 5.

"No Room for Debby" *Onward* 19 Dec 1954, 801-3, 805-6, 814-5.

"Rescue at Niska Bay" *Weekend* 2 (13 Dec 1952), 20-1.

"A Rifle for Big Boy" *SW* 20 Sept 1952, II:5.

"The Shop Whistle" *Onward* 4 July 1954, 420-2.

Shipman, Warde‡

"A Birthday Party" *Missionary Monthly* 25 (Nov 1950), 506-7.

Shirinian, Lorne (1945-)

THE KEY AND OTHER STORIES St. Jean, P.Q.: Manna, 1977.

"Armen Khatchian" *Key* (1977), 26-31.

"Arrival" *Key* (1977), 1-5.

"The Artist" *Key* (1977), 43-7.

"The Group" *Key* (1977), 32-5.

"Kevork at Geghart" *Key* (1977), 13-7.

"The Key" *Key* (1977), 52-6.

"Mother Armenia on the Statue to Victory and the Tour-Guide in the Matenadaron" *Key* (1977), 6-10.

"Radio Yerevan" *Key* (1977), 48-51.

"Soccer and Poetry" *Key* (1977), 40-2.

"Tavlu on Aragats" *Key* (1977), 18-25.

"When an Elephant Escapes" *Key* (1977), 11-2.

"Working the Walkways of Shahumian Street or The Oldest Profession in Armenia" *Key* (1977), 36-9.

Shirley, John‡

"Modern Transmutations of the Alchemist" *Story So Far* 5 (1978), 163-8.

Shook, Karen‡

[Untitled] *UCR* 1981-82, 39-40.

Shore, Lulu M.†
"The Old Injun Grave" *Echoes* No. 233 (Christmas 1958), 4, 25.
"Party Line" *Echoes* No. 224 (Aut 1956), 9, 25.

Shore, Michael M.J.
O CANADA, CANADA: SHORT STORIES Sherbrooke: Éditions Naaman, 1983.
"Caution: Causes Drowsiness and Dulls the Senses" *O Canada, Canada* (1983), 43-8.
"*Die welt von Gestern*" *O Canada, Canada* (1983), 49-54.
"Like After the Flood" *O Canada, Canada* (1983), 69-75.
"O Canada, Canada" *O Canada, Canada* (1983), 55-62.
"Please Papa, Take Us Home" *O Canada, Canada* (1983), 27-41.
"Running a Marathon, Climbing a Mountain" *O Canada, Canada* (1983), 63-7.

Shore, Mitch‡
"The Arab Market" *Images* 1:3 (Feb 1980), 6.
"The Arab Market" *Exist re* 1:1 (Oct 1980), 6.
"When I Was Seven"*Images* Oct 1982, 7.

Short, Leslie‡
"The Microscope" *Either/Or* No. 11 (Spr-Sum 1971), [1 p].

Showell, Rob‡
"The White Cadillac" *Dime Bag* [No. 18] Fiction Issue 1 (Mar 1977), 17-21.

Shrier, Howard
"I for an Eye" *Saturday Night at the Forum* (1981), 81-94.

Shtogryn, David†
"Another Morning" *Read Ch* 2:1 (Spr 1983), 58-63.

Shubik, Irene‡
"The Nightmare" *Undergrad* Mar 1950, 24-5.

Shulman, Guy†
"Time and Time Again" *JCF* No. 21 (1977-78), 61-72.

Shulman, Martin‡
"The Things I Did Last Summer" *New Breed* 14 (July 1983), 8.

Shuster, Schoel‡
"Old Story Revised" *Forge* 1967, 53.

Sibum, Norm‡
"The Real Tennessee Waltz" *Lit Storefront News* No. 21 (Feb 1980), 5-8.

Sidran, Maxine (1943?-)†
"The Best Horn Player in the World" *Title Unknown* (1975), 11.

Siebrasse, Glen
"Minutes from a Malingerer's Diary" *CF* 44 (Nov 1964), 185-6.

Siegal, Lois†
"The Nose" *NJ* Nos. 7/8 (1976), 91-2.

Sifton, John‡
"Burning Bright" *Quarry* 21:4 (Aut 1972), 44-9.

Sigal, Mark‡
"A Ring Thru His Nose" *Bakka* No. 6 (Fall 1977), 51-4.

Siggins, Marjorie‡
"I Don't Know What I'm Doing Here" *Fifth Page* 1964, 9-10.

Sigurdson, Helen†
"Pioneer Mother" *Ice Can* 12:1 (Aut 1953), 29-31, 54-5.

Sigurdson, Paul A. (1927-)
"Battle" *JCF* No. 23 (1979), 33-43.
"Battle" *Ice Can* 38:3 (Spr 1980), 7-14.
"The Image" *Ice Can* 27:2 (Win 1968), 34-6.
"Obverse" *Ice Can* [33:2] (Win 1974), 55-8. 60, 62.
"The Rolling-Pin Rodeo" *Pier Spr* 6:4 (Aut 1981), 46-54.
"Sawdust" *Ice Can* 36:4 (Sum 1978), 15-7.
"Shall I Compare Thee" *NeWest R* 2:10 (June 1977), 6-7.

Sigurgeirson, W.J.†
"The Arrowhead" *Prism* 2:1 (Fall 1960), 23-31.

Silarajs, Juris‡
"Mutti, Mutti" *TUR* 83:1 (Fall 1969), 18-9.

Sileika, Antanas
"The Silencing" *Antig R* No. 47 (Aut 1981), 31-3.

Silver, Isaac‡
"Army Flynn's Great Idea" *Undergrad* Spr 1963, 1-4.
"Melvyn Hondrich's Night Visitor" *Undergrad* Spr 1963, 30-4.

Silverwind, J.‡
"Jesus" *Industrial Sabotage* No. 14 [Mar 1983], [1 p].

Silvester, Reg (1945-)
"Berserk in a Waterbed" *Dand* 6 [n.d.], 63-5.
"Fish-Hooks" *Sundogs* (1980), 120-3.
"The Girl Who Stood Out from the Crowd" *Fid* No. 115 (Fall 1977), 12-4.
"I Love You, I Love You, I Do" *Fid* No. 115 (Fall 1977), 10-1.
"The Magnificent Coloured Dildo" *Fid* No. 115 (Fall 1977), 7-9.
"New West Testament" *Freelance* 8:5 (May 1977), 20-4.
"The Real Harry" *Fid* No. 135 (Jan 1983), 69-73.
"The Real Harry" *CBC* [Edm] "Alberta Anthology" 27 Aug 1983.

Simas, Richard†
"Joaquin Murietta Slept Here" *Prism* 20:4 (Sum 1982), 49-58.
"Joaquin Murietta Slept Here" *Metavisions* (1983), 207-16.

Simmer, Ron‡

"She Locked the Door" *Potlatch* No. 2 (Apr 1964), 19-28.

Simmie, Lois (1932-)

GHOST HOUSE Moose Jaw: Coteau Books, 1976.

"The Chair by the Window" *Ghost House* (1976), 49-54.

"Cobwebs and Eleanor" *NeWest R* 4 (Sept 1978), 8-9.

"Emily" *Smoke Signals* 3 (1978) [Based on *SWG* survey response].

"Emily" *Sundogs* (1980), 124-30.

"Emily" *Canadian Short Fiction Anthology* 2 (1982), 66-71.

"Ghost House" *Ghost House* (1976), 7-17.

"Ghost House" *Smoke Signals* 2 [date unknown] [Based on *SWG* survey response].

"Margaret Has a Real Mean Laugh" *Ghost House* (1976), 19-25.

"Margaret Has a Real Mean Laugh" *Inquiry into Literature* 1 (1980), 61-7.

"Margaret Has a Real Mean Laugh" *100% Cracked Wheat* (1983), 4-11.

"Red Shoes" *Saskatchewan Gold* (1982), 38-50.

"Romantic Fever" *Grain* 7:3 [1979], 18-25.

"Romantic Fever" *Best of Grain* (1980), 170-7.

"A Shortage of Mourners" *Smoke Signals* (1974), 1-7.

"A Shortage of Mourners" *Ghost House* (1976), 31-8.

"The Wedding Guest" *Ghost House* (1976), 41-5.

Simmons, David R.‡

"One Day in the Editor's Office" *Van Streets* 1:1 (Spr 1982), [3 pp].

Simmons, Margaret†

"The Appraiser" *Pres Record* 98 (Oct 1974), 10-1.

Simons, Beverley (1938-)

"The Beauty" *Blewointmentpress* 9:1 (June 1967), [9 pp].

Simpson, Doug‡

"Kensington Rabbit" *Gram* 5 [1979-80], 3-7.

"Pigs" *Gram* 5 [1979-80], 20-4.

Simpson, Gregg†

"Arabesque" *Lodgistiks* No. 1 (Oct 1972), 19-20.

"The Road Back" *Lodgistiks* 1:3 (Jan 1975), [7 pp].

Simpson, Leo (1934-)

THE LADY AND THE TRAVELLING SALESMAN Ed. Henry Imbleau Ottawa: Univ.
of Ottawa Press, 1976.

"The Barren Land" *CBC "Anthology"* 25 Aug 1966.

"The Cahershannon Heresy" *Lady and the Travelling Salesman* (1976), 103-8.

"The Case of the Friendly Teller" *Mont* 35 (Nov 1961), 55-7.

"The Ferris Wheel" *72: New Canadian Stories* 9-29.

"The Ferris Wheel" *Lady and the Travelling Salesman* (1976), 45-65.

"The Ivy-Covered Manner" *Lady and the Travelling Salesman* (1976), 117-27.

"Just a Few Minor Changes" *Mont* 36 (June 1962), 19-20.

"The Lady and the Travelling Salesman" *75: New Canadian Stories* 9-41.

"The Lady and the Travelling Salesman" *Lady and the Travelling Salesman* (1976), 1-29.

"The Lady and the Travelling Salesman" *Best Modern Canadian Short Stories* (1978), 144-65.

"Night and Morning Wounds" *Lady and the Travelling Salesman* (1976), 31-43.

"Recipe for a Rebel" *Lady and the Travelling Salesman* (1976), 67-72.

"The Savages" *73: New Canadian Stories* 144-73.

"The Savages" *Lady and the Travelling Salesman* (1976), 73-101.

"The Savages" *Canadian Literature in the 70's* (1980), 39-65.

"A Single to El Paso" CBC "*Anthology*" 9 Feb 1962.

"A Single to El Paso" *Lady and the Travelling Salesman* (1976), 109-16.

"A Summer Girl" CBC "*Anthology*" 17 Dec 1977.

"The Viking Professor Strikes Back" *Mont* 36 (Mar 1962), 36-7.

"The West Door" *Small Wonders* (1982), 109-23.

Simpson, Robert N.†

"Gloria, Ray, and Tammy" *Pier Spr* 8:4 (Aut 1983), 41-7.

"Gold and Age" *Mam* 6:4 (Win 1983-84), [5 pp].

Simpson, S. J.‡

"The Drag Scene" *20 Cents* 3:1/2 (Apr 1969), [3 pp].

Simpson, Valerie†

"There'll Never Be Another You" *Outset* 1974, 150-4.

Sims, Burt

"Benefit of Doubt" *MM* 64 (1 May 1951), 12-3, 34-5, 37-8.

"Let's Marry for Your Money" *MM* 63 (1 Nov 1950), 10-1, 35-6, 38-9.

Simser, Guy‡

"Fate Has a Concave Face" *AA* 61 (Sept 1970), 54-9, 61-2, 64.

Sinclair, G.B.†

"The Sun-Cot" *Writing* No. 1 (Sum 1980), 11-4.

Sinclair, Gerri (1948-)

"The Hoist" *Room* 7:4 (1982), 15-22.

"The Hoist" *Metavisions* (1983), 47-52.

Sinclair, Kathryn (1940-)

"The Golden Dragon" *Rubaboo* 2 (1963) [Based on editorial note to "The Long Wind" in *West of Fiction*].

"The Long Wind" *Isaac Asimov's Science Fiction Mag* 6 (June 1982), 41-50.

"The Long Wind" *West of Fiction* (1983), 25-35.

Sinclair, Michael P.‡

"The Keep" *Raven* No. 9 (Nov 1960), 9-13.

Sing, Gerri‡

"Christmas Eve" *Eclipse* No. 4 (1977), 7.

Singer, Barnett

"Aunt Zelda's Marriage" *Viewpoints* [12:1] (Sum 1981), 44-50.
"Cleaning Ladies and Asthma, Bedwetting and Money: From a (Proustian?) Memoirs of a Toronto Bourgeois" *JD* Sum 1981, 40-4.
"Datona's Complaint(s)" *JD* Sum 1982, 28-34, 36, 38, 40, 42, 44.
"A Game for Experts" *Quarry* 23:2 (Spr 1974), 36-9.
"To Each His Own Saviour" *JD* Hanukah 1979, 31-4.

Singer, R.S.‡

"Gone with the Winding Sheet" *Scar Fair* 6 (1979), 35-8.

Singleton, Norman M.‡

"A Shortage of Christmas" *Images About Manitoba* 1:3 (Fall-Win 1976), 26-9.

Sirluck, K.‡

"Prose Piece" *UCR* Spr 1975, 37.

Sirluck, Lesley†

"Sacred Heart" *CF* 35 (Jan 1956), 225-7.

Sister Thomas – *See* Thomas, Sister.

Sivertson, L. Margaret

"Timothy" *Alberta Writers Speak* 1960, 33-5.

Siwiec, Peter John†

"The Eve of St. Agnes" *Don't Steal This Book* (1974), 91-3.

Skelton, Robin (1925-)

"A Case of Conformity" *Des* 11:4/12:1 Nos. 30/31 (1980-81), 62-8.
"The Illusion" *Rainshadow* (1982), 191-8.
"The Man Who Sang in His Sleep" *CFM* No. 39 (1981), 10-6.
"A Matter of Vision" *Was R* 15:2 (Fall 1980), 36-41.
"Paper Boy" *Antioch R* 38 (1980), 474-8.
"Portrait of Duck" *Mal R* No. 50 (Apr 1979), 88-94.

Skeoch, Alan‡

"Full Circle" *Forum* (OSSTF) 9 (Feb-Mar 1983), 23, 26.
"What About Wounded Ducks, Dad?" *Forum* (OSSTF) 7 (Oct-Nov 1981), 157 [Dialogue].

Skey, Olga

"Cups of Coffee" *Undergrad* Spr 1952, 12-4.
"Dishonesty" *Undergrad* Aut 1951, 19-22.
"Journey by Underground" *Tam R* No. 27 (Spr 1963), 37-43.
"The New Bug" *Alphabet* No. 9 (Nov 1964), 19-24.
"The Wallet" *Undergrad* Aut-Win 1952, 17-20.

Skey, Patricia†

"The Secret Lust of a Mansewife" *UC Observer* Jan 1978, 29-30.

Skilbeck, William‡

"The Call" *Generation* Spr 1968, 9.

Skinner, Norman "Doc" (1912-)
STORY TELLER AND CERTIFIED LIAR Cobalt: Highway Book Shop, 1976.
"Caramat Train Wreck" *Story Teller* (1976), 71-2.
'The Dam Builders" *Story Teller* (1976), 63-4.
"A Dependable Guide" *Story Teller* (1976), 5-6.
"Eggflation" *Story Teller* (1976), 29-30.
"Election News from the Pagwa Outhouse Sentinel" *Story Teller* (1976), 13-4.
"Emergency Street Lighting" *Story Teller* (1976), 21-2.
"Father's Day Gift" *Story Teller* (1976), 69-70.
"Gold Medals and Holy Night" *Story Teller* (1976), 7-9.
'The Hound Magee" *Story Teller* (1976), 1-3.
"How to Grow Hair on a Pumpkin" *Story Teller* (1976), 27-8.
"Ice Fishing" *Story Teller* (1976), 75-6.
"An Ice Folly" *Squatch J* No. 13 (June 1982), 46-7.
"Meat Inspection" *Story Teller* (1976), 73-4.
"Metric" *Story Teller* (1976), 18-20.
"Moose Watch?????" *Story Teller* (1976), 47-8.
"Nellie" *Story Teller* (1976), 65-6.
"News from the Pagwa Outhouse Sentinel" *Story Teller* (1976), 14-5.
"Snowmobiling" *Story Teller* (1976), 41.
"Television" *Story Teller* (1976), 49-50.
"Turnabout" *Story Teller* (1976), 51-2.
"Welfare" *Story Teller* (1976), 67-8.
"We're Forever Blowing Bubbles" *Story Teller* (1976), 26.
"Whereinhellzamoose?????" *Story Teller* (1976), 23-5.

Sky, Steven†
"Skip's Blue Ink" *NJ* Nos. 7/8 (1976), 86-8.

Slabotsky, David (1943-)
'The Angel of Death" *JD* Sum 1975, 73.
'The Angel of Death" *JD* Hanukah 1983, 23.
"At the Bottom of a River" *JD* Sum 1975, 72-3.
"At the Bottom of a River" *JD* Hanukah 1983, 25-7.
'The Betrayal" *JD* Hanukah 1983, 8.
'The Carp" *JD* Hanukah 1983, 4.
'The Death of Rabbi Yoseph" *Can R* 1:4 (Nov-Dec 1974), 8-10.
'The Death of Rabbi Yoseph" *JD* Hanukah 1983, 33-7.
"Go to Sleep" *JD* Sum 1975, 73.
"Haayim Gold" *JD* Rosh Hashanah 1980, 30-2.
"Hershel Dov" *JD* Rosh Hashanah 1980, 48-9.
'In the Time of Two Letters" *JD* Sum 1975, 72.
'In the Time of Two Letters" *JD* Hanukah 1983, 24.
'The Killing of Haayim Gold" *CBC [Van] "Hornby Collection"* 31 Mar 1979.
'The Killing of Haayim Gold" *CBC [Van] "Hornby Collection"* 10 Oct 1981.
'The Marvellous Prayer Shawl" *JD* Sum 1975, 73.
'The Marvellous Prayer Shawl" *JD* Hanukah 1983, 20.
'The Mind of Genesis" *JD* Sum 1975, 74.
'The Mind of Genesis" *JD* Hanukah 1983, 31-2.
'The Mouse and the Fish" *JD* Hanukah 1983, 6.
"A Pair of Tigers" *JD* Hanukah 1983, 5.

"The Pear Forest" *JD* Hanukah 1983, 7.
"The Solution" *JD* Sum 1975, 73.
"The Solution" *JD* Hanukah 1983, 22.
"The Wandering Jew" *JD* Sum 1975, 73-4.
"The Wandering Jew" *JD* Hanukah 1983, 28-30.
"Weeds and Wild Grass" *JD* Hanukah 1980, 22-3 [Also on CBC (editorial note)].

Slade, Charles‡
"Country Music Singer" *Origins* 8:3 (Sept 1978), 22-4.

Slade, Mark‡
"The Drop" *Roothog* (1981), 73-86.
"Samples of Dandelion wine" *Repos* No. 26 (Sum 1979), 6-17.

Sladek, Robert‡
"Black Snow" *Twig* 1977, [3 pp].

Sladen, Kathleen (1904-)
"The Crystal Wall" *Onward* 25 Dec 1966, 6-7.

Slater, Ian (1941-)
"The High Board" *CBC* 1970 [Based on survey response].
"The Hunt" *CBC* 1970 [Based on survey response].

Slater, Keith‡
"A Time to Be Born" *Nw J* No. 26 (1982), 61-7.

Slaughter, R.W [Bill]
"The Primary Cause" *Can Wings* 18 (Dec 1976), 16-8.

Slepokura, Orest‡
"Up at the Hospital" *Thumbprints* No. 2 (Spr 1975), [3 pp].

Sloan, Doug†
"But Not in Anger ... " *Antig R* No. 50 (Sum 1982), 65-74.

Sloman, Fred
"The Keys to the Car" *MM* 66 (1 July 1953), 18, 47-9.
"Petruchio" *SW* 8 Jan 1955, I:4.
"Silver Fish" *Echoes* No. 198 (Spr 1950), 17, 28, 41.
"Take Me Home Again, Irene" *MM* 68 (17 Sept 1955), 32-3, 74-9.

Slonkowitz, Richard‡
"Meeting Burroughs Half-Way" *Alive* 3:5 No. 24 [1972], 5-6.

Slote, D.C.‡
"Death of the Moth" *Folio* 5:1 [Jan 1951], [4 pp].
"Exit" *Folio* 4:2 [Apr 1950], [3 pp].
"Impressionable" *Folio* 4:1 [Jan 1950], [3 pp].
"Lake of Glass" *Folio* 5:2 (Apr 1951), [3 pp].

Smale, Kenneth
"Rise and Fall of the Tiger's Paw Judo Club" *JCF* 3:1 (Win 1974), 38-43.
"Rise and Fall of the Tiger's Paw Judo Club" *Great Canadian Sports Stories* (1979), 79-96.

Small, Bryan R.†
"Harold Pagoda in Hollywood" *CFM* No. 4 (Aut 1971), 25-8.

Smalley, Ralph D.‡
"A Conversation" *Creative Campus* 1961, 54-8.

Smallwood, James L.‡
"The Persistent Doe" *CF* 30 (Oct 1950), 155-6.

Smart, William J.
"Beautiful Woman" *Antig R* No. 35 (Aut 1978), 53-70.
"The Char-Person" *Read Ch* 1:2 (Sum 1982), 16-30.
"The Sleepover" *Chat* 53 (Oct 1980), 50-1, 72, 74, 78, 80-2.
"Up North" *Fid* No. 131 (Jan 1982), 3-12.

Smith, A.J.M.
"In Praise of Older Men" by Anna Alopecia *SN* 81 (Jan 1966), 24, 26-7.

Smith, Carl‡
"Borne to Err in All We Do" *Amethyst* 4:1 (Aut 1964), 14-5.

Smith, Charley‡
"Why the Sun?" *Scar Fair* 2 (1974-75), [3 pp].

Smith, Colonel [pseudonym]
"As Rumor Had It" *Titmouse R* 1:1 (1972), 38.
"The Great Mystic" *Titmouse R* 1:1 (1972), 39.
"Name Your Poison" *Titmouse R* 1:1 (1972), 38.

smith, d.c [sic]‡
"How Mule Jackson Got Killed" *event* 6:2 [1966], 9-23.

Smith, David John
"Bus Number 6" *Prism* 14:3 (Win 1975), 74-8.
"A Cigarette Holder, a Paycheque and Henry at the Ritz" *JCF* Nos. 17/18 (1976), 17-24.
"Georgie's Fun Palace" *Des* 9:3/10:1 Nos. 22/23 (1978-79), 79-85.

Smith, Don†
"Stone Narcissus" *Forge* 1950, 19-23.

Smith, Donna Lee Moore‡
"Mrs. Foster's Walk" *AA* 69 (Jan 1979), 70-1, 73-4.
"A Place of Her Own" *AA* 67 (Feb 1977), 58-61.

Smith, Edmund Arthur†
"Bush" *Fid* No. 85 (May-June-July 1970), 79-81.

Smith, Gary†
"Just Crazy" *Quarry* 3 [1954?], 14-9.

Smith, Graham‡
"The Great Wall of China Time 'X' " *First Encounter* 8 (1977-78), 24-5.

Smith, Harriet Grahame†
"Growing Pains" *Onward* Sept 1964, 3-5.
"Growing Pains" *Onward* 15 Oct 1967, 3-5, 13.
"A Lady Named Bones" *Christian Home* 8 (June 1967), 14-6.
"The Scholarship" *Onward* 30 May 1965, 3-4, 10.

Smith, Ian‡
"And the Wind Blows Free" *Tyro* 1962, 32-8.

Smith, James W.‡
"Parables for at Least a Milkman (Scenario for an Absurd Comic Strip)" *WCR* 8:2 (Oct 1973), 27-9.
"This Parliament of Fears ... " *Alive* No. 42 [n.d.], 27.

Smith, Jessie Hazard
"Farm Lands Disappear" *Alberta Writers Speak* 1960, 36-8.

Smith, Jim‡
"Adult Novels" *Rampike* 3:1 (1983), 40.
"Erostratus" *Alive* No. 35 [1974], 13.

Smith, Joyce M.†
"Home for Christmas" *Saskatchewan Homecoming* (1971), 163-7.
"The Well" *Saskatchewan Homecoming* (1971), 151-4.

Smith, Judi
"Family Portrait" *Grain* 9:4 (Nov 1981), 16.
"The Lepidopterist" *JCF* No. 20 (1977), 17-20.
"No Flowers for Ole" *Canadian Short Fiction Anthology* (1976), 165-73 [Same author?].
"She Held the World on the Tip of Her Nose" *Grain* 9:4 (Nov 1981), 17.

Smith, Kathlyn‡
"Cassia" *Acta Vic* 74:4 (Feb 1950), 16-7.

Smith, Lee Ann‡
"Chance Encounter" *Driftwood* 1979, 27.

Smith, Lorne‡
"The Partnership" *North* 19 (July-Aug 1972), 26-7.

Smith, Marion†
"The Simple Truth" *Klanak Islands* (1959), 49-57.

Smith, Marnie‡
"How Babies Are Made" *Pedestal* 6:4 [n.d.], 6-7.

Smith, Marvin (1953-)
"Adding It Up" *event* 3:3 [n.d.], 49-52.
"Fence" *event* 3:1 [1973], 74-80.

Smith, Max‡
"All in the (Canadian) Family" *UC Observer* Feb 1973, 23 [Parody].

Smith, Michael†
"The Relay Race" *File* 4:4 (Fall 1980), 34-9.

Smith, Michael (1946-)
"Angel Children" *CBC "Anthology"* 16 Nov 1974
"Angel Children" *Tam R* No. 65 (Mar 1975), 43-51.
"Blood and Thunder" *Fid* No. 116 (Win 1978), 47-52.
"Concrete" *CBC "Anthology"* 3 Jan 1976.
"The Crows Above the Maple Bush" *JCF* 3:1 (Win 1974), 30-3.
"Meeting Caspar Miller" *Was R* 9:2 (Fall 1974), 55-62.
"The Star" *CFM* No. 15 (Aut 1974), 87-96.
"Stranded" *CBC "Anthology"* 27 Jan 1979.
"Town and Country" *Toronto Short Stories* (1977), 231-8.

Smith, Murray†
"The Day Levesque Got In" *Antig R* No. 43 (Aut 1980), 69-84.
"Deborah" *Los* No. 8 (Mar 1982), 30-43.
"The Greeks" *Quarry* 27:3 (Sum 1978), 16-26.

Smith, Olive Gertrude‡
"An Ounce of Prevention" *Bluenose* 2:3 (Win 1977-78), 14-7.

Smith, P. Louise‡
" 'Explanations' " *TUR* 94:2 (Apr 1981), 18-20.
"Group" *TUR* 95:1 (Jan 1982), 34-9.
"November 11, 10:30 am" *TUR* 95:2 (Spr 1982), 36-9.

Smith, Ralph F.†
"Room 713" *Grain* 11:3 (Aug 1983), 41-6.
"Snagged in the Deep Water" *Saskatchewan Gold* (1982), 235-44.

Smith, Ray (1941-)
CAPE BRETON IS THE THOUGHT-CONTROL CENTER OF CANADA
Toronto: House of Anansi Press, 1969.
"Cape Breton Is the Thought-Control Center of Canada" *Tam R* No. 45 (Aut 1967), 39-53.
"Cape Breton Is the Thought-Control Center of Canada" *New Romans* (1968), 18-30.
"Cape Breton Is the Thought-Control Center of Canada" *Cape Breton* (1969), 19-35.
"Cape Breton Is the Thought-Control Center of Canada" *Seeing Through Shuck* (1972) [Based on survey response].
"Cape Breton Is the Thought-Control Center of Canada" *Stories from Atlantic Canada* (1973), 210-24.
"Colours" *Prism* 8:2 (Aut 1968), 43-57.

"Colours" *Cape Breton* (1969), 1-17.
"Colours" *Sixteen by Twelve* (1970), 205-18.
"A Cynical Tale" *Cape Breton* (1969), 43-5.
"A Cynical Tale" *Narrative Voice* (1972), 185-6.
"A Cynical Tale" *Modern Canadian Stories* (1975), 236-8.
"The Dwarf in His Valley Ate Codfish" *Cape Breton* (1969), 99-107.
"The Dwarf in His Valley Ate Codfish" *Great Canadian Short Stories* (1971), 325-33.
"The Galoshes" *Cape Breton* (1969), 65-98.
"The Galoshes" *Story So Far* (1971), 82-108.
"Passion" *Cape Breton* (1969), 37-41.
"Passion" *Breakthrough Fictioneers* (1973), 203-6.
"Peril" *Cape Breton* (1969), 47-63.
"Peril" *Narrative Voice* (1972), 187-200.
"Raphael Anachronic" *Cape Breton* (1969), 109-21.
"Raphael Anachronic" *Fiction of Contemporary Canada* (1980), 45-51.
"Smoke" *Cape Breton* (1969), 123-35.
"Smoke" *East of Canada* (1976), 80-91.
"Symbols in Agony, a Canadian Short Story" *JCF* 1:2 (Spr 1972), 18-24.

Smith, Rich‡
"And the Last Man Will Have to Dig His Own Grave (quando fiam uti chelidon)" *Alive* 2:9 [Sept 1971], 39-40.
"Elsa" *Alive* 2:5 (Apr 1971), 3.

Smith, Richard S.‡
"Say It Again, Sam: The Lighthearted Narrative of How a Man Came to Grips with His Loss of Hearing" *Deaf Can* 7:8 (Aug 1982), 6-9.

Smith, Robert†
"The Dispossessed" *JCF* 2:4 (Fall 1973), 18-22.

Smith, Robert F. (1934-)
"The Acid Test" *Mission Mag* 5:2 (1981), 3-6.
"For the Suffering" *Mission Mag* 7:1 (1983), 8-11.
"This Little Child of Mine" *UC Observer* Dec 1979, 18-9.
"The Way of Life" *Mission Mag* 7:2 (1983), 6-8.

Smith, Rod†
"The Leper" *Antig R* No. 24 (Win 1975), 9-13.
"The Painted Room" *Antig R* No. 23 (Aut 1975), 9-12.

Smith, Roderick Wallis‡
"The Painted Room" *Snowmobiles Forbidden* (1971), 77-80.

Smith, Ron
"Along the Road Down Home" *Alive* 3:5 No. 24 [1972], 13-5.
"The Plimsoll Line" *Mal R* No. 46 (Apr 1978), 46-58.
"Shade" *Rainshadow* (1982), 81-91.

Smith, Rosamond†

"Decent Burial" *Amethyst* 3:1 (Fall 1963), [5 pp].

"The Sea Chest" *Amethyst* 3:2 (Win 1964), 25-31.

"The Strange Tale of Alexander Priffle" *Amethyst* 2:1 (Aut 1962), 33-5.

Smith, Sharon†

"Gertrude's Ring" *Story So Far* 2 (1973), 111.

"A Night in Kap" *Story So Far* 3 (1974), 91-2.

Smith, Stanley Noel‡

"The Olde Order Changeth" *Can Golden West* 13:5 [n.d.], 13-5.

Smith, Steve

RITUAL MURDERS Winnipeg: Turnstone Press, 1983.

"Chenille" *Rampike* 3:2 [1983?], 37.

"Chenille" *Ritual Murders* (1983), 5-8.

"Cinema" *Ritual Murders* (1983), 41-5.

"Darkroom" *Rampike* 3:1 (1983), 43.

"Darkroom" *Ritual Murders* (1983), 17-20.

"The Deal" *Ritual Murders* (1983), 25-9.

"Dry Vermouth" *Ritual Murders* (1983), 21-4.

"Exotic Dancer" *Per* No. 6 (Fall 1979), 29-35.

"Exotic Dancer" *Ritual Murders* (1983), 47-58.

"Fifth Row" *Ritual Murders* (1983), 9-12.

"Perfume" *Ritual Murders* (1983), 31-9.

"Subway" *Ritual Murders* (1983), 13-6.

"Three Cigarettes" *Des* 11:1/2 Nos. 27/28 (1980), 195-6.

"Three Cigarettes" *Ritual Murders* (1983), 1-4.

Smolkin, Rosalie‡

"A Paying Guest Is Not a Boarder" *Undergrad* Spr 1962, 18-20.

Smyth, Brian‡

"Joey" *Kaleidoscope* 1954-55, 18-9.

Smyth, Donna E.

"Birdman" *This* 12 (Oct 1978), 36-9.

"The Cat's Rat" *Matrix* Nos. 6/7 (1978), 75-82.

"The Chair-Man Speaks" *event* 4:3 [1974?], 7-11.

"Chickens" *Was R* 9:2 (Fall 1974), 3-16.

"Chrome Yellow" *CFM* No. 9 (Win 1973), 32-9.

"The Day Picasso Died in Saskatoon" *Matrix* 1:1 (Spr 1975), 18-9.

"The Death of a Cow" *Grain* 6:2 [1978], 46-54.

"Genesis Reprise" *Atlantis* 1:2 (Spr 1976), 128-38.

"Interior Scene: She, He, and Joe" *Antig R* No. 13 (Spr 1973), 69-76.

"Lamb" *Prism* 13:3 (Spr 1974), 102-6.

"Prairie Krishna" *Grain* 3:1 [1975], 40-7.

"Quilt" *Fireweed* No. 12 (1981), 41-4.

"The Temptation of Leafy" *Prism* 17:2 (Fall 1978), 136-44.

Smyth, Jacqui (1960-)
"Glass Doesn't Burn" *Camrose R* No. 5 [n.d.], 11-4.
"Rootcellar" *Prairie Fire* 4:4 (Mar-Apr 1983), 23-5.
"White Moments" *CF* 63 (Nov 1983), 28-31.

Smyth, W. Ross‡
"The Tall-Tale Cook" *Pedantics* 1965, 59-62.

Smythe-Chenier, Roslyn†
"Criminal Lawyer" *Mont Writers' Forum* [2:9] (Sept-Oct 1980), 6-9.

Snider, James G.‡
"Down to a Sunless Sea" *Edge* No. 6 (Spr 1967), 85-96.

Snowden, Robert‡
"The Theatre Door" *UCR* Spr 1975, 38-40.

Snyder, Richard‡
"A Late Decorum for De Koven Street" *Fid* No. [76] (Spr 1968), 49-57.

Soderstrom, Mary (1942-)
"Homecoming" *Chat* 48 (Nov 1975), 57, 88, 90, 92, 94, 96.
"I'm Sorry Mrs. Strauss" *Role of Woman in Canadian Literature* (1975), 54-9.

Solly, Bill‡
"Early Snow" *Muse* 61:1 (Dec 1951), 20-1.
"Headbeat" *Muse* 60:4 (Apr 1951), 18-24.
"Hello, Young Trout" *Muse* 62:1 (Spr 1953), 25-8.
"Lizzy" *Muse* 59:3 (Mar 1950), 7-10.
"The Night Witch" *Muse* 62:1 (Spr 1953), 7-10.
"Solitaire" *Muse* 60:3 (Feb 1951), 23-5.
"Thrice" *Muse* 60:1 (Nov 1950), 19-20.
"The Vine" *Muse* 59:4 (Apr 1950), 26-9.

Solman, Mel†
"Moby Dickman and the Jewish Question or Jonah and the Whale (Revised)"
Can J Chron R May 1975, 98.

Solo, N [pseudonym]
"The Private I" *Beaver Bites* 1:6 (30 July 1976), [1 p] [Humour].

Somerton, Ruby P.
"The Steal" *Atl Guardian* 10 (Aug 1953), 24-7.

Somerville, Christine Bryce†
"First Move" *Onward* 15 Oct 1961, 6-7, 14 [Semi-fictional].
"Jonathan Street" *Onward* 17 July 1960, 451.

Somerville, Janet†
"Taking Auntie Out of Her Own Filth" *Fid* No. 131 (Jan 1982), 22-3.

Sorenstein, Louise†
"The Station" by Louise Stein *event* 6:1 [1977], 54-6.

Sorestad, Glen (1937-)
"The Investments of Lars Ollefssen" *CSSM* 1:2 (Apr 1975), 29-33.
"It Bodder Me" *Nw J* No. 17 (1980), 72-7.
"It Bodder Me" *Sundogs* (1980), 131-8.

Sotelo, Ruben‡
"Ballin' Jack" *Communicator* 5:4 [n.d.], 20-2.
"The Seventh Star" *Communicator* 5:1 (Feb-Mar 1976), 22-8.

Southgate, A.†
"It Was a Bad Winter" *Prism* 13:3 (Spr 1974), 30-41.

Sowton, Ian (1929-)
"Daddy Plumkin's Icebox" *CBC* 1954 [Based on survey response].
"The Penance of Pierre" *Undergrad* Spr 1952, 7-11.

Spafford, Fran‡
"The Headstone" *Pier Spr* 1:2 (Spr 1977), 40-4.

Spalding, A.E.†
"A Wolf Among the Caribou" *JCF* 3:3 (1974), 12-5.

Spalding, Alec‡
"Of Death, Sin, and the Devil" *Creative Campus* 1958, 17-21.

Spanier, Muriel
"Ever See a Girl with a Painted Guitar?" *MM* 67 (15 June 1954), 20-1, 74-6.

Sparks, Richard‡
"Carousel" *2 O'Clock Rap* 4 (1975), 68-75.
"A Meeting of Two Neighbours" *Old Nun* 1:1 [n.d.], 12-4.

Sparling, Sharon
"The Chinese Coat" *SN* 97 (Oct 1982), 46-51.
"The Chinese Coat" *Coming Attractions* (1983), 92-107.
"Diminuendo" *Coming Attractions* (1983), 108-16.
"A Hinge of Possibilities" *Coming Attractions* (1983), 117-38.

Speak, Dorothy†
"Cracker Jack" *Dand* 8:2 (1981), 51-8.
"Crinolines" *Prairie J Can Lit* No. 1 (Fall 1983), 3-15.

Spector, Teresa†
"It's Called Security" *Mont Writers' Forum* 1:6 (Mar 1979), 8-11.

Spelius, Carol‡
"Substitute Santa" *Deaf Can* 3:6 (Nov-Dec 1978), 22-4.

Spence, Ian A.†
"Certified Undesirable" *Prism* 18:2 (Win 1979-80), 78-92.
"For Laughs" *Popular Illusion* No. 3 (Jan 1978), [5 pp].

"Nada – When You're Running Low on Style" *VWFP/Revue* 1:1 (Spr 1975), 1, 7.
"Rosary" *VWFP/Revue* 1:6 (Aug 1975), 16.
"Time Off" *Canadian Short Fiction Anthology* (1976), 175-87.

Spencer, Elizabeth (1921-)

SHIP ISLAND AND OTHER STORIES New York/Toronto: McGraw-Hill, 1968.
THE STORIES OF ELIZABETH SPENCER Toronto/New York: Doubleday, 1981.
"The Absence" *New Yorker* 42 (10 Sept 1966), 53-4.
"The Absence" *Stories* (1981), 221-4.
"The Adult Holiday" *New Yorker* 41 (12 June 1965), 35-6.
"The Adult Holiday" *Stories* (1981), 117-20.
"The Atwater Fiancée" *Mont* 37 (Sept 1963), 24-6.
"The Atwater Fiancée" CBC "*Anthology*" 15 Dec 1963.
"A Bad Cold" *New Yorker* 43 (27 May 1967), 38-9.
"A Bad Cold" *Stories* (1981), 267-71.
"[A?] Beautiful Day for the Wedding" *Redbook* 119 (Sept 1962), 48-9[+?] [Based on RGPL].
"The Bufords" *McCall's* 94 (Jan 1967), 76-7, 124, 126 [As "Those Bufords"].
"The Bufords" *Stories* (1981), 231-41.
"A Christian Education" *Atlantic Monthly* 233 (Mar 1974), 73-4.
"A Christian Education" *Stories* (1981), 327-31.
"The Day Before" *Ship Island* (1968), 165-73.
"The Day Before" *Stories* (1981), 225-30.
"The Eclipse" *New Yorker* 34 (12 July 1958), 25-30.
"The Eclipse" *Stories* (1981), 11-21.
"The Finder" *New Yorker* 46 (23 Jan 1971), 30-9.
"The Finder" *Stories of the Modern South* (1978), 308-26.
"The Finder" *Stories* (1981), 291-308.
"First Dark" *New Yorker* 35 (20 June 1959), 31-40.
"First Dark" *Stories from The New Yorker* 1950-1960 (1960), 413-30.
"First Dark" *Prize Stories: O'Henry Awards* 1960 237-56.
"First Dark" *Ship Island* (1968), 1-27.
"First Dark" *Stories* (1981), 23-40.
"The Fishing Lake" *New Yorker* 40 (29 Aug 1964), 24-5.
"The Fishing Lake" *Ship Island* (1968), 129-36.
"The Fishing Lake" *Stories* (1981), 111-5.
"The Girl Who Loved Horses" *Ont R* No. 10 (Spr-Sum 1979), 5-20.
"The Girl Who Loved Horses" *Pushcart Prize 5* (1980), 320-37.
"The Girl Who Loved Horses" *Stories* (1981), 413-29.
"Go South in the Winter" *JCF* No. 23 (1979), 44-7.
"Go South in the Winter" *Stories* (1981), 315-9.
"I, Maureen" *76: New Canadian Stories* 70-98.
"I, Maureen" *Stories* (1981), 341-62.
"I, Maureen" *Penguin Book of Modern Canadian Short Stories* (1982), 337-58.
"Indian Summer" *Southern R* 14 (1978), 560-79.
"Indian Summer" *Stories* (1981), 381-400.
"Instrument of Destruction" *Mississippi R* 1:1 (1972), 47-53.
"Instrument of Destruction" *Stories* (1981), 309-14.
"Jean-Pierre" *New Yorker* 57 (17 Aug 1981), 30-40.

"Jean-Pierre" *82: Best Canadian Stories* 138-60.

"Jean-Pierre" *Prize Stories: O'Henry Awards* 1983 108-27.

"Judith Kane" *Ship Island* (1968), 67-91.

"Judith Kane" *Stories* (1981), 243-59.

"A Kiss at the Door" *Southern R* 8 (1972), 676-80.

"A Kiss at the Door" *Stories* (1981), 321-4.

"The Little Brown Girl" *New Yorker* 33 (20 July 1957), 27-9.

"The Little Brown Girl" *Ship Island* (1968), 155-64.

"The Little Brown Girl" *Stories* (1981), 3-9.

"Madonna" *Hudson R* 36 (1983), 272-8.

"Moon Rocket" *McCall's* 88 (Oct 1960), 80-1[+?] [Based on RGPL].

"Moon Rocket" *Stories* (1981), 53-62.

"Mr. McMillan" *Southern R* 11 (1975), 205-11.

"Mr. McMillan" *Stories* (1981), 333-9.

"The Name of the Game" *McCall's* 99 (Sept 1972), 95, 112, 114, 117-8.

"On the Gulf" *Delta R* [date unknown] [Based on *Stories*].

"On the Gulf" *Stories* (1981), 279-82.

"Pilgrimage" *Virginia Q R* 26 (1950), 393-404.

"The Pincian Gate" *New Yorker* 42 (16 Apr 1966), 50-2.

"The Pincian Gate" *Stories* (1981), 121-6.

"Port of Embarkation" *Atlantic Monthly* 239 (Jan 1977), 69-71.

"Port of Embarkation" *78: Best Canadian Stories* 134-40.

"Port of Embarkation" *Stories* (1981), 407-11.

"Prelude to a Parking Lot" *Southern R* 12 (1976), 454-69.

"Prelude to a Parking Lot" *77: Best Canadian Stories* 130-51.

"Prelude to a Parking Lot" *Stories* (1981), 363-79.

"Presents" *Shenandoah* 22:2 (Win 1971), 68-73.

"Presents" *Stories* (1981), 273-8.

"The Puzzle Poem" *Hudson R* 36 (1983), 265-72.

"The Search" *79: Best Canadian Stories* 122-8.

"The Search" *Chat* 52 (Apr 1979), 62-3, 78, 80, 83 [also entitled "The Search"].

"The Search" *Stories* (1981), 401-6.

"Sharon" *New Yorker* 46 (9 May 1970), 36-9.

"Sharon" *Stories* (1981), 282-90.

"Ship Island: The Story of a Mermaid" *New Yorker* 40 (12 Sept 1964), 52-6, 58, 60, 63, 65-6, 69-70, 72, 74, 76, 79-80, 82, 84, 86, 91-2, 94.

"Ship Island: The Story of a Mermaid" *Prize Stories: O'Henry Awards* 1966 87-112.

"Ship Island: The Story of a Mermaid" *Ship Island* (1968), 29-66.

"Ship Island: The Story of a Mermaid" *Stories* (1981), 85-110.

"A Southern Landscape" *New Yorker* 36 (26 Mar 1960), 28-34.

"A Southern Landscape" *Ship Island* (1968), 137-54.

"A Southern Landscape" *Love Stories* (1975), 350-9.

"A Southern Landscape" *Stories* (1981), 41-52.

"To the Watchers While Walking Home" *Ont R* No. 16 (Spr-Sum 1982), 71-4.

"To the Watchers While Walking Home" *83: Best Canadian Stories* 92-6.

"To the Watchers While Walking Home" *Metavisions* (1983), 32-5.

"The Visit" *Prairie Schooner* 38 (1964), 95-108.

"The Visit" *Best American Short Stories* 1965 299-311.

"The Visit" *Ship Island* (1968), 111-28.

"The Visit" *Stories* (1981), 73-84.
"The White Azalea" *Texas Q* 4:4 (Win 1961), 112-7.
"The White Azalea" *Ship Island* (1968), 93-103.
"The White Azalea" *Stories* (1981), 63-70.
"Wisteria" *Ship Island* (1968), 105-10.
"Wisteria" *Stories* (1981), 261-5.

Spencer, Susan†
"Goodbye" *Room* 8:1 (1983), 63.

Spera, Roman‡
"Atop the Hill of Anzop" *Simcoe R* No. 1 (Win 1976), 33-5.

Sperdakos, Deane
"The Rain Gets In" *Versus* No. 3 (Spr 1977), 47-56.
"Renaming the Streets in Any Jerusalem" *Grain* 5:2 [1977], 14-9.
"RNA" *Mont Writers' Forum* 1:10 (July-Aug 1979), 18-21.

Spettigue, Douglas O. (1930-)
MANY MANSIONS Ed. Leo Simpson Ottawa: Uuniv. of Ottawa Press, 1976.
"Asters for Teddie" *NR* 4:5 (June-July 1951), 2-8.
"Asters for Teddie" *CBC* 1951 [Based on survey response].
"Asters for Teddie" *Canadian Short Stories* (1952), 88-94.
"Carnival of the Animals" *Atlantic Monthly* 203 (Apr 1959), 121-7.
"Carnival of the Animals" *Many Mansions* (1976), 55-65.
"Charlie's Dog" *CBC* Feb 1953 [Based on survey response].
"Conversation with a German" *Many Mansions* (1976), 7-21.
"Early Summer" *Quarry* 16:2 (Jan 1967), 33-8.
"Edge of Christmas" *Fid* No. 80 (May-June-July 1969), 13-23.
"Edge of Christmas" *Many Mansions* (1976), 45-54.
"Green Green Grass" *Many Mansions* (1976), 1-5.
"The Haying" *CBC "Wednesday Night"* Nov 1953 [Based on survey response].
"The Haying" *Stories from Canada* (1969), 116-41.
"The Haying" *New Canadian Writing* 1969 93-102.
"The Haying" *Die Weite Reise* (1974), 58-69 [As "Die Heuernte"; trans. Gerhard Bottcher].
"The Haying" *Many Mansions* (1976), 121-30.
"The Hayloft" *CBC* Aut 1956 [Based on survey response].
"In the Yellow Circle" *Folio* 1952 [Based on survey response].
"Lena" *Many Mansions* (1976), 97-111.
"Many Mansions" *Many Mansions* (1976), 23-43.
"Old Frank" *New Canadian Writing* 1969 67-75.
"Old Frank" *Many Mansions* (1976), 89-96.
"Pity the Poor Piper" *Fourteen Stories High* (1971), 69-83.
"Pity the Poor Piper" *Many Mansions* (1976), 67-80.
"Spring Song" *CBC "Life and Letters"* Aug 1966 [Based on survey response].
"Spring Song" *New Canadian Writing* 1969 76-83.
"Spring Song" *Many Mansions* (1976), 81-7.
"The Truck" *Tam R* No. 18 (Win 1961), 29-35.
"The Truck" *New Canadian Writing* 1969 84-91.
"The Truck" *Many Mansions* (1976), 113-20.

Spicer, Irene T.‡
"Cabin in the Clearing" *AA* 53 (Apr 1963), 76-7, 79.

Spicer, Jack‡
"The Scroll-Work on the Casket" *Is* No. 8 (1970), [1 p].

Spivak, Michael†
"Mary, Mother of God" *Fid* No. 62 (Fall 1964), 56-60.
"Secret of the Trade" *Tam R* No. 29 (Aut 1963), 56-65.

Spray, Carole‡
"The Man Who Plucked the Gorbie" *AA* 66 (July 1976), 18-9.

Sproxton, Birk
"Bitches Like Toe-Jam" *Grain* 11:2 (May 1983), 31-7.

Spruyt, Jo-Ann†
"Famine" *Muskeg R* 5 [n.d.], 12-7.

Sribniak, Mervin‡
"The Battle for Borshch" *Uk Can* 8 (15 Feb 1954), 8 [Listed under "Humour and Satire"].
"Twas the Day After Christmas" *Uk Can* 8 (1 Jan 1954), 7 [Satire].

Sroka, Bill†
"Whatever the Cost" *Northern Ontario Anthology* 2 (1978), 42-4.

St. Arnaud, Ray‡
"On the Lane" *March* [1] (Spr 1962), 12-5.

St. Jacques, Elizabeth
"Chestnuts in the Sky" *Our Family* 25 (Oct 1973), 22-3.
"Don't Worry! Don't Cry!" *Our Family* 28 (Sept 1976), 20-3.

St. Pierre, Paul (1923-)
SMITH AND OTHER EVENTS: STORIES OF THE CHILCOTIN Toronto: Doubleday, 1983.
"Cabin Fever" *Smith* (1983), 255-72.
"A Day with a Deer, a Bear and Norah Smith" *Smith* (1983), 47-73.
"December Nilsen" *Smith* (1983), 201-17.
"Dry Storm" *Smith* (1983), 25-46.
"The Education of Phyllisteen" *Smith* (1983), 219-54.
"Frenchie's Wife" *Smith* (1983), 273-98.
"How to Run the Country" *Smith* (1983), 135-99.
"The Last Day of Violence" *Smith* (1983), 111-34.
"Ol Antoine's Wooden Overcoat" *Smith* (1983), 1-23.
"The Owner of the Gang" *Smith* (1983), 93-109.
"Sale of One Small Ranch" *Smith* (1983), 299-318.
"Sarah's Copper" *Smith* (1983), 75-92.

Stacey, Ann‡
"The Hanging of Eleanor Fairbairn" *Edmonton Journal* Fri, 28 May 1965, 60-1.

Stacey, Jean

"The Boat Builder" *Newfoundland Stories and Ballads* 17:2 [date unknown] [May be pre-1950. Based on *Doryloads*].

"The Boat Builder" *Doryloads* (1974), 188-93.

"Just Today" *From This Place* (1977), 138-42.

"The Slippers" *Nfld Q* 66:2 (Win 1968), 30-2.

" 'Uncle' Andrew" *Nfld Q* 67:1 (Christmas 1968), 12.

"Waiting for Michael" *Scruncheons* 1:1 (1972), 40-5.

Stackhouse, H.M.

"Back from Outer Space" *Onward* 24 Apr 1955, 258-9, 270.

"Back from Outer Space" *Onward* 26 Sept 1965, 3-4, 14.

"Back from Outer Space" *Rapport* Apr 1971, 9-11.

Stambaugh, Sara (1936-)

"The Cider Barrel" *Des* 10:1 Nos. 22/23 (1978-79), 86-93.

"Down Below Where the Animals Live" *White Pelican* 5:1 (1975), 3-12.

"The Fresh Air Child" *Fid* No. 117 (Spr 1978), 5-13.

"Holy Mary Mother of God" *Dand* 7:1 (1980), 10-20.

"How Lena Got Set Back" *Des* Nos. 11/12 (Spr-Sum 1975), 100-3.

"Hunting Season" *Des* No. 14 (Sum 1976), 33-6.

"The King of the Glass Mountain" *event* 11:1 (1982), 40-50.

"Old Eby" *Des* 8:3 No. 19 (1977), 78-83.

Stange, Ken

"Back in the Garden Again (for Teilhard de Chardin)" *Blind Windows* No. 2 [1979], [4 pp].

"Growing Things" *Antig R* No. 49 (Spr 1982), 108-10 [Listed as poem].

"The Importance of Music" *Writ* No. 12 (1980), 24-5.

"Misplaced" *Northern Ontario Anthology* 1 (1977), 58-60.

"Mister These at the Theatre" *Antig R* No. 32 (Win 1978), 11-5.

"Old Theodore These Is Wont to Wheeze" *Dand* 4 (Win 1978), 32-7.

"Seven Day's Out" *CFM* No. 17 (Spr 1975), 20-6.

"A Slice of Mister These's Life" *Scrivener* 4:1 (Win 1983), 11-5.

"There Are Places" *Fid* No. 117 (Spr 1978), 53-6.

"These Ways Work" *Los* No. 5 (1977), 20-5.

Staniforth, Richard†

"After the Tommy Gun" *UTR* 1:1 (Spr 1977), 24-6.

"Montcalm's Last Tour of Old Quebec" *event* 6:1 [1977], 49-53.

"Road's End" *Writ* No. 7 (Fall 1975), 23-8.

"Rural Education" *Writ* No. 13 (1981), 60-5.

"Subject Sees Beyond Nullification" *Writ* No. 4 (Spr 1972), 22-6.

"Zulu" *Writ* No. 8 (1976), 56-62.

Stanko, Barbara‡

"The Doodler" *Images About Manitoba* 1:4 (Spr-Sum 1977), 5-7.

Stanley-Porter, Caroline‡

"In Search of Rosa" *TUR* 75:1 (Nov 1961), 8-10.

"Rebecca's Tree" *TUR* 75:3 (Mar 1962), 7-9.

Stanley-Porter, David‡
"Completing" *TUR* 65:2 (Jan 1953), 22-9.
"The Man Who Died" *TUR* 63:3 (Feb 1951), 14-5.
"A Married Couple" *TUR* 65:1 (Dec 1952), 8-15.
"A Matter of Time and Place" *Varsity Lit Issue* Wed, 11 Feb 1953, 3, 5-6.
"Through a Glass Darkly" *TUR* 63:2 (Aut 1950), 17-8.

Stanners, Virginia‡
[Untitled] *Muse* 70 (1961), 23-4.

Staples, Elizabeth‡
"How the Monkey Got His Tail" *Acta Vic* 77:1 (Nov 1952), 24.

Staples, Ralph S.
"Brothers – A Story with a Moral" *Can Labour* 1:4 (July 1956), 24-5.

Starr, M.‡
"The Tale of the Lion" *My Golden West* 3 (Christmas 1967), 14-5.

Statius [pseudonym]
"Gladiator's Gift" *Folio* 16:2 (Spr 1964), 5-12.

Staubitz, Arthur
"The Clock Puncher" *FH* 24 Apr 1952, 24-5.
"Hudson's Bay Sable" *Onward* 21 Jan 1962, 10-2.
"The Hunting Knife" *Rapport* May 1969, 34-5.
"Mission Indian" *Onward* 23 Oct 1960, 676-8.
"Wild Trees Calling" *Onward* 26 Mar 1961, 201-3.
"Wilderness Train Home" *Onward* 28 Aug 1960, 548-9, 555.

Stedingh, Wayne
"Solitaire" *Prism* 10:2 (Aut 1970), 73-9.

Steel, Lisa‡
"Talking Tongues: Lovespeak" *Image Nation* No. 25 (Sum 1982), [5 pp] [With French translation by Susanne de Lotbinière-Harwood].

Steele, Harwood (Elmes Robert) (1897-1978)
THE RED SERGE: STORIES OF THE ROYAL CANADIAN MOUNTED POLICE Toronto: Ryerson Press, 1961.
" 'Beaned with Bottle' " *Red Serge* (1961), 233-47.
"A Couple of Caribou" *Red Serge* (1961), 182-99.
"A Dog Won't Lie" *Red Serge* (1961), 78-100.
" 'Have Done My Best' " *Red Serge* (1961), 248-65.
"A Little and Certain Compass" *Red Serge* (1961), 151-61.
"The Little Red Devil and the Deep Blue Sea" *Red Serge* (1961), 64-77.
"Lunatic Patrol" *Red Serge* (1961), 110-30.
"Mighty Mean Indian" *Red Serge* (1961), 220-32.
"The Missing Link" *Red Serge* (1961), 131-50.
"The Monster and the 'Mountie' " *Red Serge* (1961), 162-81.
"Ordeal by Fire" *Red Serge* (1961), 56-63.
"Pal" *Red Serge* (1961), 200-19.

"The Race for Molly Scott" *Red Serge* (1961), 31-55.
"The Red Serge of Courage" *Red Serge* (1961), 1-19.
"Sir Galahad and the 'Bad Man' " *Red Serge* (1961), 20-30.
"A Working Partnership" *Red Serge* (1961), 101-9.

Steele, Tedd†
"We Stand on Guard" *Toronto Star* Sun, 23 Oct 1983, D5.

Steen, David T.‡
"The Closet" *Vanguard* Feb 1971, 13-5, 20-1.

Stefco, Karen†
"Peter and Concern" *Posh* [n.d.], [2 pp].

Steffler, George‡
See also Steffler, George and Holterman, Anne.
"Brother Fugitive" *Alive* No. 169 (3 Oct 1980), 2-5, 11-2, 14.
"Collisions" *Alive* No. 154 (29 Sept 1979), 16-9.
"Death and Life" *Alive* No. 155 (6 Oct 1979), 15-8.
"Guerrilla Warfare" *Alive* No. 147 (11 Aug 1979), 16-7.
"Losing a Friend" *Alive* No. 148 (18 Aug 1979), 16-8.
"A New Friend" *Alive* No. 149 (25 Aug 1979), 12-4.
"A Real Education" *Alive* No. 146 (4 Aug 1979), 13-5.
"Saving Someone's Skin" *Alive* No. 151 (8 Sept 1979), 14-6.
"Thieves" *Alive* No. 150 (1 Sept 1979), 12-4.
"Winkle" *Alive* No. 153 (22 Sept 1979), 16-8.

Steffler, George and Holterman, Anne‡
See also Steffler, George.
"The Final Chapter of Cinderella" *Alive* No. 109 (15 Apr 1978), 8-10.

Steiger, Mary‡
"The Best of Both Worlds" *Smoke Signals* 4 [date unknown] [Based on *SWG* survey response].

Stein, David Lewis (1937-)
CITY BOYS Ottawa: Oberon Press, 1978.
"Back Where I Can Be Me" *Imp* 2:3/4 (1973), 135-43.
"Back Where I Can Be Me" *City Boys* (1978), 113-20.
"California, Here I Come" *SN* 97 (Sept 1982), 50-2, 54-6.
"Charlie Chan and Number One Son" *Varsity* Fri, 18 Mar 1960, 2-3.
"Charlie Chan and Number One Son" *New Canadian Writing 1968* 5-17.
"The Coin Tossers" *Undergrad* Spr 1960, 41-5.
"The Coin Tossers" *Exchange* 1:1 (Nov 1961), 17-8.
"Fresh Disasters" *SN* 92 (June 1977), 26-8, 30-3, 35-6.
"Fresh Disasters" *CBC "Anthology"* 10 Sept 1977.
"Fresh Disasters" *City Boys* (1978), 148-71.
"Fresh Disasters" *Spice Box* (1981), 286-302.
"Goodbye, Charlie" *Tam R* No. 19 (Spr 1961), 51-60.
"The Huntsman" *Undergrad* Mar 1957, 34-40.
"The Huntsman" *CBC "Anthology"* 18 Feb 1958.
"The Huntsman" *New Canadian Writing 1968* 18-27.

"The Hunstman" *Kaleidoscope* (1972), 116-25.
"The Huntsman" *Die Weite Reise* (1974), 273-84 [As "Der Jùger"; trans. Gerhard Bottcher].
"In There" *CBC "Anthology"* 27 Nov 1976.
"In There" *City Boys* (1978), 172-86.
"Joie de Vivre" *Reflections* 1960 36-41.
"Joie de Vivre" *Exchange* 2:3 (Feb-Mar 1962), 12-5.
"Marvin, Marvin" *City Boys* (1978), 37-96 [Novella?].
"Morning for Grant Macadam" *Undergrad* Spr 1960, 46-52.
"The Night of the Little Brown Men" *SN* 82 (Mar 1967), 29-31.
"The Night of the Little Brown Men" *New Canadian Writing* 1968 50-63.
"The Night of the Little Brown Men" *City Boys* (1978), 97-112.
"Noblesse Oblige" *Undergrad* Spr 1959, 5-7.
"The Old Lady's Money" *New Canadian Writing* 1968 28-49.
"The Old Lady's Money" *Toronto Short Stories* (1977), 239-59.
"The Salesmen" *Reflections* 1958 15-20.
"The Salesmen" *Tam R* No. 11 (Spr 1959), 45-9, 51-4.
"The Soldiers in the Park" *Undergrad* Aut 1958, 28-31.
"Spring Morning" *Tam R* No. 28 (Sum 1963), 60-7.
"The Suicide of Alexander Jakubovic" *Jargon* No. [1] (1958-59), 23-7.
"The Working Class" *CF* 63 (July 1983), 19-21, 25-9.

Stein, Philip‡

"the dreamer" *Prism* (Mont) Fall 1965, 18.
"the son" *Prism* (Mont) Fall 1965, 18.

Stein, Rhoda Elizabeth Playfair

"The Affair of Able Willie" *FH* 1 May 1958, 16-7.
" 'And It Came to Pass ... ' " *Onward* 23 Dec 1956, 817-9, 830-1.
" 'And It Came to Pass ... ' " *Onward* 18 Dec 1966, 3-5, 14.
"And Then There Was One" *Annals* 86 (May 1972), 138[+?] [Based on survey response].
"The Bargain-Counter Don't-Miss Gift-Wrapped Christmas" *Rapport* Dec 1970, 7-10.
"Bend in the Road" *Dal R* 44 (1964), 307-11.
"Birthday Present" *Onward* 16 Oct 1966, 3-5.
"But I Won't Marry You My Pretty Maid" *Fair Lady* (S Afr) 1975 [Based on survey response].
"But I Won't Marry You My Pretty Maid" *Annals* 90 (June 1976), 144[+?] [Based on survey response].
"Cat and Me" *Onward* 10 Jan 1965, 12-3.
"The Changeless Things" *Onward* 20 Dec 1959, 806-8, 810-1.
"Christmas Miracle" *Can Messenger* 86 (Dec 1976), 18-9.
"Cinderella Couldn't Lose" *Can Messenger* 83 (Sept 1973), 12-4.
"The Coffee House" *Impact* (U.S.) Mar 1972, 48[+?] [Based on survey response].
"Colour Me Doubtful" *West Prod* 23 Feb 1967, 7[+?] [Based on survey response].
"Corsage for Lena" *FH* 15 Feb 1951, 22-3.
"A Day in the Life of Rosa" *Can Messenger* 85 (Nov 1975), 12-3, 15.
"Decision" *CHJ* Mar 1952, 18-9, 27-8, 37, 40-3.
"Deep in the Heart of Christmas" *Onward* 21 Dec 1958, 801-3, 813.

"The Detour" *Can Messenger* 88 (Nov 1978), 12-3, 18.

"A Different Drummer" *Can Messenger* 84 (Jan 1974), 16-7, 20.

"Don't Fence Them In" *Home Life* (U.S.) Nov 1965, 9[+?] [Based on survey response].

"Don't Gimme That Maybe Next Year Bit ... " *Annals* 86 (Apr 1972), 104[+?] [Based on survey response].

"The Doughnut Bag" *Can Messenger* 87 (Apr 1977), 12-4.

"Eve of the Wedding" *CHJ* July 1957, 29, 32.

"For a Loaf of Bread" *Impact* (U.S.) Dec 1971, 37[+?] [Based on survey response].

"For the Love of Linda" *FH* 2 Sept 1954, 20-1, 27.

"For Want of a Nail" *Rapport* May 1970, 7-10.

"For Want of a Nail" *Home Life* (U.S.) 25 (Feb 1971) [Based on survey response].

"For Want of a Nail" *Fair Lady* (S Afr) 1976 [Based on survey response].

"The Fruit of Their Devices" *Rapport* May 1971, 10-3.

"Generation Gap Memo" *Annals* 91 (Apr 1977), 116[+?] [Based on survey response].

"Getting to Know You" *Rapport* Nov 1970, 9.

"A Girl Like Connie" *Rapport* Nov 1968, 28-32.

"The Girl Who Wasn't Pretty" *FH* 23 June 1960, 18-9, 24.

"The Good Neighbour" *Onward* 12 Aug 1962, 3-5, 9.

"The Happening" *Home Life* (U.S.) 24 (May 1970), 34[+?] [Based on survey response].

"The Happy House" *SW* 17 Mar 1962, 19-21, 26-7.

"Her Own Affair" *Onward* 24 Mar 1962, 3-5, 11.

"Hey! Hey! Anybody Listening? Anybody Care?" *Annals* 89 (Oct 1975), 284[+?] [Based on survey response].

"Hey You! Guess Who?" *West Prod* 18 Nov 1965, 7[+?] [Based on survey response].

"His Wonders to Perform" *FH* 21 Dec 1950, 22-3.

"His Wonders to Perform" *Onward* 5 Dec 1965, 3-4, 11.

"Ho All Ye Campers" *West Prod* 29 July 1965 [Based on survey response].

"Homecoming" *Christian Home* (U.S.) 10 (Oct 1951), 14[+?] [Based on survey response].

"The House That Jack Built" *Rapport* June 1971, 22-5.

"How a Life Line Grew" *Annals* 92 (Mar 1978), 82[+?] [Based on survey response].

"How Bobby Found the Christ Child" *Baptist Leader* (U.S.) 16:9 (Dec 1954), 20[+?] [Based on survey response].

"If I Had a Hammer ... " *Rapport* Jan 1970, 8-10.

"If It's Real, It'll Be There Monday" *Rapport* Mar 1971, 24-6.

"If It's Real, It'll Be There Monday" *With* (U.S.) 6 (Mar 1973), 5[+?] [Based on survey response].

"If It's Real, It'll Be There Monday" *Impact* (U.S.) 1973 [Based on survey response].

" ... Iss Skin Deep" *Onward* 26 Sept 1965, 13-4 [Non-fiction?].

"It's All In-Law Family" *West Prod* 31 Aug 1967, 2[+?] [Based on survey response].

"It's What You Do with It" *West Prod* 8 July 1965, 7[+?] [Based on survey response].

"Journey to Jordan" *Christian Home* 2 (Sept 1961), 10-3.

"Just the Two of Us" *Story World* (U.K.) 26 June 1976, 3[+?] [Based on survey response].

"The Key" *Story World* (U.K.) 1 Nov 1975, 3[+?] [Based on survey response].

"The Key" *Can Messenger* 85 (Apr 1976), 12-4.

"The Labyrinth" *Fair Lady* (S Afr) 1974 [Based on survey response].

"Last Journey for Jasper Holler" *QQ* 67 (1961), 537-46.

"The Least of These" *Onward* 62 (24 Aug 1952), 529-31, 542-3.

"Lesson for Elizabeth" *Woman's Illustrated* (U.K.) 37 (27 Nov 1954), 8[+?] [Based on survey response].

"Like Father, Like Son" *Story World* (U.K.) 5 Oct 1974, 27[+?] [Based on survey response].

"Love Affair" *FH* 26 July 1951, 20.

"Love Sometimes Means Having to Say Goodbye" *Can Messenger* 84 (May 1974), 18-9.

"Love Sometimes Means Having to Say Goodbye" *Fair Lady* (S Afr) 1974 [Based on survey response].

"M Is for Problem – Mine" *West Prod* 20 May 1965, 7[+?] [Based on survey response].

"Madame Zahini and the Queen of Hearts" *Echoes* No. 224 (Aut 1956), 6-7, 22.

"Magic Moments" *Story World* (U.K.) 14 May 1977, 3[+?] [Based on survey response].

"Marcie" *Red Star Weekly* (U.K.) 17 Jan 1976, 10[+?] [Based on survey response].

"Margaret ... a Pearl" *CHJ* Aug 1954, 11, 90-1, 93-4, 97-8.

"Minnows and Flat-Bottomed Boats" *West Prod* 5 Aug 1976, 7[+?] [Based on survey response].

"Mr. Denby and the Rose Bush" *FH* 21 Feb 1952, 24-5.

"Mr. Rafferty's True Love" *FH* 31 Dec 1953, 16, 21.

"The New Girl" *Story World* (U.K.) 24 July 1976, 3[+?] [Based on survey response].

"Now About My Operation" *West Prod* 14 Oct 1965, 3[+?] [Based on survey response].

"On Assignment" *Annals* 91 (Oct 1977), 290[+?] [Based on survey response].

"On Christmas Eve" *Onward* 22 Dec 1963, 3-4, 6.

"On the Outside Looking In" *Story World* (U.K.) 31 July 1976, 3[+?] [Based on survey response].

"On the Outside of the Pit" *Onward* 15 Mar 1964, 3-4, 11.

"On the Outside of the Pit" *Onward* 17 Mar 1968, 3-4, 14.

"Once Upon a Summer" *FH* 22 May 1952, 24-5.

"One for the Money" *Dal R* 51 (1971-72), 571-8.

"A Pilgrim's Progress" *Annals* 91 (July-Aug 1977), 230[+?] [Based on survey response].

"A Place for Us" *Red Star Weekly* (U.K.) 29 Aug 1981, 24[+?] [Based on survey response].

"The Price of a Dream" *FH* 17 Mar 1955, 26-7, 35.

"The Prodigal" *Christian Living* (U.S.) 21 (Feb 1974), 10[+?] [Based on survey response].

"Promise of the Forsythia" *Christian Life* (U.S.) 38 (Nov 1976), 25[+?] [Based on survey response].

"Promises to Keep" *Story World* (U.K.) 20 Aug 1977, 2[+?] [Based on survey

response].

"Queen of Hearts" *Story World* (U.K.) 16 July 1977, 5[+?] [Based on survey response].

"Ready or Not" *Rapport* Oct 1970, 7-10.

"The Red Dress" *Home Life* (U.S.) May 1955, 3[+?] [Based on survey response].

"Return of the Prodigal" *Can Messenger* 82 (May 1972), 12-4.

"Second Chance" *Christian Living* (U.S.) 24 (Nov 1977), 4[+?] [Based on survey response].

"She Hadn't Changed a Bit" *FH* 20 Dec 1956, 10-1.

"Sir Launcelot Wore Blue Jeans" *Onward* 31 Aug 1958, 545-8.

"A Sister for Susanna" *Onward* 29 Dec 1957, 817-9, 830.

"Something Meaningful" *Can Messenger* 80 (Oct 1970), 12-3, 22.

"The Star That Showed the Way" *FH* 24 Dec 1959, 12-3, 30.

"A Step in the Right Direction" *Annals* 91 (Sept 1977), 256[+?] [Based on survey response].

"Summer School" *Onward* 31 July 1966, 3-4, 10.

"They Shall Mount Up with Wings" *Annals* 92 (May 1978), 134[+?] [Based on survey response].

"This Is the Day" *Annals* 93 (July-Aug 1979), 210[+?] [Based on survey response].

"A Time of Asking" *Rapport* May 1969, 11-3.

"The Time of the Singing of Birds" *QQ* 75 (1968), 147-54.

"The Time of the Singing of Birds" *Link* (U.S.) 31 (Apr 1973), 45[+?] [Based on survey response].

"The Time of the Singing of Birds" *Annals* 89 (May 1975), 142[+?] [Based on survey response].

"To One He Gave Ten" *Annals* 87 (May 1973), 151[+?] [Based on survey response].

"Too Late Tomorrow" *Rapport* Mar 1969, 27-30.

"The Town That Cares" *West Prod* 16 Mar 1972, 5[+?] [Based on survey response].

"The Treasure Hunt" *Can Messenger* 88 (Feb 1978), 12-3, 17, 20.

"Troubles of Everett Mitchell" *West Prod* 11 July 1957, 14[+?] [Based on survey response].

"Twelve Days of Christmas" *CHJ* Dec 1954, 20-1, 26-7, 29, 32-4.

"Unconditional Christmas" *West Prod* 21 Dec 1972, 5[+?] [Based on survey response].

"The Unconditional Christmas" *Link* (U.S.) 31 (Dec 1973), 40[+?] [Based on survey response].

"The Unintentional Angel" *FH* 31 Dec 1953, 16, 21.

"A Way of Caring" *Red Star Weekly* (U.K.) 11 Mar 1978, 29[+?] [Based on survey response].

"Welcome to My World" *West Prod* 28 Oct 1971, 2[+?] [Based on survey response].

"What Can Be Built on Hate?" *Can Messenger* 85 (Apr 1975), 12-4, 18.

"What Do I Do on Mondays?" *Onward* 13 June 1965, 12-3.

"Whatever Happened to Sandra" *Fair Lady* (S Afr) 1971 [Based on survey response].

"When Your Heart Sings" *Red Star Weekly* (U.K.) 27 Oct 1973, 30[+?] [Based on survey response].

"Where the Heart Is" *Christian Home* (U.S.) 11 (May 1952), 7[+?] [Based on survey response].

"The White Rose" *Norsk Ukeblad* (Norway) No. 30 (July 1955), 9[+?] [As "Tre Hvite Roser"; based on survey response].

"Who Is Twisting My Arm?" *Can Messenger* 83 (May 1973), 14-5.

"Wisdom Built Her House" *Annals* 89 (June 1975), 167[+?] [Based on survey response].

"With Expectant Spirits" *Annals* 88 (Feb 1974), 38[+?] [Based on survey response].

"A World Apart" *Story World* (U.K.) 21 Aug 1976, 18[+?] [Based on survey response].

"Your Brother Came with Guile" *Annals* 90 (July-Aug 1976), 228[+?] [Based on survey response].

Steinberg, Janice‡

"Scapes / Spaces" *Communicator* 8:4 [n.d.], [3 pp].

Steinfeld, J.J. (1946-)

THE APOSTATE'S TATTOO Charlottetown: Ragweed Press, 1983.

"Amnesia (or Mnemosyne Is a *Kurveh*)" *JD* Rosh Hashanah 1982, 2-8, 10.

"Andy Goldman's Conversion" *JD* Sum 1981, 2-6.

"The Apostate's Tattoo" *JD* Sum 1981, 22-4.

"The Apostate's Tattoo" *Apostate's Tattoo* (1983), 66-74.

"A Beautiful Woman" *Origins* 12:2 (Sum 1982), 49-64.

"A Beautiful Woman" *Apostate's Tattoo* (1983), 86-96.

"The Bet" *JD* Rosh Hashanah 1982, 12-4, 16.

"The Blue Jays versus the Black Douglases" *Origins* 12:2 (Sum 1982), 26-34.

"The Building of Yankel Rabinowitz" *JD* Sum 1981, 28-31.

"A Bullet for Perlmutter" *Origins* 12:2 (Sum 1982), 35-48.

"A Bullet for Perlmutter" *Apostate's Tattoo* (1983), 21-32.

"The Chess Master" *Apostate's Tattoo* (1983), 123-33.

"Disfigurement" *Antig R* No. 50 (Sum 1982), 15-25.

"The Heart" *JD* Hanukah 1981, 32-5.

"*Playboy* and the Bar Mitzvah Boy" *JD* Hanukah 1981, 42-5.

"In the Room Where Dying Is Complete" *Rubicon* No. 2 (Win 1983-84), 7-19.

"The Kidney Question in Quebec" *JD* Rosh Hashanah 1982, 18-22.

"The Making of a Writer" *Pot Port* 4 (1982-83), 19-22.

"Martin Buber and the Yankee" *JD* Rosh Hashanah 1982, 32-5.

"Missing Limbs and Love" *Apostate's Tattoo* (1983), 75-85.

"One of Hypermnestra's Sisters" *Apostate's Tattoo* (1983), 7-20.

"PENALTY FOR MISUSE – $20" *Apostate's Tattoo* (1983), 115-22.

"Prosperity" *Origins* 12:1 (Apr 1982), 28-50.

"Safe at Home" *Can Lit R* No. 2 (Sum 1983), 104-13.

"The Sailor's Attic" *Quarry* 31:2 (Spr 1982), 22-9.

"Saturday Afternoon" *New Q* 3:3 (Fall 1983), 51-61.

"The Squaw's Professor" *Origins* 11:3 (Win 1981), 63-74.

"The Suicide Inspector" *Apostate's Tattoo* (1983), 54-65.

"The Surprise Party" *Apostate's Tattoo* (1983), 105-14.

"The Tea Leaves of Madame Angelica" *Origins* 12:2 (Sum 1982), 18-25.

"A Television-Watching Artist" *Apostate's Tattoo* (1983), 33-41.

"Trillium" *Apostate's Tattoo* (1983), 42-53.

"Voices" *Apostate's Tattoo* (1983), 97-104.
"Weintraub's Education" *JD* Rosh Hashanah 1982, 24-6, 28, 30.
"The Writer's Room" *Pot Port* 5 (1983-84), 22-4.

Steinhauer, C.‡
"An 'I' Narrative" *Mandala* 1971, 65-7.

Steltner, Elke
" 'And Still She Cries, Bonnie Boys Are Few' " *BC Monthly* 3:6/7 (Apr-May 1977), [6 pp].

Stemo, L. Johanne (1910-)
"All Clear Land" *FH* 6 May 1954, 28-9, 37.
"The Bad Year" *FH* 9 Nov 1950, 26-7.
"The Courting of Jenny" *MM* 65 (15 Apr 1952), 18, 40-3.
"The Courting of Jenny" *Short Story International* 1 No. 6 (Apr 1964), 83-96.
"The Day Mama Went to Work" *CHJ* Dec 1957, 29, 45-7.
"The Education of the Adamses" *FH* 3 May 1951, 22-3, 30.
"The Foreigners" *FH* 24 Oct 1963, 52, 55.
"Guns Are for Men" *MM* 65 (1 Sept 1952), 18, 34-7.
"The One Who Played God" *Echoes* No. 217 (Christmas 1954), 41-2.
"The Roots of the Heart Grow Deep" *Chat* 27 (Feb 1954), 17, 53-8.
"Was He My Brother" *Diversions* 4:1 (1973), 30-6.
"The Year That Christmas Passed Us By" *Can Messenger* 90 (Jan 1980), 8-9.
"You Can't Steal Happiness" *Chat* 28 (May 1956), 17, 77-82.

Stenson, Bill‡
"Three Golden Dukes" *From an Island* 1978, 26-9.

Stenson, Frederick (1951-)
"Arlene" *SN* 95 (Jan-Feb 1980), 32-7.
"Arlene" *Three Times Five* (1983), 87-96.
"Delusions of Agriculture" *SN* 96 (Nov 1981), 52-4, 56, 58, 60-1.
"Diving for Pleasure" *Miss Chat* 14 (3 Feb 1977), 60-1, 78-80.
"The Duel" *Miss Chat* 12 (13 Mar 1975), 82-5.
"The Interview" *Can R* 4:1 (Feb 1977), 20.
"The Lesson of Fitzroy" *Miss Chat* 13 (11 Mar 1976), 92-3, 95-8.
"The Lesson of Fitzroy" *Three Times Five* (1983), 65-73.
"Lover" *Three Times Five* (1983), 74-9.
"Quiet Sunday" *Alberta Diamond Jubilee Anthology* (1979), 162-5.
"Round and Smooth" *Chat* 55 (Oct 1982), 119, 190-1, 196, 200, 202.
"Snapshots" *Miss Chat* 13 (2 Sept 1976), 69, 80-1.
"Teeth" *Edmonton Mag* 3 (Jan 1982), 29-30, 35, 37, 39.
"Teeth" *Three Times Five* (1983), 55-64.
"Teeth" *West of Fiction* (1983), 13-23.
"The Zeus Cave" *Three Times Five* (1983), 80-6.

Stephen, Sid‡
"Barn Cats" *Arts Man* 1:2 (Mar-May 1977), 30-2.

Stephens, Ian‡
   "Marc Courvois and the Football Men" *New Mitre* 85 (1980), 43-4.
   "Moonstone People" *New Mitre* 1976, 14-6.
   [Untitled] *New Mitre* 1975, 10-1.
   [Untitled] *New Mitre* 1975, 29-30.

Stephens, John‡
   "Legend of Pomona Mills" *Thornhill Month* 5 (Dec 1983), 5, 7.
   "The Menorah and the Manger" *Thornhill Month* 4 (Dec 1982), 5.
   "The Party" *Thornhill Month* 3 (Feb 1982), 5 [Humour].

Stephenson, Michael†
   "The Oldest Trick in the World" *Alfred Hitchcock* 25 (16 June 1980) [Based on Cook].
   "The Pack" *Nw J* No. 24 (1981), 60-4.
   "The Peacemaker" *Read Ch* 1:1 (Spr 1982), 71-4.
   "Please Mister Mac" *AA* 66 (Apr 1976), 17-9.
   "The Trick" *Black Cat* No. 6 (1982), 13-24.
   "The Ultimate Tranquilizer" *Alfred Hitchcock* 18 (Nov 1973), 110-5.
   "The World's Greatest Detective" *Read Ch* 1:1 (Spr 1982), 75-85.

Stephenson, Paula
   "The Hollowed Halls of Learning" *Northern Ontario Anthology* 1 (1977), 45-8.

Sterling, Sharon (1955-)
   "Elly's Dad" *Br Out* 6:4 (1979), 32-4.

Stern, Sandor‡
   "Exaltation" *Varsity* Fri, 18 Mar 1960, 7, 4.

Stevens, Irene†
   "The Way It Might Have Been" *Living Message* 79 (Dec 1968), 8-9.

Stevens, Peter (1927-)
   "April Street and After" *JD* Hanukah 1972, 48-55.
   "Bath" *Connexion* No. 4 [n.d.], [2 pp].
   "Package" *WCR* 5:2 (Oct 1970), 16-7.

Stevens, R. Jean†
   "Zack" *CSSM* 1:4 (Oct 1975), 1-3.

Stevens-Guille, Peter‡
   "A Sense of Value" *Liontayles* Win 1967, 22-5.

Stevenson, David†
   "The Doctor and the Ghost" *Green's* 10:3 (Spr 1982), 79-85.
   "The Integrating Machine" *Green's* 10:1 (Aut 1981), 74-9.

Stevenson, Gillian
   "Going Home" *Outset* 1974, 159-65.
   "Last Day" *Outset* 1973, 158-64.

Stevenson, Joan‡
"The Feminist" *Alive* No. 157 (20 Oct 1979), 15.
"Knowing History – Knowing Struggle" *Alive* No. 148 (18 Aug 1979), 14-6.
"Magic Twigs" *Alive* No. 159 (17 Nov 1979), 16.
"May Day" *Alive* No. 134 (5 May 1979), 18-9.
"Some Lessons Learned" *Alive* No. 133 (28 Apr 1979), 13-9.
"Starting Off on the Right Foot" *Alive* No. 170 (Jan 1981), 8-9.

Stevenson, Louis†
"My Brother's Keeper" *Repos* [No. 34] (1981), 18-26.

Stevenson, Roberta†
"Willows" *Raven* 2 [No. 4] (Spr 1957), 13-4.

Stevenson, S. Warren†
"Woe to the Caroche" *Forge* 1954, 67-70.

Steward, A.W.‡
"Daniel III" *Public Affairs* 15:3 (Spr 1953), 18-24.

Steward, Hartley‡
"And That's the Truth" *Fifth Page* 1964, 33-6.

Stewart, Alan‡
"NkwasiasEm YE Dina" *Writ* No. 5 (Spr 1973), 93-105.

Stewart, Alec M. (1950?-)‡
"The Editor" *Stardust* 3:2 (Spr 1981), 51-4.

Stewart, Anne L.†
"The Legacy" *Can Messenger* 91 (Feb 1981), 8-9.
"The Loss" *Can Messenger* 92 (Oct 1982), 8-9.
"Marlborough Street" *Living Message* 93 (Oct 1982), 19-21 [Same author?].
"Passport to Tomorrow" *Can Messenger* 90 (May 1980), 8-9.
"Perspective" *Can Messenger* 86 (June 1976), 12-3, 19.

Stewart, Cherie‡
"Earthquake" *Diversions* 5:1 (1975), 5-17.
"Earthquake" *Room* 1:2 (Sum 1975), 2-14.

Stewart, Cybel M.‡
"Miracle at Midnight" *UC Observer* Dec 1978, 12-3.

Stewart, Dave‡
"Unity in Struggle" *Alive* No. 72 (9 Apr 1977), 4-5.

Stewart, Irene‡
"The Ribbon" *Fid* No. 123 (Fall 1979), 89-98.

Stewart, Jocelyn‡
"The Bride Elect" *Mandala* 1978, 20-1.

Stewart, Molly‡
"Work Boots and Carpet" *AA* 63 (July 1973), 19-21.

Stewart, Scott†
"Seasons of a Flowers" *New Q* 2:2 (Sum 1982), 55-7.

Stewart, Valerie†
"A Flickering Sunspot" *Our Family* 25 (Mar 1973), 26-8.

Stewart, Vel. C.
"Revenge" *CSSM* 3:1 (Win 1977), 53-7.

Stewart-Richmond, Effie†
"Two-Way Stretch" *Alberta Writers Speak* 1964, 9-16.

Stickland, Eugene†
"How the West Was Won" *Sundogs* (1980), 139-43.
"Red Dreams, Blue Dreams" *Saskatchewan Gold* (1982), 286-92.

Stilwell, Arthur
"The Children's Hour" *Companion* [38] (Sept 1963), 8-12.
"The Door" *Companion* [39] (Feb 1964), 9-13.
"Ersatz Erotica" *Edmonton Journal* Fri, 10 May 1968, 59.
"Farewells Exchanged Beside a Train" *Onward* 1 Sept 1963, 10-1, 15.
"Giant Pike" *Stories with John Drainie* (1963), 99-105.
"Grandfather's Oak" *Onward* 8 Aug 1965, 4-5, 10.
"The Harvest of Years" *Onward* 31 Mar 1962, 6-7, 11-2.
"Holidays Can Be Fun – Even for Frustrated Father" *Companion* 37 (July-Aug 1962), 16-21.
"How to Dispose of Old Furniture" *Onward* 25 Nov 1962, 12 [Humour?].
"How to Dispose of Old Furniture" *Onward* 12 Feb 1967, 12.
"It's Hard to Grow Up" *Companion* 36 (Nov 1961), 19-23.
"Old Nick Kuzloski's Great Church Episode" *Companion* 36 (Jan 1961), 11-5.
"The Painting" *CG* 79 (Mar 1960), 61-4.
"Pop Was a Good 'Scout' " *Companion* [38] (May 1963), 16-9.

Stirling, Richard†
"The Photograph" *WWR* 2:3 No. 7 (1982), 9-16.

Stock, B.C.‡
"In Secula Seculorum" *Probe* 1:1 (1960), 7-8.

Stock, B.E.‡
"She Wakes at Midnight" *Mam* 1:2 [n.d.], [2 pp].

Stockanes, Anthony E.‡
"About the Man Who Married a Much Younger Woman Who Took Care of Him in His Declining Years, Nursing Him Through the Flu" *Dreamweaver* 1:2 (Sum [1980]).

Stockdale, J.C.†
"Better to Burn" Scruncheons 1:2 (Sept 1973), 27-32.
"Better to Burn" *Fid* No. 99 (Fall 1973), 35-40.

Stockdale, J[ohn]. C.
"Helga" *Intervales* [No. 1] (1959), 33-5.
"I Thought I Saw a Pussy Cat" *Intervales* No. 2 (1960), 37-9.

Stocks, Andy‡
"The Sudbury Bush: A Gypsy George Story" *Ostara* [n.d.], 52-6.

Stodola, Lori‡
"Rudy's Kite" *CBC "Alberta Anthology"* 30 Oct 1982.

Stokes, Denis‡
"The Place" *UCR* Spr 1980, 34-6.

Stokes, Marian‡
"The Air That We Breathe" *Portico* [1:1] (Mar 1977), 21-3.

Stone, A.C.†
"Auction" *Green's* 4:4 (Sum 1976), 94-8.
"Decision Day" *Green's* 9:4 (Sum 1981), 22-5.
"The Last Great Joke of Gilhooley Jones" *Green's* 1:4 (Sum 1973), 31-2.
"A Matter of Timing" *Green's* 4:1 (Aut 1975), 23-7.

Stone, Charles†
"Samuel James Williams" *Quarry* 4 (Spr 1955), 21-4.
"The Trouble with Eddie" *Quarry* 9 (Mar 1960), 21-3.

Stone, Larry‡
"The Duke in Toronto" *Sheet* 1:2 (Sept 1960), 13-4.

Stone, Louise‡
"Emma and the Sabbath Day" *CF* 31 (May 1951), 35, 37.

Stone, P. Anne†
"Seeing Double" *Writing* No. 4 (Win 1981-82), 33-7.
"What He Expected" *Was R* 16:1 (Spr 1981), 31-9.

Stone, Patricia†
"The Reel World" *Antig R* No. 46 (Sum 1981), 19-32.
"The Thin Edge" *Room* 8:3 (1983), 46-57.

Stortz, Joan (1920-)
"The Ancient Newsmonger" *Living Message* 89 (Nov 1978) [?] [Based on survey response].
"Grains of Sand" *Interior Voice* [No. 3?] (Jan 1983) [Based on survey response].
"Lobster Trap" *Senior American* (U.S.) Feb 1981 [Based on survey response].

Story, Alice
"15 Marley Place" *Applegarth's Folly* No. 2 (1975), 37-53.
"The Next Victim" *Twelve Newfoundland Short Stories* (1982), 85-92.

Story, Gertrude (1929-)

THE WAY TO ALWAYS DANCE Saskatoon: Thistledown Press, 1983.

"An Affair of the Heart" *West Producer* [1963?] [Based on survey response].

"At a Party It Doesn't Pay to Laugh Too Much" *NeWest R* 6 (Sept 1980), 11-2.

"Aunt Hoffer and the Highlanders" *CBC* [1967?] [Based on survey response].

"The Best Laid Plans" *West Producer* [1964?] [Based on survey response].

"Black Velvet" *Way to Always Dance* (1983), 49-56.

"But You Ought to Ask the Bride" *Can Ethnic Studies* 14:1 (1982), 103-8.

"Car of Maroon" *CA & B* 55:2 (Feb 1980), 16-8.

"Das Engelein Kommt" *Sundogs* (1980), 144-50.

"Das Engelein Kommt" *Grain* 8:3 (Nov 1980), 34-9.

"Das Engelein Kommt" *CBC* "Anthology" 18 Dec 1982 [Based on survey response].

"Das Engelein Kommt" *83: Best Canadian Stories* 49-58.

"Dress of Yellow" *West Producer* [1961?] [Based on survey response].

"Dress of Yellow" *CBC* [1969?] [Based on survey response].

"A Fair Beginning" *Way to Always Dance* (1983), 14-22.

"For Everything, a Season" *West Producer* [1964?] [Based on survey response].

"For Everything, a Season" *CBC* [1966?] [Based on survey response].

"Four-Finger Pete and the Yella Deer" *CBC* [1965?] [Based on survey response].

"Four-Finger Pete and the Yella Deer" *CBC* [1966?] [Based on survey response].

"A Friend in Need" *West Producer* [1968?] [Based on survey response].

"The Good Day" *CBC* [1967?] [Based on survey response].

"Habakkuk Hoffer and the Haunted Harpsichord" *CBC* [1968?] [Based on survey response].

"Harmonious Hoffer and His Hairless Hired Hand" *CBC* [1967?] [Based on survey response].

"Harpocrates Hoffer and the Heedless Harangue" *Smoke Signals* 3 (1978) [Based on survey responses].

"Henrietta Hoffer and the Hapless Heifer" *CBC* [1971?] [Based on survey response].

"Herodotus Hoffer and the Unilingual Hound" *CBC* [1969?] [Based on survey response].

"Hialeah Hoffer and the Walleyed Mare" *CBC* [1968?] [Based on survey response].

"Hialeah Hoffer and the Walleyed Mare" *100% Cracked Wheat* (1983), 41-9.

"A Higher Learning" *Way to Always Dance* (1983), 107-19.

"Hoffer and the Horned Dilemma" *West Producer* [1967?] [Based on survey response].

"Hoffer and the Horned Dilemma" *CBC* [1968?] [Based on survey response].

"Hottentot Hoffer and His Last Hope of Heaven" *CBC* [1974?] [Based on survey response].

"Hottentot Hoffer and His Last Hope of Heaven" *West Producer* [1975?] [Based on survey response].

"Hottentot Hoffer and His Last Hope of Heaven" *100% Cracked Wheat* (1983), 222-8.

" 'A Man's a Man,' and All That" *West Producer* [1964?] [Based on survey response].

"A Matter of Custom" *West Producer* [1963?] [Based on survey response].

"A Matter of Custom" *CBC* [1968?] [Based on survey response].

"Never Be A-Scared to Dance" *Camrose R* No. 4 [n.d.], 12-5.
"Of Mice, and Men, and Mores" *CBC* [1968?] [Based on survey response].
"Pease Porridge Hot" *West Producer* [1965?] [Based on survey response].
"Pembroke O'Connell and the Purple Pig" *CBC* [1967?] [Based on survey response].
"The Picnic" *Dand* 7:2 (1980), 13-8.
"Sarah's Easter Offering" *West Producer* [1961?] [Based on survey response].
"The Smiths of Swanson" *West Producer* [1965?] [Based on survey response].
"The Summer Visitor" *Dand* 9:2 (1982), 13-22.
"The Summer Visitor" *Saskatchewan Gold* (1982), 86-95.
"Swan Song" *Grain* 8:1 [1980], 23-7.
"This Above All" *West Producer* [1964?] [Based on survey response].
"A Time of New Beginning" *West Producer* [1963?] [Based on survey response].
"To Choose to Dance" *Way to Always Dance* (1983), 120-30.
"To Do and to Endure" *FH* 16 Mar 1967, 42.
"Too Long, Too Long, No Dance" *Way to Always Dance* (1983), 78-91.
"The Trials of P. G. O'Ryan" *CBC* [1967?] [Based on survey response].
"Uncle Hoffer and the Hat" *CBC* [1966?] [Based on survey response].
"What Is, Is" *Way to Always Dance* (1983), 92-106.
"What Makes Two, Makes Three" *Way to Always Dance* (1983), 57-77.
"When There's to Be No Moon" *Way to Always Dance* (1983), 36-48.
"The Whitest of Feathers" *Way to Always Dance* (1983), 23-35.

Stothers, Margaret‡
"Dead Dogs and Americans" *NeWest R* 5 (Nov 1979), 10.
"M.S. Remission" *Dand* 7:1 (1980), 31-4.

Strandebo, Sandra‡
"Wussams" *CBC [Van] "Hornby Collection"* 30 Jan 1982.

Strandlund, Wayne‡
"Winter Palace" *Introductions from an Island* 1971, 24-9.

Stratford, Philip
"Congratulations ... Father?" *CF* 37 (June 1957), 55-6.

Strickland, Edward†
"Atelier Oeuf: Lune" *Imp* 2:1 (Aut 1972), 28-31.
"War and Peace: A Novel in Three Books" *Des* No. 10 (Win 1974), 43-5.

Strom, Martha‡
"Requisition 23 Men" *CBC "Alberta Anthology"* 29 Oct 1983.

Strong, Aaron†
"One Morning" *Scrivener* 4:2 (Sum 1983), 24-5.

Strum, Gary‡
"Night Duty" *Communicator* 10:3 [n.d.], 41-4.

Stuart, James‡

"The Beauty of El Poeta" *Forge* Feb 1957, 46-8.
"The Perpendicular Sun" *Forge* Dec 1957, 17-9.
"Pervasion" *Forge* Dec 1954, 31-3.

Stubbs, Judy‡

" 'Welcome-Back-to-Society' " *Pedantics* 1965, 77-8.

Stuckey, Jo‡

"Mr. Bentham, I Presume?" *UC Gargoyle* 4 (27 Jan 1958), 2.

Sturdy, Giles‡

"Fragments of a Continent" *TUR* 79:1 (Oct-Nov 1965), 7-10.
"The Myth of the Black Mountain" *TUR* 78:4 (Mar 1965), 10-5.

Sturdy, John Rhodes

"Anniversary" *MM* 64 (1 Apr 1951), 19, 50-2, 58.
"Benjy and the Killer Whale" *SW* 7 Jan 1967, 28-31.
"Blind Spot" *SW* 5 May 1962, 8-10, 12.
"The Captain's Decision" *SW* 2 June 1956, I:7, 9.
"Change of Locale" *Weekend* 3 (3 Jan 1953), 8-9.
"Christening for Uncle Ethan" *SW* 12 Jan 1952, II:5.
"Efficiency Test" *Weekend* 3 (5 Dec 1953), 28-9, 50, 52.
"Evening on the Town" *Weekend* 4 (1 May 1954), 14, 46, 48, 51.
"Fight on the Beach" *SW* 19 May 1962, 13-5.
"The Fish Are Where You Find Them" *SW* 3 July 1965, 12-3, 30.
"The Homburg Hat" *Weekend* 4 (24 Apr 1954), 8-9, 41, 50.
"How's the Weather?" *Weekend* 3 (20 June 1953), 10-1.
"Last Cruise of Summer" *SW* 10 Mar 1962, 8-11.
"A Matter of Dimensions" *Weekend* 4 (23 Jan 1954), 8, 18, 21.
"Momma Rich's Pastrami" *SW* 19 Sept 1959, 16, 34.
"The Nurse" *SW* 13 Dec 1952, I:8, 12.
"Oh, Danny Boy" *Weekend* 1 (24 Nov 1951), 24-5, 32.
"The Railroad Builder" *SW* 18 Aug 1962, 10-3, 17.
"The Resident" *Weekend* 3 (14 Mar 1953), 20-2.
"The Secession of Deer Island" *SW* 2 Aug 1958, 15, 44.
"Still Brightly Shines the Light" *SW* 8 Jan 1966, 10-1, 13.
"Switcheroo" *SW* 18 June 1966, 8-11.
"Take Me Out to Dinner" *Weekend* 2 (20 Sept 1952), 12-3.
"The Third Bullet" *Weekend* 1 (8 Sept 1951), 16, 44-5.
"The Town Where I Was Born" *Weekend* 4 (4 Sept 1954), 10-1, 29, 32.
"Trail's End" *SW* 19 Sept 1953, I:6.
"Wind and Fire" *SW* 18 Aug 1956, II:1, 12.
"Winter Flight" *SW* 28 Jan 1956, I:9.
"A Wreath for Pennant Annie" *SW* 7 July 1956, II:5, 12.
"A Yukon Man" *SW* 20 Apr 1963, 10-2, 17.

Sturgeon, Brad‡

"One Persian Night Before the Fall" *UTR* 7 (Spr 1983), 28, 30-2.

Sturmanis, Dona

"Death of a President" by Dona Crane *VWFP/Revue* 1:1 (Spr 1975), 6, 8.

"Oh, Won't You Ever See the Error of Your Wicked, Wicked Ways" *Canadian Short Fiction Anthology* (1976), 195-202.

"The Personal Commitment of Cosmic Leonard" by Dona Crane *VWFP/Revue* 1:5 (July 1975), 12, 20.

"She Emerged Fresh from the Bathroom" *Br Out* 4:3 (July-Aug 1977), 30-2.

Such, Peter

"Floating Bears" *Imp* 2:3/4 (1973), 47-59.

"Last Year Another Pyramid Fell Down" *Des* 10:3/4 Nos. 25/26 (1979), 141-55.

"Mosaic in Montmartre" *Seven* [n.d.], [5 pp].

"The Reef" CBC *"Anthology"* 12 Aug 1972.

"Snow Job" CBC *"Anthology"* 19 Jan 1974.

Sudbury, Harold A.J.‡

"The Game of War" *Scar Fair* 4 (1976-77), 16-22.

"Home Sweet Home" *Scar Fair* 1 (1973-74), 9-12.

Sullivan, D.H.†

"Apples" *Matrix* Nos. 6/7 (1978), 4-13.

"The Grid" *Evidence* No. 10 (1967), 81-8.

"The Separator" *CF* 46 (Mar 1967), 275-7.

Sullivan, Edward‡

"The Kings of Lokasena" *WWR* 1:1 (Spr 1976), 66-71.

Sullivan, Jordan‡

"The Secret" *Varsity* Thu, 13 Dec 1956, 7.

Summerhayes, Don‡

"The Day I Hit Alvin" *Muse* 61:1 (Dec 1951), 5-7.

"Like a Little Princess" *Muse* 62:1 (Spr 1953), 12-6.

"Lover" *Muse* 60:1 (Nov 1950), 10-3.

"Oasis" *Muse* 60:3 (Feb 1951), 5-7.

"A Place to Die" *Muse* 60:4 (Apr 1951), 5-7.

Summers, Anthony J.‡

"Bones" *Pulp* 3:5 (15 Sept 1975), [1].

"Crumbs" *Pulp* 3:5 (15 Sept 1975), [1].

"Dog Meat" *Titmouse R* No. 7 [n.d.], 59.

"A Tribute to All the Dagwood Bumstead's in America" *Pulp* 3:5 (15 Sept 1975), [1-2].

Summers, Dave‡

"The Julie Watcher" *Quest for a Common Denominator* 1:1 (Spr 1977), [8 pp].

Summers, M[ark]. D.†

"The Curator" *Toronto Star* Sun, 6 Nov 1983, D6.

Summers, Merna (1933-)
    CALLING HOME Ottawa: Oberon Press, 1982.
    THE SKATING PARTY Ottawa: Oberon Press, 1974.
    "The Bachelors" *Skating Party* (1974), 42-59.
    "The Blizzard" *73: New Canadian Stories* 23-44.
    "The Blizzard" *Skating Party* (1974), 5-30.
    "Calling Home" *Calling Home* (1982), 32-63.
    "Calling Home" *Matrix* No. 15 (Spr-Sum 1982), 48-68.
    "City Wedding" *Calling Home* (1982), 64-76.
    "Hooking Things" *Dand* 7:2 (1980), 26-47.
    "Hooking Things" *Calling Home* (1982), 77-102.
    "A Pailful of Partridges" *Calling Home* (1982), 103-26.
    "Portulaca" *Skating Party* (1974), 60-74.
    "Ronnie So Long at the Fair" *Calling Home* (1982), 5-31.
    "The Skating Party" *Skating Party* (1974), 100-20.
    "The Skating Party" *New Worlds* (1980), 32-46.
    "The Skating Party" *West of Fiction* (1983), 79-94.
    "Threshing Time" *Nimrod* 23:1 (1979), 25-38 [Based on AHI].
    "Threshing Time" *Calling Home* (1982), 127-49.
    "Wee Tommy Devlin and the Chocolate Pudding" *Skating Party* (1974), 31-41.
    "Willow Song" *Skating Party* (1974), 75-99.
    "Willow Song" *Horizon* (1977), 178-93.

Sumpter, Judy†
    "Journey Through Fear" *From 231* [1:1] (Spr 1972), 1-7.

Surette, Debbie‡
    "Anna" *First Encounter* 12 (1981-82), 14.

Surguy, Phil‡
    "Notes from the Topsoil" *Potlatch* No. 6 (Mar 1966), 11-21.

Surtees, Lawrence‡
    "Toronto: Just Another City? Or Read the Signs" *Scar Fair* 5 (1977-78), 28-34.

Sutherland, Barry†
    "Adam" *CFM* No. 10 (Spr 1973), 75-93.
    "Installment Plan" *Introductions from an Island* 1972, 31-9.

Sutherland, David‡
    "Decree Absolute" *TUR* 63:4 (Mar 1951), 18-9.
    "The Harmon Bequest" *TUR* 65:1 (Dec 1952), 19-22.

Sutherland, Fraser (1946-)
    "Beginnings" *Pot Port* 2 (1980-81), 4.
    "Brassières" *CFM* Nos. 30/31 (1979), 196-201.
    "Brassières" *Illusion One* (1983), 119-25.
    "Breathing" *Inner Space* No. [1] (Spr 1969), [3 pp].
    "Dejeuner sur l'herbe" *NJ* No. 4 (June 1974), 20-6.
    "The Impenetrables (Parody)" *Halcyon* 12 (Win 1966-67), 34-6.
    "In Hospital" *Antig R* No. 20 (Win 1974), 21-2.
    "In the Village of Alias" *Pot Port* 5 (1983-84), 6-10.

"It Used to Be a Nice Neighbourhood" *Halcyon* 12 (Win 1966-67), 37-40.
"A Night at the Opera" *CFM* No. 11 (Aut 1973), 72-4.
'Patricia" *Antig R* No. 20 (Win 1974), 23-4.
'Patricia" *Short Short Stories* (1983), 15-7 [Based on survey response].
"Pears" *UWR* 16:2 (Spr-Sum 1982), 50-5.
"Pears" *Metavisions* (1983), 201-6.
"The Sacred Glow" *JCF* 2:4 (Fall 1973), 14-5.
"Scenario" *Alive* 2:8 (July-Aug 1971), 37-9.
"Wilderness Wild – A Sexual Saga of the Canadian North" *CFM* No. 15 (Aut 1975), 54-61.
"Wilderness Wild – A Sexual Saga of the Canadian North" *Magic Realism* (1980), 37-44.

Sutherland, Robert†
"Adam Clark, the Covenanter of Glenim" *Pres Record* Apr 1951, 114, 128.

Sutherland, Ronald (1933-)
"White Christmas in Montreal" *JCF* 2:1 (Win 1973), 16-8.

Sutterfield, Allen
"At Pharaoh's" *Cap R* No. 13 (1978), 5-7.

Svendsen, Linda (1954-)
'The Adviser" *Second Impressions* (1981), 173-8.
"Afternoon at the Lido" *Room* 3:4 (1978), 2-19.
"Esso" *80: Best Canadian Stories* 162-77 [Also entitled "Gas Pumps"].
"Esso" *Seventeen* 41 (Sept 1982), 166-7, 183, 193.
"Exercises" *Second Impressions* (1981), 135-51.
"Gas Pumps" *Miss Chat* 16 (Mar 1979), 88-9, 98, 102, 104, 106 [Also entitled "Esso"].
"Heartbeat" *Atlantic Monthly* 248 (Oct 1981), 85-91.
"Heartbeat" *Prize Stories: O'Henry Awards* 1983 270-84.
"Marine Life" *Second Impressions* (1981), 152-61.
"Marine Life" *Prairie Schooner* 56:2 (Sum 1982), 45-54.
"Origami" *Second Impressions* (1981), 162-72.
"Who He Slept By" *Atlantic Monthly* 246 (July 1980), 70-2, 74-7.
"Who He Slept By" *81: Best Canadian Stories* 128-44.

Svingen, Anne†
"Circus" *Saskatchewan Homecoming* (1971), 107-8.

Svoboda, Terese‡
"Aisle" *Titmouse R* 1:2 (Win 1972), 46.
'The Harvesters" *Was R* 8:2 (Fall 1973), 13-7.
'Pizza Piece" *Titmouse R* 1:2 (Win 1972), 46-7.

Swan, Ed‡
"Invented in a Blizzard of Words" *Pulp* 5:5 (1 May 1979), [1-3].

Swan, Mary‡
"Anna" *Fid* No. 109 (Spr 1976), 68-77.
"A Long Time Ago" *Quarry* 25:3 (Sum 1976), 28-35.

Swan, Rhoda H.†

"The One Hundred and Fifty Livres of Guillaume Couillard" *Echoes* No. 227 (Sum 1957), 4-5, 9.

Swan, Susan (1945-)

UNFIT FOR PARADISE Toronto: Christopher Dingle, 1982.
"Dante in the Laundromat" *Unfit for Paradise* (1982), 56-9.
"Fort Liquordale" *Unfit for Paradise* (1982), 31-7.
"Getting Your Money's Worth" *Des* 11:4/12:1 Nos. 30/31 (1980-81), 48-52.
"Getting Your Money's Worth" *Unfit for Paradise* (1982), 1-6.
"A Holiday in the Doom Future" *Unfit for Paradise* (1982), 60-7.
"Hot Feet in Puerto Rico" *Unfit for Paradise* (1982), 7-12.
"The Last of the Golden Girls" *SN* 92 (Mar 1977), 54-9.
"The Life and Times of Theresa Turkey" *Weekend* 27 (8 Oct 1977), 9.
"The Man Doll" *Des* 13:4 No. 38 (Fall 1982), 65-71.
"The Men" *Chat* 50 (Feb 1977), 35, 62.
"Slumming in Maui" *Unfit for Paradise* (1982), 49-55.
"The Sunshine Girl and the Shah" *Unfit for Paradise* (1982), 13-7.
"Two for Trinidad" *Unfit for Paradise* (1982), 38-48.
"Unfit for Paradise" *Unfit for Paradise* (1982), 18-25.
"The Waterbed Syndrome" *Title Unknown* (1975), 6-7, 34.
"Young and Gay" *Unfit for Paradise* (1982), 26-30.

Swann, Anahid‡

"They Sewed My Mother to Her Bed" *Mandala* 1972, 47-8 [Non-fiction?].

Swartz, Jill

"After the Yarn Is Spun" *Mal R* No. 66 (Oct 1983), 89-98.
"Carved by My Knife" *Grain* 11:3 (Aug 1983), 28-32.

Swayze, J.F.

"Family Plot" *FH* 24 Sept 1964, 34, 52.

Sweatman, Margaret†

"Angels and Other People" *Room* 8:1 (1983), 50-62.

Sweeney, Alistair‡

"Alice in Godfreyland or The Metamorphosic Dynamics of Relaxed Morality" *TUR* 79:4 (Apr 1966), 20-2.

Sweeney, Clive R.†

"Sacrifice" *Alpha* 4:3 (Spr 1980), 21, 34.

Sweet, Jean‡

"The Great Submarine Chase" *AA* 62 (Feb 1972), 12-3.

Swenson, Alan‡

"Eclipse" *Fid* No. 77 (Aut 1968), 9-29.

Swerdfegger, Enid‡

"New Birth" *Quarry* 7 (Mar 1958), [3 pp].

Swift, B.A.‡
"Cimon" *Prism* (Mont) 1967, 57-62.

Sylvie, Sylvia†.
"The Mourner" *Fifth Page* 1963, 8-13.
"The Mourner" Campus Canada Nov 1963, 28-9, 45.

Symon, John‡
"One Last Log" *Stump* 2:2 (Fall 1978), 31-3.

Symons, Harry (1893-)
THE BORED MEETING Toronto: Ryerson Press, 1951.
"The Bath, Country Fashion" *Bored Meeting* (1951), 54-64.
"The Bored Meeting" *Bored Meeting* (1951), 1-15.
"Denture Adventure" *Bored Meeting* (1951), 77-91.
"Have You Seen My Operation?" *Bored Meeting* (1951), 65-76.
"Humbug" *Bored Meeting* (1951), 92-105.
"Operation Elevator" *Bored Meeting* (1951), 106-21.
"Sabbath Victorian" *Bored Meeting* (1951), 30-53.
"Step Well Down to the Rear of the Car, Please!" *Bored Meeting* (1951), 16-29.

Szanto, George (1940-)
SIXTEEN WAYS TO SKIN A CAT Vancouver: Intermedia Press, 1977.
"The Beginning" *Sixteen Ways* (1977), 33-7.
"The Celebrated Case of Brother Sebastian" *Sixteen Ways* (1977), 91-100.
"Diversions" *Sixteen Ways* (1977), 73-80.
"Dog" *Antig R* No. 25 (Spr 1976), 71-7.
"Dog" *Sixteen Ways* (1977), 65-8.
"Fidelio" *Sixteen Ways* (1977), 55-8.
"The Fly Swatter" *Sixteen Ways* (1977), 28-32.
"For the Record" *Sixteen Ways* (1977), 69-71.
"Fort Triumph" *Sixteen Ways* (1977), 59-64.
"A Good Pair of Hands" *Sixteen Ways* (1977), 87-9.
"Mom" *Sixteen Ways* (1977), 5-8.
"The Partners" *Sixteen Ways* (1977), 49-50.
"Parts" *Antig R* No. 22 (Sum 1975), 9-14.
"Parts" *Sixteen Ways* (1977), 39-42.
"Pure Research" *Sixteen Ways* (1977), 81-5.
"A Season in Love" *Sixteen Ways* (1977), 9-27.
"Sixteen Ways to Skin a Cat" *Sixteen Ways* (1977), 1-4.
"Snowbilia" *Fid* No. 117 (Spr 1978), 90-8.
"Submission: Of Plenary Sub-Committee 26 [Logistics] Report of the League" *Sixteen Ways* (1977), 51-3.
"The Television Watcher" *Sixteen Ways* (1977), 43-8.

Sznajder, Rick‡
"Carnal Stings" *Gram* 9:1 (Fall 1983), 45-7.

Szumigalski, Anne (1922-)
"A Fable" *Writers News Man* No. 4 (Dec 1978), [1 p].
"A Fable" *Sundogs* (1980), 151-2.
"Story" *CA & B* 55:4/56:1 (Sum-Fall 1980), 30-1.
[Untitled] *Smoke Signals* 4 [date unknown] [Based on *SWG* survey response].

Taaffe, Gerald (1927-)
"The Assassination" *CBC "Anthology"* 8 Jan 1972.
"The Assassination" *CFM* No. 15 (Aut 1974), 4-13.
"Colors" *CFM* No. 39 (1981), 30-43.
"Colors" *Illusion One* (1983), 83-98.
"The Impressario" *Tam R* No. 65 (Mar 1975), 61-84.
"The Invisible Worm" *CBC "Anthology"* 11 Oct 1969.
"Kicking" *North American R* 262:3 (Fall 1977), 44-8.
"The Office Party" *CBC "Anthology"* 15 Mar 1975.
"The Office Party" *North American R* 261:1 (Spr 1976), 30-5.
"Pommagne Party" *CBC "Anthology"* 6 Oct 1961.
"Pommagne Party" *Tam R* No. 24 (Sum 1962), 51-64.

Tackaberry, Ivy‡
"Don't Wash, Shave, or Comb Your Hair – Just Move!" *Pier Spr* 1:1 (Aut 1976), 67-8.
"Melvin" *Pier Spr* 1:1 (Aut 1976), 52.
[Untitled] *Pier Spr* 1:2 (Spr 1977), 36-7.
"What Price Culture?" *Pier Spr* 1:2 (Spr 1977), 33-5.

Tadich, Alex Sasha‡
"The Reversal" *Generation* 1971, [4 pp].

Tagg, Geoff‡
"Saturday Morning" *CSSM* 1:4 (Oct 1975), 23-5.

Tagney, Paul‡
"The Beautiful Black Psalm That Farewell Was Always Meant to Be" *Tide* No. 1 [1968?], [5 pp].
"October 28, 1968" *Tide* 2:1 (Jan 1969), [1 p].

Tait, Elizabeth‡
"Hetty's Pound Party" *Onward* 16 Dec 1956, 808-10.
"The Kind-Hearted Mischief" *Onward* 23 June 1957, 392-4.
"The Mill" *Onward* 2 Dec 1956, 776-8.
"The Old Minister" *Onward* 18 Nov 1956, 742-3, 747.
"The School Teacher" *Onward* 4 Nov 1956, 708-9, 718-9.
"The Trail of the Serpent" *Onward* 1 Sept 1957, 548-50.

Tait, John (1896?-1955)
GRANDMA TAKES A HAND Toronto: Ryerson Press, 1956.
"Fish Story" *Weekend* 3 (27 June 1953), 38.
"Grandma and the Booming Bass" *FH* 13 Sept 1951, 26-7, 34.
"Grandma and the Booming Bass" *Grandma Takes a Hand* (1956), 65-76.

"Grandma and the Career Girl" *FH* 12 Nov 1953, 28-9.
"Grandma and the Dark Angel" *FH* 30 Sept 1954, 20-1.
"Grandma and the Flighty Flora" *FH* 8 May 1952, 24-5, 33.
"Grandma and the Flighty Flora" *Grandma Takes a Hand* (1956), 88-100.
"Grandma and the Godly Hamish" *FH* 8 Feb 1951, 26-7.
"Grandma and the Godly Hamish" *Grandma Takes a Hand* (1956), 24-35.
"Grandma and the Great Science" *FH* 21 Sept 1950, 26-7.
"Grandma and the Great Science" *Grandma Takes a Hand* (1956), 1-11.
"Grandma and the Love-Blind" *FH* 1 Sept 1955, 18-9, 27.
"Grandma and the Love-Blind" *Grandma Takes a Hand* (1956), 142-55.
"Grandma and the Maid Forlorn" *FH* 6 Dec 1951, 22-3, 32.
"Grandma and the Maid Forlorn" *Grandma Takes a Hand* (1956), 77-87.
"Grandma and the Man of Mettle" *FH* 14 May 1953, 24-5, 56.
"Grandma and the Misogamist" *FH* 15 July 1954, 16-7, 23.
"Grandma and the Misogamist" *Grandma Takes a Hand* (1956), 127-41.
"Grandma and the Plum Tree" *FH* 17 May 1951, 22-3.
"Grandma and the Plum Tree" *Grandma Takes a Hand* (1956), 47-55.
"Grandma and the Plunker" *FH* 19 Oct 1950, 26-7.
"Grandma and the Prideful Lady" *FH* 12 Mar 1953, 28-9, 36.
"Grandma and the Prideful Woman" *Grandma Takes a Hand* (1956), 114-26 [same as above?].
"Grandma and the Public Nuisance" *FH* 3 Mar 1955, 22-4.
"Grandma and the Sassenach" *FH* 28 Dec 1950, 16-7, 23.
"Grandma and the Sassenach" *Grandma Takes a Hand* (1956), 12-23.
"Grandma and the Spoiled Brat" *FH* 7 Aug 1952, 20-1, 48.
"Grandma and the Spoiled Brat" *Grandma Takes a Hand* (1956), 101-13.
"Grandma and the Stalled Bride" *FH* 6 Mar 1952, 28-9, 35.
"Grandma and the Stour Cart" *FH* 25 Feb 1954, 28-9.
"Grandma and the Tappit Hen" *FH* 2 Aug 1951, 16-7.
"Grandma and the Tappit Hen" *Grandma Takes a Hand* (1956), 56-64.
"Grandma and the Unmerry Christmas" *FH* 24 Dec 1953, 10-1.
"Grandma and the Unwelcome Stranger" *FH* 23 Dec 1954, 14-5.
"Grandma and the Wee Pest" *FH* 19 Apr 1951, 28-9, 56.
"Grandma and the Wee Pest" *Grandma Takes a Hand* (1956), 36-46.
"Grandma and the Wife-Beater" *FH* 28 July 1955, 18-9, 27.
"Made in Heaven" *FH* 27 July 1950, 16-7.
"Silence Is a Weapon" *FH* 11 Jan 1950, 18-9.
"You Can't Beat Herring" *Weekend* 4 (5 June 1954), 41.

Takashima, Shizuye‡

"Exiled" *Canadian Stories of Action and Adventure* (1978), 35-44.

Talbot, Charlene‡

"Cat in the Room" *AA* 55 (Sept 1964), 79-80.

Tamminga, Frederick W.†

"Autobiography of a Quarter-Day Fly" *Vanguard* July-Aug 1974, 13-5.
"The Benediction" *Fid* No. 107 (Fall 1975), 33-46.
"He Grabbed a Pig and ... " *JCF* No. 22 (1978), 13-8.

Tanaka, Tammy‡
"The Snake" *March* [3] (Mar 1964), 20-4.

Tancred, Peta†
"The Two of Them" *Forge* Dec 1957, 8-13.

Tanner, Adrian
"White Night" *Blewointmentpress* 5:1 (Jan 1967), [1 p].

Tansey, Barbara
"The Wedding" *Stories to Read Again* (1965), 167-75.

Taquine, Pascale‡
"Up from the Mattress" *Br Out* 1:2 (June-July 1974), 30-2.

Tata, Saam [pseudonym?]
"Mother Goosed (If Roch Carrier Had Written Old Mother Hubbard)" *JCF* 3:4 (1975), 31-3.

Tataryn, David‡
"The Ace" *Stump* Spr 1981, 16-21.

Tauber [pseudonym]
"A Just and Appropriate Ending" *Echo* (Van) No. 1 (Fall 1975), 11-9.

Taylor, Angus M.†
"The Ceiling Game" *Writ* No. 4 (Spr 1972), 59-61.

Taylor, Bruce D.S.†
"The Acrimonious Cloud" *Scrivener* 1:1 (Spr 1980), 10-1.

Taylor, Charles†
"The Education of Aubrey de Lapp" *Quarry* 4 (Spr 1955), 25-9.
"Incident in Islington" *Quarry* 5 (Spr 1956), 5-10.
"Nicole" *Quarry* 4 (Spr 1955), 7-14.

Taylor, Constance Gurd†
"Another Treason" *Current Assets* (1973), 8-18.
"Prisoner in Venice" *Time Pieces* (1974), 69-82.
"Supper at Lompere's" *Current Assets* (1973), 56-68.

Taylor, Cora‡
"The Screams of the Horses" CBC "Alberta Anthology" 6 Nov 1982.

Taylor, Darien‡
"Fringe" *Acta Vic* 104:1 (Spr 1980), 7-8.

Taylor, Dave‡
"The Rest of the Way to the Factory" *Communicator* 8:2 (Mar-Apr 1979), [3 pp].

Taylor, Esther
"The Stubborn Woman" *FH* 25 Mar 1954, 28-9.

Taylor, James A.‡
"To Tell the Truth" *UC Observer* Apr 1979, 14-5.

Taylor, Jeremy‡
"The Killing of Mrs. Kittywall" CBC *"Anthology"* 3 Jan 1970.

Taylor, Jim†
"The Ditch" *Iron* No. 7 (1969), 37-8.

Taylor, Kate‡
"Rings" *UCR* 1980-81, 12.

Taylor, Lorna‡
[Untitled] *Alpha* 2:1 (Sept 1972), 10-1.

Taylor, Melville
"The Flag" *Uk Can* 7 (1 July 1953), 7-8.
"Pola" *NF* 1:3 (Fall 1952), 17-8.

Taylor, Pat‡
"The Bowl" *Mandala* 1968, 61-6.

Taylor, Perry†
"The Blue Bear" *Matrix* No. 12 (Win 1981), 67-78.
"A Fragmentary Argument" *Mandala* 1969, 61-6.
"The Reverend's Cosmos" *Mandala* 1969, 53-9.

Taylor, Richard†
"Broken Harmony" *Quarry* 31:4 (Aut 1982), 6-9.

Tchir, Mary†
"Beastie" *Quarry* 9 (May 1960), 25.

Teare, Dave‡
"Fern Hill Revisited" *Mam* 6:4 (Win 1983-84), [2 pp].

Tedford, Ingrid‡
"Amelio's" *CF* 48 (June 1968), 62-4.

Teed, Roy†
"Lonely Road" *CSSM* 3:1 (Win 1977), 14-6, 68-71.

Teicher, Mark (1948-)
"Auntie Intellectual" *Moose R* 2:1 (1979), 47-51.
"My First Fire" *Matrix* No. 13 (Spr-Sum 1981), 27-31.

Teichroeb, Kevin‡
"Jambalaya" *UCR* Win 1983, 17.

Teitel, Jay (1949-)
"A Foreword" *SN* 92 (May 1977), 30-4, 36, 38, 41-2, 44-5.
"The Goal" *Weekend* 27 (31 Dec 1977), 11-2.
"Gorman" *TL* June 1978, 41, 108-9.

"His Only Person" *SN* 93 (Mar 1978), 36, 41-2, 44-6.
"The Last Game" *TL* Mar 1980, 36, 52, 101-3.
"The Love Letter" *TL* Dec 1977, 56, 92, 157-64.
"A Sense of Justice" *JD* Rosh Hashanah 1973, 44-53.
"The Surprise" *JD* Passover 1975, 4-7, 10-3, 16-21.

Teitelbaum, Marshall A.
"Confessions of a Novice" *Edge* No. 2 (Spr 1964), 55-67.

Teleky, Richard†
"After School" *Des* 12:4/13:1/2 Nos. 34/35/36 (1981-82), 164-7.
"After School, 2" *Des* 14:2 No. 40 (Spr 1983), 111-3.
"After School, 3" *Des* 13:4 No. 38 (Fall 1982), 72-4.
"Not in China" *Quarry* 31:4 (Aut 1982), 21-31.
"Pavane for a Dead Princess" *Des* 11:4/12:1 Nos. 30/31 (1980-81), 10-6.

Telford, A.‡
"Observations" *Ichor* No. 1 (Win 1980), 33-7.

Templeton, Alan‡
"Beach Dogs" *CF* 59 (Mar 1980), 28-9.

Templeton, Bill
"Then But the Always Now" *Catalyst* No. 2 (Spr 1968), 22-9.

Templeton, Wayne
"Old Fred" *WCR* 14:3 (Jan 1980), 18-22.

Templeton, Wayne†
"The Witness" *Antig R* No. 43 (Aut 1980), 55-61.

Tench, C.V.
"The Big One" *CG* 79 (Nov 1960), 39-43.
"Feud in the Chilcotin" *CG* Aug 1958, 14, 37-8.
"Grizzly Gold" *Mont* 30 (July 1956), 54-7.
"The Head of Baisano" *Mont* 30 (Jan 1956), 58-9.
"Nine Must Die" *NHM* 51 (Feb 1950), 8-9, 20-1.
"Nine Must Die" *SW* 15 Aug 1953, II:6.
"Partners" *Challenge* 19 (28 May 1950), 5-6, 10-2.
"Quits" *Challenge* 19 (15 Jan 1950), 2-4, 11.
"Rocket Riches" *Challenge* 19 (23 July 1950), 4-5, 11.
"When the Wolves Laughed" *Onward* 21 Aug 1955, 535, 543.
"The Woman Within" *CG* 78 (Aug 1959), 37-40.

Tenenbaum, Gerald‡
"Dialogism" *Prism* (Mont) 1958, 9-11.
"A Short February Story" *Prism* (Mont) 1958, 35-40.

Tens, Johnny‡
"History Account" *Pulp* 2:11 (1 Aug 1974), [1 p].
"The Last Night in Town" *Pulp* 2:22 (1 Mar 1975), [2 pp].

Tetramariner, Elessar
"The Game" *Portico* 3:2/3 [1979], 49-56, 78-91.

Thacker, P.‡
"The Poem" *Forum* (OSSTF) 2 (Dec 1975), 205-9.

Thatcher, Philip†
"Alleluia, Mrs. Jones" *CBC [Van] "Hornby Collection"* 30 Jan 1982.
"At the Threshold" *Matrix* No. 15 (Spr-Sum 1982), 9-15.

Thayer, Nancy
"The Genius" *Cap R* No. 5 (Spr 1974), 25-8.
"On a Rainy Day" *Br Out* 1:5 (Nov-Dec 1974), 20-1, 45.
"Spending the Morning in Paradise" *Room* 1:1 (Spr 1975), 41-8.

Theriault, Pierre‡
"You Were Wrong" *Outlook* Jan-Mar 1983, 6-9.

Thériault, Yves (1916-)
"Ambroise, the Whale and Gabrielle" *Weekend* 3 (22 Aug 1953), 8.
"Antoine's Mountain" *Weekend* 3 (19 Sept 1953), 38.
"The Bequest" *MM* 70 (6 July 1957), 26, 38-9.
"Bull Neck" *Weekend* 3 (7 Mar 1953), 16-7, 21, 32.
"The Caruso Recording" *SW* 14 Aug 1954, I:7.
"The Case of the Gray Moose" *FH* 5 Apr 1956, 26-7, 43.
"Don't Skin the Bear Before He's Dead" *FH* 4 Sept 1958, 20-1.
"Flash Flood" *FH* 12 July 1956, 20-1, 29.
"Half-Breed Wife" *FH* 19 Nov 1953, 28-9.
"Jeannette" *Canadian Short Stories* (1952), 177-83.
"Jeannette" *Kanadische Erzähler der Gegenwart* (1967), 163-70 [Trans. Armin Arnold].
"Jeannette" *French Canadian Experience* (1979), 62-9.
"The Little Witch and the Big Logger" *Weekend* 2 (30 Aug 1952), 12-3.
"The Pearl Necklace" *Weekend* 5 (7 May 1955), 16-7, 31, 35.
"Ramook and the Debt" *FH* 16 Sept 1954, 28-9.
"Ramook and the Medicine" *FH* 21 Apr 1955, 28-9.
"Ramook and the Royal Visitor" *FH* 18 Nov 1954, 24-5, 32.
"The Rice Ball" *FH* 26 June 1952, 20-1.
"Secret Weapon" *FH* 7 June 1951, 18-9.
"A Sneeze Is a Sneeze" *FH* 5 July 1951, 18.
"Spring Thaw" *Weekend* 5 (30 Apr 1955), 13-5.
"The Stone Rose" *Chat* 34 (Sept 1961), 40, 52, 54, 56-9.
"The Sunday Gun" *Weekend* 4 (3 July 1954), 38.
"The Ten-Inch Feet" *Weekend* 4 (2 Jan 1954), 22.
"To Stand on the Brink" *FH* 27 Sept 1951, 22.
"The Trespasser" *FH* 20 Mar 1958, 28-30.

Therion – *See* Anderson, Thomas.

Thibaudeau, Colleen (1925-)

"All About the Concours in the Rue des Lices and Present Tense for Friends Long Absent" *Applegarth's Folly* No. 2 (1975), 88-97.

"The City Underground" *Canadian Short Stories* (1952), 128-35.

"How to Know the True Prince" *Alphabet* No. 1 (Sept 1960), 69-80.

"The Last Promenade" *QQ* 64 (1958), 517-20.

"One Afternoon" *Undergrad* Win 1953, 9-12.

"The Summer Camp Incident" *CF* 30 (May 1950), 36, 38-9.

"The Toronto Girls" *CBC* "Anthology" 30 Dec 1958.

Thom, Marion†

"A Ticket to the Symphony" *Br Out* 6:1 (1979), 30-1.

Thomas, Alan‡

"The Last Bus" *Scar Fair* 9 (1982), 11-4.

Thomas, Audrey (1935-)

LADIES AND ESCORTS Ottawa: Oberon Press, 1977.

REAL MOTHERS Vancouver: Talonbooks, 1981.

TEN GREEN BOTTLES Indianapolis: Bobbs-Merrill, 1967.

TEN GREEN BOTTLES Ottawa: Oberon Press, 1977.

TWO IN THE BUSH AND OTHER STORIES Toronto: McClelland & Stewart, 1981.

"The Albatross" *Ten Green Bottles* (1967), 75-97.

"The Albatross" *Ten Green Bottles* (1977), 76-97.

"The Albatross" *Two in the Bush* (1981), 49-70.

"Aquarius" *CBC* "Anthology" 30 Jan 1971.

"Aquarius" *Fid* No. 91 (Fall 1971), 3-12.

"Aquarius" *Contemporary Voices* (1972), 168-75.

"Aquarius" *Ladies and Escorts* (1977), 5-18.

"Aquarius" *Personal Fictions* (1977), 128-38.

"Aquarius" *Best Modern Canadian Short Stories* (1978), 15-23.

"Aquarius" *Two in the Bush* (1981), 109-22.

"Aunt Hettie James and the Gates of the New Jerusalem" *Ten Green Bottles* (1967), 131-44.

"Aunt Hettie James and the Gates of the New Jerusalem" *Ten Green Bottles* (1977), 129-41 [As "Aunt Hettie James & the Gates of the New Jerusalem"].

"Clean Monday, or Wintering in Athens" *Cap R* No. 13 (1978), 68-87.

"Compulsory Figures" *True North/Down Under* No. 1 (1983), 35-8.

"Crossing the Rubicon" *SN* 95 (July-Aug 1980), 34-6, 38-41.

"Crossing the Rubicon" *Real Mothers* (1981), 155-68.

"Crudités" *Writing* No. 2 (Win 1980-81), 27-30.

"Degrees" *Small Wonders* (1982), 125-43.

"Dejeuner sur l'herbe" *Real Mothers* (1981), 139-54.

"Elephants to Ride Upon" *Ten Green Bottles* (1967), 117-30.

"Elephants to Ride Upon" *Ten Green Bottles* (1977), 115-28.

"Elevation" *SN* 98 (Jan 1983), 50-3.

"Galatea" *CBC* "Anthology" 6 Dec 1980.

"Galatea" *Real Mothers* (1981), 35-46.

"Green Stakes for the Garden" *Cap R* No. 5 (Spr 1974), 33-7.

"Green Stakes for the Garden" *Ladies and Escorts* (1977), 81-7.

"Green Stakes for the Garden" *Two in the Bush* (1981), 177-83.
"Green Stakes for the Garden" *Anthology of Canadian Literature in English 2* (1983), 399-402.
"Harry and Violet" *CBC "Anthology"* 18 Nov 1978.
"Harry and Violet" *SN* 94 (May 1979), 66-72.
"Harry and Violet" *Real Mothers* (1981), 61-74.
"If One Green Bottle ... " *Ten Green Bottles* (1967), 1-13.
"If One Green Bottle ... " *Modern Stories in English* (1975), 362-70.
"If One Green Bottle ... " *Ten Green Bottles* (1977), 5-16.
"If One Green Bottle ... " *Two in the Bush* (1981), 7-18.
"In the Bleak Mid-Winter" *Real Mothers* (1981), 75-88.
"Initram" *Cap R* No. 7 (Spr 1975), 38-54.
"Initram" *Ladies and Escorts* (1977), 88-107.
"Initram" *Personal Fictions* (1977), 161-75.
"Initram" *Two in the Bush* (1981), 185-204.
"Initram" *Anthology of Canadian Literature in English 2* (1983), 402-14.
"Joseph and His Brother" *Ladies and Escorts* (1977), 19-30.
"Joseph and His Brother" *Two in the Bush* (1981), 123-34.
"Kill Day on the Government Wharf" *CBC "Anthology"* 23 Oct 1971.
"Kill Day on the Government Wharf" *Stories from Pacific & Arctic Canada* (1974), 57-68.
"Kill Day on the Government Wharf" *Role of Woman in Canadian Literature* (1975), 103-14.
"Kill Day on the Government Wharf" *Ladies and Escorts* (1977), 31-43.
"Kill Day on the Government Wharf" *Personal Fictions* (1977), 139-48.
"Kill Day on the Government Wharf" *Canadian Short Stories 3* (1978), 280-93.
"Kill Day on the Government Wharf" *Two in the Bush* (1981), 135-47.
"The Man with Clam Eyes" *Interface* 5:2 (Feb 1982), 11-2.
"A Monday Dream at Alameda Park" *Cap R* No. 7 (Spr 1975), 25-37.
"A Monday Dream at Alameda Park" *Here and Now* (1977), 135-46.
"A Monday Dream at Alameda Park" *Ladies and Escorts* (1977), 116-31.
"A Monday Dream at Alameda Park" *Two in the Bush* (1981), 205-20.
"The More Little Mummy in the World" *Cap R* Nos. 8/9 (Fall-Spr 1975-76), 36-48.
"The More Little Mummy in the World" *76: New Canadian Stories* 38-52.
"The More Little Mummy in the World" *Ladies and Escorts* (1977), 132-46.
"The More Little Mummy in the World" *Personal Fictions* (1977), 149-60.
"The More Little Mummy in the World" *Two in the Bush* (1981), 221-35.
"Natural History" *CBC "Anthology"* 14 June 1980.
"Natural History" *Real Mothers* (1981), 23-34.
"Omo" *Ten Green Bottles* (1967), 45-74.
"Omo" *Four Hemispheres* (1971), 256-75.
"Omo" *Ten Green Bottles* (1977), 47-75.
"Omo" *Two in the Bush* (1981), 19-47.
"One Green Bottle" *CBC "Anthology"* 18 Jan 1980.
"One Is One and All Alone" *Ten Green Bottles* (1967), 99-116.
"One Is One and All Alone" *Ten Green Bottles* (1977), 98-114.
"Out in the Midday Sun" *TL* Jan 1980, 32, 59-64.
"Out in the Midday Sun" *Real Mothers* (1981), 89-100.
"Rapunzel" *74: New Canadian Stories* 43-51.

"Rapunzel" *Ladies and Escorts* (1977), 71-80.
"Rapunzel" *Fiction of Contemporary Canada* (1980), 23-31.
"Real Mothers" *Chat* 54 (Oct 1981), 76, 179, 182, 184, 186, 188, 190.
"Real Mothers" *Real Mothers* (1981), 9-22.
"Realities" CBC "Anthology" 21 Oct 1972.
"Salon des Refusés" *Ten Green Bottles* (1967), 165-82.
"Salon des Refusés" *Ten Green Bottles* (1977), 161-77.
"Salon des Refusés" *Two in the Bush* (1981), 91-107.
"Spring Break" *Chat* 54 (Mar 1981), 40-1, 122-4, 128.
"Still Life with Flowers" *Ten Green Bottles* (1967), 15-28.
"Still Life with Flowers" *Ten Green Bottles* (1977), 17-30.
"Tear Here" *Ladies and Escorts* (1977), 108-15.
"Ted's Wife" *Real Mothers* (1981), 47-60.
"Ted's Wife" *SN* 96 (Apr 1981), 84-6, 89, 91-2.
"Ted's Wife" *British Columbia: A Celebration* (1983), 189-93.
"Three Women and Two Men" CBC "Anthology" 9 Oct 1976.
"Three Women and Two Men" *Ladies and Escorts* (1977), 147-59.
"Timbuktu" *Cap R* No. 13 (1978), 31-66.
"Timbuktu" *Real Mothers* (1981), 101-38.
"Two in the Bush" CBC "Anthology" 5 Oct 1974.
"Two in the Bush" *Cap R* No. 7 (Spr 1975), 63-86.
"Two in the Bush" *Ladies and Escorts* (1977), 44-70.
"Two in the Bush" *Two in the Bush* (1981), 149-75.
"A Winter's Tale" *Ten Green Bottles* (1967), 145-64.
"A Winter's Tale" *Ten Green Bottles* (1977), 142-60.
"A Winter's Tale" *Two in the Bush* (1981), 71-89.
"Xanadu" *Ten Green Bottles* (1967), 29-44.
"Xanadu" *Ten Green Bottles* (1977), 31-46.
"Xanadu" *Stories Plus* (1979), 187-97.
"Xanadu" *West of Fiction* (1983), 232-43.

Thomas, Barrie‡
"The Silence" *Contempo* 3 (Nov-Dec 1972), 14-5.

Thomas, Bill‡
"Please Take Your Partners" *Introductions from an Island* 1974, 28-34.

Thomas, Brian‡
"Interlude" *Creative Campus* 1958, 8-10.

Thomas, John‡
"Whole Story" *Exile* 2:2 (1974), 125-9.

Thomas, K.A.‡
"Paradigm" *Chiaroscuro* 8 (1964), 9-15.

Thomas, Keith‡
"Teddy" *Undergrad* Mar 1950, 28-33.

Thomas, Martha Banning
"The Alarm Clock" *AA* 51 (Jan 1961), 73.
"Minding His Neighbour's Business" *AA* 49 (Mar 1959), 53-6.
"The Red Knife" *AA* 52 (Sept 1961), 65-8.
"A Reg'lar Whip" *AA* 54 (Sept 1963), 77.
"The Rochester Burner" *AA* 51 (July 1961), 25-30.
"A Whale of a Time" *AA* 52 (June 1962), 59-60, 62-3.

Thomas, Peter
"Like Kafka" *Fid* No. 89 (Spr 1971), 32-4.
"A Love Story" *WCR* 5:3 (Jan 1971), 20-2.
"Roses at Noon" *Fid* No. 119 (Fall 1978), 17-28.
"The Strength of Ten" *CBC "Anthology"* 2 July 1977.

Thomas, Randy
"There Was Toronto" *Imp* 2:1 (Aut 1972), 20-2.

Thomas, Richard†
"From Automatism to Zymosis" *Evidence* No. 3 (Fall 1961), 54-60.

Thomas, Sister
"For Those Who Care" *Skylark* 5:2 (Win/Jan 1969), 18-27.
"Unless the Grain of Wheat Die" *Skylark* 2:1 [date unknown], 25 [Based on index].

Thomas, W.K.†
"Latin for Six" *Was R* 7:2 (Fall 1972), 74-84.
"Talk Show" *JCF* No. 24 [1979], 52-66.

Thompsett, Dennis‡
"Stockings and Sugarplums" *From 231* 1:2 (Dec 1972), 11-5.

Thompson, B.‡
"Class" *Pedestal* 4:6 (July 1972), 10.
"I Wonder Why They Took the Icons" *Pedestal* 5:6 (Oct 1973), 4 [Non-fiction?].
"Old Times" *Pedestal* 4:3 (Mar 1972), 2.
"Peanut Butter" *Pedestal* 4:5 (May 1972), 12-3.
"There Once Was This Nice Policeman" *Pedestal* 4:8 (Oct 1978), 10-1.

Thompson, Dave‡
"Flood Tide" *Repos* No. 15 (Sum 1975), 1-3.

Thompson, Don‡
"The Bug (A Cinemagram)" *Quarry* 22:2 (Spr 1973), 47-50.
"The Hammer (A Cinemagram)" *Quarry* 22:2 (Spr 1973), 44-7.

Thompson, Doretta A.‡
"The Witness" *Des* 11:1/2 Nos. 27/28 (1980), 163-8.

Thompson, Dorothy M.‡
"Night in Acadia" *AA* 56 (July 1966), 11-3.

Thompson, George C.‡
"The Snake Lady" *AA* 53 (Sept 1962), 33-5.

Thompson, Henrietta†
"Maggie" *Repos* No. 14 (Spr 1975), 15-20.
"The Matador" *Repos* No. 10 (Spr 1974), 44-50.
"Me and Curley" *Repos* No. 16 (Aut 1975), 54-60.
"Me and My Sister" *Repos* No. 11 (Sum 1974), [14 pp].

Thompson, James†
[Untitled] *event* 6:1 [1977], 57-9.

Thompson, John R.‡
"The Tree" *Des* 8:3 No. 19 (1977), 68-74.

Thompson, Kent††
"On the Beach" *Volume* 63 No. 1 (Dec 1963), 20.

Thompson, Kent (1936-)
SHOTGUN AND OTHER STORIES Fredericton: New Brunswick Chapbooks, 1979.
"All Manner of Lies" *CBC "Anthology"* 10 Jan 1981 [Based on survey response].
"Among Women" *Axiom* 2:4 (May 1976), 34-8.
"Among Women" *Shotgun* (1979), 66-72.
"Because I Am Drunk" *Quarry* 18:3 (Spr 1969), 37-47.
"Because I Am Drunk" *Narrative Voice* (1972), 222-32.
"Because I Am Drunk" *Shotgun* (1979), 7-17.
"The Better Gift" *Story So Far* 5 (1978), 171-4.
"A Bloody Pair" *New Edinburgh R* No. 61 (Spr 1983), 11 [Based on survey response].
"The Broken Bottle: A Suicide for Barbara Ann Shea" *CBC "Anthology"* 19 Feb 1972.
"The Broken Bottle: A Suicide for Barbara Ann Shea" *UWR* 7:2 (Spr 1972), 80-90.
"Class of '49; Class of '54" *CFM* No. 8 (Aut 1972), 64-78.
"Coming Home" *Small Wonders* (1982), 145-55.
"The Complicated Camera: Jeremy and Greta" *UWR* 5:2 (Spr 1970), 98-106.
"The Complicated Camera: Jeremy and Greta" *Best Little Magazine Fiction* 1971 334-44.
"Crossing" *Intercourse* Nos. 12/13 (Jan 1970), 33-7.
"The Death of Comedy" *Tam R* No. 49 (1969), 33-41.
"The Death Party" *Fid* No. 93 (Spr 1972), 89-100.
"Ella's Father" *Bluenose* 4:4 (Feb 1980), 8.
"End of an Era" *79: Best Canadian Stories* 129-37.
"End of an Era" *Shotgun* (1979), 48-53.
"Getting Caught" *Miss Chat* 15 (Nov 1978), 82-3, 86, 88, 90, 92.
"Getting Saved" *CBC "Anthology"* 20 Sept 1980.
"Good Water, Good Water" *Axiom* 1:4 (Spr 1975), 24-7.
"Green Things" *Tam R* No. 80 (Spr 1980), 62-71.
"Green Things" *81: Best Canadian Stories* 145-56.
"Hero, O Heroine" *Tam R* No. 57 (1971), 44-59.

"Holiday Haven" *CBC "Anthology"* 13 Sept 1980.
"I Live in Canada" *Fid* No. 93 (Spr 1972), 80-8.
"I Live in Canada" *Shotgun* (1979), 18-26.
"A Local Hanging" *CF* 61 (Dec-Jan 1981-82), 24-5, 28.
"A Local Hanging" *CBC* 22 Sept 1981 [Based on survey response].
"Mad Indian at the Hockey Game" *WCR* 4:2 (Fall 1969), 25-8.
"Mall Shopping" *CFM* No. 26 (Aut 1977), 8-14.
"The Man Who Cried Faith" *New Campus R* (U.S.) 1 (May 1966), 2-8 [Based on survey response].
"A Mother's Cry" *CBC "Anthology"* 6 Sept 1980 [Title based on survey response].
"Norris' Hat" *ArtsAtlantic* 3:3 (Sum 1981), 35, 48-9.
"Oldest Rookie in the League" *December Nos. 1/2* (Dec 1971), 45-50 [Based on survey response].
"Perhaps the Church Building Itself" *CBC "Anthology"* 28 Feb 1976.
"Perhaps the Church Building Itself" *77: Best Canadian Stories* 152-68.
"Perhaps the Church Building Itself" *Shotgun* (1979), 86-96.
"Perhaps the Church Building Itself" *Stories Plus* (1979), 202-13.
"Pillars and a View of the River" *SN* 92 (Nov 1977), 94-6, 99-100, 102, 104.
"The Pilot" *78: Best Canadian Stories* 117-33.
"The Pilot" *Shotgun* (1979), 54-65.
"The Problems of a Truancy" *Narrative Voice* (1972), 209-21.
"The Problems of a Truancy" *Shotgun* (1979), 73-85.
"Professor Kingblatt's Prediction" *AA* 59 (Nov 1968), 29-30, 32, 34.
"Professor Kingblatt's Prediction" *Kaleidoscope* (1972), 4-9.
"Professor Kingblatt's Prediction" *Singing Under Ice* (1974), 30-6.
"Professor Kingblatt's Prediction" *Maritime Experience* (1975), 112-7.
"Promises" *Quarry* 31:2 (Spr 1982), 4-8.
"Robbing Motels" *Atl Insight* 2 (June 1980), 94.
"Shotgun" *SN* 90 (July-Aug 1975), 41-8.
"Shotgun" *Canadian Short Stories 3* (1978), 295-311.
"Shotgun" *Shotgun* (1979), 97-107.
"Some Things I Won't Do" *SN* 91 (Nov 1976), 74-8.
"Still Life Composition: Woman's Clothes" *Fourteen Stories High* (1971), 60-8.
"Systems" *Quarry* 23:2 (Spr 1974), 20-35.
"Translation" *QQ* 79 (1972), 495-502.
"Two Photographs" *Axiom* 3:3 (June 1977), 22-4, 26-7, 54, 59.
"Two Photographs" *Shotgun* (1979), 37-47.
"An Unfinished Television Script Entitled: 'Window on the Revolution' " *Prism* 10:1 (Sum 1970), 130-7 [Also entitled "Window on the Revolution"].
"What Costume Shall the New Man Wear?" *Fid* No. 93 (Spr 1972), 70-9.
"What Costume Shall the New Man Wear?" *Shotgun* (1979), 27-36.
"Who Was It Who Danced at Eaton's Catalogue Store?" *AA* 62 (Jan 1972), 18-9, 50-3.
"Window on the Revolution" *Stories from Atlantic Canada* (1973), 190-9 [Also entitled "An Unfinished Television Script Entitled: 'Window on the Revolution' "].
"Window on the Revolution" *Stubborn Strength* (1983), 83-90.

Thompson, Ray T.†
"All Is Right – Now" *Lib* 30 (Apr 1953), 32-3.

Thompson, Tim‡
"Alice in Parliament" *UC Gargoyle* 4 (27 Jan 1958), 3.

Thomson, E.W.‡
"Drafted" *NF* 3:2 (Sum 1954), 33-8.

Thomson, Jean C.‡
"Quiet Terror" *Undergrad* Spr 1951, 19-27.

Thomson, Pat‡
"Baptism" *UC Gargoyle* 25 (16 Dec 1980), 8.

Thordarson, Evans
"Making a Sale" *Grain* 1:1 (June 1973), 30-7.

Thorne, Lynne†
"Charlie Cirabossie: A Very Important Man" CBC *"Anthology"* 8 May 1971.
"Hazlitt" *CFM* No. 1 (Win 1971), 82-8.
"The Prisoner" *Prism* 8:2 (Aut 1968), 123-6.

Thornley, Gary C.‡
"Adventures in the Vacuum" *Potlatch* No. 4 (Jan 1965), 1-14.

Thornton, Madeleine – *See* Green, H. Gordon.

Thorpe, Carole Anne‡
"Two Out of" *Multiple Choices* (1975), 47-53.

Thorpe, Patricia‡
"A Friend for Molly" *Spear* 6 (Feb-Mar 1977), 33-4, 46.

Throng, Mary‡
"Professor Islam Has a Lovely Smell" *White Pelican* 2:4 (Fall 1972), 45-54.

Thurlow, Ann†
"The Mark" *Waves* 9:1 (Aut 1980), 24-31.

Tia [pseudonym]
"Big Momma Always Wanted a Daughter" *Pedestal* 3:9 (Oct 1971), 7.

Tierney, Barry‡
"Out of the Yellow Splotch, a Vital Sun" *Story So Four* (1976), 216-7.

Tierney, Bill†
"Fallen Angels" *Antig R* No. 18 (Sum 1974), 97-104.

Tierney, Jean‡
"Allegro con Fuoco" *Halcyon* 10:1 (1964), 32-5.
"Lebreton Flats" *CF* 45 (Apr 1965), 13-4.

Tierney, Patrick‡
"My Long Past Midnight Yonge Street" *TUR* 93:1 (Jan 1980), 29-31.

Tigchelaar, Peter‡
"A Story Shortly" *Pulp* 1:5 (15 Jan 1973), [2].

Tiger, Lionel‡
"Go – -, Young Man, Move, East, West, North, South" *Yes* 2:1 (Apr 1957), [1 p].
"Shane Horton Died on Mount Royal" *Forge* Mar 1959, 38-40.

Tilberg, Mary†
"Danny's Mouse" *Har* 4:7 No. 27 (Apr 1980), 94-6, 100-1, 103.

Tillinghast, David‡
"People Are Always the Limiters of Happiness" *QQ* 80 (1973), 239-41.

Timmerman, Peter‡
"A Limited Vision" *TUR* 85:2 (Feb 1972), 7-8.
"Waiting" *TUR* 84:3 (Sum 1971), 18-9.

Tinsley, Ted†
"All That Was Left ... " *Uk Can* 4 (1 Apr 1950), 3.
"Coffee Puzzle" *Uk Can* 8 (15 Mar 1954), 5 [Humour].
"Just Keep Smiling" *Uk Can* 8 (1 Apr 1954), 3 [Humour].

Tipping, M.T.‡
"The Child – The Man" *JCF* Nos. 31/32 (1981), 124-35.

Tisdall, Douglas‡
"The Unhappy Reed" *TUR* 71:5 (Sum 1958), 36-8.
"The Wine of Harvest and the Bread of Worship" *TUR* 71:5 (Sum 1958), 38-9.

Tock, Bill‡
"The Hunters" *New Mitre* No. 1 (1971), 15-21.

Todd, Beatrice
"A Doctor of the North" *Alberta Writers Speak* 1964, 92-7.
"A Race with the River" *Alberta Writers Speak* 1967, 84-91.

Todd, Lynn
"Calmly, Calmly" *Stories with John Drainie* (1963), 124-8.
"Divided Spoils" *Stories with John Drainie* (1963), 54-8.

Todd, R. Dave‡
"The End of the World" *Intervales* [No. 3 (1963?)], 12-5.

Todd, Richard‡
"The Mailman" *Alpha* 4:3 (Spr 1980), 5, 13, 23, 31.

Todkill, Anne†
"Modernism at the Beach" *Quarry* 31:2 (Spr 1982), 69-72.

Toft, Joseph†
"Pumpkin" *Alphabet* No. 13 (June 1967), 18-29.

Toland, George‡
"Robert Giles Passes On" *NF* 1:3 (Fall 1952), 8-12.

Tolboom, Wanda Neil
"The Legend of Ben's Rock" *Atl Guardian* 9 (Aug 1952), 11-5.

Tolton, Cameron‡
"Neighbours Known" *Acta Vic* 82:2 (Feb 1958), 27-9.

Tomkinson, Grace‡
"Emmeline's Own" *AA* 49 (Jan 1959), 49-53.

Tomkinson, Joan‡
"The Goldfish Pool" *AA* 48 (May 1958), 79-82, 84.
"A Matter of Luck" *AA* 52 (Apr 1962), 47, 49-50.
"Never the Same Again" *AA* 49 (Apr 1959), 51-7.
"A Night on the Town" *AA* 54 (Sept 1963), 27-30, 32.

Tonkin, Doris Farmer†
"Safe Lodging" *Can Lifetime* 4 (Sept-Oct 1974), 27-8.

Tonner, Thomas H.†
"The Ship Flower" *Voices Down East* [1976], 42.

Toole, David‡
"Underbelly" *CBC [Van] "Hornby Collection"* 20 Jan 1979 ["Monodrama"].

Topliff, Delores‡
"Exultation and Despair" *UC Gargoyle* [10] (Jan 1964), [2 pp].

Torgov, Morley (1928-)
A GOOD PLACE TO COME FROM Toronto: Lester and Orpen, 1974.
"Being Prepared" *Good Place to Come From* (1974), 63-7.
"Café Society" *Good Place to Come From* (1974), 73-100.
"A Good Place to Come From" *Good Place to Come From* (1974), 1-5.
"The Guest Speaker" *Good Place to Come From* (1974), 53-62.
"The House on the Rock" *Good Place to Come From* (1974), 152-73.
"The Lawyer" *Good Place to Come From* (1974), 115-22.
"The Making of a President, 1944" *Good Place to Come From* (1974), 139-51.
"The Messiah of Second-Hand Goods" *Good Place to Come From* (1974), 174-86.
"The Messiah of Second-Hand Goods" *Spice Box* (1981), 135-43.
"Of Life and Love in a '41 DeSoto" *Good Place to Come From* (1974), 127-38.
"Press Pressure" *Good Place to Come From* (1974), 101-14.
"Queen Street" *Good Place to Come From* (1974), 6-18.
"Room and Keyboard" *Good Place to Come From* (1974), 38-52.
"The Salesman" *Good Place to Come From* (1974), 68-72.
"Semper Paratus, Semper Fidelis, Semper Annie" *Good Place to Come From* (1974), 19-37.
"Up in Smoke" *Good Place to Come From* (1974), 123-6.

Torgov, Sarah‡
 "Knight Moves" *UCR* Spr 1977, 28-30.
 "Lenny's Dessert" *UC Gargoyle* 1 (19 Sept 1977), 2.

Torney, Roy Hamblin
 "The Warbler's Song" *event* 9:2 (1980), 42-9.

Torrie, John‡
 "Out of the Woodwork" *Communicator* 9:1 [n.d.], [1 p].

Toryn, Ann‡
 "Kinswoman" *Inprint* 2:3 [n.d.], 10.

Tourbin, Dennis‡
 "I Remember Seeing My Grandfather's House and Grapevines" *20 Cents* 4:5/6 (June 1970), [3 pp].
 "Please Don't Kill My Cricket!!! or, Sometimes It's Hard to Shut Those Things Off" *20 Cents* 4:3 (Mar 1970), [1 p].
 "The Port Dalhousie Stories" *OPT* 6:8 (Oct 1979), 7.
 "Saturday, Sunday, or Does It Really Matter Anyway??!!" *20 Cents* 4:4 (Apr 1970), [1 p] [Prose poem?].

Townshend, Elizabeth Morison‡
 "The Secluded Lot" *Stories with John Drainie* (1963), 1-7.
 "The Secluded Lot" *Crossroads* 2 (1979), 97-103.

Toye, Bob‡
 "Fear and the Night" *Folio* 5:2 (Apr 1951), [4 pp].

Trail, Joy‡
 "This Is the Day" *AA* 60 (Jan 1970), 45-6.

Trainor, Peter‡
 "The Countdown" *Communicator* 5:1 (Feb-Mar 1976), 11-4.

Trehey, John P.
 "Shipwreck" *Atl Guardian* 8 (Aug 1951), 16-20.

Treit, Dallas Robert
 "Crow in the High Woods" *Mal R* No. 10 (Apr 1969), 73-85.

Tremaine, William‡
 "Full Circle" *Folio* 13:2 (Spr 1961), 3-9.

Tremblay, Carol‡
 "Peter!" *Alive* 2:1 (Dec 1970), 20-1.

Tremblay, M.M.‡
 "Elephantitus" *Stump* Spr 1981, 1-6.

Tremblay, Mildred
"Lily and the Salamander" *Cap R* No. 21 (1982), 30-41.
"Lily and the Salamander" *Rainshadow* (1982), 199-210.
"Mahogany Fever" *CFM* Nos. 45/46 (1982-83), 15-24.
"The Maid" *Stump* 1:2 (Fall 1977), 52-8.

Trembley, Georges†
"I Am a Wizard" *Alive* 1:3 (Feb [1970]), [1 p].
"The Jason Sphere (A Tragi-Come-Dram in 21 Parts Dedicated to Everyone)" *Alive* 2:8 (July-Aug 1971), 34-6.

Trethewey, Eric
"The Grammar of Silence" *Fid* No. 109 (Spr 1976), 32-49.
"One More Passage to India" *Fid* No. 112 (Win 1977), 23-42.

Trifon, Louis – *See* Kilodney, Crad.

Trimble, Alberta C.
"Be Yourself" *CHJ* Apr 1955, 32, 72-5.

Trommeshauser, Dietmar†
"Slices" *Writing* No. 3 (Sum 1981), 35-8.

Trotter, Zöe Pauline (? -1962)
"I Remember – Christmas" *Echoes* No. 209 (Christmas 1952), 5, 23, 25.
"The Moccasins" *Echoes* No. 238 (Spr 1960), 14-5, 20.

Trower, Peter
"High Country Burn" *Rain Chr* No. 6 [n.d.], 50-4.
"Sojurn at Junkie Log" *Rain Chr* No. 3 [n.d.], 144-51 [Non-fiction?].

Truckey, Don†
"Lover" *Gas Rain* 3 (1979), 34-41.
"Revelation" *Gas Rain* [1] (Mar 1977), 32-6.

Trueman, Stuart
"Bap-Bap-Bap" *Weekend* 3 (26 Sept 1953), 11.
"Carry Me Back to Old Hypochondria" *AA* 62 (Apr 1972), 26-8.
"The Man Who Caught the Fish" *Weekend* 2 (31 May 1952), 30.

Truhlar, Richard
"Dump" *Des* 10:1 Nos. 22/23 (1978-79), 94-103.
"The Life and Work of Chapter Seven" *Blind Windows* No. 1 (1979), [3 pp].
"Tattoo" *Des* 10:3/4 Nos. 25/26 (1979), 101-6.
"Tattoo" *Writing* No. 4 (Win 1981-82), 7-8.

Truss, Jan
"Caged In" *Alberta Diamond Jubilee Anthology* (1979), 155-60.
"Does a Hippopotamus Have Whiskers?" *NeWest R* 6 (Mar 1981), 8-10 [As "Cry Baby Cry"; excerpt].
"My Daughter's Teacher" *Chat* 45 (June 1972), 39, 79-80, 82-5.

"Patterns of Progress" *CSSM* 2:4 (Fall 1976), 3-6.
"The Phallus" *Dand* 4 (Win 1978), 13-20.
"Talking Back" *CBC [Edm] "Alberta Anthology"* 6 Nov 1982.

Tsigane – *See* Baerstein, Tsigane.

Tsubouchi, David‡
"In the Jungle" *York Lit Series* No. 3 (Win 1971), 20-1.

Tucker, James L. (1957-)
"The Room" *Mal R* No. 64 (Feb 1983), 165-72.

Tudor, Kathleen
"And I a Smiling Woman" *CBC "Anthology"* 17 Nov 1979.
"Do You Believe?" *Antig R* No. 52 (Win 1983), 79-84.
"How 'Ja Do Today" *Pot Port* 4 (1982-83), 44.
"Mrs. McKay from White Plains" *Living Message* 91 (June 1980), 21-4.
"The Triumph" *Sift* No. 6 (Spr 1980), 3-11.
"Washday" *Atlantis* 6:1 (Fall 1980), 61-4.

Tufts, Martyn‡
"Stairway to Hell" *Folio* 5:1 [Jan 1951], [2 pp].

Tupper, Dorothy
"Wild Dogs" *Boreal* No. 7 (1977), 115-8.

Tupper, Hibbert T.†
"Too Ledders from Joe" *Read Ch* 1:2 (Sum 1982), 5-7.

Turley, Steve‡
"In Padua" *Pulp* 2:9 (15 June 1974), [1 p].

Turnbull, J.G.‡
"The Eaves of Houses" *Undergrad* Aut 1951, 25-8.

Turnbull, J.R.‡
"Parting" *Acta Vic* 76:2 (Dec 1951), 25-7.

Turnbull, Robert O.†
"The Document" *CSSM* 2:2 (Spr 1976), 9, 11-3.
"The Night the Bear Bit Albert" *CSSM* 1:2 (Apr 1975), 1-5.

Turner, Lois‡
"Guido" *Revue* 2 No. 1 (1976), 34-41.
"A Woman and Her Husband" *Canadian Short Fiction Anthology* (1976), 205-12.

Turner, Mark‡
"An Autumn Day" *Outlook* 4:4 (Apr 1976), 27-8.

Turner, Ron‡
"Eldorado" *Acta Vic* 83:3 (Jan 1959), 20-1.
"Great Perturbations" *Acta Vic* 82:1 (Nov 1957), 29-32.

Tutlis, John
"A Number, Quit the Number, It Might Be Sd, Of Years Ago" *BC Monthly* 3:9 (June 1978), 22-4 [Prose poem?].

Tweedie, Robert A.‡
"She Who Laughs Last" *AA* 53 (Feb 1963), 56, 58-60.

Twelftree, George – *See* Hough, N.C.

Tyhurst, Rob†
"Grace" *CFM* No. 9 (Win 1973), 40-1.

Tyhurst, Robert†
"Romancero Gitano" *Quarry* 30:3 (Sum 1981), 46-8.

Tymon, Gerry‡
"Home Sweet Home" *Dime Bag* No. 9 (Apr 1973), [5 pp].

Tynan, D.‡
"Mae West Fantasy" *Pulp* 3:2 (15 June 1975), [1 p].

Tyson, D.A.L.‡
"Going to See Mr. Winters" *Alpha* 3:1 (Fall 1978), 5, 10.

Tyson, Donald
"The Glen of the Green Woman" *Black Cat* 1:3 (Hallowe'en 1981), 17-22.

Uckeed, Iben F. [pseudonym]
"For the Sake of Auld Lang Syne" *Hibiscus Dawn* No. 8 (15 Jan 1968), 2-3.

Uda, Lowell
"Clever Old Men" *Pulp* 2:1 (1 Jan 1974), [2 pp].

Uhlman, Fred†
"Fable VI" *Antig R* 1:1 (Spr 1970), 81-4.

Ulmer, E.†
"Come in Joey" *CHJ* Dec 1955, 20-1, 38-40, 44, 46.

Unwin, Peter†
"Eugene" *Waves* 10:4 (Spr 1982), 22-3.
"The Wolves" *Ichor* No. 2 (1981), 39-42.

Upton, Paul‡
"From the White Line" *March* 2 (1963), 24.

Urbas, Jeannette
"Seventeen" *Mudpie* 4:8 (Oct 1983), 10-1.

Uriarte, Steven K.‡
"Repentants" *Acta Vic* 106:1 (Fall 1981), 46-54.

Urquhart, Donald‡
"The Lake" *Acta Vic* 75:4 (Mar 1951), 44-5.

Urquhart, Jane (1949-)
"Five Wheelchairs" *CFM* No. 39 (1981), 55-71.
"Five Wheelchairs" *Illusion One* (1983), 127-45.
"Seven Confessions" *CFM* No. 44 (1982), 57-84.
"Storm Glass" *Metavisions* (1983), 97-102.
"Storm Glass" *Mal R* No. 64 (Feb 1983), 106-12.

Ursan, Sheonaid†
"Bleeding Nail Polish" *Prism* 15:2/3 (Sum-Fall 1976), 182-5.

Ursell, Barbara (1943-)
"Cousin Victor" *Smoke Signals* 2 [date unknown] [Based on *SWG* survey response].
"Saved" *JCF* 2:1 (Win 1973), 29-32.

Ursell, Geoffrey
"Fat" *Sundogs* (1980), 153-65.
"Polo Park" *NeWest R* 4 (Nov 1978), 8-9.
"Underground" *Quarry* 30:3 (Sum 1981), 37-44.

Usukawa, Saeko†
"One of a Series" *Story So Far* 2 (1973), 110.

Utsal, Tony‡
"From *Quest for a Checkmate*, A Short Story" *Tit* No. 2 (Sum 1961), [7 pp] [Probable excerpt].

UU, David
"Biography" *Industrial Sabotage* No. 8 [Nov 1982], [1 p] [Prose poem?].
"Black Fly" *BC Monthly* 5:3 (Apr 1981), 13-5.
"Close Encounter" *Toybox* No. 8 (Nov 1983), [4 pp].
"The Deviant" *Industrial Sabotage* No. 14 [Mar 1983], [1 p].
"Even Fingers Sing in the Lamp" *Canadian Short Fiction Anthology* (1976), 213-6.

V., I.F.
"A Lesson in 'Democracy' " *Uk Can* 7 (1 Sept 1953), 5 [Satire].

Valeriote, Paul‡
"A Story" *Alive* 2:7 No. 17 (June 1971), 28-9.

Valero, Senja‡
"Abigail Snopes and the King of Spades" *Green's* 4:1 (Aut 1975), 52-61.

Valgardson, W.D. (1939-)
BLOODFLOWERS Ottawa: Oberon Press, 1973.
GOD IS NOT A FISH INSPECTOR Ottawa: Oberon Press, 1975.
RED DUST Ottawa: Oberon Press, 1978.
"An Act of Mercy" *Dal R* 51 (1971), 413-22.

"An Act of Mercy" *Bloodflowers* (1973), 23-33.

"An Afternoon's Drive" *UWR* 8:1 (Fall 1972), 67-76.

"An Afternoon's Drive" *Bloodflowers* (1973), 63-72.

"The Baseball Game" *Winnipeg Stories* (1974), 91-100.

"Bear" *God Is Not a Fish Inspector* (1975), 111-25.

"Beyond Normal Requirements" CBC "Anthology" 23 July 1977.

"Beyond Normal Requirements" *Red Dust* (1978), 5-15.

"Bloodflowers" *Tam R* No. 55 (1970), 34-42, 44-53.

"Bloodflowers" *Best American Short Stories* 1971 329-46.

"Bloodflowers" *Bloodflowers* (1973), 5-22.

"Bloodflowers" *Sunlight & Shadows* (1974), 203-20.

"Bloodflowers" *Best Modern Canadian Short Stories* (1978), 301-15.

"Bloodflowers" *Canadian Short Stories 3* (1978), 313-35.

"Bloodflowers" *Copyright Canada* (1978), 121-34.

"Bloodflowers" *Best Canadian Short Stories* (1981), 254-71.

"Bloodflowers" CBC "Stereo Sound Stage" 30 Oct 1982 [Based on survey response].

"Bloodflowers" CBC "Sunday Matinee" 6 Mar 1983 [Based on survey response].

"Brothers" *Bloodflowers* (1973), 34-52.

"The Burning" *AA* 61 (Oct 1970), 64-72.

"The Burning" *Bloodflowers* (1973), 82-90.

"The Burning" *Sense of Place* (1979), 259-69 [Based on survey response].

"The Burning" CBC 1981 [Based on survey response].

"A Business Relationship" *God Is Not a Fish Inspector* (1975), 126-33.

"A Business Relationship" *Fid* No. 105 (Spr 1975), 58-64.

"A Business Relationship" *Fiddlehead Greens* (1979), 200-8.

"A Business Relationship" *Connections 3* (1982), 198-204 [Based on survey response].

"The Call" *Alphabet* No. 12 (Aug 1966), 18-21.

"Capital" *God Is Not a Fish Inspector* (1975), 79-90.

"Celebration" *UWR* 11:2 (Spr-Sum 1976), 96-106.

"Celebration" *Red Dust* (1978), 87-103.

"The Cossack" *Fid* No. 83 (Jan-Feb 1970), 22-8.

"The Couch" *Sat Eve Post* 249 (Apr 1977), 52, 84-8.

"The Couch" *Water* [n.d.], 108-15.

"Crazy Times" *Nw J* No. 21 (1982), 54-72.

"The Curse" *Antig R* No. 8 (Win 1972), 11-23.

"The Curse" *Bloodflowers* (1973), 99-111.

"December Bargaining" *Fid* No. 112 (Win 1977), 104-15.

"December Bargaining" *Red Dust* (1978), 34-47.

"December Bargaining" *Stories Plus* (1979), 229-39.

"Dominion Day" *Fid* No. 89 (Spr 1971), 64-72.

"Dominion Day" *Stories from Western Canada* (1972), 194-204.

"Dominion Day" *Bloodflowers* (1973), 53-62.

"The Edge of the Garden" *Fid* No. 69 (Fall 1966), 52-7.

"First Flight" *Fid* No. 92 (Win 1971), 67-74.

"First Flight" *Bloodflowers* (1973), 73-81.

"God Is Not a Fish Inspector" *WCR* 8:1 (June 1973), 3-9.

"God Is Not a Fish Inspector" *God Is Not a Fish Inspector* (1975), 5-18.

"God Is Not a Fish Inspector" *Stories Plus* (1979), 219-29.

"God Is Not a Fish Inspector" *Fireweed* (U.K.) 9 (June 1979), 20-1 [?] [Based on survey response].

"God Is Not a Fish Inspector" *Writer's Workshop* (1982), 102-11 [Based on survey response].

"God Is Not a Fish Inspector" *Anthology of Canadian Literature in English 2* (1983), 535-41.

"Granite Point" *JCF* 3:2 (1974), 24-30.

"Granite Point" *God Is Not a Fish Inspector* (1975), 34-51.

"Granite Point" CBC *"Saturday Stereo Theatre"* 29 Oct 1983 [Based on survey response].

"Hunting" *74: New Canadian Stories* 97-110.

"Hunting" *God Is Not a Fish Inspector* (1975), 19-33.

"Hunting" *Modern Canadian Stories* (1975), 221-35.

"Hunting" *Horizon* (1977), 226-36.

"Identities" *Canadian Short Fiction Anthology 2* (1982), 50-2.

"In Manitoba" *Prism* 13:2 (Win 1973), 128-40.

"In Manitoba" *God Is Not a Fish Inspector* (1975), 64-78.

"In Manitoba" *Timarit Mals Oq Mennigar* 1975, 139-59 [As "I Manitoba"; in Icelandic; trans. J. Bjarman; based on survey response].

"In Manitoba" *Utvarp Reykjavik, rikis utvarpid* (Ice) 11 June 1977 [As "I Manitoba"; radio broadcast; based on survey response].

"In Manitoba" *Sinn Und Form* (Ger) (Mar-Apr 1981), 396-407 [Based on survey response].

"The Job" *QQ* 78 (1971), 572-8.

"The Job" CBC *"Anthology"* 4 Nov 1972.

"The Job" *Bloodflowers* (1973), 91-8.

"A Manitoba Accident" CBC *[Winn]* May 1980 [Based on survey response].

"A Matter of Balance" CBC *"Anthology"* 7 June 1980.

"A Matter of Balance" *Penguin Book of Modern Canadian Short Stories* (1982), 503-13.

"The Novice" *God Is Not a Fish Inspector* (1975), 103-10.

"The Old Man's Story" *Ice Can* 19:4 (Sum 1961), 38-41.

"On Lake Therese" *Bloodflowers* (1973), 112-22.

"A Place of One's Own" *Tam R* No. 71 (Sum 1977), 21-41.

"A Place of One's Own" *Red Dust* (1978), 48-72.

"A Place of One's Own" *Penguin Book of Canadian Short Stories* (1980), 421-40.

"A Private Comedy" *UWR* 9:2 (Spr 1974), 64-73.

"A Private Comedy" *God Is Not a Fish Inspector* (1975), 91-102.

"Red Dust" *QQ* 82 (1975), 572-86.

"Red Dust" *Red Dust* (1978), 104-25.

" 'Remember How We Dressed When We Were Teenagers'?" *Ice Can* 27:2 (Win 1968), 38-9.

"The Revolutionary" *Grain* 3:2 [1975], 4-9.

"Saturday Climbing" *Rainshadow* (1982), 13-22.

"Saturday Climbing" *Chat* 55 (May 1982), 56, 188, 192, 194, 196.

"Saturday Climbing" *West of Fiction* (1983), 3-11.

"Saved" *Antig R* No. 16 (Win 1974), 43-54.

"Saved" *God Is Not a Fish Inspector* (1975), 52-63.

"Skald" *JCF* No. 20 (1977), 5-16.

"Skald" *Red Dust* (1978), 16-33.

"Skald" *More Stories from Western Canada* (1980), 198-214.

"Skald" *Heartland* (1983), 61-73.

"Snow" *Mal R* No. 33 (Jan 1975), 97-103.

"Snow" *Moderne Erzähler der Walt: Kanada* (1976), 363-71 [As "Schnee"; trans. Walter Riedel].

"Trees" *Ont R* No. 4 (Spr-Sum 1976), 87-96.

"Trees" *77: Best Canadian Stories* 23-36.

"Trees" *Red Dust* (1978), 73-86.

van Daele, Christa (1951?-)†

"De Grassi Street" *Makara* 2:4 [1977], 33-5.

"The Dossier" *Miss Chat* 13 (11 Mar 1976), 90-1, 98-101.

van der Beek, John‡

"A Father's Love" *Muse* 67 (1958), 34-5.

van der Heuvel, M.F.‡

"Teachings" *Stump* Fall-Win 1982, 1-2.

van der Mark, Christine (1917-)

"Khyber Bride" *Chat* 36 (June 1963), 24, 48-9, 52-3.

Van Dyck, Henry Clayton‡

"The C.P.R. Clairvoyant" *Chel J* 3 (July-Aug 1977), 181-4.

van Every, Janet†

"Ah Tria Humpelbein" *Onward* 26 Apr 1959, 258-60, 267.

"The Black Umbrella" *Onward* 17 Sept 1961, 8-11, 15.

"The Quiet Tree" *Onward* 27 Mar 1960, 193-5, 206.

van Fraassen, Bas‡

"The Next Song" *Fid* No. 111 (Fall 1976), 33-5.

"St. Xaviera" *Poetic License* 1:6 (Jan 1979), 4-9 [Sketch?].

van Herk, Aritha (1954-)

"Fear of Death Will Not Disturb Me" *Aurora* 1979 110-20.

"It's Incredible" *Gas Rain* 2 (1978), 19-24.

"A Minor Loss" *Gas Rain* [1] (Mar 1977), 41-3.

"Never Sisters" *More Stories from Western Canada* (1980), 61-9.

"Never Sisters" *West of Fiction* (1983), 170-6.

"A Night Alive" *Alive* No. 27 [1973], 17.

"The Road Out" *Miss Chat* 14 (3 Feb 1977), 58-9, 76-8.

"Saint Peter" *Alberta Diamond Jubilee Anthology* (1979), 255-61.

"Stationed" *NeWest R* 3 (May 1978), 6-7.

"Transitions" *Miss Chat* 15 (Aug 1978), 38, 93-4, 96.

"A Woman of Moderate Temperament" *Getting Here* (1977), 1-14.

Van Luven, John‡

"The New Neighbour" *Talon* [1:1 (n.d.)], [2 pp].

van Luven, Lynne
"Sorting Things Out" *CBC [Edm]* "*Alberta Anthology*" 29 Nov 1980.
"The Wind" *Whetstone* Spr 1974, [2 pp].

Van Newkirk, Allen‡
"Act" [?] *Is* No. 5 (1968), [4 pp].

van Norman, Brian‡
"The Cattle Walker" *Wee Giant* 3:2 (1980), 26-8.
"The Warrior" *Wee Giant* 5:2 (1982), 19-21, 24-34.

van Varsefeld, Gail†
"Mother's Day Massacre" *Room* 7:3 (1982), 31-49.
"The Same Old Story" *Quarry* 29:4 (Aut 1980), 75-9.

van Vliet, Brigitte†
"The Day" *Can Messenger* 85 (Sept 1975), 12-3.
"Prepare Him Room" *Our Family* 31 (Dec 1980), 26-7.

van Wert, W.F.†
"The Man with the Umbrella" *Antig R* No. 36 (Win 1979), 31-45.

Vance, Bruce.
MOONRISE Don Mills: Thomas Nelson & Sons, 1970 [Based on CBIP].

Vandenbosch, Peter†
"Fine and Unusual Games" *Prism* 10:1 (Sum 1970), 70-80.

Vanderhaeghe, Gary – *See* Vanderhaeghe, Guy.

Vanderhaeghe, Guy (1951-)
MAN DESCENDING: SELECTED STORIES Toronto: Macmillan, 1982.
THE TROUBLE WITH HEROES AND OTHER STORIES Ottawa: Borealis Press, 1983.
"And No Man Could Bind Him" *Chel J* 6 (Jan-Feb 1980), 22-8.
"Cafe Society" *NeWest R* 6 (Nov 1980), 5-6.
"Cafe Society" *Trouble with Heroes* (1983), 36-42.
"Cages" *Prism* 20:1 (Aut 1981), 9-23.
"Cages" *Man Descending* (1982), 99-118.
"Dancing Bear" *Chel J* 2 (Nov-Dec 1976), 287-97.
"Dancing Bear" *Sundogs* (1980), 166-79.
"Dancing Bear" *Man Descending* (1982), 171-86.
"Drummer" *NeWest R* 7 (Oct 1981), 11-5.
"Drummer" *Man Descending* (1982), 81-98.
"Drummer" *100% Cracked Wheat* (1983), 64-87.
"The Expatriates' Party, or Je Me Souviens" *Aurora* 1980 138-59.
"The Expatriates' Party, or Je Me Souviens" *Man Descending* (1982), 149-70.
"Going to Russia" *Interface* 5 (Apr 1982), 52-4.
"Going to Russia" *Man Descending* (1982), 119-28.
"Happy Jack" *Grain* 2:1 [1974], 5-13.
"He Scores! He Shoots!" *Matrix* No. 13 (Spr-Sum 1981), 3-15.
"How the Story Ends" *Dand* 8:1 (1981), 34-50.

"How the Story Ends" *Man Descending* (1982), 51-68.
"The King Is Dead" *Was R* 13:2 (Fall 1978), 43-53.
"The King Is Dead" *Trouble with Heroes* (1983), 8-18.
"Lazarus" *Chel J* 2 (May-June 1976), 125-8.
"Lazarus" *Trouble with Heroes* (1983), 43-50.
"Little David Play on Your Harp" by Gary Vanderhaeghe *Smoke Signals* (1974), 18-27.
"Magic Circles" *Smoke Signals* 4 [date unknown] [Based on *SWG* survey response].
"Man Descending" *Aurora* 1978 5-17.
"Man Descending" *Man Descending* (1982), 187-200.
"No Man Could Bind Him" *Trouble with Heroes* (1983), 19-35.
"Parker's Dog" *Saskatchewan Gold* (1982), 188-201.
"Parker's Dog" *Fid* No. 132 (Apr 1982), 61-9.
"Parker's Dog" *Trouble with Heroes* (1983), 61-70.
"The Prodigal" *JCF* No. 21 (1977-78), 5-14.
"The Prodigal" *Trouble with Heroes* (1983), 51-60.
"Reunion" *Man Descending* (1982), 37-50.
"Reunion" *SN* 97 (Mar 1982), 46-51.
"Reunion" *Best American Short Stories* 1983 255-68.
"Sam, Soren and Ed" *JCF* Nos. 31/32 (1981), 5-31.
"Sam, Soren, and Ed" *Man Descending* (1982), 201-30.
"Snell" *Quarry* 30:1 (Win 1981), 48-52.
"A Taste for Perfection" *Man Descending* (1982), 129-48.
"The Trouble with Heroes" *Trouble with Heroes* (1983), 1-7.
"The Watcher" *CFM* Nos. 34/35 (1980), 97-124.
"The Watcher" *Man Descending* (1982), 1-36.
"What I Learned from Caesar" *Mal R* No. 49 (Jan 1979), 110-20.
"What I Learned from Caesar" *80: Best Canadian Stories* 178-91.
"What I Learned from Caesar" *Man Descending* (1982), 69-80.

Vanderlip, Brian‡
"The Magician" *Nebula* No. 14 (1980), 52-3.

Vandersluis, Cebea Shirley (1932-)
"All That Glitters" *Outset* 1973, 165-9.

Vannin, Ellan‡
"The Birthday Card" *AA* 48 (July 1958), 69.
"The Birthday Card" *Atlantic Advocate's Holiday Book* (1961), 68-9.
"Coffee Break" *AA* 52 (Nov 1961), 34.

Varney, Edwin‡
"In One Ear and out the Other" *Canadian Short Fiction Anthology* (1976), 217.

Vassanji, M.G.‡
"Waiting for the Goddess" *Tor S Asian R* 1:2 (Sum 1982), 78-83.

Vaughan, J.B.†
"Chaws" *CSSM* 2:2 (Spr 1976), 41-3.
"Joe's Apple Tree" *CSSM* 2:4 (Fall 1976), 16-9.

Vaughan, Lantry‡
"First Snow" *Repos* No. 9 (Win 1974), 37-49.

Vaughan-James, Martin
"The Mole" *Story So Far* 3 (1974), 67-75.

Veall, A.R.‡
"A Fishy Fable" *Forum* (OSSTF) 3 (Mar 1977), 92.

Vegman, Jean†
"The Abortive Ulcer" *Mam* 3:1 (Spr 1979), [3 pp].

Veighey, Rose‡
"The Wedding" *Undergrad* 1964, 7-9.

Venus Disturbed – *See* Disturbed, Venus [pseudonym].

Verhoeven, Clemetus‡
"Two Paintings at an Exhibition" *Rude* Prelim No. 1 (Spr 1978), [3 pp].

Verkoczy, Elizabeth
"The Haunted Realm of the Humber River" *Black Cat* 1:2 (July-Aug 1981), 55-9.
"Stanislaw's Clocks" *Black Cat* 1:3 (1981), 41-4.

Verleye, wj‡
"Lips" *CSSM* 3:1 (Win 1977), 66.

V[ernell]., Mark‡
"A Matter of the Heart" *Hibiscus Dawn* No. 9 (29 Jan 1968), 1-2.
"The Strangers" *Hibiscus Dawn* No. 7 (11 Dec 1967), 3-4.

Verner, Shakie‡
"A Pixy Tale" *Communicator* 7:1 [n.d.], [1 p].

Vernon, Lorraine (1921-)
"Blossoms" *Prism* 16:2 (Fall 1977), 127-9.
"The Dry Sea" *Nebula* No. 16 (1980), 11-6.
"Frankie" *event* 10:1 (1981), 16-20.
"Granny's Garden" *Scrivener* 4:1 (Win 1983), 25-7.
"In Her Best Black" *Antig R* No. 48 (Win 1982), 87-92.
"Love Letter to a Friend" *Harvest* No. 4 (June 1978), 7-12.
"The Paper Jesus" *Alphabet* No. 13 (June 1967), 30-3.
"Victoria Regina" *Da Vinci* No. 5 (Aut 1977), 22-5.

Vertolli, Lou†
"The Accomplice" *Mam* 6:1 (Sum 1982), [3 pp].
" 'Arf-and-Arf' – A Look at the R.C.M.P." *Communicator* 10:1 [n.d.], [2 pp].
"Lessons" *Harvest* No. 13 (June 1982), 5-13.
"Papa's Games" *Antig R* No. 42 (Sum 1980), 47-51.
"Quietly Awakened" *Portico* 4:1 (1980), 19-26.
"The Speaking Engagement" *Simcoe R* No. 10 (Spr 1981), 54-6.
"The Subway Ride" *Read Ch* 1:1 (Spr 1982), 41-5.
"Yearly Visit" *Green's* 10:2 (Win 1982), 84-7.

Vesey, Tom‡
"Memoir of a Grim Night in Cleveland (Ohio)" *TUR* 94:2 (Apr 1981), 3-5.

Via, Jody‡
"Me and Another Kid" [?] *Pulp* 4:9 (1 Sept 1977), [1].

Vicari, Patricia (1936-)
"The Mountain" by Pat House *TUR* 70:1 (Nov 1957), 14-8.
"Music Is Water" by Pat House *TUR* 69:1 (Nov 1956), 14-22.
"Music Is Water" *Fid* No. 58 (Fall 1963), 30-41.

Vichert, Gordon‡
"Overheard" *Muse* 64:1 (1955), 5-6.

Vigneault, Ruth‡
"An End and a Peace" *New Mitre* No. 1 (1971), 27-8.

Vincent, Barbara‡
"You Can Get Anything You Want ... " *20 Cents* 3:5/6 (June 1969), [2 pp].

Vintcent, Brian‡
"The Tour Lady" *TUR* 75:1 (Nov 1961), 34-7.
"Two Memories of Mid-Winter for Tony" *TUR* 76:3 (Jan 1963), 16-24.

Vipond, Alva†
"The Plaster Saint" *Lib* 29 (Mar 1952), 30-1, 58-60.

Virgo, Sean (1940-)
THROUGH THE EYES OF A CAT: IRISH STORIES Victoria: Sono Nis Press, 1983.
WHITE LIES AND OTHER FICTIONS Toronto: Exile Editions, 1980.
"Arkendale" *White Lies* (1980), 41-62.
"Arkendale" *Penguin Book of Modern Canadian Short Stories* (1982), 441-61.
"Bandits" *White Lies* (1980), 9-26.
"Brother Dael's New Year" *Through the Eyes of a Cat* (1983), 49-62.
"Deathbed" *White Lies* (1980), 141-50.
"Guess Who I Saw in Paris?" *White Lies* (1980), 83-100.
"The Hanging Man" *Mal R* No. 63 (Oct 1982), 20-8.
"The Hanging Man" *Through the Eyes of a Cat* (1983), 14-21.
"Haunt" *CFM* No. 6 (Spr 1972), 17-26.
"Haunt" *CBC "Anthology"* 17 Nov 1973.
"Haunt" *Stories from Pacific & Arctic Canada* (1974), 144-57.
"Haunt" *Illusion One* (1983), 25-36.
"Home and Native Land" *75: New Canadian Stories* 121-30.
"Home and Native Land" *Mal R* No. 45 (Jan 1978), 104-8.
"Home and Native Land" *Best American Short Stories* 1979 39-43.
"Horsey Horsey" *Through the Eyes of a Cat* (1983), 22-6.
"Interact" *White Lies* (1980), 75-81.
"Ipoh" *White Lies* (1982), 27-40.
"Kapino" *Rainshadow* (1982), 160-9.
"Ludwig" *Imp* 3:2 [n.d.], 29-31.
"Mother Holly" *White Lies* (1980), 101-7.

"Mother Holly" *Rain Chr* 6 [n.d.], 11-6.
"On This Good Ground" *Mal R* No. 63 (Oct 1982), 12-5.
"On This Good Ground" *Through the Eyes of a Cat* (1983), 6-9.
"Les Rites" *Exile* 6:1/2 (1979), 147-62.
"Les Rites" *White Lies* (1980), 109-24.
"Samaritan" *CFM* No. 14 (Sum 1974), 22-45.
"Shan Val Mhór" *Mal R* No. 63 (Oct 1982), 15-20.
"Shan Val Mhór" *Through the Eyes of a Cat* (1983), 1-5.
"Through the Eyes of a Cat" *Mal R* No. 63 (Oct 1982), 28-50.
"Through the Eyes of a Cat" *Through the Eyes of a Cat* (1983), 27-48.
"Tinker Tale" *Mal R* No. 63 (Oct 1982), 8-11.
"Tinker Tale" *Through the Eyes of a Cat* (1983), 10-3.
"Vagabonds" *White Lies* (1980), 63-73.
"White Lies" *Mal R* No. 43 (July 1977), 100-14.
"White Lies" *White Lies* (1980), 125-40.

Visserman, Taede W.†
"McFee's Bee Tree" *Har* 5:4 No. 32 (Dec 1980), 61, 95-8.

Vizinczey, Stephen (1933-)
"Crime and Sentiment" *Winter's Tales* 13 (1967), 98-121.
"Crime and Sentiment" *Best for Winter* (1979), 287-301.
"Scotch Mist" *CBC "Anthology"* 12 Feb 1960.

Vlahov, Ed
"Garash and the Halfbreed" *CSSM* 3:1 (Win 1977), 8-13.
"Pops and the Donland's Flat" *Contact* 3:4 (Win 1974), 46-8.

Volodarsky, Vladimir V.†
"Dunkirk" *Was R* 13:1 (Spr 1978), 41-52.

von Fuchs, Richard‡
"The Doll That Did Everything" *Harbinger* 1 Sept 1968, 10.

Vorres, Ian‡
"The Cactus Trail to Canada (A Tragic Autobiography)" *TUR* 66:2 (Christmas 1953), 14-9.
"Countess Anastasia Perini-Hughes" *TUR* 67:1 (Nov 1954), 12-7.
"Crocodile Across the Window" *TUR* 68:1 (Nov 1955), 11-3.
"Fräulein Húffenheimer's Canadian Summer" *TUR* 67:4 (Mar 1955), 21-7.
"The Lady and the Windmill" *TUR* 68:2 (Dec 1955), 17-23.

Vulpe, Nicola‡
"Cigarette" *Wee Giant* 5:2 (1982), 35-8.

W.R.C. – *See* C., W.R.

W.S. – *See* S., W.

Waddington, Miriam (1939-)

SUMMER AT LONELY BEACH AND OTHER STORIES Oakville: Mosaic Press/Valley Editions, 1982.

"Breaking Bread in Jerusalem" *Fid* No. 162 (Sum 1980), 34-44.

"Breaking Bread in Jerusalem" *Summer at Lonely Beach* (1982), 74-84.

"Day in the Sun" *Summer at Lonely Beach* (1982), 31-3.

"Far from the Snows of Winter" *Summer at Lonely Beach"* (1982), 21-30 [Also entitled "A Long Way from Home"].

"Farewells at Four O'Clock" *Summer at Lonely Beach* (1982), 38-40.

"Habit of Love" *Chat* 45 (Sept 1972), 51, 73-6.

"The Hallowe'en Party" *Summer at Lonely Beach* (1982), 16-20.

"The Honeymoon House" *Imp* No. 1 (1971), 17-22.

"The Honeymoon House" *Summer at Lonely Beach* (1982), 50-4.

"I'm Lonesome for Harrisburg" *Summer at Lonely Beach* (1982), 85-6.

"The Last Rehearsal" *Imp* 2:3/4 (1973), 111-7.

"The Last Rehearsal" *Summer at Lonely Beach* (1982), 34-7.

"A Long Way from Home" *JCF* 3:4 (1975), 34-8 [Also entitled "Far from the Snows of Winter"].

"A Mixed Marriage" *CF* 44 (Aug 1964), 109-11.

"A Mixed Marriage" *Summer at Lonely Beach* (1982), 8-15.

"A Place of Witches" *Summer at Lonely Beach* (1982), 45-9.

"A Silence All Too Long" *Summer at Lonely Beach* (1982), 64-73.

"Summer at Lonely Beach" *QQ* 63 (1956), 358-65.

"Summer at Lonely Beach" *Winnipeg Stories* (1974), 58-67.

"Summer at Lonely Beach" *Summer at Lonely Beach* (1982), 1-7.

"Waldemar" *QQ* 70 (1963), 223-32.

"Waldemar" *Summer at Lonely Beach* (1982), 55-63.

"The Water Cooler" *Summer at Lonely Beach* (1982), 41-4.

Waddington, Patrick.

"The Street That Got Mislaid" *Canadian Short Stories* (1952), 185-90.

"The Street That Got Mislaid" *Cavalcade of the North* (1958), 456-60.

"The Street That Got Mislaid" *Canadian Humour and Satire* (1976), 60-6.

"The Street That Got Mislaid" *Contexts 2* (1981), 260-3.

Wadds, Susan‡

"Oblique Angles" *CCWQ* 5:2/3 (1983), 6-8.

Wade, Jennifer A.

"The Kite" *Diversions* 5:1 (1975), 33-5.

Wagley, Stephen‡

"Pinecoffin's Complaint" *TUR* 90:1 (Sept 1976), 25-9.

"When" *TUR* 90:2 (Dec [1976]), 37-45.

Wahl, W.‡

"Udine" *Acta Vic* 94:4 (Apr 1970), 8-10.

Wait, Harvey J.

"Disarmament" *CSSM* 2:4 (Fall 1976), 7-8.

"Hadrian's Wall" *CSSM* 2:3 (Sum 1976), 57-9.

"The Ultimate Experience" *CSSM* 2:2 (Spr 1976), 7-8.

Wakefield, Carol†

"The Dawning of Joanna or Maybe Johanna?" *Toronto Star* Sun, 24 Oct 1982, D5.

"Hello, Pleased to Meet You" *Miss Chat* 14 (3 Feb 1977), 42, 75.

Wakeham, Pius Joseph

A BOOK OF NEWFOUNDLAND STORIES St. John's: Long Brothers, 1955 [Based on Miller].

TWENTY NEWFOUNDLAND STORIES St. John's: Long Brothers, 1953 [Based on Miller].

Waldman, Wendy‡

"Arla" by Jo-Anne Woodman *Writers News Man* No. 1 [July 1978], [5 pp].

"Monday's Child" *Writers News Man* Nos. 8/9 (Aug 1979), [4 pp].

Walker, Alan‡

"Fun Aboard Mutlow" *Varsity Lit Issue* Fri, 13 Dec 1963, 10-1.

"Gold Is the Sun" *Acta Vic* 86:1 (Aut 1961), 11-4.

"Marwolaeth" *Acta Vic* 85:3 (Feb 1961), 2-3.

Walker, Brian L.

"A Day in Autumn 1970" *Fresh Grease* (1971), 59-70.

Walker, Craig‡

"Wednesday Night" *Scar Fair* 7 (1979-80), 10-5.

Walker, Dan†

"The Formula" *Skylark* 11:2 (Win 1975), 63-4.

Walker, David (1911-)

STORMS OF OUR JOURNEY AND OTHER STORIES Toronto: Collins, 1963.

"Bait for a Tiger" *Sat Eve Post* 224 (14 June 1952), 35, 61-2, 64-6.

"Bait for a Tiger" *Saturday Evening Post Stories* 1952 260-74.

"Break for Freedom" *Sat Eve Post* 224 (27 Oct 1951), 31, 122, 124, 126, 128-9, 131-2.

"The Country of His Mother's People" *Storms of Our Journey* (1963), 53-69.

"Death Stood Behind Him" *Sat Eve Post* 223 (14 Oct 1950), 35, 105, 107-8, 111-2, 114-5.

"The Eternal Tournament" *Sat Eve Post* 222 (22 Apr 1950), 35, 48, 53-4, 56.

"Giant of the Reekie" *Storms of Our Journey* (1963), 221-37.

"Journey in the Dark" *Saturday Evening Post Stories* 1958 [Based on SSI].

"McKinney's Leap" *Storms of Our Journey* (1963), 238-55.

"Mr. Butter's Ocean Crossing" *Storms of Our Journey* (1963), 70-87.

"My Friend, My Enemy" *AA* 49 (Dec 1958), 29-30, 33-4, 36.

"The New and the Old" *Storms of Our Journey* (1963), 108-27.

"News at Wrigley" *SW* 9 May 1953, I:6.

"Old Warrior" *Storms of Our Journey* (1963), 201-17 [Also entitled "The Foolish Hunter"].

"Panic Over the Atlantic" *Sat Eve Post* 222 (21 Jan 1950), 26, 104, 106, 109.

"Professor Gabriel Gunn" *Storms of Our Journey* (1963), 88-107.

"Ruddy Admirals" *Storms of Our Journey* (1963), 128-45.

"The Stalking of Sheila" *Sat Eve Post* 224 (17 Nov 1951), 28, 121-2, 124-7.

"Still Waters" *SW* 19 July 1952, I:5, 9.
"Storms of Our Journey" *Book of Canadian Short Stories* (1962), 215-43.
"Storms of Our Journey" *Storms of Our Journey* (1963), 17-52.
"Summertime Adventure" *Saturday Evening Post Stories* 1955 243-58.
"Tiger of Timbala" *Storms of Our Journey* (1963), 163-200.
"Village Panther" *Storms of Our Journey* (1963), 149-62.
"The Woman Who Wanted to Go Home" *Sat Eve Post* 223 (30 Dec 1950), 28-9, 50-1.

Walker, Doris†
"Their Last Supper" *CSSM* 3:1 (Win 1977), 21-3.

Walker, Jim – *See* Green, H. Gordon.

Walker, Joan
"City Boys Are Different" *Chat* 27 (Apr 1954), 18, 109-12.

Walker, John‡
"Gifts" *Contact* 3:2 (Spr 1974), 13.

Walker, Mirian†
"Estelle the Louder" *Parole* No. 1 [1981?], [1 p].
"Hartfeld" *Parole* No. 2 [1981?], [1 p].
"Letter to Prince" *Parole* No. 1 [1981?], [1 p] [Non-fiction?].

Wall, Richard‡
"Revenge" *Gaillardia* No. 3 (Spr 1964), 8-10.

Wallace, Carl†
"Chaleur Corner" *Intervales* [No. 1] (1959), 47-54.

Wallace, Ian‡
"Mister Watcher" *Talon* [2:1] (Aut 1964), 9-16.

Wallace, Jack [pseudonym]
"The Shepherdess" *Waterloo R* 2:1 (Sum 1959), 18-25.

Wallace, Milton – *See* Green, H. Gordon.

Wallach, Ira
"Death Opens the Mail" *Beaver Bites* 1:7 (Oct 1976), 50-1.

Walsh, Donna‡
"What's a Fella Gonna Do?" *Katharsis* 2:1 (Spr 1969), 32-4.

Walsh, Elizabeth‡
[Untitled] *Writing Group Pub* 1970-71, 39-43.

Walsh, Hugh†
"How I Fucked Up My Life" *Writ* No. 15 (1983), 88-94.
"Just a Nuisance" *WWR* 2:4 (1983), 55-60.
"Life in the General Sense" *Origins* 11:2 (June 1981), 43-50.

Walsh, Patrick†
"Finally I Admit I Have a Knob on My Nose" *Antig R* 1:2 (Sum 1970), 51-60.
"The Meatball Method Journal" *Antig R* 1:3 (Aut 1970), 51-60.

Walsh, Scott†
"I.D." *Quarry* 32:2 (Spr 1983), 42-9.

Walter, H. and Bond, E.H.†
"Dan Mills" *Forge* 1954, 66.

Walters, Harold Neal (1947-)
"The Diet" *Nfld Q* 76:1 (Spr 1980), 11-3.
"The Dwarf" *Nfld Q* 69:2 (Oct 1972), 15-6.
"The Engagement" *Nfld Q* 70:2 (Nov 1973), 33-5.
"Igloo" *Nfld Q* 73:1 (Win 1977), 5, 7-9.
"In the Customs of Men" *Nfld Q* 70:4 (Sum 1974), 12-5.
"Molly's Moose" *Nfld Q* 74:4 (Win 1979), 44, 46-8.
"Not Much Later Than Now" *Nfld Q* 73:2 (Sum 1977), 37, 39, 41-2.
"Poor Little Fellow" *Nfld Q* 69:1 (July 1972), 36-8.
"Portrait Family" *Nfld Q* 75:1 (Spr 1979), 42-4.
"The Sow's Ears" *Nfld Q* 75:4 (Win 1980), 45-8.
"The Sow's Ears" *Visions from the Edge* (1981), 204-11.
"The Sow's Ears" *Twelve Newfoundland Stories* (1982), 93-102.
"The Throwback" *Nfld Q* 71:3 (Mar 1975), 5-9.
"A Trip to Sea" *Nfld Q* 71:4 (Sum 1975), 34-6, 38, 40.

Waltner-Toews, David (1948-)
"Boysenberry Jam" *Har* 3:8 No. 20 (July 1979), 86, 94.
"The Hot Volunteer" *Chel J* 3 (May-June 1977), 125-30.
"A Land Never Promised" *Grain* 5:1 [1977], 15-23.
"A Land Never Promised" *Best of Grain* (1980), 23-31.
"On Call at Christmas: The Dedicated Vet" *The Probe* (Univ of Saskatchewan) Dec 1976, 15-9 [Based on survey response].
"Saturday Night Milk Fever" *Har* 5:3 No. 31 (Oct 1980), 66, 115-6, 122, 130.
"A Sunny Day in Canada" *Fid* No. 115 (Fall 1977), 15-23.
"A Sunny Day in Canada" *Fiddlehead Greens* (1979), 186-99.
"A Sunny Day in Canada" *More Stories from Western Canada* (1980), 277-89.
"Three Days in the Revolution" *Miss Chat* 14 (5 May 1977), 54, 100, 104, 114, 116, 118, 120-1, 124, 126.
"Uncle Ed, the Mennonite Gorilla" *Grain* 6:3 [1978], 17-29.

Walz, Reinhard
"Callekato's Routine of Waking Up" by Reinhard *CFM* Nos. 2/3 (Spr-Sum 1971), 39-41.
"Mary Magdalene" by Reinhard *CFM* No. 1 (Win 1971), 80-1.
"Proof of Angels" *CFM* No. 12 (Win 1974), 9-24.

Wangersky, Russell‡
"Alone at Blue Lake" *Alpha* Spr 1982, 18-9.
"When Evening Falls" *Alpha* 7:2 (Apr 1983), 9-12.

Wansley, David.
ALL FOR MARGARITA AND OTHER STORIES Ottawa: Datwas Press, 1982.
"All for Margarita" *All for Margarita* (1982), 11-22.
"Gypsy Reverie" *All for Margarita* (1982), 23-6.
"The Littlest Thing" *All for Margarita* (1982), 31-48.
"Tomohrik" *All for Margarita* (1982), 51-90 [Novella?].
"Wine-Red Begonia" *All for Margarita* (1982), 27-9.

Wanzell, Grant‡
"Holy-Fast By-the-Sea: An Urban Fable" *City Mag* 1:1 (Oct 1974), 28-30.

Ward, Bob†
"Fat and Lazy" *Uk Can* 15 (1 Mar 1961), 16.
"A Millionaire" *Uk Can* 10 (15 Mar 1956), 10 [Satire].
"Spreading It Around ... " *Uk Can* 10 (15 Nov 1956), 16 [Humour].

Ward, Don†
"The Game" *Targya* 1:1 [n.d.], [3 pp].
"The War" *Targya* 1:2 (Fall 1973), 28-30.

Ward, Evelyn†
"The Old Canal" *Seagull* 1:1 (Aut 1979), 15-6.

Ward, Jean‡
"Mens Sana ... " *Creative Campus* 1962, 51-8.

Ward, Norman
"The Changing of the Fossils on Parliament Hill" *Mont* 32 (Aug 1958), 22-3.
"The Churchill Touch" *Mont* 36 (Apr 1962), 42-3.
"Double Time on Sunday" *Mont* 37 (May 1963), 18-9.
"Double Time on Sunday" *100% Cracked Wheat* (1983), 240-6 [As "Double Time for Sundays"].
"*King Lear* at Home" *QQ* 80 (1973), 410-2.
"*King Lear* at Home" 100% Cracked Wheat (1983), 293-7.
"A Meeting of Minds" 100% Cracked Wheat (1983), 129-33.
"The Molecular Defenestrator" *Mont* 39 (May 1965), 26-7.
"Secession North" *NeWest R* 5 (June 1980), 9.
"The Three Day Week" *Mont* 33 (May 1959), 24-5.

Wardill, William
"The Valediction" *Saskatchewan Writing* 2 (1963), 52-61.

Ware, Colin‡
"A Good Time" *Scar Fair* 4 (1976-77), 23-31.

Ware, Ron‡
"Mai" *Was R* 4:2 (1969), 53-8.

Wark, Wendy‡
"One Too Many" *Pulp* 4:7 (1 July 1977), [4].

Warney, Thomas†.
"The Alchemist" *Floorboards* No. 4 (Aut 1970), 15-7 [Originally broadcast on CBC].
"The Alchemist" *Alive* 2:3 (Feb 1971), 19-21.

Warr, Ernest†
"The Cad" *Contact* 2:11 (Fall 1973), 12-3.

Warren, Diane‡
"White Houses" *Saskatchewan Gold* (1982), 13-22.

Warren, Faith‡
"The Day Radishes Crowned a Cross" *UC Observer* June 1973, 26-7.

Wasmuth, Lorla‡
"explosions" *Pulp* 1:2 (1 Dec 1972), [1].

Wassall, Irma‡
" 'Quit Walking on Your Face!' " *CF* 40 (Sept 1960), 133-6.

Wasserman, J.F.‡
"Soaring" *event* 2:3 [1973], 68-75.

Waterfall, Don E.‡
"Annals" *Acta Vic* 88:2 [1964], 19-23.
"The Reunion" *Acta Vic* 87:1 [1962], 5-8.
"The Storm" *Acta Vic* 86:2 (Spr 1962), 33-5.
"The Vision of Fire" *Acta Vic* 88:1 [1963], 11-2.

Waterhouse, John†
"Corbett's Shaft" *Mont* 31 (Jan 1957), 58-62.
"The Hollow Men" *Forge* 1951, 15-22.
"The Hollow Men" *NR* 5:6 (Feb-Mar 1953), 19-28.
"Miss Hilary" *Forge* 1954, 71-3.
"The Small, Gentle House of Bertram Camm" *British Columbia* (1961), 424-32.

Waterston, Don†
"Hijack!" *Edmonton Journal* Fri, 29 Dec 1967, 18.

Watling, Jay†
[Untitled] Fragment *Evidence* No. 6 [n.d.], 5-13.

Watmough, David (1926-)
ASHES FOR EASTER & OTHER MONODRAMAS Vancouver: Talonbooks, 1972.
FROM A CORNISH LANDSCAPE Padstow, U.K.: Lodenek Press, 1975 [Based on survey response].
LOVE & THE WAITING GAME London: Dennis Dobson, 1978 [Based on survey response].
LOVE & THE WAITING GAME Ottawa: Oberon Press, 1975.
"All at Sea" *Waves* 9:3 (Spr 1981), 7-33.
"All Kinds of Harvesting" *Love & the Waiting Game* (1975), 5-15.
"Ashes" *Cornish R* No. 21 (Sum 1972) [Based on survey response].

"Ashes" *Cornish Short Stories* (1976) [Based on survey response].

"Ashes for Easter" *Ashes for Easter* (1972), 168-80.

"Bell Bottoms on Plymouth Hoe" *Love & the Waiting Game* (1975), 93-111.

"Beyond the Mergansers, Above the Salal" *CFM* No. 20 (Win 1976), 53-63.

"Black Memory" *Ashes for Easter* (1972), 111-30.

"Black Memory" *On the Line* (1981), 47-57.

"Closeted" *Waves* 10:4 (Spr 1982), 12-8.

"Closeted" *British Columbia: A Celebration* (1983), 202-5.

"Cousin Petherick" *CBC "Anthology"* 5 July 1975.

"Cousin Petherick & the Will" *WCR* 8:3 (Jan 1974), 33-9.

"Cousin Petherick & the Will" *Cornish R* No. 25 (Win 1974) [Based on survey response].

"Cousin Petherick & the Will" *CBC "Anthology"* 5 Apr 1975.

"Cousin Petherick & the Will" *Love & the Waiting Game* (1975), 135-50.

"The Cross-Country Run" *Origins* 11:1 (Mar 1981), 12-26.

"Dark Murmurs from Burns Lake" *JCF* No. 33 (1981-82), 45-58.

"Fathers & Sons" *Love & the Waiting Game* (1975), 151-60.

"A First Death" *Ashes for Easter* (1972), 19-27.

"A First Job" *Ashes for Easter* (1972), 61-85.

"Flies, Lizards and Bonar Law" *Love & the Waiting Game* (1975), 16-22.

"Fury" *Mal R* No. 63 (Oct 1982), 141-56.

"Fury" *83: Best Canadian Stories* 126-45.

"Giuletta" *Love & the Waiting Game* (1975), 112-34.

"In the Mood" *Ashes for Easter* (1972), 47-60.

"Love & the Waiting Game" *Love & the Waiting Game* (1975), 23-36.

"Nelly Moriarty and the Jewish Question" *Matrix* No. 12 (Win 1981), 3-15.

"One & All" *Zivot* (Yugo) 1982 [In Serbo-Croat; based on survey response].

"Return of the Native" *Love & the Waiting Game* (1975), 77-92.

"Rosemary" *Love & the Waiting Game* (1975), 51-64.

"Rosemary" *CBC "Anthology"* 24 Apr 1976.

"Sacred & Secular" *Ashes for Easter* (1972), 28-46.

"Scar Tissue" *Ashes for Easter* (1972), 86-110.

"Seduction" *Love & the Waiting Game* (1975), 65-76.

"Shipwreck" *Ashes for Easter* (1972), 155-67.

"Terminus Victoria" *SN* 91 (May 1976), 60-6.

"The Time of the Wind" *Love & the Waiting Game* (1975), 37-50.

"Trading in Innocence" *Ashes for Easter* (1972), 9-18.

"Tynehead: Another Zoo Story" *CBC [Van] "Hornby Colletion"* 2 Jan 1982.

"Wickanninish Memory" *Ashes for Easter* (1972), 131-54.

Watson, Barry‡

"Antigonish" *TUR* 64:4 (Mar 1952), 17-9.

"The Moral" *TUR* 64:2 (Dec 1951), 19-22.

"An Old-Fashioned Christmas" *TUR* 65:3 (Feb 1953), 31-42.

"A Time and a Place" *TUR* 67:1 (Nov 1954), 22-30.

"The Uncanny Case of Professor Graubergundstein" *TUR* 66:1 (Nov 1953), 7-11.

Watson, Edward A.‡

"A Strange, Obscure Revenge" *Connexion* 1:2 (Apr 1969), [6 pp].

Watson, John
"A Letter from a Girl Called Elsie" *MM* 64 (1 Jan 1951), 16, 42-4.

Watson, Robert‡
'The Blue Period" *Prism* (Mont) 4 (1961), 1-5.

Watson, Scott (1950-)
STORIES Vancouver: Talonbooks, 1974.
"A Family Secret" *Stories* (1974), 23-31.
'The Night-Sucker" *Stories* (1974), 43-9.
"Notes" *Gay Tide* 1:3 (Nov 1973), 5.
'The Prisoner of Sex" *Stories* (1974), 15-21.
'The Red Moth" *Stories* (1974), 33-42.
"Voice without Words" *Stories* (1974), 7-14.

Watson, Sharon‡
"Cliche" *Eclipse* [No. 1] [n.d.], 29-31.

Watson, Sheila
FOUR STORIES Toronto: Coach House Press, 1979.
"And the Four Animals" *Anthology of Canadian Literature in English* 2 (1983), 2-3.
"Antigone" *Tam R* No. 11 (Spr 1959), 5-13.
"Antigone" *Canadian Century* (1973), 574-81.
"Antigone" *Open Letter* 3rd Ser No. 1 [1975], 26-32.
"Antigone" *Literature in Canada* (1978), 375-82.
"Antigone" *Four Stories* (1979), 37-48.
"Antigone" *Fiction of Contemporary Canada* (1980), 53-61.
'The Black Farm" *QQ* 63 (1956), 202-13.
'The Black Farm" *Stories from Western Canada* (1972), 205-17.
'The Black Farm" *Open Letter* 3rd Ser No. 1 [1975], 16-25.
'The Black Farm" *Four Stories* (1979), 19-36.
'Brother Oedipus" *QQ* 61 (1954), 220-8.
'Brother Oedipus" *Open Letter* 3rd Ser No. 1 [1975], 9-15.
'Brother Oedipus" *Four Stories* (1979), 7-18.
'Brother Oedipus" *Penguin Book of Modern Canadian Short Stories* (1982), 35-42.
'The Rumble Seat" *Open Letter* 3rd Ser No. 1 [1975], 33-40.
'The Rumble Seat" *Four Stories* (1979), 49-62.

Watson, Wilfred
"Collage" *Literary R* (U.S.) 8 (1965), 503-10.
'Four Times Canada Is Four" *Alphabet* No. 7 (Dec 1963), 58-82.
'Four Times Canada Is Four" *Rainshadow* (1982), 211-35.
'The Lice" *Prism* 2:1 (Fall 1960), 34-57.
'The Lice" *Stories from Western Canada* (1972), 240-67.
'The Lice" *Not to Be Taken at Night* (1981), 108-36.
'The Lice" *West of Fiction* (1983), 341-64.

Watson, William‡
'The Gift" *Edmonton Journal* Sat, 22 Aug 1964, 4.

Watt, Belle†
"Cleo's Christmas" *Alberta Writers Speak* 1969, 29-32.

Watt, Frank W. (1927-)
"Desolation" *CF* 61 (May 1981), 20-1, 24-8.
"Desolation" *82: Best Canadian Stories* 161-85.
"I Am Dying, Egypt" *Mal R* No. 44 (Oct 1977), 55-65.
"A Jar in Tennessee" *QQ* 83 (1976), 613-21.
"The Offering" *Quarry* 26:2 (Spr 1977), 18-26.
"An Oxford Anecdote" *CF* 55 (Dec-Jan 1975-76), 23-6.
"Revenge" *Fid* No. 112 (Win 1977), 93-103.
"Saturday" *Chat* 49 (May 1976), 47, 64, 66, 68, 70, 72.

Watt, Kathy‡
"Seeds" *Snowmobiles Forbidden* (1971), 106-8.

Watt, Sholto
"Conversation Piece" *Weekend* 3 (7 Mar 1953), 34.
"Elena" *Weekend* 3 (11 Apr 1953), 36.
"First Encounter" *Weekend* 3 (28 Mar 1953), 9.
"I Walked Away Singing" *Weekend* 2 (20 Sept 1952), 46.
"Sailor You Fix" *MM* 64 (1 July 1951), 32.
"Sailor You Fix" *SN* 66 (14 Aug 1951), 22-3.
"Two Sisters" *Weekend* 4 (15 May 1954), 52.
"Victoria Eighteen" *Weekend* 3 (30 May 1953), 38.

Watters, Doug‡
"Three Untitled Pieces" *Story So Far* 3 (1974), 121-4.

Watts, John‡
"Gin and Tonic" *TUR* 73:2 (Dec 1959), 16-22.
"The Lodger" *TUR* 74:4 (Sum 1961), 26-9.
"The Playground" *TUR* 73:5 (Sum 1960), 21-7.

Waugh, Thomas L.†
"Asking and Telling – A Discussion of Theory" *Volume 63* No. 1 (Dec 1963), 43-8.

Waverman, George‡
"Capistrano's Last Stand" *Migdal* Sept 1977, 3.

Wawrow, Leszek‡
"Returning" *Echo* (Tor) 2:2 (Win 1970-71), 20.

Waywitka, Anne B.†
"Auction Sale" *Edmonton Journal* Wed, 10 Feb 1965, 4.
"The Curse" *Edmonton Journal* Wed, 12 June 1968, 16-7, 62 [Condensed].
"One Good Turn" *Edmonton Journal* Thu, 4 Mar 1965, 4 [Non-fiction?].

Wear, Robert Delattin‡
"Happy Soon and the Itinerant Muralist" *75: New Canadian Stories* 193-205.

Webb, Christine
"Portraits" *Aurora* 1979 199-213.

Webb, Clifford‡
"The Grecian Urn" *Folio* 4:1 [Jan 1950], [3 pp].

Webb, Donna-Marie
"The Demon in My Mind" *Mandala* 1976, 26.
[Untitled] *Mandala* 1976, 6-7.

Webb, F.W.†
"The Tent Peg" *Legion* 28 (Feb 1954), 31.

Webb, Mary‡
"Foetus" *Prism* (Mont) 1958, 41-4, 46.

Webber, Frances†
"House by the Gorge" *Lifetime* 3 (July-Aug 1973), 4-6.
"Sun Sea and Sand" *Can Lifetime* 4 (July-Aug 1974), 31-2.
"Wild Haven" *Can Lifetime* 4 (Jan-Feb 1974), 31-2.

Webber, Franklyn Millard
TWENTY PEBBLES AND OTHER STORIES New York: Pageant Press, 1955 [Based on Miller].

Webster, Jackie‡
"The Legacy" *AA* 67 (Nov 1976), 45-7.

Weekes, Mary L.†
"Bleeding the Army" *CF* 32 (Aug 1952), 112-4.

Wees, Frances Shelley (1902-19?)
"And Come What May" *CHJ* Mar 1956, 24, 75-6, 78-80.
"Pride of the Rain" *SW* 9 Mar 1963, 10-3.
"Rude Awakening" *Chat* 23 (Apr 1950), 15, 18-20, 22-3, 24.
"We're Going to Have a Wonderful Christmas" *Chat* 27 (Dec 1955), 11, 49-53, 57.

Wegner, Diana‡
"Holy Night" *Mandala* 1971, 57-60.

Weidmark, M.‡
"Small Feminine Feet" *Alpha* 3:1 (Fall 1978), 24.

Weil, Alexandra‡
"Cafe Society: Lunch with Louis at Le Rendezvous" *Avenue* No. 5 (May-June 1982), 42-3.

Weiner, Andrew (1949-)
"Comedians" *Fantasy and Science Fiction* 56 (Feb 1979), 114-24.
"Empire of the Sun" *Again, Dangerous Visions* (1972), 721-6.
"Getting Near the End" *Proteus* (1981), 211-42.
"The Housing Problem" *Leisureways* 1 (Nov 1982) [Based on survey response].

"Invaders" *Isaac Asimov's Science Fiction Mag* 7 (Oct 1983), 60-75.
"The Letter" *Fantasy and Science Fiction* 63 (Nov 1982), 128-39.
"Lost Alaskan Terminal Retreat Blues" *Quarry* 30:3 (Sum 1981), 5-15.
"On the Ship" *Fantasy and Science Fiction* 64 (May 1983), 85-98.
"One More Time" *Chrysalis* 10 (1983), 56-65.
"Takeover Bid" *Twilight Zone* 3:2 (June 1983), 77-81.
"The Third Test" *Interzone* 1:2 (Sum 1982), 16-20.

Weingarten, Roger‡
"Gabriel Boldt's Narrative" *Rune* 1:1 (Spr 1974), 56-60.

Weintraub, Claire‡
'The Waterbugs Never Drown, Mother" *Potlatch* No. 3 (Nov 1964), 7-15.

Weintraub, Ruth Claire†
"A Twig from the Judas" *Prism* 6:2 (Aut 1966), 115-29.

Weinzweig, Helen (1915-)
"Causation" *Small Wonders* (1982), 157-60.
"Circle of Fifths" *SN* 91 (Oct 1976), 57-63.
"Hold That Tiger" *TL* Nov 1980, 64, 139-41, 143, 145, 147.
"Hold That Tiger" *Spice Box* (1981), 258-68.
"The Homecoming" *CBC "Anthology"* 4 Aug 1979.
"L'Envoi" *CF* 61 (Nov 1981), 24-6.
'The Means" *Tam R* No. 70 (Win 1977), 54-67.
"My Mother's Luck" *CBC "Anthology"* 12 Feb 1976.
"My Mother's Luck" *JD* Passover 1977, 4-8.
"My Mother's Luck" *Fireweed* No. 12 (1981), 11-20.
"Quadrille" *JD* Rosh Hashanah 1975, 12-6.
"Quadrille" *JD* Rosh Hashanah 1983, 10-4.
"Surprise!" *CF* 47 (Mar 1968), 276-9.
'Treble Clef" *Imp* 2:2 (Win 1973), 36-46.
"View from the Roof" *JD* Sum 1972, 42-51.
"What Happened to Ravel's *Bolero*?" *Fid* No. 132 (Apr 1982), 7-11.

Weir, Chuck‡
"Gimmie Back My Blood!" *Uk Can* 6 (15 June 1952), 10.
"Heigh Ho, Wheesly!" *Uk Can* 6 (15 May 1952), 16.
"Joining the Army" *Uk Can* 5 (1 Jan 1951), 12 [Satire].
"Man vs. Mouse" *Uk Can* 6 (1 Mar 1952), 11.

Weir, John†
"Compensation" *Uk Can* 7 (1 July 1953), 6 [Non-fiction?].
"Golden Hands in Chains" *Uk Can* 7 (15 Oct 1953), 8.
'Her Inheritance" *Uk Can* 7 (1 Aug 1953), 6.
"Johnny's Triumph" *Uk Can* 7 (15 Aug 1953), 6.
"Marko Firman's Good Luck" *Uk Can* 7 (15 July 1953), 7 [Non-fiction?].
"Sam Hotzman's Emancipation" *Uk Can* 7 (1 Sept 1953), 7.

Weir, Marie‡
"An Ear for an Ear" *Deaf Can* 5:5 (May 1980), 13-6.

Weir, Terence‡
"Clowns" *Los* No. 6 (1980), 41-2.

Weiss, Allan (1956-)
"The Animals" *Flow* Win [1975?], [2 pp].
"Jean Béliveau Was No. 4" *Loomings* 1:1 (1979), 2-12.
"Satanesque" *Fantasy & Terror* 1:6 (1974), 24-8.
"Satanesque" *Year's Best Horror Stories* 3 (1975), 98-108.
"Tuparosh" *Space and Time* No. 40 (Jan 1977), 14-20.

Weiss, Anne Marie
"The Greenhouse" *From an Island* 10:1 [n.d.], 47.
"Paper Airplanes" *From an Island* Feb 1979, 16-7.

Weiss, H.‡
"As Time Goes By" *From an Island* Feb 1979, 29.

Welland, Jon
"Cell Walls" *Pot Port* 3 (1981-82), 35-7.

Welland, Judith†
"Tullugak" *Prism* 13:2 (Win 1973), 85-93.

Wells, Donald W.‡
"The Red Picture" *Inside* No. 1 [Oct 1964], 8-10.

Welsh, Torrey‡
"The Narcissus" *Inside* No. 4 [Jan 1965], 12-6.

Welykopolsky, Luba‡
"Bloodstone" *Writ* No. 4 (Spr 1972), 56-8.
"Eroica" *Writ* No. 3 (Win 1972), 18-20.
"How to Cure Insomnia" *Writ* No. 3 (Win 1972), 20-3.
"A Lesson in Geography" *Writ* No. 3 (Win 1972), 16-8.

Wen, William‡
"Beaches" *Scar Fair* 8 (1981), 57-60.

Werner, Gerrie‡
"Happily Hooked on a Sailboat" *Better Boating* 12 (Feb 1976), 18-22.

West, Alexa
"For You" *WCR* 17:1 (June 1982), 3.

West, David S.†
"Uncle Harry Is Dead" *Canadian Short Fiction Anthology* 2 (1982), 41-7.

West, Kent‡
"Two Is a Crowd" *Seraph* 1964, 27-9.

West, Linda‡
"The Lilac Charade" *Pier Spr* 1:2 (Spr 1977), 49-53.
"Woman on Wheels" *Pier Spr* [No. 3] (Win 1978), 43-7.

West, Rosalie‡
"Independence and Mrs. Pettigrew" *Stories with John Drainie* (1963), 22-9.

Westhues, Kenneth‡
"The Train Ride" *Alive* No. 48 (Apr 1976), 10-1.

Weston, Oleste†
"The Monkey's Story" *Writing* No. 1 (Sum 1980), 37.

Wetmore, Andrew
"Andrew Downs Goes to the Big City" *Bluenose* 2:3 (Win 1977-78), 30-2.
"Bergman Agonistes" *QQ* 81 (1974), 586-95.
"Friday Is Tuna" *AA* 65 (Nov 1974), 46-7.
"A Letter in the Mail-Star" *Alpha* Mar 1977, 3, 6-8.
"Owe, Canada" *QQ* 79 (1972), 225-9.
"Owe, Canada" *Patriot (Univ of Alberta)* 30 May 1974 [Based on editorial note in *Visions from the Edge*].
"Owe, Canada" *Visions from the Edge* (1981), 174-7.
"The Railway Station" *Voices Down East* [1973], 6-7.

Wetmore, W. Gordon†
"The Bigger They Come" *Amethyst* 1:1 (Spr 1962), 17-21.
"The Day of Curtis Daws" *Amethyst* 3:1 (Fall 1963), [10 pp].
"The Green Mushroom" *Amethyst* 2:1 (Aut 1962), 12-4.
"When Old Friends Meet" *Amethyst* 2:3 (Spr 1963), 41-4.

Wexler, Jerry (1950-)
"Alleywalk" *Antig R* No. 42 (Sum 1980), 11-6.
"The Bequest" *Antig R* No. 41 (Spr 1980), 53-73.
"The Bequest" *Saturday Night at the Forum* (1981), 36-55.
"Lament for a Son" *JD* Sum 1981, 33-5.
"A Small Crime" *Mont R* 1:1 (Spr-Sum 1979), 39.
"A Small Crime" *JD* Sum 1981, 26.

Wexler, Steve (1943-)
"Bool Sheet on the Scissor Maniac of Mexico City" *Canadian Short Fiction Anthology 2* (1982), 122-5.

Weyland, John‡
"Old Giulo Returns" *CF* 37 (Aug 1957), 110-1.

Wharton, Calvin†
"South Pacific" *Writing* No. 3 (Sum 1981), 29-30.

Wharton, Maurice‡
"The Last Mugging" *Spear* 7 (Oct-Nov 1977), 38-40.

Whealen, Barbara
"Now Playing" *Forum (OSSTF)* 6 (May-June 1980), 111-2 [See note, 6 (Oct 1980), 151].

Wheatley, Bill – *See* Green, H. Gordon.

Wheatley, Patience†
"Antiphon for Telephone and Typewriter" *Mam* 2:4 (Win 1978), [4 pp].
"A Communication" *Was R* 11:2 (Fall 1976), 39-51.
"Humouresque" *Mam* 4:3 (Aut 1980), [4 pp].
"La Langue d'Oc" *Green's* 6:3 (Spr 1978), 36-43.
"Leaving the Province" *Mam* 4:1 [1980], [3 pp].
"Mr. Mackenzie King" *Fid* No. 115 (Fall 1977), 106-13.
"Mr. Mackenzie King" *Fiddlehead Greens* (1979), 163-75.

Wheatley, Thelma†
"The Room without a Window" *Room* 8:3 (1983), 2-9.
"Wedding of the Year" *Chat* 55 (Nov 1982), 58, 137, 140, 144.

Wheeler, Frances†
"Deirdre" *Creative Campus* 1957, 28-31.
"Seascape" *Creative Campus* 1958, 2-4.
"We Three" *New Voices* (1956), 137-40.
"When a Mother Dies" *Lib* 35 (Nov 1958), 40, 52, 54.

Whelau, Ruth‡
"Pages from a Diary" *UTR* 1:1 (Spr 1977), 19-21.

Wheler, Eleanor (1900-)
"Father Sweeney and the Miracles" *Island Women* (1982), 126-8.

Wherry, Matthew‡
"Monday Afternoon" *Region* No. 6 [n.d.], [6 pp].

White, Alison‡
"The Gift" *From an Island* 1978, 6-9.

White, E.B [?]
"The Hour of Letdown" *Beaver Bites* 1:7 (Oct 1976), 42-3.

White, Howard
"The Day Joey Came" *Rain Chr* No. 6 [n.d.], 29-33.

White, Marilyn
"Letter to Jeanne Pierre S." *UWR* 12:2 (Spr-Sum 1977), 35-9.
"The Near-Sighted Swimmer" *CFM* No. 17 (Spr 1975), 59-64.

White, Nanci†
"The Great Canadian Novel" *Miss Chat* 9 (10 Aug 1972), 103, 108-9.

White, Sheila
"Gems of the Collection" *Beaver Bites* 2:1 (Jan 1977), 20-1.

Whitehead, Lee M.†
"Rooted" *Dal R* 61 (1981), 469-75.

Whiteley, [Capt.] George C.‡
"St Mary's Keys: A Story of the Supernatural" *Mar Adv* 44 (July 1954), 13-4.
"St Mary's Keys: A Story of the Supernatural" *Nfld Q* 57:2 (June 1958), 4-5.

Whiteway, Louise‡

"All's Well That Ends Well" *Nfld Q* 69:3 (Dec 1972), 14-5 [Non-fiction?].

Whiteway, Mary Mercer – *See* Cave, Gladys M. and Whiteway, Mary Mercer.

Whitford, Margaret Ann†

"Black Sacrifice" *Onward* 15 Apr 1962, 3-4, 10.
"Black Sacrifice" *Onward* 18 Sept 1966, 3-4.
"Every Moment Counts" *Onward* 2 Apr 1967, 3-5.
"A Friend in Ebony" *Onward* 17 May 1959, 308-10.
"The Great Charlie Walden" *Rapport* Apr 1970, 31-4.
"The Greatest of These ... " *Onward* 17 Nov 1963, 6-7, 11.
"Judge Not ... " *Onward* 16 Apr 1961, 248-9.
"The Man Inside" *Onward* 12 Feb 1961, 97-9.
"A Matter of Principle" *Onward* 2 Aug 1959, 484-5.
"My Sister's Keeper" *Onward* 29 Mar 1964, 3-4, 11.
"Silent Witness" *Onward* 1 Oct 1961, 6-7, 14.
"A Study in Black and White" *Onward* 30 Nov 1958, 762-3, 765.
"Truth's Way" *Onward* 29 Nov 1959, 754-6.
"Weep Together, Friends" *Rapport* Sept 1969, 14-6.
"Who Is My Neighbour?" *Onward* 22 Feb 1959, 121-3, 127.
"Whose Child Is This?" *Onward* 7 May 1967, 3-4, 14.

Whitman, Ruth‡

"Forty Dollar Doll" *AA* 49 (Dec 1958), 19-23.

Whittall, A.‡

"The Conquest" *Prism* (Mont) No. 2 (1956), 58-60.

Whyte, Jon†

"Francine" *Inside* 2:1 [n.d.], 12-4.
"Peter Pond, His True Confession" *Stories from Western Canada* (1972), 35-40.
"The Wall" *Inside* 2:3 [n.d.], 11-5.

Wickens, A. Gordon‡

"Griffin in the Garden" *AA* 53 (Oct 1962), 23, 25-6.

Wiebe, Armin (1948-)

"Audee, Nobah Naze" *NeWest R* 8 (Sum 1983), 10-3.
"The Courage to Cry" *CSSM* 2:4 (Fall 1976), 53-5.
"Flypaper" *Grain* 5:3 [1977], 9-13.
"Molecular Theory" *Alive* No. 27 [1973], 20.
"Oata, Oata" *Fid* No. 137 (Oct 1983), 59-72.
"The Rightmaker" *Writers News Man* 3:3 (July 1981), [10 pp].
"The Rightmaker" *Can Ethnic Studies* 14:1 (1982), 120-6.
"Twa Corbies" *Writers News Man* 3:5 (Dec 1981), [11 pp].

Wiebe, Rudy H. (1934-)

ALBERTA: A CELEBRATION Ed. Tom Radford. Photographs by Harry Savage Edmonton: Hurtig, 1979.
THE ANGEL OF THE TAR SANDS AND OTHER STORIES Toronto: McClelland & Stewart, 1982.

WHERE IS THE VOICE COMING FROM? Toronto: McClelland & Stewart, 1974.

"After Thirty Years of Marriage" *CF* 58 (Oct-Nov 1978), 36-40.

"After Thirty Years of Marriage" *Alberta* (1979), 165-76.

"After Thirty Years of Marriage" *Angel of the Tar Sands* (1982), 167-77.

"All on Their Knees" *Mennonite* 83 (17 Dec 1968), 778-83 [Based on survey response].

"All on Their Knees" *Mennonite Brethern Herald* 10 (3 Dec 1971), 2-6 [Based on survey response].

"All on Their Knees" *Where Is the Voice Coming From?* (1974), 73-85.

"All on Their Knees" *Angel of the Tar Sands* (1982), 18-30.

"Along the Red Deer and the South Saskatchewan" *Prism* 12:3 (Spr 1973), 47-56.

"Along the Red Deer and the South Saskatchewan" *Where Is the Voice Coming From?* (1974), 113-23.

"Along the Red Deer and the South Saskatchewan" *Personal Fictions* (1977), 105-15.

"Along the Red Deer and the South Saskatchewan" *Wild Rose Country* (1977), 18-30.

"Along the Red Deer and the South Saskatchewan" *Great Canadian Adventure Stories* (1979), 53-64.

"Along the Red Deer and the South Saskatchewan" *Canadian Literature in the 70's* (1980), 69-78.

"Along the Red Deer and the South Saskatchewan" *Angel of the Tar Sands* (1982), 31-41.

"The Angel of the Tar Sands" *Alberta* (1979), 131-4.

"The Angel of the Tar Sands" *Mennonite Brethern Herald* 1980 [Based on survey response].

"The Angel of the Tar Sands" *Angel of the Tar Sands* (1982), 188-91.

"Black Vulture" *Mennonite* 82 (20 June 1967), 410-5 [Based on survey response].

"Black Vulture" *Der Bote* 44 (27 June – 11 July 1967), 11; 11; 11 [As "Der Schwarze Geier"; trans. Ingrid Janzen; based on survey response].

"Black Vulture" *Christian Living* 14 (July 1967), 20-5 [Based on survey response].

"Black Vulture" *Mennonite Brethern Herald* 6 (21 July 1967), 2-6.

"Bluecoats on the Sacred Hill of the Wild Peas" *Star Spangled Beaver* (1971), 46-54.

"Bluecoats on the Sacred Hill of the Wild Peas" *Where Is the Voice Coming From?* (1974), 103-11.

"Chinook Christmas" *NeWest R* 4:4 (Dec 1978), 8-9, 12.

"Chinook Christmas" *Alberta* (1979), 65-75.

"Chinook Christmas" *Angel of the Tar Sands* (1982), 7-17.

"The Darkness inside the Mountain" *Alberta* (1979), 135-41.

"The Darkness inside the Mountain" *Edmonton Mag* 1 (Mar 1980), 38-41.

"The Darkness inside the Mountain" *Angel of the Tar Sands* (1982), 116-22.

"The Darkness inside the Mountain" *West of Fiction* (1983), 150-5.

"Did Jesus Ever Laugh?" *Fid* No. 84 (Mar-Apr 1970), 40-52.

"Did Jesus Ever Laugh?" *Stories from Western Canada* (1972), 176-92.

"Did Jesus Ever Laugh?" *Where Is the Voice Coming From?* (1974), 57-71.

"Did Jesus Ever Laugh?" *Angel of the Tar Sands* (1982), 152-66.

"The Fish Caught in the Battle River" CBC "Anthology" 16 Oct 1971.

"The Fish Caught in the Battle River" White Pelican 1:4 (Fall 1971), 33-7.

"The Fish Caught in the Battle River" Where Is the Voice Coming From? (1974), 125-33.

"The Fish Caught in the Battle River" Angel of the Tar Sands (1982), 69-77.

"From Montreal, 1848" Alberta (1979), 195-6.

"The Funny Money of 1980" Alberta (1979), 106-9.

"Games for Queen Victoria" SN 91 (Mar 1976), 60-7.

"Games for Queen Victoria" CBC "Anthology" 4 Sept 1976.

"Games for Queen Victoria" More Stories from Western Canada (1980), 130-51.

"Games for Queen Victoria" Angel of the Tar Sands (1982), 42-60.

"The Good Maker" Mennonite Brethern Herald 18 (16 Feb 1979), 7-10 [Based on survey response].

"The Good Maker" Angel of the Tar Sands (1982), 178-87.

"The Grand Pursuit of Big Bear" Fid No. 95 (Fall 1972), 3-12.

"Growing Up in Rosebud" Alberta (1979), 104-5.

"A History of the New World" Alberta (1979), 99-103.

"Home for Night" NeWest R 1:9 (Apr 1976), 6-7, 9.

"Hunting McDougall" Fid No. 108 (Win 1976), 17-24.

"In the Beaver Hills" Aurora 1978 71-80.

"In the Beaver Hills" Alberta Diamond Jubilee Anthology (1979), 281-8.

"An Indication of Burning" CFM Nos. 32/33 (1979-80), 150-64.

"An Indication of Burning" Angel of the Tar Sands (1982), 123-40.

"Lake Isle of Innisfree" Alberta (1979), 40-2.

"Lake Isle of Innisfree" CBC [Edm] "Anthology" [?] [date unknown] [Based on survey response].

"The Midnight Ride of an Alberta Boy" Lib 33 (Sept 1956), 22, 64, 66.

"Millstone for the Sun's Day" Tam R No. 44 (Sum 1967), 56-64.

"Millstone for the Sun's Day" Narrative Voice (1972), 242-8.

"Millstone for the Sun's Day" Where Is the Voice Coming From? (1974), 37-44.

"Millstone for the Sun's Day" Story and Structure (1981) [Based on survey response].

"The Naming of Albert Johnson" QQ 80 (1973), 370-8.

"The Naming of Albert Johnson" Stories from Pacific & Arctic Canada (1974), 265-77.

"The Naming of Albert Johnson" Where Is the Voice Coming From? (1974), 145-55.

"The Naming of Albert Johnson" Frontier Experience (1975), 28-41.

"The Naming of Albert Johnson" Personal Fictions (1977), 116-26.

"The Naming of Albert Johnson" Canadian Short Stories 3 (1978), 337-51.

"The Naming of Albert Johnson" Stories from the Canadian North (1980), 159-69.

"The Naming of Albert Johnson" Angel of the Tar Sands (1982), 88-99.

"The Naming of Albert Johnson" Anthology of Canadian Literature in English II (1983), 366-73.

"Oolulik" Story-Makers (1970), 275-92.

"Oolulik" Where Is the Voice Coming From? (1974), 87-102 [Originally chapter from First and Vital Candle (1966)].

"Oolulik" Angel of the Tar Sands (1982), 100-15.

"Over the Red Line" Mennonite 82 (18 July 1967), 464-7 [Based on survey response].

"Over the Red Line" *Der Bote* 44 (18-25 July 1967), 11; 11 [As "Über die rote Linie"; trans. Ingrid Janzen; based on survey response].

"Over the Red Line" *Christian Living* 14 (Aug 1967), 20-3 [Based on survey response].

"Over the Red Line" *Mennonite Brethern Herald* 6 (8 Sept 1967), 4-6 [Based on survey response].

"The Power" *New Voices* (1956), 128-33.

"Scrapbook" *Where Is the Voice Coming From?* (1974), 13-8.

"Scrapbook" *Sense of Place* (1979), 141-7 [Based on survey response].

"Someday Soon, Before Tomorrow" *Where Is the Voice Coming From?* (1974), 27-36.

"Son of McDougall" CBC "Anthology" 24 Feb 1973.

"There's a Muddy Road" *Where Is the Voice Coming From?* (1974), 45-55.

"There's a Muddy Road" *Angel of the Tar Sands* (1982), 141-51.

"They Just Won't Believe" CBC [Edm] "Anthology" [?] [Based on survey response].

"Tudor King" *Christian Living* 11 (Dec 1964), 10-1, 31-2 [Based on survey response].

"Tudor King" *Where Is the Voice Coming From?* (1974), 19-25.

"Tudor King" *Best Modern Canadian Short Stories* (1978), 90-5.

"Tudor King" *Childhood and Youth in Canadian Literature* (1979), 46-52.

"Wash This Sand and Ashes" CBC "*Anthology*" 1 Mar 1969.

"The Well" *Der Bote* 44 (15-22 Aug 1967), 11-2; 11 [As "Der Brunnen"; in German; trans. Ingrid Janzen; based on survey response].

"The Well" *Mennonite* 82 (15 Aug 1967), 502 [Based on survey response].

"The Well" *Christian Living* 14 (Sept 1967), 20-3 [Based on survey response].

"The Well" *Mennonite Brethern Herald* 6 (6 Oct 1967), 4-6 [Based on survey response].

"The Well" *Pluck* 1:2 (Spr 1968), 31-6.

"Where Is the Voice Coming From?" *Fourteen Stories High* (1971), 112-21.

"Where Is the Voice Coming From?" *Narrative Voice* (1972), 249-56.

"Where Is the Voice Coming From?" *Where Is the Voice Coming From?* (1974), 135-43.

"Where Is the Voice Coming From?" *Modern Stories in English* (1975), 415-23.

"Where Is the Voice Coming From?" *Moderne Erzühler der Walt: Kanada* (1976), 319-30 [As "Die rùtselhafte Stimme"; trans. Helfried Seliger].

"Where Is the Voice Coming From?" *Horizon* (1977), 35-42.

"Where Is the Voice Coming From?" *Personal Fictions* (1977), 73-81.

"Where Is the Voice Coming From?" *Literature in Canada* (1978), 558-66.

"Where Is the Voice Coming From?" *Fiction of Contemporary Canada* (1980), 85-93.

"Where Is the Voice Coming From?" *Angel of the Tar Sands* (1982), 78-87.

"The Year We Gave Away the Land" *Weekend* 27 (9 July 1977), 14-6.

"The Year We Gave Away the Land" *Alberta* (1979), 197-205.

"The Year We Gave Away the Land" *Angel of the Tar Sands* (1982), 61-8.

Wieler, Diane†

"The Visit" *Northern Mosaic* 2 (Sept 1982), 10.

Wight, Gudrun‡

"The Front Room" CBC "*Alberta Anthology*" 11 Oct 1980.

Wigle, Wil
"Slow Burn" *NJ* No. 3 (1973), 13-9.

Wilcox, E.H.‡
"The Game" *Mandala* 1976, 41-2.

Wild, Paula‡
"Thanksgiving" *West People* No. 206 (6 Oct 1983), 2.

Wildeman, Marlene
"Six Weeks" *Common Ground* (1980), 148-73.

Wiley, Gerry‡
"92 Lowther Avenue" *Acta Vic* 80:1 (Nov 1955), 16-7.

Wiley, Tom – *See* Hossick, Hugh and Wiley, Tom.

Wilford, Marjorie‡
"Granma Goes on Strike" *AA* 67 (Jan 1977), 40-1, 43.

Wilkin, Greg‡
"Native Waters" *UCR* Spr 1980, 55-61.

Wilkins, Charles†
"A Recollection of the Boneyard" *CBC* "*Anthology*" Aut 1981 [Based on Prairie Fire].
"A Recollection of the Boneyard" *Prairie Fire* 4:3 (Jan-Feb 1983), 9-19 [As "The Gravediggers"; excerpt].

Wilkins, Devon
"CARRY ON FEISAL!" A COLLECTION OF POEMS AND SHORT STORIES FOR CHRISTMAS Orangeville: privately printed, 1982 [Based on CBIP].

Wilkinson, David H.‡
"The Feminine Touch" *Driftwood* [No. 1] (Apr 1973), 57-60.
"Mollie" *Driftwood* [No. 1] (Apr 1973), 17-21.

Wilkinson, Don
"Domestic Quarrel" *FH* 26 Apr 1956, 26-7, 42.

Wilkinson, Myler†
"The Connection" *Pier Spr* 7:2 (Spr 1982), 15-21.
"What He Saw" *Prism* 20:1 (Aut 1981), 25-31.

Wilks, David‡
"Illation" *Fifth Page* 1964, 3-8.
"The Pocket" *Fifth Page* 1964, 37-48.

Will, Ray†
"Esther" *Green's* 1:3 (Spr 1973), 29-31.
"The Most Fragile Kite" *Dal R* 52 (1972), 273-9.

Willard, D.
"Blind Date" *Beaver Bites* 1:2 (15 Apr 1976), [1 p].

Willer-Cavers, Chris‡
"The Empty Seat" *Mandala* 1970, 61-3.

Williams, Catherine R.‡
"To Feed the Soul" *AA* 65 (Apr 1975), 32-3.

Williams, D.S.‡
"You Can't Kill All the Flies" *Earth and You* 4 Nos 19/20 [n.d.], 25-37.

Williams, Dave†
"Airbum + Stinkbird = Wiser Man" *Can Wings* 15 (June 1973), 4, 18-9, 25.
"Beyond the Sight of Man" *Can Wings* 16 (Nov 1974), 17-8.
"Cubby Little Planes on Hot Windy Days" *Can Wings* 16 (June 1974), 8-9, 19.
"The Joke That Had the Last Laugh" *Can Wings* 15 (Nov-Dec 1973), 14, 20.
"The Least of Things" *Can Wings* 17 (Mar 1975), 18-9.
"Skating Along on Carburator Ice" *Can Wings* 16 (July 1974), 18-9.

Williams, David (1945-)
"Buffalo Hunt" *QQ* 81 (1974), 43-58.
"Picking Roots" *JCF* 3:3 (1974), 20-8.
"Shades" *Contempora* (U.S.) Win 1972, 20-1 [Based on survey response].
"Stubble Burning" *JCF* 2:4 (Fall 1973), 39-43.
"The Supper Guest" *Winnipeg Stories* (1974), 125-30.

Williams, Flos Jewell
"Nothing but Money" *Weekend* 1 (10 Nov 1951), 14, 41-4.

Williams, John‡
"The Bracelet" *Intervales* [No. 1] (1959), 23-8.

Williams, M.A.†
"Eleanora Duse at the Sauna" *CFM* Nos. 2/3 (Spr-Sum 1971), 42-5.
"What They Eat at Georgie's House" *CFM* Nos. 2/3 (Spr-Sum 1971), 45-6.

Williams, Margaret†
"Graveyards Are Interesting Places" *From* 231 2:1 (Sept 1973), 1-5.

Williams, Marian
"I Stole the Lilacs" *Chat* 40 (Mar 1967), 36-7, 51-3, 55-6, 60.
"It's Still a Gentleman's Game" *CG* 80 (Feb 1961), 62-4.
"Keep Your Head Down Ginny" *SW* 15 June 1957, 28-9.
"The Nest" *Chat* 37 (July 1964), 15, 34, 40-1.
"The 'Nothing' Christmas" *Chat* 38 (Dec 1965), 25, 56-60.

Williams, Sandra‡
"3 Stories" *In Store* No. 1 (Apr 1969), 4; 5; 6-8 [Stories are untitled but numbered].

Williams, Vera B.†
"An Account of a Skirmish" *Room* 1:1 (Spr 1975), 4-11.
"Henry's Paradox" *Fireweed* Nos. 3/4 (Sum 1979), 102-3.
"A Matter of Style" *CFM* No. 22 (Sum 1976), 11-24.
"A Spring Fancy" *Room* 2:2/3 (1976), 92-4.

Williams, Warren‡
"Passchendaele" *Stet* Mar 1961, 14-7.

Williams, Wayne‡
"A Tale of a Male's Friend" *Halcyon* 13 (Win 1967-68), 46.
"Tea or Coffee, with or without Sugar, and Perhaps a Bit of Lemon" *Halcyon* 12 (Win 1966-67), 45-6.

Williamson, Anne‡
"Breakthrough" *AA* 69 (Apr 1979), 89-90, 92.

Williamson, B.J.†
"Window Dressing" *Chel J* 5 (Jan-Feb 1979), 23-5.

Williamson, David (1934-)
"The Advisor" *JCF* 3:1 (Win 1974), 35-7.
"Courting in 1957" *Winnipeg Stories* (1974), 7-22.

Williamson, Moncrieff (1915-)
"Closed Circuit" *Katharsis* 1971, [5 pp].

Williamson, O.T.G.
"Horning In" *Stories with John Drainie* (1963), 169-74.

Williamson, Rossa (1897-1966)
"[A?] Dependable Man?" *Woman's Home Companion* 81 (Feb 1954), 40-1[+?] [Based on RGPL].
"The Moment" *CHJ* Apr 1955, 14, 82-5.
"Old Woman" *NHM* 51 (Mar 1950), 10-1, 18.
"The Pink Hat" *Winnipeg Stories* (1974), 77-90.
"The Pink Hat" *Inquiry into Literature* 2 (1980), 249-50 [Excerpt].
"Pink Princess" *CG* 83 (Dec 1964), 29-30.
"The Rice Bowl" *SW* 26 Nov 1960, 34-5, 44-5.
"Sloane Bradshaw's Wife" *SW* 11 Nov 1950, I:1, 4.
"Tickets for Two" *SW* 12 Jan 1963, 6-7, 17.
"The Trouble with You Girls" *Chat* 25 (Mar 1952), 14, 56, 58, 60-1, 63, 65.
"The Wonderful Day" *Chat* 26 (Nov 1953), 19, 83-8.

Willis, Stephen‡
"The Adventures of a Flutist or How to Drown in Your Own Condensation" *Folio* 19:1 (Fall 1966), 6-7.

Willison, Evelyn A.†
"The Homestead and the Heart" *Alberta Writers Speak* 1967, 48-53.
"Mutiny at Pine Flats" *Alberta Writers Speak* 1969, 80-5.

Willison, Gladys A.
"The Lendrum Story" *Alberta Writers Speak* 1969, 68-73.

Willows, Joan‡
"Declarations" *WWR* 1:2 (Win 1977), 29-32.

Wills, Charles‡
"Lessons on Passing Away" *Bridle of Glass* (1973), 22-32.

Wills, Claire‡
"Permanent Wave" *Raven* No. 5 (Dec 1957), 17-22.

Wilmot, Eleanor†
"Everett" *Pulp Mill* (1977), 31-9.

Wilputte, Earla (1959-)
"Intersection" *Scar Fair* 8 (1981), 13-8.
"Jung Love" *Scar Fair* 7 (1980), 21-2.

Wilson, Angus C.†
"The Last Elf" *Beyond the Fields We Know* No. 1 (Aut 1978), 10-5.

Wilson, Barbara‡
"History & Physical: Mrs. Wishart" *Pulp* 4:14 (15 Jan 1978), [1-3].

Wilson, Betty
See also Wilson, Betty and Gillese, John Patrick.
"Kaspar's Antelope" *Singing Under Ice* (1974), 170-7.
"Where's the Spirit?" *Edmonton Journal* Wed, 18 Dec 1963, 4.
"White Mountains in the Moon" *Wild Rose Country* (1977), 65-9.
"White Mountains in the Moon" *Alberta Diamond Jubilee Anthology* (1979), 210-4.

Wilson, Betty and Gillese, John Patrick
See also Gillese, John Patrick; Wilson, Betty.
"Turning Twelve" *FH* 8 Mar 1956, 26-7, 37.
"Turning Twelve" by Betty Wilson and Jeff Challers *Our Family* 18 (Mar 1966), 20-4.

Wilson, Budge (1927-)
"The Leaving" CBC *"Anthology"* 1981 [Based on survey response].
"The Metaphor" *Chat* 56 (Oct 1983), 86, 120, 122, 125-6, 130, 132, 136.
"Three Voices" *Chat* 56 (Feb 1983), 60-1, 79-80, 82, 86.

Wilson, Colleen‡
"Approaching" *Introductions from an Island* 1972, 40-2.

Wilson, Don†
"The Tale of the Upright Man" *CFM* No. 21 (Spr 1976), 42-7.
"The Zealot" *CSSM* 2:1 (Jan 1976), 1-3.

Wilson, Elizabeth‡

"The Shell" *TUR* 72:2 (Dec 1958), 9-10.

"A View of Toledo" *TUR* 72:1 (Nov 1958), 26-8.

Wilson, Ethel D. (1888-1980)

MRS. GOLIGHTLY AND OTHER STORIES Toronto: Macmillan, 1961.

"Beware the Jabberwock, My Son ... Beware the Jubjub Bird" *Mrs. Golightly* (1961), 147-82.

"Beware the Jabberwock, My Son ... Beware the Jubjub Bird" *CJOR* (Van) 6 Aug 1962.

"The Birds" *NR* 7:1 (Oct-Nov 1954), 24-7.

"The Birds" *Mrs. Golightly'* (1961), 61-5.

"The Corner of X and Y Streets" *Mont* 32 (Sept 1958), 44-5, 47.

"The Corner of X and Y Streets" *Mrs. Golightly* (1961), 85-8.

"A Drink with Adolphus" *Tam R* No. 16 (Sum 1960), 5-16.

"A Drink with Adolphus" *Mrs. Golightly* (1961), 66-79.

"Fog" *Mrs. Golightly* (1961), 97-105.

"Fog" *Oxford Anthology of Canadian Literature* (1973), 518-24.

"Fog" *Urban Experience* (1975), 77-85.

"Fog" *British Columbia: A Celebration* (1983), 154-6.

"From Flores" *Mrs. Golightly* (1961), 34-44.

"From Flores" *Ten for Wednesday Night* (1961), 44-55.

"From Flores" *British Columbia: A Celebration* (1983), 177-80.

"God Help the Young Fisherman" *Mrs. Golightly* (1961), 45-8.

"God Help the Young Fisherman" *Inquiry into Literature* 4 (1980), 17-20.

"Haply the Soul of My Grandmother" *Mrs. Golightly* (1961), 17-28.

"Haply the Soul of My Grandmother" *British Columbia* (1961), 560-70.

"Haply the Soul of My Grandmother" *Canadian Short Stories 2* (1968), 9-22.

"Haply the Soul of My Grandmother" *Contemporary Voices* (1972), 176-82.

"Mr. Sleepwalker" *Mrs. Golightly* (1961), 126-46.

"Mr. Sleepwalker" *Canadian Winter's Tales* (1968), 150-72.

"Mr. Sleepwalker" *Not to Be Taken at Night* (1981), 165-84.

"Mrs. Golightly and the First Convention" *Canadian Short Stories* (1952), 151-64.

"Mrs. Golightly and the First Convention" *Cavalcade of the North* (1958), 196-205.

"Mrs. Golightly and the First Convention" *Mrs. Golightly* (1961), 1-16.

"Mrs. Golightly and the First Convention" *Great Canadian Short Stories* (1971), 75-88.

"Mrs. Golightly and the First Convention" *Canadian Humour and Satire* (1976), 42-56.

"Mrs. Golightly and the First Convention" *Great Canadian Adventure Stories* (1979), 169-83.

"Simple Translation" *SN* 76 (23 Dec 1961), 19.

"Simple Translation" *Read Dig* 80 (Apr 1962), 88, 90-1 [As "Journey to a Fair Land"; condensed].

"Till Death Us Do Part" *Mrs. Golightly* (1961), 183-93.

"Till Death Us Do Part" *Modern Canadian Stories* (1966), 63-72.

"To Keep the Memory of So Worthy a Friend" *New York Reporter* 13 Dec 1956, 35-6 [Sketch? Based on ABCMA].

"To Keep the Memory of So Worthy a Friend" *Mrs. Golightly* (1961), 89-96.

"Truth and Mrs. Forrester" *Mrs. Golightly* (1961), 111-25.

"A Visit to the Frontier" *Tam R* No. 33 (Aut 1964), 55-65.
"A Visit to the Frontier" *Stories from Western Canada* (1972), 1-12.
"A Visit to the Frontier" *Frontier Experience* (1975), 106-17.
"The Window" *Tam R* No. 8 (Sum 1958), 3-16.
"The Window" CBC *"Anthology"* 23 Dec 1958.
"The Window" *Best American Short Stories* 1959 381-94.
"The Window" *Mrs. Golightly* (1961), 194-209.
"The Window" *Evolution of Canadian Literature in English* (1973), 14-23.
"The Window" *Stories from Pacific & Arctic Canada* (1974), 34-48.
"The Window" *Best Modern Canadian Short Stories* (1978), 39-49.
"The Window" *Literature in Canada* (1978), 64-75.
"The Window" *Transitions 2* (1978), 189-200.
"The Window" *Anthology of Canadian Literature in English 1* (1982), 336-45.
"You'll Never Get Away" *Chat* 33 (Mar 1960), 34, 106, 110-4, 116-7, 120.

Wilson, J.D.‡
"Heraclitus Bathes" *UCR* Spr 1976, 41-2.

Wilson, Jack Lowther (1924-)
"Among the Old Singers" *Antig R* No. 47 (Aut 1981), 37-44.
"A Dinner Party" *CF* 44 (Sept 1964), 137-8.
"Of Mulcahy and Fiddlesticks" *QQ* 83 (1976), 405-12.
"Once upon a Century" *Waves* 10:4 (Spr 1982), 26-32.
"Perhaps It Never Was" *QQ* 71 (1964), 334-40.
"Roast Beef's the Thing to Eat" *QQ* 72 (1966), 651-6.
"Singing" *Tam R* No. 37 (Aut 1965), 47-53.
"The Sunday Man" *CF* 46 (May 1966), 29-32.
"The Waiting" *QQ* 65 (1958), 448-58.

Wilson, Jane E.‡
"The Warranty" *Abegweit R* 3:1 (Spr 1980), 64-70.

Wilson, John‡
"No Such Liberty" *TUR* 69:2 (Dec 1956), 10-5.
" 'When in Rome ... ' " *TUR* 68:3 (Feb 1956), 14-7.

Wilson, Kathleen‡
"A Walk" *Diversions* 5:1 (1975), 60.

Wilson, Laurence M.†
THE DICTAPHONE (A SHORT STORY) Chibougamau: Bull Moose Press, 1961.

Wilson, Marglamb‡
"A Fine White Powder" *Quarry* 32:2 (Spr 1983), 16-24.
"Gordon" *Waves* 10:1/2 (Sum-Fall 1981), 32-5.

Wilson, P.M.‡
"Our Trespasses" *TUR* 66:3 (Feb 1954), 24-7.
"A Way of Life" *TUR* 66:4 (Mar 1954), 24-7.

Wilson, Paul†
"2-Key Din-Din" *Freelance* Nov 1979, 13-4.

Wilson, Peter‡
"Bid by Bid" *Kaleidoscope* 1956-57, 13-5.

Wilson, Wendy‡
"Metamorphosis" *Simcoe R* No. 1 (Win 1976), 10-1.

Winans, A.D.‡
"Stuff and Nonsense" *Titmouse R* 1:2 (Win 1972), 37-42.

Wind, Chris†
"Double Exposure" *event* 12:2 (1983), 116-22.

Windish, Rainier Mario‡
"A Portrait of Rain and Steambath in New Colours" *Prism* 3:2 (Win 1962), 34-9.

Windley, Carol†
"Moths" *event* 12:2 (1983), 18-30.

Wing, Sandy
"Casualties" *Matinees Daily* (1981), 9-23.
"Comet on a String" *Los* No. 8 (Mar 1982), 1-15.
"Lessons in Biology" *Saturday Night at the Forum* (1981), 9-25.

Winkler, Donald†
"The Dancing Lesson" *Cyclic* 1:4 (1967), 1-2.
"A Day in the Life of the Jester" *CF* 56 (Oct 1976), 20.
"Variations" *CF* 56 (Oct 1976), 19.

Winn, Janet Bruce‡
"Dried Rose Petals in a Silver Bowl" *Evidence* No. 10 (1967), 4-11.

Winslow, Natalie‡
"The Fascinating Art of Babcockery" *AA* 47 (July 1957), 63-5.

Winter, Barbara‡
"Acquaintance" *Acta Vic* Spr 1975, 18-9.

Winter, Jack†
"15 U.B." *CF* 41 (Apr 1961), 14-6 ["a pantomime"].
"Portrait of a Lady" *Forge* Feb 1957, 45.
"Portrait of the Artist" *Forge* Dec 1956, 30.
"Untimely Death" *CBC "Anthology"* 25 Mar 1978.

Winter, Judy
"Claire" *Mal R* No. 50 (Apr 1979), 27-36.
"A Deer in the Forest" *Quarry* 32:2 (Spr 1983), 34-41.

Winter, Keith†
"Feathers for Breakfast" *Touchstone* No. 2 (Sept 1965), 22-8.

Winter, Mae‡
"Aalik" *Edmonton Culture Vultue* 1:2 (24 Oct 1975), 23-7.

Wiseman, Adele (1928-)
"The Country of the Hungry Bird" *JCF* Nos. 31/32 (1981), 136-9.
"Duel in the Kitchen" *MM* 74 (7 Jan 1961), 23, 74, 76-9 [Also entitled "On Wings of Tongue"].
"On Wings of Tongue" *Modern Canadian Stories* (1966), 271-86 [Also entitled "Duel in the Kitchen"].
"On Wings of Tongue" *Heartland* (1983), 151-65.

Wiseman, Mrs. C.
"A Glimpse That Changed a Life" *War Cry* [21 Dec] 1957, 14.
"Walls Are No Barrier" *Home Leaguer* 2 (Dec 1954), 6.

Wishart, Ian‡
"Industrial Peace: A Story" *TUR* 65:4 (Mar 1953), 9-14.

Witherington, Paul‡
"Gonedaddy" *Was R* 10:2 (Fall [1975]), 56-65.

Witte, Alton Jr.‡
"Night" *Alive* No. 32 [1973], 49.

Witte, Darlene‡
"The Smile" *CBC "Alberta Anthology"* 20 Nov 1982.

Wittrup, Jenny‡
"Sarry" *Contact* 3:2 (Spr 1974), 3-5.

Witvoet, Bert†
"The Gospel According to Wiebe's Brother" *Vanguard* 11:2 (Mar-Apr 1981), 16-8.
"Rendezvous on a Drafty Corner" *Vanguard* 10:1 (Jan-Feb 1980), 13-5.

Wolczuk, Alice†
"A Can of Paint" *Pulp Mill* (1977), 63-8.

Wolfe, Miriam‡
"The Language of Love" *North* 14 (July-Aug 1967), 37-8.

Wolfe, Morley (1928-)
"The Angel and the Prostitute" *Undergrad* Spr 1951, 12-4.
"For Those Who Remain" *Undergrad* Aut 1950, 10-3.

Wolfe, Norine‡
"Introduction to a Corpse" *Driftwood* No. 2 (1974), 41-4.

Wolfe, Patrick (1952?-)†
"Battling" *Grain* 4:1 [1976], 12-7.
"The Game" *CSSM* 1:3 (July 1975), 23-5.

Wolfe, Roy I.‡

"The Fishing Rod" *CBC "Anthology"* 13 Dec 1955.

"My Uncle Yankin and the Rock of God" *CBC "Anthology"* 5 Apr 1955.

Wolfson, Ken‡

"Playing the Game" *Fifth Page* [1969?], 20-5.

Wolper, Roy S.‡

"Happy Like a White Squash" *Quarry* 16:1 (Oct 1966), 14-20.

"A Vacation" *Was R* 1:1 (1966), 62-73.

Wong, Henry†

"All My Love, Louisa" *WWR* 2:3 No. 7 (1982), 78-83.

Wood, Herbert

"For the Sake of the Children" *Home Leaguer* 13 (Dec 1965), 8-9, 13.

"Night Visitor" *War Cry* 25 Dec 1965, 4-5, 16-7.

"Sunrise on the Mountainside" *War Cry* 25 Mar 1967, 4-5, 17.

Wood, Kerry (1907-)

"Acres Apart" *Weekend* 1 (10 Nov 1951), 18-9.

"Apples and the Fabulous Fortune" *SW* 31 Mar 1951, I:3-4.

"Bettylou and the Caribou" *Onward* 12 Oct 1958, 648-51.

"The Blind Deer" *FH* 14 Feb 1952, 24.

"Busy as a Beaver" *Onward* 19 Feb 1956, 116-7, 126-7.

"Christmas Concert" *Onward* 18 Dec 1955, 801-3, 805.

"Come Back Again" *Onward* 8 Nov 1959, 714-5 [Also entitled "Come Back Again, Johnny].

" 'Come Back Again, Johnny' " *SW* 15 Sept 1951, II:5.

"The Curse" *Onward* 24 Oct 1954, 677-8.

"Day for a Boy" *Onward* 4 May 1958, 282-4 [Non-fiction?].

"Docherty's Gone" *QQ* 59 (1952-53), 464-70.

"Donito and His Quest" *Echoes* No. 203 (Sum 1951), 5-6, 29-30.

"The Dynamite Horse" *CG* Jan 1954, 8, 46-9.

"Eskimo Spring" *CG* Dec 1955, 6, 30.

"Family Picnic" *Onward* 26 June 1960, 404-7.

"The Faraway Lady" *FH* 8 Jan 1953, 24-5.

"The Feather Bonnet" *Onward* 28 Mar 1965, 4.

"Flames at Dusk" *Onward* 1 June 1958, 340-1 [Non-fiction?].

"Fred and the Goose" *Onward* 11 Oct 1959, 641-3 [Non-fiction?].

"Fred and the Goose" *Onward* 4 Oct 1964, 11-3.

"The Gardener" *FH* 16 Oct 1952, 28-9, 33.

"Go Alone, Johnny" *Onward* 22 Apr 1962, 8-10.

"The Hungry Son" *Onward* 4 Dec 1955, 769-71.

"Indian Honor" *Edmonton Journal* Mon, 10 Aug 1964, 4.

"Jubilee Meeting" *Onward* 22 Jan 1956, 52-3, 62-3.

"The Killer Bronc" *FH* 14 Feb 1952, 24.

"The Lady Bronc" *FH* 1 Feb 1951, 18-9, 27.

"The Land Grows Love" *CG* Mar 1951, 11, 65-6, 68.

"Low Note in the Night" *Alberta Diamond Jubilee Anthology* (1979), 34-7.

"Man and Animal" *Onward* 2 Sept 1962, 3-4.

"Man and Animal" *Onward* July 1967, 3-4.
"The Parson's New Church" *CG* Sept 1951, 14, 58, 60-1.
"The Parson's Tongue" *CG* Feb 1951, 9, 46-9.
"The Peace of O-hoo" *CG* Feb 1950, 10, 58-62.
"The Picnic and the Gun" *Onward* 2 Sept 1956, 564-5.
"The Picnic and the Gun" *Onward* 9 June 1963, 10-1.
"Poacher's Game" *CG* 85 (Sept 1966), 43-4.
"Poacher's Game" *Ave Maria* 105 (20 May 1967), 24-7.
"Polly at the Fair" *CG* Oct 1951, 10, 47-50.
"The Quiet Place" *Onward* 10 Jan 1954, 17-9, 23-4.
"Rogue Male" *Mont* [43] (Nov 1969), 12-5, 17.
"A Scarf for a Maiden" *FH* 25 Aug 1955, 18-9.
"The Starting Day" *CG* Oct 1954, 8, 56-9.
"The Stick Maker" *CG* Mar 1956, 12, 55-6.
"The Stick Maker" *Onward* 13 Mar 1960, 166-7, 174-5.
"The Tartaned Hootlet" *CG* Jan 1958, 15, 36.
"The Tartaned Hootlet" *Onward* 1 July 1962, 5-7, 12.
"The Thief" *Onward* 2 Jan 1955, 5-6.
"The Thief" *Onward* 4 Mar 1962, 13-4.
"The Unmelodious Jailbird" *Echoes* No. 206 (Spr 1952), 5, 18-20.
"The Wild Horse" *CG* July 1956, 12, 30-2.
"Workaday Cowboy" *Cowboys, Cowboys, Cowboys* (1950) [Based on SSI].
"Workaday Cowboy" *FH* 10 Aug 1950, 16-7.

Wood, Margaret‡
"She Was No Lady" *Better Boating* 11 (Feb 1975), 18-20.

Wood, Margaret E.†
"The Holiday" *Can Messenger* 84 (Dec 1974), 17.
"No Holly and No Ivy" *Can Messenger* 87 (Dec 1977), 18-9.

Wood, Ted (1931-)
SOMEBODY ELSE'S SUMMER Toronto/Vancouver: Clarke, Irwin, 1973.
"All the Care in the World" *Somebody Else's Summer* (1973), 64-75.
"American Primitive" *Somebody Else's Summer* (1973), 152-6.
"American Primitive" *Inquiry into Literature* 3 (1980), 69-73.
"As Advertised" *Chat* 50 (May 1977), 45, 95-6, 98-9.
"Bed and Breakfast" *Somebody Else's Summer* (1973), 78-83.
"The Best-Laid Plan" *Somebody Else's Summer* (1973), 96-114.
"The Cucumber Contract" *CBC "Anthology"* 9 Oct 1971.
"The Cucumber Contract" *Somebody Else's Summer* (1973), 116-28.
"The Cure" *Chat* 49 (Apr 1976), 51, 65-6, 70, 72, 74, 76.
"Dependents" *Somebody Else's Summer* (1973), 158-69.
"The Expert" *CBC "Anthology"* 12 Jan 1962.
"First Taste of Apples" *Mont* 35 (Mar 1961), 28-32.
"The Fish" *Tam R* No. 49 (1969), 48-59.
"The Fun of the Fair" *Mont* 36 (Mar 1962), 31-3.
"George" *CBC "Anthology"* 23 June 1973 [Also entitled "Out of the Rain"].
"Got to Travel On" *CBC "Anthology"* 22 Nov 1969.
"Got to Travel On" *Somebody Else's Summer* (1973), 54-63.
"Here's Looking at You" *Somebody Else's Summer* (1973), 130-6.

"The Jackdaws" *Mont* 34 (July 1960), 17, 38-41.
"The Jackdaws" *CBC "Anthology"* 17 Mar 1961.
"Kinder Than the Sea" *CBC "Anthology"* 29 July 1972.
"Kinder Than the Sea" *Somebody Else's Summer* (1973), 24-38.
"Load of Trouble" *Stories from Across Canada* (1966), 56-66.
"The Man Who Shot Trout" *CBC "Anthology"* 6 Dec 1975.
"The Music Maker" *Mont* 35 (June 1961), 28-31.
"Out of the Rain" *Somebody Else's Summer* (1973), 14-23 [Also entitled "George"].
"Out of the Rain" *Sunlight & Shadows* (1974), 132-9.
"Points of View" *CBC "Anthology"* 2 Feb 1974.
"A Present for Alice" *Somebody Else's Summer* (1973), 84-94.
"Promises to Keep" *Chat* 48 (Nov 1975), 52, 107-13.
"A Quiet Life" *SN* 95 (Nov 1980), 56-8, 60, 63-5.
"The Sales Pitch" *Somebody Else's Summer* (1973), 40-52.
"The Slippery Slide" *Mont* 40 (Nov 1966), 26-7.
"Sombody Else's Summer" *Somebody Else's Summer* (1973), 2-12.
"Susan" *Somebody Else's Summer* (1973), 170-88.
"That Second Cup of Coffee" *Somebody Else's Summer* (1973), 138-51.
"The Time of Hummingbirds" *Chat* 47 (Nov 1974), 52, 84-6.
"Victims" *Chat* 56 (Jan 1983), 40, 83-4, 86, 88, 90.

Wood, Vicki†
"The Day I Caught a Thief" *Alpha* 1:2 (Nov 1976), 5-6.

Woodbury, Mary†
"Colour Me Woman" *JCF* 4:3 No. 15 (1975), 15-21.
"Smoke Screen" *New Q* 2:4 (Win 1983), 69-72.

Woodcock, Don‡
"The Wolf" *Outdoor Can* 3 (May-June 1975), 40, 44-5.

Woodman, Jo-Anne – *See* Waldman, Wendy.

Woodman, Marion†
"Christo Mente Maria" *Alphabet* No. [11] (Dec-Mar 1965-66), 45-52.

Woods, Hanford – *See* Dawson, Fielding and Woods, Hanford.

Woods, Patricia†
"Change of Viewpoint" *CSSM* 2:1 (Jan 1976), 10-1.

Woodsworth, Glenn‡
[Untitled] *Adder* 1:1 [1961?], 5-6.

Woodsworth, Nick‡
"Melville Should Have Had It So Good" *Choice Parts* (1976), 58-66.

Woodward, Gordon (1921-)
"The Edge of Sound" *New Voices* 2 (1955), 211-26.
"Escape to the City" *MM* 69 (17 Mar 1956), 26-7, 32-4, 36-8.
"Escape to the City" *Best American Short Stories* 1957 331-45.

"The Night Drivers" *Paris R* No. 18 (Spr 1958), 95-103.
"The Night Drivers" *CBC "Anthology"* 24 Mar 1959.
"A Sound of Fury" *Accent* (U.S.) 15 (1955), 201-10.
"Tiger! Tiger!" *Canadian Short Stories* (1952), 170-91.
"Tiger! Tiger!" *Ten for Wednesday Night* (1961), 170-91.
"The Woolen Gloves" *Chat* 32 (Dec 1959), 26, 75-80, 82.

Woodward, Kathryn‡
"Cadillac at Atonement Creek" *Common Ground* (1980), 81-93.

Woolaver, Lance†
"The Fox Farm" *Fid* No. 99 (Fall 1973), 64-72.

Wooley, John‡
"The Return of Mr. Mystery" *Dreamweaver* 2:1 [n.d.], 9-10.

Wooley, Michael†
"The Arrested Ones" *Mont Writers Forum* 2:1 (Oct 1979), 8-12.
"Art Really's Armour" *Mont Writers' Forum* 2:4 (Jan 1980), 8-15.

Worthington, Avis‡
"The Island" *Prism* 2:4 (Sum 1961), 26-32.

Wreggitt, Andrew
"Rodeo" *Repos* Nos. 21/22 (Win-Spr 1977), 17-20.
"Shaman" *event* 9:2 (1980), 32-41.
"Stampede" *Prism* 17:1 (Sum 1978), 214-20.
"The Thief" *VWFP/Revue* 1:3 (May 1975), 14, 19.

Wright, A. Colin†
"Night Train to Cologne" *JCF* No. 33 (1981-82), 5-17.
"Only Fair" *Dal R* 60 (1980), 405-14.
"Unknown" *Waves* 12:1 (Fall 1983), 37-40.

Wright, Blair Orville‡
"The Clerk and the Squire" *Musical Oxygen and Vegetable Torsos* (1970), 5-13.

Wright, Bruce S.‡
"The Gull Rock Light Affair" *AA* 63 (Jan 1973), 25-8, 30.

Wright, D.B.†
"The Perfect Paper" *Bluenose* 4:4 (Feb 1980), 16.

Wright, David J.‡
"And Look at Me Now" *AA* 61 (Jan 1971), 62-5, 67-70.

Wright, Douglas†
"Ding! Dong! the Angst Is Dead" *WWR* 2:1 (1980), 65-72.
"Father's Day Gift" *WWR* 1:4 (Fall 1979), 11-5.
"Little Suicides" *WWR* 2:2 (1981), 85-9.
"Vancouver at Toronto" *WWR* 1:1 (Spr 1976), 4-8.
"Work in Progress" *Grain* 5:3 [1977], 22-8 [Excerpt?].

Wright, Eric‡
"Mac" *Creative Campus* 1957, 20-5.

Wright, Kip†
"Daddy" *Words from Inside* 1971, [3 pp].

Wright, Ritta†
"Seeing Is Believing" *AA* [66] (Dec 1975), 25-7.

Wuorio, Eva-Lis (1918-)
ESCAPE IF YOU CAN: 13 TALES OF THE PRETERNATURAL New York: Viking Press, 1977.
"Call Off Your Cats" *Chat* 28 (Feb 1955), 13, 24-6, 28.
"Call Off Your Cats" *Northern Lights* (1960), 523-30.
"The Caprice" *Weekend* 3 (10 Oct 1953), 38.
"The Dance of the Petrified People" *Escape If You Can* (1977), 62-72.
"A Day on the Thames" *SW* 9 Dec 1961, 8-11, 28.
"The Dog in the Window" *Escape If You Can* (1977), 50-6.
"The Falling Trick" *Escape If You Can* (1977), 80-7.
"A Haunted House" *Escape If You Can* (1977), 73-9.
"Heikki and the Little Bear" *Escape If You Can* (1977), 88-97.
"Honeymoon with Death" *Chat* 29 (Mar 1957), 74-6.
"The House from the Eleventh Floor" *Escape If You Can* (1977), 11-21.
"The Human Hand" *Escape If You Can* (1977), 57-61.
"I Hear Them Call" *Escape If You Can* (1977), 1-10.
"Mr. Grunt" *Escape If You Can* (1977), 22-30.
"Mystery at San Roque" *Weekend* 5 (9 Apr 1955), 21, 23, 32.
"Rara Avis" *Escape If You Can* (1977), 40-9.
"Through the Arch" *Escape If You Can* (1977), 106-16.
"Winds for Sale" *Escape If You Can* (1977), 31-9.
"You Can't Take It with You" *Escape If You Can* (1977), 98-105.

Wur, Kenneth‡
"The Empty Fathom" *Mandala* 1978, 44-6.

Wuth, Beatrice‡
"Twylla" *CBC "Alberta Anthology"* 27 Sept 1980.

Wyatt, Rachel (1929-)
"Everything's Turning Up Rosie" *Chat* 50 (Feb 1977), 52-3, 73-7.
"For Christmas, a Decision" *Chat* 46 (Dec 1973), 37, 56, 58, 60-2.
"For Christmas: Her Own Space" *Chat* 48 (Dec 1975), 48-9, 102, 104, 106.
"Fragments of Dreams" *CBC "Anthology"* 27 Mar 1976.
"Genevieve" *Chat* 47 (Aug 1974), 31, 50-3.
"No More the Pink-Dress Girl" *Chat* 45 (Apr 1972), 38, 52-3.
"Please, Lady Bluebird Painter" *CBC "Anthology"* 27 Dec 1975.
"Please, Lady Bluebird Painter" *Br Out* 6:3 (1979), 10-1.
"Postcard View" *Writing* No. 6 (Spr 1983), 3-6.
"The Third Poinsettia" *Chat* 45 (Dec 1972), 27, 44, 46-9.
"Verdict" *Chat* 48 (Oct 1975), 63, 120, 122-7.
"You Owe Me Something" *Chat* 48 (Apr 1975), 28-9, 84-9.

Wycham, John‡
"Meeting at Milk Market" *CBC "Anthology"* 2 Jan 1971.

Wylie, Betty Jane (1931-)
"Amputation" *CBC "Anthology"* 25 June 1977.

Wylie, Lillian MacKinnon‡
"Mom's Apple Pie" *Legion* 27 (Mar 1953), 12-3.

Wynand, Derk (1944-)
ONE COOK, ONCE DREAMING Vancouver: Sono Nis Press, 1980.
"The Anchoress" *CBC [Van] "Hornby Collection"* 20 Oct 1979.
"The Barmaid" *Mal R* No. 50 (Apr 1979), 242-3.
"The Break" *Jeopardy* 6 (1970), 45-7 [Based on survey response].
"The Cook and His Wife" *Mal R* No. 50 (Apr 1979), 237.
"The Cook's Wife" *Canadian Short Fiction Anthology* 2 (1982), 126.
From *ONE COOK, ONCE DREAMING CFM* No. 18 (Sum 1975), 87-92.
From *ONE COOK, ONCE DREAMING* CBC "Anthology" 1 May 1976.
From *ONE COOK, ONCE DREAMING CFM* No. 22 (Sum 1976), 4-10.
From *ONE COOK, ONCE DREAMING NJ* Nos. 7/8 (1976), 21-31.
From *ONE COOK, ONCE DREAMING Waves* 5:2/3 (Spr 1977), 47-50.
From *ONE COOK, ONCE DREAMING Grain* 7:1 [1979], 48-53.
From *ONE COOK, ONCE DREAMING CFM* Nos. 30/31 (1979), 50-2.
"Ghost Story" *CBC [Van] "Hornby Collection"* 3 June 1978.
"Ghost Story" *CFM* No. 43 (1982), 33-40.
"Hermit" *Mal R* No. 50 (Apr 1979), 238-9.
"Picture of a Hero" *Mal R* No. 50 (Apr 1979), 239-42.
"Return Journey" *Rainshadow* (1982), 236-49.
"Return Journey" *Tam R* Nos. 83/84 (Win 1982), 106-18.
"The Veteran" *Illusion Two* (1983), 111-6.

Wyse, A. David†
"Fly Paper (An Intransitive Tale)" *Grain* 9:1 (Feb 1981), 31-3.
"An Introduction to the Life and Times of Ian Edward Judd" *Des* 14:5 No. 43
(Win 1983-84), 98-105.
"Screen Test" *Grain* 11:2 (May 1983), 54-60.
"Thermopylae" *Grain* 9:1 (Feb 1981), 48-52.

Wyse, Marion (1952-)
"The Flesh, the Enemy" *Goblin* 104 (Mon, 31 Oct 1983), 6-7.

Wysong, Pippa B.‡
"Someday" *UC Gargoyle* 26 (3 Mar 1982), 9.

Xanthippe [pseudonym]
"The Job" *Outset* 1973, 175-81.

Yamamoto, Karen, E.
"Alfie's Song" *Companion* 46 (Sept 1983), 21-4.
"The Butterfly" *Companion* 46 (Oct 1983), 11-3.
"Pop Bottle Sadie" *Companion* 46 (June 1983), 22-5, 30.

Yanofsky, Joel†
"Ghost Stories" *Prism* 17:2 (Fall 1978), 147-76.
"Saving Grace" *Fid* No. 126 (Sum 1980), 69-103.

Yates, J. Michael (1938-)
FAZES IN ELSEWHEN: NEW AND SELECTED FICTION Vancouver: Intermedia Press, 1976.
MAN IN THE GLASS OCTOPUS Vancouver: Sono Nis Press, 1968.
SIGNAL DRIFT Vancouver: Intermedia, 1976 [Based on CBIP].
THE ABSTRACT BEAST Vancouver: Sono Nis Press, 1971.
"And Two Percent Zero" *Abstract Beast* (1971), 149-56.
"And Two Percent Zero" *CFM* Nos. 2/3 (Spr-Sum 1971), 47-51.
"And Two Percent Zero" *Fazes in Elsewhen* (1976), 70-3.
"The Broadcaster" *Man in the Glass Octopus* (1968), 24-44.
"The Broadcaster" *Fazes in Elsewhen* (1976), 20-33.
"Concerning a Temple" *Was R* 1:2 (1966), 6-10.
"Concerning a Temple" *Man in the Glass Octopus* (1968), 47-51.
"Concerning a Temple" *Fazes in Elsewhen* (1976), 137-9.
"De Fabrica" *Abstract Beast* (1971), 99-105.
"De Fabrica" *CFM* No. 1 (Win 1971), 6-9.
"De Fabrica" *Fazes in Elsewhen* (1976), 88-90.
"The Elsewhen Homilies" *Mal R* No. 50 (Apr 1979), 144-5.
"Feathers for Oberschreiberschriftsellermeister" *Fazes in Elsewhen* (1976), 34-6.
"A Fighting" *Man in the Glass Octopus* (1968), 69-70.
"A Fighting" *Fazes in Elsewhen* (1976), 136.
"God of the World" *Man in the Glass Octopus* (1968), 71-4.
"God of the World" *Fazes in Elsewhen* (1976), 133-4.
"The Hierodule" *Abstract Beast* (1971), 13-9.
"The Hierodule" *Fazes in Elsewhen* (1976), 157-60.
"The Hunter Who Loses His Human Scent" *Man in the Glass Octopus* (1968), 52-61.
"The Hunter Who Loses His Human Scent" *New Encounter with Canada* (1969), 129-39.
"The Hunter Who Loses His Human Scent" *Fazes in Elsewhen* (1976), 39-44.
"I, Quixote, Librarian" *Man in the Glass Octopus* (1968), 67-8.
"I, Quixote, Librarian" *Fazes in Elsewhen* (1976), 45.
"An Inquest into the Disappearance and Possible Death of (the Late) Sono Nis, Photographer" *Man in the Glass Octopus* (1968), 77-109.
"An Inquest into the Disappearance and Possible Death of (the Late) Sono Nis, Photographer" *Fazes in Elsewhen* (1976), 111-31.
"Jugs" by Jean-Luc McGillicutty *CFM* Nos. 2/3 (Spr-Sum 1971), 54-6.
"Latrodectus Shoicetans" *CFM* No. 11 (Aut 1973), 8-15.
"Latrodectus Shoicetans" *Fazes in Elsewhen* (1976), 100-4.
"Man in the Glass Octopus" *Was R* 1:2 (1966), 5-6.
"Man in the Glass Octopus" *Man in the Glass Octopus* (1968), 65-6.
"Man in the Glass Octopus" *Fazes in Elsewhen* (1976), 46.

"The Man of Qualifications" *Man in the Glass Octopus* (1968), 75-6.

"The Man of Qualification" *Fazes in Elsewhen* (1976), 135.

"Mysteries of the Man Who Walks and the Man Who Watches the Walker" *CFM* No. 8 (Aut 1972), 38-54.

"Mysteries of the Man Who Walks and the Man Who Watches the Walker" *Fazes in Elsewhen* (1976), 144-56.

"Mysteries of the Man Who Walks and the Man Who Watches the Walker" *Magic Realism* (1980), 155-72.

"A Naive and Straightforward Narrative" *Abstract Beast* (1971), 223-33.

"A Naive and Straightforward Narrative" *Fazes in Elsewhen* (1976), 105-10.

"Of Sequential Things" *Fazes in Elsewhen* (1976), 85-6.

"On the Problem of Narcissus" *Fazes in Elsewhen* (1976), 87.

"The Passage of Sono Nis" *Man in the Glass Octopus* (1968), 15-23.

"The Passage of Sono Nis" *Tam R* No. 46 (Win 1968), 40-7.

"The Passage of Sono Nis" *Fazes in Elsewhen* (1976), 13-8.

"The Passage of Sono Nis" *Foreign Fictions* (1978), 41-50.

"Philodendron" *Abstract Beast* (1971), 185-91.

"Philodendron" *BC Lib Q* 35:1 (July 1971), 32-3, 35-6.

"Philodendron" *Fazes in Elsewhen* (1976), 67-9.

"Pile" *Abstract Beast* (1971), 253-70.

"Pile" *Fazes in Elsewhen* (1976), 74-84.

"Realia" *BC Lib Q* 36:1 (July 1972), 35-64.

"Realia" *Fazes in Elsewhen* (1976), 47-66.

"The Sinking of the Northwest Passage" *Abstract Beast* (1971), 55-69.

"The Sinking of the Northwest Passage" *event* 1:3 (Win 1972), 28-39.

"The Sinking of the Northwest Passage" *Stories from Pacific & Arctic Canada* (1974), 95-107.

"The Sinking of the Northwest Passage" *Fazes in Elsewhen* (1976), 91-9.

"The Sinking of the Northwest Passage" *Fiction of Contemporary Canada* (1980), 63-74.

"Smokestack in the Desert" *Man in the Glass Octopus* (1968), 45-6.

"Smokestack in the Desert" *Fazes in Elsewhen* (1976), 19.

"Something Is Nothing" *Cave* (N.Z.) No. 3 (Feb 1973), 18-22.

"Something Is Nothing" *Mundus Artium* 8:2 (1975), 33-7.

"Something Is Nothing" *75: New Canadian Stories* 94-100.

"Something Is Nothing" *Fazes in Elsewhen* (1976), 140-3.

"Virgin and Child" by Jean-Luc McGillicutty *CFM* Nos. 2/3 (Spr-Sum 1971), 52-3.

"Vita Somnium Breve" by Jean-Luc McGillicutty *CFM* Nos. 2/3 (Spr-Sum 1971), 53-4.

"Water Rising" *Man in the Glass Octopus* (1968), 62-4.

"Water Rising" *Fazes in Elsewhen* (1976), 37-8.

Yates, Joan‡

"Want to Make a Trade?" *Can Golden West* 12 (Fall 1976), [11].

Yeandle, Ruth A.†

"Irish Persuasion" *Pres Record* 96 (May 1972), 7-8.

Yee, Paul

"Prairie Night 1939" *WCR* 16:1 (Sum 1981), 24-8.

Yelin, Shulamis (1913-)

"Denie Needs a Tonic" *Viewpoints* 9:1 (1975), 63-5.

"Shekspir Was Jewish" *Viewpoints* 8:4 (1974), 59-61 [Non-fiction?].

Yellon, R.A.‡

"The Sport of Gods" *Forge* 1966, 47-53.

Yeomans, Edward†

"Each Fall" *Alphabet* No. 2 (July 1961), 4-12.

Yip, Tom‡

"Dream" *Scar Fair* 8 (1981), 77.

York, Tom‡

"The Miners' Christmas Eve" *UC Observer* 15 Dec 1968, 16-7 [Non-fiction?].

Yost, Elwy (1925-)

"The Brothers Hurst" *Bakka* No. 6 (Fall 1977), 69-76, 78-80.

Youmans, Stella‡

"It's Never Too Late" *Northern Ontario Anthology* 1 (1977), 37.

Young, David (1946-)

See also d'Or, Vic and Young, David.

INCOGNITO Toronto: Coach House Press, 1982.

"Albino Cockroaches" *Per* No. 6 (Fall 1979), 21-2.

"An American in Madrid" *Blow Up* 2:11 (Feb 1981), [1 p].

"The Concentration Camp" *Incognito* (1982), 49-63.

"Counting Combinations" *Story So Far* 3 (1974), 97-108.

"The Dancer and the Dance" *Incognito* (1982), 23-33.

"Entering the Strobe" *Per* No. 6 (Fall 1979), 25-6.

"Gilbert and Sullivan vs. Tom and Jerry" *Writing* No. 1 (Sum 1980), 19-20.

"Gilbert and Sullivan vs. Tom and Jerry" *Incognito* (1982), 43-8.

"Heart of My Heart" *Incognito* (1982), 35-41.

"A Hint of Fizz" *Per* No. 6 (Fall 1979), 22-5.

"The Ice Book" *Story So Four* (1976), 218-23.

"The Ice Book" *Fiction of Contemporary Canada* (1980), 163-9.

"Iron-On David" *Iron II* No. 20 (1978), [3 pp].

"Laughter at Dawn" *Incognito* (1982), 183-225.

"The Man in the Iron Mask" *Incognito* (1982), 91-106.

"Mondo Pocono" *Incognito* (1982), 121-39.

"Ocean Dream" *Writ* No. 4 (Spr 1972), 66-7.

"Of Mice and Men" *Incognito* (1982), 167-81.

"Overword Herds (A Martian Main Street)" *Writ* No. 4 (Spr 1972), 65-6.

"Palimpsest" *Incognito* (1982), 271-7.

"Paradise Lost" *Incognito* (1982), 229-69.

"The Patented Finishing Hold" *Per* No. 6 (Fall 1979), 26-8.

"Rusty Taps" *OPT* 4:7 (Oct 1977), 1.

"Rusty Taps" *Incognito* (1982), 111-9.

"Spotting: A Case History" *Per* No. 1 (Spr 1977), 33-41.

"Spotting: A Case History" *Imp* 7:2/3 (Win 1979), 20-1, 59.

"Spotting: A Case History" *Incognito* (1982), 149-65.

"Swingbox" *New Voices* (1956), 1-11.
"Tabula Rasa" *Incognito* (1982), 11-21.
"Three Falls" *Incognito* (1982), 65-89.
"Tom Tom's Sh-Sh-Shady Bend's Ol' Geezer Easter Special" *Story So Far* 2 (1973), 78-81.
"Vivian" *Per* No. 3 (Spr 1978), 49-56.
"Where Were You?" *OPT* 4:7 (Oct 1977), 1.
"Where Were You?" *Incognito* (1982), 141-7.

Young, Debbie‡
"Burned" *Stump* 4:1/2 (Spr 1980), 1-2.

Young, George†
"My Uncle Jack" *Waves* 7:3 (Spr 1979), 4-6.

Young, Geraldine†
"Tar Paper Walls" *Whetstone* Spr 1973, 40-2.

Young, Ian‡
"The Red Room" *Acta Vic* 94:3 (Feb 1970), 11-3.
"The Umbrella Man" *Acta Vic* 90:2 (Dec 1965), 36.
"What Happened at Websters" *Acta Vic* 91:1 (Nov 1966), 23-4.

Young, Nora‡
"Static" *UCR* 1982-83, 23.

Young, Pamela‡
"In the Sun Room" *TUR* 93:2 (Apr 1980), 43-5.

Young, Roland‡
"Entertainer" *Portico* 1:2 [n.d.], 14-31.

Young, Scott (1918-)
WE WON'T BE NEEDING YOU, AL: STORIES OF MEN AND SPORTS
Toronto: Ryerson Press, [1968].
"The Bean Ball" *American Mag* 150 (July 1950), 38-41, 130-4.
"The Bean Ball" *We Won't Be Needing You, Al* [1968], 122-40.
"Big Deal" *SW* 12 Sept 1953, II:3, 12.
"The Boy Who Threw a Snowball at Santa" *Chat* 24 (Dec 1951), 10, 28-32, 34.
"A Bust for Henry" *Weekend* 2 (22 Nov 1952), 10-1, 25, 27, 34.
"Christmas Letter" *Lib* 29 (Dec 1952), 24, 52-4, 56-8.
"City Girl's Game" *CHJ* Aug 1954, 16, 26-33.
"Crazy Over Horses" *Weekend* 2 (16 Aug 1952), 16-7.
"The Critical Young Man" *Sat Eve Post* 223 (3 Feb 1951), 20, 45, 48, 51.
"Dangerous Ice" *Argosy Book of Sports Stories* (1953) [Pre-1950? Based on SSI].
"Dead Duck!" *American Mag* 158 (Nov 1954), 121-36 [Based on RGPL].
"The Delegate from Saskatoon" *Chat* 26 (June 1953), 21, 46-9, 54-6, 66-8.
"An Englishman in Town" *We Won't Be Needing You, Al* [1968], 105-21.
"Fury at Irishman's Lake" *FH* 15 July 1953, 20-1, 26-7.
"Goodbye Grandpa" *FH* 16 Feb 1956, 24, 38.
"Goodbye Grandpa" *We Won't Be Needing You, Al* [1968], 141-52.
"Grudge Game" *American Mag* 154 (Oct 1952), 36-7, 77-82.

"Honest Woman" *CHJ* Aug 1952, 9, 26-32.

"Love Call" *Weekend* 3 (18 July 1953), 10-1.

"Mabel's Rainbow" *CHJ* July 1950, 11, 41, 43-4, 47, 50-1.

"Maloney's Last Stand" *Argosy Book of Sports Stories* (1953) [Pre-1950? Based on SSI].

"The Mastermind" *Collier's* 131 (4 Apr 1953), 42-7.

"Meeting by Moonlight" *Lib* 30 (July 1953), 17, 41-4, 46.

"The Old Doc" *FH* 5 Apr 1951, 24-5, 51.

"The Old Doc" *Stories to Read Again* (1965), 177-92.

"One Man to a Marriage" *American Mag* 157 (Feb 1954), 36-7[+?] [Based on RGPL].

"One Man to a Marriage" *FH* 11 Dec 1958, 24, 26.

"The Pinch Hitter" *Collier's* 128 (7 July 1951), 29, 49-51.

"The Pinch Hitter" *We Won't Be Needing You, Al* [1968], 90-104.

"Player Deal" *Collier's* 127 (20 Jan 1951), 30, 47-9.

"Player Deal" *FH* 31 Jan 1957, 12-3, 28-9.

"Player Deal" *We Won't Be Needing You, Al* [1968], 36-53.

"The Punishment of Ordinary Angel Blobs" *Lib* 30 (Sept 1953), 36-7, 56-7.

"A Real Tribute" *Weekend* 4 (10 July 1954), 10-1, 22.

"The Reluctant Inventor" *Collier's* 129 (7 June 1952), 20[+?] [Based on RGPL].

"The Reluctant Inventor" *FH* 18 Oct 1956, 28-30.

"The Runaway" *Weekend* 3 (21 Feb 1953), 10-1.

"The Samaritan" *Lib* 30 (Jan 1954), 25, 38-9.

"Seven Parts of a Ball Team" *Collier's* 125 (6 May 1950), 20-1, 46-7.

"Seven Parts of a Ball Team" *Scholastic* 58 (16 May 1951), 19-21, 28-9, 31.

"Seven Parts of a Ball Team" *We Won't Be Needing You, Al* [1968], 54-71.

"Trouble-Shooter Takes a Mate" *SW* 18 Feb 1956, II:6.

"The Turning-Point" *CHJ* Dec 1950, 22-3, 57, 60-5, 67.

"Vacancy in Goal" *Collier's* 125 (28 Jan 1950), 26-7, 55-6.

"Vacancy in Goal" *We Won't Be Needing You, Al* [1968], 16-35.

"White Musky" *Collier's* 127 (5 May 1951), 18-9, 62.

"White Musky" *Cavalcade of the North* (1958), 550-8.

"White Musky" *We Won't Be Needing You, Al* [1968], 1-15.

"White Musky" *Writers and Writing* (1981), 40-52.

"[The?] Winning Play" *American Mag* 149 (Feb 1950), 38-41 [Based on RGPL].

Young, Wenda (1940-)

"Scenes Before Breakfast" *Antig R* No. 39 (Aut 1979), 49-57.

"The Swimmer" *Pot Port* 3 (1981-82), 28-30.

"Three" *Antig R* No. 53 (Spr 1983), 113-20.

Young, William†

"Evolution" *Prism* 16:2 (Fall 1977), 146-51.

Youngberg, Gail‡

"In Search of Vice" *Acta Vic* 82:2 (Feb 1958), 20-2.

Younger, Bill‡

"The Awakening" *Pedantics* 1965, 73.

Younie, John†
"Vacation" *CSSM* 1:3 (July 1975), 49-51.

Zacharias, Judy‡
"In His Father's Book of Names for Boys, Teilo Means a Bright Pupil" *Potlatch* No. 5 (Dec 1965), 1-5.

Zaget, Bill†
"Manx" *Outset* 1974, 166-76.

Zaiss, David
"The Blind Munchies" *CFM* No. 4 (Aut 1971), 47-8.

Zakanas, Paul‡
"Golden Apples Are Delicious" *Quarry* 22:1 (Win 1973), 12-9.

Zalan, Magda
"Rehearsal in Rome" *JCF* No. 23 (1979), 19-32.

Zehr, Pat
"Mary Ann" *event* 7:2 (1978), 120-3.

Zeigler, Robert†
"Morrocco" *Voices Down East* [1973], 20-1.

Zend, Robert (1929-1985)
"Buttonhold" *Exile* 4:2 (1977), 112-3.
"The Heavenly Game" *Exile* 2:2 (1974), 54.
"The Key" *Exile* 2:2 (1974), 57-67 ["By Robert Zend and Jorge Luis Borges"].
"Little Nothings" *Exile* 4:2 (1977), 110.
"Meeting" *Exile* 2:2 (1974), 46.
"The Miracle" *Exile* 2:2 (1974), 44-5.
"The Rock" *Exile* 2:2 (1974), 40-1.
"Taviella" *Exile* 4:2 (1977), 117-20.
"Tusha and Time" *Rampike* 3:2 [1983?], 23.
"World's Greatest Poet" *Exile* 2:2 (1974), 55-6.

Zielonka, Allan‡
"White Rock Mine" *Undergrad* Spr 1963, 16-7.

Zieroth, Dale (1946-)
"For Sale" *NeWest R* 5 (May 1980), 8-9.
"The Hill" *Quarry* 20:1 (Win 1971), 23-7.
"Jeremey, His Arrangements" *73: New Canadian Stories* 74-88.
"Teepee" *CBC [Van] "Hornby Collection"* 6 Dec 1980.

Zietlow, E.R.
"The Old Woman Who Read to Her Houseplants" *Revue* 2 No. 1 (1976), 64-71.
"Silver" *JCF* 3:2 (1974), 31-5.
"Waiting" *Canadian Short Fiction Anthology* (1976), 219-30.

Zilber, Jacob (1924-)

"The Be Hive" *event* 1:2 (Fall 1971), 67-71.
"Icarus" *Carleton Miscellany* 1:4 (Fall 1960), 93-5.
"Justice" *December (U.S.)* 12:1/2 (1970), 88-9.
"The Price of Admission" *Prism* 2:4 (Sum 1961), 43-55.
"The Prince" *Tam R* No. 16 (Sum 1960), 37-46.
"A Riddle for Children" *event* 2:1 [1972], 63-5.
"The Slicing Machine" *Fid* No. 51 (Win 1962), 40-4.
"Souvenirs" *Prism* 3:3 (Spr 1962), 18-20.

Zimmer, Ron‡

"Kaleidoscope" *Raven* No. 10 (Mar 1962), 8-15.

Zimmerman, Susan†

"The Gift" *Fireweed* No. 1 (Aut 1978), 63.
"The Journal" *This – Media Free Times* 1:2 (Spr 1974), [10 pp].
"Yard Sale" *UTR* 2:1 (Spr 1978), 17.
"Yard Sale" *Matrix* No. 8 (Win 1979), 44-5.

Zimmmerman, Ian†

"Some Mornings I Wake Up" *Grain* 10:4 (Nov 1982), 20-9.

Zinkewich, Muriel‡

"A Romance" *Muse* 66 (1957), 13-6, 30.
"Send Me Red Roses" *Muse* 65 (1956), 21-4.

Zinober, Richard‡

"Night at the Arena" *Inscape* 13:1 (Fall 1976), 58-64.

Ziolkowski, Carmen†

"Jane's Christmas Eve" *Living Message* 82 (Dec 1971), 26-7 [Children's?].
"A Matter of Communication" *Polished Pebbles* (1974), 65-8.
" 'Why Didn't I Listen to You?' " *Companion* 33 (July- Aug 1970), 28-30.

Znaimer, Moses (1942-)

"God's House" *Forge* [24]:1 (Feb 1962), 13-4.

Zogby, Mark†

"The Long Shot" *Cyan Line* No. 2 (Fall 1976), 29-40.

Zonailo, Carolyn (1947-)

"Auto-Da-Fe" *BC Monthly* 3:6/7 (Apr-May 1977), [2 pp] [Also entitled "Making It"].
"Loss" *Waves* 7:2 (Win 1979), 15-6.
"Making It" *Canadian Short Fiction Anthology 2* (1982), 85-7 [Also entitled "Auto-Da-Fe"].
"Of Gardens" *Lit Store News* Nos. 26/27 (July-Aug 1980), 6-8.
"The Park" *BC Monthly* 3:6/7 (Apr-May 1977), [2 pp].

Zonko [pseudonym]
"Comedian for the Birds" by Neurosurgery *Writing* No. 2 (Win 1980-81), 6.
"Long Live the Assassin of the Murderer Peanut Brain" *Writing* No. 5 (Spr 1982), 21-2.
"A Pair of Aces" *Cap R* No. 7 (Spr 1975), 7-8.

Zucker, Rickie‡
"Are Flowers Jewish?" *Contact* 3:4 (Win 1974), 56-9.

Zwarts, Janice Blue‡
"The Intrusion of Mrs. Harvison" *Dal R* 61 (1981), 337-47.

PART III: TITLE INDEX

The Abortive Ulcer · *Vegman, Jean*
About a Small Town and a Girl · *Rodgers, Bob*
About an Old Man · *Berenyi, Yulika*
About Bert Israel · *Nemiroff, Greta Hofmann*
About Effie · *Findley, Timothy*
About Face · *Ravel, Aviva*
About Geneva · *Gallant, Mavis*
About Memorials · *Nowlan, Alden*
About Norad and Santa · *Gershenovitz, N. David*
About Old Ladies · *Pickett, Libby*
About Stars · *Lebel, John*
About the Brown Paper Bags · *Sandor, Karl*
About the Man Who Married a Much Younger Woman Who Took Care of Him in
His Declining Years, Nursing Him Through the Flu · *Stockanes, Anthony E.*
Above Two Forks: Sunday, February 11, 1917 · *Clark, D.M.*
Abracadabra · *Rikki [Erica Ducornet]*
Abraham Muscovitch's Michael · *Rosenberg, Elsa*
Abram Came Out of a February Blizzard · *Dumbrille, Dorothy*
The Absence · *Spencer, Elizabeth*
The Absence of a Hole · *MacLennan, Toby*
Absolutely, Absolutely · *Lucas, Victor*
Absolutely Nothing · *Filter, Reinhard*
AbsTRACTION · *Decker, Ken*
The Abyss · *Cameron, Eric*
The Academician · *Kadey, Carroll*
Acceptance of Their Ways · *Gallant, Mavis*
Accident · *Munro, Alice*
The Accident · *Gallant, Mavis*
The Accident · *Rousanoff, Nicholas*
The Accident Business · *Dickinson, Don*
Accident-Prone · *Harrison, E.W.*
Accidents · *Shields, Carol*
The Accolade · *Fowke, H. Shirley*
The Accomplice · *Vertolli, Lou*
The Accordian · *McLaren, Floris*
According to Your Cloth · *Govier, Katharine*
An Account of a Skirmish · *Williams, Vera B.*
An Account of Clara's Passing · *Kelly, Marjorie*
Accounting · *Ross, Veronica*
The Ace · *Tataryn, David*
Ace Up His Sleeve · *Chambers, John*
The Achilles' Truth · *Jirgins, Karl E.*
Achziv · *Sherman, Kenneth*
The Acid Is Lousy in Vancouver · *Horwood, Harold*
The Acid Is Shitty in Vancouver · *Horwood, Harold*
The Acid Test · *Smith, Robert F.*
Acme Art & Sailboat Company / 'Tell Them Fetch' · *Maxwell, Ward*
The Acorn · *Harvey, Jennifer A. Becks*
Acquaintance · *Winter, Barbara*
Acquired Airs on Ailing High Street · *Acheson, Cavan*

Acres Apart · *Wood, Kerry*
The Acrimonious Cloud · *Taylor, Bruce D.S.*
Acrobat · *McElroy, Gil*
Across Country · *Reynolds, Helen Mary Greenwood Campbell*
Across Symphony Hall · *Koerte, Helen*
Across the Margin · *Arscott, David*
Across the River · *Misfeldt, James*
Across the Threshold of the Dark Night · *Gibbs, Robert*
Act [?] · *Van Newkirk, Allen*
Act of a Hero · *Garner, Hugh*
Act of Apostacy (The Boy Next Door) · *Galloway, Priscilla*
An Act of Contrition · *Nowlan, Alden*
The Act of Creation · *Fairley, Bruce*
An Act of God · *Ledbetter, Ken*
An Act of Love · *MacMillan, Gail*
An Act of Mercy · *Valgardson, W.D.*
An Act of Piety · *Elliott, George*
Actaeon · *Burnett, Virgil*
Action · *Liu, Ron*
Action: Smile. Promise a Real Letter Next Time. Really Do · *Randall, Margaret*
The Actor · *Fraser, Raymond*
The Actress and the Bishop · *Shields, Bill*
Acts of Love · *Knechtel, Mary Beth*
Ada · *Gibson, Margaret*
Ada and the Raccoon · *Cooper, Bob*
Adam · *Sutherland, Barry*
Adam Clark, the Covenanter of Glenim · *Sutherland, Robert*
Adam on the Art of Dying · *Helwig, David*
Ada's Desire · *Harrison, A.S.A.*
'Add to -' · *Burnell, Ethel D.*
Adding It Up · *Smith, Marvin*
Addressing the Assassins · *Rooke, Leon*
Adieu Marie · *Carrier, Jean-Guy*
The Adjustment · *Babb, Audrey W.*
The Admiral · *Cave, Gladys M.*
The Admission · *Blaine, Eric*
Adolpho's Disappeared and We Haven't a Clue Where to Find Him · *Rooke, Leon*
The Adopted Family · *Briffett, Isabel*
Adrian and Oliver · *Henighan, Stephen*
Adrift · *Rivest, Phil*
Adua · *Browne, Paul Cameron*
An Adult Education · *Cuevas, Ernesto*
The Adult Holiday · *Spencer, Elizabeth*
Adult Novels · *Smith, Jim*
Adult Student · *Brandis, Maxine*
Advanced Oboe Problems · *Kilodney, Crad*
The Advent · *Dempster, Barry*
The Advent of Gopher · *Barker, Bessie M.*
The Adventure of the Annexationist Conspiracy · *Batten, Jack and Bliss, Michael*
The Adventure of the French Bathroom · *Forer, Anne*

Adventures in the Vacuum · *Thornley, Gary C.*

The Adventures of a Flutist or How to Drown in Your Own Condensation · *Willis, Stephen*

The Adventures of Brenda Lady Coal-Sampler · *Huxley, Brenda*

The Adventures of Chaim Pferd · *Melamet, Max*

The Adventures of Pocketman · *Bell, Don*

The Adviser · *Svendsen, Linda*

The Advisor · *Williamson, David*

An Affair in Yemen · *Hancock, Ronald Lee*

The Affair of Able Willie · *Stein, Rhoda Elizabeth Playfair*

An Affair of Frogs · *Dickinson, George*

The Affair of Gormley's Cow · *Gardner, W.W.*

An Affair of the Heart · *Story, Gertrude*

An Affair of the Heart · *Green, H. Gordon*

An Affair of Honour · *Quinton, Maurice*

African Violets · *Connor, Will*

after an anonymous french novelist · *G.D.*

After Batoche · *MacNeill, James A.*

After Birth Sketches · *Hindmarch, Gladys*

After Dinner Butterflies · *Cohen, Matt*

After Great Pain, a Formal Feeling · *Ewing, Betty Moore*

After Hours · *Burns, Mary*

After Many Days · *Bushell, Sidney*

After May 20th · *Henderson, Keith*

After Not Having Quite Enough · *Hogg, Bob*

After School, 2 · *Teleky, Richard*

After School, 3 · *Teleky, Richard*

After School · *Teleky, Richard*

After September · *Austin, Don*

After the Ball · *McNamara, Eugene*

After the Ceremony · *Kawano, Roland*

After the Darkness - The Dawn · *Lapp, Eula C.*

After the Events of Caesar · *Bailey, Don*

After the Fall · *Hospital, Janet Turner*

After the Season · *Hodgins, Jack*

After the Sirens · *Hood, Hugh*

After the Story · *Barclay, Byrna*

After the Tommy Gun · *Staniforth, Richard*

After the Yarn Is Spun · *Swartz, Jill*

After These Years! · *McFadden, Isobel*

After Thirty Years of Marriage · *Wiebe, Rudy H.*

Afterbirth · *Schermbrucker, Bill*

Afterglow · *Briffett, Isabel*

Afterglow · *Percy, H.R.*

The After-Life · *Saari, Oliver E.*

The Afterlife of Ishmael · *Atwood, Margaret*

Aftermath · *Doyle, Terence E.*

Aftermath of Revolution · *Bloom, Clement*

An Afternoon · *Crerar, Tom*

Afternoon at the Lido · *Svendsen, Linda*

An Afternoon at the Zoo · *Ritts, Mort*
The Afternoon Holds Manifold Promises · *Bialik, H.G.*
Afternoon in a Different Place · *Margoshes, Dave*
Afternoon Men · *MacLean, Kenneth*
Afternoon of Love · *Hoogstraten, Vinia*
Afternoon on a Kettle Lake · *Donaldson, Andrew*
Afternoon Shift · *Boyle, Harry J.*
An Afternoon's Drive · *Valgardson, W.D.*
Aga Dawn · *Schermbrucker, Bill*
again Noire · *Bullock, Michael*
Agatha and Homer · *Read, David*
Agathe · *Keeling, Nora*
The Age of Insolence · *Green, H. Gordon*
The Agent of Language · *Fawcett, Brian*
Aggie · *Brewster, Elizabeth*
Agnes and the Cobwebs · *Rooke, Leon*
The Agony of Being Alive · *Kutlesa, Joso*
The Agreement · *Arnold, Ricky*
Agriculture · *Kilodney, Crad*
Ah! May the Red Rose · *Grantmyre, Barbara*
Ah Love! Ah Fraternity Life · *Shepanski C[arl].L.*
Ah Tria Humpelbein · *van Every, Jane*
Ah Youth, Ah Joy! · *Parr, John*
Ahbrose C. Friendly and the Free World · *Fisher, Paul*
Ahead the Road Is · *Matyas, Cathy*
The Air That We Breathe · *Stokes, Marian*
Air Vent · *Peters, Mac*
Airbum + Stinkbird = Wiser Man · *Williams, Dave*
Airplanes · *Russell, Ted*
Aisle · *Svoboda, Terese*
Akudlik: The Half-Way House · *Crispin, Jane*
The Alabaster Box · *Edwards, Mary Kay*
The Alamo Plaza · *Rooke, Leon*
The Alarm Clock · *Thomas, Martha Banning*
Alarm Clock Dreams · *Donovan, Rita*
The Albatross · *Thomas, Audrey*
Albino Cockroaches · *Young, David*
The Alchemist · *Warney, Thomas*
Alcoholic Liquor · *Russell, Ted*
The Alec · *Person, Lloyd*
Aleth · *Burnett, Virgil*
Alexander's Letters, Continued · *Burdick, Steven*
Alfie's Song · *Yamamoto, Karen, E.*
Algebra Slippers · *Russell, Ted*
Ali · *Riordan, Michael*
The Alibi · *Green, H. Gordon*
Alice · *Douglas, Molly*
Alice in Godfreyland or The Metamorphosic Dynamics of Relaxed Morality · *Sweeney, Alistair*
Alice in Justiceland · *Falstaff, Jake*

Alice in Parliament · *Thompson, Tim*
Alice Is · *Dragland, Stan*
An Alien Flower · *Gallant, Mavis*
Alienation of Affection · *Hoogstraten, Vinia*
Aliens · *Powning, Beth*
Aliya · *Kutlesa, Joso*
Alkali Dust · *Cain, Tom*
All a Star Should Be · *Scott, Margerie*
All About the Concours in the Rue des Lices and Present Tense for Friends Long
Absent · *Thibaudeau, Colleen*
All at Sea · *Watmough, David*
All But My Ninth Birthday · *Roberts, Tom*
All Clear Land · *Stemo, L. Johanne*
All Expenses Paid · *Barnard, Leslie Gordon*
All for Love · *Dabydeen, Cyril*
All for Margarita · *Wansley, David*
All for the Children · *Murphy, Marylynn*
All He Needed · *Corps, Doreen*
All Her Own · *Edwards, Mary Kay*
All I Know About Incest · *Mason, Mike*
All in a Day · *Poy, Adrienne*
All in a Days' Work · *Renaud, Denise*
All in the Family · *Smith, Max*
All in the Winter's Cold · *Marshall, Joyce*
All Is Not Gold · *Green, H. Gordon*
All Is Right - Now · *Thompson, Ray T.*
All Kinds · *Currie, Robert*
All Kinds of Harvesting · *Watmough, David*
All Kinds of People · *Rosenfeld, Rita*
All Life from the Sea · *Edwards, Caterina*
All Manner of Lies · *Thompson, Kent*
All My Love, Louisa · *Wong, Henry*
All My Loves · *Scott, Margerie*
All Night Gas Bar · *Hekkanen, Ernest*
All on Their Knees · *Wiebe, Rudy H.*
All Our Tomorrows · *Lees, Margaret*
All Over Now · *Gibson, Margaret*
All Sales Final · *Bailey, Don*
All That Glitters · *Vandersluis, Cebea Shirley*
All That I Can Give · *Russell, Sheila MacKay*
All That Long Summer · *Molnar, Anne*
All That Was Left ... · *Tinsley, Ted*
All the Care in the World · *Wood, Ted*
All the Fun of the Fair · *Peter, John D.*
All the Gay Days · *Garner, Hugh*
All the Leaves Blow Around · *Derksen, Jim*
All the Local News · *Russell, Ted*
All the Lonely People · *Callaghan, Barry*
All the Queen's Horses · *Hutchins, Hazel J.*
All the Room in the World · *Daem, Mary and Deeder, Peg*

All the Time in the World · *Miller, J. Kit*
All the World's Crazies · *Purdy, Brian*
All Through the Night · *Murdoch, Benedict Joseph*
Allan · *Reigo, Ants*
Allegory · *Crow, S.*
An Allegory for Our Times · *Bacque, James*
An Allegory of Man's Fate · *Hood, Hugh*
Allegro con Fuoco · *Tierney, Jean*
Alleluia, Mrs. Jones · *Thatcher, Philip*
Allergy · *Alford, Norman*
All-Expense Tour · *Barnard, Leslie Gordon*
Alleywalk · *Wexler, Jerry*
The Alligator Report - with Questions for Discussion · *Kinsella, W.P.*
Allison and the Visitor · *Diadick, Cynthia*
Allophone · *Filip, Raymond*
All's Well That Ends Well · *Whiteway, Louise*
The All-Star Game · *Noonan, Gerald*
Almost a War · *Green, H. Gordon*
Almost All for Love · *Armstrong, Patricia*
Almost Like Dead · *Goldman, Alvin*
The Almost Meeting · *Kreisel, Henry*
Almost Train Time · *Cushing, Daniel*
The Almost-Didn't · *Clifton, Merritt*
The Alms · *Botting, Gary*
Alone! · *Burnell, Ethel D.*
Alone at Blue Lake · *Wangersky, Russell*
Alone in the Empire · *Schoemperlen, Diane*
Along a Dusty Road · *McNichol, Philip*
Along Came Love · *Clare, John P.*
Along the Red Deer and the South Saskatchewan · *Wiebe, Rudy H.*
Along the Road Down Home · *Smith, Ron*
Along the Snake-Fence Way · *Branden, Vicki*
Alpha · *Moen, Arlo M.*
Altar of Faith · *Gillese, John Patrick*
Aluminum Pots · *O'Connell, Dorothy*
The Aluminum Tub · *Ravel, Aviva*
Always a Motive · *Ross, W.E. Dan*
Always Look Back · *Colville, C.*
Am I My Brother's Keeper? · *O'Mahoney, Bob*
Amarie Can Camp · *Denisoff, Dennis*
Amaryllis · *Engel, Marian*
Amazing Grace · *Cohen, Matt*
Ambroise, the Whale and Gabrielle · *Theriault, Yves*
Ambulance Blues Note · *Ford, Cathy*
The Ambush · *Bird, Will R.*
Amelio's · *Tedford, Ingrid*
Amen, Charlie's Harvest · *James, Jean*
The American · *Carrier, Jean-Guy*
The American Boots · *Andre-Czerniecki, Marion*
An American Dressage Rider · *Ostrow, Joanna*

An American in Madrid · *Young, David*
American Primitive · *Wood, Ted*
The Amherst Ghost · *Evans, J.A.S.*
Amid the Alien Corn · *Gibbons, Maurice*
Amid the Glory · *Conly, Susan*
Amigo · *McWhirter, George*
Amitville Rip-Off · *MacLaurin, Douglas*
Amma · *Saunders, Charles R.*
Amnesia · *Steinfeld, J.J.*
Among My Souvenirs · *O'Connell, Dorothy*
Among the Dead · *Blaise, Clark L.*
Among the Lost · *Marshall, Joyce*
Among the Old Singers · *Wilson, Jack Lowther*
Among the Ruins · *Boyko, Elvina*
Among the Sharks · *Horwood, Harold*
Among the Trees of the Park · *Helwig, David*
Among Women · *Thompson, Kent*
Amory Hawkes · *Powning, Beth*
Amory Was Released Today · *Kohane, Jack*
Amputation · *Wylie, Betty Jane*
Amputations · *Jones, R.J.*
The Amulet · *Plaut, W. Gunther*
The Amusement Centre · *Moore, Elwin*
Analytica Number Two · *Sheils, Terry*
Anarchy · *Behrens, Peter*
The Anatomy of a Muskicide · *Power, John*
anatomy of melancholy · *Bullock, Michael*
The Anchoress · *Wynand, Derk*
Anchovies · *Carson, Bryan*
The Ancient and Honorable Art of Wool-Gathering · *Copithorne, Agnes*
The Ancient Newsmonger · *Stortz, Joan*
Ancistrodon Priscivorus: Albion Gunther Jones and the Water Viper/Number Five in a Series of River Stories · *Rooke, Leon*
And a Sea Bird Calling · *Barnard, Leslie Gordon*
And All His Wealth Was Wandering · *Boyle, Harry J.*
And All the Forbidden Tomorrows · *Russell, Sheila MacKay*
And Always the Same Story · *Potrebenko, Helen*
And Be My Love · *Currie, Doris M.*
And Bells Did Ring · *Izzard, Douglas M.*
And Come What May · *Wees, Frances Shelley*
And Counting for the Knockdowns, George Bannon · *Doyle, Dan*
And Gladly Teach ... · *Burnett, Eileen*
And I a Smiling Woman · *Tudor, Kathleen*
And I But a Poor Mermaiden · *Paterson, O.P.*
And Ice ... Mast High ... · *Grantmyre, Barbara*
... And in the Morning · *Briffett, Isabel*
And It Came to Pass · *MacGregor, Tony*
'And It Came to Pass ...' · *Stein, Rhoda Elizabeth Playfair*
And Look at Me Now · *Wright, David J.*
And Mae Flowered · *Horne, Lewis B.*

And No Man Could Bind Him · *Vanderhaeghe, Guy*
And None to Spare · *Fines, Beatrice E.*
And Nothing Was Left · *Larmour, Anne*
And on My Left · *McAiney, Phil*
And So It Goes · *Grushko, Brenda*
And So to Bed · *Callaghan, Barry*
'And Still She Cries, Bonnie Boys Are Few' · *Steltner, Elke*
And Susie Makes Three · *Ross, W.E. Dan*
And That's the Truth · *Steward, Hartley*
And the Four Animals · *Watson, Sheila*
... And the Greatest of These · *Green, H. Gordon*
And the Green Hills Laugh · *Inglis, Jean*
And the Last Man Will Have to Dig His Own Grave · *Smith, Rich*
And the Lawns All Glistening · *Rowdon, Larry*
And the Legs All Dangling Down-O · *Doyle, Dan*
And the Wind Blows Free · *Smith, Ian*
And Then There Was One · *Stein, Rhoda Elizabeth Playfair*
'And There Came Wise Men' · *Govan, Margaret*
And They Lived Happily Ever After · *McCracken, Melinda*
And Two Percent Zero · *Yates, J. Michael*
... And What's More, My Visitors Have Scaly Tails · *MacFadden, Patrick*
And With Two Such Husbands · *Bereshko-Hunter, Ludmilla* [pseudonym]
Andanta, Ma Non Troppo · *Jackson, J. Graham*
Andante · *Crandall, Kathy*
Andrew and Mr. Cat · *Grawbarger, Josephine*
Andrew Downs Goes to the Big City · *Wetmore, Andrew*
Andromeda's Child · *Peterson, Barry*
Andy · *Babic, Loranne*
Andy Goldman's Conversion · *Steinfeld, J.J.*
Anemone · *Powell, Dorothy M.*
Angakok of Kiglapait · *Cockerill, A.W.*
Angel · *Gaston, Bill*
The Angel and the Prostitute · *Wolfe, Morley*
Angel Children · *Smith, Michael*
Angel in a Red Dress · *Ringland, Mary*
The Angel of Death · *Slabotsky, David*
The Angel of the Tar Sands · *Wiebe, Rudy H.*
Angels and Other People · *Sweatman, Margaret*
Animal Noises · *Mathews, Lawrence*
An Animal Tale · *Bell, Wade*
Animal U · *Davies, Robertson*
The Animals · *Weiss, Allan*
Anita in Love · *Kutlesa, Joso*
Anita's Dance · *Engel, Marian*
Anna, Unpretty · *Marcellin, Philip*
Anna · *Swan, Mary*
Annabelle and the Doctor · *MacDonald, Dorothy*
Annals · *Waterfall, Don E.*
Anne in the Meadows · *Murray, Joan*
Annerl · *Kreisel, Henry*

Annie · *Heyward, Helen*
Annie d'Entremont's Dream · *Gerard, Lance*
Annie Gets Her House · *Blythe, Aleata E.*
Annieism & the American Way · *Evans, Christopher Dudley*
Annie's Apple · *Howard, Randy*
Annie's Daughter · *Knox, Claire Neville and Lûsse, Georginna*
[The?] Anniversary · *Barnard, Leslie Gordon*
The Anniversary · *Harasym, Sally*
Anniversary Gift · *Barker, Bessie M.*
Anniversary House · *Clarke, Gwendoline P.*
Annuit Coeptis and Doorknobs in My Ear Generally · *Kilodney, Crad*
The Annulment · *Keel, Joan*
Anointed with Oils · *Nowlan, Alden*
An Anonymous Letter · *Kreisel, Henry*
Another Boy · *Daniels, D.S.*
Another Christ · *Hughes, Philip B.*
Another Day, Another Dollar · *Garner, Hugh*
Another Desperate Cry · *MacSween, R.J.*
Another Drunken Indian · *Gazey, Marilyn*
Another Fable · *Harasymiw, Bohdan*
Another Form of the Riddle · *MacKinnon, Donald*
Another Friend for Mr. Duck · *McWhirter, George*
Another Morning · *Shtogryn, David*
Another Movie · *Schermbrucker, Bill*
Another One · *Conger, Lesley*
Another Sad Day at the Edge of the Empire · *Guppy, Steve*
Another Season · *Dampf, Michael*
Another Spring, Another Dream · *Linder, Norma West*
Another Sunrise · *Green, H. Gordon*
Another Time, Another Place · *Jackson, J. Graham*
Another Train to Pakistan · *Cowasjee, Saros*
Another Trap · *Gill, Stephen*
Another Treason · *Taylor, Constance Gurd*
Anticipation · *D'Alfonso, Antoine*
Antics of the Insane · *Dabydeen, Cyril*
Antigone · *Watson, Sheila*
Antigonish · *Watson, Barry*
Antiphon for Telephone and Typewriter · *Wheatley, Patience*
Antique Gertie Laughed · *Hekkanen, Ernest*
Antoine's Mountain · *Theriault, Yves*
The Ants · *Bénéteau, Marcel*
The Ant's Dream · *Gilbert, Lara*
Any Dumb Bunny · *MacIntosh, Keitha K.*
Any Game You Want · *Sharman, Vincent*
'Any Kind of Agent' · *Pugsley, Edmund E.*
Any Shepherds for Tea? · *Fraser, Catharine*
Any Time at All · *Marshall, Joyce*
Anybody Home? · *Callaghan, Barry*
Anyone Will Do · *Rule, Jane*
Anyone's Autobiography · *Chometsky, Harvey*

694

Anything Can Happen at Christmas · *Buckler, Ernest*
Anything You Want · *Barnard, Leslie Gordon*
The Apartment Hunter · *Moore, Brian*
Apartment Hunting in the East End · *Austin, Don*
Aphelion · *Brooks, Eunice*
Apocalypse Later · *Begamudre, Ven*
Apogee · *Robinson, Spider*
Apologia for the LRT · *Martini, Clem*
The Apostate · *Crowe, David*
The Apostate's Tattoo · *Steinfeld, J.J.*
Appetites · *Collins, R.G.*
The Apple · *Briffett, Isabel*
Apple Autumn · *Freiberg, Stanley*
The Apple Doesn't Fall Far from the Tree · *Faessler, Shirley*
the apple tree · *Bullock, Michael*
Apples · *Sullivan, D.H.*
Apples and the Fabulous Fortune · *Wood, Kerry*
The Applicant · *Monk, Douglas*
The Appraiser · *Simmons, Margaret*
The Apprentice · *Kennon, Janie*
Approaching · *Wilson, Colleen*
The Apricot Story · *McConnell, Alice*
Apricots · *Brierly, Jim*
April Fish · *Gallant, Mavis*
An April Hour · *Jarvis, June N.*
April Is the Cruelest Month ... · *Katz, Bernard*
April Street and After · *Stevens, Peter*
Aquarius · *Thomas, Audrey*
The Arab Market · *Shore, Mitch*
The Arab Steed · *Foster, Thelma H.*
An Arab Up North · *Newman, C.J.*
Arabesque · *Simpson, Gregg*
Aradia · *Brockway, R.W.*
Ararat · *Riches, Brenda*
Arbiter of Spring · *Humphries, Tom*
Arboretum · *Balk, Christianne*
Arbre de Décision · *Bowering, George*
The Archaeologist on the Anatolian Plateau · *Laflamme, Guy*
Archie · *Clegg, Robin*
The Architect · *Mirolla, Michael*
Architects of the Youth · *Nemiroff, Greta Hofmann*
The 'Arctic Cat' · *Castillo, Charles*
Are Flowers Jewish? · *Zucker, Rickie*
Are People Monkeys? · *McNamee, James*
Are There Any Shoes in Heaven? · *Kogawa, Joy*
Are You What You Are? · *Oikawa, Dulce*
'Arf-and-Arf' - A Look at the R.C.M.P. · *Vertolli, Lou*
Arguments · *Russell, Ted*
Aria da Capo · *Helwig, David*
Aria for Araby · *Grantmyre, Barbara*

Ariadne's Sister · *Dobbs, Bryan*
The Ark · *Nagal, Peter*
Arkendale · *Virgo, Sean*
Arla · *Waldman, Wendy*
The Arlberg Adventure · *Schreiber, H.E.*
Arlene · *Stenson, Frederick*
Arlene in One Day Land · *Nugent, Olive*
Armagma Polareddon · *Hammell, Steven Dale*
Armando Rodrigues · *Leitao, Lino*
Armand's Rabbit · *Keeling, Nora*
The Armchair Revolutionary · *Pickersgill, Alan G.*
Armen Khatchian · *Shirinian, Lorne*
Arms and the Poltroon · *Mills, John*
Army Flynn's Great Idea · *Silver, Isaac*
Arni Laxdal · *Barton, Marie*
Arnold · *Holden, Helene F.*
Arnold and Fonzie · *Jolowski, Wendy*
Arnold's Secrets · *Rivard, Ken*
Arnuk · *Mowat, Farley*
Arny Was Always Talking, See · *Ross, James*
Around About Midnight · *Kari, Briar*
Around Theatres · *Hood, Hugh*
The Arrest · *Evanier, David*
The Arrested Ones · *Wooley, Michael*
Arrival · *Shirinian, Lorne*
Arrivederci, Evelyn · *Hoffer, Sorryl*
The Arrowhead · *Sigurgeirson, W.J.*
'Arry, 'Arry, Quite Contrary · *Fountain, Eileen*
The Art of Kissing · *Richler, Mordecai*
Art of Song · *Braitman, Stephen*
The Art of the Late Essay · *Bryson, Ruth*
The Art of the Novel · *McNamara, Eugene*
The Art of Walking · *Lee, David*
Art Really's Armour · *Wooley, Michael*
Arthur and the Labrat · *Law, Charles*
The Artist · *Maycock, Marjorie*
Artist Anonymous · *Boszin, Andrew*
The Artist Who Went to Heaven · *Green, H. Gordon*
Artistic Artifice · *Knapp, G.L.*
Artsy-Craftsy · *Garner, Hugh*
As Advertised · *Wood, Ted*
As Fair Flowers Fade · *Olsen, Hank*
As I Lay Dying: Faulkner Revisited · *Henderson, Margaret S.*
As It Should Be · *MacMillan, Gail*
As Long as It's the Truth · *Rother, James*
As Loved Our Fathers · *Corbett, Isabel Scott*
... As Other Men Are · *McDonald, Ruth*
As Others See Us · *Green, H. Gordon*
As Others See Us · *Nowlan, Alden*
As Rumor Had It · *Smith, Colonel* [pseudonym]

As the Twig Is Bent · *Marsh, Wade*
As Time Goes By · *Weiss, H.*
As We Are · *Behrens, Peter*
As We Forgive · *Jarvis, June N.*
As You Would Have Them Do unto You · *Rigby, Carle A.*
As Young as She Felt · *Andrus, David A.*
Asa Sigmundsson: Holiday · *Gunnars, Kristjana*
The Ascension · *Cameron, William*
Ascrololidan · *Andrews, Louise*
Ashes · *Watmough, David*
Ashes for Easter · *Watmough, David*
Ashes to Ashes · *Hospital, Janet Turner*
Ash-heels · *Branden, Vicki*
Asking and Telling - A Discussion of Theory · *Waugh, Thomas L.*
Asparagus · *Shaw, Joan Fern*
The Assassin · *Schweers, Gordon*
The Assassination · *Taaffe, Gerald*
The Assassins of Don Chucho · *McWhirter, George*
The Assembly · *Gallant, Mavis*
Assembly Line · *Currie, Robert*
The Assertion of Jordan Lemke · *Gunn, Genni*
Assorted Mooseheads · *Orser, Forrest D.*
The Assumption of Gilbert Penrose · *Bradley, Alan*
Asters for Teddie · *Spettigue, Douglas O.*
Astral Sonic · *Carlson, Chuck*
Astronomy · *Quarrington, Paul*
Astypalaian Knife · *Johnston, George*
Asylum · *Illidge, Paul*
At a Party It Doesn't Pay to Laugh Too Much · *Story, Gertrude*
At Approximately Three P.M.... · *Henighan, Tom*
at dusk / just when / the Light is filled with birds · *Gault, Connie*
At Dusk the Sound: The Story of a Boy and a Dog · *Fulford, Robin*
At Home · *Brown, Barbara A.*
At Home on McGill Street · *Purdy, Al*
At Hunter River · *Rigelhof, T.F.*
At Night · *Emberly, Kenneth*
At Peace · *Copeland, Ann* [pseudonym]
At Pharaoh's · *Sutterfield, Allen*
At Spring Melt · *Hoffman, Edith*
At Station Melville · *Mills, John*
At Sunnyside Villa · *Creal, Margaret*
At the Birdbath · *Scott, John*
At the Bottom of a River · *Slabotsky, David*
At the Burning Ghat · *Forbes, Greg*
At the Cottage · *Roddy, William*
At the Count of Ten · *Jones, Barbara*
At the Edge · *Hogan, Robert*
At the Edge of the Woods · *Nowlan, Alden*
At the Empress Hotel · *Cohen, Matt*
At the End of Summer · *Ellis, Keith*

At the End of the Lane · *Bedard, Michael*
At the End of the Line · *Ireland, Ann*
At the Foot of the Hill, Birdie's School · *Hodgins, Jack*
At the Going Down of the Sun and in the Morning · *McNamara, Eugene*
At the Insanity Factory · *Gabrielli, John*
At the Lake · *Blaise, Clark L.*
At the Organ · *Bushell, Sidney*
At the Other Place · *Munro, Alice*
At the Symphony · *Rosenthal, Peter*
At the Threshold · *Thatcher, Philip*
At the Threshold of the Known · *Kaye, Aaron S.*
At the Top of the Cliff · *Powell, Dorothy M.*
At the Upper Pool · *Bushell, Sidney*
At Your Own Peril · *Dabydeen, Cyril*
The Atavists · *Kernaghan, Eileen*
Atelier Oeuf: Lune · *Strickland, Edward*
The Atheist · *Freethy, Dyved*
Athens · *Anderson, Jim*
Athens: The Knitting Party · *MacEwen, Gwendolyn*
Atlas Carries the Heavy Load · *McNamee, James*
Atonement · *Govan, Margaret*
Atop the Hill of Anzop · *Spera, Roman*
The Attendant · *Itwaru, Arnold*
Attention · *Hodgins, Norris*
the attic · *Bullock, Michael*
The Atwater Fiancée · *Spencer, Elizabeth*
Auction · *Stone, A.C.*
Auction Sale · *Waywitka, Anne B.*
Audee, Nobah Naze · *Wiebe, Armin*
The Audition · *Park, Lisa*
Auf Wiedersehen Sweetheart · *Lynch, Gerald*
August · *Gallant, Mavis*
August Heat · *A.J.N.*
August Nights · *Hood, Hugh*
August Not Over · *Sanford, Claire*
An August Wind · *Itani, Frances*
Augustin's Wife · *Kaal, Hans*
the aunt · *Heath, Terence*
Aunt Addie's Xmas Caper · *Byrne-Wood, Margaret*
Aunt Aggie's Last Escapade · *Dybvig, Leslie*
Aunt Annie and Uncle Bert · *Goudie, Elizabeth*
Aunt Di · *Downes, G.V.*
Aunt Di: A Tale of the Twenties · *Downes, Gwladys*
Aunt Disappears · *Gill, Stephen*
Aunt Emily Tells a Story · *Case, Geraldine*
Aunt Hettie & the Gates of the New Jerusalem · *Thomas, Audrey*
Aunt Hettie James and the Gates of the New Jerusalem · *Thomas, Audrey*
Aunt Hoffer and the Highlanders · *Story, Gertrude*
Aunt Lil · *Allison, Rosemary*
Aunt Linnie's Lantern · *Barker, Bessie M.*

Aunt Marion's House · *Kirkwood, Hilda*
Aunt Rose and Uncle Freidle · *Rikki [Erica Ducornet]*
Aunt Sophy · *Russell, Ted*
Aunt Sophy's Predicament · *Russell, Ted*
Aunt Sophy's Return · *Russell, Ted*
Aunt Violet and the Rain and the Dead Flowers · *MacCallum, Russell*
Aunt Zelda's Marriage · *Singer, Barnett*
Auntie Bones Becomes a Canadian · *Gray, Kitty*
Auntie Intellectual · *Teicher, Mark*
Auntie Minnie · *Birch-Jones, Sonia*
Auntie Minnie and the Goy · *Birch-Jones, Sonia*
Aurora/Anna Marie · *Byrnes, Terence*
Austin · *Ondaatje, Michael*
The Authentic Apologue, or The Maladroit Iconoclast Exposed · *Croutch, Leslie A.*
Authority Figures · *O'Connell, Dorothy*
An Authority on Racing · *Dickie, Francis*
the autobiographer · *Bullock, Michael*
An Autobiography · *Gallant, Mavis*
Autobiography of a Poppy · *Lovell, R.G.*
Autobiography of a Quarter-Day Fly · *Tamminga, Frederick W.*
The Autobiography of an Ocean Fucker · *Kardok, Butch*
The Autobiography of Mervyn Rose · *Bell, Don*
The Autobiography of Pax Balanski · *Hassan, Ray*
Auto-Da-Fe · *Zonailo, Carolyn*
Automobile Soft Legs · *Browne, Paul Cameron*
Autumn · *Sakamoto, Kerri*
Autumn and Fear · *de Vries, Anne*
Autumn Appointment · *Brown, Mae Hill*
Autumn Breezes · *Blythe, Aleata E.*
An Autumn Day · *Gubins, Indra*
Autumn Episode · *Jeffels, Ronald R.*
Autumn Idyll · *Abrams, Tevia*
The Avalanche · *Braune, Elizabeth*
Ave Atque Vale: A Malediction · *Lil [pseudonym]*
Avis de Vente · *Marshall, Joyce*
Avita · *Lewis, Brian Wyndham*
Avoidance Coping · *Mayer, Natalia*
The Awakening · *Younger, Bill*
A-Walkin & A-Talkin · *Armstrong, Patricia*
An Awfully Mature Person · *Pereira, Helen*
The Axe · *Lamb, Ken*
An Axe-Handle · *Bushell, Sidney*
The Axeman · *Cunningham, Shaun*
Aya-oo · *Hendry, Peter*

B. Greenwood · *MacLaurin, Douglas*
Baba · *Serwylo, Ray*
Babe and the Birds and Bees · *Annett, R. Ross*

Babe and the Bully · *Annett, R. Ross*
Babe and the Cattle Thief · *Annett, R. Ross*
Babe and the Hungry Soldier · *Annett, R. Ross*
Babe in Disgrace · *Annett, R. Ross*
Babe Prays for a Miracle · *Annett, R. Ross*
Babe's Christmas Wish · *Annett, R. Ross*
Babe's New Dog · *Annett, R. Ross*
Babe's Strange Illness · *Annett, R. Ross*
Babe's Surprise · *Annett, R. Ross*
Babies, Babies, Everywhere · *Barker, Bessie M.*
The Baby · *Campbell, Wanda Blynn*
Baby Face · *Sheard, Sarah*
A Baby for Rosanne · *Maclean, Muriel*
The Baby Needs a Pair of Shoes · *Bruner, Arnold*
Baby Snooky Comes Back · *Lypchuk, D.*
The Baby-Sitter · *Sanderson, Helen*
Babysittin' · *Russell, Ted*
Bachelor Brother · *Bird, Will R.*
The Bachelors · *Summers, Merna*
The Bachelor's Dilemma · *Callaghan, Morley*
Back Alley Lord · *Chuley* [pseudonym]
Back Door · *Paluk, William*
Back from Outer Space · *Stackhouse, H.M.*
Back Home · *Dean, Maureen*
Back in the Alley · *Lenoir-Arcand, Christine*
Back in the Garden Again · *Stange, Ken*
The Back Room · *Copeland, Ann* [pseudonym]
back to the tree · *Bullock, Michael*
Back Where I Can Be Me · *Stein, David Lewis*
Background of Blowing Topsail · *Klebeck, William J.*
Backhanded Inducement · *Murdoch, Benedict Joseph*
Backlash in the Oil Patch · *Morritt, Hope*
The Bad · *Bauer, Nancy*
A Bad Cold · *Spencer, Elizabeth*
Bad Day at the Bank · *Madden, Peter*
Bad Girl · *Herbert, John*
Bad Hand · *Bauer, Nancy*
Bad Santa Claus · *Beauvais, Ronald*
A Bad Scene · *Bankier, William*
The Bad Trip · *Braithwaite, J. Ashton*
The Bad Weed · *Annett, William S.*
The Bad Year · *Stemo, L. Johanne*
Badla - Revenge! · *Bruneau, Bernard*
A Bag of Cherries · *Metcalf, John*
A Bagful of Holes · *Annand, Alan M.*
Baggage · *Ogle, Robert Joseph*
Bagging Bunnies · *Power, John*
Bait for a Tiger · *Walker, David*
Bait for Bachelors · *Findlay, David K.*
Bakery Boys · *Kilodney, Crad*

The Baking Powder Tin · *Armstrong, Patricia*
the bald head · *Bullock, Michael*
Baldur's Death · *Kushner, Donn*
The Ball · *Atwood, Joan-Mary*
The Ballad of Al Shadow · *Fones, Robert*
The Ballad of the Public Trustee · *Kinsella, W.P.*
Ballast · *Hodgins, Norris*
Ballin' Jack · *Sotelo, Ruben*
The Balloon · *Richler, Mordecai*
the balloons · *Heath, Terence*
The Ballroom · *Mason, Mike*
Ballygennon Revisited · *Burns, R.*
Bambinger · *Richler, Mordecai*
A Band Aid Kite · *Roberts, Kevin*
Bandit · *Roseborough, Ron*
Bandit of the Marsh · *Gillese, John Patrick*
Bandits · *Virgo, Sean*
The Bank Clerk · *Russell, G.E.*
Bank Holiday · *Partington, David*
The Bannard Stone · *Hawkes, Mark S.*
The Banquet · *Reid, Robert W.*
Bap-Bap-Bap · *Trueman, Stuart*
A Baptism · *Guareschi, Giovanni*
Baptizing · *Munro, Alice*
Barancumbay · *Blake, Dorothy*
Barbara Ramsden with a Fancy 'R' · *Danard, Joan*
A Barbed Hook · *Jamie* [pseudonym]
Barbed Wire and Balloons · *Alford, Edna*
the barber of seville bank · *Bullock, Michael*
Barbers and Lovers · *Cohen, Leonard*
The Barclay House · *Bruns, Ina*
Bard Sinister · *Hewitt, Molly*
Bardon Bus · *Munro, Alice*

The Bare Facts · *Brunt, R.J.*
Bare Ruined Choirs · *Montagnes, Anne*
Barefoot · *Pitman, Teresa*
The Bargain · *Browne, Tom*
The Bargain Boat · *Goodwin, Debi Awde*
The Bargain Ox · *Gillese, John Patrick*
A Bargain with Fate · *Green, H. Gordon*
The Bargain-Counter Don't-Miss Gift-Wrapped Christmas · *Stein, Rhoda Elizabeth Playfair*
The Barge · *Easton, Alan*
The Barking of Dogs · *Purdy, Brian*
The Barmaid · *Wynand, Derk*
The Barn · *Ondaatje, Michael*
Barn Cats · *Stephen, Sid*
Barney · *Sangwine, Jean*
Barnyard Socialism · *Anonymous*
The Baroque Ensemble · *Hospital, Janet Turner*

The Barren Land · *Simpson, Leo*
Barriers · *Harris, Marcia*
Barry's Bay · *Dempster, Barry*
The Bars and the Bridge · *Buckler, Ernest*
Bartle's Brook · *Russell, Ted*
Base Born · *Callow, Sherry*
Baseball at Renfrew · *Johnston, Stella*
The Baseball Game · *Valgardson, W.D.*
the basement · *Heath, Terence*
Basement Lullaby · *Selvon, Samuel*
The Basilisk · *Elflandsson, Galad*
A Basket of Apples · *Faessler, Shirley*
Basket of Strawberries · *Munro, Alice*
The Bath, Country Fashion · *Symons, Harry*
Bath · *Stevens, Peter*
Bath Oil · *Anonymous*
The Bather · *Hekkanen, Ernest*
Batman and the Communist Party · *Cameron, Donald*
The Batter Was Scratched · *Gower, Richard*
The Battered Tome · *Ravel, Aviva*
The Battle · *Hancock, Ronald Lee*
The Battle for Borshch · *Sribniak, Mervin*
Battle in the Swamp · *Gillette, Agnes*
Battle of the Atlantic · *Ronald, George*
The Battle of the Biscuits · *Barker, Bessie M.*
The Battle of the Budget · *Green, H. Gordon*
The Battleford Incident · *Dnieper, Robert D.*
Battling · *Wolfe, Patrick*
A Bauble for Bernice · *Bailey, Don*
The Bauer-Hirsch Law of Survival or The Hazards of Living · *Fielden, Charlotte*
Baum, Gabriel, 1935- ( ) · *Gallant, Mavis*
Baxter Jack · *Dronyk, Levi*
Bay Bridge · *Miller, Stephen*
Bay Rum · *Schull, Joseph J.*
Bayonet · *Enwright, William*
Be a Listener · *Cade-Edwards, Eileen*
Be Good · *Herbert, John*
The Be Hive · *Zilber, Jacob*
Be My Love Always · *Cunningham, Louis Arthur*
Be Thyself · *McCarthy, Anne*
Be Yourself · *Trimble, Alberta C.*
Beach · *Anonymous*
Beach Dogs · *Templeton, Alan*
The Beachcomber · *Briffett, Isabel*
Beached · *Roberts, Tom*
Beaches · *Wen, William*
Beacon on the Beach · *Shipley, Nan*
The Bean Ball · *Young, Scott*
'Beaned with Bottle' · *Steele, Harwood*
Beans & Binoculars · *Kilodney, Crad*

Beanut and the Seder · *Nathans, Elyeh*
The Bear · *Brierly, Jim*
A Bear Escape · *Doyle, Bill*
A Bear for Punishment · *Fines, Beatrice E.*
The Bear in the Blueberries · *Morris, Doris M.*
The Bear in the Orchard · *Nowlan, Alden*
A Bear Named Sue · *Green, H. Gordon*
The Bear Story · *McLeod, Murdoch*
The Bear Walker · *Evans, J.A.S.*
The Bear Went Over the Mountain · *Larsen, Carl*
Bearing Christmas Gifts · *Edmonds, Edward L.*
Bears Aren't So Dumb · *MacKrow, Jack*
The Bears' Club Concert · *Branden, Vicki*
The Bear's Paw · *Copeland, Ann* [pseudonym]
Beast of Prey · *Green, H. Gordon*
The Beast That Couldn't Be · *Mayse, Arthur*
Beastie · *Tchir, Mary*
Beastly Story · *Mezei, Stephen*
Beat No Drums for Him · *Drew, Wayland*
The Beating · *Allan, Ted*
Beatrice · *Flood, Cynthia*
La Beau Sha Sho · *Campbell, Maria*
Beautiful Bev Caldwell · *Graham, Hugh*
The Beautiful Black Psalm That Farewell Was Always Meant to Be · *Tagney, Paul*
Beautiful Country, Burn Again · *McNamara, Eugene*
[A?] Beautiful Day for the Wedding · *Spencer, Elizabeth*
The Beautiful Lie · *Green, H. Gordon*
The Beautiful Tide · *Fletcher, Peggy*
Beautiful Woman · *Smart, William J.*
The Beauty · *Simons, Beverley*
Beauty Like a Rose · *Nelson, Harold*
The Beauty of El Poeta · *Stuart, James*
A Beaver Tale · *Kilodney, Crad*
Beaverbrook in Love · *Choyce, Lesley*
Bebe's Place · *Gallant, Mavis*
Because I Am Drunk · *Thompson, Kent*
Because I Needed to Know · *Bailey, Don*
Because of a Dream · *Gillese, John Patrick*
Because of the War · *Levine, Norman*
Becoming · *McColl, William E.*
The Bed · *Irvine, R.B.*
Bed and Breakfast · *Wood, Ted*
Bedlamb Pasture · *Casselman, Bill*
Beds · *Hodgins, Norris*
Bedtime · *Hollingshead, Greg*
Bedtime Story · *G[ladstone]., J[ames].*
Bee Cause · *Gilliam, John*
The Bee Teasers · *Murdoch, Benedict Joseph*
The Beechnut Eaters · *Branden, Vicki*
The Beef Curry · *Metcalf, John*

The Beekeeper and His Wife · *Plourde, Marc*
Been a Bad Winter · *Allen, Glen*
Beer and Skittles · *Moyer, Carolyn*
Beer Bottle Hill · *Currie, Robert*
Before His Very Eyes · *Nowlan, Alden*
Before I Go · *Green, H. Gordon*
Before Sundown · *Blaise, Clark L.*
Before the Fall · *Ross, Gary*
Before the Sun Goes Down · *Sharman, Vincent*
The Beggar · *Peters, Mac*
The Beggar at Bedford · *Hawrelko, John*
The Beggar in the Bulrush · *Rooke, Leon*
The Beggar Maid · *Munro, Alice*
Beginner's Luck · *Geitzler, Fran*
The Beginning · *Szanto, George*
A Beginning and an Ending · *Coward, Mary Ann*
Beginnings · *Cooper, Mel*
The Beguiled [A Gentle Ghost Story] · *Marsh, Audrey*
Behind Every Successful Pope · *McLaughlin, Peter*
Behind the Eight Ball Again · *Johnson, Eric*
Behind the Humming Bird · *Selvon, Samuel*
Behind the Nightengale Smile · *Russell, Sheila MacKay*
Behind the Wall · *Hancock, Ronald Lee*
Being Prepared · *Torgov, Morley*
Belgium Avenue · *Marshall, Joyce*
Believe and You Shall See · *Duloff, Nick*
Belinda · *Nelson, Elizabeth*
Belinda's Seal · *Rosta, Helen J.*
Belinda's Story · *Estabrook, Barry*
The Bell · *Bemrose, John*
Bell Bottoms on Plymouth Hoe · *Watmough, David*
Bella · *Munro, Kate*
Bella Cleans the Closets · *Johnston, Nandy*
Belladonna · *Michaluk, Gary*
The Bellatrix Report · *Quinlan, Judith*
Belle in Winter · *Butala, Sharon*
The Bell-Ringers · *Roddan, Samuel*
Bells Are Ringing · *de Vries, Anne*
Beloved · *Boyko, Elvina*
The Beloved Dissenter · *Campbell, Betty*
Beloved in the Bath, This Is My Beloved · *Rooke, Leon*
Below the Bridge · *Partridge, Basil*
Belts · *Linkovich, Stanley*
Ben · *Graham, Tammy*
The Ben Hur Chariot Race · *Lewis, David E.*
Bend in the Road · *Stein, Rhoda Elizabeth Playfair*
Beneath the Smoking Lady · *Milliken, Ross*
The Benediction · *Tamminga, Frederick W.*
Benefit of Doubt · *Sims, Burt*
Benjamin · *Bauer, Nancy*

Benjy and the Killer Whale · *Sturdy, John Rhodes*
Benny, the War in Europe, and Myerson's Daughter Bella · *Richler, Mordecai*
Benny · *Powning, Beth*
Benny and the Mermaid · *Barnard, Leslie Gordon*
The Bequest · *Theriault, Yves*
The Bequest · *Briffett, Isabel*
Bereft · *Ravel, Aviva*
Bergman Agonistes · *Wetmore, Andrew*
Bernadette · *Gallant, Mavis*
Bernard Goes to a Party · *Pegis, Jessica*
Berserk in a Waterbed · *Silvester, Reg*
Bertha and Bill · *Fraser, Raymond*
Berty Simpson · *Pope, Pat*
Beryl · *Metcalf, John*
The Best Dog That Ever Was · *LeMay, Bonnie*
Best Falling Dead · *Sherrin, Robert G.*
The Best Fishing Hole in B.C. · *Hockley, Vernon*
Best Friend · *Rosta, Helen J.*
The Best Gift of All · *Pillar, Mabel*
The Best Horn Player in the World · *Sidran, Maxine*
The Best Ice in Quebec · *Filip, Raymond*
The Best Is Yet to Be · *C., W.R.*
The Best Laid Plans · *Story, Gertrude*
The Best Lay I Ever Had · *Newman, C.J.*
Best Left Unsaid · *Belknap, Shane*
The Best Man · *Jasiura, Barbara*
The Best of Both Worlds · *Steiger, Mary*
The Best of Enemies · *Green, Robert*
Best Partner a Man Ever Had · *Haig-Brown, Roderick*
The Best Years of Their Live · *Harris, John Norman*
The Best-Laid Plan · *Wood, Ted*
The Bet · *Steinfeld, J.J.*
Beth Gulert · *Dragland, Stan*
The Betrayal · *Slabotsky, David*
Betrothal · *Ryga, George*
Betta Splendor · *Sandler, Robert*
The Better Gift · *Thompson, Kent*
Better Have a Cigar, Judge! · *Anonymous*
Better Homes and Gardens · *O'Connell, Dorothy*
A Better Life · *Byrnes, Terence*
Better Off Dead · *Marriott, J. Anne*
The Better Part of Surprise · *Ohm, Vibeke*
A Better Place Than Home · *Munro, Alice*
Better Than the Streets · *McHardy, Vincent*
Better Times · *Gallant, Mavis*
Better to Burn · *Stockdale, J.C.*
Betting Sam's Last Bet · *Dybvig, Leslie*
Betty · *Atwood, Margaret*
Betty Earns a Nickname · *Mulkin, Grace*
Bettylou and the Caribou · *Wood, Kerry*

Betty's Big Moment · *Ross, [W.E.] Dan and Ross, Charlotte*
Betty's Empty Arms · *Bole, J. Sheridan*
Between · *McNamara, Eugene*
Between Lives · *Ross, Veronica*
Between Me and the Dark · *Blackburn, Robert*
between monday and friday courage grows · *Dennis, Michael*
Between the Fall and the Flood · *Brewster, Elizabeth*
Between the Headboard and the Foot · *Dampf, Michael*
Between the Kisses and the Wine · *Glover, Douglas H.*
Between the Pillars · *Johnsen, Hank*
Between Zero and One · *Gallant, Mavis*
Beware of the Dog · *Reynolds, Dickson*
Beware the Jabberwock, My Son ... Beware the Jubjub Bird · *Wilson, Ethel D.*
Beyond a Crimson Morning · *Ryga, George*
Beyond a Destiny · *Beck, J.P.*
Beyond Normal Requirements · *Valgardson, W.D.*
Beyond the Foothills · *Pittman, Al*
Beyond the Horizon · *Jelinek, Vera*
Beyond the Mergansers, Above the Salal · *Watmough, David*
Beyond the Rising Sun · *Bryant, Cullene*
Beyond the Sight of Man · *Williams, Dave*
Beyond Words · *Alford, Norman*
Bharat Mata Ki Jai · *Cowasjee, Saros*
Bharta · *McFadden, Isobel*
Bianca · *Hosein, Clyde*
A Bibliography for Gordon Lockhead · *Persky, Stan*
Bic the Bull · *Fergusson, Anne*
Bicultural Angela · *Hood, Hugh*
the bicycle · *Heath, Terence*
Bicycle Story · *Engel, Marian*
Bicycles Swings Baseball Cards · *Schoutsen, John*
The Bicyclist · *Kleiman, Edward*
Bid by Bid · *Wilson, Peter*
The Big Bird Theory · *McLure, Bruce*
Big Bo · *MacLaurin, Douglas*
Big Boys Shouldn't Cry · *Allan, Ted*
The Big Bunco · *Bankier, William*
Big Deal · *Young, Scott*
Big Elephants Are No Longer Relevant · *Moore, Brian*
The Big Game Fisherman in Florida · *Godfrey, Dave*
A Big Hand for Danny · *Lees, Gene*
Big Joe's Alibi · *Annett, R. Ross*
Big Joe's Dilemma · *Annett, R. Ross*
The Big Leagues · *Bowering, George*
The Big Lie That Won · *Brydges, Stewart*
Big Mike · *Gillese, John Patrick*
Big Momma Always Wanted a Daughter · *Tia [pseudonym]*

The Big Moonlight Dance Cruise · *McNamara, Eugene*
Big Newf · *Green, H. Gordon*
The Big One · *Tench, C.V.*
[The?] Big Orphan Boy · *Gillese, John Patrick*
Big Spender from the West · *Findlay, David K.*
The Big Time · *O'Connell, Dorothy*
The Bigger They Come · *Wetmore, W. Gordon*
The Biggest Bridge in the World · *Mathews, Robin D.*
The Big-Time Spender · *Gordon, Betty*
The Bikers · *Sharpe, David*
Bikers Are Hard on the Digestion · *MacLaurin, Douglas*
Biking in Foreign Countries · *Mars, Jan*
Bill · *Battistuzzi, Richard*
Bill Grant Goes West · *Higham, John*
Billets Doux · *Fagan, Cary*
Billiards · *Osborne, J.T.*
Bill's Bride · *Carlton, Edna P.*
Billy and the Bears · *Evans, Dorothy*
Billy Haskell's Hanging · *Nations, Opal L.*
Billy the Bladge · *Anonymous*
Billy the Kid Is Dead · *Barbour, Sharon*
Bim · *Lûsse, Georgina*
Binary Dysfunction · *Godfrey, Dave*
Binary Lovers · *Arnason, David*
Bingo the Oh-Shit Game · *Haiven, Larry*
The Binoculars · *MacFarlane, John L.*
Biographical Notes · *Rooke, Leon*
A Biography · *Holden-Lawrence, Monica*
The Bird · *Blancher, Lew*
The Bird and the Boulder · *Koncel, Mary Aleta*
Bird Hitch-Hiking · *Ford, Cathy*
A Bird in the House · *Laurence, Margaret*
Bird Shadow · *Bowman, Martin*
The Bird-Healer · *Nemiroff, Greta Hofmann*
Birdie · *Allan, Ted*
The Birdlady · *Bauer, Frances*
Birdman · *Smyth, Donna E.*
The Birds · *Reid, James*
The Birds and the Bells in Bobby's Tower - A Parable · *Hayes, Diana*
The Bird-Winged Truck Driver · *Keeling, Nora*
Birth · *Dickson, Barry*
Birth and Death and the Whole Damn Thing · *O'Connell, Dorothy*
The Birth Control King of Upper Volta · *Rooke, Leon*
Birth of a Hero · *McCourt, Edward A.*
Birth of a Legend · *Kendrick, N.H.*
The Birth of My Father · *Collier, Diana G.*
The Birthday · *Petrie, Heather*
A Birthday Cake Forever · *Newman, Frank*
The Birthday Card · *Vannin, Ellan*
The Birthday Gift · *Booker, Jean*

A Birthday in Reverse · *Ross, W.E. Dan*
Birthday Journey · *Darling, Fran*
A Birthday Party · *Shipman, Warde*
Birthday Present · *Stein, Rhoda Elizabeth Playfair*
The Birthmark · *Alford, Edna*
Birthright · *Holley, Melvin*
Bisexual Man · *MacCormack, Terrance*
The Bishop · *Salminiw, Stephen*
A Bit of Butter · *Grantmyre, Barbara*
A Bit of Music · *Burton, Rosemary*
Bitches Like Toe-Jam · *Sproxton, Birk*
Biting the Dogs · *Amprimoz, Alexandre*
biting the dust · *Bullock, Michael*
Bitter Blood · *Dabydeen, Cyril*
Bitter Harvest · *Russell, Sheila MacKay*
Bitter Is Our Loss · *Lilla, Peter J.*
Bitter with the Sweet · *Owen, George*
Black 6 on Red 7 · *Johnson, Vera D.*
Black and White and Red All Over · *Garner, Hugh*
A 'Black Cat' Crossed Their Path · *Larmour, Anne*
Black Chute · *McLean, Anne*
Black Cockerel · *Marchaelle, Ilona*
The Black Cross · *Berketa, Raymond*
Black Currants · *Russell, Ted*
The Black Dog · *Herbart, Elizabeth*
the black engine · *Bullock, Michael*
Black Eyes Almond Skin ... · *Itani, Frances*
Black Falls · *McLean, Anne*
The Black Farm · *Watson, Sheila*
Black Fisherman · *Haig-Brown, Roderick*
Black Fly · *UU, David*
black horse, white horse · *Bullock, Michael*
The Black House · *Pacey, Desmond*
Black Is the Colour · *Ryga, George*
Black Is White · *Krakovsky, Shel*
Black Jack Taylor · *Johnson, C.D. Paisley*
the black knight and the green woman · *Bullock, Michael*
black lightning · *Bullock, Michael*
Black Memory · *Watmough, David*
Black Mountain · *Bergren, Myrtle*
The Black Queen · *Callaghan, Barry*
Black Rock Sunker · *Brown, Cassie*
Black Sacrifice · *Whitford, Margaret Ann*
Black Sheep! Black Sheep! · *Green, H. Gordon*
The Black Silk Dress · *Branden, Vicki*
Black Snow · *Sladek, Robert*
The Black Swans of the Loch Lothlomond · *Hammell, Steven Dale*
Black to Checkmate · *Fisher, Gale*
The Black Tom · *Hekkanen, Ernest*
The Black Umbrella · *van Every, Jane*

Black Velvet · *Story, Gertrude*
Black Vulture · *Wiebe, Rudy H.*
Black Wampum · *Kinsella, W.P.*
Blackbird and the Poet · *Rummel, Erika*
Blackie · *Gaunt, Laura*
Blackout · *Forest, Alan*
The Blacksmith Shop Caper · *Kinsella, W.P.*
Blame It on the Snow · *Buckler, Ernest*
The Blank-Faced People of Iden Moor · *Fones, Robert*
Blaze · *Dyba, Kenneth*
Bleeding · *Johnson, Linda Wikene*
Bleeding Nail Polish · *Ursan, Sheonaid*
Bleeding the Army · *Weekes, Mary L.*
Blending · *Sakamoto, Kerri*
Blessed Are the Deviates: A Post-Therapy Check-Up on My Ex-Psychiatrist · *Riordan, Michael*
Blessed Are the Meek · *Campbell, Alphonsus P.*
The Blessed Virgin · *Johnson, Carol*
The Blind Beggar · *Konoval, Karin*
Blind Date · *Willard, D.*
The Blind Deer · *Wood, Kerry*
Blind Eyes to See · *Burnell, Ethel D.*
Blind Justice · *Power, John*
'The Blind Leading the Blind' · *Burnell, Ethel D.*
Blind Man's Bluff · *Bristow, Susan*
The Blind Munchies · *Zaiss, David*
Blind Spot · *Sturdy, John Rhodes*
Blind Trade · *Crowell, Bill*
Blinded by Selfishness · *Ross, [W.E.] Dan and Ross, Charlotte*
The Blinding of André Maloche · *Mowat, Farley*
The Blizzard · *Kerr, Elizabeth*
Blizzard in the Banana Belt · *Mowat, Farley*
Blizzard Warning · *Annett, R. Ross*
The Block · *Riddell, John*
The Blockade Runners · *Hazell, Mary*
The Blonde and the Fifteen Little Girls · *MacCormack, Terrance*
Blood and the Northern Lights · *Bevan, Alan*
Blood and Thunder · *Smith, Michael*
The Blood in Their Veins · *Mowat, Farley*
The Blood Is on the Cup · *Ireland, Ann*
A Blood Named Charcoal · *Minions, Stephen*
Blood on His Hands · *Mayse, Arthur*
The Bloodfish · *Browne, Paul Cameron*
Bloodflowers · *Valgardson, W.D.*
Bloodstone · *Welykopolsky, Luba*
A Bloody Pair · *Thompson, Kent*
Blossoms · *Vernon, Lorraine*
Blow Job · *Knechtel, Mary Beth*
Blow Your Horn · *Ryan, Maxwell*
Blue · *Annan, A.C.*

Blue Apes · *Gotlieb, Phyllis*
The Blue Bear · *Taylor, Perry*
The Blue Blouse · *Gould, Florence*
the blue bush · *Bullock, Michael*
A Blue Day · *Martens, Debra*
The Blue Door · *L'Abbé-Jones, Pauline*
Blue Glass and Flowers · *Engel, Marian*
The Blue Gown · *Daem, Mary and Deeder, Peg*
The Blue Guitar · *Kroetsch, Robert*
the blue halo · *Bullock, Michael*
The Blue Heron · *Dagg, Mel*
Blue Jacket, Blue Jeans · *Copeland, Violet*
The Blue Jays versus the Black Douglases · *Steinfeld, J.J.*
The Blue Lamp · *Rubia, Geraldine*
Blue Milk · *Blythe, Aleata E.*
Blue Mountain Majesty · *Erne, Andy*
The Blue Period · *Watson, Robert*
The Blue Planet · *de Marco, Don*
Blue Ring · *Julian, Marilyn*
The Blue Souwester · *Pacey, Desmond*
The Blue Stool · *Bailey, Betty*
Blue Streams, Yellow Dandelion · *Bartolini, D[onna]*
The Blue Taffeta Dress · *Day, Peggy*
Bluebeard · *Nations, Opal L.*
Bluebeard's Egg · *Atwood, Margaret*
Blueberries · *Ross, Gary*
Bluecoats on the Sacred Hill of the Wild Peas · *Wiebe, Rudy H.*
The Bluefish · *Bruce, Hubert*
Bluenose in Toronto · *MacDonald, David*
Blues for Some Gamblers · *Pineo, Mari*
Blues for Tommy · *Grossman, Rita*
Bluto's Blues · *Allen, Robert*
'Bo · *Christy, Jim*
Boarding a French Vessel · *Cowasjee, Saros*
The Boat · *MacLeod, Alistair*
The Boat Builder · *Stacey, Jean*
The Boat Ride · *Goulden, Ron*
The Boat That Never Sailed · *Murphy, Capt. Leo C.*
The Boathouse Question · *Gould, Jan*
The Boats · *Cull, David*
Boats Should Be Seen and Not Heard · *Ames, Bill*
Bobby & the Fire Chief · *Armstrong, Patricia*
Bobby's Story · *Knechtel, Mary Beth*
Bobrowski · *Milander, Mary Ellen*
The Body · *Arnason, David*
Body No. 15 · *Schoemperlen, Diane*
A Bohemian in the Underworld · *Fisher, Michael J.*
Boiled Chicken · *Levine, Norman*
Boiled Owl · *Elford, Jean*
The Bolshevik and the Wicked Witch · *Harris, John Norman*

The Bomb · *Ready, William B.*
Bomb Shelters · *Fawcett, Brian*
Bombs Away · *Adair, Victor*
Le Bon Dieu of Jacques Hillaire · *Green, H. Gordon*
Bonaventure · *Gallant, Mavis*
Bonded · *Hodes, Barbara Thal*
Bonds · *Das, Satya*
A Bone to Pick · *Gotlieb, Phyllis*
Bones · *Summers, Anthony J.*
Bones Blues · *Garnet, Eldon*
Boneset · *Bauer, Nancy*
Bonfire · *Bauer, Nancy*
Bonfire on the Beach · *Cook, Gregory M.*
Une Bonne Fète de Noël · *Reid, Robert W.*
The Book · *Bedard, Michael*
The Book Maker · *Shantz, Brenda*
A Book of Birds · *Alexander, R.W.*
The Book of Life, God's Album · *Engel, Marian*
The Book of Pins · *Findley, Timothy*
The Book of the Architects · *MacLennan, Toby*
The Book That I Wrote While I Lived · *Kilodney, Crad*
The Bookkeeper's Wife · *Hosein, Clyde*
Books in the Bush · *Fines, Beatrice E.*
The Bookworm · *Plourde, Marc*
Bool Sheet on the Scissor Maniac of Mexico City · *Wexler, Steve*
Boom · *Ohs, Darrel*
Boots · *Hood, Hugh*
Booze and Music · *Kellythorne, Walt*
The Border · *Mathews, Lawrence*
Border Bride · *Shipley, Nan*
Border Crossing · *Armstrong, Sean*
Border Incident · *Lemm, Richard*
Border of Deceit · *Hazell, Mary*
The Bored Meeting · *Symons, Harry*
Borges and I · *Glennon, Lorraine*
Born Again · *Clifton, Merritt*
Born Indian · *Kinsella, W.P.*
Born of Lemmon · *Kaal, Hans*
The Born Salesman · *Grant, John*
Borne to Err in All We Do · *Smith, Carl*
The Bosom of the Family · *Rule, Jane*
The Bosun and the Blonde · *Ames, Bill*
The Bottle · *Riddell, John*
The Bottle Depot · *Adby, Zara*
The Bottle Queen · *Kinsella, W.P.*
Bottled Roses · *Madott, Darlene*
The Bottleneck · *Ross, W.E. Dan*
Bottles · *Pittman, Al*
The Bottomless Purse · *Gray, John*
The Boughwolfen · *Pittman, Al*

the boulder and the lake · *Bullock, Michael*
The Bouncer/Bus-Driving Therapy Man · *MacLaurin, Douglas*
Bound by Gold Chains · *Gardner, W.W.*
Boundary Line · *Kelly, Joy*
Boundary Lines · *Birdsell, Sandra*
A Bouquet of Roses · *Pereira, Helen*
The Bow Is Always Drawn · *Dybvig, Leslie*
The Bowl · *Taylor, Pat*
The Bowl of Fruit · *Murray, Don*
The Box · *Moldofsky, Mitch*
The Box of Fudge · *Marshall, Joyce*
A Box of July · *Moritz, Janet*
Boxes · *Linder, Norma West*
A Boy, a Girl and a Sunday · *Johnson, Myron*
The Boy and Annharrod · *McCadden, Mike*
The Boy and the Girl · *Govan, Margaret*
The Boy and the Mountain · *Carney, Robert*
The Boy and the Wolf · *Pickersgill, Edward*
The Boy in the Barn · *Bardsley, Alice*
The Boy in the Dream · *Conger, Lesley*
A Boy in the House · *de la Roche, Mazo*
The Boy in the Picture · *Clement, John*
The Boy Next Door · *Galloway, Priscilla*
The Boy Next Door · *Sangster, Hazel*
The Boy Nobody Wanted · *Russell, Sheila MacKay*
Boy on Fire · *Duggan, Robert*
Boy on His Conscience · *Mayse, Arthur*
Boy Scouts on Luau · *Hlynsky, David*
A Boy Went Out One Evening · *Morgan, Caroline*
The Boy Who Didn't Play Baseball · *MacMillan, Gail*
The Boy Who Insisted · *Ferstrom, Ken*
The Boy Who Roared Like a Man · *Dobb, Ted*
The Boy Who Smiled · *Ross, Stuart*
The Boy Who Threw a Snowball at Santa · *Young, Scott*
The Boy Who Was Lucky · *Doyle, Nancy*
The Boy Who Went on Strike · *Green, H. Gordon*
The Boy Who Wouldn't Give Up · *Green, H. Gordon*
The Boy Who Wouldn't Learn · *Green, H. Gordon*
Boy with a Wicked Tongue · *Green, H. Gordon*
[The?] Boy with the Big Tongue · *Green, H. Gordon*
'Boychick': A Fable · *Drache, Sharon*
Boylan Briggs Salutes the New Cause · *Choyce, Lesley*
Boys and Girls · *Munro, Alice*
Boys at Play · *Moore, J.P.*
A Boy's Castle · *Mann, Kay*
Boys Will Be Boys · *Davidson, Carol E.*
Boysenberry Jam · *Waltner-Toews, David*
The Bracelet · *Williams, John*
A Bracelet and a Telegram · *Chevraux, Sharleen*

Brackley and the Bed · *Selvon, Samuel*
The Braggart · *George, Thomas*
Brain Dust · *Cohen, Matt*
The Brand · *Kishkan, Theresa*
Brandywine · *Leggett, Catharine*
Brassières · *Sutherland, Fraser*
Brave Harvest · *Knox, Olive*
The Brave Music of a Distant Drum · *Baker, Rita*
Brave New Year · *Madison, Grant*
Bravery · *Russell, Ted*
The Bravest Boat · *Lowry, Malcolm*
Bread · *Atwood, Margaret*
Bread and Butter · *Barker, Bessie M.*
Bread and Jam · *Bailey, Don*
The Bread That Didn't Return · *Green, H. Gordon*
Bread-Making · *Hodgins, Norris*
The Break · *Wynand, Derk*
Break and Enter · *Rooke, Leon*
Break for Freedom · *Walker, David*
A Break for Lester · *Reinhardt, Jean*
Break No Hearts This Christmas · *Engel, Marian*
Breakdown · *Arscott, David*
Breakfast at Minnie's Pit · *Schroeder, Andreas*
Break-In · *Holland, Kerry*
Breaking · *Halliday, David*
Breaking Bread in Jerusalem · *Waddington, Miriam*
Breaking Free · *Bankier, William*
Breaking Horses · *Butala, Sharon*
Breaking Off · *Hood, Hugh*
Breaking Point · *Macdonald, Carmel*
Breakthrough · *Williamson, Anne*
Break-Up · *Beech, Doreen*
Breathing · *Sutherland, Fraser*
Brébeuf · *Browne, Paul Cameron*
The Breed · *Salter, C.R.B.*
Brian Tattoo: His Life and Times · *Gibson, Margaret*
Brian the Bull · *McLean, Rachel*
The Briar Way · *Bedard, Michael*
Bricks, Boards and Books · *Harvey, Jennifer A. Becks*
The Bride Elect · *Stewart, Jocelyn*
Bride of the Vodyanyk · *Derevanchuk, Gordon*
The Bride's Crossing · *O'Hagan, Howard*
The Bridesmaid · *Beck, Rosalie*
The Bridge · *Ferrier, Ian*
The Bridge Builder · *Higham, C.M.M.*
The Bridge Builders · *Briffett, Isabel*
The Bridge of Fear · *Bruneau, Bernard*
The Bridge on the Scraw · *Coney, Michael G.*
The Bridgeman · *Henderson, Catherine*
Bridges · *Huggan, Isabel*

Brief · *Porkolab, Gyorgy*
Brief Candle · *Friesen, Victor Carl*
A Brief Discourse on Human Affections · *Green, Galen*
Brief Encounter · *Anonymous*
A Brief His-Story of Mental Health · *Laturnus, Ted*
Brief Love Affair · *Nolan, Gladys*
Bright, Agile, Impassable and Subtle · *McNamara, Eugene*
Bright Flowers for Elsie · *Cash, Gwen*
Bright Green Plants · *Fagan, Cary*
Bright Wire · *Schoemperlen, Diane*
Brightest Star in the Dipper · *Garner, Hugh*
The Brilliant Mr. Budge · *Meyers, Leonard W.*
Bring Back the Bands, Please · *Hekkanen, Ernest*
Bringing Home the Bacon · *Reykdal, Art*
The Brink of Destruction · *Gourlay, Elizabeth*
The Broad Back of the Angel · *Rooke, Leon*
The Broadcaster · *Yates, J. Michael*
Broadway Matinée · *Hershorn, Ruth*
The Brocade Sofa · *Fines, Beatrice E.*
Broken · *Black, Karen*
The Broken Bottle: A Suicide for Barbara Ann Shea · *Thompson, Kent*
Broken Field · *Keyes, John*
A Broken Game · *Boyarsky, Abraham*
Broken Glasses · *MacSween, R.J.*
The Broken Globe · *Kreisel, Henry*
The Broken Hand · *Gant, Eric W.*
Broken Harmony · *Taylor, Richard*
The Broken Hole · *Schoutsen, John*
Broken Horn · *Gillese, John Patrick*
The Broken Reed · *Howard, Richard*
Broken Teeth · *Lee, Sky*
The Brook · *Briffett, Isabel*
Brother, Can You Spare a Crime? · *Bankier, William*
Brother and Sister · *Rule, Jane*
Brother André, Père Lamarche and My Grandmother Eugenie Blagdon · *Hood, Hugh*
Brother Dael's New Year · *Virgo, Sean*
Brother Fugitive · *Steffler, George*
Brother Jim and the Case of the Vanishing Ham · *Morris, Doris M.*
Brother Oedipus · *Watson, Sheila*
Brother Simon · *Dow, John*
Brotherly Love · *Johnston, George*
Brothers · *Perks, Megan*
Brothers by the Wall · *Hutton, William Finlay*
The Brothers Hurst · *Yost, Elwy*
Brothers - A Story with a Moral · *Staples, Ralph S.*
Brough, as in Rough · *Bankier, William*
Broward Dowdy · *Blaise, Clark L.*
Brown Coat · *Clarke, Gwendoline P.*
the brown dog · *Heath, Terence*

714

Brown Penny · *Cooke, Walter*
Bruno · *O'Connell, Dorothy*
A Brush with Manet · *Purdy, Brian*
The Bubbe; the Zayde · *Rosenfeld, Rita*
Bubble Bath for Two · *Hibberd, Dale*
The Bubble · *Briffett, Isabel*
The Bubble Gum King · *Mitchell, Ken*
Bubeh Meisse · *Fielden, Charlotte*
Bucket of Roses · *Barnard, Leslie Gordon*
Buckshot for Strays · *Lifeso, E.L.*
Buddha at the Laundromat: A Parable · *Choyce, Lesley*
Buddies · *Narvey, Fred*
Budgets · *Hodgins, Norris*
Buffalo and Fish Pie · *Schroeder, Elizabeth G.*
Buffalo Hunt · *Williams, David*
Buffalo Jump · *Kinsella, W.P.*
Bufo, a Grandmother Toad · *Mulkin, Grace*
The Bufords · *Spencer, Elizabeth*
The Bug · *Thompson, Don*
Bug-Bearing for Fun and Profit · *Howard, Randy*
The Bugler of Nippombara · *Green, H. Gordon*
Build Me a Monument · *Baldridge, Mary Humphrey*
The Builders · *Dales, Walter A.*
Building a Fire Under Peterson · *Rooke, Leon*
The Building of the Ship · *Freiberg, Stanley*
The Building of the Wall · *Freiberg, Stanley*
The Building of Yankel Rabinowitz · *Steinfeld, J.J.*
Bukowski Sunrise · *Holley, T.M.*
the bull · *Bullock, Michael*
Bull and Tulip · *Robson, Merrilee*
Bull Loose · *Green, H. Gordon*
The Bull Moose · *Russell, Ted*
The Bull Moose · *Russell, Ted*
Bull Neck · *Theriault, Yves*
The Bulldogs All Have Rubber Teeth · *Korber, Freda*
The Bulldozer That Went Away · *Randall, Nora Delahunt*
A Bullet for Perlmutter · *Steinfeld, J.J.*
Bullets Are for Catching · *Nicks, W. Frederick*
Bulls of the Resurrection · *Lowry, Malcolm*
The Bully · *Reaney, James*
Bully on the Beach · *Mayse, Arthur*
The Bullying Ones · *Sears, Dennis T. Patrick*
The Bundle · *Bereska, Brigette*
Bungalo and the Python · *Bunner, Freda Newton*
The Bungalow · *Alford, Norman*
Bunk Beds · *O'Connell, Dorothy*
The Bunkhouse · *Cook, Michael*
Bunkhouse Betty · *Jackson, Pat*
Burgled · *Rothschild, Robert P.*
The Burgundy Weekend · *Gallant, Mavis*

The Burial · *Dempster, Barry*
Burial of the Dead · *Fawcett, Brian*
The Buried Letter · *Ekbaum, Salme*
The Buried Life · *McCauley, Glenn*
The Burn · *McWhirter, George*
Burned · *Young, Debbie*
The Burning · *Schleich, David*
Burning Bright · *Sifton, John*
Burning Chrome · *Gibson, William*
The Burning Crusade of Andrew McNorran · *French, Doris*
Burning Man · *Blaise, Clark L.*
The Burnt Forest · *MacSween, R.J.*
Burnt Roses · *MacRae, Jacquelyn*
Burnt Umber · *Ehrlich, Hilari*
Burst of a Birdheart · *Itani, Frances*
The Bus · *Peters, Cliff*
Bus #77 · *Huggan, Isabel*
Bus Number 6 · *Smith, David John*
Bus Ride · *Bruns, Ina*
Bus Trapping in Ottawa · *Setkowicz, Libby*
Bus Trip to Almora · *Ogle, Robert Joseph*
Bush · *Smith, Edmund Arthur*
Bush Angel · *Knox, Olive*
Bushwhacker's Christmas · *Gillese, John Patrick*
Bushy: Tale of a Squirrel · *Kemeny, Eva*
Business · *Julian, Marilyn*
The Business Manager · *Redant, Julia*
The Business of the Blinds · *Daem, Mary and Deeder, Peg*
A Business Relationship · *Valgardson, W.D.*
A Bust for Henry · *Young, Scott*
Buster · *Carisbrooke, Stephen*
Buster and the Blue Dahlia · *Dyba, Kenneth*
Busy as a Beaver · *Wood, Kerry*
Busy Signal · *Bloom, David*
'But ...' · *MacMillan, Gail*
But Always April · *Madison, Grant*
But for the Grace of God · *LeBourdais, Isabel*
But I Won't Marry You My Pretty Maid · *Stein, Rhoda Elizabeth Playfair*
But in a Fiction, in a Dream of Passion ... · *Lassen, Judy*
But Not for Keeps · *Coates, Eleanor*
But Not in Anger ... · *Sloan, Doug*
But Thou Go By · *Powell, Marilyn*
But You · *Can Get a Man with a Gun* · *Cadogan, Elda*
But You Ought to Ask the Bride · *Story, Gertrude*
The Butchering · *Carlton, Edna P.*
The Butchers · *Hannant, Larry*
A Buttercup for Uncle Lennie · *Birch-Jones, Sonia*
Butterflies · *Kinsella, W.P.*
The Butterfly · *Kraintz, Dona*
The Butterfly Ball · *McClung, Nellie*

The Butterfly Ward · *Gibson, Margaret*
The Butternut Tree · *Brennan, Reg*
Buttonhold · *Zend, Robert*
The Buttonhole · *Littlejohn, Helen*
Buying a Watch for Billy's Christmas · *Major, Kevin*
The Buzz Barrett Story · *Bruns, Ina*
The Buzzer · *Doyle, Nancy*
Bwala Li Mwesu · *Saunders, Charles R.*
By a Frozen River · *Levine, Norman*
By Any Other Name: A Holiday Romance · *Buckler, Ernest*
By Power of Scalpel · *Day, Gene*
By the Eyes You Can Always Tell · *Rosenfeld, Rita*
By the Light of the Heliotrope Barbell · *Kent, Valerie*
By the Neck Until Dead · *Bankier, William*
By the Richelieu · *Levine, Norman*
By the River · *Hodgins, Jack*
By the Sea · *Cairns, A.T.*
Bye Baby Bunting · *Rosta, Helen J.*

C.N. - Northern Route · *Fergusson, Anne*
The C.P.R. Clairvoyant · *Van Dyck, Henry Clayton*
The Cab Business · *Potrebenko, Helen*
Cabbagetown Overkill: The Story of One Man's Search for a Scene of the Ultimate
Crime · *McCubbin, Terrence*
The Cabin · *Plaskett, John*
Cabin at the Wolf · *Dehaas, David*
Cabin Fever · *Miles, Christine*
Cabin in the Clearing · *Spicer, Irene T.*
Cabines Sur Mer · *Jelliffe, Vaughn*
The Cactus Trail to Canada · *Vorres, Ian*
The Cad · *Warr, Ernest*
The Caddy Pervert · *MacLaurin, Douglas*
Cadence · *Bruce, Charles T.*
Cadillac at Atonement Creek · *Woodward, Kathryn*
Cadillacs and Chevies Don't Mix · *Hekkanen, Ernest*
The Cafe · *Finlay, Michael*
Café Le Dog · *Cohen, Matt*
Cafe Society · *Vanderhaeghe, Guy*
Cafe Society: Lunch with Louis at Le Rendezvous · *Weil, Alexandra*
The Cage · *Nowlan, Alden*
Caged In · *Truss, Jan*
Cages · *Vanderhaeghe, Guy*
The Cahershannon Heresy · *Simpson, Leo*
CAIN[n] · *Hargreaves, H.A.*
Cajolery · *Gallant, Cathy*
Cakes, Piles and Pianos · *LeCorre, Kathryn*
Cal Teck's Last Stand · *Lownsbrough, John*
Calaban's Last Journey · *Grace, Gregory*
Calamitous Courtship · *Armstrong, Patricia*

California, Here I Come · *Stein, David Lewis*
The Call · *Skilbeck, William*
A Call in December · *Nowlan, Alden*
A Call in the Fog · *Brandis, Maxine*
Call Me Anytime · *Brown, Joy*
Call Me Belladonna · *Rooke, Leon*
Call Me Merrydell · *Kidney, Dorothy Boone*
Call of the Sea · *Roddan, Samuel*
Call Off Your Cats · *Wuorio, Eva-Lis*
Call Ruby · *Hurley, Richard A.*
Callekato's Routine of Waking Up · *Walz, Reinhard*
The Caller · *Margoshes, Dave*
Calling Home · *Summers, Merna*
The Calling of the Loons · *Laurence, Margaret*
Calmly, Calmly · *Todd, Lynn*
Calves · *Hodgins, Norris*
Calypso in London · *Selvon, Samuel*
Calypsonian · *Selvon, Samuel*
Camilla · *Dominskyj, Marianne*
Camp Chiclet · *O'Connell, Dorothy*
Camp Daze · *Graham, Ferne*
The Camp Director's Wife · *Ross, Gary*
A Campaign for Mr. Arrowman · *Sheldon, Michael*
Campaigns · *Krause, Pat*
Camping Trip · *Roberts, Kevin*
Can I Count You In? · *Faessler, Shirley*
A Can of Paint · *Wolczuk, Alice*
'Can We Help'? · *Burnell, Ethel D.*
Can You Wear Earrings in the Woods? · *Randall, Nora Delahunt*
Canada Made Me · *Levine, Norman*
Canada's Crucial Role in Europe · *Anonymous*
Canada's National Magazine · *Gilbert, Gerry*
Canada - The Land of Golden Opportunity · *McKay, Jacqueline*
Canadiaiana · *Harrison, Elizabeth*
Canadian Culture · *Kinsella, W.P.*
A Canadian Custom · *Kilodney, Crad*
The Canadian Diaspora · *Avery, Martin*
A Canadian Education · *Cook, Hugh*
A Canadian Parable · *Hutchison, Bruce*
The Canadian Road · *Daniels, D.S.*
The Canadian Saga · *Hutchison, Bruce*
A Canadian Story · *Kouhi, Elizabeth*
A Canadian Upbringing · *Levine, Norman*
Canadian Writers in Bulgaria · *Livesay, Dorothy*
Canary Bird · *Schonfeld, Marcia*
Cancer of the Testicles · *Evanier, David*
The Candidate · *Pacey, Desmond*
Candles · *Priest, Robert*
Cane Is Bitter · *Selvon, Samuel*
Canine Sun · *Dabydeen, Cyril*

Canoe Trip · *Gudjonson, Eric*
Canyon · *Johnson, Linda Wikene*
A Cap for Steve · *Callaghan, Morley*
Cape Breton Is the Thought-Control Center of Canada · *Smith, Ray*
Cape Breton Picnic · *MacKinnon, Lilian Vaux*
Capistrano's Last Stand · *Waverman, George*
Capital · *Valgardson, W.D.*
Capital Punishment: Notes of a Willing Victim · *Riordan, Michael*
The Caprice · *Wuorio, Eva-Lis*
The Caprice Hotel · *Harris, Janice*
The Captain · *Hayward, Colin J.*
Captain Earmuff and His Little Party · *Ross, Stuart*
Captain Joe · *McCormack, Eric*
Captain of the Comet · *Shipley, Nan*
Captain Rafferty · *Garner, Hugh*
Captain Stephen Hawco · *Janes, Percy*
The Captain Wore His Scarf · *Davidson, John*
The Captain's Decision · *Sturdy, John Rhodes*
The Captain's Son · *Rikely, Dan*
The Captive · *Mitchell, Nick*
The Captive Niece · *Gallant, Mavis*
The Car · *Bell, Don*
A Car Is Just Like an Eating Baby · *Dabydeen, Cyril*
Car of Maroon · *Story, Gertrude*
Caramat Train Wreck · *Skinner, Norman Doc*
Caraway · *Kinsella, W.P.*
Caraway Seed Cake · *Lynn, Eunice*
Carcajou · *Harrington, Michael F.*
the carcasses · *Bullock, Michael*
The Card in the Window · *Hamilton, D.E.*
The Card Player · *Benstead, Steven*
Cardboard Soldier · *McDougall, Colin M.*
The Cardinal's Levee · *Ryan, Patricia*
'Careless Memories' · *Guillet, Valerie*
Careless Talk · *Gallant, Mavis*
the caretaker · *Heath, Terence*
Caribou · *Moyle, Frank F.*
The Carillon · *Marriott, J. Anne*
Carnal Stings · *Sznajder, Rick*
Carnival of the Animals · *Spettigue, Douglas O.*
Carolina's Legacy · *Bolin, Janet*
Carolling When We Were Kids · *Ewing, Eleanor*
Carols for Miss Hedley · *Fines, Beatrice E.*
Carousel · *Sparks, Richard*
The Carp · *Slabotsky, David*
Carpenters and Kings · *Burley, Margaret F.*
A Carpet of Roses · *Burles, Mary Jo*
The Carpet People · *Currie, Doris M.*
A Carriage Affair · *Harding, John*
the carrot · *Bullock, Michael*

Carry Me Back to Old Hypochondria · *Trueman, Stuart*
Carter Fell · *Bowering, George*
The Caruso Recording · *Theriault, Yves*
Carved by My Knife · *Swartz, Jill*
Carving · *Eikenberry, Gary*
Casablanca Revisited · *Litman, Jane*
Case A-7 · *Dewdney, Christopher*
The Case Is Altered · *Dragland, Stan*
The Case of Cassandra Dop · *Marshall, Joyce*
A Case of Conflict · *Russell, Sheila Mackay*
A Case of Conformity · *Skelton, Robin*
A Case of Innocence · *Henriques, Alexandra*
A Case of Non-Involvement · *Duncan, Leslie*
A Case of Sour Grapes · *Olson, Ruth*
The Case of the 7 Note Song · *Havelock, Ray*
The Case of the Friendly Teller · *Simpson, Leo*
The Case of the Gray Moose · *Theriault, Yves*
The Case of the Infrequent Visitor · *Oldham, Robert*
The Case of the Royal Arctic Theatrical · *Oldham, Robert*
The Case of the Shattered Eggshell · *Johansen, John*
The Case of the Silent Witness · *Ross, W.E. Dan*
The Case of the Stiff-Necked Saints · *Green, H. Gordon*
The Case of the Trout in the Milk · *Matthews, William*
The Case of the Yellow Corpse · *McCarthy, Len*
Casebook · *Ross, W.E. Dan*
Cash-Flow Cameron · *MacLaurin, Douglas*
Cashing a Cheque in Cabbagetown · *Plantos, Ted*
Cassia · *Smith, Kathlyn*
Cassie · *Copeland, Ann* [pseudonym]
Castle in the Snow · *Ross, W.E. Dan*
The Castle of Patrick O'Flynn · *Boyle, Harry J.*
Castles · *Lyn, Dennis*
Casualties · *Wing, Sandy*
the cat · *Bullock, Michael*
Cat #400 · *Avery, Martin*
Cat and Me · *Stein, Rhoda Elizabeth Playfair*
Cat Call · *Rebus, Philip*
The Cat Came Back · Margoshes, Dave
Cat in My Irises · *Elgaard, Elin*
Cat in the Room · *Talbot, Charlene*
The Cat Killer · *Rooke, Leon*
The Cat Screamed · *Drachman, Wolf*
The Cat That Went to Trinity · *Davies, Robertson*
The Cat with a Woman's Eyes · *Green, H. Gordon*
The Cat with the Yaller Face · *Pollett, Ron*
Cat Women on Mars · *Denisoff, Dennis*
Catalogue Christmas · *Bushell, Sidney*
The Catalyst · *McConnell, William C.*
Catapult to the Stars · *Coney, Michael G.*

The Catch · *Guppy, Steve*
Catch a Nigger by the Toe · *Samotie, Bill*
Catcher in the Wry · *Ritter, Erika*
Catching Hell · *Foster, Graeme*
Catharsis · *Collier, Diana G.*
The Cat-Hater · *Harvey, Jennifer A. Becks*
The Cathedral · *Battistuzzi, Richard*
Catherine and the Winter Wheat · *Hughes, Philip B.*
Catholics, Catholics, Ring the Bell · *Gibbs, Robert*
Cat's Best Friend · *Beachey, Anne*
Cats Have Kittens · *Glover, Douglas H.*
The Cat's Rat · *Smyth, Donna E.*
Catskinners Paradise · *Johnson, G. Bertha*
the cattle · *Bullock, Michael*
Cattle Call · *Bankier, William*
The Cattle Walker · *van Norman, Brian*
Caught in the Web · *Sawyer, Robert*
Causation · *Weinzweig, Helen*
Cause for Alarm · *Fontaine, Patricia*
The Cause for War · *Fox, Gail*
Caution: Causes Drowsiness and Dulls the Senses · *Shore, Michael M.J.*
Cautionary Fable · *Powell, Derek Reid*
Cave of the Mother of the Moon · *MacLennan, Toby*
the cavern · *Bullock, Michael*
The Ceiling Game · *Taylor, Angus M.*
The Celebrated Case of Brother Sebastian · *Szanto, George*
Celebration · *Conly, Susan*
Celebration on East Houston Street · *Ludwig, Jack*
Celia Behind Me · *Huggan, Isabel*
Celina · *Shepherd, R.W.*
Cell Walls · *Welland, Jon*
The Cellars of Buffalo Junction · *Armstrong, Patricia*
Cement · *Choyce, Lesley*
Cemetery · *Shaw, Joan Fern*
The Cemetery Club · *Blostein, David*
Centennial Comes to Purple Hill · *Hendrickson, Magda*
Centennial Portrait · *Euringer, Fred*
The Centipede's Dilemma · *Robinson, Spider*
Ceramic Meanderings · *Freeman, Michael*
The Ceremony of Innocence · *Gordon, George*
Ceremony of Innocence · *Brandis, Marianne*
A Certain Age · *Miller, Kathleen D.*
A Certain Light · *Bruce, John*
Certified Undesirable · *Spence, Ian A.*
The Cesar Franck Story · *Kilodney, Crad*
C'est Drôle la Langue Anglaise · *Bell, Don*
C'est Voulu · *Bankier, William*
Chad: Its Rise, Its Age, Its Fall · *Hawthorn, Margaret*
Chaddeleys and Flemings: 1. Connection · *Munro, Alice*
The Chair · *Boyarsky, Abraham*

Chair by the Window · *Beckett, Judith*
The Chair-Man Speaks · *Smyth, Donna E.*
Chaleur Corner · *Wallace, Carl*
The Chalice of the Lord's Supper · *McConnell, Alice*
The Chalk Circle · *Bedard, Michael*
The Challenge · *Butts, Ed P.*
Chameleon · *Schermbrucker, Bill*
Champagne Barn · *Levine, Norman*
Champion Takes Inventory · *Ross, Stuart*
Champions · *Fawcett, Brian*
A Chance Encounter · *Gough, Bruce*
Chance Meeting · *Sheldon, Michael*
Chance Meeting in an Elevator · *McLaren, Floris*
The Chancers · *Porter, Eugene Gordon*
A Change in Circumstances or Fanny's Courtship: A Romance · *Cooper, Mel*
A Change of Air · *Pletz, Joan*
A Change of Heart · *Grimster, Ellen*
A Change of Life · *Margoshes, Dave*
Change of Locale · *Sturdy, John Rhodes*
Change of Perspective · *Bauchman, Rosemary*
A Change of Scene · *McNamara, Eugene*
Change of Scenery · *Hodgins, Jack*
A Change of Season · *Royston, Carol*
Change of Viewpoint · *Woods, Patricia*
The Changeless Things · *Stein, Rhoda Elizabeth Playfair*
The Changeling · *Hood, Hugh*
Changes · *Gilliam, John*
Changing for the Worse · *McLean, Anne*
The Changing of Enoch · *Briffett, Isabel*
The Changing of the Fossils on Parliament Hill · *Ward, Norman*
Channel of Violence · *O'Reilly, Patrick*
A Chant for One Voice · *Horwood, Harold*
Chantal · *Filip, Raymond*
Chapperwell's Secret · *McKinley, Philip*
The Character and I · *Mills, Elizabeth*
Character Sketch · *Beattie, Elizabeth*
Characters · *Munro, Alice*
Charlie · *Richards, David Adams*
Charlie Chan and Number One Son · *Stein, David Lewis*
Charlie Cirabossie: A Very Important Man · *Thorne, Lynne*
Charlie's Dog · *Spettigue, Douglas O.*
Charlotte · *Redant, Philip D.*
The Charlottetown Banquet · *Davies, Robertson*
Charm · *Jackson, J. Graham*
Charmaine and the Wizard · *Howard, Randy*
The Char-Person · *Smart, William J.*
Charting a New Course · *Chappell, Constance*
Chasers · *Manson, Sharon*
Chasing After Carnivals · *Hekkanen, Ernest*
Chassidic Song · *Kreisel, Henry*

A Chat with God · *Lalor, George T.*
Chatham's Flying Saucer · *Fraser, Raymond*
Chaws · *Vaughan, J.B.*
The Cheat · *Bird, Will R.*
Checkers · *Mackenzie, Alan*
Checkpoint · *Hazell, Mary*
Cheering Section · *Govan, Margaret*
The Cheese Stands Alone · *Beghtol, Claire*
Cheiron Came · *Drepaul, Joe*
Chemical Row · *Grieveson, Brian*
Chenille · *Smith, Steve*
The Cheque · *Green, H. Gordon*
Cherries · *Kirk, Donald*
Cherries Jubilee · *Bowie, Douglas*
The Cherry-Wood Chair · *Barker, Bessie M.*
The Chess Master · *Steinfeld, J.J.*
The Chess Match · *Hood, Hugh*
The Chess Player · *Chevreau, Jonathan*
Chestnuts in the Sky · *St. Jacques, Elizabeth*
Chez le Notaire · *Deblois, Diane*
Chez Nous · *Harvey, Jennifer A. Becks*
Chez Sergei · *Nemiroff, Greta Hofmann*
The Chicken Dancer · *Kinsella, W.P.*
Chicken Peddlar · *Rosenfeld, Rita*
Chicken Soup · *Birch-Jones, Sonia*
The Chicken Story Part V · *Itter, Carole*
The Chicken Who Thought He Was People · *Branden, Vicki*
Chickens · *Hodgins, Norris*
Chief Mahnomen · *Knox, Olive*
A Child, One Night · *Cowie, Marilyn*
Child · *Brown, Jean E.*
The Child and the Boy · *Richards, David Adams*
A Child Bride Grows Up · *Lenoir-Arcand, Christine*
Child in Love · *McConnell, Alice*
The Child Is Now · *Atwood, Margaret*
Child Language · *Goulden, Alban*
Child of Fury · *Fromhold, J.*
The Child Who Was Free · *Loisier, Mary Jane*
A Childhood Incident · *Hood, Hugh*
The Children · *Booth, Luella S.*
The Children and the Pedant · *Jasper, Lori*
The Children Are Crying · *Birdsell, Sandra*
The Children Green and Golden · *Metcalf, John*
The Children of Pan · *Jakober, Marie*
The Children's Hour · *Stilwell, Arthur*
A Child's Flower · *Humphries, Tom*
A Child's Story of the Hill · *Dennis, Ian*
The Child - The Man · *Tipping, M.T.*
China · *Lowry, Malcolm*
China Bay · *MacFarlane, Duncan*

The China Shepherdess · *Beresford-Howe, Constance*
The China Teapot · *Fines, Beatrice E.*
the chinaman · *Heath, Terence*
La Chincha · *Rikki [Erica Ducornet]*
Chinchilla for a Hot Afternoon · *Hlynsky, David*
The Chinese Coat · *Sparling, Sharon*
A Chinese Fable · *Kelly, Gary*
Chinese Freemasons and the Dart Coon Club · *Ker, H.*
Chinese Gold · *Avery, Martin*
The Chinese Lover · *Coulbeck, Art G.*
The Chinese Madonna · *Gaul, Avery*
The Chinese Music Box · *Koerte, Helen*
The Chinook · *Mahoney, Tracy*
Chinook Christmas · *Wiebe, Rudy H.*
Chip on the Shoulder · *Green, H. Gordon*
The Chipmunk · *Grantmyre, Barbara*
A Chippy Little Number · *Cameron, Donald*
The Chiseler · *Kadey, Carroll*
[A?] Chit of a Girl · *Barnard, Margaret E. and Barnard, Leslie Gordon*
The Chocolate Easter Rabbit · *McCallum, Gary*
The Choice · *Caverhill, Austin*
The Choirboy · *Bankier, William*
Choose Your Partners · *Buckler, Ernest*
Choosing a Second Career · *Narvey, Fred*
The Chord That Was Lost · *Hicks, John V.*
The Chowkidar · *Cowasjee, Saros*
The Christened · *P[onomarenko], F[rancis]*
The Christening · *Bergren, Myrtle*
The Christening at Dhu Varren · *Green, H. Gordon*
Christening for Uncle Ethan · *Sturdy, John Rhodes*
A Christian Education · *Spencer, Elizabeth*
Christmas · *Livesay, Dorothy*
Christmas and Mr. Smith · *Asquith, Glenn H.*
Christmas and White Roses · *Guderian, Evelyn*
Christmas at Home · *Barnard, Margaret E. and Barnard, Leslie Gordon*
Christmas at Sulpher for the Lonely Brigade · *Hughes, Robert*
The Christmas Bird · *Backmeyer, LaDonna Breidford*
Christmas Blues · *Korowiakowski, Eugeniuz*
Christmas Came to Pearl Street · *Elford, Jean*
Christmas Candle · *Conn, Desmond*
The Christmas Candlestick · *Brandis, Marianne*
The Christmas Card Hustler · *McFadden, David*
A Christmas Carol · *Liggett, C.J.*
A Christmas Carol Update · *Nicol, Eric*
The Christmas Carols' Annual Meeting · *Elianna [pseudonym]*
Christmas Comes to Deer Lick Creek · *Browne, Tom*
Christmas Comes to Nor'East Tickle · *Bond, F. Fraser*
Christmas Concert · *Wood, Kerry*
Christmas Crisis · *Russell, Sheila MacKay*
The Christmas Deer · *Cosier, Anthony*

Christmas Eve · *Sing, Gerri*
Christmas Eve Decision · *Ross, W.E. Dan*
A Christmas Eve in the Thirties · *Boyle, Harry J.*
A Christmas Fable · *Rooke, Leon*
A Christmas Fantasy · *Langevin, John*
A Christmas for Grandmother · *Nowlan, Michael O.*
The Christmas Gift · *McLean, Rachel*
Christmas Goose · *Grantmyre, Barbara*
Christmas Grace · *Malley, Michael*
The Christmas Hat · *MacKinnon, Lilian Vaux*
Christmas Homecoming · *Anonymous*
The Christmas House · *Peterson, Phyllis Lee*
Christmas Is an Uproar · *Green, H. Gordon*
Christmas Is for Secrets · *Beck, Norma Jean*
Christmas Is the Spirit · *Green, H. Gordon*
Christmas Lay Away · *Morritt, Hope*
Christmas Letter · *Young, Scott*
Christmas Lost and Found · *Cohen, Matt*
Christmas Magic · *Armstrong, Patricia*
Christmas Memories · *Bushell, Sidney*
Christmas Miracle · *Stein, Rhoda Elizabeth Playfair*
A Christmas Mouse · *Helwig, David*
The Christmas of Donegan's Brawl · *Green, H. Gordon*
The Christmas of the Last Partridge · *Green, H. Gordon*
Christmas on Manitoulin · *Linder, Norma West*
Christmas on the Flats · *Curran, Kitty*
A Christmas Pageant · *Euringer, Fred*
Christmas Patrol · *Haig-Brown, Roderick*
Christmas Presents · *Govan, Margaret*
Christmas Problem for Ruff · *Ross, [W.E.] Dan and Ross, Charlotte*
Christmas Revisited · *Hunter, Mary Alice*
The Christmas Star · *Asquith, Glenn H.*
A Christmas Story · *Brown, Miranda*
The Christmas Story I Tell My Children · *Green, H. Gordon*
The Christmas Tree · *Halonen, H.*
Christmas Under a Pale Green Sky · *Novak, Barbara*
The Christmas-Cake Doll · *Gillespie, Joan*
Christo Mente Maria · *Woodman, Marion*
Christopher · *Drayton, Geoffrey*
Chrome Yellow · *Smyth, Donna E.*
Chronic Offender · *Robinson, Spider*
A Chronicle · *Crerar, T.H.*
The Chronicle of Alexandra Atherton · *Clayton, Thomas*
Chronicles · *Bauer, Nancy*
Chrysalid · *Rosenfeld, Rita*
Chrysanthemum Transplanted · *Beattie, Jessie L.*
The Chub · *Green, H. Gordon*
Chuck Covered the Churches · *Reynolds, Helen Mary Greenwood Campbell*
The Church and the Union · *MacKenzie, Wayne O.*
Church Going Down · *Green, H. Gordon*

Churchgoin' · *Russell, Ted*
The Churchill Touch · *Ward, Norman*
The Cicada and the Cockroach · *McWhirter, George*
Ciceronia Graduateth · *Atwood, Joan-Mary*
Cicero's Disease · *Morrell, Dave*
The Cider Barrel · *Stambaugh, Sara*
Cigarette · *Vulpe, Nicola*
A Cigarette Holder, a Paycheque and Henry at the Ritz · *Smith, David John*
The Cigarette Pack · *Cook, Gregory M.*
Cimon · *Swift, B.A.*
Cinderella Couldn't Lose · *Stein, Rhoda Elizabeth Playfair*
Cinema · *Smith, Steve*
The Circle · *Burns, Mary*
The Circle of a Jumper · *Davidson, John Hugh*
Circle of Ashes · *Coulbeck, Art G.*
Circle of Confusion · *Dronyk, Levi*
Circle of Fifths · *Weinzweig, Helen*
The Circle of Love · *Avery, Martin*
The Circle Unbroken · *Lyman, Katharine*
The Circular Lady · *Daniel, Michael*
Circus · *Svingen, Anne*
Citizens of That Country · *Dobb, Ted*
Citrus Flaked Sunshine · *Barrington, John*
City Boys Are Different · *Walker, Joan*
The City Cousin · *Marriott, J. Anne*
City Date · *Cook, Gregory M.*
City Dreams · *MacKay, Jed*
City Girl's Game · *Young, Scott*
City of Angus · *MacMillan, Angus*
The City of Eyes · *MacSween, R.J.*
The City of the Dead · *Anonymous*
City the Insects Invade · *Browne, Paul Cameron*
The City Underground · *Thibaudeau, Colleen*
City Wedding · *Summers, Merna*
Civilities · *Rooke, Leon*
The Civilizing Influence · *Barry, P.S.*
Claire · *Winter, Judy*
The Clairvoyant · *Bauer, William A.*
The Clam-Digger · *Bowering, George*
Clamtorts and Hippocrumps · *Doyle, Dan*
Clara · *Baker, Rita*
Clara Smiling · *Riches, Brenda*
Class · *Thompson, B.*
Class Extinction · *Hutchison, David*
Class of 1948 · *Levine, Norman*
Class of 1949 · *Levine, Norman*
Class of '49; Class of '54 · *Thompson, Kent*
A Class of New Canadians · *Blaise, Clark L.*
Class Warfare · *Fraser, D.M.*
Classical Portrait · *Gustafson, Ralph B.*

The Cloud-Watcher · *Dales, Walter A.*
Clove · *Nations, Opal L.*
Clown · *Cook, Hugh*
The Clown Doll · *Quaggin, Alison*
Clowns · *Weir, Terence*
The Club · *Anonymous*
A Club for Anyone · *Bruneau, H.*
Clue to Retire · *Camp, Merle*
The Clumsy One · *Buckler, Ernest*
Clyde Langdon, In Word, Indeed · *Deneau, Denis Phillippe*
C'mon, Get That Hair Cut! · *Ryan, Josephine*
The CN Tower · *McFadden, David*
the coach · *Heath, Terence*
Coach Onion · *Diamond, Marc*
The Coal-Oil Kids · *Hutchinson, Rosemary*
Coasting · *Lewis, Jennifer*
The Coat · *Sakamoto, Kerri*
Cobbler's Children · *Barford, Grace L.*
Cobra · *Green, H. Gordon*
Cobwebs and Eleanor · *Simmie, Lois*
Cock-Eyed Optimists · *O'Connell, Dorothy*
The Cocks Are Crowing · *Levine, Norman*
The Cocoon · *Briffett, Isabel*
Cocoons · *Mason, Harriet*
Coffee Break · *Baldridge, Mary Humphrey*
Coffee for the Bailiff · *Harding, Cy*
The Coffee House · *Stein, Rhoda Elizabeth Playfair*
Coffee Puzzle · *Tinsley, Ted*
The Coffee Shop · *Fisher, Peter*
Coffins · *Kemp, Penny*
The Cohen in Cowan · *Callaghan, Barry*
The Coin Tossers · *Stein, David Lewis*
The Coke Machine · *Forbes, Greg*
The Colander · *Mills, John*
Cold Christmas in Kent County · *Hughes, Philip B.*
Cold Duty Watch · *Morris, Neil K.*
A Cold Frosty Morning · *Fraser, Raymond*
The (c)old Grey Blue · *Gilbert, Gerry*
The Cold Honeymoon Wind · *Armstrong, Patricia*
Cold Weather · *Russell, Ted*
Coldpaw's Country · *Gillese, John Patrick*
Colds · *Hodgins, Norris*
Cole Slaw · *Dybvig, Leslie*
Collage · *Watson, Wilfred*
The Collapse of Empires · *Collier, Diana G.*
the collection · *Heath, Terence*
The Collector · *Clarke, Austin C.*
Collector's Choice · *Heuchert, T.M.*
Collector's Items · *Baltensperger, Peter*
A Collector's Piece · *Eames, David*

The College · *Kinsella, W.P.*
College Street Turnaround · *Christy, Jim*
College Town Restaurant · *Fraser, Raymond*
Collisions · *Steffler, George*
The Colonel · *Helwig, David*
The Colonel's Child · *Gallant, Mavis*
The Colonial Bishop's Visit · *Leitao, Lino*
The Color of My True Love's Hair · *Foster, Malcolm*
Colors · *Taaffe, Gerald*
Colour Me Doubtful · *Stein, Rhoda Elizabeth Playfair*
Colour Me Woman · *Woodbury, Mary*
The Colour of Crowd · *Luckhurst, Elizabeth*
The Coloured Pencils · *Amiel, Barbara*
Colours · *Smith, Ray*
The Colours of Summer · *Bruce, John*
The Colours of War · *Cohen, Matt*
The Colt · *Hunking, Diane*
Colt Headstone · *Foster, Dennis*
Columbus and the Fat Lady · *Cohen, Matt*
Columbus Hits the Shoreline Rag · *Dorsey, Candas Jane*
Columbus Hotel · *Fawcett, Brian*
Combination · *Reinl, Constance and Jakob, Conrad*
'Come Back Again, Johnny' · *Wood, Kerry*
Come Back Again · *Wood, Kerry*
Come Back to Grenada · *Selvon, Samuel*
Come Down, Come Down: A Faery Fantasy · *Drew, N. John*
Come Fly with Me · *McCarthy, Anne*
Come in Joey · *Ulmer, E.*
Come On and Play War · *Gibbs, Robert*
Come on Back to the Party · *Hale, Barrie*
Comedian for the Birds by Neurosurgery · *Zonko* [pseudonym]
Comedians · *Weiner, Andrew*
Comet on a String · *Wing, Sandy*
Comfort Me with Apples · *Brewster, Elizabeth*
A Comic Book Heroine · *Murphy, Sarah*
Comic Books · *Russell, Ted*
Coming Back Out · *Boon, F.M.*
Coming Home · *O'Connell, Dorothy*
The Coming of Age · *Nowlan, Alden*
The Coming of Night · *Fausett, J.C.*
The Coming of the Barbarians · *Fawcett, Brian*
The Coming of the Wild Flowers · *Boston, Stewart*
The Coming Out · *Dinniwell, Douglas*
Coming Out Is a Long Time · *Fuller, Arthur*
Coming Out Party · *Garner, Hugh*
Coming to an End · *Horwood, Harold*
Coming to Grips with Lucy · *McWhirter, George*
Coming Up Clean · *Emberly, Kenneth*
Coming Up for Air · *Milner, Philip*
Command Performance · *Hunter, Bruce*

Conversations with Ruth · *Rooke, Leon*
Conversations with Ruth: The Farmer's Tale · *Rooke, Leon*
Conversations with the Little Table · *Davies, Robertson*
The Conversion · *Ghan, Linda*
The Conversion of Willie Heaps · *Garner, Hugh*
The Convert · *Ashcroft, Sheila*
Convincing Professor Brindle About Flying Saucers · *Kilodney, Crad*
The Cook and His Wife · *Wynand, Derk*
The Cookburning Woodstove · *Bacque, James*
Cookie · *Fraser, Raymond*
The Cookie Crumbles · *Lane, William*
The Cook's Wife · *Wynand, Derk*
Cool Water · *Bailey, Arn*
Cool-Calm-and Collected · *Knapp, G.L.*
Cooling · *Glen, John*
The Coon · *Alexander, R.W.*
The Coon Caper · *Power, John*
Cooper · *Hollingshead, Greg*
Co-Owner of Theoretical 'Toutou' · *Egyedi, Bela*
Copenhagen · *Marshall, Joyce*
The Coquette · *Carroll, Elizabeth*
Corbett's Shaft · *Waterhouse, John*
Corinna · *Roberts, Dorothy*
Corky · *Cunningham, Louis Arthur*
The Corn Beef Madeleine · *Engel, Howard*
The Corner of X and Y Streets · *Wilson, Ethel D.*
The Cornfield · *Linder, Norma West*
Cornfield with Crows · *Ritchie, Ian*
Cornucopia · *Dyba, Kenneth*
Corny McCarthy's Culture Shock · *Keane, Mary*
Coronation Extra · *Paterson, O.P.*
The Corporate Secretary · *Rowland, Jon*
Corsage for Lena · *Stein, Rhoda Elizabeth Playfair*
Cosmic Strip · *Oughton, John*
The Cossack · *Valgardson, W.D.*
The Cost of Living · *Sherman, Kenneth*
Cottage Gothic · *Avery, Martin*
The Couch · *Valgardson, W.D.*
The Cougar at Old Tie Camp · *Bergren, Myrtle*
Could Be I'm Romantic · *Barnard, Leslie Gordon*
Could We Visit Grace · *Lund, Mary*
The Councillor · *Armstrong, Patricia*
The Countdown · *Trainor, Peter*
The Counter Earth · *MacLean, Kenneth*
Countercheck · *MacMaster, Rowland*
The Counterfeiter · *Howard, Richard*
Counterpart · *McQuinn, Maureen*
Counterpoint · *Creal, Margaret*
Countess Anastasia Perini-Hughes · *Vorres, Ian*
The Countess Asked Us to Tea · *McCormick, Frances*

Countess Isobel and the Torturer · *Glassco, John*
Counting Combinations · *Young, David*
Countries · *Harvor, Beth*
The Country · *McWhirter, George*
Country Club · *Batten, Jack*
The Country Doctor · *Kilodney, Crad*
Country Mouse and City Mouse · *Schilling, Rita*
Country Music · *Bell, Wade*
Country Music Singer · *Slade, Charles*
The Country of His Mother's People · *Walker, David*
The Country of the Hungry Bird · *Wiseman, Adele*
Country Style · *Harvey, Jennifer A. Becks*
A Country Weekend · *Dickinson, Mary Lou*
Coupal Street · *Byrnes, Terence*
A Couple and a Cow · *Duncan, Leslie*
A Couple of Caribou · *Steele, Harwood*
A Couple of Dimes · *Annett, R. Ross*
A Couple of Guys · *Schermbrucker, Bill*
A Couple of Quiet Young Guys · *Garner, Hugh*
The Courage Corsage · *Briffett, Isabel*
The Courage of Catherine Schubert · *Rice, Greg*
The Courage to Cry · *Wiebe, Armin*
Courting in 1957 · *Williamson, David*
The Courting of Jenny · *Stemo, L. Johanne*
Courtship · *Novak, Barbara*
The Courtship of Cassie Barrett · *Bruns, Ina*
The Courtship of Uncle Janos · *Marlyn, John*
Cousin Petherick · *Watmough, David*
Cousin Petherick & the Will · *Watmough, David*
Cousin Victor · *Ursell, Barbara*
The Covenant · *McKay, Muriel Saint*
Cowboy · *Shein, Brian*
The Cow's in the Corn · *Morris, Doris M.*
The Cow-Woman · *Allingham, Aari*
Coyote · *Johnson, Linda Wikene*
The Coyote Hunter · *Shields, Roy*
CP 59 · *Godfrey, Dave*
Crab Traps · *Gould, Jan*
The Crack · *Folkes. David*
Cracked Wheat - 1 · *Cook, Hugh*
Cracker Jack · *Speak, Dorothy*
The Crack-Up · *Kutlesa, Joso*
The Cranberry Stain · *Ammeter, A.E.*
Crane · *Jardine, Paula*
Cranes Fly South · *McCourt, Edward A.*
Cranstone enters the darkness · *Bullock, Michael*
Crawl of the Open Road · *Cooper, Bill*
The Crayfish Festival · *Granewall, Christine*
Crazy Dobbs · *Fines, Beatrice E.*
Crazy Joe · *Allan, Ted*

Crazy Old Woman · *Bankier, William*
Crazy Over Horses · *Young, Scott*
Crazy Times · *Valgardson, W.D.*
Cream. Or: The Holy Trinity in the Kingdom of Heaven · *Rikki [Erica Ducornet]*
Cream in My Coffee · *Philipp, Rowland*
Cream of the Crop · *Owen, George*
Creation Story · *McLaughlin, Peter*
The Creative Affair · *Lever, Bernice*
The Creative Crowd · *Dillon, Norma*
The Creator Has a Master Plan · *Bowering, George*
The Creator of the One-Fingered Lily · *Evanier, David*
Creature at Night · *Fitzpatrick, Brenda*
Credit · *Mitton, M. Anne*
'The Credit Shall Be Yours' · *Raddall, Thomas H.*
Cree Boy · *Price, C.B.*
Creeping Vine · *Nelson, Bert*
Creeps · *MacTavish, Grant*
Cressida Got Nothing on This Kid · *Doyle, John*
The Crevasse · *Briffett, Isabel*
The Cricket Match · *Selvon, Samuel*
A Cricket Match in Grenada · *Hood, Esther*
Crime and Sentiment · *Vizinczey, Stephen*
The Crime of Fergus McKim · *Green, H. Gordon*
Crime Wave in Pigeon Inlet · *Russell, Ted*
Criminal Lawyer · *Smythe-Chenier, Roslyn*
Crimson Lake · *Dyba, Kenneth*
Crinolines · *Speak, Dorothy*
The Crisis Summer · *Russell, Sheila MacKay*
Critical Mess · *Dodd, Alan*
The Critical Young Man · *Young, Scott*
Crocodile Across the Window · *Vorres, Ian*
the crocodile and the serpent · *Bullock, Michael*
Crocus at the Coronation · *Mitchell, W.O.*
Cromac's Charabanc · *McWhirter, George*
The Crooked Knife · *Shields, Bill*
A Crooked Rib · *Farah, Nuruddin*
Crosby · *Hood, Hugh*
The Cross and the Shopping Bag · *Holman, Lloyd*
The Cross Is Bent · *Clarke, H.D.*
The Cross of David · *Kizik, Andy*
Cross the Road · *Ball, John*
The Cross-Country Run · *Watmough, David*
Crossing · *Lange, Gerald*
Crossing France · *Gallant, Mavis*
Crossing the Rubicon · *Thomas, Audrey*
Crossroads · *Bell, John*
[The?] Crossroads · *Gillese, John Patrick*

The Crosswalk · *Fines, Beatrice E.*
Cross-Word · *Margoshes, Dave*
Crow · *Gourlay, Elizabeth*
Crow in the High Woods · *Treit, Dallas Robert*
Crow Jane's Blues · *Callaghan, Barry*
Crow Moon · *Engel, Marian*
The Crow Sits High in the Lilac Tree · *MacIntosh, Keitha K.*
Crow Takes the M's · *Munro, Jane*
Crowgull · *Greenway, Rex*
The Crowing Hen · *Green, H. Gordon*
The Crows Above the Maple Bush · *Smith, Michael*
Crows Nest · *McLeod, Murdoch*
Crucifixions · *O'Connell, Dorothy*
Crud Story · *Jordan, Godfrey*
Crudités · *Thomas, Audrey*
Cruising · *Easton, Alan*
Cruising on the Queen E · *Hutchinson, Rosemary*
Crumbs · *Summers, Anthony J.*
Crush · *Burnard, Bonnie*
A Crust of Bread · *Cameron, Eric*
the cry · *Bullock, Michael*
A Cry from the Heart · *Day, Peggy*
A Cry of Love · *Russell, Sheila MacKay*
Cry of the Heart · *Cates, Helen*
Cry 'Warlock' Softly Angel · *Harper, Richard C.*
Crying at the Kitchen Table · *O'Connell, Dorothy*
The Crying of the Loons · *Laurence, Margaret*
The Crystal Ball · *Briffett, Isabel*
Crystal Pillow · *Kleiman, Edward*
The Crystal Rose Dream · *de Creszenzo, Marianne*
The Crystal Wall · *Sladen, Kathleen*
Crystle's Tree · *Birdsell, Sandra*
Cuban Heels · *Russell, Ted*
Cubby Little Planes on Hot Windy Days · *Williams, Dave*
The Cucumber Contract · *Wood, Ted*
Cuiseine Francais [sic] · *Govier, Katharine*
The Cuish · *Edweirdo [pseudonym]*
Cuixmala · *Penner, Judith*
Cul de Sac · *Bevan, Alan*
Culinary Confusion · *Harvey, Jennifer A. Becks*
The Culler · *Scammell, A.R.*
The Culling Board · *Scammell, A.R.*
The Cultivated Carib · *Selvon, Samuel*
Culture Shock: Yesterday's Dreams, Tomorrow's Nightmares · *Jirgins, Karl E.*
Cunard · *Jones, Grania*
A Cup of Sugar · *Briffett, Isabel*
Cupboard Love · *Green, Robert*
Cupid and the Carefree Lady · *Gillese, John Patrick*
Cupid Wears No Halo · *Green, H. Gordon*
Cupid's Rifle · *Dales, Walter A.*

Cups · *Belserene, Paul*
Cups of Coffee · *Skey, Olga*
Cura Pastoralis · *Hood, Hugh*
The Curator · *Summers, M[ark]. D.*
The Cure · *Perrault, Ernest G.*
The Cure of the Lawyer's Wife · *Bartlett, Brian*
A Curiosity · *Rosqui, Carolyn*
The Curious Holdup at Longhorn Creek · *Green, H. Gordon*
A Curious Toast · *Loomer, L.S.*
Curling · *Russell, Ted*
The Curse · *Waywitka, Anne B.*
The Curse of the Bana-Gui · *Saunders, Charles R.*
The Curse of the Manitou Wapow · *Johnson, G. Bertha*
the curtain · *Bullock, Michael*
Curtain Up · *Birch-Jones, Sonia*
Curtains · *Hosein, Clyde*
The Customer Is Always Right · *Garner, Hugh*
Customer Service · *Ibbitson, John*
Cut! · *Baar, Anita*
Cut, Print · *Blaise, Clark L.*
Cut Flowers: A Rape Story · *Ford, Cathy*
Cut Me a Slice and Make It Thin · *Bailey, Don*
Cut Off at the Broken Arms · *de Barros, Paul*
The Cut-Glass Pickle Dish · *Field, L.L.*
Cutworms · *Hodgins, Norris*
cycle · *Bullock, Michael*
Cycloids: Two Wheels · *Julian, Marilyn*
'Cyclone' Taylor and the Case of Armada Base III · *Duffin, Ken*
The Cynic · *Russell, Ted*
A Cynical Tale · *Smith, Ray*
Cynthia Loves You · *Nowlan, Alden*
Cypernetics at Home · *Davis, Lois McLean*
The Czech Dog · *Hardy, W.G.*

'Daddy' · *Bailey, Arn*
Daddy Plumkin's Icebox · *Sowton, Ian*
Daddy's Gone a-Hunting · *Gilbert, Gerry*
Daedalus in the Underworld · *Allen, Peter*
The Daffodils · *Pastachuk, Pauline A.*
Daft Davie · *Nielsen, Angela F.*
The Dainties · *McCracken, Melinda*
Daisy · *Booker, Jean*
The Dam · *Ogle, Robert Joseph*
The Dam Builders · *Skinner, Norman Doc*
The Damnation of Jed Staley · *Lawrence, S.A.M.*
Dan Mills · *Walter, H. and Bond, E.H.*
Dance, Dance, Wherever You May Be · *Bauer, Nancy*
The Dance · *Nielson, Dorise*
Dance for the Devil · *McCourt, Edward A.*

Dance Me Outside · *Kinsella, W.P.*
The Dance of the Bells · *Henry, Ann Maude*
Dance of the Dolls · *Butts, Ed P.*
The Dance of the Happy Shades · *Munro, Alice*
Dance of the Happy Shades · *Munro, Alice*
The Dance of the Petrified People · *Wuorio, Eva-Lis*
Dancehall · *Haggerty, Joan*
The Dancer · *Govier, Katharine*
The Dancer and the Dance · *Young, David*
The Dancers · *Aass, Jane*
Dancers at Night · *Richards, David Adams*
'A Dancer's Foot' · *Purdy, Debra M.*
Dancing Bear · *Vanderhaeghe, Guy*
Dancing Girls · *Atwood, Margaret*
The Dancing Lesson · *Winkler, Donald*
The Dancing Master · *Dorsey, Candas Jane*
Dancing the Night Away · *Choyce, Lesley*
Dancing with Cuckoo-Gee · *Morrissette, George*
Dandelions · *Metcalf, John*
Dandy · *Janes, Percy*
danger · *Bullock, Michael*
Danger Canyon · *Findlay, David K.*
Danger in the Desert · *Anonymous*
The Dangerfields · *Mitchell, Ken*
Danger - Girl at Work · *Harvey, Jennifer A. Becks*
The Dangerous Age · *Green, H. Gordon*
Dangerous Enterprise · *Bankier, William*
Dangerous Enterprises · *Bankier, William*
Dangerous Fish · *Dempster, Barry*
Dangerous Ice · *Young, Scott*
Dangerous Mission · *Hawkins, David Geoffrey*
The Dangerous One · *Munro, Alice*
Dangerous Women · *Rooke, Leon*
The Dangers of Travel for Young Females · *Carson, Ann*
Daniel · *Horodezky, Zeporah*
Daniel III · *Steward, A.W.*
Daniel O'Keefe and Jo · *Phillips, Bluebell Stewart*
Danny Fire · *Hildebrandt, Gloria*
Danny's Mouse · *Tilberg, Mary*
Danny's Sister · *Diamond, Marc*
Dante in the Laundromat · *Swan, Susan*

The Dappled Mares · *Gudjonson, Eric*
Darby McGee's Fairy: A Subject for Ridicule · *MacArthur, F.H.*
Dark · *Hodgins, Norris*
The Dark Ages · *McCoy, Sarah*
Dark Angel, Pale Fire · *Gibson, Margaret*
Dark Armies · *Moon, Bryan*
Dark Glasses · *Hood, Hugh*
Dark Intruder · *Kilodney, Crad*
Dark Laughter · *Callaghan, Barry*

Dark Mirror · *Cameron, Eric*
Dark Murmurs from Burns Lake · *Watmough, David*
Dark Odyssey of Soosie · *Mowat, Farley*
Dark of the Storm · *Perkins, Vincent*
Dark Places · *Murdie, Donna Haggarty*
Dark Pursuit · *Cunningham, Louis Arthur*
Dark River · *Briffett, Isabel*
Dark Secrets · *Ross, Veronica*
The Dark Wood · *Hospital, Janet Turner*
The Darkest Day · *Green, H. Gordon*
The Darkest Time · *Buckler, Ernest*
darkness · *Bullock, Michael*
The Darkness inside the Mountain · *Wiebe, Rudy H.*
The Darkroom · *Lippert, Laura*
Darling I Have Found Myself in You · *Kelly, M.T.*
A Dartmoor Incident · *Blacock, Mary*
Das Engelein Kommt · *Story, Gertrude*
The Date · *Robinson, Joan*
A Date with Dora · *McLaren, Floris*
Datona's Complaint(s) · *Singer, Barnett*
Daughter of Kings · *Conger, Lesley*
Daughter of Tantaley · *Irvine, R.B.*
Daughters · *Gunnery, Sylvia C.*
Dave · *Baillie, Janice*
Davey, Dear · *Powell, Dorothy M.*
David · *Barrett, Alan John*
David in Gath · *Roskies, Ruth*
David's Wall Dream · *Richardson, Eamon*
Dawn at the Sleepy-Dust Motel · *Clark, D.M.*
The Dawn of the Gothic Period · *Mandrake, Jill*
The Dawning of Joanna or Maybe Johanna? · *Wakefield, Carol*
The Day · *van Vliet, Brigitte*
The Day After · *Hekkanen, Ernest*
The Day After Death · *Bedard, Michael*
The Day After They Shot the Bear · *de Barros, Paul*
A Day at the Front, a Day at the Border · *Harvor, Beth*
A Day at the Springs · *Brown, Robert*
A Day at the Zoo · *Hanson, Hart*
The Day Auntie Became a Zombie · *Harris, Walter*
The Day Before · *Spencer, Elizabeth*
The Day Begins · *Rooke, Leon*
A Day by the Ocean, a Night on the Town · *Ewing, Wain*
Day Eight: Morning and Afternoon · *Bain, Dena*
The Day Elvis Presley Died · *Kelly, Dermot*
Day for a Boy · *Wood, Kerry*
The Day for a Fish · *Hancock, Ronald Lee*
A Day for Remembering · *Jarvis, June N.*
The Day Frank Schoonover Died · *Bell, John*
The Day God Died for Benny · *Bergren, Myrtle*
The Day Granddad Quit the Sea · *Barnhouse, D.P.*

The Day the Boys Wore Ties · *Gower, Richard*
The Day the Computer Went Wild · *Doyle, Nancy*
The Day the Cow Ate Cake · *Holman, Lloyd*
The Day the Dog Bit Jimmy Sadler · *Loomer, Frank*
The Day the Magician Came to Town · *Lewis, David E.*
The Day the Queen Came to Minnicog · *Bacque, James*
The Day the War Ended · *Nemiroff, Greta Hofmann*
The Day They Set Out · *Harris, Beverly*
The Day They Threw Eggs at Ringo Starr · *Burrs, Mick*
The Day They Took Our Town Away · *Oman, Alan*
The Day Time Stopped Standing Still · *Hlynsky, David*
A Day to Remember · *Doyle, Nancy*
The Day Travers Lost His Pills · *Green, Robert*
A Day with a Deer, a Bear and Norah Smith · *St. Pierre, Paul*
Daybreak at Pisa: 1945 · *Findley, Timothy*
Daydreamers · *Kosar, Rochell*
Daydreams · *Matson, Marshall*
The Days Are Longer · *Hill, Kathy*
Days Before Tomorrow · *Murdoch, Benedict Joseph*
A Day's Journey · *Anonymous*
The Days of 1963, '64, '65 ... · *Robertson, Strowan*
Days of Innocence and Truth · *Leigh, Mildred*
The Days of Winter Yet to Come · *Carrier, Jean-Guy*
The Days of Youth Are Long · *Galloway, Priscilla*
A Day's Work · *Peabody, George*
Daze in the Life of Jimmy D · *Schoen, Frank N.*
De Fabrica · *Yates, J. Michael*
De Grassi Street · *van Daele, Christa*
De Z-shore · *Coleman, Victor and Young, David A.*
The Deacon's Tale · *Rooke, Leon*
Dead Centre · *Duffin, Ken*
Dead Dogs and Americans · *Stothers, Margaret*
Dead Duck! · *Young, Scott*
Dead Flies · *Langlais, Richard*
Dead Man's Coppers · *Green, H. Gordon*
Dead Man's Run · *Mayse, Arthur*
Dead Meat · *Lee, Pamela*
The Dead Sun · *MacSween, R.J.*
Dead Ted Snuff ... Puff Piece · *Hlynsky, David*
Dead to the World · *Hargreaves, H.A.*
The Deadhead · *Gardner, W.W.*
Deadline for Love · *Russell, Sheila MacKay*
The Deadly Whispers · *Ross, W.E. Dan*
The Deaf Penalty · *Ellis, Harry*
Deafiness & Daffiness · *Ellis, Harry*
The Deal · *Smith, Steve*
A Deal's a Deal · *Dobinson, George*
Dean Pretty and the Dragon · *Harris, John*
Dear Baby · *Graham, Ferne*
Dear Daria · *Kiperchuk, Helen*

Dear Earth · *Shaw, Irene*
Dear God! Eternity · *Carson, Susan*
Dear Joanne · *Bowie, Douglas*
Dear Metronome · *Reaney, James*
Dear Mom · *Rae, George Menendez*
Dear Mum, How're You Doing? · *Mosher, Edith*
Dear Santa · *Buckler, Grant*
Dear Trails in Tzityonyana · *Rooke, Leon*
Death · *Giffin, David A.*
Death and Dr. Landrin · *Freiberg, Stanley*
Death and Life · *Steffler, George*
Death and the Farmer · *Benger, JoAnne*
Death and the Maiden · *Klein, Jack*
Death at Bridport Inlet · *Harington, C.R.*
Death at Thanksgiving · *Chafe, Fred*
Death by Fetish · *Lockhart, Laurie*
Death by Seniority · *Grills, Barry W.*
Death Came and Whispered in My Ear: Live · *Margoshes, Dave*
Death in an Evacuation Camp of One Who Never Saw Japan · *Sakamoto, Kerri*
Death in Jukun · *Saunders, Charles R.*
A Death in October · *Mathews, Lawrence*
Death in the Autumn · *Carlisle, Eric*
Death in the Toy Parade · *Johnson, Vera D.*
Death Is a Bus That Can't Slow Down · *MacIntosh, Keitha K.*
Death Is Always Part of Dinner · *Campbell, Wanda Blynn*
Death of a Canadian Writer · *Kilodney, Crad*
The Death of a Cow · *Smyth, Donna E.*
The Death of a Dog · *Kyte, Ernest C.*
Death of a Dream · *Gill, Stephen*
Death of a Friend · *Cohen, Matt*
Death of a Guppy · *Cohen, Matt*
The Death of a Loving Man · *Jackson, J. Graham*
The Death of a Precocious Poet · *MacMann, Samuel Lavalliere*
Death of a President · *Sturmanis, Dona*
Death of an Unknown Hamburgher · *Davies, P.*
The Death of Arthur Rimbaud · *Mathews, Lawrence*
The Death of Buddy Holly · *McNamara, Eugene*
The Death of Charlie Bender · *Longstaff, Bill*
The Death of Comedy · *Thompson, Kent*
The Death of Justin Thatcher · *Sexton, J.D.*
The Death of Mr. Lee · *Donaldson, Allan*
A Death of One's Own · *Ludwig, Jack*
The Death of Rabbi Yoseph · *Slabotsky, David*
The Death of the Cat · *Marriott, J. Anne*
The Death of the Coyote · *Annett, William S.*
The Death of the Lute · *Cronenberg, David*
The Death of the Marionettes · *Dunn, C.A.*
Death of the Moth · *Slote, D.C.*
Death of the Wild Goose · *Boszin, Andrew*
The Death of Tom McGuire · *Kelly, M.T.*

Death on Rewind · *Penney, Lloyd*
Death Opens the Mail · *Wallach, Ira*
The Death Party · *Thompson, Kent*
Death Ray · *Keel, Joan*
Death Stood Behind Him · *Walker, David*
Death Was the Glass · *Ludwig, Jack*
Death Wore a Long Red Sock · *Elford, Jean*
Deathbed · *Virgo, Sean*
Death-Bed Gamble · *Lacy, Ed*
The Death's Head · *Appleby, Margaret A.*
Debate on a Rainy Afternoon · *Mukherjee, Bharati*
Debbie · *Randall, Elizabeth*
Deborah · *Smith, Murray*
The Debt · *Briffett, Isabel*
The Debunker · *Govan, Margaret*
Debut · *Harvey, Jennifer A. Becks*
December Bargaining · *Valgardson, W.D.*
December Nilsen · *St. Pierre, Paul*
Decent Burial · *Smith, Rosamond*
A Decent Man · *Green, H. Gordon*
The Deceptions of Marie-Blanche · *Gallant, Mavis*
Decision · *Dent, David*
Decision Day · *Stone, A.C.*
The Declaration of Independence · *Hutton, Bill*
Declarations · *Willows, Joan*
The Decline and Fall of the Emergency World-Salvation and Conquest Club ·
Fedorowicz, Jan
Declining Westward: A Romantic Outline · *Holley, T.M.*
The Decoy for Ducks · *Findlay, David K.*
Decree Absolute · *Sutherland, David*
Dedication · *Adler, Naomi*
Deep in the Heart of Christmas · *Stein, Rhoda Elizabeth Playfair*
Deep Inside Woodwards · *Harrison, Kim*
Deep Roots · *McKay, Muriel Saint*
The Deep Treasure · *Conly, Susan*
A Deer in the Forest · *Winter, Judy*
The Deer Slayer · *Branden, Vicki*
Deer Trails in Tzityonyana · *Rooke, Leon*
Deerslayer · *Helwig, David*
Defensive Moves · *Bankier, William*
Deflowered & Debauched · *Mark, Norm*
Defy the Night · *Kroetsch, Robert*
Degrees · *Thomas, Audrey*
Deirdre · *Wheeler, Frances*
Deirdre Dickens · *Konoval, Karin*
Deja Vu · *Galloway, Priscilla*
Dejeuner sur l'herbe · *Thomas, Audrey*
The Delegate from Saskatoon · *Young, Scott*
Delegate's Outing · *Sheldon, Michael*
Delia · *Blake, Dorothy*

The Delicate Balance · *Blue, Janice*
The Delicate Situation · *Green, H. Gordon*
Delinquent? · *Baum, Esther*
The Deliverance of Armand · *Rother, James*
Delta · *Enemark, Brett*
Delusions of Agriculture · *Stenson, Frederick*
Dem Ole Mosquito Blues · *Anonymous*
Demeter's Daughter · *Riches, Brenda*
The Demon · *Reid, Robert W.*
A Demon for a Decoy · *Bird, Will R.*
The Demon in My Mind · *Webb, Donna-Marie*
The Demonstration · *Mark, Norm*
Den of Thieves · *Bankier, William*
The Denial · *Auersperg, Ruth*
Denie Needs a Tonic · *Yelin, Shulamis*
Dennet & the Fiddler · *de Lint, Charles*
Dénouement · *Keith, John*
Denture Adventure · *Symons, Harry*
The Departed · *Halliday, David*
The Departure · *Cull, David*
A Dependable Guide · *Skinner, Norman Doc*
[A?] Dependable Man? · *Williamson, Rossa*
Dependents · *Wood, Ted*
Deputy Bell · *Scobie, Stephen*
The Deputy Sheriff · *Bowering, George*
Der Traum · *Pelz, Bud*
The Derrick · *Cosier, Anthony*
Dervish · *Mason, Mike*
Descent · *Enemark, Brett*
Descent of Woman · *Horwood, Harold*
Descent to a Temperate Valley · *MacFadden, Patrick*
Descriptions · *Rensby, Harry*
The Deserter · *Boyer, Agnes*
Desire · *Rikki [Erica Ducornet]*
A Desire to Dance · *Nicholson, Maureen*
Desmoulins among the Olive Groves · *Cummer, Don*
Desolation · *Watt, Frank W.*
Despair of Nothing · *Kushmelyn, Christina*
The Desperate People · *Mowat, Farley*
The Destiny of Man · *Glover, Douglas H.*
Destiny's Child · *Gillese, John Patrick*
Destroying Angel · *Cameron, Eric*
The Destruction of Main Street · *Lavoie, Edgar*
The Detachment Man · *Macdonald, H.J.*
Details from the Canadian Mosaic · *Minni, C.D.*
Determination · *Gill, Stephen*
The Detour · *Stein, Rhoda Elizabeth Playfair*
Detroit Poison · *Sherman, Tom*
Deux Croissants · *McPhee, Brian*
The Devastating Effect of the Toronto Transit Strike on the Artistic Development

of Canada and Probably the Western World · *Mezei, Stephen*
The Deviant · *UU, David*
The Devil and the Disciple · *Hardin, Herschel*
The Devil and the Steeple Builder · *Heriteau, Jacqui*
The Devil Came to Trinidad · *Erskine, J.S.*
The Devil Dance on Orleans · *Anonymous*
Devil Dog! · *Gillese, John Patrick*
The Devil Lives in a Grey Stone House · *MacIntosh, Keitha K.*
The Devil Was Aboard · *Mayse, Arthur*
Devil's Advocate · *Bankier, William*
The Devil's Treasure · *Green, H. Gordon*
Devious Strangers · *Rooke, Leon*
Dew · *Elgaard, Elin*
Dialogism · *Tenenbaum, Gerald*
A Dialogue · *Hrynkiw, Oreste*
A Dialogue Concerning the Moon · *Harris, John*
Dialogue of Two Teachers · *Daquano, R.*
Dialogue with Egomaniacal Man · *Mitchell, Jeanine*
The Dialogues of Fane · *Payerle, George*
The Diamond · *Carlton, Edna P.*
Diamond Solitaire · *Hoffer, Fannie*
Diamonds · *Carrier, Jean-Guy*
Diamonds and Coaldust · *Kennedy, Cliff F.*
Diamonds in the Sky · *Clare, John P.*
Diamonds of Vengeance · *Clarke, Andrew C.*
Diamonds Threaded Yellow · *Darling, John*
Diana Betrayed · *M[agalis]., E[laine].*
Diaper Talk · *Humphries, Tom*
The Diary · *Milligan, Doris*
The Diary Fragments of Joseph Ahlmahn · *Hunter, Brad*
Diary from France · *Harrison, Elizabeth*
Diary of an Executioner · *Neufeld, Bob*
Diary of an Executive · *Job, Pat*
The Diary of Anna Stairs: Being the Real Life Observations of a Canadian Lady
Living in Montreal a Century Ago · *Disher, I. Scott*
Diary of the Pilot · *Goldstein, Allan*
Dic Mihi de Nostra, Quae Sentis, Vera Puella · *Currie, Sheldon*
Dickens Digested · *Davies, Robertson*
A Dicker to Spare · *Osborne, J.T.*
The Dictator · *Austin, Don*
Dictionaries · *Russell, Ted*
Did Dolly Say 'Mama'? · *Michaelson, Dave*
Did He Who Made the Lamb Make Thee? · *Arthur, Harry*
Did Jesus Ever Laugh? · *Wiebe, Rudy H.*
Did You Ever Eat a Sheep's Nose? · *Itani, Frances*
Did You Ever Think ... · *Kerslake, Susan*
Did You Ever Think? · *Ogle, Robert Joseph*
Did You Ever Want to Raise Bees ... ? · *Fitzpatrick, Helen*
Dido Flute, Spouse to Europe · *Gallant, Mavis*
Die Happy · *Blostein, David*

Die Now and Life Later · *Beasley, B.J.*
The Diet · *Walters, Harold Neal*
Die welt von Gestern Shore, Michael
The Difference · *McLeod, E. Vessie*
The Difference Between Good and Evil · *Berger, David*
A Different Cup of Tea · *Peters, Gregory J.*
A Different Drummer · *Stein, Rhoda Elizabeth Playfair*
Different Perspectives · *Murdoch, Benedict Joseph*
Different Summer · *Barnard, Margaret E. and Barnard, Leslie Gordon*
Different Thanksgiving · *Briffett, Isabel*
A Difficult Birth · *Cronenberg, David*
Difficult Choice · *Barnard, Margaret E.*
The Dig · *Ohodbok, Ted*
Digestive System · *McFarlane, Greg*
The Digger · *Bradford, Robert*
Dilemma · *Drachman, Wolf*
The Dilettantes · *Levine, Norman*
The Dilletantes · *Levine, Norman*
A Dilly of a Job · *Mitchell, Sylvia Elizabeth Fisher*
Dilys O'Connor · *Birch-Jones, Sonia*
The Dimensions of a Shadow · *Munro, Alice*
Diminuendo · *Sparling, Sharon*
Dimitri · *Hewko, Kati*
Dimitri: An Unfinished Portrait · *Friedman, Irena*
Dimitrios the Greek · *McDonald, Donna*
Dina Pyros · *Rule, Jane*
Ding! Dong! the Angst Is Dead · *Wright, Douglas*
Dingo Hunter · *Hubbard, Dexter*
Dinner in Chile · *Davies, Ann*
The Dinner Party · *Melfi, Mary*
Dinner with an Old Man · *Green, H. Gordon*
Dinner with Gordon Blue · *Moorhouse, Eliza*
Dinner with the Swardians · *Rooke, Leon*
Diplomacy · *Corps, Doreen*
The Diplomats · *Branden, Vicki*
A Diptera Chronicle · *Luxton, Stephen*
Direction · *Hodgins, Norris*
Directions · *Collins, David M.*
The Director's Assistant · *Borsman, Carolyn*
Dirty Face Pete · *Anonymous*
Dirty Kid and Colonel Boogie · *Dybvig, Leslie*
Dirty Laundry · *Bailey, Don*
Disarmament · *Wait, Harvey J.*
The Disarrayed · *Hekkanen, Ernest*
The Disciple · *Morris, Richard*
Discord · *Quayle, Marjorie*
Discoveries · *Seaton, Jean Q.*
Discovery · *Parsons, Sandra*
The Discovery of Bismuth · *Kilodney, Crad*
The Discovery of Canada · *Butler, J.E.P.*

The Double Four Poster Bed · *Morritt, Hope*
A Double Gin · *Burns, Robert A. McA.*
Double Happiness · *O'Neil, Ernie*
Double Role · *Robb, Frank*
Double Solitaire · *Clare, John P.*
A Double Thread · *Ravel, Aviva*
Double Time for Sundays · *Ward, Norman*
Double Time on Sunday · *Ward, Norman*
Double-Riding, Robbing the Chapel and Singing in the Cemetery · *Kelly, Dermot*
Doubles · *Cook, George*
The Doughnut Bag · *Stein, Rhoda Elizabeth Playfair*
The Doulton Man · *Blostein, David*
Down among the Wallabies · *Collins, David M.*
Down at the Point · *McNamara, Eugene*
Down Below Where the Animals Live · *Stambaugh, Sara*
Down in the Valley · *Rose, Mildred A.*
Down on the Farm · *Bourne, Stephen R.*
Down the Main · *Selvon, Samuel*
Down the Road · *McNamara, Eugene*
Down Tickle · *Bushell, Sidney*
Down to a Sunless Sea · *Snider, James G.*
The Dowry Man · *Birch-Jones, Sonia*
Dr. Don · *Kinsella, W.P.*
Dr. Ed's Last Sleigh Ride · *Baird, K.A.*
Dr. Temple Is Dead · *Bankier, William*
Dr John H Watson: The Dead-Headed League · *McAllister, Lesley*
Drafted · *Thomson, E.W.*
The Drag Scene · *Simpson, S. J.*
Drag the Man Down! · *Mayse, Arthur*
The Dragon · *Govier, Katharine*
The Dragon and the Flower · *Noble, Dennis E.*
the dragonfly · *Bullock, Michael*
The Drain Commissioner's Christmas · *Green, H. Gordon*
The Drama Festival · *Russell, Ted*
Drapes · *McFadden, David*
Drawing the Pillow · *Itani, Frances*
A Drawn Blind · *Callaghan, Barry*
The Dreadwood · *Bedard, Michael*
The Dream · *Caesar, Floyd*
The Dream and the Triumph · *Buckler, Ernest*
A Dream Hat for Easter · *Cade-Edwards, Eileen*
The Dream House · *Fagan, Cary*
Dream Island · *Itani, Frances*
dream life of the ant · *Bullock, Michael*
The Dream Master · *Bedard, Michael*
A Dream of Blood · *Marriott, J. Anne*
The Dream of Hopeless White · *Bankier, William*
A Dream of Horses · *Barr, Allan*
A Dream of Isfahan · *Hospital, Janet Turner*
[A?] Dream of the South Seas · *Conger, Leslie*

The Dream Path · *Bedard, Michael*
Dream Sequence · *Lash, Timothy*
[A?] Dream So Real · *Peterson, Phyllis Lee*
Dream Three Hundred · *Sherrin, Robert G.*
Dreamboat · *Moore, Brian*
The Dreamer · *Sheppard, John*
The Dreamers · *Raddall, Thomas H.*
dreaming water · *Bullock, Michael*
Dreamland and Other Poems · *Cummer, Don*
Dreams · *Kinsella, W.P.*
Dreams & Sleep · *Ross, Veronica*
Dreams for Doctor Freud · *Gauthier, Guy*
Dreams in the Marketplace · *Rummel, Erika*
Dreams of Freedom, Dreams of Need · *Dalton, Sheila*
The Dreams of Harry S · *Gabori, Susan*
Dreams of Men and Women · *Newman, C.J.*
Dream-Visions · *Horne, Lewis B.*
The Dress · *Lewis, Jennifer*
A Dress for a Dance · *Burles, Mary Jo*
Dress of Yellow · *Story, Gertrude*
Dressmakin' · *Russell, Ted*
Dried Rose Petals in a Silver Bowl · *Winn, Janet Bruce*
Driftwood Notes · *Murray, Heather*
Driftwood of the Pacific · *Fischer, Gretl Kraus*
The Driller · *Cullen, Burke*
A Drink of Water · *Selvon, Samuel*
A Drink with Adolphus · *Wilson, Ethel D.*
Drinking Bitter · *Riis, Sharon*
Drinking It Up · *Fawcett, Brian*
The Drive · *Langston, Corrine*
The Driver · *Keeling, Nora*
Driving Home in the Rain · *Heide, Christopher*
Driving Toward the Moon · *Kinsella, W.P.*
The Drop · *Slade, Mark*
'Drop One, Pick One' · *Burnell, Ethel D.*
Drought · *Rashley, R.E.*
The Drowned Girl · *McNamara, Eugene*
The Drowning · *Kenny, George*
Drowning Gophers · *Adams, Ian*
The Drowsy Shopper · *Gabel, Miriam*
Drugstore Cowboy · *Harrison, John Kent*
The Drummer · *Shaw, Paul G.*
The Drummer of All the World · *Laurence, Margaret*
Drummer's Rock · *Cave, Gladys M. and Whiteway, Mary Mercer*
The Drunk · *Dickey, Len*
Dry Graves · *Muir, John Dapray*
Dry Media · *Riches, Brenda*
The Dry Sea · *Vernon, Lorraine*
Dry Spots · *Heble, Ajay*
Dry Storm · *St. Pierre, Paul*

Dry Vermouth · *Smith, Steve*
Dual Warning · *Bauchman, Rosemary*
'Ducdame' · *Ferrier, Mary Jane*
The Duchess · *Baker, Cynthia*
the duck · *Bullock, Michael*
Duck Blind · *Bushell, Sidney*
Duck Story · *Rosser, Ken*
The Ducks · *Haas, Diana*
The Dude, the Warden and the Marvel Lake Kid · *Marty, Sid*
Dud's Place · *Powell, Dorothy M.*
The Duel · *Stenson, Frederick*
Duel in the Kitchen · *Wiseman, Adele*
Duel in the Smokehouse · *Hubbard, Dexter*
Duet for Solo Yang · *Bailey, Bruce*
Duet for Two Lovers and an Abandoned Suite · *John, Beno*
Duffy's Last Contract · *Bankier, William*
Duh · *Kilodney, Crad*
The Duke in Toronto · *Stone, Larry*
Dulse · *Munro, Alice*
The Dumb Look · *O'Connell, Dorothy*
The Dumb Writer · *Glendenning, Donald*
Dumbo Nelson · *Fraser, D.M.*
The Dummy Was Alive · *Bartlett, Brian*
Dump · *Truhlar, Richard*
Dunkirk · *Volodarsky, Vladimir V.*
Dunn's Wife · *Greenway, Rex*
The Duplicate Cheque · *Banting, Meredith*
During Mass · *Fraser, Raymond*
During the Fall · *Albert, Maxine*
Dust · *Hodgins, Norris*
Dust of the Ages: A Hyperbolic Fabulist Essay · *Balon, Brett*
Dust to Dust · *McWhinnie, Jill*
The Dwarf · *Walters, Harold Neal*
The Dwarf in His Valley Ate Codfish · *Smith, Ray*
Dwell in Heaven, Die on Earth · *Garner, Hugh*
Dwight Makes Right · *Redant, Philip D.*
The Dying · *Payerle, George*
Dying Metaphors · *McFadden, David*
Dynamite Duggan's Courtship · *Gillese, John Patrick*
The Dynamite Horse · *Wood, Kerry*

E.R.A. · *Findley, Timothy*
E Equals MC Squared · *Garner, Hugh*
Each Asparagus Is an Angel · *Amprimoz, Alexandre*
Each Fall · *Yeomans, Edward*
Each Man Is an Island · *Rockman, Arnold*
the eagle and its reflection · *Bullock, Michael*
The Eagle's Eye · *MacSween, R.J.*
The Eagles Soar · *Ballantine, Emile*

Eanna · *Clark, Isabel*
An Ear for an Ear · *Weir, Marie*
An Ear to a Knot Hole · *Fremlin, Gerald*
Earl Schapiro Sends His Best Regards · *Petty, Chris*
Early April · *Nichol, bp*
Early Early Early One Morning · *Clarke, Austin C.*
Early Impressions · *Amprimoz, Alexandre*
The Early Life of King Lionfeather · *Lord Jupiter* [pseudonym]
Early Loves of Angus Gordon · *Cameron, John Cullen*
Early Morning Exile · *Jirgins, Karl E.*
An Early Morning Message · *Gould, Jan*
Early Morning Rabbits · *Metcalf, John*
Early Snow · *Solly, Bill*
Early Summer · *Spettigue, Douglas O.*
Ears to Hear · *Lockhart, Laurie*
Earth Moving · *Kroetsch, Robert*
Earth Station · *Decker, Ken*
Earthquake · *Stewart, Cherie*
East End · *Lennick, D.*
An Easter Carol · *Clarke, Austin C.*
Easter for Stephen Carley · *Barker, Bessie M.*
Easter Legacy · *Pitcher, Arthur*
Easter Morning on Tinker Island · *Ash, Fred*
Easter Passage · *Observer* [pseudonym]
The Easter Spirit · *Branden, Vicki*
Easter Sunday · *Koerte, Helen*
The Easter-Egg House · *McLaughlin, Lorrie*
The Eastmill Reception Centre · *Metcalf, John*
The Easy Child · *Friedman, Irena*
Easy Come, Easy Go · *Clare, John P.*
Eating Crow · *Power, John*
The Eaves of Houses · *Turnbull, J.G.*
An Eavesdropper · *Cyr, Rita*
The Ebb Tide of Peader O'Meara · *Sandbrook, Betty M.*
Ebbe & Hattie · *Bowering, George*
Ebbe's Roman Holiday · *Bowering, George*
Ebony Blueprint · *Miller, Ivie*
An Echo for Frances · *Barker, Bessie M.*
The Echo of a Metronome · *Bell, John*
Echoes from Gethsemane · *Hayward, Colin J.*
The Echoing Hills · *Buckler, Ernest*
Eckankar · *McFadden, David*
Eclipse · *Swenson, Alan*
Economics · *Crowe, Eleanor*
Economists and Eggs · *O'Connell, Dorothy*
Ecstasy of Clara Hobson · *Koerte, Helen*
An Ecumenical Challenge · *Julien, Florence*
Ed Wheeling · *Lewis, David E.*

Edge of Christmas · *Spettigue, Douglas O.*
The Edge of Friday Night · *Fisher, Jennifer*
Edge of Innocence · *Ryan, Josephine*
The Edge of Sound · *Woodward, Gordon*
Edge of the Circle · *Fines, Beatrice E.*
The Edge of the Cornfield · *Braun, Lois*
The Edge of the Garden · *Valgardson, W.D.*
The Edge of Town · *Munro, Alice*
Edie · *Anderson, Jay*
Edinburgh Vellomaniacs · *Buckie, Robert C.*
Editing Job in a Fake Park · *McCubbin, Terrence*
The Editor · *Stewart, Alec M.*
'Edmonton, I Said,' I Said, Repeating What I Said · *Mathieson, Ken*
Edna Pike, on the Day of the Prime Minister's Wedding · *Hodgins, Jack*
The Educated Couple · *Buckler, Ernest*
Educating Mary · *Hood, Hugh*
Education · *Russell, Ted*
The Education of Aubrey de Lapp · *Taylor, Charles*
The Education of Phyllisteen · *St. Pierre, Paul*
The Education of the Adamses · *Stemo, L. Johanne*
Edvard and Katrina · *Rooke, Constance*
Edward Allen Falls in Love · *Metcalfe, B[rian].R.*
Edward and Georgina · *McCormack, Eric*
Edward VII · *Amernic, Jerry*
Eelskins · *Russell, Ted*
The Effect of Narcissism on Form and Content · *Field, L.L.*
The Effects of Drought · *Ritter, Judy*
Efficiency Test · *Sturdy, John Rhodes*
The Efficient Intellectual · *McGrath, Patrick*
The Egg · *Newlove, John*
The Egg Poems Were Conceived ... · *Rosenblatt, Joe*
Egg Whites and Yolks · *Higo, T.K.*
Eggflation · *Skinner, Norman Doc*
Eggs · *Hodgins, Norris*
the eggshells · *Bullock, Michael*
Ego Game · *Koerte, Helen*
Egotizm · *Charles, Barry*
Eight Prunes ... or Three? · *Grantmyre, Barbara*
Eighteen · *Caesar, Floyd*
Einstein and the Little Lord · *Davies, Robertson*
Einstein and This Admirer · *Ludwig, Jack*
Einstellung · *Browne, Robert*
The Eisenhower Years · *Hutton, Bill*
El Dorado · *Minni, C.D.*
El Toro · *Hancock, Ronald Lee*
Elah · *Shaw, Joan Fern*
the elderly gentleman and the tattered hag · *Bullock, Michael*
Eldorado · *Turner, Ron*
Eleanora Duse at the Sauna · *Williams, M.A.*
Election News from the Pagwa Outhouse Sentinel · *Skinner, Norman Doc*

Electric Rose · *Rikki [Erica Ducornet]*
Electrico Utensilo · *Kinsella, W.P.*
Elegy for a Sergeant · *Donaldson, Allan*
Elegy in Ice · *Humphries, Tom*
The Element Follows You Around, Sir! · *Lowry, Malcolm*
Elena · *Watt, Sholto*
Elephant and Colosseum · *Lowry, Malcolm*
Elephant He Go Come Here Plenty · *Godfrey, Dave*
Elephantiasis · *Fraser, D.M.*
Elephantitus · *Tremblay, M.M.*
Elephants to Ride Upon · *Thomas, Audrey*
The Elephant-Shaped Perfume Bottle · *Reid, Dennis*
Elevation · *Thomas, Audrey*
The Elevator · *Kinsella, W.P.*
The Elevator Man · *Holberg, Darlyne*
Elisabeth Rides Again · *Scott, Gail*
Elizabeth · *Crawford, Joyce*
Ella's Father · *Thompson, Kent*
Ellen Denby's Husband · *MacLeod, Gladys M.*
Elliott's Disorder · *Doyle, Judith*
Elly's Dad · *Sterling, Sharon*
Elmer · *Flatt, Mary*
Eloise · *Kelly, M.T.*
Elsa · *Smith, Rich*
The Elsewhen Homilies · *Yates, J. Michael*
The Elsinor SquiresStudy in Danish; or, The Castle of Fear · *Bamford, Wendy*
The Elves · *Hughes, J. McK.*
The Embrace of Death · *Harris, Walter*
The Embroidery of Chao Li · *Ross, W.E. Dan*
The Emerald City · *Fraser, Keath*
Emergency Call · *Ross, [W.E.] Dan and Ross, Charlotte*
An Emergency Case · *Gallant, Mavis*
Emergency Street Lighting · *Skinner, Norman Doc*
The Emigrant - A Christmas Story · *English, L.E.F.*
Emile · *Beattie, Jessie L.*
Emily · *Simmie, Lois*
Emma · *Robinson, Gail*
Emma and the Sabbath Day · *Stone, Louise*
Emmeline's Own · *Tomkinson, Grace*
'Emovora' · *Holden, Helene F.*
Empire of the Sun · *Weiner, Andrew*
Empires of the Air · *Austin, Don*
The Employee · *Dyce, Peter*
The Empty Fathom · *Wur, Kenneth*
The Empty Gun · *Jeggerings, Ronald*
The Empty Lot · *Pugsley, Judith*
The Empty Room · *Craig-James, Janet*
The Empty Seat · *Willer-Cavers, Chris*

The Empty Tomb · *Govan, Margaret*
Emulation · *Acks, Daniel*
En Ontario Batinge · *Carrier, Jean-Guy*
The Enactment · *Miller, Robert*
The Enchanted Bookshop · *Cunningham, Louis Arthur*
An Enchanted Christmas · *Cuthand, John*
The Enchantment · *Harvor, Beth*
Encore · *Morrissey, Philip*
Encore for Strings · *Moore, Charlotte*
Encounter · *Macey, Anne Louise*
Encounter of an Emotional Kind · *Rosenberg, Flash*
Encounter with a Fool · *Moncrieff, Charles*
Encounters with the Element Man · *Atwood, Margaret*
The End · *Cohen, Matt*
An End and a Peace · *Vigneault, Ruth*
The End of a War · *Livesay, Dorothy*
End of an Era · *Appleton, Hilary*
The End of Braycourt · *Millard, Peter T.*
The End of Canada Week /78 · *Osborne, J.T.*
The End of It · *Hood, Hugh*
End of Loneliness · *Russell, Sheila MacKay*
The End of Something · *Callaghan, Barry*
The End of Summer · *Brown, Dorothy Howe*
End of Summer . *Dagg, Mel*
The End of the City · *Perrault, Ernest G.*
The End of the Game · *Linder, Norma West*
The End of the Line · *McGrath, Patrick*
The End of the Revolution and Other Stories · *Rooke, Leon*
The End of the Road · *Funke, Carl*
The End of the Romance · *Halliday, David*
The End of the Rope · *Green, H. Gordon*
The End of the Spiral · *Sherman, Tom*
The End of the Summer · *Hallett, Susan*
The End of the Tunnel · *MacMillan, Gail*
The End of the World · *Todd, R. Dave*
An Ending, a Beginning · *Bailey, Don*
The Ending of Journeys · *Horne, Lewis B.*
The Ending Up Is the Starting Out · *Clarke, Austin C.*
Endings and Beginnings · *McFadden, Isobel*
The Endless Ripples · *Russell, Sheila MacKay*
Ends and Means · *Howard, Randy*
The Endurance Test · *Johnson, A.L.*
Enemies of the People · *Moore, Brian*
Enemies of the State · *Notar, Stephen*
The Enemy · *Marshall, Joyce*
The Engagement · *Walters, Harold Neal*
The Engagement Book · *Hedges, Doris*
England · *Morton, Colin*
The Englander and Our Hans · *Ens, Alvin G.*
The English Bobby in Canada · *Brennan, Frank*

English for Foreigners · *Levine, Norman*
The English Girl · *Levine, Norman*
The English Lesson · *Huntington, Terry*
An Englishman in Town · *Young, Scott*
Enigma · *Gill, Stephen*
Enigma in Ebony · *Birney, Earle*
The Enlightenment of Mrs. Simpson · *Fisher, Chris*
Enrique · *Plaut, W. Gunther*
Ensemble · *Cosier, Anthony*
Enter One in Sumptuous Armor · *Lowry, Malcolm*
Entering the Strobe · *Young, David*
Enterprise · *Kearns, Lionel*
Entertainer · *Young, Roland*
Entertaining · *Bridger, Steve*
The Entertainment · *McWhirter, George*
Entropy, Atlas, and the Tortoise · *Bain, Dena*
Entropy · *McNamara, Eugene*
The Envoys · *Reid, Robert W.*
Envy · *Doyle, Judith*
Eolin · *Lewis, Murray*
The Epic of Petit Trudeau · *Hutchison, Bruce*
Episode · *Birdsell, Sandra*
Epistle of Wilderness · *Gunnars, Kristjana*
Epistle to Cindy-Sue · *Chamish, Barry*
An Epitaph for Mrs. Parker · *McConnell, Gail A.*
Equal Opportunities · *Mitcham, Peter*
Equality · *Hamill, Tom*
Equimeat: A Three-Year Run to the Wire · *McDougall, Joseph Easton*
The Equivalent · *Bird, Will R.*
Eraser's Dilemma · *Selvon, Samuel*
'Erbert Winch · *Grantmyre, Barbara*
the erection · *Heath, Terence*
Eric the Red · *Bailey, Don*
Ernest McCaudle · *Blakeston, Oswell*
Ernestine · *Mirolla, Michael*
Ernst in Civilian Clothes · *Gallant, Mavis*
Eroica · *Welykopolsky, Luba*
The Erosion of Privacy in the New Age or Caged on a Stage with No Place to Hide
· *Boston, Stephen*
Erostratus · *Smith, Jim*
Errands · *Browne, Paul Cameron*
Erratic · *Drew, Wayland*
Ersatz Erotica · *Stilwell, Arthur*
The Eruption of Albert Wingate · *Buckler, Ernest*
Escape · *Douglas, D.A.*
Escape! · *McKeever, Harry Paul*
The Escape Artist · *O'Brien, Bill T.*
Escape by Night · *Hazell, Mary*
Escape from My Winter Pent House · *Godfrey, Dave*
Escape to the City · *Woodward, Gordon*

755

Escape Money · *Gillese, John Patrick*
Escapism · *Garnet, Eldon*
Escargots · *Amprimoz, Alexandre*
ESCHAR · *Decker, Ken*
Eschatology · *Fraser, D.M.*
Escrebiscortion · *McDougall, Bill*
Eskimo Spring · *Wood, Kerry*
Especially Worthy · *Gillese, John Patrick*
Essence of Marigold · *Brewster, Elizabeth*
Essex North's First and Last Rock 'N' Roll Star · *Root, Thomas A.*
Esso · *Svendsen, Linda*
Estelle the Louder · *Walker, Mirian*
Esther · *Will, Ray*
Esther: A Spring Sketch · *Schermbrucker, Bill*
The Estuary · *Metcalf, John*
Et in Arcadia · *Branden, Vicki*
The Eternal Mystery · *Gill, Stephen*
The Eternal Prospector · *Anonymous*
The Eternal Tournament · *Walker, David*
Ethel and the Pink Lady's Slippers · *Anderson, Helen E [or W.]*
Ethelbert Comes to Call · *Barker, Bessie M.*
The Ethics of Survival · *McNamara, Eugene*
The Etiquette of Invisible Eating · *Nations, Opal L.*
Eugene · *Unwin, Peter*
Eulogy for Don · *Rorke, Michael J.*
Euphoria · *Ryan, E. Anne*
Europe by Satellite · *Gallant, Mavis*
Eva · *Porter, Helen*
Eve · *Bemrose, John*
The Eve of St. Agnes · *Siwiec, Peter John*
Eve of the Wedding · *Stein, Rhoda Elizabeth Playfair*
Evellyn · *Riddington, Bruce*
Even as the Fortress Walls · *Doyle, Nancy*
Even Dying Takes a Long Time · *Harrison, Devin*
Even Fingers Sing in the Lamp · *UU, David*
Even I Will Carry · *Perry, Cecil*
Even Machines Break Down · *Atkinson, George*
Evening and Night · *Howard, Randy*
Evening at Home · *Rooney, Frances*
The Evening Bells · *A.N.P [pseudonym]*
Evening Courses · *Ravel, Aviva*
Evening in Brussels · *Green, H. Gordon*
An Evening in the Life of Harold Brunt · *Marshall, Tom*
An Evening in Two Voices · *Schoemperlen, Diane*
Evening on the Town · *Sturdy, John Rhodes*
Evening Out · *Bartley, Jim*
Evening Scrub Football in Greece · *Lambert, Rick*
The Evening Star · *Knox, Olive*
An Evening Walk · *Malt, Rick*
An Evening with Emily · *Cogswell, Fred*

An Evening with Reynard Rhomboid · *MacFadden, Patrick*
An Evening with Sholom Aleichem · *Kreisel, Henry*
Evening without Clark Gable · *Allen, Robert Thomas*
The Event · *McGorman, Don*
Events at Headland Cottage · *Bankier, William*
Events Leading to My Departure · *Hogan, Robert*
Ever Build a House? · *Corbett, Edward Annand*
Ever See a Girl with a Painted Guitar? · *Spanier, Muriel*
Everett · *Wilmot, Eleanor*
The Everlasting Arms · *Evans, Allen Roy*
Everlasting Life · *Edwards, Caterina*
Everlasting Love · *Dabydeen, Cyril*
Every Day of His Life · *Hodgins, Jack*
Every Good Gift · *Carlton, Edna P.*
Every Moment Counts · *Whitford, Margaret Ann*
Every Morning Is Christmas · *Horwood, Harold*
Every Night Is Boat Race Night · *McCourt, Edward A.*
Every Piece Different · *Hood, Hugh*
Every Time I Write a Story, Someone Dies ... · *Levine, Norman*
Everybody Comes in Handy · *Schull, Joseph J.*
Everybody Else Is Running · *Curtis, Margaret*
Everybody Gets Something Here · *Mitchell, Ken*
Everybody Wants to Be a President · *Melamet, Max*
Everyday Life in the Twentieth Century · *McFadden, David*
An Everyday Morning · *Barbeau, Malcolm*
Everyman's Uncle Fred · *Seajay* [pseudonym]
Everyone a Loser · *Blythe, Aleata E.*
Everyone Agreed Miss Prue Was a Sharp Old Gal · *Morris, Doris M.*
Everyone Is Someone · *Kay, Margaret B.*
Everyone Knows That! · *Ross, W.E. Dan*
Everything Must Be Sold · *Newman, C.J.*
Everything Will Be Wonderful · *Mawson, Anthony R.*
Everything's Turning Up Rosie · *Wyatt, Rachel*
Eve's Child · *Schmekel, Suzan*
Evesham · *Green, H. Gordon*
The Evidence · *Findlay, David K.*
The Evil Man · *Gant, Eric W.*
Evolution, Fox, and Associates · *Paratte, Henri Dominique*
Evolution · *Young, William*
The Evolution of Harry · *Davis, R.*
Exactly 1,000.00 · *Carney, Dora*
Exaltation · *Stern, Sandor*
Exam · *Dyba, Kenneth*
The Examination · *Fraser, D.M.*
An Excellent Specimen · *Fawcett, Patrick*
Excelsior · *Presant, Joan*
Excerpt from a Letter to a Friend · *Millikin, Brenda*
Excerpts from Bogart's Diary · *Halliday, David*
Excerpts from Gérarde's Diary · *Jackson, J. Graham*
Excerpts from Journal · *Itter, Carole*

F*A*I*R*Y F*I*N*G*E*R · *Rikki [Erica Ducornet]*
A Fable · *Harasymiw, Bohdan*
The Fable Frogs of Seigo Slough · *Hicks, John V.*
The Fable of the Ant and the Grasshopper · *Hood, Hugh*
Fable One · *Anonymous*
Fable VI · *Uhlman, Fred*
Fables I: The Garden · *Govier, Katharine*
Fables IV: The Dancer · *Govier, Katharine*
Fables of Faubus · *MacLean, James F.*
The Fabric of a Dream · *Malag, Oonagh*
The Fabulous Eddie Brewster · *Blaise, Clark L.*
The Fabulous Journey · *O'Hagan, Howard*
the face · *Bullock, Michael*
Face into the Wind · *MacMillan, Beatrice*
The Face of Crime · *Green, H. Gordon*
The Face of Death · *MacSween, R.J.*
The Face of Georges Jacques Danton · *Cummer, Don*
The Face of God · *Anderson, G.S.*
The Face of Innocence · *Beresford-Howe, Constance*
Faces · *Coull, Barry*
A Fact of Life · *Russell, Sheila MacKay*
Fact or Fiction or Whatever · *Anonymous*
The Facts of Life · *Peterson, Phyllis Lee*
The Facts of the Matter · *Kudrick, Sylvia*
Fade Out · *Kent, Valerie*
Fadeaway · *Ancevich, Jon*
Fading · *Doyle, Judith*
Failure · *Moore, Elwin*
The Fair, the Foul & the Foolish · *de Lint, Charles*
The Fair · *Carroll, Elizabeth*
A Fair Beginning · *Story, Gertrude*
Fair Harbour My Eye · *Hindmarch, Gladys*
A Fairy · *Bouvette, Robin*
The Fairy Princess & the Feet of Clay · *Armstrong, Patricia*
Fairy Tale · *Cromwell, Liz*
Faith and the Blind Man's Symphony · *Ketchen, Susan*
Faith of Our Fathers · *MacMillan, Gail*
A Faithful Friend · *Hekkanen, Ernest*
The Faithful Goose · *Fowke, H. Shirley*
The Fall · *Buchar, Frank*
Fall Cleaning · *Alford, Edna*
The Fall Guy · *Garner, Hugh*
The Fall of a City · *Nowlan, Alden*
The Fall of a Sparrow · *Helwig, David*
A Fall of Birds · *Jeffels, Ronald R.*
A Fall of Sparrows · *Luxton, Stephen*
The Fall of the Ariadne · *Bell, John Leslie*
The Fall of the House That Jack Built · *Engel, Marian*
Fall with the Rain · *Bankier, William*
Fallen Angels · *Tierney, Bill*

The Fallen Dust · *MacKenzie, Eric*
Fallen Leaves · *Deane, Christopher*
Fallen Rock · *Neal, Ellen*
The Fallen Sheep · *Bryson, David*
Falling for Mavis · *Percy, H.R.*
Falling in Love · *Birdsell, Sandra*
Falling Stars · *Breingan, J.N.*
falling tree · *Bullock, Michael*
The Falling Trick · *Wuorio, Eva-Lis*
Fallings from Us, Vanishings · *Hood, Hugh*
A False Moustache · *Margoshes, Dave*
False to Your Calling · *Cathcart, Graham*
Fame · *Copeland, Ann* [pseudonym]
Familiar · *Denby, Netha K.*
Familiar Runner · *Dempster, Barry*
The Family · *Schwartz, Judith*
Family Allowance · *Engel, Marian*
Family Man · *Perrault, Ernest G.*
The Family Meal · *Fox, Gail*
Family Picnic · *Wood, Kerry*
Family Plot · *Swayze, J.F.*
Family Portrait · *Smith, Judi*
Family Reunion · *Boston, Stephen*
The Family Rock Star · *Kelly, Dermot*
Family Sacraments · *Leone, Nicole*
A Family Secret · *Watson, Scott*
Family Ties · *Beghtol, Claire*
Family Trait · *Pugsley, Edmund E.*
The Family Tree · *Briffett, Isabel*
Family Ways · *Bradshaw, Colleen*
Famine · *Spruyt, Jo-Ann*
Famous Cases of Defenestration · *Livesey, Margot*
A Famous Egyptologist · *Ebbeson, Barbara*
Famous Players · *Hollingshead, Greg*
The Fancy Green Jacket · *Blythe, Aleata E.*
Fancy Yancy · *O'Connell, Dorothy*
Fane · *Payerle, George*
The Fane of the Grey Rose · *de Lint, Charles*
Fangus · *O'Connell, Dorothy*
Fanshawe Park · *Bryon, Judi*
The Fantasy · *Craig, Cheryl Lynne*
Fantasy and Circumstance · *Gunnery, Sylvia C.*
Fantasy Child · *Grieveson, Brian*
Fantasy Coming True · *Dotto, Lydia*
Far Above Rubies · *Fines, Beatrice E.*
Far from the Snows of Winter · *Waddington, Miriam*
Far Out, Man · *Davis, Sheila*
A Far Place Home · *Dabydeen, Cyril*
Far Thunder · *Melen, Terrance*
The Faraway Lady · *Wood, Kerry*

Fare Well, a Long Farewell · *Kaey, Arden*
Farewell, Beatles · *Green, H. Gordon*
Farewell, Dear Lady · *Peterson, Phyllis Lee*
Farewell, Little Flying Squirrel · *Gillese, John Patrick*
The Farewell · *Fasick, Laura*
A Farewell for Mr. Moran · *Gillese, John Patrick*
Farewell to Moss Lake · *Brewster, Elizabeth*
Farewell to Mr. Moran · *Gillese, John Patrick*
Farewells at Four O'Clock · *Waddington, Miriam*
Farewells Exchanged Beside a Train · *Stilwell, Arthur*
Farm Lands Disappear · *Smith, Jessie Hazard*
The Farmer Element · *Plourde, Marc*
The Farmer's Daughter or Theology in a Nutshell · *Campbell, Angelena H.*
The Farmer's Heart · *Bole, J. Sheridan*
Farming: The Ontario Line Fences Act · *Akenson, Donald Harmon*
Farming Scientific · *Branden, Vicki*
The Farnsworth Collection · *Morrison, Harold R.W.*
Far-Off Event · *Evans, Allen Roy*
the fart · *Heath, Terence*
The Fascinating Art of Babcockery · *Winslow, Natalie*
Fast Miracles · *Dempster, Barry*
Fat · *Ursell, Geoffrey*
Fat Albert · *Collins, Michael*
Fat and Furry · *Clark, Jennifer*
Fat and Lazy · *Ward, Bob*
Fat Cat · *Ohm, Vibeke*
The Fat Farm Fiasco · *O'Connell, Dorothy*
The Fat Lady · *Paris, Anne Porter*
Fata Morgana · *Kinsella, W.P.*
The Fatal Error · *Hekkanen, Ernest*
The Fatality · *Bolen, Dennis E.*
Fate Has a Concave Face · *Simser, Guy*
The Fate of Other People · *Doyle, Nancy*
Fate or Coincidence · *Gill, Stephen*
Fate Smiled the Other Way · *Green, H. Gordon*
The Father · *Lake, Rhody*
Father and the Schoolteacher · *Green, H. Gordon*
The Father · *Garner, Hugh*
Father Came from Boston · *Gillese, John Patrick*
Father Instinct · *Engel, Marian*
father lamonte · *Inglis, Patricia*
Father Malleus · *Marchand, Philip*
Father Moran's Trick · *Hubbard, Dexter*
Father Murphy's Dilemma · *Loomer, L.S.*
Father Shannon's Nest Egg · *Duncan, M.M.*
Father Sweeney and the Miracles · *Wheler, Eleanor*
Father to the Rescue · *Luckhurst, Margaret*
Father Was a Fancier · *Green, H. Gordon*
Fathers & Sons · *Watmough, David*
Fathers and Daughters · *McNamara, Eugene*

Father's Boy · *Livesay, Dorothy*
Father's Day Gift · *Wright, Douglas*
A Father's Love · *van der Beek, John*
Fatigue · *Gottlieb, Paul*
Fauna Free Press · *Redbourne, Ray* [probable pseudonym]
Fausta · *Burnett, Virgil*
The Favour · *Campbell, Wanda Blynn*
The Fawn · *Kinsella, W.P.*
The Fear · *Horne, Lewis B.*
Fear and the Night · *Toye, Bob*
Fear and Trembling · *Bankier, William*
Fear Continued · *Sheard, Sarah*
A Fear in the Night · *Blaylock, Susan*
Fear of Death Will Not Disturb Me · *van Herk, Aritha*
Fear of Miracles · *Riis, Sharon*
The Fearful Heart · *Marcuse, Katherine*
Feast Days and Others · *Levine, Norman*
The Feast of Christ the King · *Doyle, Donna*
Feastdays and Others · *Levine, Norman*
The Feather Bonnet · *Wood, Kerry*
Feathers · *Kinsella, W.P.*
Feathers for Breakfast · *Winter, Keith*
Feathers for Oberschreiberschriftsellermeister · *Yates, J. Michael*
February · *Bowell, Don*
February Mama · *Hood, Hugh*
February Morning · *Potrebenko, Helen*
The Feeble Virtue · *McConnell, Alice*
A Feed of July Herring and New Potatoes · *Petrie, M. Ann*
The Feeder · *Rushton, Alfred*
the feel · *Heath, Terence*
Feeling My Way Forward · *Bauer, Nancy*
Feet · *Engel, Marian*
Feet of Clay · *Branden, Vicki*
Feldman vs. Buchalter: A New World Parable · *Kleiman, Edward*
Felix's Pheasant · *Naglin, Nancy*
A Fellow of Christhouse · *Pacey, Desmond*
The Feminine Touch · *Wilkinson, David H.*
The Feminist · *Stevenson, Joan*
Feminist Blues · *Dalton, Sheila*
Fence · *Friesen, Victor Carl*
The Fenians Are Coming · *Branden, Vicki*
Fern · *Bauer, William A.*
Fern Hill Revisited · *Teare, Dave*
The Ferris Wheel · *Simpson, Leo*
The Festival · *Redant, Philip D.*
Festival du Poulet · *Butler, Paula*
A Fetish for Love · *Laurence, Margaret*
Feud · *Mirolla, Michael*
The Feud and the Fire · *Armstrong, Patricia*
Feud in the Chilcotin · *Tench, C.V.*

The Final Solution · *Haskins, David*
The Final Twist · *Bankier, William*
Finally I Admit I Have a Knob on My Nose · *Walsh, Patrick*
Finals · *Krause, Pat*
Finchley's Folly · *Mole, Elsie Hadden*
Find a Friend · *Ross, W.E. Dan*
Find the Sun · *Jakober, Marie*
The Finder · *Spencer, Elizabeth*
'Finding Peace of Mind' · *Burnell, Ethel D.*
Fine and Unusual Games · *Vandenbosch, Peter*
Fine Water for a Sloop · *Rooke, Leon*
A Fine White Powder · *Wilson, Marglamb*
The Finest Hour · *Peterson, Phyllis Lee*
The Finger · *Persky, Stan*
Fingers, Fingers · *Sandor, Karl*
Finishing Touch · *Choyce, Lesley*
The Finny Monster · *Mayse, Arthur*
Fiona the First · *Kinsella, W.P.*
Fire · *MacEwen, Gwendolyn*
Fire in the Jungle · *McAuliffe, Edward*
The Fire Mountain · *Anonymous*
Fire Weed · *Dagg, Mel*
Fire with Fire · *Price, Anna Mae*
the firebird and the arrow · *Bullock, Michael*
The Fire-Proof Doors · *Gaul, Avery*
The Firing · *Murray, Rona*
The Firing Squad · *McDougall, Colin M.*
The Firmament of Time · *Cleland, Elizabeth*
First, They Got Luke · *Melmer, J.R.*
The First Canadian · *Porter, Loraine*
First Catch Your Crook · *Paterson, O.P.*
The 'First Christmas' · *Sherwood, Roland H.*
A First Class Funeral · *Birch-Jones, Sonia*
The First Crocus · *Livesay, Dorothy*
First Dark · *Spencer, Elizabeth*
First Date · *Beck, Norma Jean*
First Day at School · *Green, H. Gordon*
The First Day of June: I Turn Seventeen · *Madott, Darlene*
The First Day of Summer · *Mitchell, Edith*
The First Day of the World · *Rooke, Leon*
A First Death · *Watmough, David*
First Encounter · *Watt, Sholto*
The First Encountering of Mr. Basa-Basa and His Excellency, Ling Huo · *Godfrey, Dave*
First Encounters with the Opposite Sex · *Levine, Norman*
The First Ever Use of the Comparison Test in Advertising History · *Heavisides, Martin*
First Flight · *Fountain, Eileen*
[The?] First Garden · *Gillese, John Patrick*
A First Job · *Watmough, David*

The First Journey · *Beck, J.P.*
The First Kiss · *Kimmett, Deborah*
First Love · *Ord, Douglas*
First Love/Last Love · *Rule, Jane*
The First Mate Takes Over · *Hayes, Anne*
The First Millionaire · *Carriere, Marguerite*
First Move · *Somerville, Christine Bryce*
First Names and Empty Pockets · *Kinsella, W.P.*
The First of Further Adventures of John J. McCary · *Garnet, Eldon*
The First of November · *Jeffries, Pat*
First Person Regular · *Fitzgerald, Judith*
First Publication 'Lost' Kafka Manuscript · *Rooke, Leon*
First She Killed Him ... · *Dickinson, Mary Lou*
The First Snow · *Sears, Janet*
The First Son, and the Second · *Margoshes, Dave*
The First Stone · *Green, H. Gordon*
First Taste of Apples · *Wood, Ted*
First Thursday of the Month · *Plourde, Marc*
The First Time I Left Home · *Richler, Mordecai*
First Trials · *Livesay, Dorothy*
The First Trip Up · *Kelly, M.T.*
The First Vision · *Evans, J.A.S.*
The First Wall · *Carson, Bryan*
First Winter · *Murdoch, Nancy Clegg*
Firstie · *McWhirter, George*
the fish · *Bullock, Michael*
Fish and Brewis · *Scammell, A.R.*
The Fish Are Where You Find Them · *Sturdy, John Rhodes*
The Fish Caught in the Battle River · *Wiebe, Rudy H.*
A Fish for Mr. Waddington · *Knox, Claire Neville*
A Fish Out of Water · *Knapton, Lucy*
Fish Story · *Tait, John*
Fish That Go Bump in the Night · *Power, John*
The Fisherman · *Rodgers, Joan*
The Fishermen That Walk Upon the Beach · *Gray, Charles*
The Fishes Hornpipe · *Harding, John*
Fishface's Leg · *Hamilton, Patricia*
Fish-Hooks · *Silvester, Reg*
Fishing for the Bottom of the Lake · *Richards, John*
The Fishing Lake · *Spencer, Elizabeth*
The Fishing Rod · *Wolfe, Roy I.*
A Fishing Trip · *Mandryk, Ted*
A Fishy Fable · *Veall, A.R.*
A Fistful of Love · *Pederson, Steven*
A Fitting Place · *Bell, John*
The Five Cent Piece · *Cadogan, Elda*
Five Cents · *Shepherd, R.W.*
Five Dialogues on the Subject of Contemporary Literature · *Ord, Douglas*
Five Fingers, No Thumb · *Goede, William*
The Five O'Clock Train · *Scarfe, Eunice*

Five Oral Reports on the Death of a Friend · *Rooke, Leon*
Five Times a Father · *MacIntosh, Keitha K.*
Five to a Hand · *Alford, Edna*
Five Wheelchairs · *Urquhart, Jane*
The Five Wills of Rory McTavish · *Green, H. Gordon*
Fivesight · *Robinson, Spider*
Five-Twenty · *Addario, Frank*
The Fix · *Purdy, Brian*
The Flag · *Taylor, Melville*
The Flags · *McWhirter, George*
The Flame of Faith · *Elliott, Noreen*
Flames at Dusk · *Wood, Kerry*
Flame's Family · *Gillese, John Patrick*
Flash Flood · *Theriault, Yves*
Flash Harry & the Daughters of Divine Light · *Roberts, Kevin*
A Flash of Pink · *Cranton, Judy*
The Flat on Rue Chambord · *Elflandsson, Galad*
Flat-Mate · *Holmes, Ken*
The Flesh, the Enemy · *Wyse, Marion*
Flicker Vertigo · *Doyle, Judith*
A Flickering Sunspot · *Stewart, Valerie*
Flies, Lizards and Bonar Law · *Watmough, David*
The Flies in the Glass · *Plourde, Marc*
Flight · *Morrison, Robert*
Flight 272 · *Ogle, Robert Joseph*
Flight at Freeze-Up · *Ringland, Mary*
Flight from Christmas · *Anonymous*
Flight from Courage · *Green, H. Gordon*
The Flight of the Flying Coffins · *Russell, Lawrence*
A Flight to Montreal · *Finnigan, Joan*
Flim-Flam Man · *Doyle, Dan*
The Flirtatious Phantom of Montreal · *Sheldon, Michael*
The Flitting Bird · *Bergren, Myrtle*
The Flitting of the · *Nancy Gay · Hill, Kay*
Floater · *Glover, Douglas H.*
Floating Bears · *Such, Peter*
The Flood · *Ritchie, Ian*
Flood Tide · *Thompson, Dave*
Flood Time · *Horne, Lewis B.*
Floors · *Hodgins, Norris*
Florentine Letourneau · *Mathews, Robin D.*
The Florentine Table · *Nebbs, Margaret*
Florian's Apocalypse · *Fedorowicz, Jan*
The Flout What Kilt Foster · *Ross, Stuart*
Flower Girl · *Brewster, Elizabeth*
Flower Piece · *Cunningham, Louis Arthur*
The Flower Pot · *Saltzburg, Joan*
the flower that started the day · *Bullock, Michael*
The Flowering of Miss Ellen · *Cowan, Connie*
Flowers for the Dead · *Duncan, Frances*

Flowers for the Teacher · *Bauchman, Rosemary*
Flowers for Weddings and Funerals · *Birdsell, Sandra*
Flowers from the Sky · *Saunders, Gary L.*
Flowers in Haunted Castles · *Linder, Norma West*
Flowers in His Eyes · *Rolheiser, Ronald*
The Flowers of Spring · *Gallant, Mavis*
Flowers That Bloom in the Spring · *Metcalf, John*
The Flowers That Killed Him · *Ross, Sinclair*
The Flowers You Did Not Bring Me · *Doyle, Nancy*
Flux · *Rooke, Leon*
A Fly Buzzing · *Connolly, Jacqueline*
Fly Paper · *Wyse, A. David*
The Fly Swatter · *Szanto, George*
Flycatcher · *Bowering, George*
Flying · *Coleman, Victor and Young, David A.*
Flying a Red Kite · *Hood, Hugh*
The Flying Cat · *Fones, Robert*
Flying Fish · *Godfrey, Dave*
Flying Fish · *Kreiner, Philip*
The Flying Saucers Have Taken Off · *Sharp, Daryl*
A Flying Start · *Gallant, Mavis*
Flying Things · *Guppy, Steve*
A Flying Visit · *Cameron, Eric*
Flypaper · *Wiebe, Armin*
Foetus · *Webb, Mary*
Fog · *Flatt, Mary*
Foggy · *O'Connell, Dorothy*
The Folding Bed · *Rikki [Erica Ducornet]*
The Followers · *McWhirter, George*
Fontanelle · *Crowell, Peter*
Food · *Mathews, Lawrence*
Food for Poetry · *Boorman, Sylvia*
The Food of Love · *Branden, Vicki*
Food People · *Byrnes, Terence*
The Fool · *Irvine, Connie*
Fool's Errand · *Nagorsen, Ross*
Fool's Paradise · *Barnard, Leslie Gordon*
Football · *Russell, Ted*
Foot-in-Field Story · *Rooke, Leon*
Foot-in-Mouth · *O'Connell, Dorothy*
Footloose and Fiancee Free · *Green, H. Gordon*
For 3 Nights Only · *Schull, Joseph J.*
For a Few Beers · *Rivard, Ken*
For a Loaf of Bread · *Stein, Rhoda Elizabeth Playfair*
For a New Life · *McKie, Florence*
For a Piece of Bread · *Gubins, Indra*
For Auld Lang Syne · *Levine, Norman*

For Better or for Worse · *Hansen, Frances E.*
For Better or Worse · *Reinhardt, Jean*
For Christmas, a Decision · *Wyatt, Rachel*
For Christmas: Her Own Space · *Wyatt, Rachel*
For Crying Out Loud · *Barnard, Leslie Gordon*
For Elaine · *MacIntyre, Wendy*
For Every Man an Island · *Porter, Helen*
For Everything, a Season · *Story, Gertrude*
For Galois, Linda, Pam and Me · *John, Beno*
For Laughs · *Spence, Ian A.*
For Leather or Worse · *Jaffe, Sherrill*
For Love of Denise · *Hughes, Philip B.*
For Love of Eleanor · *Rooke, Leon*
For Love of Gómez · *Rooke, Leon*
For Love of Madeline · *Rooke, Leon*
For Maggie · *Bole, J. Sheridan*
For October · *Millette, Richard*
For Pete's Sake · *Bird, Tom*
For Sale, Reasonable · *Borgese, Elizabeth Mann*
For Sale · *Zieroth, Dale*
For Sale - One Pair of Golf Clubs · *Quain, Hamilton*
For Sunshine · *Barrick, Steve*
For the Love of Linda · *Stein, Rhoda Elizabeth Playfair*
For the Love of Marcy · *Green, H. Gordon*
For the Love of Yackie Sculler · *MacIntosh, Keitha K.*
For the Record · *Szanto, George*
For the Sake of Auld Lang Syne · *Uckeed, Iben F* [pseudonym]
For the Sake of the Children · *Wood, Herbert*
For the Suffering · *Smith, Robert F.*
For Their Sport · *Mitcham, Peter*
For Those Who Care · *Thomas, Sister*
For Those Who Remain · *Wolfe, Morley*
For True Harmony · *Hallawell, Nancy*
For Want of a Nail · *Stein, Rhoda Elizabeth Playfair*
For Whom the Horses Run · *Allan, Ted*
For You · *West, Alexa*
For Your Own Good · *Anonymous*
For Zoltan, Who Sings · *Kinsella, W.P.*
Forbesy · *Engel, Marian*
The Forbidden Bay · *Esdaille, Daphne*
The Forbidden Island · *Mayse, Arthur*
Forbidden Words · *Bacque, James*
Forced Labour · *Amprimoz, Alexandre*
Forced Out · *Sherrin, Robert G.*
The Forces · *Garen, Robert*
Forecast: Wet! · *Beck, Norma Jean*
The Foreigner · *Nowlan, Alden*
Foreigner in the Family · *Brandis, Maxine*
The Foreigners · *Stemo, L. Johanne*
The Forest · *Kinsella, W.P.*

The Forest and the Man · *Hamilton, John*
Forester · *Dickinson, Mary Lou*
Forever a Secret · *Blythe, Aleata E.*
Forever Clouds · *Millisor, Guy*
Forever Dreaming · *Rosenfeld, Rita*
Forever Too Late · *Gillese, John Patrick*
Forever Young · *Conger, Lesley*
A Foreword · *Teitel, Jay*
Forget That Grapefruit; Here Come the Midgets · *Kilodney, Crad*
The Forgetful Bride · *Dales, Walter A.*
Forgiveness in Families · *Munro, Alice*
Form Notes Toward a Jewish Poem · *Sherman, Joseph*
Forms and Fragments · *Kemp, Penny*
The Formula · *Walker, Dan*
Forsaking All Others · *Fines, Beatrice E.*
Fort Liquordale · *Swan, Susan*
Fort Orders · *Bird, Will R.*
Fort Triumph · *Szanto, George*
Fortune Lies Westward · *Carriere, Marguerite*
Forty Dollar Doll · *Whitman, Ruth*
The Forty Dollar Plan · *Gillen, Kathleen Mollie*
Forward · *Melfi, Mary*
Foster and His Dummy · *MacMillan, Alex*
The Foul Trophy · *Easton, Alan*
The Found Boat · *Munro, Alice*
The Foundation of This House · *Bauer, Nancy*
The Foundering of Squatchberry · *Lavoie, Edgar*
Four California Deaths · *Bowering, George*
Four into One Goes Once · *Barnard, Leslie Gordon*
Four Jobs · *Bowering, George*
Four Kinds of Fantasy · *Avery, Martin*
The Four Letter Word · *James, Janet Craig*
Four Little Words · *Elliott, George*
Four Loves · *Moore, Peter*
Four Men and a Box · *Barnard, Leslie Gordon*
The Four Seasons · *Gallant, Mavis*
Four Sisters · *MacEwen, John A.*
Four Stations in His Circle · *Clarke, Austin C.*
Four Times Canada Is Four · *Watson, Wilfred*
Four Walls · *Garber, Lawrence*
Four Words · *Ross, W.E. Dan*
Four-Finger Pete and the Yella Deer · *Story, Gertrude*
Fourmidable · *McLaughlin, Peter*
The Four-Sky-Thunder Bundle · *Kinsella, W.P.*
Fourteen Stories · *Gilbert, Gerry*
Fowl Supper · *Riley, Wilma L.*
The Fox · *Gardner, Jigs*
The Fox Farm · *Woolaver, Lance*
Fox Fever · *Power, John*
A Fox Is Where You Find Him · *Gillese, John Patrick*

Foxblood · *Martin, Gwyn*
Foxes · *Rikki [Erica Ducornet]*
Foxfire and Paradox · *Rawdon, Michael*
Foxtails · *Dyba, Kenneth*
The Fragile Surpriser · *Govan, Margaret*
Fragility · *Shields, Carol*
Fragment · *Hagan, Derek [pseudonym]*
Fragment of a Single Mind · *Jasper, Lori*
A Fragmentary Argument · *Taylor, Perry*
Fragmentation · *Hill, Deborah*
Fragments · *Gillis, Susan*
Fragments from a Photo Album · *Madott, Darlene*
Fragments of a Bed/Ridden Man · *Babineau, Brian*
Fragments of a Continent · *Sturdy, Giles*
Fragments of a Hologram Rose · *Gibson, William*
Fragments of a Treaty Forever · *Mitchell, Marsha*
Fragments of Dreams · *Wyatt, Rachel*
Francesco · *Berger, Harvey*
Francine · *Whyte, Jon*
Francis Wiper's Ailment · *Plourde, Marc*
Frank About Farming · *Bole, J. Sheridan*
Frankie · *Vernon, Lorraine*
'Franz' · *Cohen, Matt*
The Fraser River · *Rae, Donna*
Fräulein Húffenheimer's Canadian Summer · *Vorres, Ian*
Frayed · *Currie, Robert*
Fred · *O'Connell, Dorothy*
Fred and the Goose · *Wood, Kerry*
Fred as Told by Friend of Fred · *Mahoney, Owen*
Fred Gets the Point · *Dixon, Kevin*
Freddy Makes It Snow · *Marks, Arlene F.*
Freddy Nothing · *Breslow, Maurice*
Freddy Rules the Waves · *Rutt, Edwin*
Freddy's Sister · *Plourde, Marc*
Fred's Resurrection · *Pegler, Arthur*
Free Associations · *Kalman, Judy*
A Free Country · *Robinson, Rudy O.*
Free for a While · *Pils [pseudonym]*
The Free Man · *Scobie, Stephen*
Free Samples · *McFadden, David*
Free Speech · *Ross, Mary Lowrey*
The Freedom of Slaves · *Katz, Bruce*
The Freedom of the Cage · *Bonellie, Janet*
Freeman's Cheesecake · *Dennis, Ian*
The Freeway · *Schroeder, Andreas*
French Baseball · *MacDonald, David*
French Crenellation · *Gallant, Mavis*
A French Girl to Stay · *McWhirter, George*
Frenchie's Wife · *St. Pierre, Paul*
Frescoed with Angels · *Johnson, G. Bertha*

Fresh Air · *Nella* [pseudonym]
Fresh Air and Westward Expansion · *Davidson, Craig*
The Fresh Air Child · *Stambaugh, Sara*
Fresh Disasters · *Stein, David Lewis*
A Fresh Tale · *Rosqui, Carolyn*
The Freshie Frolic · *Krause, Pat*
Friday, the 13th · *Pinsent, John C.*
Friday at the Travelodge · *Mann, Judy*
The Friday Everything Changed · *Hart, Anne*
Friday Is Tuna · *Wetmore, Andrew*
Friday Night and Saturday Morning · *Melen, Terrance*
friday night at the project and tenuous relationships reaching to long island ·
Lord, Peter
Fridrik Sveinsson: Mice · *Gunnars, Kristjana*
The Friend · *Fawcett, Brian*
A Friend for Margaret · *Nowlan, Alden*
A Friend for Molly · *Thorpe, Patricia*
A Friend in Ebony · *Whitford, Margaret Ann*
A Friend in Need · *Story, Gertrude*
A Friend of Beau's · *Barnard, Leslie Gordon*
[A?] Friend of Beau's · *Barnard, Leslie Gordon*
A Friend of Mine · *Moore, Brian*
Friend of My Youth · *Branden, Vicki*
Friend of the Family · *Ringland, Mary*
The Friendly Fog · *Legate, John*
The Friendly Ones · *Gillese, John Patrick*
Friends · *Iserman, Jenny*
Friends Always · *Fielding, Cheryl*
Friends and Relations · *Hood, Hugh*
Friends of a Friend · *Rosenfeld, Rita*
Friendship · *Rikki [Erica Ducornet]*
Friendship and Libation · *Rooke, Leon*
Friendship and Property · *Rooke, Leon*
Friendship and Rejuvenation · *Rooke, Leon*
Fringe · *Taylor, Darien*
Frisco ... · *Anonymous*
Froba Fraxler · *Barry, Lisa*
The Frog · *Hedley, Peter*
the frogs · *Bullock, Michael*
From a Death to a View · *Peter, John D.*
From a High Thin Wire · *Clark, Joan*
From a Seaside Town · *Levine, Norman*
From Adam Never Had One · *Riches, Brenda*
From Automatism to Zymosis · *Thomas, Richard*
From Flores · *Wilson, Ethel D.*
From Frank's Diary · *Read, Bob*
From Gabrielle Street to Mountain Heights · *Phillips, Bluebell Stewart*
From Gamut to Yalta · *Gallant, Mavis*
From Here to Where · *DeCampo, Paul*
From · *One Cook, Once Dreaming · Wynand, Derk*

Funny Ghosts · *Dabydeen, Cyril*
The Funny Man · *Hunter, Beth L.*
The Funny Money of 1980 · *Wiebe, Rudy H.*
A Funny Thing Happened · *Bankier, William*
Für Elise Before the War · *McIver, Emily Hollis*
Furniture · *Sarah, Robyn*
The Furniture of Home · *Rule, Jane*
Further Adventures of a Cross Country Man · *Rooke, Leon*
Fury · *Watmough, David*
Fury at Irishman's Lake · *Young, Scott*
The Future of Little Banana · *Costello, Kevin*
Future Tense · *Schoemperlen, Diane*
Fyodor's Bears · *Rikki [Erica Ducornet]*

G. Truehart, Man's Best Friend · *McNamee, James*
Gabriel Boldt's Narrative · *Weingarten, Roger*
The Gadfly Stung Me · *Kreiner, Philip*
The Gag of the Century · *Bankier, William*
Gaily Comes My Love · *Lawrence, Dorothy Elderkin*
Gain Through Loss · *Burnell, Ethel D.*
Gainfully Employed in Canada · *Kilodney, Crad*
Gal Souzy · *Luckhurst, Elizabeth*
Galatea · *Erskine, J.S.*
Galatic-Toc · *Scheider-Livesley, Richard*
Gall · *Riches, Brenda*
Gallstones · *Duncan, Frances*
The Galoshes · *Smith, Ray*
The Gamble of Past Years · *Babstock, George*
The Game · *Ward, Don*
A Game for Experts · *Singer, Barnett*
The Game of Chance · *Johnson, G. Bertha*
A Game of Chess · *Briffett, Isabel*
A Game of Errors · *Bankier, William*
The Game of Limping · *Newman, C.J.*
The Game of Love · *Brennan, Anthony*
A Game of Touch · *Hood, Hugh*
The Game of War · *Sudbury, Harold A.J.*
A Game or Three · *Henderson, Keith*
Game Over Lightly · *Johnson, Chris*
A Game with Adonis · *Grills, Barry W.*
Games · *Collins, David M.*
Games for Queen Victoria · *Wiebe, Rudy H.*
The Gamin on the Island Ferry · *Bowering, George*
Gang Warfare: A Love Story · *Fawcett, Brian*
Gap for the Circle · *Dungey, Christopher*
Gaps · *Minni, C.D.*
The Garage Sale · *Copeland, Ann [pseudonym]*
Garash and the Halfbreed · *Vlahov, Ed*
Garbage Man John · *Benger, JoAnne*

Garbage Run · *Hutchinson, Rosemary*
The Garbageman Is Drunk · *Acorn, Milton*
The Garden · *Livingston, Marilyn*
The Garden at Louveciennes · *Livesey, Margot*
The Garden · *Briffett, Isabel*
Garden of Earthly Delights · *Mitchell, Ken*
The Garden of Eloise Loon · *Alford, Edna*
Garden of the Sun · *Bonellie, Janet*
The Garden on the Point · *Pollett, Ron*
The Garden Patch · *Browne, Paul Cameron*
Gardens · *Jackson, J. Graham*
The Gardner Canal Goat · *McLeod, Murdoch*
The Gargoyle · *Redmond, Chris*
Gargoyle · *Kemp, Penny*
The Gas Bag · *Allen, Robert Thomas*
Gas Pumps · *Svendsen, Linda*
The Gas Saver · *Green, H. Gordon*
The Gate · *Field, Ann*
The Gates · *Andre-Czerniecki, Marion*
The Gates of Hell · *Kaminsky, Helen*
The Gateway to Now · *Coney, Michael G.*
Gathen a Balka · *MacCallum, Russell*
Gather Them In · *Campbell, Angelena H.*
Gathering In · *Rawdon, Michael*
A Gathering of Riddles · *McLaughlin, Peter*
Gatsby and Oranges · *Graham, Tammy*
Gatsby's Smile · *Rooke, Constance*
Gauze · *Rifka, Ruth*
The Gay Tragedy · *Forest, Alan*
The Gayo and the Leeofite Tree · *Richman, Sharon Lea*
Gazette Boy · *McGoogan, Kenneth*
Geese · *Russell, Ted*
A Gem of a Day · *Kwasny, Barbara J.*
Gems of the Collection · *White, Sheila*
Gene and the Horses · *Gentleman, Dorothy Corbett*
General Dahl · *Plourde, Marc*
The General Secretary · *Cowasjee, Saros*
Generation Gap · *Edmonds, Edward L.*
Generation Gap Memo · *Stein, Rhoda Elizabeth Playfair*
The Generation of Hunters · *Godfrey, Dave*
Genesis Reprise · *Smyth, Donna E.*
Genesis Revisited · *B., Jane*
Genevieve · *Wyatt, Rachel*
the genie · *Bullock, Michael*
The Genius · *Enwright, William*
Gentle as Flowers Make the Stones · *Metcalf, John*
Gentle Like a Cyclone · *Annett, R. Ross*
Gentle Rain · *Earle, Kathleen*
A Gentle Shove · *Shilvock, Margaret*
The Gentle Wind · *Inglis, Jean*

Geography of the House · *Metcalf, John*
Geometry & Dream · *Russell, Lawrence*
George, the TXI Model · *Feinstein, Robert*
George · *Rosta, Helen J.*
George and Lisbeth · *Christie, Michael*
George and the Lonely Hearts · *Scott, Margerie*
George Comes Down · *Mason, Mike*
George Hurd's Problem · *Ross, W.E. Dan*
George Twospot · *Hancock, Ronald Lee*
Georgie · *Maeers, Esther*
Georgie's Fun Palace · *Smith, David John*
Geranium! · *Currie, Robert*
The Geraniums · *MacMillan, Gail*
Gerard Markle · *Orenstein, Brent*
Gerardus · *Burnett, Virgil*
Germ · *Paragot* [pseudonym]
Germ Warfare · *MacNeill, James A.*
A German Lunatic on Top of the CPR Building · *Arnason, David*
The Gernsback Continuum · *Gibson, William*
Gertrude's Ring · *Smith, Sharon*
Get into the Woods · *Field, Roger*
Get on Board, Sinners · *Gibbs, Robert*
Gethin and Horace Go to Market · *Corrigall, Melodie Joy*
Getting Away from Home · *Levine, Norman*
Getting Caught · *Thompson, Kent*
Getting Married, Just Like Everyone Else · *Ross, Veronica*
Getting Near the End · *Weiner, Andrew*
Getting Off on the Right Foot · *Dobson, Sydney*
Getting Ready · *Haskins, David*
Getting Saved · *Thompson, Kent*
Getting the Hang of It · *Byrnes, Terence*
Getting the Picture · *Copeland, Ann* [pseudonym]
Getting the Word · *Carpenter, David*
Getting to Know Rachel · *Chappell, Constance*
Getting to Know You · *Stein, Rhoda Elizabeth Playfair*
Getting to Sleep · *Fraser, Raymond*
Getting to Williamstown · *Hood, Hugh*
Getting Up · *Oliver, Michael Brian*
Getting Your Goat · *Lynch, Gerald*
Getting Your Money's Worth · *Swan, Susan*
The Ghost · *Leitao, Lino*
The Ghost Dancers · *Greenway, Rex*
Ghost House · *Simmie, Lois*
A Ghost in the House · *Clamp, Murray*
Ghost of Legend · *Dehaas, David*
The Ghost of Reddleman Lane · *Pacey, Desmond*
Ghost Stories · *Yanofsky, Joel*
Ghost Story · *Wynand, Derk*
The Ghost Town · *Kingsbury, Donald*
Ghost Town Dog · *Evans, Hubert*

The Ghost Who Vanished by Degrees · *Davies, Robertson*
The Ghost Whose Name Was Change · *Daem, Mary*
Ghostkeeper · *Lowry, Malcolm*
Ghosts · *Schoutsen, John*
Ghosts Are Old-Fashioned · *Cropps, Marjorie E.*
Ghosts at Jarry · *Hood, Hugh*
Ghosts in Garter Belts · *Miller, J. Kit*
Ghosts in the Alley · *Morris, Cathy*
A Ghost's Sense of Humour · *Harrison, Edelmera*
Ghost-Town Dog · *Evans, Hubert*
The Giant · *Harris, John*
Giant of the Reekie · *Walker, David*
Giant Pike · *Stilwell, Arthur*
Giants · *Fawcett, Brian*
The Giant's Tomb · *Dale, Mark*
The Gift · *Green, H. Gordon*
A Gift at Parting · *Evans, Hubert*
The Gift Box · *Nimchuk, Michael John*
Gift for a Stubborn Son · *Green, H. Gordon*
The Gift of Fire · *Parr, D. Kermode*
A Gift of Ivory · *Hughes, Philip B.*
The Gift of Maggie · *Riskin, Mary W.*
Gift of Oranges · *Fines, Beatrice E.*
Gift of Prometheus · *MacIntosh, Keitha K.*
A Gift of Stamps · *Charney, Anne*
The Gift of the Bear · *Hummell, Steven*
The Gift of the Fairies · *Bedard, Michael*
A Gift of Trust · *Antoshewski, Anne-Marie*
A Gift of Wishes · *Percy, H.R.*
Gifts · *Walker, John*
Gifts: 'It's Only Money' · *Levine, Norman*
Gilbert and Sullivan vs. Tom and Jerry · *Young, David*
Gills · *Matta, John*
Gilman's Last Joke · *Morison, Scot*
Gimmie Back My Blood! · *Weir, Chuck*
Gimmie Shelter · *Jansen, Dagmar*
Gin and Goldenrod · *Lowry, Malcolm*
Gin and Tonic · *Watts, John*
Gingerbread Boy · *Gotlieb, Phyllis*
The Gingerbread House · *Mack, Dorothy*
'The Gingeriascope' · *Drache, Sharon*
Ginny, and the Dog · *Baldridge, Mary Humphrey*
the giraffe who turned purple · *Bullock, Michael*
The Girl Above the Mantle · *Armstrong, Patricia*
A Girl and a Dummy and the Dummy's Best Friend · *Rooke, Leon*
the girl at the bus stop · *Bullock, Michael*
A Girl Called Monday Morning · *Phillips, Bluebell Stewart*
The Girl from Gault Road · *Ross, [W.E.] Dan and Ross, Charlotte*
Girl from Peace River · *Green, H. Gordon*
The Girl from the Maritimes · *Easton, Alan*

The Girl I Left Behind · *Green, H. Gordon*
Girl in a Blue Shirtwaist · *Engel, Marian*
[A?] Girl in Lilac Time · *Gillese, John Patrick*
The Girl in the White Dress · *Currie, Robert*
A Girl Like Connie · *Stein, Rhoda Elizabeth Playfair*
The Girl Next Door · *Levine, Norman*
A Girl of Reputation · *Engel, Marian*
Girl on the Beach · *Harvey, Jennifer A. Becks*
The Girl on the Olive Oil Can · *Schwartz, Alvin*
The Girl on the Shore · *Graham, Tammy*
The Girl on the Square · *Barnard, Leslie Gordon*
Girl Stealer · *Mayse, Arthur*
The Girl Suddenly Found Luck · *Ross, W.E. Dan*
The Girl That Men Forgot · *McLaughlin, Lorrie*
The Girl That Ran Away · *Murray, Joan*
The Girl to Kill For · *Kelly, Dermot*
The Girl Who Collected Husbands · *Rooke, Leon*
The Girl Who Had Accidents · *Findlay, David K.*
The Girl Who Loved Children · *Jordan, Zoe*
The Girl Who Loved Horses · *Spencer, Elizabeth*
The Girl Who Made Good · *Russell, Sheila MacKay*
The Girl Who Made Time · *Rooke, Leon*
The Girl Who Stood Out from the Crowd · *Silvester, Reg*
The Girl Who Sweeps the Porch · *Kawalilak, Ron A.*
The Girl Who Turned into a Bird · *Dalton, Sheila*
The Girl Who Understood · *Green, H. Gordon*
The Girl Who Wasn't Pretty · *Stein, Rhoda Elizabeth Playfair*
The Girl Who Went to Mexico · *Nowlan, Alden*
The Girl Who Wore the Diamonds · *Brown, Joy*
Girl with a Grudge · *Mayse, Arthur*
The Girl with the Baby Arms · *Burningham, Bradd*
Girls, Like White Birds · *Bankier, William*
The Girls · *Ross, Veronica*
The Girls' Picnic · *Branden, Vicki*
Girls' Talk · *Lenardson, Paula*
Giuletta · *Watmough, David*
Give a Little Extra · *Cade-Edwards, Eileen*
Give It a Shot · *Clarke, Austin C.*
Give Me Back My Rags · *MacCormack, Terrance*
Give Me Love · *Daem, Mary*
Give Me Your Answer, Do · *Mitchell, Ken*
Give the Bride a Kiss, George · *McNamee, James*
Give Us This Day: And Forgive Us · *Clarke, Austin C.*
The Giver without a Gift · *Elford, Jean*
Giving Birth · *Atwood, Margaret*
Giving Up the Ghost · *Bowerman, Pearson*
The Glace Bay Miner's Museum · *Currie, Sheldon*
Glad Eastertide · *Edwards, Mary Kay*
Gladiator's Gift · *Statius [pseudonym]*
Glance in the Mirror · *Buckler, Ernest*

Glasgow · *Mayoff, Steven*
The Glass · *Hulet, William*
Glass Appetite · *Schull, Christiane*
Glass Bodies · *Campbell, Craig*
Glass Doesn't Burn · *Smyth, Jacqui*
The Glass Door · *Dick, Jane*
Glass Eyes and Chickens · *Cohen, Matt*
The Glass House · *Livesay, Dorothy*
The Glass Lampshade · *Cooper, Mel*
Glass of Beer · *Jake*
A Glass of Cognac · *Hancock, Ronald Lee*
The Glass of Water · *Massel, Dona Paul*
The Glass Roses · *Nowlan, Alden*
The Glass Slippers · *Atwood, Margaret*
the glass thimble · *Bullock, Michael*
The Glass Wall · *Russell, Sheila MacKay*
Glass-Blowing · *Hodgins, Norris*
The Glassy Essence · *MacLean, Kenneth*
The Glen of the Green Woman · *Tyson, Donald*
Glenda and the Painter · *Johnson, S.*
Glenda Working · *Rooke, Constance*
A Glimpse of Eden · *Harvey, Jennifer A. Becks*
A Glimpse That Changed a Life · *Wiseman, Mrs. C.*
Glimpses in the Fields · *Bartlett, Brian*
Gloops · *Bain, Dena*
Gloria, Ray, and Tammy · *Simpson, Robert N.*
Gloria · *Brody, Leslie*
The Glories of Greece · *Gould, Jan*
The Glorious Life and Death of Don Fernando de Soto · *Mays, John Bentley*
The Glory and the Grief · *Doyle, Nancy*
Glox, Equaling Honeycoo · *Kilodney, Crad*
Gnome's Dome · *Austen, Doug*
Go, Go, Go! · *Green, Robert*
Go - - , Young Man, Move, East, West, North, South · *Tiger, Lionel*
Go Alone, Johnny · *Wood, Kerry*
Go an' Play in the Traffic · *Dabydeen, Cyril*
Go Away, Baby · *Barnard, Margaret E.*
Go Gomez! · *O'Connell, Dorothy*
Go South in the Winter · *Spencer, Elizabeth*
Go to Sleep · *Slabotsky, David*
Go with Gladness · *Grier, Dave*
The Goal · *Teitel, Jay*
The Goat-Man · *Baker, Helen*
Goat's Grace · *Dobb, Ted*
The Goblin and the Student · *Lazarus, John*
God, Burgers and French Fries to Go · *Nations, Opal L.*
God and Doc Murphy · *Morris, Doris M.*
God and Grandfather · *Miller, Angela*
God Bless You · *Leddy, Joseph*
God Doesn't Sleep · *Bruneau, Bernard*

God Has Manifested Himself unto Us As Canadian Tire · *Hood, Hugh*
God Help the Young Fisherman · *Wilson, Ethel D.*
God Is a Plant · *Dennis, Ian*
God Is an Iron · *Robinson, Spider*
God Is Not a Fish Inspector · *Valgardson, W.D.*
God of the World · *Yates, J. Michael*
God Works in a Mysterious Way · *Shepherd, Harvey L.*
Goddamned War · *Heide, Reg*
Goddess · *Brennan, T. Casey*
Godman's Master · *Laurence, Margaret*
God's Country · *Clark, Joan*
Gods' Death · *Crompton, Susan*
God's House · *Znaimer, Moses*
God's Lake Voice · *Pugsley, Edmund E.*
Gods Must Yield · *Robertson, Strowan*
God's Rooster · *Green, H. Gordon*
Goin' Home · *Russell, Ted*
Going Ashore · *Gallant, Mavis*
Going Away · *Clark, D.M.*
Going Back · *Holdstock, P.J.*
Going Buggy · *Edwards, N.*
Going Down · *Clark, Ross*
Going for Broke · *Rooke, Leon*
Going Home · *Moore, Peter*
Going on Alone · *Dempster, Barry*
Going Out as a Ghost · *Hood, Hugh*
Going to Bed · *Atwood, Margaret*
Going to Ground · *Power, John*
Going to India · *Blaise, Clark L.*
Going to Russia · *Vanderhaeghe, Guy*
Going to See Mr. Winters · *Tyson, D.A.L.*
Going to See the Baba · *Krueger, Lesley*
Going West · *Dempsey, Ian*
Gold · *Briffett, Isabel*
Gold and Age · *Simpson, Robert N.*
The Gold Brick · *Green, H. Gordon*
The Gold Dust Dancing Through the Flame · *Rodgers, Gordon*
Gold Is the Sun · *Walker, Alan*
Gold Medals and Holy Night · *Skinner, Norman Doc*
Golden Anniversary · *Graham, Ferne*
The Golden Ant · *Pooley, Richard*
Golden Apples Are Delicious · *Zakanas, Paul*
The Golden Dragon · *Sinclair, Kathryn*
the golden emporer · *Bullock, Michael*
The Golden Gift of Grey · *MacLeod, Alistair*
Golden Girl · *Hospital, Janet Turner*
The Golden Goose · *Briffett, Isabel*
Golden Hands in Chains · *Weir, John*
The Golden Jubilee Citizen · *Mitchell, W.O.*
A Golden Land of Summer Enchantment · *Parr, John*

The Golden Rule · *de Villiers, Marq*
The Golden Thread · *Copeland, Ann* [pseudonym]
The Golden Trees · *Bryden, Ronald*
The Golden Wedding · *Green, H. Gordon*
Golden Whore of the Heartland · *Cohen, Matt*
Golden Windows · *Hoaken, Gail*
Goldenrod · *Haensel, Regine G.*
Goldfish and Other Elements · *Schell, Winston G.*
Goldfish and Other Summer Days · *Gibson, Margaret*
The Goldfish Pool · *Tomkinson, Joan*
Goldie · *Kinsella, W.P.*
Goldtooth Jimmy's Last Cup of Tea · *Michaels, Edward L.*
Golfing with the Old Man · *Fawcett, Brian*
Golgotha by the Sea · *Howard, Randy*
Gone Home · *Gledhill, Robert*
Gone Is My Fear of Sailing · *Greene, Anna*
Gone Three Days · *Hood, Hugh*
Gone with the Winding Sheet · *Singer, R.S.*
Gonedaddy · *Witherington, Paul*
Gonna Come and Get You in a Taxi, Honey · *Potrebenko, Helen*
Gooch · *Kinsella, W.P.*
A Good Catch · *Cameron, Eric*
Good Citizen · *Harley, Peter*
The Good Day · *Story, Gertrude*
A Good Day for a Parade · *Alford, Edna*
Good Deed · *Gallant, Mavis*
Good Dirt · *Ogle, Robert Joseph*
Good for You, Mrs. Feldesh · *Marlyn, John*
A Good Heart Dies · *Green, Shane*
The Good Hope · *Pacey, Desmond*
A Good Job - For a Girl · *Potrebenko, Helen*
The Good Lieutenant · *Campbell, Alphonsus P.*
The Good Listener · *Hood, Hugh*
The Good Maker · *Wiebe, Rudy H.*
Good Morning · *Kemp, Penny*
The Good Neighbour · *Stein, Rhoda Elizabeth Playfair*
The Good Old Days · *Multamaki, Ellen*
A Good Pair of Hands · *Szanto, George*
Good People · *Hodder, Uda*
A Good Place to Come From · *Torgov, Morley*
The Good Samaritan · *Briffett, Isabel*
The Good Samartian of the Sea · *Chappell, Constance*
Good Sir, Take My Advice and Do Not Die · *Nowlan, Alden*
A Good Swift Kick · *McWhirter, George*
The Good Tenor Man · *Hood, Hugh*
The Good Thief · *Mayse, Arthur*
A Good Time · *Ware, Colin*
A Good Time in the Old Town · *Collier, Diana G.*
Good Times - Bad Times · *Saunders, Les*
A Good Trick on Hens · *Johnston, George*

Good Value · *Ross, W.E. Dan*
Good Water, Good Water · *Thompson, Kent*
The Good Wife · *Fulford, Robert*
The Good Works Spirit · *Briffett, Isabel*
Good-by in Silence · *Mayse, Arthur*
Good-by Myra · *Munro, Alice*
Goodbye, Charlie · *Stein, David Lewis*
Goodbye, Northwest · *Horner, Bill*
Goodbye, Pam · *Dempsey, Jane*
Goodbye · *Spencer, Susan*
Good-bye Bibi · *Amprimoz, Alexandre*
[The?] Good-bye Gift · *Gillese, John Patrick*
Goodbye Grandpa · *Young, Scott*
Goodbye Grannie · *McConnell, Alice*
Goodbye John · *McLaughlin, Lorrie*
Goodbye Prince · *Buckler, Ernest*
Goodbye to All That · *Margoshes, Dave*
Goodnight Muse · *Bowser, Sara*
Goofy's Tits · *Raum, Elizabeth*
Goose Moon · *Kinsella, W.P.*
Gooseberry Twist · *Rushton, Bethany K.*
Goosefeathers · *Leveson, E.R.*
Gordie · *Davidson, Bill*
Gordon · *Wilson, Marglamb*
Gorg: A Detective Story · *Nichol, bp*
Gorman · *Teitel, Jay*
The Gospel According to Wiebe's Brother · *Witvoet, Bert*
The Gospel Woods · *Freiberg, Stanley*
Gossip: The Birds That Flew, the Birds That Fell · *Godfrey, Dave*
Got to Travel On · *Wood, Ted*
Gotta See That Man · *Heath, Martin*
A Gourdful of Glory · *Laurence, Margaret*
Government, Farming, and Water Sports · *Estill, Lyle*
A Government Grant at Last · *Carlson, Chuck*
The Government Man and the Indian or Is a Little Bit Really Better Than Nothing at All? · *Pinay, Donna*
Grace · *Tyhurst, Rob*
Grace & Faigel · *Levine, Norman*
Grace in the Bar · *Robson, Merrilee*
The Gradual Day · *Marshall, Joyce*
Graduation Day · *Ancevich, Jon*
Graffito · *Eisler, Ken*
A Grain of Manhood · *Gotlieb, Phyllis*
Grains of Sand · *Stortz, Joan*
The Gramaphone · *Dickson, Doris*
The Grammar of Silence · *Trethewey, Eric*
Grampa's Mistakes · *Russell, Ted*
Grampa's Only Sickness · *Russell, Ted*
The Grand Day · *Petersen, Olive MacKay*
Le Grand Déménagement · *Hood, Hugh*

Grand Finale · *Sawyer, Constance*
Grand Performance · *Fothergill, Robert J.*
The Grand Pursuit of Big Bear · *Wiebe, Rudy H.*
A Grand View of the Dog · *Guss, Joseph*
The Grandchildren · *Johnston, Basil H.*
Granddad's Futile Trip · *MacArthur, F.H.*
Grande Prairie · *Sheard, Sarah*
The Grandfather · *Burley, Margaret F.*
Grandfather's House · *Jones, Gerald*
Grandfather's Oak · *Stilwell, Arthur*
Grandfer's Deepfreeze · *Paterson, O.P.*
Grandma · *Ahmad, Iqbal*
Grandma and the Booming Bass · *Tait, John*
Grandma and the Career Girl · *Tait, John*
Grandma and the Dark Angel · *Tait, John*
Grandma and the Flighty Flora · *Tait, John*
Grandma and the Godly Hamish · *Tait, John*
Grandma and the Great Science · *Tait, John*
Grandma and the Love-Blind · *Tait, John*
Grandma and the Maid Forlorn · *Tait, John*
Grandma and the Man of Mettle · *Tait, John*
Grandma and the Misogamist · *Tait, John*
Grandma and the Plum Tree · *Tait, John*
Grandma and the Plunker · *Tait, John*
Grandma and the Prideful Woman · *Tait, John*
Grandma and the Public Nuisance · *Tait, John*
Grandma and the Sassenach · *Tait, John*
Grandma and the Spoiled Brat · *Tait, John*
Grandma and the Stalled Bride · *Tait, John*
Grandma and the Stour Cart · *Tait, John*
Grandma and the Tappit Hen · *Tait, John*
Grandma and the Unmerry Christmas · *Tait, John*
Grandma and the Unwelcome Stranger · *Tait, John*
Grandma and the Wee Pest · *Tait, John*
Grandma and the Wife-Beater · *Tait, John*
Grand'mere · *Scott, Margerie*
Grandmother · *Itani, Frances*
The Grandmother · *Cameron, Anne*
Grandpa · *Anonymous*
Grandpa Loved His Muzzle Loader · *North, Phil*
Grandpa Salem Talks Sail · *Morris, Flip*
Grandpa Saul · *Birch-Jones, Sonia*
The Grange · *Kirby, Ilona*
The Granite Club · *Hood, Hugh*
Granite Point · *Valgardson, W.D.*
Granma Goes on Strike · *Wilford, Marjorie*
Granny Grant · *Burnell, Ethel D.*
Granny Not! · *Ellis, Harry*

782

Granny Wins Canada · *Pope, Helen Hofmann*
Granny's Art · *Bird, Will R.*
Granny's Garden · *Vernon, Lorraine*
The Grant Game · *O'Connell, Dorothy*
The Grass · *Margoshes, Dave*
Grass Burning · *Dyroff, Jan Michael*
Grasshopper, Grasshopper · *Oliver, Michael Brian*
Grassi Place · *Allen, Robert Thomas*
The Grateful Tree · *Loftus, Peggy*
The Grates of Heaven · *Culliford, Clair*
The Grave by the Fig · *Schermbrucker, Bill*
The Grave of the Famous Poet · *Atwood, Margaret*
The Gravel Pile · *Duncan, Frances*
The Graveyard Shift · *Lavigne, Jean-Luc*
Graveyards Are Interesting Places · *Williams, Margaret*
The Great Atlantis Lotto · *Murray, Walter*
Great Aunt Harriett and the Red Ribbon Bull · *MacIntosh, Keitha K.*
Great Aunt Selina · *Farmer, Bernard J.*
The Great Banff Mountain Climbing Scandal · *Harris, Walter*
The Great Bear Expedition · *Hancock, Ronald Lee*
Great Big Boffs They Are · *Mitchell, Ken*
Great Blue Heron · *Hodgins, Jack*
The Great Canadian Novel · *White, Nanci*
The Great Charlie Walden · *Whitford, Margaret Ann*
A Great Day · *Hutchison, Bruce*
The Great Debate at Squid Tickle · *Harrington, Michael F.*
The Great Dog Race · *Johnson, G. Bertha*
The Great Electrical Revolution · *Mitchell, Ken*
Great Escapes · *O'Connell, Dorothy*
The Great Fall Supper · *Gray, Roberta B.*
The Great Film Night · *Pengelley, M.B.*
The Great Garbage Strike · *Legault, Donald*
The Great Intendant Plays St. Nick · *Dybvig, Leslie*
[The?] Great Man · *Barnar, Leslie Gordon*
The Great Man · *Gillese, John Patrick*
The Great Mouser of Wright Street · *Schweiger, Karol*
The Great Mystic · *Smith, Colonel* [pseudonym]
A Great Night for Hospitals · *Purdy, Brian*
Great Perturbations · *Turner, Ron*
The Great Queen Is Amused · *Davies, Robertson*
The Great Rosedale Beauty Contest · *Harris, Walter*
The Great Sanitary Landfill Debate · *Lavoie, Edgar*
The Great Speckled Bird · *Ireland, Ann*
The Great Submarine Chase · *Sweet, Jean*
The Great Wall of China Time 'X' · *Smith, Graham*
A Great Whore · *Butler, Juan*
The Greater Good · *MacLeod, Alistair*
The Greatest of These · *Green, H. Gordon*

The Greatest of These ... · *Whitford, Margaret Ann*
The Greatest Show on Earth · *de Barros, Paul*
The Greatest Thing · *Dorland, Keith R.*
The Grecian Urn · *Webb, Clifford*
The Greek Poetess · *Baliozian, Ara*
The Greeks · *Smith, Murray*
Green Blades of Grass · *Keeling, Nora*
Green Candles · *Kinsella, W.P.*
A Green Child · *Hood, Hugh*
Green Christmas · *Plant, R.C.*
The Green Far Hills · *Bird, Will R.*
Green Felt Blues · *Dronyk, Levi*
The Green Fox · *Kohut, Michael*
Green Ghosts · *Massey, G. Merrin*
the green girl · *Bullock, Michael*
Green Goddess · *Gormann, Adele M.*
Green Green Grass · *Spettigue, Douglas O.*
Green Ideas · *Avery, Martin*
Green Lake and Moose Point · *Boissonneau, Alice*
Green Leaves Falling · *Barnard, Leslie Gordon*
The Green Light · *Millard, Peter T.*
The Green Mushroom · *Wetmore, W. Gordon*
Green Pastures · *Buyukmihci, Hope Sawyer*
The Green Pickle · *Ariano, David*
Green Stakes for the Garden · *Thomas, Audrey*
Green Things · *Thompson, Kent*
Green Thumbs · *O'Connell, Dorothy*
The Greenhouse · *Weiss, Anne Marie*
Greenspan's Studio · *Kleiman, Edward*
Greenwich Village Blues · *Evanier, David*
Gregor Strassen · *Hutton, William Finlay*
Gregory · *Mandryk, Ted*
Grendel Greene · *Archer, Rodney*
Greta · *Burns, Mary*
The Greta Script · *Bailey, Don*
Gretel · *Beer, R.M.*
The Grey Goose · *Grawbarger, Josephine*
Grey Noon of Madness · *Easson, Bruce*
The Grid · *Sullivan, D.H.*
Grids and Doglegs · *Blaise, Clark L.*
Grief · *Kelly, M.T.*
Grieve for the Dear Departed · *Moore, Brian*
Griff! · *Clarke, Austin C.*
Griffin in the Garden · *Wickens, A. Gordon*
The Grindstone Man · *Fagan, Cary*
Grippes and Poche · *Gallant, Mavis*
Grizzly Gold · *Tench, C.V.*
Grizzly Mountain · *Burnard, Bonnie*

Groceries · *Gray, Hal*
Grogery Pack Tells About the Real Compleat Angler · *Anonymous*
The Grooviest Thing · *Maynard, Rona*
Grotesques · *Copeland, David*
Ground Level · *Bradbury, Esme*
The Ground Rod · *Mann, Judy*
The Groundhog · *Bailey, Don*
Group · *Smith, P. Louise*
Growing Pains · *Smith, Harriet Grahame*
Growing Things · *Stange, Ken*
Growing Up in Rosebud · *Wiebe, Rudy H.*
Growing Up Rosie · *Krueger, Lesley*
Grownups Get So Muddled · *Armstrong, Patricia*
The Grub Box · *Russell, Ted*
Grudge Game · *Young, Scott*
Grunda Mist · *Archer, Rodney*
Guardian Angel · *Layton, Boschka*
Gudfinna, Bells · *Gunnars, Kristjana*
Guerrilla Warfare · *Steffler, George*
Guess Who I Saw in Paris? · *Virgo, Sean*
The Guest · *Guthro, Lisa*
The Guest Speaker · *Torgov, Morley*
Guests and Fish · *Hobart, Virginia*
Guidance · *Evanier, David*
The Guide · *Nowlan, Alden*
Guido · *Turner, Lois*
Guilt · *Lambert, Elizabeth M.*
Guilt on the Lily · *Buckler, Ernest*
The Guilty Stain · *Mayse, Arthur*
The Guitar Lady · *Bradley, Esme*
The Guitar Man · *Cropas, Nyna*
Gull · *Bennett, Michael*
The Gull Rock Light Affair · *Wright, Bruce S.*
Gum Chewing Angel · *Edwards, Mary Kay*
Gumphy · *Gould, Jan*
The Gun Closet · *Ferris, Thomas*
Gun Law: The Judgment of Billy's Partner · *Haig-Brown, Roderick*
Gun Law: The Red-Headed Woman's Judgment · *Haig-Brown, Roderick*
Gundegar · *Burnett, Virgil*
Gunfight · *Scobie, Stephen*
The Gunfighter · *Nowlan, Alden*
Guns Are for Men · *Stemo, L. Johanne*
Gussy and the Boss · *Selvon, Samuel*
Gusto · *Corbett, Lenore M.*
A Guy Named Riley · *Annett, R. Ross and Annett, William S.*
The Guy with the Eyes · *Robinson, Spider*
Guys, Drinking · *Currie, Robert*
Gypsy Fiddler · *Green, H. Gordon*

Gypsy Reverie · *Wansley, David*
The Gyro Effect · *Hutchinson, Bobby*
The Gyroscope · *Sheils, Terry*

Haayim Gold · *Slabotsky, David*
Habakkuk Hoffer and the Haunted Harpsichord · *Story, Gertrude*
Habeus Corpus · *Shantz, Brenda*
Habit of Love · *Waddington, Miriam*
Habits · *Hodgins, Norris*
Had a Wife · *Hindmarch, Gladys*
Had Another · *Hindmarch, Gladys*
Had Myself a Merry Little Christmas · *Anonymous*
Hades Revisited · *Euringer, Fred*
Hadley and the First Child · *Donnell, David*
Hadrian's Wall · *Wait, Harvey J.*
Haggerty and the Big One · *Linder, Norma West*
Haggerty Serves His Special · *Linder, Norma West*
Hail · *Maltman, Kim*
Hail to the Chief · *Allister, Will*
Hailing a Cab · *Mandryk, Ted*
Hainesville Is Not the World · *Nowlan, Alden*
Hair Grows Half an Inch Every Month · *Kunnas, Susan*
Hair Jewellery · *Atwood, Margaret*
Hair on My Chest · *Klebeck, William J.*
The Haircut · *Fraser, Ross*
The Hair-Do · *Cormack, Barbara Villy*
Hake Massacre · *Choyce, Lesley*
Half a Bass Is Better Than No Love at All · *Greene, Anna*
Half a Grapefruit · *Munro, Alice*
Half a Worm · *Elgaard, Elin*
Half an Oaf · *Robinson, Spider*
The Half Husky · *Laurence, Margaret*
Half Truths · *Choyce, Lesley*
Half-Breed · *Hutchison, Bruce*
Half-Breed Wife · *Theriault, Yves*
Half-Breeds · *Bedard, Fran*
Halfdán Sigmundsson: Guest · *Gunnars, Kristjana*
The Half-Husky · *Laurence, Margaret*
Half-Past Eight · *Alford, Edna*
Halfway House · *Cappon, Cormac Gerald*
Halfway to the Mountain · *Barnhouse, D.P.*
Haliburton · *Percy, H.R.*
Halldor Thorgilsson: Crossroads · *Gunnars, Kristjana*
Hallowe'en · *Gibbs, Betty*
The Hallowe'en Party · *Waddington, Miriam*
Hamburger Heaven · *Bailey, Don*
The Hammer · *Thompson, Don*
Hammie and the Black Dean · *Clarke, Austin C.*
The Hamper · *Johnson, L.P.V.*

The Hamster Cage · *Kogawa, Joy*
the hand · *Bullock, Michael*
Hand in Glove with an Old Hat · *Dewdney, Christopher*
The Hand in the Dark · *Bowes, Margaret*
The Hand of the King · *Elflandsson, Galad*
The Hand on My Breast · *Clark, Joan*
Hand to Hand · *Gilliam, John*
The Handicap · *Kleiman, Edward*
The Handicap Was Blackmail · *Morrow, Mark*
Hands · *Cobban, William*
Hang Out Your Washing on the Siegfried Line · *Sawai, Gloria*
The Hanged Man · *Cohen, Matt*
The Hanging Man · *Virgo, Sean*
The Hanging of Eleanor Fairbairn · *Stacey, Ann*
Hanging Out with the Magi · *Rooke, Leon*
Hannibal the Great · *Duncan, M.M.*
Haply the Soul of My Grandmother · *Wilson, Ethel D.*
The Happening · *Pearson, Ailsa*
Happening on the Left · *Campbell, Ronald*
The Happiest Days · *Metcalf, John*
The Happiest Easter · *Briffett, Isabel*
The Happiest Man in the World · *Garner, Hugh*
The Happiest Man in Town [?] · *Garner, Hugh*
Happily Ever After · *Choyce, Lesley*
Happily Hooked on a Sailboat · *Werner, Gerrie*
Happiness · *Corwin, Phillip*
Happiness Is Not a Home · *Russell, Sheila MacKay*
The Happiness Pill · *Dobbs, Kildare R.E.*
Happiness You Can Count On · *Bankier, William*
Happy Birthday, an April Caprice · *Grantmyre, Barbara*
Happy Birthday Little Anarchist · *O'Brien, Bill T.*
Happy Birthday to You · *Barnard, Leslie Gordon*
Happy Endings · *Atwood, Margaret*
The Happy House · *Stein, Rhoda Elizabeth Playfair*
Happy Is the Man · *Bushell, Sidney*
Happy Jack · *Vanderhaeghe, Guy*
Happy Landing · *Seaman, Kathleen*
Happy Like a White Squash · *Wolper, Roy S.*
The Happy Smile · *Lewko, Judy*
Happy Soon and the Itinerant Muralist · *Wear, Robert Delattin*
The Happy Warrior · *Dobbs, Kildare R.E.*
The Happy Wife · *Partridge, Shirley*
Happy's Christmas · *Percy, H.R.*
The Harbinger · *McWhirter, George*
Harbinger: A Romantic Tale · *Schaub, Michael*
the harbour · *Bullock, Michael*
the hard · *Heath, Terence*
Hard Cash · *Scammell, A.R.*
Hard Decision · *McFadden, Isobel*
A Hard Pull · *Bergren, Myrtle*

787

Hard Tack for Mr. Calder · *Parr, D. Kermode*
Hard to Bear · *Murdoch, Benedict Joseph*
Hard to Swallow · *Power, John*
The Hard Way · *Barnard, Leslie Gordon*
The Harder the Worse · *Forrest, Bob*
The Hard-Headed Collector · *Godfrey, Dave*
Hard-Luck Stories · *Munro, Alice*
The Hard-Working Garbage Men of Cleveland · *Kilodney, Crad*
A Hare-Raisin' Experience · *Power, John*
Harlequins of the Night · *Ayre, John*
Harley Talking · *Hood, Hugh*
The Harmon Bequest · *Sutherland, David*
Harmonious Hoffer and His Hairless Hired Hand · *Story, Gertrude*
The Harness · *Buckler, Ernest*
Harness of Memory · *Fines, Beatrice E.*
Harold · *Jalava, Jarmo*
Harold and the Dragon · *Denoon, Ann*
Harold in Heaven · *Morton, Alex*
Harold Pagoda in Hollywood · *Small, Bryan R.*
Harold Winters · *Shepherd, R.W.*
Harpocrates Hoffer and the Heedless Harangue · *Story, Gertrude*
The Harpoon · *Barnard, Leslie Gordon*
Harrier · *Griggs, Terry*
Harriet · *Lewis, David E.*
Harry, the Businessman, Meets a Bag Lady · *Nielsen, Angela F.*
Harry · *Rikely, Dan*
Harry and Violet · *Thomas, Audrey*
Harry the Dream · *Hollingshead, Greg*
Harry the Hound Goes to Town · *McLean, Rachel*
Harry the Starman · *Kleiman, Edward*
Harry the Tiger Enters His Fiftieth Year · *Rooke, Leon*
The Harrying of Bokalewski · *Helwig, David*
Hartfeld · *Walker, Mirian*
Harvest · *Peterson, Barry*
Harvest Blessed · *Kelly, Marjorie*
Harvest of Love · *McDonald, Ruth*
The Harvest of Years · *Stilwell, Arthur*
The Harvester · *Kroetsch, Robert*
The Harvesters · *Svoboda, Terese*
The Has-Been · *Russell, Sheila MacKay*
Hasta La Vista · *Grieveson, Brian*
Hastings Jungle Vancouver · *Horne, Marcel*
The Hat · *Buffoono* [pseudonym]
A Hat for Billy Jim · *Conger, Lesley*
Hat Pandowdy · *Rooke, Leon*
The Hateful Suitor · *Green, H. Gordon*
Hatred Needs a Friend · *Molinaro, Ursula*
The Hatted Mannequins of 54th Street · *Rooke, Leon*
Hauling Away a Lighter · *Ellis, Harry*
Haunt · *Virgo, Sean*

The Haunted Dancers · *Mayse, Arthur*
A Haunted House · *Wuorio, Eva-Lis*
The Haunted Realm of the Humber River · *Verkoczy, Elizabeth*
Haunted Ship · *Mayse, Arthur*
Haute Couture · *Oliver, Michael Brian*
Have a Little Decency · *Hekkanen, Ernest*
Have a Nice Day · *Potrebenko, Helen*
'Have Done My Best' · *Steele, Harwood*
Have Gun, Will Shoot · *Russell, Sheila MacKay*
Have I Got a Picture for You · *O'Connell, Dorothy*
Have You Ever Killed a Spider? · *Friedman, Irena*
Have You Got a Rag · *Dagg, Mel*
Have You Seen Jesus? · *Bowering, George*
Have You Seen My Operation? · *Symons, Harry*
A Haven for the Aged · *Duncan, Leslie*
Having Eyes to See · *Green, H. Gordon*
The Hawk · *Dick, George*
Hayaqwas and the Cross · *Conger, Lesley*
The Hayfield · *Bowering, George*
The Haying · *Spettigue, Douglas O.*
The Hayloft · *Spettigue, Douglas O.*
Haynes, the Machine, and Maud · *Rushton, Alfred*
Hazlitt · *Thorne, Lynne*
He & I · *Minni, C.D.*
He Couldn't Argue with a Conscience · *Ryan, Josephine*
He Grabbed a Pig and ... · *Tamminga, Frederick W.*
He Had a Dog Once · *Carrier, Jean-Guy*
He Just Adores Her · *Hood, Hugh*
He Looked Around · *Dickinson, Mary Lou*
He Married for Murder · *Johnson, Vera D.*
He Raises Me Up · *Blaise, Clark L.*
He Said, Parenthetically · *Currie, Sheldon*
He Said · *Browne, Colin*
He Scores! He Shoots! · *Vanderhaeghe, Guy*
He Speaks to Me of Alphonse · *Hajes, A.J.*
He Wanted Adventure · *Eaton, Lucy Ellen*
He Was Almost My Baby · *Lee, Thirza M.*
He Who Laughs · *Lehman, Paul R.*
He Wished He Could Be Real · *Pogue, Lucille*
The Head · *Hughes, Gail*
Head in the Clouds · *Green, H. Gordon*
The Head of Baisano · *Tench, C.V.*
Headbeat · *Solly, Bill*
Heading into Winter · *Sarah, Robyn*
Headlights · *Campbell, Wanda Blynn*
Headlights in the Rain · *Powell, Dorothy M.*
Headofficestuff · *Anonymous*
Heads, Tails, or the Coin · *Paul & Jim*
The Headstone · *Spafford, Fran*
Headway · *Lazarus, Emma* [pseudonym]

The Healer · *Sanderson, James*
Healing · *Fraser, Keath*
Healing Hands · *Chappell, Constance*
The Health Bootleggers · *Parr, D. Kermode*
Healthy · *Hill, David*
Heard in the Echo · *Beattie, Jessie L.*
The Heart · *Steinfeld, J.J.*
Heart Attack ... Quien Sabe? · *Ogle, Robert Joseph*
The Heart Has Its Reasoning · *Pepper, Leila*
Heart of My Heart · *Young, David*
Heart of the Family · *Conger, Lesley*
The Heart Surgeon · *Kleiman, Edward*
Heart Trouble · *Harvor, Beth*
Heart-Aches Column Answered: Native Witchdoctor Performs Operation · *Eisen-bichler, Konrad*
Heartbeat · *Svendsen, Linda*
The Heart-Broken Lady · *Kutlesa, Joso*
Hearts and Flowers · *Moore, Brian*
The Heat of Summer · *Helwig, David*
Heat of the Light · *Butler, Douglas*
Heather from Swanage · *Helwig, David*
The Heatherington Murder Case · *Nowlan, Alden*
Heaven-57 · *Gilbert, Michael A.*
Heaven Help Us · *Gustafson, Ralph B.*
Heaven to Betsy · *McKim, Audrey*
The Heavenly Game · *Zend, Robert*
Hebel · *Kerslake, Susan*
Hector · *Perkin, Darlene*
Heigh Ho, Wheesly! · *Weir, Chuck*
The Height of a Boy · *Green, H. Gordon*
The Height of a Lad · *Green, H. Gordon*
Heikki and the Little Bear · *Wuorio, Eva-Lis*
Heil! · *Brown, Randy*
Heir to the Land · *Boas, Max*
The Heiress · *Harris, C.K.*
Helen · *Gustafson, Ralph B.*
Helen Mary and the Stranger · *Bird, Will R.*
Helga · *Stockdale, J[ohn]. C.*
Hell, No! We Won't Go · *MacLaurin, Douglas*
The Hell of It All · *Fenerty, Ron*
The Hell Raising Church Raiser · *Dybvig, Leslie*
Hello, Mrs. Newman · *Levine, Norman*
Hello, Out There · *Nowlan, Alden*
Hello, Pleased to Meet You · *Wakefield, Carol*
Hello, Young Trout · *Solly, Bill*
Hello and Goodbye · *Cameron, Eric*
Hello Boating! Goodbye Arnold · *Morris, Flip*
Hello Bobbins · *Powell, Dorothy M.*
The Helmet · *Pomroy, Christopher*
Help! · *Hoffman, Edith*

Help! Murder!   ·   *Hunter, Mary Alice*
Help Me, Hepplewhite   ·   *Hart, Anne*
Help Wanted   ·   *Cameron, Eric*
The Helper   ·   *Packer, Miriam*
A Helping Hand   ·   *Pritchard, Allan E.*
Hemispheres   ·   *Cruess, Jim*
'Hemo'   ·   *Grisak, Garry*
Henbane and a Tablespoon of Violets   ·   *Hoogstraten, Vinia*
Henrietta & and the Green Man   ·   *Jackson, J. Graham*
Henrietta Hoffer and the Hapless Heifer   ·   *Story, Gertrude*
Henrietta the Porcupine   ·   *Harvey, Kay L.*
Henry   ·   *McLaughlin, Paul*
Henry Finds the Roar   ·   *Blanchet, W. Wylie*
Henry Smoot's Practical Joke   ·   *Dougherty, Dan*
Henry's Birthday   ·   *Angus, Iris*
Henry's Paradox   ·   *Williams, Vera B.*
Henye   ·   *Faessler, Shirley*
Her Achilles Heel   ·   *Selvon, Samuel*
Her Boy   ·   *Bjarnason, Bogi*
Her Dear Deluded Daughter   ·   *Green, H. Gordon*
Her Father's Daughter   ·   *Horne, Lewis B.*
Her First Apartment   ·   *Brewster, Elizabeth*
Her Highness   ·   *Robertson, Strowan*
Her House   ·   *Hosein, Clyde*
Her Inheritance   ·   *Weir, John*
Her Last Visit Home   ·   *Gillese, John Patrick*
Her Moment of Fulfillment   ·   *Russell, Sheila MacKay*
Her Name Is Susan   ·   *Drylie, William*
Her Own Affair   ·   *Stein, Rhoda Elizabeth Playfair*
Her Salvation   ·   *Clark, Joan*
Her Story   ·   *Malone, Doreen*
Her Uncle   ·   *Hocking, Beverly*
Her Wonders to Perform   ·   *Currie, Sheldon*
Heraclitus Bathes   ·   *Wilson, J.D.*
Herb Cook's Breakfast   ·   *Sandman, John*
Here Are Some More Snaps   ·   *McFadden, David*
Here Be Dragons   ·   *Halstead, P.G.*
'Here Comes the Canada Council'   ·   *Fones, Robert and Nations, Opal L.*
Here Is No Water   ·   *Howard, Richard*
Here Too - They Serve   ·   *Burnell, Ethel D.*
Here We Go Round the Prickly Pear   ·   *Riddell, Bill*
Here's Looking at You   ·   *Wood, Ted*
Heresy for Carnivores and Golfers   ·   *McWhirter, George*
Heritage   ·   *Garside, Allan E.*
Herman   ·   *Petrie, Graham*
The Hermit   ·   *Burch, Mark A.*
Hero, O Heroine   ·   *Thompson, Kent*
The Hero   ·   *McKay, Muriel Saint*
The Hero Despite Himself   ·   *Hughes, Philip*
The Hero Who Was Scared of Cows   ·   *Green, H. Gordon*

Herodotus Hoffer and the Unilingual Hound · *Story, Gertrude*
Heroes · *Harlow, Robert*
The Heron Pool Fight · *Branden, Vicki*
Heronwood · *Mills, John*
Hershel Dov · *Slabotsky, David*
'He's a Stubborn Man' · *Morris, Doris M.*
Hester and the Special Fund · *Linder, Norma West*
Heteronyms · *Fones, Robert*
The Hetherington Murder Case · *Nowlan, Alden*
Hetty's Pound Party · *Tait, Elizabeth*
Hexagonal Throughput · *Decker, Ken*
The Hex-Man of Croaker's Hole · *Mayse, Arthur*
Hey! Hey! Anybody Listening? Anybody Care? · *Stein, Rhoda Elizabeth Playfair*
Hey You! Guess Who? · *Stein, Rhoda Elizabeth Playfair*
Heyfitz · *Cohen, Matt*
Hhar'ani · *Filter, Reinhard*
Hialeah Hoffer and the Walleyed Mare · *Story, Gertrude*
The Hidden Eye · *Kellythorne, Walt*
Hidden Treasure · *Beauvais, Ronald*
The Hidden Truth · *Leitao, Lino*
Hide and Seek · *Sanderson, James*
Hiding · *Kerlikowske, Elizabeth*
Hiding Place · *Bowie, Douglas*
The Hierodule · *Yates, J. Michael*
High Altitude · *Barnard, Leslie Gordon*
The High Board · *Slater, Ian*
High Button Shoes · *Parks, Milton*
High Country Burn · *Trower, Peter*
High Fidelity · *Robinson, Spider*
High Finance · *Anonymous*
The High Snow · *Bacque, James*
High Speed Interchange · *de Barros, Paul*
High Walls · *McEwen, Maud*
A Higher Learning · *Story, Gertrude*
The Higher Things · *Flatt, Mary*
Highway 69 Is Disappearing · *Jirgins, Karl E.*
Highway Three · *Bowering, George*
Hijack! · *Waterston, Don*
The Hill · *Zieroth, Dale*
Hills Are Like Blue Eyes · *Mason, Mike*
Him · *Floras, John*
Himmler, Hotshot and Dandy · *Keeling, Nora*
The Hindu Goan · *Leitao, Lino*
A Hinge of Possibilities · *Sparling, Sharon*
A Hint of Danger · *Bankier, William*
A Hint of Fizz · *Young, David*
A Hint of Poochiness · *Barker, Bessie M.*
Hippies' Child · *Graham, Ferne*
Hippopotamus · *Greenwood, Gail*
The Hippy Summer · *MacIntosh, Keitha K.*

The Hire · *Browne, Paul Cameron*
The Hired Man · *McCourt, Edward A.*
Hiroko Writes a Story · *McFadden, David*
His Alone · *Brown, Randy*
His Eyes in the Storm · *Harding, John*
His Family · *Itani, Frances*
His Father's Medals · *Cowasjee, Saros*
His First Hard Knock · *Monckton, M.E.*
his flashing eyes, his floating hair · *Branden, Vicki*
His Last Gift · *Burnell, Ethel D.*
His Mother · *Gallant, Mavis*
His Mother's Son · *Russell, Sheila MacKay*
His Move · *Johnson, Ruth*
His Native Place · *Nowlan, Alden*
His Nemesis · *Dyke, Dave Hart*
His Only Person · *Teitel, Jay*
His Story · *Rehlinger, Oliver*
His Weakness · *Price, C.B.*
His Wonders to Perform · *Stein, Rhoda Elizabeth Playfair*
The Historian · *Austin, Don*
Historical Fiction · *Clark, Joan*
Histories · *Schoemperlen, Diane*
History · *Sherman, Kenneth*
History & Physical: Mrs. Wishart · *Wilson, Barbara*
History Account · *Tens, Johnny*
The History Lesson · *Harris, Fredie Steve*
The History of England, Part Four · *Rooke, Leon*
History of Poets: Benny Goodman · *Coleman, Victor and Young, David A.*
History of the Canadian West · *Bell, Wade*
A History of the New World · *Wiebe, Rudy H.*
The History of the World · *Kilodney, Crad*
The Hitch Hiker · *Mercer, P.F.*
Hitch Hype · *Coleman, Victor and Young, David A.*
A Hitch in Time · *Cameron, Eric*
Hitch-Hiker · *Mitton, Roger*
Hitch-Hiking · *Dewsnap, David*
Hitler Argentine Journal · *King, Earl*
Hitting the Charts · *Rooke, Leon*
Ho All Ye Campers · *Stein, Rhoda Elizabeth Playfair*
Hobby · *Cooper, Jas E.*
Hobe · *Burns, Richard M.*
The Hobo Tea · *Armstrong, Patricia*
Hockey and the Bald-Headed Great Aunts · *Avery, Martin*
Hockey Etiquette · *McIlroy, Kimball*
A Hockey Game · *Boyarsky, Abraham*
Hockey Night in Canada Jr. · *Avery, Martin*
Hockey Wife · *McIlroy, Kimball*
Hoffer and the Horned Dilemma · *Story, Gertrude*
Hofritz · *Rikki [Erica Ducornet]*
The Hoist · *Sinclair, Gerri*

Hold That Tiger · *Weinzweig, Helen*
Hold Your Tongue · *Haig-Brown, Roderick*
The Holding Jar · *Fagan, Cary*
Holdup! · *Moore, Brian*
The Holdup · *Lappin, Ben*
Hold-Up at Castleborough · *Craigie, Alexander*
The Hole · *Kinsley, William*
The Hole in the Hill · *Mitchell, Sylvia Elizabeth Fisher*
The Hole - Thing · *Goulden, Ron*
Holiday, My Bone · *Gunnars, Kristjana*
The Holiday · *Wood, Margaret E.*
Holiday 'Ad Lib' · *Matthews, Sandy*
Holiday Eve · *Barnard, Leslie Gordon*
Holiday Father · *Begamudre, Ven*
Holiday for Mum · *Harvey, Jennifer A. Becks*
Holiday Haven · *Thompson, Kent*
Holiday in Five Rivers · *Selvon, Samuel*
A Holiday in the Doom Future · *Swan, Susan*
Holidays · *Ogle, Robert Joseph*
Holidays Can Be Fun - Even for Frustrated Father · *Stilwell, Arthur*
Holiday's End · *Fagan, Cary*
The Hollow Men · *Waterhouse, John*
The Hollow Tree · *Briffett, Isabel*
The Hollowed Halls of Learning · *Stephenson, Paula*
The Holocaust Remembrance Service · *Avery, Martin*
The Holy Man · *Hood, Hugh*
Holy Mary Mother of God · *Stambaugh, Sara*
Holy Night · *Wegner, Diana*
The Holy Roller Empire · *Clark, Joan*
Holydays · *Gentleman, Kirstie*
Holy-Fast By-the-Sea: An Urban Fable · *Wanzell, Grant*
Homage · *Allen, M.E.*
Homage to Axel Hoeniger · *Drew, Wayland*
The Homburg Hat · *Sturdy, John Rhodes*
Home · *O'Hagan, Denis*
Home Again · *Kerpneck, Harvey*
Home and Native Land · *Missio, Aldo G.*
Home Base · *Ringwood, Gwen Pharis*
Home Country · *Collins, David M.*
Home for Christmas · *Smith, Joyce M.*
Home for Night · *Wiebe, Rudy H.*
Home from the Hill · *Jones, G.H.J.*
Home Front · *Donaldson, Allan*
Home Grown in the East End · *Powell, Marilyn*
The Home Handyman · *Duncan, Frances*
Home Is the Sailor · *Barnard, Leslie Gordon*
Home Life · *Andrews, Marke*
Home Movie · *Rule, Jane*
Home Movies · *Rooke, Constance*
Home No More Home to Me · *Branden, Vicki*

Home on the Midnight · *Dales, Walter A.*
Home Place · *Fines, Beatrice E.*
Home Sweet Home · *Sudbury, Harold A.J.*
Home the Warrior · *Green, H. Gordon*
Home Thoughts from Abroad · *Engel, Marian*
The Home Waltz · *Ketchen, Susan*
Homecoming · *Nichols, Mark*
Homecoming: A Memory of Europe After the Holocaust · *Kreisel, Henry*
The Homemaker · *Briffett, Isabel*
Homer's Door · *Euringer, Fred*
The Homestead · *Haig-Brown, Roderick*
The Homestead and the Heart · *Willison, Evelyn A.*
Homestead Honeymoon · *Curran, Kitty*
Homunculus · *Cary, Joseph*
Honest Woman · *Young, Scott*
Honestly, It's Nothing · *Cooper, Audrey*
A Honeymoon · *Dempsey, Ian*
The Honeymoon House · *Waddington, Miriam*
Honeymoon with Death · *Wuorio, Eva-Lis*
Honeymoonland · *Rapoport, Janis*
Honeysuckle and Snickadoodles · *Owen, George*
the honeywagon · *Heath, Terence*
The Honolulu Sun · *Rosenfeld, Rita*
The Honourable Man · *Rasmussen, Anita*
Hoofbeats in the Night · *Fitzpatrick, Eva*
The Hook, the Eye and the Whip · *Coney, Michael G.*
A Hook into the Rough · *Helwig, David*
Hook Line and Mrs. Sinclair · *Hayes, Ada*
Hooker · *Halliday, David*
Hooking Things · *Summers, Merna*
Hooray for No System · *Green, H. Gordon*
Hop Sing · *Donnelly, John F.*
Hope · *Percy, H.R.*
Hopfstadt's Cabin · *Kinsella, W.P.*
Hopkins · *Rose, Bob*
Hormone Pills · *MacNair, Janet*
Horning In · *Williamson, O.T.G.*
Horrid Upheavals · *Harvey, Jennifer A. Becks*
Horror Comics · *Atwood, Margaret*
Horror in the Black Hills · *Saunders, Charles R.*
Horse · *Glover, Douglas H.*
The Horse Buster · *Kowal, Victor*
A Horse Called Bill · *Greenwood, Joan*
Horse Collars · *Kinsella, W.P.*
Horse Power · *Lemna, D.F.*
A Horse Ride · *McWhirter, George*
Horse Sense · *Cameron, Eric*
Horse Tales · *Mosher, Edith*
The Horse That Left His Mark · *Mosher, Edith*
Horse Thieves · *Grennan, William*

The Horse Wrangler · *Sears, Dennis T. Patrick*
The Horseman and the Red Columns · *Pelargos, Anna*
Horses Make Me Sad · *MacDonald, Deborah*
Horses of the Night · *Laurence, Margaret*
Horses of the Sun · *Redmond, Tess*
Horsey Horsey · *Virgo, Sean*
The Horticulturalist · *Harvey, Jennifer A. Becks*
Hospital Visit · *Dey, Myrna*
Hoss and the Man-Eating Wolverines · *Wiley, Tom*
Hoss and the Yuk-Chick-toes · *Hossick, Hugh and Wiley, Tom*
Hostess · *Copeland, Ann* [pseudonym]
Hostility · *Dyer, Evelyn*
Hot Day · *Chen, Jean*
Hot Feet in Puerto Rico · *Swan, Susan*
Hot Line · *Kilodney, Crad*
Hot Supper · *Corbett, Isabel Scott*
The Hot Volunteer · *Waltner-Toews, David*
Hottentot Hoffer and His Last Hope of Heaven · *Story, Gertrude*
The Hound Magee · *Skinner, Norman Doc*
The Hounds of Barkerville · *Bauer, William A.*
The Hour of Letdown · *White, E.B [?]*
An Hour to Wait · *Garner, Hugh*
A House · *Dillon, Norma*
House by the Gorge · *Webber, Frances*
A House by the Sea · *Park, John*
A House for Senora Lopez · *Ross, James*
The House from the Eleventh Floor · *Wuorio, Eva-Lis*
A House Full of Women · *Brewster, Elizabeth*
House Guest · *Rule, Jane*
House of Cards · *Julian, Marilyn*
House of Glass · *Humphries, Tom*
House of Ice · *Fleury, Val* [pseudonym]
The House of Jimmy Yee · *Longstaff, Bill*
The House of Make-Believe · *Liman, Claude*
House of the Whale · *MacEwen, Gwendolyn*
The House on Tenth · *Bowering, George*
The House on the Island · *Laurent, Lucien*
The House on the Rock · *Torgov, Morley*
The House on the Top of the Hill · *Doyle, Nancy*
The House Opposite · *Blakeston, Oswell*
House Proud · *Robinson, Joan*
The House That Jack Built · *Stein, Rhoda Elizabeth Playfair*
The House Where My Heart Lives · *Clare, John P.*
A House with a Past · *Mosher, Edith*
Housekeeper · *Rule, Jane*
Houses · *Kellythorne, Walt*
The Housewife's Dilemma · *Kollonay. Georgina*
The Housing Problem · *Weiner, Andrew*
How a Birthday Was Passed and a Sorrow Set · *Horne, Lewis B.*
How a Life Line Grew · *Stein, Rhoda Elizabeth Playfair*

How a Man Ought to Die · *Green, H. Gordon*
How Babies Are Made · *Smith, Marnie*
How Bamford-Gordon Abolished the Income Tax · *Gray, John*
How Beautiful Is the Rain · *Barnard, Margaret E. and Barnard, Leslie Gordon*
How Beautifully Blue the Sky the Glass is Rising Very High Continue Fine I Hope
I May ... · *Davidson, Craig*
How Bobby Found the Christ Child · *Stein, Rhoda Elizabeth Playfair*
How Can I Lose, Doc? · *O'Neil, Ernie*
How Casey Lost His Girl · *Nimchuk, Michael John*
How Could I Do That? · *Munro, Alice*
How Crocus Got Its Seaway · *Mitchell, W.O.*
How Cuchulainn Went on the Glooscap Trail · *Paratte, Henri Dominique*
How Darkness Came to Carcosa · *Elflandsson, Galad*
How Delsing Met Frances & Started to Write a Novel · *Bowering, George*
How Does a Barn Fall Down? · *Olson, Sheree-Lee*
How Fame Was Thrust Upon Me · *King, Florence*
How I Became a Jew · *Blaise, Clark L.*
How I Became a Vampire · *Pratt, Terry*
How I Became an Englishman · *Garner, Hugh*
How I Became Champ · *Christy, Jim*
How I Came to Canada · *Belserene, Paul*
How I Fucked Up My Life · *Walsh, Hugh*
How I Got Cured: A Testimonial · *Baerstein, Tsigane*
How I Lost My Mind · *Baycroft, Perry*
How I Met My Husband · *Munro, Alice*
How I Won the Medal in Vietnam or I Like Nuts in My Chocolate Bar · *Dickson,
Barry*
How It Feels · *Hindmarch, Gladys*
How It Happens · *Sanderson, Helen*
How 'Ja Do Today · *Tudor, Kathleen*
How Lena Got Set Back · *Stambaugh, Sara*
How Much a Pound · *Green, H. Gordon*
How Much a Pound? · *Green, H. Gordon*
How Much Do You Pay for the Sun · *Graham, Robert*
How Mule Jackson Got Killed · *smith, d.c [sic]*
How My Auntie Became Prime Minister · *Harris, Walter*
How My Auntie Communed with the Ghost of Mackenzie King · *Harris, Walter*
How Not to Buy a Horse · *Epps, Bernard*
How Pittsburgh Returned to the Jungle · *Long, Haniel*
How She Go, Johnny? · *Reid, Iris R.*
How the Earth Gave Birth to Fire · *Pooley, Richard*
How the Hungry Are Fed · *Bauer, William A.*
How the Monkey Got His Tail · *Staples, Elizabeth*
How the Raiders Are Doing · *Rooke, Leon*
How the Story Ends · *Vanderhaeghe, Guy*
How the West Was Won · *Stickland, Eugene*

How the Woman's Generation Movement Freed Heleda Bang from Her Tortures
and Brought Midnight Oil to the Old Folks on Oa · *Rooke, Leon*
How Things Are · *Pollock, Sharon*
How Three Little Pigs Were Baptized · *Keefe, K.B.*
How to Compile a Dictionary · *Sarna, Lazar*
How to Cure Insomnia · *Welykopolsky, Luba*
How to Dispose of Old Furniture · *Stilwell, Arthur*
How to Grow Hair on a Pumpkin · *Skinner, Norman Doc*
How to Handle Women · *McNamee, James*
How to Invent a Better Egg Timer · *Ellis, Harry*
How to Know the True Prince · *Thibaudeau, Colleen*
How to Live with People · *Cade-Edwards, Eileen*
How to Punctuate a Date: For Better or for Worse · *Cairns, Malcolm*
How to Run the Country · *St. Pierre, Paul*
How to Sell Insurance · *Nowlan, Alden*
How to Watch Television · *Sherman, Tom*
How Was Your Day? · *MacMillan, Gail*
How Well We Filled the Wilderness · *Sarah, Robyn*
Howard · *Lord, J. Barry*
The Howard Parker Montcrief Hoax · *McNamara, Eugene*
Howie · *Brown, Mae Hill*
How's the Traffic on Bloor Street? · *Dickinson, Mary Lou*
How's the Weather? · *Sturdy, John Rhodes*
The Hoyer · *Alford, Edna*
The Huckemeyer Story · *Johnson, Vera D.*
The Hudson River · *Harvor, Beth*
Hudson's Bay Sable · *Staubitz, Arthur*
Hugh Hood's Version of 'Diddle Diddle Dumpling' · *Hood, Hugh*
Hugues · *Burnett, Virgil*
The Human Factor · *Rosenman, John B.*
The Human Hand · *Wuorio, Eva-Lis*
Humble Pie · *Buckler, Ernest*
Humbly, for Fyodor · *Nowlan, Alden*
Humbug · *Symons, Harry*
The Humour and the Frustration · *Pitsch, Terry*
Humouresque · *Wheatley, Patience*
Humphrey's Christmas · *de Lint, Charles and Harris, MaryAnn*
A Hundred Things Forgotten · *Helwig, David*
A Hungarian Rhapsody · *Friedman, Irena*
Hunger · *Roberts, Dorothy*
The Hungry Son · *Wood, Kerry*
Hunky · *Garner, Hugh*
The Hunstman · *Stein, David Lewis*
The Hunt · *Green, H. Gordon*
The Hunt · *Slater, Ian*
The Hunter · *Frey, Lilly*
the hunter and the flower · *Bullock, Michael*
The Hunter Who Loses His Human Scent · *Yates, J. Michael*
Hunters · *Ross, Veronica*
Hunter's Death · *Andrews, Donald*

Hunters in the Night · *McConnell, Shane*
Hunters Lost · *Jensen, Kevin*
The Hunter's Waking Thoughts · *Gallant, Mavis*
Hunting · *Valgardson, W.D.*
The Hunting Knife · *Staubitz, Arthur*
Hunting License · *Evans, Lewis*
Hunting McDougall · *Wiebe, Rudy H.*
The Hunting of the Snerk · *Lavoie, Edgar*
Hunting Season · *Rosta, Helen J.*
The Huntsman · *Stein, David Lewis*
Hurricane Hazel · *Atwood, Margaret*
Hurt · *Nowlan, Alden*
the husband · *Halliday, David*
Husband and Wife Gratten · *Richards, David Adams*
Husbands · *Hodgins, Norris*
Husbands Are for Keeping · *Ryan, Josephine*
The Hutterites · *Russell, Sheila Mackay*
the hydra · *Bullock, Michael*
The Hydrophobia Stunt · *McConnell, Shane*
The Hypocrite · *Dreschel, Andrew*

I, Maureen · *Spencer, Elizabeth*
I, Myself · *Pat [pseudonym]*
I, Quixote, Librarian · *Yates, J. Michael*
I.D. · *Walsh, Scott*
I a Wino · *Anonymous*
I Always Knew There Was a Lord · *Gibbs, Robert*
I Am a Poet · *Horst, Roger*
I Am a Wizard · *Trembley, Georges*
I Am Dying, Dying · *Jackson, J. Graham*
I Am Dying, Egypt · *Watt, Frank W.*
I Am for the Birds · *Schull, Joseph J.*
I Ask Myself · *Birdsell, Sandra*
I Became a Ghost · *Jelinek, Vera*
I Called to My Mother · *Dille, Carolyn*
I Can't Figure Anything Out Anymore but Then I Never Could Am I Doing What
I Ought to or Merely What I Should? · *Carson, Bryan*
I Do, I Do or, The Energy for Bloodsport · *Aylen, John*
I Don't Know What I'm Doing Here · *Siggins, Marjorie*
I Don't Want to Know Anyone Too Well · *Levine, Norman*
I Don't Want You Back · *Pemberton, Prim*
I Dreamed I Saw the Queen Last Night · *Cohen, Matt*
I Fled Him Down the Nights · *Bruneau, Bernard*
I for an Eye · *Shrier, Howard*
I Found a Thing to Do · *Sheps, David*
I Got Your Card About the Chickadees · *McLaughlin, Peter*
I Gotta Get Outta Here · *Hindmarch, Gladys*
I Hanging On, Praise God! · *Clarke, Austin C.*
'I Have a Letter for Mr. Frenchman ... ' · *Rutland, R.B.*

I Have Died. She Lives · *Avery, Martin*
I Hear a Tambourine · *Jackson, Carl*
I Hear Them Call · *Wuorio, Eva-Lis*
I Just Don't Know · *Millson, Larry*
I Just Heard from Helen Again · *Sheard, Sarah*
I Knew Queen Victoria's Sister · *Anderson, Mavis*
I Know What I Like · *Currie, Robert*
I Know Where I'm Going · *Baker, Rita*
I Like Chekhov · *Levine, Norman*
I Live in Canada · *Thompson, Kent*
I Love Dragon Lady · *Hollingshead, Greg*
I Love People · *Phillips, R.A.J.*
I Love You, I Love You, I Do · *Silvester, Reg*
I Meet the Major · *Moore, Thomas*
I Must Be Going · *Margoshes, Dave*
An 'I' Narrative · *Steinhauer, C.*
I Prefer Dogs ... · *McDougall, Joseph Easton*
I Remember · *Cowasjee, Saros*
I Remember Aunt Linda · *Jarvis, June N.*
I Remember Buckshot · *Green, H. Gordon*
I Remember El Stomacho · *O'Brien, Richard*
I Remember Horses · *Kinsella, W.P.*
I Remember Miss Jean Murdock · *Lewis, David E.*
I Remember Seeing My Grandfather's House and Grapevines · *Tourbin, Dennis*
I Remember You · *Mofina, R.H.*
I Remember - Christmas · *Trotter, Zoë Pauline*
'I Reserve the Right ...' · *Barker, Bessie M.* ·
i saw cortez in the streets of the city · *Austin, Don*
I Saw Them in Love, Peter and Sue · *Chatupa, James*
I See Something, It Sees Me · *Engel, Marian*
I Shot an Arrow in the Air · *Hendrie-Quinn, J.*
I Should Explain About Sally · *Clark, Matthew*
I Stole the Lilacs · *Williams, Marian*
I Think They Were Laughing at Me · *Rodgers, Gordon*
I Thought I Saw a Pussy Cat · *Stockdale, J[ohn]. C.*
I Walked Away Singing · *Watt, Sholto*
I Want My Mother · *Amprimoz, Alexandre*
I Want to Be Free · *Anonymous*
I Wanted to Call You · *Austin, Don*
I Was a Teen-Age Slumlord · *Kinsella, W.P.*
I Was Here First! · *Burnell, Ethel D.*
I Will Never Forget You Ernie Frigmaster · *Rikki [Erica Ducornet]*
I Wonder Why They Took the Icons · *Thompson, B.*
I Work in the City · *Hekkanen, Ernest*
Ibena · *Rooke, Leon*
Icarus · *Zilber, Jacob*
Ice and 'Baccy · *Russell, Ted*
Ice and Ducks · *Russell, Ted*
The Ice Book · *Young, David*
Ice Carnival · *Clemmer, E.F.*

The Ice Cream Man · *Pope, Dan*
The Ice Dream Parlor · *Bowman, Brian*
Ice Fishing · *MacLean, Robert*
The Ice Floes · *Kirkwood, Hilda*
An Ice Folly · *Skinner, Norman Doc*
The Ice Forest · *Marriott, J. Anne*
The Ice House · *Freiberg, Stanley*
The Ice House Gang · *Rooke, Leon*
The Ice Road · *Barker, H.T.*
The Ice Wagon Going Down the Street · *Gallant, Mavis*
Ice-Elation · *Foley, Mark*
the icehouse · *Heath, Terence*
Icicle · *Boates, Bob*
I'd Bale It · *Godfrey, Dave*
I'd Have Kicked Her Out · *Rosenfeld, Rita*
The Idealist · *Barnard, Murray*
Identities · *Valgardson, W.D.*
Identity · *Ezrin, Bob*
The Idiot Lady · *Atkinson, Keith*
Idiots · *Ledbetter, Ken*
The Idyllic Summer · *Munro, Alice*
Idylls of the King: A Newfoundland Version · *Cahill, Brian*
If Gauthier Should Read This · *Novak, Barbara*
If God Hadn't Intended Man to Fly, He Would Have Given Him Roots · *Bennett, A.*
If He Hollers Let Him Go · *Lamb, Murray*
If I Had a Hammer ... · *Stein, Rhoda Elizabeth Playfair*
If I Were Einstein or Wittgenstein or Poe · *Austin, Don*
If I'm Here, Imagine Where They Sent My Luggage · *Sawyer, Robert*
If It's Real, It'll Be There Monday · *Stein, Rhoda Elizabeth Playfair*
If Jill Hadn't Taken · *Schendlinger, Mary*
If Lost Return to the Swiss Arms · *Rooke, Leon*
If One Green Bottle ... · *Thomas, Audrey*
If There Is No Gate · *Rule, Jane*
If Thine Eye Offend Thee · *Callaghan, Michael*
If Thy Brother Offend Thee ... · *Jess, Cameron*
If We Make It Through the Winter · *Easley, Shirley-Dale*
If Winter Come · *Martin, Peter G.*
If Winter Comes · *Selvon, Samuel*
If You Ask for a Fish · *Eaton, Lucy Ellen*
If You Hum Me a Few Bars I Might Remember the Tune · *Bailey, Don*
If You Love Me Meet Me There · *Rooke, Leon*
If You Went to the River Why Were You Not Baptized? · *Rooke, Leon*
If You Wish upon a Star · *Beachey, Anne*
IGA Days · *Hollingshead, Greg*
Igloo · *Walters, Harold Neal*
Ignorance Is Not Bliss · *Green, H. Gordon*
I-grec Is Y: Autonomie · *Bell, Gay*
The Iguana · *Jonas, George*
'I'll Be Seeing You!' · *Hodgins, Norris*

I'll Bring You Back Something Nice · *Levine, Norman*
I'll Never Forget Miss Lemon · *Harvey, Kay L.*
I'll Never Let You Go · *Garner, Hugh*
I'll See You Again · *Garner, Hugh*
I'll Take Archie · *McKay, Muriel Saint*
Illation · *Wilks, David*
Illiana Comes Home · *Kinsella, W.P.*
The Illness · *Horne, Lewis B.*
The Illusion · *Skelton, Robin*
Illusions of Young Men · *Brewster, Elizabeth*
The Illustrator · *Johnson, Linda Wikene*
I'm a Big Girl Now · *Burke, James*
I'm a Presbyterian, Mr. Kramer · *Hosein, Clyde*
I'm Annoyed with Freud · *Owen, George*
I'm Beginning to Lose My Humanity · *Boyle, John C.*
I'm But a Stranger Here · *Hardy, W.G.*
I'm Dreaming of Rocket Richard · *Blaise, Clark L.*
I'm Free! I'm Free! · *Hollingshead, Rosemary*
I'm Lonesome for Harrisburg · *Waddington, Miriam*
I'm Not Desparate [sic] · *Hood, Hugh*
I'm Sorry · *Cade-Edwards, Eileen*
I'm Sorry Mrs. Strauss · *Soderstrom, Mary*
I'm Still Here · *Ross, Veronica*
I'm Still Losing My Humanity · *Boyle, John C.*
The Image · *Bentley, Allen*
Image 1 · *Roberts, Terence*
Image 2 · *Roberts, Terence*
The Image and the Girl · *Rakosy, Susan*
Image in the Shattered Mirror · *Fagan, Cary*
The Image Is Like That, It Started Out of a Simple Light · *Anastacio, Michael*
Image without Flaw · *Hanson, Esther Schneider*
Images. From a Moving Railway Car · *Godfrey, Dave*
Images · *Munro, Alice*
Images for the Horsemen · *Leyden, Douglas*
The Imaginary Soldier · *Nowlan, Alden*
Imagination's Wings · *Ranson, Dave*
Imaro and the Giant Kings · *Saunders, Charles R.*
An Imitation of Two Men · *McWhirter, George*
The Immigrant · *Croutch, Leslie A.*
Immigrants at the Dump · *Powning, Beth*
Immolation · *Duncan, Frances*
The Immortal Quest · *Bankier, William*
Immortality · *Gugeler, Fritz*
The Immortals · *Kleiman, Edward*
Impatience · *Elgaard, Elin*
'The Impenetrables' · *Sutherland, Fraser*
Imperatives · *Flood, Cynthia*
The Importance of Music · *Stange, Ken*
The Importance of Patsy McLean · *Hodgins, Jack*
An Important Change in My Outlook on Life as a Result of Two Events That Took

In Plain Words · *Laudon, H.V.*
In Point of Fact · *Gustafson, Ralph B.*
In Praise of Older Men · *Smith, A.J.M.*
In Praise of Professionals · *Amprimoz, Alexandre*
In Pursuit of the Maraschino · *Garber, Lawrence*
In Quebec City · *Levine, Norman*
In Retrospect: The Going · *Edwards, Lionel*
In Search of a Portfolio · *O'Connell, Dorothy*
In Search of Graham Greene · *Clemence, Esme*
In Search of Inspiration · *Cohen, Matt*
in search of Noire · *Bullock, Michael*
In Search of Perfection · *Baltensperger, Rita*
In Search of Rosa · *Stanley-Porter, Caroline*
In Search of Vice · *Youngberg, Gail*
In Season · *Campbell, Wanda Blynn*
In Secula Seculorum · *Stock, B.C.*
In Sickness and in Health ... · *Fontaine, Patricia*
In Silent Desperation · *Bristow, Susan*
In Small Towns, Everybody Knows · *Armstrong, Patricia*
In Spite of the War · *Plimbley, Pat*
In the Attic of the House · *Rule, Jane*
In the Basement of the House · *Rule, Jane*
In the Beaver Hills · *Wiebe, Rudy H.*
In the Beginning · *Marlatt, Daphne*
In the Bleak Mid-Winter · *Thomas, Audrey*
In the Blood · *Rosta, Helen J.*
In the Boot · *Mason, Mike*
In the Bright of the Moon · *Doyle, Nancy*
In the Country · *Robertson, E.*
In the Crowd's Image · *Melfi, Mary*
In the Cultural Warehouse · *Kilodney, Crad*
In the Culture Warehouse · *Kilodney, Crad*
In the Customs of Men · *Walters, Harold Neal*
In the Dark · *Crowther, Joan*
In the Dark Gymnasium of a Warm Spring Night · *Dodge, William*
In the Darkness of the Light · *Hofbauer, Pat*
In the Distant Singing Guts of the Moment · *Godfrey, Dave*
In the Fall · *MacLeod, Alistair*
In the Final Sounds of Play · *Furey, L.J.*
In the Finland Woods · *Nowlan, Alden*
In the Forests of the Night · *Rose, Mildred A.*
In the Garden · *Rooke, Leon*
In the Gatineaus · *Rigelhof, T.F.*
In the House Next Door · *Bankier, William*
In the Ingle Nook · *Blakeston, Oswell*
In the Jungle · *Tsubouchi, David*
In the Lazaretto · *Marcellin, Philip*
In the Lobby of the Phaedra · *Ross, Stuart*
in the log · *Bullock, Michael*
In the Long Run · *Boyle, John*

In the Midst of Life · *Marshall, Joyce*
In the Mood · *Watmough, David*
In the Moon's Sphere · *Howard, Richard*
In the Museum · *McNamara, Eugene*
In the Museum of Evil · *Hodgins, Jack*
In the New House · *Holz, Cynthia*
In the New World · *Hekkanen, Ernest*
In the Night Season · *Chambers, Doug*
In the Park · *MacSween, R.J.*
In the Pocket · *Foran, Charles*
In the Prison · *Bedard, Michael*
In the Room Where Dying Is Complete · *Steinfeld, J.J.*
In the Shadow of Her Sister · *Fines, Beatrice E.*
In the Shadows · *Madsen, Margaret*
In the Spell of Its Breathing · *Bloomfield, W.M.*
In the Spotlight · *O'Connell, Dorothy*
In the Sun Room · *Young, Pamela*
In the Time of Two Letters · *Slabotsky, David*
In the Tunnel · *Gallant, Mavis*
In the Village of Alias · *Sutherland, Fraser*
In the Warm-Up Hut - A View of Mirabel Airport · *Richardson, Peter*
In the Wilderness · *Goulden, Alban*
In the Woods · *Beneteau, Marcel*
In the Yellow Circle · *Spettigue, Douglas O.*
In There · *Stein, David Lewis*
In This Age of Chess · *Richards, David Adams*
In This Day and Age · *Lennox, Gary*
In This Illumined Large, the Veritable Small · *Rawdon, Michael*
In This Sign Conquer · *Mundy, Bill*
In Touch · *Deane, Christopher*
In Transit · *Gallant, Mavis*
In Winter - In Writing · *Payerle, George*
In Youth Is Pleasure · *Gallant, Mavis*
The Inaugural Meeting · *Kinsella, W.P.*
Incendiaries · *Hood, Hugh*
Incest · *Clifton, Merritt*
The Incident · *Mallon, Jane*
Incident in Islington · *Taylor, Charles*
Incident in the Place d'Armes · *Shepherd, Harvey L.*
Incident with a Racoon · *Plourde, Marc*
Incidents on a Trolley That Didn't Make the Newspapers the Following Day ·
Sherrin, Robert G.
The Incomplete Messenger · *Carr, Roberta*
Incomprehensible Visiting · *Bauer, Nancy*
The Incorrigible McGillicutty · *McGoogan, Kenneth*
The Incredible Carollers · *Moore, Brian*
The Incredible German · *Bird, Will R.*
Independence and Mrs. Pettigrew · *West, Rosalie*
The Independent One · *Green, H. Gordon*
The Independent Woman · *Govier, Katharine*

India · *Griggs, Terry*
The Indian, the Dancer and the Sailor · *Arnason, David*
The Indian Amulet · *McKim, Eleanor*
Indian Christmas Carol · *Marquis, Helen*
Indian 'Cinderella' · *Anonymous*
The Indian Giver · *McKay, Fortesque*
Indian Givers · *Fletcher, Peggy*
An Indian Hand · *Keith, Sarah*
Indian Honor · *Wood, Kerry*
Indian Princess · *Jiles, Paulette*
Indian Struck · *Kinsella, W.P.*
Indian Summer · *Spencer, Elizabeth*
An Indian Tale of Birch Bark, Musk-Rat Tails & Rabbits Ears · *McKay, Fortesque*
Indians Don't Cry · *Kenny, George*
The Indians of the Southwest · *Hutton, Bill*
An Indication of Burning · *Wiebe, Rudy H.*
[The?] Indispensable Woman · *Conger, Lesley*
Industrial Peace: A Story · *Wishart, Ian*
Inertia · *Hodgins, Norris*
The Inevitable Decision · *Green, H. Gordon*
Infants, Dogs and Teachers · *Kanitz, Walter*
Infidelity · *Nowlan, Alden*
Infinite Variation · *Hargreaves, H.A.*
Influential Citizen · *Lee, Carroll H.*
The Ingenuity of Trapper Jim · *Gomery, Percy*
An Inglorious Affair · *Percy, H.R.*
The Inheritance · *Jakober, Marie*
Inheriting the Earth · *Choyce, Lesley*
Iniquities of the Fathers · *Horwood, Harold*
The Initiate · *MacIntyre, Wendy*
The Initiation of Akasa · *Coney, Michael G.*
Initram · *Thomas, Audrey*
the ink · *Heath, Terence*
The Inkwell · *Mitchell, Ethel Golden*
Inland Beach · *Creal, Margaret*
Inner Beauty · *Mezei, Stephen*
Inner Circle · *Friesen, Zara*
An Inner Parlour · *Heyd, Ruth*
The Innermost One · *Nowlan, Alden*
The Innkeeper · *Pearson, Phyllis*
The Innkeeper's Wife · *Gesner, Claribel*
Innocence · *Peter, John D.*
The Innocence of Rasputin · *Rosenfeld, Rita*
An Inquest into the Disappearance and Possible Death of Sono Nis, Photographer
· *Yates, J. Michael*
Insanity · *Dust, Julian*
the insect · *Bullock, Michael*
Insect Collecting · *Rosenfeld, Rita*
Inside Out · *Rosenberg, Flash*
Inside Passage · *Sherrin, Robert G.*

The Inside Story · *Hospital, Janet Turner*
Inside the Easter Egg · *Engel, Marian*
Inside the Glass Hospital · *Osborne, J.T.*
Inside the Square: A Fragment · *Nunn, Robert*
The Inside Window · *Conger, Lesley*
Insignificant Invasion · *McDermid, Doug*
The Insignificant Young Man · *Govan, Margaret*
Inspections · *O'Connell, Dorothy*
The Inspector · *Boyarsky, Abraham*
The Inspiration of Gustave Morose · *Ades, Terry*
Installment Plan · *Sutherland, Barry*
Instant · *Elgaard, Elin*
Institutions · *Marriott, J. Anne*
Instructing the Young · *Madott, Darlene*
The Instrument of Death · *Jackson, Philip*
Instrument of Destruction · *Spencer, Elizabeth*
Insula Insularum · *Atwood, Margaret*
The Insult · *Callaghan, Morley*
The Integrating Machine · *Stevenson, David*
The Intellectual · *Kanurkas, Irene*
Interact · *Virgo, Sean*
Intercede for Us, Auntie Chayele · *Faessler, Shirley*
An Interest in Bears · *Fawcett, Brian*
Interface · *Brown, Ron*
Interim · *Horne, Lewis B.*
Interior Scene: She, He, and Joe · *Smyth, Donna E.*
Interlude · *Chertkoff, Gary*
'Interlude at Rainbow' · *Arrol, Ed*
Interlude in Black and White · *Garner, Hugh*
Intermediaries · *Kinsella, W.P.*
Internal Combustion · *Lemm, Richard*
International Incident · *Blesse, Landry*
An Interruption · *Clifford, Wayne*
Intersection · *Mackenzie, Alan*
Intersections · *Beghtol, Claire*
Interstice · *Ritter, Judy*
The Interview · *Donohue, Patrick*
Interview: Humphrey Bogart · *Halliday, David*
Interview on an April Afternoon · *Gilbert, Michael A.*
Interview with Humphrey Bogart · *Halliday, David*
An Intimate Letter · *Roberts, Tom*
Into His Own Country · *McFadden, Isobel*
Into the Daylight · *Meltzer, Edmund S.*
Into the Future Life · *Poesiat, Bart*
Into the Sunset · *Beattie, Jessie L.*
The Intolerable Statue · *Rooke, Richard*
Introduction to a Corpse · *Wolfe, Norine*
An Introduction to the Life and Times of Ian Edward Judd · *Wyse, A. David*
The Intruder · *Blythe, Aleata E.*
The Intrusion of Mrs. Harvison · *Zwarts, Janice Blue*

Invaders · *Weiner, Andrew*

The Invalid · *Harvey, Jennifer A. Becks*

The Invasion of Don Mills by Enemy Forces · *Krueger, Lesley*

Invasion of Privacy · *Atchison, Michael*

Invasions '79 · *Hodgins, Jack*

Invented in a Blizzard of Words · *Swan, Ed*

Invention for Shelagh · *Rule, Jane*

Inventory · *Boles, Rachel*

Investigation · *Jacob, John*

The Investments of Lars Ollefssen · *Sorestad, Glen*

The Invisible Worm · *Taaffe, Gerald*

An Invitation to Join · *Clarke, Austin C.*

Involuntary Man's Laughter · *Robinson, Spider*

the invulnerable ovoid aura: a first report on an epoch-making scientific experiment · *Bullock, Michael*

IOU One Life · *Bankier, William*

Ipoh · *Virgo, Sean*

Irina · *Gallant, Mavis*

An Irish Chip · *Inglis, George*

Irish Persuasion · *Yeandle, Ruth A.*

The Iron Age · *Powell, Robert*

The Iron Men · *Mowat, Farley*

The Iron Mikado · *Hockley, Vernon*

The Iron Stone · *de Lint, Charles*

Iron Wheels · *Itani, Frances*

Iron Woman · *Rooke, Leon*

Iron-On David · *Young, David*

Ironstone Chalice · *Barker, Bessie M.*

The Iroquois Hotel · *McFadden, David*

The Irritant · *Kadey, Carroll*

Is a Good Thing · *Barnard, Leslie Gordon*

Is Anyone Out There Working · *Fuhringer, Sandy*

Is Oakland Drowning? · *Blaise, Clark L.*

Is Oft Interred · *Grantmyre, Barbara*

Is Scientific Thought Outrunning Common Sense · *Sherman, Tom*

Is Stealing a Girl Really Stealing? · *Hughes, Philip B.*

Is That All There Is? · *Ogle, Robert Joseph*

Is There a Balm in Gilead · *Bauer, Nancy*

Is There a Killer in the House? · *Bankier, William*

Is This All You Think About? · *Kalman, Judy*

Isabeau · *Burnett, Virgil*

Isis Returns · *Hauser, Gwen*

Island · *Cairns, A.T.*

Island Funeral · *Ross, Veronica*

Island of the Innocents · *Horwood, Harold*

Island of the Nightengales · *Edwards, Caterina*

Island Saga · *Briffett, Isabel*

Isolated Incidents · *Mukherjee, Bharati*

Isolation · *Russell, Ted*

The Isolation Booth · *Hood, Hugh*

It's Not What You Think · *Armour, Heather*
Its Own Reward · *Percy, H.R.*
It's Roses All the Way · *Booth, Luella S.*
It's So Peaceful in the Country · *Carlton, Edna P.*
It's Still a Gentleman's Game · *Williams, Marian*
It's Too Late · *Matyas, Cathy*
It's Very Dark by Six · *Conger, Lesley*
It's What You Do with It · *Stein, Rhoda Elizabeth Playfair*
I've Always Felt Sorry for Decimals · *Gibbs, Robert*
'I've Found the Friend' · *Burnell, Ethel D.*
I've Got a Secret · *Lonneberg, Lyle R.*
I've Got It Made · *Metcalf, John*
I've Got to Tell You, Darling · *Barnard, Margaret E. and Barnard, Leslie Gordon*
The Ivy-Covered Manner · *Simpson, Leo*
IZZY · *Richler, Mordecai*

Jack and 'Whiskey Jack' · *Rivers, J. Scott*
Jack High · *Gillese, John Patrick*
Jack of Hearts · *Huggan, Isabel*
Jack O'Lantern · *Brown, Crombie*
Jack Ronald Told the Lord · *Ross, James*
The Jackdaws · *Wood, Ted*
The Jacket · *Morton, Lionel*
The Jackhammer · *Kinsella, W.P.*
Jack's Dream · *Halliday, David*
Jacks or Better, Jokers Wild · *Garner, Hugh*
Jackson, Doing His Rounds · *Ross, James*
Jacob's Ladder · *Briffett, Isabel*
Jade · *Read, Elfreida*
The Jade Planet · *Rikki [Erica Ducornet]*
Jaffer's Chicken · *Leitao, Lino*
Jake · *Haggerty, Joan*
Jake's Fortune · *Donnelly, Maggie*
Jambalaya · *Teichroeb, Kevin*
Jamboree · *McNamara, Eugene*
James Learns the Pipes · *Crowell, Bill*
Jane · *McAllister, Lesley*
Jane's Christmas Eve · *Ziolkowski, Carmen*
Janice · *Cohen, Matt*
Janitors & Kitchen Staff · *Kilodney, Crad*
The Janitor's Wife · *Fraser, Raymond*
January 1983 · *Curry, John W.*
January Slump · *Currie, Doris M.*
japanese roses · *Bullock, Michael*
Japonica · *Peter, John D.*
A Jar in Tennessee · *Watt, Frank W.*
The Jardine Exhibition · *Fraser, D.M.*
Jaribu · *Browne, Paul Cameron*
Jarvey and the Dolphin · *Bruce, Charles T.*

Jason and the Swan · *Paratte, Henri Dominique*
Jason Crull · *Croutch, Leslie A.*
The Jason Sphere · *Trembley, Georges*
A Jaundiced Liver · *MacSween, R.J.*
Jay's Aviary · *Bartlett, Brian*
A Jazz Story · *Murray, Joan*
Jean Beliveau Was No. 4 · *Weiss, Allan*
Jean Pierre Robichaud · *Cosier, Anthony*
Jeanie · *Beattie, Jessie L.*
Jean-Marc · *Shiach, Allan*
Jeanne · *Beresford-Howe, Constance*
Jeannette · *Theriault, Yves*
Jeannine · *Packer, Miriam*
Jean-Pierre · *Spencer, Elizabeth*
Jed · *Holt, Patricia*
Jeff Was a Mind Reader · *Green, H. Gordon*
The Jellybean · *Pugsley, Edmund E.*
The Jellyfish: An Old Story Retold · *Kishibe, Kaye*
Jennifer Jane · *Foord, Isabelle*
Jenny and the Witnesses · *Fletcher, Peggy*
Jeremey, His Arrangements · *Zieroth, Dale*
Jeremiah Proosky · *Drache, Sharon*
Jeremy · *Ramsden, J.D.*
Jeremy's Choice · *Levin, Malcolm A.*
Jericho's Brick Battlements · *Laurence, Margaret*
Jeroboam Henley's Debt · *Saunders, Charles R.*
Jerome · *Latta, William*
Jerry · *Ross, James*
Jerusalem & Home · *Avery, Martin*
Jesus · *Silverwind, J.*
Jesus Creep · *Currie, Sheldon*
Jesus Exploited · *Barbusse, Henri*
Jethro Noddy · *Russell, Ted*
Jettatura · *Rooke, Leon*
Jeux d'Ete · *Gallant, Mavis*
The Jew Boy · *Graham, Robert*
Jewboy! · *Newman, Sol*
The Jewel Studded Comb · *Chisholm, Bennett*
The Jeweller · *Hosein, Clyde*
The Jewish Buddha · *Evanier, David*
Jews Are Women · *Gould, Terry*
Jezebel Jessie · *Boyle, Harry J.*
Jimmy · *Ariano, Vera Nanson*
Jimmy Came Flying In · *Miller, J. Kit*
Jimmy Turner's Secret File · *Bartram, Gerald*
Jinja · *Ross, Brian*
The Jinker · *Schull, Joseph J.*
The Jinx · *Green, H. Gordon*
Jo Cancel Half a Line · *Ryan, Josephine*
Jo Portugais · *Macdonald, John Geddie*

Joaquin Murietta Slept Here · *Simas, Richard*
The Job · *Kinsella, W.P.*
Job Experience: Telephone Soliciting · *Chapman, Sheila*
Job Hunting · *Richler, Mordecai*
Job of the Ghetto · *Reinhartz, Henia*
Job Search · *Decker, Ken*
A Job with a Future · *Annett, R. Ross*
The Job-Haunt · *Egyedi, Bela*
Jodi in a Life Not Hers · *Luckevich, Rosanne*
Joe · *Rigutto, William*
Joe Kennedy's Dream · *Maher, Paul*
Joe Pynoo Sees It Through · *Deally, Margaret*
Joe's Apple Tree · *Vaughan, J.B.*
Joe's Secret Plan · *Annett, R. Ross*
Joey · *Smyth, Brian*
The Jogger · *Moelaert, John*
John · *Kaiser, Terry*
The John Brown · *Rajkumar, Ken*
John Cabot · *Russell, Ted*
John Cat · *Kinsella, W.P.*
John Gilder's Argument · *Green, H. Gordon*
John Grant Becomes a Minister · *Hill, O. Mary*
John K. Sugarue's First Million · *Green, H. Gordon*
John the Baptist · *Dow, John*
John Womble's Second Dream · *Ayre, Robert H.*
Johnny · *Bryant, Alan J.*
Johnny Mnemonic · *Gibson, William*
Johnny Skunk · *Devore, Roy*
Johnny Swanson's Debt · *Shipley, Nan*
Johnny the Pear · *Pollett, Ron*
Johnny's Game · *Fawcett, Brian*
Johnny's Triumph · *Weir, John*
Johnson and the Cascadura · *Selvon, Samuel*
Joie de Vivre · *Stein, David Lewis*
The Joining I · *Devaney, Dan*
The Joining II · *Devaney, Dan*
Joining the Army · *Weir, Chuck*
The Joke That Had the Last Laugh · *Williams, Dave*
Jokemaker · *Kinsella, W.P.*
Jokers Are Wild · *Devereaux, Bob*
Jolson Sings Again · *Evanier, David*
Jonah II · *Fleming, Morag*
Jonathan Street · *Somerville, Christine Bryce*
Jones' End · *Rooke, Leon*
Jorinda and Jorindel · *Gallant, Mavis*
Josef and the Jellybean · *Shea, Dorothy J.*
Joseph · *Allen, Dale*
Joseph and His Brother · *Thomas, Audrey*
joseph and t · *David, Jack*
Joseph's Dilemma · *Ryan, Josephine*

The Joshua Levine Cassettes: Numbers 1, 4, 11, 14, 18, 23 · *Lampert, Gerald*
The Journal · *Zimmerman, Susan*
The Journal of Glory Maxwell · *Schoemperlen, Diane*
A Journal of Mona · *McLean, Anne*
The Journals · *Ireland, Ann*
The Journey · *Gunn, Walter*
Journey ... · *Gifford* [pseudonym]
Journey Around My Skull · *Rosenberg, Elsa*
Journey Back to Love · *Barnard, Leslie Gordon*
Journey Before Spring · *Crowe, Keith*
Journey by Underground · *Skey, Olga*
Journey for Abner · *Gray, Lillian Collier*
Journey Home · *Duncan, W.T.*
Journey in Darkness · *Ostenso, Martha*
journey in search of a shell · *Bullock, Michael*
Journey in the Dark · *Walker, David*
Journey Inland · *Dagg, Mel*
A Journey of Love · *Goodman, Lynn*
Journey Through Fear · *Sumpter, Judy*
Journey to Jordan · *Stein, Rhoda Elizabeth Playfair*
Journey to Light · *Bardsley, Alice*
Journey to Nowhere · *Lane, John*
Journey to the Lake · *Birdsell, Sandra*
Journeyman · *Hurlbut, Eric*
Journeys · *Cohn, Marlene*
Journey's End · *Abelsen, Terry*
The Journeys of Eugene · *Miller, Malcolm*
Journeys Through Bookland · *Dragland, Stan*
Joust in Eight Rounds · *Mills, John*
Joy · *Rule, Jane*
The Joy of Elevated Thoughts · *Harding, John*
Joy Ride · *Briffett, Isabel*
Joyful Christmas · *Gane, Margaret Drury*
The Joyride · *Jess, Cameron*
Juan Fortune · *Nations, Opal L.*
Jubilee · *Copeland, Ann* [pseudonym]
Jubilee Meeting · *Wood, Kerry*
Judas Iscariot as Seen by Simon, the Zealot · *Dow, John*
Judge Not · *Borrell, Helen*
Judge Not ... · *Whitford, Margaret Ann*
Judgement · *Butts, Ed P.*
The Judge's Sermon · *Bushell, Sidney*
The Judgment of Paris · *Kaal, Hans*
Judith Kane · *Spencer, Elizabeth*
Judy · *Pflug, Ursula*
Judy & the Archivist · *Bell, Wade*
Jug and Bottle · *Ross, Sinclair*
Juggler · *Dobb, Ted*
Jugs · *Yates, J. Michael*
A Jukebox in the Kitchen · *Nowlan, Alden*

Julian · *Burns, Jim*
Julie · *Burnett, Virgil*
The Julie Watcher · *Summers, Dave*
The Jump · *Lonneberg, Lyle R.*
Jumping Jackie · *Lenoir-Arcand, Christine*
June · *McKay, Jean*
June the 30th, 1934 · *Lowry, Malcolm*
The Junebugs · *Reyto, Martin*
Jung and Freud in America · *Donnell, David*
Jung Love · *Wilputte, Earla*
Jungle · *Rikki [Erica Ducornet]*
Jungle Station · *Lunn, Richard*
Junk · *MacDonald, John E.C.*
The Junk Dealer · *Freiberg, Stanley*
A Jury Has to Eat · *Rebel, Hermann*
Just a Few Minor Changes · *Simpson, Leo*
Just a Moment · *Bolger, William Neil*
Just a Nuisance · *Walsh, Hugh*
Just a Picosecond! · *Avery, Martin*
Just a Simple Story · *Courchesne, Peter*
Just a Whim · *Gordon, Betty*
A Just and Appropriate Ending · *Tauber [pseudonym]*
Just Another Bureaucrat · *Kenny, George*
Just Another Guy Out for a Ride on His Bike · *Burke, Brian*
Just Baloney Story · *Cacchioni, Mark*
Just Because These Words · *Hindmarch, Gladys*
Just Before the Bastille Fell · *Cummer, Don*
Just Between Two Worlds · *Ross, J.D.*
Just Crazy · *Smith, Gary*
Just Dessert · *Robinson, Spider*
Just for Fun · *Dalrymple, A.J.*
Just for the Night · *McNamara, Eugene*
Just for the Sport · *Hawryluk, Paul*
Just Friends · *Black, Karen*
Just in Memory · *Kosacky, Helen*
Just Jessica · *Hushlak, Mary Ann*
Just Keep Smiling · *Tinsley, Ted*
Just Like Her Mother · *Callaghan, Morley*
Just Like Li Po · *Kelsey, Robin*
Just Like Sisters · *McLaughlin, Lorrie*
Just Like the Orient Express · *McGorman, Don*
Just One Room · *Goldman, Hazel*
Just Pooling Around · *Power, John*
Just the Two of Us · *Stein, Rhoda Elizabeth Playfair*
Just to Be Content · *Lamb, Marcia*
Just Today · *Stacey, Jean*
Just Too Careless · *Ross, W.E. Dan*
Just Two Old Men · *Metcalf, John*

Just Two or Three · *Bole, J. Sheridan*
Justice · *Macey, Anne Louise*
The Justice of the Red Queen · *Phillips, Fred H.*

Kafka's Ghosts · *Mirolla, Michael*
Kaladar · *Gillette, Agnes*
Kaleidoscope · *Zimmer, Ron*
Kamloops Baby · *Greenwood, Joan*
Kapino · *Virgo, Sean*
Karelia Suite · *Hall, Edwin*
Kaspar's Antelope · *Wilson, Betty*
Kate · *Minsos, Susan*
Katy · *Rapoport, Nessa*
Katy and the Nest Egg · *Creighton, Norman*
Katydid · *Kent, Valerie*
Kazabazua · *Firestone, Catherine*
The Keep · *Sinclair, Michael P.*
Keep a Green Bough in the Heart, and the Singing Bird Will Come · *Briffett, Isabel*
Keep Away from Laura · *Callaghan, Morley*
Keep Your Head Down Ginny · *Williams, Marian*
The Keeper of Error · *Filson, Bruce K.*
Keeper of the Legend · *Rowdon, Larry*
The Keeper of the Vineyard · *Pope, Dan*
Keeping Fit · *Cohen, Matt*
Keepsake · *McHardy, Vincent*
A Keg of Herring for Linnea · *Hanson, Esther Schneider*
Keizersgracht 69 · *Neil, Al*
Kelpie Rapids · *Roberts, Theodore Goodridge*
Kensington Rabbit · *Simpson, Doug*
Kevin and Stephanie · *Nowlan, Alden*
Kevork at Geghart · *Shirinian, Lorne*
The Key · *Shirinian, Lorne*
Key to Rosemary · *Barnard, Margaret E.*
Key to the House · *Shipley, Nan*
Keys and Watercress · *Metcalf, John*
The Keys to the Car · *Sloman, Fred*
Khyber Bride · *van der Mark, Christine*
Kibanda Ya Kufa · *Saunders, Charles R.*
A Kick at the Couch · *O'Connell, Dorothy*
Kicking · *Taaffe, Gerald*
The Kid · *McQuillan, Pat*
The Kid and the Stick · *Penfold, Russ*
The Kid in the Stove · *Kinsella, W.P.*
The Kid Network · *O'Connell, Dorothy*
The Kid Who Got Pushed Around All His Life · *Hutton, Bill*
The Kidnapper · *Kinsella, W.P.*
The Kidney Question in Quebec · *Steinfeld, J.J.*
Kiki · *Laflamme, Guy*
Kildonan Park · *Narvey, Fred*

Kill Day on the Government Wharf · *Thomas, Audrey*
The Kill Man · *Hyland, Gary*
The Killdeer Nest · *Krueger, Lesley*
Killer · *MacLaurin, Douglas*
The Killer Bronc · *Wood, Kerry*
The Killer Dyke and the Lady · *Rule, Jane*
The Killers · *Garth, Richard*
The Killing of Colin Moosefeathers · *Kinsella, W.P.*
The Killing of Haayim Gold · *Slabotsky, David*
The Killing of Mrs. Kittywall · *Taylor, Jeremy*
The Killing of Nelson John · *Hosein, Clyde*
Killing Time · *Currie, Robert*
The Kilmarnovian Revolution · *Shapiro, Frederic*
A Kind, Beautiful, Understanding Mother · *Kutlesa, Joso*
A Kind Husband · *Horne, Lewis B.*
A Kind of Education · *Kirkwood, Hilda*
A Kind of Feeling · *Dabydeen, Cyril*
The Kind of Guy · *Chamish, Barry*
A Kind of Joy · *Furey, L.J.*
A Kind of Miracle · *Levine, Norman*
A Kind of Mordent · *Knight, David*
The Kind of Story Your Mother Would Love · *Ford, Cathy*
Kinder Than the Sea · *Wood, Ted*
The Kind-Hearted Mischief · *Tait, Elizabeth*
The Kindness · *Grantmyre, Barbara*
The King · *Jonas, George*
King Andy · *Meadow, Barry*
King David · *Russell, Ted*
King David and Jethro · *Russell, Ted*
King David's Family Allowance · *Russell, Ted*
King David's Winter Outfit · *Russell, Ted*
The King Enjoys His Own Again · *Davies, Robertson*
King Folly · *Burnett, Virgil*
The King Is Dead · *Vanderhaeghe, Guy*
King Kong and the Mouse · *Mitchell, Sirjy*
King Lear at Home · *Ward, Norman*
King of Spades · *Rodman, Hyman*
The King of Spain's Daughter · *Briffett, Isabel*
King of the Castle · *Linder, Norma West*
The King of the Glass Mountain · *Stambaugh, Sara*
King on a Rock · *Black, Simon*
The King Over the Water · *McCourt, Edward A.*
The King Who Had No Tongue · *Green, H. Gordon*
Kingbird · *Hollingshead, Greg*
A Kingly Thing · *de Lint, Charles*
A King's Daughter · *Harvey, Jennifer A. Becks*
The King's Gift · *Govan, Margaret*
The King's Jester · *Orbeliani, Andre*
The King's Justice · *Govan, Margaret*
The Kings of Lokasena · *Sullivan, Edward*

Kingsmere · *MacEwen, Gwendolyn*
Kinswoman · *Toryn, Ann*
Kirby's Gander · *Gillese, John Patrick*
Kirkwood, Missouri · *Rose, Bob*
Kirsty · *Powell, Dorothy M.*
The Kiss · *Murray, Joan*
The Kiss and the Moonshine · *Johnston, Basil H.*
A Kiss at the Door · *Spencer, Elizabeth*
The Kiss of Krushchev · *Davies, Robertson*
Kiss the Devil Goodbye · *Rooke, Leon*
Kisses · *Campbell, Wanda Blynn*
The Kissing Man · *Elliott, George*
The Kitchen Curtains · *Dybvig, Leslie*
Kitchen Knives · *Dampf, Michael*
The Kitchen Window View · *Sherman, Tom*
The Kite · *Wade, Jennifer A.*

A Kitel · *Drache, Sharon*
The Kites · *Fletcher, Peggy*
The Kite's Tale · *Briffett, Isabel*
Kitsilano · *Evans, D.G.*
kitten among the bulrushes · *Bullock, Michael*
The Kittlings · *Gillese, John Patrick*
Kitty · *Milner, Philip*
Kitty's Kitchen · *Briffett, Isabel*
Kleckner · *Parley, Kay*
Klee · *Holmes, Ken*
The Kneeling of the Cattle · *Nowlan, Alden*
The Knife · *Alexander, Joan*
The Knight and the Maiden · *Kenyon, Nancy*
Knight Moves · *Torgov, Sarah*
Knit for Tatt - the Tale of a Snail · *Hulse, Louise*
Knock, Knock · *Anderson, Jim*
Knock on Wood · *Selvon, Samuel*
the knock-out · *Heath, Terence*
Knowing Anna · *Barnhouse, D.P.*
Knowing History - Knowing Struggle · *Stevenson, Joan*
The Knowing Moment · *Poy, Adrienne*
Kolla, Ticks · *Gunnars, Kristjana*
The Komedy Kabaret · *Avery, Martin*
Kopochus 1825 · *Richards, David Adams*
Kotzko Was a Writer Who Did Not Write · *Kelsey, Robin*
Kovack Bros. · *Dyba, Kenneth*
Kozicki & the Living Dog · *Dickinson, Don*
The Krazy World of Crad Kilodney · *Kilodney, Crad*
Kristbjorg's Story in the Black Hills · *Lowry, Malcolm*
Kristen · *McColl, Earla-Kim*
Kristy · *Russell, Sheila MacKay*
Kru and the Mammoth · *MacKenzie, Blake*
The Kumbh Fair · *Ahmad, Iqbal*
Kwame Bird Lady Day · *Godfrey, Dave*

L.O.V.E. · *Emkeit, Ron L.*
A La Recherche d'Arbuthnot · *Murray, David*
Lab Technician · *Potrebenko, Helen*
Labor Day Dinner · *Munro, Alice*
The Labour · *Hawkins, Susan C.*
Labour of Love · *Pope, Suzanne*
The Labyrinth · *Stein, Rhoda Elizabeth Playfair*
The Labyrinthine Investigations of Fane · *Payerle, George*
The Ladadantë · *Gilbert, Anne*
The Ladder · *Lawrence, Charles M.*
Ladders · *Hodgins, Norris*
The Ladies · *Marriott, J. Anne*
Ladies Always Carry · *Margoshes, Dave*
Ladies and Gentlemen, the Fabulous Barclay Sisters! · *Hodgins, Jack*
Lady, Make Up Your Mind · *Findlay, David K.*
The Lady · *Gould, Jan*
The Lady and the Cop · *Knapp, G.L.*
The Lady and the Doctor · *MacNeill, James A.*
The Lady and the Labourer · *Armstrong, Patricia*
The Lady and the Servant · *Levine, Norman*
The Lady and the Travelling Salesman · *Simpson, Leo*
The Lady and the Windmill · *Vorres, Ian*
The Lady Bronc · *Wood, Kerry*
Lady Craig · *Cameron, John Cullen*
Lady for a Day · *McDonald, Ruth*
Lady Godiva's Horse · *Rooke, Leon*
The Lady in the Schiaparelli Shoes · *Bauer, Frances*
Lady in Waiting · *Arnason, David*
The Lady Lamp and the Fisherman · *Marshalore* [pseudonym]
The Lady Loved Music · *Owen, George*
A Lady Named Bones · *Smith, Harriet Grahame*
Lady of the Lake · *Margoshes, Dave*
Lady of the Ocean · *Burns, Mary*
Lady of Windigo Hills · *Gillese, John Patrick*
The Lady on the Limb · *Leitch, Adelaide*
Lady T · *MacLaurin, Douglas*
The Lady Was a Horse Thief · *Armstrong, Patricia*
The Lady Who Fought at the Siege of Jerusalem · *Horwood, Harold*
Lady with a Cold · *Grantmyre, Barbara*
The Laird of Skid Row · *MacLaurin, Douglas*
The Lake · *Urquhart, Donald*
Lake Isle of Innisfree · *Wiebe, Rudy H.*
Lake of Glass · *Slote, D.C.*
Lake of Spirits · *Lewis, Leda M.*
The Lake That Didn't Like Us · *Earl, Lawrence*
Lamb · *Smyth, Donna E.*
Lamb in the Thicket · *Briffett, Isabel*
Lament · *Mitchell, Mary*
Lament for a Son · *Wexler, Jerry*
Lament for a Writer · *Atman* [pseudonym]

Lamentation · *Malik, Cynthia*
L'Amour est fini · *Chushingura [pseudonym]*
The Lamp · *Mayse, Arthur*
The Lamp of El Azimair · *Moore, Brian*
Lamplight and Rocking Chairs · *Mosher, Edith*
The Land Grows Love · *Wood, Kerry*
A Land Never Promised · *Waltner-Toews, David*
Land of Heart's Desire · *Cameron, Eric*
Land of the Dying · *Graham, Ferne*
Land of the Free · *Campbell, Ronald*
The Land of Un · *McAllister, Lesley*
Land without Mills · *Flood, Robert J.*
The Land-Grabber · *Annett, R. Ross*
The Lane · *Campion, Bridget*
Langston, Ladycloud, and the Horse That Swam Side-Stroke · *MacNeill, James A.*
The Language of Love · *Wolfe, Miriam*
La Langue d'Oc · *Wheatley, Patience*
The Lantern · *Briffett, Isabel*
Lapsang and Oolong · *Harvor, Beth*
A Large K in Kill · *Dempster, Barry*
Lark Song · *Kinsella, W.P.*
L'Arrivee · *Browne, Colin*
Larry · *Gallant, Mavis*
Larry the Lobster · *Burnley, John*
The Lass from Cape Breton · *Green, H. Gordon*
The Last Act · *Birch-Jones, Sonia*
The Last Act Was Deadly · *Bankier, William*
Last Armistice Day · *Coughlan, Jack*
The Last Beginning. The Last! The Last! · *Newman, C.J.*
The Last Bell · *Nowlan, Michael O.*
The Last Bridge · *Grant, Leslie H.*
The Last Bus · *Martin, Sheila*
The Last Cadenza · *Carey, Barbara*
Last Call · *Owen, D.M.*
The Last Canadian Dreidel Maker · *Hertz, Kenneth V.*
The Last Christmas · *Engel, Marian*
The Last Climb · *Livesay, Dorothy*
The Last Coin · *Carr, Grace*
The Last Cowboy · *Abbott, Douglas*
Last Cruise of Summer · *Sturdy, John Rhodes*
The Last Dancer · *Horne, Lewis B.*
Last Day · *Stevenson, Gillian*
The Last Day Before My Father's Holiday · *Heide, Christopher*
Last Day of All · *Barnard, Margaret E. and Barnard, Leslie Gordon*
The Last Day of Violence · *St. Pierre, Paul*
Last Days · *Mardon, Caroline*
Last Delivery Before Christmas · *Buckler, Ernest*

The Last Dinner · *Lambert, Elizabeth M.*
The Last Door · *Peterson, Phyllis Lee*
The Last Easter · *Hildebrandt, Gloria*
The Last Elf · *Wilson, Angus C.*
The Last Fifteen Minutes · *Ringwood, Gwen Pharis*
The Last Fix · *Halliday, David*
The Last Friday of Every Month · *Engel, Howard*
The Last Gamble · *Gillese, John Patrick*
The Last Game · *Teitel, Jay*
The Last Great Joke of Gilhooley Jones · *Stone, A.C.*
The Last Happy Wife · *Engel, Marian*
The Last Hour of Irena Baronovitch · *Hannaford, Nigel*
The Last Hunt · *Gillese, John Patrick*
The Last Husky · *Mowat, Farley*
The Last Interview with Crad Kilodney · *Kilodney, Crad*
Last Job · *Bartley, Allan*
Last Journal · *Hoolboom, Michael*
The Last Journey · *Boyd, Robert*
Last Journey for Jasper Holler · *Stein, Rhoda Elizabeth Playfair*
The Last Kiss · *Beller, Jacob*
The Last Laugh · *Burkman, Kay*
The Last Lesson · *Roddan, Samuel*
The Last Long Summer · *Kellythorne, Walt*
Last Mission · *Schull, Joseph J.*
The Last Moment · *Mahood, Maurice*
The Last Monday · *Holloway, Robin*
The Last Mugging · *Wharton, Maurice*
The Last Night in Town · *Tens, Johnny*
Last Night on Lombard Street · *Jacobs, William*
The Last of Her Sons · *Nowlan, Alden*
The Last of the Czars · *Livesay, Dorothy*
The Last of the Dodos · *Rankin, Joyce*
The Last of the Golden Girls · *Swan, Susan*
The Last of the Pioneers · *Fines, Beatrice E.*
The Last One · *Dehaas, David*
Last One Home Sleeps in the Yellow Bed · *Rooke, Leon*
The Last One to Know · *Bankier, William*
'The Last Page' · *Burnell, Ethel D.*
The Last Present · *Green, H. Gordon*
The Last Prisoner · *Engkent, Garry*
The Last Promenade · *Thibaudeau, Colleen*
The Last Rehearsal · *Waddington, Miriam*
The Last Resort · *Cole, David*
Last Respects · *Riskin, Mary W.*
The Last River · *Cassidy, Sky*
The Last Rose · *Shepherd, Helen*
The Last Run of the Ten-Twenty · *Bell, John Leslie*
Last Scene Fishing · *Salminiw, Stephen*
The Last Secrets of Omega · *Kilodney, Crad*
The Last Shall Be First?? · *Mawhinney, Hal*

Last Spring · *Peterson, Phyllis Lee*
The Last Struggle for Life · *Amprimoz, Alexandre*
The Last Summer · *Rogers, Jeanne*
Last Summer of Youth · *McNamara, Eugene*
The Last Supper · *MacLaurin, Douglas*
The Last Sweet Summer · *Linder, Norma West*
Last Tears of Boyhood · *Conner, Orville*
The Last Time I Saw Paris · *Moes, Peter*
A Last Tribute · *F.C.N* [pseudonym]
The Last Trick · *Bird, Will R.*

The Last Trip · *Galbraith, Mary*
Last Tuesday, Valkeria · *Reid, Jeffrey*
Last Writing of an Unknown Officer of -th Regiment Found Dead Near Aachen,
May 3, 1945 · *Metcalfe, B[rian].R.*
Last Year Another Pyramid Fell Down · *Such, Peter*
The Last Young Man · *Edwards, Caterina*
Late Arrival · *Barnett, S.M.*
Late Bloom · *Anderson, Alberta*
Late Blooming · *Bushell, Sidney*
A Late Decorum for De Koven Street · *Snyder, Richard*
Late Lunch in Car 19 · *Hudson, Noel*
The Late Man · *Schroeder, Andreas*
A Late Socialization · *Potrebenko, Helen*
The Latehomecomer · *Gallant, Mavis*
The Latest Advance · *Mandrake, Jill*
The Latest Island News · *Gould, Jan*
The Latest 'Noos' from By-Pass Cove · *Anderson, Evelyn*
Latin for Six · *Thomas, W.K.*
Latrodectus Shoicetans · *Yates, J. Michael*
Lauchie and Liza and Rory · *Currie, Sheldon*
Laughing Chaz · *Bankier, William*
The Laughing Wood · *Ferguson, Rosemary*
Laughter at Dawn · *Young, David*
Laughter on 3rd Street · *Neil, Al*
Laundromat Devotions · *Mason, Mike*
The Laundry Room · *Dampf, Michael*
Laura Secord - Canadian Author Interview · *Rushton, Alfred*
L'avenir degagé, l'avenir engagé · *Friedman, Irena*
Lawbreaker · *Sharma, D.T.*
The Lawnmower · *Bowering, George*
The Lawyer · *Torgov, Morley*
The Lawyer's Letter · *Green, H. Gordon*
Laying on with Macduff · *Eastoe, Derek*
Lazar Cat · *Amprimoz, Alexandre*
Lazarus · *Vanderhaeghe, Guy*
Lead Kindly Light · *McEwan, Lily*
the leaf · *Bullock, Michael*
A Leaf for Everything Good · *Elliott, George*
A Leak in the Roof · *Rentz, Kenneth G.*
Leaps · *McGillivary, Judy*

Less and Less Human · *Henderson, Keith*
The Lesser Canada · *Coultrey, Peter*
The Lesson · *Kidd, Roberta*
A Lesson for Albert · *Barnard, Leslie Gordon*
Lesson for Elizabeth · *Stein, Rhoda Elizabeth Playfair*
A Lesson for Miss Randell · *Ross, W.E. Dan*
A Lesson for the Teacher · *Green, H. Gordon*
A Lesson in Character · *Green, H. Gordon*
A Lesson in Dance · *Cook, Hugh*
A Lesson in 'Democracy' · *V., I.F.*
A Lesson in Geography · *Welykopolsky, Luba*
Lesson in Humiliation · *Green, H. Gordon*
Lesson in Love · *Curran, Kitty*
A Lesson in Sympathy · *Dybvig, Leslie*
The Lesson of Fitzroy · *Stenson, Frederick*
Lessons · *Vertolli, Lou*
Lessons in Biology · *Wing, Sandy*
Lessons in Geometry · *Noonan, Gerald*
Lessons on Passing Away · *Wills, Charles*
Let It Be · *Douglas, Molly*
Let It Be Ellen · *McDougall, Colin M.*
Let Love Come After · *Green, H. Gordon*
Let Me Always Love · *Greene, Elizabeth*
Let Me Bury My Dead · *Doyle, Nancy*
Let Me Call You Sweetheart · *Henley, Patricia*
Let Me Cherish This Child · *Conger, Lesley*
Let Me Love You · *Russell, Sheila MacKay*
Let Not the Sun Go Down · *Gardner, W.W.*
Let Sleeping Dogs Lie: A Barney Messerschmidt Mystery by Dachshund Hamster
· *Robinson, Brad*
Let the Fox Go Free · *Fines, Beatrice E.*
Let Us Remember · *McLellan, Pat*
Let's All Go Round the Bend · *Blakeston, Oswell*
Let's Go Shopping · *Drache, Sharon*
Let's Have a Function · *Flury, Kay*
Let's Make Music · *Drache, Sharon*
Let's Marry for Your Money · *Sims, Burt*
The Letter · *Oborne, Louise Margaret*
The Letter · *Gillese, John Patrick*
A Letter from a Girl Called Elsie · *Watson, John*
Letter from America · *Percy, H.R.*
Letter from Home · *Armstrong, Patricia*
A Letter from Jerusalem · *Boyarsky, Abraham*
Letter from Matt Arthur's Fishpond · *Heide, Christopher*
Letter from Mrs. H. Watkins · *Mitchell, Jeanine*
Letter from Sakaye · *Mitchell, Beverly*
letter from the country · *M., C.R.*
The Letter I Would Have Written You · *Miraglia, Anne Marie*
A Letter in the Mail-Star · *Wetmore, Andrew*
Letter of Rejection · *MacLeod, Mildred*

Letter to a Friend · *Madott, Darlene*
Letter to Anne · *Bailey, Don*
Letter to Aunt Sophy · *Russell, Ted*
A Letter to History Teachers · *Arnason, David*
Letter to Jeanne Pierre S. · *White, Marilyn*
Letter to My Father · *Green, H. Gordon*
Letter to Nigeria · *Fawcett, Heather*
Letter to Prince · *Walker, Mirian*
Letter to Time · *Agetees, George*
The Letter Writer · *Rosenfeld, Rita*
The Letters · *Fraser, D.M.*
Letters for Abel · *Bird, Will R.*
Letters from Another Country · *Kennon, Janie*
'Letters Without Ending' · *Harvey, Jennifer A. Becks*
letterset · *Riddell, John*
A Liberal Education · *Richler, Mordecai*
The Librarians · *Kushner, Donn*
The Lice · *Watson, Wilfred*
Licence to Live · *Krause, Pat*
Licking Up Honey · *Rooke, Leon*
Liddle Black Boy · *Nason, Colleen*
The Lie · *McDonald, Ruth*
Lies · *Conger, Lesley*
Lies in Search of the Truth · *Harvor, Beth*
Lies My Father Told Me · *Allan, Ted*
The Life and Death of Morning Star · *Pacey, Desmond*
Life and Times · *Nowlan, Alden*
The Life and Times of Theresa Turkey · *Swan, Susan*
The Life and Work of Chapter Seven · *Truhlar, Richard*
The Life in a Day · *Martin, Rob*
A Life in Laundry · *Kenyon, Linda*
Life in the General Sense · *Walsh, Hugh*
Life Is a Three and Two Changeup · *Hopson, Brett*
The Life of a Poet · *Keeler, Judy*
The Life of Riley · *Bunner, Freda Newton*
The Life of Robert Oomer · *Fawcett, Brian*
Life on a Gram Scale · *Fuller, Arthur*
Life on the Roof · *McLean, Anne*
Life on This Planet · *Cohen, Matt*
The Life Preserve · *Rushton, Alfred*
Life with the Prime Minister · *Hollingshead, Greg*
Life's a Ball · *Rosenfeld, Rita*
Ligature and Competition · *Decker, Ken*
Light · *Downie, Glen R.*
The Light at the End of the Cave · *McCallum-Morash, Gordon*
A Light in the Night · *Ross, Veronica*
The Light of My Father · *Evanier, David*
Light Shining Out of Darkness · *Hood, Hugh*
Light Through the Leaves · *Palomba, Laura*
Light Traveller · *Hannant, Larry*

The Lighted Windows · *Shipley, Nan*
A Lighter Shade of Green · *Anonymous*
The Lightning Bolt · *Bedard, Michael*
Lightning Struck My Dick · *Kilodney, Crad*
Like a Curve in a Waterfall · *Bauer, Nancy*
'Like a Hinge on a Gate' · *Schermbrucker, Bill*
Like a Little Princess · *Summerhayes, Don*
Like a Man · *Currie, Robert*
Like a Roe or a Young Hart · *Foley, James*
Like After the Flood · *Shore, Michael M.J.*
Like Father, Like Son · *Stein, Rhoda Elizabeth Playfair*
Like Heaven · *Percy, H.R.*
Like in a Book · *Sangster, Allan*
Like Kafka · *Thomas, Peter*
Like Leading a Lamb · *Cranton, Judy*
Like Sisters · *Maclean, Muriel*
Like Superman or the Shadow · *Oliver, Michael Brian*
Like the Earth and the Rain · *Russell, Sheila MacKay*
Like with a Preacher · *Annett, R. Ross*
A Likely Story · *Kilodney, Crad*
The Lilac Charade · *West, Linda*
Lilian · *Rule, Jane*
Lilith · *Bergman, Brian*
A Lilly of the Fields · *MacMillan, Gail*
Lily and the Salamander · *Tremblay, Mildred*
Lima without Ears · *Casper, Claudia*
Limbo · *Powning, Beth*
A Limited Vision · *Timmerman, Peter*
The Limits of the Natural World · *MacLennan, Toby*
The Limper · *Briffett, Isabel*
Lin · *Hart, Kathy*
Lincoln - Man or Myth? · *Collins, Michael*
Linda Star · *Kinsella, W.P.*
Linda's Brush with the Lake · *Shipley, Nan*
The Line · *Phillips, Bluebell Stewart*
The Line Fence · *Buckler, Ernest*
Line of Steel · *Briffett, Isabel*
Lines Don't Lie · *Armstrong, Patricia*
Lines from a Judgement · *Ellis, A.*
Links · *Burns, Mary*
Lion in the Lane · *Powell, Dorothy M.*
Lion of the Afternoon · *Moore, Brian*
A Lion Skin · *Armstrong, Dorothy L.*
The Lion Sleeps · *Bass, Jack A.*
The Lioness · *Riordan, Michael*
Lions · *Morash, Gordon*
Lion-Taming for Beginners · *Ballantine, Andrew Campbell*
Lips · *Verleye, wj*
Lisa's Tale · *Lovering, Virginia*
The List · *Rule, Jane*

The List of Dreams · *McFadden, David*
Listen, Oh Listen! · *MacMillan, Gail*
Listen · *Macdonald, Lynne*
Listen Now · *Avison, Margaret*
Listen to This Train · *Laver, Sue*
The Listener · *Barker, Bessie M.*
The Listeners · *Elliott, George*
Listening In · *Byrnes, Terence*
Listing · *Denby, Netha K.*
A Literary History of Anton · *Cohen, Matt*
A Little and Certain Compass · *Steele, Harwood*
Little Arrow · *Ison, Olivine*
The Little Boats · *Cunningham, James*
Little Boxes · *Drache, Sharon*
Little Boy Lost · *Govan, Margaret*
The Little Brown Girl · *Spencer, Elizabeth*
A Little Child Shall Lead Them · *Carr, Jo-Ann*
Little David Play on Your Harp · *Vanderhaeghe, Guy*
Little Deaths · *Blostein, David*
A Little Folk Tale for Pro-Lifers · *Handler, Denyse*
The Little Ghost · *Ringwood, Gwen Pharis*
The Little Girl and the Moth · *Kent-Barber, Rosemary*
A Little Girl in a Pink Dress · *Pardy, Maryn*
Little Girls Giggling · *Green, H. Gordon*
The Little Green Book · *Fay, Michael*
Little Green Flowers · *Kent, Valerie*
The Little Green Hat · *Barnard, Leslie Gordon*
The Little Hunter · *Hendry, Peter*
Little Joe and the Mounties · *Ringwood, Gwen Pharis*
Little Joe on the Spot · *Annett, R. Ross*
Little Joe on Trial · *Annett, R. Ross*
Little Joe vs. the Blackmailer · *Annett, R. Ross*
Little Joe's Revenge · *Annett, R. Ross*
The Little Lamp · *Briffett, Isabel*
A Little Lesson in Honesty · *Ross, W.E. Dan*
The Little Mademoiselle · *Russell, Sheila MacKay*
The Little Men · *Selvon, Samuel*
Little Mo 'Gets Religion' · *Montour, Enos T.*
The Little Mother · *Briffett, Isabel*
Little Nothings · *Zend, Robert*
Little Orville Andy · *Gnonscentz, Phulloph [pseudonym]*
A Little Patience · *Duncan, Helen*
A Little Protection · *Currie, Robert*
The Little Red Devil and the Deep Blue Sea · *Steele, Harwood*
The Little Red Hat · *MacIntosh, Keitha K.*
Little Red Riding Hood · *Fraser, Jim*
The Little Siren · *Erskine, J.S.*
Little Suicides · *Wright, Douglas*
A Little to the Left of Centre · *Bailey, Don*
Little Unknown · *Mills, Elizabeth*

The Little War of the Roses · *Green, H. Gordon*
The Little White Cloud · *Roper, Florence*
The Little White Girl · *Marshall, Joyce*
Little White Lie · *Green, H. Gordon*
Little Willie · *Deacove, James*
The Little Witch and the Big Logger · *Theriault, Yves*
A Little World So Big · *Conger, Lesley*
The Little Yorkie · *Bird, Will R.*
The Littlest Rubby · *Shein, Brian*
The Littlest Sinner · *Green, H. Gordon*
The Littlest Thing · *Wansley, David*
Livability Test · *Humphries, Tom*
Lived in Full · *Harvey, Jennifer A. Becks*
The Lived-In Look · *Innis, Mary Quayle*
Lives of Maple Sugar/La Vie du sucre d'érable · *Forbes, Greg*
Lives of the 400,000 · *Avery, Martin*
Lives of the Poets · *Atwood, Margaret*
The Living Christmas Tree · *Brandis, Maxine*
Living in a Personality · *Barnes, M.R.*
Living in England · *Levine, Norman*
The Living Link · *Ogle, Robert Joseph*
The Living Quarter · *Schwartz, Judith*
Living Room · *Rosta, Helen J.*
Living Waters · *Evans, Hubert*
Lizzie's Curator · *Murray, Joan*
Lizzy · *Solly, Bill*
Lo Fat Speaks · *Marsh, Audrey*
The Load · *Cull, David*
Load Every Rift with Ore · *Rooke, Leon*
Load of Trouble · *Wood, Ted*
Loading Deep · *Easton, Alan*
The Loaf of Bread · *Lees, Margaret*
The Loaves and Fishes · *Briffett, Isabel*
Lobster Soufflée · *Drache, Sharon*
Lobster Trap · *Stortz, Joan*
Local Champ · *Robinson, Spider*
Local Color · *Campbell, Alphonsus P.*
A Local Hanging · *Thompson, Kent*
Local Initiatives · *Harris, John*
Local Minister Goes Berserk - Sings, Tap Dances at Altar · *Records, Sally*
Localized Peculiarities · *Sebastian, John*
The Lock · *Jess, Cameron*
Lock the Doors, Lock the Windows · *Cuevas, Ernesto*
The Locked Door · *McCourt, Edward A.*
Locked Out of Christmas · *Elford, Jean*
Locomotive · *Lonneberg, Lyle R.*
Locus of Control · *Freeman, Jonathan*
The Locust Keeper · *Petrie, Graham*
The Lodger · *Watts, John*
The Loggers · *Levesque, Anne*

Loggin' · *Russell, Ted*
Logic · *Kilodney, Crad*
London to Ottawa · *Gill, Stephen*
London Walk · *Moore, Robert*
The Londonderry Air · *Garner, Hugh*
The Londoner · *Mathews, Robin D.*
The Lone Cabin Mystery · *Brockie, William*
The Lone Igloo · *Evans, Allen Roy*
The Loneliest Man · *Hetherington, Laurie*
The Loneliness of the Long Distance Writer · *Choyce, Lesley*
Lonely as a Cloud · *Brandis, Marianne*
The Lonely Blues · *O'Connell, Dorothy*
Lonely Monarch · *Gillese, John Patrick*
The Lonely One · *Leitch, Adelaide*
The Lonely Quiet · *Dowling, Tom*
Lonely Road · *Teed, Roy*
A Lonely Time of Day · *Reambeault, Mary*
A Lonely Walk · *Corbett, Eva*
A Lonely Woman Afraid of Mirrors · *Dampf, Michael*
Lonesome Bus · *Bergren, Myrtle*
Lonesome Canary · *Kofman, Anni*
A Lonesome Pine · *Martin, J.L.*
Lonesome Summer · *Curran, Kitty*
Long, Long After School · *Buckler, Ernest*
The Long, Long Mile · *Burles, Mary Jo*
Long Ago, Far Away · *Peter, John D.*
Long Ago and Far Away · *McLeod, E. Vessie*
A Long and Lonely Ride · *Porter, Helen*
Long Before Detroit · *Branden, Vicki*
The Long Corridor · *Philipp, Rowland*
Long Distance Tragedies · *Barb, Michael*
The Long Fall · *Brown, Betty*
The Long Feud · *Mosher, Edith*
The Long Gravel Road · *Moser, Marie*
A Long Hard Walk · *Findley, Timothy*
The Long Journey · *Bennett, Warren*
Long Journey Home · *Ross, W.E. Dan*
A Long Labor · *Grills, Barry W.*
Long Live the Assassin of the Murderer Peanut Brain · *Zonko* [pseudonym]
Long Long Ago · *Donaldson, Anne*
The Long Lost Love · *Green, H. Gordon*
The Long March · *O'Connell, Dorothy*
The Long Night · *Johnson, Vera D.*
A Long Night's Journey into Day · *Longfield, Kevin*
The Long Road Home · *Briffett, Isabel*
The Long Road to Christmas · *Lee, Carroll H.*
The Long Shot · *Zogby, Mark*
A Long Story · *Host, Fred*
A Long Time Ago · *Swan, Mary*
A Long Time Dying · *Mintz, Chavah*

Long View · *Barker, Bessie M.*
The Long Walk Home · *Jenson, Carole*
A Long Way from Home · *Waddington, Miriam*
The Long Way Home · *Hagey, Mary*
The Long Weekend of Louis Riel · *Nichol, bp*
The Long Wind · *Sinclair, Kathryn*
The Long Winter · *Ruberto, Roberto*
Longboat · *Ketcheson, Doug*
A Longer Life · *Dabydeen, Cyril*
The Longest Hour · *Clarkson, Vi*
Longhouse · *Kinsella, W.P.*
Lonnie Comes Home · *Nowlan, Alden*
Look Here! · *Decker, Ken*
Look Man, I Love You · *Horwood, Harold*
Look What They're Doing · *Renner, Vivian*
Look Who's Laughing · *Barnard, Margaret E. and Barnard, Leslie Gordon*
Looking Down from Above · *Hood, Hugh*
Looking for a Girl in an Orange Flower Dress · *Howell, Bill*
Looking for Bessie · *Allan, Ted*
Looking for Ebbe · *Bowering, George*
Looking for Love · *McClintock, Norah*
Looking Up · *Gormley, Nancy K.*
The Looking-Glass Child · *Dominskyj, Marianne*
The Lookout Stone · *Krause, Pat*
Loon Lake · *Metcalfe, William*
The Loons · *Laurence, Margaret*
The Loon's Egg · *Dolan, Douglas*
Loon's Landing · *Briffett, Isabel*
Loose Change · *Cohen, Matt*
Loose Ruck · *Mitchell, Ken*
Loose Shoes · *Miller, J. Kit*
... loosers, weepers [sic] · *Duggan, Edwin J.*
Lord Newmountain's Love · *Nyberg, Wayne*
Lord of Lightning · *Derevanchuk, Gordon*
'The Lord Used Me!' · *Burnell, Ethel D.*
Lords of the Night · *Fletcher, Peggy*
The Lord's Supper · *Copeland, Ann* [pseudonym]
Lorenzo the Inventor · *Bankier, William*
Los Machos/The He-Men · *Korowiakowski, Eugeniuz*
Losers, Finders: Strangers at the Door · *Findley, Timothy*
Losers · *Fawcett, Brian*
Losers Sometimes Win · *Ross, W.E. Dan*
Losers Weepers · *Garner, Hugh*
Losing a Friend · *Steffler, George*
Losing Ground · *Schoemperlen, Diane*
The Loss · *Stewart, Anne L.*
The Loss of the Marquess of Queensbury · *Fawcett, Brian*
Lost · *Glassco, Hugh*
Lost Alaskan Terminal Retreat Blues · *Weiner, Andrew*
Lost and Found · *Goodale, Don*

The Lost and Found Canary · *Briffett, Isabel*
The Lost Cowhand · *Hoogstraten, Vinia*
Lost for Words · *Harvey, Jennifer A. Becks*
Lost Friendship · *Kenny, George*
The Lost Girl · *Pacey, Desmond*
Lost in the Barren Lands · *Mowat, Farley*
Lost in the Rain Forest · *Kean, Alex*
The Lost Key · *Jaffe, Sherrill*
The Lost Man's Tale · *Oakey, Shaun*
The Lost Pigeon of East Broadway · *Evanier, David*
The Lost Salt Gift of Blood · *MacLeod, Alistair*
The Lost Sheep · *Givner, Joan*
the lost wind · *Bullock, Michael*
The Lost World · *Helwig, David*
The Lost-and-Found Home · *Briffett, Isabel*
Lots of Room in Hell · *Peter, John D.*
Lot's Wife · *Nations, Opal L.*
The Lottery Ticket · *Booker, Jean*
Louder Than Words · *Cusack, Pauline*
Louella and Grandma · *Russell, Ted*
Louise · *Bruns, Ina*
Loulou; or, The Domestic Life of the Language · *Atwood, Margaret*
Lou - The Skating Butcher · *Burke, Leah*
The Lovable Thief · *Beck, Norma Jean*
Love, a Lunenberger, and Rappie Pie · *Hubbard, Dexter*
Love, Lost and Found · *Clement, John*
Love & the Waiting Game · *Watmough, David*
Love Affair · *Stein, Rhoda Elizabeth Playfair*
Love Among the Bookstacks · *Hornborg, Sten*
Love and Ambrose · *Allaby, Ian*
love and the mist · *M., C.R.*
The Love Bug · *(R)rose, Barbara [sic]*
Love by the Book · *Cameron, Donald*
Love Call · *Young, Scott*
Love Casts Out Fear · *Pearson, Phyllis*
Love Comes Home Again · *Findlay, David K.*
Love Feast · *Abnett, Eileen*
Love Finds a Way · *Evans, Allen Roy*
Love for Learning: A Tale of Passion and Poetry · *Cook, George*
A Love for the Infinite · *Cohen, Matt*
The Love Gods · *Gillese, John Patrick*
Love Has Its Reasons · *Currie, Doris M.*
Love in a Flash · *Conger, Lesley and Aaron, Michael*
Love in a Very Cold Climate · *Horwood, Harold*
Love in the Attic · *Layton, Boschka*
Love in the Park · *McConnell, William C.*
Love Is a Funny Thing · *McLaughlin, Lorrie*
Love Is a Growing Thing · *Fines, Beatrice E.*
Love Is a Long Shot · *Allan, Ted*
Love Is Always an Accident · *Green, H. Gordon*

Love Is an Active Verb · *Henry, Cam*
Love Is for Christmas · *Powell, Dorothy M.*
Love Is for Everyone · *Scott, Margerie*
Love Is for the Birds · *McDougall, Colin M.*
Love Is Sometimes Having to Say Goodbye · *Stein, Rhoda Elizabeth Playfair*
Love Is the Best Gift · *Powell, Dorothy M.*
Love Is the Reason · *Fitzpatrick, Helen*
Love Is the Surest Gamble · *Bruce, Charles T.*
Love Letter · *Nowlan, Alden*
Love Letter 37 Minos/Calgary · *Dyba, Kenneth*
The Love Letter · *Gillese, John Patrick*
Love Letter to a Friend · *Collier, Diana G.*
Love Letters · *Mezei, Stephen*
Love Letters: A Docu-Drama of the Sixties · *Kostash, Myrna*
Love Must Say 'No' · *Adelaide, Sister Mary*
The Love of Bride Crowdy · *Bird, Will R.*
The Love of Limpy Joe · *Green, H. Gordon*
Love on a 22-Footer · *Greene, Anna*
Love Sometimes Means Having to Say Goodbye · *Stein, Rhoda Elizabeth Playfair*
A Love Story · *Thomas, Peter*
Love Story for Ma · *Dales, Walter A.*
The Love Story of Mr. Alfred Wimple · *O'Hagan, Howard*
Love That Hair · *Koncel, Mary Aleta*
Love Those Lenses · *Peters, A.W.M.*
Love with Hammer and Nails · *Findlay, David K.*
The Loved Ones Bit · *Baker-Pearce, Mike*
Love-In at Trevor Station · *Jakober, Marie*
A Lovely Bottle of Wine · *Bankier, William*
A Lovely Day · *Baker, Rita*
A Lovely Place to Visit · *Hart, Anne*
Lover · *Summerhayes, Don*
Lover Bounce High · *Nimchuk, Michael John*
Lover Come Back · *Green, H. Gordon*
A Lover Needs a Guitar · *Lewis, David E.*
Lovers · *Ashcroft, Sheila*
Lover's Leap · *McLeod, Murdoch*
Love-Song to Palinurus · *Kishkan, Theresa*
Loving Carbon · *Sakhuja, Minnie A.*
Low Note in the Night · *Wood, Kerry*
Lower Than the Angels · *Halliday, David*
Loyalty · *Harwood, Mary*
Lucilla: A Fable · *Ohm, Vibeke*
The Luck · *Peter, John D.*
The Luck of Miss Tina · *Lûsse, Georgina*
The Luck of the Kid · *Barnard, Leslie Gordon*
The Luckiest of Them All · *Fetherling, Doug*
The Lucky Coins · *Forer, Mort*
Lucky Guy · *McIlroy, Kimball*
The Lucky Lady · *Callaghan, Morley*
Lucky Sign · *Hoogstraten, Vinia*

Lucy · *Garner, Hugh*
Lucy and Minnie · *Faessler, Shirley*
Ludwig · *Virgo, Sean*
Luggage · *Rikki [Erica Ducornet]*
Luggage Fire Sale · *Cohen, Leonard*
Lukey's Boat · *Harrington, Michael F.*
Lulu of the D'Isturbed: A Poor Woman · *Chatterton, John*
Lumberman's Brawl · *Green, H. Gordon*
Lunatic Patrol · *Steele, Harwood*
Lunch · *Rikki [Erica Ducornet]*
Lunch and Native Wit and ... · *M., H.M.*
Lunch Conversation · *Ondaatje, Michael*
Lunch Counter · *Reinart, Ustun*
Lunch Under Cover · *Kent, Valerie*
Lusawort's Meditation · *McCormack, Eric*
Lust Lodge · *McKinnon, Barry*
Lutist · *Riddington, Bruce*
Lydia Growing Up · *Murray, Joan*
The Lynx and the Wolves · *Rowland, Judith*

M.C. · *Plaut, W. Gunther*
M.S. Remission · *Stothers, Margaret*
M Is for Problem - Mine · *Stein, Rhoda Elizabeth Playfair*
Ma Kwet's Present · *Price, C.B.*
Mabel's Rainbow · *Young, Scott*
Mac · *Wright, Eric*
Macaroni Lost · *Barta, John*
Macaronia, Moussaka and Baklava and a Little Bit of Retsina Too · *Hadzipetros, Sophia*
Macedonia's Revenge · *Dunn, J.M.*
The Machinators · *Carey, Barbara*
The Machine · *Hawrelko, John*
The Machine Age · *Holloway, Robin*
Mad Adventure in a Hotel in Bangkok · *Hoffman, Michael*
Mad Indian at the Hockey Game · *Thompson, Kent*
The Mad River · *Glover, Douglas H.*
The Mad River Blues Song · *Glover, Douglas H.*
The Mad Snickerer · *O'Connell, Dorothy*
The Mad Woman · *Leitao, Lino*
Madame Bovary's Training Bra · *Anonymous*
Madame Eglantine · *Engel, Marian*
Madame Hortensia, Equilibriste · *Engel, Marian*
Madame Palanina · *Brown, Randy*
Madame Zahini and the Queen of Hearts · *Stein, Rhoda Elizabeth Playfair*
Made in Canada · *McNamara, Eugene*
Made in Heaven · *Tait, John*
Madeline's Birthday · *Gallant, Mavis*
Mademoiselle Paul · *Mencher, M.B.*
Madman's Logic · *Green, H. Gordon*

Madonna · *Spencer, Elizabeth*
Mae · *Copeland, David*
Mae West Fantasy · *Tynan, D.*
Maelstrom of Madness · *Gallant, Jimmy*
Magdalen · *Boyington, Lauren*
Magdalena · *Ross, Veronica*
Magette · *Rogers, Allan*
Maggie · *Thompson, Henrietta*
Maggie Was Game · *Mosher, Edith*
The Magic Brain of Sigismund Gantzoff · *Sheldon, Michael*
The Magic Carnival · *Helwig, David*
The Magic Carpet · *Briffett, Isabel*
The Magic Circle · *Briffett, Isabel*
Magic Circles · *Vanderhaeghe, Guy*
Magic Hat · *Callaghan, Morley*
The Magic Ingredient · *Nelson, Elizabeth*
Magic Juice · *Russell, Lawrence*
The Magic Life · *Henry, Ann Maude*
Magic Moments · *Stein, Rhoda Elizabeth Playfair*
Magic Moments Moonglow · *Duncan, Frances*
The Magic Monastery · *Copeland, Ann* [pseudonym]
Magic Realism · *Cameron, Donald*
The Magic Root · *MacIntosh, Keitha K.*
Magic Twigs · *Stevenson, Joan*
Magic Words · *Mackintosh, James*
The Magician · *Kent, Valerie*
Magicians · *Harvor, Beth*
The Magician's Last Act · *Eley, Bonita Bishop*
The Magnet · *Garner, Hugh*
The Magnificent Coloured Dildo · *Silvester, Reg*
The Magnificent Conspiracy · *Robinson, Spider*
The Magnolia Tree · *Grantmyre, Barbara*
Magpie · *Rosta, Helen J.*
Mahal · *Hosein, Clyde*
Mahogany Fever · *Tremblay, Mildred*
Mah-sei-nahe-gun (The Letter) · *Mombourquette, Michael*
Mai · *Ware, Ron*
The Maid · *Tremblay, Mildred*
The Maiden · *Harrop, Gerry*
The Maidservant · *McLaughlin, Peter*
Mai-Kulala · *Saunders, Charles R.*
Mail · *Ogle, Robert Joseph*
Mail Day for Amelia · *Scammell, A.R.*
Mail Order · *Murray, Aase*
The Mailman · *Todd, Richard*
The Mailman on R.R. #2 · *Boyle, Harry J.*
Mail-Order Bride · *Armstrong, Patricia*
The Main Event · *Bankier, William*
Main Mast · *Ross, James*
Mainly Because of the Meat · *Porter, Helen*

Maisie · *Ferns, John*
The Major Advance · *Govan, Margaret*
Make a Joyful Noise · *Peter, John D.*
Make Mine Vanilla · *Garner, Hugh*
Make-Believe Mother · *Powell, Dorothy M.*
Makin' Out: Sunday · *Ettinger, John*
Making a Killing with Mama Cass · *Bankier, William*
Making a Living · *M., M.*
Making a Sale · *Thordarson, Evans*
Making It · *Gibson, Margaret*
Making It · *Zonailo, Carolyn*
Making Light of the Love in the Moon · *Harris, John*
Making Love to Pulu · *Mezei, Stephen*
The Making of a Man · *Bird, Will R.*
The Making of a President · *Hancock, Ronald Lee*
The Making of a Writer · *Steinfeld, J.J.*
Making Up · *Bailey, Don*
Making Up the Distance · *Fawcett, Brian*
Le Mal de l'Air · *Fraser, Keath*
Malcolm and Bea · *Gallant, Mavis*
Male Guest · *Jeffels, Ronald R.*
Mall Shopping · *Thompson, Kent*
Mallardville Monologues · *McLean, Anne*
Malliardus · *Burnett, Virgil*
The Mallorcan Concerto · *Hancock, Ronald Lee*
Maloney's Last Stand · *Young, Scott*
Malta · *McIntosh, Don*
The Maltese Cross · *Mills, John*
The Maltese Mistress · *Braun, Lois*
The Maltese Piano · *McCourt, Edward A.*
Mama Goose · *Rooke, Constance*
Mama Says to Tell You She's Out · *Garner, Hugh*
Mama Tuddi Done Over · *Rooke, Leon*
Mammita's Garden Cove · *Dabydeen, Cyril*
a man, a girl and a door · *Bullock, Michael*
Man, in England, You've Just Got to Love Animals · *Selvon, Samuel*
Man About Hobbiton · *Oldham, Robert*
Man Against Machine · *Heather, H.M.*
Man Against Mouse · *Humphries, Tom*
A Man and an Older Man · *Greenstone, Gerry*
Man and Animal · *Wood, Kerry*
a man and his dog · *Bullock, Michael*
A Man and His Dream · *Nadia [pseudonym]*
The Man and His Wife · *Nations, Opal L.*
Man and His World · *Blaise, Clark L.*
Man and Lightning · *Nations, Opal L.*
Man and Snowman · *Buckler, Ernest*
The Man and the Cat · *Derksen, Jim*
The Man and the Four-Eyed Dog · *McKenzie, Earl*
The Man and the Vulture · *Nations, Opal L.*

Man at the Window · *Ross, Edeet*
The Man Behind the News · *Palmer, John*
Man Descending · *Vanderhaeghe, Guy*
The Man Doll · *Swan, Susan*
The Man Dynasty · *Patterson, Jayne*
A Man for the Drink · *McCourt, Edward A.*
The Man from Headless Valley · *Acorn, Milton*
The Man from Mars · *Atwood, Margaret*
Man from Nowhere · *Armstrong, Patricia*
Man from the Past · *Fines, Beatrice E.*
The Man Had a Wife · *Reiter, David Phillip*
Man in a Cannon · *Christie, Jack*
Man in the Black Magic Box · *Sherrin, Robert G.*
The Man in the Blue Vest · *Plaut, W. Gunther*
The Man in the Elevator · *Armstrong, Patricia*
Man in the Glass Octopus · *Yates, J. Michael*
The Man in the Iron Mask · *Young, David*
The Man in the Marsh · *Green, H. Gordon*
Man in the Mirror · *Booth, Luella S.*
The Man in the Moore · *MacEwen, Gwendolyn*
A Man in the Park · *Hawson, Joan*
The Man in the Street · *Bryden, Ronald*
The Man in the Street Scene · *Dybvig, Leslie*
Man in Vacuum · *Dornan, Chris*
The Man Inside · *Whitford, Margaret Ann*
A Man Is Born · *Gillese, John Patrick*
The Man Nance Married · *Barnard, Leslie Gordon*
Man of Destiny · *Partington, David*
A Man of His Word · *Pugsley, Edmund E.*
The Man of Qualifications · *Yates, J. Michael*
Man of Steel · *Green, H. Gordon*
The Man of the Hour · *Bankier, William*
man on a bicycle · *Bullock, Michael*
The Man on the Mountain · *Perkins, Ralph A.*
Man or Woman · *Blythe, Aleata E.*
The Man Sitting in Place Pigalle · *Hancock, Ronald Lee*
Man Versus Machine · *Rymer, John E.*
Man vs. Mouse · *Weir, Chuck*
The Man Who Believed in Christmas · *Cameron, Eric*
The Man Who Came and Went · *Medovoy, George*
The Man Who Caught the Fish · *Trueman, Stuart*
The Man Who Conquered Davy Crockett · *Gray, John*
The Man Who Couldn't Forgive · *Green, H. Gordon*
The Man Who Cried Faith · *Thompson, Kent*
The Man Who Did Not Watch the Olympics · *Brockway, R.W.*
The Man Who Died · *Stanley-Porter, David*
The Man Who Divorced His Wife Because She No Longer Looked Like Marilyn Monroe · *Dalton, Sheila*
The Man Who Found God Through Suffering · *Rentz, Kenneth G.*
The Man Who Found Happiness: A Fable · *Lambert, Elizabeth M.*

The Man Who Found Himself · *Briffett, Isabel*
The Man Who Got Sick · *Edwards, F.D.*
The Man Who Had a Clear Conscience · *Osman, R.B.*
The Man Who Hated Children · *Green, H. Gordon*
The Man Who Killed Hemingway · *Fox, Gail*
The Man Who Knew Everything · *Kellythorne, Walt*
The Man Who Liked Women · *Carey, Pauline*
The Man Who Lived Out Loud · *Elliott, George*
The Man Who Lost His Credit · *Green, H. Gordon*
The Man Who Loved a Pig · *Shields, Roy*
The Man Who Loved Cadillacs · *Gower, Richard*
The Man Who Loved Elizabeth Taylor · *Marshall, Tom*
The Man Who Loved Mrs. Norman Torque · *Milner, Philip*
the man who loved Rusty Iron · *Bullock, Michael*
the man who loved trees · *Bullock, Michael*
The Man Who Met an Angel · *Dempster, Barry*
The Man Who Plucked the Gorbie · *Spray, Carole*
The Man Who Rebuilt Butterflies · *Allen, Robert*
The Man Who Refused to Watch the Academy Awards · *Evanier, David*
The Man Who Remembered Inhumanity: A Space Age Tale · *Carter, Dyson*
The Man Who Sang in His Sleep · *Skelton, Robin*
The Man Who Saw the Sea-Serpent · *McLaren, Floris*
The Man Who Shot Trout · *Wood, Ted*
The Man Who Sold Prayers · *Creal, Margaret*
The Man Who Stopped Talking · *Radu, Kenneth*
The Man Who Thought of Everything · *Foley, Brendan*
The Man Who Wanted to Be a Spaniard · *McWhirter, George*
The Man Who Waved the Flag · *Green, H. Gordon*
The Man Who Went Before · *Green, H. Gordon*
The Man Who Worked for Joe the Barber · *Barnard, Leslie Gordon*
the man with burning hair · *Bullock, Michael*
The Man with Clam Eyes · *Thomas, Audrey*
The Man with the Bad Bladder · *Harris, John*
The Man with the Briefcase · *Haig-Brown, Roderick*
The Man with the Many Barns · *Green, H. Gordon*
The Man with the Musical Tooth · *Garner, Hugh*
The Man with the Notebook · *Levine, Norman*
The Man with the Umbrella · *van Wert, W.F.*
Mana · *Dobb, Ted*
Mandi · *Layton, Max*
Mandrillo · *Rosenblatt, Joe*
The Mango Tree · *Selvon, Samuel*
Manifesto · *Morrice, Hugh*
Manifesto A · *Rooke, Leon*
The Manila Folder · *Plaut, W. Gunther*
The Manipulators · *Murdoch, Benedict Joseph*
A Manitoba Accident · *Valgardson, W.D.*
Manitou Motors · *Kinsella, W.P.*
La Manivelle · *Percy, H.R.*
Maniwaki Mon Amour · *Carrier, Jean-Guy*

Mankiewitz Won't Be Bowling Tuesday Nights Anymore · *Kinsella, W.P.*
Mankipoo · *Percy, H.R.*
A Manly Heart · *Garner, Hugh*
The Mannequin · *Pauwels, Germaine*
Mannequin's Love · *Peters, Mac*
Manoeuvre of Trapper Jim · *Gomery, Percy*
the manor house · *Bullock, Michael*
'A Man's a Man,' and All That · *Story, Gertrude*
Man's Best Friend · *Harris, John*
A Man's Got to Lie Once in a While · *Johnson, Vera D.*
A Man's Integrity · *Green, H. Gordon*
Mansion, Magic, and Miracle · *Horne, Lewis B.*
A Mantle for Maria · *Ryder, Huia*
Manuel · *Copland, Alfred*
Manuel's Shark · *Horwood, Harold*
Manx · *Zaget, Bill*
Many Are the Brave · *Gardner, W.W.*
Many Mansions · *Spettigue, Douglas O.*
The Manya · *Coney, Michael G.*
Marble Halls · *Patterson, Phyllis*
The Marble King · *Horse, Benjamin* [pseudonym]
Marbles of the Dancing Floor · *Grant, William J.*
Marc Courvois and the Football Men · *Stephens, Ian*
Marcel · *Ritts, Mort*
March Mo(u)rning · *Davison, Marion*
Marching to Praetoria · *Fraser, D.M.*
Marcie · *Stein, Rhoda Elizabeth Playfair*
Marco in Paradise · *Kinsella, W.P.*
Margaret · *Gibson, William*
Margaret ... a Pearl · *Stein, Rhoda Elizabeth Playfair*
Margaret Has a Real Mean Laugh · *Simmie, Lois*
Margaret MacWilliams · *Sharp, [Mrs.] Bryce*
Margaret's Baby · *Moore, Brian*
Margot: 1969 · *Ewing, Betty Moore*
Maria B · *Andre-Czerniecki, Marion*
Maria Rising · *Hoffos, Signe*
Maria's Older Brother · *Gaston, Bill*
Marie · *Govier, Katharine*
Marie Tyrell · *Fraser, D.M.*
Marilyn · *Naylor, C. David*
Marilyn Monroe Didn't Have a Date One Saturday Night · *McCaughna, David*
Marina Island · *Murray, Rona*
Marinade · *McWhirter, George*
Marine Life · *Svendsen, Linda*
Mario · *MacKinnon, Bernard*
Marion Fernleigh Takes a Walk · *Endres, Robin Belitsky*
The Mariposa Hunting Excursion · *Chatterton, John*
Marjorie · *Prokopchuk, Ivan*
The Mark · *Mills, Elizabeth*
Mark Brown's Moccasins · *Briffett, Isabel*

Marked by Fire · *Rigby, Carle A.*
Marko Firman's Good Luck · *Weir, John*
Marks · *Elgaard, Elin*
Marlborough Street · *Stewart, Anne L.*
Marrakesh · *Munro, Alice*
Marriage · *O'Leary, Denyse*
Marriage a-la-mode Orlick Miller · *Ludwig, Jack*
The Marriage Breaker · *Russell, Sheila MacKay*
Marriage Is a Dangerous Sport · *Findlay, David K.*
Marriage Is a Lonely Game · *Russell, Sheila MacKay*
Marriage Makes Three · *Russell, Sheila MacKay*
Marriages Are Made · *Barnard, Leslie Gordon*
Marriages Are Made in Heaven · *Plexman, A. Constance*
A Married Couple · *Stanley-Porter, David*
Marry Anger: An Unfinished Satire · *M [pseudonym]*
Marrying the Hangman · *Atwood, Margaret*
Mars · *Mathews, Lawrence*
The Mars Bar · *Israel, Inge*
Marsha · *Goodeve, Patrick R.*
Marshallene at Work · *Engel, Marian*
Marshallene on Rape · *Engel, Marian*
Martha · *Peterson, Phyllis Lee*
Martha Gets an Outing · *Morgan. Bernice*
Marti Roch · *Bankier, William*
Martin Berman and Son · *Linder, Norma West*
Martin Buber and the Yankee · *Steinfeld, J.J.*
Martin Gilmer's Hour · *Briffett, Isabel*
Martin McGuire's Vomitorium · *Lewis, David E.*
Marty Was Sitting Gracelessly in the Corner (Oblique[)] · *Daurio, Beverley*
The Marvellous Prayer Shawl · *Slabotsky, David*
The Marvelous Gift · *Berg, Sharon*
Marvin, Marvin · *Stein, David Lewis*
Marwolaeth · *Walker, Alan*
Mary, Go Call the Cattle Home · *Rowdon, Larry*
Mary, Mother of God · *Spivak, Michael*
Mary · *Murray, Joan*
Mary Ann · *Zehr, Pat*
Mary Duncan · *Hollingshead, Greg*
Mary Ellen · *Julian, Marilyn*
Mary Magdalene · *Walz, Reinhard*
Mary Polowy · *Dobb, Ted*
Mary Poppins Took a Trip · *Joe [pseudonym]*
Mary's Mother · *Keeling, Nora*
Ma's Easter Hat · *Bird, Will R.*
The Mask · *Bedard, Michael*
Mask of Beaten Gold · *Laurence, Margaret*

The Mask of the Bear · *Laurence, Margaret*
A Masked Ball · *Burnett, Virgil*
Masked Bandit in the Henhouse · *Mosher, Edith*
The Masked Buddha · *Mitchell, Ken*
Masquerade · *Hedges, Doris*
The Master Approach · *Glucksman, Trevor*
Master Bo-Lu at Rest · *Rigelhof, T.F.*
The Mastermind · *Young, Scott*
The Masterpiece · *Fahlman, Jean*
Masterpiece Avenue · *Fraser, D.M.*
The Matador · *Thompson, Henrietta*
The Match · *Melfi, Mary*
Match-Boxes · *Bowering, George*
The Matchmaker · *Pollett, Ron*
Material · *Munro, Alice*
The Mathematician · *Dewdney, Keewatin*
Mathematics for the Lonely · *Dales, Walter A.*
Matherstruck · *Hough, N.C.*
Matt · *Livesay, Dorothy*
Matt Dillon, Inspector Erskine and Joe Mannix Go to College · *Parr, John*
A Matter for Spike · *Bruce, Charles T.*
A Matter of Balance · *Valgardson, W.D.*
A Matter of Climate · *Maher, Paul*
A Matter of Communication · *Ziolkowski, Carmen*
A Matter of Conviction · *Barker, Bessie M.*
A Matter of Custom · *Story, Gertrude*
A Matter of Dimensions · *Sturdy, John Rhodes*
A Matter of Directions · *Greene, Elizabeth*
A Matter of Horse Sense · *Barnard, Leslie Gordon*
A Matter of Indifference · *Norman, Colin*
A Matter of Logic · *Laub, Marshall*
A Matter of Luck · *Kushner, Donn*
A Matter of Necessity · *Hodgins, Jack*
A Matter of Principle · *Sale, Peter*
A Matter of Propriety · *Oikawa, Dulce*
A Matter of Small Importance · *Norman, Colin*
A Matter of Stature · *Carriere, Monique and Rene*
A Matter of Style · *Williams, Vera B.*
A Matter of Survival · *Gerstenberger, Donna*
A Matter of Taste · *Ross, W.E. Dan*
A Matter of the Heart · *V[ernell], Mark*
A Matter of Time and Place · *Stanley-Porter, David*
A Matter of Timing · *Stone, A.C.*
A Matter of Transportation · *Grantmyre, Barbara*
A Matter of Trust · *Fines, Beatrice E.*
A Matter of Vision · *Skelton, Robin*
Matthew · *Dow, John*
Matthew and Chauncy · *Phillips, Edward O.*
Matt's Great Day · *Chappell, Constance*
Matty and Rose · *Sapergia, Barbara*

Mau to Lew: The Maurice Ravel - Lewis Carroll Friendship · *Gallant, Mavis*
Maureen O'Hara with Pimples · *Rifka, Ruth*
Maurice · *DeFaveri, Ivan*
May Day · *Stevenson, Joan*
May Day Rounds: Renfrew County · *Finnigan, Joan*
May I Have This Dance? · *Peroff, Donya*
The May Irwin-John C. Rice Kiss · *McNamara, Eugene*
May Sleep Be with You · *Graves, Phil*
May the Best Man Win! · *Barnard, Leslie Gordon*
May Wine · *Lennon, Pauline*
Maybe Later It Will Come Back to My Mind · *Faessler, Shirley*
Maybe Next Year · *Blythe, Aleata E.*
Maybe Tomorrow · *McKinnon, Wayne Francis*
Maybe Tomorrow I'll See It All from Heaven · *Mandrake, Jill*
Maynard's Mistake · *Foxcroft, Wm.*
The Mayor · *Case, James G.*
Mayor Boswell's Campaign · *Levin, Malcolm A.*
The Maze · *Rosta, Helen J.*
McCafferty's 100,000 · *Blythe, Aleata E.*
McCloskey's Plan · *Barrick, Geoffrey*
The McCrimmons · *Boissonneau, Alice*
McDuff's Last Case · *Ellis, Harry*
McFee's Bee Tree · *Visserman, Taede W.*
The McGuffin · *Kinsella, W.P.*
McKinney's Leap · *Walker, David*
Me · *Austin, Don*
Me Against the World · *Fahlman, Jean*
Me and Another Kid [?] · *Via, Jody*
Me and Charlie and the Concentrated Ground · *Romuld, Conrad*
Me and Curley · *Thompson, Henrietta*
Me and MacCracken · *Laflamme, Guy*
Me and My Sister · *Thompson, Henrietta*
Me Name? · *Keene, Peggy*
A Meal of Flippers · *Saunders, Gary L.*
The Meaning of Meaning · *Norman, Colin*
The Means · *Weinzweig, Helen*
The Measure of a Man · *Fines, Beatrice E.*
A Measure of Rooms · *Schleich, David*
Meat Balls Tomorrow · *Barnard, Margaret E.*
Meat Inspection · *Skinner, Norman Doc*
The Meatball Method Journal · *Walsh, Patrick*
The Mechanic · *Harrison, A.S.A.*
Mechanical Therapy · *Foley, Sheila*
The Meddlers · *Dybvig, Leslie*
The Medicine Line · *MacNeill, James A.*
The Medicine Woman · *McCourt, Edward A.*
Meditation in an Emergency · *Kemp, Penny*
Medusa · *Baliozian, Ara*
Mees and L'Amour · *Scott, Margerie*
Meesh · *Ludwig, Jack*

Meet Mr. Santa Claus · *Mitchell, Sylvia Elizabeth Fisher*
Meet My Lovely Daughter · *Dales, Walter A.*
The Meeting · *Beauvais, Ronald*
Meeting at Milk Market · *Wycham, John*
Meeting Burroughs Half-Way · *Slonkowitz, Richard*
Meeting by Moonlight · *Young, Scott*
Meeting Caspar Miller · *Smith, Michael*
Meeting Mr. Camp · *Herbert, John*
A Meeting of Minds · *Duffin, Ken*
A Meeting of Two Neighbours · *Sparks, Richard*
Megan · *Itani, Frances*
Megan's Vampire · *Heatley, Marney*
Melancholy Elephants · *Robinson, Spider*
Melinda · *Hill, Doug*
Mellie's Poem · *Rofihe, Rick*
(a mellowdrama) · *Bell, Wade*
Melody for a Bull · *Hicks, John V.*
Melody on a Ferry · *Grantmyre, Barbara*
Melting · *Davies. Kevin*
Melville Should Have Had It So Good · *Woodsworth, Nick*
Melvin · *MacMillan, Ian*
Melvin Arbuckle's First Course in Shock Therapy · *Mitchell, W.O.*
Melvyn Hondrich's Night Visitor · *Silver, Isaac*
A Member of the Department · *Byrnes, Terence*
A Member of the Family · *Marlyn, John*
Memo to Nobody · *Grant, Peter*
Memoir: To Guy · *Keeling, Nora*
Memoir of a Grim Night in Cleveland · *Vesey, Tom*
Memoirs of a Cross-Country Man · *Rooke, Leon*
Memoirs of a Girl · *Lenoir-Arcand, Christine*
Memoirs of a Gunfighter · *French, Richard*
Memoranda for an Illuminated Manuscript · *Lillard, Charles*
Memorial · *Munro, Alice*
A Memorial Day · *Boyarsky, Abraham*
Memorial for Old Doc · *Hubbard, Dexter*
Memories of Love and War · *Hobbs, Gillian*
Memories of Mervyn · *Linder, Norma West*
The Memory · *Alsop, Wayne*
Memory Lapse at the Waterfront · *Pflug, Ursula*
A Memory of Gideon · *Gillese, John Patrick*
A Memory of Judith Waring · *Gillese, John Patrick*
A Memory of Ottawa · *Levine, Norman*
A Memory of the Conservatory · *Budra, Paul*
Memphis · *Dabydeen, Cyril*
A Memsahib's Confession · *Dobbs, Kildare R.E.*
The Men · *Swan, Susan*
Men and the Moon · *Geitzler, Fran*
Men Are Only People · *Barnard, Margaret E.*
Men in My Life · *Shaw, Joan Fern*
Men Like Summer Snow · *Horwood, Harold*

Men of Genius · *Hutchison, Bruce*
Men Wanted · *Conway, Maggie*
The Menace · *Doyle, Nancy*
The Menace of Mr. Samson · *Roberts, Dorothy*
A Menace to Society · *Allan, Ted*
Mene Mene Tekel Upharsin · *Seay, Karen*
The Menorah and the Manger · *Stephens, John*
Men's Rights · *Russell, Ted*
Mens Sana ... · *Ward, Jean*
The Mentally Disturbed Astronomers of Cincinnati · *Kilodney, Crad*
The Merchant of Heaven · *Laurence, Margaret*
Mercury · *Dragland, Stan*
Mercy Killing · *Goldstein, Ethel*
Meredith and the Lousy Latin Lover · *Engel, Marian*
Merely Modern · *Furey, L.J.*
Mergers · *Horne, Lewis B.*
The Mermaid on His Stomach · *Irvine, R.B.*
Merry Christmas, Mrs. Cohen · *Rosenberg, Elsa*
The Merry Maid & Miss Chance · *Roberts, Kevin*
Merry-Go-Round · *Furey, L.J.*
Mert Strikes Back · *Pickersgill, Edward*
The Mesmerizing Artist · *Kadey, Carroll*
Message · *Caldwell, Cal*
The Message Garden · *Barker, Bessie M.*
Message to the Architect of the Revolution · *Sandor, Karl*
Messages · *Rowland, Jon*
The Messiah · *Kuti, John*
The Messiah of Second-Hand Goods · *Torgov, Morley*
Metamorphosis · *Galemba, Ronald S.*
The Metamorphosis of Mr. Thims: A Modern Fable · *Fowke, H. Shirley*
Metamorphosis - Six Years · *Dyce, Peter*
The Metaphor · *Wilson, Budge*
Meteors of Wishing, with Long Tails of Guilt · *Lemm, Richard*
The Meterman, Caliban, and Then Mr. Jones · *Callaghan, Morley*
The Method · *Kremberg, Rudy*
Methuselah to Disaster in One Hour · *Hoogstraten, Vinia*
Metik · *Goodyear, Cyril*
Metric · *Skinner, Norman Doc*
Metric Patrol · *Mehren, Peter and Mehren, Kay Gullickson*
Meyer Kempel's Garden · *Arato, Rona*
Miami · *Kushner, Donn*
Michael · *Portras, Daniel R.*
Michael and All the Angels · *Blostein, David*
Michael in Branches · *Crowell, Peter*
Michael Rode His Dream Aboard · *Rosenfeld, Rita*
Michael's Story · *Kalman, Judy*
A Michelangelo Among Tailors · *Minni, C.D.*
Michlias · *Morton, Mark*
The Microscope · *Short, Leslie*
Middens · *Kishkan, Theresa*

Middle Children · *Rule, Jane*
The Middletown Begonias · *Matcham, Linda*
Mid-May's Eldest Child · *Alford, Edna*
A Midnight Clear · *Anco, Rich*
Midnight in the Afternoon · *Green, H. Gordon*
Midnight Mike · *Mayse, Arthur*
Midnight Moons · *Kosacky, Helen*
The Midnight Ride of an Alberta Boy · *Wiebe, Rudy H.*
Midnight Special · *Black, Lampman*
Midnight Sun · *Grieveson, Brian*
Midnight Trousers · *Kilodney, Crad*
Midsummer Feast · *Rosta, Helen J.*
Midsummer Gladness · *Guy, Ray*
Midsummer Night's Dream · *Moogk, Margeurite E.*
A Midsummer's Nightmare or Like It or Lump It · *Beilin, Elaine*
Mid-Winter · *Kishkan, Theresa*
Midwinter Night's Dream · *Mairghread [pseudonym]*
Mightier Than the Sword · *Carlton, Edna P.*
A Mighty Echo · *Hutchison, Bruce*
Mighty Mean Indian · *Steele, Harwood*
The Mighty Mr. Grundy: A Cautionary Tale for Little People · *Partington, David*
A Mighty Vision · *Dabydeen, Cyril*
A Migrant Christmas · *Rule, Jane*
The Migrant Man · *Briffett, Isabel*
Mike · *Carr, Jo-Ann*
Mikla-Sakan · *Moore, Brenda*
The Mikveh Man · *Drache, Sharon*
Mildred · *Baker, Kent*
Mile Eighteen · *Schermbrucker, Bill*
Mile-High Lemon Meringue Pie · *Baker, Steven*
Milestone · *Ravel, Aviva*
The Military Hospital · *Gotlieb, Phyllis*
The Mill · *DeBeck, Brian*
Millie, 'Ears,' and the Supreme Test · *McRae, Garfield*
A Millionaire · *Ward, Bob*
Millstone for the Sun's Day · *Wiebe, Rudy H.*
The Millyard · *Garratt, James*
A Mime with Two Sounds · *Moses, Daniel*
Mina and Clare · *Engel, Marian*
Mind and Matter · *Pearcey, Lillian*
The Mind of Genesis · *Slabotsky, David*
Mind Trip · *Mikolasch, Andrew*
Minding His Neighbour's Business · *Thomas, Martha Banning*
The Mind's Eye · *Ashcroft, Sheila*
The Miners' Christmas Eve · *York, Tom*
A Miner's Victory · *McClure, Mary*
Miniature Color Television · *Ellis, Harry*
Mini-Marts · *Avery, Martin*
The Minister and the Murderess · *Quaggin, Alison*
The Ministry of the League of Mercy · *Burnell, Ethel D.*

The Mink Jacket · *Harvey, Jennifer A. Becks*
Minnie and the Moocher · *Duncan, M.M.*
Minnie's Christmas Gift · *Blythe, Aleata E.*
Minnie's Gift · Blythe, Aleata E.
Minnows and Flat-Bottomed Boats · *Stein, Rhoda Elizabeth Playfair*
A Minor Loss · *van Herk, Aritha*
Minstrel Show · *Beirnes, Peggy*
Minutes from a Malingerer's Diary · *Siebrasse, Glen*
The Miracle · *Johnston, Basil H.*
Miracle at Indian River · *Nowlan, Alden*
Miracle at Malcolm's Cove · *Linder, Norma West*
Miracle at Midnight · *Stewart, Cybel M.*
Miracle at Ram River · *Ison, Olivine*
The Miracle at Saint Xavier · *Paterson, O.P.*
Miracle at the Andovers · *Murray, Rona and Glay, George Albert*
The Miracle Drug · *Finnigan, Joan*
A Miracle for Christmas · *Mackenzie, Sophie*
The Miracle of the Piebald Nightie · *Logan, Dorothy E.*
Miracle Refused · *Govan, Margaret*
The Miracle Worker · *McHardy, Vincent*
Miranda · *Morgan. Bernice*
Miriam · *McRae, Garfield*
Miriam's Quest · *Chappell, Constance*
Mir''michi Squash · *Heckbert, Steve*
Mirror, Alberta · *Scobie, Stephen*
Mirror, Mirror · *Halliday, David*
The Mirror · *Dominskyj, Marianne*
Mirror Images · *Finnigan, Joan*
Mirror Mirror Off the Wall · *Kerslake, Susan*
Mirror/rorriM, Off the Wall · *Robinson, Spider*
Miscarriage · *Copeland, Ann* [pseudonym]
Mischief · *Munro, Alice*
Misfit and Miracle · *Julien, Florence*
Miskwabia Lake · *Garratt, James*
The Misogge Parler · *Lynch, Gerald*
Misplaced · *Stange, Ken*
The Miss · *Hogg, Bob*
Miss Banister and the Horseman · *McGorman, Don*
Miss Cork · *Hoaken, Gail*
Miss Darby's Room · *Drew, Wayland*
Miss French · *Dawson, Virginia Douglas*
Miss Hansell · *Lewis, David E.*
Miss Higgins Goes to Summer School · *Curran, Kitty*
Miss Hilary · *Waterhouse, John*
Miss Hubbard Went to the Cupboard · *Findlay, David K.*
A Miss Is as Good as a Mile · *Grace, Peter*
Miss Jane's Other World · *Fletcher, Peggy*
Miss Mellowes · *Parr, John*
Miss Minnie · *Jordan, Marjorie*
Miss Poke's Search for Love · *Fletcher, Peggy*

Miss Sullivan in Her Element · *Dynan, Margaret*
Miss Thames and Miss Findlay · *Purdy, Brian*
Miss Wistan's Promise · *Rule, Jane*
The Misses York · *Pacey, Desmond*
Missing Limbs and Love · *Steinfeld, J.J.*
The Missing Link · *Steele, Harwood*
The Missing Missile · *Bankier, William*
Missing Person · *Carew, Captain John*
Mission · *Copeland, Ann* [pseudonym]
Mission Improbable · *Ellis, Harry*
Mission Indian · *Staubitz, Arthur*
Mission John · *Colby, Elsie Wilson*
Missy · *Rikki [Erica Ducornet]*
The Mist · *MacDonald, Ray*
The Mistake · *Forgie, Diane*
Mister These at the Theatre · *Stange, Ken*
Mister Watcher · *Wallace, Ian*
Mister Whitford One Sunday Evening · *Plourde, Marc*
The Mists Are Rising · *Richards, Helen*
The Misunderstood · *Morrison, Margaret*
Mite Pitkin · *Dybvig, Leslie*
Mix a Little Murder in the Wine, Dear · *Harris, Walter*
A Mixed Marriage · *Waddington, Miriam*
The Mixture as Before · *Bourjeaurd, Jean*
The Mix-Up · *Harvey, Jennifer A. Becks*
MM 80 · *Phills, O.*
Mme. Petitpas and the German Invaders · *Scott, Margerie*
The Moabitess · *Gallant, Mavis*
The Mob · *Kadey, Carroll*
Mobile Homes · *Decker, Ken*
Moby Dickman and the Jewish Question or Jonah and the Whale · *Solman, Mel*
The Moccasin Telegraph · *Kinsella, W.P.*
The Moccasins · *Trotter, ZIe Pauline*
The Model Boat · *Hancock, Ronald Lee*
A Model Lover · *Percy, H.R.*
Modern Communication · *Duncan, Frances*
A Modern Prodigal's Return · *Burnell, Ethel D.*
Modern Transmutations of the Alchemist · *Shirley, John*
Modernism at the Beach · *Todkill, Anne*
Mokelumne Hill · *Marlatt, Daphne*
The Mole · *Vaughan-James, Martin*
The Molecular Defenestrator · *Ward, Norman*
Molecular Theory · *Wiebe, Armin*
Molecular-Clock-Evaluation · *Decker, Ken*
Mollie · *Wilkinson, David H.*
Molly and the Stone Beads · *Bush, Helen*

Molly Goes on an Expedition · *Bush, Helen*
Molly's Moose · *Walters, Harold Neal*
Molly's New Hat · *Riley, Wilma L.*
Mom · *Szanto, George*
The Moment · *Williamson, Rossa*
A Moment as Dionysus · *MacMann, Samuel Lavalliere*
A Moment in the Life of Bonzo the Cat · *Butts, Allan Richard*
Moment of Decision · *Hoogstraten, Vinia*
Moment of Glory · *Green, H. Gordon*
Moment of Impulse · *Green, H. Gordon*
A Moment of Love · *Pacey, Desmond*
Moment of Revelation · *Ross, W.E. Dan*
A Moment of Truth · *Russell, Sheila MacKay*
The Moment Prior · *Hudson, Noel*
Momentous Prospects: A Myth · *Schutzman, Steve*
Moments of Most Madness · *Duffin, Ken*
Momma Rich's Pastrami · *Sturdy, John Rhodes*
Momma Will Hear You · *Hyatt, Murray*
Mom's Apple Pie · *Wylie, Lillian MacKinnon*
Mona Lisa · *MacCormack, Terrance*
The Monarch · *Browne, Paul Cameron*
Monarchs · *Kemp, Penny*
Monday Afternoon · *Wherry, Matthew*
A Monday Dream at Alameda Park · *Thomas, Audrey*
A Monday Dream at Alameida Park · *Thomas, Audrey*
Monday Is a Bad Day · *Dalton, Sheila*
Monday of the Sixth Week · *Govier, Katharine*
Monday's Child · *Waldman, Wendy*
Mondo Pocono · *Young, David*
Mondrian Skin · *Mason, Mike*
Money Really Isn't Everything · *Barford, Grace L.*
Mongrel and the Bear · *Hammell, Steven Dale*
Monique · *Nowlan, Alden*
The Monitor, in the Voice of I · *Sherman, Tom*
The Monkey · *Miller, Malcolm*
Monkey in the Cockpit · *Hubbard, Dexter*
The Monkey Lover · *Rikki [Erica Ducornet]*
Monkey Tricks · *Powning, Beth*
The Monkey's Story · *Weston, Oleste*
The Monkey's Uncle · *Lerman, Arlene*
the monolith · *Bullock, Michael*
Monologue · *Gaddes, Sara*
Monologue by a Photographer · *Govier, Katharine*
Monologue for Three · *MacInnes, Ron*
Monsieur Pantouffles · *Peterson, Phyllis Lee*
The Monster · *Halfpenny, Tonia*
The Monster and the 'Mountie' · *Steele, Harwood*
Monster Baby · *Harvor, Beth*
Montage · *McWhirter, George*
Montcalm's Last Tour of Old Quebec · *Staniforth, Richard*

Morning-Afternoon-Infinity · *Brown, Barbara A.*
Morninglory Tears · *Feindel, Michael*
Mornings, or I Don't Want to Go to the Country · *Holden, Helene F.*
Moroccan Exports · *Grieveson, Brian*
Morris; · *Bhaiya* · *Hosein, Clyde*
Morrocco · *Zeigler, Robert*
Mortality · *O'Connell, Dorothy*
Mortimer Griffin, Shalinsky, and How They Settled the Jewish Question · *Richler, Mordecai*
Mosaic in Montmartre · *Such, Peter*
Moses to the Waterwork · *McWhirter, George*
The Moslem Wife · *Gallant, Mavis*
Mosquito Story · *Baltensperger, Peter*
Most Beautiful Night · *McLaughlin, Lorrie*
The Most Beautiful Shoulders · *Herbert, John*
The Most Beautiful Skates in the World · *MacIntosh, Keitha K.*
The Most Fragile Kite · *Will, Ray*
The Most Unforgettable Character I Have Met · *MacKrow, Jack*
A Most Unusual Winter · *Kingsley, F [pseudonym]*
Mostly Sunny Today · *Roberts, Dorothy*
The Moth · *Martin, Peter G.*
The Mother · *Ferns, John*
Mother and Father Talk of Going South · *Fraser, Keath*
Mother and Mrs. O'Reilly · *Kirkwood, Hilda*
Mother and the Ice Storm · *Green, H. Gordon*
Mother Armenia on the Statue to Victory and the Tour-Guide in the Matenadaron · *Shirinian, Lorne*
Mother Goose Acres - 1973 · *Kalb, Sandra*
Mother Goosed · *Tata, Saam [pseudonym?]*
Mother Holly · *Virgo, Sean*
Mother Is the Necessity of Invention · *Jeffrey, David L.*
Mother of Us All · *Dabydeen, Cyril*
Mother Tucker's Yellow Duck · *Kinsella, W.P.*
Motherhood · *Mitton, M. Anne*
The Mother-in-Law · *Livesay, Dorothy*
The Mother-in-Law · *Green, H. Gordon*
Mothers, Daughters: Barriers, Borders · *Nemiroff, Greta Hofmann*
Mothers · *Powning, Beth*
A Mother's Cry · *Thompson, Kent*
The Mother's Dance · *Kinsella, W.P.*
Mother's Day · *Sawai, Gloria*
Mother's Day Massacre · *van Varsefeld, Gail*
Mother's Day Visit · *Gagnon, Christine*
Mother's Hideaway · *Brock, Paul*
A Mother's Love · *Anonymous*
Mother's Milk · *Gibson, Margaret*
Mother's Pets Are Very Old · *Dedels, Dorothy M.*
Moths · *Windley, Carol*
The Motor Car · *Clarke, Austin C.*
The Mountain · *Goulden, Alban*

The Mountain · *Vicari, Patricia*
Mountain in No Zone and Friends · *Kosacky, Helen*
A Mountain Journey · *O'Hagan, Howard*
The Mountain of Death · *Mayse, Arthur*
Mountains & Rivers & an Arctic Sea · *Bell, Wade*
the mountie · *Heath, Terence*
The Mourner · *Cameron, Zita*
The Mourners · *Duncan, George*
The Mourning Dead · *Greenway, Eric*
The Mouse and the Fish · *Slabotsky, David*
The Mouse and the Sparrow · *Garner, Hugh*
Mousse · *Gallant, Mavis*
Mouthful · *Dabydeen, Cyril*
Move Over, Shepherds · *Graham, Ferne*
The Movie · *Arnason, David*
The Movies · *Browne, Colin*
Moving Day · *Garner, Hugh*
Moving In · *Harvey, Jennifer A. Becks*
Moving On · *Rule, Jane*
The Moving Story of a Last Confession · *Bruneau, Bernard*
Moving to Moss Lake · *Brewster, Elizabeth*
Moving to the Country · *MacDonald, David*
Moving with the Times · *Rosenfeld, Rita*
Mozy · *Reyto, Martin*
Mr. Arc-En-Ciel · *MacKenzie, Brenda*
Mr. Atkinson's Bats · *Green, H. Gordon*
Mr. Bentham, I Presume? · *Stuckey, Jo*
Mr. Butter's Ocean Crossing · *Walker, David*
Mr. Carew's Contract · *Barnard, Leslie Gordon*
Mr. Cohen's Leprechaun · *Peterson, Phyllis Lee*
Mr. Day · *Cairns, John C.*
Mr. Deacon · *Eikenberry, Gary*
Mr. Denby and the Rose Bush · *Stein, Rhoda Elizabeth Playfair*
Mr. Dimmler · *Gehl, John*
Mr. Elephant's Magnificent Moment · *Dobbs, Kildare R.E.*
Mr. Greene · *Phillips, Edward O.*
Mr. Grunt · *Wuorio, Eva-Lis*
Mr. Hammamacher and the Evil Eye · *Moore, Brian*
Mr. Hetherington's Patrons · *Quaadri, Muhammad*
Mr. Hor. Brunose Considers Marriage · *Ellis, Patrick*
Mr. Image · *Harris, John*
Mr. Jensen · *Boissonneau, Alice*
Mr. Jonathan's Suit · *Briffett, Isabel*
Mr. Lewis Saved My Soul · *Boake, Mildred*
Mr. Ling and the Petunias · *Harvey, Jennifer A. Becks*
Mr. Lorda's Secret · *Bradbury, Patricia*
Mr. Mackenzie King · *Wheatley, Patience*
Mr. McMillan · *Spencer, Elizabeth*
Mr. Mendel and the Other Side · *Kanner, Alexis*
Mr. Mole · *MacCallum, Russell*

Mr. Monahan's Revenge · *Green, H. Gordon*
Mr. Naseltoes and Mr. Lapidarius · *Carroll, Jean*
Mr. Nicholson's Spendid Adventure in Bigamy · *Ayre, Robert H.*
Mr. Nightengale · *Russell, Sheila MacKay*
Mr. Noad · *Glassco, John*
Mr. Pernouski's Dream · *Hodgins, Jack*
Mr. Prigg Inherits the Earth · *Dunn, Keller*
Mr. Rafferty's True Love · *Stein, Rhoda Elizabeth Playfair*
Mr. Saldanha · *Leitao, Lino*
Mr. Sleepwalker · *Wilson, Ethel D.*
Mr. Smith and Incredible Grace · *Kenyon, Nancy*
Mr. Smudge Takes a Dip · *Nations, Opal L.*
Mr. Soon · *Richler, Mordecai*
Mr. Stanley P. U. Smart · *Read, David*
Mr. Tilton Comes Through · *Gillies, Glorya*
Mr. Vertigo Tackles Inflation · *McDougall, Joseph Easton*
Mr. Waverly and Slippery Jake · *Armstrong, Patricia*
Mr. Whitey · *Kinsella, W.P.*
Mr. Willis and the Heavenly Twins · *Harvey, Jennifer A. Becks*
Mr. Woodford's Legacy · *LeMay, Bonnie*
Mr & Mrs Cassandra Brown · *Jackson, J. Graham*
Mr Eugenides' Geometrical Dog Bone · *Schwartz, Judith*
Mrs. Absalom · *Marriott, J. Anne*
Mrs. Brennan's Secret · *Kroetsch, Robert*
Mrs. Cobbett's Secret · *Bushell, Sidney*
Mrs. Cross and Mrs. Kidd · *Munro, Alice*
Mrs. Dolan's Ride · *Briffett, Isabel*
Mrs. Foster's Walk · *Smith, Donna Lee Moore*
Mrs. George · *Grantmyre, Barbara*
Mrs. Golightly and the First Convention · *Wilson, Ethel D.*
Mrs. Kollin · *Butt, Grace*
Mrs. Lumner · *Cohen, David*
Mrs. MacLean and the Governor-General · *Murray, Joan*
Mrs. Magennis · *Jones, Paul*
Mrs. Malloy · *Donohue, Patrick*
Mrs. Martin's Day · *Goodwin, Mary*
Mrs. Mary 'awkins Takes Her Winnin's · *Fountain, Eileen*
Mrs. McKay from White Plains · *Tudor, Kathleen*
Mrs. Miller Goes to Ottawa · *Anderson, Helen E [or W.]*
Mrs. Mills' Morning · *Joslyn, Linda*
Mrs. Morgan · *Penman, Margaret*
Mrs. Mucharski and Her Princess · *Keefer, Janice Kulyk*
Mrs. Newton · *de Cointet, Guy*
Mrs. Pepper, O.B.E. · *DeWitt, Ross*
Mrs. Pierson · *Cosseboom, Ray*
Mrs. Plews · *Bradley, Alan*
Mrs. Popsovitch, the Pig, and the Paragon · *Mills, Elizabeth*
Mrs. Quinton, Your Son ... · *Johnson, Jane*
Mrs. Rankin · *McAlpine, Mary*

Mrs. Rose and the Waterfall · *Carey, Pauline*
Mrs. Spy · *Livesay, Dorothy*
Mrs. T. and Her Boarder · *McIntosh, Don*
Mrs. Thomas and the Pink Straw Hat · *Powell, Evelyn Jones*
Mrs. Trudeau's Diary · *Clement, Bill*
Mrs Polinov · *Layton, Irving*
Mrs Watchimacallit · *Anonymous*
Mt. Currie Rodeo, Mt. Currie, B.C. · *Croll, Mike*
Much Ado · *Briffett, Isabel*
Much in Little · *Burnell, Ethel D.*
Much Is Forgiven · *Martin, Carl*
Mud Digger · *Pugsley, Edmund E.*
Mud Lake: If Any · *Godfrey, Dave*
Muddy Waters · *Byrnes, Slim*
Mui · *Gillette, Agnes*
Mulatto Girl · *Cook, Gregory M.*
The Mulberry Bush · *O'Neill, Paul*
Muldoon's Cove · *Russell, Ted*
Mules · *Fawcett, Brian*
Mumma · *Dyba, Kenneth*
The Mural · *Davey, Frank*
Murchison's Moose · *Fines, Beatrice E.*
The Murder · *Ross, Stuart*
Murder After the Matinée · *Phillips, Fred H.*
Murder at Eight Bells · *Parr, D. Kermode*
Murder of a Candidate for a Post-Doctorate Degree · *Halliday, David*
Murder of a Man · *Asplund, Susan*
The Murder of Agatha Christie · *McCaffery, Steve*
Murder on the Northumberland Ferry · *Leclair, Elizabeth*
The Murder That Saved a Marriage · *Ericsson, Sue*
[The?] Murderer · *Barnard, Leslie Gordon*
Muriuki's Mother · *Schermbrucker, Bill*
Murk IV Meets Watson the Benedict · *Hollyer, Cameron*
The Murphy Touch · *Murdoch, Benedict Joseph*
The Murphys Don't Stay Licked · *Murdoch, Benedict Joseph*
The Muscle · *Callaghan, Barry*
The Museum · *Lawson, Eric*
The Museum of Man · *Dagg, Mel*
Museum Piece · *Fodor, T.C.*
Mushrooms for a Stroganoff · *Friedman, Irena*
Music, When Soft Voices Die · *Grantmyre, Barbara*
Music · *Behrens, Peter*
The Music Festival · *Mitton, M. Anne*
Music for a Wet Afternoon · *Bell, Wade*
Music Is Water · *Vicari, Patricia*
The Music Lesson · *Adamson, Regmore*
The Music Maker · *Wood, Ted*
The Music on the Barge · *Avery, Martin*
Musical Hell · *Layton, Boschka*
Musical Ride · *Morton, Colin*

Musician · *Riches, Brenda*
Musings of an Old Lady · *O'Brien, Olive*
Muskie Madness · *Power, John*
The Muskokians · *Avery, Martin*
The Mutation · *Flynn, Nore*
Mutiny at Pine Flats · *Willison, Evelyn A.*
Mutti, Mutti · *Silarajs, Juris*
My Ainsel' · *de Lint, Charles*
My Auntie's Christmas Flight to the Moon · *Harris, Walter*
My Babysitter · *Cook, Gregory M.*
My Belgian Straw Hat · *Scott, Margerie*
My Biographer · *Morton, Lionel*
My Birthday Party · *Boyarsky, Abraham*
My Blonde Tiger · *Birdsell, Sandra*
My Book · *Pullen, Charles*
My Brother, My Keeper · *Mathews, Robin D.*
My Brother · *Bailey, Don*
My Brother Ki · *Russell, Ted*
My Brother Solomon, the Bible, and the Bicycle · *Newman, C.J.*
My Brother's Keeper · *Stevenson, Louis*
My Brother's Killer · *Bankier, William*
My Career with the Leafs · *Fawcett, Brian*
My Case of Fleeting Fever Fame, or How I Stopped Worrying and Learned to Love Fatal Diseases · *Duncan, Leslie*
My Child, My Son, MY! · *Lewis, Leda M.*
My Children Bring the Sun · *Delver, Emily*
My Country Wrong · *Rule, Jane*
My Cousin Ned and the Canadian Ethos · *Cahill, Brian*
My Cup Runneth Over · *Roddan, Samuel*
My Daughter's Teacher · *Truss, Jan*
My Dear Dr. Pinkham · *Bell, Wade*
My Early Musical Career · *Lewis, David E.*
My Fate · *Christy, Jim*
My Father, with Both Hands · *Hollingshead, Greg*
My Father and the Book Agent · *Armstrong, Patricia*
My Father the Fiddler · *Nowlan, Alden*
My Father's Fancy · *Percy, H.R.*
My Father's House · *Rule, Jane*
My Father's Inventions · *Allan, Ted*
My Father's Tailor · *Bauer, Walter*
My Fiancée · *Boyarsky, Abraham*
My First Canadian Christmas · *Bruns, Ina*
My First Fire · *Teicher, Mark*
My Friend, My Enemy · *Walker, David*
My Friend Andrew · *Kay, Margaret B.*
My Friend Gossip · *Green, H. Gordon*
My Friend Julio · *Purdy, Al*
My Friend Mrs. Wallis · *Field, Nancy*
My Girl and the City · *Selvon, Samuel*
My Grandmother · *Heath, Jean*

Mystery at San Roque · *Wuorio, Eva-Lis*
Mystery at the Henderson Shipping Company · *Danys, Ruth*
Mystery in Marin · *Dawson, Fielding and Woods, Hanford*
A Mystery of Roses · *Linder, Norma West*
The Mystery of the Missing Penelope · *Bankier, William*
Mystery on the Collection Plate · *Green, H. Gordon*
The Mystic Adventurer · *Kutlesa, Joso*
Mystras: The Search for the Great White Horse · *MacEwen, Gwendolyn*
Myth and Mistake · *Garber, Lawrence*
The Myth of Joel Ickerman · *Layton, Max*
The Myth of Serpentarius · *Boyko, Elvina*
The Myth of the Black Mountain · *Sturdy, Giles*
Mythical Beasts · *Ross, James*

Nada, Nada y Nada · *Latimer, Hugh*
Nada - When You're Running Low on Style · *Spence, Ian A.*
Nadya Visits Washington · *Hopwood, V.G.*
The Nagger · *Hubbard, Dexter*
Nail, Nail on the Wall · *Marlyn, John*
Nailing Down Pornography · *Rogal, Stan*
Nai-Nai · *Cameron, Anne*
A Naive and Straightforward Narrative · *Yates, J. Michael*
The Name of the Game · *Spencer, Elizabeth*
A Name to Remember · *Mayse, Arthur*
Name Your Poison · *Smith, Colonel* [pseudonym]
Nameless Age · *Roberts, Joy*
The Namesake · *Madott, Darlene*
The Naming of Albert Johnson · *Wiebe, Rudy H.*
Nan Finds a Cure · *Daem, Mary*
Nana · *Murray, Rona*
Nanabozho and the Song: A New Northern 'Legend' · *Reid, Dorothy M.*
The Nanook in the Stone · *MacMillan, William*
Nanuk · *Laurence, Margaret*
Nanuk ... the King! · *Black, Simon*
Napoleon's Member · *Lipman, Robert*
Narcissus · *Brown, Randy*
Narcissus Consulted · *Rooke, Leon*
Nareth the Questioner · *de Lint, Charles*
Narrative #7 · *Judy, Stephanie*
Natalia, Lady of Culture · *Martens, Debra*
Natalie Said · *Pletz, Joan*
Natasha Rombova · *Pomeroy, Graham*
Nation, Nation · *Fraser, Keath*
Nationalism · *Engel, Marian*
The Native Albertan · *Delaney, John*
A Native Son · *Mofina, R.H.*
Native Waters · *Wilkin, Greg*
Natura Finds a Husband · *Bilovus, Linda*
Natural History · *Rikki [Erica Ducornet]*

The Natural Man · *Dickinson, Don*
The Nature of the Beast · *Anderson, Thomas*
Nature Woman · *Green, H. Gordon*
Nazis, Communists, Presbyterians & Jews in Norman Bethune's Hometown · *Avery, Martin*
NBSS: The Ugly Brothers · *Avery, Martin*
A Near Miss · *Hood, Hugh*
The Nearness of Grace · *Powell, Dorothy M.*
The Near-Sighted Swimmer · *White, Marilyn*
The Necessary Evil · *Barnes, Bill [William J.?]*
Necessity Is the Pimp of Invention · *John, Beno*
The Necessity of Billy · *McWhirter, George*
Needle in a Grove · *Eccleston, K.*
The Needle's Eye · *Harvor, Beth*
Negatives · *Coombes, Blaine*
Negotiations · *O'Connell, Dorothy*
The Negotiator · *Laub, Marshall*
Neighbor · *Reinhardt, Jean*
Neighbors · *Friesen, Victor Carl*
Neighbors and Peculiar Sheep · *McFadden, Isobel*
The Neighbour Man · *Briffett, Isabel*
Neighbours Known · *Tolton, Cameron*
The Neilson Chocolate Factory · *Friedman, Irena*
Nellie · *Skinner, Norman Doc*
Nellie Went Away · *Barnard, Margaret E.*
Nellie's Mistake · *Harrison, A.S.A.*
Nelly Moriarty and the Jewish Question · *Watmough, David*
The Nephew · *Doubt, Bryan*
Neptune's Way · *Brandis, Marianne*
Nero's Immortal Soul · *de Meulles, Richard*
The Nest · *Williams, Marian*
A Nest of Dolls · *Brewster, Elizabeth*
The Nesting Instinct · *Findlay, David K.*
Nests · *Kinsella, W.P.*
the net · *Bullock, Michael*
Nettles into Orchids · *Buckler, Ernest*
The Neurotic's Handbook · *Austin, Don*
Neuton's Law · *Malt, Rick*
Never a Cross Word · *Lûsse, Georgina*
Never a Fire Bird · *Findlay, David K.*
Never Be A-Scared to Dance · *Story, Gertrude*
Never Bet on a Dead Horse · *Bauer, William A.*
Never but Once the White Tadpole · *Rooke, Leon*
Never Forge a Valentine · *Drylie, William*
Never Go to Dinner · *Hanson, Hart*
Never Lonely · *Elliott, Larry*
Never Seek to Destroy · *Dymant, Margaret*
Never Sisters · *van Herk, Aritha*
Never So Happy · *Marriott, J. Anne*
Never the Loser · *Reinhardt, Jean*

Never the Same Again · *Tomkinson, Joan*
The New and the Old · *Walker, David*
The New and Wonderful Land · *Hennessey, Michael*
New Associations · *Barker, Bessie M.*
A New Beginning · *Milne, Lynda*
New Birth · *Swerdfegger, Enid*
New Blood · *Haig-Brown, Roderick*
The New Bridge · *Dewsnap, David*
New Brunswick Mourning · *Eby, Robert E.*
The New Bug · *Skey, Olga*
New Citizens · *Barker, Bessie M.*
New Country · *Hood, Hugh*
New Day Dawning · *Fines, Beatrice E.*
a new direction · *Bullock, Michael*
A New Dress for Maggie · *Grenon, Joan*
The New Enemy · *Loring, Frances Woolaver*
A New Friend · *Steffler, George*
The New Girl · *Stein, Rhoda Elizabeth Playfair*
New Living Quarters · *Christy, Jim*
The New Lords · *Monserrate, Angela*
New Love for Leopold · *Barker, Bessie M.*
The New Neighbour · *Van Luven, John*
The New Pair of Shoes · *Nations, Opal L.*
The New Road · *Fines, Beatrice E.*
The New Source · *Nolan, Gladys*
New Star in the Heavens · *Parr, John*
A New Start · *Govier, Katharine*
A New Strike Out Record for Every Day · *Rooke, Leon*
A New Volunteer · *Newberry, Sterling*
New West Testament · *Silvester, Reg*
New Year's Day · *Murray, Rona*
New Year's Eve · *Gallant, Mavis*
A New Year's Morning on Bloor Street · *Godfrey, Dave*
New Year's Resolutions · *Russell, Ted*
The Newbridge Sighting · *Fraser, Raymond*
The Newest Profession · *Gotlieb, Phyllis*
A New-Found Ecstasy · *Kleiman, Edward*
The Newfoundland Boat That Never Sailed · *Murphy, Capt. Leo C.*
A Newfoundland Christmas · *Briffett, Isabel*
Newfoundland Night · *Godfrey, Dave*
News · *Briar, Matthew*
News at Wrigley · *Walker, David*
News from the Pagwa Outhouse Sentinel · *Skinner, Norman Doc*
The News Vendor · *Mirolla, Michael*
The Newspaper · *Austin, Don*
The Next Day · *Kawano, Roland*
Next Door Neighbours · *O'Connell, Dorothy*
The Next Song · *van Fraassen, Bas*
Next Table Over · *Green, H. Gordon*
Next Thing Was Kansas City · *Moore, Brian*

Next to Godliness · *Branden, Vicki*
Next to the Raspberries · *Lazier, Ann*
The Next Victim · *Story, Alice*
Next Week This Time · *Hart, Anne*
Next Year Country · *Humphries, Tom*
Niagara Fall · *Sharpe, David*
A Nice Cold Beer · *Roberts, Kevin*
Nice White Ones · *Paterson, O.P.*
A Nicer Story By the 'B' Road · *Rooke, Leon*
The Nicest Neighbour · *Katz, Bruce*
Nicholas Bratzlavet · *Koerte, Helen*
Nickel and Dime · *Christy, Jim*
Nicodemus · *Dow, John*
Nicole · *Taylor, Charles*
Nietzsche, No. 69 · *Mondiale* [pseudonym]
The Nigger-Jack Tree · *Gaston, Clifford*
Night · *Witte, Alton Jr.*
A Night Alive · *van Herk, Aritha*
Night and Day · *Perozak, Helen Irene*
Night and Morning Wounds · *Simpson, Leo*
Night at the Arena · *Zinober, Richard*
A Night at the Opera · *Sutherland, Fraser*
Night Call · *Rule, Jane*
Night Caller · *B., Jane*
The Night Clerk · *Chaisson, Michael*
Night Creatures · *Pope, Dan*
The Night Diefenbaker Stood on Guard · *Lewis, David E.*
The Night Drivers · *Woodward, Gordon*
Night Driving · *Eikenberry, Gary*
Night Duty · *Strum, Gary*
Night Edition · *Avison, Margaret*
Night Errand · *Bruneau, Bernard*
Night Exercise · *Petrie, Graham*
Night Feeding · *Flood, Cynthia*
Night Games · *Currie, Robert*
The Night Grandma Swam the Lake · *Clare, John P.*
The Night I Played Chicken with Eddy · *Mosher, Edith*
Night in Acadia · *Thompson, Dorothy M.*
Night in Gethsemanie · *Howe, Thomas C.*
A Night in Kap · *Smith, Sharon*
Night in the Big Swamp · *Anonymous*
The Night Is Black and Orange Fire · *Duffin, Ken*
The Night Is Long · *Frith, Alex*
Night Junction · *Dobbs, Kildare R.E.*
The Night Manny Mota Tied the Record · *Kinsella, W.P.*
The Night McLeish Went Dry · *Green, H. Gordon*
The Night of Farbror Pelle's Ghost · *Hanson, Esther Schneider*
Night of Testing · *Evans, Hubert*
The Night of the Big Gale · *Fletcher, Peggy*
The Night of the Decree · *Green, H. Gordon*

Night of the Golden Moon · *Alaric, Harvey B.*
The Night of the Little Brown Men · *Stein, David Lewis*
The Night of the Longest Day · *Johnston, J.D.*
The Night of the Three Kings · *Davies, Robertson*
The Night of the Thunder Pump · *Green, H. Gordon*
The Night of the Valkings · *de Lint, Charles*
Night of the Wolves · *Haig-Brown, Roderick*
Night on the Mountain · *Rutledge, Leo*
A Night on the Town · *Lewis, David E.*
Night Out · *Linkovich, Stanley*
Night Patrol · *McCourt, Edward A.*
Night Prayers · *Callaghan, Barry*
Night Rider on a Pale Horse · *Elflandsson, Galad*
Night School · *Scammell, A.R.*
Night Shift · *Brennan, Frank*
Night Sweepers · *Ranger, Ruth*
The Night the Arcturians Landed · *Dornan, Chris*
The Night the Bear Bit Albert · *Turnbull, Robert O.*
The Night the Earth Opened · *Bruneau, Bernard*
The Night the French Chef Came to Dinner · *Musgrave, Susan*
The Night the Mountains Crumbled · *Bruneau, Bernard*
Night Thoughts · *Place, Rosalind*
A Night to Remember · *Guthro, Lisa*
Night Train · *Friedman, Irena*
Night Train to Cologne · *Wright, A. Colin*
Night Travellers · *Birdsell, Sandra*
Night Tripper · *Godfrey, Dave*
Night Visitor · *Wood, Herbert*
The Night Walk · *Purdy, Brian*
Night Watch · *Green, H. Gordon*
The Night We Swished the Barrel · *Lewis, David E.*
The Night Witch · *Solly, Bill*
Night with No Moon · *Gillese, John Patrick*
Night World · *Murray, Rona*
The Nightengale Touch · *Ringland, Mary*
Nightfall · *Gasparini, Len*
Nightfear · *Elflandsson, Galad*
The Nightlamp · *Browne, Paul Cameron*
Nightmare · *Nicol, John*
Nightmare Hotel · *Riddell, John*
Nightmare in Retrospect · *Aihoshi, Susan M.*
the nightmares · *Bullock, Michael*
Nights · *Pope, Dan*
Nights and Mornings · *Pope, Dan*
The Night-Sucker · *Watson, Scott*
The Nightwalk · *Payerle, George*
Nihilism or Insanity: The Strange Life of Ichabod Oise · *Cohen, Matt*
Nika, a Tale of the Surf · *Deane, James*
Nine Is a Desperate Age · *Lewis, David E.*
Nine Must Die · *Tench, C.V.*

Nine O'Clock Lift · *Cormack, Barbara Villy*
Nine to Five · *Arrell, Leigh*
Nineteen Seventy Five · *McLean, Anne*
Nineteen-Eleven · *McNamara, Eugene*
The Nino's Eyes · *Mortenson, Constance*
The Ninth of May · *Eric, P.*
A Nip in the Air · *Donovan, Robert E.*
The Nipple · *Rikki [Erica Ducornet]*
NkwasiasEm YE Dina · *Stewart, Alan*
NLG X✻B · *Anonymous*
'No, Jerry, Don't Do It' · *Ross, Stuart*
No Apology Needed · *Green, H. Gordon*
No Band for Aunt Polly · *Green, H. Gordon*
No Bargain Today · *Green, H. Gordon*
No Black Envy · *Lagnado, Robert*
No Broken Stones · *Rolheiser, Kenneth*
No Challenge Needed · *Murdoch, Benedict Joseph*
No Cheese · *Hindmarch, Gladys*
No Choice · *Lenoir-Arcand, Christine*
No Country for Old Men · *McCormack, Eric*
No Divorce · *Knox, Olive*
No End to Winter · *Kemp, Penny*
No Excitement · *Pugsley, Edmund E.*
No Flour in the Barrel · *Fines, Beatrice E.*
No Flowers for Ole · *Smith, Judi*
No Fuss! · *Price, C.B.*
No Glamor in Glasses · *Armstrong, Patricia*
No Habla Espanol · *McAllister, Lesley*
No Holly and No Ivy · *Wood, Margaret E.*
No Hope · *Milne, J.G.*
No Humming of Wires · *Coombs, Vera*
No Individual · *Milligan, Jim*
No Love Required · *Green, H. Gordon*
No Mail Today · *Philipovich, Marion*
No Man Could Bind Him · *Vanderhaeghe, Guy*
No Man's Castle · *Micros, Marianne*
No Man's Land · *LeVay, John*
No More Bargains · *Rule, Jane*
NO MORE MESSAGES PLEASE stop · *McIntosh, Robin*
No More Songs About The Suwanee · *Garner, Hugh*
No More Than Disguise · *Birch, Paul*
No More the Pink-Dress Girl · *Wyatt, Rachel*
No Nerve to Lose · *Pugsley, Edmund E.*
No No No No No · *Bowering, George*
No One Ever Told Me · *Johnston, Nandy*
No One Is Bigger · *Roberts, Kevin*
No One's Fault · *Carrier, Jean-Guy*
No Photos Please · *Green, H. Gordon*
No Place for a Woman · *Knox, Olive*
No Place for Basking · *Murdoch, Benedict Joseph*

No Place to Hide · *Browne, Tom*
No Prophet Now · *Conlon, Jim*
No Raisins for Katrina · *Devlin, Ivan Hope*
No Renewal · *Robinson, Spider*
No Room · *Rilsky, Nika*
No Room for Debby · *Shipley, Nan*
No Room for Sentiment · *Green, H. Gordon*
No Special Reason · *Biderman, Ruth*
No Such Liberty · *Wilson, John*
No Thrill for Nancy · *Armstrong, Patricia*
No Time for Christmas · *Fletcher, Peggy*
No Time for Jerry · *MacNeill, James A.*
No Time for Listening · *Cade-Edwards, Eileen*
No Time to Talk · *Barnard, Leslie Gordon*
No Whistle Slow · *Rooke, Leon and Constance*
Noah's Ark · *Jensen, LeRoy*
The Nobleman · *Green, H. Gordon*
Noblesse Oblige · *Stein, David Lewis*
Nobody, but Nobody, Underhells Gimbel's [sic] · *Klein, Jack*
Nobody Ever Knew · *Armstrong, Patricia*
Nobody Likes to Be Lonely · *Robinson, Spider*
Nobody Told the Fish · *Faulknor, Cliff*
Nobody Walks Nowadays · *Johnston, Nandy*
Nobody's Business · *Jaffe, Sherrill*
Nobody's Going Anywhere! · *Hood, Hugh*
Nobody's Notebook · *McWhirter, George*
Nobody's Women · *Cameron, Anne*
Nocturne · *Masters, Ian*
Noire's dialogues · *Bullock, Michael*
Noire's eyes · *Bullock, Michael*
Noise and No Victory · *Godfrey, Dave*
Noman · *MacEwen, Gwendolyn*
No-Movement · *Buckle, Daphne*
None But the Lonely · *Barnard, Leslie Gordon*
None Genuine without This Signature or Peaches in the Bathtub · *Hood, Hugh*
Nonno Liked to Sleep · *Amprimoz, Alexandre*
The 'Non-Returned' Man · *Redant, Philip D.*
The Non-Taxable Loves of Mrs. Ollenberger · *Hughes, Philip B.*
Noon Hour · *Allen, Glen*
Noota and the Pilot · *Boyd, Robert*
Nor Cake, Either · *Holmes, Rex*
Nor Did Anyone Call After Him · *Carrier, Jean-Guy*
Nordegg · *Dyba, Kenneth*
Norman's Chinese Junk · *Kelsey, Robin*
Normy Chalks His Cue · *Plantos, Ted*
Norris' Hat · *Thompson, Kent*
North · *Blaise, Clark L.*
A North American Education · *Blaise, Clark L.*
North by North by North · *Sherrin, Robert G.*
North by North West · *Dixon, J.*

North End Faust · *Kleiman, Edward*
Northern Chimera · *Garratt, James*
A Northern Christmas Story · *Bauer, George*
Northern Light · *Marshman, Paul*
Northern Lights and Other Local Phenomena · *Gould, Jan*
The Nose · *Siegal, Lois*
Nostalgia · *Marshall, Lloyd*
Not a Medical Emergency · *Jensen, Phyllis*
Not a Through Street · *Marsh, Wade*
Not a Word · *Sherman, Kenneth*
Not Again? · *Arn, Robert*
Not an Ordinary Wife · *Rule, Jane*
Not Even Silence · *Pickersgill, Alan G.*
Not Everybody Can Live in Israel · *Ravel, Aviva*
Not Fade Away · *Robinson, Spider*
Not Far from the Borders of the Indian Ocean · *Rooke, Leon*
Not for Zenocrate Alone · *Grainger, Thomas*
Not How You Play the Game · *Blackwell, M.H.*
Not in China · *Teleky, Richard*
Not in the News · *Briffett, Isabel*
Not Like This · *Bolin, Janet*
Not Much in the Pulpit · *Green, H. Gordon*
Not Much Later Than Now · *Walters, Harold Neal*
Not Only of Words · *Amprimoz, Alexandre*
Not Quiet Cricket · *Clarke, Bob*
Not Quite New Shop · *Barnard, Leslie Gordon*
Not That I Care · *Garner, Hugh*
Not the Marrying Kind · *Brown, Joy and Davidson, John*
Not the Marrying Kind · *Green, H. Gordon*
Not Who She Was What She Did · *Morton, Colin*
Not with a Bang · *Hobbs, Gillian*
Not Yet ... Not Yet · *Bent, Foster*
A Note from Jimmy · *Helwig, David*
A Note on Gallows Humour · *Nowlan, Alden*
A Note on the Academic Life · *McNamara, Eugene*
Notebook Entries · *Persky, Stan*
Notes · *Watson, Scott*
Notes Beyond a History · *Blaise, Clark L.*
Notes for an Impossible Fiction · *Amprimoz, Alexandre*
Notes for the Twelfth of May · *Collins, David M.*
Notes from a Diary #6 · *Halliday, David*
Notes from a Suicide Diary · *Morrison, Harold R.W.*
Notes from the Topsoil · *Surguy, Phil*
Notes on a Blemish · *Keyes, John*
Notes on Singer Isle · *Horodezky, Zeporah*
Notes to a Novel · *Copps, Robert*
Notes Toward a Plot for an Unwritten Short Story · *Nowlan, Alden*
Nothing at Face Value · *Gane, Margaret Drury*
Nothing Bothers Me · *Bailey, Don*
Nothing but Money · *Williams, Flos Jewell*

Nothing but the Truth · *Cadogan, Elda*
The 'Nothing' Christmas · *Williams, Marian*
Nothing Happened to Matt · *Peter, John D.*
Nothing Is Simple · *Hindmarch, Gladys*
Nothing New Under the Sun · *Gillese, John Patrick*
Nothing to It · *Harvey, Jennifer A. Becks*
Nothing to Lose · *Bankier, William*
A Nova Scotia Jewellery Theft and It's Tragic Denouement [sic] · *Blake, Ruth*
A Novel · *Kawalilak, Ron A.*
November, Georgian Bay · *Fuchs, Terry*
November · *Hodgins, Norris*
November 1, 1979 · *Hocking, Beverly*
November 11, 10:30 am · *Smith, P. Louise*
November Nose Job · *Mason, Mike*
The Novice · *Valgardson, W.D.*
Novillero · *Dickinson, Don*
The Novitiate · *Howarth, Jean*
Now About My Operation · *Stein, Rhoda Elizabeth Playfair*
Now It Can Be Told · *Hillhouse, Gordon*
Now Playing · *Whealen, Barbara*
Now There Was Today · *Russell, Sheila MacKay*
Now Voyager · *Miller, Kathleen D.*
Nowadays Clancy Can't Even Sing · *Jarman, Mark*
Nowhere But Yesterday · *Blythe, Aleata E.*
Nowhere to Come From · *Pickersgill, Alan G.*
Nowhere Waving Back · *Dybvig, Leslie*
N'Tu-Nusu Ya Chikanda · *Saunders, Charles R.*
Nude Therapy · *Cowasjee, Saros*
A Number, Quit the Number, It Might Be Sd, Of Years Ago · *Tutlis, John*
Number 1 · *Inman, P.*
Numbers One Through Thirty of One Thousand Notes While Passing Between the
Silent Borders of Your Country and Mine · *Rooke, Leon*
The Nun · *Gilmore, R.V.*
The Nun in Nylon Stockings · *Garner, Hugh*
nunc dimitus · *Johnstone, Rick*
The Nurse · *Paterson, Katherine*
The Nurse from Outer Space · *Cohen, Matt*
Nursery Tale · *Radu, Kenneth*
Nuts and Bolts · *Kilodney, Crad*
Nuts to Knots · *Ames, Bill*

The O.H. · *Avery, Martin*
O.T. Necrapala · *Amprimoz, Alexandre*
O Canada, Canada · *Shore, Michael M.J.*
O Happy Melodist! · *Hood, Hugh*
O Lasting Peace · *Gallant, Mavis*
O Sad, Lost, Gone and Never-to-Be-Found · *Boas, Max*
O Take Me as I Am · *Porter, Helen*
O What Venerable & Reverend Creatures · *Butala, Sharon*

The Oak Door · *Blue* [pseudonym]
The Oak King's Daughter · *de Lint, Charles*
The Oarsman and the Seamstress · *MacEwen, Gwendolyn*
Oasis · *Summerhayes, Don*
Oata, Oata · *Wiebe, Armin*
The Oath · *Doyle, Nancy*
Obasan · *Kogawa, Joy*
Obeah in the Grove · *Selvon, Samuel*
the obelisk · *Bullock, Michael*
Obits for Picasso · *Purdy, Brian*
Obituary · *Livesey, Margot*
Obligatory Tit Time · *Kilodney, Crad*
Oblique Angles · *Wadds, Susan*
Observant Night Man · *Dybvig, Leslie*
Observations · *Telford, A.*
Observations of a Street Walker · *Adler, Eric*
The Obstetrical Eye · *Holmes, Nancy*
Obverse · *Sigurdson, Paul A.*
The O'Carroll Archipelago · *de Santana, Hubert*
An Occasion · *Morris, Roberta*
The Occasional Rise and Fall of Mitch Moley · *Jenoff, Marvyne*
Ocean Dream · *Young, David*
Ocean of Flies · *Fitchette, James*
October · *Murphy, Bruce*
October 28, 1968 · *Tagney, Paul*
October 30, 1946 · *Allen, Guy B.*
October Days on the Alouette · *Neil, Al*
October Leaves · *Riddell, John*
October Monday · *Fenton, Terry*
october thursday inattention · *Needles, K. Reed*
Octoberfire · *MacNeill, James A.*
The Octopus · *Briffett, Isabel*
Ode to a Poetess · *Edgar, Keith*
An Ode to the Night · *Haley, Peter*
The Odour of Incense · *Pacey, Desmond*
Of Agonizing and Organizing · *O'Connell, Dorothy*
Of Children in the Foliage · *Green, Terence M.*
Of Death, Sin, and the Devil · *Spalding, Alec*
Of Dreams and Other Fools · *Baltensperger, Peter*
Of Ducks and Death · *Godfrey, Dave*
Of Eastern Newfoundland, Its Inns & Outs · *Dorn, Ed*
Of Fear and Love · *Russell, Sheila MacKay*
Of Gardens ... · *Barrett, Alan John*
Of Gardens · *Zonailo, Carolyn*
Of Generations · *Campbell, Wanda Blynn*
Of Happiness and Despair, We Have No Measure · *Hofsess, John*
Of Laws and Compasses · *Hughes, Philip B.*
Of Life and Love in a '41 DeSoto · *Torgov, Morley*
Of Mice, and Men, and Mores · *Story, Gertrude*
Of Mice and Men · *Young, David*

Of Mulcahy and Fiddlesticks · *Wilson, Jack Lowther*
Of Passion · *Dampf, Michael*
Of Physical Culture · *Bushell, Sidney*
Of Rats and Snakes · *Amprimoz, Alexandre*
Of Saints, Hags, and Martyrs · *Lenoir-Arcand, Christine*
Of Sequential Things · *Yates, J. Michael*
Of the Fathers · *Doyle, Nancy*
Of the Temple in the City of the Burning Spire · *de Lint, Charles*
Of Times Past: A Wine Warp · *Jeffels, Ronald R.*
Of Tongue or Pen · *Pastachuk, Pauline A.*
Of Truth and Shadows · *Clifton, Merritt*
Of Young and Cold Nights · *MacDonald, D.G.*
Off the Prairie · *Robinson, C.R.*
Off the Track · *Moore, Brian*
An Offer of Freedom · *Baerstein, Tsigane*
Offer of Immortality · *Davies, Robertson*
The Offering · *Watt, Frank W.*
The Office · *Munro, Alice*
The Office Party · *Taaffe, Gerald*
Office Worker's Dreams · *Kilodney, Crad*
Officer 19826 · *Andrews, Louise*
The Officer and the Woman · *Murray, Rona*
Offload on TAP · *Richardson, Peter*
Off-Season · *Ross, Gary*
Off-shore Wind · *Barnard, Leslie Gordon*
Offspring · *Anonymous*
Oh! To Be an Expatriate · *Levine, Norman*
Oh, Beautiful · *Margoshes, Dave*
Oh, Bury Me Next to Sol Kosslitsky · *Mogelon, Alex*
Oh, Danny Boy · *Sturdy, John Rhodes*
Oh, Dear, What Can the Matter Be? · *MacNeill, James A.*
Oh, My Lovely Kimi · *Joslyn, Linda*
Oh, Sylvia · *Harris, Beverly*
Oh, That Virgin Hair · *Gould, Jan*
Oh, Think of the Home Over There · *Gibbs, Robert*
Oh, Won't You Ever See the Error of Your Wicked, Wicked Ways · *Sturmanis, Dona*
Oh Jocelyn, My Friend · *Marshall, Joyce*
Oh Rupert, Dear, We Love You · *McLaughlin, Lorrie*
Oh Sunny California · *Kent, Valerie*
The Oil Baptists of the Indignants · *Ancevich, Jon*
Oil Barrel · *Douma, Felix*
Okay, Mr. Z · *Barnard, Leslie Gordon*
Ol Antoine's Wooden Overcoat · *St. Pierre, Paul*
Ol' Biggy · *Marshall, Rand D.*
Ol' Buck and the Buckpassers · *Power, John*
Old Age Gold · *Lum, Leslie*
An Old Book of Poems Authored by My Brother · *McFadden, David*
Old Bottles · *Bowering, George*
The Old Bread Truck · *McRae, Garfield*

Old Bull · *Briffett, Isabel*
An Old Bush Pilot Flies Again · *Dinniwell, Douglas*
The Old Canal · *Ward, Evelyn*
Old Charlie · *Cook, Michael*
The Old Charm · *Ross, Veronica*
Old Chris · *Hendry, Peter*
Old Comrades · *Pullen, Charles*
The Old Corn Broom · *McKee, Barbara*
Old Crow · *Lennox, Kathy*
Old Dan · *Phillips, Bluebell Stewart*
The Old Doc · *Young, Scott*
Old Eby · *Stambaugh, Sara*
Old Enough to Quit? · *Murdoch, Benedict Joseph*
The Old Farmhouse · *O'Donnell, Al*
Old Flame · *Green, H. Gordon*
Old Folks at Home · *Allen, Heather*
Old Frank · *Spettigue, Douglas O.*
Old Fred · *Templeton, Wayne*
The Old Friends · *Gallant, Mavis*
Old Giulo Returns · *Weyland, John*
The Old Grey Blues · *Gilbert, Gerry*
Old Harry and the Fourth Commandment · *Briffett, Isabel*
The Old House · *Gillies, Glorya*
The Old House Was Being Eaten · *Carson, Bryan*
Old Hunter · *McKellar, Iain*
The Old Injun Grave · *Shore, Lulu M.*
Old Jim Spenders · *Ringland, Ruth R.*
Old Johnstone's Exit · *Gillese, John Patrick*
The Old Lady's Money · *Stein, David Lewis*
Old Love · *A.A.*
Old Magora · *Purdy, Brian*
Old Maid's Children · *Green, H. Gordon*
Old Man, Young Man, Old Man's Son · *Green, H. Gordon*
Old Man · *Geitzler, Fran*
The Old Man and the Mountain · *Currie, Doris M.*
The Old Man and the Tree · *O'Toole, John R.*
Old Man Carver · *Ipellie, Alootook*
Old Man of the Cape · *Freiberg, Stanley*
The Old Man of the Mountains · *Dakin, Laurence*
The Old Man of the Sea · *Briffett, Isabel*
Old Man Stories · *Kroetsch, Robert*
The Old Man's Laughter · *Garner, Hugh*
The Old Man's Seeds · *Hutchison, Bruce*
The Old Man's Story · *Valgardson, W.D.*
Old Mattresses and New Coffins · *Brass, Peter*
The Old Minister · *Tait, Elizabeth*
Old Miss Armstrong · *Courrin, Elva*
Old Mossback · *MacNintch, John E.*
Old Mrs. Dirks · *Friesen, Victor Carl*
Old Nick Kuzloski's Great Church Episode · *Stilwell, Arthur*

Old Pangburn & the Walking Crayfish · *Hudson, Noel*
The Old Pauline · *Brown, Crombie*
Old Photographs · *McKay, Jean*
The Old Place · *Gallant, Mavis*
the old priest hailed me stay · *Gnarowski, Michael*
Old Red · *Garber, Lawrence*
Old Rounders Never Die, They Just Steal Away · *MacLaurin, Douglas*
Old Sam · *Ryga, George*
An Old Secret · *MacSween, R.J.*
Old She · *Blythe, Aleata E.*
The Old Skinner · *Primrose, Tom*
Old Snoot · *Elgaard, Elin*
An Old Soldier · *Marston, Tom*
Old Soldiers Also Die · *McAllister, Clare*
Old Story Revised · *Shuster, Schoel*
An Old Tale · *Murray, Rona*
Old Theodore These Is Wont to Wheeze · *Stange, Ken*
Old Tim Doherty and the Cumbersome Law · *Green, H. Gordon*
Old Times · *Thompson, B.*
Old Trevor · *Blythe, Aleata E.*
Old Warrior · *Walker, David*
An Old Witch Remembers · *Dalton, Sheila*
The Old Woman · *Marshall, Joyce*
An Old Woman Raging in the Face of Extinction · *Guertin, John*
The Old Woman Who Lived in a Boathouse · *Hindmarch, Gladys*
The Old Woman Who Read to Her Houseplants · *Zietlow, E.R.*
The Olde Order Changeth · *Smith, Stanley Noel*
Older Than Methuselah · *Morritt, Hope*
Oldest Rookie in the League · *Thompson, Kent*
The Oldest Trick in the World · *Stephenson, Michael*
Old-Fashioned · *Rae, Donna*
An Old-Fashioned Christmas · *Watson, Barry*
Old-Fashioned Games · *Russell, Ted*
An Old-Fashioned Girl · *Dalton, Sheila*
Oldman's Last Ride · *Egyedi, Bela*
Ole and the Fate of Man · *Dybvig, Leslie*
Ole and the Irishman · *Dybvig, Leslie*
O'Leary's Crack · *Mathews, Lawrence*
Oli Andras · *Arnason, David*
An Olive Branch · *Engel, Marian*
The Olive Eaters · *Rooke, Leon*
Oliver Loon · *Kelly, M.T.*
Olives Under the Table · *Pinder, Leslie Hall*
Olivia: A Short Story · *Buswell, Shirley*
Olivia's Disappointment · *Harding, Mark*
Olympia: The Runners · *MacEwen, Gwendolyn*
Olympic Hawks and Doves · *Filip, Raymond*
Om · *McCutcheon, Ken*
Ominous Stranger · *Humble, Jacquelyn*
Omnia Vincit Amor · *Linder, Norma West*

Omo · *Thomas, Audrey*
Omphale · *Burnett, Virgil*
On a Moroccan Roof · *Hancock, Ronald Lee*
On a Quiet Winter's Morn · *Keith, Allen*
On a Rainy Day · *Thayer, Nancy*
On a Snowy Sunday · *Bole, J. Sheridan*
On a Sunday Afternoon · *Marriott, J. Anne*
... on Thursday in autumn like today and that's the truth · *Jasper, Lori*
On an Airless Satellite · *Almon, Bert*
On an April Morning · *Margoshes, Dave*
On Assignment · *Stein, Rhoda Elizabeth Playfair*
On Being Left-Handed · *Boyd, Josephine*
On Being Mental · *Shein, Brian*
On California Street · *Flood, Cynthia*
On Call at Christmas: The Dedicated Vet · *Waltner-Toews, David*
On Christmas Eve · *Stein, Rhoda Elizabeth Playfair*
On Directness of Statement in the Bush · *Razzolini, Dante*
On Friday · *Bartley, Allan*
On Going · *McLaughlin, Peter*
On His Majesty's Service · *Boston, Stewart*
On Honey Dew Hath Fed · *Ripley, John*
On Lake Therese · *Valgardson, W.D.*
On Living Alone · *Hall, Elaine D.*
On My Return from Hell · *Oszeusko, Cornelia*
On One Leg · *Clarke, Austin C.*
On One Side of Silence · *McNamara, Eugene*
On Our Way to the Flea-Market · *Bailey, Don*
On Parle Par Coeur · *Currie, Sheldon*
On Reading the Rockies/Reaching Susan Musgrave · *Halliday, David*
On Seeing 'A Clockwork Orange' · *Pugsley, Judith*
On Sheep · *Kropp, Paul*
On Summer Lawns · *Carey, Barbara*
On the Antler · *Proulx, Annie*
On the Avenue · *Anonymous*
On the Beach · *Thompson, Kent*
On the Bus · *Fraser, Raymond*
On the Corner · *Lambert, Claudia*
On the Crow's Nest Pass · *McLeod, Murdoch*
On the Dharmsala Road · *Forbes, Greg*
On the Edge of a World · *Callaghan, Morley*
On the Edge of the Knife · *Peters, C.M.*
On the Gulf · *Spencer, Elizabeth*
On the Halves · *Russell, Ted*
On the Hoof · *Johnson, G. Bertha*
On the Lane · *St. Arnaud, Ray*
On the Life of a Bull · *Kaye, Aaron S.*
On the Outside Looking In · *Stein, Rhoda Elizabeth Playfair*
On the Outside of the Pit · *Stein, Rhoda Elizabeth Playfair*
On the Point · *Flood, Cynthia*
On the Problem of Narcissus · *Yates, J. Michael*

On the River · *Godfrey, Dave*
On the Road · *Ross, Veronica*
On the Roman Road · *Pacey, Desmond*
On the Ship · *Weiner, Andrew*
On the Shooting of a Beaver · *Kenny, George*
On the Sidewalk · *Dobbs, Kildare R.E.*
On the Way · *Rule, Jane*
On the Way Home · *LeDain, Gerald*
On This Good Ground · *Virgo, Sean*
On Welsh and Names · *Collins, Pamela*
On Wings of Tongue · *Wiseman, Adele*
On with the New in France · *Gallant, Mavis*
Once a Rebel · *Hendry, Peter*
Once Bitten, Twice Shy · *Lutely, A.B.*
Once He Started Looking · *Ross, Veronica*
Once in a Quiet Neighbourhood · *Duncan, Frances*
Once Living in a Healthy State of Paranoia · *Sherman, Tom*
Once More into the Breach · *Reynolds, Allan B.*
Once There Was an Ordinary Boy · *McLeod, Joseph*
Once upon a Century · *Wilson, Jack Lowther*
Once Upon a Summer · *Stein, Rhoda Elizabeth Playfair*
Once Upon a Time · *Langille, Mary*
Once Upon a Time in a City · *Nations, Opal L.*
Once Upon a Train · *McAiney, Phil*
Ondine · *Nightengale, Christine*
One, Two, Three Little Indians · *Garner, Hugh*
One & All · *Watmough, David*
One Afternoon · *Haley, J.H.*
One Angry Man · *Petersen, Olive MacKay*
One Aspect of a Rainy Day · *Gallant, Mavis*
One Blue Velvet Dress · *Petersen, Olive MacKay*
One Christmas Eve · *Moffat, Allan*
One Christmas Star · *Barker, Bessie M.*
One Clear Sweet Clue · *Bankier, William*
One Cold Bright Afternoon · *Nowlan, Alden*
One Day at Ponds · *Mitchell, Chris*
One Day in March · *Ripley, Richard*
One Day in the Editor's Office · *Simmons, David R.*
One Day's Peace · *Bergren, Myrtle*
One Easter Lily · *Barker, Bessie M.*
One Easy Lesson · *Nelson, Harold*
One Enemy · *McLellan, Pat*
One Evening · *Helwig, David*
One Fish, Two Fish · *Rose, Ellen*
One Foot Before Moscow · *Kristen, Marti*
One for Cupid · *Metcalf, John*
One for the Master · *Doyle, Dan*
One for the Money · *Stein, Rhoda Elizabeth Playfair*
One for the Road · *Garner, Hugh*
One Frog Held Out · *Fothergill, Robert J.*

One Good Turn · *Waywitka, Anne B.*
One Goose · *Rosta, Helen J.*
One Green Bottle · *Thomas, Audrey*
One Hot Day · *Evans, J.A.S.*
The One Hundred and Fifty Livres of Guillaume Couillard · *Swan, Rhoda H.*
One Hundred Dollars · *Radu, Kenneth*
One Is One and All Alone · *Thomas, Audrey*
One Last Log · *Symon, John*
One Left Turn Too Many · *Clement, Steve*
One Lesson to Learn · *Green, H. Gordon*
One Like Her · *Liontos, Demitri*
One Man to a Marriage · *Young, Scott*
One Man's Family Feud · *Green, H. Gordon*
One Master · *Shaw, Hugh*
One Mile of Ice · *Garner, Hugh*
One Mile Run · *Manzer, Ronald*
One More for the Practical Cats · *Euringer, Fred*
One More Passage to India · *Trethewey, Eric*
One More Time · *Weiner, Andrew*
One Morning · *Strong, Aaron*
One Morning in June · *Gallant, Mavis*
One of a Series · *Usukawa, Saeko*
One of Hypermnestra's Sisters · *Steinfeld, J.J.*
One of Our Agents Is Missing · *Jacob, John*
One of the Boys · *Booth, Luella S.*
One of the Family · *Briffett, Isabel*
'One of the Lads ... ' · *Bowen, Roger*
One of These Days · *Cameron, Eric*
One of Those Days · *McLaughlin, Lorrie*
One of Us · *Alford, Norman*
One Owner, Low Mileage · *Hood, Hugh*
One Persian Night Before the Fall · *Sturgeon, Brad*
One Saturday · *Porter, Helen*
One Saturday in June · *Lea, Irene Barbara*
One September Afternoon · *Nowlan, Alden*
One Shining Moment · *Russell, Sheila MacKay*
One Sixty-Six Dash Two · *Robertson, Don*
One Special Present · *Nowlan, Michael O.*
One Story, Two Tales · *Fawcett, Brian*
One Summer · *Cameron, Eric*
One Sweet Day · *Buckler, Ernest*
The One Talent · *Briffett, Isabel*
One Thing After Another · *Pyper, C.B.*
One Tide Over · *Schroeder, Andreas*
One Too Many · *Wark, Wendy*
One Too Many Mornings · *Margoshes, Dave*
One Up for the Tories · *Hambling, Jack*
A One Way Dialogue · *Butts, Ed P.*
One Way North and South · *Hood, Hugh*
One Way Ticket · *Caulfield, Johanne*

One Way to Skin a Cat · *McCarthy, Len*
The One Who Asked · *Marshall, Joyce*
The One Who Played God · *Stemo, L. Johanne*
The One-Eyed Rabbit and the Fistulated Dog · *Friedman, Peter*
The Ones We Never See · *Collective, April*
The One-Star Jew · *Evanier, David*
The One-Way Ticket · *Chanady, Amaryll B.*
Onkle Janos · *Marlyn, John*
Only a Child · *Baltensperger, Rita*
The Only Albino at the Bus Stop · *Hlynsky, David*
The Only Decent Light · *Mason, Mike*
Only Fair · *Wright, A. Colin*
Only God, My Dear · *Engel, Marian*
Only If You Get Caught · *Bankier, William*
The Only Place on Earth · *Foros, Adam*
Only the Children · *Harper, Mandy*
Only the Dead Are Neutral · *Gillese, John Patrick*
The Only Woman Who Ever Puzzled Me · *Grantmyre, Barbara*
Ookpik's Winter · *Chabot, Nikki*
Oolulik · *Wiebe, Rudy H.*
Open Air Haircut with a Fat Canada Goose · *Egyedi, Bela*
The Open Door · *Briffett, Isabel*
Open for Business · *Gunn, William* [pseudonym]
the open gate · *Bullock, Michael*
Open Heart · *Ross, Gary*
Open House · *Briar, Matthew*
Open Line · *Hodgins, Jack*
Opened in Error. Please Forward · *Lauder, Scott*
An Opening Day · *Godfrey, Dave*
The Opening of a Door · *Nowlan, Alden*
Operation Cordelia · *Gool, Reshard*
Operation Elevator · *Symons, Harry*
Operation Oliver · *Leitch, Adelaide*
Operation Smoothie · *Anonymous*
The Operator · *Born, A.J.*
Opportunity · *Leyland, M.*
Option to Sell · *Hendry, Peter*
Optional Prefaces · *Dampf, Michael*
Options · *O'Connell, Dorothy*
Or Take a Tramp Steamer · *Purdy, Brian*
The Oracle · *Ristich, David*
Oral History: The Deacon's Tale · *Rooke, Leon*
The Orange Bridge · *Mason, Mike*
Orange Cripple · *Dyba, Kenneth*
An Orange from Portugal · *MacLennan, Hugh*
The Orange Tree · *Grant, Dorothy*
Orbituary · *Cheesbrough, E.*
Orchids After Midnight · *Collier, Diana G.*
Ordeal · *Acheson, James Dean*
Ordeal by Fire · *Steele, Harwood*

The Ordeal of Jimmy Robicheau · *Choyce, Lesley*
Ordeal of Jimmy Robicheau · *Choyce, Lesley*
Orest Kulak's Wonderful New Wheat · *Sapergia, Barbara*
Organ Recital · *Baliozian, Ara*
Organic Living · *Gould, Terry*
Organization · *Cuevas, Ernesto*
Origami · *Svendsen, Linda*
Origin Unknown · *Appleford, R. Duncan*
The Originator · *Graham, T.*
Orion · *Kavanagh, Patrick*
Orphans' Progress · *Gallant, Mavis*
Ortona Again · *Brooks, Eunice*
Oscar · *McGoogan, Kenneth*
Oscar Wants to Know · *Quin, Mike*
The Oslund House · *Donnelly, John F.*
Osmeck · *Layton, Irving*
The Osoyoos Indians Picket Highway 97 at OK Falls and Then Decide to
Take the Government to Court · *Persky, Stan*
Oswiecim · *Kirk, Heather*
Othello's Affair with the Civil Service · *Hendry, Peter*
The Other Beach · *Richler, Mordecai*
The Other Family · *Bannerji, Himani*
The Other Half · *Deane, Christopher*
Other Men Make the · *Hindmarch, Gladys*
Other Men Make the [sic] · *Hindmarch, Gladys*
The Other Paris · *Gallant, Mavis*
Other People's Troubles · *Hodgins, Jack*
The Other Rock · *Bontron, Frances*
The Other Side of the Street · *Livesay, Dorothy*
The Other War · *Dickinson, Don*
The Other Woman · *Green, H. Gordon*
The Other Woman · *Kent, Valerie*
The Others · *Goulden, Alban*
The Otherside Incident · *MacNeill, James A.*
Ottawa · *Scott, Gail*
The Ottawa Valley · *Munro, Alice*
Ottawa's First Sidewalk Cafe · *Lappin, Ben*
An Ounce of Cure · *Munro, Alice*
An Ounce of Prevention · *Smith, Olive Gertrude*
Our American · *O'Connell, Dorothy*
Our Ballast Is Old Wine · *McConnell, William C.*
Our Bull Barcelona · *Bruns, Ina*
Our Club · *Frost, Bean*
Our Father · *Deane, Christopher*
Our Home Was a Haven · *Gillese, John Patrick*
Our Inheritance: Struggle Ever, Capitulation Never! · *Collective, April*
Our Lady of All the Distances · *Harvor, Beth*
Our Last Respects · *Bruneau, H.*
Our Little Chamber Concerts · *Hospital, Janet Turner*
Our Man on Everest · *McCourt, Edward A.*

Our Mr. Benson · *Metcalf, John*
Our Mysterious Neighbour · *McRobbie, Genevieve*
Our Natural Resources · *Russell, Ted*
Our Neighbors the Nuns · *Garner, Hugh*
Our Passion Lit the Night · *Cohen, Matt*
Our Super-pet's About to Pop · *Cole, Patricia*
Our Town · *Schoemperlen, Diane*
Our Trespasses · *Wilson, P.M.*
Ours Is the Cause of All Mankind · *Cinquant, Peter*
Ours to Discover · *Sawyer, Robert*
Out for Lunch · *Gollan, Don*
Out in Chinguacousy · *Godfrey, Dave*
Out in the Midday Sun · *Thomas, Audrey*
The Out Islands · *Graham, Michael R.*
Out of Control · *Abelsen, Terry*
Out of Order · *Long, Charles*
Out of Sight Out of Love · *Clare, John P.*
Out of the Blue · *Plourde, Marc*
Out of the Cradle Endlessly Rocking · *Michener, Wendy*
Out of the Doll's House · *di Michele, Mary*
Out of the Forest · *Holloway, Robin*
Out of the Rain · *Wood, Ted*
Out of the Silence · *Findley, Timothy*
Out of the Storm · *Beattie, Jessie L.*
Out of the Storm - A Bear · *Carew, Captain John*
Out of the Window · *Brackett, Dawnold*
Out of the Woods · *Rigelhof, T.F.*
Out of the Woodwork · *Torrie, John*
Out of the Yellow Splotch, a Vital Sun · *Tierney, Barry*
Out the Mirror · *Hollingshead, Greg*
Out to Lunch · *Miller, J. Kit*
Out West with Lady Sutton-Smith · *Carlson, Chuck*
The Outboard · *Faulknor, Cliff*
The Outcast · *Bruneau, Bernard*
The Outdoor Motor · *Scammell, A.R.*
The Outer Berth · *Briffett, Isabel*
Outfoxed · *Burnett, Eileen*
The Outhouse · *Shaw, Joan Fern*
The Outing · *Itter, Carole*
Outlander · *Rule, Jane*
The Outlaw · *Green, H. Gordon*
The Outlaw · *Ross, Sinclair*
Outlaw Dog · *Mayse, Arthur*
The Outlaw Hounds · *Hedlin, Ralph*
Outport Homecoming · *Pitcher, Arthur*
Outports · *Russell, Ted*
Outremont · *Behrens, Peter*
Outside · *Pope, Elizabeth*
Outside the Structure · *Beattie, Jessie L.*
Outside the Window · *Kenny, Wade*

A Pair of Deuces · *Garner, Hugh*
The Pair of Gloves · *Marshall, Joyce*
A Pair of Peacocks · *Ready, William B.*
A Pair of Tigers · *Slabotsky, David*
A Pair of White Buck Shoes · *Reeve, Phyllis*
Pal · *Steele, Harwood*
Pale Beneath His Tan · *Miller, J. Kit*
Paleface Potlatch · *Peter, John D.*
Palimpsest · *Young, David*
Pòll Thorlòksson: Bloodletter · *Gunnars, Kristjana*
Pan American Announces · *Drepaul, Joe*
Panache · *Kinsella, W.P.*
Pandemonium in the Cockpit · *Easton, Alan*
Panic Over the Atlantic · *Walker, David*
Panic · *Green, H. Gordon*
Panther · *Glover, Douglas H.*
Paolo and Renata · *Gallant, Mavis*
Papa and Angus · *Duncan, M.M.*
Papa Passes Judgment · *Hedlin, Ralph*
Papa's Games · *Vertolli, Lou*
Papa's Girl · *Grantmyre, Barbara*
Paper · *Hodgins, Norris*
Paper Airplanes · *Weiss, Anne Marie*
Paper Boy · *Skelton, Robin*
Paper Dolls · *Chryssoulakis, Mary*
Paper Doom · *Hutchinson, Alice*
Paper Hangover · *Hockin, Louise*
The Paper Jesus · *Vernon, Lorraine*
Paper Roses · *Ravel, Aviva*
The Paper Spike · *Gustafson, Ralph B.*
The Paperboy · *Johannson, Robert D.*
The Paper-Spike · *Gustafson, Ralph B.*
Pappa Falconi · *Hamilton, Harry*
Parable of Paragraphs · *Nemiroff, Greta Hofmann*
The Parable of Sourdough · *Lee, Carroll H.*
The Parable of the Rutted Road · *Lee, Carroll H.*
The Parable of the Seventh Seal · *Kearns, Lionel*
The Parable of the Three Brothers · *MacMillan, Ian*
A Parable on a Parable · *Sandor, Karl*
Parables for at Least a Milkman · *Smith, James W.*
Parade · *Fletcher, Peggy*
Parade Square · *Faivre, Regine*
Paradigm · *Thomas, K.A.*
Paradise · *Cameron, John Cullen*
Paradise Lost? · *Kee, Kathy*
Paradise Lost · *Young, David*
Paradise Mislaid · *Home, Elizabeth*
Paradise Retained · *Hood, Hugh*
Parallel Lines · *Donovan, Rita*
The Paraphernalia of Consolation · *Harvor, Beth*

Parasites of the Wasteland · *McLaughlin, Hilary*
Parasites · *Rikki [Erica Ducornet]*
Parchment · *Mason, Mike*
The Parents of Pop · *Hale, Barrie*
Paris: April · *Mathews, Robin D.*
The Parish House · *McGrath, Robin*
The Park · *Henry, Ann Maude*
Park Benches · *Briffett, Isabel*
Parkdale Farm · *Jones, Clive*
Parker's Dog · *Vanderhaeghe, Guy*
Parker's Elect · *Neufeld, K. Gordon*
The Parking Lot Attendant · *Bailey, Don*
Parkin-Jewell · *Mencher, M.B.*
Parliament Hill · *Ogle, Robert Joseph*
Parquette · *Baltensperger, Peter*
The Parrot · *Aspler, Tony*
Parrot in a Pew · *Briffett, Isabel*
The Parson's New Church · *Wood, Kerry*
The Parson's Tongue · *Wood, Kerry*
The Part He Sees His Country · *Dickinson, Don*
Participation · *McConnell, Alice*
A Particular Journey · *Levine, Norman*
Parting · *Turnbull, J.R.*
The Partisans · *Bell, Leslie*
The Partner · *Holden, Helene F.*
The Partners · *Nicks, W. Frederick*
The Partnership · *Smith, Lorne*
Parts · *Szanto, George*
Parts of the Eagle · *Kinsella, W.P.*
Parts of the Story · *Goulden, Alban*
Party · *Moynihan, Robert*
Party Below · *Bell, Roger*
Party Crowd · *Russell, Sheila MacKay*
Party Discipline or Why I Flunked the Kantian Test · *Bloom, L.S.*
The Party Dress · *Percy, H.R.*
Party Line · *Shore, Lulu M.*
Partying · *Phinney, Richard*
Pas de Deux · *Govier, Katharine*
A Passable Likeness · *Percy, H.R.*
Passage · *Metcalfe, B[rian].R.*
Passage by Water · *Clark, Joan*
The Passage of Sono Nis · *Yates, J. Michael*
Passage to Infinity · *Procunier, Peter*
Passchendaele · *Williams, Warren*
The Passenger · *Knowles, Rebecca*
Passengers · *Madott, Darlene*
The Passing · *Jameson, Hazel*
The Passing of a Primitive · *Haig-Brown, Roderick*
The Passing of Issy Hersh · *Richler, Mordecai*
Passion · *Smith, Ray*

A Passover Eve · *Heine, Henrich*
Passport · *Plaut, W. Gunther*
Passport to Tomorrow · *Stewart, Anne L.*
Past ... Incomplete · *Russell, Sheila MacKay*
Past Forgotten · *MacSween, R.J.*
The Past People · *Schroeder, Andreas*
Pastoral Romance · *Ord, Douglas*
Pat Frank's Dream · *Cohen, Matt*
Pat Hebert · *Carrier, Jean-Guy*
Pat Murphy Faces Up to It · *Murdoch, Benedict Joseph*
Pat Murphy Takes Command · *Murdoch, Benedict Joseph*
Pat Murphy Tries Psychology · *Murdoch, Benedict Joseph*
Pat Pendleton's Disastrous Invention · *Green, H. Gordon*
Patata Frita · *Puff* [pseudonym]
Patent Applied For · *O'Connor, John*
The Patented Finishing Hold · *Young, David*
the path · *Bullock, Michael*
The Path to Haydon Pool · *Colson, Theodore*
A Pathan Soldier · *Gill, Stephen*
The Patient Will Recover · *Morrison, Harold R.W.*
Patricia · *Sutherland, Fraser*
Patrick O'Malley Sheds His Coat · *Dybvig, Leslie*
The Patriot · *Jess, Cameron*
The Patriot · *Orrell, Herbert M.*
The Patriot Game · *Hennessey, Michael*
A Patriotic Ballad · *Roberts, Dorothy*
Patrol · *McIlroy, Kimball*
Patsies for Purchases · *Brockmann, Frieda*
A Pattern of Silver Strings · *de Lint, Charles*
Patterns · *Mitchell, W.O.*
Patterns of Change · *Okun, Nicole*
Patterns of Progress · *Truss, Jan*
Paudeen's Riddle · *McLaughlin, Peter*
Paul · *Anonymous*
Paul and Phyllis · *Marshall, Joyce*
Paul Bunyan · *McEwan, Tom*
Pavane for a Dead Princess · *Teleky, Richard*
Pavlochenko's · *Mitchell, Ken*
The Pawn Ticket · *Phillips, Fred H.*
Payday · *Ross, Veronica*
A Paying Guest Is Not a Boarder · *Smolkin, Rosalie*
Paying the Piper · *Kushner, Donn*
The Payment of Little Debts · *Gould, Terry*
The Pay-Off · *Annett, R. Ross*
The Pea Patch · *Hiscock, Reid*
The Peace of O-hoo · *Wood, Kerry*
The Peace of Utrecht · *Munro, Alice*
Peace on Earth! · *Pastachuk, Pauline A.*
The Peacemaker · *Stephenson, Michael*
A Peach Tree on Lincoln Street · *Carver, Patricia*

Peaches · *Browne, Elisa Beth*
The Peachstone · *Momson, G. Robert*
Peanut Butter · *Thompson, B.*
Peanut Butter Hero · *Armstrong, Patricia*
The Pear Forest · *Slabotsky, David*
Pearl · *Buckland, D.*
The Pearl Necklace · *Theriault, Yves*
Pearls Before Swine · *Krzeczunowicz, Sarah*
The Pearls of Li Pong · *Ross, W.E. Dan*
Pears · *Sutherland, Fraser*
Pease Porridge Hot · *Story, Gertrude*
The Peashooter · *Neil, Al*
A Peculiar Botanical Deficiency · *Peloquin, George*
Peculiar Inspector Carstairs · *Green, Robert*
Peeling Labels · *La Haye, Marguerite*
The Peeper · *Maloney, Elizabeth*
The Peeping Dog · *Green, Robert*
The Peeping Game · *Green, Robert*
The Peeping Tom · *Kushner, Donn*
The Peggy · *Bowman, Russell*
Peggy and the Olivers · *Horne, Lewis B.*
The Pelly, the Powder and the Snake · *Browne, Paul Cameron*
Pembroke O'Connell and the Purple Pig · *Story, Gertrude*
PENALTY FOR MISUSE - $20 · *Steinfeld, J.J.*
Penance · *Kinsella, W.P.*
The Penance of Pierre · *Sowton, Ian*
Pender's Visions · *Glover, Douglas H.*
Penelope's Dog · *Dragland, Stan*
Penny on a Sky Horse · *Coney, Michael G.*
Peonies and Bleeding Hearts · *Dey, Myrna*
People Are Always the Limiters of Happiness · *Tillinghast, David*
People Die · *Hogan, Robert*
People from Away · *Bruce, Charles T.*
People of the Twilight · *Mozel, Howard B.*
The People on the Shore · *Findley, Timothy*
People Remaining · *Rensby, Harry*
People Talk Too Much · *Barnard, Leslie Gordon*
The People Who Were Not There · *Horne, Lewis B.*
The People Wrote It · *Acorn, Milton*
Pepper · *Morton, Lionel*
Pepra · *Birdsell, Sandra*
The Perambulating Pastor · *Hedlin, Ralph*
Perchance to Dream · *Derevanchuk, Gordon*
Percheron Girl · *Carriere, Marguerite*
Perfect · *Rikki [Erica Ducornet]*
The Perfect Catch · *Gane, Margaret Drury*
The Perfect Couple · *Shewchun, Joan*
A Perfect Fit · *Schryver, Frank*
The Perfect Game · *Lowther, Pat*
The Perfect Night · *Hood, Hugh*

The Perfect Paper · *Wright, D.B.*
The Perfect Parent · *Riskin, Mary W.*
The Perfect Segment: An Allegory of Undergraduate Life · *Holland, James* [pseudonym]
A Perfect Setting · *Brewster, Elizabeth*
A Perfect Stranger · *O'Connell, Dorothy*
The Perfect Widow · *Maslowski, Alina*
The Perfectionist · *Morris, Doris M.*
A Perfectly Nice Man · *Rule, Jane*
Perfidia · *Aldridge, Mary-Catherine*
Perfume · *Smith, Steve*
The Perfume Sea · *Laurence, Margaret*
The Pergola · *Colson, Theodore*
Perhaps a Myth · *Cheshire, John*
Perhaps It Never Was · *Wilson, Jack Lowther*
Perhaps the Church Building Itself · *Thompson, Kent*
Peril · *Smith, Ray*
The Peril of Two Carat · *Flynn, Nore*
The Perils of the Double Sign · *Davies, Robertson*
The Period of Soon · *Corrigall, Melodie Joy*
Period Piece · *Dunn, Tim*
The Periodic Stranger's Hand · *MacLennan, Toby*
Permanent · *MacCallum, Russell*
Permanent Wave · *Wills, Claire*
The Perpendicular Sun · *Stuart, James*
Persecution Mania · *O'Fadlain, Sean*
Persia Awakening · *Ross, Veronica*
Persimmon · *Riches, Brenda*
The Persistent Doe · *Smallwood, James L.*
The Personal Commitment of Cosmic Leonard · *Sturmanis, Dona*
The Personality Box · *Osser, Harry*
Perspective · *Gillese, John Patrick*
Perspective · *Stewart, Anne L.*
Pervasion · *Stuart, James*
The Pest · *Conger, Lesley*
The Pet Mouse · *Emkeit, Ron L.*
Petals · *Fawcett, Brian*
Pete · *Horst, Roger*
The Petek · *Plaut, W. Gunther*
Peter! · *Tremblay, Carol*
Peter & John: Two Cameos · *Jackson, J. Graham*
Peter and Concern · *Stefco, Karen*
Peter Pond, His True Confession · *Whyte, Jon*
Peter Rabbit · *Nella* [pseudonym]
Peter Smiley's Influence · *LeDain, Gerald*
The Peter Stories · *Hindmarch, Gladys*
Peter's Boat · *Joyce, F.N.*
Pete's Rubbers · *Peterson, Phyllis Lee*
Pete's Story - A Chronicle of Galactic Lust and High Drama · *Dowright, George Oliver*

Petits Fours · *McKibbon, Mollie Pearce*
Petra Goggin's Letter · *Carlson, Chuck*
Petrified · *Drachman, Wolf*
Petruchio · *Sloman, Fred*
Petruniach · *Harley, Jorda Anne*
Petty Thievery · *Scott, Gail*
Pétur Arnason, Roundup · *Gunnars, Kristjana*
PFSD · *Bell, Mackenzie*
A Phable of Phool's Paradise Tale of Compassionate Phlim-Phlam · *Ellis, Harry*
The Phallus · *Truss, Jan*
Phantase · *Enwright, William*
Phantom Foot · *Gotlieb, Phyllis*
Phantom Hill · *Gardner, W.W.*
Phantoms · *Bell, Wade*
Pharma · *Shainblum, Mark*
The Phase · *Gibson, Margaret*
Pheasants in the Corn · *Godfrey, Dave*
Pheidippides Was Not a Family Man · *Hutchinson, Bobby*
Philip · *Dow, John*
The Philistine · *Hardy, W.G.*
Philodendron · *Yates, J. Michael*
The Philosopher of the People · *Boyarsky, Abraham*
The Philosopher's Stone · *Scobie, Stephen*
The Philosophical Dodge · *Cameron, Donald*
Philosophy of Design · *Anonymous*
Phobia · *Bougie, Blaine*
Phoenix, Phoenix, Light & Fire · *Ross, James*
Phoenix · *Marcellin, Philip*
Phonecall · *O'Rourke, David*
The Phoner · *Rushton, Alfred*
Phonsie, the Unfortunate Wooer · *Currie, Doris M.*
A Photograph, in Black and White · *Friedman, Irena*
The Photograph · *Stirling, Richard*
A Photograph of Man · *Heide, Christopher*
The Photographer · *Munro, Alice*
'Physician, Heal Thyself' · *Egner, Brian*
The Physicist and the Poet · *Hancock, Ronald Lee*
Piano Blues · *McKenna, Brian J.*
Picaroon · *Burnett, Virgil*
The Piccolo · *Raelo, Juan*
Picker · *Murray, Joan*
Picking Roots · *Williams, David*
Pickles · *Hodgins, Norris*
The Pickling of Guingin · *Geddes, Gary*
Pickup at Twilight · *Carriere, Marguerite*
The Picnic · *Macdonald, Helen*
The Picnic and the Gun · *Wood, Kerry*
The Picture · *Merz, Sandra*
Picture of a Hero · *Wynand, Derk*
A Picture of the Virgin · *Kinsella, W.P.*

Pipes · *Mitchell, Sylvia Elizabeth Fisher*
A Piping from the Sea · *Bigalow, Mary*
Pipistrello · *Hrynkiw, Oreste*
A Pirate Called the 'Sea Owl' · *Freeman, T.J.*
The Pirates of Copper River · *Mayse, Arthur*
The Pit · *Garber, Lawrence*
Pit Lamping · *Kinsella, W.P.*
The Pit Whence Ye Are Digged · *Davies, Robertson*
The Pitcher · *Hood, Hugh*
Pitcher Has a Rubber Nose · *Heble, Ajay*
The Pitchman · *Maude, Phil*
Pity the Poor Piper · *Spettigue, Douglas O.*
Pius Blindman Is Coming Home · *Kinsella, W.P.*
A Pixy Tale · *Verner, Shakie*
Pizza Piece · *Svoboda, Terese*
Place · *Graham, Gary*
A Place for Us · *Stein, Rhoda Elizabeth Playfair*
A Place in This House · *Carey, Barbara*
A Place of Her Own · *Smith, Donna Lee Moore*
The Place of His Hiring · *Eibel, Deborah*
A Place of One's Own · *Valgardson, W.D.*
The Place of Stones · *Saunders, Charles R.*
A Place of Witches · *Waddington, Miriam*
A Place to Belong · *MacIntosh, Keitha K.*
A Place to Die · *Summerhayes, Don*
A Place to Land · *Duffin, Ken*
A Place to Stay · *Morton, Lionel*
A Place Where There Is No Darkness · *Ellison, Joanne*
The Place Whereon Thou Standest · *Dickinson, George*
Places I've Never Been · *Hood, Hugh*
The Plague · *Roger, Robin*
The Plague Children · *Hodgins, Jack*
A Plague of Armadillos · *Dance, James Michael*
Le plaidoyer d'une folle hommage; Strindberg · *Marshall, Linda*
Plain Jane · *Brock, Paul*
A Plain Story · *Hough, N.C.*
The Plan · *Leonhardt, Richard A.*
A Plan Is a Plan · *Dabydeen, Cyril*
The Planned Returning · *Daem, Mary*
Plant Light and Las Vegas · *Ewing, Wain*
The Plaster Saint · *Vipond, Alva*
A Plate of Spaghetti · *Doyle, Dan*
Plaudits · *Browne, Paul Cameron*
A Plausible Story · *Layton, Irving*
Play, Fellow · *Hull, Raymond*
Play and Pay · *Homer, Daniel Scott*
Play for the Lady · *Bankier, William*
Play It Again, Eddy · *Hart, Michael*
Playboy · *Krause, Pat*

Playboy and the Bar Mitzvah Boy · *Steinfeld, J.J.*
Player Deal · *Young, Scott*
The Playgirl · *Russell, Sheila MacKay*
The Playground · *Watts, John*
Playing Ball · *Brenna, Dwayne*
Playing Ball on Hampstead Heath · *Richler, Mordecai*
Playing the Game · *Wolfson, Ken*
The Playmate · *Laub, Marshall*
The Play's the Thing · *MacSween, R.J.*
Plaza Del Loma · *Reid, Dennis*
Pleasant Dreams · *Browne, Norman G.*
Please! Help Me! · *Chambers, Patrick*
Please, Lady Bluebird Painter · *Wyatt, Rachel*
Please, Teacher · *Carlton, Edna P.*
Please Don't Kill My Cricket!!! or, Sometimes It's Hard to Shut Those Things Off ·
Tourbin, Dennis
Please Mister Mac · *Stephenson, Michael*
Please Papa, Take Us Home · *Shore, Michael M.J.*
Please Take Your Partners · *Thomas, Bill*
The Pleasures of Competition · *MacCormack, Terrance*
The Pleasures of Love · *McFadden, David*
A Pledge for Bobby Ellis · *Kent, Christopher*
A Pleroma of Cousins · *Bauer, Nancy*
The Plight of Ellen · *Heywood, Rosalie*
The Plight of the Vociferous Clamour Unlimited · *Caloren, Fred*
The Plimsoll Line · *Smith, Ron*
Plitochny Chay · *Kon, Louis*
The Plouffes Visit Toronto · *Lemelin, Roger*
the plough and the mice · *Bullock, Michael*
Plucked · *Marseillin, Philip*
Plumbers Can Dish It Out Too · *Irvine, R.B.*
Plums Are Important Perhaps · *Belfry, Chris*
Plut's Discover · *Hekkanen, Ernest*
Poacher's Game · *Wood, Kerry*
Poaching · *Power, John*
The Pocket · *Wilks, David*
The Poem · *Thacker, P.*
Poem for the Blind · *Green, H. Gordon*
A Poem Is a Sort of Subway Token · *Bailey, Don*
A Poet and a Star · *Oudecek, Madia*
The Poet with the Perfect Reputation · *Bruchovsky, Olga*
The Poetry of Politics · *Hebb, Marian*
The Poetry Reading · *Lea, Joseph William*
Poetry Workshop · *Brooks, Eunice*
The Point · *Gridly, Verity*
Point of Origin · *Green, H. Gordon*
A Point of View · *Radu, Kenneth*
The Pointillistic · *Courchesne, Peter*
Points of View · *Wood, Ted*
The Poker Game · *Pratt, Terry*

Pola · *Taylor, Melville*
The Polar Passion · *Bartlett, Brian*
Polarities · *Atwood, Margaret*
the police · *Heath, Terence*
Policeman's Lot · *Bankier, William*
A Polished Boo-or-Two · *Glendenning, Donald*
Poll 101 · *Alford, Edna*
Polly at the Fair · *Wood, Kerry*
Polly Wants a Cracker · *Kent, Valerie*
Polo Park · *Ursell, Geoffrey*
The Polychromatic Murmurs · *Coleman, Victor and Fones, Robert*
The Polymerised Woman · *Edinborough, Arnold*
Pommagne Party · *Taaffe, Gerald*
Pomp and Circumstances · *Currie, Sheldon*
Pompadex · *Sengmueller, Fred*
Ponchontas · *Browne, Paul Cameron*
The Pond · *Greenway, Eric*
The Pond Place · *Bruce, Charles T.*
The Pony · *Lambert, Elizabeth M.*
Poodles John · *Callaghan, Barry*
The Pool · *McAllister, Lesley*
Pool of Paradise · *Bedard, Michael*
Poor Albert Floated When He Died ... · *Burnford, Sheila*
Poor Franzi · *Gallant, Mavis*
Poor Is Powerful · *O'Connell, Dorothy*
Poor Little Fellow · *Walters, Harold Neal*
The Poor Moriartys · *Laurence, Elsie Fry*
The Poor People's Bugle · *O'Connell, Dorothy*
Pop Bottle Sadie · *Yamamoto, Karen, E.*
PoP PoP · *Kent, Valerie*
Pop Psychology · *Mezei, Stephen*
Pop Was a Good 'Scout' · *Stilwell, Arthur*
The Pope's Emissary · *Rooke, Leon*
Poppin' the Question · *Russell, Ted*
Pops and the Donland's Flat · *Vlahov, Ed*
Pop's Springtime Fancy · *Annett, R. Ross*
A Population of Birds · *Braun, Lois*
The Porcupine Murders · *Atwood, Margaret*
Pork College · *Kilodney, Crad*
Pork College Heroes · *Kilodney, Crad*
Pork College Lethargy · *Kilodney, Crad*
Pork College Mystery · *Kilodney, Crad*
The Pork-Pie Hat · *Higgins, D.W.*
Porky Proctor's Downfall · *Harris, John Norman*
Porridge and Silver · *Flood, Cynthia*
Porridge and Tears · *Loomer, Frank*
The Port Dalhousie Stories · *Tourbin, Dennis*
Port of Embarkation · *Spencer, Elizabeth*
The Port of No Return · *Barrett, Herb*
Portable Cities · *Austin, Don*

Prairie Romance · *Ostenso, Martha*
Prairie Spring · *Creal, Margaret*
The Prankster Finds Solitude · *Diamond, Marc*
Pravlijica · *Person, A.D [pseudonym]*
Pray for Sylvia · *Birdsell, Sandra*
Pray for Sylvia · *Birdsell, Sandra*
Preacher for the Day · *Dickinson, George*
The Preacher's Kid · *La Haye, Marguerite*
Precious Amber · *Macdonald, Elizabeth*
Precision, Perception and an Oil Drum · *Arscott, David*
The Predators · *Hutton, William Finlay*
Predictions of Ice · *Hood, Hugh*
Preface · *Challis, John*
Preface to His Memoirs · *Morton, Murray*
Preliminary Pages for a Work of Revenge · *Moore, Brian*
Prelude and Theme · *Fraser, D.M.*
Prelude to a Big Night · *Hoogstraten, Vinia*
Prelude to a Parking Lot · *Spencer, Elizabeth*
Prelude to New Year's Eve · *Lenoir-Arcand, Christine*
Preludes · *Amprimoz, Alexandre*
Premature Departures · *Hale, Barrie*
The Premeditated Death of Samuel Glover · *Garner, Hugh*
A Premier Preserve · *Power, John*
Premonition · *MacKinnon, Brian*
Preparations · *Redmond, Chris*
Prepare Him Room · *van Vliet, Brigitte*
Preparing for the Worst · *Richler, Mordecai*
Preparing the Foundations · *Gilliam, John*
Preponderance of the Great · *Kome, Penney*
The Presence in the Grove · *Phillips, Alan*
Presences · *Helwig, David*
The Present · *Lee, Dennis*
A Present for a Baby · *Fidler, Vera*
A Present for Alice · *Wood, Ted*
Present for Jimmy · *Boyle, Harry J.*
Present for Mary · *Pumphrey, Ron*
A Present for Miss Merriam · *Buckler, Ernest*
A Present for My Mother · *Hubbard, Dexter*
A Present from an Angel · *Hoogstraten, Vinia*
Present State of Pompeii · *Lowry, Malcolm*
Present Tense Floating · *Lynch, Gerald*
Presents · *Spencer, Elizabeth*
Presents from the Sea · *Carson, Bryan*
Preserves · *Riches, Brenda*
The President · *Boyarsky, Abraham*
Press Pressure · *Torgov, Morley*
Pretend Dinners · *Kinsella, W.P.*
A Pretentious Tale · *Percy, Carol*
The Prettiest Woman in Town · *Green, H. Gordon*
Pretty Boy · *Metcalf, John*

Pretty Plumbing · *O'Connell, Dorothy*
The Price · *Bruneau, Bernard*
The Price of a Cup of Coffee · *Hunt, Reg*
The Price of a Dream · *Stein, Rhoda Elizabeth Playfair*
[The?] Price of a Hat · *Gillese, John Patrick*
The Price of a Piano · *Gillese, John Patrick*
The Price of Admission · *Zilber, Jacob*
The Price of Peace · *MacKinnon, Malcolm*
Pride Comes Before a Fall · *Ablett, Pauline*
The Pride of Horsechester · *Miller, John G.*
The Pride of Man · *Margoshes, Dave*
Pride of the Rain · *Wees, Frances Shelley*
Pride to the Last Prune · *Dybvig, Leslie*
The Primary Cause · *Slaughter, R.W [Bill]*
The Prince · *Halliday, David*
The Prince of Peace · *Clifton, Merritt*
Prince Sam and Princess Spray-Me-Not · *Reid, Peter*
Princess · *Brasen, Terese*
The Princess and the Wild Ones · *Mitchell, W.O.*
Print on the Wall · *Gould, Jan*
The Printed Word · *Geitzler, Fran*
Priscilla · *Bauer, Nancy*
The Prism · *Briffett, Isabel*
Prison Essays · *Goulden, Alban*
The Prisoner · *Thorne, Lynne*
Prisoner in Venice · *Taylor, Constance Gurd*
Prisoner of Conscience · *Carey, Barbara*
The Prisoner of Sex · *Watson, Scott*
The Prisoner's Dilemma · *Rogal, Stan*
Privacies · *Itani, Frances*
Private Affair · *Green, H. Gordon*
A Private Comedy · *Valgardson, W.D.*
The Private Executioner · *Janes, Percy*
The Private I · *Solo, N [pseudonym]*
A Private Place · *Marshall, Joyce*
Private Property · *Hunter, Bruce*
A Private Sorrow · *Abnett, Eileen*
Privates · *Frew, Glenn*
Privilege · *Munro, Alice*
Privileged Information · *Choyce, Lesley*
The Privy Council · *MacSween, R.J.*
Pro Tem · *Bird, Will R.*
Probably Over Thirty · *Hall, Christopher W.*
The Problem · *Dampf, Michael*
The Problem of the Woman's Point of View · *Hara, John T.*
The Problem Shop · *Rooke, Leon*
The Problem Sister · *Ross, [W.E.] Dan and Ross, Charlotte*
Problem(s) in Paradise · *Coburn, Marion*
The Problems of a Truancy · *Thompson, Kent*
The Process · *Edenson, Jerry*

Protectors of the Race · *Carson, Ann*
Protonics · *Filter, Reinhard*
Providence · *Munro, Alice*
Prowlers · *Callaghan, Barry*
Proxy · *Day, Gene and Jack, Gale*
Prue · *Munro, Alice*
Prying · *Blaise, Clark L.*
the psalmist · *Heath, Terence*
A Psychological Story · *Powell, Marilyn*
Ptarmigan · *Graham, Robert*
P'tit Village · *Itani, Frances*
The Pub · *Schroeder, Andreas*
The Public Good · *Choyce, Lesley*
Puck Among the Tea Biscuits · *Fay, Michael*
Puddin' and Pie · *Courchesne, Peter*
The Pueget Sound · *Miller, J. Kit*
A Puff of Smoke · *Kratis, Diana*
Pulp · *Coleman, Victor*
The Pulwharskie Dragon · *Moore, Elwin*
Pumpkin · *Toft, Joseph*
Pumpkin Lady · *Linder, Norma West*
Pun-Dit · *Sawyer, Robert*
The Punishment of Ordinary Angel Blobs · *Young, Scott*
A Punk Christmas · *Kelly, Dermot*
The Puppet People · *Jamieson, Kevin*
The Puppet Show · *Rule, Jane*
The Purchased Letter · *Bjarnason, Bogi*
The Pure Diamond Man · *Laurence, Margaret*
Pure Research · *Szanto, George*
The Pure Wound · *Roberts, Kevin*
The Purest Profit · *Carrier, Jean-Guy*
Purgatory · *Sarah, Robyn*
Puritan · *Lord, Barry*
The Purple Garters · *Kadey, Carroll*
The Purpose of the Exercise · *Gane, Margaret Drury*
Purring · *Hodgins, Norris*
the pursuing river · *Bullock, Michael*
the pursuit · *Bullock, Michael*
Push · *Matyas, Cathy*
A Push for Cupid · *Collins, Michael*
Pushing Fifty · *McNamara, Eugene*
Push-me Pull-you · *Kerslake, Susan*
Put Away Your Bugle, Soldier · *Hughes, Philip B.*
Put This Dream on My Charge Account · *Brauer, Joanna*
Putting It Together · *Reid, John*
The Puzzle Poem · *Spencer, Elizabeth*
Pyotr's Story · *Robinson, Spider*
The Pyramid · *McNeil, Beatrice*
Pyramidalis · *Bell, Marion*
Pyrotechnic · *Mann, Ted*

Pythagoras · *D'Arrigo, Stephen*
A Python of the Gaspé · *Godfrey, Dave*
The Pyx · *Bruneau, Bernard*

Quadrille · *Weinzweig, Helen*
The Quality of Courage · *Ross, W.E. Dan*
The Quality of Mercy · *Ammeter, A.E.*
Quality Stock · *Kalman, Judy*
Qu'Appelle Christmas 1885 · *Gosselin, Madeleine*
Quarantine · *McWhirter, George*
Quarantine Christmas · *Bushell, Sidney*
The Quarry · *Harris, John*
Quebec: A Whimsical Speculation · *Buller, Herman*
Quebec on a Sunday · *Roskies, Ruth*
The Quebec Prison · *Fraser, Raymond*
The Queen · *McLaughlin, Peter*
Queen Constance · *Burnett, Virgil*
Queen Death · *Burnett, Virgil*
Queen Elizabeth II, Seduced · *McFadden, David*
A Queen in Thebes · *Laurence, Margaret*
Queen of Hearts · *Stein, Rhoda Elizabeth Playfair*
The Queen of Ireland · *Branden, Vicki*
Queen Street · *Torgov, Morley*
Queen Street #23 Soundings · *Ireland, Ann*
The Queen Who Walked on Stilts · *Foster, Thelma H.*
Queenie · *Harris, Beverly*
The Queen's Hat · *Kinsella, W.P.*
The Queen's Marys · *Gration, Gwen*
The Queen's Scout · *Morton, Colin*
The Queer · *Potrebenko, Helen*
The Queer Ones · *Green, H. Gordon*
Quest · *Philipp, Rowland*
The Quest Theme in Canadian Literature · *Carson, Bryan*
A Question · *Anonymous*
The Question Mark · *Cameron, Eric*
A Question of Class Solidarity · *Burnley, John*
A Question of Command · *Moore, Brian*
A Question of Faith · *Green, H. Gordon*
A Question of Motive · *Dobbs, Kildare R.E.*
Question of Need · *Green, H. Gordon*
A Question of Numbers · *Marshall, Joyce*
A Question of Outlook · *Arscott, David*
A Question of Style · *Brewster, Elizabeth*
Questions · *Morrison, Harold R.W.*
Questions and Answers · *Gallant, Mavis*
The Quick · *Shier, James*
Quick Canada · *Bowering, George*
Quicksilver · *Howard, Dorothy*

Quidnunc · *Bondy, Roger*
'Quiet! Please' · *MacKinnon, Lilian Vaux*
Quiet Chat · *Engel, Howard*
The Quiet Conscience · *Dybvig, Leslie*
Quiet Enough My Life of Late · *Rooke, Leon*
Quiet Hour · *Merrow, Adin*
The Quiet House · *Barnard, Leslie Gordon*
A Quiet Life · *Burns, Robert A. McA.*
A Quiet Little Dinner · *Ritter, Erika*
Quiet Months and Years · *Carrier, Jean-Guy*
The Quiet Peasant · *Ladoo, Harold Sonny*
The Quiet Place · *Wood, Kerry*
Quiet Sunday · *Stenson, Frederick*
Quiet Terror · *Thomson, Jean C.*
The Quiet Town · *Ross, W.E. Dan*
The Quiet Tree · *van Every, Jane*
A Quiet Weekend · *Drew, Mabel E.*
Quietly Awakened · *Vertolli, Lou*
Quietus · *Anderson, Tonia*
The Quilt · *Curry, Julia*
Quinsey Pursues a Butterfly · *Griffin, George*
'Quit Walking on Your Face!' · *Wassall, Irma*
A Quite Incredible Dance · *Kinsella, W.P.*
Quits · *Tench, C.V.*
Quoth the Raven · *Robison, Ruth*
qwertyuiop · *Schull, Joseph J.*

Rabbit · *Campbell, Wanda Blynn*
Rabbit Done Run, Seymour Went Away and Rosacoke's Got the Blues · *Margoshes, Dave*
The Rabbit Hunt · *Price, C.B.*
Rabbits · *Russell, Ted*
Rabbit-Skinning · *Holz, Cynthia*
The Race · *Green, H. Gordon*
The Race · *McQueen-Darcie, Margaret*
A Race for Freedom · *Gold, Artie and Nations, Opal L.*
The Race for Molly Scott · *Steele, Harwood*
The Race for the Love of Mizpah Jenkins · *Hockley, Vernon*
A Race with the River · *Todd, Beatrice*
Racism Is Not Debatable! · *Burnley, John*
The Radiant Twinnie · *Rikki [Erica Ducornet]*
Radio Cafe · *Horse, Benjamin* [pseudonym]
Radio Yerevan · *Shirinian, Lorne*
A Rage for Order · *Ross, James*
Rags, Clothes, Bottles · *Allan, Ted*
Rags of a Saint · *Anonymous*
The Raid · *Levin, Malcolm A.*
The Railroad Builder · *Sturdy, John Rhodes*
the railway station · *Bullock, Michael*

the railway track and the canal · *Bullock, Michael*
Rain, Rain, Rain · *Gaetz, Jamie*
the rain · *Bullock, Michael*
Rain All Day · *Dabydeen, Cyril*
Rain at Night · *Honsinger, Robert*
The Rain Check · *Littlejohn, Helen*
The Rain Child · *Laurence, Margaret*
The Rain Forest · *Duncan, Frances*
The Rain Gets In · *Sperdakos, Deane*
The Rain Guage · *Caldnell, Jack*
Rain on the Roof · *Bailey, Don*
Raindrops · *Poulakakis, Matt*
Raindrops Kept Falling on Their Heads · *Sharp, Dorothy*
The Rainstorm · *Garvin, Guy C.*
A Rainy Afternoon in a French Port · *Mitchell, Donald M.*
Rainy Days · *Draayer, Ken*
Raising the Cougar · *McWhirter, George*
Raising the Dead · *Baerstein, Tsigane*
Ralphie at the Races · *Selvon, Samuel*
Ramook and the Debt · *Theriault, Yves*
Ramook and the Medicine · *Theriault, Yves*
Ramook and the Royal Visitor · *Theriault, Yves*
The Ramp · *Riddell, John*
Ramsey Taylor · *Richards, David Adams*
Random Error · *McCormack, Marilyn*
Rannulf Robertson · *Sessford, Ken*
A Rap at the Door · *Bjarnason, Bogi*
Rape Fantasies · *Atwood, Margaret*
The Rape of Maysie Weekend · *Boston, Stewart*
Raphael Anachronic · *Smith, Ray*
Rapunzel, Rapunzel · *Bankier, William*
Rapunzel · *Thomas, Audrey*
Rara Avis · *Wuorio, Eva-Lis*
Raspberry Vinegar · *Shaw, Joan Fern*
the rat · *Bullock, Michael*
The Rat and the Goose · *Euringer, Fred*
The Rat Game · *Butts, Ed P.*
Rat Racist · *Filip, Raymond*
Rate of Descent · *Doyle, Judith*
The Rattlesnake · *Amprimoz, Alexandre*
The Rattlesnake Express · *Kinsella, W.P.*
raven and fir tree · *Bullock, Michael*
The Raven's Nest · *Horwood, Harold*
Ravioli · *Crowell, Peter*
Raw Materials · *Atwood, Margaret*
The Rawleigh Man · *Luce-Kapler, Rebecca*
Ray Bradley · *Inkster, Tim*
R-Day · *Phillips, Jack H.*
Re Union · *Bowering, George*
Reach for an Angel · *Barnard, Margaret E.*

Reading, Writing and Two Red Braids · *MacIntosh, Keitha K.*
A Reading from Whitman · *Matheson, Graeme*
The Reading of Signs · *Bauer, William A.*
Ready for Everything · *Douglas, Gilean*
Ready or Not · *Stein, Rhoda Elizabeth Playfair*
A Real Education · *Steffler, George*
Real Estate · *Riddell, John*
The Real Harry · *Silvester, Reg*
A Real Lady · *O'Connell, Dorothy*
Real Mothers · *Thomas, Audrey*
The Real Mrs. Hunter · *Sandman, John*
Real Roger · *Ober, Harold*
Real Stars · *McCracken, Melinda*
The Real Tennessee Waltz · *Sibum, Norm*
A Real Tribute · *Young, Scott*
The Real World of Peregrine Hull · *Dempsey, Jane*
Realia · *Yates, J. Michael*
Realities · *Thomas, Audrey*
reality is · *Bullock, Michael*
Rear Them Right · *Henderson, Charles, Jr.*
Reason Enough · *Mintz, Helen*
The Reason Is Love · *Fitzpatrick, Helen*
The Reason Why · *Anonymous*
A Reasonable Man · *Byrnes, Terence*
Rebecca · *Hildebrandt, Gloria*
Rebecca's Tree · *Stanley-Porter, Caroline*
Rebel Mother · *Ryan, Josephine*
Rebellion of Brill · *Annett, William S.*
The Rebellion of Young David · *Buckler, Ernest*
Rebellion on Euclid Avenue · *Atwood, Joan-Mary and Holt, Muriel*
Rebirth · *Lockau, Kevin*
Recherches · *Morrell, Dave*
Recipe for a Rebel · *Simpson, Leo*
Reciprocal · *Salter, Geoff*
The Recital · *Huser, Glen*
Reclining Nude · *Daurio, Beverley*
Recognition · *Bowen, Robert O.*
A Recollection · *Gallant, Mavis*
A Recollection of the Boneyard · *Wilkins, Charles*
Recollections of the Toronto Works Department · *Hood, Hugh*
Recollections of the Works Department · *Hood, Hugh*
The Reconcilement · *Heard, F.E.*
The Reconciliation of Calan McGinty · *Choyce, Lesley*
A Record of Past Failures · *Cairncross, Larissa*
The Recruit · *Lemond, Edward*
Recruiting · *Meredith, Rita*
Recuperation at Nantucket · *Halbus, Mary*
The Recurrence · *Bailey, Don*
Red · *Fowlie, Barry*
Red and Green Make Brown · *Sherman, Tom*

The Red and Green Pony · *Acorn, Milton*
The Red Ball · *Bell, John Leslie*
Red Barn, Interior · *Helwig, David*
Red Beard's quest · *Bullock, Michael*
The Red Bikini · *Cameron, Eric*
The Red Dory · *McKay, Muriel Saint*
Red Dreams, Blue Dreams · *Stickland, Eugene*
The Red Dress · *Stein, Rhoda Elizabeth Playfair*
Red Dress - 1946 · *Munro, Alice*
Red Dust · *Valgardson, W.D.*
The Red Fox · *Black, Lampman*
A Red Haired Girl on a White Horse · *Kleiman, Edward*
The Red Horses · *Jelinek, Vera*
The Red Iris · *Horne, Lewis B.*
Red Is for Quiet · *Green, H. Gordon*
Red Is for the Quiet · *Green, H. Gordon*
The Red Knife · *Thomas, Martha Banning*
The Red Leaf · *Dunham, Lynne*
A Red Letter Day · *James, Richard*
Red Light, Green Light · *Jacobs, M. Culross*
Red Lights · *Beller, Jacob*
The Red Living Room · *Knudsen, Joyce*
Red Menace · *Richler, Mordecai*
The Red Moth · *Watson, Scott*
Red Muffins · *Hollingshead, Greg*
The Red Painting · *Israel, Inge*
The Red Picket · *Deane, James*
The Red Picture · *Wells, Donald W.*
Red Racer · *Garner, Hugh*
Red Ribbon · *Marshall, Carolyn*
Red Ribbons · *Loggie, Margaret L.*
The Red Room · *Young, Ian*
Red Scarf for Christmas · *Furlong, Harry*
Red Sequins on Markham Street · *Shaw, Joan Fern*
The Red Serge of Courage · *Steele, Harwood*
Red Shoes · *Simmie, Lois*
The Red Silk Dress · *Beattie, Jessie L.*
Red Tarnation · *Crowell, Bill*
The Red Velvet Dress · *Oki, Henry*
The Redman's Burden · *Dybvig, Leslie*
The Reef · *Such, Peter*
The Reel World · *Stone, Patricia*
Reflections · *Ford, James*
Reflections of Madeleine · *Errat, M.*
Reflections of Sartre · *Ashcroft, Sheila*
Reflections on a Commuter · *Dyce, Peter*
Reflections onto a Golden Life · *Brodzki, Marek*
The Reforming of McGregor · *Perrault, Ernest G.*
The Refuge · *Doyle, Nancy*
Refuge of Insulted Saints · *Davies, Robertson*

The Refugee · *Donaldson, Allan*
Refugee on the River · *Gillese, John Patrick*
Regeneration · *Kroeker, Ben*
A Reg'lar Whip · *Thomas, Martha Banning*
The Regulars and the Fisher King · *Campbell, Donald*
Rehearsal in Rome · *Zalan, Magda*
The Reincarnation Pool · *Sharpe, David*
The Reindeer Buyer · *Downey, Fairfax*
Reinhardt · *Armstrong, George*
The Rejection · *Gallant, Mavis*
Rejections · *Lush, Richard M.*
Relations · *Rosenfeld, Rita*
The Relaxed Anarchist · *Austin, Don*
The Relay Race · *Smith, Michael*
Release · *Fox, Joseph*
The Relic · *Kolding, Sigrid*
Relief · *Blaise, Clark L.*
The Religion of the Country · *Hodgins, Jack*
The Reluctant Dog Catcher · *McRobbie, Genevieve*
The Reluctant Genius · *Branden, Vicki*
The Reluctant Inventor · *Young, Scott*
The Reluctant Mousekeeper · *Henderson, Dorothy*
The Remaining Years · *Etco, Mildred*
'Remember How We Dressed When We Were Teenagers' · *Valgardson, W.D.*
Remember Love · *Machniak, Carol*
Remember Neelie · *Henderson, Catherine*
Remember Sappho · *Potter, Esther Holm*
Remember When · *Fines, Beatrice E.*
Remember Woody · *Cade-Edwards, Eileen*
Remembered April · *Bushell, Sidney*
Remembered Forms · *Birch, David*
The Remembered Lake · *Frog, Simon*
Remembering · *Murray, Rona*
Remembering Annie · *Covey, Eva Alice*
Remembering Newfoundland · *Maher, Paul*
Remembrance · *McIntosh, Dave*
Remembrance Day, 2010 A.D. · *MacLennan, Hugh*
Remembrance Day · *Deane, Christopher*
The Remission · *Gallant, Mavis*
Remus Where Are You? · *McCubbin, Terrence*
Renaissance · *Cairns, John C.*
Renaming the Streets in Any Jerusalem · *Sperdakos, Deane*
Renascence · *Lambert, Barbara*
Render unto Caesar ... · *Scammell, A.R.*
The Rendezvous · *Percy, H.R.*
A Rendezvous in the Bathtub · *Kaal, Hans*
Rendezvous on a Drafty Corner · *Witvoet, Bert*
Renee · *Hartman, Matt*
Renovations · *O'Hearn, Audrey*
Rent Please · *Purdy, Brian*

Return to Eden · *Hamilton, John*
Return to Pork College · *Kilodney, Crad*
Return to P'yongyang · *d'Easum, Lille*
Return to Redvale · *Gillese, John Patrick*
Returning · *Wawrow, Leszek*
The Reunion · *Waterfall, Don E.*
Reveillon · *Carrier, Jean-Guy*
Revelation · *Truckey, Don*
Revelation from a Smoky Fire · *Davies, Robertson*
The Revenge · *Powell, Derek Reid*
The Revenge of Eddie Reeser · *Hollingshead, Greg*
Revenge Sequence · *Ross, Stuart*
The Reverend's Cosmos · *Taylor, Perry*
The Reversal · *Tadich, Alex Sasha*
Revival Preacher · *Redant, Philip D.*
Revolution on the Gatineau · *Green, H. Gordon*
The Revolutionary · *Valgardson, W.D.*
[The?] Revolving Door · *Barnard, Leslie Gordon*
Reward · *Moore, Brian*
Rex Morgan, M.D. · *Shein, Brian*
The Rhinestone Cow · *Read, Mary*
Rhoda & Julia · *Keeling, Nora*
Rhys · *Burnett, Virgil*
Rib of Eve · *Epps, Bernard*
The Ribbon · *Stewart, Irene*
Ricardo and the Flower · *Bowering, George*
The Rice Ball · *Theriault, Yves*
The Rice Bowl · *Williamson, Rossa*
Rice Pudding · *Eaton, John*
The Rich Girls of Rosedale · *Gane, Margaret Drury*
The Rich Young Ruler · *Govan, Margaret*
Richard · *Butts, Ed P.*
Richard de la Bonnevoie's Pet Monkeys · *Hill, Larry*
[The?] Riches of Charity · *Gillese, John Patrick*
The Richest Man in Canada · *Lewis, David E.*
The Richest Woman in Town · *McNamee, James*
Riconoscenza · *Greene, Elizabeth*
A Riddle for Children · *Zilber, Jacob*
The Riddle of the Viking Bow · *Mowat, Farley*
The Ride · *Goulden, Alban*
A Ride for Life · *Clink, Beatrice*
The Ride Home · *Pereira, Helen*
Ride in the Night · *Conroy, Tom*
Riders Incognito · *Deindorfer, Gary*
The Ridiculous Proposal · *Moore, Brian*
Riding the Rails · *Krenz, Reynold*
A Rifle Can Shoot Far · *de Barros, Paul*
A Rifle for Big Boy · *Shipley, Nan*
The Right Age · *Beresford-Howe, Constance*
Right Back Where I Started From · *Kostash, Myrna*

The Right Market · *Chamish, Barry*
The Right to Be Socially Responsible · *Sasse, Joyce and Dow, Janet*
The Right to Life · *Harper, A.W.J.*
The Right to Live · *Doyle, Nancy*
The Right Wife for George · *Gillese, John Patrick*
Rightly Call the Nymph · *Marshall, Joyce*
The Rightmaker · *Wiebe, Armin*
The Ring · *Campbell, Marjorie*
The Ring: A Tale of Chedabucto Bay · *Bushell, Sidney*
Ring Around the Rosie · *Bailey, Don*
The Ring of Brodgar · *de Lint, Charles*
The Ring That Held a Curse · *MacArthur, F.H.*
A Ring Thru His Nose · *Sigal, Mark*
Ringa Ringa Rosie · *Levine, Norman*
Ring-a-Ring o' Roses · *Elgaard, Elin*
Ringa-Ringa-Rosie · *Levine, Norman*
A Ringer's Circle · *Dabydeen, Cyril*
Rings · *Taylor, Kate*
Rings and Things · *Fontaine, Patricia*
the rinkhut · *Heath, Terence*
A Rinky Dinky Do · *Nowlan, Alden*
Rio · *Campbell, D.A.*
Rioter, Harbour Grace, Boxing Day, 1883 · *Butts, Ed P.*
Rip · *Browne, Paul Cameron*
Rise and Fall of the Tiger's Paw Judo Club · *Smale, Kenneth*
The Rise of the Poet · *Russell, Lawrence*
Rita Maguire's Vermilion Dress · *Lynch, Gerald*
The Rite · *Hekkanen, Ernest*
Rite of Passage · *Orford, Mena*
Rites · *Riches, Brenda*
Rite of Passage · *Orford, Mena*
The Rites of Spring · *Bush, Pamela*
The Ritual · *Nason, Colleen*
The Rival · *Cameron, Eric*
The Rivals · *Barnhouse, D.P.*
River · *Reid, Dennis*
The River Behind Things · *Hood, Hugh*
River People · *Graham, Kathleen*
River Reckoning · *Evans, Hubert*
River Two Blind Jacks · *Godfrey, Dave*
[A?] Riverful of Stars · *Gillese, John Patrick*
The Rivers Run to the Sea · *Hicks, John V.*
RNA · *Sperdakos, Deane*
The Road · *Blythe, Aleata E.*
the road and the rock · *Bullock, Michael*
The Road Back · *Simpson, Gregg*
Road Games · *Bowering, George*
The Road Out · *van Herk, Aritha*
The Road Runner · *Mills, John*
A Road through Summer Fields · *Helwig, David*

Road to Nowhere · *Baker, Rita*
The Road to Oblivion · *Nicks, W. Frederick*
The Road to Rankin's Point · *MacLeod, Alistair*
The Road to Stardom · *Cowasjee, Saros*
The Road to the Graveyard · *Flood, Cynthia*
Road to True Worth · *Ross, W.E. Dan*
Road to Victory · *Parks, F.M.*
The Road without a Name · *Bankier, William*
Road's End · *Staniforth, Richard*
Roadshow · *Horne, Lewis B.*
Roast Beef's the Thing to Eat · *Wilson, Jack Lowther*
The Robbery · *Gasgoyne, R.*
Robbing Motels · *Thompson, Kent*
Robert, standing · *Metcalf, John*
Robert: A Mirror Image · *Dominskyj, Marianne*
Robert and Nancy · *Marshall, Tom*
Robert Giles Passes On · *Toland, George*
The Robert Wagner Chorale and the Three Wise Men · *Keyes, John*
Robins · *Hodgins, Norris*
Robinson Crusoe · *Russell, Ted*
The Rochester Burner · *Thomas, Martha Banning*
The Rock · *Geitzler, Fran*
The Rock Garden · *Birdsell, Sandra*
The Rock Man · *Akins, Russell*
Rockefeller Center · *Evanier, David*
The Rocket Guns · *Dworkin, Martin S.*
Rocket Riches · *Tench, C.V.*
The Rocks · *Garvie, Peter*
The Rocks at the Bottom of the Lake · *McFadden, David*
Rock's Last Role · *Bankier, William*
Rocky · *Evans, Hubert*
Rocky and the Philosopher · *Shepanski C[arl].L.*
Rocky Road to Romance · *Armstrong, Patricia*
Rodeo · *Wreggitt, Andrew*
Roditi · *Bullock, Michael*
Rodrigo's Dream · *Berry, David*
Rod's Pound of Flesh · *Armstrong, Patricia*
Roger Ash or The Year We Built the Golf Course · *Schermbrucker, Bill*
Roger-Case #39807 · *de Yoe, Judy*
Roget's Thesaurus · *Fraser, Keath*
Rogue Male · *Wood, Kerry*
Roll Call · *Plaskett, John*
Roll Over, Beethoven · *Langhout, Mary*
Roll-Downs & Pin-Heads · *Horne, Marcel*
The Roller Rink · *Schroeder, Andreas*
Rolling Down the Bowling Green · *Christie, Michael*
The Rolling-Pin Rodeo · *Sigurdson, Paul A.*
A Romance · *Zinkewich, Muriel*
Romance for Vivienne · *McCourt, Edward A.*
The Romance of the Beekeeper · *Cahill, Brian*

Romance of the Children · *Adams, Richard*
The Romance of the Plastic Rose · *Dennis, Ian*
Romancero Gitano · *Tyhurst, Robert*
Romancin' · *Russell, Ted*
Romantic Fever · *Simmie, Lois*
The Romantic Idiot · *Disturbed, Venus* [pseudonym]
Romeo MacClean and the Dishwasher · *Gower, Richard*
A Romp with Comp · *Armstrong, Patricia*
Ron · *Shapiro, David*
Rona's Complaint · *Govier, Katharine*
Ronnie So Long at the Fair · *Summers, Merna*
The Roofer's Guarantee · *Hoffman, Edith*
Rooftop and Below · *Ritchie, Ian*
Rookie Centre · *McIlroy, Kimball*
A Room, a Light for Love · *Elliott, George*
The Room · *Haskins, David*
Room 101 · *Fletcher, Peggy*
Room 713 · *Smith, Ralph F.*
Room and Keyboard · *Torgov, Morley*
The Room Dweller · *Potrebenko, Helen*
A Room Full of Research Assistants · *Horse, Benjamin* [pseudonym]
A Room High Over the City · *Helwig, David*
Room with a View · *Carlton, Edna P.*
A Room with Flowers · *Helwig, David*
The Room without a Window · *Wheatley, Thelma*
The Rooming House · *Frey, Cecelia*
The Roommates · *Partridge, Shirley*
Rooms · *Pollman, Olaf*
Root Hog · *Harris, John*
Rootcellar · *Smith, Jacqui*
Rooted · *Whitehead, Lee M.*
A Rooted Sorrow · *Pratt, Terry*
Roots · *Chiu, Mabel*
The Roots of the Heart Grow Deep · *Stemo, L. Johanne*
A Rope to Hang a Man · *McCourt, Edward A.*
The Rorqual · *Bazley, Walter*
Rory Peter's Last Run · *MacDonald, David*
Rosamunda · *Davis, Frances*
Rosary · *Spence, Ian A.*
The Rose · *MacMillan, Gail*
Rose and the Red Stallion · *Harris, John*
A Rose By Any Other Name · *Futhey, John F.*
Rose Coloured Glasses · *Clark, Joan*
A Rose for Johnny Dan · *Briffett, Isabel*
A Rose for Minnie Mullet · *Grantmyre, Barbara*
A Rose for Tomorrow · *Green, H. Gordon*
The Rose Garden · *Frey, Cecelia*
A Rose Is a Rose · *Craig, Jean Carol*
Rosemary · *Watmough, David*
Roses Are Red · *Flood, Cynthia*

Roses at Noon · *Thomas, Peter*
Roses for Mickey · *Barnard, Margaret E. and Barnard, Leslie Gordon*
Roses for Mother's Day · *Hubbard, Dexter*
Rosie · *Kaiser, Terry*
Rosie Was a Good Old Dog · *Annand, Alan M.*
Rosi-ka's Ankles · *Nemiroff, Greta Hofmann*
Rough Sketch · *Coombes, Blaine*
Round and Smooth · *Stenson, Frederick*
Round Trip Ticket · *Avery, Martin*
The Round-About Will · *Briffett, Isabel*
Rounded with a Sleep · *Lynch, Gerald*
Routine · *Page, William*
'Rover St. Patrick Murphy' · *Morris, Doris M.*
A Rowboat, a Submarine · *Hocking, Beverly*
Royal Beatings · *Munro, Alice*
The Royal Dirge · *Eades, Murray*
The Royal Oak · *Grantmyre, Barbara*
Royal Visit · *Roberts, Kevin*
Ruben · *Choyce, Lesley*
The Ruby · *Grant, Katharine*
Ruddy Admirals · *Walker, David*
Rude Awakening · *Wees, Frances Shelley*
Rudy's Kite · *Stodola, Lori*
Rue de Lille · *Gallant, Mavis*
Ruffed Up · *Power, John*
A Rugged Knight · *Murdoch, Benedict Joseph*
The Rugger Look · *Avery, Martin*
Ruin · *Kent, Peter*
Ruin and Wrack · *Marshall, Joyce*
A Ruined Maid · *Kushner, Donn*
A Ruler of Mind · *Mackenzie, Alan*
The Rules · *Kerslake, Susan*
Rum Along the Imjin · *Murphy, Aralt*
Rum Compass · *Easton, Alan*
Rum in the Pudding · *Pollett, Ron*
Rum Sky Rum Sun · *Johnstone, Rick*
The Rumble Seat · *Watson, Sheila*
Rumbly Cove · *Russell, Ted*
Rumination · *Hodgins, Norris*
Rumours of War · *Nowlan, Alden*
Run, Run, as Fast as You Can · *Horne, Lewis B.*
Run Bertie Run! · *Bird, Tom*
Run Children · *Baker, Rita*
Run for Your Life · *Lukiv, Dan*
Run Like the Devil · *Kremberg, Rudy*
Run Son, Run · *Morritt, Hope*
The Runaway · *Ross, Sinclair*
The Runaway Bride · *Carriere, Marguerite*
The Run-Away Holiday · *Briffett, Isabel*
Runaway Orphan · *Mayse, Arthur*

Runaway Reindeer · *Rayson, Ruth*
The Runner · *Kinsella, W.P.*
The Runner - A Satire · *Cushing, Leo*
Running · *Friedman, Tom*
Running a Marathon, Climbing a Mountain · *Shore, Michael M.J.*
Running Along · *Sewell, John*
Running Back to Saskatoon · *Sandman, John*
Running Laughing · *Curtis, Mary*
Running Out of Breath · *Sexton, Siobhan*
Running the Rapids · *McLeod, Murdoch*
Rupert Preston's Bad Year · *Choyce, Lesley*
Rupertsland · *Kreiner, Philip*
Rural Education · *Staniforth, Richard*
A Rural Place · *Richards, David Adams*
The Ruse · *Fipps, Mohammed Ulysses*
Rush Hour · *Lord, Barry*
Rusty at McClintock's · *Lawson, David*
Rusty Taps · *Young, David*
Ruth · *Dyba, Kenneth*
Ruth and Rosebud · *Engel, Marian*

The Sabbath · *Boyarsky, Abraham*
The Sabbath After · *Langer, Howie*
Sabbath Victorian · *Symons, Harry*
A Sabbath Walk · *Levine, Norman*
Saboo · *Richman, Sharon Lea*
The Saboteur · *Barnard, Leslie Gordon*
Sabras · *Friedman, Irena*
Sacred & Secular · *Watmough, David*
The Sacred Glow · *Sutherland, Fraser*
Sacred Heart · *Sirluck, Lesley*
Sacred Mushrooms of Canada · *Baerstein, Tsigane*
The Sacrifice · *Micros, Marianne*
The Sad Beauty of Children · *Horne, Lewis B.*
A Sad Story · *Lippert, Laura*
Safe at Home · *Steinfeld, J.J.*
Safe in the Arms · *Richards, David Adams*
Safe in the Arms of Jesus · *Birdsell, Sandra*
Safe Lodging · *Tonkin, Doris Farmer*
A Safe Route on Eighty-Third Street · *Evanier, David*
Safety-Pin · *Cunningham, James*
Saga of a Strange Valley · *Gillese, John Patrick*
The Saga of Joe Sable · *Hickman, Tom*
The Saga of Susie · *Gillese, John Patrick*
Saga of the Sauerkraut Juice · *Hubbard, Dexter*
Saga of the Sow · *Barker, Bessie M.*
The Sage of Susie · *Gillese, John Patrick*
Sagitta · *Jones, R[ichard].*
The Sailboat · *Morton, Lionel*

A Sailboat in the Sky · *Reid, John*
The Sailboats · *MacLean, James S.*
Sailing to Istanbul · *Hepworth, Brian*
The Sailor and the Snow Princess · *Percy, H.R.*
A Sailor from Holland · *Reynolds, Helen Mary Greenwood Campbell*
Sailor in the Chair · *Percy, H.R.*
Sailor You Fix · *Watt, Sholto*
The Sailor's Attic · *Steinfeld, J.J.*
The Saint · *Crerar, Tom*
Saint George the Lucky Dragon · *Samuel, George*
Saint Peter · *van Herk, Aritha*
Salad Days · *Hurley, Joan Mason*
Sale of One Small Ranch · *St. Pierre, Paul*
The Sales Pitch · *Wood, Ted*
The Salesman · *Torgov, Morley*
The Salesman's Son Grows Older · *Blaise, Clark L.*
A Salesman's Son Grows Older · *Blaise, Clark L.*
The Salesmen · *Stein, David Lewis*
Sally · *Hails, Anna*
Sally Go 'Round the Roses · *Dorsey, Candas Jane*
Sally's Misadventures and Mine · *Lewis, David E.*
Salmon · *Hudson, Noel*
Salmon and Trout · *Russell, Ted*
Salmon Run · *Roberts, Kevin*
Salon des Refuses · *Thomas, Audrey*
Salt, Bitter Sea · *Dexter, Laura M.*
The Salt Garden · *Atwood, Margaret*
The Salt Mines · *Engel, Marian*
The Salt of Life · *Bristow, Susan*
Salty Dog · *Field, L.L.*
Salvador the Serendipitous Seer · *Crawford, Terry*
Salvage · *Marshall, Joyce*
Salvage Drive · *Krause, Pat*
Salvation · *Clark, Joan*
The Salvation of Paddy O'Flynn · *Fowke, H. Shirley*
Salvation on Queen Street · *Linkovich, Stanley*
Sam, Soren, and Ed · *Vanderhaeghe, Guy*
Sam & Anna · *Burman, Jack*
Sam Hotzman's Emancipation · *Weir, John*
The Samaritan · *Ibsen, Norman*
The Same Old Bridge · *Rollins, D.S.*
Same Old Stories · *Grainger, Louise*
The Same Old Story · *van Varsefeld, Gail*
The Same Thing · *Margoshes, Dave*
Same Truck, Different Driver · *Dagg, Mel*
Samples of Dandelion wine · *Slade, Mark*
Sampson and Delilah · *Currie, Doris M.*
Samuel James Williams · *Stone, Charles*
San Francisco - Hong Kong · *Newman, C.J.*
Sanabitur Anima Mea · *Currie, Sheldon*

Sanctuary · *Luider, Lyanda*
Sand · *Bruce, Charles T.*
The Sand Banks · *Drew, Mabel E.*
Sand Castle · *Powell, Dorothy M.*
The Sandals · *Loewy, Ilse*
The Sandcastle · *MacEwen, John A.*
Sanders · *Horst, Roger*
The Sandman of Goville · *Kent, Armoral*
The Sandpile · *Rosta, Helen J.*
The Sandpit · *Browne, Paul Cameron*
Sandstone Animals · *Dyba, Kenneth*
The Sandwich Generation · *Rule, Jane*
Sanford · *Jones, Michael*
Santa Claus · *Russell, Ted*
Santa Claus Jones · *Callaghan, Morley*
The Santa Claus Syndrome · *Engel, Marian*
Santa Snatched · *Glunna, J.C.*
Santa's Village · *Avery, Martin*
Saplings · *Dekker, Frieda*
Sarah · *Edwards, Caterina*
Sarah & Wellington · *Fullerton, Barbara*
Sarah Skimple · *Russell, Ted*
Sarah's Cod Liver Oil · *Lampert, Gerald*
Sarah's Copper · *St. Pierre, Paul*
Sarah's Easter Offering · *Story, Gertrude*
Sardine Sandwiches · *Cockrell, Patricia M.*
Sari in the Kitchen · *Russell, Sheila MacKay*
The Sarnean: A Definition · *McWhirter, George*
Saror, House of Gold · *Luchsinger, Gabriel*
Sarry · *Wittrup, Jenny*
Sarsfield Bridge · *Foran, Charles*
Saskatchewan Hero · *Garner, Hugh*
Sasquatch · *Chappus, Peggy Rae*
Sassafras Tea · *Bolin, Janet*
Sassenach · *Moore, Brian*
Satanesque · *Weiss, Allan*
Satan's Children · *Robinson, Spider*
The Satie Church · *Bell, Wade*
Satire on Sanity · *Hannam, Appleton*
Satori · *Bailey, Bruce*
Saturation Point · *Linder, Norma West*
Saturday, Sunday, or Does It Really Matter Anyway??!! · *Tourbin, Dennis*
Saturday · *Gallant, Mavis*
Saturday Afternoon · *Marsh, Wade*
Saturday Climbing · *Valgardson, W.D.*
Saturday Collection · *Dobb, Ted*
Saturday Matinee and Me · *Fulford, Susan*
Saturday Morning · *Tagg, Geoff*
Saturday Night, Bean Night · *Ross, Veronica*
Saturday Night · *Ross, Sinclair*

Saturday Night Dance · *Clark, Joan*
Saturday Night Game · *Friedman, Irena*
Saturday Night in Yugoslavia · *Kellythorne, Walt*
Saturday Night Milk Fever · *Waltner-Toews, David*
A Saturday Night Out in the Country · *Malloch, Bruce*
Saturday Swim · *Phillips, Alan*
Saturn Is My Home · *Margoshes, Dave*
Sauce for the Goose · *Green, H. Gordon*
Sauerkraut Please · *Meldrum, Vernon*
The Savages · *Simpson, Leo*
Saved · *Valgardson, W.D.*
Saved by the Bells · *Lee, Carroll H.*
Saving Grace · *Yanofsky, Joel*
The Saving of Sister Oothout · *Colson, Theodore*
Saving Someone's Skin · *Steffler, George*
The Saviour · *Andre-Czerniecki, Marion*
Saviours · *Flechtman, Wilfred*
Sawdust · *Huggan, Isabel*
Sawdust Mama · *Grantmyre, Barbara*
Sawkey and the Status Symbol · *Grantmyre, Barbara*
Sawkey Mullet Collects a Debt · *Grantmyre, Barbara*
Say It Again, Sam: The Lighthearted Narrative of How a Man Came to
Grips with His Loss of Hearing · *Smith, Richard S.*
Say It with Food · *Engel, Marian*
'Say Mom Know What Happened in School Today?' · *Cathcart, L.M.*
Scab · *Lee, Bibi*
The Scaffold · *MacMaster, Rowland*
Scandal in the Village · *Peterson, Phyllis Lee*
Scapes / Spaces · *Steinberg, Janice*
Scar Tissue · *Percy, H.R.*
A Scarf for a Maiden · *Wood, Kerry*
Scarlet, Scarlet · *Moser, Marie*
Scarlet Ibis · *Atwood, Margaret*
The Scarlet Jacket and the Middy Blouse · *Dinn, Elizabeth*
Scarlet Ribbons · *Corrigall, Melodie*
The Scarlet Trail · *Godsell, Philip H.*
the scarlet woman · *Bullock, Michael*
Scarlett's Web · *Earle, Ruthven*
Scars · *Kinsella, W.P.*
Scenario · *Jones, Miriam*
Scenarios · *Kilodney, Crad*
A Scene · *Bailey, Bruce*
Scenes Before Breakfast · *Young, Wenda*
Scenes from Montreal Life III: Bicultural Angela · *Hood, Hugh*
Scenes of the Alhambra · *Hogan, Robert*
The Scent of Cedars · *Galloway, David R.*
Scent of Gold · *Hazell, Mary*
the scent of honey · *Bullock, Michael*
Scent of Magnolias · *Breen, Melwyn*
Schadenfroh · *Sherrin, Robert G.*

The Seagull · *Mason, Kim*
The Sea-Haven · *Buckle, Daphne*
Seamus and the Crow · *Lynch, Gerald*
Seamus and the Windy Day · *Anonymous*
Sean O'Leary and the Swede · *Dybvig, Leslie*
The Search · *Campbell, Betty*
The Search by 'Jorge Luis Borges' · *Harrow, K.J.*
The Search for Christmas · *Govan, Margaret*
A Search for More Than a Strawberry Sister · *McLaughlin, Jeffrey*
The Search for Sarah Grace · *McNamara, Eugene*
The Search for Strangler Sweeney · *Hockley, Vernon*
The Search for the New Child · *Manning, Dorothy*
The Search - A Sketch · *Cote, J. Richard*
The Searcher · *Haig-Brown, Roderick*
The Searchers · *Spencer, Elizabeth*
Searching for the Blue Heron · *Robson, Nora*
Seas to Armageddon ... and Beyond · *Hancock, Anthony*
Seascape · *Wheeler, Frances*
A Season for Sharks · *Julian, Marilyn*
A Season in Limbo · *Glassco, John*
A Season in Love · *Szanto, George*
A Season of Calm Weather · *Hood, Hugh*
The Season of Perfect Works · *Mayne, Lise Guyanne*
Seasons of a Flowers · *Stewart, Scott*
Seaweed & Song · *Rule, Jane*
Secession North · *Ward, Norman*
The Secession of Deer Island · *Sturdy, John Rhodes*
The Secluded Lot · *Townshend, Elizabeth Morison*
Second Best · *McDonald, Ruth*
The Second Car · *O'Brien, Peter*
Second Chance · *Stein, Rhoda Elizabeth Playfair*
The Second Coming of Julian the Magician · *MacEwen, Gwendolyn*
Second Cousin Once Removed · *Barclay, Byrna*
Second Harvest · *Beattie, Jessie L.*
Second Honeymoon · *Buller, Betty*
Second Life · *Mountford, Charles*
The Second Mile · *Briffett, Isabel*
The Second Mrs. Lindsay · *Beresford-Howe, Constance*
Second Person · *Jeffrey, Neil*
The Second Round · *Russell, Ted*
The Second Round · *Russell, Ted*
Second Sight · *Lavoie, Stephanie*
Second Spring · *MacLeod, Alistair*
Second Thoughts · *Hawryluk, Paul*
Second Wife · *LeBourdais, Isabel*
Second Wind · *Avery, Martin*
Secrecy · *MacSween, R.J.*
The Secret · *Bach, Kathleen*
Secret Admirer · *Harvey, Jennifer A. Becks*
The Secret Lust of a Mansewife · *Skey, Patricia*

The Secret Mission · *Fox, C.M.*
The Secret of the Kugel · *Richler, Mordecai*
Secret of the Trade · *Spivak, Michael*
The Secret Pitch · *McIlroy, Kimball*
Secret Places · *Livesey, Margot*
The Secret Weapon · *O'Connell, Dorothy*
The Secretary Bird · *Rule, Jane*
Secrets · *Hamm, Mark*
The Secrets of Jonathan Coates · *Desjardins, Phil*
Secrets of the Human Heart · *Kutlesa, Joso*
Seduction · *Watmough, David*
The Seduction of Molly McGee · *Amernic, Jerry*
The Seduction of Queen Elizabeth II · *McFadden, David*
See No Evil · *Avery, Martin*
See the Dark · *Gasparini, Len*
See What Jeff Says · *Barnard, Margaret E. and Barnard, Leslie Gordon*
See You in September · *Garner, Hugh*
The Seed · *Green, H. Gordon*
the seed filament · *Bullock, Michael*
Seeds · *Watt, Kathy*
Seeds for the Sonata of Birds · *Amprimoz, Alexandre*
Seeing and Touching · *Ellis, Keith*
Seeing Double · *Stone, P. Anne*
Seeing Is Believing · *Wright, Ritta*
Seeing Strangers · *Horne, Lewis B.*
Seeking Carefully with Tears · *Bauer, Nancy*
Seguin's Last Train · *Carrier, Jean-Guy*
The Seizure · *Blaise, Clark L.*
Selected Episodes from an Empty Diary · *Nyberg, Wayne*
Selected Works · *Hart, Don*
A Selection from the Private Records of the Late Deceased Dr. O'Faolan
Umna n'Atura, Humanist · *Anonymous*
Selective Service · *Evanier, David*
Self Made Man · *Gillese, John Patrick*
Self-Portrait · *Dust, Julian*
Self-Portrait: The Welcome · *Moffatt, Greg*
The Selling of Heaven: A Folktale · *Rooke, Leon*
The Semi-Omnipotent Engine · *Sharpe, David*
Semi-Private · *McDonald, Ruth*
Semper Paratus, Semper Fidelis, Semper Annie · *Torgov, Morley*
The Senator · *Plantos, Ted*
Send Me Back Sunday · *Crouse, Paul*
Send Me Red Roses · *Zinkewich, Muriel*
Send Not to Know · *Fraser, D.M.*
Senor Pinedo · *Gallant, Mavis*
Sense · *Aylen, John*
The Sense of an Ending · *Blaise, Clark L.*
A Sense of Awareness · *Mercer, Michael*
A Sense of Justice · *Teitel, Jay*
A Sense of Myself · *Brown, Betty*

Sense of Place · *Graham, Gary*
A Sense of Remembrance · *Goldie, Olive*
A Sense of Responsibility · *Evanier, David*
A Sense of Value · *Stevens-Guille, Peter*
A Sense of Wonder · *Burnell, Ethel D.*
The Sense She Was Born With · *Kinsella, W.P.*
The Sen-Sen Kid Dreams of Heaven · *Newlove, John*
A Sensible Man · *Armstrong, Patricia*
Sensible Susan · *Perkin, Darlene*
The Sentence · *Hager, Carl*
A Sentimental Journey · *Greer, David*
A Sentimental Love-Story · *Harris, Christopher*
Sentimental Meetings · *Cohen, Matt*
The Sentinel · *Brulotte, Gaetan*
The Sentry · *Cowasjee, Saros*
Separating · *Hodgins, Jack*
The Separation · *Mobley, Carla*
The Separator · *Sullivan, D.H.*
September Wedding · *McLaughlin, Lorrie*
sera · *Bullock, Michael*
A Serbian Dance · *Boyarsky, Abraham*
Seredonia · *Fraser, D.M.*
Sergeant Froissart · *Kadey, Carroll*
The Sermon on the Mount Redone · *Carrier, Jean-Guy*
Serpents' Teeth · *Robinson, Spider*
The Serving of Mushrooms · *Evans, J.A.S.*
Settin' on a Gold Mine · *Dodd, Barrie*
Setting Traps · *Legault, Donald*
Settings for a Love Poem · *Schoemperlen, Diane*
The Settlement · *Gibb, Alice M.*
The Settler · *Carson, Jane*
The Settler from Stettler · *Faulknor, Cliff*
Settling a Score · *Goldberg, Harvey*
Seven Confessions · *Urquhart, Jane*
Seven Day's Out · *Stange, Ken*
Seven Parts of a Ball Team · *Young, Scott*
Seven Seas · *McFadden, David*
Seven Words' Worth · *Linder, Norma West*
Seven Years Later · *Brooks, Eunice*
Seventeen · *Urbas, Jeannette*
The Seventh Star · *Sotelo, Ruben*
Seventy-Two Hours · *Brown, Isobel*
Severing the Ties · *Kruberg, Galina*
The Sewn Picture · *Mays, John Bentley*
The Sex Life of Accident Victims · *Austin, Don*
Seymour · *Richler, Mordecai*
Shade · *Smith, Ron*
Shades · *Williams, David*
Shadow Box · *Sharpe, David*
The Shadow Fighter · *Anonymous*

Shadow Fruit · *Kennedy, Thomas*
Shadow in the Morning · *Deneau, Denis Phillippe*
The Shadow of the Rock · *Green, H. Gordon*
Shadows · *Priest, Paul B.*
Shadows in the Sand · *Baltensperger, Peter*
Shadows in the Snow Storm · *Anderson, Dagny*
Shake the Green Leaf off the Tree · *Rowdon, Larry*
A Shakespearian Tragedy · *Dickie, Allan*
Shale and Rock · *McConnell, William C.*
Shall I Compare Thee · *Sigurdson, Paul A.*
Shaman · *Wreggitt, Andrew*
The Shameless Wooing of Clarence Patterson · *McNamee, James*
Shamus Rafferty's Famous Dog · *Green, H. Gordon*
Shan Val Mhór · *Virgo, Sean*
Shane Horton Died on Mount Royal · *Tiger, Lionel*
Shangri-la on the Peace · *Hollingshead, Archie*
The Shape of the White Waves · *Kaminsky, Helen*
Shared Accommodation · *Bailey, Don*
Sharon · *Spencer, Elizabeth*
A Sharp Curve · *Pope, Sandra*
Sharp Rock Inlet · *Fuchs, Terry*
Shattered Idol · *Rose, Mildred A.*
Shawnigan · *Hart, Kathy*
S/he · *Dunn, James*
She Broke Up with Him and Then I Broke Up with Him · *Agetees, George*
She Emerged Fresh from the Bathroom · *Sturmanis, Dona*
She Fell Asleep Sunbathing Outside Her Apartment Building · *Austin, Don*
She Hadn't Changed a Bit · *Stein, Rhoda Elizabeth Playfair*
She Held the World on the Tip of Her Nose · *Smith, Judi*
She Locked the Door · *Simmer, Ron*
She Wakes at Midnight · *Stock, B.E.*
She Wanted to Hear the Bagpipes · *Burnell, Ethel D.*
She Was No Lady · *Wood, Margaret*
She Who Laughs Last · *Tweedie, Robert A.*
A Sheaf of Wheat · *Almond, Paul*
The Sheepherder · *Goulden, Alban*
The Sheffield Candlesticks · *Rooke, Constance*
Shekspir Was Jewish · *Yelin, Shulamis*
The Shell · *Wilson, Elizabeth*
The Shell Collector · *Horwood, Harold*
She'll Love Again · *Green, H. Gordon*
Shell Out · *Shepherd, R.W.*
Shelley the Sensitive Plant · *Nichols, Don*
Shelter for Nelson · *Branden, Vicki*
A Shelter from the Rain · *Garner, Hugh*
Sheltered Life · *Life* [pseudonym]
Shelved · *Nathan, Norman*
Shông: The Growing Upwards · *Cropas, Nyna*
The Shepherdess · *Wallace, Jack* [pseudonym]
The Shepherd's Revolt · *Dickinson, Don*

A Sherbrooke Street Man · *Hood, Hugh*
Sherlock Holmes' Great Canadian Adventure · *Batten, Jack and Bliss, Michael*
The 'Shine Can · *Dorman, Alexander*
the shingle arrow gun · *Heath, Terence*
The Shining Houses · *Munro, Alice*
Ship Ahoy! · *Pollett, Ron*
The Ship Flower · *Tonner, Thomas H.*
A Ship in the Night · *Foster, Chris*
Ship Island: The Story of a Mermaid · *Spencer, Elizabeth*
The Ship That Was Late · *Mayse, Arthur*
Ship to Shore · *Brennan, Anthony*
Shipwreck · *Trehey, John P.*
Shirley · *Ludwig, Jack*
Shirley's Workaday Witness · *Riman, Arthur*
The Shirt Off My Back · *Jackson, J. Graham*
Shivaree · *Brewster, Elizabeth*
Shock Treatments · *Knight, Ann*
The Shoe · *Burnley, John*
The Shoe and the Future · *Bruchovsky, Olga*
Shoe Fly Pie · *Rooke, Leon*
Shoeless Joe · *Kinsella, W.P.*
Shoeless Joe Jackson Comes to Iowa · *Kinsella, W.P.*
Shoes · *Hosein, Clyde*
Shoes for Dancing · *Rubia, Geraldine*
Shoe-String Playboy · *Briffett, Isabel*
Shoo, Flu, Don't Bother Me · *MacIntosh, Keitha K.*
Shooting It · *Keyes, John*
Shooting the Breeze on St. Urbain · *Richler, Mordecai*
Shooting the Bull: The Need of Change · *Reykdal, Art*
Shoot-Out at Dead Dog Gulch · *Kilodney, Crad and Nations, Opal L.*
The Shop Whistle · *Shipley, Nan*
Shore of Desire · *Mandrake, Jill*
Short Circuit · *Annesley, Fred*
Short Cut for Mr. Poppin · *Barnard, Leslie Gordon*
A Short Fair History of a Family · *Gordon, Jaimy*
A Short February Story · *Tenenbaum, Gerald*
A Short Hagiography of Old Quebec · *Bowering, George*
A Short History of Prophylactics · *McCubbin, Terrence*
A Short Love Story · *Gallant, Mavis*
A Short Short Story · *Hindmarch, Gladys*
A Short Story · *Gore, Anita*
Short Story · *Birdsell, Sandra*
A Short Story Celebrating the Day of Public School Integration, New Orleans, La.
Song by Gov. Jimmy Davis, Entitled: 'You Are My Sunshine' · *Rooke, Leon*
The Short Visit Home · *Horne, Lewis B.*
A Short Visit to Heaven · *Anonymous*
A Short Walk Home · *Garner, Hugh*
A Shortage of Christmas · *Singleton, Norman M.*
A Shortage of Mourners · *Simmie, Lois*
A Shorte Tale Concerning a Woeful Warlock · *Bates, Hilary*

Shortly After the Incident on the Haifa-Tel Aviv Road · *Ross, Edeet*
Shorts Story · *Price, Flo*
A Shot in the Arm · *Phillips, Fred H.*
A Shot to Remember · *Scammell, A.R.*
Shotgun · *Thompson, Kent*
Should Auld Acquaintance · *Buckler, Ernest*
A Shout of Joy · *Bauer, Nancy*
The Shoveller · *Bartley, Allan*
Show and Tell · *Elford, Jean*
Show Business · *Creighton, Dave*
Show Me the Feast · *Fagan, Cary*
The Show Off · *Russell, Ted*
Showdown · *Kostash, Myrna*
Shower Baths · *Hodgins, Norris*
Shower of Gold · *Gustafson, Ralph B.*
Shower Parade · *Browne, Colin*
A Shudder of Wings · *Ross, W.E. Dan*
Shy Boy - Shy Girl · *Barker, Bessie M.*
Siblings · *Copeland, Ann* [pseudonym]
Sic Transit Gloria Mundi · *MacMaster, Rowland*
A Sick Call · *Nowlan, Alden*
Sick Leave · *Corse, Murray*
The Sickbed · *Schendlinger, Mary*
The Sickness · *Kawalilak, Ron A.*
Side Effects · *Godfrey, Dave*
Sidetrack · *Bolger, William Neil*
Sidewalk Blues: A Great Canadian Tragedy · *Flatt, Mary*
Sidonia · *Phillips, Bluebell Stewart*
Siegfried's Memoirs · *Gallant, Mavis*
Sighing: From the Diary of Jane Queale · *Chapman, Marie*
The Sight · *Moore, Brian*
Sightseers in Death Valley · *Rule, Jane*
Sigiri: Palace in the Sky · *Fraser, Keath*
The Sign · *Brask, Per K.*
[The?] Sign of the Swami · *Gillese, John Patrick*
A Sign of the Times · *Buckler, Ernest*
Sign Posts · *Krause, Pat*
The Sign That Never Changed · *Briffett, Isabel*
The Signal · *Arscott, David*
A Signal at Crossings · *Bremner, Lary*
The Signature · *Hosein, Clyde*
Significant Moments in the Life of My Mother · *Atwood, Margaret*
Signing the 'A' Form · *McAllister, Clare*
Sigurdur the Fisherman · *Palsson, Gestur*
The Silence · *Thomas, Barrie*
A Silence All Too Long · *Waddington, Miriam*
Silence Is a Weapon · *Tait, John*
The Silencing · *Sileika, Antanas*
The Silent Goose · *Blenkin, Dorothy M.*
Silent Movie · *Brewster, Elizabeth*

Silent Music · *Callaghan, Barry*
The Silent Star of Stratford · *Johnson, Vera D.*
Silent Witness · *Whitford, Margaret Ann*
A Silk Hat from Denmark · *Green, H. Gordon*
Silvana and Eliot · *Kutlesa, Joso*
Silver · *Zietlow, E.R.*
The Silver Bit of Potential · *Mills, Elizabeth*
Silver Bugles, Cymbals, Golden Silks · *Hood, Hugh*
Silver Chief · *Downer, Don*
The Silver Drum · *Green, H. Gordon*
Silver Fish · *Sloman, Fred*
The Silver King · *Perrault, Ernest G.*
'The Silver Lining' · *Burnell, Ethel D.*
Silver Streams · *Pilowsky-Santos, Judith*
Silverthorn · *Hodgins, Jack*
Sima · *Delahanty, C.E.*
Simmering · *Atwood, Margaret*
Simon · *Holz, Cynthia*
Simon's Luck · *Munro, Alice*
A Simple Fellow · *Bergren, Myrtle*
A Simple Story · *Hladzuk, Veronica*
Simple Translation · *Wilson, Ethel D.*
The Simple Truth · *Smith, Marion*
Simplicity in Life or The Pastries · *Bermiller, Arthur*
SIN: A Parable · *Julian, Marilyn*
The Sin Eater · *Atwood, Margaret*
The Sin of Jimmy Lincoln · *Green, H. Gordon*
Sing Me No Love Songs, I'll Say You No Prayers · *Rooke, Leon*
The Singapore Hotel · *Hood, Hugh*
Singin' Carols · *Russell, Ted*
Singing · *Wilson, Jack Lowther*
The Singing Drum · *Saunders, Charles R.*
The Singing Rabbi · *Avery, Martin*
Single and Available · *Leznoff, Glenda*
Single Gents Only · *Metcalf, John*
A Single Scrambled · *Hindmarch, Gladys*
A Single to El Paso · *Simpson, Leo*
The Singular Sisters · *Jenoff, Marvyne*
Sinister Isn't Always Left · *Kidder, John*
The Sinking of the Northwest Passage · *Yates, J. Michael*
The Sinners of Shilone · *Campbell, Angelena H.*
The Sins of Tomas Benares · *Cohen, Matt*
Sip into the Past · *Burnett, Eileen*
Sir Galahad and the 'Bad Man' · *Steele, Harwood*
Sir John's Bed · *Hutchison, Bruce*
Sir Launcelot Wore Blue Jeans · *Stein, Rhoda Elizabeth Playfair*
The Sister · *Boyarsky, Abraham*
Sister Ann of the Cornfields · *Kinsella, W.P.*
A Sister for Susanna · *Stein, Rhoda Elizabeth Playfair*
Sister of the Bride · *McLaughlin, Lorrie*

Sisterhood · *Copeland, Ann* [pseudonym]
Sisters · *Cooper, Anne*
Sisyphus in Winter · *Rooke, Leon*
Six Chicken Flight · *Blum, Vicki*
six daffodils · *Bullock, Michael*
Six Feet of Frayed Rope · *Reynolds, Helen Mary Greenwood Campbell*
Six of One · *Harvey, Jennifer A. Becks*
Six Weeks · *Wildeman, Marlene*
Sixteen Ways to Skin a Cat · *Szanto, George*
Sixteen-Year-Old Susan March Confesses to the Innocent Murder of All
the Devious Strangers Who Would Drag Her Down · *Rooke, Leon*
Sixth Sense · *Coney, Michael G.*
Skald · *Valgardson, W.D.*
Skating Along on Carburator Ice · *Williams, Dave*
The Skating Party · *Summers, Merna*
The Skeleton Coast · *Saunders, Charles R.*
The Skeleton in Grandpa's Closet · *Green, H. Gordon*
Sketch · *Murray, Joan*
A Sketch of a Junk Pile · *Hancock, Ronald Lee*
Sketches for a Story · *Kishkan, Theresa*
Skin · *Jenoff, Marvyne*
Skin Deep · *Lyngseth, Joan*
The Skinflint · *Marriott, J. Anne*
A Skink in My Jewel Box · *Grimster, Ellen*
the skipper · *Bullock, Michael*
Skipper Joe's Trip to St. John's · *Russell, Ted*
Skipper the Sniffer · *Mikolasch, Andrew*
Skipper Zeke Sets All Right · *Briffett, Isabel*
The Skippers · *Allen, Robert*
Skipping the Facts of Life · *Cooper, Jas E.*
Skip's Blue Ink · *Sky, Steven*
Skirmish at Crater Alphonsus · *Dornan, Chris*
Sky Music · *Evans, Allen Roy*
Skye · *Kerslake, Susan*
Skye Hill · *Kelley, Brian*
The Skylark and the Nightengale · *Giddings, Alice*
Sladislavus Buyeth a House · *Atwood, Joan-Mary*
Slammer · *Neil, Al*
The Slap · *Leitao, Lino*
The Slaughterhouse · *Joffre, Jeffrey*
Slave October · *Ramsden, Doug*
Slave to Tradition · *Clovis, An*
Slaves · *Kinsella, W.P.*
Sleep · *Rikki [Erica Ducornet]*
Sleepers · *Bennett, Jennifer*
Sleeping Jesus and the Scavengers · *Arnason, David*
The Sleepover · *Smart, William J.*
A Slice · *Matas, Margaret Dwyer*
A Slice of Bread · *Logan, Dorothy E.*
Slice of Life · *Heavisides, Martin*

A Slice of Mister These's Life · *Stange, Ken*
Slices · *Trommeshauser, Dietmar*
The Slicing Machine · *Zilber, Jacob*
Slide · *McRae, Robert*
Slingshot · *Heble, Ajay*
The Slippers · *Stacey, Jean*
The Slippery Slide · *Wood, Ted*
Slipping on the Same Step Twice · *Heble, Ajay*
Sloane Bradshaw's Wife · *Williamson, Rossa*
Slocan Days · *McLeod, Murdoch*
The Sloop · *Bruce, Charles T.*
The Slough · *Briffett, Isabel*
A Slow and Steady Decline · *Bristow, Susan*
Slow Burn · *Wigle, Wil*
Slug · *Fawcett, Brian*
Slumming in Maui · *Swan, Susan*
The Small, Gentle House of Bertram Camm · *Waterhouse, John*
The Small Birds · *Hood, Hugh*
The Small Black Hat · *Broy, Evelyn J.*
A Small Crime · *Wexler, Jerry*
Small Feminine Feet · *Weidmark, M.*
A Small Film · *Bacque, James*
The Small Hours · *Nowlan, Alden*
Small Mercies · *Harvor, Beth*
A Small Piece of Blue · *Levine, Norman*
The Small Rain · *Helwig, David*
A Small Thing · *Armstrong, Patricia*
A Small Tone · *Horne, Lewis B.*
Small World · *Purdy, Brian*
Smallboatmen · *Kennedy, F.M.*
Smalltown · *Hogg, Bob*
Smart Pig · *Rose, Bob*
The Smartest Dog in Town · *Green, H. Gordon*
Smashing · *Andrews, Bill*
Smashing Capital · *Gregg, John*
... Smell a Fool · *Gabris, Linda*
The Smell of Dust · *Curran, Kitty*
The Smell of Green · *Chaplan, Lucille Singer*
The Smell of Wintergreen · *Porter, Helen*
Smelts · *Battley, Mark R.*
The Smile · *Witte, Darlene*
Smile for the Crying Basket · *Gould, Jan*
The Smile of the Mortician · *Chalmers, John W.*
The Smiths of Swanson · *Story, Gertrude*
Smoke · *Smith, Ray*
Smoke Gets in Your Eyes · *Leibowitz, Fred*
Smoke in the Hills · *Bergren, Myrtle*
Smoke Screen · *Woodbury, Mary*
Smoked Out · *Ravel, Aviva*
Smoked Oysters · *Lewis, David E.*

Smokestack in the Desert · *Yates, J. Michael*
Smote Plums · *Nishimura, Wendy*
Smudge · *Mackintosh, James*
The Smugglers · *Riddell, John*
Snagged in the Deep Water · *Smith, Ralph F.*
The Snake · *Tanaka, Tammy*
the snake and the spring · *Bullock, Michael*
Snake Charmer · *Lenoir-Arcand, Christine*
The Snake in the Wall · *Gould, Jan*
The Snake Lady · *Thompson, George C.*
Snake-Eyes · *Peter, John D.*
Snakes · *Russell, Ted*
Snapshot · *Rooke, Constance*
Snapshot: The Third Drunk · *Cameron, Donald*
Snapshots · *Stenson, Frederick*
Sneaker Week · *O'Connell, Dorothy*
Sneakers · *Kaufman, Pat*
A Sneeze Is a Sneeze · *Theriault, Yves*
Snell · *Vanderhaeghe, Guy*
Snicker-Snack, Crying Wolf · *Castillo, Charles*
The Sniper · *Graham, Robert*
Snippet · *Daurio, Beverley*
Snips and Snaps · *Augustine, Wilma*
Snoring · *Hodgins, Norris*
Snotbox · *Fawcett, Brian*
Snow · *MacEwen, Gwendolyn*
Snow and Solitaire · *Rosta, Helen J.*
Snow Fall · *Dawe, Tom*
Snow Hole · *Fairley, Bruce*
Snow Job · *d'Or, Vic and Hutton, Bill*
The Snow Man · *Carlyle, Andrew*
The Snow Man · *Nemiroff, Greta Hofmann*
Snow on Flat Top · *Marshall, Joyce*
Snow Trail · *Mitchell, Sylvia Elizabeth Fisher*
The Snow Walker · *Mowat, Farley*
Snowball · *Connolly, Jacqueline*
Snowbilia · *Szanto, George*
Snowbound · *Hutchins, Hazel J.*
Snowbound Christmas Train · *Sayer, Frank*
Snowflake, Snowflake · *Babineau, Brian*
The Snowflake · *Dewdney, Keewatin*
The Snowman · *Dickinson, Jim*
Snowmobiling · *Skinner, Norman Doc*
Snowmoon · *Rogers, Beth*
Snow-Shadow Man · *Russell, Lawrence*
Snowstorm · *Leggett, Catharine*
So Close · *Maar, John Zeljko*
So Foolish Was I · *McDonald, Ruth*
So It's My Fault? · *Gould, Terry*
So Long, Cabbagetown · *Plantos, Ted*

So Many Children · *Carrier, Jean-Guy*
So Many Have Died · *Marshall, Joyce*
So Many 'If's · *McLeod, E. Vessie*
So Much a Word · *Barnard, Leslie Gordon*
So Much for Stukynamud · *Cameron, Eric*
So Much for That · *Norman, Colin*
'So Nice of You to Come' · *Ogle, Robert Joseph*
So Now I'll Tell You · *Green, H. Gordon*
So Small a Thing · *Barnard, Leslie Gordon*
So Soft, So White · *Newlove, John*
So the Little Girl Knows · *Bodie, Blake*
So Wide the Sea · *Barnard, Margaret E. and Barnard, Leslie Gordon*
Soap and Water · *Birch-Jones, Sonia*
the soap builders · *Bullock, Michael*
Soap-and-Water Charity · *Barker, Bessie M.*
Soaring · *Wasserman, J.F.*
The Sob in the Silence · *Green, H. Gordon*
Sobbing Through the Day: Part Two · *Fasick, Laura*
The Sobering of Joshua, the Shuswap · *Bastow, E.*
Soberman's Release · *Sherman, Kenneth*
Soccer and Poetry · *Shirinian, Lorne*
The Social · *Bushell, Sidney*
A Social Disease, So to Speak · *Jackson, Marni*
Social Leopard · *Barnhouse, D.P.*
Social Walls · *Bernhardt, Peter*
The Society of Jesus · *Daly, Michael E.*
Socks · *Campbell, Wanda Blynn*
Sofer S'tm · *Drache, Sharon*
The Soft Answer · *Green, H. Gordon*
Soft Places on the Main · *Agetees, George*
Soft Shell · *Frey, Cecelia*
The Soft Summer Air · *Gordon, Jane*
Sojurn at Junkie Log · *Trower, Peter*
Solace Stone · *Moyer, Carolyn*
The Soldier · *Misfeldt, James*
A Soldier Returns · *Halbus, Frank W.*
The Soldiers in the Park · *Stein, David Lewis*
A Solemn Deal · *Pugsley, Edmund E.*
The Solid-Gold Lie · *Bankier, William*
Soliloquy of a Common Man · *Davitt, F.G.*
Solipsist · *Gleeson, Sean*
Solitaire · *Solly, Bill*
A Solitary Ewe · *Hood, Hugh*
Solitary Stroll · *Landreth, Tomas*
Solo · *Anderson, Gwendolyn*
Solo Dive · *Novak, Barbara*
The Solution · *Slabotsky, David*
Solution: Rob a Bank · *Sheldon, Michael*
The Soma Building · *Harris, Beverly*
Sombody Else's Summer · *Wood, Ted*

Some Are So Lucky · *Garner, Hugh*
Some Day I'll Love You · *Clare, John P.*
Some Day We'll Go · *Barnard, Leslie Gordon*
'Some Enchanted Evening' · *Malcolm, Susan*
Some Essential Points About Fish · *Fernie, Lynne*
Some Evidence of Foxing · *de Barros, Paul*
Some Grist for Mervyn's Mill · *Richler, Mordecai*
Some Have Called Thee Mighty and Dreadful · *Hospital, Janet Turner*
Some Lessons Learned · *Stevenson, Joan*
some mornings · *Riches, Brenda*
Some Mornings I Wake Up · *Zimmmerman, Ian*
Some Neighborhood!! · *Ellis, Harry*
Some Never Know · *Ransom, Else*
Some Notes on Three Mongoloid Configurations · *Leon, John A.*
Some of His Best Friends · *Horwood, Harold*
'Some of the Street in' · *Finnigan, Joan*
Some People Have No Sense of Humour · *O'Connell, Dorothy*
Some People Will Tell You the Situation at Henny Penny Nursery Is Getting
Intolerable · *Rooke, Leon*
Some People's Grandfathers Give Them Cigarettes to Smoke · *Ringwood, Gwen
Pharis*
Some People's Luck · *Bergren, Myrtle*
Some Recent Developments in the High Cost of Government · *Cheesbrough, E.*
Some Things Are True · *Fawcett, Brian*
Some Things I Won't Do · *Thompson, Kent*
Some Trip This Is Going to Be · *Hindmarch, Gladys*
Some Will Never Quit · *Fenerty, Ron*
Somebody Has to Buy the New York Times · *Brodie, Blake*
Somebody Owes Me Money · *Sellers, Peter*
Someday · *Wysong, Pippa B.*
Someday Soon, Before Tomorrow · *Wiebe, Rudy H.*
Someone Else's · *Livesey, Margot*
Someone They Know · *Moore, Brian*
Someone Who Understands · *Fletcher, Peggy*
Someone with Such a Future · *Bradbury, Patricia*
Somer-Sault · *Lindsey, Robert*
Something Better Than This · *Gaitskill, Mary*
Something Close to Joy · *Linder, Norma West*
Something Evil This Way Comes · *Kinsella, W.P.*
Something for Nothing · *Callaghan, Morley*
Something for Olivia's Scrapbook I Guess · *Helwig, David*
Something Happened Here · *Levine, Norman*
Something I Do · *Riis, Sharon*
Something in Common · *Bettison, Margaret*
Something Is Nothing · *Yates, J. Michael*
Something I've Been Meaning to Tell You · *Munro, Alice*
Something Meaningful · *Stein, Rhoda Elizabeth Playfair*

Something Mysterious Has Arrived · *Holt, Maria*
Something Old, Something New · *Baldwin, Laura*
Something Out There · *Bauer, Nancy*
Something Special · *Reid, Helen B.*
Something to Eat · *Illidge, Paul*
Something to Go On · *Russo, Leonard*
Something to Grin At · *McWhirter, George*
Something to Live By · *Green, H. Gordon*
Something to Think About · *Kinsella, W.P.*
Something's Going On · *Hindmarch, Gladys*
Sometime - Later - Not Now · *Findley, Timothy*
Sometimes a Draw Will Do · *Rensby, Harry*
Sometimes Andy Mathison Has Some Great Ideas · *Cameron, Anne*
Sometimes English, Sometimes French · *Levine, Norman*
Sometimes I Feel Like Going Down · *Lambert, Rick*
Sometimes I Forget · *Kevin, George*
Sometimes Revenge Comes Quickly · *Morritt, Hope*
Sometimes You Choose - Win or Lose · *Scott, Lynn*
Somewhere My Love · *Fagan, Cary*
Somewhere Over the Rainbow · *Perozak, Helen Irene*
Somnambulism · *Kadey, Carroll*
The Somnolent · *Dutton, Paul*
the son · *Stein, Philip*
Son of McDougall · *Wiebe, Rudy H.*
Song · *Caruso, Barbara*
Song in the Night · *Carew, Captain John*
Song of Araby · *McFee, Oonah*
The Song of Sarne · *McWhirter, George*
Song of Sixpence · *Selvon, Samuel*
The Song of the Reindeer · *Gunnars, Kristjana*
The Songs · *Marten, Anna*
Songs Beyond Recall · *Humphries, Tom*
Sonny Boy · *Burkman, Kay*
Sons and Mothers · *Gourlay, Elizabeth*
The Sons of Lear · *Ayre, John*
Sooner or Later · *Branden, Vicki*
The Sorcerer · *Reid, Peter*
Sorrows of the Flesh · *Huggan, Isabel*
Sorry, My Wife Doesn't Live Here · *Lee, Carroll H.*
The Sorry Papers · *Bailey, Don*
Sorting Things Out · *van Luven, Lynne*
SOS from Mei Wong · *Ross, W.E. Dan*
Sospiri · *Robinson, Brad*
Sottish Solomon · *Anonymous*
Soufflés Need Support · *Boyd, Josephine*
Soul of a Rabbit · *Green, H. Gordon*
Soul Search · *Robinson, Spider*
The Soul Thirsts · *Schermbrucker, Bill*
The Sound · *Hollingshead, Greg*
The Sound of a Horn · *Harlow, Robert*

Sound of Christmas · *McLeod, E. Vessie*
A Sound of Fury · *Woodward, Gordon*
The Sound of Hollyhocks · *Garner, Hugh*
The Sound of the Singing · *Laurence, Margaret*
The Sound of Thunder · *Horwood, Harold*
The Sound of Waves · *Choy, Wayson S.*
The Sounding Brass · *Fitzpatrick, Helen*
The Sour Apple Tree · *Richards, Mabel*
Sour Gas · *Benger, JoAnne*
Sour Notes from the Portuguese · *Pereira, Helen*
South · *Blaise, Clark L.*
South End Avenue · *Bruce, Charles T.*
South of Montreal · *Levine, Norman*
South Pacific · *Wharton, Calvin*
Southern Exposure · *Ibsen, Norman*
A Southern Landscape · *Spencer, Elizabeth*
Southern Style · *McIlroy, Kimball*
Souvenir · *Miller, Glenn*
Souvenirs · *Zilber, Jacob*
Soviet Jewellery · *Avery, Martin*
A Sow's Ear · *O'Connell, Dorothy*
The Sow's Ears · *Walters, Harold Neal*
Space · *Harrop, Gerry*
Space Greens · *Chard, Jean Marie*
Space in the Heart · *Morris, Doris M.*
Spaces · *Martineau, Barbara Halpern*
Spadina Time · *Cohen, Matt*
Spanish Jack · *Fraser, Raymond*
The Spanish Lady · *Munro, Alice*
Spanish Oranges · *Rikki [Erica Ducornet]*
Spans · *Bowering, George*
The Spark Plug Thief · *Plourde, Marc*
The Sparrow · *Pierterse, Cecilia*
The Sparrow of Bethlehem · *Bole, J. Sheridan*
The Sparrows · *Livesay, Dorothy*
Sparrows on a Roof · *Bri_ett, Isabel*
The Speaker · *Riddell, John*
Speakez-vous the Engleesho? · *Harvey, Jennifer A. Becks*
The Speaking Engagement · *Vertolli, Lou*
Spearheads · *Haig-Brown, Roderick*
Special · *Mazei, Stephen*
The Special · *Shein, Brian*
Special Cargo · *Easton, Alan*
A Special Case · *Evans, Hubert*
A Special Girl for Him · *Dales, Walter A.*
A Special Kind of Magic · *Birch-Jones, Sonia*
A Special Madonna · *Ross, W.E. Dan*
A Special Occasion · *Plantos, Ted*

The Specialist · *Foster, David*
Speck's Idea · *Gallant, Mavis*
Spectacular · *Carr, Roberta, with William Grant and Joe Koegh*
The Spectator · *Shannon, Norman*
The Spectre of Art · *d'Or, Vic and Nations, Opal L.*
The Spell of the Distant Drum · *Laurence, Margaret*
The Spell of the Ex · *Adamson, Arthur*
The Spell of the Snow Crater · *Barnard, Margaret E. and Barnard, Leslie Gordon*
Spelling · *Munro, Alice*
The Spencers · *Barnard, Margaret E.*
Spencerville · *Dust, Julian*
Spending the Morning in Paradise · *Thayer, Nancy*
The Sphincter · *McWhirter, George*
Spice-Cake · *Lynch, Gerald*
Spider · *Clement, Bill*
Spider Road · *Margeson, John*
Spike · *Ross, Sinclair*
Spike the Spider · *Campion, Bridget*
Spikenard Root · *Bauer, Nancy*
Spill of Guilt · *Garner, Hugh*
The Spinster · *Garner, Hugh*
Spirit Level · *Green, H. Gordon*
The Spirit of the Bank of Lower Canada · *Sheldon, Michael*
A Spirited Encounter · *Percy, H.R.*
The Spiritual Life of Sari Green · *Cohen, Annette*
Spiritus Mundu · *Goodchild, Peter*
Spit Delaney's Island · *Hodgins, Jack*
Splurge · *Moulton, Donna*
The Splurge of Charlie Harris · *Dybvig, Leslie*
Spooker · *Brown, Dorothy Howe*
The Spool of Wire · *Melfi, Mary*
The Sport of Gods · *Yellon, R.A.*
The Sportive Center of Saint Vincent de Paul · *Hood, Hugh*
The Sportsman · *Hendry, Peter*
A Spot for Elizabeth · *Daem, Mary*
Spotting: A Case History · *Young, David*
Spreading It Around ... · *Ward, Bob*
Spring · *Shaw, Paul G.*
Spring Break · *Thomas, Audrey*
Spring Cleaning · *Mason, Mike*
Spring Comes · *Russell, Sheila MacKay*
Spring Comes to Ksirocambi · *Friedman, Irena*
A Spring Fancy · *Williams, Vera B.*
Spring Gale · *Manicom, David [pseudonym]*
Spring Is for the Lambs · *Pollett, Ron*
Spring Manoeuvres · *Butterwick, Jessie*
Spring Morning · *Stein, David Lewis*
Spring Song · *Rockwell, Vance*
Spring Song of the Frogs · *Atwood, Margaret*
Spring Thaw · *Theriault, Yves*

Spring Time · *Craig-James, Janet*
Spring Tournaments · *Krause, Pat*
Spring Water · *Callaghan, Barry*
The Sprout · *Marlatt, Daphne*
Square Nails · *Barker, Bessie M.*
The Square Peg · *Brifflett, Isabel*
Squashed Spruce · *Elgaard, Elin*
Squaw Fish Story · *Price, C.B.*
The Squaw's Professor · *Steinfeld, J.J.*
The Squirrel · *Duncan, Frances*
The Squirrel Tale · *Gerrond, Mike*
Squirrels and Summer Flowers · *Allan, Ted*
St. Jose[p]h Asylum: Fall 1915 · *Clark, D.M.*
St. Joseph's Marvellous Boilers · *Morris, Doris M.*
St. Patrick's Day Cabane ; Sucre · *Filip, Raymond*
St. Xaviera · *van Fraassen, Bas*
St Mary's Keys: A Story of the Supernatural · *Whiteley, [Capt.] George C.*
Staff Only · *Cowasjee, Saros*
Stage Struck · *MacNeill, James A.*
The Stained Glass Window · *Flury, Kay*
The Stairs: A Parable · *Brockenshire, Frank*
Stairway to Hell · *Tufts, Martyn*
The Stalking of Sheila · *Walker, David*
Stalled · *Rooke, Leon*
The Stallion · *Arscott, David*
Stampede · *Wreggitt, Andrew*
Stan · *Hay, Elizabeth*
Standard of Living · *Briffett, Isabel*
Standing in for Nita · *Rooke, Leon*
Standing Up · *Conde, Carole and Beveridge, Karl*
Standing Up to It · *Murdoch, Benedict Joseph*
The Stand-Off · *Jess, Cameron*
Stanislaw's Clocks · *Verkoczy, Elizabeth*
Stan's Complaint · *Plantos, Ted*
The Star · *Smith, Michael*
Star Bright · *Marriott, J. Anne*
The Star Heart · *Priest, Robert*
Star Performance · *Findlay, David K.*
The Star Shines Down · *Mitchell, Sylvia Elizabeth Fisher*
The Star That Showed the Way · *Stein, Rhoda Elizabeth Playfair*
The Star That Was · *Green, H. Gordon*
The Star Wench · *Dewar, Andrew*
The Star-Cross · *Johnson, Carol*
Star-Crossed · *Callaghan, Mary C.*
A Starfish · *Austin, Don*
Starring the Giraffe · *Heble, Ajay*
The Starry Night Sky · *Keefer, Janice Kulyk*
Stars, Moons · *Harvor, Beth*

The Stars at Night · *Rosenfeld, Rita*
Starscape · *Olsen, Hank*
Starthinker 9 · *Coney, Michael G.*
Starting Again on Sherbrooke Street · *Hood, Hugh*
The Starting Day · *Wood, Kerry*
Starting Off on the Right Foot · *Stevenson, Joan*
A State of Mind · *Scully, Greg*
State Visit · *Radu, Kenneth*
A Statement from Inside the Cultural Industrial Compound · *Sherman, Tom*
Static · *Young, Nora*
Station Break · *Garner, Hugh*
The Station · *Sorenstein, Louise*
Stationed · *van Herk, Aritha*
A Statue · *Knox, Gary*
The Statues Taken Down · *Gallant, Mavis*
Stay Me with Flagons · *Cottrell, Terence Lloyd*
Staying · *Bailey, Bill*
Staying with the Dream · *Barclay, Byrna*
The Steal · *Somerton, Ruby P.*
Stealin' the Holes · *Russell, Ted*
Steam Room · *Levson, Elliott H.*
The Steamer Trunk · *Bedard, Michael*
Steel Man · *MacLean, Robert*
Stella · *Marriott, J. Anne*
'Step' for Short · *Annett, R. Ross*
A Step in the Right Direction · *Stein, Rhoda Elizabeth Playfair*
A Step into Courage · *Buckaway, Catherine M.*
Step Off into Darkness · *Jubb, D.E.*
Step Well Down to the Rear of the Car, Please! · *Symons, Harry*
Stephen · *Kishkan, Theresa*
Step-'n-a-half · *Garner, Hugh*
The Steps · *McKevitt, Garry*
Stereo · *Horne, Lewis B.*
Steveston 1926 · *Evans, Hubert*
Stewart's Time · *Potrebenko, Helen*
Stewed Chicken Night · *Rifka, Ruth*
The Stick Maker · *Wood, Kerry*
Sticklebacks · *MacDonald, David*
The Stick-Maker · *Wood, Kerry*
Sticks · *Crowe, Eleanor*
The Stigmata · *Hart, William*
Still Brightly Shines the Light · *Sturdy, John Rhodes*
Still Close to the Island · *Dabydeen, Cyril*
Still Life · *Krahn, Ruth*
Still Life Composition: Woman's Clothes · *Thompson, Kent*
Still Life in Leather · *Emberly, Kenneth*
Still Life of Lilac Blossoms · *Blostein, David*
Still Life with Flowers · *Gourlay, Elizabeth*
Still Waters · *MacDonald, Margaret*
Stilts · *Abbey, Lloyd*

Sting · *Klebeck, William J.*
The Stirring Mouse · *Barker, Bessie M.*
A Stitch in Time · *Lisle, Glenn*
Stockings and Sugarplums · *Thompsett, Dennis*
Stockpiling · *Allen, Heather*
The Stoker · *Graham, Tammy*
Stolen Christmas · *Mayse, Arthur*
Stolen Moments · *d'Or, Vic and Young, David*
Stolen Money · *Annett, R. Ross*
Stolen Roans · *Mitchell, Ken*
Stone · *Riches, Brenda*
Stone in the Field · *Munro, Alice*
Stone Narcissus · *Smith, Don*
The Stone Room · *Hildebrandt, Gloria*
The Stone Rose · *Theriault, Yves*
The Stoneboat and the Bride · *Fines, Beatrice E.*
Stone-Cutter · *Gibson, Shirley Mann*
Stones · *Birdsell, Sandra*
Stony's Elfin Visitors · *Magnusson, K.*
Stood-Up Date · *Garner, Hugh*
The Stool · *McLaughlin, Peter*
Stop Bath · *Boire, Gary*
The Stop Sign · *Gould, Jan*
Stop the Press · *Murphy, D.T.*
Stopover · *Bruchovsky, Olga*
Stopped · *Sharpe, David*
Stories without Ending · *McFadden, Isobel*
The Storm · *Waterfall, Don E.*
The Storm: Killarney Lake, Alberta, 1915 · *Moser, Marie*
Storm at Flatlands · *Phillips, Bluebell Stewart*
Storm Centre · *Russell, Sheila MacKay*
Storm Glass · *Urquhart, Jane*
Stormraven · *de Lint, Charles*
Storms of Our Journey · *Walker, David*
Story · *Pickersgill, Ron*
The Story About a Sculptor · *Oudecek, Madia*
A Story for All Hallows Eve · *Hobbs, Gillian*
A Story for Jane · *Sanderson, James*
Story for Sunday · *Munro, Alice*
A Story from the Polar Bear Capital · *Nagorsen, Ross*
The Story I Never Heard · *Amprimoz, Alexandre*
Story in Force · *Niffenson, Harvey*
The Story of a Birth · *Bannerji, Himani*
The Story of a Cat · *Newlove, John*
The Story of a Film · *Keeler, Judy*
The Story of a Nurse · *Govan, Margaret*
Story of a Poor Man · *Kennon, Janie*
The Story of Alton Finney · *Hollingshead, Greg*

The Story of Anne · *McFadden, David*
The Story of Gethin and Horace · *Corrigall, Melodie Joy*
The Story of How Doctor Dalton Solved the Mystery About Who Killed Old Sleezer: A Murder Mystery · *Carson, Bryan*
The Story of Icarus, the Boy Who Wanted to Fly; or a Portrait of the Artist as a Young Bird · *Nevitt, Brian*
The Story of Jenny · *McLaren, Floris*
The Story of Jimmy Wracker · *Ristich, David*
The Story of Joe Canoe · *Koerte, Helen*
The Story of Max · *Miller, Samuel*
The Story of Millicent · *Armstrong, Patricia*
story of my life · *Bullock, Michael*
A Story of the Renaissance · *Cosier, Anthony*
Story One · *Scanlon, Margaret*
A Story or Something · *Ellis, Harry*
A Story Shortly · *Tigchelaar, Peter*
Story Story · *Hollingshead, Greg*
The Story Teller · *Foley, Mark*
Story That Saw Defeat · *Dempster, Barry*
Stove Pipes · *Lifeso, E.L.*
The Stowaway · *Harris, John Norman*
The Stragglers · *Kroetsch, Robert*
Straight Poker · *Cohen, Matt*
Straight Talk · *Pugsley, Edmund E.*
Stranded · *Smith, Michael*
A Strange, Obscure Revenge · *Watson, Edward A.*
The Strange Aberration of Mr. Ken Smythe · *Metcalf, John*
The Strange Affair of Reno Brown and Mama Tuddi · *Rooke, Leon*
The Strange Awakening · *Pomeroy, Elsie*
The Strange Boy · *Knudsen, Joyce*
Strange Cargo · *Hollingshead, Greg*
The Strange Case of Rev. Mr. Gow · *Maher, Paul*
Strange Comfort Afforded by the Profession · *Lowry, Malcolm*
A Strange Day · *Jeffries, Pat*
The Strange Death of Sam Fletcher · *Clare, John P.*
Strange Fruit · *Johnson, Carol*
Strange Honour · *Capelovitch, Ed*
Strange Music · *Cameron, Eric*
The Strange Tale of Alexander Priffle · *Smith, Rosamond*
A Strangeness of Habit, a Twist of Mind · *Carrier, Jean-Guy*
The Stranger · *Ringland, Mary*
Stranger and Pilgrim · *Bauer, Nancy*
Stranger in My House · *MacMillan, Gail*
A Stranger in Paradise · *Nemiroff, Michael*
Stranger in Taransay · *Mowat, Farley*
A Stranger in the House · *Eisenbichler, Konrad*
Stranger on Pistol Creek · *Roberts, Theodore Goodridge*
A Stranger to Remember · *Bruns, Ina*
The Stranger Who Made His Mark · *Ross, W.E. Dan*
The Strangers · *V[ernell], Mark*

Strangers on a Lonely Journey · *Powell, Dorothy M.*
Strangulation · *McWhirter, George*
the strap · *Heath, Terence*
Strategies · *Collins, David M.*
Straw Flowers · *Millet, Aynes*
The Straw Stack Room · *Mitchell, Sylvia Elizabeth Fisher*
the strawberries · *Heath, Terence*
Strawberries and Marshmallows · *O'Connell, David*
The Strawberry Field · *Mathews, Robin D.*
The Strawberry Man · *Barker, Bessie M.*
A Stray Cat at the Window · *Patterson, Anne*
The Stray Cats of District Saint-Louis · *Lawson, David*
Strays · *Friedman, Irena*
Streak Mosaic · *Scobie, Stephen*
The Stream · *Rutkis, S.*
The Street · *Green, H. Gordon*
Street Musician · *Lemm, Richard*
Street Plays in the Village of Black Houses · *Amprimoz, Alexandre*
Street Scenes · *Eikenberry, Gary*
The Street That Got Mislaid · *Waddington, Patrick*
Streetcar, Streetcar, Wait for Me · *Helwig, David*
Streetcars, School and Sunday Matinees · *MacRae, Allan*
The Streetcomber · *Janes, Percy*
The Strength of Ten · *Thomas, Peter*
The Stretcher Bearers · *Garner, Hugh*
Stretching a Point · *Duffin, Ken*
Strictly for the Birds · *Grantmyre, Barbara*
The Strictly Private Secretary · *McLaughlin, Lorrie*
Strike · *Balma, Donna*
Strike Sketch · *Bury, J. Colbrook*
The Strikem Flag · *Price, C.B.*
Strings · *Kinsella, W.P.*
the strip · *Heath, Terence*
The Stroke · *Horne, Lewis B.*
Stroke of Twelve · *Heckbert, Steve*
Strom's Father · *Esterholm, Jeff*
Strong Fences · *Sharp, Edith Lambert*
The Strong Man · *Briffett, Isabel*
The Strongbox · *Browne, Paul Cameron*
Stubble Burning · *Williams, David*
Stubborn As They Come · *Green, H. Gordon*
Stubborn Like His Pa · *Bird, Will R.*
The Stubborn Woman · *Taylor, Esther*
Stubborn's No Name · *Green, H. Gordon*
Stud · *Mason, Mike*
Student, Petty Thief, TV Star · *Bowering, George*
The Student · *Hancock, Ronald Lee*
the student and the lobster · *Bullock, Michael*
The Student Prince · *Moon, Bryan*
Studies of the Ilanga District · *Dobbs, Kildare R.E.*

Study · *Kellythorne, Walt*
A Study in Black and White · *Whitford, Margaret Ann*
A Study in Geometry · *Bancroft, Marjory*
Study in Self-Consciousness #2 · *Daly, Thomas*
Studying Causes Schizophrenia · *Lepage, Ramon*
Stuff and Nonsense · *Winans, A.D.*
The Stuff Dreams Are Made Of · *Clark, Joan*
Stuffed Horses · *Bowering, George*
Stumblebum · *Garner, Hugh*
The Stump · *Buyukmihci, Hope Sawyer*
Stumps · *Keeler, Judy*
Stupidity Has Come to the Plains · *Bell, Wade*
The Sturgeon · *Bell, Wade*
Styx · *Riches, Brenda*
Su Chen · *Findlay, David K.*
Subject: Centaur · *Gray, John*
Subject Sees Beyond Nullification · *Staniforth, Richard*
Sublet · *Engel, Marian*
The Submarine · *Govan, Margaret*
Submission: Of Plenary Sub-Committee 26 [Logistics] Report of the League ·
Szanto, George
The Substitute · *Rousanoff, Nicholas*
Substitute Groom · *Findlay, David K.*
Substitute Santa · *Spelius, Carol*
Subterranean Cognizance · *Jirgins, Karl E.*
The Subtle Touch · *Burles, Mary Jo*
Subway · *Smith, Steve*
The Subway Ride · *Vertolli, Lou*
Success Story · *Ravel, Aviva*
The Succession · *Israel, Charles E.*
The Successor · *Hekkanen, Ernest*
Successor to Laura · *Barnard, Leslie Gordon*
Such As It Is · *Hindmarch, Gladys*
Such Bright Ideas · *Barnard, Leslie Gordon*
Suckers · *Green, Robin*
Sucking In: A Fable · *Kitcher, W.H.C.*
The Sudbury Bush: A Gypsy George Story · *Stocks, Andy*
The Sudden Door · *Govan, Margaret*
Sudden Squalls · *Krause, Pat*
Suddenly, Last Leaf · *Elgaard, Elin*
Suddenly Last Spring · *Doyle, Nancy*
Suddenly Very Quiet · *Falconer, Roger*
Sue Solomon · *Sagaris, Lake*
Suffer Little Children · *Carroll, Elizabeth*
Suffer the Little Children · *Kawalilak, Ron A.*
Sufferin' Steelheads · *Power, John*
The Suffering · *Morris, Dorothy M.*
Sufficient unto the Day · *McLellan, Helen*
Sugarpops and Razorblades · *Crowell, Peter*
The Suicide · *Kuipers, Jelte*

The Suicide Inspector · *Steinfeld, J.J.*
A Suicide Note · *MacMillan, Ian*
The Suicide of Alexander Jakubovic · *Stein, David Lewis*
Suicide on Skis · *Findlay, David K.*
Suicide Seeds · *Amprimoz, Alexandre*
The Suicide Tower · *Bhatia, June*
The Suicide-Proof Leprechaun · *MacLaurin, Douglas*
Suitable Employment · *Marriott, J. Anne*
The Suitcase · *Giesbrecht, Vern*
The Suitcase Man · *DeWitt, Ed*
Suites and Single Rooms, with Bath · *Hood, Hugh*
Suits · *Kinsella, W.P.*
sumiko · *Bullock, Michael*
Summary · *Leitao, Lino*
Summer · *Sallows, Roy*
Summer: Vancouver · *Bowering, George*
The Summer Afternoon · *Cunningham, James*
A Summer Afternoon Boat Ride · *Oliver, Michael Brian*
A Summer Afternoon with the North End Buccaneers · *Kleiman, Edward*
Summer at Lonely Beach · *Waddington, Miriam*
The Summer Cabin · *Conger, Lesley*
The Summer Camp Incident · *Thibaudeau, Colleen*
Summer Course · *Anderson, Fred*
Summer Crossings · *Cohen, Matt*
Summer Dawn on Loon Lake · *Kenny, George*
A Summer Girl · *Simpson, Leo*
Summer Hunting Grounds · *Nichols, Jane*
Summer in Cleveland · *Martinich, Aloysius*
Summer Journey · *Crabtree, Peter*
Summer Loves · *Mezei, Stephen*
Summer Mournings, 1959 · *Harvor, Beth*
The Summer My Grandmother Was Supposed to Die · *Richler, Mordecai*
The Summer My Mother Died · *Moore, Thomas*
Summer Night · *Rutty, Lorimer*
Summer of '42 Retold · *Popkin-Clurman, Esther*
Summer of Monsters · *Hammell, Steven Dale*
Summer Play · *Carlton, Edna P.*
Summer Scene · *Schoemperlen, Diane*
Summer School · *Stein, Rhoda Elizabeth Playfair*
Summer Soldiers · *Ritter, Erika*
Summer Stock · *Buckler, Ernest*
Summer Storm · *McKim, Audrey*
Summer Tempest · *Moller, Margaret*
The Summer the Wind Fell · *La Haye, Marguerite*
A Summer to Sing - A Summer to Cry · *Horne, Lewis B.*
Summer Vacation · *Chryssoulakis, Mary*
The Summer Visitor · *Story, Gertrude*
Summercamp · *Moore, Peter*
The Summerhouse · *Peterson, Phyllis Lee*
A Summer's Ending · *McRae, Garfield*

Suppose Your Mother · *FitzSimmons, Edward Peter*
Supreme · *Etheridge, David*
A Sure Footed Dream · *Bond, Eric Gary*
Sure Things Are for the Birds · *Morrow, Mark*
Sure Wish Somehow · *Katz, Barry*
Surfaces or Remembering · *Rikki [Erica Ducornet]*
Surprise! · *Weinzweig, Helen*
The Surprise · *Kutlesa, Joso*
A Surprise for Babe · *Annett, R. Ross*
Surprise for Maria · *Harvey, Jennifer A. Becks*
The Surprise Party · *Steinfeld, J.J.*
Surrender · *Bruce, Charles T.*
Survival · *Butts, Ed P.*
Survival of the Fittest · *Dybvig, Leslie*
The Survivor · *Kent, Duncan*
Survivors · *Flannigan, Rod*
Susan · *Berger, Joanne*
Susanna, Susanna! · *Coney, Michael G.*
Susie Baby! · *Fitzpatrick, Helen*
Susie Q² · *Green, Terence M.*
Suspense · *Bruce, Charles T.*
The Suspicious Stranger · *Annett, R. Ross*
Suzie Baby · *Fitzpatrick, Helen*
Sveinborg Sigfsdttir: Grasses · *Gunnars, Kristjana*
A Swallow Bellies Turn · *Gordon, John*
The Swami · *Ogle, Robert Joseph*
The Swamp · *Davis, Pat*
The Swamp Pool · *Jelinek, Vera*
Swamp Wise · *Hembrow, J.A.*
The Swan · *Peterson, Barry*
Swan Song · *Marshall, Christina*
Swan Song for Sir Craigie · *Green, H. Gordon*
The Sweater · *Maag, Trudy*
Swede · *Lemm, Richard*
The Swedes Who Never Went Back · *Bergren, Myrtle*
The Sweep · *Haig-Brown, Roderick*
Sweet Babby · *Branden, Vicki*
Sweet Comic Valentine · *Linder, Norma West*
Sweet Grass · *Kerslake, Susan*
Sweet Hell · *Kuschinski, Charles*
Sweet Potatoes · *Lee, Arthur*
Sweet Scent of Spring · *Branden, Vicki*
The Sweet Smell of Flowers · *Ford, Cathy*
The Sweet Taste of Revenge · *Morritt, Hope*
Sweet Trick · *McHardy, Vincent*
The Sweetness of Life · *Fraser, D.M.*
A Sweet-Smelling Savour · *Bushell, Sidney*
The Swell Party · *O'Connell, Dorothy*
The Swept Place · *Alford, Norman*
Swiles · *Russell, Ted*

The Swim · *Brown, Julia*
The Swimmer · *Grant, William J.*
Swimming · *Hodgins, Norris*
Swimming Out, Swimming Back · *Helwig, David*
the swimming trunks · *Heath, Terence*
Swim-Suits · *Hodgins, Norris*
Swing Session · *Krause, Pat*
Swingbox · *Young, David*
Swinging Doors · *Lee, Thirza M.*
The Swinging Headhunter · *Evanier, David*
The Swiss Bell Ringers · *Sears, Dennis T. Patrick*
Switcheroo · *Sturdy, John Rhodes*
The Sword · *Hosein, Clyde*
Sybille at Twenty · *Read, Ranee R.*
Sylvan Hart · *Hyatt, Paul*
Symbols in Agony, a Canadian Short Story · *Smith, Ray*
symmetry · *Bullock, Michael*
Symphonies That Sing · *Scupham, Peter*
The Synns · *Rushton, Alfred*
Synopados · *Deacove, James*
Synopsis of an Irishman's Love Affair · *Green, H. Gordon*
Systems · *Thompson, Kent*
Syzygy · *Kinsella, W.P.*

T.V. · *Russell, Ted*
The Tabasco Caper · *Coulbeck, Art G.*
Tableau · *Radu, Kenneth*
The Tables Turned · *Bjarnason, Bogi*
Tabula Rasa · *Young, David*
A Tactical Exigency · *Lee, Ron*
The Tagger · *Browne, Linda*
Tags · *Russo, Leonard*
the tail · *Heath, Terence*
Tail of the Female · *Clark, Joan*
Tailfeather · *Hall, Christopher W.*
Tainted Data · *Kilodney, Crad*
Take Care of Linda · *French, Doris*
Take Me Home Again, Irene · *Sloman, Fred*
Take Me Out to Dinner · *Sturdy, John Rhodes*
Take Two Aspirins ... · *Gale, Kay*
Takeover Bid · *Weiner, Andrew*
Taking a Chance · *Madden, Peter*
Taking Auntie Out of Her Own Filth · *Somerville, Jane*
Taking Cover · *Fraser, Keath*
Taking Hamish by Surprise · *MacKinnon, Lilian Vaux*
Taking Her Shot · *Mouré, Erin*
Taking It from the Top · *Bremner, Lary*
The Taking of Lake Shutney · *Hekkanen, Ernest*
A Tale from Life on the Danforth · *Cooper, Audrey*

Tale of a Kinsman · *Lamb, Murray*
A Tale of a Male's Friend · *Williams, Wayne*
Tale of a Modern Xmas, Neither Sentimentality nor Festive Tradition · *Creighton, Dave*
Tale of a Mouse · *Burville, Victor*
A Tale of Tangle Who Has Many Names · *de Lint, Charles*
The Tale of the Illicit Ape · *Kome, Penney*
The Tale of the Lion · *Starr, M.*
The Tale of the Ratcatcher's Daughter · *Guppy, Steve*
The Tale of the Upright Man · *Wilson, Don*
A Tale of Two Chalahs · *Shifrin, Len*
A Tale Which Holdeth Children from Play · *Bowering, George*
A Tale with No Women · *Bronson, A.A.*
A Tale without a Donkey · *Narvey, Fred*
Talent · *Grills, Barry W.*
The Talents · *Carlton, Edna P.*
Tales from a · *Pensione · Creal, Margaret*
Tales from the Quarter · *Garber, Lawrence*
Talk · *Selvon, Samuel*
Talk of Life · *Lockhart, Laurie*
Talk Show · *Thomas, W.K.*
Talking Back · *Truss, Jan*
The Talking Hearing Aid · *Argondezzi, Vincent*
Talking Tongues: Lovespeak · *Steel, Lisa*
Talking Vagabond Blues · *Borkowski, Maria*
The Talks · *Bratton, Mark*
Tall Cowboys and True · *Scott, Gail*
The Tall Grass · *Dyba, Kenneth*
Taller Than His Tall Self · *Doyle, Nancy*
The Tallest Jewish Basketball Player in the World · *Hedley, Leslie*
The Tallest Tree · *Ross, W.E. Dan*
The Tall-Tale Cook · *Smyth, W. Ross*
Tallyho Toronto · *Rutt, Edwin*
Tamar Ferouin Amongst the Savages · *Frey, Cecelia*
The Tamarack Tree · *Fines, Beatrice E.*
The Taming of Mrs. O'Leary · *Sample, Maureen*
Tammie's Shoe Box · *Gillen, Beth*
Tangiers February · *Phillips, Neal*
A Tangle of Voices · *Itani, Frances*
Tangled Web · *Hargreaves, H.A.*
The Tangles of Neaera's Hair · *Gustafson, Ralph B.*
A Tantrum Is a Tantrum Is a Tantrum · *Person, Lloyd*
The Tape Recorder · *McDonald, Ruth*
Taped · *Engel, Marian*
Tapestry · *Boyko, Elvina*
A Tapestry of Dreams · *Elflandsson, Galad*
Tar Paper Walls · *Young, Geraldine*
Target 2124 · *Gray, Charles*
The Tartaned Hootlet · *Wood, Kerry*
A Taste for Perfection · *Vanderhaeghe, Guy*

The Taste of Ice Cream · *Brown, Horace*
The Taste of the Earth · *Mitton, M. Anne*
The Taste of Wool · *Rubia, Geraldine*
The Taste of Wyoming Sadness · *Bonneville, Francois A.*
The Tattered Lapel · *Bjarnason, Bogi*
Tattoo · *Truhlar, Richard*
The Tattooed Woman · *Engel, Marian*
Tauf Aleph · *Gotlieb, Phyllis*
Taviella · *Zend, Robert*
Tavlu on Aragats · *Shirinian, Lorne*
The Taxi · *Grant, Lois*
Taxi Drivers Don't Cry · *Potrebenko, Helen*
TBDF: Transborder Data Flow · *Sherman, Tom*
The Tea · *Mitton, M. Anne*
The Tea Leaves of Madame Angelica · *Steinfeld, J.J.*
Tea or Coffee, with or without Sugar, and Perhaps a Bit of Lemon · *Williams, Wayne*
Tea Party · *Mounie, Ruth*
Tea with Katherine Mansfield's Sister · *Harvor, Beth*
Tea with Miss Mayberry · *Garner, Hugh*
Tea with Relations · *Garvie, Peter*
The Teacher · *Lynch, John*
The Teacher Wasn't Pretty · *Branden, Vicki*
Teachers · *MacNeil, Mike*
Teachings · *van der Heuvel, M.F.*
the team · *Heath, Terence*
Team Play · *Gilliam, John*
Team Town · *Daurio, Beverley*
Tear Here · *Thomas, Audrey*
Tearin' Her Down · *Percy, H.R.*
Tea-Room · *Brodsky, Myrtle*
Tears for Father's Day · *Green, H. Gordon*
Tears for Peace · *Edwards, Hope*
Tears in the Afternoon · *Hunt, Edward*
The Tears of Things · *Forbes, Joyce T.*
Tea-Time · *Geauch, Agnes*
Techniques of Living · *Davies, Joanne H.*
Ted of All People's · *Chappell, Constance*
Ted Slaumwhite's Garden · *Heide, Christopher*
Teddy · *Thomas, Keith*
Teddy Bear and the Pregnant Parallel · *Nimchuk, Michael John*
Ted's Wife · *Thomas, Audrey*
Tee Vee Man · *Hargreaves, H.A.*
Teen-Age Sixty · *Bryant, Cullene*
Teepee · *Zieroth, Dale*
Teeth · *O'Connell, Dorothy*
The Teeth of My Father · *Metcalf, John*
The Telegram · *Browne, Colin*
Teleological - With Chicken Meat · *Kilodney, Crad*
A Telephone Booth · *Kenny, Wade*

The Telephone Call · *Harris, Bob*
Telephones · *Avery, Martin*
Television · *Cohn, Judith*
A Television Drama · *Rule, Jane*
The Television Watcher · *Szanto, George*
A Television-Watching Artist · *Steinfeld, J.J.*
Tell It to J. Edgar Hoover · *Purdy, Brian*
Tell Me, Would You Get Married Again? · *Cameron, Donald*
Tell Me · *Lever, Bernice*
Tell Me the Jokes I Know · *Pemberton, Prim*
Tell Me What You See · *Kennedy, Daniel*
Tell Me Yes or No · *Munro, Alice*
The Temper · *McCormack, Eric*
Temple and Car · *Anonymous*
The Temple of the Unicorn · *Brandis, Marianne*
The Temple of Their Gods · *Bell, John Leslie*
The Temple Visitor · *Rushton, Alfred*
Temporarily Yours · *Sands, E.*
A Temporary Arrangement · *Gould, Jan*
A Temporary Obsession · *Daurio, Beverley*
Le Temps des Citrouilles: A Story for Michael · *Jackson, J. Graham*
The Temptation of Ian · *Green, H. Gordon*
The Temptation of Leafy · *Smyth, Donna E.*
Tempted, Tried, and True · *Baker, Cynthia*
Ten Sketches · *Itter, Carole*
The Tenant · *Eng, Rose*
Tender Island · *Mitchell, Jeanine*
The Tender Leaf · *Deneau, Denis Phillippe*
The Tender Moment in Life · *Kutlesa, Joso*
The Tender View · *Fines, Beatrice E.*
The Ten-Inch Feet · *Theriault, Yves*
The Tennis Court Oath · *Fawcett, Brian*
Tent by the Sea · *Bartlett, Brian*
The Tent Peg · *Webb, F.W.*
Tenth Medal · *Russell, Nancy Ellen*
Tents for the Gaudy-Dancers · *Engel, Marian*
The Ten-Year Gap · *Russell, Sheila MacKay*
The Tepee · *O'Hagan, Howard*
Terminal Case · *Bruneau, Bernard*
A Terminal Report · *Harding, John*
Terminus: A New Beginning · *Jackson, J. Graham*
Terminus Victoria · *Watmough, David*
A Terrible Discontent · *Callaghan, Barry*
The Terrible Fate of Joshua Sibbs · *Drew, Wayland*
The Terrible Secret of M. Laroche · *Cunningham, Louis Arthur*
The Terrible Temper of Kathy O'Mara · *Mayse, Arthur*
A Terrible Tragedy · *W.S.*
The Terrible Trap · *McNamara, Eugene*
Territory · *Clark, Joan*

Terror · *Gillies, Glorya*
Terror by Night · *Bruneau, Bernard*
The Tertiary Justification · *Coney, Michael G.*
The Test · *Kent-Barber, Rosemary*
Test Patterns 1-3 · *Doyle, Judith*
Testament Found in a Bureau Drawer · *Atwood, Margaret*
Testimony · *Barclay, Byrna*
Testing Ground · *McKay, Muriel Saint*
Testing Time for Tiny Tim · *Bird, Will R.*
A Text · *Amprimoz, Alexandre*
Text of a Lecture On: · *Sappol, Michael*
Thaddeus · *O'Rourke, David*
'Thank God for Wicka!' · *MacDonald, Andy*
Thank You, God · *Bushell, Sidney*
Thank You for the Lovely Tea · *Gallant, Mavis*
Thanks for Everything - Mother · *Blythe, Aleata E.*
Thanks for the Ride · *Munro, Alice*
Thanks Pal · *MacKinnon, Bernard*
Thanks to Goa Bus System! · *Leitao, Lino*
Thanksgiving · *Ross, Veronica*
Thanksgiving: Between Junetown and Caintown · *Hood, Hugh*
Thanksgiving Dinner · *Layton, Boschka*
Thanksgiving Monday: 1960 · *Julian, Marilyn*
Thanksgiving Surprise · *Green, H. Gordon*
That Boy! That Boy! · *Green, H. Gordon*
That Certain Moment · *Ross, W.E. Dan*
That Day in Spring · *Gillese, John Patrick*
That Day in the Bush · *Pacey, Desmond*
That First Million · *Morris, Doris M.*
That Good Night · *Powning, Beth*
That Great Canadian Novel · *McCluskey, John*
That Kind · *Currie, Robert*
That Lazy Neighbour Family! · *Redmond, Mary*
That Night and the Storm · *Derksen, Jim*
That Old David Copperfield Kind of Crap · *Newman, C.J.*
That Pagan Charm · *Peterson, Phyllis Lee*
That Romantic Cake · *Lee, Thirza M.*
That Second Cup of Coffee · *Wood, Ted*
That Sensual Music · *Maynard, Fredelle Bruser*
That Sort of Day · *Armstrong, Patricia*
That Special Day · *Rosenfeld, Rita*
That Summer · *Ross, Veronica*
That Summer in Auxerre · *Brewer, Jackie*
That Was a Good Year · *Clark, D.M.*
That Which Was Lost · *Green, H. Gordon*
That Year My Father Died · *Kreiner, Philip*
That Yellow Prairie Sky · *Kroetsch, Robert*
That's Entertainment! · *Goede, William*
The Thaw · *Campbell, Wanda Blynn*
The Theatre Door · *Snowden, Robert*

The Theft · *Schroeder, Andreas*
Their Last Supper · *Walker, Doris*
Theme for Diverse Instruments · *Rule, Jane*
Theme for Mother's Day · *Coulbeck, Art G.*
Then But the Always Now · *Templeton, Bill*
Then Came the Night · *Misfeldt, James*
Then There Was This Character Mona Something or Other · *McLachlin, Stella*
Then There Were None · *Evans, Allen Roy*
Theodor's Wife · *Blakeston, Oswell*
the theologue · *Heath, Terence*
Theory of Forms · *Matyas, Cathy*
Theory of the Novel · *Kelley, Paul*
'There Ain't Nobody Loves Me' · *Mosher, Edith*
There Are Damons at the Bottom of My Garden ... or, The Pythias Legend Revisited · *Howard, Richard*
There Are No Clocks in Eden · *Bonellie, Janet*
There Are No Single Causes · *Craig, Jean Carol*
There Are Places · *Stange, Ken*
There Has Never Been a Deluge · *Bauer, Walter*
There in Spirit · *Harvey, Jennifer A. Becks*
There Is a Sweetness in Decay · *Engel, Marian*
There Is a Time for Everything · *Cameron, Margaret*
There Is No Shoreline · *Birdsell, Sandra*
There Might Be Angels · *Glover, Douglas H.*
There Must Be Others ... · *Barnes, Lilly*
There Once Was This Nice Policeman · *Thompson, B.*
There Stands a Lady · *Poy, Adrienne*
There Was a Crooked Man · *Biel, Kent C.*
There Was an Old Man · *Lima, Paul*
There Was an Old Woman from Wexford · *Nowlan, Alden*
There Was Toronto · *Thomas, Randy*
There'll Never Be Another You · *Simpson, Valerie*
There's a Lot in a Name · *Murdoch, Benedict Joseph*
There's a Muddy Road · *Wiebe, Rudy H.*
There's Always a Christmas · *Lee, Thirza M.*
There's Always Room for Two More · *Johnston, Stella*
There's Been a Death · *Beghtol, Claire*
There's No Free Lunch · *Anonymous*
There's This Girl · *Clare, John P.*
Thermopylae · *Wyse, A. David*
These Are My Neighbours · *Hemingway, Grace Elton*
These Are the Bonnie Babes of the Bank of Lower Canada · *Sheldon, Michael*
These Men See · *Gardner, W.W.*
These Ways Work · *Stange, Ken*
Thessalon · *Grieveson, Brian*
They Come Here to Die · *Fraser, Raymond*
They Do Not Discriminate · *Clarke, John J.*
They Don't Even Know My Name · *Oliver, Michael Brian*
They Heard a Ringing of Bells · *Clarke, Austin C.*
They Introduced Me to My Homunculus · *Sherman, Tom*

They Just Won't Believe · *Wiebe, Rudy H.*
They Know What They're Doing · *Hindmarch, Gladys*
They Met the Test · *Chappell, Constance*
They Never Tell Anyone · *Conger, Lesley*
They Said He Was Simple · *McFarlane, Lucy*
They Sewed My Mother to Her Bed · *Swann, Anahid*
They Shall Mount Up with Wings · *Stein, Rhoda Elizabeth Playfair*
They Went Berrypicking · *Arnason, David*
They Were All Very Nice About It · *Crowe, Donald*
They Were Her Men · *Blythe, Aleata E.*
they who stood on guard · *Hawkins, William*
They're Asking for You, Bettina · *Hoffer, Sorryl*
Thibidault et Fils · *Blaise, Clark L.*
Thibideau · *McGoogan, Kenneth*
Thick and Thin · *Harvey, Jennifer A. Becks*
Thief, God, Thief · *Butts, Ed P.*
The Thief · *Friend, David*
A Thief in the House · *Green, H. Gordon*
The Thief - Fables III · *Govier, Katharine*
Thieras · *Kernaghan, Eileen*
Thieves · *Steffler, George*
Thighbones · *Engel, Howard*
The Thin Edge · *Stone, Patricia*
Thin Hands · *Carrier, Jean-Guy*
Thin Ice · *Levine, Norman*
The Thin Red Line · *Nowlan, Alden*
The Thing About Jenny · *Baltensperger, Peter*
A Thing of Beauty · *Baker, Rita*
A Thing They Wear · *Metcalf, John*
The Things I Did Last Summer · *Shulman, Martin*
Things Not Occurring Rapidly · *Austin, Don*
Things That Don't Happen · *Sarah, Robyn*
Things That Happened Before You Were Born · *Helwig, David*
Things to Say · *Biley, Bill*
Things Were Simpler Then - Or Were They? · *Maclean, Peter*
Things You Couldn't Tell · *Noonan, Gerald*
The Things You Do · *Collier, Diana G.*
The Things You Understand · *Pemberton, Prim*
Think of a Number · *Anderson, Rod*
Think of This When You Smoke Tobacco · *Porter, Ian*
The Thinker · *Longstaff, Bill*
Thinkin' in Circles · *Russell, Ted*
Thinking About One of His Stories · *Amprimoz, Alexandre*
The Third Bullet · *Sturdy, John Rhodes*
The Third Floor · *Rooke, Leon*
Third Floor Back · *Pemberton, Prim*
Third Grade Smart · *Rodger, Oxford*
The Third Grotesque · *Davidson, Craig*
The Third Nugget · *Murdoch, Benedict Joseph*
[The?] Third Party · *Conger, Lesley*

The Third Poinsettia · *Wyatt, Rachel*
The Third Safari · *Briffett, Isabel*
The Third Test · *Weiner, Andrew*
Third Time Under · *Dalton, Sheila*
Third Wind · *Berryman, J.*
The Third Wish · *Armstrong, Patricia*
Thirteen O'Clock · *Kadey, Carroll*
Thirteen Other Ways of Looking at a Blackbird · *Hogan, Robert*
Thirteen Steps · *Haskins, David*
The Thirteenth Juror · *Doyle, Nancy*
Thirty White Horses · *Garber, Daniel*
Thirty Years On · *MacKinnon, Lilian Vaux*
This Above All · *Story, Gertrude*
This Actually Happened to a Friend of Mine · *McLaughlin, Peter*
This Beautiful Star · *MacLean, Kenneth*
This Black Woman Sure Has Problems Like Hell · *Clarke, Austin C.*
This Boy in His Narrow Bed · *Sherrin, Robert G.*
This Bureaucrat Loves the Limbo · *Godfrey, Dave*
This Fell Sergeant · *Cottrell, Terence Lloyd*
This House · *Rosta, Helen J.*
This I Will Keep · *Green, H. Gordon*
This Is Blue · *Harper, Mandy*
This Is It · *Babstock, George*
This Is My Country · *MacCrimmon, Harriett M.*
This Is Our Willie · *Nowlan, Michael O.*
This Is the Day · *Stein, Rhoda Elizabeth Playfair*
This Is the Grim Season · *Galt, George*
This Is What the Sign Says: The Garbageman Is Drunk · *Acorn, Milton*
This Is What You Were Born For · *Fraser, Keath*
This Job's Been Good to Me · *Hindmarch, Gladys*
This Little Child of Mine · *Smith, Robert F.*
This Man Called Joe · *Gillese, John Patrick*
This Music to Love · *Schoemperlen, Diane*
This My Son · *Barnard, Leslie Gordon*
This Parliament of Fears ... · *Smith, James W.*
This Space · *Gallant, Mavis*
This Story Ends in a Pinegrove · *Bauer, William A.*
This Transparent Static · *Casey, Billy Lee*
This Way to the Egress · *O'Connell, Dorothy*
This World We Live: Introduction · *Russo, Leonard*
This Year at the Arabian Nights Hotel · *Richler, Mordecai*
Tho' Me and My True Love · *Gillese, John Patrick*
Thor Thorsen's Book of Days · *Horne, Lewis B.*
Thorn in the Flesh · *Cameron, Eric*
Those Blue Hills · *Misfeldt, James*
Those Bufords · *Spencer, Elizabeth*
Those Days Around the Tree-Town Corner Now · *Rooke, Leon*
Those Fabulous Barclay Sisters · *Hodgins, Jack*
Those Good Old Days of Liquid Fuel · *Coney, Michael G.*
Those New Ideas · *Russell, Ted*

Threshing Time · *Summers, Merna*
The Threshold · *Fletcher, Peggy*
Thrice · *Solly, Bill*
Through a Chestnut Clearly · *McHardy, Vincent*
Through a Dark Wood · *Garrow, Barb*
Through a Glass Darkly · *Stanley-Porter, David*
Through an Open Window · *An Eavesdropper* [pseudonym]
Through Dreaming Towns · *Horwood, Harold*
Through No Other Door · *Rodriguez, Juan*
Through Pools of Light · *Fielder, Martyn*
Through the Arch · *Wuorio, Eva-Lis*
Through the Eyes of a Cat · *Virgo, Sean*
Through the Gates of Gethsemane · *Bruederlin, Barbara*
Through the Iron Gate · *Erian, Soraja*
Through the Panama · *Lowry, Malcolm*
through the trees to the river · *Bullock, Michael*
The Throwback · *Walters, Harold Neal*
The Thumb · *Melfi, Mary*
Thunder in Autumn · *Humphries, David*
Thunderbirds · *Findlay, David K.*

Thursday Afternoon · *Newton, Marion*
Thursday Evening · *Bell, Michael*
Thursday Morning Mothers · *Schoutsen, John*
Thy Will Be Done · *Carson, Susan*
Tibs Baits Mr. Sibinoff · *Peters, Mac*
Tibs' First Communion · *Peters, Mac*
Tichara, a ndi to Ziba! · *Hurly, Paul*
Ticket to Ride · *Anonymous*
A Ticket to the Symphony · *Thom, Marion*
Tickets · *McGrath, Patrick*
Tickets for Mother's Day · *Barker, Bessie M.*
Tickets for Two · *Williamson, Rossa*
Tidals · *Elgaard, Elin*
The Tide Line · *Metcalf, John*
Tidewater Morning · *Bruce, Charles T.*
A Tie Game · *Rae, Angela*
The Tie That Binds · *Brooks, Eunice*
Ties · *Ross, Veronica*
Tiger! Tiger! · *Woodward, Gordon*
the tiger · *Bullock, Michael*
Tiger and Me · *Heatley, Marney*
The Tiger and the Zebra · *Bourbonnais, Normand*
tiger in the park · *Bullock, Michael*
The Tiger Lily · *Paolielo, Carlo*
Tiger of Timbala · *Walker, David*
Tiger Under the Palm Tree · *Peters, Cliff*
The Tiger Was a Cat · *Briffett, Isabel*
Tigermen with Spears · *Ross, Stuart*
Tiger's Tale · *Henry, Brian*
the tigress · *Bullock, Michael*

The Tiles · *Kelsey, Sheila*
'Til He Takes a Wife · *Gane, Margaret Drury*
Till Death · *MacSween, R.J.*
Till Death ... · *Durvis, J.S.*
Till Death Do Us Part · *Green, Terence M.*
Till Death Us Do Part · *Wilson, Ethel D.*
Till Human Voices Wake Us · *Nelson, Joanne L.*
Till She Find It · *Bushell, Sidney*
Till the Right One Comes Along · *Green, H. Gordon*
Tillicum Baby · *Price, C.B.*
The Tilsley Thunderbolt · *Beal, Bill*
Tilt · *Gasparini, Len*
Tim Garnet's Legacy · *Briffett, Isabel*
Timber Wolf · *Price, C.B.*
Timbuktu · *Thomas, Audrey*
A Time & a Place · *Phillips, Linda*
A Time and a Place · *Watson, Barry*
Time and Again · *Bowering, George*
Time and Tennis · *Frank, Bernhard*
Time and the Tide · *Cadogan, Elda*
Time and Tide · *Green, H. Gordon*
Time and Time Again · *Shulman, Guy*
The Time Dilator · *Penney, Lloyd*
Time Enough Tomorrow · *Clare, John P.*
Time for a Smoke · *Kitcher, W.H.C.*
A Time for Decision · *Lee, Carroll H.*
A Time for Sharing · *McFarlane, Beverley*
Time for Thinking · *Blythe, Aleata E.*
The Time I Gave Jane the Diary · *Lewis, David E.*
Time in London · *Eglitis, Joseph*
The Time Is Green · *Rodman, Hyman*
Time Is No Boundary · *Hill, D.R.*
Time Is Not Soon Enough · *F., Katharine*
Time Lost · *Moore, Peter*
Time Meant That · *Parker, Rick*
A Time of Asking · *Stein, Rhoda Elizabeth Playfair*
The Time of Death · *Munro, Alice*
The Time of Death · *Munro, Alice*
The Time of Earth · *Murdie, Donna Haggarty*
The Time of Hummingbirds · *Wood, Ted*
A Time of New Beginning · *Story, Gertrude*
A Time of Testing · *Russell, Sheila MacKay*
The Time of the Singing of Birds · *Stein, Rhoda Elizabeth Playfair*
The Time of the Spring Sun · *MacDonald, Bill*
The Time of the Wind · *Watmough, David*
A Time of Waiting · *Laurence, Margaret*
Time Off · *Spence, Ian A.*
Time Rules · *Eikenberry, Gary*
The Time Skipper Joe Knocked Off Swearing · *Butt, Grace*
A Time to Be Born · *Slater, Keith*

Time to Go · *Ahmad, Iqbal*
Time to Live · *Hawryluk, Paul*
A Time to Lose · *Misfeldt, James*
A Time to Remember · *Green, H. Gordon*
A Time to Remember · *Ryan, Maxwell*
A Time to Sow · *Mitchell, Ken*
Time to Talk · *Barnard, Leslie Gordon*
Time Waits for No One · *Phillips, Linda*
The Timeless Island · *Percy, H.R.*
Timothy · *Sivertson, L. Margaret*
Tin Ear · *Robinson, Spider*
Tinker Tale · *Virgo, Sean*
Tinsel · *Percy, H.R.*
The Tinsel Gift · *Phillips, Bluebell Stewart*
Tiny Battles · *Budra, Paul*
the tiny people · *Bullock, Michael*
The Tip · *Harvey, Jennifer A. Becks*
The Tired Heart · *Ross, W.E. Dan*
'Tis the Season to Be Jolly · *Moyer, Carolyn*
To Be a God · *Belinski, P.X.*
To Be Dead · *Bowering, George*
To Be Here · *Hindmarch, Gladys*
To Blisland · *Levine, Norman*
To Burn · *McNamara, Eugene*
To Chase a Cowboy Hat · *Harvey, Jennifer A. Becks*
To Choose to Dance · *Story, Gertrude*
To Cross the Bay · *Browne, Paul Cameron*
To Do and to Endure · *Story, Gertrude*
To Each Her Own · *Reinhardt, Jean*
To Each His Own Saviour · *Singer, Barnett*
To Every Thing There Is a Season · *MacLeod, Alistair*
To Everything There Is a Season · *Pickard, Joan*
To Feed the Soul · *Williams, Catherine R.*
To Grow into a Man · *Brandis, Maxine*
To Hell with This Cockeyed World · *Christy, Jim*
To Keep the Memory of So Worthy a Friend · *Wilson, Ethel D.*
To Kill a Ghost · *Scott, Margerie*
To Kill an Angel · *Bankier, William*
To Meet the Family · *Green, H. Gordon*
To My Daughter in Love · *Green, H. Gordon*
To One He Gave Ten · *Stein, Rhoda Elizabeth Playfair*
To Pass Through Honey · *Rosenfeld, Rita*
To Raise a Child · *Drew, Wayland*
To Run a Big Boat · *Little, C.H.*
To Set Our House in Order · *Laurence, Margaret*
To Stand on the Brink · *Theriault, Yves*
To Tell the Truth · *Taylor, James A.*
To the Bay · *Conway, Jim*
To the Castle · *Marriott, J. Anne*
To the Colour Green · *Francisci, L.*

To the Drug Store for Evale · *Doyle, Nancy*
To the Gods Below · *Hughes, Ora Wayne*
To the Stars · *Green, H. Gordon*
to the top of the tower · *Bullock, Michael*
To the Uncharted Land · *Alford, Norman*
To the Warden, So You'll Know · *MacIntyre, Rod*
To the Watchers While Walking Home · *Spencer, Elizabeth*
To Whom It May Concern · *Schoemperlen, Diane*
To Write · *Newman, P.N.*
Toba Inlet · *Bolen, Dennis E.*
The Tobacco Jar · *Osser, Harry*
Toffee Apples · *Birch-Jones, Sonia*
Toffee Apples · *Birch-Jones, Sonia*
Together Again · *McCarthy, Anne*
The Tolstoy Pitch · *Hood, Hugh*
The Tom · *Hanley, Kathleen*
Tom Swift and His Giant Spoofnik or Saved by My Pink Underwear · *Cinquant, Peter*
Tom Tom's Sh-Sh-Shady Bend's Ol' Geezer Easter Special · *Young, David*
Tom-All-Alone · *Lenoir-Arcand, Christine*
Tómas Jónasson: Jazz · *Gunnars, Kristjana*
the tomb · *Bullock, Michael*
A Tombstone or a Monument · *Bow, Jane*
Tommy, Are You with Us? · *Lamont, Margo*
Tommy Arrives · *Harrison, D.B.*
Tommy Douglas Avenue · *Hill, Gerald*
Tomohrik · *Wansley, David*
Tomorrow I'll Be TEN · *Frankel, Vera*
Tomorrow I'll Be Twenty-Eight and Old · *Birch-Jones, Sonia*
Tomorrow Will Be the Same · *Rensby, Harry*
The Tomorrow-Tamer · *Laurence, Margaret*
Tom's A-Cold · *Peter, John D.*
the tongue · *Heath, Terence*
The Tongue That Never Told a Lie · *Pollett, Ron*
Tonsilitis · *Mason, Mike*
Tony B. in the Black Cat · *Plourde, Marc*
Tony Chestnut Talking · *Decker, Ken*
Too Bad Galahad · *Cohen, Matt*
Too Bad He Went Crazy · *Plantos, Ted*
Too Big for Santa Claus · *Montour, Enos T.*
Too Early to Rise · *Orr, Edward*
Too Late to Liberate · *Layer, Ethel*
Too Late Tomorrow · *Stein, Rhoda Elizabeth Playfair*
Too Ledders from Joe · *Tupper, Hibbert T.*
Too Little! Too Late! · *Aitken, W.E.*
Too Long, Too Long, No Dance · *Story, Gertrude*
Too Long at the Fair · *Ritter, Erika*
Too Many Parts · *Engel, Marian*
Too Much Dough · *Anonymous*
Too Much Fun for Nothing · *Green, H. Gordon*

Too Much Nothing · *Fraser, D.M.*
The Too Old Man · *Jarvis, Allen*
Too Old to Quit · *Christy, Jim*
Too Soon We Grow Old · *Robinson, Spider*
Too Sweet Sorrow · *Cohen, Matt*
Too Sweet to Speak · *Green, H. Gordon*
Too Young · *Burke, James*
The Toothpick · *Oughton, John*
The Top of the Pine Tree · *Legate, John*
Torments of the Neoflight Trauma Critic · *Herbert, John*
Toro! · *Gordon, Joanna*
Toronto: Just Another City? Or Read the Signs · *Surtees, Lawrence*
Toronto Evening · *Fisher, Michael J.*
The Toronto Girls · *Thibaudeau, Colleen*
Toronto Tragedy · *Cowan, Judith*
Toronto/the War · *Donnell, David*
Torrance · *Davis, Sheila*
Tortillas for Lunch · *Corps, Doreen*
Totem · *McCarthy, Dermot*
A Touch of ... Larceny · *Anonymous*
The Touch of a Bird's Wing · *MacSween, R.J.*
Touch of a Vanished Hand · *Choyce, Lesley*
A Touch of Gentle Sorrow · *Fletcher, Peggy*
A Touch of Horse Flesh · *Elliott, Alan*
A Touch of Magic · *Harvey, Jennifer A. Becks*
A Touching of Lives · *Russell, Sheila MacKay*
Tough Boy · *Green, H. Gordon*
The Toughest Mile · *Kroetsch, Robert*
The Tour Lady · *Vintcent, Brian*
The Tour-Guide Instructor · *Newman, C.J.*
The Tourists · *Kevin, George*
Tournament · *Bain, Dena*
A Tournament with Truth · *La Haye, Marguerite*
Toutens · *Russell, Ted*
The Tower · *Fortier, Mark*
Tower of Power · *Kent, Winona*
Tower People · *Kay, Steve*
The Towers · *Bowering, George*
Town and Country · *Smith, Michael*
The Town That Cares · *Stein, Rhoda Elizabeth Playfair*
The Town Where I Was Born · *Sturdy, John Rhodes*
The Town Where Mary Lived · *Barnard, Leslie Gordon*
A Town without a Graveyard · *Creal, Margaret*
Toy Boat · *Martinich, Aloysius*
A Toy Called Peter Dog · *Metcalf, John*
The Toy Piano · *O'Reilly, Patrick*
The Toy Pilgrim · *Cohen, Matt*
The Toy That Had to Be Returned · *Lemond, Edward*
Toys · *Gill, Stephen*
Traces · *Sarah, Robyn*

Track Star · *Kenny, George*
The Tractor and the Holiday · *Lukiv, Dan*
Trade · *Cohen, Leonard*
tradewinds · *Myers, Robert*
Trading in Innocence · *Watmough, David*
Tradition Bound · *Elford, Jean*
Traffic · *Sheils, Terry*
Traffic Violation · *Bankier, William*
Tragedy at McLeod Beach · *Fisher, Mary*
Tragic Planet · *Govan, Margaret*
The Tragic Tale of Old Burwash · *Arnold, Ricky*
Trail of the Scrimshaw · *Charles, F.*
The Trail of the Serpent · *Tait, Elizabeth*
Trail's End · *Sturdy, John Rhodes*
Train · *Kenyon, Michael*
Train Blues · *Fothergill, Robert J.*
The Train Ride · *Westhues, Kenneth*
The Train Ride to Siberia: A Fable · *Burston, Daniel*
Train to Lausanne · *Gall, Glendy*
Training · *Atwood, Margaret*
Trains · *Malt, Rick*
Trains West · *Free Park* [pseudonym]
Tramonto · *Filipow, Bernard R.*
Transcript · *Doyle, Judith*
Transfer · *Shaw, Joan Fern*
Transformations · *Engel, Marian*
Transformations of the Knife · *Dolan, Douglas*
The Transistor Radio · *Khankhoje, Maya*
Transitions · *Rawdon, Michael*
Translation · *Thompson, Kent*
Transplanted · *Carriere, Marguerite*
Transplants · *Rosenfeld, Rita*
Transposition · *Birdsell, Sandra*
The Trap · *Egan, Patricia*
Trap Berth · *Scammell, A.R.*
Trapped · *Gillette, Agnes*
Trapper Jim · *Gomery, Percy*
Traps · *Butts, Ed P.*

The Trash Collector · *Grant, William J.*
Travel: Cyprus · *Kaye, Marcia*
A Travel Piece · *Atwood, Margaret*
The Traveling Nude · *Kreisel, Henry*
The Traveller · *Marston, Tom*
the traveller and his staff · *Bullock, Michael*
The Travellers · *Carroll, Elizabeth*
Travelling · *Setton, Ruth Knafo*
The Travelling Lilies · *Barker, Bessie M.*
The Travelling Nude · *Kreisel, Henry*
Travelling On · *Harvor, Beth*
Treading Water · *Gallant, Mavis*

Treadmill for a Lucky Man · *Brown, Horace*
The Treasure · *MacSween, R.J.*
The Treasure Chest · *Harvey, Jennifer A. Becks*
The Treasure Hunt · *Stein, Rhoda Elizabeth Playfair*
Treasure Trove · *Briffett, Isabel*
Treble Clef · *Weinzweig, Helen*
The Tree · *Grimster, Ellen*
Tree House · *Bailey, Don*
Tree of Life · *Owens, Rhonda*
the tree of the crows · *Bullock, Michael*
Trees · *Barker, Bessie M.*
the trees and the fish · *Bullock, Michael*
the trees and the fungi · *Bullock, Michael*
Trees Are Lonely Company · *O'Hagan, Howard*
The Tremendous Spasm of Pain · *McFadden, David*
The Trench Dwellers · *Hodgins, Jack*
The Trespasser · *Pacey, Desmond*
Trespassers Will Be Violated · *Margoshes, Dave*
Trial by Chance · *Boisvert, Michel*
Trial by Night · *Green, H. Gordon*
Trial of a Lesser Magistrate · *Dobbs, Kildare R.E.*
The Trial of Judge Axminster · *Bankier, William*
The Trials of P.G. O'Ryan · *Story, Gertrude*
Triangle · *Hughes, Ora Wayne*
A Tribute to All the Dagwood Bumstead's in America · *Summers, Anthony J.*
The Trick · *Stephenson, Michael*
Tricking the Devil · *McArthur, Dennis*
The Trier · *Dybvig, Leslie*
Trillium · *Steinfeld, J.J.*
Trio · *Lee, Kim*
Triolet · *Engel, Marian*
The Trip · *Hogg, Bob*
A Trip for Mrs. Taylor · *Garner, Hugh*
A Trip North · *Nolan, Gladys*
The Trip to Detroit · *Daunt, James*
A Trip to Sea · *Walters, Harold Neal*
A Trip to Slocum's Creek · *Briffett, Isabel*
A Trip to the Casbah · *Gibson, Margaret*
A Trip to the Coast · *Munro, Alice*
Trip without Marge · *Barnard, Leslie Gordon*
Triplex · *Anthony, George*
Tripper · *Anonymous*
Triptych · *Christopherson, Claudia*
The Triumph · *Tudor, Kathleen*
Trophies · *Seifert, Keith A.*
Tropisms · *Peterson, Barry*
The Trouble at Shelmerdines · *Branden, Vicki*

Trouble at Timothy's · *Barnard, Leslie Gordon*
Trouble on Happy Lane · *Martin, Eric*
The Trouble with Eddie · *Stone, Charles*
The Trouble with Heroes · *Vanderhaeghe, Guy*
The Trouble with Sex · *Currie, Robert*
Trouble with the Sly Pastry Chef · *Ross, W.E. Dan*
The Trouble with You Girls · *Williamson, Rossa*
Troubled Waters · *Heather, H.M.*
Troubles of Everett Mitchell · *Stein, Rhoda Elizabeth Playfair*
Troubleshooter · *Coney, Michael G.*
Trouble-Shooter Takes a Mate · *Young, Scott*
Troutin' · *Russell, Ted*
The Truant · *Michaels, Edward L.*
the truants · *Heath, Terence*
The Truck · *Spettigue, Douglas O.*
Truck Start · *Cline, Amanda*
Truck Stop · *Mundwiler, Leslie*
Truckee Your Blues Away · *Margoshes, Dave*
Truckin' · *Mitchell, Ken*
Trucks: The Fifth Wheel · *Gasparini, Len*
Truda · *Birdsell, Sandra*
Trude's Homecoming · *Egyedi, Bela*
Trudging to the City · *Browne, Tom*
True Confession · *Nowlan, Alden*
The True Eventual Story of Billy the Kid · *Nichol, bp*
The True Lover · *MacDonald, D. Lorne*
The True Measure · *Harvey, Jennifer A. Becks*
True Romance · *Lord, Peter*
True Romances · *Atwood, Margaret*
A True Story · *Levine, Norman*
The True Story of My Dentist, Dr. Mark Litvack · *Kilodney, Crad*
The Trumpet Shall Sound · *McCourt, Edward A.*
Truro/Summer/'73 · *Hay, Eldon R.*
the truth · *Heath, Terence*
The Truth About the Sasquatch · *Hockley, Vernon*
Truth and Mrs. Forrester · *Wilson, Ethel D.*
Truths or Writer's Diary · *Itani, Frances*
Truth's Way · *Whitford, Margaret Ann*
Try It On for Size · *Barnard, Margaret E. and Barnard, Leslie Gordon*
Tube Head · *Murphy, D.T.*
Tudor King · *Wiebe, Rudy H.*
Tuesday, Wednesday, Thursday · *Alford, Edna*
Tuesday · *Kaiser, Terry*
Tuktoyaktuk · *Hollingshead, Greg*
Tulips · *Hollingsworth, Margaret*
Tulips and a Hotdog · *Milander, Mary Ellen*
Tullugak · *Welland, Judith*

The Tunnel · *Chalmers, John W.*
Tuparosh · *Weiss, Allan*
The Tupper Toupee Man · *Green, Robert*
Turkey Feathers · *Bacque, James*
The Turkey Season · *Munro, Alice*
Turkhana Knives · *Saunders, Charles R.*
Turnabout · *Skinner, Norman Doc*
The Turning Point · *Cameron, Eric*
The Turning-Point · *Young, Scott*
The Turning Tide · *Beresford-Howe, Constance*
Turning Twelve · *Wilson, Betty and Gillese, John Patrick*
Turnip-o-Lantern · *Bullard, Jean*
The Turret Room · *Bedard, Michael*
The Turtle · *Fones, Robert*
Turtles · *Duncan, Francis*
Tusha and Time · *Zend, Robert*
TV or Not TV · *O'Connell, Dorothy*
TV Sets a Trap · *Drylie, William*
Twa Corbies · *Wiebe, Armin*
Twa Hornbills · *Dennis, Ian*
The Twain Shall Meet · *Boston, Stewart*
'Twas a Bumper Trip · *Babstock, George*
Twas the Day After Christmas · *Sribniak, Mervin*
Tweedledee and Tweedledum · *Faiers, Christopher*
Twelve Days of Christmas · *Stein, Rhoda Elizabeth Playfair*
Twelve Miles of Asphalt · *Garner, Hugh*
A Twentieth Century Success · *Arscott, David*
Twenty Nights in Northeast Africa · *Kenyon, Michael*
A Twig from the Judas · *Weintraub, Ruth Claire*
The Twilight of Her Youth · *Janoff, Douglas*
Twilight Time · *Palomba, Laura*
Twins · *McCormack, Eric*
Twins - A History · *Nichol, bp*
Two Afternoons: One World · *Crabtree, Peter*
The Two Bedrooms · *Roberts, Dorothy*
The Two Boats · *Barnard, Leslie Gordon*
Two Chained Jack · *Hawrelko, John*
Two Codes · *Briffett, Isabel*
Two Days Leave · *Phillips, Fred H.*
Two Episodes in the Life · *Fuchs, Terry*
Two Europeans · *Kushner, Donn*
Two for the Money · *Sheils, Terry*
Two for the Road · *Narvey, Fred*
Two for Trinidad · *Swan, Susan*
Two Gals and a Guy · *Roedde, W.A.*
two girls and a man coming and going · *Bullock, Michael*
Two Heads Are Better Than One · *Robinson, Spider*
Two Heroes · *Nichol, bp*

The Two Hills · *Bedard, Michael*
The Two Hitchhikers · *Pickersgill, Alan G.*
Two in the Bush · *Thomas, Audrey*
Two Is a Crowd · *West, Ken*
Two Lonely People · *Mitchell, M.J.*
Two Memories of Mid-Winter for Tony · *Vintcent, Brian*
Two Men from Alamein · *Bell, John Leslie*
Two Men on a Horse · *Morrow, Mark*
two men with knives · *Bullock, Michael*
The Two Millionth Customer of the Bank of Lower Canada · *Sheldon, Michael*
two monsters · *Bullock, Michael*
two moons · *Bullock, Michael*
Two Notes · *MacLeod, Robert*
Two of a Kind · *Briffett, Isabel*
The Two of Them · *Tancred, Peta*
Two Old Fools · *Fox, James J.*
Two Out of · *Thorpe, Carole Anne*
Two Pages from a Journal · *Johnstone, Rick*
Two Paintings at an Exhibition · *Verhoeven, Clemetus*
Two Part Soliloquy from the House of Love · *Cull, David*
Two Peas in a Pod · *Downs, Tommy*
The Two Philosophers · *Quin, Mike*
Two Photographs · *Thompson, Kent*
The Two Portraits · *MacSween, R.J.*
Two Questions · *Gallant, Mavis*
Two Removes · *Duclos, David*
Two Rooms · *Boyarsky, Abraham*
Two Sisters · *Allan, Ted*
Two Sisters in Geneva · *Kreisel, Henry*
Two Smiths · *Godfrey, Dave*
Two Students · *Dufresne, John*
Two Sundays · *Haynes, D.*
Two Tickets to Muskeago · *Pugsley, Edmund E.*
Two Travellers · *McWhirter, George*
Two Villages · *de Looze, L.*
Two Votaries · *Gill, Stephen*
Two Ways to Hook a Sucker · *McNamee, James*
Two Who Were One · *Mowat, Farley*
The Two Willies · *Livesay, Dorothy*
The Two Witches · *Elliott, W.M.*
Two Women · *Creal, Margaret*
Two Worlds · *Price, Ray*
Two Yellow Pails · *MacDonald, Jake*
two-four · *Freeman, Michael*
Two - From There · *Dixon, J.*
The Two-Gun Kid · *Linder, Norma West*
Two-Way Stretch · *Stewart-Richmond, Effie*
Twylla · *Wuth, Beatrice*

Tynehead: Another Zoo Story · *Watmough, David*
Typewriter · *Jirgins, Karl E.*
Tyrannosaurus Rex · *Harris, Fredie Steve*

The U.S. Chinese Immigrant's Book of the Art of Sex · *Nations, Opal L.*
Udine · *Wahl, W.*
Ugly Can Be Beautiful · *Resnick, Rae*
The Ugly Frog · *Jones, Sandra*
The Ugly Spectre of Sexism · *Davies, Robertson*
Uglypuss · *Atwood, Margaret*
The Ultimate Experience · *Wait, Harvey J.*
the ultimate poem · *Bullock, Michael*
The Ultimate Tranquilizer · *Stephenson, Michael*
Umbrella · *Julian, Marilyn*
The Umbrella Man · *Young, Ian*
The Umbrellas · *Livesey, Margot*
Unadvertised Specials · *Choyce, Lesley*
Unaware They Served · *Clare, Jim*
Unbalanced Diet · *Heble, Ajay*
An Unbidden Monologue · *Ord, Douglas*
Unbodied Souls · *Kelly, M.T.*
The Uncanny Case of Professor Graubergundstein · *Watson, Barry*
Uncertain Flowering · *Laurence, Margaret*
Uncertain Sounds · *Phillips, R.A.J.*
Uncle: Building Something · *Cosseboom, Ray*
Uncle / Heber · *Robinson, Gillian*
'Uncle' Andrew · *Stacey, Jean*
Uncle Charlie Crosses the Tracks · *Almon, Bert*
Uncle Charlie's Prize · *Blythe, Aleata E.*
Uncle Dud and the Runaway Automobile · *Hubbard, Dexter*
Uncle Dud Goes Bear Hunting · *Hubbard, Dexter*
Uncle Ed, the Mennonite Gorilla · *Waltner-Toews, David*
Uncle Harry Is Dead · *West, David S.*
Uncle Henry's Ghoster · *Puddester, John*
Uncle Herbert's Silver Moon · *Barnard, Margaret E. and Barnard, Leslie Gordon*
Uncle Hoffer and the Hat · *Story, Gertrude*
Uncle Mose Begins His Chronicles · *Russell, Ted*
Uncle Otto's Weighty Problem · *Hammarlow, Catherine*
Uncle Philbert and His Big Surprise · *Cohen, Matt*
Uncle Rebus Clean-Song · *Dutton, Paul*
Uncle Reg · *Haig-Brown, Roderick*
Uncle Sammy and Me · *Crowell, Peter*
Uncle Samuel and the Crackie · *McKay, Muriel Saint*
Uncle Samuel's Lady Love · *McKay, Muriel Saint*
Uncle T · *Moore, Brian*
The Unclouded Eyes · *Green, H. Gordon*
The Unconditional Christmas · *Stein, Rhoda Elizabeth Playfair*
Unconditional Christmas · *Stein, Rhoda Elizabeth Playfair*

Under Control · *Grieveson, Brian*
Under Glass · *Atwood, Margaret*
Under the Crab-Apple Tree · *Braven, Luisa*
Under the I · *Alford, Edna*
Under the Mistletoe · *Russell, Ted*
Under the Skin · *Beghtol, Claire*
Under the Volcano · *Lowry, Malcolm*
Under the Weather · *Fagan, Cary*
Underbelly · *Toole, David*
Underground · *Bedard, Michael*
An Underlying Sex Tragedy Written Especially for Television · *Salminiw, Stephen*
An Understanding · *Bennett, Katherine*
Understanding Eva · *Brewster, Elizabeth*
The Understanding Heart · *Russell, Sheila MacKay*
An Understated Look · *Ross, Veronica*
The Undertaker · *Purdy, Al*
The Undertaker of Ste Angele · *Peterson, Phyllis Lee*
The Undertaker's Tale · *Hill, Elizabeth*
Undertow · *Doyle, Dan*
Unearthing Suite · *Atwood, Margaret*
Uneasy Companions · *Knudsen, Joyce*
Unemployed · *Layton, Irving*
Unexpected Emergency · *Green, H. Gordon*
The Unexpected Ending · *Rothoehler, Tamara*
An Unexpected Prairie Blizzard · *Meckler, Frances*
The Unexpected Valentine · *Green, H. Gordon*
Unfinished · *Cowasjee, Saros*
An Unfinished Television Script Entitled: 'Window on the Revolution' · *Thompson, Kent*
Unfit for Paradise · *Swan, Susan*
The Unforgettable David · *Mooers, Vernon*
The Unforgiveable Sin · *Green, H. Gordon*
The Unfortunate Demise of Miss Pilk · *Frankel, Vera*
The Unhappy Medium · *Ham, R.K.*
The Unhappy Reed · *Tisdall, Douglas*
Unicorn · *Banky, Jake*
Uniformities · *Goebel, Ulf*
The Unintentional Angel · *Stein, Rhoda Elizabeth Playfair*
The Uninvited · *McDonald, Ruth*
The Unique Case of Professor Talentire · *Andre-Czerniecki, Marion*
United Nations · *Russell, Ted*
Unity in Struggle · *Stewart, Dave*
The Universal Miracle · *Cohen, Matt*
University Opening · *Russell, Ted*
The University That Never Was · *Goodall, Ray*
Unknown · *Wright, A. Colin*
Unknown Column #314 - A Totally Fictitious Allegory to Make with What You Will · *Anonymous*
An Unknown Hero · *Henderson, Jeff*
Unknown Visitor · *Ross, [W.E.] Dan and Ross, Charlotte*

Unleased Passion · *O'Connell, Dorothy*
Unleavened Bread · *Blomquist, Sonia*
Unless a Life Be ... · *Brownell, Elizabeth*
Unless the Eye Catch Fire ... · *Page, P.K.*
Unless the Grain of Wheat Die · *Thomas, Sister*
The Unlikely Matchmakers · *Parsons, Fay*
An Unmarried Man's Summer · *Gallant, Mavis*
The Unmarried Sister · *Arnason, David*
Unmasking a Bourgeois · *Blaise, Clark L.*
The Unmelodious Jailbird · *Wood, Kerry*
The Unnatural Son · *Nowlan, Alden*
The Unpredictable Point · *Fulford, Robin*
The Unprotected Border · *McNamara, Eugene*
Unravelling · *Porter, Helen*
The Unreal Country · *Downie, Jill*
An Unrestricted View · *Mannard, W.G.*
Unsealed Memo · *Pugsley, Edmund E.*
The Unseen · *Green, H. Gordon*
The Unsettling of the West · *Geddes, Gary*
Unsteady Eddie · *Mosher, Edith*
Untermensch and Kluger Kind · *Newman, C.J.*
Until Proven Innocent · *Hjorteland, Elaine*
Until the Petals Fall Off · *Oakey, Shaun*
Until We've Found the Center of the Circle · *Doyle, Dan*
Untimely Death · *Winter, Jack*
Untitled · *Pollock, Chris*
Untitled Fragment · *Watling, Jay*
Unto Death · *Morrow, Dave*
Unto One of the Least · *Bushell, Sidney*
The Untouchable Gifts · *Barker, Bessie M.*
The Unusual Marker · *Antoniak, Jane*
The Unwilling Twig · *Briffett, Isabel*
Up Ahead · *Roddy, William*
Up and Down, Round and Round · *Huggan, Isabel*
Up and Down in the Depression · *Duncan, Chester*
The Up and Downers · *Levine, Norman*
Up at the Hospital · *Slepokura, Orest*
Up from the Mattress · *Taquine, Pascale*
Up in Smoke · *Torgov, Morley*
Up in the Rainforest · *Godfrey, Dave*
Up North · *Andrus, David A.*
Up Until Now · *Linttell, Anne*
Upon Grounds of Adultery · *Cameron, Donald*
An Upright People · *Bird, Will R.*
The Uprooting · *McCourt, Edward A.*
Ups and Downs · *Harvey, Jennifer A. Becks*
The Upsetting Man · *Dybvig, Leslie*
Up-to-Date Nursery Stories · *Mather, Barry*
Upturn the Rock · *Browne, Paul Cameron*
Urban Renewal · *O'Connell, Dorothy*

Ursula · *Glover, Douglas H.*
Ursus · *O'Hagan, Howard*
Us · *Peters, A.W.M.*
Used Stars · *Harley, Peter*
Utopia Embassey Moves! · *Minor, Junius* [pseudonym]
U-Turn on University · *Doyle, Nancy*

Vacances Pax · *Gallant, Mavis*
Vacancy in Goal · *Young, Scott*
The Vacation · *Galloway, David R.*
Vacation Romance · *Ross, W.E. Dan*
Vacation-Packing · *Hodgins, Norris*
Vacations in the Sun · *Barnes, Lilly*
Vacuum · *Richmond, Jack*
Vagabonds · *Virgo, Sean*
The Valediction · *Wardill, William*
Valedictory · *Gotlieb, Phyllis*
A Valentine for Martha · *Pardy, Maryn*
The Valiant Hearts · *Carlton, Edna P.*
The Valley · *Bowering, George*
The Valley of Achor · *Colson, Theodore*
The Valley of Terror · *Mayse, Arthur*
Valley of the Shadow · *Sharpe, David*
The Valley of the Sorrows · *Elflandsson, Galad*
The Value of King David · *Russell, Ted*
the vampire · *Bullock, Michael*
A Vampire Life · *Dabydeen, Cyril*
The Van · *Mason, Mike*
Vancouver at Toronto · *Wright, Douglas*
Vanessa · *Dolman, Robert Hartley*
Vanishing Act · *Kernaghan, Eileen*
The Vanishing Lakes · *Engel, Marian*
the vanishing landscape · *Bullock, Michael*
Vanity · *Riches, Brenda*
Vanity of Vanities · *Fowke, H. Shirley*
Variations · *Howard, William*
Varieties of Exile · *Gallant, Mavis*
The Vastness of the Dark · *MacLeod, Alistair*
The Vegetarian · *MacSween, R.J.*
Velvet Apes · *Miller, J. Kit*
Venetian Glass · *Corning, Emilia*
Vera Cruz · *Hancock, Ronald Lee*
A Verb: To Love · *McNichol, Philip*
Verdict · *Wyatt, Rachel*
Verena · *Rubia, Geraldine*
Veritas, a Morality · *Kruger, Earl*
The Verlaine Symposium · *Jackson, J. Graham*
The Versatile Group · *Park, Bob*
Versions · *Dyck, E.F.*

A Very Common Condition · *Abnett, Eileen*
Very Green, Very Rubbery · *Byers, Valerie*
A Very Lame Man · *Frost, Bean*
A Very Long Swim · *Branden, Vicki*
A Very Minor Tragedy · *Hughes, Charles*
A Very Modern Person · *Itani, Frances*
A Very Special Day · *Phillips, Sharon P.*
The Veteran · *Wynand, Derk*
Vichyssoise · *Jackson, J. Graham*
vicissitudes of a couple · *Bullock, Michael*
Victim · *Sandor-Lofft, Suzanne*
Victims · *Austin, Don*
The Victims' Ball · *Mays, John Bentley*
The Victim's Joy · *Kelly, M.T.*
Victims of the Temple · *Ayre, John*
Victoria · *La Haye, Marguerite*
Victoria Day · *Rigby, Carle A.*
Victoria Eighteen · *Watt, Sholto*
Victoria Regina · *Vernon, Lorraine*
A Victory · *Jensen, Leif*
Victory Dance · *Lalonde, Wendy*
Victory Party · *Currie, Robert*
Vida · *Robertson, Strowan*
La Vie Parisienne · *Gallant, Mavis*
A View Before Nightfall · *Abnett, Eileen*
The View from the Hill · *Bennett, Bill*
View from the Roof · *Weinzweig, Helen*
The View from Uncle Dave's Window · *Howell, Bill*
A View of Toledo · *Wilson, Elizabeth*
Vigil · *Reyes, R. Ivanov*
Vigil on the Rock · *Johnson, Vera D.*
Vignette: Photographs or Portrait Showing Only Head and Shoulders with Background Shaded Off · *Bailey, Don*
Vignette - A Summer Evening · *Millons, John*
The Viking Professor Strikes Back · *Simpson, Leo*
The Village · *Ogle, Robert Joseph*
The Village Contracts 4 · *Halliday, David*
The Village The Apartment 3 · *Halliday, David*
The Village and the Old Man · *Dearborn, Dorothy E.*
The Village Dragon · *Loomer, L.S.*
The Village Inside · *Hood, Hugh*
Village Panther · *Walker, David*
Village Theatre · *Petrie, Graham*
The Village Washer · *Selvon, Samuel*
A Villain Rare · *Gibbs, Robert*
Vince Willys Strikes Again · *Parr, John*
The Vine · *Solly, Bill*
The Violation · *Huggan, Isabel*
Violent Spirit · *Rae, Donna*
Violette · *Burnett, Virgil*

953

The Violin · *Fraser, Keath*
The Violinist · *Boyarsky, Abraham*
Virgil · *Horst, Roger*
Virgin and Child · *Yates, J. Michael*
The Virgins of Po · *Elflandsson, Galad*
Virus X · *Gallant, Mavis*
Vis a Vis · *General Idea* [pseudonym]
Viscount Joshua · *Dybvig, Leslie*
Viscount Joshua Takes a Bride · *Dybvig, Leslie*
Vision · *Bain, Dena*
The Vision · *Green, H. Gordon*
A Vision of Death · *MacMann, Samuel Lavalliere*
The Vision of Fire · *Waterfall, Don E.*
A Vision of Godliness · *Robison, Wendy*
Vision of the Burning Gate · *Cuson, Tom*
The Visionary · *Logan, Gloria*
Visions · *Friedman, Irena*
Visions Before Midnight · *Garber, Lawrence*
Visions of Christ in a Wheelchair · *Schwartzman, Victor*
The Visit · *Butterworth, Judith*
Visit from the Pension Lady · *Ryga, George*
A Visit from Uncle · *Fletcher, Peggy*
Visit to an Art House · *Deindorfer, Gary*
A Visit to Her Son · *Ross, Veronica*
A Visit to the Frontier · *Wilson, Ethel D.*
A Visit with Robert · *Garner, Hugh*
Visitant · *Cairns, A.T.*
The Visitation · *Addison, B.D.*
Visitation Street · *Saible, Jane*
Visiting Aunt Alix · *Brewster, Elizabeth*
Visiting Hours · *Brewster, Elizabeth*
Visiting Miss M. · *Roberts, Nancy*
Visiting Rights · *Fletcher, Peggy*
Visiting the Grave · *Dalton, Sheila*
The Visitor · *Koncel, Mary Aleta*
Visitors · *Munro, Alice*
Vita Somnium Breve · *Yates, J. Michael*
Vive le Quebec Libre · *Pereira, Anil*
Vivian · *Young, David*
The Vivid Air · *Gustafson, Ralph B.*
The Vocation · *Campbell, Anne*
Vogel · *Cohen, Matt*
the voice · *Heath, Terence*
A Voice for Timothy Newton · *Lewis, Ruth C.*
Voice from the Past · *Green, H. Gordon*
Voice in the Wilderness · *MacNeill, James A.*
A Voice Is Heard in Ramah ... · *Robinson, Spider*
The Voice of an Angel · *Cunningham, Louis Arthur*
The Voice of Authority · *Bantjes, June*
The Voice of Cape des Loups · *Leitch, Adelaide*

The Voice of Doreen Gray · *Bankier, William*
The Voice of Emma Sachs · *Fraser, D.M.*
The Voice of the Elephant · *Blaise, Clark L.*
The Voice of the North · *Brunt, R.J.*
Voice without Words · *Watson, Scott*
Voices · *Steinfeld, J.J.*
Voices Lost in Snow · *Gallant, Mavis*
The Voices of Adamo · *Laurence, Margaret*
The Vote · *Green, H. Gordon*
A Vote for Sir Thomas · *Paterson, O.P.*
The Voters Love a Happy Family · *Conger, Lesley*
Vows · *Kinsella, W.P.*
Voyage Home · *Brewster, Elizabeth*
Voyage to Ultima Azul · *Rikki [Erica Ducornet]*
Voyage to Ultima Azul Chapter 79 · *Rikki [Erica Ducornet]*
Voyeur · *Kinsella, W.P.*
Vroom Vroom · *Findlay, David K.*

The Wacky Bunch · *Barnard, Margaret E.*
The Wager · *Browne, Paul Cameron*
The Wailing Western Wall · *Najovits, Simson R.*
The Wait · *Murphy, Kathleen*
Wait for Me · *Marshall, Joyce*
Wait Until You're Asked · *Garner, Hugh*
The Waiters · *Estabrook, Barry*
Waiting · *Kawai, Haruo*
Waiting for Aunty to Cough · *Selvon, Samuel*
Waiting for Charley · *Garner, Hugh*
Waiting for Charly · *Schartner, Adelaide*
Waiting for Halley's Comet · *Kilodney, Crad*
Waiting for · *Queen Emma · Birney, Earle*
Waiting for Michael · *Stacey, Jean*
Waiting for Mr. Big · *McColl, Len*
Waiting for Mrs. O'Malley · *Doyle, Nancy*
Waiting for Rain · *Kenyon, Linda*
Waiting for the 6:40 · *Hancock, Ronald Lee*
Waiting for the Call · *Kinsella, W.P.*
Waiting for the Goddess · *Vassanji, M.G.*
Waiting for the Postman to Knock · *Clarke, Austin C.*
Waiting for the Return of the Prodigal · *Furcha, Edward J.*
Waiting for the Storm · *Levine, Norman*
The Waiting Game · *Jeffrey, Carole-Lynn*
The Waiting Room · *Cormack, Barbara Villy*
The Waiting Time · *Birdsell, Sandra*
Waiting Up for Santa · *Scott, Moira*
The Wake · *Dickson, Barry*
Waken, Lords and Ladies Gay · *Pacey, Desmond*
Waldemar · *Waddington, Miriam*
Waldo and Willie · *Percy, H.R.*

A Walk · *Wilson, Kathleen*
The Walk Away · *Horne, Lewis B.*
A Walk by Himself · *Rule, Jane*
The Walk Home · *Grantmyre, Barbara*
A Walk in the Dark · *Bryden, John*
a walk in the dust · *Bullock, Michael*
A Walk in the Park · *Harrison, A.S.A.*
A Walk on Y Street · *Garner, Hugh*
A Walk through the Park · *Barnhouse, D.P.*
Walk Through the Valley · *McCourt, Edward A.*
A Walk to Derek's Landing - January 1935 · *Haig-Brown, Roderick*
A Walk to the Paradise Garden · *McNamara, Eugene*
Walk to the Station · *Cooperman, Stanley Roy*
Walk Well, My Brother · *Mowat, Farley*
Walker Brothers Cowboy · *Munro, Alice*
The Walker - A Mood · *Cushing, Leo*
Walking Around the City · *Metcalf, John*
the walking country · *Bullock, Michael*
Walking on Cried Rivers · *Filip, Raymond*
Walking on Water · *Munro, Alice*
Walking Round the City · *Metcalf, John*
The Walking Tree · *Percy, H.R.*
The Wall · *Milne, Sonny*
The Wallet · *Skey, Olga*
The Wallet: An Exercise in Sixties West Coast Bourgeois Realism · *Bowering, George*
Walls Are No Barrier · *Wiseman, Mrs. C.*
the walnut tree · *Bullock, Michael*
The Walrus and the Carpenter · *Bailey, Don*
The Walrus Feeders · *Rooke, Leon*
Walter · *Manzer, Ronald*
Walter Simpson's Satellite · *McIlroy, Kimball*
The Wanderer · *Klemm, Joachim*
Wanderer of the Waters · *Gillese, John Patrick*
The Wandering Jew · *Slabotsky, David*
Wands Across Dark Rooms · *Nishihata, Jesse*
Want to Make a Trade? · *Yates, Joan*
Want-Ad Lovers · *MacLaurin, Douglas*
The Wanted · *Roberts, Dorothy*
Wanted - Grandmothers with Attics · *Bunner, Freda Newton*
Wanting Picture · *Parris, Paula*
The War · *Ward, Don*
War and Peace · *Fraser, D.M.*
War and Peace: A Novel in Three Books · *Strickland, Edward*
War Baby · *Morrissette, George*
The War in the Bathroom · *Atwood, Margaret*
War of the Worlds Revisited · *Hadzipetros, Emmanuel J.*
The Warbler's Song · *Torney, Roy Hamblin*
Ward · *Bolger, William Neil*
Ward C · *Kritsch, Holly*

Warehouse Worker's Dreams · *Kilodney, Crad*
The Warlord · *Reid, Robert W.*
The Warm Wind Goes · *Fraser, Raymond*
The Warning · *O'Hagan, Howard*
Warning: Walking Can Be Dangerous · *Anonymous*
Warp & Woof · *Briffett, Isabel*
The Warranty · *Wilson, Jane E.*
The Warrior · *van Norman, Brian*
The Wart · *Eastman, Harriet*
Wartime Activities · *Selvon, Samuel*
Was He My Brother · *Stemo, L. Johanne*
Was I You - I Wouldn't · *Armstrong, Patricia*
Was Life Supposed to Be That Way · *Roitner, Joseph*
Was Socrates the First Absurdist · *Mirolla, Michael*
Was That Malcolm Lowry · *Duncan, Frances*
Wash This Sand and Ashes · *Wiebe, Rudy H.*
Washday · *Tudor, Kathleen*
The Washing Machine · *Arnason, David*
Washington Valley · *Jones, R[ichard].*
The Wasp · *Hamilton, John*
The Waste Sad Time · *Lyngseth, Joan*
The Wasted Years · *Garner, Hugh*
The Wastelander · *Percy, H.R.*
The Watch · *Blythe, Aleata E.*
A Watch and a Work-Out · *Briffett, Isabel*
Watch Out for Ronnie · *Kleiman, Edward*
Watch the Birdie · *Hultch, U.*
The Watcher · *Shiach, Allan*
The Watchers · *Conger, Lesley and Aaron, Michael*
Watches · *Hollingshead, Greg*
Watching Mother · *Mouré, Ken*
The Watchmaker · *Cohen, Matt*
Water Babies · *Harvey, Jennifer A. Becks*
The Water Ballet · *Krause, Pat*
The Water Cooler · *Waddington, Miriam*
The Water Fairy · *Gibson, Margaret*
Water in the Dust-Bowl · *Houser, Gwenyth*
The Water of Life · *Meredith, Rita*
Water Rising · *Yates, J. Michael*
Water Under the Bridge · *Heard, F.E.*
The Water Witch · *Fines, Beatrice E.*
The Waterbed Syndrome · *Swan, Susan*
The Waterbugs Never Drown, Mother · *Weintraub, Claire*
The Waterloo of Alamawa Potessa · *Branden, Vicki*
Watermelon's Funeral Oration · *Parry, Carrietta*
The Waters Close Over · *Ryan, Josephine*
The Waters of Marah · *Gardner, W.W.*
watery room · *Bullock, Michael*
The Wave · *Phinney, Richard*
The Waves · *Cull, David*

The Way Back · *Alford, Norman*
The Way Is Hard and Weary · *Johnson, Vera D.*
The Way It Ended · *Callaghan, Morley*
The Way It Might Have Been · *Stevens, Irene*
The Way It Ought to Be · *Green, H. Gordon*
The Way It Was · *Briffett, Isabel*
The Way It Was in the Summer of '31 · *Roddan, Samuel*
A Way of Caring · *Stein, Rhoda Elizabeth Playfair*
The Way of Knowledge · *Hiebert, Susan*
A Way of Life · *Wilson, P.M.*
The Way of the Sea · *McKay, Muriel Saint*
The Way of the Strong · *Cunningham, Louis Arthur*
The Way of the Transgressor · *Green, H. Gordon*
The Way of Wise Men · *Sangwine, Jean*
The Way of Wizards · *Elflandsson, Galad*
A Way Out of the Forest · *Haas, Maara*
Way Out on Life's Stormy Seas · *Gibbs, Robert*
The Way Things Are · *Helwig, David*
The Way Things Happen · *Johnston, Stella*
The Way 'Tings' Go · *Giovinazzo, William A., Jr.*
The Way to Concord · *McNamara, Eugene*
The Way We Do It Here · *Godfrey, Dave*
A Way with Women · *Gillese, John Patrick*
Ways of Going · *Dagg, Mel*
We, Who Have Never Suffered · *Richards, David Adams*
We All Begin in a Little Magazine · *Levine, Norman*
We Are All Strangers Here · *Behrens, Peter*
We Are in a Car Going Somewhere · *Nemiroff, Greta Hofmann*
We Are Many · *Newman, Peter C.*
We Are Three, Not Counting the Combine · *Filson, Bruce K.*
We Collide in Our Dreams · *Kreiner, Philip*
We Did It Ourselves · *Harvey, Jennifer A. Becks*
We Got Trouble, Captain · *Childerhose, Robert*
We Have Always Been Heroes · *Dickson, Barry*
We Have Gone to Find a Merry-Go-Round · *Gibb, Jardine*
We Just Had to Be Alone · *Callaghan, Morley*
'We Like Hugs!' · *K.E* [pseudonym]
We Need a Mother · *Burnell, Ethel D.*
We Outnumber the Dead · *Hood, Hugh*
We Stand on Guard · *Steele, Tedd*
We Three · *Wheeler, Frances*
We Took a Scooter Holiday Through the Matto Grosso · *Morron, Glen* [pseudonym]
We Two Are Now One · *Langhout, Mary*
We Were All Going Home · *Burns, Robert A. McA.*
We Won't Talk About It · *Nicol, Eric*
Weaf in the Garden · *MacDonald, William J.*
The Wealth of Nations · *Harris, John*
Wealth - Shared · *Kendall, Wallis*
Wear This for Me · *Drepaul, Joe*

958

Weariness · *MacSween, R.J.*
The Weasel · *Pacey, Desmond*
The Weasel Skin · *Bird, Will R.*
Weasels and Ermines · *Kinsella, W.P.*
The Weatherman · *Benstead, Steven*
A Weaver of Dreams · *Albatross* [pseudonym]
The Web Spinners · *Lee, Carroll H.*
The Wedding · *Reid, Dennis*
Wedding Bells · *Harvey, Jennifer A. Becks*
The Wedding Dress · *Hobbs, Gillian*
The Wedding Guest · *Simmie, Lois*
A Wedding in Toronto · *Clarke, Austin C.*
Wedding of the Year · *Wheatley, Thelma*
The Wedding of Willi Auger · *Brunt, R.J.*
Wedding on the Green · *Bird, Will R.*
The Wedding Party · *Percy, H.R.*
Wedding Review · *Gentleman, Kirstie*
The Wedding Ring · *Gallant, Mavis*
Weddin's · *Russell, Ted*
The Wednesday Circle · *Birdsell, Sandra*
Wednesday Night · *Walker, Craig*
Wednesday's Child · *Carey, Barbara*
Wee Tommy Devlin and the Chocolate Pudding · *Summers, Merna*
The Weed · *Green, H. Gordon*
Weeds and Wild Grass · *Slabotsky, David*
A Week in New York · *Cohen, Matt*
A Week in the Country · *Livesay, Dorothy*
The Weekend · *Rea, Charles*
Weep Together, Friends · *Whitford, Margaret Ann*
Weep with Me · *Clare, John P.*
The Weeping of the People · *Bauer, Nancy*
Weintraub's Education · *Steinfeld, J.J.*
Welcome · *Kenny, George*
Welcome Aboard! Champagne, My Dear? · *Ames, Bill*
Welcome Home · *Graves, Warren*
Welcome the New Pioneers · *Fines, Beatrice E.*
Welcome to My World · *Stein, Rhoda Elizabeth Playfair*
'Welcome-Back-to-Society' · *Stubbs, Judy*
Welfare · *Skinner, Norman Doc*
Well, Well, Well: Three Very Deep Subjects · *Margoshes, Dave*
The Well · *Johnston, D. Maureen*
We'll Go Hunting When I Get Home · *Carter, Shane*
The Well of the Bluebull · *Cowasjee, Saros*
We'll Wait Until Dusk · *Greenway, Rex*
A Well-Adjusted Man · *Kilodney, Crad*
We're Forever Blowing Bubbles · *Skinner, Norman Doc*
We're Going to Have a Wonderful Christmas · *Wees, Frances Shelley*
Were You the Hero? · *Green, H. Gordon*
The West Coast Trail · *Duncan, Frances*
The West Door · *Simpson, Leo*

959

What More Will the Bones Allow? · *McNamara, Eugene*
What Other Love? · *Marcuse, Katherine*
What Price Bread · *Cowasjee, Saros*
What Price Culture? · *Tackaberry, Ivy*
What Price Freedom · *Cummins, Willis*
What Price Glory? · *Heywood, Rosalie*
What Really Happened? · *Bankier, William*
What the Arrival of New York State Onions Meant to Me · *Kilodney, Crad*
What the Hell · *Morton, Colin*
What They Eat at Georgie's House · *Williams, M.A.*
What Time Is It? · *Evanier, David*
What Type Type of a Type Are You? · *Owen, George*
What Will Harry Tell the Boss? · *Porter, John*
What Would Carrie Nation Do? · *Hockley, Vernon*
Whatever Became of Becky · *MacMillan, Gail*
Whatever Happened to Sandra · *Stein, Rhoda Elizabeth Playfair*
Whatever the Cost · *Sroka, Bill*
What's a Fella Gonna Do? · *Walsh, Donna*
What's a Fellow Gonna Do? · *Gallant, Donna*
What's Been Happening to God's Kingdom Since 1914? · *Coleman, Victor*
What's This Agoosto? · *Birney, Earle*
Whatsis Name · *Carrier, Jean-Guy*
Wheat Over the Hill · *Gillese, John Patrick*
The Wheel · *Heller, Sheryl*
The Wheel Chair Pusher · *Miller, Samuel*
The Wheelchair Pusher · *Boyarsky, Abraham*
Wheelchair Sonata · *Kent, Valerie*
When · *Wagley, Stephen*
When a Man Follows a Dream · *Gillese, John Patrick*
When a Mother Dies · *Wheeler, Frances*
When an Elephant Escapes · *Shirinian, Lorne*
When Christmas Came to Cape St. Anthony · *Grenfell, Wilfred T.*
When Dry Summers End · *Horne, Lewis B.*
When Evening Falls · *Wangersky, Russell*
When Evergreens Brown · *McHardy, Vincent*
When Every Woman Looked Like Regina Lee · *Howard, Blanche M.*
When Everything Is Allowed · *Allan, Ted*
When Father Couldn't Say Grace · *Green, H. Gordon*
When Fishermen Meet · *Avery, Martin*
When Freddy Brought the Cream · *Fines, Beatrice E.*
When Greek Meets Greek · *Selvon, Samuel*
When Hamish Hung Up His Kilt · *Green, H. Gordon*
When He Arrived Home · *Hammond, Arthur*
When He Was Free and Young and He Used to Wear Silks · *Clarke, Austin C.*
When I Am King, Dilly Dilly · *Cummer, Don*
'When I Put Out to Sea' · *Morritt, Hope*
When I Was Seven · *Shore, Mitch*
When I Was Seventeen · *Bergren, Myrtle*
When in Rome · *Amprimoz, Alexandre*
'When in Rome ... ' · *Wilson, John*

When It Happens · *Atwood, Margaret*
When It Rains · *Lynch, Gerald*
When It Rains in the Sunshine, a Witch Is Getting Married · *Dabydeen, Cyril*
When Jacob Fletcher Was a Boy · *Elliott, George*
When John Brown and I Were Young · *Madott, Darlene*
When Love Is Forever ... · *Knox, Olive*
When Morning Came · *Higham, John*
When Morning Comes · *Nepszy, Geraldine*
When My Uncle Was the Messiah · *Allan, Ted*
When No One Was Watching · *Leduc, Gäetane*
When Old Age Shall This Generation Waste · *Branden, Vicki*
When Old Friends Meet · *Wetmore, W. Gordon*
When Polyhistoricism Receded · *Kilodney, Crad*
When Satan Goes Home for Christmas · *Davies, Robertson*
When She Comes Over · *Pacey, Desmond*
When Swimmers on the Beach Have All Gone Home · *Rooke, Leon*
When the Bough Breaks · *Rosta, Helen J.*
When the Boys Come Home · *Korber, Freda*
When the Foundations Shake · *MacSween, R.J.*
When the Lamp Is Shattered · *Rowdon, Larry*
When the Letter Came Back · *Clarke, Austin C.*
When the Long Sheeps Gallop · *Engkent, Garry*
When the Moon Is Full · *Fletcher, Peggy*
When the Power Failed · *Barker, Bessie M.*
When the Roll Is Called Up Yonder · *Green, H. Gordon*
'When the Saints Come Marching In' · *Murray, Joan*
When the Snake Bites the Sun · *Ogle, Robert Joseph*
When the Wolves Laughed · *Tench, C.V.*
When the Women Went on Strike · *Cadogan, Elda*
When There's to Be No Moon · *Story, Gertrude*
When We Saw a Sign · *Horne, N.R.*
When We Were Nearly Young · *Gallant, Mavis*
When Winter Came · *Potrebenko, Helen*
When Winter Comes ... · *Philipp, Rowland*
When You Give Your Heart · *Conger, Lesley*
When Your Heart Sings · *Stein, Rhoda Elizabeth Playfair*
When Your Mother Comes to Visit · *Crowell, Peter*
Where Are You Susanna Brown · *Ross, Veronica*
Where Fades the Thin Line · *Beattie, Jessie L.*
'Where Is Harvey Now?' · *Sandor, Karl*
Where Is My Wandering Car Tonight? · *Duffie, Archie*
Where Is the Voice Coming From? · *Wiebe, Rudy H.*
Where Lilies Bloom Free · *Cade-Edwards, Eileen*
Where Motley Is Worn · *Brandis, Marianne*
Where My Cowboy Boots Have Been · *Anonymous*
Where Seldom Is 'Herd' a Discouraging Word · *Decker, Ken*
Where the Devil Would Have His Horns · *Birch, Frank*
Where the Heart Is · *Stein, Rhoda Elizabeth Playfair*
Where the Irish Are · *Gillese, John Patrick*
Where the Myth Touches Us · *Hood, Hugh*

Where the Wild Things Are · *Kinsella, W.P.*
Where the Wild Thyme Blows · *Briffett, Isabel*
Where There's a Will · *Grimster, Ellen*
Where They Are · *Hindmarch, Gladys*
Where Two or Three Are Gathered Together · *Brown, Allan*
Where Were You? · *Young, David*
Where Will It All End · *Bankier, William*
Whereinhellzamoose????? · *Skinner, Norman Doc*
Where's Charlie? · *Margoshes, Dave*
Where's the Spirit? · *Wilson, Betty*
Whether Clarence Lowry Was Here · *Browne, Colin*
Which Christmas Was He Most Dear? · *Gesner, Claribel*
Which One Are You? · *Dickinson, Mary Lou*
Which Way to Go · *Hindmarch, Gladys*
While Shepherds Watched · *Parr, James*
The Whip Smuggler · *Rigby, Carle A.*
The Whirlabout · *Fay, Michael*
Whirlpool · *Ablack, Vera*
[A?] Whisper. A Kiss · *Conger, Lesley*
Whiskeyjack · *Austin, Jeremy*
Whisky Jack · *Hutchison, Bruce*
a whispering · *Bullock, Michael*
The Whispering Machine · *Bruns, Ina*
Whispers · *Brown, Gordon*
Whistle, Daughter, Whistle · *Itter, Carole*
The Whistle Blows at Five · *Garvin, Guy C.*
The Whistler · *Rosenfeld, Rita*
Whistling · *Ross, Veronica*
White and Other Colours · *Pitt-Brooke, Linda*
The White Azalea · *Spencer, Elizabeth*
The White Cadillac · *Showell, Rob*
The White Canoe · *Mowat, Farley*
White Christmas in Montreal · *Sutherland, Ronald*
The White Coffin · *Bowering, George*
The White Dress · *Currie, Robert*
The White Eye · *MacSween, R.J.*
The White Flag · *Geddes, Gary*
white gloves · *Bullock, Michael*
The White Horse · *O'Hagan, Howard*
White Houses · *Warren, Diane*
White Is for Brides · *Peterson, Phyllis Lee*
The White Jeep · *Johnson, Linda Wikene*
The White Kitten · *Conger, Lesley*
White Knight to King's Pawn · *Drummond, R. Jill*
White Land, Blue Toe · *Parr, John*
White Lies · *Virgo, Sean*
The White Lilacs · *Buyukmihci, Hope Sawyer*
White Man's Everything · *Countryman, Glenn*
White Meadows · *Barnard, Leslie Gordon*
White Moments · *Smyth, Jacqui*

White Mountains in the Moon · *Wilson, Betty*
White Musky · *Young, Scott*
The White Mustang · *McCourt, Edward A.*
The White Nicotine · *Murray, Joan*
White Night · *Tanner, Adrian*
White Otter Castle · *Barr, Elinor*
The White Peacock · *Briffett, Isabel*
The White Rabbit · *Cook, Hugh*
White Rabbits · *Klebeck, William J.*
The White Ravine · *Rae, Donna*
White Rock Mine · *Zielonka, Allan*
The White Rose · *Stein, Rhoda Elizabeth Playfair*
White Running Shoes · *Kinsella, W.P.*
the white sheet and the couple · *Bullock, Michael*
White Silence · *Ross, Veronica*
The White Sky · *Scobie, Stephen*
White Spot · *Egyedi, Bela*
The White Squirrel · *Campbell, Sheila*
The White Tornado · *McKay, Jean*
White Wail · *Schreiber, H.E.*
The White Walrus · *Briffett, Isabel*
The White Wolf · *Kropp, Josefa*
The White-Cane Wreck 'Em Derby · *MacLaurin, Douglas*
Whitecaps · *Foran, Charles*
Whiteout · *Arscott, David*
The Whitest of Feathers · *Story, Gertrude*
Whither Thou Goest ... · *Edwards, Mary Kay*
Whither Thou Goest · *Graham, Ferne*
Who Can Avoid a Place? · *McFadden, David*
Who Do You Think You Are? · *Munro, Alice*
Who Gets What? · *Babstock, George*
Who He Slept By · *Svendsen, Linda*
Who Is My Neighbour? · *Whitford, Margaret Ann*
Who Is Twisting My Arm? · *Stein, Rhoda Elizabeth Playfair*
Who Jew You · *Martinich, Aloysius*
Who Said There Ain't No Heaven · *Earl, Lawrence*
Who Steals My Face? · *Bankier, William*
Who Walked with Kings · *McCourt, Edward A.*
Who Was It Who Danced at Eaton's Catalogue Store? · *Thompson, Kent*
Who Was the Greatest Writer Who Ever Lived? · *Nowlan, Alden*
Who Was the Woman of the Glove? · *Gray, John*
Who Would Marry a Riverman? · *Kroetsch, Robert*
Whole Story · *Thomas, John*
The Wholesome One · *Boorman, Sylvia*
Whomsoever I Shall Kiss · *Broadfoot, J.B.*
The Whopper · *Mosher, Edith*
Whorts · *Russell, Ted*
Who's Afraid of the Planning Committee? · *Fines, Beatrice E.*
Whos Paying for This Call · *Hood, Hugh*
Who's Your Pal? · *Hutton, Bill*

Whose Child Is This? · *Whitford, Margaret Ann*
Why a Judaeo-Christian Philosophy That Knows So Much About the Nature of God Knows So Little About the Nature of Jack B. Wood · *Rooke, Leon*
Why Agnes Left · *Rooke, Leon*
Why Did 6 Old Friends Kill Themselves? · *Donovan, Terry*
Why Did It Happen to Me? · *Price, Ray*
'Why Didn't I Listen to You?' · *Ziolkowski, Carmen*
Why Didn't You Use a Plunger? · *Clarke, Austin C.*
Why Do You Lie? · *Bailey, Don*
Why Do You Live So Far Away? · *Levine, Norman*
Why Don't We Ask First? · *Cade-Edwards, Eileen*
Why Don't You Love Me · *Hollingshead, Greg*
Why Fade These Children of the Spring · *Gault, Connie*
Why I Am Here Where I Am Talking to You Like This · *Rooke, Leon*
Why I Never Went to University · *Green, H. Gordon*
Why No Familiar Tune? · *McWhirter, George*
Why Raymond Joined the Navy · *Irvine, R.B.*
Why Should I Have Been There? · *Novack, Deborah*
Why Should I? · *Rackham, Ruth*
Why the Big Computer Broke Down Processing Census Returns from the Parish of St. Marys, York County, N.B. · *Munroe, Rolf*
Why the Devil - Mule? · *Kent, Valerie*
Why the Sun? · *Smith, Charley*
Why We Killed Mackee · *Robinson, Peter*
Whyntcha Write Happy Stories? · *Holz, Cynthia*
Wickanninish Memory · *Watmough, David*
Wicked Am I? · *Birch-Jones, Sonia*
The Wicked Fleeth · *Gardner, W.W.*
The Wickedness of Rubin Broome · *Howell, Bill*
Wider and Deeper · *Gzowski, Peter J.*
A Wider Window · *Barker, Bessie M.*
The Widow · *Pettijohn, Constance*
The Widower Bird · *Helwig, David*
The Widower · *Munro, Alice*
Widow's Aid · *Grantmyre, Barbara*
The Widow's Dilemma · *Morrison, Margaret*
The Widow's Kid · *Mayse, Arthur*
Widow's Sanctuary · *Horne, Lewis B.*
Widow's Walk · *Drew, Wayland*
The Wife · *Halliday, David*
Wife Beater · *Green, H. Gordon*
A Wife for Antonio · *Hubbard, Dexter*
A Wife for Pop · *Annett, R. Ross*
A Wife Runs Away · *Armstrong, Patricia*
The Wife Sawed in Half · *Julian, Marilyn*
The Wife Who Was Really a Slave · *Green, H. Gordon*
Wild Dogs · *Tupper, Dorothy*
The Wild Goose · *Buckler, Ernest*
Wild Grapes and Chlorine · *Bowering, George*
Wild Harmony · *Bow, Jane*

Wild Haven · *Webber, Frances*
The Wild Horse · *Wood, Kerry*
Wild Horses · *Glover, Douglas H.*
The Wild Plum Tree · *Birdsell, Sandra*
Wild Swans · *Munro, Alice*
Wild Trees Calling · *Staubitz, Arthur*
Wildcat · *McLellan, Pat*
Wildcat 13 · *Gillese, John Patrick*
A Wilderness Lesson · *Boyd, Robert*
Wilderness Marriage · *Coleman, Thelma*
Wilderness Train Home · *Staubitz, Arthur*
Wilderness Wife · *Armstrong, Patricia*
Wilderness Wild - A Sexual Saga of the Canadian North · *Sutherland, Fraser*
Wildlife Studies · *Avery, Martin*
The Wildness in Her · *Mayse, Arthur*
Will · *Copeland, Ann* [pseudonym]
A Will to Fail · *Greenbaum, Jonathan*
Will Ye Let the Mummers In? · *Nowlan, Alden*
Will You Go Hunt, My Lord? · *Shein, Brian*
Will You Love Me Tomorrow? · *Fines, Beatrice E.*
Will You Show Me a Light, Lad · *Green, H. Gordon*
Willi · *Gallant, Mavis*
William · *Mitchell, Ken*
Willie · *Flatt, Mary*
Willie the Squowse · *Allan, Ted*
Willis · *Matheson, Shirlee Smith*
Willow, Weep for Me · *Notar, Stephen*
Willow Song · *Summers, Merna*
Willows · *Stevenson, Roberta*
Willy · *Daem, Mary*
The Wind · *van Luven, Lynne*
Wind and Fire · *Sturdy, John Rhodes*
The Wind Blows Around · *Clifton, Merritt*
The Wind Climber · *Branden, Vicki*
the windmill · *Bullock, Michael*
The Window · *Glay, George Albert*
Window Dressing · *Williamson, B.J.*
Window on the Revolution · *Thompson, Kent*
Window People · *Bailey, Don*
Window Slammer · *Barnard, Leslie Gordon*
Window-Pane · *Nipp, Dora*
Windows · *Morgan. Bernice*
Windows & She · *Clifton, Merritt*
Winds for Sale · *Wuorio, Eva-Lis*
Winds of Change · *Coulton, Doris*
Winds of Despair · *Holland, Marjorie*
Winds of Wrath · *Johnson, G. Bertha*

Windward Summer · *Barnard, Leslie Gordon*
The Wine of Harvest and the Bread of Worship · *Tisdall, Douglas*
Wine-Red Begonia · *Wansley, David*
Wings · *Bowering, George*
Wing's Chips · *Gallant, Mavis*
Wings in the Night · *Barrick, Steve*
Wings in the Wind · *Powell, Dorothy M.*
Wings Over Antar · *de Lint, Charles*
Wings Over Dumottan · *Dafoe, Christopher*
Wings Over Pigeboogwek · *Goodwin, Irene Lloyd*
Winkle · *Steffler, George*
The Winner · *Hood, Hugh*
Winner Take Nothing · *Austin, Don*
Winners and Losers · *Helwig, David*
Winner's Circle · *Linder, Norma West*
Winnifred Longden's Commercial Crusade · *Field, L.L.*
[The?] Winning Play · *Young, Scott*
Winning the Whitefish of the Weekend · *Power, John*
Winter. Moving Just Inside the Door · *Marlatt, Daphne*
Winter Carnival · *Avery, Martin*
Winter Day · *Hanson, R.D.*
Winter Dog · *MacLeod, Alistair*
Winter Flight · *Sturdy, John Rhodes*
Winter Friday · *Palomba, Laura*
Winter Has a Lovely Face but Isn't Summer Hell · *Rooke, Leon*
Winter Hill · *C., J.H.*
Winter Is Lovely, Isn't Summer Hell · *Rooke, Leon*
Winter Morning Long Ago · *Campbell, Marjorie*
Winter of Content · *Filip, Raymond*
The Winter of the Daffodils · *Helwig, David*
Winter Palace · *Strandlund, Wayne*
The Winter Stiffs · *Godfrey, Dave*
Winter Vacation · *Mottadelli, Irene*
Winter Wedding · *Powell, Dorothy M.*
Winter Wind · *Munro, Alice*
Wintergreen - Evergreen · *MacNeill, James A.*
Wintering in Victoria · *Rooke, Leon*
Wintering Over · *Byrnes, Terence*
Wintering Place · *King, Carol*
Winter's End · *Rowell, Carolyn*
Winter's Rains and Ruins · *Brewster, Elizabeth*
A Winter's Tale · *Thomas, Audrey*
Winthrop into the Flesh of Piano · *Salminiw, Stephen*
Wisdom Built Her House · *Stein, Rhoda Elizabeth Playfair*
Wise One of Windigo Hills · *Gillese, John Patrick*
Wise Woman · *Howarth, Jessmin*
The Wish · *Bell, Mackenzie*
Wish on a Star, Silas · *Mosher, Edith*
Wisteria · *Spencer, Elizabeth*
the witch · *Heath, Terence*

Witch Doctor · *MacSween, R.J.*
The Witch in the Woods · *Hancock, Ronald Lee*
The Witch Tree · *Bedard, Michael*
Witch's Power · *Bird, Will R.*
With a Capital T · *Gallant, Mavis*
With a Heart on Her Sleeve · *Eaton, Jean*
With Every Child · *Powell, Dorothy M.*
With Expectant Spirits · *Stein, Rhoda Elizabeth Playfair*
With Love, Father · *Rose, Mildred A.*
With Palms and Scattered Garments · *Edwards, David R.*
Withdrawal Sym-phonies · *Scott, Gail*
Without Fear or Favor · *Hutchison, Bruce*
Without Glory · *Barkhouse, Joyce C.*
Without Her · *Sandor, Karl*
Without Malice, the American Way · *Fetherling, Doug*
Without Prefix · *McWhirter, George*
Without Sound · *Nagal, Peter*
Without the Trimmings · *Hiebert, Susan*
The Witness · *Templeton, Wayne*
Witness for the Crown · *Green, H. Gordon*
Witness in a Lesson · *Govan, Margaret*
The Witnesses · *Kushner, Donn*
Wives, New Wives, and Mothers · *Horne, Lewis B.*
The Wizard of Danbury Wood · *Bedard, Michael*
Wizard's Bounty · *de Lint, Charles*
Woe to the Caroche · *Stevenson, S. Warren*
A Woeful Pageant of the Seventh Age · *Bauer, William A.*
The Wolf, the Fox and the Fishmonger · *Leyerle, John*
The Wolf · *Woodcock, Don*
A Wolf Among the Caribou · *Spalding, A.E.*
Wolf at the Door · *Paxton, Maureen*
Wolf King's Mate · *Gillese, John Patrick*
Wolf Poses as Grandmother - He Attacks, Rapes Young Redhead · *Fraser, Raymond*
The Wolf Pup · *Conger, Lesley and Aaron, Michael*
Wolf Tracks · *Dienheim, Anthony* [pseudonym]
The Wolf Who Did · *Day, T.*
Wolfbane Fane · *Payerle, George*
Wolf's Day in Court · *Hennessey, Michael*
The Wolves · *Unwin, Peter*
The Wolves and the Heathens · *Matheson, Shirley Smith*
The Wolves of the Devil · *Crawford, Terry*
Woman Alone · *Gillese, John Patrick*
The Woman Alone Thing · *Bailey, Don*
A Woman and Her Dog · *McFadden, David*
A Woman and Her Husband · *Turner, Lois*
The Woman and the Wolf · *Mowat, Farley*
The Woman at Bore Light · *Gaul, Avery*

The Woman Beautiful · *Nations, Opal L.*
A Woman Can't Wait Too Long · *Bird, Will R.*
A Woman Crossing the Street · *Friedman, Irena*
The Woman from Columbia · *Rooke, Leon*
The Woman He Left to Die · *Mowat, Farley*
A Woman in Love · *Armand, Dorothy*
The Woman in the Control Room · *Bankier, William*
A Woman Is Sleeping by the Lake with Her Small Son and Baby · *Lill, Wendy*
The Woman Luli Sent Me · *Allan, Ted*
A Woman of Her Age · *Ludwig, Jack*
A Woman of Moderate Temperament · *van Herk, Aritha*
A Woman of Some Beauty · *MacMann, Samuel Lavalliere*
Woman on Hill · *Bartlett, Brian*
The Woman on the Bench · *Drew, Mabel E.*
Woman on Wheels · *West, Linda*
A Woman to Pity · *Harvey, Jennifer A. Becks*
The Woman Who Bred Them for War · *Hudson, Noel*
The Woman Who Got On at Jasper Station · *O'Hagan, Howard*
The Woman Who Talks to Canada Geese · *Barclay, Byrna*
The Woman Who Wanted No Love · *Green, H. Gordon*
The Woman Who Wanted to Go Home · *Walker, David*
The Woman Whose Child Fell from the Tower · *Godfrey, Dave*
Woman with Corpse: Study for Fiction No. 1 · *Fortier, Mark*
The Woman with the BBC Voice · *Clarke, Austin C.*
The Woman Within · *Tench, C.V.*
A Woman's Touch · *Copeland, Ann* [pseudonym]
The Women · *Boissonneau, Alice*
Women in Battle · *Sanderson, Vi*
The Women in His Life · *Barker, Bessie M.*
Women Who Wanted No Love · *Green, H. Gordon*
The Wonder of Light · *Hansen, Laurence*
A Wonder of Wishes · *Percy, H.R.*
The Wonderful Conspiracy · *Robinson, Spider*
A Wonderful Day · *Burnell, Ethel D.*
The Wonderful Dreams of My Saintly Father · *Roddan, Samuel*
The Wonderful Years · *Peterson, Phyllis Lee*
Wood · *Munro, Alice*
Wood Pile · *DeFaveri, Ivan*
The Woodcutter's Third Son · *Hood, Hugh*
The Wooden Indian · *Cuevas, Ernesto*
Wooden Ships · *Gillespie, William D.*
Wooden Wings of Ste. Angele · *Peterson, Phyllis Lee*
The Wooden Woman · *Crispin, Jane*
Woods and Waters Wild · *de Lint, Charles*
[The?] Woodlot · *Barnard, Leslie Gordon*
Woodsedge · *Bedard, Michael*
The Woodworker or, The Man Who Refinished His Wife · *Naylor, C. David*
Wood-Worms and Walnuts · *LeCorre, Kathryn*
the woolen garment · *Bullock, Michael*
The Woolen Gloves · *Woodward, Gordon*

Woolsey · *Assmann, Winny*
Woorden Op Een Vensterbank · *Rule, Jane*
A Word Problem · *Masterton, Richard*
Words, Words, Words Is the Future · *Clarke, Austin C.*
Words and Hands · *Kalman, Judy*
Words Are for the Birds · *Owen, George*
Words for the Winter · *Blaise, Clark L.*
Words for Winter · *Blaise, Clark L.*
Words of Glass · *Newman, C.J.*
Work Boots and Carpet · *Stewart, Molly*
Work in Progress · *Wright, Douglas*
Workaday Cowboy · *Wood, Kerry*
Working Blind · *Rooke, Leon*
The Working Class · *Stein, David Lewis*
A Working Paper · *Carlson, Chuck*
A Working Partnership · *Steele, Harwood*
Working the Transport · *Selvon, Samuel*
Working the Walkways of Shahumian Street or The Oldest Profession in Armenia
· *Shirinian, Lorne*
Working Wife and Mother · *Cameron, Anne*
Workmen Not Ashamed · *Carlton, Edna P.*
Works and Days · *FitzSimmons, Edward Peter*
The World Again · *Marshall, Joyce*
A World Apart · *Stein, Rhoda Elizabeth Playfair*
The World of Men · *Marcellin, Philip*
The World's Dullest Story · *Kilodney, Crad*
The World's Fastest Flying Tuba · *Ford, Frederic C.*
The World's Greatest Detective · *Stephenson, Michael*
World's Greatest Poet · *Zend, Robert*
Worm in the Apple · *Maynard, Fredelle Bruser*
The Worm That Lived · *Deane, James*
The Worry Wart · *Faulknor, Cliff*
The Worst Is Not · *Colucci, Joseph*
Worst Thing Ever · *Hood, Hugh*
Wot de Hell Ah Go do? · *Dean, Darryl*
The Wow Sound of the Prairie · *Fetherling, Doug*
The Wrath of Zeus · *Partington, David*
A Wreath for Pennant Annie · *Sturdy, John Rhodes*
The Wrench · *McLellan, Pat*
Wrinkled Desert · *Maxted, Randolph*
Writ on Water · *Garber, Lawrence*
Write of Passage · *Quinlan, Judith*
The Writer · *MacMillan, Ian*
A Writer in the Family · *MacCormack, Terrance*
The Writer of a Fact of Life · *Doran, J.*
Writer-in-Residence · *Coyne, John*
[A?] Writer Remembers · *Gillese, John Patrick*
Writer's Block · *McGrath, Patrick*
A Writer's Eye · *de Barros, Paul*
The Writer's Nose · *MacCormack, Terrance*

The Yellow Light Road · *Pickersgill, Edward*
The Yellow Rose · *Bergren, Myrtle*
Yellow Scarf · *Kinsella, W.P.*
The Yellow Sweater · *Garner, Hugh*
The Yellowest Xmas Tree · *Brunt, R.J.*
Yellowknife · *Hay, Elizabeth*
Yenteh · *Newman, C.J.*
Yes, Aunt Sophy, There Is · *Russell, Ted*
Yes, Young Daddy · *Chin, Frank*
Yeshua X · *Gotlieb, Phyllis*
Yesterday · *Perkin, Darlene*
Yesterday and Forever · *Bowers, Rick*
Yesterday's Child · *Friesen, Victor Carl*
Yesterday's Ship · *Belcourt, Lesley Tarrant*
Yesterday's Tomboy · *Mayse, Arthur*
Yo-Ho Yo-Ho · *Lonneberg, Lyle R.*
Yonge Street · *Halliday, David*
You · *Raglon, Rebecca*
You Are a Bastard Mr. Death · *Amprimoz, Alexandre*
You Are Very Much on My Mind · *Newman, C.J.*
You Better Not Pout · *Mitchell, Ken*
You Can Get Anything You Want ... · *Vincent, Barbara*
You Cannot Judge a Pumpkin's Happiness by the Smile Upon His Face · *Rule, Jane*
You Can't Beat Herring · *Tait, John*
You Can't Get Out · *Deneau, Denis Phillippe*
You Can't Get There from Here · *McNamara, Eugene*
You Can't Kill All the Flies · *Williams, D.S.*
You Can't Steal Happiness · *Stemo, L. Johanne*
You Can't Take It with You · *Wuorio, Eva-Lis*
You Cant Trust Anyone These Days · *Baker, Rita*
You Can't Trust Farmers · *Armstrong, Patricia*
You Don't Understand · *Humphries, Tom*
You Gave Me Hyacinths · *Hospital, Janet Turner*
You Get to Know People · *Barnard, Leslie Gordon*
You Get What You Deserve · *Bankier, William*
You Gotta Stay Ahead · *Anonymous*
You Have to Learn to Fly · *McCracken, Melinda*
You Haven't Really Lost a Daughter · *Cronenberg, David*
You Know What Thought Did · *Gibbs, Robert*
You Make Your Own Breaks · *Dempsey, Jane*
You Never Ast Me Before · *Garner, Hugh*
You Never Give Me Flowers · *Moore, Brian*
You Never Heard? · *Barnard, Leslie Gordon*
You Never Know · *Hollingshead, Greg*
You Never Told Me You'd Been to Mexico · *Malik, Cynthia*
You Never Walk Alone · *Gillese, John Patrick*
You Owe Me Something · *Wyatt, Rachel*
You Went Away · *Peterson, Phyllis Lee*
You Were Wrong · *Theriault, Pierre*

You Wouldn't Talk Like That If You Were Dead · *Richler, Mordecai*
You Wouldn't Want To · *Hindmarch, Gladys*
You'll Get the Rest of Him Soon · *Elliott, George*
You'll Never Get Away · *Wilson, Ethel D.*
You'll Never Have to Take Me Home Again · *Burnell, Ethel D.*
You'll Never Make It, Phillip · *Quast, Jeanette*
You'll Remember Mercury · *Dorsey, Candas Jane*
Young and Gay · *Swan, Susan*
A Young Artist's Dreams · *Oudecek, Madia*
Young Blood Must Have Its Course, Lad and Every Dog His Day · *Hill, Edward*
The Young Chatelaine · *Briffett, Isabel*
Young Dr. Trail · *Foster, W.B.*
Young Man in a Hurry · *Barnard, Margaret E.*
Young Man's Fancy · *Barnard, Leslie Gordon*
Young Men Will Do It · *Griffin, George*
Young Moment · *Madison, Grant*
The Younger Brother · *Gill, Stephen*
Younger Days · *Collicott, George*
Youngsters · *Russell, Ted*
Your Brother Came with Guile · *Stein, Rhoda Elizabeth Playfair*
Your Father and I · *Rule, Jane*
Your Green Coat · *Newman, C.J.*
Your Witness · *Potter, Chris*
You're a Taker · *Ritter, Erika*
You're New Here, Eh? · *Ericsson, Sue*
You're Their Mother · *Anonymous*
You're Very Young · *Barnard, Margaret E. and Barnard, Leslie Gordon*
Youth and Innovations · *Mills, Elizabeth*
Youthful Friendship · *Rolheiser, Ronald*
The Yo-Yo Champ · *Amprimoz, Alexandre*
A Yukon Man · *Sturdy, John Rhodes*
Yule Get Yours · *Anonymous*
Yusuf and Maria · *Dobbs, Kildare R.E.*
Yvonne · *Cameron, John Cullen*

Zack · *Stevens, R. Jean*
The Zeal of Thine House · *Baker, Mark*
The Zealot · *Wilson, Don*
Zeballos, B.C. · *Hindmarch, Gladys*
Zeppi's Machine · *Selvon, Samuel*
The Zeus Cave · *Stenson, Frederick*
Zina's Version · *Horne, Lewis B.*
The Zoo · *Callaghan, Will N., Jr.*
Zoomates · *Lenoir-Arcand, Christine*
Zou Zou and the Preacher · *Arrol, Ed*
Zulu · *Staniforth, Richard*